Teacher's Edition

PRENTICE HALL

HISTORY OF OUR WORLD
The Early Ages

In association with

DK

Discovery CHANNEL SCHOOL

PEARSON

Prentice Hall

Boston, Massachusetts
Upper Saddle River, New Jersey

Program Consultants

Heidi Hayes Jacobs

Heidi Hayes Jacobs has served as an education consultant to more than 1,000 schools across the nation and abroad. Dr. Jacobs serves as an adjunct professor in the Department of Curriculum on Teaching at Teachers College, Columbia University. She has written two best-selling books and numerous articles on curriculum reform. She received an M.A. from the University of Massachusetts, Amherst, and completed her doctoral work at Columbia University's Teachers College in 1981. The core of Dr. Jacobs's experience comes from her years teaching high school, middle school, and elementary school students. As an educational consultant, she works with K–12 schools and districts on curriculum reform and strategic planning.

Michal L. LeVasseur

Michal LeVasseur is the Executive Director of the National Council for Geography Education. She is an instructor in the College of Education at Jacksonville State University and works with the Alabama Geographic Alliance. Her undergraduate and graduate work were in the fields of anthropology (B.A.), geography (M.A.), and science education (Ph.D.). Dr. LeVasseur's specialization has moved increasingly into the area of geography education. Since 1996 she has served as the Director of the National Geographic Society's Summer Geography Workshops. As an educational consultant, she has worked with the National Geographic Society as well as with schools and organizations to develop programs and curricula for geography.

Senior Reading Consultants

Kate Kinsella

Kate Kinsella, Ed.D., is a faculty member in the Department of Secondary Education at San Francisco State University. A specialist in second-language acquisition and adolescent literacy, she teaches coursework addressing language and literacy development across the secondary curricula. Dr. Kinsella earned her M.A. in TESOL from San Francisco State University and her Ed.D. in Second Language Acquisition from the University of San Francisco.

Kevin Feldman

Kevin Feldman, Ed.D., is the Director of Reading and Early Intervention with the Sonoma County Office of Education (SCOE) and an independent educational consultant. At the SCOE, he develops, organizes, and monitors programs related to K–12 literacy. Dr. Feldman has an M.A. from the University of California, Riverside, in Special Education, Learning Disabilities and Instructional Design. He earned his Ed.D. in Curriculum and Instruction from the University of San Francisco.

Acknowledgments appear on pages 575–578, which constitute an extension of this copyright page.

Copyright © 2005 by Pearson Education, Inc., publishing as Pearson Prentice Hall, Boston, Massachusetts 02116.
All rights reserved. Printed in the United States of America. This publication is protected by copyright, and permission should be obtained from the publisher prior to any prohibited reproduction, storage in a retrieval system, or transmission in any form or by any means, electronic, mechanical, photocopying, recording, or likewise. For information regarding permission(s), write to: Rights and Permissions Department, One Lake Street, Upper Saddle River, New Jersey 07458.

MapMaster™ is a trademark of Pearson Education, Inc.
Pearson Prentice Hall™ is a trademark of Pearson Education, Inc.
Pearson® is a registered trademark of Pearson plc.
Prentice Hall® is a registered trademark of Pearson Education, Inc.
Discovery Channel School® is a registered trademark of Discovery Communications, Inc.

DK is a registered trademark of Dorling Kindersley Limited.
Prentice Hall World Studies is published in collaboration with DK Designs, Dorling Kindersley Limited, 80 Strand, London WC2R ORL. A Penguin Company.

ISBN 0-13-130772-X
45678910   08 07 06 05

Cartography Consultant

DK Andrew Heritage

Andrew Heritage has been publishing atlases and maps for some 25 years. In 1991, he joined the leading illustrated nonfiction publisher Dorling Kindersley (DK) with the task of building an international atlas list from scratch. The DK atlas list now includes some 10 titles, which are constantly updated and appear in new editions either annually or every other year.

PRENTICE HALL

HISTORY OF OUR WORLD

Don't miss these powerful teacher timesavers!

Teacher's Edition Step-by-step guide for teachers ensures that objectives are met, provides reading strategies, makes point-of-use suggestions for using resources, and offers differentiated instruction.

Teaching Resources

All-in-One Teaching Resources Everything you need to teach in one location—including lesson plans, worksheets, and tests—making it easy to find materials, prep for class, and teach exciting lessons.

TeacherExpress CD-ROM Powerful lesson planning, resource management, testing, and an interactive Teacher's Edition, all in one place, make class preparation quick and easy!

Academic Reviewers

Africa
Barbara B. Brown, Ph.D.
African Studies Center
Boston University
Boston, Massachusetts

Ancient World
Evelyn DeLong Mangie, Ph.D.
Department of History
University of South Florida
Tampa, Florida

Central Asia and
the Middle East
Pamela G. Sayre
History Department,
   Social Sciences Division
Henry Ford Community College
Dearborn, Michigan

East Asia
Huping Ling, Ph.D.
History Department
Truman State University
Kirksville, Missouri

Eastern Europe
Robert M. Jenkins
Center for Slavic, Eurasian and
   East European Studies
University of North Carolina
Chapel Hill, North Carolina

Latin America
Dan La Botz
Professor, History Department
Miami University
Oxford, Ohio

Medieval Times
James M. Murray
History Department
University of Cincinnati
Cincinnati, Ohio

North Africa
Barbara E. Petzen
Center for Middle Eastern Studies
Harvard University
Cambridge, Massachusetts

Religion
Charles H. Lippy, Ph.D.
Department of Philosophy
   and Religion
University of Tennessee
   at Chattanooga
Chattanooga, Tennessee

Russia
Janet Vaillant
Davis Center for Russian
   and Eurasian Studies
Harvard University
Cambridge, Massachusetts

South Asia
Robert J. Young
Professor Emeritus
History Department
West Chester University
West Chester, Pennsylvania

United States and Canada
Victoria Randlett
Geography Department
University of Nevada, Reno
Reno, Nevada

Western Europe
Ruth Mitchell-Pitts
Center for European Studies
University of North Carolina
   at Chapel Hill
Chapel Hill, North Carolina

Reviewers

Sean Brennan
Brecksville-Broadview Heights
   City School District
Broadview Heights, Ohio

Stephen Bullick
Mt. Lebanon School District
Pittsburgh, Pennsylvania

William R. Cranshaw, Ed.D.
Waycross Middle School
Waycross, Georgia

Dr. Louis P. De Angelo
Archdiocese of Philadelphia
Philadelphia, Pennsylvania

Paul Francis Durietz
Social Studies
   Curriculum Coordinator
Woodland District #50
Gurnee, Illinois

Gail Dwyer
Dickerson Middle School,
   Cobb County
Marietta, Georgia

Michal Howden
Social Studies Consultant
Zionsville, Indiana

Rosemary Kalloch
Springfield Public Schools
Springfield, Massachusetts

Deborah J. Miller
Office of Social Studies,
   Detroit Public Schools
Detroit, Michigan

Steven P. Missal
Newark Public Schools
Newark, New Jersey

Catherine Fish Petersen (Retired)
East Islip School District
Islip Terrace, New York

Joe Wieczorek
Social Studies Consultant
Baltimore, Maryland

HISTORY OF OUR WORLD

Develop Skills

Use these pages to develop your reading, writing, and geography skills.

Focus on History

Learn about the geography, history, and cultures of the world from the beginnings of history to our world today.

Unit 5 Age of Encounter 390

- Learn map skills with the MapMaster Skills Handbook.
- Practice your skills with every map in this book.
- Interact with every map online and on CD-ROM.

Maps and illustrations created by DK help build your understanding of the world. The DK World Desk Reference Online keeps you up to date.

The World Studies Video Program takes you on field trips to study countries around the world.

The World Studies Interactive Textbook online and on CD-ROM uses interactive maps and other activities to help you learn.

Special Features

Literature

Explore the mythology of ancient Greece and the legends of King Arthur

Focus On

**Learn more about the people in world history—
their lives, their adventures, and the places in
which they lived.**

Skills for Life

Learn skills that you will use throughout your life.

See how social studies has fascinating links to

Links

other disciplines.

Links Across Time

Links Across the World

Links to Art

Links to Economics

Links to Government

Links to Language Arts

Citizen Heroes

Meet people who have made a difference in their civilization or society.

Target Reading Skills

Chapter-by-chapter reading skills help you read and understand social studies concepts.

DK Eyewitness Technology

Detailed drawings show how technology shapes places and societies.

Discovery Channel School

Explore the geography, history, and cultures of the world.

Maps and Charts

MAP✦MASTER™

MAP✦MASTER™ Interactive

Go online to find an interactive version of every MapMaster™ map in this book. Use the Web Code provided to gain direct access to these maps.

How to Use Web Codes:

1. Go to **www.PHSchool.com**.

2. Enter the Web Code.

3. Click Go!

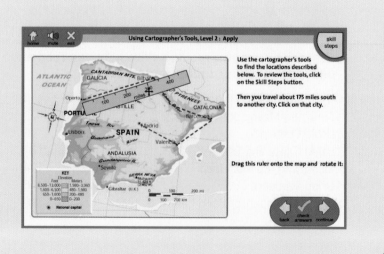

Charts, Graphs, and Tables

NCLB Implications for Social Studies

The No Child Left Behind (NCLB) legislation was a landmark in educational reform designed to improve student achievement and create a fundamental shift in American education. In the essay that follows, we will explore the implications of NCLB on social studies curriculum, instruction, assessment, and instructional programs.

Facts about NCLB

The No Child Left Behind Act of 2001 (NCLB) calls for sweeping educational reform, requiring all students to perform proficiently on standardized tests in reading, mathematics, and (soon to be added) science by the year 2014. Under NCLB, schools will be held accountable for students' academic progress. In exchange for this accountability, the law offers more flexibility to individual states and school districts to decide how best to use federal education funds. NCLB places an emphasis on implementing scientifically proven methods in teaching reading and mathematics, and promotes teacher quality. It also offers parental choice for students in failing schools.

Effects on Curriculum, Instruction, and Assessment

Since the primary focus of NCLB is on raising the achievement of students in reading and mathematics, some educators have wondered how it relates to social studies. Some teachers have expressed concerns that since NCLB does not require yearly testing of social studies, state and school districts may decide to shift resources and class time away from teaching social studies. However, NCLB considers the social studies areas of history, geography, economics, and government and civics to be core academic subjects. Many states are requiring middle grades social studies teachers to be highly qualified in history and geography in order to comply with the principle of improving teacher quality in NCLB.

NCLB sets the goal of having every child meet state-defined education standards. Since social studies educators have been leaders in the development of standards-based education and accountability through student testing over the past decade, many state and local districts have their own standards and assessments for social studies already in place. Assessment, including screening, diagnostic, progress-monitoring—including end-of-year, end-of-schooling, grade level, district, and state testing—and large-scale assessments, will continue to play a significant role in shaping social studies curriculum and instruction in the near future.

Integrating Reading into Social Studies Instruction

Due to the increased emphasis on reading and mathematics required by NCLB, social studies teachers may be called on to help improve their students' reading and math skills. For example, a teacher might use a graph about exports and imports to reinforce math skills, or a primary source about a historical event to improve reading skills. The connection between reading and social studies is especially important. Since many state and local assessments of reading require students to read and interpret informational texts, social studies passages are often used in the exams. Therefore, social studies teachers may assist in raising reading scores by integrating reading instruction into their teaching of social studies content.

Implications for Instructional Programs

The environment created by the NCLB legislation has implications for instructional programs. In keeping with the spirit of NCLB, social studies programs should clearly tie their content to state and local standards. Programs should also provide support so that all students can master these standards, ensuring that no child is left behind. An ideal instructional program is rooted in research, embeds reading instruction into the instructional design, and provides assessment tools that inform instruction—helping teachers focus on improving student performance.

Prentice Hall Response

We realize that raising the achievement level of all students is the number one challenge facing teachers today. To assist you in meeting this challenge, Prentice Hall enlisted a team of respected consultants who specialize in middle grades issues, reading in the content areas, and geographic education. This team created a middle grades world studies program that breaks new ground and meets the changing needs of you and your students.

With Prentice Hall, you can be confident that your students will not only be motivated, inspired, and excited to learn world studies, but they will also achieve the success needed in today's environment of the No Child Left Behind (NCLB) legislation and testing reform.

In the following pages, you will find the key elements woven throughout this World Studies program that truly set it apart and assure success for you and your students.

Teacher's Edition Contents in Brief

Research on Effective Reading Instruction

Why do many students have difficulty reading textbooks? How can we help students read to learn social studies? In the pages that follow, we examine the research on the challenge of reading textbooks; explain the direct, systematic, and explicit instruction needed to help students; and then show how Prentice Hall has responded to this research.

What is skilled reading?

Recent research (Snow et al., 2002) suggests that skillful and strategic reading is a long-term developmental process in which "readers learn how to simultaneously extract and construct meaning through interaction with written language." In other words, successful readers know how to decode all kinds of words, read with fluency and expression, have well-developed vocabularies, and possess various comprehension strategies such as note-taking and summarizing to employ as the academic reading task demands.

Many students lack reading skills

Sadly, many secondary students do not have solid reading skills. In the early years, students read mainly engaging and accessible narratives, such as stories, poems, and junior biographies. But in the upper elementary years, they shift toward conceptually dense and challenging nonfiction, or expository texts. It is no accident that the infamous "Fourth-Grade Slump" (Chall, 2003; Hirsch 2003)—a well-documented national trend of declining literacy after grade four—occurs during this time. The recent National Assessment of Educational Progress (NAEP, 2002) found that only 33 percent of eighth-grade students scored at or above the proficient level in reading.

Even students quite skilled in reading novels, short stories, and adolescent magazines typically come to middle school ill-equipped for the rigors of informational texts or reading to learn. They tend to dive right into a social studies chapter as if reading a recreational story. They don't first preview the material to create a mental outline and establish a reading purpose. They have not yet learned other basic strategies, including reading a section more than once, taking notes as they read, and reading to answer specific questions.

Dr. Kate Kinsella
Reading Consultant for
History of Our World
Department of Secondary Education
San Francisco State University, CA

Dr. Kevin Feldman
Reading Consultant for
History of Our World
Director of Reading and Early Intervention
Sonoma County, CA

"Even students quite skilled in reading novels, short stories, and adolescent magazines typically come to middle school ill-equipped for the rigors of informational texts or reading to learn."

The unique demands of textbooks

The differences between textbooks and the narratives students are used to reading are dramatic. The most distinctive challenges include dense conceptual content, heavy vocabulary load, unfamiliar paragraph and organizational patterns, and complex sentence structures. Academic texts present such a significant challenge to most students that linguists and language researchers liken them to learning a foreign language (Schleppegrell, 2002). In other words, most secondary students are second language learners: they are learning the academic language of informational texts!

Effective reading instruction

Research illustrates that virtually all students benefit from direct, systematic, and explicit instruction in reading informational texts (Baker & Gersten, 2000). There are three stages to the instructional process for content-area reading:

    (1) before reading: instructional frontloading;

    (2) during reading: guided instruction;

    (3) after reading: reflection and study.

Before reading

Placing a major emphasis on preteaching, or "front-loading" your instruction—building vocabulary, setting a purpose for reading, and explicitly teaching students strategies for actively engaging with the text—helps you structure learning to ensure student success (see Strategies 1 and 2 on pages T36-T37). Frontloading strategies are especially critical in mixed-ability classrooms with English language learners, students with special needs, and other students performing below grade level in terms of literacy.

During reading

In guided instruction, the teacher models approaches for actively engaging with text to gain meaning. The teacher guides students through the first reading of the text using passage reading strategies (see Strategies 3-7 on pages T37-T39), and then guides discussion about the content using participation strategies (see Strategies 8-11 on pages T39-T41). Finally, students record key information in a graphic organizer.

After reading

During the reflection and study phase, the teacher formally checks for student understanding, offers remediation if necessary, and provides activities that challenge students to apply content in a new way. To review the chapter, students recall content, analyze the reading as a whole, and study key vocabulary and information likely to be tested.

References

Baker, Scott and Russell Gersten. "What We Know About Effective Instructional Practices for English Language Learners." *Exceptional Children*, 66 (2000):454–470.

Chall, Jeanne S. and Vicki A. Jacobs. "Poor Children's Fourth-Grade Slump." *American Educator* (Spring 2003):14.

Donahue, P.L., et al. *The 1998 NAEP Reading Report Card for the Nation and the States* (NCES 1999-500). Washington, D.C.: U.S. Department of Education, Office of Education Research and Improvement, National Center for Education Statistics, 1999.

Grigg, W.S. et al. *The Nation's Report Card: Reading 2002* (NCES 2003-521). Washington D.C.: U.S. Department of Education, Institute of Education Sciences, National Center for Education Statistics, 2003.

Hirsch, E.D., Jr. "Reading Comprehension Requires Knowledge—of Words and the World." *American Educator* (Spring 2003):10-29.

Kinsella, Kate, et al. *Teaching Guidebook for Universal Access.* Upper Saddle River, NJ: Prentice Hall, 2002.

Schleppegrell, M. "Linguistic Features of the Language of Schooling." *Linguistics and Education*, 12, no. 4 (2002): 431–459.

Snow, C., et al. *Reading for Understanding: Toward an R&D Program in Reading Comprehension.* Santa Monica, California: The Rand Corporation, 2002.

Putting Research Into Practice

Prentice Hall enlisted the assistance of Dr. Kate Kinsella and Dr. Kevin Feldman to ensure that the new middle grades world history program would provide the direct, systematic, and explicit instruction needed to foster student success in reading informational texts. To help students rise to the challenge of reading an informational text, *History of Our World* embedded reading support right into the student text.

Embedded Reading Support in the Student Text

Before students read

- **Objectives** set the purpose for what students will read.
- **Target Reading Skill** for the section is explained.
- **Key Terms** are defined up front with pronunciation and part of speech.

During the section

- **Target Reading Skill** is applied to help students read and understand the narrative.
- **Key Terms** are defined in context, with terms and definitions called out in blue type.
- **Reading Checks** reinforce students' understanding by slowing them down to review after every concept is discussed.
- **Caption Questions** draw students into the art and photos, helping them to connect the content to the images.

After students read

- **Section Assessment** revisits the **Key Terms**, provides an opportunity to master the **Target Reading Skill**, allows student to rehearse their understanding of the text through the **Writing Activity**.

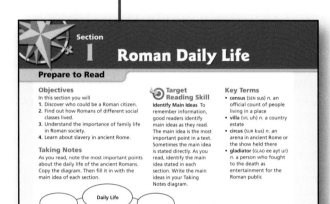

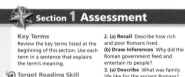

Gladiators wore helmets for protection.

Putting Research Into Practice

History of Our World offers teachers guidance in direct, systematic, and explicit reading instruction. The instructional sequence in the Teacher's Edition explicitly guides you in the use of effective strategies at each stage of the instructional process.

Reading Instruction in *History of Our World* Teacher's Edition

Before Reading

Every lesson plan begins with suggestions that help you integrate frontloading strategies into your teaching. Build Background Knowledge activates and builds prior knowledge. Set a Purpose for Reading prompts students to predict and anticipate content and motivates students to engage with the text. Preview Key Terms helps students learn Key Terms to understand the text. Target Reading Skill models a reading strategy to help students gain meaning from the text. Vocabulary Builder gives teachers definitions and sample sentences to help teach high-use words.

During Reading

In the "Instruct" part of the lesson plan, you can use suggestions for getting students actively engaged in the text. Guided Instruction clarifies high-use words, applies a passage-reading strategy to promote text comprehension, and guides discussion to construct meaning. Independent Practice prompts students to reread and take notes in the graphic organizer provided to rehearse understanding.

After Reading

The lesson plan closes with specific strategies for the reflection and study phase after reading is completed. Monitor Progress checks students' note taking, and verifies students' prereading predictions. Assess and Reteach measures students' recall of content and provides additional instruction if needed. Review Chapter Content promotes retention of key concepts and vocabulary.

Integrated Reading Resources

The *History of Our World* program provides instructional materials to support the reading instruction in the Teacher's Edition.

The **All-in-One Unit Booklets in the Teaching Resources** provides reading instruction support worksheets, such as a Reading Readiness Guide, Word Knowledge, and Vocabulary Development.

Students can use the **Reading and Vocabulary Study Guide** (English and Spanish) to reinforce reading instruction and vocabulary development, and to review section summaries of every section of the student text.

Research on Differentiated Instruction

It's basic, but it's true—not all our students learn in the same manner and not all our students have the same academic background or abilities. As educators, we need to respond to this challenge through the development and utilization of instructional strategies that address the needs of diverse learners, or the number of children who "fall through the cracks" will continue to rise (Kame'enui & Carnine, 1998).

Providing universal access

Universal access happens when curriculum and instruction are provided in ways that allow all learners to participate and to achieve (Kinsella, et al., 2002). Teachers who teach in heterogeneous, inclusive classrooms can provide universal access by modifying their teaching to respond to the needs of typical learners, gifted learners, less proficient readers, English language learners, and special needs students. Many of these learner populations benefit from extensive reading support (see pages T18-T21).

It is also critical to properly match the difficulty level of tasks with the ability level of students. Giving students tasks that they perceive as too hard lowers their expectations of success. However, giving students assignments that they think are too easy, undermines their feelings of competence (Stipek, 1996). Therefore, it is important for a program to give teachers leveled activities that allow them to match tasks with the abilities of their individual students.

When students connect to and are engaged with the content, comprehension and understanding increase. Technology, such as online activities, can provide an ideal opportunity for such engagement. It also can be used to provide additional opportunities to access content. For example, a less proficient reader may reinforce understanding of a key concept through watching a video. A complete social studies program makes content available in a variety of formats, including text, audio, visuals, and interactivities.

> "Universal access happens when curriculum and instruction are provided in ways that allow all learners to participate and to achieve (Kinsella, et al., 2002)."

Kame'enui, Edward and Douglas Carnine. *Effective Teaching Strategies that Accommodate Diverse Learners.* Upper Saddle River, NJ: Prentice Hall, 1998.

Kinsella, Kate, et al. *Teaching Guidebook for Universal Access.* Upper Saddle River, NJ: Prentice Hall, 2002.

Stipek, D.J. "Motivation and Instruction," in R.C. Clafee and D.C. Berlinger (Eds.), *Handbook of Educational Psychology.* New York: Macmillan, 1996.

Putting Research Into Practice

Prentice Hall recognizes that today's classrooms include students with diverse backgrounds and ability levels. Accordingly, the *History of Our World* program was designed to provide access to the content for all students. The program provides both the instructional materials to meet the learning needs of all students and the guidance you need to accommodate these needs.

Differentiated Instruction in the Teacher's Edition

The Teacher's Edition was designed to make it easy for teachers to modify instruction for diverse learners. Teaching strategies, provided by Dr. Kate Kinsella and Dr. Kevin Feldman, to help you modify your teaching are incorporated into every lesson plan. Specific activities help you differentiate instruction for individual students in five categories—less proficient readers, advanced readers, special needs students, gifted and talented, and English language learners. Resources are identified as being appropriate for use by each of these categories. All resources are also assigned a level—basic, average, and above average—so you know exactly how to assign tasks of appropriate difficulty level.

All-in-One Teaching Resources

Everything you need to provide differentiated instruction for each lesson, including reading support, activities and projects, enrichment, and assessment—in one convenient location.

World Studies Video Program

Students will benefit from our custom-built video program—the result of an exclusive partnership with Discovery Channel School—making content accessible through dynamic footage and high-impact stories.

Student Edition on Audio CD

The complete narrative is read aloud, section by section, providing extra support for auditory learners, English language learners, and reluctant readers. Also available is the Guided Reading Audio CD (English/Spanish), containing section summaries read aloud.

Interactive Textbook—The Student Edition Online and on CD-ROM

The Interactive Textbook allows students to interact with the content, including reading aids, visual and interactive learning tools, and instant feedback assessments.

Differentiated Instruction

For Less Proficient Readers [L1]
Have students read the section in the Reading and Vocabulary Study Guide. This version provides basic-level instruction in an interactive format with questions and write-on lines.
Chapter 4, Section 1, **Latin America Reading and Vocabulary Study Guide**, pp. 42–44

For Special Needs Students [L1]
Have students read the section as they listen to the recorded version on the Student Edition on Audio CD. Check for comprehension by pausing the CD and asking students to share their answers to the Reading Checks.
Chapter 4, Section 1, **Student Edition on Audio CD**

Learn about how natural hazards affect life in Mexico.

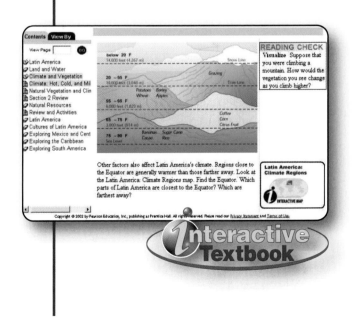

Research on Geographic Literacy

As the *Geography for Life: National Geography Standards* (1994) state, "There is now a widespread acceptance among the people of the United States that being literate in geography is essential if students are to leave school equipped to earn a decent living, enjoy the richness of life, and participate responsibly in local, national, and international affairs." A middle grades social studies program needs to help teachers produce students who are literate in geography.

Geographic literacy defined

Results for the 2001 National Assessment of Educational Progress (NAEP) Geography assessment show that the average scores of fourth- and eighth-grade students have improved since 1994. The average score of twelfth-grade students, however, has not changed significantly. In order to make the critical leap from basic geography skills to the kind of geographic literacy needed by the twelfth grade and beyond, a program must teach both geography content and geography skills, and then help students think critically. Geography content is made up of the essential knowledge that students need to know about the world. Geography skills are the ability to ask geographic questions, acquire and analyze geographic information, and answer these questions. To be truly literate in geography, students must be able to apply their knowledge and skills to understand the world.

Elements for success in middle grades

Students in the elementary grades don't always get enough training in geography. In order to help all students gain a base upon which to build middle grades geographic literacy, a program should introduce basic geography skills at the beginning of the school year.

The quality of maps is also vital to the success of a middle grades world studies program. Maps must be developmentally appropriate for middle grades students. They should be clean, clear, and accurate. Maps should be attractive and present subject matter in appealing ways, so that students *want* to use them to learn.

Another element that can lead to success is the incorporation of technology into the teaching and learning of geography, specifically the Internet. Research has shown that 8th grade students with high Internet usage scored higher in geography (NAEP, 2001).

U.S. Department of Education, Office of Educational Research and Improvement, National Center for Education Statistics, National Assessment of Educational Progress (NAEP), 2001 Geography Assessment.

Andrew Heritage
Head of Cartography
Dorling Kindersley (DK)

"Maps should be attractive and present subject matter in appealing ways, so that students *want* to use them to learn."

Putting Research Into Practice

Prentice Hall partnered with DK—internationally known for their dynamic atlases—to develop the *History of Our World* program. DK's Andrew Heritage and his world-renowned cartography team designed all maps, resulting in stunning, high quality maps that are middle grades appropriate.

The MapMaster™ System

History of Our World offers the first interactive geography instruction system available with a world studies textbook.

Introduce Basic Map Skills

The MapMaster™ Skills Handbook, a DK-designed introduction to the basics, brings students up to speed with a complete overview at the beginning of every book.

Build Geographic Literacy with Every Map

Scaffolded questions start with questions that require basic geography content and skills, and then ask students to demonstrate geographic literacy by thinking critically about the map.

Activate Learning Online

MapMaster™ Interactive—online and on CD-ROM—allows students to put their knowledge of geography skills and content into practice through interactivities.

Extend Learning with DK

• **DK World Desk Reference Online** is filled with up-to-date data, maps, and visuals that connect students to a wealth of information about the world's countries.

• **DK Compact Atlas of the World** with MapMaster™ Teacher's Companion provides activities to introduce, develop, and master geography and map skills.

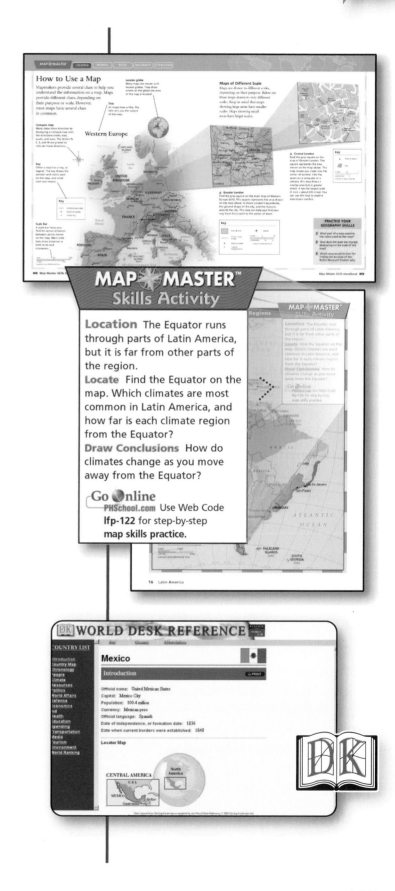

Research on Assessment

Meeting the NCLB challenge will necessitate an integrated approach to assessment with a variety of assessment tools. With the spotlight now on *improving* student performance, it is essential to use assessment results to inform instruction.

Assessments Tools for Informing Instruction

The key to success is using a variety of assessment tools coupled with data analysis and decision making. Teachers work with information coming from four kinds of assessment.

Screening assessments are brief procedures used to identify at-risk students who are not ready to work at grade level.

Diagnostic assessments provide a more in-depth analysis of strengths and weaknesses that can help teachers make instructional decisions and plan intervention strategies.

Progress-monitoring assessments (sometimes referred to as benchmark tests) provide an ongoing, longitudinal record of student achievement detailing individual student progress toward meeting end-of-year and end-of-schooling, grade level, district, or state standards.

Large-scale assessments, such as state tests and standardized tests, are used to determine whether individual students have met the expected standards and whether a school system has made adequate progress in improving its performance.

Ongoing Assessment

Daily assessment should be embedded in the program before, during, and after instruction in the core lessons. Legitimate test preparation experiences also should be embedded in the program. Test preparation involves teaching students strategies for taking tests, such as eliminating answers, reading comprehension, and writing extended response answers.

Eileen Depka
Supervisor of Standards and Assessment
Waukesha, WI

"Meeting the NCLB challenge will necessitate an integrated approach to assessment with a variety of assessment tools."

Putting Research Into Practice

Prentice Hall developed the *History of Our World* program with a variety of assessment tools, including ongoing assessment in the student text.

Assessments for Informing Instruction

History of Our World was designed to provide you with all four kinds of assessment.

- **Screening test** identifies students who are reading 2-3 years below grade level.

- **Diagnostic tests** focus on skills needed for success in social studies, including subtests in geographic literacy, visual analysis, critical thinking and reading, and communications skills, as well as vocabulary and writing.

- **Benchmark tests**, to be given six times throughout the year, monitor student progress in the course.

- **Outcome test**, to be administered at the end of the year, evaluates student mastery of social studies content standards.

Ongoing Assessment

- **Student Edition** offers section and chapter assessments with questions building from basic comprehension to critical thinking and writing.

- **Test Prep Workbook** and **Test-taking Strategies with Transparencies** develop students' test-taking skills and improve their scores on standardized tests.

- **ExamView® Test Bank CD-ROM** allows you to quickly and easily develop customized tests from a bank of thousands of questions.

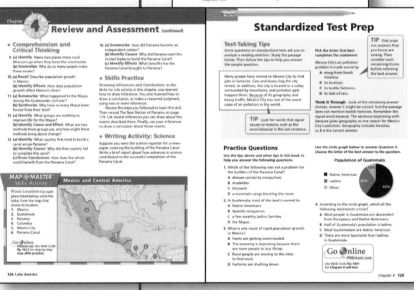

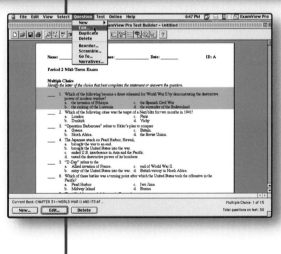

History of Our World Skills Scope and Sequence

History of Our World contains a comprehensive program of core skills. Each skill is taught in every book of the series. A Target Reading Skill is located at the beginning of each chapter and expanded upon in each section within the chapter. Core skills are also taught either in the "Skills for Life Activity" in the Student Edition, or in a "Skills Mini Lesson" in the Teacher's Edition. In addition, worksheets for the students' use in completing each skill are located in the All-in-One Unit Booklets in the Teaching Resources. The chart below lists the skills covered in *History of Our World* and the chapter or chapters in which each skill is taught.

History of Our World Analysis Skills	SE	TE
Analyzing Graphic Data	Ch. 4	Ch. 4
Analyzing Images		Chs. 2, 15
Analyzing Primary Sources	Ch. 7	Ch. 13
Clarifying Meaning	Chs. 2, 11, 16	Chs. 2, 11, 16
Comparing and Contrasting	Ch. 9	Chs. 9, 11
Distinguishing Fact and Opinion	Ch. 14	Ch. 14
Drawing Inferences and Conclusions	Ch. 6	Ch. 6
Identifying Cause and Effect/Making Predictions	Chs. 1, 4, 9, 13, 15	Chs. 4, 12, 13, 15
Identifying Frame of Reference and Point of View	Ch. 15	Chs. 2, 6, 15
Identifying Main Ideas/Summarizing	Chs. 2, 5, 9, 12, 17	Chs. 5, 9, 12, 17
Making Valid Generalizations	Ch. 5	Chs. 5, 10
Problem Solving		Ch. 13
Recognizing Bias and Propaganda	Ch. 16	Chs. 7, 16
Sequencing	Chs. 6, 14	Chs. 6, 8, 12, 14
Supporting a Position	Ch. 17	Chs. 16, 17
Synthesizing Information	Ch. 8	Chs. 3, 8
Transferring Information From One Medium to Another		Ch. 5
Using the Cartographer's Tools		Chs. 1, 9, 11
Using Context	Ch. 3	Ch. 3
Using the Reading Process	Chs. 1, 10	Chs. 1, 10
Using Reliable Information	Ch. 11	Chs. 4, 11
Using Special-Purpose Maps	Ch. 2	Ch. 2
Using Word Analysis	Ch. 8	Ch. 8

Pacing Options

History of Our World offers many aids to help you plan your instruction time, whether regular class periods or block scheduling. Section-by-section lesson plans for each chapter include suggested times, based on the 36-week course configuration below. Teacher Express CD-ROM will help you manage your time electronically.

Pacing Options		18-week unit	36-week unit
Chapter 1	Section 1	2	3
	Section 2	2	3
	Section 3	2	3
Chapter 2	Section 1	1	2
	Section 2	1	2
	Section 3	1	2
	Section 4	2	3
	Section 5	2	4
Chapter 3	Section 1	1	2
	Section 2	1	2
	Section 3	1	2
	Section 4	2	3
	Section 5	2	4
Chapter 4	Section 1	1	2
	Section 2	1	2
	Section 3	2	2
	Section 4	2	3
Chapter 5	Section 1	1	3
	Section 2	1	2
	Section 3	2	2
	Section 4	2	4
Chapter 6	Section 1	1	3
	Section 2	1	4
Chapter 7	Section 1	1	4
	Section 2	2	4
	Section 3	2	4
Chapter 8	Section 1	1	3
	Section 2	1	3
Chapter 9	Section 1	1	4
	Section 2	2	3
	Section 3	2	3

Pacing Options		18-week unit	36-week unit
Chapter 10	Section 1	2	3
	Section 2	1	3
	Section 3	2	3
Chapter 11	Section 1	2	3
	Section 2	2	4
	Section 3	2	4
Chapter 12	Section 1	2	3
	Section 2	1	4
	Section 3	2	4
Chapter 13	Section 1	2	4
	Section 2	1	4
	Section 3	2	4
Chapter 14	Section 1	1	2
	Section 2	1	4
	Section 3	2	4
	Section 4	2	3
Chapter 15	Section 1	1	4
	Section 2	1	2
	Section 3	2	2
	Section 4	2	4
Chapter 16	Section 1	2	4
	Section 2	1	3
	Section 3	1	3
Chapter 17	Section 1	2	3
	Section 2	2	3
	Section 3	2	3
	Section 4	1	3
Total Number of Days		**90**	**180**

Correlation to *Geography for Life,* the National Geography Standards

On the following pages, *Prentice Hall History of Our World* is correlated with *Geography for Life*, the National Geography Standards. These standards were prepared in response to the Goals 2000, Educate America Act, by the Geography Education Standards Project. Participating in the project were the American Geographical Society, the Association of American Geographers, the National Council for Geographic Education, and the National Geographic Society. Concepts and skills contained in the Geography Standards are incorporated throughout the program. This correlation list areas in which the standards are directly addressed.

Standard	History of Our World
The World in Spatial Terms	
Standard 1 Use maps and other geographic representations, tools, and technologies to acquire, process, and report information from a spatial perspective.	MapMaster Skills Handbook, 1:2, 2:1, 2:2, 2:3, 2:5, 3:1, 3:2, 3:5, 4:1, 4:4, 5:1, 5:3, 5:4, 7:2, 7:3, 8:1, 8:2, 9:2, 9:3, 10:1, 10:2, 12:1, 12:2, 13:1, 13:2, 13:3, 14:1, 15:1, 15:4, 16:1, 17:2
Standard 2 Use mental maps to organize information about people, places, and environments in a spatial context.	MapMaster Skills Handbook, 1:1–3, 2:4, 3:1, 4:1, 8:2, 12:3, 14:1, Skills for Life: Ch. 3, Review and Assessment: Chs. 1, 3
Standard 3 Analyze the spatial organization of people, places, and environments on Earth's surface.	MapMaster Skills Handbook, 1:2, 1:3, 2:1, 2:2, 2:4, 2:5, 3:1, 3:2, 3:5, 4:1, 4:3, 4:4, 5:1, 5:3, 5:4, 6:1, 7:2, 7:3, 8:1, 8:2, 9:2, 9:3, 12:3, 14:1, 16:1, Skills for Life: Chs. 3, 5, Focus On: Chs. 4, 5, 6, Review and Assessment: Chs. 2, 5
Places and Regions	
Standard 4 Understand the physical and human characteristics of places.	MapMaster Skills Handbook, 1:1–3, 2:1, 2:2, 2:4, 3:1, 3:2, 3:4, 3:5, 4:1, 4:3, 4:4, 6:1, 6:2, 7:1, 8:1–2, 9:1–3, 10:1, 11:1–3, 12:1–3, 14:1, 15:1, Focus On, Chs. 1–4, 6, 8, Review and Assessment: Chs. 1–4, 6–9
Standard 5 Understand that people create regions to interpret Earth's complexity.	MapMaster Skills Handbook, 1:3, 2:1, 3:1, 4:1, 5:1, 6:1, 8:1, 11:1, 12:2, 13: 3, 14:4, 15:1, 16:3, Review and Assessment: Chs. 1, 2, 5
Standard 6 Understand how culture and experience influence people's perception of places and regions.	MapMaster Skills Handbook, World Overview, 1:1–3, 2:1–5, 3:1, 3:3, 3:4, 3:5, 4:1, 4:3, 4:4, 5:1, 5:3, 5:4, 5:5, 6:1, 8:1, 12:3, 16:2, Skills for Life: Ch. 5, Focus On: Chs. 1, 4, Review and Assessment: Chs. 1–17
Physical Systems	
Standard 7 Understand the physical processes that shape the patterns of Earth's surface.	MapMaster Skills Handbook, 1:1, 2:1, 3:1, 4:1, 5:1, 6:1, 8:1, 11:1, 12:3, Skills for Life: Ch. 5, Review and Assessment: Chs. 2, 3, 4
Standard 8 Understand the characteristics and spatial distribution of ecosystems on Earth's surface.	MapMaster Skills Handbook, 1:1–3, 2:1, 3:1, 4:1, 5:1, 11:1, 13:1, 14:2, Focus On: Chs. 1, 2, Review and Assessment: Chs. 1, 2, 3

Correlation to *Geography for Life*, the National Geography Standards (continued)

Standard	History of Our World
Human Systems	
Standard 9 Understand the characteristics, distribution, and migration of human populations on Earth's surface.	MapMaster Skills Handbook, 1:1–3, 2:1, 2:2, 2:4, 2:5, 3:1, 3:2, 3:5, 4:1, 4:3, 4:4, 5:1, 5:3, 5:4, 6:1–2, 7:1–3, 10:2, 11:1, 11:3, 12:1, 12:3, 14:1, 16:2, 17:1, 17:4, Focus On: Chs. 3, 4, 7, Review and Assessment: Chs. 1–17
Standard 10 Understand the characteristics, distribution, and complexity of Earth's cultural mosaics.	MapMaster Skills Handbook, 1:1–3, 2:1–5, 3:1–5, 4:1–4, 5:1–4, 6:1–2, 7:1–3, 8:1–2, 9:1–2, 10:3, 11:3, 12:1, 14:5, 15:2, 16:2, 17:1–4, Focus On: Chs. 1–17, Skills for Life: Chs. 2 4, 6, Review and Assessment: Chs. 1–17
Standard 11 Understand the patterns and networks of economic interdependence on Earth's surface.	MapMaster Skills Handbook, 1:1, 1:3, 2:1, 2:2, 2:4, 3:1, 3:2, 3:5, 5:4, 6:1–2, 7:1–3, 8:1–2, 9:1, 10:1, 12:2, 13:1, 13:3, 14:2, 16:1, 16:2, 17:1–4, Skills for Life, Ch. 5, Focus On: Chs. 3, 4, 7, 10, 14, 17, Review and Assessment: Chs. 1–17
Standard 12 Understand the processes, patterns, and functions of human settlement.	MapMaster Skills Handbook, 1:1–3, 2:1, 2:2, 2:4, 2:5, 3:1, 3:2, 3:4, 3:5, 4:1, 4:4, 5:1, 5:3, 5:4, 6:1–5, 7:1, 7:2, 7:3, Skills for Life: Ch. 5, Focus On: Chs. 3, 4, 6, Review and Assessment: Chs. 1–7
Standard 13 Understand how the forces of cooperation and conflict among people influence division and control of Earth's surface.	2:1, 2:2, 2:4, 2:5, 3:1, 3:4, 3:5, 4:1–4, 5:1, 5:2, 5:3, 5:4, 6:1, 7:2, 7:3, 10:2, 11:3, 13:2, 14:3, 15:4, 17:1–4, Focus On: Chs. 4, 5
Environment and Society	
Standard 14 Understand how human actions modify the physical environment.	1:1–3, 2:1, 2:2, 3:1, 3:2, 3:3, 3:4, 4:1, 4:4, 5:1, 5:2, 5:3, 8:2, 11:3, 12:1–3, 14:1, 14:3, 17:1–3, Focus On: Chs. 2, 3, 7, 16, 17
Standard 15 Understand how physical systems affect human systems.	1:1–3, 2:1, 2:4, 3:1, 3:4, 4:1, 5:1, 6:1, 8:1, 8:2, 10:2, 12:2, Skills for Life: Chs. 3, 5, Focus On: Ch. 2, Review and Assessment: Chs. 1–7
Standard 16 Understand the changes that occur in the meaning, use, distribution, and importance of resources.	1:1–3, 2:1, 2:2, 2:3, 2:4, 3:1, 3:2, 3:4, 3:5, 4:4, 5:3, 5:4, 6:1, 8:1, 8:2, 9:3, 10:1, 11:3, 12:1–3, 13:1–3, 14:2, 16:3, Review and Assessment: Chs. 1, 5
The Uses of Geography	
Standard 17 Understand how to apply geography to interpret the past.	MapMaster Skills Handbook, 1:1–3, 2:1, 2:2, 2:4, 3:1, 3:2, 3:5, 4:1, 4:3, 4:4, 5:1, 5:3, 5:4, 6:1, 7:3, 8:1, 10:1–2, 11:1, 12:1, 12:3, 13:1–3, 16:1, 17:1, 17:3, Review and Assessment, Chs. 1–17
Standard 18 Understand how to apply geography to interpret the present and plan for the future.	MapMaster Skills Handbook, 1:1–3, 2:1, 2:4, 2:5, 3:1, 3:4, 4:1, 4:4, 5:2, 11:3, Review and Assessment: Ch. 1

Correlation to the NCSS Curriculum Standards

On the following pages *Prentice Hall History of Our World* is correlated with *Expectations of Excellence*, the Curriculum Standards for Social Studies. These standards were developed by the National Council for the Social Studies to address overall curriculum design and comprehensive student performance expectations.

Standard	History of Our World
Performance Expectations 1: Culture	
• compare similarities and differences in the ways groups, societies, and cultures meet human needs and concerns • explain how information and experiences may be interpreted by people from diverse cultural perspectives and frames of reference • explain and give examples of how language, literature, the arts, architecture, other artifacts, traditions, beliefs, values, and behaviors contribute to the development and transmission of culture • explain why individuals and groups respond differently to their physical and social environments and/or changes to them on the basis of shared assumptions, values, and beliefs • articulate the implications of cultural diversity, as well as cohesion, within and across groups	MapMaster Skills Handbook, 1:1–3, 2:1–5, 3:1–5, 4:1–4, 5:1–4, 6:1–2, 7:1–3, 8:1–2, 9:1–3, 12:1–3, 13:1–3, 14:1–3, 15:1–4, 16:1–3, 17:1–4, Focus On: Chs. 1–17, Review and Assessment: Chs. 1–17
Performance Expectations 2: Time, Continuity, and Change	
• demonstrate an understanding that different scholars may describe the same event or situation in different ways but must provide reasons or evidence for their view • identify and use key concepts such as chronology, causality, change, conflict, and complexity to explain, analyze, and show connections among patterns of historical change and continuity • identify and describe selected historical periods and patterns of change within and across cultures • identify and use processes important to reconstructing and reinterpreting the past • develop critical sensitivities regarding attitudes, values, and behaviors of people in different historical contexts • use knowledge of facts and concepts drawn from history, along with methods of historical inquiry, to inform decision-making about and action-taking on public issues	MapMaster Skills Handbook, 1:1–3, 2:1–5, 3:1–5, 4:1–4, 5:1, 5:2, 5:4, 6:1–2, 7:1–3, 8:1–2, 9:1, 9:3, 10:1–4, 11:1–3, 12:1–3, 13:1–2, 14:1–4, 15:1–4, 16:1–3, 17:1–4, Focus On: Chs. 1, 2, 4, 6, 7, 8, 10, 12, 17, Review and Assessment: Chs. 1–17
Performance Expectations 3: People, Places, and Environment	
• elaborate mental maps of locales, regions, and the world that demonstrate understanding of relative location, direction, size, and shape • create, interpret, use, and distinguish various representations of the earth • use appropriate resources, data sources, and geographic tools to generate, manipulate, and interpret information • estimate distance, calculate scale, and distinguish geographic relationships • locate and describe varying landforms and geographic features and explain their relationship with the ecosystem • describe physical system changes and identify geographic patterns associated with them • describe how people create places that reflect cultural values and ideals • examine, interpret, and analyze physical and cultural patterns and their interactions • describe ways that historical events have been influenced by, and have influenced, physical and human geographic factors in local, regional, national, and global settings • observe and speculate about social and economic effects of environmental changes and crises resulting from natural phenomena • propose, compare, and evaluate alternative uses of land and resources in communities, regions, nations, and the world	MapMaster Skills Handbook, 1:1–3, 2:1–5, 3:1, 3:2, 3:4, 3:5, 4:1, 4:4, 5:1, 5:3, 5:4, 6:1–2, 7:1–3, 8:1–2, 9:1, 9:3, 10:1, 11:1–2, 12:1–3, 13:1–3, 14:1–3, 15:1, 15:4, 16:1, 17:1, 17:2, Skills for Life: Chs. 3, 5, Focus On, Chs. 2, 3, 4, 6, 17, Review and Assessment: Chs. 1–17

Correlation to the NCSS Curriculum Standards *(continued)*

Standard	History of Our World
Performance Expectations 4: Individual Development and Identity	
• relate personal changes to social, cultural, and historical contexts • describe personal connections to place—as associated with community, nation, and world • describe the ways family, gender, ethnicity, nationality, and institutional affiliations contribute to personal identity • relate such factors as physical endowment and capabilities, learning, motivation, personality, perception, and behavior to individual development • identify and describe ways regional, ethnic, and national cultures influence individuals' daily lives • identify and describe the influence of perception, attitudes, values, and beliefs on personal identity • identify and interpret examples of stereotyping, conformity, and altruism • work independently and cooperatively to accomplish goals	1:1, 2:1, 2:3, 2:4, 2:5, 3:2, 3:3, 3:4, 3:5, 4:1–4, 5:1–4, 6:1–2, 7:1–3, 8:1–2, 9:1, 9:3, 10:3, 11:1, 11:3, 12:1–3, 14:1–2, 15:1–4, 16:1–3, 17:1–4, Focus Ons: 4, 6, 7, 10, 11,12, 13, 14, 17, Review and Assessment: Chs. 1–17
Performance Expectations 5: Individuals, Groups, & Institutions	
• demonstrate an understanding of concepts such as role, status, and social class in describing interactions of individuals and social groups • analyze group and institutional influences on people, events, and elements of culture • describe the various forms institutions take and the interactions of people with institutions • identify and analyze examples of tensions between expressions of individuality and group or institutional efforts to promote social conformity • identify and describe examples of tensions between belief systems and government policies and laws • describe the role of institutions in furthering both continuity and change • apply knowledge of how groups and institutions work to meet individual needs and promote the common good	1:3, 2:1-5, 3:2, 3:3, 3:4, 3:5, 4:1–4, 5:1–4, 6:1, 6:2, 8:1–2, 9:1–3, 11:1, 11:3, 12:1–3, 14:1–4, 15:1–4, 16:1–3, 17:1–4, Focus On: 1, 2, 4, 7, 15, 17, Review and Assessment: Chs. 1–17
Performance Expectations 6: Power, Authority, and Governance	
• examine persistent issues involving the rights, roles, and status of the individual in relation to general welfare • describe the purpose of government and how its powers are acquired, used, and justified • analyze and explain ideas and governmental mechanisms to meet needs and wants of citizens, regulate territory, manage conflict, and establish order and security • describe the ways nations and organizations respond to forces of unity and diversity affecting order and security • identify and describe the basic features of the political system in the United States, and identify representative leaders from various levels and branches of government • explain conditions, actions, and motivations that contribute to conflict and cooperation within and among nations • describe and analyze the role of technology as it contributes to or helps resolve conflicts • explain how power, role, status, and justice influence the examination of persistent issues and social problems • give examples and explain how governments attempt to achieve their stated ideals at home and abroad	1:3, 2:2, 2:3, 2:4, 3:2, 3:5, 4:1, 4:4, 5:1, 5:2, 5:3, 6:1, 6:2, 7:2, 7:3, 8:1, 8:2, 9:1, 9:3, 10:1–2, 11:2, 11:3, 12:2, 13:1–3, 14: 1, 14:4, Review and Assessment, Chs. 1–4, 6–14

Correlation to the NCSS Curriculum Standards *(continued)*

Standard	History of Our World
Performance Expectation 7: Production, Distribution, and Consumption	
• give examples of ways that economic systems structure choices about how goods and services are to be produced and distributed • describe the role that supply and demand, prices, incentives, and profits play in determining what is produced and distributed in a competitive market system • explain differences between private and public goods and services • describe a range of examples of the various institutions that make up economic systems • describe the role of specialization and exchange in the economic process • explain and illustrate how values and beliefs influence different economic decisions • differentiate among various forms of exchange and money • compare basic economic systems according to who determines what is produced, distributed, and consumed • use economic concepts to help explain historical and current events in local, national, or global concepts • use economic reasoning to compare different proposals for dealing with contemporary social issues	2:1, 2:2, 2:4, 3:1, 3:2, 3:4, 3:5, 4:4, 5:3, 5:4, 6:1, 7:3, 8:1, 9:1, 9:3, 10:1, 11:2, 11:3, 13:1, 15:2, 16:3, 17:4, Review and Assessment: Chs. 1, 2, 5, 6, 7, 8, 9, 11, 15, 16, 17
Performance Expectation 8: Science, Technology, and Society	
• examine and describe the influence of culture on scientific and technological choices and advancement • show through specific examples how science and technology have changed peoples' perceptions of their social and natural world • describe examples in which values, beliefs, and attitudes have been influenced by new scientific and technological knowledge • explain the need for laws and policies to govern scientific and technological applications • seek reasonable and ethical solutions to problems that arise when scientific advancements and social norms or values come into conflict	1:1–3, 2:1, 2:2, 2:3, 2:4, 3:1–5, 4:1, 5:1, 5:3, 5:4, 6:1, 6:2, 7:3, 8:2, 9:3, 10:1, 10:4, 11:2, 11:3, 12:2, 13:1, 13:3, 14:1, 15:2, 15:4, 16:1, Focus On: Chs. 2, 4, 15
Performance Expectation 9: Global Connections	
• describe instances in which language, art, music, and belief systems, and other cultural elements can facilitate global understanding or cause misunderstanding • analyze examples of conflict, cooperation, and interdependence among groups, societies, and nations • describe and analyze the effects of changing technologies on the global community • explore the causes, consequences, and possible solutions to persistent contemporary and emerging global interests • describe and explain the relationships and tensions between national sovereignty and global interests • demonstrate understanding of concerns, standards, issues, and conflicts related to universal human rights • identify and describe the roles of international and multinational organizations	1:1–3, 2:2, 2:3, 2:4, 2:5, 3:2, 3:4, 3:5, 4;1–4, 5:2, 5:3, 5:4, 6:1, 6:2, 7:2, 7:3, 8:1–2, 9:2, 9:3, 10:1, 11:1–3, 12:2, 13:1, 13:3, 15:1, 15:2, 16:1–3, 17:1–4, Focus Ons: Chs. 1, 5, 6, 7, 15, 16, Review and Assessment: Chs. 1–17

Correlation to the NCSS Curriculum Standards *(continued)*

Standard	History of Our World
Performance Expectation 10: Civic Ideals and Practices	
• examine the origins and continuing influence of key ideals of the democratic republican form of government, such as individual human dignity, liberty, justice, equality, and rule of law • identify and interpret sources and examples of the rights and responsibilities of citizens • locate, access, analyze, organize, and apply information about selected public issues—recognizing and explaining multiple points of view • practice forms of civic discussion and participation consistent with the ideals of citizens in a democratic republic • explain and analyze various forms of citizen action that influence public policy decisions • identify and explain the roles of formal and informal political actors in influencing and shaping public policy and decision-making • analyze the influence of diverse forms of public opinion on the development of public policy and decision-making • analyze the effectiveness of selected public policies and citizen behaviors in realizing the stated ideals of a democratic republican form of government • explain the relationship between policy statements and action plans used to address issues of public concern • examine strategies designed to strengthen the "common good," which consider a range of options for citizen action	2:3, 3:4, 4:4, 5:2, 6:1, 6:2, 7:1, 8:1, 11:3, 13:1–3, 14:1–3, 15:4, 17:3, Focus On: Ch. 8

Instructional Strategies for Improving Student Comprehension

In response to today's environment of the NCLB legislation and testing reform, Prentice Hall asked Dr. Kate Kinsella and Dr. Kevin Feldman to provide specific instructional strategies you can use to improve student comprehension. Their guidance informed the development of the *History of Our World* Teacher's Edition. The lesson plans in this Teacher's Edition incorporate the following instructional strategies to enhance students' comprehension.

There is no single magical strategy that will solve all of the difficulties students encounter in reading challenging content area texts. Secondary students in mixed-ability classrooms depend on teachers to use a consistent set of research-informed and classroom-tested strategies in a patient and recursive manner—not the occasional or random use of different strategies. Students will not become skillful readers of content area texts in a week or two of instruction. However, when teachers engage students in the consistent use of a well-chosen set of content reading strategies appropriately matched to the demands of the text and the students' level of knowledge, their ability to comprehend difficult grade level texts will be dramatically enhanced.

Strategy 1: Set a Purpose for Reading

This program has two types of activities designed to help students set a purpose for reading:
an Anticipation Guide and a KWL chart. The two types rotate by section.

A. Anticipation Guide

Purpose: To focus students' attention on key concepts, and guide them to interact with ideas in the text

1. Distribute the *Reading Readiness Guide*. Read each statement aloud, and then ask students to react to the statements individually and in groups, marking their responses in the Before Reading column.

2. Use the worksheet as a springboard for discussing the section's key concepts as a unified class. Refrain from revealing the correct responses at this time, to avoid taking away the need for them to read the text.

3. Have students read the section with the purpose of finding evidence that confirms, disproves, or elaborates each statement in the *Reading Readiness Guide.*

4. After students finish reading, have them return to the statements and mark the After Reading column on their worksheets. Have them locate information from the text that supports or disproves each statement.

5. Discuss what the class has learned and probe for any lingering confusion about key concepts.

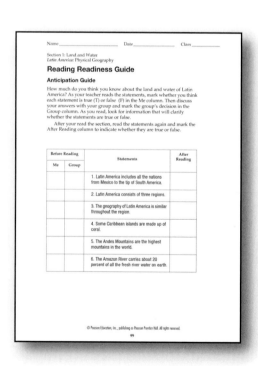

B. KWL

Purpose: To engage students before, during, and after reading

The KWL worksheet guides students to recall what they **K**now, determine what they **W**ant to learn, and identify what they **L**earn as they read.

1. Distribute the *Reading Readiness Guide*. Brainstorm with the group about what they already know about the topic. List students' ideas on the board. Encourage students to generate questions at points of ambiguity.

2. Students then list pieces of information they already know and questions they want to answer in the first two columns of their worksheets.

3. As students read the section, ask them to note information that answers their questions or adds to what they know.

4. After reading, facilitate a class discussion about what the students have learned. Clarify any lingering confusion about key concepts.

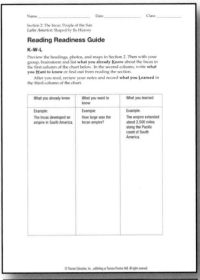

Strategy 2: Teach High-Use Academic Words

Purpose: To teach students words used often in academic texts, beyond the content-specific Key Terms

How to Do It

1. Have students rate how well they know each word on their *Word Knowledge* worksheets. Tell them there is no penalty for a low rating.

2. Survey students' ratings to decide which words need the most instruction.

3. Provide a brief definition or sample sentence for each word. (See Vocabulary Builder at the beginning of each section for definitions and sample sentences.) Rephrase your explanation, leaving out the word and asking students to substitute it aloud.

4. Work with students as they fill in the "Definition or Example" column of their *Word Knowledge* worksheets.

5. Point out each word in context as you read the chapters. Consider allowing students to earn extra credit if they use a word correctly in class discussion or assignments.

Strategy 3: Oral Cloze

Purpose: To help students read actively while the teacher reads aloud

How to Do It

1. Choose a passage and direct students to "read aloud silently using their inner voices." Be sure students understand reading is an active process, not simply a listening activity, and their job is to follow along—eyes riveted to each word, saying the words to themselves as you read aloud.

2. Tell students to be on their "reading toes," for you will be leaving out an occasional word and their task is to chorally supply the word.

3. The first few times you use the Oral Cloze, demonstrate by telling the students in advance what word you will be leaving out, directing them to read the word at the right time. Practice this a few times until they have the feel for the procedure. Leave out fewer words as students become more familiar with the Oral Cloze and require less direction to remain focused during teacher read alouds.

Strategies for Improving Student Comprehension (continued)

Strategy 4: Choral Reading

Purpose: To have students attend to the text in a non-threatening atmosphere

How to Do It

1. Choose a relatively short passage.

2. Tell students that you will all read the text aloud at once. Direct students to "keep your voice with mine" as they read.

3. Read the passage slowly and clearly.

4. Have students read the text again silently.

Strategy 5: Structured Silent Reading

Purpose: To give students a task as they read silently to increase their attentiveness and accountability

How to Do It

1. Assign a section to read silently. Pose a question for the whole class to answer from their silent reading, such as the Reading Check question at the end of each subsection. Model how one thinks while reading to find answers to a question.

2. When students get used to reading to answer the Reading Check question, pose more in-depth questions, progressing from factual recall to questions that stimulate interpretive or applied thinking.

3. Teach students to ask and answer their own questions as they read. Model this process by reading a section aloud and asking and answering your own questions as you read.

4. After the students have finished reading, engage the class in a brief discussion to clarify questions, vocabulary, and key concepts.

Strategy 6: Paragraph Shrinking

Purpose: To increase comprehension during reading

How to Do It

1. Partner struggling students with more proficient students and assign a manageable portion of the text.

2. Ask one member of each pair to identify the "who or what" the paragraph is about and tell the other.

3. Have the other member of the pair identify important details about the "who or what" and tell the other.

4. Ask the first member to summarize the paragraph in fifteen to twenty words or less using the most important details. The second member of the pair monitors the number of words and says "Shrink it!" if the summary goes over twenty words.

5. Have the partners reverse roles and continue reading.

6. Discuss the reading as a class to make sure students' paragraphs have correctly hit upon the main ideas of the passage.

Strategy 7: ReQuest (Reciprocal Questioning)

Purpose: To ask and answer questions during reading to establish a purpose for reading and monitor one's own comprehension

How to Do It

1. Prepare students to read by doing the section's Build Background Knowledge, Set a Purpose for Reading, and Preview Key Terms activities.

2. Begin reading a brief portion of the text aloud. Ask and answer your own questions about the text, progressing from recall to critical thinking questions.

3. After modeling this question and response pattern with a brief passage, ask students to read the next section of the text. Tell students that they will be taking turns asking you questions about what they read, and you will answer their questions, just like you modeled for them.

4. Ask students to read the next section. Inform them that you will be asking them questions about the section and they will be answering your questions.

5. Continue to alternate between student-generated questions and teacher-generated questions until the entire designated passage has been read. As students become used to the strategy, they gradually assume more responsibility in the process.

6. When the students have read enough information to make predictions about the remainder of the assignment, stop the exchange of comprehension questions. Instead, ask prediction questions, such as, "What do you think will be discussed in the next section? Why do you think so?"

7. Assign the remaining portion for students to read silently. Then lead a wrap-up discussion of the material.

Strategy 8: Idea Wave

Purpose: To engage students in active class discussions

How to Do It

1. Pose a question or task.

2. Give students quiet time to consider what they know about the topic and record a number of responses.

3. Whip around the class in a fast-paced and structured manner (e.g. down rows, around tables), allowing as many students as possible to share an idea in 15 seconds or less.

4. After several contributions, if there tends to be repetition, ask students to point out similarities in responses rather than simply stating that their idea has already been mentioned.

Strategies for Improving Student Comprehension *(continued)*

Strategy 9: Numbered Heads

Purpose: To engage students in active class discussions

How to Do It

1. Seat students in groups of four and number off one through four (if possible, combine established partners to form groups of four).

2. After giving the discussion prompt, allow students to discuss possible responses for an established amount of time.

3. Remind students to pay close attention to the comments of each group member because you will be randomly selecting one student to represent the best thinking of the entire group.

4. Call a number (one through four), and ask all students with that number to raise their hands, ready to respond to the topic at hand in a teacher-directed, whole-class discussion.

5. Add comments, extend key ideas, ask follow-up questions, and make connections between individual student's comments to create a lively whole-class discussion.

6. Provide any summary comments required to ensure that all students understand critical points.

Strategy 10: Think-Write-Pair–Share

Purpose: To engage students in responding to instruction

How to Do It

1. **Think**—Students listen while the teacher poses a question or a task related to the reading or classroom discussion. The level of questions should vary from lower level literal to higher order inferential or analytical.

2. **Write**—Provide quiet thinking or writing time for students to deal with the question, and go back to the text or review notes. Have students record their ideas in their notebooks.

3. **Pair/Share**—Cue students to find a partner and discuss their responses, noting similarities and differences. Teach students to encourage one another to clarify and justify responses.

4. Randomly call on students to share during a unified class discussion after they have all rehearsed answers with their partners.

5. Invite any volunteers to contribute additional ideas and points of view to the discussion after calling on a reasonable number of students randomly.

6. Direct students to go back to notes and add any important information garnered during the partner and class discussions.

Strategy 11: Give One, Get One

Purpose: To foster independent reflection and peer interaction prior to a unified class discussion

How to Do It

1. Pose a thought-provoking question or a concrete task to the class.

2. Allow three to five minutes of quiet time for students to consider what they may already know about the topic and jot down a number of potential responses.

3. Ask students to place a check mark next to the two or three ideas that they perceive as their strongest and then draw a line after their final idea to separate their ideas from those that they will gather from classmates.

4. Give students a set amount of time (about eight to ten minutes) to get up from their seats and share ideas with classmates. After finding a partner, the two students exchange papers and first quietly read each other's ideas. They discuss the ideas briefly, then select one idea from their partner's list and add it to their own, making sure to accurately copy the idea alongside the partner's name.

5. When one exchange is completed, students move on to interact with a new partner.

6. At the end of the exchange period, facilitate a unified class discussion. Call on a volunteer to share one new idea acquired from a conversation partner. The student whose idea has just been reported then shares the next idea, gleaned from a different conversation partner.

Professional Development

For more information about these strategies, see the end of each chapter's Interleaf.

Objectives

- Learn how to read nonfiction critically by analyzing an author's purpose, distinguishing between facts and opinions, identifying evidence, and evaluating credibility.

Prepare to Read

Build Background Knowledge L2

Write the phrase "Don't believe everything you read" on the board. Ask students to brainstorm examples that illustrate the saying. Provide a few simple examples to get them started (*tall tales, advertisements.*)

Instruct

Reading Informational Texts L2

Guided Instruction

- Tell students that they must actively evaluate the information in most of the nonfiction they read.

- Read the sample editorial on this page aloud. Tell students that an editorial expresses a person's opinion. Ask students to consider why the author wrote this editorial. (*The author expresses the opinion that the proposal to build the new shopping center should have been approved.*) Ask **How might this purpose affect what the editorial says?** (*The author may present information in the best possible light to prove his or her belief.*)

- Another important step in evaluating nonfiction is distinguishing between facts and opinions. Ask each student to write one fact and one opinion, on any subject, in their notebooks. Use the Idea Wave strategy (TE, p. T39) to get students to share their facts and opinion. If students have incorrectly categorized examples, help them to see why.

Reading Informational Texts

Reading a magazine, an Internet page, or a textbook is not the same as reading a novel. The purpose of reading nonfiction texts is to acquire new information. On page M18 you'll read about some ⊙ Target Reading Skills that you'll have a chance to practice as you read this textbook. Here we'll focus on a few skills that will help you read nonfiction with a more critical eye.

Analyze the Author's Purpose

Different types of materials are written with different purposes in mind. For example, a textbook is written to teach students information about a subject. The purpose of a technical manual is to teach someone how to use something, such as a computer. A newspaper editorial might be written to persuade the reader to accept a particular point of view. A writer's purpose influences how the material is presented. Sometimes an author states his or her purpose directly. More often, the purpose is only suggested, and you must use clues to identify the author's purpose.

Distinguish Between Facts and Opinions

It's important when reading informational texts to read actively and to distinguish between fact and opinion. A fact can be proven or disproven. An opinion cannot—it is someone's personal viewpoint or evaluation.

For example, the editorial pages in a newspaper offer opinions on topics that are currently in the news. You need to read newspaper editorials with an eye for bias and faulty logic. For example, the newspaper editorial at the right shows factual statements in blue and opinion statements in red. The underlined words are examples of highly charged words. They reveal bias on the part of the writer.

> More than 5,000 people voted last week in favor of building a new shopping center, but the opposition won out. The margin of victory is irrelevant. Those radical voters who opposed the center are obviously self-serving elitists who do not care about anyone but themselves.
>
> This month's unemployment figure for our area is 10 percent, which represents an increase of about 5 percent over the figure for this time last year. These figures mean unemployment is getting worse. But the people who voted against the mall probably do not care about creating new jobs.

RW History of Our World

- Tell students that identifying evidence is another way to read nonfiction critically. Ask students to look again at the facts highlighted in the sample editorial. **Does the evidence presented in these facts convince you that building a new shopping center is a good idea?** (*The evidence is incomplete—the author has not shown that the new shopping center would solve the unemployment problem.*)

- Tell students that analyzing an author's purpose, distinguishing between fact and opinions, and identifying evidence are all ways to evaluate the credibility of the author. Tell students to look at the checklist for evaluating Web sites. Ask students to think about Web sites they have visited. Do those Web sites pass the checklist's test? Why or why not?

Identify Evidence

Before you accept an author's conclusion, you need to make sure that the author has based the conclusion on enough evidence and on the right kind of evidence. An author may present a series of facts to support a claim, but the facts may not tell the whole story. For example, what evidence does the author of the newspaper editorial on the previous page provide to support his claim that the new shopping center would create more jobs? Is it possible that the shopping center might have put many small local businesses out of business, thus increasing unemployment rather than decreasing it?

Evaluate Credibility

Whenever you read informational texts, you need to assess the credibility of the author. This is especially true of sites you may visit on the Internet. All Internet sources are not equally reliable. Here are some questions to ask yourself when evaluating the credibility of a Web site.

☐ Is the Web site created by a respected organization, a discussion group, or an individual?

☐ Does the Web site creator include his or her name as well as credentials and the sources he or she used to write the material?

☐ Is the information on the site balanced or biased?

☐ Can you verify the information using two other sources?

☐ Is there a date telling when the Web site was created or last updated?

Reading and Writing Handbook **RW1**

Independent Practice

Ask students to bring in an editorial from the local newspaper, or distribute copies of an appropriate editorial. Ask students to critically assess their editorial by analyzing the author's purpose; underlining facts and circling opinions in the text of the editorial; summarizing the evidence presented in the editorial; and finally drawing a conclusion about the credibility of the editorial.

Monitor Progress

Pair students and have them share their editorial assessments. Ask them to explain the reasoning behind the conclusions they drew about the editorial's credibility. Circulate and offer assistance as needed.

Assess and Reteach

Assess Progress L2
Collect students' papers and review their assessments.

Reteach L1
If students are struggling, tell them to approach the task by asking themselves the following questions as they read a piece of nonfiction: **Why** did the author write this? **How** has the author made his or her points, using facts or opinions? **What** evidence has the author used to support the main idea? **Who** is the author, and what sources has he or she used?

Extend L3
To extend this lesson, tell students to turn to the Table of Contents in the Student Edition and pick a chapter name that intrigues. Then, ask them to search the Internet and find two Web sites about the chapter's topic. Finally, ask them to use the checklist on this page to evaluate each Web site and compare the two in terms of credibility.

Differentiated Instruction

For Advanced Readers L3
Draw students' attention to the checklist under the heading "Evaluate Credibility." Ask students to create a similar checklist for analyzing an author's purpose, distinguishing between fact and opinion, and identifying evidence.

For Special Needs Students L1
If special needs students are having trouble making the distinction between facts and opinions, partner them with more proficient students to do the *Distinguishing Fact and Opinion* lesson on the Social Studies Skill Tutor CD-ROM.

⊙ Distinguishing Fact and Opinion, **Social Studies Skill Tutor CD-ROM**

Objectives

- Use a systematic approach to write narrative, persuasive, expository, and research essays.

Prepare to Read

Build Background Knowledge   L2

As a group, brainstorm all the ways that people use writing to communicate. Start them with these examples: labeling a folder, writing an email. Conduct an Idea Wave (TE, p. T39) and write students' responses on the board. Tell them that people often write to express ideas or information. Give them *Four Purposes for Writing* and tell them to keep it in their notebooks for future reference.

All in One History of Our World Teaching Resources, Reading and Writing Skills Handbook *Four Purposes for Writing,* p. 3

Instruct

Narrative Essays   L2

Guided Instruction

- Tell students that narrative essays tell a story about their own experiences. Discuss the steps listed in the Student Edition.

- Choose an event in your own life (or invent one) such as visiting friends in another city. Write your topic on the board and model how to list details *(what the trip was like, what you did while you were there, what your friends are like.)* Cross out the least interesting details.

- Think aloud as your form your topic into a sentence that conveys the main idea of your essay.

- Tell students that you will go on to flesh out the details into a colorful story.

Independent Practice

- Tell students to write a narrative essay about a recent positive experience. Have student pairs brainstorm topics.

Writing for Social Studies

Writing is one of the most powerful communication tools you will ever use. You will use it to share your thoughts and ideas with others. Research shows that writing about what you read actually helps you learn new information and ideas. A systematic approach to writing—including prewriting, drafting, revising, and proofing—can help you write better, whether you're writing an essay or a research report.

Narrative Essays

Writing that tells a story about a personal experience

1 Select and Narrow Your Topic

A narrative is a story. In social studies, it might be a narrative essay about how an event affected you or your family.

2 Gather Details

Brainstorm a list of details you'd like to include in your narrative.

3 Write a First Draft

Start by writing a simple opening sentence that conveys the main idea of your essay. Continue by writing a colorful story that has interesting details. Write a conclusion that sums up the significance of the event or situation described in your essay.

4 Revise and Proofread

Check to make sure you have not begun too many sentences with the word *I.* Replace general words with more colorful ones.

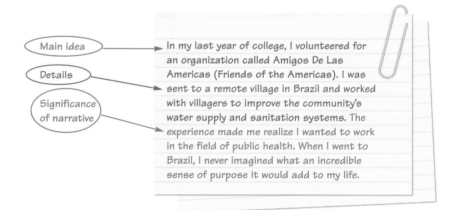

Main idea → In my last year of college, I volunteered for an organization called Amigos De Las Americas (Friends of the Americas). I was

Details → sent to a remote village in Brazil and worked with villagers to improve the community's water supply and sanitation systems. The

Significance of narrative → experience made me realize I wanted to work in the field of public health. When I went to Brazil, I never imagined what an incredible sense of purpose it would add to my life.

- Give students *Writing to Describe* to help them write their essays. After they have written the body of their essay, give them *Writing the Conclusion* to help them complete it.

All in One History of Our World Teaching Resources, Reading and Writing Handbook *Writing to Describe,* p. 4; Writing the Conclusion, p. 5

Monitor Progress

Have students share their drafts with their partners. Give them *Using the Revision Checklist* and ask them to review their partners' papers.

All in One History of Our World Teaching Resources, Reading and Writing Skills Handbook, *Using the Revision Checklist,* p. 6

Persuasive Essays

Writing that supports an opinion or position

1 Select and Narrow Your Topic

Choose a topic that provokes an argument and has at least two sides. Choose a side. Decide which argument will appeal most to your audience and persuade them to understand your point of view.

2 Gather Evidence

Create a chart that states your position at the top and then lists the pros and cons for your position below, in two columns. Predict and address the strongest arguments against your stand.

3 Write a First Draft

Write a strong thesis statement that clearly states your position. Continue by presenting the strongest arguments in favor of your position and acknowledging and refuting opposing arguments.

4 Revise and Proofread

Check to make sure you have made a logical argument and that you have not oversimplified the argument.

Main Idea → It is vital to vote in elections. When people vote, they tell public officials how to run the government. Not every proposal is carried

Supporting (pro) argument

Opposing (con) argument → out; however, politicians do their best to listen to what the majority of people want.

Transition words → Therefore, every vote is important.

Reading and Writing Handbook **RW3**

Guided Instruction

- Tell students that the purpose of writing a persuasive essay is to convince other people to believe your point of view. However, you must use solid, reliable evidence and arguments to make your points.

- Model the thought process by pointing out how the writer presents his or her argument in the paragraph on this page.

Independent Practice

- Tell students to write a persuasive essay about a topic that is important to them. Have students form pairs. One student in each pair should state his or her position. The other student then shares opposing arguments, which the first student should refute in his or her essay. Then the pairs switch roles.

- Give students *Writing to Persuade* to help them write their essays.

  All in One **History of Our World Teaching Resources,** Reading and Writing Skills Handbook, Writing to Persuade, p. 7

Monitor Progress

If students are having trouble structuring their paragraphs, give them *Structuring Paragraphs* and *Creating Paragraph Outlines* to provide a framework.

  All in One **History of Our World Teaching Resources,** Structuring Paragraphs, p. 8; Creating Paragraph Outlines, p. 9

Differentiated Instruction

For Less Proficient Readers   L1

Tell students to use looping to help them focus on a topic. Have them follow these steps: Write freely on your topic for about five minutes. Read what you have written and circle the most important idea. Write for five minutes on the circled idea. Repeat the process until you isolate a topic narrow enough to cover well in a short essay.

Expository Essays L2

Guided Instruction
- Read the steps for writing expository essays with students.
- Tell students that the graphic organizer example given on the Student Edition page is for a cause and effect expository essay. They might use a Venn diagram for a compare and contrast essay and a flow-chart for a problem and solution essay.
- Model how to create a topic sentence from the information in the cause and effect graphic organizer. *(Sample topic sentence: In Mexico, several factors are causing rural families to move from the countryside to the city.)*
- Create a brief outline showing how you will organize the paragraphs in your essay.

Independent Practice
Tell students to write an expository essay based on a recent current event. Have them brainstorm ideas with a partner, then choose which type of essay best suits their topic (cause and effect, compare and contrast, or problem and solution.) Give them *Writing to Inform and Explain* and *Gathering Details* to help them start drafting their essays.

All in One History of Our World Teaching Resources, Reading and Writing Skills Handbook, *Writing to Inform and Explain*, p.10; *Gathering Details*, p. 11

Monitor Progress
If students are struggling with their essays, give them *Writing a Cause-and-Effect Essay* or *Writing a Problem-and-Solution Essay.*

All in One History of Our World Teaching Resources, Reading and Writing Skills Handbook, *Writing a Cause-and-Effect Essay*, p. 12; *Writing a Problem-and-Solution Essay*, p. 13

Research Papers L2

Guided Instruction
Go over the steps for writing a research paper carefully. Ask students to share questions about the process, using the Idea Wave structured engagement strategy (p. T39). Answer any questions they might have.

Reading and Writing Handbook

Expository Essays

Writing that explains a process, compares and contrasts, explains causes and effects, or explores solutions to a problem

1 Identify and Narrow Your Topic
Expository writing is writing that explains something in detail. It might explain the similarities and differences between two or more subjects (compare and contrast). It might explain how one event causes another (cause and effect). Or it might explain a problem and describe a solution.

2 Gather Evidence
Create a graphic organizer that identifies details to include in your essay.

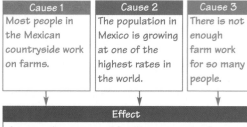

Cause 1	Cause 2	Cause 3
Most people in the Mexican countryside work on farms.	The population in Mexico is growing at one of the highest rates in the world.	There is not enough farm work for so many people.

Effect

As a result, many rural families are moving from the countryside to live in Mexico City.

3 Write Your First Draft
Write a topic sentence and then organize the essay around your similarities and differences, causes and effects, or problem and solutions. Be sure to include convincing details, facts, and examples.

4 Revise and Proofread

Research Papers

Writing that presents research about a topic

1 Narrow Your Topic
Choose a topic you're interested in and make sure that it is not too broad. For example, instead of writing a report on Panama, write about the construction of the Panama Canal.

2 Acquire Information
Locate several sources of information about the topic from the library or the Internet. For each resource, create a source index card like the one at the right. Then take notes using an index card for each detail or subtopic. On the card, note which source the information was taken from. Use quotation marks when you copy the exact words from a source.

Source #1
McCullough, David. *The Path Between the Seas: The Creation of the Panama Canal, 1870-1914.* N.Y., Simon and Schuster, 1977.

3 Make an Outline
Use an outline to decide how to organize your report. Sort your index cards into the same order.

Outline
I. Introduction
II. Why the canal was built
III. How the canal was built
   A. Physical challenges
   B. Medical challenges
IV. Conclusion

Differentiated Instruction

For Gifted and Talented L3
Tell students that a verb is in active voice when the subject performs the action named by the verb. A verb is in passive voice when the subject undergoes the action named by the verb.

Give these examples:

Passive voice: The house is being painted by my sister and me.

Active voice: My sister and I are painting the house.

Tell students that using the active voice whenever possible will make their writing more dynamic and concise.

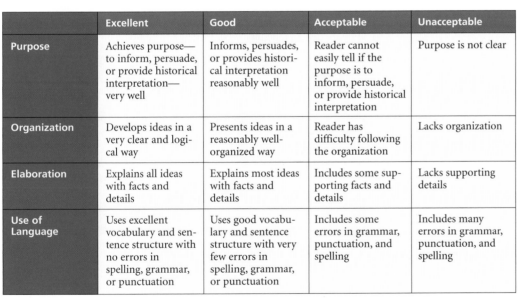

> **Introduction**
> **Building the Panama Canal**
> Ever since Christopher Columbus first explored
> the Isthmus of Panama, the Spanish had been
> looking for a water route through it. They wanted
> to be able to sail west from Spain to Asia without
> sailing around South America. However, it was not
> until 1914 that the dream became a reality.

> **Conclusion**
> It took eight years and more than 70,000
> workers to build the Panama Canal. It
> remains one of the greatest engineering
> feats of modern times.

④ Write a First Draft
Write an introduction, a body, and a conclusion. Leave plenty of space between lines so you can go back and add details that you may have left out.

⑤ Revise and Proofread
Be sure to include transition words between sentences and paragraphs. Here are some examples:

To show a contrast—*however, although, despite.*

To point out a reason—*since, because, if.*

To signal a conclusion—*therefore, consequently, so, then.*

Evaluating Your Writing
Use this table to help you evaluate your writing.

	Excellent	**Good**	**Acceptable**	**Unacceptable**
Purpose	Achieves purpose—to inform, persuade, or provide historical interpretation—very well	Informs, persuades, or provides historical interpretation reasonably well	Reader cannot easily tell if the purpose is to inform, persuade, or provide historical interpretation	Purpose is not clear
Organization	Develops ideas in a very clear and logical way	Presents ideas in a reasonably well-organized way	Reader has difficulty following the organization	Lacks organization
Elaboration	Explains all ideas with facts and details	Explains most ideas with facts and details	Includes some supporting facts and details	Lacks supporting details
Use of Language	Uses excellent vocabulary and sentence structure with no errors in spelling, grammar, or punctuation	Uses good vocabulary and sentence structure with very few errors in spelling, grammar, or punctuation	Includes some errors in grammar, punctuation, and spelling	Includes many errors in grammar, punctuation, and spelling

Reading and Writing Handbook **RW5**

Differentiated Instruction

For English Language Learners L2
To help students understand the tasks you have given them, provide them with an example of a well-executed essay from a different class or a previous year. The example essay should be well written and organized but not above grade level. You could look for and save good examples each year you teach.

Independent Practice
- Have students consider topics for a research paper. Give them *Choosing a Topic* to help them learn how to evaluate potential topics.

  All in One History of Our World Teaching Resources, Reading and Writing Skills Handbook, *Choosing a Topic,* p. 14

- Once students have selected a topic, tell them they will need facts to support their ideas. Give them *Using the Library, Summarizing and Taking Notes,* and *Preparing Note Cards* to help them start their research.

  All in One History of Our World Teaching Resources, Reading and Writing Skills Handbook, *Using the Library,* p. 15; *Summarizing and Taking Notes,* p. 16 *Preparing Note Cards,* p. 17

Monitor Progress
Give students *Writing an Introduction* and *Writing the Body of an Essay* to help them write their essays.

  All in One History of Our World Teaching Resources, Reading and Writing Skills Handbook, *Writing an Introduction,* p. 18; *Writing the Body of an Essay,* p. 19

Assess and Reteach

Assess Progress L2
Ask student to pick the best essay they have written so far and evaluate it using the rubric on this page.

Reteach L1
Collect students' essays and self-evaluations. Meet with students to go over good points and areas for improvement. Revisit each type of essay as needed with the whole class.

Extend L3
To extend this lesson, tell students there are many other different types of writing. Have them complete *Writing for Assessment* and *Writing a Letter* to learn about two more types of writing.

  All in One History of Our World Teaching Resources, Reading and Writing Skills Handbook, *Writing for Assessment,* p. 20; *Writing a Letter,* p. 21

MapMaster Skills Handbook
Step-by-Step Instruction

Objective
- Identify and define the five themes of geography.

Prepare to Read

Build Background Knowledge L2

Assign students to small groups and give them five minutes to write a definition of geography. Then write the five themes of geography on the board. Remind students that a theme is an important underlying idea. As a class, decide which parts of their definitions go under each of the geography themes. For example, "landforms" would fall under the theme of place.

Instruct

Five Themes of Geography L2

Guided Instruction
- Divide the text using the headings and ask students to read the pages using the Structured Silent Reading technique (TE, p. T38). Clarify the meanings of any unfamiliar words.

- Ask students to give the relative locations of their home.

- Mention the popularity of different kinds of ethnic foods in the United States. Ask **What theme of geography are these foods a good example of?** (*movement*) Encourage students to name other examples of the movement of cultural traditions from one region to another.

- Discuss the climate in your area. Ask **How does the environment affect how we live?** (*affects dress, travel, sports and other recreational activities, the way homes are built*)

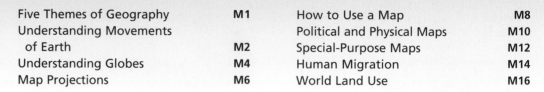

MAP MASTER™ SKILLS HANDBOOK

CONTENTS

Go Online PHSchool.com Use Web Code **lap-0000** for all of the maps in this handbook.

Five Themes of Geography

Studying the geography of the entire world is a huge task. You can make that task easier by using the five themes of geography: location, regions, place, movement, and human-environment interaction. The themes are tools you can use to organize information and to answer the where, why, and how of geography.

LOCATION

1 Location answers the question, "Where is it?" You can think of the location of a continent or a country as its address. You might give an absolute location such as 22 South Lake Street or 40° N and 80° W. You might also use a relative address, telling where one place is by referring to another place. *Between school and the mall* and *eight miles east of Pleasant City* are examples of relative locations.

▲ **Location**
This museum in England has a line running through it. The line marks its location at 0° longitude.

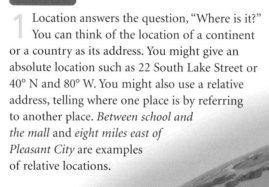

M MapMaster Skills Handbook

Differentiated Instruction

For English Language Learners L1

Students may find it difficult to pronounce some of the multisyllable words in this section such as *relative, environment, interaction, government, signature,* and *communicate.* Show students how to break down these words into smaller parts to help them sound out the pronunciation.

For Advanced Readers L3

Have students find articles in newspapers or magazines that illustrate the five themes of geography. Have students underline the relevant sections and identify the theme or themes they illustrate. Suggest that students create a bulletin board to share their examples with the class.

REGIONS

2 Regions are areas that share at least one common feature. Geographers divide the world into many types of regions. For example, countries, states, and cities are political regions. The people in any one of these places live under the same government. Other features, such as climate and culture, can be used to define regions. Therefore the same place can be found in more than one region. For example, the state of Hawaii is in the political region of the United States. Because it has a tropical climate, Hawaii is also part of a tropical climate region.

MOVEMENT

4 Movement answers the question, "How do people, goods, and ideas move from place to place?" Remember that what happens in one place often affects what happens in another. Use the theme of movement to help you trace the spread of goods, people, and ideas from one location to another.

PLACE

3 Place identifies the natural and human features that make one place different from every other place. You can identify a specific place by its landforms, climate, plants, animals, people, language, or culture. You might even think of place as a geographic signature. Use the signature to help you understand the natural and human features that make one place different from every other place.

INTERACTION

5 Human-environment interaction focuses on the relationship between people and the environment. As people live in an area, they often begin to make changes to it, usually to make their lives easier. For example, they might build a dam to control flooding during rainy seasons. Also, the environment can affect how people live, work, dress, travel, and communicate.

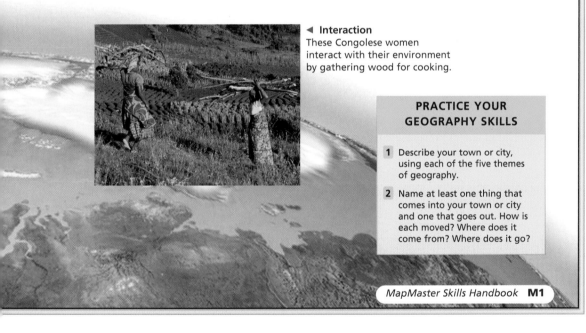

◀ **Interaction**
These Congolese women interact with their environment by gathering wood for cooking.

PRACTICE YOUR GEOGRAPHY SKILLS

1 Describe your town or city, using each of the five themes of geography.

2 Name at least one thing that comes into your town or city and one that goes out. How is each moved? Where does it come from? Where does it go?

MapMaster Skills Handbook **M1**

Independent Practice
Partner students and have them complete *The Five Themes of Geography*.

AII in One **History of Our World Teaching Resources,** MapMaster™ Teacher's Companion, *The Five Themes of Geography*, p. 1

Monitor Progress
As students complete the worksheet, circulate to make sure that individuals comprehend the material. Provide assistance as needed.

Assess and Reteach

Assess Progress   L2
Have students complete the questions under Practice Your Geography Skills.

Reteach   L1
Help students create a concept web that identifies the five themes of geography. Start filling in blank *Transparency B17: Concept Web* to model how to identify information to clarify each theme. For example, under Regions students might write "share common feature such as government, climate, culture." Encourage students to refer to their webs to review the themes.

History of Our World Transparencies, *Transparency B17: Concept Web*

Extend   L3
To extend the lesson, ask students to find out about any plans for new buildings, highways, or other types of construction in your area. Ask students to predict how these changes will affect the community's environment.

Answers

PRACTICE YOUR GEOGRAPHY SKILLS

1. Answers should include an example of each of the five themes that relates to your community.

2. Students' answers should provide examples of goods, ideas, or things that move into and out of your community.

Objective

- Explain how the movements of Earth cause night and day, as well as the seasons.

Prepare to Read

Build Background Knowledge **L2**

Remind students that while the Earth revolves around the sun, it also rotates on its own axis. Review the meanings of "revolve" and "rotate" in this context. Ask students to brainstorm ways that the Earth's revolving and rotating might affect their lives. Conduct an Idea Wave (TE, p. T39) to generate a list of ideas.

Instruct

Understanding Movements of Earth **L2**

Guided Instruction

- Read the text as a class using the Oral Cloze technique (TE, p. T37). Explain that the illustrations on pages M2 and M3 show the information in the text visually. Clarify the meanings of any unfamiliar words.

- Ask students **How does Earth rotating on its axis cause day and night?** *(It is daytime on the side of Earth facing the sun, while the side facing away from the sun is dark.)*

- Ask **How does the tilt of Earth affect seasons?** *(The farther away a part of Earth is from the sun's rays, the colder it is.)*

Independent Practice

Partner students and have them complete *Understanding the Movements of the Earth.*

All in One History of Our World Teaching Resources, MapMaster™ Teacher's Companion, *Understanding Movements of the Earth,* p. 2

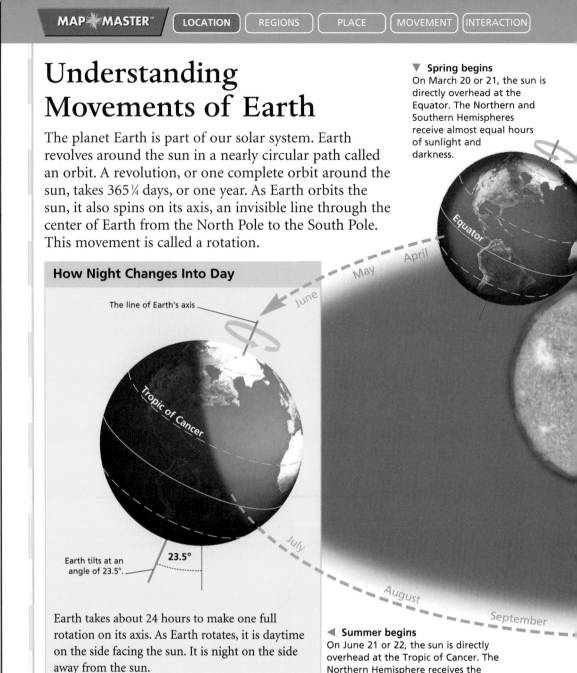

Understanding Movements of Earth

The planet Earth is part of our solar system. Earth revolves around the sun in a nearly circular path called an orbit. A revolution, or one complete orbit around the sun, takes 365 ¼ days, or one year. As Earth orbits the sun, it also spins on its axis, an invisible line through the center of Earth from the North Pole to the South Pole. This movement is called a rotation.

How Night Changes Into Day

The line of Earth's axis

Tropic of Cancer

Earth tilts at an angle of 23.5°.   **23.5°**

Earth takes about 24 hours to make one full rotation on its axis. As Earth rotates, it is daytime on the side facing the sun. It is night on the side away from the sun.

▼ **Spring begins**
On March 20 or 21, the sun is directly overhead at the Equator. The Northern and Southern Hemispheres receive almost equal hours of sunlight and darkness.

Equator

May   April
June
July
August   September

◄ **Summer begins**
On June 21 or 22, the sun is directly overhead at the Tropic of Cancer. The Northern Hemisphere receives the greatest number of sunlight hours.

M2 MapMaster Skills Handbook

Background: Links Across Place

Sunrise and Sunset Most people have heard the saying "The sun rises in the east and sets in the west." However, the sun does not ever actually change position. Every day, Earth rotates on its axis so that as each region faces the sun, it experiences day. The rotation continues so that as a region turns away from the sun, it experiences night. The sun stays in the same place. A person viewing sunrise or sunset is really seeing Earth's slow turn on its axis, not the sun rising or setting.

The Seasons

Earth's axis is tilted at an angle. Because of this tilt, sunlight strikes different parts of Earth at different times in the year, creating seasons. The illustration below shows how the seasons are created in the Northern Hemisphere. In the Southern Hemisphere, the seasons are reversed.

PRACTICE YOUR GEOGRAPHY SKILLS

1 What causes the seasons in the Northern Hemisphere to be the opposite of those in the Southern Hemisphere?

2 During which two days of the year do the Northern Hemisphere and Southern Hemisphere have equal hours of daylight and darkness?

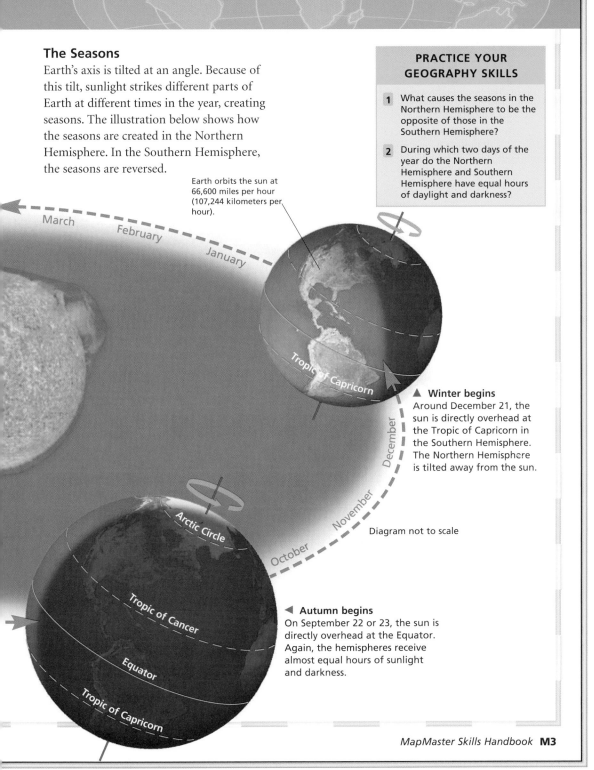

Earth orbits the sun at 66,600 miles per hour (107,244 kilometers per hour).

▲ **Winter begins**
Around December 21, the sun is directly overhead at the Tropic of Capricorn in the Southern Hemisphere. The Northern Hemisphere is tilted away from the sun.

Diagram not to scale

◄ **Autumn begins**
On September 22 or 23, the sun is directly overhead at the Equator. Again, the hemispheres receive almost equal hours of sunlight and darkness.

MapMaster Skills Handbook **M3**

Monitor Progress

As students do the worksheet, circulate to make sure individuals comprehend the key concepts. Provide assistance as needed.

Assess and Reteach

Assess Progress L2
Have students complete the Practice Your Geography Skills questions.

Reteach L1
If students are having trouble understanding these concepts, create a model to demonstrate Earth's revolution. Use a foam ball to represent Earth. Insert a pencil through the ball to represent Earth's axis, labeling the ends "North Pole" and "South Pole." Draw the Equator perpendicular to the axis. Place a light source in the center of a table to represent the sun. Then tilt the ball at a slight angle and move it around the light to mimic Earth's revolution. Have students notice the point at which each pole is nearest the sun and identify what season it would be in each hemisphere.

Extend L3
To extend the lesson, ask students to consider Earth's relationship to its satellite, the Moon. Ask them to research on the Internet to answer these questions: "Does the Moon rotate like Earth? Does the Moon revolve around Earth as Earth revolves around the sun?"

Answers

PRACTICE YOUR GEOGRAPHY SKILLS

1. The seasons are reversed in the Northern Hemisphere and Southern Hemisphere because Earth is tilted. When one hemisphere is tilted towards the sun, the other hemisphere is tilted away from the sun.

2. September 22–23 and March 20–21

Objectives

- Understand how a globe is marked with a grid to measure features on Earth.
- Learn how to use longitude and latitude to locate a place.

Prepare to Read

Build Background Knowledge **L2**

Tell students that in this lesson, they will learn how to use globes. Ask students what it would be like to see Earth from a spacecraft. Discuss the shape that students would see. Then discuss why a globe is a more accurate rendering of Earth than a flat map. Point out that a globe is like a model car in that it is a small version of something larger. If a globe is available, have students examine it.

Instruct

Understanding Globes **L2**

Guided Instruction

- Read the text as a class using the Oral Cloze technique (TE, p. T37). Have students study the illustrations carefully.

- Ask **What line of latitude divides the Northern and Southern Hemispheres?** *(the Equator)* **At what degrees latitude is this line?** *(0°)*

- Ask **Where do the lines of longitude come together?** *(at the North and South Poles)* **What is the name of the meridian at 0 degrees?** *(Prime Meridian)*

- Have students look at the global grid on *Color Transparency HOW 3: The Global Grid.* Ask **What is the global grid?** *(a pattern of lines formed where the parallels of latitude and meridians of longitude cross)* **What continent in the Eastern Hemisphere does the 100E° meridian pass through?** *(Asia)*

  History of Our World Transparencies, *Color Transparency HOW 3: The Global Grid.*

Understanding Globes

A globe is a scale model of Earth. It shows the actual shapes, sizes, and locations of all Earth's landmasses and bodies of water. Features on the surface of Earth are drawn to scale on a globe. This means that a small unit of measure on the globe stands for a large unit of measure on Earth.

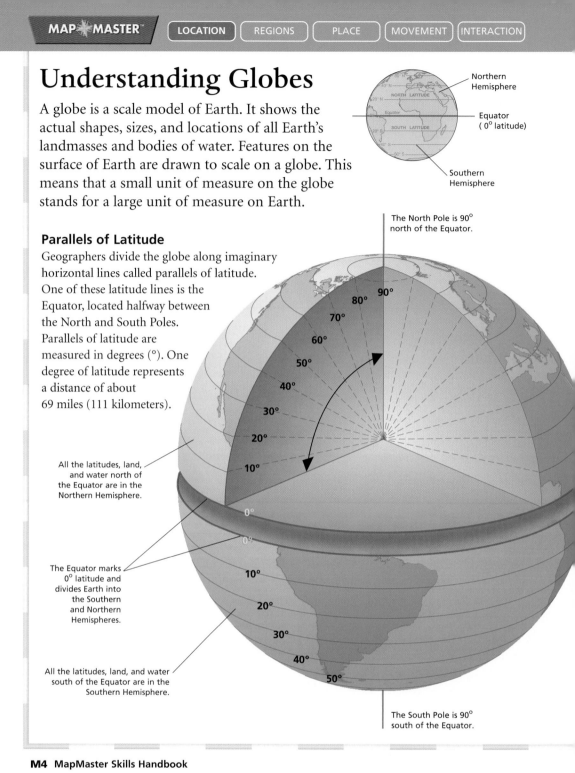

Parallels of Latitude

Geographers divide the globe along imaginary horizontal lines called parallels of latitude. One of these latitude lines is the Equator, located halfway between the North and South Poles. Parallels of latitude are measured in degrees (°). One degree of latitude represents a distance of about 69 miles (111 kilometers).

Northern Hemisphere

Equator (0° latitude)

Southern Hemisphere

The North Pole is 90° north of the Equator.

90°
80°
70°
60°
50°
40°
30°
20°
10°
0°

All the latitudes, land, and water north of the Equator are in the Northern Hemisphere.

The Equator marks 0° latitude and divides Earth into the Southern and Northern Hemispheres.

All the latitudes, land, and water south of the Equator are in the Southern Hemisphere.

10°
20°
30°
40°
50°

The South Pole is 90° south of the Equator.

M4 MapMaster Skills Handbook

Background: Links Across Time

The First Globes Historians believe that the first globe may have been made in the second century B.C. by a Greek geographer known as Crates of Mallus. The mathematician Ptolemy represented Earth as a globe in his written works in the second century A.D. In late 1492 Martin Behaim made a terrestrial globe that although inaccurate by today's knowledge, reflected the best geographical knowledge of the time. This globe still exists and is on display in Behaim's hometown of Nuremberg, Germany.

Meridians of Longitude

Geographers also divide the globe along imaginary vertical lines called meridians of longitude, which are measured in degrees (°). The longitude line called the Prime Meridian runs from pole to pole through Greenwich, England. All meridians of longitude come together at the North and South Poles.

PRACTICE YOUR GEOGRAPHY MAP SKILLS

1 Which continents lie completely in the Northern Hemisphere? In the Western Hemisphere?

2 Is there land or water at 20° S latitude and the Prime Meridian? At the Equator and 60° W longitude?

All the longitudes, land, and water west of the Prime Meridian are in the Western Hemisphere.

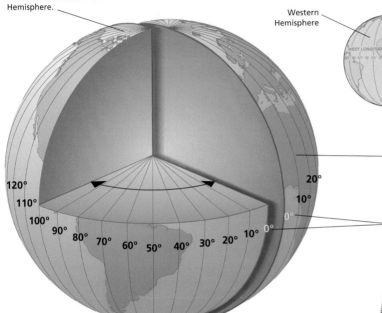

Western Hemisphere

WEST LONGITUDE   EAST LONGITUDE

Eastern Hemisphere

Prime Meridian (0° longitude)

All the longitudes, land, and water east of the Prime Meridian are in the Eastern Hemisphere.

The Prime Meridian marks 0° longitude and divides the globe into the Eastern and Western Hemispheres.

120° 110° 100° 90° 80° 70° 60° 50° 40° 30° 20° 10° 0°

20° 10° 0°

The Global Grid

Together, the pattern of parallels of latitude and meridians of longitude is called the global grid. Using the lines of latitude and longitude, you can locate any place on Earth. For example, the location of 30° north latitude and 90° west longitude is usually written as 30° N, 90° W. Only one place on Earth has these coordinates—the city of New Orleans, in the state of Louisiana.

▲ **Compass**
Wherever you are on Earth, a compass can be used to show direction.

READ BEARING

SILVA SYSTEM TYPE 7 NL

MapMaster Skills Handbook **M5**

Differentiated Instruction

For Less Proficient Readers L1
For students having difficulty understanding the concept of a global grid, give them *Understanding Grids* and help them complete it. Then follow up with *Using a Grid*.

All in One History of Our World Teaching Resources, MapMaster™ Teacher's Companion, *Understanding Grids*, p. 5; *Using a Grid*, p. 6

For Advanced Readers L3
Have students complete *Comparing Globes and Maps*. Then ask them to make a chart showing the pros and cons of these two ways of representing Earth.

All in One History of Our World Teaching Resources, MapMaster™ Teacher's Companion, *Comparing Globes and Maps*, p. 3

Independent Practice

Have students work in pairs to complete *Understanding Hemispheres* and *Understanding Latitude and Longitude.*

All in One History of Our World Teaching Resources, MapMaster™ Teacher's Companion, *Understanding Hemispheres*, p. 4; *Understanding Latitude and Longitude*, p. 7

Monitor Progress

As students do the worksheets, circulate to make sure pairs understand the key concepts. Show *Color Transparency HOW 2: The Hemispheres* to help students.

History of Our World Transparencies, *Color Transparency HOW 2: The Hemispheres*

Assess and Reteach

Assess Progress L2
Have students answer the questions under Practice Your Geography Skills.

Reteach L1
Use the DK Atlas activity *Understanding Latitude and Longitude* to review these skills with students. Have students complete the activity in pairs.

All in One History of Our World Teaching Resources, MapMaster™ Teacher's Companion, *DK Compact Atlas of the World Activity: Understanding Latitude and Longitude,* p. 65

Extend L3
To extend the lesson, have students complete *Using Latitude and Longitude.* Then have students use the map and with a partner, play a game of Can You Find …? Each partner takes a turn giving the coordinates for a place on the map and the other partner must name the place.

All in One History of Our World Teaching Resources, MapMaster™ Teacher's Companion, *Using Latitude and Longitude,* p. 7

Answers

PRACTICE YOUR GEOGRAPHY SKILLS

1. Northern Hemisphere: North America; Europe; Western Hemisphere: North America; South America

2. water; land

Objectives

- Compare maps of different projections.

- Describe distortions in map projections.

Prepare to Read

Build Background Knowledge L1

In this lesson, students will learn how cartographers depict Earth on a two-dimensional map. Remind students that if they were traveling in a spaceship, they would see Earth as a globe. Ask if they could ever see the entire Earth at one time from space. Help students recognize that a flat map is the only way to see all of Earth at one time.

Instruct

Map Projections L2

Guided Instruction

- Read the text as a class using the Choral Reading technique (TE, p. T38). Direct students to look at the relevant maps after you read each section together. Follow up by having students do a second silent reading.

- Help students locate Greenland on the Mercator and Robinson maps. Ask **What difference do you notice in the way Greenland is shown?** (*It appears much larger on the Mercator map.*) **How would you explain this?** (*The Mercator is a same-shape map and the shapes toward the poles are enlarged.*)

- Ask **Where does the distortion usually occur on an equal-shape map?** (*at the edges of the map*)

- Have students compare Antarctica on the three projections. (*It is largest and most distorted on the Mercator map; smallest on the equal-area map; covers the entire bottom edge of the Robinson map.*)

Map Projections

Maps are drawings that show regions on flat surfaces. Maps are easier to use and carry than globes, but they cannot show the correct size and shape of every feature on Earth's curved surface. They must shrink some places and stretch others. To make up for this distortion, mapmakers use different map projections. No one projection can accurately show the correct area, shape, distance, and direction for all of Earth's surface. Mapmakers use the projection that has the least distortion for the information they are presenting.

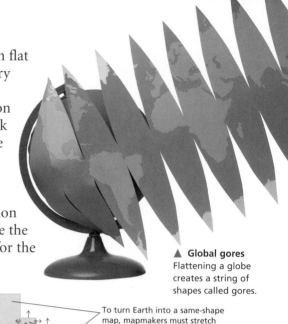

▲ **Global gores**
Flattening a globe creates a string of shapes called gores.

Same-Shape Maps

Map projections that accurately show the shapes of landmasses are called same-shape maps. However, these projections often greatly distort, or make less accurate, the size of landmasses as well as the distance between them. In the projection below, the northern and southern areas of the globe appear more stretched than the areas near the Equator.

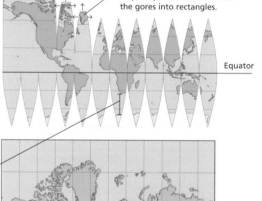

To turn Earth into a same-shape map, mapmakers must stretch the gores into rectangles.

Equator

Stretching the gores makes parts of Earth larger. This enlargement becomes greater toward the North and South Poles.

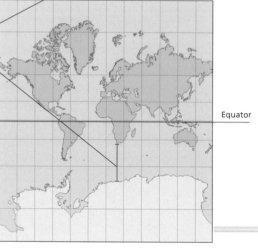

Mercator projection ▶
One of the most common same-shape maps is the Mercator projection, named for the mapmaker who invented it. The Mercator projection accurately shows shape and direction, but it distorts distance and size. Because the projection shows true directions, ships' navigators use it to chart a straight-line course between two ports.

Equator

Differentiated Instruction

For Special Needs Students L1

If students have difficulty understanding why distortion occurs, draw a simple picture on an orange. Then have students try to peel the orange in one piece. Challenge students to place the peel flat on a piece of paper without any tears and spaces. Talk about what happens to the drawing. Explain that mapmakers face this same challenge when drawing Earth on a flat paper.

For Gifted and Talented L3

Have students complete *Great Circles and Straight Lines*. Then ask them to use their completed page and a globe to explain the concept of great circles to the class.

All in One **History of Our World Teaching Resources,** MapMaster™ Teacher's Companion, *Great Circles and Straight Lines*, p. 10

Equal-Area Maps

Map projections that show the correct size of landmasses are called equal-area maps. In order to show the correct size of landmasses, these maps usually distort shapes. The distortion is usually greater at the edges of the map and less at the center.

PRACTICE YOUR GEOGRAPHY SKILLS

1 What feature is distorted on an equal-area map?

2 Would you use a Mercator projection to find the exact distance between two locations? Tell why or why not.

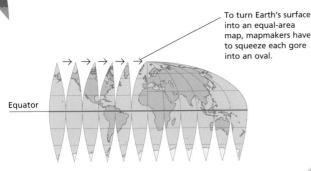

To turn Earth's surface into an equal-area map, mapmakers have to squeeze each gore into an oval.

Equator

The tips of all the gores are then joined together. The points at which they join form the North and South Poles. The line of the Equator stays the same.

North Pole

Equator

Robinson Maps

Many of the maps in this book use the Robinson projection, which is a compromise between the Mercator and equal-area projections. The Robinson projection gives a useful overall picture of the world. It keeps the size and shape relationships of most continents and oceans, but distorts the size of the polar regions.

South Pole

The entire top edge of the map is the North Pole.

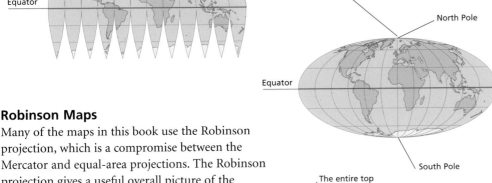

The map is least distorted at the Equator.

Equator

The entire bottom edge of the map is the South Pole.

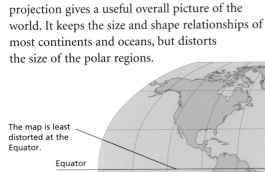

MapMaster Skills Handbook **M7**

Independent Practice

Have students work with partners to complete *Understanding Projection*.

All in One **History of Our World Teaching Resources,** MapMaster™ Teacher's Companion, *Understanding Projection,* p. 9

Monitor Progress

As students do the worksheet, circulate to make sure individuals comprehend the key concepts. Provide assistance as needed.

Assess and Reteach

Assess Progress L2

Have students complete the Practice Your Geography Skills questions.

Reteach L1

Use *Maps with Accurate Shapes: Conformal Maps* and *Maps with Accurate Areas: Equal-Area Maps* to help students go over the information in the lesson. Model thinking for each question and partner students to complete each page together. Circulate to provide explanations and help as students work.

All in One **History of Our World Teaching Resources,** MapMaster™ Teacher's Companion, *Understanding Projection,* p. 9; *Maps with Accurate Shapes: Conformal Maps,* p. 11; *Maps with Accurate Areas: Equal-Area Maps,* p. 12

Extend L3

To extend the lesson, ask students to complete *Maps with Accurate Direction: Azimuthal Maps.* Then have students write a sentence or two describing the different projections they have learned about.

All in One **History of Our World Teaching Resources,** MapMaster™ Teacher's Companion, *Understanding Projection,* p. 9; *Maps with Accurate Directions: Azimuthal Maps,* p. 14

Background: Biography

Gerardus Mercator The Mercator projection takes its name from a Flemish geographer, Gerhard Kremer (1512–1594). Kremer, who used the Latin form of his name, Gerardus Mercator, wrote books on ancient geography and cartography. He made his first world map in 1538. In 1554 he made a map of Europe. In 1568, the first map using the Mercator projection bearing his name appeared. Mercator also began an atlas of his maps which was finished by his son and published in 1594.

Answers

PRACTICE YOUR GEOGRAPHY SKILLS

1. shapes
2. No; the Mercator projection distorts distances.

Objective

■ Identify and use the parts of a map.

Prepare to Read

Build Background Knowledge `L1`

In this lesson, students will learn about the practical aspects of maps. Ask students to name reasons that they might use a map; for example, to find directions, boundaries, distances. Conduct an Idea Wave (TE, p. T39) to generate a list of ideas. List the ideas on the board.

Instruct

How to Use a Map `L2`

Guided Instruction

■ Divide the text and captions in the lesson using the headings and ask students to read the pages using the Structured Silent Reading strategy (TE, p. T38). Remind students to use the illustrations to acquire additional understanding. Refer to the list on the board, then ask students which map part (key, compass rose, scale, symbol, title) would be helpful in using a map for a specific purpose.

■ Ask **What is the purpose of a compass rose?** *(to show directions)*

■ Talk about how the three maps show different amounts of Earth's surface. Ask **Which map shows the largest area?** *(Western Europe)* **Which map shows the smallest area?** *(Central London)*

■ Ask **What are some symbols that you might find on a map key?** *(border, national capital, city, airport, park, point of interest)*

Independent Practice

Partner students and have them complete *Using the Map Key* and *Using the Compass Rose.*

All in One **History of Our World Teaching Resources,** MapMaster™ Teacher's Companion, *Understanding Projection,* p. 9; *Using the Map Key,* p. 15; *Using the Compass Rose,* p. 16

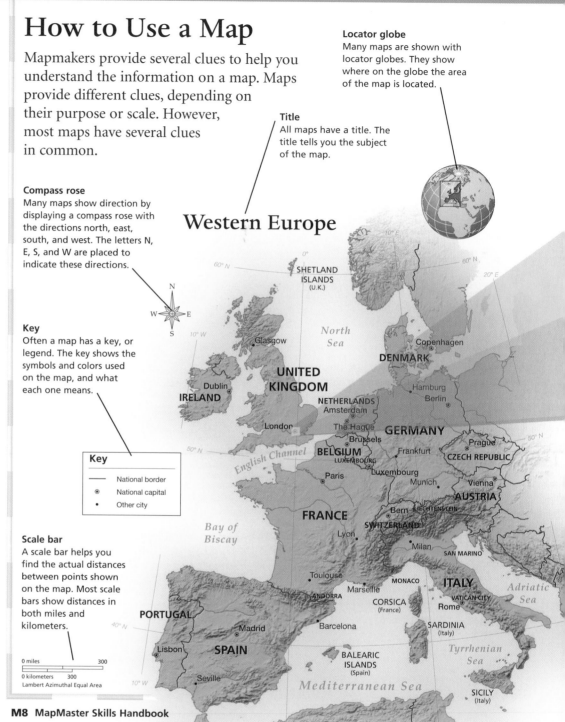

MAP MASTER™ LOCATION REGIONS PLACE MOVEMENT INTERACTION

How to Use a Map

Mapmakers provide several clues to help you understand the information on a map. Maps provide different clues, depending on their purpose or scale. However, most maps have several clues in common.

Locator globe
Many maps are shown with locator globes. They show where on the globe the area of the map is located.

Title
All maps have a title. The title tells you the subject of the map.

Compass rose
Many maps show direction by displaying a compass rose with the directions north, east, south, and west. The letters N, E, S, and W are placed to indicate these directions.

Key
Often a map has a key, or legend. The key shows the symbols and colors used on the map, and what each one means.

Scale bar
A scale bar helps you find the actual distances between points shown on the map. Most scale bars show distances in both miles and kilometers.

Key
—— National border
⊛ National capital
• Other city

M8 MapMaster Skills Handbook

Differentiated Instruction

For Less Proficient Readers `L2`

If students have difficulty recalling the purposes of different parts of a map, have them make a table using each map part as a heading. Under each heading, help students list the important function or functions of that map part. Suggest that students refer to their table when they are working with maps.

For English Language Learners `L1`

Some of the words in the lesson, such as *symbol* and *scale,* may be unfamiliar to students acquiring English. Have students identify difficult words, look them up in the dictionary, and write sentences explaining what the terms mean.

Maps of Different Scales

Maps are drawn to different scales, depending on their purpose. Here are three maps drawn to very different scales. Keep in mind that maps showing large areas have smaller scales. Maps showing small areas have larger scales.

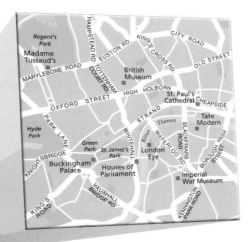

▲ **Greater London**
Find the gray square on the main map of Western Europe (left). This square represents the area shown on the map above. It shows London's boundaries, the general shape of the city, and the features around the city. This map can help you find your way from the airport to the center of town.

▲ **Central London**
Find the gray square on the map of Greater London. This square represents the area shown on the map above. This map moves you closer into the center of London. Like the zoom on a computer or a camera, this map shows a smaller area but in greater detail. It has the largest scale (1 inch represents about 0.9 mile). You can use this map to explore downtown London.

Key

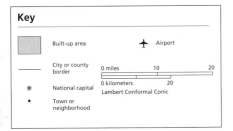
- ■ Point of interest
- ◤ Park

0 miles   0.5   1
0 kilometers   1

Key
- ▨ Built-up area
- ✈ Airport
- — City or county border
- ⊛ National capital
- • Town or neighborhood

0 miles   10   20
0 kilometers   20
Lambert Conformal Conic

PRACTICE YOUR GEOGRAPHY SKILLS

1 What part of a map explains the colors used on the map?

2 How does the scale bar change depending on the scale of the map?

3 Which map would be best for finding the location of the British Museum? Explain why.

Monitor Progress

Circulate around the room as students complete the worksheets. Make sure that individuals comprehend the material. Provide assistance as needed.

Assess and Reteach

Assess Progress L2
Have students complete the questions under Practice Your Geography Skills.

Reteach
Some DK Atlas Activities will be helpful in reteaching the lesson. Give students more practice using these concepts by doing the activities for *Using the Map Key; Using the Compass Rose;* and, *Using the Map Scale.*

All in One **History of Our World Teaching Resources,** MapMaster™ Teacher's Companion, *Understanding Projection*, p. 9; *DK Compact Atlas of the World Activity: Using the Map Key*, p. 67; *DK Compact Atlas of the World Activity: Using the Compass Rose*, p. 68; *DK Compact Atlas of the World Activity: Using the Map Scale*, p. 69

Extend L3
To extend the lesson, have students complete *Comparing Maps of Different Scale* and *Maps with Accurate Distances: Equidistant Maps.*

All in One **History of Our World Teaching Resources,** MapMaster™ Teacher's Companion, *Comparing Maps of Different Scale*, p. 18; *Maps with Accurate Distances: Equidistant Maps*, p. 13

Answers

PRACTICE YOUR GEOGRAPHY SKILLS

1. key

2. Maps showing large areas have smaller scales. Maps showing small areas have larger scales.

3. the map of Central London; it shows the streets in more detail and includes the British Museum as a point of interest

Objectives

- Understand and use political maps.
- Understand and use physical maps.

Prepare to Read

Build Background Knowledge **L1**

Tell students that they will learn about political maps and physical maps in this lesson. Explain that a political map is one that shows the boundaries and cities of an area as established by its people. Physical maps show information about the physical features of the area. These physical features would exist whether people lived in a place or not.

Instruct

Political Maps **L2**
Physical Maps **L2**

Guided Instruction

- Read the text as a class using the Choral Reading technique (TE, p. T38) and ask students to study the map.

- Ask students to identify what river forms the boundary between Zimbabwe and South Africa. (*Limpopo River*). Then ask them to name at least two capitals on the Mediterranean Sea. (*Tripoli, Algiers, Tunis*)

- Read the text with the class and draw students' attention to the map and its key.

- Explain that sea level is the average height of the ocean's surface; sea level is at zero elevation. Ask students what color represents sea level on the map key. (*dark green*)

- Have students find the Qattara Depression. Ask **What is its elevation?** (*from 0 to 650 feet*)

- Ask **What is the difference between elevation and relief?** (*Elevation is the height of land above sea level while relief shows how quickly the land rises or falls.*)

Answers

PRACTICE YOUR GEOGRAPHY SKILLS

1. solid line, star in a circle, dot
2. Luanda

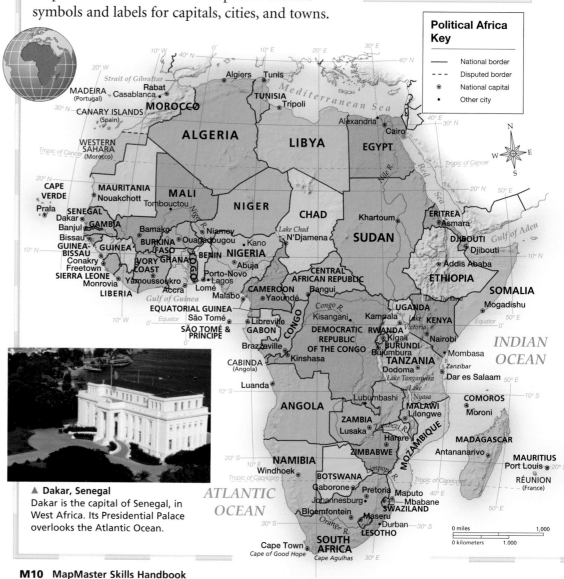

Political Maps

Political maps show political borders: continents, countries, and divisions within countries, such as states or provinces. The colors on political maps do not have any special meaning, but they make the map easier to read. Political maps also include symbols and labels for capitals, cities, and towns.

PRACTICE YOUR GEOGRAPHY SKILLS

1 What symbols show a national border, a national capital, and a city?

2 What is Angola's capital city?

Political Africa Key

— National border
- - - Disputed border
⊛ National capital
• Other city

▲ Dakar, Senegal
Dakar is the capital of Senegal, in West Africa. Its Presidential Palace overlooks the Atlantic Ocean.

M10 MapMaster Skills Handbook

Background: Global Perspectives

Africa's Highest Peaks Africa's two highest mountains are both extinct volcanoes that rise near the equator on the eastern part of the continent. The tallest mountain, Kilimanjaro in Tanzania, reaches 19,340 feet (5,895 meters) at its highest point. Although snow covers its peaks, farmers raise coffee and plantains on the lower southern slopes of Kilimanjaro. Africa's second highest mountain is Mt. Kenya at 17,058 feet (5,199 meters) located in central Kenya. Like Kilimanjaro, it is snowcapped in its highest regions. Both Kilimanjaro and Mt. Kenya are attractions for mountain climbers from all over the world.

Physical Maps

Physical maps represent what a region looks like by showing its major physical features, such as hills and plains. Physical maps also often show elevation and relief. Elevation, indicated by colors, is the height of the land above sea level. Relief, indicated by shading, shows how sharply the land rises or falls.

PRACTICE YOUR GEOGRAPHY SKILLS

1 Which areas of Africa have the highest elevation?

2 How can you use relief to plan a hiking trip?

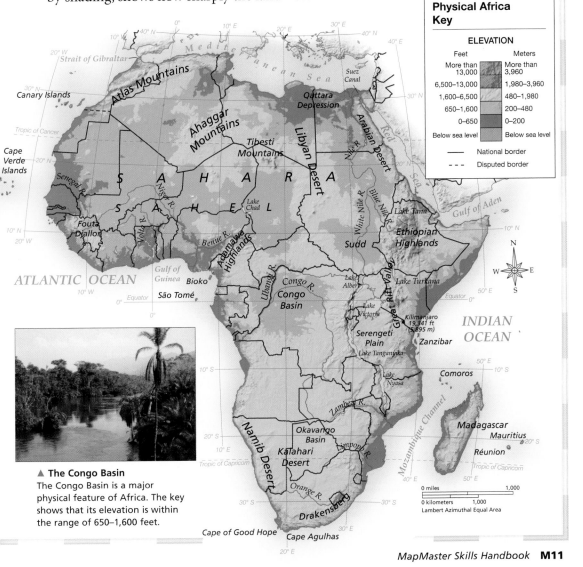

Physical Africa Key

ELEVATION

Feet		Meters
More than 13,000		More than 3,960
6,500–13,000		1,980–3,960
1,600–6,500		480–1,980
650–1,600		200–480
0–650		0–200
Below sea level		Below sea level

— National border
- - - Disputed border

▲ The Congo Basin
The Congo Basin is a major physical feature of Africa. The key shows that its elevation is within the range of 650–1,600 feet.

MapMaster Skills Handbook **M11**

Differentiated Instruction

For Special Needs Students L1
Reuse *Reading a Political Map* to help students understand the features of a political map. Point to the symbol for a national border in the key, then trace the borders of several countries. Invite students to trace others.

All in One History of Our World Teaching Resources, MapMaster™ Teacher's Companion, *Reading a Political Map,* p. 19

For Advanced Readers L3
Challenge students to explore the concepts of relief and elevation further by completing *Relief on a Map* and *Maps of the Ocean Floor.*

All in One History of Our World Teaching Resources, MapMaster™ Teacher's Companion, *Relief on a Map,* p. 22; *Maps of the Ocean Floor,* p. 23

Independent Practice
Have students complete *Reading a Political Map, Reading a Physical Map* and *Elevation on a Map* working with partners.

All in One History of Our World Teaching Resources, MapMaster™ Teacher's Companion, *Reading a Political Map,* p. 19; *Reading a Physical Map,* p. 20; *Elevation on a Map,* p. 21

Monitor Progress
As students complete the worksheets, circulate around the room to make sure individuals understand the key concepts. Provide assistance as needed.

Assess and Reteach

Assess Progress L2
Have students answer the questions under Practice Your Geography Skills on pages M10 and M11.

Reteach L1
Use the DK Atlas Activities *Reading a Political Map* and *Reading a Physical Map* to review the concepts in this lesson.

All in One History of Our World Teaching Resources, MapMaster™ Teacher's Companion, *DK Compact Atlas of the World Activity: Reading a Political Map,* p. 71; *DK Compact Atlas of the World Activity: Reading a Physical Map,* p. 72

Extend L3
To extend the lesson, have students fill in the name of each country and its capital on the outline maps *North Africa, West and Central Africa,* and *East and Southern Africa.* Also, ask them to use colors and shading to indicate the Atlas Mountains, the Ethiopian Highlands, the Congo Basin, and the Namib Desert.

All in One History of Our World Teaching Resources, MapMaster™ Teacher's Companion, *Outline Map 22: North Africa,* p. 104; *Outline Map 23: West and Central Africa,* p. 105; *Outline Map 24: East and Southern Africa,* p. 106

Answers

PRACTICE YOUR GEOGRAPHY SKILLS

1. mountains; the areas with the purple or brown coloring

2. It can help you find out how the land rises and falls.

Objectives

- Understand and use climate maps.
- Understand and use language maps.

Prepare to Read

Build Background Knowledge   L1

Ask students to think of as many meanings for the word *special* as they can. Tell them that maps can be special too. Ask **What do you think a special-purpose map might show?** List suggestions on the board.

Instruct

Special-Purpose Maps: Climate   L1

Guided Instruction

- Ask students to read the text using the Structured Silent Reading strategy (TE, p. T38). Point out that the map shows Bangladesh, Bhutan, Nepal, and parts of Myanmar and Pakistan as well as India.

- Point out the map and key. Ask **What areas have a tropical wet climate?** *(area along the southern western coast; eastern part of Bangladesh)*

Independent Practice

Partner students and have them complete *Reading a Climate Map.*

All in One **History of Our World Teaching Resources,** MapMaster™ Teacher's Companion, *Reading a Climate Map,* p. 24

Monitor Progress

As students complete the worksheet, circulate around the room to make sure individuals comprehend the key concepts. Provide assistance as needed.

Answers

PRACTICE YOUR GEOGRAPHY SKILLS

1. the key
2. No cities are shown in the arid or semi-arid regions.

Special-Purpose Maps: Climate

Unlike the boundary lines on a political map, the boundary lines on climate maps do not separate the land into exact divisions. For example, in this climate map of India, a tropical wet climate gradually changes to a tropical wet and dry climate.

PRACTICE YOUR GEOGRAPHY SKILLS

1 What part of a special-purpose map tells you what the colors on the map mean?

2 Where are arid regions located in India? Are there major cities in those regions?

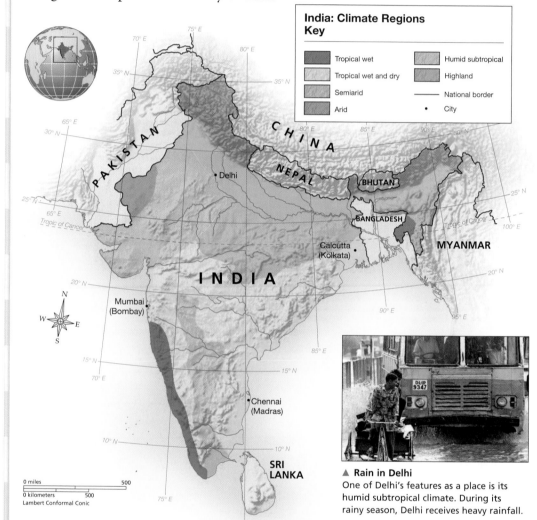

India: Climate Regions Key

- Tropical wet
- Tropical wet and dry
- Semiarid
- Arid
- Humid subtropical
- Highland
- ── National border
- • City

▲ **Rain in Delhi**
One of Delhi's features as a place is its humid subtropical climate. During its rainy season, Delhi receives heavy rainfall.

0 miles 500
0 kilometers 500
Lambert Conformal Conic

M12   **MapMaster Skills Handbook**

Differentiated Instruction

For English Language Learners   L1
If students are unfamiliar with words in the lesson, help them identify and look up those words in the dictionary. For example: *arid*—adj. having little or no rainfall; dry *humid*—adj. having a lot of water; damp *semi*—adj. part or partially

Follow up by having students determine the meaning of *semiarid.*

For Gifted and Talented Students   L3
Give students *Reading a Climate Graph.* Ask students to compare the information in the graph with the information on the map above. Ask them to write a sentence synthesizing about the climate of Mumbai.

All in One **History of Our World Teaching Resources,** MapMaster™ Teacher's Companion, *Reading A Climate Graph,* p. 43

Special-Purpose Maps: Language

This map shows the official languages of India. An official language is the language used by the government. Even though a region has an official language, the people there may speak other languages as well. As in other special-purpose maps, the key explains how the different languages appear on the map.

PRACTICE YOUR GEOGRAPHY SKILLS

1 What color represents the Malayalam language on this map?

2 Where in India is Tamil the official language?

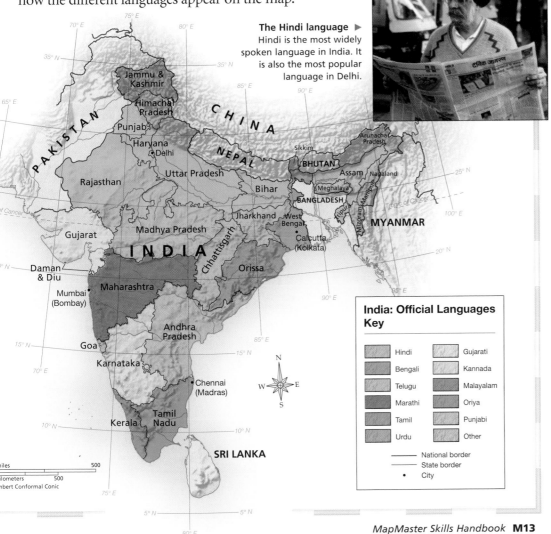

The Hindi language ▶ Hindi is the most widely spoken language in India. It is also the most popular language in Delhi.

India: Official Languages Key

Hindi	Gujarati
Bengali	Kannada
Telugu	Malayalam
Marathi	Oriya
Tamil	Punjabi
Urdu	Other

—— National border
—— State border
• City

MapMaster Skills Handbook **M13**

Background: Daily Life

The Hindi Language Hindi is the official language of India and is the primary language for about 300 million people. Hindi is the written form of Hindustani that is used by Hindus. English is also spoken by many Indians and is considered the language of politics and commerce. However, the diversity of the country is reflected in the enormous number of languages spoken there, more than 1,500 in all. Ten of India's major states are organized along linguistic lines, and the Indian constitution recognizes 15 regional languages.

Special-Purpose Maps: Language L2

Guided Instruction
- Read the text as a class. Draw students' attention to the map and its key.

- Have students consider the diversity of official languages. Ask **Why might it be important for a country to have a common language in addition to regional ones?** *(Communication is easier with a common language.)*

Independent Practice

Have students work with partners to read another special purpose map, *Reading a Natural Vegetation Map*.

All in One History of Our World Teaching Resources, MapMaster™ Teacher's Companion, *Reading a Natural Vegetation Map*, p. 28

Monitor Progress

As students complete the worksheet, circulate around the room and make sure individuals understand key concepts. Provide assistance as needed.

Assess and Reteach

Assess Progress L2
Have students answer the questions under Practice Your Geography Skills on pages M12 and M13.

Reteach L1
To help students understand how to use a special purpose map, have them practice the skill using *Analyzing and Interpreting Special Purpose Maps*.

⦿ Analyzing and Interpreting Special-Purpose Maps, **Social Studies Skills Tutor CD-ROM**

Extend L3
Have students learn about another type of special-purpose map by completing *Reading a Time Zone Map*. Then ask students to find out the time zones in India and create their own time zone map, using *Outline Map 26: South Asia: Political*.

All in One History of Our World Teaching Resources, MapMaster™ Teacher's Companion, *Reading a Time Zone Map*, p. 26; *Outline Map 26: South Asia: Political*, p. 108

Answers

PRACTICE YOUR GEOGRAPHY SKILLS

1. dark pink
2. southeast India

MapMaster Skills Handbook **M13**

Objectives

- Learn why people migrate.
- Understand how migration affects environments.

Prepare to Read

Build Background Knowledge　L1

Remind students that they studied the theme of movement earlier in this unit. Brainstorm with students why people move from place to place, particularly those who move from one country to another. Use Numbered Heads (TE, p. T40) to generate ideas.

Instruct

Human Migration　L2

Guided Instruction

- Divide the text using the headings and ask students to read the pages using the Partner Paragraph Shrinking technique (TE, p. T38). Clarify the meanings of any unfamiliar words.

- Have students look at the map. Ask **From what European countries did people migrate to the Americas in the years between 1500-1800?** (*Portugal, Spain, France, Netherlands, England*)

- Ask **Where did the French settle in Latin America?** (*French Guiana and Haiti*) **Which European country had the most possessions in the Americas?** (*Spain*)

- Ask **Why were some Africans forced to migrate?** (*They were imported as slaves from their homeland. Europeans wanted them to work on the land they claimed in the Americas.*)

Human Migration

Migration is an important part of the study of geography. Since the beginning of history, people have been on the move. As people move, they both shape and are shaped by their environments. Wherever people go, the culture they bring with them mixes with the cultures of the place in which they have settled.

Explorers arrive ▼
In 1492, Christopher Columbus set sail from Spain for the Americas with three ships. The ships shown here are replicas of those ships.

▲ Native American pyramid
When Europeans arrived in the Americas, the lands they found were not empty. Diverse groups of people with distinct cultures already lived there. The temple-topped pyramid shown above was built by Mayan Indians in Mexico, long before Columbus sailed.

Migration to the Americas, 1500–1800

A huge wave of migration from the Eastern Hemisphere began in the 1500s. European explorers in the Americas paved the way for hundreds of years of European settlement there. Forced migration from Africa started soon afterward, as Europeans began to import African slaves to work in the Americas. The map to the right shows these migrations.

Map labels:
ATLANTIC OCEAN
NEW SPAIN (Spain)
Mexico City
Caribbean Sea
Panama City
DUTCH GUIANA (Netherlands)
NEW GRENADA (Spain)
FRENCH GUIANA (France)
Amazon R.
PERU (Spain)
Lima
Cuzco
BRAZIL (Portugal)
Potosí
RIO DE LA PLATA (Spain)
Concepción
Buenos Aires
0 miles 1,000
0 kilometers 1,000
Wagner VII

Differentiated Instruction

For Less Proficient Readers　L1

Review with students the meaning of "push" and "pull" factors in terms of human migration. Model for students how to make a table with the headings Push and Pull. Then work with students to list as many factors as they can under each heading.

For Advanced Readers　L3

Have students complete *Analyzing Statistics*. When they have finished, have them write a paragraph explaining how economic and social statistics are related to "push" and "pull" factors.

All in One **History of Our World Teaching Resources,** MapMaster™ Teacher's Companion, *Analyzing Statistics,* p. 47

SCOTLAND
IRELAND ENGLAND
FRANCE NETHERLANDS
EUROPE
PORTUGAL SPAIN
MOROCCO
WALO **AFRICA**
Saint-Louis
Fort James
Cacheu AKAN STATES
Elmina BENIN
Axim Accra
Congo R.
Congo Basin
KONGO
Luanda
Benguela
ATLANTIC OCEAN

Niger R.

Migration to Latin America, 1500–1800 Key

⬅ European migration
⬅ African migration
— National or colonial border
⋯ Traditional African border
▨ African State

▨ Spain and possessions
▨ Portugal and possessions
▨ Netherlands and possessions
▨ France and possessions
▨ England and possessions

PRACTICE YOUR GEOGRAPHY SKILLS

1 Where did the Portuguese settle in the Americas?

2 Would you describe African migration at this time as a result of both push factors and pull factors? Explain why or why not.

"Push" and "Pull" Factors

Geographers describe a people's choice to migrate in terms of "push" factors and "pull" factors. Push factors are things in people's lives that push them to leave, such as poverty and political unrest. Pull factors are things in another country that pull people to move there, including better living conditions and hopes of better jobs.

▲ **Elmina, Ghana**
Elmina, in Ghana, is one of the many ports from which slaves were transported from Africa. Because slaves and gold were traded here, stretches of the western African coast were known as the Slave Coast and the Gold Coast.

Independent Practice

Have students work with partners to complete *Reading a Historical Map*. Have students be ready to explain how the movement of European groups changed the map of Africa. (*Much of Africa was colonized by Europeans.*)

⊠ **in** **One** **History of Our World Teaching Resources,** MapMaster™ Teacher's Companion, *Reading a Historical Map,* p. 29

Monitor Progress

As students complete the worksheet, circulate around the room to make sure individuals comprehend the key concepts. Provide assistance as needed.

Assess and Reteach

Assess Progress L2

Have students complete the questions under Practice Your Geography Skills.

Reteach L1

Help students make an outline of the lesson. Show *Transparency B15: Outline* as a model. Then work with students to identify the main points. Encourage students to refer to their outlines to review the material.

📖 **History of Our World Transparencies,** *Transparency B15: Outline*

Extend L3

To extend the lesson, have students complete *The Global Refugee Crisis*. Then ask them to choose a specific region on the graph and find out more about refugees from one country in that region.

Go **Online**
PHSchool.com **For:** Environmental and Global Issues: *The Global Refugee Crisis*
Visit: PHSchool.com
Web Code: lbd-2001

Answers

PRACTICE YOUR GEOGRAPHY SKILLS

1. Brazil

2. most likely push factors because people were forced to leave; the need for workers in the Americas was a pull factor although it was the Europeans who responded to it by importing Africans as slaves

Objectives

- Understand and use a land use map.

- Learn how land use and economic structures are linked.

Prepare to Read

Build Background Knowledge L1

Discuss with the class the ways that people in your community are using land. For example, is all the land used for homes? How much is used for commercial purposes? What kinds? Are there farms or manufacturing facilities? Point out that communities in all parts of the world use land in different ways.

Instruct

World Land Use L2

Guided Instruction

- Read the text as a class using the Oral Cloze strategy (TE, p. T37). Follow up by having students do a second silent reading. Encourage students to study the map and photographs.

- Talk about the difference between commercial and subsistence farming. Have them look closely at the photographs on pages M16 and M17. Ask **How do the tools and equipment people use differ in these types of farming?** (*Large power machines are used in commercial farming; hand tools are used in subsistence farming*) **Why might people use more land in commercial farming?** (*Machines make it possible to cultivate more land. The more land cultivated, the more sales possible.*)

- Ask **What color represents nomadic herding on this map?** (*light purple*) **In what parts of the world is this an economic activity?** (*Africa, Asia*)

- Ask **Why might some parts of the world have little or no land use activity?** (*Land and/or climate might not be suitable for farming or other activity.*)

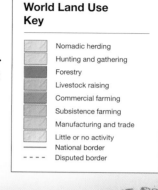

World Land Use

People around the world have many different economic structures, or ways of making a living. Land-use maps are one way to learn about these structures. The ways that people use the land in each region tell us about the main ways that people in that region make a living.

World Land Use Key

	Nomadic herding
	Hunting and gathering
	Forestry
	Livestock raising
	Commercial farming
	Subsistence farming
	Manufacturing and trade
	Little or no activity
——	National border
- - - -	Disputed border

▲ **Wheat farming in the United States**
Developed countries practice commercial farming rather than subsistence farming. Commercial farming is the production of food mainly for sale, either within the country or for export to other countries. Commercial farmers like these in Oregon often use heavy equipment to farm.

Levels of Development

Notice on the map key the term *subsistence farming*. This term means the production of food mainly for use by the farmer's own family. In less-developed countries, subsistence farming is often one of the main economic activities. In contrast, in developed countries there is little subsistence farming.

▲ **Growing barley in Ecuador**
These farmers in Ecuador use hand tools to harvest barley. They will use most of the crop they grow to feed themselves or their farm animals.

NORTH AMERICA

SOUTH AMERICA

```
0 miles              2,000
0 kilometers         2,000
Robinson
```

M16 MapMaster Skills Handbook

Background: Global Perspectives

Agriculture Almost 50 percent of the world's population is occupied in agriculture. A much higher proportion of this is in Third World countries where dense populations, small land holdings, and traditional techniques predominate. In areas where there is intense cultivation using people and animals but few machines, the yield is low in relation to the output of energy. In leading food producing countries such as the United States, industrial farms make use of new technology and crop specialization to increase output.

▲ **Growing rice in Vietnam**
Women in Vietnam plant rice in wet rice paddies, using the same planting methods their ancestors did.

PRACTICE YOUR GEOGRAPHY SKILLS

1 In what parts of the world is subsistence farming the main land use?

2 Locate where manufacturing and trade are the main land use. Are they found more often near areas of subsistence farming or areas of commercial farming? Why might this be so?

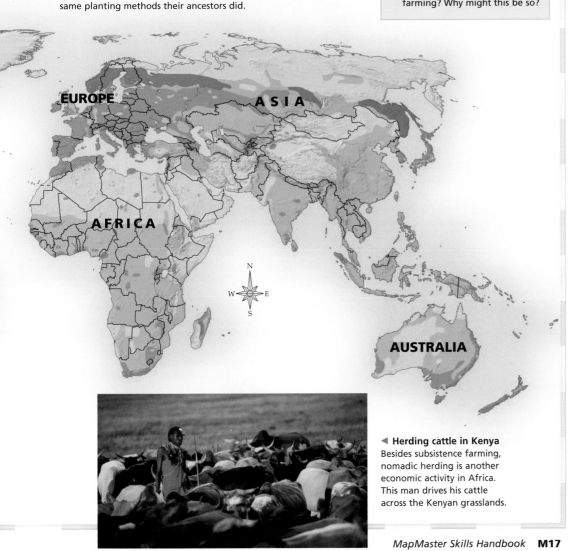

EUROPE

ASIA

AFRICA

AUSTRALIA

◄ **Herding cattle in Kenya**
Besides subsistence farming, nomadic herding is another economic activity in Africa. This man drives his cattle across the Kenyan grasslands.

MapMaster Skills Handbook **M17**

Independent Practice

Partner students and have them complete *Reading an Economic Activity Map.* Have students be ready to offer explanations for how the economic activity in Somalia might affect the lives of people there.

All in One History of Our World Teaching Resources, MapMaster™ Teacher's Companion, *Reading an Economic Activity Map,* p. 30

Monitor Progress

Circulate around the room as students complete the worksheet to make sure individuals comprehend the key concepts. Provide assistance as needed.

Assess and Reteach

Assess Progress   L2

Have students complete the questions under Practice Your Geography Skills.

Reteach   L1

Help students make a table to identify kinds of land use. Draw a model on the board for students to follow. Use these headings: Nomadic Herding, Forestry, Livestock Raising, Commercial Farming, Subsistence Farming, Manufacturing and Trade. Under each heading, help students write a short explanation. Then have students find one or two places on the map in their books where that activity takes place.

Extend   L3

To extend the lesson, have students complete *Reading a Natural Resources Map.* Point out that this map shows mineral resources. Then ask students to write a paragraph relating mineral resources to land use.

All in One History of Our World Teaching Resources, MapMaster™ Teacher's Companion, *Reading a Natural Resources Map,* p. 25

Differentiated Instruction

For English Language Learners   L3
Students may find it difficult to pronounce some of the multisyllable words in this section such as *nomadic, subsis-* *tence, commercial,* and *forestry.* Model how to break down these words into smaller parts to help students sound out the pronunciation.

Answers

PRACTICE YOUR GEOGRAPHY SKILLS

1. Africa, Asia, South America

2. areas of commercial farming; both manufacturing and trade and commercial farming require technology which is found in developed countries

MapMaster Skills Handbook **M17**

Teaching the Target Reading Skills

The Prentice Hall *History of Our World* program has interwoven essential reading skills instruction throughout the Student Edition, Teacher's Edition, and ancillary resources.

Student Edition The *History of Our World* Student Edition provides students with reading skills instruction, practice, and application opportunities in each chapter within the program.

Teacher's Edition The *History of Our World* Teacher Edition supports your teaching of each skill by providing full modeling in each chapter's interleaf and modeling of the specific sub-skills in each section lesson.

All in One Teaching Resources The *History of Our World* All-in-One Teaching Resources provides a worksheet explaining and supporting the elements of each Target Reading Skill. Use these to help struggling students master skills, or as more practice for every student.

How to Read Social Studies

Target Reading Skills

The Target Reading Skills introduced on this page will help you understand the words and ideas in this book and in other social studies reading you do. Each chapter focuses on one of these reading skills. Good readers develop a bank of reading strategies, or skills. Then they draw on the particular strategies that will help them understand the text they are reading.

Target Reading Skill
Using the Reading Process Previewing can help you understand and remember what you read. You will practice using the reading process in these chapters: **Chapter 1, Chapter 10**

Target Reading Skill
Clarifying Meaning In these chapters, you will use several skills to clarify the meaning of a word or an idea. **Chapter 2, Chapter 11, Chapter 16**

Target Reading Skill
Using Context In this chapter, you will practice using context clues to help you understand the meaning of unfamiliar words. **Chapter 3**

Target Reading Skill
Using Cause and Effect You will practice recognizing cause and effect to help you understand relationships among the situations and events you are reading about. **Chapter 4, Chapter 13, Chapter 15**

Target Reading Skill
Identifying the Main Idea The main idea of a section or paragraph is the most important point, the one you want to remember. In these chapters, you will practice identifying both stated and implied main ideas and identifying supporting details. **Chapter 5, Chapter 9, Chapter 17**

Target Reading Skill
Using Sequence Understand sequence—the order in which a series of events occurs—helps you to remember and understand events. You will practicing using sequence in these chapters. **Chapter 6, Chapter 14**

Target Reading Skill
Making Comparisons and Contrasts When you compare, you examine the similarities between things. When you contrast, you look at the differences. You will practice making comparisons and contrast is this chapter. **Chapter 7**

Target Reading Skill
Using Word Analysis You can analyze words to determine their meanings. In this chapter, you will practice using word parts (such as roots, prefixes, and suffixes) and recognizing word origins. **Chapter 8**

Assessment Resources

Use the diagnosing readiness tests from **AYP Monitoring Assessments** to help you identify problems before students begin to study the Ancient World.

Determine students' reading level and identify challenges:

📄 Screening Tests, pp. 1–11

Evaluate students' verbal skills:

📄 Critical Thinking and Reading Tests, pp. 25–34

📄 Vocabulary Tests, pp. 45–52

📄 Writing Tests, pp. 53–60

HISTORY OF OUR WORLD
The Early Ages

To understand today's world, we must learn about its past. Ancient civilizations laid strong foundations for modern cultures. The early ages of world history have added greatly to those cultures. In this book, you will learn how the ideas, events, and people of those early ages have shaped our lives.

Guiding Questions

The text, photographs, maps, and charts in this book will help you discover answers to these Guiding Questions.

1. **Geography** How did physical geography affect the development and growth of societies around the world?

2. **History** How did each society's belief system affect its historical accomplishments?

3. **Culture** What were the beliefs and values of people in these societies?

4. **Government** What types of governments were formed in these societies and how did they develop?

5. **Economics** How did each society develop and organize its economic activities?

Project Preview

You can also discover answers to the Guiding Questions by working on projects. Several project possibilities are listed on page 502 of this book.

Guiding Questions

- This book was developed around five Guiding Questions about world history. They appear on the reduced Student Edition page to the left. The Guiding Questions are intended as an organizational focus for the book. The Guiding Questions act as a kind of umbrella under which all of the material falls.

- You may wish to add your own Guiding Questions to the list in order to tailor them to your particular course.

- Draw students' attention to the Guiding Questions. Ask them to write the questions in their notebooks for future reference.

- In the Teacher's Edition, each section's themes are linked to a specific Guiding Question at the beginning of each chapter. Then, an activity at the end of the chapter returns to the Guiding Questions to review key concepts.

Project Preview

- The projects for this book are designed to provide students with hands-on involvement in the content area. Students are introduced to some projects on page 502.

- *Book Projects* give students directions on how to complete these projects, and more.

   All in One **History of Our World Teaching Resources,** Book Projects

- Assign projects as small group activities, whole-class projects, or individual projects. Consider assigning a project at the beginning of the course.

Assess students' social studies skills:

- Geographic Literacy Tests, pp. 13–20
- Visual Analysis Tests, pp. 21–24
- Communications Tests, pp. 35–44

The *History of Our World* program provides instruction and practice for all of these skills. Use students' test results to pinpoint the skills your students have mastered and the skills they need to practice. Then use *Correlation to Program Resources* to prescribe skills practice and reinforcement.

- Correlation to Program Resources, pp. 64–77

Toward Civilization

Unit Overview

In Chapter 1, students will learn about early human culture in the Stone Age, the development of farming during the New Stone Age, and the growth of the first civilizations. Chapter 2 provides a detailed overview of civilizations in the Fertile Crescent, including Babylonia, Assyria, and Mesopotamia.

Monitoring Student Progress

After students have completed Chapter 2, administer Benchmark Test 1, the first of six benchmark tests provided to assess students' progress toward mastery of the National Geography Standards.

The Report Sheet for this test will identify which objectives or standards students have mastered and where they need additional work. It also correlates to the appropriate sections in the Reading and Vocabulary Study Guide, where students can get additional review as needed.

AYP Monitoring Assessment Resources

Determine students' progress toward mastery of the National Geography Standards.

   📖 *Benchmark Test 1,* **AYP Monitoring Assessments,** pp. 81–86

Use the Report Sheet to identify which standards your students have mastered, where they need more work, and where they can get additional help.

   📖 *Report Sheet, Benchmark Test 1,* **AYP Monitoring Assessments,** p. 125

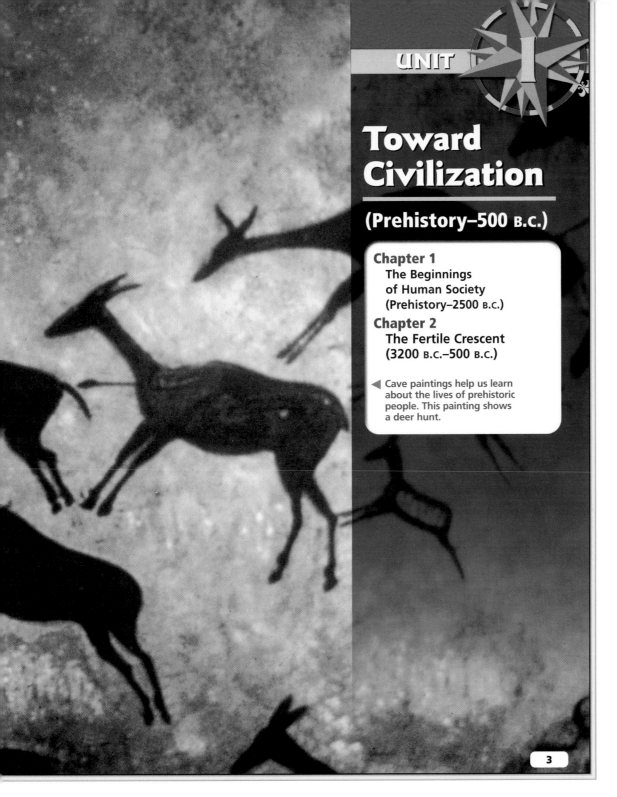

Toward Civilization

(Prehistory–500 B.C.)

◀ Cave paintings help us learn about the lives of prehistoric people. This painting shows a deer hunt.

3

Using the Visual

Ask students to study the picture on pp. 2–3. Tell students that the picture shows a cave painting made by people who lived thousands of years ago. Ask students what the painting shows about how early humans lived. *(The painting shows that early humans hunted animals with bows and arrows.)* Discuss with students how cave paintings have left a valuable record of prehistoric times.

The Beginnings of Human Society

Overview

1 Section 1 — Geography and History
1. Learn what tools are used to understand history.
2. Find out about the connections between geography and history.

2 Section 2 — Prehistory
1. Discover how hunter-gatherers lived during the Stone Age.
2. Learn about the beginning of farming.

3 Section 3 — The Beginnings of Civilization
1. Find out about the advantages people gained from settling down in one place.
2. Learn about the growth of early cities.
3. Understand how the first civilizations formed and spread.

Discovery CHANNEL SCHOOL Video

The First Great Migration
Length: 5 minutes, 6 seconds
Use with Section 2
This video segment explores the migration of ancient people from Africa to Asia and beyond. The segment discusses how climate influenced this movement.

Technology Resources

Go Online
PHSchool.com

Students use embedded Web codes to access Internet activities, chapter self-tests, and additional map practice. They may also access Dorling Kindersley's Online Desk Reference to learn more about each country they study.

Interactive Textbook

Use the Interactive Textbook to make content and concepts come alive through animations, videos, and activities that accompany the complete basal text—online and on CD-ROM.

PRENTICE HALL TeacherEXPRESS
Plan • Teach • Assess

Use this complete suite of powerful teaching tools to make planning lessons and administering tests quicker and easier.

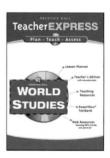

Reading and Assessment

Reading and Vocabulary Instruction

⟳ Model the Target Reading Skill

Reading Process Reading actively helps students retain knowledge and become better readers. One way of reading actively is to preview and think about the text *before reading*.

Model this skill by thinking about the chapter aloud:

This chapter's title is *The Beginnings of Human Society*, and I will be learning about how human society began. The first section is called *Geography and History*. I wonder what the relationship between the geography and history of an area is. I'll read the section to find out.

The second section is called *Prehistory*. What does *prehistory* mean exactly? It includes *history*, which is the subject of this course. I predict that in this section, I'll find out what *prehistory* means.

The third section is called *The Beginnings of Civilization*. I have heard the word *civilization* before, and I know it relates to societies of people. A beginning, of course, means the start of something. How did civilizations begin? I'll read this section to find out.

Use the following worksheets from All-in-One Unit 1 History of Our World Teaching Resources (pp. 20–22) to support this chapter's Target Reading Skill.

Vocabulary Builder
High-Use Academic Words

Use these steps to teach this chapter's high-use words:

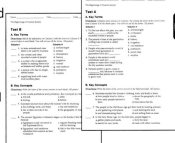

1. Have students rate how well they know each word on their Word Knowledge worksheets (All-in-One Unit 1 History of Our World Teaching Resources, p. 23).

2. Pronounce each word and ask students to repeat it.

3. Give students a brief definition and sample sentence (provided on TE pp. 7, 13, and 21).

4. Work with students as they fill in the "Definition or Example" column of their Word Knowledge worksheets.

Assessment

Formal Assessment

Test students' understanding of core knowledge and skills.

Chapter Tests A and B, All-in-One Unit 1 History of Our World Teaching Resources, pp. 37–42

Customize the Chapter Tests to suit your needs.

Exam*View*® Test Bank CD-ROM

Skills Assessment

Assess geographic literacy.

MapMaster Skills, Student Edition, pp. 5, 15, 26

Assess reading and comprehension.

Target Reading Skills, Student Edition, pp. 8, 14, 22 and in Section Assessments

Chapter 1 Assessment, History of Our World Reading and Vocabulary Study Guide, p. 15

Performance Assessment

Assess students' performance on this chapter's Writing Activities using the following rubrics from All-in-One Unit 1 History of Our World Teaching Resources.

Rubric for Assessing a Writing Assignment, p. 35

Rubric for Assessing a Journal Entry, p. 36

Assess students' work through performance tasks.

Small Group Activity: Simulation: Analyzing "Ancient" Objects, All-in-One Unit 1 History of Our World Teaching Resources, pp. 26–29

Online Assessment

Have students check their own understanding.

Chapter Self-Test

4b

Section 1 **Geography and History**

 2 periods, 1 block (includes Skills for Life)

Social Studies Objectives
1. Learn what tools are used to understand history.
2. Find out about the connections between geography and history.

Reading/Language Arts Objective
Learn how to set a purpose for reading.

Prepare to Read	**Instructional Resources**	**Differentiated Instruction**
Build Background Knowledge Discuss how scientists learned about the Iceman's life. **Set a Purpose for Reading** Have students evaluate statements on the *Reading Readiness Guide.* **Preview Key Terms** Teach the section's Key Terms. **Target Reading Skill** Introduce the section's Target Reading Skill of **setting a purpose for reading.**	**All in One Unit 1 History of Our World Teaching Resources** **L2** Reading Readiness Guide, p. 9 **L2** Preview and Set a Purpose, p. 20	**Spanish Reading and Vocabulary Study Guide** **L1** Chapter 1, Section 1, pp. 7–8 ELL

Instruct	**Instructional Resources**	**Differentiated Instruction**
Understanding History Discuss how archaeologists study prehistory. **Target Reading Skill** Review **how to set a purpose for reading.** **Linking Geography and History** Ask about the relationship between geography and history.	**All in One Unit 1 History of Our World Teaching Resources** **L2** Guided Reading and Review, p. 10 **L2** Reading Readiness Guide, p. 9 **History of Our World Transparencies** **L2** Section Reading Support Transparency HOW 53	**All in One Unit 1 History of Our World Teaching Resources** **L2** Skills for Life, p. 25 AR, GT, LPR, SN **Teacher's Edition** **L1** For Special Needs Students, TE p. 8 **Spanish Support** **L2** Guided Reading and Review (Spanish), p. 4 ELL

Assess and Reteach	**Instructional Resources**	**Differentiated Instruction**
Assess Progress Evaluate student comprehension with the section assessment and section quiz. **Reteach** Assign the Reading and Vocabulary Study Guide to help struggling students. **Extend** Extend the lesson by assigning a literature reading.	**All in One Unit 1 History of Our World Teaching Resources** **L2** Section Quiz, p. 11 **L3** The Iceman, pp. 31–32 Rubric for Assessing a Writing Assignment, p. 35 **Reading and Vocabulary Study Guide** **L1** Chapter 1, Section 1, pp. 6–8	**History of Our World Transparencies** **L3** Transparency B20: Timeline AR, GT **Teacher's Edition** **L1** For Special Needs Students, TE p. 11 **Spanish Support** **L2** Section Quiz (Spanish), p. 5 ELL **Social Studies Skills Tutor CD-ROM** **L1** Sequencing ELL, LPR, SN

Key
L1 Basic to Average   **L3** Average to Advanced
L2 For All Students

LPR Less Proficient Readers
AR Advanced Readers
SN Special Needs Students

GT Gifted and Talented
ELL English Language Learners

Section 2 Prehistory

 2 periods, 1 block (includes Focus on Hunters and Gatherers)

Social Studies Objectives
1. Discover how hunter-gatherers lived during the Stone Age.
2. Learn about the beginning of farming.

Reading/Language Arts Objective
Learn how to make predictions to help you remember what you read.

Prepare to Read	**Instructional Resources**	**Differentiated Instruction**
Build Background Knowledge Have students brainstorm how life changed for people during the Stone Age. **Set a Purpose for Reading** Have students begin to fill out the *Reading Readiness Guide*. **Preview Key Terms** Teach the section's Key Terms. **Target Reading Skill** Introduce the section's Target Reading Skill of **predicting**.	**All in One Unit 1 History of Our World Teaching Resources** L2 Reading Readiness Guide, p. 13 L2 Preview and Predict, p. 21	**Spanish Reading and Vocabulary Study Guide** L1 Chapter 1, Section 2, pp. 9–10 ELL

Instruct	**Instructional Resources**	**Differentiated Instruction**
Stone Age Hunting and Gathering Discuss hunters and gatherers. **Target Reading Skill** Review **predicting**. **The Beginning of Farming** Ask questions about and discuss the way farming developed.	**All in One Unit 1 History of Our World Teaching Resources** L2 Guided Reading and Review, p. 14 L2 Reading Readiness Guide, p. 13 **History of Our World Transparencies** L2 Section Reading Support Transparency HOW 54 **History of Our World Video Program** L2 The First Great Migration	**All in One Unit 1 History of Our World Teaching Resources** Rubric for Assessing a Writing Assignment, p. 35 **History of Our World Transparencies** L1 Transparency B15: Outline ELL, LPR, SN **Teacher's Edition** L1 For Less Proficient Readers, TE p. 16 L2 For English Language Learners, TE pp. 16, 18 **Student Edition on Audio CD** L1 Chapter 1, Section 2 ELL, LPR, SN **Spanish Support** L2 Guided Reading and Review (Spanish), p. 6 ELL

Assess and Reteach	**Instructional Resources**	**Differentiated Instruction**
Assess Progress Evaluate student comprehension with the section assessment and section quiz. **Reteach** Assign the Reading and Vocabulary Study Guide to help struggling students. **Extend** Extend the lesson by assigning a MapMaster Skills Activity.	**All in One Unit 1 History of Our World Teaching Resources** L2 Section Quiz, p. 15 L3 Reading a Natural Vegetation Map, p. 30 Rubric for Assessing a Journal Entry, p. 36 **Reading and Vocabulary Study Guide** L1 Chapter 1, Section 2, pp. 9–11	**Spanish Support** L2 Section Quiz (Spanish), p. 7 ELL

Key
L1 Basic to Average   L3 Average to Advanced   LPR Less Proficient Readers   GT Gifted and Talented
L2 For All Students   AR Advanced Readers   ELL English Language Learners
                                                SN Special Needs Students

Section Lesson Planner

4d

Section 3 The Beginnings of Civilization

 2 periods, 1 block (includes Chapter Review and Assessment)

Social Studies Objectives
1. Find out about the advantages people gained from settling down in one place.
2. Learn about the growth of early cities.
3. Understand how the first civilizations formed and spread.

Reading/Language Arts Objective
Learn how to ask questions to help you remember what you have read.

Prepare to Read	**Instructional Resources**	**Differentiated Instruction**
Build Background Knowledge Ask students to preview and form two questions about the reading. **Set a Purpose for Reading** Have students begin to fill out the *Reading Readiness Guide*. **Preview Key Terms** Teach the section's Key Terms. **Target Reading Skill** Introduce the section's Target Reading Skill of **asking questions**.	**All in One Unit 1 History of Our World Teaching Resources** **L2** Reading Readiness Guide, p. 17 **L2** Preview and Ask Questions, p. 22	**Spanish Reading and Vocabulary Study Guide** **L1** Chapter 1, Section 3, pp. 11–12 ELL

Instruct	**Instructional Resources**	**Differentiated Instruction**
Advantages of a Settled Life Discuss food surpluses and the causes of population growth. **Target Reading Skill** Review **asking questions**. **The Growth of Cities** Discuss early cities. **The First Civilizations** Discuss how inventions and trade helped civilization form and spread.	**All in One Unit 1 History of Our World Teaching Resources** **L2** Guided Reading and Review, p. 18 **L2** Reading Readiness Guide, p. 17 **History of Our World Transparencies** **L2** Section Reading Support Transparency HOW 55	**All in One Unit 1 History of Our World Teaching Resources** **L3** Small Group Activity: Simulation: Analyzing "Ancient" Objects, pp. 26–29 AR, GT **L3** Enrichment, p. 24 AR, GT **Teacher's Edition** **L3** For Gifted and Talented Students, TE p. 22 **L3** For Advanced Readers, TE p. 22 **Spanish Support** **L2** Guided Reading and Review (Spanish), p. 8 ELL

Assess and Reteach	**Instructional Resources**	**Differentiated Instruction**
Assess Progress Evaluate student comprehension with the section assessment and section quiz. **Reteach** Assign the Reading and Vocabulary Study Guide to help struggling students. **Extend** Extend the lesson by assigning a writing activity.	**All in One Unit 1 History of Our World Teaching Resources** **L2** Section Quiz, p. 19 **L3** Writing to Inform and Explain, p. 33 Rubric for Assessing a Writing Assignment, p. 35 **L2** Vocabulary Development, p. 34 **L2** Word Knowledge, p. 23 **L2** Chapter Tests A and B, pp. 37–42 **Reading and Vocabulary Study Guide** **L1** Chapter 1, Section 3, pp. 12–14	**Spanish Support** **L2** Section Quiz (Spanish), p. 9 ELL **L2** Chapter Summary (Spanish), p. 10 ELL **L2** Vocabulary Development (Spanish), p. 11 ELL

Key
L1 Basic to Average   **L3** Average to Advanced
L2 For All Students

LPR Less Proficient Readers
AR Advanced Readers
SN Special Needs Students

GT Gifted and Talented
ELL English Language Learners

Professional Development

Reading Background

Previewing and Prereading

This chapter's Target Reading Skill asks students to preview each section and set a purpose for reading. Students who do a brief, preliminary reading of complex material are in a strategic position to take control of their learning and comprehension. Previewing helps students consider what they already know about a topic they will be studying and gives some idea of what a text selection is about before they read it. Previewing also helps students identify the text structure and develop a mental framework for ideas to be encountered in the text. This can help them in formulating a more realistic reading and study plan.

Follow the steps below to teach students how to preview and preread.

1. Tell students that previewing will help them identify the text structure and develop a mental outline of ideas they will encounter in the text.
2. List the various text features you will be previewing in the order in which you would like students to examine them: section title, text headings, introduction, list of key terms, questions or tasks in the reading selection, photographs, drawings, maps, charts and other visuals in the text. Focus students' attention on some of these items, or ask them to look at all of the items.
3. Prompt students to reflect after examining various text features. They may ask themselves questions, such as: What is this reading selection about? What are some key words I will learn? How should I tackle this reading and divide up the task?

Structuring Paragraphs

One active way of helping students learn how to form well-written paragraphs is to rearrange the sentences in a paragraph and have students put them back in the correct order.

Have students work in pairs or groups. Write each sentence from a paragraph in the Student Edition on a separate strip of paper. Mix up the strips and ask students to arrange them into a well-ordered paragraph. Remind students to look for main ideas, details, and transition words.

Try the exercise with this paragraph from page 21.

Farming was much harder work than hunting and gathering. However, it had far greater rewards. People who produced their own food could have a steady supply of food year-round. This meant they no longer had to travel from place to place. People often even had a food surplus—more than what is needed. Surplus food could be stored for use at another time.

World Studies Background

The Importance of Grains

One key in the link between the beginning of agriculture and population growth was the domestication of grains. Foods such as wheat, rye, barley, rice, and corn provided enough nutrition to form the bulk of people's diets in ancient societies. The existence of such foods helped support large populations. In the early Americas, for example, although there were a number of early domesticated crops such as peppers and avocados, these foods alone were not substantial enough to support large populations. Only when early Americans began to grow corn did villages begin to form.

Ur and the Great Flood

The concept of a great flood is present in the literature of many peoples. The Biblical book of Genesis tells the story of Noah's Ark. One of the first great Mesopotamian works of literature relates a tale of a similar flood that tested the faith and courage of a hero named Utnapishtim. Scientific evidence indicates that the first settlers of Ur, one of the first cities in the world, were wiped out by a great flood, such as the one described in these stories.

Infoplease® provides a wealth of useful information for the classroom. You can use this resource to strengthen your background on the subjects covered in this chapter. Have students visit this advertising-free site as a starting point for projects requiring research.

 Use Web code **lbd-2100** for **Infoplease®**.

Guiding Questions

Remind students about the Guiding Questions introduced at the beginning of the book.

Section 1 relates to **Guiding Question ①** **How did physical geography affect the growth of ancient civilizations?** *(Egyptian civilization was built on the banks of the Nile River, which floods yearly and deposits fertile soil on its banks. Egyptian farmers used the Nile to grow enough crops to feed people living in the cities, making civilization possible.)*

Section 2 relates to **Guiding Question ②** **What historical accomplishments is each civilization known for?** *(Early humans created stone tools, learned how to use fire, began farming, and trained animals.)*

Section 3 relates to **Guiding Question ④** **How did ancient people develop governments?** *(Farming allowed people in ancient times to settle in one place rather than travel according to the seasons. Populations grew, settlements developed into villages and towns, and some of these towns grew into cities. Growing cities with more and more people required governments to keep order, provide services, settle disputes, and manage public building and irrigation projects.)*

⟳ Target Reading Skill

In this chapter, students will learn and apply the reading skill of previewing to understand and remember what they read. Use the following worksheets to help students practice this skill:

All in One Unit 1 History of Our World Teaching Resources, *Preview and Set a Purpose,* p. 20; *Preview and Predict,* p. 21; *Preview and Ask Questions,* p. 22

The Beginnings of Human Society

Chapter Preview

In this chapter you will find out how archaeologists learn about the past. You will also learn about the connections between geography and history.

Section 1
Geography and History

Section 2
Prehistory

Section 3
The Beginnings of Civilization

 Target Reading Skill

Reading Process In this chapter you will focus on previewing to help you understand and remember what you read.

▶ Cave painting from about 5000 B.C., Argentina

Bibliography

For the Teacher
Fagan, Brian M. *Ancient Lives: An Introduction to Archaeology and Prehistory, Second Edition.* Prentice Hall, 2003.
Fowler, Brenda. *Iceman.* Random House, 2000.
Robbins, Manuel. *Collapse of the Bronze Age: The Story of Greece, Troy, Israel, Egypt, and the Peoples of the Sea.* Author's Choice Press, 2001.

For the Student
L1 Brookes, Philip. *From the Stone Age to the Space Age.* Lorenz Books, 2003.
L2 Panchyk, Richard. *Archaeology for Kids: Uncovering the Mysteries of Our Past.* Chicago Review Press, 2001.
L3 Chrisp, Peter. *Ancient Egypt (DK Revealed).* Dorling Kindersley Publishing, 2002.

MAP MASTER™ Skills Activity

Early Migration of Modern Humans

0 miles 5,000
0 kilometers 5,000
Robinson

NORTH AMERICA
Bering Land Bridge
EUROPE
ASIA
AFRICA
SOUTH AMERICA
AUSTRALIA

Arctic Circle
Tropic of Cancer
Equator
Tropic of Capricorn
Antarctic Circle

KEY

→ Migration of modern humans

■ Landmasses as of 18,000 B.C.

This map shows the shapes of the continents during the last ice age.

Movement Modern humans may have originated more than 100,000 years ago in Africa before spreading to other parts of the world. This migration most likely took place over many thousands of years. **Identify** What landmass did modern humans cross to travel from Asia into North America? **Infer** Why did the migration of humans from Africa to the rest of the world take place so slowly? Explain your answer.

Go Online PHSchool.com Use Web Code **lbp-2111** for step-by-step map skills practice.

Chapter 1 **5**

MAP MASTER™ Skills Activity

- Point out to students that the map shows the continents as they were as of 18,000 B.C. Encourage them to compare the map to the map on pages 506–507 of their textbook and to take note of the differences.

- Have students study the migration of modern humans in North and South America. Have them write a sentence or two explaining how people spread across the two continents.

Go Online PHSchool.com Students may practice their map skills using the interactive online version of this map.

Using the Visual   L2

Reach Into Your Background Draw students' attention to the caption accompanying the picture on pages 4–5.

Discuss the visual with your students. Ask them to think of other kinds of ancient art they may be familiar with, such as that done by ancient Egyptians or ancient Greeks. Then ask them to speculate how paintings such as those pictured on pages 4–5 might have been made, by whom, and for what purpose. Have students share their ideas with the class.

Answers

MAP MASTER™ Skills Activity **Identify** the Bering Land Bridge **Infer** Possible answer: Because all traveling was done on foot throughout the wilderness, migration from Africa to the rest of the world was a slow process.

Chapter Resources

Teaching Resources
- L2 Vocabulary Development, p. 34
- L2 Skills for Life, p. 25
- L2 Chapter Tests A and B, pp. 37–42

Spanish Support
Spanish Letter Home, p. 3
- L2 Spanish Chapter Summary, p. 10
- L2 Vocabulary Development, p. 11

Media and Technology
- L1 Student Edition on Audio CD
- L1 Guided Reading Audio CDs, English and Spanish
- L2 Social Studies Skills Tutor CD-ROM
- **ExamView® Test Bank CD-ROM**

Discovery CHANNEL SCHOOL History of Our World Video Program

Interactive Textbook

PRENTICE HALL

TeacherEXPRESS™ Plan · Teach · Assess

Objectives

Social Studies

1. Learn what tools are used to understand history.
2. Find out about the connections between geography and history.

Reading/Language Arts

Learn how to set a purpose for reading.

Prepare to Read

Build Background Knowledge **L2**

Tell students that in this section they will find out how we learn about ancient peoples. Read the paragraphs on page 6 aloud and then have students look at all of the images on pages 6–7. Ask students to answer this question: **How did scientists piece together the Ice Man's story?** Use the Think-Write-Pair-Share strategy (TE, p. T40) to generate theories.

Set a Purpose for Reading **L2**

- Preview the Objectives.

- Read each statement in the *Reading Readiness Guide* aloud. Ask students to mark the statements true or false.

  All in One **Unit 1 History of Our World Teaching Resources**, *Reading Readiness Guide*, p. 9

- Have students discuss their statements in pairs or groups of four, and then mark their worksheets again. Use the Numbered Heads participation strategy (TE, p. T40) to call on students to share their group's perspective.

Vocabulary Builder
Preview Key Terms **L2**

Pronounce each Key Term, then ask the students to say the word with you. Provide a simple explanation such as, "Studying geography can include learning about the physical features, such as mountains and lakes, in a certain part of the world."

Prepare to Read

Objectives

In this section you will
1. Learn what tools are used to understand history.
2. Find out about the connections between geography and history.

Taking Notes

As you read, look for details that tell how people learn about the past. Copy the concept web below, and use it to record your findings. Add more ovals as needed.

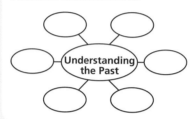

Understanding the Past

Target Reading Skill

Preview and Set a Purpose When you set a purpose for your reading, you give yourself a focus. Before you read this section, preview the headings and pictures to find out what the section is about. Then set a purpose for reading this section. Your purpose might be to find out about the study of history, or to learn about the connections between geography and history. Finally, read to meet your purpose.

Key Terms

- **history** (HIS tuh ree) *n.* written and other recorded events of people
- **prehistory** (pree HIS tuh ree) *n.* time before writing was invented
- **archaeologist** (ahr kee AHL uh jist) *n.* a scientist who examines objects to learn about the human past
- **oral traditions** (AWR ul truh DISH unz) *n.* stories passed down by word of mouth
- **geography** (jee AHG ruh fee) *n.* the study of Earth's surface and the processes that shape it

---

A scientist recovers the body of the ancient Iceman from a glacier in the Alps.

He is called the Iceman. His frozen body was found in a mountain pass in the Alps, on the Italian-Austrian border in Europe.

Two hikers discovered the Iceman by chance in 1991. His body and possessions were taken to a laboratory, where scientists learned more about him. His clothing, tools, and his body were well preserved. They provided clues about the Iceman's life and death. Scientists used these clues to build a story of his life. To learn how the Iceman died, see the Links to Science on the next page.

Scientists determined that the Iceman lived about 5,000 years ago, in about 3000 B.C. The Iceman's finely stitched animal skins showed that he probably came from a community that included people who were skilled in sewing.

The most important clue about the Iceman's life was his copper ax. Copper was the first metal used by Europeans, beginning about 4000 B.C. The ax left no doubt that the Iceman lived after people had learned to use copper. In many ways, the story of the Iceman helps us to understand the story of our past.

6 History of Our World

Target Reading Skill **L2**

Preview and Set a Purpose Point out the Target Reading Skill. Tell students that setting a purpose before they start reading can help them read more effectively.

Model setting a purpose by looking at the main head and sub-heads on pp. 8–9 and developing the following focus: I will read this section for the purpose of understanding different methods of learning about early history.

Give students *Preview and Set a Purpose.* Have them complete the activity in their groups.

All in One **Unit 1 History of Our World Teaching Resources**, *Preview and Set a Purpose*, p. 20

Understanding History

The scientists' curiosity about the Iceman's life was natural. As human beings, we are curious about our earliest origins. What was life like many thousands of years ago?

Before and After Writing About 5,000 years ago, peoples in Southwest Asia and in Africa developed systems of writing. They began to keep written records of their experiences. These developments marked the beginning of **history,** the written and other recorded events of people. By adding the prefix *pre-*, which means "before," you form the word *prehistory*. **Prehistory** is the time before history. Prehistory is the period of time before writing was invented.

Prehistory: Digging Up the Past To learn about life in prehistoric times, scientists must rely on clues other than written records. **Archaeologists** (ahr kee AHL uh jists) are scientists who examine objects to learn about past peoples and cultures. They sift through the dirt of prehistoric camps to find bones, tools, and other objects. These objects may tell them something about the people who lived there. For example, the size of stone spear points shows what kinds of game the people hunted. To kill big game, such as bears, hunters had to use large, heavy spear points. Such points, however, would not work very well with birds and small animals.

Links to
Science

Cause of Death At first, scientists believed that the Iceman had frozen to death. But ten years after the discovery of the Iceman, scientists found an arrowhead lodged in his shoulder. Later, they found a knife wound on his hand. Now scientists believe the Iceman may have died from injuries he received during an armed struggle.

The stone amulet, above, is similar to the one found with the Iceman. The knife and its grass case, left, were among his belongings.

A museum model of the Iceman, right, shows how he may have dressed.

Instruct

Understanding History L2

Guided Instruction

- **Vocabulary Builder** Clarify the high-use words **community, curiosity,** and **record** before reading.

- Read Understanding History, using the Choral Reading technique (TE, p. T38).

- Discuss the challenges of learning prehistory. *(There is no written record of events.)*

- Ask students **How is an archaeologist like a detective?** *(The archaeologist must piece together clues to find out what happened in the past.)*

Independent Practice

Ask students to create the Taking Notes graphic organizer on a blank piece of paper. Then have them fill in five of the empty circles with examples of what they have just learned about ways to understand the past. Briefly model what kind of information to record.

Monitor Progress

As students fill in the graphic organizer, circulate and make sure individuals are choosing the correct details. Provide assistance as needed.

Links

Read the **Links to Science** on this page. Ask students **Why did scientists change their minds about the Iceman's cause of death?** *(They found a knife wound on his hand and an arrowhead lodged in his shoulder.)*

Vocabulary Builder

Use the information below to teach students this section's high-use words.

High-Use Word	Definition and Sample Sentence
community, p. 6	*n.* a group of people living in the same area who share common interests The **community** wanted to raise money for a new library.
curiosity, p. 7	*n.* the desire to learn To satisfy my **curiosity,** I went to find out more.
record, p. 7	*n.* something written down to preserve knowledge She kept a diary so there would be a written **record** of her life.
deposit, p. 9	*v.* to place on or put into He **deposited** money into his bank account.

Set a Purpose As a follow up, ask students to answer the Target Reading Skill question on this page of the Student Edition. (*Studying oral traditions is one method used to learn about history.*)

Linking Geography and History ⬛L2

Guided Instruction

- **Vocabulary Builder** Clarify the high-use word **deposit** before reading.

- Read Linking Geography and History. As students read, circulate and make sure individuals can answer the Reading Check question.

- Discuss how geography helps us learn about history. (*The geography of an area can give clues about ancient people who lived there.*)

- Ask students **What kinds of positive and negative effects might geography have had on the way people lived in different places?** (*Good soil in certain places allowed great civilizations to grow. Areas with poor soil or not much water supported little population.*)

Independent Practice

Ask students to fill in the last empty circle on the Taking Notes graphic organizer with one example they have just learned of a way to understand the past.

Monitor Progress

- Show *Section Reading Support Transparency HOW 53* and ask students to check their graphic organizers individually. Go over key concepts and clarify key vocabulary as needed.

  📖 **History of Our World Transparencies,** *Section Reading Support Transparency HOW 53*

- Tell students to fill in the last column of the *Reading Readiness Guide*. Probe for what they learned that confirms or invalidates each statement.

  All in One Unit 1 History of Our World Teaching Resources, *Reading Readiness Guide,* p. 9

Answers

✓ **Reading Check** Oral traditions can provide information about a society's way of life.
Draw Conclusions Communities can use the past to shape the present and future.

Prehistoric rock painting in South Africa

⏩ **Set a Purpose** **Target Skill** If your purpose is to learn about the study of history, how does reading about oral traditions help you to achieve your purpose?

History: A Record in Writing Historians do not rely only on the objects discovered by archaeologists to learn about the past. They also study the written records of human life and accomplishments to understand a society—its wars, its religion, and its rulers, among other things. Historians also look at what other groups living at the same time wrote about that society.

A Record of the Spoken Word The written records studied by historians often began as **oral traditions,** stories passed down by word of mouth. Oral traditions can include a family's history, such as stories of parents, grandparents, and great-grandparents. They can also tell stories about heroes or events in the past.

Oral traditions are still an important part of many societies today. Not all oral stories are historically accurate. Stories often change as they are told and retold. Like myths and legends, they often contain facts mixed with personal beliefs and exaggerations about heroes. Still, oral traditions tell how a society lived and what the people considered important.

✓ **Reading Check** Why are historians interested in oral traditions?

Carrying on a Tradition
In West Africa, a professional storyteller called a griot (GREE oh) keeps oral traditions alive.
Draw Conclusions
How does a community benefit from knowing about its recent and ancient past?

8 History of Our World

Differentiated Instruction

For Special Needs Students ⬛L1
Have students create flash cards of words that they encounter frequently as they read. Model how to write a word on one side of a card and its definition on the other side. Encourage students to use a dictionary if they need help defining the words.

Background: Links Across Place

African Griots and American Rap Music
The African griots' style of telling epic histories is similar to the storytelling heard in American rap music. In rap, a performer does not actually sing, but rather tells a story in spoken words, often to a quick, rhythmic beat. Rap began in New York City in the late 1970s and has gained popularity throughout the world.

Linking Geography and History

Knowing when something happened is important. Understanding why historic events took place is also important. To do this, historians often turn to **geography**, the study of Earth's surface and the processes that shape it. Geography also refers to the features of a place, including its climate, landscape, and location. Knowing the connections between geography and history is often the key to understanding why events happened. Weather patterns, the water supply, and the landscape of a place all affect the lives of the people who live there. For example, to explain why the ancient Egyptians developed a successful civilization, you must look at the geography of Egypt.

A farm in Egypt's Nile delta

Egyptian civilization was built on the banks of the Nile River in Africa. Each year the Nile flooded, depositing soil on its banks. Because the soil was rich, Egyptian farmers could grow enough crops to feed the large numbers of people in the cities. That meant everyone did not have to farm, so some people could perform other jobs that helped develop the civilization. Without the Nile and its regular flooding, Egyptian civilization would not have become so successful.

 **Reading Check** Give one example of geography's effect on history.

Section 1 Assessment

Key Terms
Review the key terms at the beginning of this section. Use each term in a sentence that explains its meaning.

Target Reading Skill
How did having a reading purpose help you understand this section?

Comprehension and Critical Thinking
1. (a) Recall What do scientists study to learn about prehistory?
(b) Generalize What do we know about societies that leave behind written records?

(c) Draw Inferences Analyze the clothes you wear and the things you carry to school. What do they say about your life? How does your story compare to the Iceman's story?
2. (a) Identify Name some examples of familiar geographic features.
(b) Explain How can geography help us to understand history?
(c) Identify Cause and Effect What effect has geography had on the way people in your community live?

Writing Activity
Ask a classmate to share a story with you. The story should be about an important event in the person's life. Write the story from your classmate's point of view.

For: An activity on archaeology
Visit: PHSchool.com
Web Code: lbd-2101

Chapter 1 Section 1 **9**

Writing Activity
Use the *Rubric for Assessing a Writing Assignment* to evaluate students' stories.

 **All in One Unit 1 History of Our World Teaching Resources,** *Rubric for Assessing a Writing Assignment,* p. 35

Go Online
PHSchool.com Typing in the Web Code when prompted will bring students directly to detailed instructions for this activity.

Objective

Learn how to use timelines.

Prepare to Read

Build Background Knowledge L2

Ask students to define the word *chronology*. (*the order that events happened*) Then ask them to brainstorm reasons why knowing the order of a set of events might be important. (*gives perspective, helps students identify causes and effects of events*)

Instruct

Using Timelines L2

- Read the steps to Using Timelines as a class and write the instructions on the board.

- Practice the skill by constructing a timeline on the board as a class. Model each skill step by having 10–15 volunteers write their birthdays on the board, including the month, day, and year, and labeling the date with their first name. Then help students arrange the dates in chronological order, determine the time span, determine the intervals, and give the timeline an appropriate title.

- Ask students to identify topics from the chapter that might make good timeline subjects.

Independent Practice

Assign *Skills for Life* and have students complete it individually.

All in One Unit 1 History of Our World Teaching Resources, *Skills for Life,* p. 25

Monitor Progress

As students are completing the *Skills for Life* worksheet, check to make sure they understand the skill steps.

 # Using Timelines

A wall painting from the ancient city of Knossos, Greece, founded in 2500 B.C.

The post above was used to secure the reins on an animal's harness. It is from the ancient city of Ur, founded in 3500 B.C. in Mesopotamia.

When you study history, you must learn about many different events and the dates on which they occurred. However, a whole page filled with dates can be hard to follow. For that reason, writers often use a simple diagram called a timeline. A timeline shows the order in which events happened. At a glance, a timeline can give you a picture of a certain time period.

Learn the Skill

Refer to page 11 as you follow the steps below.

1 **Read the title of the timeline.** The title tells you what the timeline will show.

2 **Determine the time span.** Look at the beginning and the endpoint of the timeline to determine the time span. If the timeline shows ancient history, it is sometimes divided into two parts. The dates on the left side are marked with the letters *B.C.* The dates on the right side are marked with the letters *A.D.* The letters *B.C.* are an abbreviation of "before Christ" and refer to the years before Jesus' birth. The letters *A.D.* mean "anno Domini," which is Latin for "in the year of our Lord." The letters *A.D.* refer to the time after Jesus' birth.

Notice that with *B.C.*, you count backward. The numbers get larger as you go backward in time. Also note the letter *c.* before some dates. An abbreviation for the Latin word *circa*, *c.* means "about." Historians often use *circa* or *c.* before dates.

3 **Determine the intervals of time.** A timeline is divided into intervals of time that are marked by vertical lines. Determine how many years occur between the vertical lines. Timelines that show a long span of time have longer intervals, such as 100 or 1,000 years. Timelines that show a short span of time have shorter intervals, such as 10 or 20 years.

4 **Study the events on the timeline.** Each event has a date and is connected to the timeline by a dot and a line. Notice when each event happened. Be sure to notice whether a date has more than one event.

10 History of Our World

Practice the Skill

Use the timeline below to practice the skill.

1 Find the title of the timeline. Based on the title, do you think this timeline will show a long or a short time span?

2 Determine the time span. Find the beginning of the timeline at the left. Notice that the first date is followed by B.C. Next, find the endpoint of the timeline. Notice that the last date is preceded by A.D. What is the span of time between these two dates?

3 Determine the intervals. Look at the dates marked by vertical lines on the timeline. How far is one date from another?

4 Study the events on the timeline. Notice the kinds of events that are shown and whether they are connected. How can you tell whether some events occurred closer together than others? Look at the abbreviations used with the dates on this timeline. Why is the event "Jesus is born" an important event to show on this particular timeline?

Apply the Skill

Turn to the table titled Early Cities on page 22. Create a timeline based on the information in the table. Follow the steps you used to practice this skill to help you create your timeline.

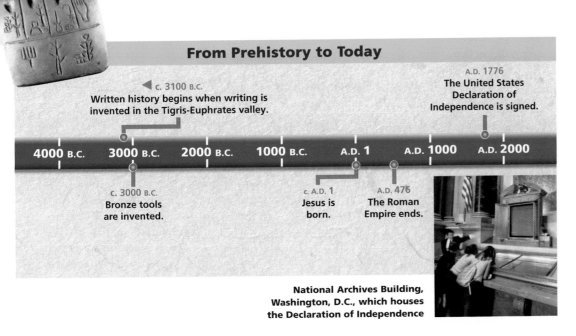

From Prehistory to Today

- ◄ c. 3100 B.C. Written history begins when writing is invented in the Tigris-Euphrates valley.
- c. 3000 B.C. Bronze tools are invented.
- c. A.D. 1 Jesus is born.
- A.D. 476 The Roman Empire ends.
- A.D. 1776 The United States Declaration of Independence is signed.

4000 B.C. | 3000 B.C. | 2000 B.C. | 1000 B.C. | A.D. 1 | A.D. 1000 | A.D. 2000

National Archives Building, Washington, D.C., which houses the Declaration of Independence

Chapter 1 **11**

Assess and Reteach

Answer
Apply the Skill

Timelines should include a title, time span, dates, and place each city's founding date in the correct order.

Objectives

Social Studies

1. Discover how hunter-gatherers lived during the Stone Age.
2. Learn about the beginning of farming.

Reading/Language Arts

Learn how to make predictions to help you remember what you read.

Prepare to Read

Build Background Knowledge　L2

In this section, students will learn about how early people lived. Have students preview the section to find three ways people's lives changed during the Stone Age. Use the Give One, Get One participation strategy (TE, p. T41) to generate responses. *(Possible responses: discovered fire, settled new areas, began farming, domesticated animals)*

Set a Purpose for Reading　L2

■ Preview the Objectives.

■ Form students into pairs or groups of four. Distribute the *Reading Readiness Guide.* Ask students to fill in the first two columns of the chart. Use the Numbered Heads participation strategy (TE, p. T40) to call on students to share one piece of information they already know and one piece of information they want to know.

All in One **Unit 1 History of Our World Teaching Resources,** *Reading Readiness Guide,* p. 13

Vocabulary Builder
Preview Key Terms　L2

Pronounce each Key Term, then ask the students to say the word with you. Provide a simple explanation such as, "A person who does not have permanent home and moves from place to place is a nomad."

Prepare to Read

Objectives

In this section you will
1. Discover how hunter-gatherers lived during the Stone Age.
2. Learn about the beginning of farming.

Taking Notes

As you read, look for details about survival during the Stone Age. Copy the table below, and use it to record your findings.

Topic	Details
Tools	
Hunting	
Gathering	
Fire	
Settlement	
Farming	
Animals	

Target Reading Skill

Preview and Predict Making predictions about your text helps you to remember what you read. Before you read this section, preview it by looking at the headings and pictures. Then predict what the text might discuss about prehistory. For example, you might predict that the text will explain important events that happened in prehistory. As you read, connect what you read to your prediction. If what you learn doesn't support your prediction, revise your prediction.

Key Terms

- **Stone Age** (stohn ayj) *n.* a period of time during which early humans made lasting tools and weapons mainly from stone; the earliest known period of human culture
- **nomad** (NOH mad) *n.* a person who has no settled home
- **fertile** (FUR tul) *adj.* rich in the substances plants need to grow well; describes soil and land
- **domesticate** (duh MES tih kayt) *v.* to adapt wild plants for human use; tame wild animals and breed them for human use

Long before humans used metal, about three and a half million years ago, a huge explosion shook a part of what is now the country of Tanzania (tan zuh NEE uh) in East Africa. A volcano spit out clouds of fine ash that fell on the surrounding land. Then rain came. It turned the blanket of ash into thick mud. Before the mud dried, two individuals walked across the landscape. As they walked, they left their footprints in the mud.

In 1976, a group of scientists looking for evidence of early humans discovered the footprints, preserved in stone. They were amazed at their find. The footprints are almost identical to those made by modern humans walking in wet sand. Such evidence may help to explain the development of our prehistoric ancestors.

Human ancestors made these footprints about 3.5 million years ago.

12 History of Our World

Target Reading Skill　L2

Predict Point out the Target Reading Skill. Tell students that making predictions about their text will help them remember what they read.

Model predicting by previewing the material on page 13. Look at the heads and visuals on the page and predict what kinds of information the paragraphs might reveal.

Think aloud: "I predict that I will learn about Stone Age hunting and gathering techniques, such as the use of certain tools and fire, by reading this page."

Give students *Preview and Predict.* Have them complete the activity in their groups.

All in One **Unit 1 History of Our World Teaching Resources,** *Preview and Predict,* p. 21

Stone Age Hunting and Gathering

A million years after the footprints were made, our human ancestors used tools. By studying these tools, we learn about the development of human culture.

Earliest Human Culture The first use of stone to create tools began the earliest known period of human culture: the Stone Age. The **Stone Age** was a period of time during which early humans made lasting tools and weapons mainly from stone. They also made tools from wood and animal bones. Scientists think that the Stone Age continued for hundreds of thousands of years, until people learned to use metal for tools.

Archaeologists divide the Stone Age into three periods: the Old Stone Age, the Middle Stone Age, and the New Stone Age. During the Old Stone Age, early humans did not yet know how to farm. They were hunter-gatherers, people who survive by hunting animals and gathering wild plants. Almost all of human prehistory took place during the Old Stone Age.

Fire! Between about 1,400,000 and 500,000 years ago, our ancestors learned how to use fire. No one knows for sure how they learned. Perhaps one day a small band of hunters saw a grass fire caused by lightning on the open plain. Although terrified by the fire, they learned how to keep it going. With fire, they could ward off dangerous animals, who were also afraid of the flames.

Finally, early humans discovered how to create fire. They probably did this by rubbing two sticks together or by striking stones together to produce a spark. The ability to create fire was an important step for our human ancestors. With this great advance, they could move to areas with colder climates.

Links to Science

How Old Is It? After archaeologists find bones, tools, or other objects, they ask themselves that question. Scientists use different tests for dating different objects. One very useful test is called radiocarbon dating. All plants and animals have tiny amounts of a substance called radiocarbon in their bodies. After they die, the radiocarbon changes into another substance. Scientists know how long this change takes. They have tests that measure how much radiocarbon remains. Scientists can then calculate the age of the material. Because the ancient comb, below, is made from the antler of a deer or an elk, radiocarbon dating could be used to determine its age.

A wildfire on the grasslands of Africa

Links

Read the **Links to Science** on this page. Ask students **What other questions do you think scientists ask about the artifacts they find?** *(Possible answers: What materials was the artifact made from? Where did it come from? What was it used for?)*

Instruct

Stone Age Hunting and Gathering   L2

Guided Instruction

- **Vocabulary Builder** Clarify the high-use words **evidence** and **ward off** before reading.

- Read Stone Age Hunting and Gathering, using the Structured Silent Reading Technique (TE, p. T38).

- Ask students **When did the Stone Age end?** (when people began using metal to make tools).

- Discuss the early methods that people used to get food. *(They hunted wild animals and gathered food growing in the wild.)*

- Ask students **What might have happened if humans had not learned to make fire?** *(They probably would not have been able to migrate to colder climates.)*

Vocabulary Builder

Use the information below to teach students this section's high-use words.

High-Use Word	Definition and Sample Sentence
evidence, p. 12	*n.* something that serves to prove or disprove information There was not enough **evidence** to prove guilt.
ward off, p. 13	*v.* to turn away Bug spray **wards off** insects.
characterize, p. 14	*v.* to describe the qualities of I would **characterize** Bill as an honest man.
pastoral, p. 15	*adj.* related to the raising of livestock The shepherd and his flock added to the **pastoral** scene.

Target Reading Skill

L2

Predict As a follow up, ask students to answer the Target Reading Skill question in the Student Edition. *(Answers will vary depending on students' predictions, but should reflect what students have read so far.)*

Guided Instruction (continued)

■ Ask students to discuss how early humans are similar to humans today. *(Like people today, early humans could survive in a variety of geographical conditions.)*

 Show students *The First Great Migration.* Ask **How did climate influence the migration of people into Asia and beyond?** *(People moved to areas in which the climate was good for farming.)*

Independent Practice

Ask students to create the Taking Notes graphic organizer on a blank piece of paper. Then have them fill in the first five rows with information they have just learned. Briefly model what details to record.

Monitor Progress

As students fill in the graphic organizer, circulate and make sure individuals are choosing the correct details. Provide assistance as needed.

Answers

√ **Reading Check** People made tools from stone, wood, and animal bones. They got food by hunting and gathering. They used fire and lived as nomads.

Predict the food supply, the weather, the time of year

Predict Based on what you have read so far, is your prediction on target? If not, change your prediction now.

Explore the first great migration.

Nomadic Herding
A young shepherd guides her flock to graze in the Taza Province of Morocco in North Africa. **Predict** *What factors might influence this nomad's decision to move her sheep from one area to another?*

14 History of Our World

Settling New Areas As our human ancestors developed the use of tools, they left their original homes in Africa. Their move may have begun as early as one million years ago. Many of our Old Stone Age ancestors were nomads. **Nomads** are people who have no settled home. They moved around to places where they thought they would find food and stayed there for several days. When they had gathered all the food around them, they moved on.

Humans eventually spread out over much of Earth. There is evidence that human ancestors were living in Asia and Europe at least 500,000 years ago. Many scientists believe that modern humans originated more than 100,000 years ago in Africa and then spread to other parts of the world. Perhaps 30,000 years ago humans crossed from Asia into North America. By 10,000 B.C., humans had reached Peru in South America. Compared with today, humans then were few in number. But as we can today, they survived in all sorts of geographical conditions. They lived in the steamy rain forests of Asia, the cold lands near the Arctic Circle, and the high altitudes of the Andes in South America.

√ **Reading Check** **What was life like during the Stone Age?**

The Beginning of Farming

For tens of thousands of years, our ancestors continued to live as hunter-gatherers. However, some societies entered the Middle Stone Age, which was characterized by the use of more refined, or advanced, tools. Those who began the practice of farming would enter the New Stone Age.

 Skills Mini Lesson

Using Cartographer's Tools L2

1. Teach the skill by pointing out that there are certain elements common to most maps. The key explains unique items that will be pointed out on the map. Most maps contain a key.

2. Help students practice the skill by looking at the map on page 15 and noting where the core area of yam production was located and in what direction it spread. *(West Africa; spread to southern Africa)*

3. Have students apply the skill by answering this question: What crop was important in South China, and in what directions did it spread? *(rice; spread south, west, and east)*

The Spread of Agriculture

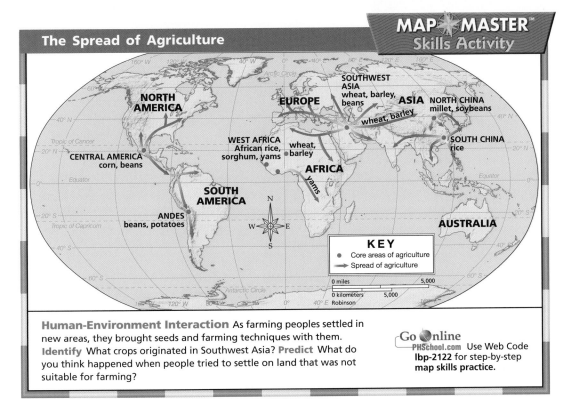

SOUTHWEST ASIA
wheat, barley, beans

EUROPE

ASIA

NORTH CHINA
millet, soybeans

wheat, barley

NORTH AMERICA

CENTRAL AMERICA
corn, beans

WEST AFRICA
African rice, sorghum, yams

wheat, barley

SOUTH CHINA
rice

AFRICA

yams

SOUTH AMERICA

ANDES
beans, potatoes

AUSTRALIA

KEY
● Core areas of agriculture
→ Spread of agriculture

0 miles 5,000
0 kilometers 5,000
Robinson

Human-Environment Interaction As farming peoples settled in new areas, they brought seeds and farming techniques with them. **Identify** What crops originated in Southwest Asia? **Predict** What do you think happened when people tried to settle on land that was not suitable for farming?

Go Online
PHSchool.com Use Web Code **lbp-2122** for step-by-step map skills practice.

Early Farmers About 11,000 years ago, people in Southwest Asia made an amazing discovery. They learned that if they planted the seeds of wild grasses, new crops of grasses would come up. Thus began the New Stone Age in Southwest Asia. It was called the New Stone Age because people began to grow their own food. They did not have to be nomads, although they still depended on stone tools. However, in many other parts of the world, the Old and Middle Stone Ages continued for many thousands of years. In some areas, Old Stone Age societies even existed into the 1900s.

At the same time that people began to grow their own food, some people became pastoral nomads. That is, they raised livestock and traveled from place to place in search of grazing areas for their animals. Many people, such as the desert-roaming Bedouins of present-day Iraq, Syria, and other areas, are still pastoral nomads.

In most societies, women were responsible for gathering plants and seeds. Therefore they may have been the first to plant seeds. Men usually were the hunters. Women began planting and harvesting their crops in the same place year after year.

Chapter 1 Section 2 **15**

The Beginning of Farming

L2

Guided Instruction

■ **Vocabulary Builder** Clarify the high-use words **characterize** and **pastoral** before reading.

■ Read The Beginning of Farming. As students read, circulate and make sure individuals can answer the Reading Check question.

■ Ask students **How did the New Stone Age begin in Southwest Asia?** *(About 11,000 years ago, people began farming to grow their own food.)*

■ Ask students **Who are pastoral nomads?** *(people who raise livestock and travel from place to place in search of grazing areas for their animals)*

■ Ask students **Why might women have been the first to plant seeds?** *(because in most societies, women were responsible for gathering the plants and seeds)*

Background: Global Perspectives

Global Climate and Agriculture For many years scientists believed that farming began in one place and spread from there throughout the world. However, recent discoveries of evidence of farming in areas as diverse as the Middle East, Thailand, and the Americas at around the same time in history have led some scientists to believe that there is no single place of origin for farming. Many experts note that the earliest evidence of farming coincides with the end of the last Ice Age. This may indicate that changes in the global climate suddenly made it easier to farm in places throughout the world.

Answers

Identify wheat, barley, beans **Predict** They probably moved on quickly to another spot.

Guided Instruction (continued)

- Discuss why farming developed differently in different parts of the world. *(The soil was more fertile in some areas than in others.)*

- Ask students **What are some advantages of domesticating animals rather than just hunting them?** *(Domesticated animals can provide a constant, renewable source of food and clothing. They can also be used in agriculture and to carry heavy loads.)*

Independent Practice

Ask students to fill in the last empty rows on the Taking Notes graphic organizer with information they have just learned.

Monitor Progress

- Show *Section Reading Support Transparency HOW 54* and ask students to check their graphic organizers individually. Go over key concepts and clarify key vocabulary as needed.

  📖 **History of Our World Transparencies,** *Section Reading Support Transparency HOW 54*

- Tell students to fill in the last column of the *Reading Readiness Guide.* Probe for what they learned that confirms or invalidates each statement.

  All in One **Unit 1 History of Our World Teaching Resources,** *Reading Readiness Guide,* p. 13

Farming Techniques

Over time, people have made important advances in farming. In Bali, Indonesia, top, farmers build terraces, or platforms, into the hillsides for growing rice. In 5000 B.C., people grew ears of corn, above left, about 1 inch (2.5 cm) long. By A.D. 1500, years of careful breeding produced much larger corn, above right, about 5 1/3 inches (13.6 cm) long. **Analyze Images** *What advantages do farmers gain from such techniques as terrace farming and plant breeding?*

Farming Around the World Some places were better for farming than others. Soil in some areas was very **fertile,** or rich in the substances that plants need to grow. Because plants also need light and warmth, areas that had long springs and summers were good places to farm. Gentle rains are important sources of water for plants. People gradually discovered that the soil, the water, and the length of the growing seasons in several places around the world were good for plants. These people took up the farming way of life.

About 9,000 years ago, Chinese farmers began planting rice and other crops. A little later in Central America, people began to grow corn, beans, and squash. The map on page 15 shows where certain crops were first planted and how their use spread.

Plant Selection While the kinds of plants grown by those first farmers are still important today, the plants looked very different then. When people first began to plant crops, they carefully chose seeds from the biggest, best-tasting plants. In doing so, they began to **domesticate** plants, or adapt wild plants for human use. Very gradually, this careful selection of seeds and roots from each crop led to the kinds of food that we eat today. The photograph of ears of corn on this page shows the domestication of corn over time.

16 History of Our World

Differentiated Instruction

For Less Proficient Readers **L1**

Have students outline the section to help them remember key points about the reading. Use the *Outline Transparency* to model creating an outline.

📖 **History of Our World Transparencies,** *Transparency B15: Outline*

English Language Learners **L2**

Have students read the section as they listen to the recorded version on the Student Edition on Audio CD. Check for comprehension by pausing the CD and asking students to share their answers to the Reading Checks.

◉ Chapter 1, Section 2, **Student Edition on Audio CD**

Answers

Analyze Images Terraces allow farmers to grow crops on slopes, while plant breeding allows them to improve their crops over time.

Raising Animals Just as humans learned to domesticate plants, they also learned to domesticate animals. During the New Stone Age, humans learned to tame wild animals and breed them for human use. The first domesticated animals may have been dogs, because they were valuable in hunting. By taming larger animals such as sheep, goats, and pigs, people developed ready sources of meat, milk, wool, and skins. Through gradual and careful breeding, herders developed animals that were gentler than their wild ancestors and provided more milk or wool. By about 2500 B.C., cattle, camels, horses, and donkeys were trained to carry heavy loads.

The Challenge of Domestication Over the course of history, humans have tried and failed to domesticate many species. Since ancient times, many animals have been captured in the wild and tamed. The people of ancient India tamed wild elephants for use in battle. Ancient Assyrians and Egyptians trained wild cheetahs for hunting. But these animals and many other species are not easy to breed in captivity. In fact, only a few species of large animals have been suitable for use in agriculture or transportation.

A caravan of camels used by nomads in Iran

✓ **Reading Check** What skills did people develop during the New Stone Age?

Section 2 Assessment

Key Terms
Review the key terms at the beginning of this section. Use each term in a sentence that explains its meaning.

⟳ **Target Reading Skill**
What did you predict about this section? How did your prediction guide your reading?

Comprehension and Critical Thinking
1. (a) **Recall** Describe how people of the Old Stone Age survived.

(b) **Infer** What important skills did people of the Old Stone Age use to find food?
(c) **Synthesize** How did survival skills change as people began to settle?
2. (a) **Identify** What marked the beginning of the New Stone Age?
(b) **Contrast** How was life in the New Stone Age different from life in the Old Stone Age?
(c) **Apply Information** What are the effects of geography and climate on farming?

Writing Activity
Suppose you are a hunter-gatherer. You think of an idea for growing your own food. Write a journal entry describing what gave you the idea, and how your idea might affect your people.

Go Online
PHSchool.com

For: An activity on the Stone Age
Visit: PHSchool.com
Web Code: lbd-2102

Chapter 1 Section 2 **17**

Writing Activity
Use the Rubric for Assessing a Writing Assignment to evaluate students' journal entries.

All in One **Unit 1 History of Our World Teaching Resources,** *Rubric for Assessing a Journal Entry,* p. 36

Go Online PHSchool.com Typing in the Web code when prompted will bring students directly to detailed instructions for this activity.

Assess Progress   L2
Have students complete the Section Assessment. Administer the *Section Quiz.*

All in One **Unit 1 History of Our World Teaching Resources,** *Section Quiz,* p. 15

Reteach   L1
If students need more instruction, have them read this section in the Reading and Vocabulary Study Guide.

📖 Chapter 1, Section 2, **History of Our World Reading and Vocabulary Study Guide,** pp. 9–11

Extend   L3
Have students learn more about early crop growth by having them complete *Reading a Natural Vegetation Map.*

All in One **Unit 1 History of Our World Teaching Resources,** *Reading a Natural Vegetation Map,* p. 30

Answer

✓ Reading Check They developed the ability to grow their own food and domesticate animals.

Section 2 Assessment

Key Terms
Students' sentences should reflect knowledge of each Key Term.

⟳ **Target Reading Skill**
Answers will vary, but should demonstrate the ability to make predictions before reading.

Comprehension and Critical Thinking
1. (a) They hunted using stone weapons, gathered wild plants, and moved around constantly in search of food. (b) the ability to find good hunting ground and knowledge of edible plants (c) They used their skills to find places to live that had good soil and experimented with different types of plants to find the ones that grew best in their area.

2. (a) people growing their own food
(b) People settled in areas to grow their own food rather than traveling constantly in search of food. (c) Geography and climate affect whether certain types of plants will grow well in an area.

Focus on Hunter-Gatherers

L2

Guided Instruction

- Have students read the paragraphs on pp. 18–19 and study the art, photo, and captions as a class.
- Ask students to name techniques scientists believe humans used to kill mammoths. *(wounded and lured into pits; attacked near watering holes; forced over bluffs)*
- Have students answer the Assessment questions in groups of two or three.

Focus On
Hunter-Gatherers

Spears ready, they hide behind rocks and trees. Their hand axes have been sharpened to a fine edge. They are hungry, and the wait seems endless. Then one of them spies the prey and gives a signal to the group. The hunt is on!

Hunter-gatherers lived in the wild. They built their own shelter and made their own clothes. They ate fruits, roots, leaves, and nuts. When they wanted meat, hunting in groups worked best.

Hunting in Groups Big game, such as the mammoth shown here, was valuable for its meat, hide, and bones. Mammoths—now extinct—thrived during the last ice age, which ended about 10,000 years ago.

Hunting big game was dangerous and required team-work. A hunter could easily be crushed by a mammoth, or speared by its sharp tusks.

Scientists have different ideas about how such game was hunted. The animals may have been wounded by spears and then lured into hidden pits and killed. Or, hunters may have attacked the animals near watering holes. Some evidence suggests that hunters would herd animals until they were forced over bluffs, falling to their deaths.

The illustration above shows the mammoth being butchered after a hunt. Once the hide was removed, it was stretched and scraped clean. Damaged weapons were then repaired and made ready for the next hunt.

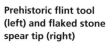

Prehistoric flint tool (left) and flaked stone spear tip (right)

18 History of Our World

Differentiated Instruction

For English Language Learners L3
Students may be unfamiliar with some of the vocabulary in this section, such as *sustained, lured, bluffs,* or *extinct.* Have them look up the words in a dictionary and create flash cards with the word on one side of the card and the definition and the part of speech on the other side. Then pair students and have them take turns quizzing each other.

Ancient Art
During the Ice Age, a time when glaciers covered much of Earth, hunter-gatherers painted animal forms and symbols on cave walls. Charcoal and other materials were used for pigments. Paintings have been found in Africa, Europe, and Australia. The painting above is from a cave in Alsace, France.

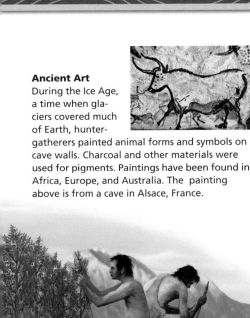

Creating Shelter
Hunter-gatherers lived in caves or human-made shelters. Long ago, hunter-gatherers in parts of Europe made huts of mammoth bones and tusks, like the model shown above. The shelters were probably covered by large animal hides. Firepits, dug into the hut floor, provided heat.

A shell and bone necklace found in Israel

Tools
Hunter-gatherers made their own tools and weapons using stone, wood, bone, and animal sinew.

A prehistoric harpoon made from reindeer bone, found in Europe

Assessment

Describe What methods did hunter-gatherers use to hunt large animals?

Infer Describe the importance of animals to the survival of hunter-gatherers long ago.

Independent Practice
Have students write a short story from the perspective of a hunter-gatherer using the information on pp. 18–19 as a guide. Students may conduct library or Internet research if they require further information about hunter-gatherers in order to write their stories. Students may accompany their stories with illustrations. Use the *Rubric for Assessing a Writing Assignment* to evaluate students' work.

All in One **Unit 1 History of Our World Teaching Resources,** *Rubric for Assessing a Writing Assignment,* p. 35

Answers

Assessment

Describe Scientists believe that hunters may have wounded animals with spears and lured them into pits, waited near watering holes to attack animals that came to drink, or herded animals until they were trapped or forced over bluffs. **Infer** Hunter-gatherers relied on animals for their food, shelter, and probably clothing.

Objectives

Social Studies

1. Find out about the advantages people gained from settling down in one place.
2. Learn about the growth of early cities.
3. Understand how the first civilizations formed and spread.

Reading/Language Arts

Learn how to ask questions to help you remember what you have read.

Prepare to Read

Build Background Knowledge ▪L2

In this section, students will learn about early civilization and the first cities. Ask students to preview the section and form two questions about early cities and civilizations. Write students' questions on the board. Allow them to use these questions to fill in the second column of their charts in the Set a Purpose for Reading activity below.

Set a Purpose for Reading ▪L2

■ Preview the Objectives.

■ Form students into pairs or groups of four. Distribute the *Reading Readiness Guide.* Ask students to fill in the first two columns of the chart. Use the Numbered Heads participation strategy (TE, p. T40) to call on students to share one piece of information they already know and one piece of information they want to know.

All in One **Unit 1 History of Our World Teaching Resources,** *Reading Readiness Guide,* p. 17

Vocabulary Builder
Preview Key Terms ▪L2

Pronounce each Key Term, then ask the students to say the word with you. Provide a simple explanation such as, "When you have an extra amount of something, it is called a surplus."

Prepare to Read

Objectives

In this section you will
1. Find out about the advantages people gained from settling down in one place.
2. Learn about the growth of early cities.
3. Understand how the first civilizations formed and spread.

Taking Notes

As you read, summarize changes that lead to the growth of civilization. Copy the chart below, and use it to record your findings.

The Growth of Civilization

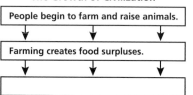

People begin to farm and raise animals.
↓
Farming creates food surpluses.
↓

 Target Reading Skill

Preview and Ask Questions Before you read this section, preview the headings and pictures to find out what the section is about. As you read, write two questions that will help you remember something important about the beginnings of civilization. For example, you might ask yourself, What is a city? Or, How did early civilizations form? Find the answers to your questions as you read.

Key Terms

- **irrigation** (ihr uh GAY shun) *n.* supplying land with water through a network of canals
- **surplus** (SUR plus) *n.* more than is needed
- **artisan** (AHR tuh zun) *n.* a worker who is especially skilled at crafting items by hand
- **civilization** (sih vuh luh ZAY shun) *n.* a society with cities, a central government, job specialization, and social classes
- **social class** (SOH shul klas) *n.* a group of people with similar backgrounds, incomes, and ways of living

Caring for irrigation trenches in Libya, North Africa

Under a fierce desert sun, long lines of people are digging a trench that will soon become a deep canal. Other people lift heavy baskets of dirt dug from the canal onto their shoulders. They dump the dirt near the river where another crew is building a huge earthen dam.

These are some of the world's first construction workers. They are building a system of **irrigation,** supplying land with water from another place using a network of canals. One person directs the work at each site. Like the big construction projects of today, this job takes teamwork.

Soon, the dam will hold back the spring floodwaters of the river. A group of people are building wooden gates in the dam. Officials will open the gates in the dry season, allowing water to flow through the canals and irrigate the growing crops. Farming techniques like this irrigation system were important in creating early communities.

20 History of Our World

◈ Target Reading Skill ▪L2

Preview and Ask Questions Point out the Target Reading Skill. Tell students that asking questions before they start reading can help them understand and remember the information they are to learn.

Model asking questions by looking at the headings and visuals on page 21 and forming two questions about the material: What caused populations to grow suddenly? What gave rise to villages and towns? As the students read the section, have them refer back to these questions to find the answers. (*surplus food; large population*)

Give students *Preview and Ask Questions.* Have them complete the activity in their groups.

All in One **Unit 1 History of Our World Teaching Resources,** *Preview and Ask Questions,* p. 22

Advantages of a Settled Life

Farming was much harder work than hunting and gathering. However, it had far greater rewards. People who produced their own food could have a steady supply of food year-round. This meant they no longer had to travel from place to place. People often even had a food **surplus**—more than what is needed. Surplus food could be stored for use at another time.

The Population Grows Having surplus food also affected the size of families. The hunting-gathering life did not allow parents to have many children. How could they feed them all? Now, food surpluses would feed many more people.

Larger families brought rapid population growth. Scientists estimate that about 10,000 years ago, the population of the world was about 5 million people, which is about the number of people living in Minnesota today. By 7,000 years ago, many people had settled into the farming life. The world's population then was as much as 20 million.

Early Villages and Towns People lived in New Stone Age farming settlements for many centuries. Gradually, as the population increased, the settlements grew into towns.

With food surpluses, people did not have to spend all their days producing food. Some people were able to switch from farming to other kinds of work. For example, some people became artisans. An **artisan** is a worker who is especially skilled in crafting items by hand. Artisans make items such as baskets, leather goods, tools, pottery, or cloth.

✓ **Reading Check** What effect did food surpluses have on people living in settlements?

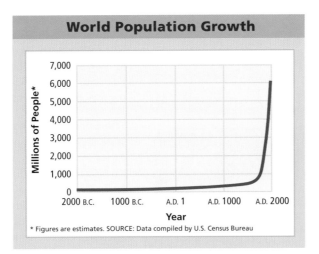

World Population Growth

*Millions of People**

* Figures are estimates. SOURCE: Data compiled by U.S. Census Bureau

Graph Skills

By A.D. 1000, the world's population had reached about 275 million.
Identify By what date had the population reached more than 6 billion?
Generalize How would you describe the rate of population growth before the year A.D. 1?

The ruins of Çatal Hüyük in Turkey, a settlement from around 7000 B.C.

Vocabulary Builder

Use the information below to teach students this section's high-use words.

High-Use Word	Definition and Sample Sentence
occupation, p. 22	*n.* job He enjoyed his **occupation** as a banker.
refine, p. 23	*v.* to improve or polish; free from unwanted material I **refined** the ideas in my paper by revising it twice.
axle, p. 23	*n.* a rod or pin on which a wheel revolves The car had two **axles**, each with two wheels.
prosperity, p. 24	*n.* economic success The country's **prosperity** led to many more jobs.

Advantages of a Settled Life L2

Guided Instruction
- Read Advantages of a Settled Life, using the Paragraph Shrinking technique (TE, p. T38).

- Discuss how food surpluses affected societies. *(Populations and settlements grew. Some people could concentrate on things other than just surviving.)*

- Ask students **Why do you think that the world's population has grown so much in the past 200 years?** *(Possible answer: The world's people have better methods of farming and greater access to food surpluses, and improved health care and living conditions.)*

Independent Practice
Ask students to create the Taking Notes graphic organizer on a blank piece of paper. Then have them fill in the last rectangle with information they have just learned about the effects of food surpluses. Briefly model what kinds of information to record.

Monitor Progress
As students fill in the graphic organizer, circulate and make sure individuals are choosing the correct details. Provide assistance as needed.

Answers
Chart Skills Identify A. D. 2000
Generalize very slow

✓ **Reading Check** Populations grew; some people were able to do work other than producing food.

Target Reading Skill

Ask Questions As a follow up, ask students to answer the Target Reading Skill question in the Student Edition. *(Questions and answers will vary, but should reflect how settlements grew into cities.)*

The Growth of Cities

Guided Instruction

- **Vocabulary Builder** Clarify the high-use word **occupation** before reading.

- Read The Growth of Cities.

- Discuss why many early cities rose up near rivers. *(The soil for farming is rich near riverbeds.)*

- Ask students **What might be an advantage of having a government to run a city?** *(Answers will vary, but should note that life would probably be more stable if a government organized people and settled disputes.)*

Independent Practice

Ask students to add additional rectangles to the graphic organizer using information from this section.

Monitor Progress

As students continue to work on the graphic organizer, circulate and make sure they are adding appropriate details. Provide assistance as needed.

Answers

Chart Skills **Identify** Ur—Iraq, c. 3500 B.C., Anyang—China, c. 1700 B.C. **Compare** They both were probably located near rivers.

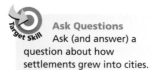

Ask Questions Ask (and answer) a question about how settlements grew into cities.

Explore the birthplaces of civilizations.

■ **Chart Skills**

Cities arose at different times in different places. Ruins from Knossos, right, are part of a palace built circa, or around, 1550 B.C. In the table, *c.* stands for *circa.* **Identify** Where were the cities of Ur and Anyang located, and when were these cities founded? **Compare** In the text, you learned about the geographic conditions in the areas where the earliest cities developed. What geographic factor do you think the cities of Ur and Anyang had in common?

The Growth of Cities

Although some farming settlements grew into cities, many others did not. Cities were more likely to develop in areas where rich soil created large surpluses of food. People also needed a dependable source of drinking water and materials to build shelters. Some of the earliest cities grew up along large rivers, such as the Nile in Egypt, the Tigris (TY gris) and Euphrates (yoo FRAY teez) in Iraq, the Huang (hwahng) in China, and the Indus (IN dus) in Pakistan. Cities grew up in these areas because the soil for farming is rich near riverbeds.

The Earliest Cities Look at the table titled Early Cities. The table shows when some of the first cities developed in Asia, Africa, and Europe. You will learn more about some of these cities later.

Early cities were different from farming villages in some important ways. Cities were larger, of course. Cities also had large public buildings. There were buildings to store surplus grain, buildings for the worship of gods, and buildings where people could buy and sell goods. In villages, most people were farmers. In cities, workers had a wide variety of occupations. Most worked at a craft. As new skills developed, so did new occupations.

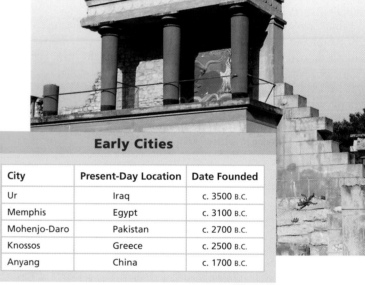

Early Cities

City	Present-Day Location	Date Founded
Ur	Iraq	c. 3500 B.C.
Memphis	Egypt	c. 3100 B.C.
Mohenjo-Daro	Pakistan	c. 2700 B.C.
Knossos	Greece	c. 2500 B.C.
Anyang	China	c. 1700 B.C.

22 History of Our World

Differentiated Instruction

For Gifted and Talented L3
Have students complete the *Small Group Activity.* Encourage them to analyze some mechanical objects, such as a calculator, and others that are simpler, such as a spoon. Encourage students to be creative.

All in One Unit 1 History of Our World Teaching Resources, *Small Group Activity: Simulation: Analyzing "Ancient" Objects,* pp. 26–29

For Advanced Readers L3
After reading the section, have students learn about ancient villages in the Alps by completing the *Enrichment* activity. Ask students to create a visual depiction of one of the villages, based on the description provided in the worksheet.

All in One Unit 1 History of Our World Teaching Resources, *Enrichment,* p. 24

Governments Form As the population of cities grew, governments formed. Governments kept order in society and provided services. They also settled disputes and managed public building and irrigation projects.

✓ **Reading Check** Along which rivers did early cities grow?

The First Civilizations

Over time, some New Stone Age societies grew into civilizations. A **civilization** is a society that has cities, a central government run by official leaders, and workers who specialize in various jobs. Writing, art, and architecture also characterize a civilization.

The Bronze Age By 6600 B.C., artisans in Europe and Asia had learned a key skill. They discovered that melting a certain rock at high temperatures would separate the metal copper from the rock. By 3000 B.C., artisans had learned to mix copper with another metal, tin, to make a mixture called bronze. Ancient peoples may have discovered bronze-making by accident. In nature, small amounts of tin are sometimes found with copper deposits. This discovery marked the beginning of the Bronze Age.

The first people to refine copper with tin had discovered a valuable new metal. Because bronze is much harder than copper, it could be used to make items more durable, or long-lasting. For example, bronze was used to make weapons, tools, helmets, and shields more durable.

Bronze Tools
Shown are half of a stone mold for pins and a bronze pin, top, from Switzerland, around 1000 B.C., and a bronze razor from Denmark, bottom. **Infer** *How are these tools signs of early civilizations?*

Trade and the Spread of Ideas Traders took valuable items such as pottery, tools and weapons, baskets, cloth, and spices to faraway cities. They traded these items for food and goods that people at home wanted.

By around 3500 B.C., some civilizations had developed a simple but amazing invention: the wheel and axle. An axle is a rod on which a wheel turns.

With the wheel and axle, trade goods could be loaded into carts and pushed through the city to market. More goods could be transported farther and more easily.

Chapter 1 Section 3 **23**

The First Civilizations L2

Guided Instruction

- **Vocabulary Builder** Clarify the high-use words **refine, axle,** and **prosperity** before reading.

- Read The First Civilizations. As students read, circulate and make sure individuals can answer the Reading Check question.

- Discuss why bronze was more useful than copper. *(It was harder and thus could be used to make harder, more long-lasting items.)*

- Ask students **Why might some people think that the wheel was one of the most important inventions in history?** *(It helped to improve trade and transportation and today is used in all kinds of transportation, such as bicycles, automobiles, trains, and even airplanes.)*

- Ask students **What role did trade play in the creation of social classes?** *(Trade brought goods and wealth to the cities. People with a similar amount of wealth were part of the same social class.)*

Independent Practice

Ask students to add more rectangles to the Taking Notes graphic organizer using the information they have just learned about the accomplishments of the first civilizations.

Monitor Progress

- Show *Section Reading Support Transparency HOW 55* and ask students to check their graphic organizers individually. Go over key concepts and clarify key vocabulary as needed.

  📖 **History of Our World Transparencies,** *Section Reading Support Transparency HOW 55*

- Tell students to fill in the last column of the *Reading Readiness Guide*. Probe for what they learned that confirms or invalidates each statement.

  All in One Unit 1 History of Our World Teaching Resources, *Reading Readiness Guide,* p. 17

Answers

✓ **Reading Check** They grew along the Nile River in Egypt, the Tigris and Euphrates in Iraq, the Huang in China, and the Indus in Pakistan.

Infer They show the ability to make tools from bronze.

Assess and Reteach

Assess Progress L2

Have students complete the Section Assessment. Administer the *Section Quiz*.

 Unit 1 History of Our World Teaching Resources, *Section Quiz,* p. 19

Reteach L1

If students need more instruction, have them read this section in the Reading and Vocabulary Study Guide.

 Chapter 1, Section 3, **History of Our World Reading and Vocabulary Study Guide,** pp. 12–14

Extend L3

Tell students that bronze-making changed the way ancient peoples lived by allowing them to make more durable tools and weapons. Ask them to consider an invention or discovery from the last 100 years that has had a large impact on the world, and have them write a paragraph explaining how it has improved peoples' lives. (*Possible topics include the Internet, computers, automobiles, and electricity.*) Give students *Writing to Inform and Explain* to help them get started on their paragraphs.

 Unit 1 History of Our World Teaching Resources, *Writing to Inform and Explain,* p. 33

Answers

Infer The bracelet tells us that the society it came from valued beautiful things, and its artisans knew how to work with metal.

✓ **Reading Check** The ability to make valuable items and to trade these items were important in the growth and spread of civilizations.

Section 3 Assessment

Key Terms

Students' sentences should reflect knowledge of each Key Term.

Target Reading Skill

Answers will vary depending on the questions students posed.

Comprehension and Critical Thinking

1. (a) They settled in communities. **(b)** Populations grew and people could focus on other jobs besides farming.

2. (a) rich soil, dependable drinking water, materials to build shelter **(b)** Cities were larger and had public buildings; people had a

greater variety of occupations; they developed governments.

3. (a) Artwork, writing, and social classes developed and trade expanded. **(b)** Some groups were more prosperous than others.

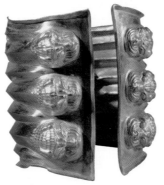

Social Status
Ancient jewelry can provide clues to the social status of its owner or to the type of artisans in a society. The decorative bracelet above comes from the area of present-day Iran. **Infer** *What does the bracelet tell us about the ancient society it came from?*

Trade over water also developed. Merchant ships now carried goods across seas and rivers. With all this travel, people of many different cultures came into contact with one another. New tools and ideas from one society soon spread to other societies as people traded information along with goods.

Social Classes Develop Growing trade links brought new prosperity to the cities. Prosperity led to another major change in society—the development of social classes. A **social class** is a group of people having similar backgrounds, incomes, and ways of living.

In the large cities, the king was the most powerful person. Next in importance were two classes of people. One class was made up of the priests of the city's religion. The other class was made up of nobles, who were government officials and military officers. Below them were the artisans, small traders, and merchants. Common workers and farmers were the lowest ranked free members of society.

Slaves, human beings owned as property by other people, formed a separate social class. Most slaves worked in cities, often as household servants and as laborers. Their status, or rank, was beneath that of free people.

✓ **Reading Check** **What skills and practices were important in the growth and spread of early civilizations?**

 ## Section 3 Assessment

Key Terms

Review the key terms at the beginning of this section. Use each term in a sentence that explains its meaning.

Target Reading Skill

What questions did you ask to help you learn or remember something about this section?

Comprehension and Critical Thinking

1. (a) Describe How did people's lives change when they began to produce their own food?

(b) Identify Effects What effects did food surpluses have on people and populations?

2. (a) Recall What resources were necessary for villages to grow into cities?

(b) Compare and Contrast What were the similarities and differences between villages and cities?

3. (a) Name What developments occurred as societies grew into civilizations?

(b) Draw Conclusions How did prosperity lead to the development of social classes?

Writing Activity

Suppose you are an early trader bringing tools and weapons made of bronze to people who have never seen bronze before. Write a speech in which you try to persuade these people to trade for your bronze goods.

> **Writing Tip** Write an opener for your speech that will grab the listener's attention. Write a list of reasons why bronze tools are better than tools made of copper. Refer to this list when writing your speech.

Writing Activity

Use the *Rubric for Assessing a Writing Assignment* to evaluate students' speeches.

 Unit 1 History of Our World Teaching Resources, *Rubric for Assessing a Writing Assignment,* p. 35

Review and Assessment

◆ Chapter Summary

Section 1: Geography and History

- The study of tools, bones, and other objects can help to explain prehistoric life.
- The development of writing marks a turning point in the story of our past.
- The geography of a place can explain why historic events happened there.

Section 2: Prehistory

- During the Old Stone Age, our ancestors survived by hunting animals and gathering plant foods.
- Gradually, our ancestors moved from Africa and spread out over much of Earth.
- During the New Stone Age, some people began to farm and to domesticate animals.

Section 3: The Beginnings of Civilization

- The advantage of a steady food supply helped early farming settlements to prosper.
- Farming settlements grew into cities because of their geographical locations.
- The first civilizations developed in cities and spread with the help of trade.

Knossos

Camel caravan

◆ Reviewing Key Terms

Fill in the blanks in Column I using the key terms from Column II.

Column I

1. Stories passed down by word of mouth are _____.

2. The _____ was the earliest known period of human culture.

3. Human ancestors learned how to _____, or tame, animals.

4. Making items such as baskets, jewelry, and pottery is the job of a(n) _____.

5. A society that has cities, a central government, and specialized workers is a(n) _____.

6. _____ is the period of time before writing was developed.

Column II

civilization
archaeologist
oral traditions
artisan
Stone Age
prehistory
domesticate
irrigation

Vocabulary Builder

Revisit this chapter's high-use words:

community	evidence	occupation
curiosity	ward off	refine
record	characterize	axle
deposit	pastoral	prosperity

Ask students to review the definitions they recorded on their *Word Knowledge* worksheets.

 Unit 1 History of Our World Teaching Resources, *Word Knowledge,* p. 23

Consider allowing students to earn extra credit if they use the words in their answers to the questions in the Chapter Review and Assessment. The words must be used correctly and in a natural context to win the extra points.

Review and Assessment

Review Chapter Content

- Review and revisit the major themes of this chapter by asking students to classify what Guiding Questions each bulleted statement in the Chapter Summary answers. Have students work in groups to match the statements with the appropriate questions. Have the groups conduct an Idea Wave (TE, p. T39) to share their answers. Refer to page 1 of the Student Edition for the text of the Guiding Questions.

- Assign Vocabulary Development for students to review Key Terms.

   All in One **Unit 1 History of Our World Teaching Resources,** *Vocabulary Development,* p. 34

Answers

Key Terms

1. oral traditions

2. Stone Age

3. domesticate

4. artisan

5. civilization

6. prehistory

Review and Assessment

Comprehension and Critical Thinking

7. (a) History is a written record of events, while prehistory occurred before there were written records. **(b)** We can study the artifacts they left behind. **(c)** They probably hunted large animals.

8. (a) They hunted and gathered food. **(b)** People started to plant seeds to grow their own food. **(c)** As people farmed, populations grew, leading to the rise of cities.

9. (a) They learned how to make tools and how to get food. **(b)** It allowed them to live in colder climates. **(c)** the development of tools and the need for more food

10. (a) Cities had growing populations, public buildings, people doing a variety of jobs, and governments. **(b)** Governments helped keep order, provide protections, settle disputes, and organize public projects. **(c)** Leaders of government were usually among the highest classes in the cities.

Skills Practice
Students' flowcharts should place the information from the text in the proper order.

Writing Activity: Science
Students' answers will vary, but should reflect accurate information about the places they have chosen.

MAP MASTER™
Skills Activity

1. A	**2.** D
3. F	**4.** B
5. C	**6.** E

Go Online PHSchool.com Students may practice their map skills using the interactive online version of this map.

Review and Assessment (continued)

◆ **Comprehension and Critical Thinking**

7. (a) Identify What is the difference between history and prehistory?
(b) Explain How can we learn about human ancestors who lived before written history?
(c) Draw Inferences Suppose that large, heavy spear points are found at a prehistoric site. What might they tell us about the human ancestors who once lived there?

8. (a) Describe How did early humans find food during the Old Stone Age?
(b) Make Generalizations What characterized the Old Stone Age, the Middle Stone Age, and the New Stone Age?
(c) Sequence What is the connection between farming and the growth of early cities?

9. (a) Recall What survival skills did our human ancestors learn throughout the Stone Age?
(b) Identify Effects How did the discovery of the use of fire affect our human ancestors?
(c) Identify Causes What developments allowed early nomads to move from Africa to many parts of the world?

10. (a) Recall Describe aspects of the earliest cities.
(b) Explain How did cities benefit from a central government?
(c) Draw Conclusions What was the relationship between government and the social classes of early civilizations?

◆ **Skills Practice**

Using Timelines In the Skills for Life activity in this chapter, you learned how to use a timeline to gain a better understanding of a certain time period. You then created your own timeline. Review the steps you follow for this skill and study the timeline on page 13. Then reread Chapter 1 looking for events that fit within the timeline span. Redraw the timeline with the additional events.

◆ **Writing Activity: Science**

Form conclusions the way archaeologists do. Choose a place you know well, such as your classroom. Then, pick two or three objects found there and make detailed notes on them. What do your notes tell you about the people who use the objects?

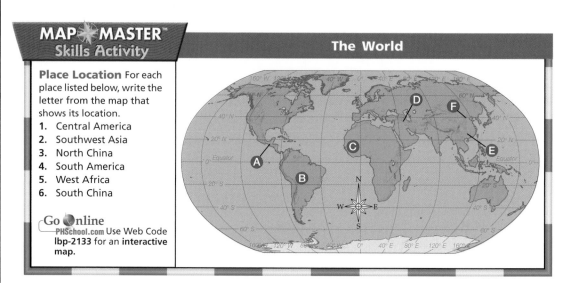

MAP MASTER™
Skills Activity

The World

Place Location For each place listed below, write the letter from the map that shows its location.
1. Central America
2. Southwest Asia
3. North China
4. South America
5. West Africa
6. South China

Go Online PHSchool.com Use Web Code **lbp-2133** for an **interactive map.**

Standardized Test Prep

Test-Taking Tips

Some questions on standardized tests ask you to analyze a reading passage for causes and effects. Read the paragraph below. Then follow the tips to answer the sample question.

The Sumer civilization arose in the region between the Tigris and Euphrates rivers. Similarly, early Egyptian civilization developed along the Nile River. Ancient China had its origins along the Huang River. <u>A fresh water supply and rich soil made these river valleys "cradles of civilization."</u>

TIP Identify the main idea, or most important point, as you read a paragraph or passage.

Pick the letter that best completes the statement.

TIP Restate this as a question: Which effect was the author writing about?

The author wrote this passage to give information about the effect of

  A geography on early civilizations.

  B agriculture on early civilizations.

  C geography on the economies of early civilizations.

  D migration on the environment.

Think It Through Start with the main idea: Early civilizations developed near rivers in many places. Keep the main idea in mind as you try to answer the question. Rivers are a part of geography, so you can eliminate B and D. Rivers do have an effect on economies, but the paragraph does not discuss that topic. The correct answer is A.

Practice Questions

Use the tips above and other tips in this book to help you answer the following questions.

1. Prehistory describes the time period before
   A people existed.
   B people used tools.
   C clothes were made from animal skins.
   D writing was invented.

2. During which time period did farming develop?
   A prehistory
   B the Old Stone Age
   C the Middle Stone Age
   D the New Stone Age

3. As food surpluses developed,
   A population growth increased.
   B towns grew into farming settlements.
   C people left the cities.
   D more artisans became farmers.

Read the passage below, and then answer the question that follows.

Oral history, while important, does not give an accurate history of a society. Stories may exaggerate or only focus on certain things. Archaeology is also incomplete. Bones and objects tell us only part of the story of the past. Any accurate history must take into account the written records of human life.

4. Which statement best reflects the main idea of the passage?
   A Historians must have written records to fully understand the past.
   B Written records are not very important.
   C Written records are almost as important as stories and archaeology.
   D Historians value oral stories the most.

Use Web Code lba-2103
for **Chapter 1 self-test.**

Standardized Test Prep

Answers

1. D

2. A

3. A

4. A

Go **Online**
PHSchool.com **Students may use the Chapter 1 self-test at PHSchool.com to prepare for the Chapter Test.**

Assessment Resources

Use Chapter Tests A and B to assess students' mastery of chapter content.

All in One **Unit 1 History of Our World Teaching Resources,** Chapter Tests A and B, pp. 37–42

Tests are also available on the **Exam*View*®** **Test Bank CD-ROM**

  ⊙ **Exam*View*® Test Bank CD-ROM**

The Fertile Crescent

Overview

 Section 1

Land Between Two Rivers
1. Find out how geography made the rise of civilization in the Fertile Crescent possible.
2. Learn about Sumer's first cities.
3. Examine the characteristics of Sumerian religion.

 Section 2

Babylonia and Assyria
1. Learn about the two most important empires of Mesopotamia.
2. Find out what characterized the Babylonian and Assyrian empires.
3. Understand how Babylonia was able to rise again after defeat.

 Section 3

The Legacy of Mesopotamia
1. Learn about the importance of Hammurabi's Code.
2. Find out how the art of writing developed in Mesopotamia.

 Section 4

Mediterranean Civilizations
1. Understand how the sea power of the Phoenicians helped spread civilization throughout the Mediterranean area.
2. Learn about the major events in the history of the Israelites.

 Section 5

Judaism
1. Learn about the basic beliefs of Judaism.
2. Find out about the effect that Judaism has had on other religions.

Petra: Secrets of the Red City
Length: 4 minutes, 39 seconds
Use with Section 1
This video segment discusses the secrets of the ancient city of Petra.

 **Technology Resources**

Go Online
PHSchool.com

Students use embedded Web codes to access Internet activities, chapter self-tests, and additional map practice. They may also access Dorling Kindersley's Online Desk Reference to learn more about each country they study.

Interactive Textbook

Use the Interactive Textbook to make content and concepts come alive through animations, videos, and activities that accompany the complete basal text—online and on CD-ROM.

PRENTICE HALL
TeacherEXPRESS™
Plan · Teach · Assess

Use this complete suite of powerful teaching tools to make planning lessons and administering tests quicker and easier.

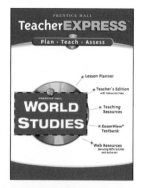

Reading and Assessment

Reading and Vocabulary Instruction

⟲ Model the Target Reading Skill

Clarifying Meaning A number of reading skills can help students to clarify the meaning of the text. Rereading and reading ahead allow students to look for unfamiliar words and terms. Paraphrasing allows students to restate ideas in words they better understand and remember. Summarizing helps students to state the main points of the passage. Model this skill by thinking aloud about this text from page 32 of the Student Edition:

Rivers of Life and Death *The Tigris and Euphrates rivers were the source of life for the peoples of Mesopotamia. In the spring, melting snow picked up tons of topsoil as it rushed down from the mountains and flooded the land. The floods left this topsoil on the plain below. Farmers grew crops in this soil. The rivers also supplied fish, clay for building, and tall, strong reeds used to make boats.*

I wonder what the subhead means. I'll read ahead. The paragraph describes how the rivers bring life to the people of Mesopotamia. The last two sentences give details about the kind of life the rivers bring. I'll reread these sentences to make sure I understand. The second and third sentences seem a little complicated, so I'll restate them: "Melted snow fills the rivers with more water than they can hold, so the rivers flood the area beside them. This covers the land with dirt from the river." Finally, I'll summarize the paragraph: "The Tigris and Euphrates rivers supplied many things that the people living near them needed."

Use the following worksheets from All-in-One Unit 1 History of Our World Teaching Resources (pp. 67–69) to support this chapter's Target Reading Skill.

Vocabulary Builder
High-Use Academic Words

Use these steps to teach this chapter's high-use words:

1. Have students rate how well they know each word on their Word Knowledge worksheets (All-in-One Unit 1 History of Our World Teaching Resources, p. 70).

2. Pronounce each word and ask students to repeat it.

3. Give students a brief definition and sample sentence (provided on TE pp. 31, 38, 44, 49, 57).

4. Work with students as they fill in the "Definition or Example" column of their Word Knowledge worksheets.

Assessment

Formal Assessment

Test students' understanding of core knowledge and skills.

Chapter Tests A and B, All-in-One Unit 1 History of Our World Teaching Resources, pp. 86–91

Customize the Chapter Tests to suit your needs.

Exam*View*® Test Bank CD-ROM

Skills Assessment

Assess geographic literacy.

MapMaster Skills, Student Edition, pp. 29, 31, 39, 49, 51, 59, 62

Assess reading and comprehension.

Target Reading Skills, Student Edition, pp. 33, 41, 44, 51, 57, and in Section Assessments

Chapter 2 Assessment, History of Our World Reading and Vocabulary Study Guide, p. 31

Performance Assessment

Assess students' performance on this chapter's Writing Activities using the following rubrics from All-in-One Unit 1 History of Our World Teaching Resources.

Rubric for Assessing a Journal Entry, p. 79

Rubric for Assessing a Timeline, p. 80

Rubric for Assessing a Caption, p. 81

Rubric for Assessing an Oral Presentation, p. 82

Rubric for Assessing a Student Poster, p. 83

Rubric for Assessing a Writing Assignment, p. 84

Rubric for Assessing a Student Poem, p. 85

Assess students' work through performance tasks.

Small Group Activity: Making an Illustrated Diagram About the Wheel, All-in-One Unit 1 History of Our World Teaching Resources, pp. 73–76

Online Assessment

Have students check their own understanding.

Chapter Self-Test

Section 1 **Land Between Two Rivers**

 2 periods, 1 block (includes Focus On Farming in Mesopotamia)

Social Studies Objectives

1. Find out how geography made the rise of civilization in the Fertile Crescent possible.
2. Learn about Sumer's first cities.
3. Examine the characteristics of Sumerian religion.

Reading/Language Arts Objective

Reread to help you understand words and ideas in the text.

Prepare to Read	**Instructional Resources**	**Differentiated Instruction**
Build Background Knowledge Discuss how geography affects the way people live. **Set a Purpose for Reading** Have students evaluate statements on the *Reading Readiness Guide.* **Preview Key Terms** Teach the section's Key Terms. **Target Reading Skill** Introduce the section's Target Reading Skill of **rereading.**	**All in One Unit 1 History of Our World Teaching Resources** L2 Reading Readiness Guide, p. 48 L2 Reread or Read Ahead, p. 67	**Spanish Reading and Vocabulary Study Guide** L1 Chapter 2, Section 1, pp. 14–15 ELL

Instruct	**Instructional Resources**	**Differentiated Instruction**
The Geographic Setting Discuss how the Fertile Crescent's geography made living there possible. **The First Cities** Have students identify features of Sumerian city-states. **Target Reading Skill** Review **rereading.** **Sumerian Religion** Discuss religion in Sumer.	**All in One Unit 1 History of Our World Teaching Resources** L2 Guided Reading and Review, p. 49 L2 Reading Readiness Guide, p. 48 **History of Our World Transparencies** L2 Section Reading Support Transparency HOW 56 **History of Our World Video Program** L2 Petra: Secrets of the Red City	**All in One Unit 1 History of Our World Teaching Resources** Rubric for Assessing a Student Poster, p. 83 **Teacher's Edition** L1 For Special Needs Students, TE p. 34 L3 For Gifted and Talented Students, TE p. 36 **Student Edition on Audio CD** L1 Chapter 2, Section 1 ELL, LPR, SN **Spanish Support** L2 Guided Reading and Review (Spanish), p. 12 ELL

Assess and Reteach	**Instructional Resources**	**Differentiated Instruction**
Assess Progress Evaluate student comprehension with the section assessment and section quiz. **Reteach** Assign the Reading and Vocabulary Study Guide to help struggling students. **Extend** Extend the lesson by assigning a Small Group Activity.	**All in One Unit 1 History of Our World Teaching Resources** L2 Section Quiz, p. 50 L3 Small Group Activity: Making an Illustrated Diagram About the Wheel, pp. 73–76 Rubric for Assessing a Journal Entry, p. 79 **Reading and Vocabulary Study Guide** L1 Chapter 2, Section 1, pp. 16–18	**Spanish Support** L2 Section Quiz (Spanish), p. 13 ELL

Key

L1 Basic to Average   L3 Average to Advanced   LPR Less Proficient Readers   GT Gifted and Talented

L2 For All Students   AR Advanced Readers   ELL English Language Learners

                                          SN Special Needs Students

Section 2 Babylonia and Assyria

 *2 periods, 1 block*

Social Studies Objectives
1. Learn about the two most important empires of Mesopotamia.
2. Find out what characterized the Babylonian and Assyrian empires.
3. Understand how Babylonia was able to rise again after defeat.

Reading/Language Arts Objective
Restate information by paraphrasing.

Prepare to Read	**Instructional Resources**	**Differentiated Instruction**
Build Background Knowledge Discuss the significance of Assyrian carvings. **Set a Purpose for Reading** Have students evaluate statements on the *Reading Readiness Guide.* **Preview Key Terms** Teach the section's Key Terms. **Target Reading Skill** Introduce the section's Target Reading Skill of **paraphrasing**.	**All in One Unit 1 History of Our World Teaching Resources** L2 Reading Readiness Guide, p. 52 L2 Paraphrase, p. 68	**Spanish Reading and Vocabulary Study Guide** L1 Chapter 2, Section 2, pp. 16–17 ELL

Instruct	**Instructional Resources**	**Differentiated Instruction**
The Two Empires of Mesopotamia Have students list the shared features of Babylonia and Assyria. **The Babylonian Empire** Ask questions about the growth of the Babylonian Empire. **The Empire of the Assyrians Babylonia Rises Again** Ask questions about the Assyrians and the second rise of Babylon. **Target Reading Skill** Review **paraphrasing**.	**All in One Unit 1 History of Our World Teaching Resources** L2 Guided Reading and Review, p. 53 L2 Reading Readiness Guide, p. 52 **History of Our World Transparencies** L2 Transparency B16: Venn Diagram L2 Section Reading Support Transparency HOW 57	**All in One Unit 1 History of Our World Teaching Resources** Rubric for Assessing a Timeline, p. 80 AR, GT **Teacher's Edition** L2 For English Language Learners, TE p. 40 L3 For Advanced Readers, TE p. 40 **Spanish Support** L2 Guided Reading and Review (Spanish), p. 14 ELL

Assess and Reteach	**Instructional Resources**	**Differentiated Instruction**
Assess Progress Evaluate student comprehension with the section assessment and section quiz. **Reteach** Assign the Reading and Vocabulary Study Guide to help struggling students. **Extend** Extend the lesson by having students research the accomplishments of Nebuchadnezzar II.	**All in One Unit 1 History of Our World Teaching Resources** L2 Section Quiz, p. 54 Rubric for Assessing a Caption, p. 81 **Reading and Vocabulary Study Guide** L1 Chapter 2, Section 2, pp. 19–21	**Spanish Support** L2 Section Quiz (Spanish), p. 15 ELL

Key
- L1 Basic to Average
- L2 For All Students
- L3 Average to Advanced
- LPR Less Proficient Readers
- AR Advanced Readers
- SN Special Needs Students
- GT Gifted and Talented
- ELL English Language Learners

Section 3 The Legacy of Mesopotamia

 *2 periods, 1 block*

Social Studies Objectives
1. Learn about the importance of Hammurabi's Code.
2. Find out how the art of writing developed in Mesopotamia.

Reading/Language Arts Objective
Use summarizing to restate key points in the text.

Prepare to Read	**Instructional Resources**	**Differentiated Instruction**
Build Background Knowledge Have students brainstorm the effects of writing on everyday life. **Set a Purpose for Reading** Have students evaluate statements on the *Reading Readiness Guide.* **Preview Key Terms** Teach the section's Key Terms. **Target Reading Skill** Introduce the section's Target Reading Skill of **summarizing.**	**All in One Unit 1 History of Our World Teaching Resources** L2 Reading Readiness Guide, p. 56 L2 Summarize, p. 69	**Spanish Reading and Vocabulary Study Guide** L1 Chapter 2, Section 3, pp. 18–19 ELL

Instruct	**Instructional Resources**	**Differentiated Instruction**
Hammurabi's Code Discuss Hammurabi's Code. **Target Reading Skill** Review **summarizing.** **The Art of Writing** Discuss the beginnings of writing in Mesopotamia.	**All in One Unit 1 History of Our World Teaching Resources** L2 Guided Reading and Review, p. 57 L2 Reading Readiness Guide, p. 56 **History of Our World Transparencies** L2 Section Reading Support Transparency HOW 58	**All in One Unit 1 History of Our World Teaching Resources** Rubric for Assessing an Oral Presentation, p. 82 AR, GT **Teacher's Edition** L1 For Less Proficient Readers, TE p. 46 L3 For Advanced Readers, TE p. 46 **Spanish Support** L2 Guided Reading and Review (Spanish), p. 16 ELL

Assess and Reteach	**Instructional Resources**	**Differentiated Instruction**
Assess Progress Evaluate student comprehension with the section assessment and section quiz. **Reteach** Assign the Reading and Vocabulary Study Guide to help struggling students. **Extend** Extend the lesson by having students research an alphabet and describe their findings in a poster.	**All in One Unit 1 History of Our World Teaching Resources** L2 Section Quiz, p. 58 Rubric for Assessing a Student Poster, p. 83 Rubric for Assessing a Writing Assignment, p. 84 **Reading and Vocabulary Study Guide** L1 Chapter 2, Section 3, pp. 22–24	**Spanish Support** L2 Section Quiz (Spanish), p. 17 ELL

Key

L1 Basic to Average   L3 Average to Advanced

L2 For All Students

LPR Less Proficient Readers
AR Advanced Readers

SN Special Needs Students
GT Gifted and Talented
ELL English Language Learners

Section 4 Mediterranean Civilizations

 2 periods, 1 block (includes Skills for Life)

Social Studies Objectives
1. Understand how the sea power of the Phoenicians helped spread civilization throughout the Mediterranean area.
2. Learn about the major events in the history of the Israelites.

Reading/Language Arts Objective
Read ahead to help clarify words and ideas.

Prepare to Read

Build Background Knowledge
Discuss oral traditions in history.

Set a Purpose for Reading
Have students evaluate statements on the *Reading Readiness Guide.*

Preview Key Terms
Teach the section's Key Terms.

Target Reading Skill
Introduce the section's Target Reading Skill of **reading ahead**.

Instructional Resources

All in One Unit 1 History of Our World Teaching Resources
- L2 Reading Readiness Guide, p. 60
- L2 Reread or Read Ahead, p. 67

Differentiated Instruction

Spanish Reading and Vocabulary Study Guide
- L1 Chapter 2, Section 4, pp. 20–21 ELL

Instruct

Phoenician Sea Power
Ask questions about the effects of sea trade and travel on the Phoenicians.

The Phoenician Alphabet
Discuss the spread of the Phoenician alphabet.

The Rise of the Israelites
Discuss the history of the Israelites.

Target Reading Skill
Review **reading ahead**.

Instructional Resources

All in One Unit 1 History of Our World Teaching Resources
- L2 Guided Reading and Review, p. 61
- L2 Reading Readiness Guide, p. 60

History of Our World Transparencies
- L2 Transparency B15: Outline
- L2 Section Reading Support Transparency HOW 59

Differentiated Instruction

All in One Unit 1 History of Our World Teaching Resources
- L2 Skills for Life, p. 72 AR, GT, LPR, SN

Teacher's Edition
- L1 For Less Proficient Readers, TE p. 50
- L1 For Special Needs Students, TE p. 51

Reading and Vocabulary Study Guide
- L1 Chapter 2, section 4, pp. 25–27 ELL, LPR, SN

Spanish Support
- L2 Guided Reading and Review (Spanish), p. 18 ELL

Assess and Reteach

Assess Progress
Evaluate student comprehension with the section assessment and section quiz.

Reteach
Assign the Reading and Vocabulary Study Guide to help struggling students.

Extend
Extend the lesson by assigning the chapter's Enrichment activity.

Instructional Resources

All in One Unit 1 History of Our World Teaching Resources
- L2 Section Quiz, p. 62
- L3 Enrichment, p. 71
  Rubric for Assessing a Student Poem, p. 85

Reading and Vocabulary Study Guide
- L1 Chapter 2, Section 4, pp. 25–27

Differentiated Instruction

Teacher's Edition
- L1 For Less Proficient Readers, TE p. 55

Spanish Support
- L2 Section Quiz (Spanish), p. 19 ELL

Social Studies Skills Tutor CD-ROM
- L1 Identifying Main Ideas ELL, LPR, SN

Key
L1 Basic to Average	L3 Average to Advanced	LPR Less Proficient Readers	GT Gifted and Talented
L2 For All Students		AR Advanced Readers	ELL English Language Learners
		SN Special Needs Students	

Section 5 Judaism

 2 periods, 1 block (includes Chapter Review and Assessment)

Social Studies Objectives

1. Learn about the basic beliefs of Judaism.
2. Find out about the effect that Judaism has had on other religions.

Reading/Language Arts Objective

Summarize to review the main points in a text.

Prepare to Read

Build Background Knowledge
Discuss how aspects of ancient Judaism affect people today.

Set a Purpose for Reading
Have students evaluate statements on the *Reading Readiness Guide.*

Preview Key Terms
Teach the section's Key Terms.

Target Reading Skill
Introduce the section's Target Reading Skill of **summarizing.**

Instructional Resources

All in One Unit 1 History of Our World Teaching Resources
- L2 Reading Readiness Guide, p. 64
- L2 Summarize, p. 69

Differentiated Instruction

Spanish Reading and Vocabulary Study Guide
- L1 Chapter 2, Section 5, pp. 22–23 ELL

Instruct

The Beliefs of Judaism
Ask questions about and discuss the beliefs of Judaism.

Target Reading Skill
Review **summarizing.**

The Effects of Judaism
Discuss the impact of Judaism on other religions.

Instructional Resources

All in One Unit 1 History of Our World Teaching Resources
- L2 Guided Reading and Review, p. 65
- L2 Reading Readiness Guide, p. 64

History of Our World Transparencies
- L2 Section Reading Support Transparency HOW 60

Differentiated Instruction

All in One Unit 1 History of Our World Teaching Resources
Rubric for Assessing a Student Poster, p. 83 AR, GT

Teacher's Edition
- L2 For English Language Learners, TE p. 59
- L3 For Gifted and Talented Students, TE p. 59

Spanish Support
- L2 Guided Reading and Review (Spanish), p. 20 ELL

Assess and Reteach

Assess Progress
Evaluate student comprehension with the section assessment and section quiz.

Reteach
Assign the Reading and Vocabulary Study Guide to help struggling students.

Extend
Extend the lesson by assigning a primary source literature reading.

Instructional Resources

All in One Unit 1 History of Our World Teaching Resources
- L2 Section Quiz, p. 66
- L3 Moses and the Ten Commandments, p. 77 Rubric for Assessing a Writing Assignment, p. 84
- L2 Vocabulary Development, p. 78
- L2 Word Knowledge, p. 70
- L2 Chapter Tests A and B, pp. 86–91

Reading and Vocabulary Study Guide
- L1 Chapter 2, Section 5, pp. 28–30

Differentiated Instruction

Spanish Support
- L2 Section Quiz (Spanish), p. 21 ELL
- L2 Chapter Summary (Spanish), p. 22 ELL
- L2 Vocabulary Development (Spanish), p. 23 ELL

Key

L1 Basic to Average	L3 Average to Advanced	
L2 For All Students		

LPR Less Proficient Readers
AR Advanced Readers
SN Special Needs Students

GT Gifted and Talented
ELL English Language Learners

Reading Background

Pre-Teaching Vocabulary

Research literature on academic vocabulary instruction indicates that effective strategies require students to go beyond simply looking up dictionary definitions or examining the context. Vocabulary learning must be based on the learner's dynamic engagement in constructing understanding.

If students are not retaining the meaning of the Key Terms or high-use words, use this extended vocabulary sequence to engage them in learning new words.

1. Present the word in writing and point out the part of speech.
2. Pronounce the word and have students pronounce the word.
3. Provide a range of familiar synonyms (or "it's like" words) before offering definitions.
4. Provide an accessible definition and concrete examples, or "showing sentences."
5. Rephrase the definition or example sentence, asking students to complete the statement by substituting the word aloud.
6. Check for understanding by providing an application task/question requiring critical thinking.

Sample instructional sequence:

1. *Myth* is a noun, a word that names a person, place, or thing.
2. Say the word *myth* after me. (Students repeat.)
3. A *myth* is like *a story* or *a legend*.
4. *Myth* means *traditional story that explains people's beliefs*. The *myth* explained how the Egyptians believed Earth was created.
5. The Egyptians explained how Earth was created in one of their _____. (Students substitute missing word.)
6. Is a newspaper article an example of a *myth*? Yes-No-Why? (Students answer the question.)

Word Wizard

Using new words outside of the classroom will also help students remember what they have learned. Set up a system in which students earn points for bringing in evidence of having heard or seen the Key Terms or high-use words outside the classroom. Suggest to students that they may find examples of words in newspapers, magazines, television, or radio.

World Studies Background

The Seven-Day Week

Evidence indicates that the Chaldeans in the New Babylonian Empire may be responsible for establishing the seven-day week. According to the Chaldeans, each of the seven astral bodies—what we know today as Saturn, Jupiter, Mars, Venus, Mercury, and the sun and the moon—represented a major Babylonian god. They believed that one of these gods watched over the people from sunrise to sunset of every day, creating a seven-day cycle.

Paleography and the Mystery of Writing

The experts who figured out the history of early Sumerian writing are people known as paleographers. Paleographers specialize in the study of ancient and medieval handwriting. Their main task is to study the language in old writings and decipher the date and place of origin.

The Canaanites

The Phoenicians, in their own language, called themselves "Kena'ani." Sometimes this is translated as "Canaanite," a term that also appears in many ancient Hebrew writings. The Hebrews believed the Canaanites were descended from Canaan, a grandson of Noah the Ark-builder.

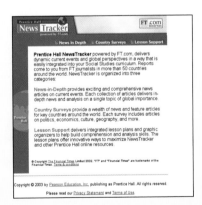

Get in-depth information on topics of global importance with **Prentice Hall Newstracker,** powered by FT.com.

 Use Web code **lbd-2200** for **Prentice Hall Newstracker.**

Guiding Questions

Remind students about the Guiding Questions introduced at the beginning of the book.

Section 1 relates to **Guiding Question** **1**
How did physical geography affect the growth of ancient civilizations? (*Fertile land made possible the rise of civilizations in the Fertile Crescent.*)

Section 2 relates to **Guiding Question** **2**
What historical accomplishments is each civilization known for? (*The Babylonians and Assyrians gained riches and land through conquest, and built grand cities.*)

Section 3 relates to **Guiding Question** **4**
How did ancient people develop governments? (*Hammurabi's code, a set of written laws, told the Babylonians how to settle conflicts in all areas of life.*)

Section 4 relates to **Guiding Question** **1**
How did physical geography affect the growth of ancient civilization? (*The great sea power of the Phoenicians and their location on the Mediterranean Sea allowed their idea of civilization to spread.*)

Section 5 relates to **Guiding Question** **3**
What were the beliefs and values of ancient peoples? (*The beliefs of the Israelites developed into Judaism, and influenced the religions of Christianity and Islam.*)

Target Reading Skill

In this chapter, students will learn and apply the reading skill of clarifying. Use the following worksheets to help students practice this skill:

All in One Unit 1 History of Our World Teaching Resources, *Reread or Read Ahead,* p. 67; *Paraphrase,* p. 68, *Summarize,* p. 69

Differentiated Instruction

The following Teacher Edition strategies are suitable for students of varying abilities.

Advanced Readers, pp. 40, 46
English Language Learners, pp. 40, 59
Gifted and Talented Students, pp. 36, 59
Less Proficient Readers, pp. 46, 50, 55
Special Needs Students, pp. 34, 51

Chapter
2

The Fertile Crescent

Chapter Preview

This chapter will introduce you to the civilizations of an ancient region of the Middle East known as the Fertile Crescent.

Section 1
Land Between Two Rivers

Section 2
Babylonia and Assyria

Section 3
The Legacy of Mesopotamia

Section 4
Mediterranean Civilizations

Section 5
Judaism

Target Reading Skill

Clarifying Meaning In this chapter you will focus on clarifying, or better understanding, the meaning of what you read.

▶ A shepherd grazes his sheep along the banks of the Euphrates River in Syria.

28 History of Our World

Bibliography

For the Teacher
Dever, William G. *Who Were the Early Israelites and Where Did They Come From?* Wm. B. Eerdmans Publishing Co., 2003.
Leick, Gwendolyn. *Mesopotamia: The Invention of the City.* Penguin, 2003.
Roberton, Henry S. *Voices of the Past: From Assyria and Babylonia.* Lost Arts Media, 2003.

For the Student
L1 French, Vivian and Collins, Ross. *Write Around the World: The Story of How and Why We Learned to Write.* Oxford University Press Children's Books, 2002.
L2 Charing, Douglas. *Judaism (Eyewitness Books).* DK Publishing, 2003.
L3 Deedrick, Tami. *Mesopotamia.* Raintree Publishers, 2002.

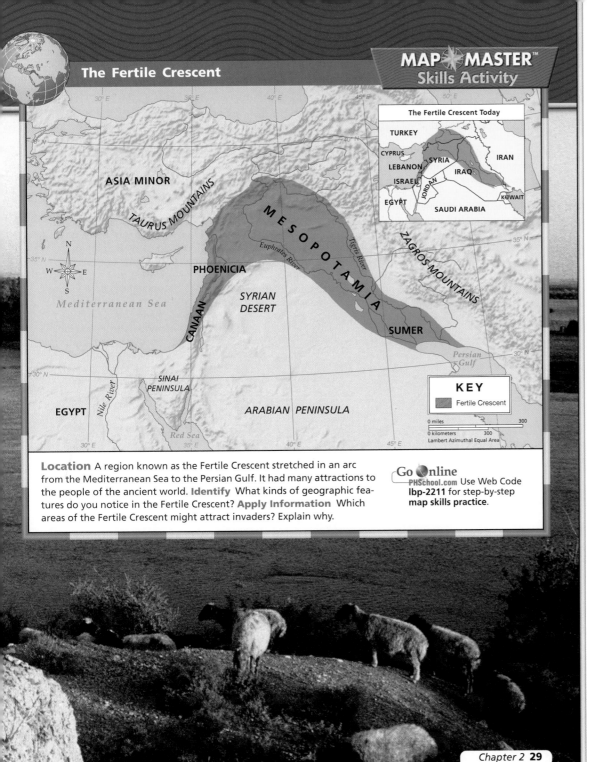

The Fertile Crescent

The Fertile Crescent Today

TURKEY
CYPRUS
LEBANON
ISRAEL
JORDAN
EGYPT
SYRIA
IRAQ
IRAN
KUWAIT
SAUDI ARABIA

ASIA MINOR

TAURUS MOUNTAINS

Euphrates River

Tigris River

MESOPOTAMIA

ZAGROS MOUNTAINS

PHOENICIA

CANAAN

Mediterranean Sea

SYRIAN DESERT

SUMER

Persian Gulf

SINAI PENINSULA

EGYPT

Nile River

Red Sea

ARABIAN PENINSULA

N W E S

KEY
Fertile Crescent

0 miles 300
0 kilometers 300
Lambert Azimuthal Equal Area

Location A region known as the Fertile Crescent stretched in an arc from the Mediterranean Sea to the Persian Gulf. It had many attractions to the people of the ancient world. **Identify** What kinds of geographic features do you notice in the Fertile Crescent? **Apply Information** Which areas of the Fertile Crescent might attract invaders? Explain why.

Go Online
PHSchool.com Use Web Code **lbp-2211** for step-by-step **map skills practice**.

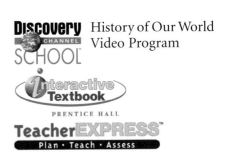

Chapter 2 **29**

- Have students trace the outline of the region and describe its shape. *(crescent)* Point out to students the connection between the name of the area *(the Fertile Crescent)* and its shape.

- Have students compare the map of the Fertile Crescent with the inset map showing the Fertile Crescent region today. Create a two-column table on the board with the headings "Fertile Crescent civilizations" and "Fertile Crescent countries." Then help the students fill in the information in the appropriate columns.

Go Online
PHSchool.com Students may practice their map skills using the interactive online version of this map.

Using the Visual ▪L2▪

Reach Into Your Background Draw students' attention to the photo and its caption on pages 28–29. Ask them to describe how the shepherd in the photo is benefiting from the river. *(The river provides water for the plants the sheep graze on, and also provides water for the sheep to drink.)* What other ways can they think of that people in the region can benefit from the river? In what ways do they use water in their daily lives? Conduct an Idea Wave (TE, p. T39) to elicit student responses.

Answers

MAP MASTER Skills Activity **Identify** rivers, gulf and sea coasts; **Apply Information** Areas along the coasts might attract invaders since they are easily reached by boat.

Chapter Resources

Teaching Resources
▪L2▪ Vocabulary Development, p. 78
▪L2▪ Skills for Life, p. 72
▪L2▪ Chapter Tests A and B, pp. 86–91

Spanish Support
▪L2▪ Spanish Chapter Summary, p. 22
▪L2▪ Spanish Vocabulary Development, p. 23

Media and Technology
▪L1▪ Student Edition on Audio CD
▪L1▪ Guided Reading Audio CDs, English and Spanish
▪L2▪ Social Studies Skills Tutor CD-ROM ExamView® Test Bank CD-ROM

Discovery CHANNEL SCHOOL History of Our World Video Program

interactive Textbook
PRENTICE HALL

TeacherEXPRESS™
Plan • Teach • Assess

Objectives

Social Studies
1. Find out how geography made the rise of civilization in the Fertile Crescent possible.
2. Learn about Sumer's first cities.
3. Examine the characteristics of Sumerian religion.

Reading/Language Arts
Reread to help you understand words and ideas in the text.

Prepare to Read

Build Background Knowledge L2
Tell students that in this section they will study the geography and people of the Fertile Crescent. Have students review the headings and visuals in the section with this question in mind: **How does geography affect the way people live?** Use the Give One, Get One participation strategy (TE, p. T41) to help encourage student participation.

Set a Purpose for Reading L2
- Preview the Objectives.
- Read each statement in the *Reading Readiness Guide* aloud. Ask students to mark the statements true or false.

  All in One Unit 1 History of Our World **Teaching Resources,** *Reading Readiness Guide,* p. 48

- Have students discuss the statements in pairs or groups of four, and then mark their worksheets again. Use the Numbered Heads participation strategy (TE, p. T40) to call on students to share their group's perspectives.

Vocabulary Builder
Preview Key Terms L2
Pronounce each Key Term, and then ask the students to say the word with you. Provide a simple example such as, "A scribe is a person who is paid to write things down."

Answer

Analyze Information They kept records for the kings and priests.

Prepare to Read

Objectives
In this section you will
1. Find out how geography made the rise of civilization in the Fertile Crescent possible.
2. Learn about Sumer's first cities.
3. Examine the characteristics of Sumerian religion.

Taking Notes
As you read, look for details about Mesopotamia and Sumer. Copy the outline below, and use it to record your findings.

> I. The geographic setting
>   A. Mesopotamia
>   1.
>   2.
>   B. The Tigris and
>   Euphrates rivers
> II.

🎯 Target Reading Skill

Reread Rereading is a strategy that can help you to understand words and ideas in the text. If you do not understand a certain passage, reread it to look for connections among the words and sentences. When you reread, you may gain a better understanding of the more complicated ideas.

Key Terms
- **scribe** (skryb) *n.* a professional writer
- **Fertile Crescent** (FUR tul KRES unt) *n.* a region in Southwest Asia; site of the first civilizations
- **city-state** (SIH tee stayt) *n.* a city that is also a separate, independent state
- **polytheism** (PAHL ih thee iz um) *n.* the belief in many gods
- **myth** (mith) *n.* a traditional story; in some cultures, a legend that explains people's beliefs

The Work of Scribes
The language on this tablet—Sumerian—is the oldest known written language. **Analyze Information** *Why were scribes important in Sumer?*

The following words from the past come from a student at one of the world's first schools. He tells what happened to him when his homework was sloppy or when he spoke without permission.

> ❝My headmaster read my tablet and said, 'There is something missing,' and hit me with a cane. . . . The fellow in charge of silence said, 'Why did you talk without permission?' and caned me.❞
>
> —*A Sumerian student*

The first known schools were set up in the land of Sumer (SOO mur) over 4,000 years ago. Sumerian schools taught boys—and possibly a few girls—the new invention of writing. Graduates of the schools became **scribes, or professional writers.** Scribes were important because they kept records for the kings and priests. Learning to be a scribe was hard work. Students normally began school at about the age of eight and finished about ten years later. The writings Sumerian scribes left behind help to tell the story of this early civilization.

🎯 Target Reading Skill L2

Reread Point out the Target Reading Skill. Tell students that rereading a passage can help them better understand words and ideas in the text.

Model using rereading to find the meaning of the word "caned" in this sentence from the quote on this page: "The fellow in charge of silence said: 'Why did you talk without permission?' and caned me." (*Rereading the last sentence before the quote reveals that caning is a type of punishment.*)

Give students *Reread or Read Ahead.* Have them complete the activity in groups.

All in One Unit 1 History of Our World **Teaching Resources,** *Reread or Read Ahead,* p. 67

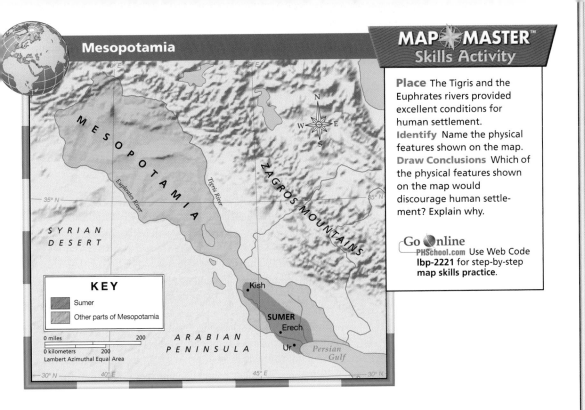

MAP MASTER™
Skills Activity

Place The Tigris and the Euphrates rivers provided excellent conditions for human settlement.
Identify Name the physical features shown on the map.
Draw Conclusions Which of the physical features shown on the map would discourage human settlement? Explain why.

Go Online
PHSchool.com Use Web Code lbp-2221 for step-by-step map skills practice.

The Geographic Setting

Sumer was located in a region called Mesopotamia (mes uh puh TAY mee uh). Look at the map titled Mesopotamia. Like the place where you live, ancient Mesopotamia had special attractions that drew people to settle there. Most important, it had rich soil and life-giving rivers. These attractions drew people who became farmers and city builders. Sumer's central location within the ancient world drew many traders from other regions. Sumer became one of the most prosperous areas of the ancient world.

The Location of Mesopotamia

Mesopotamia's name describes its location. The word *Mesopotamia* comes from Greek words that mean "between the rivers." The map above shows that Mesopotamia lies between two rivers, the Tigris and the Euphrates.

The ruins of Uruk, an ancient Sumerian city on the Euphrates River, northwest of Ur

Chapter 2 Section 1 **31**

── Vocabulary Builder ──

Use the information below to teach students this section's high-use words.

High-Use Word	Definition and Sample Sentence
fertile, p. 32	*adj.* producing much fruit or large crops, rich The high quality of the farmer's crop was due to the **fertile** land he farmed.
terrace, p. 34	*n.* a flat platform with sloping banks Farmers cut **terraces** into hills to increase the amount of farm land.
rival, p. 35	*n.* someone who tries to get the same thing as another; competitor The first place trophy was the aim of the two **rivals**.

Instruct

The Geographic Setting [L2]

Guided Instruction

- **Vocabulary Builder** Clarify the high-use word **fertile** before reading.

- Read The Geographic Setting, using the Paragraph Shrinking technique (TE, p. T38).

- Ask students **What geographical features made life in the Fertile Crescent possible?** (*rich soil and life-giving rivers*)

- Ask students **Why do you think people continued to live in the Fertile Crescent despite the threat of dangerous floods?** (*The benefits that the floods provided must have outweighed the harmful effects of occasionally destructive floods.*)

Answers

MAP MASTER Skills Activity **Identify** mountains, deserts, rivers, gulf, lakes **Draw Conclusions** Mountains and deserts generally do not encourage human settlement because of their harsh conditions.

Go Online
PHSchool.com Students may practice their map skills using the interactive online version of this map.

Independent Practice

Ask students to create the Taking Notes graphic organizer on a blank piece of paper. Then have them fill in the details about the geographic setting of the Fertile Crescent. Briefly model how to identify which details to record.

Monitor Progress

As students fill in the graphic organizer, circulate and make sure individuals are selecting the correct details. Provide assistance as needed.

Mesopotamia is part of the **Fertile Crescent,** a region in Southwest Asia that was the site of the world's first civilizations. Turn to the map titled The Fertile Crescent on page 62. To see how this region got its name, place your finger at the eastern edge of the Mediterranean Sea (med uh tuh RAY nee un) on the map. Move eastward from the Mediterranean coast to Mesopotamia. Then move southeast to the Persian Gulf. Notice that the region you've traced is shaped like a crescent moon. The rivers of this crescent-shaped region helped to make it one of the best places in Southwest Asia for growing crops.

Rivers of Life and Death The Tigris and the Euphrates rivers were the source of life for the peoples of Mesopotamia. In the spring, melting snow picked up tons of topsoil as it rushed down from the mountains and flooded the land. The floods left this topsoil on the plain below. Farmers grew crops in this soil. The rivers also supplied fish, clay for building, and tall, strong reeds used to make boats.

The floodwaters sometimes brought sorrows as well as gifts. The floods did not always happen at the same time each year. Racing down without warning, they swept away people, animals, crops, and houses. Then, the survivors would rebuild and pray that the next flood would not be so destructive.

✓ Reading Check **How did flooding rivers affect people who settled in Mesopotamia?**

Peacetime in Sumer
Around 2500 B.C., artists from the Sumerian city-state of Ur created this mosaic recording of peacetime activities. Shown are two out of the three rows of figures.
❶ The king sits facing members of the royal family at a banquet.
❷ Servants stand ready to wait upon the royal family.
❸ A musician playing a harp and a singer provide entertainment.
❹ Servants deliver animals, fish, and other items for the feast.
Infer *How do the activities shown provide clues about jobs and social classes in Ur?*

32 History of Our World

Answers

✓ Reading Check Flooding made farming, and therefore life, possible in Mesopotamia; floods also sometimes swept away people, animals, crops, and homes.

Infer Answers will vary, but students should suggest that the people in the top row are probably wealthy and of a higher social class. The people in the bottom row are servants and are part of a lower social class.

The First Cities

As farming succeeded in Mesopotamia, communities began to build up surpluses of food. In time, food surpluses encouraged the growth of cities. By 3500 B.C., some of the earliest known cities arose in the southern region of Sumer, along the Tigris and Euphrates rivers.

Independent Cities Form Although cities in Mesopotamia shared a common culture and language, they did not unite under a single ruler. Instead, they remained politically independent city-states. A **city-state** is a city that is also a separate, independent state. Each Sumerian city acted as a separate state, with its own special god or goddess, its own government, and, eventually, its own king.

A Brief Tour of a Sumerian City Public squares bustled with activity. In the marketplaces, merchants displayed goods in outdoor stalls. Musicians, acrobats, beggars, and water sellers filled the streets. For a fee, scribes wrote letters for those who could not read or write. Sumerian houses faced away from the crowded streets, onto inner courtyards where families ate and children played. On hot nights, people slept outdoors on their homes' flat roofs. Oil lamps supplied light for Sumerian homes.

✓ **Reading Check** How were the cities of Sumer governed?

Discovery SCHOOL Video Find out about the ancient city of Petra.

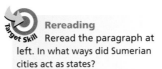
Rereading
Reread the paragraph at left. In what ways did Sumerian cities act as states?

Show students *Petra: Secrets of the Red City*. Ask **Why did the city of Petra decline?** (*Trade routes changed and the city was eventually devastated by earthquakes.*)

The First Cities L2

Guided Instruction

- Read about the earliest cities presented in The First Cities. As students read, circulate to make sure individuals can answer the Reading Check question _____.

- Using the Idea Wave participation strategy, (TE, p. T39) have students identify features of Sumerian city-states. (*City-states shared a common culture and language, but they did not unite under a single ruler; they were politically independent cities with their own traditions, gods or goddesses, laws, and governments that eventually were led by their own kings.*)

Independent Practice

Have students continue to fill in the Taking Notes graphic organizer with details about the first cities in Mesopotamia.

Monitor Progress

Allow students to continue to fill in their graphic organizers. Circulate to check that individuals are filling in the correct details. Provide assistance as needed.

⊙ Target Reading Skill L2

Rereading As a follow up, ask students to answer the Target Reading Skill question in the Student Edition. (*Each city remained politically independent, had its own special god or goddess, its own government, and its own king.*)

Background

The Standard of Ur The panel shown on pp. 32–33 is one side of an artifact that scholars call the Royal Standard of Ur. The side shown in the photo shows images of peacetime, while the opposite side shows images of war. The panel itself is made of wood that has since decayed, shell, red limestone, and lapis lazuli.

The original use for the panel remains unknown. It was found by British archaeologist Sir Leonard Woolley, who believed it was carried on a pole as a standard, a symbol representing the people it belonged to. Another theory claims that the panel may have been part of a musical instrument.

Answer

✓ **Reading Check** Each city had its own government and laws.

Sumerian Religion 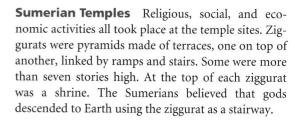 L2

Guided Instruction

- **Vocabulary Builder** Clarify the high-use words **terrace** and **rival** before reading.

- Ask students to read Sumerian Religion and have them examine the photographs on this page and the next.

- Ask students to name and describe the type of worship practiced by the Sumerians. *(Polytheism; religious practice in which people believe in many gods)*

- Ask students **Why do you think religion was so important to the Sumerians?** *(Answers will vary, but should include that Sumerians believed that gods would punish people who angered them and reward people who served them well.)*

Independent Practice

Have students complete the graphic organizer by filling in details about Sumerian religion.

Monitor Progress

- Show *Section Reading Support Transparency HOW 56* and ask students to check their graphic organizers individually. Go over key concepts and clarify key vocabulary as needed.

    History of Our World Transparencies, *Section Reading Support Transparency HOW 56*

- Tell students to fill in the last column of the *Reading Readiness Guide*. Probe for what they learned that confirms or invalidates each statement.

    All in One Unit 1 History of Our World Teaching Resources, *Reading Readiness Guide,* p. 48

Answer

Analyze Images Because it was shaped like a ladder.

Sumerian Religion

A stranger coming to a Sumerian city could easily notice a giant brick building at the heart of the city. It was the ziggurat (ZIG oo rat), the site of the temple to the main god or goddess of the city.

Sumerians placed prayer figures on altars. The eyes of the worshiping figures were made wide, as though they were fixed on the gods.

Sumerian Temples Religious, social, and economic activities all took place at the temple sites. Ziggurats were pyramids made of terraces, one on top of another, linked by ramps and stairs. Some were more than seven stories high. At the top of each ziggurat was a shrine. The Sumerians believed that gods descended to Earth using the ziggurat as a stairway.

Ancient Religious Beliefs The people of Sumer worshiped many gods and goddesses. This practice is known as **polytheism,** a belief in many gods. To understand this word, break it up into its parts. *Poly-,* a Greek prefix, means "many." *Theism* means "belief in a god or gods."

Sumerian **myths,** or stories about gods that explain people's beliefs, warned that the gods would punish people who angered them. The myths also promised rewards to people who served the gods well.

Stairway to the Heavens
This partially restored brick ziggurat was part of the ancient city of Ur. **Analyze Images** *Why do you think the Sumerians believed the gods could use the ziggurat to descend to Earth?*

Differentiated Instruction

For Special Needs Students L1
Have students read the section as they listen to the recorded version on the Student Edition on Audio CD. Check for comprehension by pausing the CD and asking students to share their answers to the Reading Checks.

⊙ Chapter 2, Section 1, **Student Edition on Audio CD**

Honoring the Gods The Sumerians honored their gods in religious ceremonies. Temple priests washed the statues of gods before and after each meal was offered. Music sounded and incense burned as huge plates of food were laid before them. In most ancient religions, the food was often eaten after it was presented to the gods. Perhaps the worshipers thought that by eating the offering, they would be taking in the qualities they admired in the gods. The religious beliefs of the Sumerians give us an idea of what was important to them. Poetry was also used to express what was important to them:

> **"**Behold the bond of Heaven and Earth, the city. . . .
> Behold . . . its well of good water.
> Behold . . . its pure canal. **"**
>
> —*A Sumerian poem*

A reconstructed musical instrument called a lyre (lyr), about 2500 B.C., from Ur

The Fall of Sumer Unfortunately for Sumer, its wealth became its downfall. Sumerian city-states fought each other over land and the use of river water. Rulers from various city-states won and lost control of all of Sumer. Around 2300 B.C., Sumer was conquered by the armies of neighboring Akkadia (uh KAY dee uh). Their ruler, King Sargon, united the Sumerian city-states and improved Sumer's government and its military. Sumer remained united for about 100 years until it dissolved once more into independent city-states. Sumer was no longer a major power after 2000 B.C. It fell to a northern rival, Babylonia, in the 1700s B.C.

✓ **Reading Check** What weakened the cities of Sumer?

Section 1 Assessment

Key Terms
Review the key terms at the beginning of this section. Use each term in a sentence that explains its meaning.

Target Reading Skill
What word or idea were you able to clarify by rereading certain passages?

Comprehension and Critical Thinking
1. (a) Recall Describe the geography of Mesopotamia.

(b) Find the Main Ideas How did Mesopotamia's geography help civilizations to develop in the area?
2. (a) Compare In what ways were Sumerian cities alike?
(b) Contrast In what ways were the cities of Sumer different?
3. (a) Explain How did Sumerians practice religion?
(b) Infer What do the religious practices of the Sumerians tell us about their values?

Writing Activity
Write a journal entry from the viewpoint of a student scribe in Sumer. Describe what you see on your walk to school.

For: An activity on Sumer
Visit: PHSchool.com
Web Code: lbd-2201

Assess and Reteach

Assess Progress　L2
Have students complete the Section Assessment. Administer the *Section Quiz*.

All in One **Unit 1 History of Our World Teaching Resources,** *Section Quiz,* p. 50

Reteach　L1
If students need more instruction, have them read this section in the Reading and Vocabulary Study Guide.

Chapter 2, Section 1, **History of Our World Reading and Vocabulary Study Guide,** pp. 16–18

Extend　L3
Have students learn more about life in Mesopotamia by completing the *Small Group Activity: Making an Illustrated Diagram About the Wheel.* Have students work together in small groups to complete the activity.

All in One **Unit 1 History of Our World Teaching Resources,** *Small Group Activity: Making an Illustrated Diagram About the Wheel,* pp. 73–76

Answers

✓ **Reading Check** Fights between city-states over use of land and river water led to frequent battles that weakened Sumer's rulers and armies.

Writing Activity
Use the *Rubric for Assessing a Journal Entry* to evaluate students' journal entries.

All in One **Unit 1 History of Our World Teaching Resources,** *Rubric for Assessing a Journal Entry,* p. 79

Go Online PHSchool.com Typing in the Web code when prompted will bring students to detailed instructions for this activity.

Section 1 Assessment

Key Terms
Students' sentences should reflect knowledge of each Key Term.

Target Reading Skill
Answers will vary but should reflect students' understanding of how to reread to clarify a word or idea.

Comprehension and Critical Thinking
1. (a) Mesopotamia, located between the Tigris and Euphrates rivers, had rich soil and plentiful water. **(b)** Abundant water and fertile soil encouraged people to settle in the area and develop civilizations.

2. (a) Sumerian cities were well developed, had high walls to keep out invaders, large temples, houses, busy shops, markets, and splendid royal palaces. **(b)** Each city was its own politically independent city-state; each had its own ruler, special gods or goddesses, and its own government.

3. (a) Sumerians worshipped at temples called ziggurats; they practiced polytheism and made sure their gods were properly cared for. **(b)** Sumerians greatly admired their gods, enjoyed food and music, and loved their cities.

Focus on Farming in Mesopotamia L2

Guided Instruction

- Ask students to read the text and study the art, photos, and captions on these pages.

- Ask students **What effects did the rivers have on the lives of the Mesopotamians?** *(The rivers were a source of both life and terrible problems for the Mesopotamians, they provided water and silt for the crops, but could also bring starvation through droughts and floods.)*

- Ask students **Why do you think local officials decided when the floodgates would be opened?** *(Possible answers: so all of the farmers would have water at the same time; to avoid having too much or not enough water.)*

- As a class, answer the Assessment questions. Allow students to briefly discuss their responses with a partner before sharing their answers with the class.

Farming the land "between the rivers" required skill and determination. The life-giving rivers could be generous one year and stingy the next. Frosts, droughts, floods, weeds, or insects could bring starvation. For survival, families worked together in farming communities. As cities rose above the Mesopotamian plain, governments created huge farms. From the river-fed land, farmers cultivated the crops—wheat, barley, cucumbers, and figs—that nourished kingdoms for many years to come.

Working the Fields Farmers in Mesopotamia were allowed a certain amount of water each year to prepare their soil for planting and to water their crops. Local officials often decided when to open the floodgates in canals, allowing water into the fields.

Farmers would let their animals graze in the wet soil, to trample and eat the weeds. The earliest farmers then broke up the soil using hand tools. This work became easier with the invention of the ox-drawn plow. After plowing, the seeds could be planted.

At first, farmers spread seeds by hand. In the 2000s B.C., they attached a funnel to the plow, as shown in the illustration, to spread the seeds easily and more evenly. After the grain was harvested, it was threshed, or pounded to separate the grain from the straw.

36 History of Our World

Differentiated Instruction

For Gifted and Talented L3
Working in pairs or groups, have students do research in the library or on the Internet to find out what kinds of crops the Mesopotamians grew. Then have each pair or group create a poster showing the crops and their uses. Poster should include photos or drawings of the type of grain, vegetable or fruit, how it was grown, and what it was used for. Use *Rubric for Assessing a Student Poster* to evaluate students' work.

All in One Unit 1 History of Our World Teaching Resources, *Rubric for Assessing a Student Poster,* p. 83

Farming Tools
Early farmers in Mesopotamia first used simple tools—sticks for plowing and stone-bladed sickles, like the one shown here, for harvesting grain. In time, more efficient tools were invented.

Assessment

Analyze Information Describe how farmers in Mesopotamia prepared the soil and planted their crops.

Draw Conclusions How did Mesopotamians improve their farming methods over time?

Pottery
The pottery made by Mesopotamians had many uses. The spouted vessel above, from about 3000 B.C., was found in Iraq. It may have been used to carry water. The cup, dated to 2200–1900 B.C., was found in Israel. It was probably used to measure grain.

Chapter 2 Section 1 **37**

Independent Practice
Have students work in pairs to create an "Instruction Manual" for growing a crop using the Mesopotamians' farming method. Students should create a list of the numbered steps, and include drawings showing each step.

Answers

Assessment

Analyze Information Local officials decided when to open the floodgates in canals which provided water for the farmers' fields; farmers let their animals graze in the wet soil to eat the weeds and spread out the salt and minerals in the silt; farmers then broke up the soil and planted the seeds.
Drawing Conclusions At first farmers broke up the soil using hand tools and spread seeds by hand; later the invention of the ox-drawn plow to break up the soil and a funnel attached to the plow to spread the seeds made the job much easier.

Chapter 2 **37**

Objectives

Social Studies

1. Learn about the two most important empires of Mesopotamia.
2. Find out what characterized the Babylonian and Assyrian empires.
3. Understand how Babylonia was able to rise again after defeat.

Reading/Language Arts

Restate information by paraphrasing.

Prepare to Read

Build Background Knowledge L2

Ask students to examine the photos of carvings of battle scenes and their captions on pages 38–39. Have students speculate about what these carvings tell about the significance of warfare in Assyrian culture. Conduct an Idea Wave (TE, p. T39) in order to generate a list of students' responses.

Set a Purpose for Reading L2

- Preview the Objectives.

- Read each statement in the *Reading Readiness Guide* aloud. Ask students to mark the statements true or false.

  All in One Unit 1 History of Our World Teaching Resources, *Reading Readiness Guide,* p. 52

- Have students discuss the statements in pairs or groups of four, then mark their worksheets again. Use the Numbered Heads participation strategy (TE, p. T40) to call on students to share their group's perspectives.

Vocabulary Builder
Preview Key Terms L2

Pronounce each Key Term, and then ask students to say the word with you. Provide a simple example such as, "A bazaar is a type of market where people buy and sell items."

Section
2 Babylonia and Assyria

Prepare to Read

Objectives

In this section you will

1. Learn about the two most important empires of Mesopotamia.
2. Find out what characterized the Babylonian and Assyrian empires.
3. Understand how Babylonia was able to rise again after defeat.

Taking Notes

As you read, note the similarities and the differences between Babylonia and Assyria. Copy the Venn diagram below, and record your findings in it.

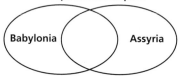

Mesopotamian Empires

Babylonia — Assyria

🎯 Target Reading Skill

Paraphrase When you paraphrase, you restate what you have read in your own words. You could paraphrase the first paragraph of this section this way: "King Sargon II of Assyria learned that two kingdoms were joining together to resist him. In 714 B.C., he attacked the weaker forces of Urartu and Zikirtu."

As you read, paraphrase or "say back" the information following each red or blue heading.

Key Terms

- **empire** (EM pyr) *n.* many territories and peoples controlled by one government
- **Babylon** (BAB uh lahn) *n.* the capital of Babylonia; a city of great wealth and luxury
- **caravan** (KA ruh van) *n.* a group of traders traveling together
- **bazaar** (buh ZAHR) *n.* a market selling different kinds of goods
- **battering ram** (BAT ur ing ram) *n.* a powerful weapon with a wooden beam mounted on wheels

King Sargon II of Assyria (center) and two officials

38 History of Our World

King Sargon II of Assyria (uh SEER ee uh) heard the news: Assyria had attacked the nearby kingdoms of Urartu and Zikirtu as planned. But the two kingdoms had then joined forces against him. How dare they resist the most powerful monarch in the world? In the summer of 714 B.C., King Sargon II set out to confront his enemies.

The two kingdoms were no match for the powerful Assyrian ruler. His armies quickly overcame the forces of Urartu and killed all who resisted. The Assyrians howled with laughter when they saw the king of Urartu fleeing on an old horse. Sargon II let him go. He knew that the defeated king would serve as a warning to others who might later be tempted to challenge the mighty Assyrians. Sargon II was one of many kings who ruled Mesopotamia after the fall of Sumer.

🎯 Target Reading Skill L2

Paraphrase Point out the Target Reading Skill. Tell students that paraphrasing, or restating information in their own words, will help reinforce the knowledge they gain from a text.

Model using paraphrasing to restate the meaning of the proverb at the end of the first paragraph on page 39. "Using my own words, I would say that this proverb means that one war often leads to another war."

Give students *Paraphrase.* Have them complete the activity in groups.

All in One Unit 1 History of Our World Teaching Resources, *Paraphrase,* p. 68

The Two Empires of Mesopotamia

The history of Mesopotamia is filled with stories of conquest. The army that could conquer Mesopotamia gained great wealth from trade and agriculture. But each new ruler became a target for another conqueror. This pattern is reflected in an old proverb, "You go and carry off the enemy's land; the enemy comes and carries off your land."

The biggest and most important Mesopotamian civilizations were the empires of Babylonia (bab uh LOH nee uh) and Assyria. An **empire** is an area of many territories and peoples that is controlled by one government. The beautiful city of **Babylon** was the center of the Babylonian empire. This empire reached its height around 1750 B.C. The Assyrians, named after the northern city of Assur, began expanding their lands in the 1300s B.C. By the 600s B.C., they controlled a large empire.

The Babylonians and the Assyrians had two things in common. In their quest for riches, they were vicious warriors. And in the enjoyment of their riches, they built grand cities where culture and learning were highly valued.

Assyrian warriors carry off goods from a defeated enemy.

✓ **Reading Check** Why was Mesopotamia a target for conquest?

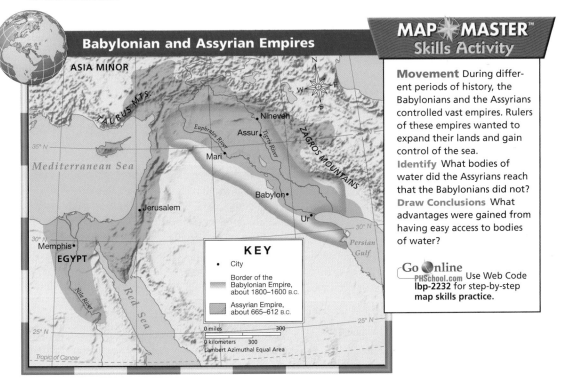

Babylonian and Assyrian Empires

ASIA MINOR
TAURUS MTS.
Nineveh
Assur
Euphrates River
Tigris River
ZAGROS MOUNTAINS
Mari
35° N
Mediterranean Sea
Babylon
Jerusalem
Ur
30° N
Persian Gulf
30° N
Memphis
EGYPT
Nile River
Red Sea
25° N

KEY
• City
Border of the Babylonian Empire, about 1800–1600 B.C.
Assyrian Empire, about 665–612 B.C.

0 miles 300
0 kilometers 300
Lambert Azimuthal Equal Area
Tropic of Cancer

MAP MASTER™ Skills Activity

Movement During different periods of history, the Babylonians and the Assyrians controlled vast empires. Rulers of these empires wanted to expand their lands and gain control of the sea.
Identify What bodies of water did the Assyrians reach that the Babylonians did not?
Draw Conclusions What advantages were gained from having easy access to bodies of water?

Go Online
PHSchool.com Use Web Code lbp-2232 for step-by-step map skills practice.

Vocabulary Builder

Use the information below to teach students this section's high-use words.

High-Use Word	Definition and Sample Sentence
conquer, p. 39	*v.* to gain control over someone or something Giving her speech in class helped her **conquer** her fear of public speaking.
expand, p. 39	*v.* to spread out or make greater in size The tire **expanded** as the air was pumped in.
invade, p. 41	*v.* to enter as an enemy The ants started to **invade** the picnic as the food was set out to eat.

Instruct

The Two Empires of Mesopotamia L2

Guided Instruction

■ **Vocabulary Builder** Clarify the high-use words **conquer** and **expand** before reading.

■ Have students read The Two Empires of Mesopotamia, using the Structured Silent Reading technique (TE, p. T38).

■ Ask students **What were the two most important empires of Mesopotamia?** (*Babylonia and Assyria*)

■ Have students list the traits that the Babylonians and the Assyrians shared. (*They both sought riches, were fierce warriors, and built grand cities where culture and learning were highly valued.*)

■ Direct students' attention to the proverb in the first paragraph. Have students discuss their interpretation of the proverb. Then, based on their interpretation, have them predict what will occur to the Babylonian and Assyrian empires.

Independent Practice

Ask students to create the Taking Notes graphic organizer on a blank piece of paper. Then have them begin to fill it in by listing information they have just learned. Briefly model how to identify which details to record using the blank *Venn Diagram Transparency*.

📖 **History of Our World Transparencies,** *Transparency B16: Venn Diagram*

Monitor Progress

As students fill in the graphic organizer, circulate and make sure that individuals are placing the information in the correct circles.

Answers

✓ **Reading Check** because rulers believed the land would bring great wealth

MAP MASTER Skills Activity **Identify** the Mediterranean Sea and the Red Sea **Draw Conclusions** Possible answer: Having access to bodies of water provides people with water to grow crops as well as access to trading routes.

Go Online
PHSchool.com Students may practice their map skills using the interactive online version of this map.

Read the **Links to Math** on this page. Ask students **How did the use of mathematics help to advance Babylonian civilization?** (*Mathematics helped Babylonians solve everyday problems, such as how to make building plans.*)

The Babylonian Empire

L2

Guided Instruction

- Ask students to read about Babylonia's growth in The Babylonian Empire. Help students to trace the borders of the Babylonian Empire by referring them back to the map on page 39. As students read, circulate and make sure that individuals can answer the Reading Check question.

- Ask students **What made Babylonia a crossroads of trade?** (*its central location*)

- Ask students **What factors led to Babylonia's early growth?** (*Its armies conquered large amounts of land; its central location led to the growth of trade; it gathered great wealth through conquest.*)

Independent Practice

Have students continue to fill in their graphic organizers by listing appropriate details in the "Babylonia" circle.

Monitor Progress

As students fill in their graphic organizers, circulate to check that individuals are filling in the correct details about Babylonia. Provide assistance as needed.

Answer

✓ Reading Check Hammurabi was a Babylonian king who created the Babylonian Empire by uniting the cities of Sumer and conquering lands all the way to Asia Minor.

Links to Math

Babylonian Mathematics
The Babylonians developed a useful system of mathematics for solving everyday problems. For example, they learned to calculate areas of geometric shapes. Such calculations were important for making building plans. Their number system was based on numbers from 1 to 60. We still divide minutes and hours into 60 parts.

The Babylonian Empire

A Babylonian king named Hammurabi (hah muh RAH bee) created the Babylonian Empire by uniting the cities of Sumer. Then he conquered lands all the way to Asia Minor, a region within the present-day country of Turkey. Find the boundaries of the empire on the map titled Babylonian and Assyrian Empires, on page 39.

A Crossroads of Trade Under Hammurabi's steady rule, the Babylonians created a system of roads throughout the empire. The roadways made travel easier, which improved communication between cities and towns. It also encouraged trade.

Babylon's location made it a crossroads of trade. Caravans, or groups of travelers, stopped in Babylon on their way to and from the cities of Sumer to the south and Assyria to the north. In the city's bazaars, or markets, shoppers could buy cotton cloth from India and spices from Egypt. Trade made Babylon rich. So did conquest.

Wealth Through Conquest A conqueror—if successful—reaped great rewards. In about 1760 B.C., Hammurabi conquered the city of Mari. He seized Mari's war chariots, weapons, and tools, which were the best in the world. But all the wealth that Babylon had gathered could not save it from conquest. By about 1600 B.C., the empire first conquered by Hammurabi had shrunk and was finally destroyed.

North of Babylon lay Assyria, a small kingdom of a few walled cities. Like Babylon, Assyria would grow into a powerful empire. But in time, it would also suffer defeat.

✓ Reading Check Who was Hammurabi and what did he accomplish?

Differentiated Instruction

For English Language Learners **L2**
Provide Spanish-speaking students with the *Guided Reading and Review (Spanish)*.

📄 *Guided Reading and Review (Spanish)*, **History of Our World Spanish Support,** p. 14

For Advanced Readers **L3**
Have students research and create a time line showing important world events from 1750 B.C. to 600 B.C. Encourage students to create simple, captioned illustrations showing conquests and cultural achievements. Use the *Rubric for Assessing a Timeline* to evaluate students' timelines.

 Unit 1 History of Our World Teaching Resources, *Rubric for Assessing a Timeline,* p. 80

The Empire of the Assyrians

The kingdom of Assyria lay in open land, making it easy for other peoples to invade. Since they were constantly defending themselves, the Assyrians became skilled warriors. About 1365 B.C., they decided the best method of defense was to attack. By 650 B.C., Assyria had conquered a large empire. It stretched across the Fertile Crescent, from the Nile River to the Persian Gulf.

Assyria's Contributions   The Assyrians were clever when it came to waging war. They invented the **battering ram,** a powerful weapon having a wooden beam mounted on wheels. Battering rams pounded city walls to rubble. Warriors used slings to hurl stones at the enemy. Expert archers were protected with helmets and armor. But most feared were the armed charioteers who slashed their way through the enemy troops.

As the empire grew, Assyria's capital of Nineveh (NIN uh vuh) became a city of great learning. It had a remarkable library that held thousands of clay tablets with writings from Sumer and Babylon. Because the Assyrians kept these records, we now know a great deal about life in early Mesopotamia.

Assyria Overthrown   The Assyrians had few friends in the lands that they ruled. Conquered peoples attempted a number of revolts against Assyrian rule. Two groups, the Medes (meedz) and Chaldeans (kal DEE unz), joined together to defeat the Assyrian Empire in 612 B.C.

✓ **Reading Check**   What were the strengths of the Assyrian Empire?

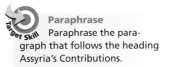
Paraphrase
Paraphrase the paragraph that follows the heading Assyria's Contributions.

Assyrian and Arab Troops in Battle
This stone panel shows Assyrian soldiers fighting Arabs mounted on camels.
① Sturdy shields protected the Assyrian soldiers.
② The Arab archers fought from swift camels.
③ The Assyrians fought from horseback and from chariots.
④ The Assyrian army was well armed and highly trained.
Predict   *Judging by what you have read about the Assyrian army, who would have won the battle shown on this carving?*

Skills Mini Lesson

Analyzing Images   L2
1. Point out that images can provide a lot of information. To gain information from the image, students should read the caption (if there is one), examine the image to determine who or what is the subject, ask themselves when and where the scene takes place, and identify the details, the mood, and the main idea of the image.

2. Help students practice the skill by looking at the photograph of the battle on this page.

3. Have students apply the skill by identifying the subject, details, mood, and the main idea of the carving.

The Empire of the Assyrians   L2
Babylonia Rises Again   L2

Guided Instruction
■ **Vocabulary Builder** Clarify the high-use word **invade** before reading.

■ Read The Empire of the Assyrians and Babylonia Rises Again.

■ Ask students **How did the Assyrians build a large empire?***(They decided that their best defense would be to attack first. These attacks gained the Assyrians a large empire.)*

■ Ask students **What events led to the second rise of Babylon?***(The Chaldeans and the Medes joined forces to defeat the Assyrian Empire. The Chaldeans then gained control over Babylonia and rebuilt the city of Babylon.)*

Independent Practice
Have students complete the graphic organizer by filling in the remaining details about Assyria and Babylonia.

Monitor Progress
■ Show *Section Reading Support Transparency HOW 57*. Go over key concepts and clarify key vocabulary as needed.

📖 **History of Our World Transparencies,** *Section Reading Support Transparency HOW 57*

■ Tell students to fill in the last column of the *Reading Readiness Guide*. Probe for what they learned that confirms or invalidates each statement.

All in One **Unit 1 History of Our World Teaching Resources,** *Reading Readiness Guide,* p. 52   L2

🔁 Target Reading Skill
Paraphrase As a follow up, ask students to complete the task in the Target Reading Skill in the Student Edition. *(Students should state the paragraph in their own words.)*

Answers
✓ **Reading Check**   The Assyrians were skilled warriors with advanced techniques of warfare; their capital, Nineveh, was a center of learning.

Predict   The Assyrians, because they had the ability to fight from a distance with slings and arrows and were protected by sturdy shields.

Assess and Reteach

Assess Progress
L2

Have students complete the Section Assessment. Administer the *Section Quiz.*

All in One **Unit 1 History of Our World Teaching Resources,** *Section Quiz,* p. 54

Reteach
L1

If students need more instruction, have them read this section in the Reading and Vocabulary Study Guide.

Chapter 2, Section 2, **History of Our World Reading and Vocabulary Study Guide,** pp. 19–21

Extend
L3

Have students learn more about the accomplishments of Nebuchadnezzar II. They can read more about him in the library or on the Internet. Then have them present their findings to the class as an oral or written report.

Answers

✓ Reading Check Nebuchadnezzar II was the king of Babylon. He rebuilt the city after the Assyrians destroyed it.

Generalize The Chaldeans showed their interest in science and learning by charting the paths of the stars and measuring the length of a year.

Section 2 Assessment

Key Terms
Students' sentences should reflect knowledge of each Key Term.

➲ Target Reading Skill
Possible answer: The Chaldeans, like other Mesopotamian empires, were threatened by stronger groups. In 539 B.C. they were defeated by Cyrus the Great, leading the Persian army. The Persians did not destroy Babylon.

Comprehension and Critical Thinking
1. (a) important Mesopotamian empires located in southwest Asia Minor **(b)** Students may suggest that this proverb describes how empires in the region were continually conquering other empires, as well as being conquered.

2. (a) The empire of Babylonia united the cities of Sumer and stretched all the way to Asia Minor; it was a great military power and a center of trade. Assyria was an empire of skilled warriors that stretched across the Fertile Crescent, from the Nile

Babylonian Globe
A clay tablet from around 500 B.C. shows a map of the world as it was known to the Chaldean Babylonians.
Generalize *How did the Chaldeans show an interest in science and learning?*

Babylonia Rises Again

Under the Chaldeans, Babylon rose again to even greater splendor. It became the center of the New Babylonian Empire.

Nebuchadnezzar, King of Babylon King Nebuchadnezzar II (neb you kud NEZ ur) rebuilt the city of Babylon, which the Assyrians had destroyed. He put up massive walls around the city for protection. He also built a gigantic palace, decorated with colored tiles. Nebuchadnezzar's royal palace was built on several terraces that rose to the height of some 350 feet (110 meters). It had a dazzling landscape of trees and gardens. According to legends, he built the gardens for his wife, who hated the dry plains of Mesopotamia.

Advances in Learning Under the rule of the Chaldeans, the New Babylonian Empire became a center of learning and science. Chaldean astronomers charted the paths of the stars and measured the length of a year. Their measurement was only a few minutes different from the length modern scientists have found. And Chaldean farmers raised "the flies that collect honey"—honey bees.

Like other Mesopotamian empires, the Chaldeans were open to attack by powerful neighbors. In 539 B.C., the New Babylonian Empire fell to the Persians, led by Cyrus the Great. But the city of Babylon was spared.

✓ Reading Check **Who was Nebuchadnezzar II?**

 Section 2 Assessment

Key Terms
Review the key terms at the beginning of this section. Use each term in a sentence that explains its meaning.

➲ Target Reading Skill
Paraphrase the last paragraph in this section.

Comprehension and Critical Thinking
1. (a) Identify What were Babylonia and Assyria and where were they located?

(b) Analyze Explain how the following proverb applies to Mesopotamia: "You go and carry off the enemy's land; the enemy comes and carries off your land."

2. (a) Recall Describe the empires of Babylonia and Assyria.
(b) Compare How were the two empires similar?

3. (a) Describe How was New Babylonia created?
(b) Conclude What do the achievements of the New Babylonian Empire tell us about what was important to the Chaldeans?

Writing Activity
Epitaphs are messages carved into tombstones. They praise and honor the deceased. Write an epitaph in remembrance of Nebuchadnezzar II.

Writing Tip Keep your message short and to the point. To get started, summarize what you know about Nebuchadnezzar II.

42 History of Our World

River to the Persian Gulf. Assyria's capital, Nineveh, became a city of great learning.

(b) Both empires covered vast amounts of territory and had strong armies.

3. (a) New Babylonia was created under the Chaldeans, after they conquered the Assyrians; King Nebuchadnezzar II rebuilt the city of Babylon. **(b)** Students may suggest that the Chaldeans valued learning and science, because they made

important advancements in astronomy and the science of timekeeping.

Writing Activity
Use the *Rubric for Assessing a Caption* to evaluate students' epitaphs.

All in One **Unit 1 History of Our World Teaching Resources,** *Rubric for Assessing a Caption,* p. 81

Section 3
The Legacy of Mesopotamia

Prepare to Read

Objectives

In this section you will
1. Learn about the importance of Hammurabi's Code.
2. Find out how the art of writing developed in Mesopotamia.

Taking Notes

As you read, look for details summarizing the achievements of Mesopotamian civilizations. Copy the table below, and record your findings in it.

The Legacy of Mesopotamia	
Hammurabi's Code	The Art of Writing

🎯 Target Reading Skill

Summarize You can better understand a text if you pause to restate the key points briefly in your own words. A good summary includes important events and details, notes the order in which the events occurred, and makes connections between the events or details.

Use the table at the left to help you summarize what you have read.

Key Terms

- **code** (kohd) *n.* an organized list of laws and rules
- **Hammurabi** (hah muh RAH bee) *n.* the king of Babylon from about 1792 to 1750 B.C.; creator of the Babylonian Empire
- **cuneiform** (kyoo NEE uh fawrm) *n.* groups of wedges and lines used to write several languages of the Fertile Crescent

Sometimes the customs and laws of other countries may seem strange to us. Imagine what it would be like to have to obey the laws set down by early civilizations.

> ❝If a man has destroyed the eye of a man of the class of gentlemen, they shall destroy his eye. If he has broken a gentleman's bone, they shall break his bone. If he has destroyed the eye of a commoner or broken a bone of a commoner, he shall pay one mina [measure of weight] of silver. If he has destroyed the eye of a gentleman's slave, or broken a bone of a gentleman's slave, he shall pay half [the slave's] price. If a gentleman's slave strikes the cheek of a gentleman, they shall cut off [the slave's] ear. ❞
>
> —from Hammurabi's Code

King Hammurabi standing before Shamash, the sun god and the god of justice

🎯 Target Reading Skill L2

Summarize Point out the Target Reading Skill. Tell students that summarizing, or briefly restating the key points in a text, can help them to better understand the text.

Model using summarizing to find the meaning of the quotation from Hammurabi's Code on this page. (*Punishment for a crime varies according to the crime itself. The level of punishment depends on the status of the criminal and the victim.*)

Give students *Summarize.* Have them complete the activity in groups.

All in One Unit 1 History of Our World Teaching Resources, *Summarize,* p. 69

Objectives

Social Studies

1. Learn about the importance of Hammurabi's Code.
2. Find out how the art of writing developed in Mesopotamia.

Reading/Language Arts

Use summarizing to restate key points in the text.

Prepare to Read

Build Background Knowledge L2

In this section students will learn of the advances made by the Mesopotamians, including the art of writing. Ask students to think about how their lives would be different without writing. Model the thought process by helping them to think of various aspects of society, such as laws, literature, and street signs that are enhanced by or dependent on writing. Use the Think-Write-Pair-Share participation strategy (TE, p. T40) to generate a list.

Set a Purpose for Reading L2

- Preview the Objectives.

- Read each statement in the *Reading Readiness Guide* aloud. Ask students to mark the statements true or false.

  All in One Unit 1 History of Our World Teaching Resources, *Reading Readiness Guide,* p. 56

- Have students discuss the statements in pairs or groups of four, and then mark their worksheets again. Use the Numbered Heads participation strategy (TE, p. T40) to call on students to share their group's perspectives.

Vocabulary Builder
Preview Key Terms L2

Pronounce each Key Term, and then ask the students to say the word with you. Provide a simple example such as, "A code tells people how they should behave."

Instruct

Hammurabi's Code   L2

Guided Instruction

- **Vocabulary Builder** Clarify the high-use word **conflict** before reading.

- Have students read Hammurabi's Code, using the Paragraph Shrinking technique (TE, p. T38).

- Ask students **Why was Hammurabi's code important?** (*Written laws meant everyone could know the rules and the punishments and they could be applied fairly.*)

- Ask students to explain what Hammurabi's Code tells us about the class system in Babylonia. (*The classes were unequal; the higher classes were more valued than the lower classes since punishments for crimes against the higher classes were more severe.*)

Independent Practice

Ask students to create the Taking Notes graphic organizer on a blank piece of paper. Then have them fill in the column labeled "Hammurabi's Code" with details that summarize it. Briefly model how to identify which details to record.

Monitor Progress

Circulate throughout the classroom to ensure that individuals are filling in their graphic organizers with the correct details. Provide assistance as needed.

⊙ Target Reading Skill   L2

Summarize As a follow up, ask students to perform the Target Reading Skill activity in the Student Edition. (*Answers will vary, but make sure students include the main point and two details in their summaries.*)

Hammurabi's Code

What kind of justice system do you think we would have if our laws were not written down? What would happen if a judge were free to make any law he or she wanted, or if the judge could give any punishment? Would people think that the laws were fair? A written **code**, or organized list of laws, helps people know what is expected of them and what punishment they will receive if they disobey a law.

We live by the idea that all laws should be written down and applied fairly. The Babylonians held similar beliefs about law. **Hammurabi** ruled Babylonia from about 1792 to 1750 B.C. He set down rules for everyone in his empire to follow. These rules are known as Hammurabi's Code. The code told the people of Babylonia how to settle conflicts in all areas of life.

Hammurabi's Code, which was based partly on earlier Sumerian codes, contained 282 laws organized in different categories. These included trade, labor, property, and family. The code had laws for adopting children, practicing medicine, hiring wagons or boats, and controlling dangerous animals.

Target Skill **Summarize** Summarize the paragraph at the right. Give the main point and two details.

This clay lion once stood guard at a Babylonian temple.

An Eye for an Eye Reread the first law from the quotation on page 43. Hammurabi's Code was based on the idea of "an eye for an eye." In other words, punishment should be similar to the crime committed. However, the code did not apply equally to all people. The harshness of the punishment depended on how important the victim and the lawbreaker were. The higher the class of the victim, the greater the penalty was. For example, an ox owner would pay half a mina of silver if the ox gored a noble. If the victim was a slave, however, the owner would pay only one third of a mina.

A person who accidentally broke a law was just as guilty as someone who meant to break the law. People who could not always control the outcome of their work, such as doctors, had to be very careful, as the following law shows:

> **❝If a surgeon performed a major operation on a citizen with a bronze lancet [knife] and has caused the death of this citizen . . . his hand shall be cut off. ❞**
>
> —from Hammurabi's Code

Vocabulary Builder

Use the information below to teach students this section's high-use words.

High-Use Word	Definition and Sample Sentence
conflict, p. 44	*n.* a disagreement A **conflict** arose between the two friends when they couldn't agree about which film to see.
document, p. 45	*n.* anything written that conveys information The American Constitution is one of the most important **documents** of American history.

Laws for Everyone You probably know many rules. There are rules for taking tests, playing ball, and living in your home. People have followed—or broken—rules for thousands of years. What, then, was the importance of Hammurabi's Code?

The laws are important to us because they were written down. With written laws, everyone could know the rules—and the punishments. Hammurabi's punishments may seem harsh to us, but they improved upon previous laws. Hammurabi's laws were not the first attempt by a society to set up a code of laws. But his laws are the first organized, recorded set that we have found.

✓ **Reading Check** What was Hammurabi's Code?

The Art of Writing

Think how much more difficult life would be if no one knew how to read and write. But writing did not suddenly appear. It took a long time for the art of writing to be developed.

Ancient Scribes Writing first developed in Mesopotamia around 3100 B.C. Long before Hammurabi issued his code, the people of Sumer had developed a system of writing. Writing met the need Sumerians had to keep records. Record keepers were very important—and busy—people in Sumer. The Sumerians' earliest written documents are records of farm animals. Since only a few people could write, it was one of the most valuable skills in the ancient world. Scribes held positions of great respect in Mesopotamia.

The scribes of Sumer recorded sales and trades, tax payments, gifts for the gods, and marriages and deaths. Some scribes had special tasks. Military scribes calculated the amount of food and supplies that an army would need. Government scribes figured out the number of diggers needed to build a canal. Written orders then went out to local officials who had to provide these supplies or workers. None of these records were written on paper, however. Paper had not yet been invented. Instead, the scribes of Mespotamia kept their notes and records on clay.

Hammurabi's Code

- If any one steal the minor son of another, he shall be put to death.
- If any one is committing a robbery and is caught, then he shall be put to death.
- If any one open his ditches to water his crop, but is careless, and the water flood the field of his neighbor, then he shall pay his neighbor corn for his loss.
- If a man adopt a child [as his] son, and rear him, this grown son cannot be demanded back again.
- If a son strike his father, his hands shall be hewn (cut) off.

■ **Chart Skills**

The table above shows five of the nearly 300 laws that make up Hammurabi's Code. At the left is a detail of the stone pillar on which the laws were carved. **Identify** Which of the laws in the table deals with the crime of kidnapping? **Generalize** What do the laws shown above tell us about the Babylonians' ideas of justice?

Links Across Time

New Discoveries In 2000, archaeologists uncovered a small stone with an unfamiliar type of ancient writing inscribed upon it. Scientists estimate that the stone, found in the present-day country of Turkmenistan, dates back to about 2300 B.C. The stone and other findings in the area indicate the existence of an ancient culture that had been entirely unknown.

Chapter 2 Section 3 **45**

The Art of Writing [L2]

Guided Instruction

■ **Vocabulary Builder** Clarify the high-use word **document** before reading.

■ Read The Art of Writing. As students read, make sure individuals can answer the Reading Check question.

■ Ask students **What did Sumerian scribes do?** *(They recorded sales and trades, tax payments, gifts for the gods, and marriages and deaths.)*

■ Ask students **What do you think are the advantages and disadvantages of writing on clay tablets?** *(Advantages— tablets can last a long time; cannot be erased; are fireproof. Disadvantages— tablets are bulky and heavy; are hard to transport; can break.)*

Links

Read the **Links Across Time** on this page. Ask students **What does evidence of writing tell us about an ancient culture?** *(Students may suggest that evidence of writing in an ancient culture indicates that the culture was developed enough to have a system to keep records.)*

Skills Mini Lesson

Identifying Frame of Reference and Point of View [L2]

1. Point of view is an opinion or perspective on an issue or topic. Frame of reference is a person's background. Some background factors are age, culture, nationality, social position, beliefs, experiences, and historical era. Frame of reference often affects point of view.

2. Have students practice the skill by identifying the point of view expressed in the law on the bottom of page 48. *(that a surgeon who causes the death of a patient deserves physical punishment)*

3. Have students compare that point of view with one people today might take. Ask how the frames of reference differ.

Answers

✓ **Reading Check** Hammurabi's Code was a set of written laws created by the Babylonian ruler Hammurabi. These laws set down rules for the people in his empire to follow and helped settle conflicts.

Chart Skills **Identify** the first law **Generalize** Their ideas of justice were harsh and every crime had a specific punishment.

Independent Practice

Have students complete the graphic organizer by filling in the remaining details about the art of writing in the appropriate column of the chart.

Monitor Progress

- Show *Section Reading Support Transparency HOW 58* and ask students to check their graphic organizers individually. Go over key concepts and clarify key vocabulary as needed.

    📖 **History of Our World Transparencies,** *Section Reading Support Transparency HOW 58*

- Tell students to fill in the last column of the *Reading Readiness Guide.* Probe for what they learned that confirms or invalidates each statement.

    All in One Unit 1 History of Our World Teaching Resources, *Reading Readiness Guide,* p. 56

Scribes sometimes enclosed a message (above) in an envelope (top) made from wet clay. As the envelope dried, it formed a seal around the tablet. A sharpened reed (below) is used to write cuneiform script on soft clay.

A Record in Clay The Tigris and the Euphrates rivers provided scribes with the clay they used to write on. Each spring, the rivers washed down clay from the mountains. Scribes shaped the soft, wet clay into smooth, flat surfaces called tablets. They marked their letters in the clay with sharp tools. When the clay dried, it was a permanent record.

The shape and size of a tablet depended on its purpose. Larger tablets were used for reference purposes. Like the heavy atlases and dictionaries in today's libraries, they stayed in one place. Smaller tablets, the size of letters or postcards, were used for personal messages. Even today, these personal tablets can be fun to read. They show that Mesopotamians used writing to express the ups and downs of everyday life:

❝This is really a fine way of behaving! The gardeners keep breaking into the date storehouse and taking dates. You yourselves cover it up and do not report it to me! Bring these men to me—after they have paid for the dates.❞

—*from a Mesopotamian tablet*

How Writing Was Invented Like most inventions, writing developed over time. Long before the Sumerians invented writing, they used shaped pieces of clay as tokens, or symbols. They used the clay tokens to keep records. Tokens could keep track of how many animals were bought and sold, or how much food had been grown. By around 3100 B.C., this form of record keeping had developed into writing.

At first, written words were symbols that represented specific objects. Grain, oxen, water, or stars—each important object had its own symbol. As people learned to record ideas as well as facts, the symbols changed. Eventually, scribes combined symbols to make groups of wedges and lines known as **cuneiform** (kyoo NEE uh fawrm). Cuneiform script could be used to represent different languages. This flexibility was highly useful in a land of many peoples.

46 History of Our World

The Development of Writing

Word	Outline Character, About 3000 B.C.	Sumerian, About 2000 B.C.	Assyrian, About 700 B.C.	Chaldean, About 500 B.C.
Sun				
God or heaven				
Mountain				

■ Chart Skills

The table at the left shows how writing based on pictures changed over time. **Identify** The simplest symbols came from which time period? **Generalize** How did the symbols for each word change over time?

Refer to the table above titled The Development of Writing. Notice how the symbols developed over time. Scholars believe that the Sumerians developed their system of writing independently. That means that they did not borrow ideas from the writing systems of other civilizations. Working independently meant that they had many decisions to make. They decided that the symbols should be set in rows, that each row should be read from left to right, and that a page should be read from top to bottom. What other languages are written this way?

✓ **Reading Check** When, where, and how did writing first develop?

Section 3 Assessment

Key Terms

Review the key terms at the beginning of this section. Use each term in a sentence that explains its meaning.

⟳ Target Reading Skill

Summarize the information in the last paragraph of this section.

Comprehension and Critical Thinking

1. (a) **Recall** What was Hammurabi's Code, and what was its purpose in ancient Babylonia?

(b) **Analyze** What does the expression "an eye for an eye" mean in relation to the laws in Hammurabi's Code?

(c) **Apply Information** Hammurabi's Code was fair in some ways and unfair in other ways. Explain.

2. (a) **Describe** What were some early uses for the art of writing?

(b) **Contrast** How do the early forms and methods of writing differ from the way we write today?

(c) **Draw Inferences** Why was the development of writing an important step in human history?

Writing Activity

Reread the quote on page 50 in which the writer complains about the gardeners. Write a law that applies to the gardeners who stole the dates. What do you think should happen to the people who didn't tell about the theft?

Go Online
PHSchool.com

For: An activity on cuneiform writing
Visit: PHSchool.com
Web Code: lbd-2203

Chapter 2 Section 3 **47**

Section 3 Assessment

Key Terms

Students' sentences should reflect knowledge of each Key Term.

⟳ Target Reading Skill

Writing developed over time. Sumerian writing may have developed independently instead of borrowing ideas from other writing systems.

Comprehension and Critical Thinking

1. (a) A written set of laws followed by Babylonians; to prevent people from breaking the rules, and to punish them if they did. (b) That the punishment equaled the crime. (c) Fair—laws were made to help people settle conflicts; unfair—laws were applied unequally depending on the victim's class.

2. (a) to keep records, create references, record personal messages (b) Today we

---

Assess and Reteach

Assess Progress　L2

Have students complete the Section Assessment. Administer the *Section Quiz*.

All in One Unit 1 History of Our World Teaching Resources, *Section Quiz*, p. 58

Reteach　L1

If students need more instruction, have them read this section in the Reading and Vocabulary Study Guide.

📖 Chapter 2, Section 3, **History of Our World Reading and Vocabulary Study Guide**, pp. 22–24

Extend　L3

Divide the class into small groups. Have each group research an alphabet used either today or in the past in a specific country or region. Have each group create a poster about that alphabet. Use the *Rubric for Assessing a Student Poster* to evaluate students' posters.

All in One Unit 1 History of Our World Teaching Resources, *Rubric for Assessing a Student Poster*, p. 83

Answers

✓ **Reading Check** Writing first developed in Mesopotamia in about 3500 B.C. At first, people drew pictures to represent what they wanted to say. Eventually, these pictures developed into a set group of symbols.

Chart Skills Identify about 3,000 B.C. **Generalize** They became more detailed.

Writing Activity

Use the *Rubric for Assessing a Writing Assignment* to evaluate students' laws.

All in One Unit 1 History of Our World Teaching Resources, *Rubric for Assessing a Writing Assignment*, p. 84

Go Online
PHSchool.com Typing in the Web code when prompted will bring students to detailed instructions for this activity.

write with letters instead of symbols; we use pens, pencils, paper, and computers instead of sharp tools and clay tablets. (c) It allowed us to clearly state laws and keep records.

Objectives

Social Studies

1. Understand how the sea power of the Phoenicians helped spread civilization throughout the Mediterranean area.

2. Learn about the major events in the history of the Israelites.

Reading/Language Arts

Read ahead to help clarify words and ideas.

Prepare to Read

Build Background Knowledge L2

Engage students in a discussion about the tradition of oral history. Explain that many stories of ancient history have reached us by being told and retold from one generation to the next. Ask students to think about what might happen to a story as it is retold over a long period of time. *(It will change slightly.)* Then ask students to think about what important development changed the way stories were told. *(writing)* Use the Idea Wave participation strategy (TE, p. T39) to elicit student responses.

Set a Purpose for Reading L2

■ Preview the Objectives.

■ Read each statement in the *Reading Readiness Guide* aloud. Ask students to mark the statements true or false.

All in One Unit 1 History of Our World Teaching Resources, *Reading Readiness Guide,* p. 60

■ Have students discuss the statements in pairs or groups of four, and then mark their worksheets again. Use the Numbered Heads participation strategy (TE, p. T40) to call on students to share their group's perspectives.

Vocabulary Builder

Preview Key Terms L2

Pronounce each Key Term, then ask students to say the word with you. Provide a simple example such as, "A famine occurs when many people are hungry because there is not enough food."

Prepare to Read

Objectives

In this section you will

1. Understand how the sea power of the Phoenicians helped spread civilization throughout the Mediterranean area.

2. Learn about the major events in the history of the Israelites.

Taking Notes

As you read, create an outline of the history of the Phoenicians and the Israelites. Copy the outline below, and record your findings in it.

> I. The Phoenicians
> A. Sea-trading power
>   1.
>   2.
> B. Phoenician alphabet
>   1.
>   2.
> II. The Israelites

Target Reading Skill

Read Ahead Reading ahead is a strategy that can help you to understand words and ideas in the text. If you do not understand a certain passage, read ahead, because a word or idea may be clarified later on. Use this strategy as you read this section.

Key Terms

• **alphabet** (AL fuh bet) *n.* a set of symbols that represent the sounds of a language

• **monotheism** (MAHN oh thee iz um) *n.* the belief in one god

• **famine** (FAM in) *n.* a time when there is so little food that many people starve

• **exile** (EK syl) *v.* to force someone to live in another country

Above, ancient vats from a site in Tel Dor, Israel, once contained purple dye of the type used by the Phoenicians. The stained pottery piece in the middle probably came from a vessel that held the dye. The purple dye comes from the glands of the murex snail, shown at the right.

While the great empire of Hammurabi was rising and falling, the people of a city on the shores of the Mediterranean Sea were becoming rich by gathering snails.

The snails collected near the coastal city of Tyre (tyr) were not ordinary snails. These snails produced a rich purple dye. Cloth made purple with the dye was highly valued by wealthy people throughout the Mediterranean region. Ships from Tyre sold the purple cloth at extremely high prices. The profits helped make Tyre a wealthy city.

48 History of Our World

Target Reading Skill L2

Read Ahead Point out the Target Reading Skill. Tell students that reading ahead is a strategy they can use to help them understand difficult words or passages in a text, because they may be clarified later on.

Model using reading ahead to help students understand this statement in the first paragraph of this page: "…the people of a city on the shores of the Mediterranean Sea were becoming rich by gathering snails." Explain that by reading ahead, students will learn how the people were getting rich. *(The second paragraph reveals that the snails produced a highly profitable dye.)*

Give students *Reread or Read Ahead.* Have them complete the activity in groups.

All in One Unit 1 History of Our World Teaching Resources, *Reread or Read Ahead,* p. 67

Phoenician Sea Power

Tyre was the major city in a region called Phoenicia (fuh NISH uh). Locate Phoenicia and its colonies on the map below. The Phoenicians' outlook was westward, toward the Mediterranean Sea and the cities that were growing around it.

Masters of Trade The Phoenicians had settled in a land that had limited, but very important, resources. Besides the snails used to dye cloth, Phoenicia had a great amount of dense cedar forests. The Phoenicians sold their dyed cloth and the wood from their forests to neighboring peoples.

As trade grew, the Phoenicians looked to the sea to increase their profits. In time, they controlled trade throughout much of the Mediterranean. From about 1100 to 800 B.C., Phoenicia was a great sea power. Phoenician ships sailed all over the Mediterranean Sea and into the stormy Atlantic Ocean. They came back from these trips with stories of horrible monsters that lived in the ocean depths. These stories helped keep other peoples from trying to compete for trade in the Atlantic.

A silver coin from Sidon showing a Phoenician galley, a ship powered by oars

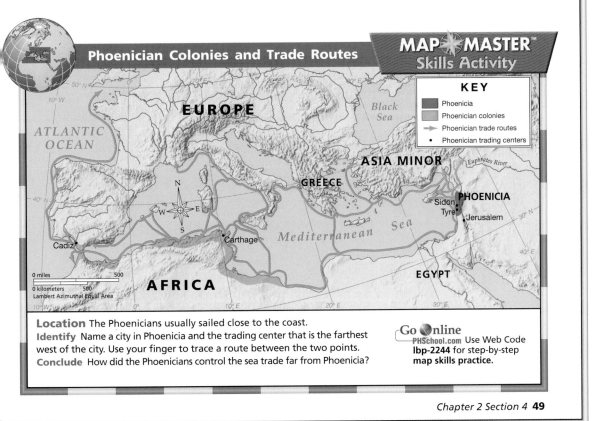

Phoenician Colonies and Trade Routes

MAP MASTER™ Skills Activity

KEY
- Phoenicia
- Phoenician colonies
- → Phoenician trade routes
- • Phoenician trading centers

EUROPE · ATLANTIC OCEAN · Black Sea · ASIA MINOR · Euphrates River · GREECE · Sidon · PHOENICIA · Tyre · Jerusalem · Carthage · Cadiz · Mediterranean Sea · AFRICA · EGYPT

0 miles 500
0 kilometers 500
Lambert Azimuthal Equal Area

Location The Phoenicians usually sailed close to the coast.
Identify Name a city in Phoenicia and the trading center that is the farthest west of the city. Use your finger to trace a route between the two points.
Conclude How did the Phoenicians control the sea trade far from Phoenicia?

Go Online PHSchool.com Use Web Code **lbp-2244** for step-by-step map skills practice.

Vocabulary Builder

Use the information below to teach students this section's high-use words.

High-Use Word	Definition and Sample Sentence
conduct, p. 50	*v.* to manage; direct It was important that he **conduct** the meeting in an organized manner.

Instruct

Phoenician Sea Power L2

Guided Instruction

- **Vocabulary Builder** Clarify the high-use word **enrich** before reading.

- Have students read Phoenician Sea Power, using the Structured Silent Reading technique (TE, p. T38).

- Ask students **Why do you think the Phoenicians looked to foreign lands and sea trade to develop their wealth?** (*They had limited resources, so they took advantage of their geographic location to expand their resources through trade.*)

- Ask students **How did the sea power of the Phoenicians help spread civilization?** (*Possible answer: As the Phoenicians traveled across the world, they could spread ideas of civilization to other places.*)

Independent Practice

Ask students to create the Taking Notes graphic organizer on a blank piece of paper. Then have them fill in the details about Phoenician sea power that they have just read. Briefly model how to identify which details to record, using the *Outline Transparency.*

📖 **History of Our World Transparencies,** *Transparency B15: Outline*

Monitor Progress

As students begin to fill in their graphic organizers, make sure individuals are using the correct details about the Phoenicians as a sea-trading power. Provide assistance as needed.

Answers

MAP MASTER™ Skills Activity **Identify** city: Sidon or Tyre; trading center: Cadiz **Conclude** The Phoenicians were able to control the sea trade by establishing trading centers along the coasts of distant places and spreading stories of the horrors facing sailors in the Atlantic Ocean.

Go Online PHSchool.com Students may practice their map skills using the interactive online version of this map.

The Phoenician Alphabet

Guided Instruction

- **Vocabulary Builder** Clarify the high-use word **conduct** before reading.

- Read about the birth and growth of the Phoenician alphabet in The Phoenician Alphabet. As students read, help individuals answer the Reading Check question.

- Ask students **How did the Phoenician alphabet spread throughout the ancient world?** *(through sea trade)*

- Have students explain why the creation of the Phoenician alphabet made writing more accessible to more people. *(Before the creation of the Phoenician alphabet, highly educated scribes controlled the power of writing, after the alphabet's creation, other people could use it as well.)*

Independent Practice

Have students continue to fill in their Taking Notes graphic organizers. Make sure they fill in details about the Phoenician alphabet.

Monitor Progress

Circulate around the classroom to make sure that individuals are choosing the correct details as they fill in their graphic organizers. Provide assistance as needed.

Answer

✓ Reading Check The Phoenicians used wood and the dye from snails to build their wealth.

✓ Reading Check The Phoenician alphabet used fewer symbols and was much easier to learn than the cuneiform script, which used symbols.

Chart Skills Identify A, D, E, H, L, M, N, O, Q, and T **Identify Effects** Other civilizations used the alphabet as the basis of their alphabets, which are used in many languages today.

Exotic Marketplaces Trade brought valuable goods from lands around the Mediterranean Sea to the Phoenician cities of Tyre and Sidon (SY dun). Bazaars swelled with foods brought from faraway places. These foods included figs, olives, honey, and spices. In the bazaars, merchants sold strange animals, such as giraffes and warthogs from Africa and bears from Europe.

The overflowing markets of Tyre awed visitors. Here is one description of Tyre's bazaars:

> **When your wares came from the seas, you satisfied many peoples. With your great wealth and merchandise, you enriched the kings of the earth.**
>
> —the Bible

✓ Reading Check What resources did the Phoenicians first use to build their wealth?

The Phoenician Alphabet

The Phoenicians relied on writing to help them conduct trade. They developed a writing system that used just 22 symbols. This system was the Phoenician **alphabet**, a set of symbols that represents the sounds of the language. It forms the basis of the alphabet used in many languages today, including English. In the Phoenician alphabet, however, each letter stood for one consonant sound.

The simple Phoenician alphabet was far easier to learn than cuneiform. Before the alphabet, only highly educated scribes were skilled in writing. Now many more people could write using the new alphabet. The alphabet simplified trade between people who spoke different languages. The Phoenician sea trade, in turn, helped the alphabet to spread.

✓ Reading Check How did the Phoenician alphabet differ from cuneiform script?

The Phoenician Alphabet

Chart Skills

The chart at the left shows the Phoenician letters that correspond to our alphabet. The symbols for A, E, I, O, and U originally represented consonant sounds. The Greeks later used the symbols to represent vowel sounds. The Phoenician stone inscription above dates to about 391 B.C. **Identify** Which letters in the Phoenician alphabet seem similar to the letters in our alphabet? **Identify Effects** How did the Phoenician alphabet affect other civilizations?

50 History of Our World

Differentiated Instruction

For Less Proficient Readers

L1

Have students read the section in the Reading and Vocabulary Study Guide. This version provides basic-level instruction in an interactive format with questions and write-on lines.

Chapter 2, Section 4, **History of Our World Reading and Vocabulary Study Guide,** pp. 25–27

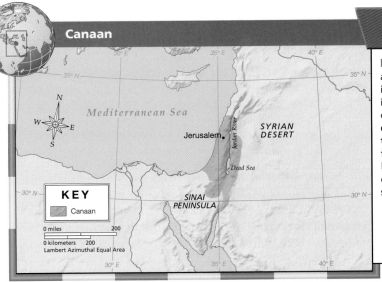

Canaan

Movement The Israelites are said to have spent 40 years in the desert of the Sinai Peninsula trying to reach the land of Canaan. **Locate** In what direction did the Israelites travel to return to Canaan from the Sinai Peninsula? **Infer** What physical features of Canaan made it suitable for settlement?

Go Online
PHSchool.com Use Web Code **lbp-2254** for step-by-step-map skills practice.

The Rise of the Israelites

South of Phoenicia, a small band of people settled in the hills around the Jordan River valley. Called Hebrews at first, they later became known as Israelites. Although the Israelites never built a large empire, they had a great influence on our civilization.

Much of what is known about the early history of the Israelites comes from stories told in the Torah (TOH ruh), or the Hebrew Bible. Historians compare biblical and other religious stories with archaeological evidence to piece together events from the past. In this way they have determined that Abraham, whose story follows, may have lived sometime between 2000 and 1500 B.C.

Abraham the Leader The Israelites traced their beginnings to Mesopotamia. For hundreds of years, they lived as shepherds and merchants who grazed their flocks outside Sumerian cities.

According to the Torah, a leader named Abraham taught his people to practice monotheism, a belief in one god. *Mono-* is the Greek prefix for "one." The Torah says that God told Abraham to leave Mesopotamia and settle elsewhere:

Read Ahead The Torah says that Abraham was told to leave Mesopotamia and settle elsewhere. Keep reading to see what that means.

❝Get you out of your country, and from your kindred [relatives], and from your father's house, to the land that I will show you. And I will make of you a great nation. ❞

—the Torah

The Rise of the Israelites L2

Guided Instruction

■ Read about the growth and movement of the Israelites in The Rise of the Israelites.

■ Ask students **What resources do scholars use to study the life of Abraham?** *(They compare biblical and other religious stories with archaeological evidence.)*

■ Have students list in chronological order the major events in the history of the Israelites. *(Abraham led his people to settle in Canaan; after a famine in Canaan, the Israelites fled south to Egypt; after a few hundred years, an Egyptian king forced them into labor; an Israelite hero named Moses led them out of Egypt and into the Sinai desert where they wandered for 40 years, during which time the Torah says they received the Ten Commandments; eventually they settled in Canaan where they established a capital and built a temple; the kingdom divided; later they were exiled to other lands.)*

🎯 Target Reading Skill L2

Read Ahead As a follow up, ask students to perform the activity of the Target Reading Skill in the Student Edition. *(According to the Torah, the Israelites were told to leave their homeland to settle in a land shown to them by God, who would make them a great nation.)*

Differentiated Instruction

For Special Needs Students L1
Have students with special needs partner with more proficient students in order to

complete the *Target Reading Skill* activity and the *MapMaster Skills Activity* on this page.

Answer

MAP ✦ MASTER™ Skills Activity **Locate** northeast
Infer The waterways were helpful for trade and farming and therefore made Canaan suitable for settlement.

Go Online
PHSchool.com Students may practice their map skills using the interactive online version of this map.

Independent Practice

Have students complete the graphic organizer by adding details about the Israelites.

Monitor Progress

■ Show *Section Reading Support Transparency HOW 59* and ask students to check their graphic organizers individually. Go over key concepts and clarify key vocabulary as needed.

📖 **History of Our World Transparencies,** *Section Reading Support Transparency HOW 59*

■ Tell students to fill in the last column of the *Reading Readiness Guide.* Probe for what they learned that confirms or invalidates each statement.

All in One Unit 1 History of Our World Teaching Resources, *Reading Readiness Guide,* p. 60

Assess and Reteach

Assess Progress L2

Have students complete the Section Assessment. Administer the *Section Quiz.*

All in One Unit 1 History of Our World Teaching Resources, *Section Quiz,* p. 62

Reteach L1

If students need more instruction, have them read this section in the Reading and Vocabulary Study Guide.

📖 Chapter 2, Section 4, **History of Our World Reading and Vocabulary Study Guide,** pp. 25–27

Extend L3

Have students learn more about King Solomon by reading and completing the *Enrichment* activity. Students may work in pairs to complete the activity.

All in One Unit 1 History of Our World Teaching Resources, *Enrichment,* p. 71

Answer

Analyze Images Students may identify the domed mosques, the large wall in the foreground, and other older buildings and ruins as features that point to Jerusalem's ancient past.

From Canaan to Egypt The Torah goes on to say that Abraham led the Israelites from Mesopotamia to settle in the land of Canaan (KAY nun). Find this region on the map titled Canaan, on page 55. According to the Torah, a famine then spread across Canaan. A **famine** is a time when there is so little food that many people starve. The famine caused the Israelites to flee south to Egypt.

In Egypt, the Israelites lived well for a few hundred years. But then, an Egyptian king forced them into labor after he grew suspicious of their power.

In the Desert According to the Torah, an Israelite leader named Moses led his people out of Egypt. The Israelites' departure from Egypt is called the Exodus (EKS uh dus). For the next 40 years, the Israelites wandered through the desert of the Sinai (SY ny) Peninsula. Locate the Sinai on the map titled Canaan. The Torah says that while in the desert, God gave the Israelites the Ten Commandments, a code of laws. Eventually, the Israelites returned to Canaan. There, over time, the Israelites moved from herding to farming and built their own cities.

Old and New Jerusalem
People have lived in Jerusalem since 1800 B.C. Today, centuries-old buildings stand near modern hospitals, apartments, and hotels. **Analyze Images** *Using clues from the photo, describe features that point to Jerusalem's ancient past.*

52 History of Our World

Background

A Holy City Followers of three of the world's major religions consider Jerusalem to be a holy city and a destination for pilgrimages. Jews regard Jerusalem, the location of two important temples that were destroyed, as the center of their religion. Jews from around the world visit the Western Wall, the only existing remains of the second temple. Worshippers slip written prayers into the cracks of the wall. Christians view Jerusalem as holy because important events in the life of Jesus took place there. Muslims consider Jerusalem to be the third holiest city after Mecca and Medina in Saudi Arabia. Muslims believe that the prophet Muhammad ascended to heaven from Jerusalem.

Settlement in Canaan As they moved farther north, the Israelites were able to settle in many parts of Canaan. They united under their first king, Saul, who defended them against their enemies. The next king, David, established his capital in the city of Jerusalem.

A Divided Kingdom After David died, his son, Solomon, inherited the kingdom. After Solomon's death, the country split into two kingdoms. The northern kingdom was called Israel. The southern kingdom took the name Judah. The divided kingdom was ripe for invasion. Its neighbor, Assyria, conquered the Israelites and gained control of Judah.

Sent Into Exile In 722 B.C., the Israelites resisted Assyrian rule. In response, the Assyrians exiled thousands of people to distant parts of their empire. To **exile** means to force people to live in another place or country. The Assyrians controlled Judah until 612 B.C., when Assyria was conquered by the Chaldeans. Judah then fell under control of the Chaldean Babylonians. Later, in 587 B.C., the King of Judah rebelled against the Chaldeans. King Nebuchadnezzar responded by destroying the capital city of Jerusalem. He exiled the people of Judah to Babylonia.

✓ **Reading Check** Who were the Israelites?

King Solomon

⭐ **Section 4 Assessment**

Key Terms
Review the key terms at the beginning of this section. Use each term in a sentence that explains its meaning.

⟳ **Target Reading Skill**
What word or idea were you able to clarify by reading ahead?

Comprehension and Critical Thinking
1. (a) Identify Who were the Phoenicians?
(b) Recall How did the Phoenicians gain their wealth and power?

2. (a) Explain What are some features of the Phoenician alphabet?
(b) Identify Effects Describe the importance of the Phoenician alphabet. How did it affect the Mediterranean world and later civilizations?

3. (a) Identify Sequence Briefly trace the history of the Israelites from the leadership of Abraham to King Solomon.
(b) Identify Central Issues What important events in the history of the Israelites were shaped by movement and by war?

Writing Activity
Reread the description of Tyre. Using what you have read, write a poetic verse about Tyre's markets. Or work with a partner to write song lyrics on the same subject.

Writing Tip Poetic verses and song lyrics don't have to rhyme, but they usually have rhythm. To supply rhythm to your verse or lyrics, it sometimes helps to think of a familiar song as you write. Match words and phrases in your verse to the beats and phrases of the music.

Answers

✓ **Reading Check** The Israelites originally came from Mesopotamia and were called Hebrews. Although they never built a large empire, they made a deep impact on our civilization.

Section 4 Assessment

Key Terms
Students' sentences should reflect knowledge of each Key Term.

⟳ **Target Reading Skill**
Students' answers will vary, but should identify a word or idea they were able to clarify by reading ahead.

Comprehension and Critical Thinking
1. (a) The Phoenicians developed an empire through trade along the coast of the Mediterranean Sea. **(b)** At first they sold wood and dye; later they gained wealth and power through trade to and from lands around the Mediterranean Sea.

2. (a) The alphabet had 22 symbols that represented the sounds of the Phoenician language; each letter stood for one consonant sound. **(b)** The Phoenician alphabet was easy to learn. As a result, its use was widespread and no longer limited to scribes. It formed the basis for the alphabet used today in many countries.

3. (a) Abraham led the Israelites from Mesopotamia to Canaan. During a famine, many Israelites fled to Egypt, where they prospered for a few hundred years but then were forced into labor. Moses led them out of Egypt. Eventually, they returned to Canaan. Kings Saul and David reclaimed Canaan and unified the Israelite nation. Israel prospered under King Solomon. **(b)** The Israelites moved to Egypt to escape a famine. When they left Egypt, they wandered in the desert for 40 years. They fought a war to regain control of Canaan and live as a united nation. Later, they divided again, and were conquered and sent into exile.

Writing Activity
Use the *Rubric for Assessing a Student Poem* to evaluate students' writing.

All in One Unit 1 History of Our World Teaching Resources, *Rubric for Assessing a Student Poem,* p. 85

Objective

Learn how to identify main ideas.

Prepare to Read

Build Background Knowledge **L2**

Conduct an Idea Wave (TE, p. T39) to ask students to identify movies they have seen recently. List these movies on the board. Then have individuals tell the main idea of the movie they have identified. Encourage students to state the main idea as clearly as possible.

Instruct

Identifying Main Ideas **L2**

Guided Instruction

- Read the steps to identify main ideas as a class and write them on the board.

- Help students learn the skill by following the steps on p. 54 as a class. Model each step in the activity by identifying the main idea of the boxed text in the Practice section. Read through the paragraph together, then have students name the key idea from each sentence and write it on the board. Develop a title for the paragraph based on the key ideas and help students transform the title into a sentence identifying the main idea of the paragraph.

Independent Practice

Assign *Skills for Life* and have students complete it individually.

All in One Unit 1 History of Our World Teaching Resources, *Skills for Life*, p. 72

Monitor Progress

As students are completing the *Skills for Life* worksheet, check to make sure they understand the skill steps. Provide assistance as needed.

 **Identifying Main Ideas**

"That movie was really confusing," Brandon said to his friend Juan as they left the theater.

"The action was great, though," said Juan. "Can you believe how much that explorer had to go through to find the treasure?"

Juan's comment gave Brandon an idea. "I guess that was the whole point of the movie—to show all the adventures they had while they tried to find the lost treasure."

Juan and Brandon were right. To understand anything you read or see, you need to identify the main idea.

Learn the Skill

These steps will explain how to find the main idea in a written paragraph or in any kind of information that carries a message or a theme.

1. **Look for an idea that all the sentences in the paragraph have in common.** In a well-written paragraph, most of the sentences provide details that support or explain a particular idea.

2. **Identify the subject of the paragraph.** You may find the subject stated in several sentences. Or, you may find the subject in a topic sentence, one sentence that tells what the paragraph is about. The subject may also be stated in a title.

3. **State the main idea in your own words.** Write one or two versions of the main idea or topic. Then reread the passage to make sure that what you wrote accurately identifies the main idea.

Practice the Skill

Read the text in the box below, and then use the steps on page 58 to identify the main idea of the text.

1. What idea do the sentences in the paragraph have in common?

2. This paragraph does not have a title, so you will need to find the sentence or sentences that state the main idea. Is there a topic sentence?

3. First, try to come up with a title for the paragraph. Then turn the title into a complete sentence that identifies the main idea.

In 1901, an archaeologist discovered a stone pillar with an ancient set of laws—Hammurabi's Code. The black stone is almost eight feet tall and more than seven feet around. At its top is a carving of Hammurabi receiving the code of laws from the Babylonian god of justice. About 3,500 lines of cuneiform characters are carved into the stone. These inscriptions are Hammurabi's Code.

Apply the Skill

Turn to page 44, and read the paragraph titled An Eye for an Eye. Follow the steps on page 54 to identify the main idea of the paragraph.

The stele, or stone pillar, on which Hammurabi's Code was written

Chapter 2 **55**

Differentiated Instruction

For Less Proficient Readers L1
Partner less proficient students with more proficient students to do Level 1 of the *Identifying Main Ideas* lesson on the Social Studies Skills Tutor CD-ROM together.

When the students feel more confident, they can move on to Level 2 alone.
◉ *Identifying Main Ideas*, **Social Studies Skills Tutor CD-ROM**

Assess and Reteach

Assess Progress L2
Ask students to do the Apply the Skill activity.

Reteach L1
If students are having trouble applying the skill steps, have them review the skill using the interactive Social Studies Skills Tutor CD-ROM.
◉ *Identifying Main Ideas*, **Social Studies Skills Tutor CD-ROM**

Extend L3
To extend the lesson, ask students to apply the skill steps to a specific paragraph or excerpt in any of the previous sections.

Answer
Apply the Skill
All the sentences describe Hammurabi's code. The second and third sentences state the main idea. Possible title: The Laws of Hammurabi's Code; The laws of Hammurabi's code stated that punishments should be similar to the crime that was committed.

Chapter 2 **55**

Objectives

Social Studies
1. Learn about the basic beliefs of Judaism.
2. Find out about the effect that Judaism has had on other religions.

Reading/Language Arts
Summarize to review the main points in a text.

Prepare to Read

Build Background Knowledge   L2

Tell students that in this section they will learn about the history and basic beliefs of Judaism. Have students review the headings and visuals in the section with this question in mind: **What aspects of Judaism influence us today?** Encourage ideas and discussion by using the Give One, Get One (TE, p. T41) participation strategy.

Set a Purpose for Reading   L2

■ Preview the Objectives.

■ Read each statement in the *Reading Readiness Guide* aloud. Ask students to mark the statements true or false.

All in One **Unit 1 History of Our World Teaching Resources,** *Reading Readiness Guide,* p. 64

■ Have students discuss the statements in pairs or groups of four, then mark their worksheets again. Use the Numbered Heads participation strategy (TE, p. T40) to call on students to share their group's perspectives.

Vocabulary Builder
Preview Key Terms   L2

Pronounce each Key Term, then ask students to say the word with you. Provide a simple example such as, "A covenant is a type of agreement that people are bound to follow."

Prepare to Read

Objectives
In this section you will
1. Learn about the basic beliefs of Judaism.
2. Find out about the effect that Judaism has had on other religions.

Taking Notes
As you read, list details that characterize Judaism. Copy the concept web below, and use it to help you summarize this section.

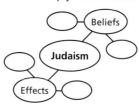

Target Reading Skill

Summarize When you summarize, you review and state, in the correct order, the main points you have read. Summarizing what you read is a good technique to help you comprehend and study. As you read, pause to summarize the main ideas about Judaism. The diagram you are using to take notes may help you to summarize.

Key Terms
- **covenant** (KUV uh nunt) *n.* a promise made by God
- **Moses** (MOH zuz) *n.* an Israelite leader whom the Torah credits with leading the Israelites from Egypt to Canaan
- **prophet** (PRAHF it) *n.* a religious teacher who is regarded as someone who speaks for God or for a god
- **diaspora** (dy AS pur uh) *n.* the scattering of people who have a common background or beliefs

Reading from the Torah

The Torah, the most sacred text of Judaism, says God made a promise to the Israelite leader Abraham:

> **I will increase your numbers very, very much, and I will make you into nations—kings will be your descendants. . . . I will be a God to you and to your [descendants].**
>
> *—the Torah*

This promise has helped shape the history of the people of Israel from ancient times to the present.

The early Israelites came to believe that God was taking part in their history. The Torah records events and laws important to the Israelites. It is made up of five books. They are called Genesis (JEN uh sis), Exodus, Leviticus (luh VIT ih kus), Numbers, and Deuteronomy (doo tur AHN uh mee). Later, Christians adopted these books as the first five books of the Old Testament. The promise that you just read is from the Book of Genesis. In Genesis, we learn of the very beginnings of Judaism.

56 History of Our World

Target Reading Skill   L2

Summarize Point out the Target Reading Skill. Tell students that summarizing can be used to help them to review and state the main points of what they have read.

Model using summarizing by reading the text on this page and then listing the main ideas. (*The early Israelites believed that their history and culture were governed by the Torah and that God took part in their history.*)

Give students *Summarize.* Have them complete the activity in groups.

All in One **Unit 1 History of Our World Teaching Resources,** *Summarize,* p. 69

The Beliefs of Judaism

To the Israelites, history and religion were closely connected. Each event showed God's plan for the Israelite people. Over time, Israelite beliefs developed into the religion we know today as Judaism. You already know that Judaism was monotheistic from its beginning. It differed from the beliefs of nearby peoples in other ways as well.

A Promise to the Israelites Most ancient people thought of their gods as being connected to certain places or people. The Israelites, however, believed that God is present everywhere. They believed that God knows everything and has complete power.

According to the Torah, God promised Abraham that his people would become kings and build nations. God said to Abraham, "I will keep my promise to you and your descendants in future generations as an everlasting covenant." Because of this **covenant,** or promise made by God, the Israelites considered themselves to be God's "chosen people." This covenant was later renewed by **Moses,** an Israelite leader who lived sometime around 1200 B.C. He told the Israelites that God would lead them to Canaan, "the promised land." In return, the Israelites had to obey God faithfully.

The Dead Sea Scrolls
The Dead Sea Scrolls (above) were discovered in 1947 in jars like the one shown at the left. The scrolls helped historians reconstruct the early history of the Israelites. **Generalize** *What is the importance of archaeological finds like the Dead Sea Scrolls?*

Summarize Summarize the paragraph at the left. Be sure to include the key points and important details about God's promise to the Israelites.

Vocabulary Builder

Use the information below to teach students this section's high-use words.

High-Use Word	Definition and Sample Sentence
generation, p. 57	*n.* a single stage in the history of a family The importance of honor was passed from **generation** to generation.
preserve, p. 60	*v.* to keep, protect, or save A museum helps **preserve** old paintings such as the Mona Lisa.

Instruct

The Beliefs of Judaism L2

Guided Instruction

■ **Vocabulary Builder** Clarify the high-use word **generation** before reading.

■ Read The Beliefs of Judaism, using the Choral Reading technique. (TE, p. T38).

■ Ask students **Into what religion did the beliefs of the Israelites develop?** *(Judaism)*

■ Have students discuss how Judaism differed from the beliefs of other nearby peoples. *(It was monotheistic; the Israelites believed that God was present everywhere and had complete power.)*

■ Ask students **According to the Torah, what was the covenant renewed by Moses between God and the Israelites?** *(God would lead the Israelites to Canaan if the Israelites obeyed God faithfully.)*

⟳ Target Reading Skill L2

Summarize As a follow up, ask students to perform the Target Reading Skill activity in the Student Edition. *(The Torah states that God promised Abraham that his people would be leaders of nations, and, therefore, the Israelites considered themselves "God's chosen people." By following Moses to the promised land and obeying God faithfully, God's covenant was renewed by the Israelites.)*

Answer

Generalize Archaeological finds such as the Dead Sea Scrolls help historians to reconstruct events from early history.

Guided Instruction (continued)

■ Ask students **What are the Ten Commandments?** *(the laws the Israelites believed God gave them)*

■ Ask students to describe the code of ethics preached to the Israelites by prophets. *(The Israelites were to live good and decent lives, protect the poor and weak, and Israelite rulers recognized that they had to obey God's law like everyone else.)*

Independent Practice

Ask students to create the Taking Notes graphic organizer on a blank piece of paper. Then have them fill in the blank circles with details they have just learned about the beliefs of Judaism. Briefly model how to identify which details to record.

Monitor Progress

As students begin to fill in their graphic organizers, make sure individuals only write details that summarize the beliefs of Judaism. Provide assistance as needed.

Before sunset on Friday evenings, Jewish women light white Shabbat candles and say a blessing.

58 History of Our World

The Ten Commandments At the heart of Judaism are the Ten Commandments. The Israelites believed that God delivered the Commandments to them through Moses. Some Commandments set out religious duties toward God. Others are rules for correct behavior. Here are some of the Commandments.

> **❝**I the Lord am your God who brought you out of the land of Egypt. . . . You shall have no other gods beside Me. . . . Honor your father and your mother, as the Lord your God has commanded. . . . You shall not murder. You shall not steal.**❞**
>
> —the Ten Commandments

In addition to the Ten Commandments, the Torah set out many other laws. Some had to do with everyday matters, such as how food should be prepared. Others had to do with crimes. Like Hammurabi's Code, many of the Israelites' laws tried to match punishments to crimes. At the same time, religious teachers called on leaders to carry out the laws with justice and mercy.

Judaism and Women Some laws protected women. One of the Commandments, for example, requires that mothers be treated with respect. But, as in many other religions, women were considered to be of lower social status than men. A man who was head of a family owned his wife and children. A father could sell his daughters into marriage. Only a husband could seek a divorce.

Early in Israelite history a few women, such as the judge Deborah, won honor and respect as religious leaders. Later on, however, women were not allowed to take part in many religious leadership roles.

Background

Deborah According to tradition, the prophet Deborah lived during the 1100s B.C. She held the highly respected position of judge and acted as an advisor to her people. Upon hearing that her people were being mistreated by the Canaanites, Deborah and another Israelite leader developed a plan to defeat the Canaanites. According to the Bible, Deborah predicted that a woman would lead the Israelites to victory. The Israelites engaged the Canaanites in battle. During the battle, a thunderstorm struck. The Canaanite chariots became stuck in the muddy battlefield. Later, a woman killed the Canaanite leader. As prophesied by Deborah, the Israelites emerged victorious over the Canaanites.

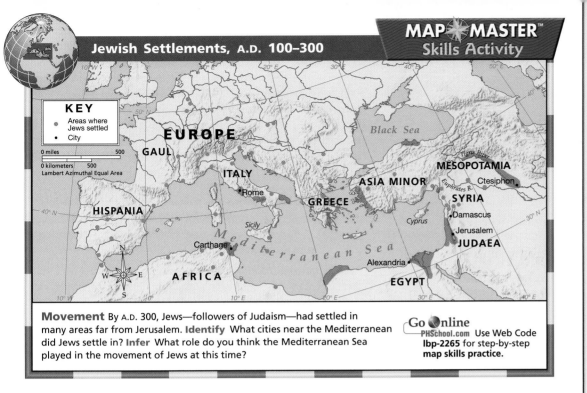

MAP MASTER™ Skills Activity

Jewish Settlements, A.D. 100–300

KEY
- • Areas where Jews settled
- • City

0 miles 500
0 kilometers 500
Lambert Azimuthal Equal Area

EUROPE
GAUL
ITALY
Rome
HISPANIA
Sicily
Carthage
AFRICA
Mediterranean Sea
Alexandria
EGYPT
GREECE
Black Sea
ASIA MINOR
Cyprus
MESOPOTAMIA
Tigris River
Ctesiphon
Euphrates R.
SYRIA
Damascus
Jerusalem
JUDAEA

Movement By A.D. 300, Jews—followers of Judaism—had settled in many areas far from Jerusalem. **Identify** What cities near the Mediterranean did Jews settle in? **Infer** What role do you think the Mediterranean Sea played in the movement of Jews at this time?

Go Online
PHSchool.com Use Web Code **lbp-2265** for step-by-step map skills practice.

Justice and Morality The history of the Israelites tells of **prophets,** or religious teachers who are regarded as speaking for God. The prophets told the Israelites how God wanted them to live. They warned the people not to disobey God's law. Disobedience could bring disaster.

Prophets preached a code of ethics, or moral behavior. They urged the Israelites to live good and decent lives. They also called on the rich and powerful to protect the poor and weak. All people, the prophets said, were equal before God. In many ancient societies, a ruler was seen as a god. To the Israelites, however, their leaders were human. Kings had to obey God's law just as shepherds and merchants did.

✓**Reading Check** What did the prophets tell the Israelites?

The Effects of Judaism

After their exile from Judah in 587 B.C., the Jews, or people who follow Judaism, saw their homeland controlled by various foreign powers, including the Romans. The Romans drove the Jews out of their homeland in A.D. 135. As a result, the Jewish people scattered to different parts of the world.

Chapter 2 Section 5 **59**

Differentiated Instruction

For English Language Learners L2
Students may have difficulty pronouncing some of the longer words in these selections, such as *rebellion, heritage, influence,* and *geographical.* Encourage students to break down these words into smaller parts to help them sound out the pronunciations.

For Gifted and Talented L3
Have students research Jewish holidays such as Passover or Hanukkah and create a poster providing information about one holiday. Use the *Rubric for Assessing a Student Poster* to evaluate students' work.

All in One Unit 1 History of Our World Teaching Resources, *Rubric for Assessing a Student Poster,* p. 83

The Effects of Judaism L2

Guided Instruction
- **Vocabulary Builder** Clarify the high-use word **preserve** before reading.

- Read The Effects of Judaism. As students read, help individuals answer the Reading Check question.

- Have students name the two major religions that were influenced by Judaism. *(Christianity and Islam)*

- Ask students to describe the impact of Judaism on Christianity and Islam. *(Like Judaism, Christianity and Islam are monotheistic religions. Followers of Islam and Christianity honor Abraham, Moses, and the prophets. They also share the moral point of view developed by the Israelites.)*

Independent Practice
Have students complete the graphic organizer by adding details about the effects of Judaism.

Monitor Progress
- Show *Section Reading Support Transparency HOW 60* and ask students to check their graphic organizers individually. Go over key concepts and clarify key vocabulary as needed.

  📖 **History of Our World Transparencies,** *Section Reading Support Transparency HOW 60*

- Tell students to fill in the last column of the *Reading Readiness Guide.* Probe for what they learned that confirms or invalidates each statement.

  All in One Unit 1 History of Our World Teaching Resources, *Reading Readiness Guide,* p. 64

Answer
✓**Reading Check** The prophets preached a code of ethics that told the Israelites how God wanted them to live.

MAP MASTER Skills Activity **Identify** Rome, Carthage, Alexandria, Jerusalem **Infer** It provided a method of transportation.

Go Online
PHSchool.com Students may practice their map skills using the interactive online version of this map.

Assess and Reteach

Assess Progress `L2`

Have students complete the Section Assessment. Administer the *Section Quiz.*

All in One Unit 1 History of Our World Teaching Resources, *Section Quiz,* p. 66

Reteach `L1`

If students need more instruction, have them read this section in the Reading and Vocabulary Study Guide.

📖 Chapter 2, Section 5, **History of Our World Reading and Vocabulary Study Guide,** pp. 28–30

Extend `L3`

Have students learn more about the Ten Commandments by reading *Moses and the Ten Commandments.* Have students work individually to complete the reading.

All in One Unit 1 History of Our World Teaching Resources, *Moses and the Ten Commandments,* p. 77

Answer

✓ **Reading Check** By living together in close communities; obeying their religious laws; worshiping at their temples; following traditions.

Section 5 Assessment

Key Terms
Students' sentences should reflect knowledge of each Key Term.

🔃 Target Reading Skill
Possible Answer: Judaism had an important impact on two other religions, Christianity and Islam.

Comprehension and Critical Thinking
1. (a) They believed God promised Abraham that his people would become kings and build nations. **(b)** to obey God faithfully **(c)** According to the Torah, based on the covenant made between God and Abraham and later renewed by Moses.

2. (a) the religious laws set forth in the Torah, including the Ten Commandments **(b)** Most ancient people believed in many gods that were connected to specific places or people; the Israelites believed in one all-powerful God that was everywhere. **(c)** Possible answer: these laws show that Israelites were concerned with honoring God above

men; with issues of right and wrong, and helping the less fortunate.

Writing Activity
Use the *Rubric for Assessing a Writing Assignment* to evaluate students' letters.

All in One Unit 1 History of Our World Teaching Resources, *Rubric for Assessing a Writing Assignment,* p. 84

After defeating the Jews in battle in A.D. 70, Roman soldiers carried off precious objects from the temple in Jerusalem.

New Settlements The Romans carried on the Jewish **diaspora** (dy AS pur uh), the scattering of a group of people, begun by the Assyrians and Chaldeans. See the map titled Jewish Settlements, A.D. 100–300, on page 59.

Wherever they settled, the Jews preserved their heritage. They did so by living together in close communities. They took care to obey their religious laws, worship at their temples, and follow their traditions. The celebration of Passover is one such tradition. It marks a time when Israelites believed their children were spared from destruction. Death "passed over" them, and they were led out of Egypt by Moses. Over time, such long-held traditions helped to unite Jews.

Effects on Later Religions Judaism had an important influence on two later religions, Christianity and Islam. Both religions have their beginnings in Judaism. Both faiths originated from the same geographical area. Both were monotheistic. Jews, Christians, and followers of Islam all honor Abraham, Moses, and the prophets. They also share the same moral point of view that the Israelites first developed.

✓ **Reading Check** How did the Jews preserve their heritage?

Section 5 Assessment

Key Terms
Review the key terms at the beginning of this section. Use each term in a sentence that explains its meaning.

🔃 Target Reading Skill
Write a summary of the last paragraph in this section.

Comprehension and Critical Thinking
1. (a) Identify What promise did the Israelites believe God made to Abraham?

(b) Explain What did God's covenant with Abraham require of the Israelites?
(c) Analyze Information Why did the Israelites believe that they were God's chosen people?

2. (a) Recall What religious laws did the Israelites follow?
(b) Compare and Contrast How does Judaism compare and contrast with the beliefs of other peoples in the ancient world?
(c) Draw Inferences What do the laws of Judaism say about the moral values of the Israelites?

Writing Activity
Suppose you have a friend who wants to learn more about Judaism. Write him or her a letter explaining the basic beliefs and history of Judaism.

> **Writing Tip** When writing a letter, remember to include the date, a salutation, or greeting, and a closing. It might help to have a specific friend in mind when you write your letter.

Review and Assessment

◆ Chapter Summary

Cuneiform tablet

Section 1: Land Between Two Rivers
- Mesopotamia's attractive location between two rivers drew people to settle there.
- Some of the earliest cities grew up in Sumer, in the region of Mesopotamia.
- Sumerians worshiped and honored many gods.

Section 2: Babylonia and Assyria
- Competing armies fought to control Mesopotamia and its desirable resources.
- The Babylonian Empire included the conquered cities of Sumer and lands reaching into Asia Minor.
- The Assyrians overthrew the Babylonians and created an even larger empire.
- The Assyrian Empire fell to the Chaldeans, who created the New Babylonian Empire under Nebuchadnezzar II.

Section 3: The Legacy of Mesopotamia
- The earliest existing set of written laws, known as Hammurabi's Code, established rules and punishments for Babylonians.
- Writing developed in Mesopotamia in about 3500 B.C., and was first used to keep records.

Section 4: Mediterranean Civilizations
- Phoenicia was a major sea power from 1100 to 800 B.C. Its wealth came from trade.
- The Phoenician alphabet forms the basis of alphabets used in English and other languages.
- The Israelites practiced monotheism and established a capital in the city of Jerusalem.

Section 5: Judaism
- The religion practiced by the Israelites was very different from other religions practiced in the ancient world.
- The Ten Commandments are the core beliefs of Judaism.
- Judaism has influenced other major religions of the world.

Babylonian statue

◆ Key Terms

Use each key term below in a sentence that shows the meaning of the term.

1. city-state
2. polytheism
3. myth
4. empire
5. caravan
6. bazaar
7. code
8. cuneiform
9. monotheism
10. famine
11. exile
12. covenant
13. prophet
14. diaspora

Chapter 2 **61**

Vocabulary Builder

Revisit this chapter's high-use words:

fertile	expand	enrich
terrace	invade	conduct
rival	conflict	generation
conquer	document	preserve

Ask students to review the definitions they recorded on their *Word Knowledge* worksheets.

All in One Unit 1 History of Our World Teaching Resources, *Word Knowledge,* p. 70

Consider allowing students to earn extra credit if they use the words in their answers to the questions in the Chapter Review and Assessment. The words must be used correctly and in a natural context to win the extra points.

Review and Assessment

Review Chapter Content

- Write each statement of the Chapter summary on the board, and ask students to identify which Guiding Question each bulleted statement in the Chapter Summary answers, using the Think-Write-Pair-Share strategy (TE. p. T40). Refer to page 1 in the Student Edition for text of Guiding Questions.

- Assign *Vocabulary Development* for students to review Key Terms.

  All in One Unit 1 History of Our World Teaching Resources, *Vocabulary Development,* p. 78

Answer

Key Terms

Students' sentences (1.–14.) should reflect knowledge of each Key Term.

Comprehension and Critical Thinking

15. (a) a region shaped like a crescent moon along the eastern edge of the Mediterranean Sea **(b)** The rivers provided water for irrigation, fish for food, and reeds and clay for building. They also deposited fertile soil good for farming when they flooded. **(c)** They were able to grow crops and trade goods with people throughout the ancient world.

16. (a) All were large empires within Mesopotamia; each society had skilled warriors, valued learning, and built wealthy cities. **(b)** Mesopotamia was near two rivers and its land was fertile. As a result, people established farming communities that then developed into cities. **(c)** One civilization would rise to power through military victories and then enjoy a period of growth and prosperity. Then, a new civilization would come along and defeat the civilization in power. This pattern repeated itself several times.

17. (a) a written set of laws. **(b)** The code told people in Babylonia how to behave and settle conflicts. **(c)** It laid the foundation for an organized set of written laws; most societies since have relied on some form of written law.

18. (a) sea traders who invented an alphabet that forms the basis for many modern alphabets **(b)** The Phoenicians developed an alphabet that represented the sounds of the language; expanded trade in the Mediterranean and exchanged goods and culture throughout the ancient world. **(c)** They improved upon the Sumerian alphabet, and created an alphabet that stood for sounds instead of words, allowing them to write a language using just 22 symbols.

19. (a) The Israelites were united under the religion of Judaism. They were monotheists, who believed that God was absolute and that they were God's "chosen people." **(b)** Students may choose to explain two of the following events: God's covenant with Abraham; the Exodus; the conquest and settlement of Canaan; the union and growth of the Israelites under Saul, David, and Solomon; or the giving of the Ten Commandments and other Hebrew laws. **(c)** Students' answers will vary depending on the event they choose.

◆ Comprehension and Critical Thinking

15. (a) Identify What is the Fertile Crescent?
(b) Apply Information Explain the importance of the Tigris and the Euphrates rivers in the Fertile Crescent.
(c) Draw Conclusions How did the geography of the Fertile Crescent help the Sumerians to prosper?

16. (a) Recall Describe the empires of Assyria, Babylonia, and New Babylonia.
(b) Identify Cause and Effect Explain how Mesopotamia's location shaped the development of its civilizations.
(c) Find the Main Ideas What patterns do you see in the rise and fall of the many civilizations in Mesopotamia?

17. (a) Define What was Hammurabi's Code?
(b) Explain What was the purpose of Hammurabi's Code?
(c) Make Generalizations What effect did Hammurabi's Code have on future civilizations?

18. (a) Name Who were the Phoenicians?
(b) Explain Describe two cultural contributions of the Phoenicians and explain their importance.

(c) Compare and Contrast How did the Phoenicians improve upon a Sumerian invention?

19. (a) Recall Who were the Israelites and what did they believe?
(b) Explain Describe two major events in the history of the Israelites.
(c) Analyze Information Choose an event from the history of the Israelites and describe its importance.

◆ Skills Practice

Identifying Main Ideas In the Skills for Life Activity, you learned how to identify main ideas. You also learned how to summarize main ideas in a brief statement. Review the steps you followed to learn this skill. Then turn to page 45 and read the three paragraphs on that page under the heading The Art of Writing. Identify the main ideas and then summarize them in a few sentences.

◆ Writing Activity: Math

Turn to the World Overview on page 3. According to the map key, how long is the time period assigned to ancient Mesopotamia? Write an explanation that describes how you arrived at your answer.

MAP MASTER™
Skills Activity

The Fertile Crescent

Place Location For each place listed below, write the letter from the map that shows its location.
1. Tigris River
2. Euphrates River
3. Mesopotamia
4. Fertile Crescent
5. Canaan
6. Mediterranean Sea

Go Online
PHSchool.com Use Web Code **lbp-2275** for an **interactive map.**

Skills Practice
Students' answers will vary. Possible summary of main ideas: Writing developed over a long period of time. The people of Sumer in Mesopotamia developed writing around 3100 B.C. Scribes were important because few people were able to write. They used writing to keep records that helped Sumerian society to function.

Writing Activity: Math
about 2,761 years; Students' explanations should indicate that they subtracted 539 from 3,300 to arrive at their answers. Use *Rubric for Assessing a Writing Assignment* to evaluate students' work.

All in One Unit 1 History of Our World Teaching Resources, *Rubric for Assessing a Writing Assignment*, p. 84

Standardized Test Prep

Test-Taking Tips

Some questions on standardized tests ask you to draw conclusions by analyzing a reading passage. Read the paragraph below. Then follow the tips to answer the sample question.

> Sumerian priests washed the statues of gods before and after each meal was offered. Music sounded and incense burned as huge plates of food were laid before them. In most ancient religions, the food was often eaten after it was presented to the gods. Perhaps the worshipers thought that by eating the offering, they would be taking in the qualities they admired in the gods.

TIP Reread if necessary before answering.

Pick the letter that best completes the statement.

TIP Use logic—or good reasoning—to choose your answer.

Which conclusion can you reach, based on the passage?

- **A** The Sumerians were not as intelligent as modern people.
- **B** Only priests were allowed into temples.
- **C** The Sumerians did not like to waste food.
- **D** Religious ceremonies were important to the Sumerians.

Think It Through You can rule out B. The passage does not say that only priests were allowed in the temples. The practices of the Sumerians may seem odd to us, but odd does not mean unintelligent. So A is not correct. The passage states that people possibly ate offerings to honor their gods. So C is not the best answer. The correct answer is D.

Practice Questions

Use the tips above and other tips in this book to help you answer the following questions.

1. Where was Mesopotamia located?
   - **A** along the Nile River
   - **B** between the Tigris and the Euphrates rivers
   - **C** in the Arabian Desert
   - **D** in present-day Egypt

2. Which civilization mastered seafaring?
   - **A** Phoenicia
   - **B** Sumer
   - **C** Assyria
   - **D** Babylonia

Read the passage below, and then answer the questions that follow.

The Assyrians invented the battering ram to tear down city walls. They trained people to hurl stones with slings, and they created special armor to protect their archers. They also perfected the skill of fighting while on horse-drawn chariots.

3. What can you conclude about the Assyrians from this passage?
   - **A** They were inexperienced warriors.
   - **B** They liked inventing new things.
   - **C** They disliked fighting.
   - **D** They had fought many wars.

4. Judaism differed from other early religions in that it
   - **A** was polytheistic.
   - **B** treated men and women equally.
   - **C** was monotheistic.
   - **D** developed in the Fertile Crescent.

Use Web Code **lba-2205** for **Chapter 2 self-test.**

Chapter 2 **63**

Unit 2

Ancient Egypt, India, and China

Unit Overview

This unit covers civilizations that developed in the Nile, Indus, and Huang river valleys. Beginning with Chapter 3, students will learn about the significant features of ancient Egypt and Nubia, two civilizations that developed in the Nile Valley. Chapter 4 provides a detailed overview of civilizations in ancient India. Chapter 5 describes the history of ancient China. When students have studied all three chapters, they will be able to compare such features as natural environment, urban development, social hierarchy, written language, belief systems, government, and economy.

Monitoring Student Progress

After students have completed Chapter 5, administer Benchmark Test 2, the second of six benchmark tests provided to assess students' progress toward mastery of the National Geography Standards.

The Report Sheet for this test will identify which objectives or standards students have mastered and where they need additional work. It also correlates to the appropriate sections in the Reading and Vocabulary Study Guide, where students can get additional review as needed.

AYP Monitoring Assessment Resources

Determine students' progress toward mastery of the National Geography Standards.

 Benchmark Test 2, **AYP Monitoring Assessments,** pp. 87–92

Use the Report Sheet to identify which standards your students have mastered, where they need more work, and where they can get additional help.

 Report Sheet, Benchmark Test 2, **AYP Monitoring Assessments,** p. 126

Ancient Egypt, India, and China

(2700 B.C.–A.D. 500)

Chapter 3
Ancient Egypt and Nubia
(2700 B.C.–500 B.C.)

Chapter 4
Ancient India
(2500 B.C.–A.D. 500)

Chapter 5
Ancient China
(1750 B.C.–A.D. 220)

◄ The Pyramids at Giza, Egypt, are one of the Seven Wonders of the Ancient World.

65

Using the Visual

Ask students to study the picture on pp. 64–65. Have students read the caption on p. 65. Ask **In what chapter will we learn more about the pyramids?** *(Chapter 3)* Tell students that the ancient Egyptians built pyramids as part of their religious belief system. Of the three pyramids at Giza (two are pictured here), the tallest is about 480 feet high. Students will learn more about pyramids in Chapter 3, Section 3.

Overview

 Section 1

The Geography of the Nile
1. Find out how the geography of the Nile changes as the river runs its course.
2. Learn about the types of communities that first appeared along the Nile, and how the Nile was used for trade.

 Section 2

The Rulers of Egypt
1. Learn about the history of kingship in ancient Egypt.
2. Find out about Egypt's accomplishments during each of the three kingdom periods.
3. Understand what characterized the rule of Egypt during the New Kingdom period.

 Section 3

Egyptian Religion
1. Learn about Egyptian gods and goddesses.
2. Find out about the Egyptians' belief in the afterlife.
3. Discover how and why the pharaohs' tombs were built.

 Section 4

Ancient Egyptian Culture
1. Find out about the everyday life of the ancient Egyptians.
2. Learn about writing in ancient Egypt.
3. Discover advances made by the Egyptians in science and medicine.

 Section 5

The Cultures of Nubia
1. Examine the relationship between Nubia and Egypt.
2. Learn about the Nubian kingdoms centered in Kerma, Napata, and Meroë.

Discovery CHANNEL SCHOOL Video

Ancient Egypt, Life on the Nile
Length: 5 minutes, 7 seconds
Use with Section 1

This video segment provides an overview of the importance of the Nile River to ancient Egyptians. The segment includes how the river influenced both the economy and religion of the region.

Technology Resources

Go Online
PHSchool.com

Students use embedded Web codes to access Internet activities, chapter self-tests, and additional map practice. They may also access Dorling Kindersley's Online Desk Reference to learn more about each country they study.

interactive Textbook

Use the Interactive Textbook to make content and concepts come alive through animations, videos, and activities that accompany the complete basal text—online and on CD-ROM.

PRENTICE HALL

TeacherEXPRESS™
Plan • Teach • Assess

Use this complete suite of powerful teaching tools to make planning lessons and administering tests quicker and easier.

Reading and Assessment

Reading and Vocabulary Instruction

🔄 Model the Target Reading Skill

Use Context Clues Tell students that using context clues, or other words they already know in a passage, can help them figure out the meaning of unfamiliar words in a text. They may find clues within the same sentence as an unfamiliar word, or in other surrounding sentences. Write the following paragraph on the board and have students use context clues to determine the meaning of the underlined words:

The pharaoh had absolute power over Egypt. Whatever he decided became law. It was thought that he controlled flooding of the Nile River. His people worshipped him like a god.

Ask students which context clues refer to the meaning of *pharaoh*. (*power, whatever he decided became law, worshipped like a god*) Model how these clues can be put together to make a definition:

"The words *power* and *law* signify that a pharaoh is a ruler, but *worshipped like a god* indicates some kind of religious status. A pharaoh must be a religious and political ruler in Egypt." Next have students choose the context clues that correspond to *absolute power* and create a definition. (*whatever he decided* is a context clue; *absolute power* means complete control)

Use the following worksheets from All-in-One Unit 2 History of Our World Teaching Resources (pp. 25–27) to support this chapter's Target Reading Skill.

Vocabulary Builder
High-Use Academic Words

Use these steps to teach this chapter's high-use words:

1. Have students rate how well they know each word on their Word Knowledge worksheets (All-in-One Unit 2 History of Our World Teaching Resources, p. 28)
2. Pronounce each word and ask students to repeat it.
3. Give students a brief definition and sample sentence (provided on TE pp. 69, 75, 81, 89, 97).
4. Work with students as they fill in the "Definition or Example" column of their Word Knowledge worksheets.

Assessment

Formal Assessment

Test students' understanding of core knowledge and skills.

> **Chapter Tests A and B,** All-in-One Unit 2 History of Our World Teaching Resources, pp. 42–47

Customize the Chapter Tests to suit your needs.
> **Exam***View* ®
> **Test Bank CD-ROM**

Skills Assessment

Assess geographic literacy.

> **MapMaster Skills,** Student Edition pp. 67, 77, 98, 102

Assess reading and comprehension.

> **Target Reading Skills,** Student Edition, pp. 70, 76, 84, 91, 99, and in Section Assessments

> **Chapter 3 Assessment,** History of Our World Reading and Vocabulary Study Guide, p. 47

Performance Assessment

Assess students' performance on this chapter's Writing Activities using the following rubrics from All-in-One Unit 2 History of Our World Teaching Resources.

> **Rubric for Assessing a Journal Entry,** p. 39
> **Rubric for Assessing a Writing Assignment,** p. 40
> **Rubric for Assessing a Student Poem,** p. 41

Assess students' work through performance tasks.

> **Small Group Activity: Making Ancient Egyptian Slate Palettes,** All-in-One Unit 2 History of Our World Teaching Resources, pp. 31–34

Online Assessment

Have students check their own understanding.

> **Chapter Self-Test**

Section 1 The Geography of the Nile

 3 periods, 1.5 blocks

Social Studies Objectives

1. Find out how the geography of the Nile changes as the river runs its course.
2. Learn about the types of communities that first appeared along the Nile, and how the Nile was used for trade.

Reading/Language Arts Objective

Use context clues to help understand the meaning of an unfamiliar word.

Prepare to Read	Instructional Resources	Differentiated Instruction
Build Background Knowledge Discuss the influence of the Nile River on Egypt and Nubia. **Set a Purpose for Reading** Have students evaluate statements on the *Reading Readiness Guide.* **Preview Key Terms** Teach the section's Key Terms. **Target Reading Skill** Introduce the section's Target Reading Skill of **using context clues.**	**All in One Unit 2 History of Our World Teaching Resources** **L2** Reading Readiness Guide, p. 6 **L2** Use Context Clues: General Knowledge, p. 25	**Spanish Reading and Vocabulary Study Guide** **L1** Chapter 3, Section 1, pp. 25–26 ELL

Instruct	Instructional Resources	Differentiated Instruction
The Course of the Nile River Ask questions about the importance of the Nile to Ancient Nubia. **Target Reading Skill** Review **using context clues.** **The Growth of Communities and Trade Along the Nile** Discuss trading in ancient Egypt and Nubia.	**All in One Unit 2 History of Our World Teaching Resources** **L2** Guided Reading and Review, p. 7 **L2** Reading Readiness Guide, p. 6 **History of Our World Transparencies** **L2** Section Reading Support Transparency HOW 61 **History of Our World Video Program** **L2** Ancient Egypt, Life on the Nile	**All in One Unit 2 History of Our World Teaching Resources** **L1** Guided Reading and Review, p. 7 ELL, LPR, SN **Teacher's Edition** **L1** For English Language Learners, TE p. 70 **L3** For Gifted and Talented, TE p. 71 **History of Our World Transparencies** **L3** Color Transparency HOW 25: Southwest Asia and North Africa: Political AR, GT **Spanish Support** **L1** Guided Reading and Review (Spanish), p. 24 ELL

Assess and Reteach	Instructional Resources	Differentiated Instruction
Assess Progress Evaluate student comprehension with the section assessment and section quiz. **Reteach** Assign the Reading and Vocabulary Study Guide to help struggling students. **Extend** Extend the lesson by assigning a Long-Term Integrated Project.	**All in One Unit 2 History of Our World Teaching Resources** **L2** Section Quiz, p. 8 Rubric for Assessing a Journal Entry, p. 39 **Reading and Vocabulary Study Guide** **L1** Chapter 3, Section 1, pp. 32–34 **PHSchool.com** **L3** For: Long-Term Integrated Projects: Creating a Multimedia Presentation: Rivers and People **Web Code:** lbd-2306	**Spanish Support** **L2** Section Quiz (Spanish), p. 25 ELL

Key
L1 Basic to Average **L3** Average to Advanced
L2 For All Students

LPR Less Proficient Readers
AR Advanced Readers
SN Special Needs Students

GT Gifted and Talented
ELL English Language Learners

Section 2 The Rulers of Egypt

 3 periods, 1.5 blocks

Social Studies Objectives
1. Learn about the history of kingship in ancient Egypt.
2. Find out about Egypt's accomplishments during each of the three kingdom periods.
3. Understand what characterized the rule of Egypt during the New Kingdom period.

Reading/Language Arts Objective
Use restatement in context to determine the meaning of an unfamiliar word.

Prepare to Read	Instructional Resources	Differentiated Instruction
Build Background Knowledge Discuss how art and architecture provides information about ancient Egypt's culture. **Set a Purpose for Reading** Have students begin to fill out the *Reading Readiness Guide*. **Preview Key Terms** Teach the section's Key Terms. **Target Reading Skill** Introduce the section's Target Reading Skill of **using context clues**.	**All in One Unit 2 History of Our World Teaching Resources** **L2** Reading Readiness Guide, p. 10 **L2** Use Context Clues: Definition/Description, p. 26	**Spanish Reading and Vocabulary Study Guide** **L1** Chapter 3, Section 2, pp. 27–28 ELL

Instruct	Instructional Resources	Differentiated Instruction
Egyptian Kingship Discuss the pharaohs and ask questions about their absolute power. **The Three Kingdoms** Discuss the accomplishments of each kingdom. **Target Reading Skill** Review **using context clues**. **Rule During the New Kingdom** Ask about the rule of Thutmose III.	**All in One Unit 2 History of Our World Teaching Resources** **L2** Guided Reading and Review, p. 11 **L2** Reading Readiness Guide, p. 10 **History of Our World Transparencies** **L2** Section Reading Support Transparency HOW 62	**History of Our World Teacher's Edition** **L3** For Advanced Readers, TE p. 77 **L1** For Less Proficient Readers, TE p. 77 **Spanish Support** **L2** Guided Reading and Review (Spanish), p. 26 ELL

Assess and Reteach	Instructional Resources	Differentiated Instruction
Assess Progress Evaluate student comprehension with the section assessment and section quiz. **Reteach** Assign the Reading and Vocabulary Study Guide to help struggling students. **Extend** Extend the lesson by assigning literature readings.	**All in One Unit 2 History of Our World Teaching Resources** **L2** Section Quiz, p. 12 **L3** In Her Own Words: Hatshepsut, Queen of Egypt c. 1500 B.C., p. 36 **L3** In Her Own Words: Ankhesenpaton, Queen of Egypt c. 1350 B.C., p. 37 Rubric for Assessing a Writing Assignment, p. 222 **Reading and Vocabulary Study Guide** **L1** Chapter 3, Section 2, pp. 35–37	**Spanish Support** **L2** Section Quiz (Spanish), p. 27 ELL

Key
L1 Basic to Average   **L3** Average to Advanced
L2 For All Students

LPR Less Proficient Readers
AR Advanced Readers
SN Special Needs Students

GT Gifted and Talented
ELL English Language Learners

Section 3 Egyptian Religion

 3 periods, 1.5 blocks (includes Focus On the Pyramid Builders)

Social Studies Objectives

1. Learn about Egyptian gods and goddesses.
2. Find out about the Egyptians' belief in the afterlife.
3. Discover how and why the pharaohs' tombs were built.

Reading/Language Arts Objective

Learn how to use context clues in surrounding words and sentences to find the meanings of unfamiliar words.

Prepare to Read	**Instructional Resources**	**Differentiated Instruction**
Build Background Knowledge Discuss the construction of the pyramids. **Set a Purpose for Reading** Have students evaluate statements on the *Reading Readiness Guide.* **Preview Key Terms** Teach the section's Key Terms. **Target Reading Skill** Introduce the section's Target Reading Skill of **using context clues.**	**All in One Unit 2 History of Our World Teaching Resources** **L2** Reading Readiness Guide, p. 14 **L2** Use Context Clues: Definition/Description, p. 26	**Spanish Reading and Vocabulary Study Guide** **L1** Chapter 3, Section 3, pp. 29–30 ELL

Instruct	**Instructional Resources**	**Differentiated Instruction**
Egyptian Gods and Goddesses Discuss the gods worshipped by ancient Egyptians. **Belief in an Afterlife** Discuss the Egyptian belief in the afterlife and the customs related to that belief. **Eyewitness Technology** Study the Great Pyramid in depth with students. **The Pharaohs' Tombs** Discuss the construction of the pyramids. **Target Reading Skill** Review **using context clues.**	**All in One Unit 2 History of Our World Teaching Resources** **L2** Guided Reading and Review, p. 15 **L2** Reading Readiness Guide, p. 14 **L2** Enrichment, p. 29 **History of Our World Transparencies** **L2** Section Reading Support Transparency HOW 63	**History of Our World Teacher's Edition** **L1** For Less Proficient Readers, TE pp. 84, 86 **L1** For Special Needs Students, TE p. 84 **History of Our World Transparencies** **L1** Transparency B6: Flow Chart ELL, LPR, SN **Spanish Support** **L2** Guided Reading and Review (Spanish), p. 28 ELL

Assess and Reteach	**Instructional Resources**	**Differentiated Instruction**
Assess Progress Evaluate student comprehension with the section assessment and section quiz. **Reteach** Assign the Reading and Vocabulary Study Guide to help struggling students. **Extend** Extend the lesson by assigning a Book Project.	**All in One Unit 2 History of Our World Teaching Resources** **L2** Section Quiz, p. 16 **L3** Book Project: Life in the Ancient World, pp. 10–12 Rubric for Assessing a Journal Entry, p. 39 **Reading and Vocabulary Study Guide** **L1** Chapter 3, Section 3, pp. 38–40	**Spanish Support** **L2** Section Quiz (Spanish), p. 29 ELL

Key

L1 Basic to Average **L3** Average to Advanced
L2 For All Students

LPR Less Proficient Readers
AR Advanced Readers
SN Special Needs Students

GT Gifted and Talented
ELL English Language Learners

Section 4 Ancient Egyptian Culture

 3 periods, 1.5 blocks (includes Skills for Life)

Social Studies Objectives
1. Find out about the everyday life of the ancient Egyptians.
2. Learn about writing in ancient Egypt.
3. Discover advances made by the Egyptians in science and medicine.

Reading/Language Arts Objective
Learn how cause and effect clues can help you understand the meaning of an unfamiliar word.

Section Lesson Planner

Prepare to Read

Build Background Knowledge
Discuss hieroglyphs and how picture symbols are used as a system of writing.

Set a Purpose for Reading
Have students begin to fill out the *Reading Readiness Guide.*

Preview Key Terms
Teach the section's Key Terms.

Target Reading Skill
Introduce the section's Target Reading Skill of **using context clues.**

Instructional Resources
All in One Unit 2 History of Our World Teaching Resources
- **L2** Reading Readiness Guide, p. 18
- **L2** Use Context Clues: Cause and Effect, p. 27

Differentiated Instruction
Spanish Reading and Vocabulary Study Guide
- **L1** Chapter 3, Section 4, pp. 31–32 ELL

Instruct

The Lives of the Egyptians
Discuss everyday life in ancient Egypt.

Writing in Ancient Egypt
Ask questions about and discuss the hieroglyphic system of writing.

Target Reading Skill
Review **using context clues.**

Science and Medicine
Discuss some of ancient Egypt's accomplishments in science and medicine.

Instructional Resources
All in One Unit 2 History of Our World Teaching Resources
- **L2** Guided Reading and Review, p. 19
- **L2** Reading Readiness Guide, p. 18

History of Our World Transparencies
- **L2** Transparency B2: Flow Chart
- **L2** Section Reading Support Transparency HOW 64

Differentiated Instruction
All in One Unit 2 History of Our World Teaching Resources
- **L2** Skills for Life, p. 30 AR, GT, LPR, SN

Teacher's Edition
- **L1** For Special Needs Students, TE p. 90
- **L1** For English Language Learners, TE p. 91
- **L3** For Gifted and Talented, TE p. 95

Student Edition on Audio CD
- **L1** Chapter 3, Section 4 ELL, LPR, SN

Assess and Reteach

Assess Progress
Evaluate student comprehension with the section assessment and section quiz.

Reteach
Assign the Reading and Vocabulary Study Guide to help struggling students.

Extend
Extend the lesson by assigning a Small Group Activity.

Instructional Resources
All in One Unit 2 History of Our World Teaching Resources
- **L2** Section Quiz, p. 20
- **L3** Small Group Activity: Making Ancient Egyptian Slate Palettes, pp. 31–34
  Rubric for Assessing a Writing Assignment, p. 40

Reading and Vocabulary Study Guide
- **L1** Chapter 3, Section 4, pp. 41–43

Differentiated Instruction
All in One Unit 2 History of Our World Teaching Resources
- **L3** Understanding Road Maps, p. 35 AR, GT

Spanish Support
- **L2** Section Quiz (Spanish), p. 31 ELL

Social Studies Skills Tutor CD-ROM
- **L1** Analyzing and Interpreting Special-Purpose Maps ELL, LPR, SN

Key
- **L1** Basic to Average **L3** Average to Advanced
- **L2** For All Students
- **LPR** Less Proficient Readers
- **AR** Advanced Readers
- **SN** Special Needs Students
- **GT** Gifted and Talented
- **ELL** English Language Learners

Section 5 The Cultures of Nubia

 3 periods, 1.5 blocks (includes Chapter Review and Assessment)

Social Studies Objectives
1. Examine the relationship between Nubia and Egypt.
2. Learn about the Nubian kingdoms centered in Kerma, Napata, and Meroë.

Reading/Language Arts Objective
Use synonyms to understand the meanings of unfamiliar words.

Prepare to Read	Instructional Resources	Differentiated Instruction
Build Background Knowledge Have students locate different regions on a map and discuss how location affects trade. **Set a Purpose for Reading** Have students evaluate statements on the *Reading Readiness Guide.* **Preview Key Terms** Teach the section's Key Terms. **Target Reading Skill** Introduce the section's Target Reading Skill of **using context clues.**	**All in One Unit 2 History of Our World Teaching Resources** **L2** Reading Readiness Guide, p. 22 **L2** Use Context Clues: Definition/Description, p. 26 **History of Our World Transparencies** **L2** Color Transparency HOW 17: Africa: Political	**Spanish Reading and Vocabulary Study Guide** **L1** Chapter 3, Section 5, pp. 33–34 ELL

Instruct	Instructional Resources	Differentiated Instruction
Nubia and Egypt Ask about and discuss the relationship between Egypt and Nubia. **The Kerma Culture** Compare and contrast Egypt and Nubia. **Target Reading Skill** Review **using context clues.** **Napata and Meroë** Discuss the kingdoms of Napata and Meroë.	**All in One Unit 2 History of Our World Teaching Resources** **L2** Guided Reading and Review, p. 23 **L2** Reading Readiness Guide, p. 22 **History of Our World Transparencies** **L2** Section Reading Support Transparency HOW 65	**History of Our World Teacher's Edition** **L3** For Advanced Readers, TE p. 98 **L1** For Less Proficient Readers, TE p. 99 **Reading and Vocabulary Study Guide** **L1** Chapter 3, Section 5, p. 44–46 ELL, LPR, SN **Spanish Support** **L2** Guided Reading and Review (Spanish), p. 32 ELL

Assess and Reteach	Instructional Resources	Differentiated Instruction
Assess Progress Evaluate student comprehension with the section assessment and section quiz. **Reteach** Assign the Reading and Vocabulary Study Guide to help struggling students. **Extend** Extend the lesson by assigning a group project.	**All in One Unit 2 History of Our World Teaching Resources** **L2** Section Quiz, p. 24 Rubric for Assessing a Writing Assignment, p. 40 Rubric for Assessing a Student Poem, p. 41 **L2** Vocabulary Development, p. 38 **L2** Word Knowledge, p. 28 **L2** Chapter Tests A and B, pp. 42–47 **Reading and Vocabulary Study Guide** **L1** Chapter 3, Section 5, pp. 44–46	**Spanish Support** **L2** Section Quiz (Spanish), p. 33 ELL **L2** Chapter Summary (Spanish), p. 34 ELL **L2** Vocabulary Development (Spanish), p. 35 ELL

Key

L1 Basic to Average	**L3** Average to Advanced	LPR Less Proficient Readers	GT Gifted and Talented
L2 For All Students		AR Advanced Readers	ELL English Language Learners
		SN Special Needs Students	

Reading Background

Simplified Outlining

When taking notes, utilizing the Power Notes strategy may help students differentiate between main ideas and details from their reading. Remind students that a Power Notes outline differs from a traditional outline in that it labels and organizes relationships among ideas in the reading. Level 1 should reflect the main idea. The following levels are details supporting either the main idea or the level it follows. Write the sample Power Notes outline on the board for the first section of the chapter.

> Level 1: The Nile River
> > Level 2: Egypt
> > > Level 3: Black Land
> > > Level 3: Red Land
> > Level 2: Nubia

Explain to students what the levels mean and how to create a Power Note outline. Have students develop their own Power Notes outline for the other sections in the chapter. Remind students that the outlines are good reference tools for answering section assessment questions or studying for quizzes and tests.

Encourage Active Participation

In this chapter, students will use the Numbered Heads Strategy to come up with and share their answers to questions. Remind students that it can be beneficial to compare their answers with those of other teams. Comparing responses provides students with other perspectives on a subject, additional answers to contemplate, and further clarification of their own answers. Below are sample language strategies to help students achieve this goal.

> *Our answer was (similar to/different from) that of team _____ because _____.*
> *We agree with team _____ that…*
> *As team _____ already pointed out, it seems like…*
> *Team _____ already mentioned…, but I would like to add that…*

World Studies Background

Controlling the Nile

Beginning around the 1800s people began to construct dams along the Nile River to control the water and improve irrigation. The most important of these dams is the Aswan High Dam, completed in 1970. While the dam has stopped the dangers to Egypt from annual flooding, some people believe that it has done more harm than good to the environment and that the Nile should remain in its natural state.

The Great Sphinx

One of the most amazing pieces of Egyptian art is the Great Sphinx, a huge limestone creation 240 feet long and 66 feet tall. In Egyptian mythology a sphinx is a creature with a lion's body and a human head. The creature also appears in Greek mythology, but with wings. Built around 2500 B.C. under the rule of King Khafre, the face of the Great Sphinx is probably a portrait of the king.

Sacred Cats

Around the year 1500 B.C. Egyptians began to domesticate cats. They were popular as pets for many Egyptian families. Cats were also useful for protecting food from vermin such as snakes and rats. Cats were so important to many Egyptians that when a pet cat died, its owners shaved their eyebrows in mourning.

Infoplease® provides a wealth of useful information for the classroom. You can use this resource to strengthen your background on the subjects covered in this chapter. Have students visit this advertising-free site as a starting point for projects requiring research.

Use Web code **lbd-2300** for **Infoplease®**.

Guiding Questions

Remind students about the Guiding Questions introduced at the beginning of the book.

Section 1 relates to **Guiding Question** ❶
How did physical geography affect the growth of ancient civilizations? *(Silt from the Nile River created rich farm land along the river's banks, allowing civilizations to develop.)*

Section 2 relates to **Guiding Question** ❹
How did ancient peoples develop governments? *(Egyptian pharoahs gave themselves absolute power over the people they ruled.)*

Section 3 relates to **Guiding Question** ❸
What were the beliefs and values of ancient peoples? *(Egyptians believed in an afterlife and in gods and goddesses that controlled nature.)*

Section 4 relates to **Guiding Question** ❷
What historical accomplishments is each civilization known for? *(heiroglyphs, determining the length of the year, using basic mathematics, developing natural remedies)*

Section 5 relates to **Guiding Question** ❶
How did geography affect the growth of ancient civilizations? *(Nubia was rich in mineral resources that it traded to Egypt.)*

🎯 Target Reading Skill

In this chapter, students will learn and apply the reading skill of cause and effect. Use the following worksheets to help students practice this skill:

All in One **Unit 2 History of Our World Teaching Resources,** *Use Context Clues: General,* p. 25; *Use Context Clues: Definition/Description,* p. 26; *Use Context Clues: Cause and Effect,* p. 27

⌐ Differentiated Instruction ¬

The following Teacher Edition strategies are suitable for students of varying abilities.

Advanced Readers, pp. 77, 98
English Language Learners, pp. 70, 91
Gifted and Talented, pp. 71, 95
Less Proficient Readers, pp. 77, 84, 86, 99
Special Needs Students, pp. 84, 90

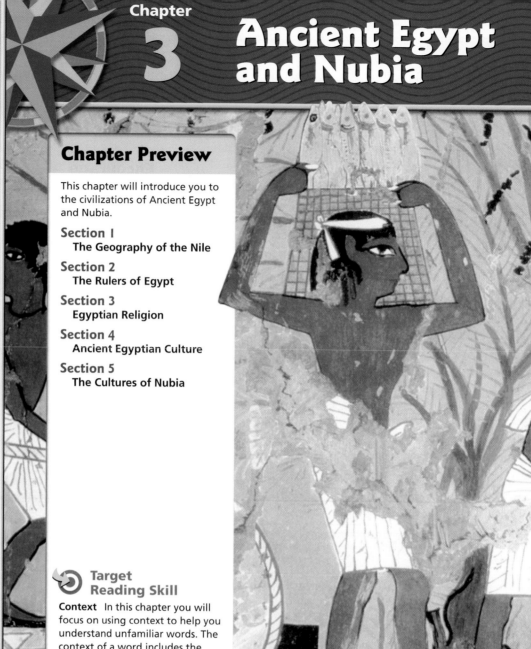

Chapter
3 Ancient Egypt and Nubia

Chapter Preview

This chapter will introduce you to the civilizations of Ancient Egypt and Nubia.

Section 1
The Geography of the Nile

Section 2
The Rulers of Egypt

Section 3
Egyptian Religion

Section 4
Ancient Egyptian Culture

Section 5
The Cultures of Nubia

🎯 Target Reading Skill

Context In this chapter you will focus on using context to help you understand unfamiliar words. The context of a word includes the words, phrases, and sentences surrounding the word.

▶ A tomb painting of Egyptian fishermen, dating from about 1292 to 1225 B.C.

Bibliography

For the Teacher

Collins, Robert O. *The Nile.* Yale University Press, 2002.

Reeves, C.N., Richard H. Wilkinson and Nicholas Reeves. *The Complete Valley of the Kings: Tombs and Treasures of Egypt's Greatest Pharoahs.* Thames and Hudson, 2002.

For the Student

L1 Morley, Jacqueline. *An Egyptian Pyramid.* Peter Bedrick Books, 2001.

L2 Russmann Ph. D., Edna R. *Nubian Kingdoms.* Franklin Watts Incorporated, 1999.

L3 Payne, Elizabeth. *The Pharoahs of Ancient Egypt.* Bt Bound, 1999.

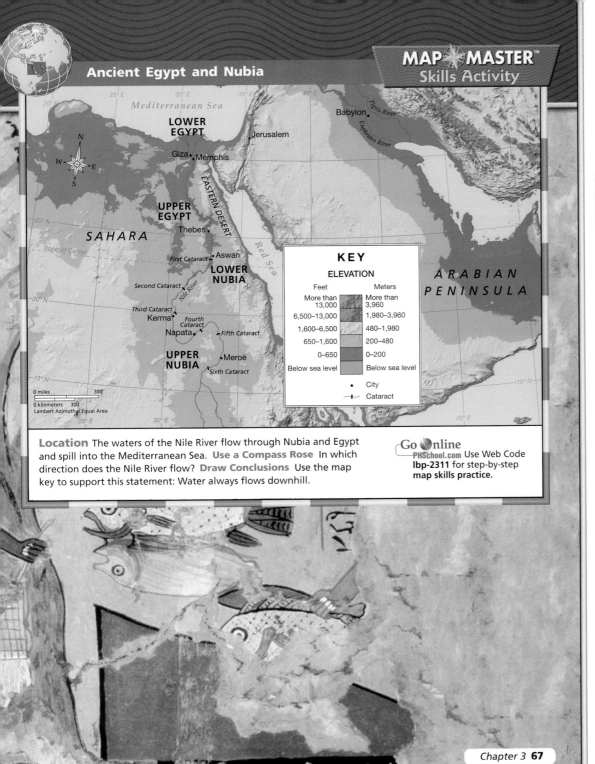

Ancient Egypt and Nubia

MAP MASTER™
Skills Activity

Mediterranean Sea

LOWER EGYPT

Jerusalem

Babylon

Giza • Memphis

Tigris River

Euphrates River

UPPER EGYPT

SAHARA

Thebes

EASTERN DESERT

Tropic of Cancer

First Cataract • Aswan

Red Sea

LOWER NUBIA

Second Cataract

Third Cataract

Nile River

Kerma •

Fourth Cataract

Napata •

Fifth Cataract

UPPER NUBIA

• Meroë

Sixth Cataract

ARABIAN PENINSULA

0 miles 300
0 kilometers 300
Lambert Azimuthal Equal Area

KEY
ELEVATION

Feet	Meters
More than 13,000	More than 3,960
6,500–13,000	1,980–3,960
1,600–6,500	480–1,980
650–1,600	200–480
0–650	0–200
Below sea level	Below sea level

• City
⌒ Cataract

Location The waters of the Nile River flow through Nubia and Egypt and spill into the Mediterranean Sea. **Use a Compass Rose** In which direction does the Nile River flow? **Draw Conclusions** Use the map key to support this statement: Water always flows downhill.

Go Online
PHSchool.com Use Web Code **lbp-2311** for step-by-step **map skills practice.**

MAP MASTER™
Skills Activity

Have students trace the flow of the Nile with their fingers from south to north and ask them to call out the names of the cities along the river as they pass them.

Go Online
PHSchool.com Students may practice their map skills using the interactive online version of this map.

Using the Visual L2

Reach Into Your Background Draw students' attention to the tomb painting on pages 66–67 and its caption. Discuss the visual and have students describe what the fishermen are doing. Ask **How do you think fishing contributed to the growth of ancient Egypt?** (*Possible answer: it provided food for the people and allowed the civilization to grow.*)

Answers

MAP MASTER™ Skills Activity **Use a Compass Rose** north **Draw Conclusions** The Nile flows from higher elevations of about 650–1,600 feet (200–480 meters) in Lower Nubia to lower elevations of about 0–650 feet (0–200 meters) where it empties into the Mediterranean Sea.

Chapter Resources

Teaching Resources
L2 Vocabulary Development, p. 38
L2 Skills for Life, p. 30
L2 Chapter Tests A and B, pp. 42–47

Spanish Support
L2 Spanish Chapter Summary, p. 34
L2 Spanish Vocabulary Development, p. 35

Media and Technology
L1 Student Edition on Audio CD
L1 Guided Reading Audio CDs, English and Spanish
L2 Social Studies Skills Tutor CD-ROM *ExamView®* Test Bank CD-ROM

DISCOVERY CHANNEL SCHOOL History of Our World Video Program

interactive Textbook

PRENTICE HALL
TeacherEXPRESS™
Plan • Teach • Assess

Section 1
Step-by-Step Instruction

Objectives

Social Studies

1. Find out how the geography of the Nile changes as the river runs its course.

2. Learn about the types of communities that first appeared along the Nile, and how the Nile was used for trade.

Reading/Language Arts

Use context clues to help understand the meaning of an unfamiliar word.

Prepare to Read

Build Background Knowledge L2

In this section students will learn about the Nile River and how it influenced ancient Egypt and Nubia. Have students preview the headings and visuals in this section with the following question in mind: **What were the benefits of living along the Nile?** Use the Idea Wave participation strategy (TE, p. T39) to generate a list.

Set a Purpose for Reading L2

■ Preview the Objectives.

■ Read each statement in the *Reading Readiness Guide* aloud. Ask students to mark the statements true or false.

> **All in One Unit 2 History of Our World Teaching Resources,** *Reading Readiness Guide,* p. 6

■ Have students discuss the statements in pairs or groups of four, then mark their guides again. Use the Numbered Heads participation strategy (TE, p. T40) to call on students to share their group's perspectives.

Vocabulary Builder
Preview Key Terms L2

Pronounce each Key Term, then ask the students to say the word with you. Provide a simple explanation such as, "Silt is rich soil usually found at the bottom of a river."

Answers

Analyze Images Gifts shown include fish, wild fowl, and vegetation.

Section 1
The Geography of the Nile

Prepare to Read

Objectives

In this section you will

1. Find out how the geography of the Nile changes as the river runs its course.

2. Learn about the types of communities that first appeared along the Nile, and how the Nile was used for trade.

Taking Notes

As you read, note the effects the Nile had on the growth of communities and trade. Copy the chart below, and use it to record your findings.

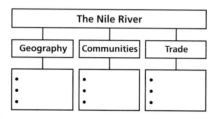

Target Reading Skill

Use Context Clues When reading, you may come across an unfamiliar word, or a word that is used in an unfamiliar way. Look for clues in the context—the surrounding words, sentences, and paragraphs—to help you understand the meaning. Look at the context for the word *sediment* on page 72 in the paragraph that begins with The Gifts of the Nile. What do you think *sediment* means?

Key Terms

• **Nubia** (NOO bee uh) *n.* an ancient region in the Nile River Valley, on the site of present-day southern Egypt and nothern Sudan

• **cataract** (KAT uh rakt) *n.* a large waterfall; any strong flood or rush of water

• **delta** (DEL tuh) *n.* a plain at the mouth of a river, formed when sediment is deposited by flowing water

• **silt** (silt) *n.* fine soil found on river bottoms

The Greek historian Herodotus (huh RAHD uh tus) wrote, "Egypt is the gift of the Nile." Herodotus explored Egypt in the 400s B.C. On his journey, he saw the life-giving waters of its great river. He traveled upriver until he was stopped by churning rapids of white water. Forced to turn back, he never found the source of the river.

Herodotus wrote down his observations of Egypt and other lands. His writings still make interesting reading today. Despite his failure to locate the source of the Nile, Herodotus had learned a basic truth: There would be no Egypt without the Nile.

River of Life
An Egyptian uses a throwstick, a sort of boomerang, to hunt for birds from his boat. **Analyze Images** *What gifts of the Nile are shown in this painting?*

68 History of Our World

Target Reading Skill L2

Use Context Clues Point out the Target Reading Skill. Tell students that information surrounding an unknown word can provide clues to the word's meaning.

Model the skill by using context clues to find the meaning of *gratitude* in the following sentences from p. 70: "By late summer the Nile spilled over its banks all the way to the delta. The floodwaters deposited a thick layer of silt, making the land ideal for farm-ing. In gratitude, the Egyptians praised Hapi, the god of the Nile…" *(The surrounding sentences and the word* praised *provide clues that* gratitude *means "thankfulness.")*

Give students *Use Context Clues: General.* Have them complete the activity in groups.

> **All in One Unit 2 History of Our World Teaching Resources,** *Use Context Clues: General,* p. 25

The Course of the Nile River

The Nile River is the world's longest river. It flows north from its sources in East Africa to the Mediterranean Sea for more than 4,000 miles (6,400 kilometers). That is about the distance from New York to Alaska. The Nile has two main sources. The Blue Nile rises in the highlands of the present-day country of Ethiopia and races down to the desert in thundering torrents. The White Nile is calmer. It begins deep in East Africa and flows northward through swamps. The two rivers meet in the present-day country of Sudan. There, the Nile begins its journey through desert lands to the Mediterranean Sea.

The Nile Through Ancient Nubia Just north of the point where the Blue Nile and White Nile meet, the Nile makes two huge bends. It forms an S shape 1,000 miles (1,600 kilometers) in length. The northern tip of the S is at the city of Aswan in Egypt. Along this stretch of the Nile was **Nubia,** an ancient region in the Nile River valley.

The Nubian section of the Nile contained six **cataracts,** or rock-filled rapids. Between the first and second cataracts was Lower Nubia. In that region, the desert and granite mountains lined the riverbanks, leaving very little land for farming. Because it rarely rained in Lower Nubia, people had to live close to the Nile for their water supply.

Farther south, between the second and sixth cataracts, lies the area that was known as Upper Nubia. In that region, rain does fall, so people could plant in the fall and then harvest in the spring. But the farmland was in a very narrow strip, no more than 2 miles (3 kilometers) wide on each side of the river.

Nubia's Resources
Nubian princes bring gifts of gold to an Egyptian ruler. **Infer** *How did geography help link the cultures of Egypt and Nubia?*

Learn about life on the Nile.

Instruct

The Course of the Nile River L2

Guided Instruction

■ **Vocabulary Builder** Clarify the high-use words **source** and **isolate** before reading.

■ Read The Course of the Nile River, using the Oral Cloze strategy (TE, p. T37).

■ Ask **Which cataracts did Lower Nubia lie between?** *(the first and second cataracts)* **Where was Upper Nubia located?** *(between the second and sixth cataracts)*

■ Discuss with students the landscape and climate of Ancient Nubia. Ask **Do you think that the flow of the Nile through this region was important to these ancient peoples? Why or why not?** *(The flow of the Nile was important because it provided a constant source of water for drinking and for farming.)* Use the Give One, Get One strategy (TE, p. T41) to involve all students in the discussion.

Show students *Ancient Egypt, Life on the Nile.* Ask **What needs did the Nile fulfill for ancient Egyptians?** *(The Nile provided a constant source of water for drinking and for farming the land. It also provided a route of access to other places where they could trade their crops for resources they needed.)*

Answer

Infer The Nile linked Nubia and Egypt. The people of Egypt and Nubia could easily travel to each other's kingdom on the Nile.

Vocabulary Builder

Use the information below to teach students this section's high-use words.

High-Use Word	Definition and Sample Sentence
source, p. 69	*n.* the point of origin of something The plumber could not locate the **source** of the leak.
isolate, p. 71	*v.* to set apart from others To prevent the spread of the disease, the sick were kept **isolated.**

Guided Instruction (continued)

- Have students describe the land of Lower Egypt. (*Fertile, marshy land made up Lower Egypt. Deserts stretched on each side of the river's green banks.*)

- Help students to compare the ancient Egyptian section of the Nile to the ancient Nubian section. Encourage students to think about the quality of the farmland in each section. (*The Egyptian section of the Nile is located farther north and does not have cataracts like the Nubian section. The Egyptian section had more fertile land than the Nubian section.*) Ask **How does Egypt's location farther north contribute to the richness of the land?** (*As the Nile flows out to sea, it deposits sediment that makes the land fertile for farming. Also, in the spring, the highlands in the north cause the Nile to flood dry lands and deposit silt in this same region.*)

⮌ Target Reading Skill

Using Context Clues As a follow up, ask students to answer the Target Reading Skill question in the Student Edition. (*Students should be able to infer that* sediment *is material deposited by water.*)

Using Context Clues In the paragraph at the right, sediment is described as being mineral rich and carried by water. If you read ahead, you will learn that silt is a kind of sediment What is the meaning of *sediment?*

The Nile Through Ancient Egypt The Nile ran for about 700 miles (1,100 kilometers) through ancient Egypt, from the First Cataract at Aswan to the Mediterranean Sea. On its way, it passed through a narrow region called Upper Egypt. This fertile strip had an average width of around 6 miles (10 kilometers) on each side of the river. In the north, the Nile spread out to form a fertile, marshy area called Lower Egypt. Deserts stretched on each side of the river's green banks.

At the end of the Nile in the north, the river split into several streams that flowed to the Mediterranean Sea. These streams formed an area called the delta. A **delta** is a plain at the mouth of a river. The flowing water deposited mineral-rich sediment. Because of this, the Nile delta contained very fertile farmland.

The Gifts of the Nile Every spring, far away in the highlands of Africa, waters began to rush downstream. As they flowed, they brought a rich, fertile sediment called silt. **Silt** is fine soil found on river bottoms. By late summer, the Nile spilled over its banks all the way to the delta. The floodwaters deposited a thick layer of silt, making the land ideal for farming. In gratitude, the Egyptians praised Hapi (HAH pea), the god of the Nile:

> **❝Hail to you, O Nile, who flows from the Earth and comes to keep Egypt alive.❞**
>
> —*ancient Egyptian prayer*

Differentiated Instruction

For English Language Learners 🄛🄸

Pair English Language Learners with native English speakers to complete the *Guided Reading and Review*. If appropriate, give English language learners *Guided Reading and Review (Spanish)* and ask them to work with their partners to answer the questions in English.

📄 *Guided Reading and Review (Spanish),* **History of Our World Spanish Support,** p. 24

🄰🄻🄻 in One **Unit 2 History of Our World Teaching Resource,** *Guided Reading and Review,* p. 7

Black Land and Red Land The ancient Egyptians called their land Kemet (KEH met), "the black land," because of the dark soil left by the Nile's floods. The timing of the floods and the height of the floodwaters might vary from year to year. But unlike the Mesopotamians, the Egyptians usually did not have to worry about flash floods. Dry years were rare in Egypt, but they could cause famine.

Beyond the fertile river banks lay the "red land," the vast desert. It spread out on either side of the river. Most of the Sahara lay to the west, and the part of the Sahara called the Eastern Desert lay to the east. These lands were not friendly to human life. They were useless for farming. Only those who knew the deserts well dared travel over this blistering-hot land.

Desert Protection The hot sands shielded Egypt and Nubia from foreign attacks. That was a protection Mesopotamia did not have. The land between the Tigris and Euphrates rivers was wide open to outsiders. The people of Mesopotamia often faced invasions. Over a period of 2,000 years, the people of ancient Egypt and Nubia faced few invasions. Yet they were not isolated. The Nile valley provided a path for trade with Central Africa. The Mediterranean Sea and the Red Sea provided access to Southwest Asia.

✓ **Reading Check** How did the people of Nubia and Egypt benefit from the geography of the region?

Geography and Civilization
In the large photo below, you can see the date palms and fields that line the Nile River near the city of Luxor. The small photo shows the desert landscape that surrounds the Nile.
Analyze Images *Compare the two photos. What are the challenges of living in the desert? What are the advantages of living along the Nile?*

Differentiated Instruction

For Gifted and Talented
L3

Have students work in pairs or small groups to create a rough map that shows the course of the Nile from East Africa to the Mediterranean Sea. Be sure they label the cataracts in ancient Nubia and Upper and Lower Egypt. Remind students to include a map key. Display *Color Transparency AW 13: Southwest Asia and North Africa: Political* to help them plot the course of the Nile River.

📖 **History of Our World Transparencies,** *Color Transparency HOW 16: Southwest Asia and North Africa: Political*

- Ask **Why did ancient Egyptians call their land Kemet?** *(Kemet means "the black land." Egyptians referred to their land this way because it was composed of the dark soil left by the Nile's floods.)* **What was the "red land?"** *(the desert that spread out on either side of the Nile)*

- Ask students **Why did the people of Egypt and Nubia face few invasions?** *(The desert shielded the civilizations from attack.)*

Independent Practice

Ask students to create the Taking Notes graphic organizer on a blank piece of paper. Then have them fill in the "Geography" section with the information they have just learned. Briefly model how to identify which details to record.

Monitor Progress

As students fill in the graphic organizer, circulate and make sure individuals are choosing the correct details. Provide assistance as needed.

Answers

Analyze Images Possible answers: Challenges faced in the desert include finding water for drinking, and being able to produce enough food to survive. Advantages to living along the Nile include easy access to drinking water, fish, and fertile farmland.

✓ **Reading Check** The ancient Egyptians and Nubians were surrounded by hot deserts that kept them isolated from invaders. However, they had waterways, such as the Nile, that provided drinking water, and allowed them to trade with other peoples and irrigate for farming.

The Growth of Communities and Trade Along the Nile L2

Guided Instruction

- Read The Growth of Communities and Trade Along the Nile. As students read, circulate and make sure individuals can answer the Reading Check question.

- Ask **How were Egyptian and Nubian communities similar?** (*Both had farming communities and traded.*)

- Discuss the ways that Egyptians and Nubians traded with other peoples. (*Egyptians traveled on the Nile and also in caravans over land to trade with other people. The Nubians traded only by land routes because of the cataracts. Like the Egyptians, they traveled in caravans.*)

Independent Practice

Ask students to complete the second and third sections of their graphic organizer with the information they have just learned.

Monitor Progress

- Show *Section Reading Support Transparency HOW 61* and ask students to check their graphic organizers individually. Go over key concepts and clarify key vocabulary as needed.

  History of Our World Transparencies, *Section Reading Support Transparency HOW 61*

- Tell students to fill in the last column of the *Reading Readiness Guide*. Probe for what they learned that confirms or invalidates each statement.

  All in One Unit 2 History of Our World Teaching Resources, *Reading Readiness,* p. 6

Links

Read the **Links Across Time** on this page. Ask students **Why do you think it was important to save the temples?** (*The temples are part of the ancient heritage of the world's people.*)

The Growth of Communities and Trade Along the Nile

Settled hunting and fishing communities may have appeared in Nubia around 6000 B.C. Unlike the communities of the Fertile Crescent that settled after taking up agriculture, the Nubians formed settlements before they began to farm. Settled farming communities began to appear in both Egypt and Nubia sometime around 5000 B.C. As these communities grew, trade also expanded.

Living Along the Nile Egypt's early farming communities settled in the delta and valley regions of the Nile. The people of the delta built villages around the fertile river beds. Their homes were built of straw or of bricks made from a mix of mud and straw. To the south, in Upper Egypt, people built scattered farming villages along the banks of the Nile.

Nubia had less farmland along the Nile than Egypt. Because of the shortage of farmland, Nubians added to their diet by fishing in the Nile and hunting ducks and other birds along its banks.

Links Across Time

Saving Monuments To control flooding, the Egyptians built the Aswan High Dam on the Nile River in the 1960s. The water held back by the dam created Lake Nasser. During its creation, Lake Nasser threatened to flood ancient monuments that had been carved in the cliffs above the Nubian Nile. Egypt, with the help of about 50 nations, saved some of the monuments. At a site called Abu Simbel, the temple of Ramses II (below) was saved. Workers cut the temple into blocks. They moved the blocks to higher ground and then rebuilt the temple.

Background: Links Across Time

Ancient and Modern Crops Farming is still an important part of life in Egypt. Farmers still rely upon the Nile to provide water for their crops, but today, systems of canals and dams along the Nile supply year-round irrigation. As in ancient Egypt, most farmland is in the Nile Valley, and the wheat and date crops that were grown by the ancient Egyptians are still major crops. Because of irrigation, modern Egypt grows some crops, such as cotton, that were not grown in ancient times. In fact, thanks to irrigation, Egypt is one of the world's major producers of cotton.

A Highway for Trade In Egypt, the Nile was used to transport goods. Ships could travel north on the Nile because it was moving downriver. But they could also sail upriver with the help of the winds that blew toward the south. Other trade links ran east across the desert to the Red Sea ports or to Mesopotamia. Caravans loaded with gold, silver, copper, and fine pottery traveled the overland trade routes. Valuable goods such as cedar from the eastern coast of the Mediterranean Sea and gold from Nubia were sold in the bazaars of Egypt's towns.

Routes Through Nubia Because of the cataracts, people could not travel through Nubia by river. Instead, the Nubians developed trade routes over land. The Nubians became famous traders of the ancient world. They carried goods from central Africa and Nubia into Egypt and southwestern Asia and brought other goods back.

One Nubian caravan that traveled into Egypt had 300 donkeys. The donkeys carried ebony wood, ivory from elephant tusks, ostrich feathers and eggs, and panther skins. Another popular object was a throwstick, a type of boomerang that Africans used for hunting.

✓ **Reading Check** How did the Nile operate as a "highway for trade"?

Nubians traded many valuable goods. This Nubian bronze mirror with a gilt silver handle, from about 700 B.C., was found in present-day Sudan.

Section 1 Assessment

Key Terms
Review the key terms at the beginning of this section. Use each term in a sentence that explains its meaning.

Target Reading Skill
Find the word *torrents* on page 69. Use context clues to find the meaning of *torrents*.

Comprehension and Critical Thinking
1. (a) Recall Describe the course of the Nile River from its source all the way to the delta.

(b) Identify Cause and Effect How did the Nile River affect the lives of the early Egyptians and Nubians?
(c) Predict If the Nile did not flood regularly, how might life along the river have been different in ancient times?
2. (a) List What kinds of trade goods passed through Nubia on their way to Egypt?
(b) Identify Effects How did the cataracts of the Nile River affect Nubian trade?
(c) Draw Conclusions How did the Nubians become famous as traders?

Writing Activity
Suppose that you are traveling along the Nile from its source to the Nile delta. Write a journal entry about the changes you notice in the river as you travel.

Go Online
PHSchool.com
For: An activity on the Nile River
Visit: PHSchool.com
Web Code: lbd-2301

Chapter 3 Section 1 **73**

Section 1 Assessment

Key Terms
Students' sentences should reflect knowledge of each Key Term.

Target Reading Skill
Students should be able to use the context clues to learn that *torrents* are fast, violent streams of water.

Comprehension and Critical Thinking
1. (a) As the White Nile in East Africa flows north, it meets the Blue Nile. The Nile then flows along the 1,000-mile stretch of land once called Nubia and through the Egyptian section of the Nile—another 700 miles—to the Mediterranean. **(b)** The Nile brought the ancient Egyptians and Nubians a constant source of water, allowing them to fish, farm, trade, and build communities along its banks. **(c)** The land might have been less fertile.

Assess Progress `L2`
Have students complete the Section Assessment. Administer the *Section Quiz*.

All in One **Unit 2 History of Our World Teaching Resources,** *Section Quiz,* p. 8

Reteach `L1`
If students need more instruction, have them read this section in the Reading and Vocabulary Study Guide.

📖 Chapter 3, Section 1, **History of Our World Reading and Vocabulary Study Guide**, pp. 32–34

Extend `L3`
Have students begin working in small groups to complete *Creating a Multimedia Presentation: Rivers and People.*

Go Online
PHSchool.com
For: Long-Term Integrated Projects:
Creating a Multimedia Presentation: Rivers and People
Visit: PHSchool.com
Web Code: lbd-2306

Answers

✓ **Reading Check** Ships could float downriver or sail upriver to the many ports along the banks of the Nile.

Writing Activity
Use the *Rubric for Assessing a Journal Entry* to evaluate students' journal entries.

All in One **Unit 2 History of Our World Teaching Resources,** *Rubric for Assessing a Journal Entry,* p. 39

Go Online
PHSchool.com Typing in the Web code when prompted will bring students directly to detailed instructions for this activity.

There might then have been less farming, less food, and, therefore, less people.

2. (a) Goods included ebony wood, ivory, ostrich feathers and eggs, panther skins, and throw-sticks. **(b)** The cataracts prevented Nubians from trading by traveling on the river, so Nubian trade routes had to be over land. **(c)** They carried their goods in huge caravans through and to many distant lands.

Section 2
Step-by-Step Instruction

Objectives

Social Studies

1. Learn about the history of kingship in ancient Egypt.
2. Find out about Egypt's accomplishments during each of the three kingdom periods.
3. Understand what characterized the rule of Egypt during the New Kingdom period.

Reading/Language Arts

Use restatement in context to determine the meaning of an unfamiliar word.

Prepare to Read

Build Background Knowledge L2

Tell students that in this section they will learn about the pharaohs and the kingdoms of Egypt. Have students preview the headings and visuals in this section with the following question in mind: **How does the art and architecture illustrate the advanced culture of ancient Egypt?** Have students engage in a Think-Write-Pair-Share activity (TE, p. T40) to share their answers.

Set a Purpose for Reading L2

■ Preview the Objectives.

■ Form students into pairs or groups of four. Distribute the *Reading Readiness Guide.* Ask the students to fill in the first two columns of the chart. Use the Numbered Heads participation strategy (TE, p. T40) to call on students to share one piece of information they already know and one piece of information they want to know.

All in One Unit 2 History of Our World Teaching Resources, *Reading Readiness Guide, Journal Entry,* p. 10

Vocabulary Builder
Preview Key Terms L2

Pronounce each Key Term, then ask the students to say the word with you. Provide a simple explanation such as, "If a teacher had absolute power over a class, she might be able to decide what students can wear to class, what they will learn, what they can eat for lunch, and even with whom they may be friends."

Section 2   The Rulers of Egypt

Prepare to Read

Objectives

In this section you will
1. Learn about the history of kingship in ancient Egypt.
2. Find out about Egypt's accomplishments during each of the three kingdom periods.
3. Understand what characterized the rule of Egypt during the New Kingdom period.

Taking Notes

As you read, look for the main ideas about ancient Egyptian rulers. Copy the diagram below, and record your findings in it.

Ancient Egyptian Rulers

Target Reading Skill

Use Context Clues When you read an unfamiliar word, you can sometimes figure out its meaning from clues in the context. Sometimes the context will restate the word. The following phrase, for example, restates the meaning of *sphinx*: "a legendary creature with a lion's body and a human head." As you read, look at the context for the word *timber* on page 78. What do you think *timber* means?

Key Terms

- **pharaoh** (FEHR oh) *n.* the title of the kings of ancient Egypt
- **dynasty** (DY nus tee) *n.* a series of rulers from the same family or ethnic group
- **absolute power** (AB suh loot POW ur) *n.* complete control over someone or something
- **regent** (REE junt) *n.* someone who rules for a child until the child is old enough to rule

A sculpture of Queen Hatshepsut as a sphinx, a legendary creature with a lion's body and a human head

She seized control of Egypt's throne and made herself **pharaoh** (FEHR oh), the title used by the kings of Egypt. Hatshepsut (haht SHEP soot) was not the only woman to rule Egypt. But the title of pharaoh was traditionally held by men. Hatshepsut took on all the responsibilities of a pharaoh. Sometimes she even wore the false beard traditionally worn by pharaohs. Like all Egyptian pharaohs, Hatshepsut controlled the wealth and power of a great civilization.

Egyptian Kingship

Hatshepsut was one of many famous Egyptian pharaohs who ruled Egypt. Some, like her, were wise. Others were careless or cruel. Egypt's fortunes rested on the strength of its pharaohs.

Target Reading Skill L2

Use Context Clues Draw student's attention to the Target Reading Skill. Tell them that sometimes they can find the meaning of an unfamiliar word restated in the same sentence in which it appears, or in a surrounding sentence.

Model the skill by reading the first paragraph on p. 75. Point out that the meaning of the word *kingdom* in this context is restated twice, once within the sentence it appears and once at the end of the paragraph.

Give students *Use Context Clues: Definition/Description.* Have them complete the activity in groups.

All in One Unit 2 History of Our World Teaching Resources, *Use Context Clues: Definition/Description,* p. 26

From Dynasty to Dynasty The history of ancient Egypt is the history of each of its dynasties. A **dynasty** is a series of rulers from the same family or ethnic group. Egypt had 31 dynasties, from about 3100 B.C. until it was conquered in 332 B.C. Historians group Egypt's dynasties into three major time periods, called kingdoms. The earliest major time period is called the Old Kingdom. Next comes the Middle Kingdom. The latest time period is called the New Kingdom. The timeline titled Major Time Periods in Ancient Egypt on page 76 shows the approximate dates of each kingdom. Remember, these kingdoms are not places. They are time periods.

The gaps between the kingdoms were times of troubles—wars, invasions, or weak rulers. These in-between periods were rare, however. For most of ancient Egyptian history, rule was stable.

Egypt Is Unified According to legend, Egypt's first dynasty began when a king named Menes (MEE neez) united Upper and Lower Egypt. Menes built a city named Memphis near the present-day city of Cairo (KY roh). From there, he ruled over the Two Lands, the name the ancient Egyptians gave to Upper and Lower Egypt. Carvings from Menes' time show a pharaoh named Narmer wearing two crowns—the white crown of Upper Egypt and the red crown of Lower Egypt. Some historians believe that Menes and Narmer may have been the same man. The unification of Egypt was the beginning of one of the most stable civilizations in history.

All-Powerful Pharaohs The pharaohs had **absolute power,** or complete control over their people. For help in making decisions, they could turn to their advisors or appeal to Ma'at, the goddess of truth. In the end, whatever the pharaoh decided became law. For example, he decided when the fields would be planted. At harvest time, he demanded crops from the workers in the fields.

The Narmer Palette
This two-sided tablet honors the unification of Upper and Lower Egypt by a king named Narmer.
❶ Narmer wears symbols of Egyptian kingship: the cone-shaped crown of Upper Egypt and a false beard and tail. He prepares to strike the enemy.
❷ The falcon represents Horus, the god of kingship.
❸ Reed plants, which grow in the Nile delta, represent Lower Egypt.
❹ A royal sandal bearer carries Narmer's shoes. **Predict** *Narmer wears a different crown on the opposite side of the tablet. What crown do you think he wears?*

Chapter 3 Section 2 **75**

Instruct

Egyptian Kingship L2

Guided Instruction

- **Vocabulary Builder** Clarify the high-use word **approximate** before reading.

- Read Egyptian Kingship, using the ReQuest technique (TE, p. T39).

- Ask students **When did Egypt's first dynasty begin?** *(about 3100 B.C., when Menes first united Upper and Lower Egypt)*

- Discuss why the text refers to pharaohs as "god-kings." *(Egyptians believed pharaohs had god-like powers, such as the power to provide floods and harvests.)*

- Ask students **Should one person be allowed to create the laws for an entire society? Why or why not?** *(Possible answers: Yes—if the ruler is wise and truly concerned about his people, he or she might provide guidance and stability for the people. No—one person cannot possibly know what is best for everyone.)*

Independent Practice

Ask students to create the Taking Notes graphic organizer on a blank piece of paper. Give guidance by suggesting they use a main idea from each of the subsections for each circle in their organizers. Help them identify the main idea of the first subsection to get them started. Then have them fill out the main idea of the second subsection on their own.

Monitor Progress

As students fill in the graphic organizer, circulate and make sure individuals are able to locate the main ideas. Help students as needed.

Vocabulary Builder

Use the information below to teach students this section's high-use words.

High-Use Word	Definition and Sample Sentence
approximate, p. 75	*adj.* nearly correct or exact The **approximate** distance from here to the store is one mile.
restore, p. 77	*v.* to put or bring back into existence or use The artist was able to **restore** the damaged sculpture.
proclaim, p. 78	*v.* to declare to be officially or formally After adding the votes, she was **proclaimed** the winner.
yield, p. 78	*v.* to surrender to the physical control of another Joe retired and **yielded** the business to his son.

Answer

Predict The crown of lower Egypt.

The Three Kingdoms L2

Guided Instruction

- **Vocabulary Builder** Clarify the high-use word **restore** before reading.

- Read about Egypt's three main time periods in The Three Kingdoms.

- Discuss the major accomplishments achieved during each kingdom. *(The Old Kingdom pharaohs kept the peace and traded with Nubia. They also imported timber to build boats and furniture. Land was irrigated and canals were built during the Middle Kingdom. Huge, powerful armies were created during the New Kingdom.)*

➔ Target Reading Skill

Use Context Clues As a follow up, ask students to answer the Target Reading Skill question in the Student Edition. *(Timber is trees used for building.)*

Major Time Periods in Ancient Egypt

c. 3100 B.C.
Egypt is unified.

c. 2686–2181 B.C.
Old Kingdom
(Dynasties 3–6)

c. 1991–1786 B.C.
Middle Kingdom
(Dynasty 12)

c. 1567–1085 B.C.
New Kingdom
(Dynasties 18–20)

3000 B.C.   2700 B.C.   2400 B.C.   2100 B.C.   1800 B.C.   1500 B.C.   1200 B.C.

Old Kingdom
- c. 2589 B.C.
Builders begin Great Pyramid.
- c. 2533 B.C.
Great Sphinx statue is completed.

Middle Kingdom
- c. 1991–1786 B.C.
Egypt expands into Lower Nubia. Literature and art flourish.

New Kingdom
- c. 1503–1482 B.C.
Queen Hatshepsut rules.
- c. 1504–1450 B.C.
Reign of Thutmose III; empire expands into Syria.

■ Timeline Skills

Notice the three time periods called kingdoms, as well as the number of years between the kingdoms. **Identify** How many dynasties ruled from 2686 to 2181 B.C.? How many ruled from 2181 to 1991 B.C.? **Infer** During which of those two time periods was Egypt most stable? Explain your answer.

Use Context Clues
Target Skill If you do not know what timber is, look for context clues. Find a restatement of the word *timber*. Then reread what the Egyptians used timber for. What is timber?

Ancient Egyptians believed that their pharaohs were the earthly form of Horus, the falcon god. Over time, pharaohs came to be connected with other gods, including the sun god Re (ray). In this way, the pharaohs were god-kings. It was the pharaoh, Egyptians believed, who provided his people with the Nile's yearly floods and the harvests that followed.

"He is the god Re whose beams enable us to see.
He gives more light to the Two Lands than the sun's disc.
He makes Earth more green than the Nile in flood.
He has filled the Two Lands with strength and life."
—*an official of ancient Egypt*

✔ **Reading Check** Who was Menes and what did he accomplish?

The Three Kingdoms

Important events and achievements marked each of Egypt's three kingdoms. The Old Kingdom was noted for its well-run system of government.

The Old Kingdom The Old Kingdom pharaohs kept the peace and traded with Nubia, with only occasional conflicts. They sent merchants to the eastern coast of the Mediterranean to find timber, trees used for building. The timber was used to make houses, boats, and furniture. Merchants may have traveled north across the Mediterranean in search of trade items.

Toward the end of the Old Kingdom, governors in the provinces began to challenge the power of the pharaohs' government. Egypt's unity crumbled, and the dynasties grew weak.

76 History of Our World

Answers
Timeline Skills Identify four; none
Infer Possible answer: Egypt was probably more stable from 2686–2181 B.C. because rulers were firmly in control of the civilization, unlike the period from 2181 to 1991 B.C. when Egypt's unity crumbled and dynasties were weak.

✔ **Reading Check** Menes was the first leader of Egypt's first dynasty. He united Upper and Lower Egypt.

Skills for Life Skills Mini Lesson

Synthesizing Information

1. Explain that when you synthesize something, you put together pieces of information to draw a conclusion.

2. Help students practice the skill by synthesizing the information in the timeline on p. 76 and the map and its caption on p. 77 to determine whether the following conclusion is true or false: Egypt expanded under the rule of Queen Hatshepsut. *(true)*

3. Have students apply the skill by using the map and timeline to answer the following question: **Who ruled Egypt when the empire was the size shown on the map?** *(Thutmose III)*

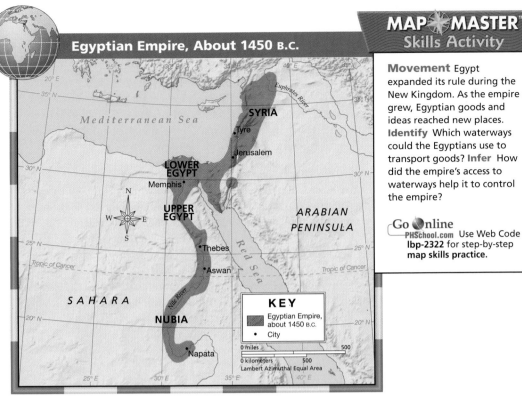

Egyptian Empire, About 1450 B.C.

MAP MASTER™
Skills Activity

Movement Egypt expanded its rule during the New Kingdom. As the empire grew, Egyptian goods and ideas reached new places. **Identify** Which waterways could the Egyptians use to transport goods? **Infer** How did the empire's access to waterways help it to control the empire?

Go Online
PHSchool.com Use Web Code lbp-2322 for step-by-step map skills practice.

KEY
▨ Egyptian Empire, about 1450 B.C.
• City

0 miles 500
0 kilometers 500
Lambert Azimuthal Equal Area

The Middle Kingdom The early rulers of the Middle Kingdom restored order and reunited the country. Pharaohs spent the nation's wealth on public works instead of on wars. For example, they constructed buildings and irrigation projects. Egypt grew even richer. However, weaker and less able rulers followed. In time, they lost control of the country to foreign invaders.

The New Kingdom Egyptian princes became strong enough to drive out the foreign invaders. This event marks the start of the New Kingdom, which began in 1567 B.C. The first pharaohs of the New Kingdom wanted to build an empire. They created huge armies of foot soldiers, mounted warriors, and charioteers. Bronze swords and body armor made the Egyptians nearly unbeatable. One New Kingdom pharaoh is of special interest to scholars. King Tutankhamen became ruler of Egypt while he was still a child. At about age 18 he died and was buried with many precious objects. An archaeologist discovered his tomb in 1922. Since then, studies of Tutankhamen's funeral treasures have taught us a great deal about the ancient Egyptians.

✓ **Reading Check** What characterized each of the three kingdoms?

A gold portrait mask was one of the many treasures found in King Tutankhamen's tomb.

Chapter 3 Section 2 **77**

Independent Practice

Tell students to continue to fill in their graphic organizers with the information they have just learned. Tell them that to add one circle each for Old Kingdom rulers, Middle Kingdom rulers, and New Kingdom rulers.

Monitor Progress

As students fill in the graphic organizer, circulate and make sure individuals are able to locate the main ideas. Provide assistance as needed.

Answers

MAP MASTER Skills Activity **Identify** The Mediterranean Sea, the Red Sea, the Euphrates River, and the Nile River. **Infer** The Egyptians were able to use the waterways to trade, which increased their wealth. They used this wealth to build powerful armies. Egyptians could also travel to other lands via the waterways to conquer them.

Go Online
PHSchool.com Students may practice their map skills using the interactive online version of this map.

✓ **Reading Check** The Old Kingdom was characterized by peace and trade with Nubia and the overthrow of the pharaoh by his governors. The construction of buildings and irrigation projects, and invasions by outside forces took place during the Middle Kingdom. The New Kingdom was marked by the building of its army and the creation of armor and weaponry.

Differentiated Instruction

For Advanced Readers L3
Have students conduct Internet and library research to learn about a pharaoh who ruled during the Old, Middle, or New Kingdom. Then have them write a brief biography about the ruler providing information such as when the pharaoh ruled, the pharaoh's major accomplishments, and any other important information.

For Less Proficient Readers L1
Have students create a table to help them organize information about the three kingdoms. Columns should be labeled Old Kingdom, Middle Kingdom, and New Kingdom. Have them paraphrase each of these subsections from the Student Edition in their tables. Circulate to make sure the students understand what they have read.

Rule During the New Kingdom

Guided Instruction

- **Vocabulary Builder** Clarify the high-use words **proclaim** and **yield** before reading.

- Read Rule During the New Kingdom. Make sure individuals can answer the Reading Check question.

- Ask students **Why was Thutmose III considered to be one of the greatest pharaohs of the New Kingdom?** *(He conquered many lands, yet he treated conquered peoples with mercy.)*

Independent Practice

Ask students to complete their graphic organizers by filling in the main ideas they have just learned.

Monitor Progress

- Show *Section Reading Support Transparency HOW 62* and ask students to check their graphic organizers individually. Go over key concepts and clarify key vocabulary as needed.

  📖 **History of Our World Transparencies,** *Section Reading Support Transparency HOW 62*

- Tell students to fill in the last column of the *Reading Readiness Guide.* Ask them to evaluate if what they learned was what they had expected to learn.

  All in One **Unit 2 History of Our World Teaching Resources,** *Reading Readiness Guide,* p. 10

Assess and Reteach

Assess Progress

L2

Have students complete the Section Assessment. Administer the *Section Quiz.*

All in One **Unit 2 History of Our World Teaching Resources,** *Section Quiz,* p. 12

Reteach

L1

If students need more instruction, have them read this section in the Reading and Vocabulary Study Guide.

📖 Chapter 3, Section 2, **History of Our World Reading and Vocabulary Study Guide,** pp. 35–37

Answer

Analyze Possible answers: the temple's size, numerous levels, and carvings

---

Deir el-Bahri, Thebes
This temple built by Queen Hatshepsut was set into a cliff on the west bank of the Nile River.

1 The lower court entrance was once planted with trees and vines.

2 Ramps lead visitors to the middle and upper levels.

3 Inside the colonnades are carvings honoring Hatshepsut's birth as well as a famous trade journey to Punt that she once sponsored. **Analyze** *What features of Hatshepsut's temple would have impressed its visitors in ancient Egypt?*

HATSHEPSUT'S TEMPLE AT DEIR EL-BAHRI

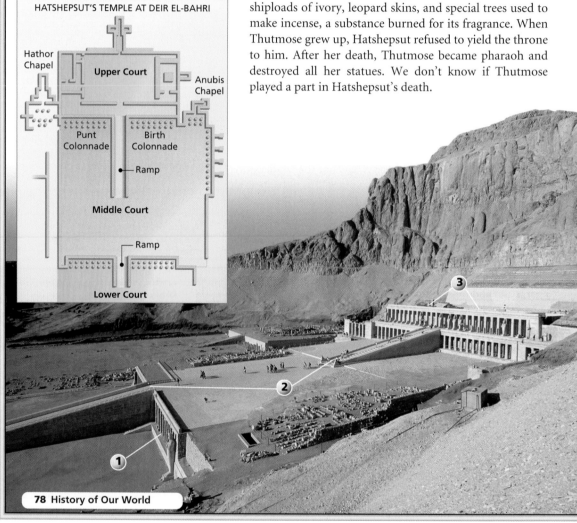

- Hathor Chapel
- Upper Court
- Anubis Chapel
- Punt Colonnade
- Birth Colonnade
- Ramp
- Middle Court
- Ramp
- Lower Court

78 History of Our World

Rule During the New Kingdom

In 1504 B.C., a child named Thutmose III (thoot MOH suh) began his reign. Because of his youth, his stepmother was appointed regent. A **regent** is someone who rules for a child until the child is old enough to rule. His stepmother was Hatshepsut, whom you read about at the beginning of this section. Not content to be regent, Hatshepsut had herself proclaimed pharaoh. She was Egypt's supreme ruler for about 15 years.

The Pharaoh Queen Hatshepsut's reign was good for Egypt. She was a bold leader who is most known for creating a time of great peace and economic success. She encouraged trade with faraway places, sending a famous expedition to the land of Punt on the east coast of Africa. Egyptian traders returned with shiploads of ivory, leopard skins, and special trees used to make incense, a substance burned for its fragrance. When Thutmose grew up, Hatshepsut refused to yield the throne to him. After her death, Thutmose became pharaoh and destroyed all her statues. We don't know if Thutmose played a part in Hatshepsut's death.

Thutmose III Rules Thutmose III became one of the greatest pharaohs of the New Kingdom. He led his army in wars against Syria and Phoenicia, in Southwest Asia. His troops advanced as far east as the Euphrates River and south into Nubia. Yet Thutmose was more than a conqueror. He was an educated man who loved to study plants. Unlike most rulers of his time, he treated those he defeated with mercy.

Ancient Egypt After the New Kingdom Toward the end of the New Kingdom, Egypt declined. Civil war left Egypt weak and poorly defended. In 332 B.C., long after the end of the New Kingdom, Egypt fell to the famous conqueror Alexander the Great of Macedonia. The Macedonians continued to rule Egypt for about 300 years.

In 51 B.C., Queen Cleopatra VII became the last Macedonian to rule Egypt. She shared the throne with other members of her family until Egypt was conquered by the Romans. Egypt became part of the Roman Empire in 31 B.C. Cleopatra suspected that the Romans would parade her through Egypt to celebrate their victory. To avoid this humiliation, she committed suicide. Egypt would not govern itself again for almost 2,000 years.

√ **Reading Check** What caused the decline of Egypt during the New Kingdom period?

Thutmose III finally assumed the throne after the death of his stepmother, Hatshepsut.

Extend ▮L3▮
Have students learn more about the rulers of Egypt by reading *In Her Own Words: Hatshepsut, Queen of Egypt c. 1500 B.C.* and *In Her Own Words: Ankhesenpaton, Queen of Egypt c. 1350 B.C.*

▮All in One▮ **Unit 2 History of Our World Teaching Resources,** *In Her Own Words: Hatshepsut, Queen of Egypt c. 1500 B.C.,* p. 36, *Ankhesenpaton, Queen of Egypt c. 1350 B.C.,* p. 37

Section 2 Assessment

Key Terms
Review the key terms at the beginning of this section. Use each term in a sentence that explains its meaning.

▶ **Target Reading Skill**
Find the word *incense* on page 78. Use context to figure out its meaning. What clues helped you to understand the meaning of *incense*?

Comprehension and Critical Thinking
1. (a) Identify What unusual powers did Egyptians believe their kings had?

(b) Link Past and Present Explain why Egypt's rulers had more authority than most rulers have today.
2. (a) Recall Describe some of the accomplishments of each of the three Egyptian kingdoms.
(b) Compare What characteristics did all three kingdoms have in common?
3. (a) Generalize Describe the New Kingdom under Thutmose III and during its later decline.
(b) Analyze Information Why do you think the pharaohs of Egypt were so successful for so long? What factors led to the decline of Egypt?

Writing Activity
Write a paragraph explaining the following statement: "Ancient Egypt was strongest when its rulers were strong."

Writing Tip Before you write, reread Section 2. Pay special attention to the parts of the text that describe Egypt's strongest pharaohs. Use the statement above as your topic sentence, the sentence that begins your paragraph.

Chapter 3 Section 2 **79**

Section 2 Assessment

Key Terms
Students' sentences should reflect knowledge of each Key Term.

▶ **Target Reading Skill**
The meaning of the word *incense*—a substance burned for its fragrance—is restated in the sentence in which it appears.

Comprehension and Critical Thinking
1. (a) the power to provide floods and the harvests that followed **(b)** Egyptians thought rulers had god-like powers and therefore hesitated to question their authority.

2. (a) Old Kingdom—pharaohs kept the peace and trade with Nubia. Middle Kingdom—irrigation and public works; New Kingdom—huge, powerful armies. **(b)** All made progress and prospered for much of the time; all were led by pharaohs.

Answer

√ **Reading Check** Civil war in Egypt left the country weak and poorly defended.

Writing Activity
Use the *Rubric for Assessing a Writing Assignment* to evaluate students' paragraphs.

▮All in One▮ **Unit 2 History of Our World Teaching Resources,** *Rubric for Assessing a Writing Assignment,* p. 40

3. (a) Thutmose III conquered many lands. The conquered were treated with mercy. The New Kingdom declined after civil war left Egyptians defenseless against foreign invasion. Egypt fell to Alexander the Great. **(b)** People believed their pharaohs were god-like. Fertile land and access to the Nile allowed Egypt to grow and prosper. But, as it grew, the pharaohs lost power. Civil war ensued.

Objectives

Social Studies

1. Learn about Egyptian gods and goddesses.
2. Find out about the Egyptians' belief in the afterlife.
3. Discover how and why the pharaohs' tombs were built.

Reading/Language Arts

Learn how to use context clues in surrounding words and sentences to find the meanings of unfamiliar words.

Prepare to Read

Build Background Knowledge L2

Ask students to look at the photos and diagrams of the Great Pyramid at Giza on page 83. Explain that these huge structures were built from large stone blocks without the benefit of trucks, cranes, or fork lifts. Ask students to describe how they would organize a group of people to move these huge stones from one place to another under these conditions. Conduct an Idea Wave (TE, p. T39) to generate responses.

Set a Purpose for Reading L2

■ Preview the Objectives.

■ Read each statement in the *Reading Readiness Guide* aloud. Ask students to mark the statements true or false.

   All in One **Unit 2 History of Our World Teaching Resources,** *Reading Readiness Guide,* p. 14

■ Have students discuss the statements in pairs or groups of four, then mark their guides again. Use the Numbered Heads participation strategy (TE, p. T40) to call on students to share their group's perspectives.

Vocabulary Builder

Preview Key Terms L2

Pronounce each Key Term, then ask the students to say the word with you. Provide a simple explanation such as, "Ancient Egyptians believed that after people die they live again in a time called the afterlife."

Prepare to Read

Objectives

In this section you will

1. Learn about Egyptian gods and goddesses.
2. Find out about the Egyptians' belief in the afterlife.
3. Discover how and why the pharaohs' tombs were built.

Taking Notes

As you read, take notes to summarize the religious beliefs and practices of the ancient Egyptians. Copy the chart below, and use it to record your notes.

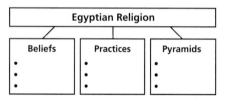

Egyptian Religion
- Beliefs
- Practices
- Pyramids

Target Reading Skill

Use Context Clues When reading, you may find a word that is unfamiliar or even a word you know that is used in an unfamiliar way. Look for clues in the surrounding words and sentences, to help you understand the meaning of the word. For example, look at the context for the word *linen* in the second paragraph on this page. Find the explanation of how linen was used in mummification. What do you think *linen* means?

Key Terms

- **afterlife** (AF tur lyf) *n.* a life after death
- **mummy** (MUM ee) *n.* a dead body preserved in lifelike condition
- **pyramid** (PIH ruh mid) *n.* a huge building with four sloping triangle-shaped sides; built as royal tombs in Egypt
- **Giza** (GEE zuh) *n.* an ancient Egyptian city; the site of the Great Pyramid

Anubis, god of the dead, tends a dead pharaoh. According to Egyptian myth, Anubis invented mummification.

As the royal family wept over the pharaoh's body, the priest chanted:

❝ You will live again. You will live forever. Behold, you will be young forever. ❞

—ancient Egyptian prayer

One hundred days had passed since the pharaoh had died. During that time, the royal officials had been carefully preparing his body. Now, they wrapped the body in many strips of fine linen and placed it in a gold-covered coffin decorated to resemble the king in all of his royal glory.

The Egyptians believed in an **afterlife,** a life after death. They said prayers during the funeral, hoping to help the pharaoh's soul on its way to the afterlife. Then the nobles and royal family followed the body as it was carried to the royal tomb. Workers closed the tomb and the mourners went home. The pharaoh's journey to the afterlife had begun.

Target Reading Skill L2

Use Context Clues Point out the Target Reading Skill. Remind students that context clues are pieces of information that help you find the meaning of an unfamiliar word.

Model the skill by reading the last paragraph on p. 80. Draw attention to the word *mourners.* Explain that students can use clues in the paragraph to find out what *mourners* means. (*The first two sentences state that Egyptians go to funerals and say prayers. The sentence in which* mourners *appears uses this term to refer to these people. Therefore,* mourners *are people who come to pay their respects and say prayers for the dead.*)

Give students *Use Context Clues: Definition/Description.* Have them complete the activity in groups.

   All in One **Unit 2 History of Our World Teaching Resources,** *Use Context Clues: Definition/Description,* p. 26

Egyptian Gods and Goddesses

Religion was an important part of daily life in ancient Egypt. The Egyptians believed that their gods and goddesses controlled the workings of nature. They built temples to honor their gods, and offered them food, gifts, and prayers.

Regional Differences Early on, Egyptian towns had their own gods and goddesses with their own temples. These included gods who were often shown as humans with animal heads. All Egyptians also worshiped certain principal gods, such as the sun god, Re and the falcon god, Horus. Over time, however, all ancient Egyptians came to believe in several groups of gods.

Important Gods The chief god of the ancient Egyptians was Amon-Re (ah mun RAY). He protected the rich and the poor alike. The Egyptians believed that Amon-Re was born each morning in the east with the sunrise. Each evening he died in the west with the setting sun. That is why the desert area to the west was believed to be the home of the dead.

Other powerful gods included Osiris (oh SY ris), the god of the living and the dead. The goddess Isis (EYE sis) was his wife. She was worshiped as the great mother who protected her children. The sky god, Horus, was their son.

✓ **Reading Check** Who was Osiris?

Egyptian Gods and Goddesses
The ancient Egyptians believed that their gods controlled life, death, and all of nature.
① Horus, the sky god and the god of kingship
② Osiris, the god of the afterlife
③ Isis, the goddess of women
④ Thoth, the god of wisdom and of writing
⑤ Amon-Re, the sun god and god of creation

Vocabulary Builder

Use the information below to teach students this section's high-use words.

High-Use Word	Definition and Sample Sentence
preserve, p. 82	*v.* to protect from harm or damage Placing it under glass will **preserve** the delicate artifact.
site, p. 85	*n.* the location of a planned structure The **site** of the new school is next to the park.

Belief in an Afterlife L2

Guided Instruction

- **Vocabulary Builder** Clarify the high-use word **preserve** before reading.

- Read about the methods in which Egyptians prepared bodies for the afterlife in Belief in an Afterlife.

- Ask students **How can you tell that ancient Egyptians believed the afterlife was much like life on Earth?** *(They entombed preserved bodies and included earthly possessions, believing that both would be useful in the afterlife.)*

- Ask students **Why do you think some Egyptians were unable to have the bodies of their loved ones mummified?** *(The process was expensive. Only wealthy Egyptians could afford it.)*

Independent Practice

Tell students to continue to fill in the first two boxes of their charts with the information they have just learned.

Monitor Progress

Organize students into pairs and have them fill in their organizers together. Encourage them to discuss the details they have chosen with their partners. Circulate to make sure students are choosing the correct details. Provide assistance as needed.

Answers

Infer King Tutankhamen; the decorative coffin indicates wealth, which implies that more necessities such as food, clothing, and furniture would be buried with the individual and available to him in the afterlife.

✓ **Reading Check** They believed that people needed their possessions in order to survive in the afterlife.

Burials, rich and poor
The decorative coffin on the right held the expensively preserved internal organs of King Tutankhamen. The reed coffin tied with rope (above), from about 1450 B.C., holds the naturally preserved body of a baby. **Infer** *According to ancient Egyptian religious beliefs, which of the two souls would enjoy a more comfortable afterlife? Explain.*

Belief in an Afterlife

Like the people of many civilizations, the ancient Egyptians believed in life after death. Evidence of this belief is often found in the art and artifacts they left behind.

Journey to the Afterlife The ancient Egyptians believed the spirits of the dead made their way to the afterlife in heavenly boats. If they had pleased the gods in this world, they joined Osiris and lived a life of ease and pleasure. They spent their days eating, drinking, and visiting with friends and family members who had died. Because the souls of the dead could not survive without food, clothing, and other items from this life, their possessions were buried with them.

During the Old Kingdom, the afterlife was thought to be only for kings and their associates. But beginning in the Middle Kingdom, people of all classes looked forward to an afterlife.

Preparing the Dead Before the building of pyramids, most Egyptians were buried in the desert in shallow pits. Egypt's climate dried out a person's remains, creating a **mummy**, the preserved body of a dead person. According to religious beliefs, the soul would leave the mummy, but return to it to receive food offerings. The preserved appearance of the body allowed it to be recognized by the person's spirit. By the time of the Fourth Dynasty, the Egyptians had begun to practice mummification, artificially preserving the bodies before burial.

Mummification was expensive and took two or three months. Workers carefully removed the organs. The body was then filled with a natural salt and stored for about 40 days. During that time, it completely dried out. Once dry, the body was cleaned and bathed in spices. It was then wrapped with long linen bandages.

While workers were preparing the mummy, artisans were busy carving the coffin. Pharaohs actually had three or four coffins. The coffins nested one inside another like boxes. The innermost coffin was usually shaped like a human body, with the dead person's face painted on the cover.

✓ Reading Check **Why did ancient Egyptians bury their dead with food and other possessions?**

Background: Links Across Time

Treasures Unearthed In 1922, an Egyptologist named Howard Carter discovered a buried staircase that led to a sealed tomb. When the tomb was opened, Carter and others in his party found fantastic treasures—items made with gold, alabaster, ebony, and other precious stones. Within the burial chamber was the greatest treasure—the mummified body of King Tutankhamen, the 18-year-old boy-king, encased in three nested coffins. The outer two were wooden but the innermost coffin was made of solid gold.

The Great Pyramid

For more than 4,000 years, the Great Pyramid at Giza stood taller than any other human-made structure in the world. About 480 feet (147 meters) high, it still stands today. It has four triangle-shaped sides and a square base.

Inside the Grand Gallery
In the 1800s, Napoleon Bonaparte of France ordered a study of the pyramids. His scientists made drawings as they passed through the Grand Gallery to the King's Chamber.

These stones spread the weight of the pyramid above, preventing the whole structure from collapsing.

Graffiti carved into these slabs records the names of the workers who built the chamber.

The pharaoh's outer coffin is larger than the entrance to the chamber, meaning that the pyramid was built around it.

Building the King's Chamber
The King's Chamber was hidden away at the heart of the Great Pyramid. The pharaoh's mummy was sealed into the chamber and lay undisturbed until grave robbers stole it.

The King's Chamber lay at the center of the pyramid.

The pharaoh's body was carried to the burial chamber through secret tunnels. Some tunnels were false, leading to dead ends.

Granite blocks sealed off the Grand Gallery route to the King's Chamber.

A temple held the pharaoh's body before burial.

ANALYZING IMAGES
What did the builders of the Great Pyramid at Giza do to keep out grave robbers?

Chapter 3 Section 3 **83**

 EYEWITNESS TECHNOLOGY

The Great Pyramid L2

Guided Instruction
Ask students to study the Great Pyramid by reading the text and captions, and examining the photo and cutaway diagrams. As a class, answer the Analyze Images question. Allow students to briefly discuss their responses with a partner before sharing answers.

Independent Practice
Another impressive Egyptian structure stands near the Great Pyramid of Giza in the desert. It is a huge monument of a mythical figure with the body of a lion and the head of a human called the Great Sphinx. Have students complete the *Enrichment* activity to learn more about the Great Sphinx of Egypt.

All in One **Unit 2 History of Our World Teaching Resources,** *Enrichment,* p. 29

Answer

ANALYZE IMAGES They hid the burial chamber deep inside the structure, and made the only access to it via secret tunnels.

The Pharaohs' Tombs L2

Guided Instruction

- **Vocabulary Builder** Clarify the high-use word **site** before reading.

- Read The Pharaohs' Tombs. As students read, circulate to make sure individuals can answer the Reading Check question.

- Discuss the pyramid building process with students. (*Stone came from quarries both near and far. Workers cut the stones into blocks, and used sleds, wooden rollers, and levers to drag and push the blocks up ramps to build the pyramids.*)

- Have students compare and contrast this site with a modern construction site. (*Similarities—A large number of workers needed, teamwork is important, construction sites can be dangerous. Differences—Today, powered equipment is used, making the labor easier than in ancient times.*)

Independent Practice

Ask students to complete the third and final box on the graphic organizer with the information they have just learned about the pyramids.

Monitor Progress

- Show *Section Reading Support Transparency HOW 63* and ask students to check their graphic organizers individually. Go over key concepts and clarify key vocabulary as needed.

    📖 **History of Our World Transparencies,** *Section Reading Support Transparency HOW 63*

- Tell students to fill in the last column of the *Reading Readiness Guide.* Probe for what they learned that confirms or invalidates each statement.

    All in One Unit 2 History of Our World Teaching Resources, *Reading Readiness Guide,* p. 14

Target Reading Skill

Using Context Clues a follow up, ask students to answer the Target Reading Skill question in the Student Edition. (*The word hauled means "moved forcefully."*)

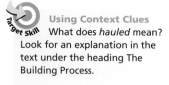

Using Context Clues What does *hauled* mean? Look for an explanation in the text under the heading The Building Process.

The Pharaohs' Tombs

The planning for a pharaoh's tomb began soon after he was crowned. The earliest royal tombs were made of mud brick. As time went on, however, tomb building became a complex art.

The Pyramids The pharaohs of the Fourth Dynasty built the largest and most famous tombs. These were the pyramids, huge buildings with four sloping triangle-shaped sides. Most of the pyramids were built during the Old Kingdom. The largest is called the Great Pyramid, built for Khufu (KOO foo), the second king of the Fourth Dynasty. The Great Pyramid was built in the ancient city of Giza. Find Giza on the map at the beginning of this chapter.

The Building Process Building the pyramids required a great deal of organization. The Great Pyramid is made up of more than 2 million stones. The average weight of each stone is 5,000 pounds (2,270 kilograms). Each stone had to be hauled up the side of the pyramid and put into its proper place.

The Great Sphinx is a portrait of King Kafre with the body of a lion. Kafre's pyramid is behind and to the right of the Sphinx.

84 History of Our World

Differentiated Instruction

For Less Proficient Readers L1

Have students work in pairs to create a word web. Inside the center circle have students write "Building the Great Pyramid." Ask them to draw six spokes extending from the circle with smaller circles at the end of each one. In each circle, ask them to answer each of the following: *Who? What? Where? When? Why? How?*

For Special Needs Students L1

Have students illustrate each step in the process of building the pyramids. Then pair them with more able partners to write captions or labels for each step.

A pyramid could take more than 20 years to build. The project began with the selection of a site on the west bank of the Nile. Remember that the west was thought to be the land of the dead. Once the site was chosen, workers cleared the ground. Engineers set the pyramid square so that the sides faced the main points of the compass—north, south, east, and west.

Workers then cut the building blocks. Stone for the inside of the pyramid came from nearby quarries. But fine stone for the outside came from farther away. Some stone came all the way from Nubia. It had to be loaded onto barges and carried to the building site either along the Nile or along canals near the Nile.

Teamwork To get the blocks of stone into place, workers used sleds, wooden rollers, and levers. They dragged and pushed the huge blocks up ramps of packed rubble to the level they were working on.

Carpenters at work, from a painting in an official's tomb

Building pyramids was dangerous work. Each year, men lost their lives, crushed by falling blocks. But the workers believed in the importance of their work. For them, building a pyramid was an act of faith. It was a way of ensuring the pharaoh's place in the afterlife.

✓ Reading Check **Why did the Egyptians build pyramids?**

Section 3 Assessment

Key Terms
Review the key terms at the beginning of this section. Use each term in a sentence that explains its meaning.

Target Reading Skill
Find the word *quarries* in the second paragraph of this page. What do you think it means?

Comprehension and Critical Thinking
1. (a) Identify What were the religious beliefs of the ancient Egyptians?

(b) Describe In what ways did the ancient Egyptians use religion to understand nature?
2. (a) Explain Why did the Egyptians mummify their dead?
(b) Analyze How do we know that the afterlife was important to the ancient Egyptians?
3. (a) Recall Why were the pharaohs concerned about the condition of their tombs?
(b) Sequence Describe how the ancient Egyptians organized the building of the pyramids.

Writing Activity
Suppose the pharaoh invites you to go with him to inspect his pyramid as it is being built. Write a journal entry describing what you see on your visit.

For: An activity on the religion of the ancient Egyptians
Visit: PHSchool.com
Web Code: lbd-2303

Chapter 3 Section 3 **85**

Section 3 Assessment

Key Terms
Students' sentences should reflect knowledge of each Key Term.

Target Reading Skill
The context shows that *quarries* are places from which rock can be extracted.

Comprehension and Critical Thinking
1. (a) Ancient Egyptians believed in several groups of gods, all of whom had control over major aspects of life. They also believed in life after death. **(b)** They believed that the gods controlled nature and therefore explained the workings of nature.

2. (a) Egyptians believed that a person's spirit would exist in the afterlife and would return to the mummified body to receive food and offerings. **(b)** Egyptians took great care to preserve bodies and create tombs to ensure a person's place and comfort in the afterlife.

3. (a) The pharaohs wanted their bodies and possessions to be safe from robbers. They may also have felt that the appearance of the tomb reflected their wealth and power. **(b)** They carried stone to the building site from quarries near and far. Then they cut building blocks from the stone. Next, they used sleds, wooden rollers, and levers to push huge blocks up ramps to the level they were working on.

Assess and Reteach

Assess Progress · L2
Have students complete the Section Assessment. Administer the *Section Quiz*.

All in One **Unit 2 History of Our World Teaching Resources,** *Section Quiz,* p. 16

Reteach · L1
If students need more instruction, have them read this section in the Reading and Vocabulary Study Guide.

Chapter 3, Section 3, **History of Our World Reading and Vocabulary Study Guide**, pp. 38–40

Extend · L3
Have students learn more about Egyptian religion and culture by beginning work on the *Book Project: Life in the Ancient World*. Assign students to work in groups to complete the project.

All in One **Unit 2 History of Our World Teaching Resources,** *Book Project: Life in the Ancient World,* pp. 10–12

Answers

✓ Reading Check The pyramids were built to serve as tombs for Egyptian pharaohs.

Writing Activity
Use the *Rubric for Assessing a Journal Entry* to evaluate students' journal entries.

All in One **Unit 2 History of Our World Teaching Resources,** *Rubric for Assessing a Journal Entry,* p. 39

Go Online PHSchool.com Typing in the Web code when prompted will bring students directly to detailed instructions for this activity.

Focus On The Pyramid Builders

L2

Guided Instruction

- Read the introductory paragraph and study the art, photos, and captions as a class.

- Ask **Why do you think some Egyptians were willing to volunteer to help build the pyramids?** (*Possible answer: They may have needed work during the flood season when they could not farm.*)

- Discuss the importance of copper to ancient Egyptians. (*Copper, fashioned into tools that could split rock, was helpful to building.*)

- Ask students **How did bread aid in the building of the pyramids?** (*Hungry pyramid-builders needed the bread for nourishment and energy.*)

- Have students work individually to answer the Assessment questions.

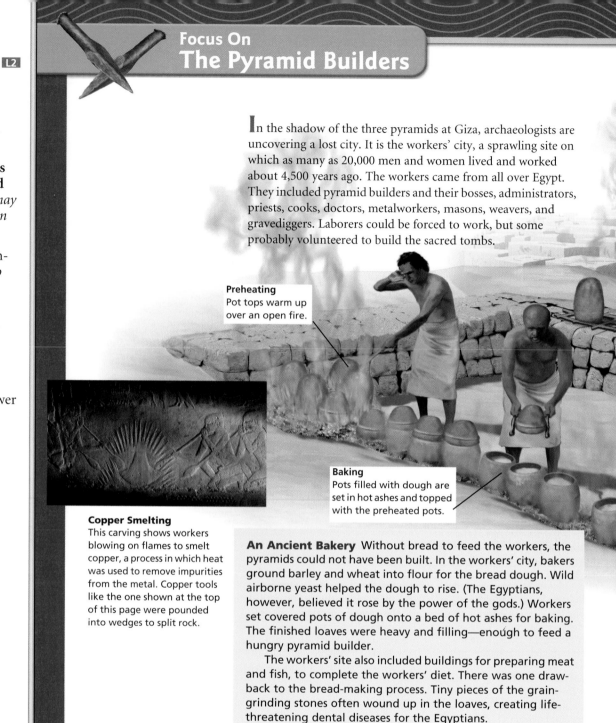

In the shadow of the three pyramids at Giza, archaeologists are uncovering a lost city. It is the workers' city, a sprawling site on which as many as 20,000 men and women lived and worked about 4,500 years ago. The workers came from all over Egypt. They included pyramid builders and their bosses, administrators, priests, cooks, doctors, metalworkers, masons, weavers, and gravediggers. Laborers could be forced to work, but some probably volunteered to build the sacred tombs.

Preheating
Pot tops warm up over an open fire.

Baking
Pots filled with dough are set in hot ashes and topped with the preheated pots.

Copper Smelting
This carving shows workers blowing on flames to smelt copper, a process in which heat was used to remove impurities from the metal. Copper tools like the one shown at the top of this page were pounded into wedges to split rock.

An Ancient Bakery Without bread to feed the workers, the pyramids could not have been built. In the workers' city, bakers ground barley and wheat into flour for the bread dough. Wild airborne yeast helped the dough to rise. (The Egyptians, however, believed it rose by the power of the gods.) Workers set covered pots of dough onto a bed of hot ashes for baking. The finished loaves were heavy and filling—enough to feed a hungry pyramid builder.

The workers' site also included buildings for preparing meat and fish, to complete the workers' diet. There was one drawback to the bread-making process. Tiny pieces of the grain-grinding stones often wound up in the loaves, creating life-threatening dental diseases for the Egyptians.

Differentiated Instruction

For Less Proficient Readers
To aid in students' comprehension of the ancient Egyptian bread-making process, have students work in pairs with more proficient readers to create a flow chart detailing the steps for making bread.

Display the *Flow Chart* transparency to provide students with a model for their charts.

📖 **History of Our World Transparencies,** Transparency B6: Flow Chart

Cooling Bread
After the bread bakes, it cools.

Making Bread Dough
Flour and water are mixed in a large terra-cotta vat.

Egyptian Medicine
In the workers' city, doctors set bones and treated a variety of ailments. Egyptians believed the household god Bes, whose statue is shown at the left, could protect them from danger.

Assessment

Identify Who were the people who lived in the lost city near the pyramids at Giza?

Infer Why was a city of workers needed to build the pyramids?

Chapter 3 Section 3 **87**

Independent Practice

Ask students to suppose they live in the city of the pyramid builders. Tell them to choose one of the professions listed in the first paragraph on p. 86 and have them write a journal entry describing a day in their life. Use *Rubric for Assessing a Journal Entry* to evaluate students' work.

All in One Unit 2 History of Our World Teaching Resources, *Rubric for Assessing a Journal Entry,* p. 39

Answers

Assessment

Identify They were the workers who helped build the pyramids. Workers included pyramid builders and their bosses, metalworkers, masons, weavers, and gravediggers.
Infer Possible answer: Many people were needed to help build the pyramids. They needed to live nearby because the process was difficult and time-consuming. These workers needed services, such as medical services, to help them survive.

Section 4
Step-by-Step Instruction

Objectives

Social Studies
1. Find out about the everyday life of the ancient Egyptians.
2. Learn about writing in ancient Egypt.
3. Discover advances made by the Egyptians in science and medicine.

Reading/Language Arts
Learn how cause and effect clues can help you understand the meaning of an unfamiliar word.

Prepare to Read

Build Background Knowledge L2

Allow students to preview the section by looking at the photos. Point out the photo of hieroglyphs on page 93, and explain that this was an early form of writing with picture symbols. Ask students if they have ever seen a rebus, which uses letters and pictures to tell a story. Then ask students to write their own short message using pictures rather than words.

Set a Purpose for Reading L2
■ Preview the Objectives.

■ Form students into pairs or groups of four. Distribute the *Reading Readiness Guide*. Ask students to fill in the first two columns of the chart. Use the Numbered Heads participation strategy (TE, p. T40) to call on students to share one piece of information they already know and one piece of information they want to know.

All in One Unit 2 History of Our World Teaching Resources, *Reading Readiness Guide,* p. 18

Vocabulary Builder
Preview Key Terms L2
Pronounce each Key Term, then ask the students to say the word with you. Provide a simple explanation such as, "Ancient Egyptians wrote on papyrus made from reeds just as we write on paper made from trees."

Prepare to Read

Objectives
In this section you will
1. Find out about the everyday life of the ancient Egyptians.
2. Learn about writing in ancient Egypt.
3. Discover advances made by the Egyptians in science and medicine.

Taking Notes
As you read, look for details about ancient Egyptian culture. Copy the flowchart below and record your findings in it.

Egyptian Culture
- Everyday Life
  - •
  - •
  - •
- Achievements
  - •
  - •
  - •

Target Reading Skill

Use Context Clues Cause-and-effect clues can help you understand the meaning of an unfamiliar word. In the following sentence, a cause-and-effect clue points to the meaning of *scattered:* When the farmer scattered the seeds, he caused them to fly and land in many directions. What do you think *scattered* means?

Key Terms
- **hieroglyphs** (HY ur oh glifs) *n.* pictures and other written symbols that stand for ideas, things, or sounds
- **papyrus** (puh PY rus) *n.* an early form of paper made from a reed plant found in the marshy areas of the Nile delta; the plant used to make this paper
- **astronomer** (uh STRAHN uh mur) *n.* a scientist who studies the stars and other objects in the sky

A high official of ancient Egypt and his wife

Uni was a high-ranking Egyptian of the Old Kingdom. His life story—a success story—is recorded in his tomb.

Uni began his career in a simple way—running a storehouse. Later, he was promoted to groundskeeper of the royal pyramid. In his job, he oversaw the delivery of stone from the quarry, the site where stone was cut, to the pyramid. Uni must have worked hard, because later he was made a general. Then, he became Governor of Upper Egypt, in charge of goods and taxes for half the kingdom. By the time of his death, Uni had become royal tutor at the palace and an honored companion of the pharaoh. Uni and many other people like him were part of everyday life in ancient Egypt.

The Lives of the Egyptians

Most of what we know about the everyday life of the Egyptians is based on paintings that cover the walls of tombs and temples. Written records also tell us much about their lives.

Target Reading Skill L2

Use Context Clues Draw students' attention to the Target Reading Skill. Explain that they can use cause-and-effect clues in the text to help them find the meaning of unfamiliar words.

Model the skill by pointing out the word *crosswise* in the last paragraph on page 91. Point out that placing the strips of papyrus *crosswise* over the previous layer of pieces that were side by side, caused the pieces to make a sheet. Students can infer that *crosswise* means "in the opposite direction of" from the cause-and-effect clue.

Give students *Use Context Clues: Cause and Effect.* Have them complete the activity in groups.

All in One Unit 2 History of Our World Teaching Resources, *Use Context Clues: Cause and Effect,* p. 27

Social Classes Historians often turn to Egyptian art to learn about the social classes of ancient Egypt. Egyptian paintings and carvings show royalty and ordinary people involved in all aspects of life. Like Uni, most Egyptians were busy and hard-working people. They also had a sense of fun and a love of beauty.

Egyptian society itself resembled a pyramid. At the very top stood the pharaoh. Beneath him was a small upper class. This group included priests, members of the pharaoh's court, and nobles who held the largest estates. The next level was the middle class, made up of merchants and skilled workers. At the base of the pyramid was by far the largest class, the peasants. Mostly, the peasants did farm labor. But they also did other kinds of labor, such as building roads and temples. A person could rise to a higher class. Generally, the way to rise was through service to the pharaoh, as Uni did.

Slavery Prisoners captured in wars were made slaves. Slaves formed a separate class, which was never very large. Egyptian society was flexible, however. Even slaves had rights. They could own personal items and inherit land from their masters. They could also be set free.

Working in Egypt
Models showing scenes from everyday life were often placed in tombs. This wood model shows workers in a bakery. **Infer** *Why do you think such scenes are useful to archaeologists?*

Chapter 3 Section 4 **89**

Citizen Heroes

Read the **Citizen Heroes** on this page. Ask students **What obstacles do you think Nekhebu had to overcome?** *(He probably needed to overcome his social class and his lack of education.)*

Instruct

The Lives of the Egyptians L2

Guided Instruction

■ **Vocabulary Builder** Clarify the high-use word **resemble** before reading.

■ Read The Lives of the Egyptians, using the ReQuest technique (TE, p. T39)

■ Ask students **How do we know what everyday life was like for Egyptians?** *(Written records and ancient Egyptian paintings and carvings that cover tomb and temple walls tell us most of what we know about their everyday lives.)*

■ Ask **Why do you think the peasant class was the largest class in ancient Egyptian society?** *(Students might suggest that because farming was so important and farmland so abundant, a large peasant class was needed. Students might also suggest that much of the two highest classes were determined by ancestry so peasants could not rise to those higher classes.)*

Vocabulary Builder

Use the information below to teach students this section's high-use words.

High-Use Word	Definition and Sample Sentence
resemble, p. 89	*v.* to be or look like We **resemble** each other so much that people often think we are sisters.
complicate, p. 91	*v.* to make complex or difficult The map was so **complicated** that we could not find the treasure.

Answer

Infer The models show archaeologists details about daily life in ancient times.

- Have students describe a typical day for peasants during the harvest. (*Men, women, and children worked in the fields from sunrise to sunset. Then villagers gathered for a feast.*)

- Ask students **Do you think that ancient Egyptians felt that women had an important place in society? Why or why not?** (*Yes, because women were able to own property, run businesses, and enter into legal contracts. They held many different important jobs and some were nobles.*)

Independent Practice

Ask students to create the Taking Notes graphic organizer on a blank piece of paper. Then have them fill in the Everyday Life section of the flow chart with the information they have just learned. Briefly model how to identify which details to record by filling in the first detail with them on the appropriate blank transparency.

📖 **History of Our World Transparencies,** *Transparency B2: Flow Chart*

Monitor Progress L2

As students fill in the graphic organizer, circulate and make sure individuals are choosing the correct details. Provide assistance as needed.

Answers

✓ Reading Check Egyptian society was organized by a class structure that resembled a pyramid. At the top was the pharaoh. Next was a small upper class made up of priests, nobles, and members of the pharaoh's court. The middle class was made up of merchants and skilled workers. The largest and lowest class was the peasants.

Conclude The woman working on the farm is most likely a peasant while the women shown with wax cones and jewelry are more likely of a wealthier class.

Lives of the Peasants Although peasants could own land, most worked the land of wealthier people. During the flood season, the peasants worked on roads, temples, and other buildings. As soon as the waters left the land, they had to plant the fields. The work had to be done quickly while the soil was still moist. One farmer plowed the black earth with a team of oxen while another followed behind, scattering the seeds.

The harvest was the busiest season for Egypt's peasants. All men, women, and older children went into the fields to gather the crops of wheat or barley. Work went on from sunrise to sunset. Once the crops were gathered, the villagers feasted. They offered food and drink to the gods in thanks for their help.

Women of Egypt Egyptian women were looked upon as living models of Isis, the wife of the god Osiris. They had most of the rights that men had. They could own property, run businesses, and enter into legal contracts. For the most part, women traveled about freely. Egyptian paintings often show them supervising farm work or hunting. And women performed many roles—from priestess to dancer.

Noble women held a special position in Egyptian society. Sometimes they were in charge of temples and religious rites. They could also use their position to influence the pharaoh. Some women acted as regents until the pharaoh was old enough to rule on his own.

✓ Reading Check **How was Egyptian society organized?**

Women's Lives
The women shown above are wearing scented wax cones on their heads. The wax melted in the heat, surrounding the women with perfume. At the right, a woman works in a field with her husband. **Conclude** *Which social classes do you think the women in the paintings belonged to? Explain your answer.*

90 History of Our World

Differentiated Instruction

For Special Needs Students L1

Pair special needs students with more able partners to create a diagram of a pyramid, showing the classes of Egyptian culture as they are described in this section.

Writing in Ancient Egypt

The records and writings left by the ancient Egyptians allow us to learn more about their culture. From these records, we know that they possessed an amazing amount of knowledge.

A New System of Writing In ancient Egypt, as in Mesopotamia, ideas were written down in picturelike symbols called hieroglyphs (HY ur oh glifs). In this script, some pictures stand for ideas or things. For example, a picture of two legs means "go." Other pictures stand for sounds. For example, a drawing of an owl stands for the "m" sound.

The Egyptians began to use hieroglyphs because they needed a way to keep track of the kingdom's growing wealth. As the Egyptian empire grew, it became necessary to create more pictures for more complicated ideas.

Writing Materials At first, the Egyptians wrote on clay and stone, as the Sumerians did. But they needed a more convenient writing surface. They found it in papyrus (puh py ruhs), an early form of paper made from a reed found in the marshy areas of the Nile delta. The plant used to make this paper is also called papyrus. To make the paper, the inner stalks of the plant were cut into narrow strips. The strips were cut to the same length and placed side by side by side in one layer. Another layer of strips was placed crosswise on top to form a sheet. Papyrus makers wet the sheet, pressed it flat, and dried it in the sun. Sap from the plant glued the strips together. Pasted side by side, the sheets formed a long strip that could be rolled up.

Hieroglyphs

A		P	
AH		F	
AY		M	or
EE		N	
U		L	
B		H	
H		Q	
S		K	
SH		T	

■ Chart Skills

The text of the *Book of the Dead* (top left) was meant to guide the dead on their journey to the afterlife. The book's hieroglyphs are written on papyrus. The table (above) shows some hieroglyphs and the sounds they stood for. **Identify** What is the hieroglyph for the "p" sound? **Analyze Images** What are some English words you could spell using the hieroglyphs in the chart?

 Use Context Clues What does *sap* mean? Look for cause-and-effect clues in the text. Sap from the plant glues the strips of papyrus together. What does that tell you about sap?

Writing in Ancient Egypt L2

Guided Instruction

■ **Vocabulary Builder** Clarify the high-use word **complicate** before reading.

■ Read about hieroglyphs in Writing in Ancient Egypt. As students read, circulate to make sure they can answer the Reading Check question.

■ Ask students **Why did Egyptians begin using hieroglyphs?** *(They needed a way to keep track of the growing empire's wealth.)*

■ Discuss the similarities and differences between hieroglyphs and our system of writing. *(Similarity—Both use symbols to stand for sounds. Differences—Some hieroglyphs are pictures; some hieroglyphs stand for entire words.)*

Independent Practice

Ask students to begin filling in the flow chart's Achievements box with the information they have just learned.

Monitor Progress

As students fill in the graphic organizer, circulate and make sure individuals are choosing the correct details. Provide assistance as needed.

↺ Target Reading Skill

Use Context Clues As a follow up, ask students to answer the Target Reading Skill in the Student Edition. *(Students can use the clues to learn that sap is a sticky substance that comes from a plant.)*

Answers

Chart Skills **Identify** a box or rectangle **Analyze Images** Answers will vary, but should show students' understanding of the sounds and appearance of the hieroglyphs illustrated.

Science and Medicine ▫L2

Guided Instruction

- Read about more of the ancient Egyptians' accomplishments in Science and Medicine.

- Have students describe how Egyptians determined the length of their year. (*As farmers, they needed to know when the Nile would flood. An astronomer discovered that it flooded whenever they saw Sirius, the Dog Star, in the sky. They saw the star once every 365 days, so 365 days became the length of their year.*)

- Ask **Why do you think Egypt was known as a land of great learning?** (*Egyptians established a system of writing and made important advances in astronomy, such as establishing the length of a year, and medicine, such as performing some surgeries and using herbs for medicine.*)

Independent Practice

Ask students to complete the Accomplishments box of the flow chart with the information they have just learned about Egyptian advances in astronomy and medicine.

Monitor Progress

- Show *Section Reading Support Transparency HOW 64* and ask students to check their graphic organizers individually. Go over key concepts and clarify key vocabulary as needed.

  📖 **History of Our World Transparencies,** *Section Reading Support Transparency HOW 64*

- Tell students to fill in the last column of the *Reading Readiness Guide*. Ask them to evaluate if what they learned was what they had expected to learn.

  All in One Unit 2 History of Our World Teaching Resources, *Reading Readiness Guide,* p. 18

Clues to the Past
The Rosetta Stone bears the same inscription in three languages. The hieroglyphs are at the stone's top, another Egyptian script called demotic is in the middle, and Greek appears at the bottom. The circled hieroglyphs (above left) spell the name of King Ptolemy V. Jean François Champollion (above right) realized that hieroglyphs stood for sounds in the Egyptian language and was able to decipher the hieroglyphs used to spell Ptolemy's name.
Generalize *Why was the translation of hieroglyphs an important discovery in the study of Egyptian history?*

92 History of Our World

Unlocking a Mystery The meaning of ancient Egypt's hieroglyphic writing was lost after the A.D. 400s. Scholars could not read the mysterious pictures. It wasn't until about 200 years ago, in 1799, that an important find took place. A soldier digging a fort near the Nile found a large black stone with three different types of writing on it. The upper part showed hieroglyphs, the middle part showed a later Egyptian script called demotic, and the lower part showed Greek letters. The stone was named the Rosetta Stone because it was found near Rosetta, a city in the Nile delta near the Mediterranean Sea.

The three texts on the stone held the same meaning. Therefore, many scholars tried to use the Greek letters on the Rosetta Stone to figure out the meaning of the hieroglyphs. But it was not an easy task. Then, in the 1820s, a young French scholar named Jean François Champollion (zhahn frahn SWAH shahm poh LYOHN) finally figured it out. When Champollion published his results, a new window onto the world of ancient Egypt opened.

✓ **Reading Check** What was the significance of the Rosetta Stone?

Science and Medicine

In addition to their developments in writing, the ancient Egyptians made important advances in such fields as astronomy and medicine. Among the people of the ancient world, Egypt was known as a land of great learning.

Keeping Track of Time Because they were an agricultural people, the Egyptians needed to be able to predict when the Nile would flood. Astronomers noticed that the Nile appeared to rise rapidly about the same time that they could see Sirius (SIHR ee us), the Dog Star, in the sky shortly before sunrise. **Astronomers are scientists who study the stars and other objects in the sky.** They worked out the average time between the appearances of the star. They found that it came to about 365 days. This became the length of their year.

Answers

✓ **Reading Check** The Rosetta Stone was important because it translated hieroglyphs into other languages so modern people could learn what the hieroglyphs meant.
Generalize The ability to translate hieroglyphs was important because it provided the history of the Egyptians that was previously unknown.

Background: Links Across Time

Ebers Papyrus In 1873, George Maurice Ebers, a German scholar, acquired one of the oldest known medical works. It was a scroll dating from about 1550 B.C. that contains some 700 folk remedies used by ancient Egyptian physicians. The papyrus shows that the Egyptians had a fairly accurate idea of the workings of the human circulatory system and the function of the heart. The papyrus also contains "cures" for everything from sore toenails to crocodile bites.

Mathematics The Egyptians used basic mathematics in finding solutions to problems they faced every day. We know they could add, subtract, multiply, and divide. We also know they used simple fractions. Mathematics helped Egyptians measure stone so that it could be cut to the proper size to build pyramids. They used geometry to measure area so that they could figure out the amount of taxes for a plot of land.

Medicine Religion and medicine were closely related in ancient Egypt. Doctors were specially trained priests who used religious practices and their knowledge of illnesses to try to heal the sick. Probably because of their work on mummies, the ancient Egyptians knew a great deal about the body. By studying the body, they learned to perform surgery. They could set broken bones and treat many minor injuries.

The Egyptians also understood herbalism, the practice of creating medicines from plants. They used these natural remedies to help ease everyday illnesses such as stomachaches and headaches. Mothers prepared their own home remedies, or cures, to reduce children's fevers. The Egyptians wrote much of their medical knowledge down on papyrus. Centuries later, the ancient Greeks and Romans used these records.

√ **Reading Check** Why was it important for the Egyptians to figure out the length of their year?

Assess and Reteach

Assess Progress [L2]
Have students complete the Section Assessment. Administer the *Section Quiz*.

All in One Unit 2 History of Our World Teaching Resources, *Section Quiz,* p. 20

Reteach [L1]
If students need more instruction, have them read this section in the Reading and Vocabulary Study Guide.

Chapter 3, Section 4, **History of Our World Reading and Vocabulary Study Guide,** pp. 41–43

Extend [L3]
To extend students' knowledge about ancient Egypt, have students create their own palettes, similar to ancient Egyptian slate palettes.

All in One Unit 2 History of Our World Teaching Resources, *Small Group Activity: Making Ancient Egyptian Slate Palettes,* pp. 31–34

Answers

√ **Reading Check** They needed to know when the waters of the Nile would flood.

Writing Activity
Use the *Rubric for Assessing a Writing Assignment* to evaluate students' work.

All in One Unit 2 History of Our World Teaching Resources, *Rubric for Assessing a Writing Assignment,* p. 40

Section 4 Assessment

Key Terms
Review the key terms at the beginning of this section. Use each term in a sentence that explains its meaning.

Target Reading Skill
Find the word *remedies* in the last paragraph in this section. Use cause-and-effect clues to figure out its meaning.

Comprehension and Critical Thinking
1. (a) Describe How were the lives of Egypt's peasants ruled by the seasons?

(b) Draw Conclusions How did the seasons affect all of Egyptian society?
2. (a) Recall Describe how the Egyptians used hieroglyphs to communicate.
(b) Analyze Information What was the importance of writing in Egyptian society?
3. (a) List What areas of science and medicine did the ancient Egyptians study?
(b) Link Past and Present How did the learning achievements of the Egyptians affect later civilizations?

Writing Activity
Suppose you are an Egyptian scribe. Write a description that shows how you use your skill in the service of the pharaoh. Then, use the table of hieroglyphs in this section to create a word.

Writing Tip Scribes kept records and accounts for the pharaohs. They also wrote prayers on the wall paintings of tombs. Think about some other work a scribe might perform for a pharaoh. Then write your description from the scribe's point of view.

Chapter 3 Section 4 **93**

Section 4 Assessment

Key Terms
Students' sentences should reflect knowledge of each Key Term.

Target Reading Skill
The context clues show that *remedies* are medicines that help ease everyday illnesses.

Comprehension and Critical Thinking
1. (a) During the flood season, the peasants worked on roads, temples, and buildings. After the flood, they planted crops and later harvested them. **(b)** Possible answer: Since the Egyptian economy was largely based on farming and trade, the flood season influenced the prosperity of the people. The harvest season was the busiest for peasants.

2. (a) Hieroglyphs were picture-like symbols that represented sounds or ideas.

Egyptians used hieroglyphs as their system of writing. **(b)** Writing enabled the people to keep track of their economy through written records and, later, enabled them to communicate more complicated ideas.

3. (a) Astronomy, herbalism, and the human body **(b)** Future civilizations used the information Egyptians learned about medicine and astronomy.

Skills for Life

Objective

Learn how to read a route map.

Prepare to Read

Build Background Knowledge   L2

Ask students whether they have ever looked at a road atlas, a bus or subway map, or a hiking or biking trail map. Have volunteers explain why and how they used such maps. Explain that these maps are all route maps. Point out that any map that shows established paths is a route map.

Instruct

Using Route Maps   L2

Guided Practice

■ Read the steps to using a route map as a class and write them on the board.

■ Practice the skill by following the steps on p. 95 as a class. Have students read the title of the map. Ask students to identify what region the map shows *(Ancient Egypt, Nubia, Syria, and Mesopotamia)*, what type of map it is *(political)*, what time period it shows *(about 1450 B.C.)*, and what the main purpose of the map is *(to show Egyptian trade routes)*. Then have students study the map key identifying what each symbol or color represents *(purple represents the Egyptian empire, red lines are trade routes, black dots are cities)*. Students should trace the paths of the routes with their finger and notice that most routes are by land, but run near waterways.

■ Help students answer the questions in Step 4 that will lead them to conclusions about the map. *(Most of the trade routes ran through the purple area because this area was within the Egyptian area and was more populated so people were more familiar with its terrain. Egyptians had to work the trade routes around bodies of water and avoid the harsh desert areas. There is no road from Thebes to Giza because they probably didn't need one since they could travel on the Nile between the two cities.)*

A silver jug from ancient Egypt

> The leader of the caravan turned and saw the storm approaching in the distance. Then he looked ahead, straining to see some glimpse of Assur. The caravan had been traveling for many days, carrying goods from Giza. Although his men were tired, the leader signaled for them to move faster. He wanted to reach the city before the storm came.
>   For years, the caravan leader had brought goods from Lower Egypt to Syria and Sumer. This particular road, however, was new to him. He hoped that they would reach Assur soon.

The leader of the caravan might have found a route map useful. Although maps did exist in ancient times, most people's knowledge of roads was passed along by word of mouth. Today, most road travel is fairly easy. You just need to know how to read a route map.

Learn the Skill

Use the following steps to read a route map.

1 **Read the title of the map, and become familiar with the map's features.** What is the purpose of the map? What type of map is it—physical or political, modern or historical, or a standard road map?

A camel caravan in the Sahara

94 History of Our World

2 **Study the key to understand its symbols.** Colors are generally used on route maps to show different routes or different types of roads.

3 **Trace routes on the map.** Using the scale of miles, you can calculate distances. A physical map will show the geographic features of a route.

4 **Interpret the map.** Draw conclusions about which routes would be fastest, safest, most scenic, or the easiest to follow.

■ Ask students to plan the fastest travel route from Giza to Kadesh. Review with students how to use the map scale if necessary.

Independent Practice

Assign *Skills for Life* and have students complete it individually.

All in One Unit 2 History of Our World Teaching Resources, *Skills for Life,* p. 30

Monitor Progress

As students are completing *Skills for Life,* circulate to make sure individuals are applying the skill steps correctly. Provide assistance as needed.

Practice the Skill

Use the steps on page 96 and the map at the right to gather and interpret information about ancient trade routes.

1 Write down the purpose of the map. What does the map show?

2 Look at the key to see information about Egyptian trade routes. Identify the purple region on the map. Find routes that travel over land and water. Identify the landmarks indicated in the map key.

3 Using the compass rose, note the general direction of the trade routes. Identify the geographic features of the routes. Look for geographic features that the routes seem to avoid.

4 Write a paragraph that draws conclusions about Egyptian trade routes. Answering these questions might help you: Why did most of the trade routes run through the purple area? How did geography influence the paths that traders took? Why does the map show no direct road connecting the major Egyptian cities of Thebes and Giza?

Egyptian Trade Routes, c. 1450 B.C.

KEY

Egyptian Empire, about 1450 B.C.
Trade route on land
Trade route on water
⊛ National capital
• Other city

Apply the Skill

Draw a map showing the route you take from your home to your school. Add a scale and a compass rose. Mark the location of your school and your home with symbols. Explain the symbols in a map key.

When you are finished, exchange maps with a classmate. Identify the symbols used in the map key. Determine the distance from your classmate's home to school.

Chapter 3 **95**

Assess Progress　L2

Ask students to do the Apply the Skill activity.

Reteach　L1

If students are having trouble applying the skill steps, have them review the skill using the interactive Social Studies Skills Tutor CD-ROM.

◉ *Analyzing and Interpreting Special-Purpose Maps,* **Social Studies Skills Tutor CD-ROM**

Extend　L3

To extend the lesson, ask students to apply the skill steps to the road map of the area around Sydney, Australia, by assigning *Understanding Road Maps.* Here they will analyze the common features of road maps including the location of cities, roads that link the cities, and distances between cities.

All in One Unit 2 History of Our World Teaching Resources, *Understanding Road Maps,* p. 35

■ As a concluding question, ask students **What do you notice about the relationship of highways to major cities?** (*There are more highways near cities, while there are more small roads as you move farther away from a major city.*)

Differentiated Instruction

For Gifted and Talented　L3

Ask students to do library or Internet research to find a map of a city they would like to visit. Tell them to choose a hotel and find its location on the city map. Then, tell them to select three points of interest or sights they would like to visit in one day. Ask them to plan the routes from their hotel to each of the sights in the most efficient way possible.

Answers

Apply the Skill

Students' maps should include the major map elements and demonstrate an understanding of the skill.

Chapter 3 **95**

Objectives

Social Studies

1. Examine the relationship between Nubia and Egypt.
2. Learn about the Nubian kingdoms centered in Kerma, Napata, and Meroë.

Reading/Language Arts

Use synonyms to understand the meanings of unfamiliar words.

Prepare to Read

Build Background Knowledge **L2**

With students, locate ancient Nubia on the map on page 69 and follow the course of the Nile River through Nubia. Then locate the region in Africa today on *Color Transparency HOW 17: Africa: Political* and show how it stretches from Khartoum in Sudan to Aswan in Egypt. Discuss how the location of Nubia between Central Africa and Egypt gave it a great advantage in bringing the products of Central Africa to Egypt, Mesopotamia, and the Greek Islands of the Aegean Sea.

📖 **History of Our World Transparencies,** *Color Transparency HOW 17: Africa: Political*

Set a Purpose for Reading **L2**

- Preview the Objectives.

- Read each statement in the *Reading Readiness Guide.* Ask students to mark the statements true or false.

  All in One **Unit 2 History of Our World Teaching Resources,** *Reading Readiness Guide,* p. 22

- Have students discuss the statements in pairs or groups of four, then mark their guides again. Use the Numbered Heads participation strategy (TE, p. T40) to call on students to share their group's perspectives.

Vocabulary Builder
Preview Key Terms **L2**

Pronounce each Key Term, then ask the students to say the word with you. Provide a simple explanation such as, "Miners dig copper ore out of the ground and then use it to make the metal used in jewelry."

Prepare to Read

Objectives

In this section you will
1. Examine the relationship between Nubia and Egypt.
2. Learn about the Nubian kingdoms centered in Kerma, Napata, and Meroë.

Taking Notes

As you read, find details on the resources and culture of ancient Nubia. Copy the table below, and fill in the columns to record your findings.

Nubia			
Relations With Egypt	Kerma	Napata	Meroë
• •	• •	• •	• •

🎯 Target Reading Skill

Use Context Clues You can use synonyms, words that have similar meanings, to figure out the meaning of an unfamiliar word. Find the synonym for *ultimate* in the following sentence: Taharka received the *ultimate* prize, the greatest honor possible. *Greatest* is a synonym for *ultimate*. As you read, look for synonyms and other context clues.

Key Terms

- **ore** (awr) *n.* a mineral or a combination of minerals mined for the production of metals
- **Lower Nubia** (LOH ur NOO bee uh) *n.* the region of ancient Nubia between the first and second Nile cataracts
- **Upper Nubia** (UP ur NOO bee uh) *n.* the region of ancient Nubia between the second and sixth Nile cataracts
- **artisan** (AHR tuh zun) *n.* a worker who is skilled in crafting goods by hand

This Egyptian bronze statue shows Pharaoh Taharka making an offering to the falcon god.

Prince Taharka of Nubia loved a good contest. He once held a 5-hour, 30-mile race across the desert. The athletes, Taharka's soldiers, ran at night to avoid the blazing heat. In the end, he gave prizes to the winners and losers alike.

In 690 B.C., Taharka himself would receive the ultimate prize: He was to be crowned king of both Nubia and Egypt. He would become the greatest ruler of his dynasty. Taharka's mother traveled 1,200 miles from Nubia north to Memphis to see her son made king. Their homeland of Nubia gave birth to some of the world's oldest cultures.

Nubia and Egypt

Archaeologists have found pottery, weapons, and jewelry at Nubian burial sites. Some of these items date to about 6000 B.C. Findings also show that trade existed among these early peoples. From about 3100 B.C., many Nubian kingdoms arose, only to die out as their rulers lost power.

96 History of Our World

🎯 Target Reading Skill **L2**

Use Context Clues Point out the Target Reading Skill. Explain to students that sometimes you can use synonyms to help you understand the meaning of an unfamiliar word.

Model the skill by writing the following sentence on the chalkboard: "The Kushite kingdom continued to expand as it spread into southern Egypt." Tell students to sup- pose they need to find the meaning of *expand.* The synonym for the word, *spread,* can help them determine that the meaning of *expand* is "to spread out or enlarge."

Give students *Use Context Clues: Definition/Description.* Have them complete the activity in groups.

All in One **Unit 2 History of Our World Teaching Resources,** *Use Context Clues: Definition/Description,* p. 26

Land of the Bow Recall that the region of Nubia was located south of ancient Egypt, beyond the first cataract of the Nile River. For most of their long history, Nubia and Egypt were peaceful, friendly neighbors. The Egyptians called Nubia Ta Sety (tah SEHT ee), the "land of the bow." They were probably referring to the Nubians' skill as archers. The Nubian archers were so skilled that Egypt hired many of them for its armies.

Valuable Resources Egypt valued Nubia for its rich mineral resources, such as gold, copper, and iron ore. An **ore** is a mineral or a combination of minerals mined for the production of metals. Because of its location, Nubia became a bridge for goods traveling between central Africa and Egypt. Early in its history, Egypt benefited from goods that came from **Lower Nubia,** the region between the first and second Nile cataracts. Later, powerful kingdoms began to rise to the south, in **Upper Nubia,** the region between the second and sixth Nile cataracts. These kingdoms rivaled Egypt for control of land. The most powerful of these kingdoms were in the cities of Kerma (KUR muh), Napata (nuh PAY tuh), and Meroë (MEHR oh ee). Find these cities on the map on page 98. These kingdoms were ruled by Kushites, people who lived in southern Nubia.

✔ **Reading Check** Why did Nubia and Egypt become rivals?

Links to
Science

Nubia and Egypt A recent discovery of a Nubian incense burner has some scientists thinking about Nubia's early relationship with Egypt. Some scientists think the object was made around 3100 B.C., or even earlier. Carved on its side are a seated king and other figures that later became the symbols of Egyptian pharaohs. Scholars are debating whether Nubia or Egypt had the first kings.

Nubian Archers
A model shows an army of Nubian archers. The Egyptians admired the Nubians' skill in archery. **Conclude** *Why was Nubia called the "land of the bow"?*

Chapter 3 Section 5 **97**

Instruct

Nubia and Egypt L2

Guided Instruction

- **Vocabulary Builder** Clarify the high-use words **refer** and **benefit** before reading.

- Read Nubia and Egypt, using the Structured Silent Reading strategy technique (TE, p. T38).

- Ask students **Why did Egyptians refer to Nubia as "the land of the bow?"** *(The Nubians were skilled archers. Egypt hired many of them for its armies.)*

- Lead a discussion about the relationship between ancient Egypt and Nubia. Use the Think-Write-Pair-Share strategy (TE, p. T40) to elicit responses. *(The relationship started as a friendly one. Egypt and Nubia traded goods and Nubians even served in Egyptian armies. Later, Egyptians and Nubians began fighting for control of each other's lands.)*

Independent Practice

Ask students to create the Taking Notes graphic organizer on a blank piece of paper. Then have them fill in the first column of the chart with the information they have just learned. Briefly model how to identify which details to record.

Monitor Progress

As students fill in the graphic organizer, circulate and make sure individuals are choosing the correct details. Provide assistance as needed.

Links

Read the **Links to Science** on this page. Ask students **Why do Nubia and Egypt share cultural ties?** *(Egypt and Nubia traded with each other and conquered each other's lands at different points in history.)*

Answers

✔ **Reading Check** Because of its strategic location, Nubia became increasingly wealthy. Three powerful kingdoms rose in Upper Nubia and began to challenge Egypt for control of the land.

Conclude Nubians were skilled archers and Nubia was therefore nicknamed "the land of the bow".

― Vocabulary Builder ―

Use the information below to teach students this section's high-use words.

High-Use Word	Definition and Sample Sentence
refer, p. 97	*v.* to relate or apply I frequently **refer** to my father as my dad.
benefit, p. 97	*v.* to receive something that helps well-being The team **benefited** from the coach's experience.
devote, p. 98	*v.* to give over to or concentrate on an activity He **devoted** all his free time to studying for the test.

The Kerma Culture

Guided Instruction

- **Vocabulary Builder** Clarify the high-use word **devote** before reading.

- Read The Kerma Culture. As students read, circulate to make sure they can answer the Reading Check question.

- Discuss the similarities and differences between the ways the dead were buried in Kerma and ancient Egypt. *(Royal burials were important in both Egypt and Kerma. In Kerma, the kings' tombs were buried in great mounds of dirt rather than pyramids. But similar to the ancient Egyptians their bodies were surrounded by gold and prized possessions.)*

- Ask students **Why did Nubian culture and Egyptian culture mix around the 1500s B.C.?** *(Egypt defeated Kerma in a war that lasted 50 years. Egypt ruled Kerma for the next 700 years during which time Nubians adopted some Egyptian ways of life.)*

Independent Practice
Ask students to fill in the Kerma column in the graphic organizer with the information they have learned about Kerma culture.

Monitor Progress
As students fill in the graphic organizer, circulate and make sure individuals are choosing the correct details. Provide assistance as needed.

Answers

MAP★MASTER Skills Activity **Locate** Gold **Identify Effects** Egypt valued Nubia's mineral resources, so they helped to create a strong trade relationship between Egypt and Nubia.

Go Online PHSchool.com Students may practice their map skills using the interactive online version of this map.

MAP★MASTER™ Skills Activity

The Kingdoms of Nubia: Resources

Human-Environment Interaction The natural resources of Nubia formed the basis of its wealth. **Locate** Which metal was found between the second and third cataracts of the Nile River? **Identify Effects** How did Nubia's metal resources affect its relationship with Egypt?

Go Online PHSchool.com Use Web Code lbp-2335 for step-by-step map skills practice.

KEY
- Kingdoms of Nubia
- • City
- Cataract
- Gold
- Copper
- Iron

First Cataract
Second Cataract
Third Cataract
Fourth Cataract
Fifth Cataract
Sixth Cataract

LOWER NUBIA
UPPER NUBIA
Kerma
Napata
Meroë

Nile River
Red Sea
Atbara River
Blue Nile River
White Nile River

0 miles 200
0 kilometers 200
Lambert Azimuthal Equal Area

The Kerma Culture

The Kushites came to power at a time when Egypt was weakening. By about 1600 B.C., the Kushite kingdom had expanded from the city of Kerma into parts of southern Egypt. These Nubians are known as the Kerma culture. Their kingdom lasted from about 2000 to 1500 B.C.

Kerma's Wealth Kerma had gained not only power but wealth, mainly from controlling the trade between Central Africa and Egypt. It was noted for its **artisans,** or workers skilled at crafting items by hand. They made highly prized, delicate pottery. Items made by Kerma artisans have been found in the tombs of pharaohs.

Like the Egyptians, the people of Kerma devoted a great deal of energy and resources to royal burials. They buried their kings in mounds of earth as large as football fields. Inside their tombs, the kings' bodies rested on top of gold-covered beds surrounded by jewelry, gold, and ivory.

A Kerma pottery bowl

98 History of Our World

Differentiated Instruction

For Advanced Readers

Remind students that they have learned much about the traditions Egyptians and Nubians practiced toward the dead. Have students work in pairs or small groups to research traditions these civilizations practiced for other important parts of life such as births, marriages, and other major life events. Encourage students to find visual information as well as written information. Ask students to prepare a poster showing what they have learned about one important Nubian or Egyptian tradition.

Conflict With Egypt Around the 1500s B.C., Egypt began to recover its strength and to reclaim control of the area. Pharaoh Thutmose I sent his armies into Nubia. After a war that lasted about 50 years, the Egyptians took control of Nubia as far south as the fourth cataract. Egypt ruled Nubia for about the next 700 years.

During this period, the Nubians adopted many Egyptian ways. They even began to worship Egyptian gods along with their own. Throughout these times of conflict and peace, people and goods continued to pass between Nubia and Egypt. The two cultures became mixed.

✓ **Reading Check** What were some characteristics of Kerma?

Napata and Meroë

South of Kerma lay the Nubian cities of Napata and Meroë, in the ancient land called Kush. After centuries of Egyptian rule, the Kushites rose again to power. Their kingdom was centered in the Nubian city of Napata and then later in Meroë.

The Capital of Napata In the late 700s B.C., Egypt was once again weak and divided. From their capital in Napata, the Kushites expanded their power into Egypt.

The Napatan kings gradually took control of more of Egypt. They moved their capital city first to Thebes and then to Memphis. By the time of Taharka, whose coronation you read about earlier, the Nubians controlled all of Egypt. The pharaohs of Egypt's Twenty-fifth Dynasty were Nubians.

The Napatan kings admired Egyptian culture. They brought back many old Egyptian ways and preserved them. They even began building pyramids in which to bury their kings. The ruins of these small Nubian pyramids can still be seen today.

The rule of the Napatan kings did not last very long. About 660 B.C., they were forced back into Nubia. They retreated to Napata and then gradually moved their capital south to Meroë. The Nubians never again controlled Egyptian land.

Monuments of Napata
The pyramids of Napata (top) and a ram statue (bottom) from the entrance to the Great Amum Temple at Napata reflect the ties between Nubian culture and Egyptian culture. **Contrast** *How do the Nubian pyramids differ from the Egyptian pyramids shown in the photo on page 86?*

Chapter 3 Section 5 **99**

⟲ **Target Skill**

Use Context Clues
Do you know what *recover* means? Find a synonym for *recover* later in the same sentence. What does it mean?

↪ **Target Reading Skill**

Use Context Clues As a follow up, ask students to answer the Target Reading Skill in the Student Edition. *(The synonym reclaim can help students determine that the meaning of recover is "to get back or claim again.")*

Napata and Meroë   L2

Guided Instruction

- Read about the other two Nubian kingdoms in Napata and Meroë.

- Discuss the ways in which Napatan kings showed their admiration for Egyptian culture. *(They brought back old Egyptian ways and preserved them. They even built pyramids in which to bury their kings.)*

- Ask students **What do you think happened to Meroë?** *(Students may suggest that Meroë was conquered by invaders and absorbed into another culture.)*

Independent Practice

Ask students to complete the third and fourth columns of the chart with details they have just learned about Napata and Meroë.

Monitor Progress

- Show *Section Reading Support Transparency HOW 65* and ask students to check their graphic organizers individually. Go over key concepts and clarify key vocabulary as needed.

   📖 **History of Our World Transparencies,** *Section Reading Support Transparency HOW 65*

- Tell students to fill in the last column of the *Reading Readiness Guide.* Probe for what they learned that confirms or invalidates each statement.

   All in One **Unit 2 History of Our World Teaching Resources,** *Reading Readiness Guide,* p. 22

Differentiated Instruction

For Less Proficient Readers   L1

If students are having trouble mastering this section's Target Reading Skill, tell them that they can use the Reading and Vocabulary Study Guide to practice the skill before they try it in the Student Edition. Have them complete this section in the Reading and Vocabulary Study Guide, then answer the Target Reading Skill question on page 101 and in the Section Assessment.

📖 Chapter 3, Section 5, **History of Our World Reading and Vocabulary Study Guide,** pp. 44–46

Answers

✓ **Reading Check** Kerma was noted for its artisans who made highly prized pottery. The people of Kerma devoted a lot of energy to royal burials. The Kerma lost a 50-year war with Egypt and came under its control. It then began adopting some aspects of Egyptian culture.

Contrast Possible answer: The angle of the Egyptian pyramids seem to be less steep than that of the Nubian pyramids.

Assess and Reteach

Assess Progress L2

Have students complete the Section Assessment. Administer the *Section Quiz.*

All in One **Unit 2 History of Our World Teaching Resources,** *Section Quiz,* p. 24

Reteach L1

If students need more instruction, have them read this section in the Reading and Vocabulary Study Guide.

 Chapter 3, Section 5, **History of Our World Reading and Vocabulary Study Guide,** pp. 44–46

Extend L3

Form student groups into three large groups and assign one of the three Nubian kingdoms to each group. Ask students to conduct research to find out more about the people and customs of the kingdom. Each group should prepare an oral presentation with visuals, such as photos and maps.

Answer

✓ Reading Check The people of Meroë used iron ore to make weapons and tools.

Section 5 Assessment

Key Terms

Students' sentences should reflect knowledge of each Key Term.

 Target Reading Skill

Students can use the synonym *goods* to help them understand that *articles* means "items for sale" in this sentence.

Comprehension and Critical Thinking

1. (a) At first, they were friendly and traded goods. In time, they became competitive, struggling over power and control of the land. **(b)** The Nubians adopted many Egyptian gods and traditional ceremonies. Many Nubian artifacts were found in tombs of Egyptian pharaohs.

The Women of Nubia
Women held very high status in Nubian society. Most often, the children of the ruler's sister would be next in line for the throne. Compared to Egypt, Nubia had many more women as rulers. In ancient artwork, the queens of Meroë have large and powerful figures. The queens were considered ideal beauties, and their weight reflected their wealth and rank.

The Capital of Meroë   After moving south of Egypt's reach, the Nubians founded a royal court in the ancient city of Meroë. This city was located on the Nile between the fifth and sixth cataracts. It became the center of an empire that included much of Nubia. It also stretched south into central Africa.

The rocky desert east of Meroë held large deposits of iron ore. The Nubians used the ore to make iron weapons and tools. Iron plows allowed them to produce generous supplies of food. Iron weapons allowed them to control trade routes that ran all the way to the Red Sea. There they traded goods from central Africa for articles from India, the Arabian Peninsula, and Rome. Meroë grew rich from this trade.

Today, Meroë remains largely a mystery. The Nubians of Meroë created their own system of hieroglyphic writing. Scholars have so far been unable to fully understand these hieroglyphics, which are found on the temples and tombs of the kingdom.

Meroë began to weaken in the A.D. 200s, and it fell to the African kingdom of Axum in the next century. Features of Nubian culture, however, have lasted for 3,500 years. To this day, Nubian styles of pottery, furniture, jewelry, braided hairstyles, and clothing survive among people of the modern-day African country of Sudan.

✓ Reading Check   How did the people of Meroë use iron ore?

Section 5 Assessment

Key Terms
Review the key terms at the beginning of this section. Use each term in a sentence that explains its meaning.

Target Reading Skill
Find *articles* in the second paragraph on this page. If it is used in an unfamiliar way, find a synonym to understand its meaning.

Comprehension and Critical Thinking
1. (a) Explain What was the relationship between Egypt and Nubia?

(b) Apply Information How did the Nubians and the Egyptians borrow from each other's cultures?
2. (a) Recall What were the resources of Kerma?
(b) Identify the Main Idea What part did Kerma's wealth play in its conflict with Egypt?
3. (a) Explain How are the histories of Napata and Meroë tied to Egypt?
(b) Link Past and Present What signs of Nubian culture exist in Africa today? Do you think present-day Africans are likely to be interested in Nubian culture? Explain why or why not.

Writing Activity
List the names of the three major Nubian cities you learned about in this section. Write a brief description of each of the cities, and include its importance in the history of Nubia.

Writing Tip Before you begin, reread Section 5. As you read, look for important details about each city of Nubia. Your list should include the most important and most interesting details. Refer to the list when you write your description.

---

2. (a) the work of its artisans and its geography **(b)** Because Kerma was wealthy when Egypt was weak, Kerma was able to conquer and expand into southern Egypt.

3. (a) Napata conquered Egypt at a weak point in its history. Napatan rule restored and preserved many old Egyptian ways. Egypt traded with both Meroë and Napata, benefiting from their resources. **(b)** Nubian culture can still be found in styles of pottery, furniture, jewelry, and fashion.

They would be interested in Nubian culture because it was part of Africa's history and remnants may still exist in their culture today.

Writing Activity
Use the *Rubric for Assessing a Writing Assignment* to evaluate students' work.

All in One **Unit 2 History of Our World Teaching Resources,** *Rubric for Assessing a Writing Assignment,* p. 40

3 Review and Assessment

◆ Chapter Summary

Section 1: The Geography of the Nile

- Beginning from two sources, the Nile flows northward in a varied course until it reaches the Mediterranean Sea.
- The Nile provided the ancient Egyptian and Nubian peoples with water, food, and fertile soil.
- The Nile River and its valley were central trade routes for the ancient Egyptians and Nubians.

Section 2: The Rulers of Egypt

- Egyptian kings had absolute power and were thought to be gods.
- Ancient Egypt prospered during three major time periods, the Old Kingdom, the Middle Kingdom, and the New Kingdom.
- After Hatshepsut died, Thutmose III rose to power and became one of the greatest pharaohs of the New Kingdom.

Section 3: Egyptian Religion

- Egyptians were deeply religious and believed in several gods and goddesses.
- Egyptians believed in life after death and carefully prepared their dead for the afterlife.
- Pharaohs began the long, difficult process of building their tombs as soon as they came into power.

Hunting in ancient Egypt

Section 4: Ancient Egyptian Culture

- The Egyptian social order resembled a pyramid, with the pharaoh at the top, and the largest class, the peasants, at the base.
- The ancient Egyptians used a pictorial writing system similar to that used in Mesopotamian civilization.
- Egyptians also studied the stars and practiced medicine.

Section 5: The Cultures of Nubia

- Throughout its history, Nubia was both a friend and a rival of Egypt.
- The Nubian kingdom of Kerma was known for its skilled artisans.
- The people of Meroë were the first Africans to work with iron.

Nubian Pharaoh and falcon god

◆ Key Terms

Match the definitions in Column I with the key terms in Column II.

Column I

1. a strong rush of water
2. a skilled worker
3. a series of rulers from the same family
4. a picturelike symbol
5. a building with four triangle-shaped sides
6. minerals mined for the production of metal
7. fertile soil deposited by flooding rivers

Column II

A ore
B dynasty
C pyramid
D artisan
E hieroglyph
F cataract
G silt

Chapter 3 **101**

Review Chapter Content

- Review and revisit the major themes of this chapter by asking students to classify what Guiding Question each bulleted statement in the Chapter Summary answers. Have students work in groups to classify the statements. Use the Numbered Heads strategy (TE, p. T40) to have the groups share their answers in a group discussion. Refer to page 1 in the Student Edition for the text of the Guiding Questions.

- Assign *Vocabulary Development* for students to review Key Terms.

  All in One **Unit 2 History of Our World Teaching Resources,** *Vocabulary Development,* p. 38

Vocabulary Builder

Revisit this chapter's high-use words:

source	yield	refer
isolate	preserve	benefit
approximate	site	devote
restore	resemble	
proclaim	complicate	

Ask students to review the definitions they recorded on their *Word Knowledge* worksheet.

All in One **Unit 2 History of Our World Teaching Resources,** *Word Knowledge,* p. 28

Consider allowing students to earn extra credit if they use the words in their answers to the questions in the Chapter Review and Assessment. The words must be used correctly and in a natural context to win the extra points.

Answers

Key Terms

1. F
2. D
3. B
4. E
5. C
6. A
7. G

Comprehension and Critical Thinking

8. (a) The Nile flows north from its sources in East Africa to the Mediterranean Sea. The Nubian section of the Nile is characterized by cataracts and little land that is available for farming. The Egyptian section of the Nile is characterized by fertile farm land, including the marshy areas and deltas at the mouth of the Mediterranean. **(b)** The desert kept out invaders from foreign lands. **(c)** The river benefited surrounding civilizations by providing water for drinking and irrigation, and its floods made surrounding land fertile. Sometimes it hurt civilizations when unexpected floods ruined villages.

9. (a) During the Old Kingdom timber was brought in to build houses, boats and furniture. The Middle Kingdom was marked by progress in irrigation and the building of a canal between the Nile and the Red Sea. During the New Kingdom powerful armies were built. **(b)** The pharaohs made all the laws and had absolute power. The people saw the pharaoh as god-like—more than their leader, the pharaoh was often thought to be responsible for all the forces of nature. **(c)** Hammurabi and the pharaohs were similar in their desire to conquer surrounding lands. Both developed the laws their people would follow.

10. (a) The pyramids were the burial places for the bodies of pharaohs. **(b)** Religion was a way of explaining the forces of nature, such as the flooding of the Nile. **(c)** The ancient Egyptians believed that the afterlife was the place where they would be rewarded for living a good life on earth.

11. (a) The ancient Egyptians provided the foundation for surgery and the use of herbal medicines. They also created their own system of writing, as well as tools for measurement. Finally, Egyptian astronomers were responsible for determining the length of a year to be 365 days. **(b)** Answers will vary. Possible answer: Establishing the length of a year has provided the foundation for a system of time by which all of humanity lives.

12. (a) Each civilization had many resources to offer the other in trade. Both civilizations were also successful on their own—a war had the potential of ruining the civilizations. **(b)** Egyptian and Nubian civilizations lasted longer than the Assyrian and Babylonian civilizations. Possible reason: Nubia and Egypt were protected from some invaders by vast desert whereas the Babylonian and

---

◆ Comprehension and Critical Thinking

8. Recall Describe the geography of the Nile River and the lands that surround it.
(a) Explain Why did the people of Egypt and Nubia consider their deserts to be a blessing?
(b) Identify Effects In what ways did the Nile river affect ancient civilizations?

9. List Name and describe the three major periods in ancient Egyptian history.
(a) Describe What was the role of the pharaoh in Egyptian government and society?
(b) Compare and Contrast Compare the pharaohs' rule of Egypt with Hammurabi's rule of Babylonia. How are the rulers similar or different?

10. (a) Identify What was the purpose of the pyramids in ancient Egypt?
(b) Generalize Why was religion so important to the people of ancient Egypt?
(c) Analyze Why did the idea of the afterlife appeal to the ancient Egyptians?

11. (a) Recall List the accomplishments of the ancient Egyptians.
(b) Conclude Choose one accomplishment of the ancient Egyptian civilization and describe its importance.

12. (a) Explain Why was it in the interests of Egypt and Nubia to maintain friendly relations?
(b) Compare and Contrast Compare the length of time Egypt's and Nubia's civilizations lasted with that of the Assyrians and the Babylonians. How do you account for the differences?

◆ Skills Practice

Using Route Maps In the Skills for Life lesson in this chapter, you learned how to analyze and interpret route maps. You also learned how to create your own route map.

Review the steps for this skill. Using your route map, complete the following: (a) Add another route between your home and your school. It could be a shortcut, or a longer route. (b) Explain the advantages and disadvantages of your alternate route.

◆ Writing Activity: Language Arts

Think about the Nile River and how important it was to the ancient Egyptians and Nubians. Then write a poem about the Nile, from the point of view of an ancient Egyptian or Nubian.

The poem can be in any form, rhyming or unrhyming. Be sure to include details that show the importance of the river. Reread Section 1 to refresh your memory on the geography of the Nile.

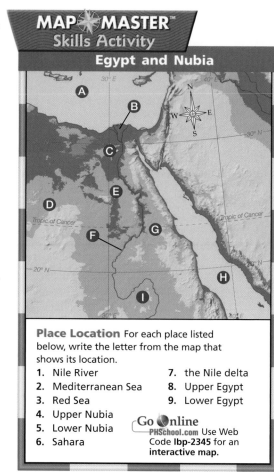

MAP MASTER™ Skills Activity

Egypt and Nubia

Place Location For each place listed below, write the letter from the map that shows its location.

1. Nile River
2. Mediterranean Sea
3. Red Sea
4. Upper Nubia
5. Lower Nubia
6. Sahara
7. the Nile delta
8. Upper Egypt
9. Lower Egypt

Go Online PHSchool.com Use Web Code **lbp-2345** for an interactive map.

Assyrian empires lay in an open land which others could be easily invaded. Also, they did not fight each other.

Skills Practice

Students' maps and alternate routes will vary. They should reflect an understanding of the skill.

Writing Activity: Language Arts

Answers will vary. Poems should reflect knowledge of the Nile River and its importance as a source of water for drinking and farming and as a trade route.

Use the *Rubric for Assessing a Student Poem* to evaluate students' poems.

All in One Unit 2 History of Our World Teaching Resources, *Rubric for Assessing a Student Poem,* p. 41

Standardized Test Prep

Test-Taking Tips

Some questions on standardized tests ask you to draw conclusions by analyzing a table. Study the table below. Then follow the tips to answer the sample question.

BUILDING THE GREAT PYRAMID	
Number of blocks	2 million
Weight of each block	5,000 pounds
Height of pyramid	450 feet
Time to build	about 20 years

Pick the letter that best completes the statement.

The information in the table could be used to show the

A ~~importance of the Nile River in Egypt.~~

B division of Egyptian society into classes.

C ~~cruelty of the Egyptian pharaohs.~~

D organization and skills of the Egyptians.

Think It Through All of the information in the table has to do with the construction of the pyramids. You can rule out answer A, because it has to do with the river. You can eliminate C, because it has to do with the characteristics of the pharaohs. Of B and D, which answer has the most to do with the construction of the pyramids? The answer is D. It states correctly that the pyramids show the organization and skill of the Egyptians.

TIP Preview the question first and think about it as you study the table.

TIP Eliminate answer choices that don't make sense. Then decide which remaining choice is BEST.

Practice Questions

Use the tips above and other tips in this book to help you answer the following questions.

1. Why did the Nubians develop trade routes over land?

   A Cataracts on the Nile River limited travel.

   B The Egyptians tended to attack by boat.

   C Nubians had no ship-building skills.

   D Travel in the desert was easy.

Study the table below, and then answer the question that follows.

Ancient Civilizations

Location	Time Span
Ancient Mesopotamia	About 3300 – 539 B.C.
Ancient Egypt	About 3100 – 31 B.C.
Ancient Nubia	About 3100 B.C. – A.D. 350

2. Which sentence accurately describes the information in the table?

   A All ancient civilizations ended before A.D. 1.

   B The civilizations of Mesopotamia began after those of Egypt and Nubia.

   C The civilizations of ancient Egypt and Nubia both lasted about 1,000 years.

   D Several ancient civilizations lasted thousands of years.

3. Egyptian society was pyramid-shaped, with

   A the pharaoh at the top and peasants at the bottom.

   B the pharaoh at the top and priests at the bottom.

   C priests at the top and no peasants.

   D priests and peasants at the top.

Use Web Code **lba-2305** for **Chapter 3 self-test.**

1. F	**2.** A
3. H	**4.** I
5. G	**6.** D
7. B	**8.** E
9. C	

Go Online PHSchool.com Students may practice their map skills by using the interactive online version of this map.

Standardized Test Prep

Answers

1. A

2. D

3. A

Go Online PHSchool.com Students may use the Chapter 3 self-test on PHSchool.com to prepare for the Chapter Test.

Assessment Resources

Use Chapter Tests A and B to assess students' mastery of chapter content.

All in One **Unit 2 History of Our World Teaching Resources,** *Chapter Tests A and B,* pp. 42–47

Tests are also available on the Exam-*View®* Test Bank CD-ROM.

⊙ **Exam*View*® Test Bank CD-ROM**

Ancient India

Overview

Section 1

The Indus and Ganges River Valleys
1. Learn about India's geographic setting.
2. Find out about life in an ancient city of the Indus River valley.
3. Examine the rise of a new culture in the Indus and Ganges river valleys.

Section 2

Hinduism in Ancient India
1. Find out about the beginnings of Hinduism.
2. Learn about the teachings of Hinduism.
3. Examine the many paths to truth in Hinduism.

Section 3

The Beginnings of Buddhism
1. Learn about the Buddha and his teachings.
2. Find out how Buddhism was received inside and outside India.

Section 4

The Maurya Empire
1. Learn about the rise of the Maurya Empire.
2. Understand the effects of Asoka's leadership on the Maurya Empire.

Discovery CHANNEL SCHOOL Video

The Maurya Elephant Army
Length: 4 minutes, 31 seconds
Use with Section 4

This video segment explores the Maurya Empire and the importance of the elephant in both trade and defense. The segment provides details on how this animal was used as a beast of burden as well as a powerful military weapon.

Technology Resources

Go Online
PHSchool.com

Students use embedded Web codes to access Internet activities, chapter self-tests, and additional map practice. They may also access Dorling Kindersley's Online Desk Reference to learn more about each country they study.

Interactive Textbook

Use the Interactive Textbook to make content and concepts come alive through animations, videos, and activities that accompany the complete basal text—online and on CD-ROM.

PRENTICE HALL
TeacherEXPRESS
Plan • Teach • Assess

Use this complete suite of powerful teaching tools to make planning lessons and administering tests quicker and easier.

Reading and Assessment

Reading and Vocabulary Instruction

⟳ Model the Target Reading Skill

Cause and Effect Tell students that learning to identify causes and effects in their reading can help them understand and analyze relationships between situations or events. Mastering this skill can help students realize *why* something happened as well as *what* happened. Model identifying causes and effects using the following selection from page 117 of the Student Edition:

According to Hindu belief, the actions of a person in this life affect his or her fate in the next. Good behavior is always rewarded. Bad behavior is always punished.

Think aloud: "I know that this selection describes causes and effects because it talks about what will happen as a result of a person's actions. The first sentence contains the word *affect*, which gives me a hint as to what is the cause and what is the effect. I see that a person's actions in this life cause his or her fate to be a certain way. The following sentence summarizes which actions cause which effects: "Good behavior causes a person to be rewarded, and bad behavior causes a person to be punished. As I read the chapter, I will look for more causes and effects."

Use the following worksheets from All-in-One Unit 2 History of Our World Teaching Resources (pp. 67–70) to support this chapter's Target Reading Skill.

Vocabulary Builder
High-Use Academic Words
Use these steps to teach this chapter's high-use words:

1. Have students rate how well they know each word on their Word Knowledge worksheets (All-in-One Unit 2 History of Our World Teaching Resources, p. 71)

2. Pronounce each word and ask students to repeat it.

3. Give students a brief definition and sample sentence (provided on TE pp.107, 115, 120, 127).

4. Work with students as they fill in the "Definition or Example" column of their Word Knowledge worksheets.

Assessment

Formal Assessment
Test students' understanding of core knowledge and skills.

Chapter Tests A and B, All-in-One Unit 2 History of Our World Teaching Resources, pp. 90–95

Customize the Chapter Tests to suit your needs.
Exam*View*®
Test Bank CD-ROM

Skills Assessment
Assess geographic literacy.
MapMaster Skills, Student Edition pp. 105, 107, 122, 128, 132

Assess reading skills.
Target Reading Skills, Student Edition, pp. 106, 114, 119, 126 and in Section Assessments

Chapter 4 Assessment, History of Our World Reading and Vocabulary Study Guide, p. 60

Performance Assessment
Assess students' performance on this chapter's Writing Activities using the following rubric from All-in-One Unit 2 History of Our World Teaching Resources.

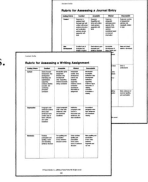

Rubric for Assessing a Writing Assignment, p. 86
Rubric for Assessing an Oral Presentation, p. 87
Rubric for Assessing a Journal Entry, p. 88
Rubric for Assessing a Caption, p. 89

Assess students' work through performance tasks.
Small Group Activity: Making a Map of Mohenjo-Daro, All-in-One Unit 2 History of Our World Teaching Resources, pp. 74–77

Online Assessment
Have students check their own understanding.
Chapter Self-Test

Section 1 The Indus and Ganges River Valleys

 2 periods, 1 block (includes Focus On Mohenjo-Daro)

Social Studies Objectives
1. Learn about India's geographic setting.
2. Find out about life in an ancient city of the Indus River valley.
3. Examine the rise of a new culture in the Indus and Ganges river valleys.

Reading/Language Arts Objective
Use causes and effects to understand relationships among situations or events.

Prepare to Read	**Instructional Resources**	**Differentiated Instruction**
Build Background Knowledge Use the section's headings and visuals to discuss how geography affected people's lives in ancient India. **Set a Purpose for Reading** Have students evaluate statements on the *Reading Readiness Guide*. **Preview Key Terms** Teach the section's Key Terms. **Target Reading Skill** Introduce the section's Target Reading Skill of **identifying causes and effects**.	**All in One Unit 2 History of Our World Teaching Resources** L2 Reading Readiness Guide, p. 52 L2 Identify Causes and Effects, p. 67	**Spanish Reading and Vocabulary Study Guide** L1 Chapter 4, Section 1, pp. 36–37 ELL

Instruct	**Instructional Resources**	**Differentiated Instruction**
India's Geographic Setting Discuss India's geography and its influence on the people there. **Target Reading Skill** Review **identifying causes and effects**. **Life in the Indus River Valley** Ask questions about and discuss Mohenjo-Daro. **A New Culture Arises** Discuss the cultures of India.	**All in One Unit 2 History of Our World Teaching Resources** L2 Guided Reading and Review, p. 53 L2 Reading Readiness Guide, p. 52 **History of Our World Transparencies** L2 Section Reading Support Transparency HOW 66	**All in One History of Our World Teaching Resources** L3 Small Group Activity: Making a Map of Mohenjo-Daro, pp. 74–77 AR, GT **Teacher's Edition** L1 For English Language Learners, TE p. 108 L1 For Less Proficient Readers, TE p. 108 L3 For Gifted and Talented, TE pp. 109, 112 **Student Edition on Audio CD** L1 Chapter 4, Section 1 ELL, LPR, SN **Spanish Support** L2 Guided Reading and Review (Spanish), p. 36 ELL

Assess and Reteach	**Instructional Resources**	**Differentiated Instruction**
Assess Progress Evaluate student comprehension with the section assessment and section quiz. **Reteach** Assign the Reading and Vocabulary Study Guide to help struggling students. **Extend** Extend the lesson by assigning an Activity Shop Lab.	**All in One Unit 2 History of Our World Teaching Resources** L2 Section Quiz, p. 54 L3 Activity Shop Lab: Rivers That Flood, pp. 78–79 Rubric for Assessing a Writing Assignment, p. 86 **Reading and Vocabulary Study Guide** L1 Chapter 4, Section 1, pp. 48–50	**Spanish Support** L2 Section Quiz (Spanish), p. 37 ELL

Key
L1 Basic to Average	L3 Average to Advanced	LPR Less Proficient Readers	GT Gifted and Talented
L2 For All Students		AR Advanced Readers	ELL English Language Learners
		SN Special Needs Students	

Section 2 Hinduism in Ancient India

 *2 periods, 1 block*

Social Studies Objectives

1. Find out about the beginning of Hinduism.
2. Learn about the teachings of Hinduism.
3. Examine the many paths to truth in Hinduism.

Reading/Language Arts Objective

Learn to identify cause-and-effect signal words.

Prepare to Read	**Instructional Resources**	**Differentiated Instruction**
Build Background Knowledge Compare and contrast Hinduism and ancient Egyptian religion. **Set a Purpose for Reading** Have students evaluate statements on the *Reading Readiness Guide*. **Preview Key Terms** Teach the section's Key Terms. **Target Reading Skill** Introduce the section's Target Reading Skill of recognizing cause-and-effect signal words.	**All in One Unit 2 History of Our World Teaching Resources** **L2** Reading Readiness Guide, p. 56 **L2** Recognize Cause-and-Effect Signal Words, p. 68	**Spanish Reading and Vocabulary Study Guide** **L1** Chapter 4, Section 2, pp. 38–39 ELL

Instruct	**Instructional Resources**	**Differentiated Instruction**
The Beginnings of Hinduism Discuss the Hindu religion. **The Teachings of Hinduism** **The Practice of Hinduism** Discuss the idea of reincarnation and how Hindus believe they can find truth. **Target Reading Skill** Review using cause and effect.	**All in One Unit 2 History of Our World Teaching Resources** **L2** Guided Reading and Review, p. 57 **L2** Reading Readiness Guide, p. 56 **History of Our World Transparencies** **L2** Section Reading Support Transparency HOW 67	**All in One Unit 2 History of Our World Teaching Resources** **L3** Savitri: A Tale of Ancient India, pp. 80–83 AR, GT **Teacher's Edition** **L1** For Less Proficient Readers, TE p. 116 **L1** For Special Needs Students, TE p. 116 **L3** For Advanced Readers, TE p. 117 **L1** For English Language Learners, TE p. 117 **Spanish Support** **L1** Guided Reading and Review, p. 38 ELL

Assess and Reteach	**Instructional Resources**	**Differentiated Instruction**
Assess Progress Evaluate student comprehension with the section assessment and section quiz. **Reteach** Assign the Reading and Vocabulary Study Guide to help struggling students. **Extend** Have students research Hindu gods and goddesses and prepare and conduct a presentation for the classes.	**All in One Unit 2 History of Our World Teaching Resources** **L2** Section Quiz, p. 58 Rubric for Assessing an Oral Presentation, p. 87 Rubric for Assessing a Writing Assignment, p. 86 **Reading and Vocabulary Study Guide** **L1** Chapter 4, Section 2, pp. 51–53	**Spanish Support** **L2** Section Quiz (Spanish), p. 39 ELL

Key

L1 Basic to Average   **L3** Average to Advanced   LPR Less Proficient Readers   GT Gifted and Talented
L2 For All Students   AR Advanced Readers   ELL English Language Learners
                                                        SN Special Needs Students

Section 3 The Beginnings of Buddhism

 2 periods, 1 block (includes Skills for Life)

Social Studies Objectives

1. Learn about the Buddha and his teachings.
2. Find out how Buddhism was received inside and outside India.

Reading/Language Arts Objective

Understand that an effect may have multiple causes.

Prepare to Read	**Instructional Resources**	**Differentiated Instruction**
Build Background Knowledge Discuss the elements of life that are important in Buddhism. **Set a Purpose for Reading** Have students evaluate statements on the *Reading Readiness Guide.* **Preview Key Terms** Teach the section's Key Terms. **Target Reading Skill** Introduce the section's Target Reading Skill of recognizing multiple causes.	**All in One Unit 2 History of Our World Teaching Resources** L2 Reading Readiness Guide, p. 60 L2 Recognize Multiple Causes, p. 69	**Spanish Reading and Vocabulary Study Guide** L1 Chapter 4, Section 3, pp. 40–41 ELL

Instruct	**Instructional Resources**	**Differentiated Instruction**
The Buddha and His Teachings Ask questions about and discuss the Buddha and his teachings. **Target Reading Skill** Review **recognizing multiple causes**. **Buddhism Inside and Outside India** Discuss the spread of Buddhism.	**All in One Unit 2 History of Our World Teaching Resources** L2 Guided Reading and Review, p. 61 L2 Reading Readiness Guide, p. 60 **History of Our World Transparencies** L2 Section Reading Support Transparency HOW 68	**All in One Unit 2 History of Our World Teaching Resources** L3 A Great Asian Thinker, p. 84 AR, GT L2 Skills for Life, p. 73 AR, GT, LPR, SN **Teacher's Edition** L3 For Advanced Readers, TE p. 122 **Spanish Support** L2 Guided Reading and Review (Spanish), p. 40 ELL

Assess and Reteach	**Instructional Resources**	**Differentiated Instruction**
Assess Progress Evaluate student comprehension with the section assessment and section quiz. **Reteach** Assign the Reading and Vocabulary Study Guide to help struggling students. **Extend** Extend the lesson by assigning an Enrichment activity.	**All in One Unit 2 History of Our World Teaching Resources** L2 Section Quiz, p. 62 L3 Enrichment, p. 72 Rubric for Assessing a Journal Entry, p. 88 **Reading and Vocabulary Study Guide** L1 Chapter 4, Section 3, pp. 54–56	**Spanish Support** L2 Section Quiz (Spanish), p. 41 ELL

Key

L1 Basic to Average   L3 Average to Advanced
L2 For All Students

LPR Less Proficient Readers
AR Advanced Readers
SN Special Needs Students

GT Gifted and Talented
ELL English Language Learners

Section 4 The Maurya Empire

 2 periods, 1 block (includes Chapter Review and Assessment)

Social Studies Objectives
1. Learn about the rise of the Maurya Empire.
2. Understand the effects of Asoka's leadership on the Maurya Empire.

Reading/Language Arts Objective
Understand that a cause may produce several effects.

Prepare to Read	Instructional Resources	Differentiated Instruction
Build Background Knowledge Use the section's headings and visuals to discuss the rulers of the Maurya Empire. **Set a Purpose for Reading** Have students evaluate statements on the *Reading Readiness Guide*. **Preview Key Terms** Teach the section's Key Terms. **Target Reading Skill** Introduce the section's Target Reading Skill of **understanding effects.**	**All in One Unit 2 History of Our World Teaching Resources** **L2** Reading Readiness Guide, p. 64 **L2** Understand Effects, p. 70	**Spanish Reading and Vocabulary Study Guide** **L1** Chapter 4, Section 4, pp. 42–43 ELL

Instruct	Instructional Resources	Differentiated Instruction
The Rise of the Maurya Empire Ask questions about and discuss the Maurya Empire and its leader, Chandragupta. **Asoka's Leadership** Discuss the Maurya Empire under the rule of Asoka. **Target Reading Skill** Review **understanding effects.**	**All in One Unit 2 History of Our World Teaching Resources** **L2** Guided Reading and Review, p. 65 **L2** Reading Readiness Guide, p. 64 **History of Our World Transparencies** **L2** Section Reading Support Transparency HOW 69 **World Studies Video Program** **L2** The Maurya Elephant Army	**Teacher's Edition** **L3** For Advanced Readers, TE p. 129 **Spanish Support** **L2** Guided Reading and Review (Spanish), p. 42 ELL

Assess and Reteach	Instructional Resources	Differentiated Instruction
Assess Progress Evaluate student comprehension with the section assessment and section quiz. **Reteach** Assign the Reading and Vocabulary Study Guide to help struggling students. **Extend** Extend the lesson by having students research the art of the Maurya Empire.	**All in One Unit 2 History of Our World Teaching Resources** **L2** Section Quiz, p. 66 Rubric for Assessing a Writing Assignment, p. 86 Rubric for Assessing a Caption, p. 89 **L2** Vocabulary Development, p. 85 **L2** Word Knowledge, p. 71 **L2** Chapter Tests A and B, pp. 90–95 **Reading and Vocabulary Study Guide** **L1** Chapter 4, Section 4, pp. 57–59	**Spanish Support** **L2** Section Quiz (Spanish), p. 43 ELL **L2** Chapter Summary (Spanish), p. 44 ELL **L2** Vocabulary Development (Spanish), p. 45 ELL

Key
L1 Basic to Average **L3** Average to Advanced
L2 For All Students

LPR Less Proficient Readers
AR Advanced Readers
SN Special Needs Students

GT Gifted and Talented
ELL English Language Learners

Reading Background

Word Wizard

Students can often master new vocabulary more easily if they can see how it is applied to everyday life. Have students make a list of the Key Terms and high-use words from the chapter. Then have them take the list home and see how many examples they can find of these words being used in current magazines and newspapers. Offer students bonus points for every accurate example they bring in.

Structuring Paragraphs

Using a standard framework for writing paragraphs can help students write assignments that are effective and to the point. Ask students to write a paragraph using the following guidelines:

1. Begin with a topic sentence.
2. Add 3 to 5 examples with transition words.
3. Include a summary sentence.

Remind students to vary sentence length and structure. Model the assignment by providing students with a topic sentence, three examples, transition words, and a summary.

Topic Sentence: Hinduism is one of the world's oldest religions.

Examples: There have been many great Hindu religious leaders. More than 850 million people in India are Hindu, and Hindu beliefs have influenced many other religions.

Summary Sentence: Hinduism continues to be one of the world's most important religions.

Sharing Key Concepts

Ask each student to explain one key concept, Key Term, or high-use word on a note card. Then have students form two concentric circles. Students on the inside circle should pair with the student facing them on the outside circle. Each pair should explain their concepts to each other using their cards. The two students can ask each other questions to make sure both students understand. Students then trade cards and the outside circle moves clockwise one person. Repeat the process until students end up with their original cards.

World Studies Background

Climbing the Himalayas

The Himalayas have fascinated people for thousands of years. Once it was thought impossible for anyone to climb to the top of these great mountains. In 1953 climbers successfully reached the top of Mount Everest—the tallest peak in the Himalayas and the world. Since then, improved mountain-climbing gear has enabled many people to climb these mountains. Still, the Himalayas remain very dangerous. Dozens of climbers have died trying to reach the summit of Mount Everest, including eight men who were caught in a blizzard in 1996.

The Sacred Cow

In Hindu cultures the milk cow is considered a sacred animal, not to be slaughtered or eaten.

Some Hindu literature associates the cow with goddesses. At one point in Hindu history, the killing of a milk-producing cow was considered the equivalent of murdering a Brahman, a member of the highest caste. Today the legality of killing cows is a divisive political issue in India.

Infoplease® provides a wealth of useful information for the classroom. You can use this resource to strengthen your background on the subjects covered in this chapter. Have students visit this advertising-free site as a starting point for projects requiring research.

 Use Web code **lbd-2400** for **Infoplease®**.

104g

Use some or all of the following ideas or terms for the activity:

monsoon	Indus River Valley	Aryans
caste	Vedas	Hinduism
Upanishads	reincarnation	dharma
ahimsa	Buddhism	nirvana
Maurya Empire	Chandragupta	Asoka

Reading Passages Strategically

In this chapter, students will use the Choral Reading strategy to engage them in actively reading the chapter. Remember that the following tips can help improve the effectiveness of the Choral Reading strategy:

1. Make sure that students say the words with you, without lagging behind or racing ahead in their speech.
2. Use only short passages of less than 500 words.
3. Follow the choral reading with a silent reading of the same passage to allow students to review the materials silently now that they have heard the content.

Scaffolding Tip

When asking students questions about the text, first ask questions to which the answer can be clearly found in the text. Then ask more difficult questions that require students to make their own interpretations based on the easier questions. For example, you might ask students, "What do Hindus believe?" and "What do Buddhists believe?" After students have answered these questions, ask them, "In what ways are Buddhism and Hinduism similar and in what ways are they different?"

Buddhism and Nuns

At first, the Buddha only allowed men to become priests or monks. Later he allowed some women to become nuns. As Buddhism spread throughout the world, different countries adopted different forms of the faith that often reflected local cultural beliefs. In some countries, such as Thailand, Sri Lanka, and Myanmar, Buddhist nuns are no longer accepted because some people believe only men should be members of the clergy.

Expanding India Through Marriage

To spread his kingdom, Chandragupta used not only his vast army but also the political benefits of marriage. Around A.D. 308 he married Princess Kumaradevi of the Licchavi people. The Licchavis controlled north Bihar and Nepal. The marriage united the kingdoms of Chandragupta and the Licchavis into a powerful new alliance. Gold coins from the era show King Chandragupta and Queen Kumaradevi on one side and the Licchavi people on the other.

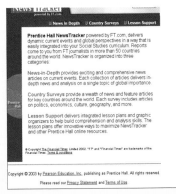

Get in-depth information on topics of global importance with **Prentice Hall Newstracker,** powered by FT.com.

 Use Web code **lbd-2401** for **Prentice Hall Newstracker.**

Chapter 4

Guiding Questions

Remind students about the Guiding Questions introduced at the beginning of the book.

Section 1 relates to **Guiding Question** ⑤
How did physical geography affect the growth of ancient civilizations? *(Ancient civilizations in India had little contact with the rest of Asia due to the barriers formed by mountains and the Arabian Sea. The Indus River valley had fertile farmland that helped early civilizations grow.)*

Section 2 relates to **Guiding Question** ②
What were the beliefs and values of ancient peoples? *(Hinduism developed from the blending of Aryan culture with existing Indian culture.)*

Section 3 relates to **Guiding Question** ⑤
What were the beliefs and values of ancient peoples? *(Siddhartha Guatama spread the teachings of Buddhism in ancient India. Over time Buddhism died out in India but it spread to many other parts of the ancient world.)*

Section 4 relates to **Guiding Question** ⑤
How did ancient peoples develop governments? *(Chandragupta ran the Maurya Empire as an absolute ruler. His son Asoka, later ruled using Buddhist principles.)*

Target Reading Skill

In this chapter, students will learn and apply the reading skill of cause and effect. Use the following worksheets to help students practice this skill:

All in One Unit 2 History of Our World Teaching Resources, *Identify Causes and Effects* p. 67; *Recognize Cause-and-Effect Signal Words,* p. 68; *Recognize Multiple Causes,* p. 69; *Understand Effects,* p. 70

Differentiated Instruction

The following Teacher Edition strategies are suitable for students of varying abilities.

Advanced Readers, pp. 117, 122, 129
English Language Learners, pp. 108, 117
Gifted and Talented, pp. 109, 112
Less Proficient Readers, pp. 108, 116
Special Needs Students, p. 116

Chapter 4 Ancient India

Chapter Preview

This chapter will introduce you to the geography and civilizations of ancient India.

Section 1
The Indus and Ganges River Valleys

Section 2
Hinduism in Ancient India

Section 3
The Beginnings of Buddhism

Section 4
The Maurya Empire

Target Reading Skill

Cause and Effect In this chapter you will learn how to focus on identifying the cause-and-effect relationships in your text. Identifying causes and effects will give you a deeper understanding of the text.

▶ Somnath Temple, Gujarat, India

Bibliography

For the Teacher
Keay, John. *India: A History.* Grove/Atlantic Inc., 2001.
Armstrong, Karen. *Buddha.* Viking Press, 2001.
Thapar, Romila. *Asoka and the Decline of the Mauryas.* Oxford University Press, 1998.

For the Student
L2 Parker, Victoria. *The Ganges.* Raintree Publishers, 2003.
L2 Platt, Richard and Melanie Rice. *Crusades: The Battle for Jerusalem.* DK Publishing, 2001.
L3 Demi, Hitz. *Buddha.* Henry Holt and Company, Inc., 1996.

Ancient India

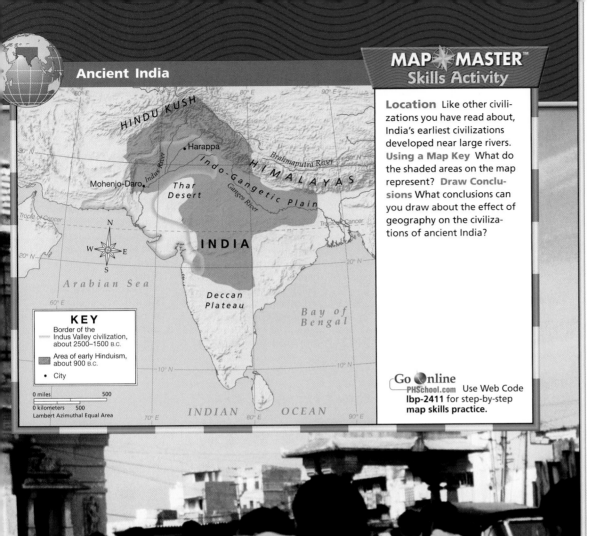

HINDU KUSH

HIMALAYAS

Indo-Gangetic Plain

Brahmaputra River

Indus River

Ganges River

•Harappa

Mohenjo-Daro•

Thar
Desert

INDIA

Arabian Sea

Deccan
Plateau

Bay of
Bengal

Tropic of Cancer

INDIAN OCEAN

KEY
— Border of the
Indus Valley civilization,
about 2500–1500 B.C.

▨ Area of early Hinduism,
about 900 B.C.

• City

0 miles 500
0 kilometers 500
Lambert Azimuthal Equal Area

MAP MASTER™
Skills Activity

Location Like other civilizations you have read about, India's earliest civilizations developed near large rivers. **Using a Map Key** What do the shaded areas on the map represent? **Draw Conclusions** What conclusions can you draw about the effect of geography on the civilizations of ancient India?

Go Online PHSchool.com Use Web Code **lbp-2411** for step-by-step **map skills practice.**

MAP MASTER™
Skills Activity

Draw students' attention to the northern border of the area of early Hindiusm that is shaded on the map. Ask them to identify the two natural features that mark this border *(the Hindu Kush and the Himalayas).* Discuss why early Hinduism may not have expanded past this border. *(It was difficult to carry the teachings of Hinduism across these tall mountains.)* **L1**

Go Online PHSchool.com Students may practice their map skills using the interactive online version of this map.

Using the Visual **L2**

Reach Into Your Background Draw students' attention to the photograph on pp. 104–105 and its caption. Ask students to infer what religion might be practiced at this temple based on the section titles found on p. 104 *(Buddhist or Hindu).* Explain that it is a Hindu temple and that they will learn more about Hinduism in this chapter.

Answers

MAP MASTER™ Skills Activity **Use a Map Key** the area of early Hinduism, about 900 B.C. **Draw Conclusions** Ancient civilizations arose near the Indus River where people had a source of water nearby for farming. Hinduism could not spread beyond the geographical barriers of the Hindu Kush and the Himalayas.

Chapter Resources

Teaching Resources
L2 Vocabulary Development, p. 85
L2 Skills for Life, p. 73
L2 Chapter Tests A and B, pp. 90–95

Spanish Support
L2 Spanish Chapter Summary, p. 44
L2 Spanish Vocabulary Development, p. 45

Media and Technology
L1 Student Edition on Audio CD
L1 Guided Reading Audio CDs, English and Spanish
L2 Social Studies Skills Tutor CD-ROM
ExamView® Test Bank CD-ROM

DISCOVERY CHANNEL SCHOOL History of Our World Video Program

Interactive Textbook

PRENTICE HALL
TeacherEXPRESS™
Plan • Teach • Assess

Objectives

Social Studies

1. Learn about India's geographic setting.
2. Find out about life in an ancient city of the Indus River valley.
3. Examine the rise of a new culture in the Indus and Ganges river valleys.

Reading/Language Arts

Use causes and effects to understand relationships among situations or events.

Prepare to Read

Build Background Knowledge L2

In this section students will learn about some of the geography, climate, and culture of ancient India. Have students preview the headings and visuals in the section with this question in mind: **How did the geography of the region affect the lives of people in ancient India?** Provide a few simple examples to get students started. Use the Idea Wave strategy (TE, p. T39) to solicit answers.

Set a Purpose for Reading L2

- Preview the Objectives.

- Read each statement in the *Reading Readiness Guide* aloud. Ask students to mark the statements true or false.

  All in One **Unit 2 History of Our World Teaching Resources,** *Reading Readiness Guide,* p. 52

- Have students discuss the statements in pairs or groups of four, then mark their worksheets again. Use the Numbered Heads participation strategy (TE, p. T40) to call on students to share their group's perspectives.

Vocabulary Builder
Preview Key Terms L2

Pronounce each key term, then ask students to say the word with you. Provide a simple explanation such as, "A caste can be a group of people who do the same work, such as carpentry or acting."

Prepare to Read

Objectives

In this section you will

1. Learn about India's geographic setting.
2. Find out about life in an ancient city of the Indus River valley.
3. Examine the rise of a new culture in the Indus and Ganges river valleys.

Taking Notes

As you read, create an outline of this section. The outline below has been started for you.

> I. India's geographic setting
>   A. Monsoon climate
>   1.
>   2.
>   B.
>   1.
>   2.
> II. Life in the Indus River valley

Target Reading Skill

Identify Causes and Effects Determining causes and effects can help you understand the relationships among situations or events. A cause makes something happen. An effect is what happens. For example, millions of years ago the Indian landmass crashed into Asia. Think of this as a cause. The effect was the formation of mountains.

Key Terms

- **subcontinent** (SUB kahn tih nunt) *n.* a large landmass that juts out from a continent
- **monsoon** (mahn SOON) *n.* a strong wind that blows across East Asia at certain times of the year
- **citadel** (SIT uh del) *n.* a fortress in a city
- **migrate** (MY grayt) *v.* to move from one place to settle in another area
- **caste** (kast) *n.* a social class of people

The land of India is separated from the rest of the world by a great wall. Rising along India's northern border, the wall is more than 1,500 miles (2,400 kilometers) long and nearly 5 miles (8 kilometers) high. The wall is not made of stone or bricks. It is a wall of snow-capped peaks and icy glaciers. This great barrier is the Himalayas, the highest mountain range in the world.

The Himalayas

106 History of Our World

Target Reading Skill L2

Identify Causes and Effects Point out the Target Reading Skill. Explain that a cause makes something happen and an effect is what happens.

Model the skill by pointing out the cause-and-effect relationship in the following sentence: "With a surplus of food, the population in the Indus Valley grew." (*Cause: surplus of food; Effect: the population in the Indus valley grew.*)

Give students *Identify Causes and Effects*. Have them complete the activity in groups.

All in One **Unit 2 History of Our World Teaching Resources,** *Identify Causes and Effects,* p. 67

India's Geographic Setting

Stretching south from the Himalayas, the kite-shaped land of India juts out from Asia into the Indian Ocean. Geographers refer to India as a **subcontinent,** or a large landmass that juts out from a continent.

For centuries, geography limited the contact the people of the Indian subcontinent had with the rest of the world. Turn to the map titled Ancient India on page 107. Notice how the Himalaya and the Hindu Kush mountain ranges separate India from the rest of Asia. The Bay of Bengal, the Indian Ocean, and the Arabian Sea limit contact with lands to the east and west. These mountains and waters have been a major influence on the history and culture of the land.

A Climate of Monsoons India's climate is dominated by the **monsoons,** strong winds that blow across the region at certain times of the year. Look at the map below titled India: Monsoons. From October to May, the winter monsoon blows from the northeast, spreading dry air across the country. Then, in the middle of June, the wind blows in from the Indian Ocean. This summer monsoon picks up moisture from the ocean. It carries rains that drench the plains and river valleys daily.

Links to Science

The Creation of the Himalayas Millions of years ago, all of today's continents were part of a single continent called Pangaea (pan JEE uh). Then Pangaea slowly broke apart. Eventually, India broke loose from Africa and began moving northeast. About 55 million years ago, India began crashing into Asia. The force of the collision pushed up layers and layers of rock to form the Himalayas.

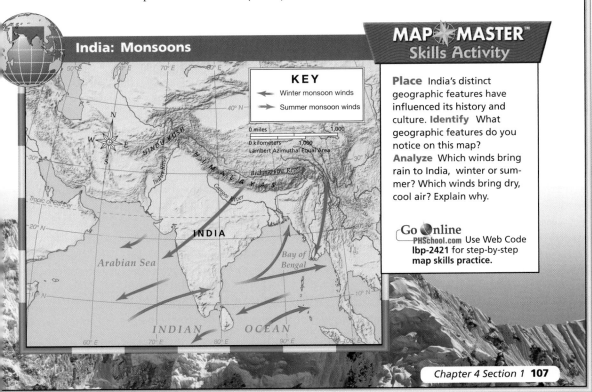

India: Monsoons

MAP MASTER™ Skills Activity

KEY
→ Winter monsoon winds
→ Summer monsoon winds

0 miles 1,000
0 kilometers 1,000
Lambert Azimuthal Equal Area

Place India's distinct geographic features have influenced its history and culture. **Identify** What geographic features do you notice on this map? **Analyze** Which winds bring rain to India, winter or summer? Which winds bring dry, cool air? Explain why.

Go Online PHSchool.com Use Web Code **lbp-2421** for step-by-step map skills practice.

Vocabulary Builder

Use the information below to teach students this section's high-use words.

High-Use Word	Definition and Sample Sentence
dominate, p. 107	*v.* to have a major influence The aroma of apple pie **dominated** the kitchen.
barrier, p. 108	*n.* something that prevents passage or separates places The fence acts as a **barrier** between the neighbors' yards.
flourish, p. 108	*v.* to grow and succeed The perfect summer weather allowed the garden to **flourish.**
fashion, p. 109	*v.* to shape or mold A carver **fashioned** the wood into a spoon.

Links

Read the **Links to Science** on this page. Ask **What two landmasses collided to form the Himalayas?** *(India and Asia)*

Instruct

India's Geographic Setting   L2

Guided Instruction

- **Vocabulary Builder** Clarify the high-use words **dominate** and **barrier** before reading.

- Read India's Geographic Setting using the Choral Reading technique (TE p. T38).

- Ask students **What mountain ranges separate India from Asia?** *(the Himalayas and the Hindu Kush)*

- Ask students **How has India's geographic setting affected the life of its people?** *(Mountains served as barriers between India's people and the rest of Asia; people depend on the monsoons for growing crops, but crops and homes can be damaged if there is too much rain; pathways in mountains serve as avenues for migration and invasion.)*

Answers

MAP MASTER Skills Activity **Identify** Answers should include the Himalayas and Hindu Kush mountains and the Indus, Ganges, and Brahmaputra rivers; **Analyze** Summer winds bring rain to India because they blow in from the ocean so they carry moist air. Winter winds bring dry air because they blow in from the interior of Asia and do not pick up moisture.

Go Online PHSchool.com **Students may practice their map skills using the interactive online version of this map.**

Independent Practice

Have students begin creating the outline described in Taking Notes. Have them use a roman numeral for the main head, India's Geographic Setting, and capital letters for the subheads, such as A Climate of Monsoons. Students should use numbers for supporting details. Help them identify the supporting details for the first subhead to get them started.

Monitor Progress

As students complete their outlines, circulate and make sure individuals are setting up their outlines correctly. Provide assistance as needed.

◉ Target Reading Skill

Identify Causes and Effects As a follow up, ask students to answer the Target Reading skill question in the Student Edition. (*Cause—The monsoon is late or weak. Effect—Crops die. Cause—Crops die. Effect—famine; Cause—the monsoon brings too much rain. Effect—deadly floods*)

Life in the Indus River Valley L2

Guided Instruction

- **Vocabulary Builder** Clarify the high-use words **flourish** and **fashion** before reading.

- Ask students to read Life in the Indus River Valley.

- Ask students **What was the location of Mohenjo-Daro?** (*along the banks of the Indus River*)

- Discuss with students what life was like in Mohenjo-Daro. (*The city was very busy, with shops lining the streets. Traders came from far away to buy and sell goods. People lived in homes that opened onto courtyards. Children played with toys and pets, and adults enjoyed games and music.*)

Answers

✓ **Reading Check** Winter monsoons bring dry air to India, while summer monsoons bring rain.

Compare Possible answer: Merchants today often use labels and logos to identify their goods, just as the merchants of Mohenjo-Daro used seals.

◉ Identify Causes and Effects

What cause-and-effect relationships are described in the paragraph at the right?

The people of India depend on summer monsoons to provide life-giving rain. If the monsoon is late or weak, crops die, causing famine. If it brings too much rain, overflowing rivers may cause deadly floods.

Barriers and Pathways Although the mountains separate India from other lands, they do have openings. For thousands of years, passes through the Hindu Kush mountain range have served as highways for migration and invasion. The earliest people of northern India probably entered the Indus River valley through these pathways.

Great rivers begin in the mountains. The Indus (IN dus) River crosses the Himalayas and empties into the Arabian Sea. The Ganges (GAN jeez) River flows from the Himalayas into the Bay of Bengal. Fed by melting snow and rain, the Indus and Ganges rivers cut through the mountains. They flow across northern India and make farming possible in the river valleys.

✓ **Reading Check** How do winter monsoons differ from summer monsoons?

Life in the Indus River Valley

From the rich soil of the Indus valley, early farmers harvested a surplus of wheat and other grains. With a surplus of food, the population grew. Some villages grew to become cities. From around 2500 to 1500 B.C., well-planned cities flourished in the valley. Two such cities were Harappa (huh RAP uh) and Mohenjo-Daro (moh HEN joh DAH roh), both located in present-day Pakistan. To find these cities, return to the map titled Ancient India on page 105. Mohenjo-Daro was the larger of the two cities, and it lay along the banks of the Indus River.

Stone Seals
Merchants of Mohenjo-Daro may have used seals like these to identify their goods.
Compare *How do these seals compare to the ways that present-day merchants identify their goods?*

Ancient City Planners The ruins of Mohenjo-Daro show how carefully the city was planned. To help protect it from floods, the city was built above ground level. Homes and workshops made up one side of the city. Public buildings stood on the other side. Streets separated these regular blocks of homes and buildings. The city's highest point served as a **citadel,** or **fortress.** Built on a high mound of earth, the citadel was probably enclosed by a high brick wall. This wall would have protected the city's most important buildings, including a storehouse for grain and a bath house.

108 History of Our World

Differentiated Instruction

For English Language Learners L1

Pair native English-speaking students with English learners and have them read India's Geographic Setting together. Encourage students to answer each other's questions about the material. Circulate and ask students questions about the material to be sure they understand what they have read.

For Less Proficient Readers L1

Have students read the text of India's Geographic Setting as they listen to the Student Edition on Audio CD. Pause the CD after each subsection and ask the students if they have any questions about what they have read.

◉ Chapter 4 Section 1, **Student Edition on Audio CD**

108 *History of Our World*

Unlike most other cities of the time, Mohenjo-Daro had a drainage system. Clay pipes ran under the brick streets. They carried waste from homes and public buildings away from the city. Outside the city, canals ran along the Indus River, which often flooded. The canals helped to control flooding by catching overflow from the river. The water was then directed where it was most needed.

A mythical animal on a stone seal

Life in Mohenjo-Daro In Mohenjo-Daro, merchants and artisans sold their wares from shops that lined the streets. Carts loaded with grain rolled through the city. Traders came from as far away as Mesopotamia to buy and sell precious goods. The citizens of Mohenjo-Daro lived in homes that opened onto courtyards. Children played with toys and pets. Adults enjoyed games and music. Artisans fashioned jewelry and bright cotton clothing for the people to wear.

The language of the people is still a mystery. Their writings appear on square seals, but experts have not yet been able to figure out what the symbols mean. The form of government and the religion of Mohenjo-Daro are also unknown. No royal tombs or great temples have been found. But evidence found in the city's ruins suggests that the people had a number of gods.

Ancient City
The baked-brick ruins of Mohenjo-Daro are in the present-day country of Pakistan. **Analyze Images** *How does the photograph below suggest that Mohenjo-Daro was probably a crowded city?*

Guided Instruction (continued)

■ Ask students to compare what life was like in Mohenjo-Daro with what life is like today. *(Possible answer: The children of Mohenjo-Daro played with toys and pets like many children do today.)*

■ Ask students **Why do you think scientists know little about the religion and government of Mohenjo-Daro?** *(They have not found the ruins of tombs or temples and they cannot figure out the system of writing which may have described the city's religion and government.)*

Independent Practice
Have students continue the next section of their outlines as they read Life in the Indus River Valley.

Monitor Progress
Ask students to pair up with a partner and share their outlines. Circulate to make sure students continue to follow the proper format and provide appropriate supporting details. Assist students as needed.

Differentiated Instruction

For Gifted and Talented L3
Assign students to groups of four and have them complete the *Small Group Activity* in which they will create a map of Mohenjo-Daro.

All in One **Unit 2 History of Our World Teaching Resources** *Small Group Activity: Making a Map of Mohenjo-Daro,* pp. 74–77

Answer

Analyze Images Possible answer: The remains of the buildings are crowded together suggesting that they had to use as much space as they could to accommodate the population.

A New Culture Arises L2

Guided Instruction

- Have students read about Aryan culture in A New Culture Arises. As students read, circulate and make sure individuals can answer the Reading Check question.

- Ask students **How did Aryan culture arise in India?** *(Aryans migrated from central Asia to India. Their horse-drawn chariots scared local people and helped the Aryans gain power. The local people began to adopt some Aryan ways of life.)*

- Ask students to list the benefits and disadvantages of the caste system. *(Example of an advantage: the society was very organized and everyone filled an important societal role. Examples of disadvantages: people always had to do the same work as their parents regardless of their interests; there was no way to progress to a higher class.)*

Independent Practice

Have students complete their outlines as they read A New Culture Arises.

Monitor Progress

- Show *Section Reading Support Transparency HOW 66* and ask students to check their outlines individually. Go over key concepts and clarify key vocabulary as needed.

    History of Our World Transparencies, *Section Reading Support Transparency HOW 66*

- Tell students to fill in the last column of their *Reading Readiness Guides.* Probe for what they learned that confirms or invalidates each statement.

    All in One Unit 2 History of Our World Teaching Resources, *Reading Readiness Guide,* p. 52

Answers

Generalize Farmers provided the food people needed to survive and be able to settle in one place.

✓ **Reading Check** around 2000 B.C.

Farming the Indus Valley
In Ladakh, India, farming is part of an ancient tradition. **Generalize** *How did farmers help make civilization possible in the Indus valley?*

A Mysterious Decline   Around 2000 B.C., Indus valley farmers began to abandon their land. The climate may have changed, turning the fertile soil into desert. Or great earthquakes may have caused floods that destroyed the canals. Without enough food, people began to leave the cities of the Indus valley. Between 2000 and 1500 B.C., newcomers from the north entered the valley. These newcomers eventually gained power throughout the region.

✓ **Reading Check**   **When did the Indus valley civilization begin to decline?**

A New Culture Arises

The newcomers called themselves Aryans (AYR ee unz), which in their language meant "noble" or "highborn." They **migrated,** or moved, from their homelands in central Asia. For several centuries, waves of these nomadic herders swept into India.

The Aryans drove horse-drawn chariots that helped them gain power. The chariots overwhelmed the enemy's slow-moving foot soldiers and settled populations. In time, local people adopted the language and some of the beliefs of the Aryans. Gradually, a new Aryan culture developed. This culture combined the traditions of the original inhabitants with ideas and beliefs brought by the newcomers. Marriages between members of the two groups created a mixed population.

Aryan Culture Spreads   This new culture first developed in the northern Indus valley. Gradually, it spread into the Ganges valley to the east, where people also adopted the Aryan language. By about 800 B.C., the people of northern India had learned to make tools and weapons out of iron. With iron axes, these people cleared areas of the thick rain forests of the northeast. There they built farms, villages, and even cities.

110 History of Our World

Skills for Life Skills Mini Lesson

Using Reliable Information   L2

1. Teach the skill by explaining the steps to determine if information is reliable. Step 1: Determine if the information can be verified against other sources. Step 2: Check the author's qualifications and methods. Step 3: Determine why the author is writing, and if the author has any biases.

2. Help students practice the skill by having them reread the section Aryan Life.

3. Have students complete the steps to determine if the Vedas are reliable. *(By completing the steps, students may determine that the Vedas are probably reliable in some topics, but should be read with caution.)*

Aryan Life Most of what we know of early Aryan life comes from religious books called Vedas, which means "knowledge." The Vedas tell us that the earliest Aryans were herders and warriors who lived in temporary villages. Often on the move, these people did not at first build cities or spacious homes.

The Aryans organized their society around three classes. Aryan priests, called Brahmans, performed religious services and composed hymns and prayers. Ranked below them was a class of warriors and nobles. Next came the artisans and merchants. Gradually, a low-ranking fourth class was formed. It was made up of farm workers, laborers, and servants.

The Social Order By 500 B.C., there was a strict division of classes. Europeans later called it the caste system. At first, each **caste,** or class, performed special duties. Under the caste system, people always had to stay in the caste of their parents. Over time, the caste system became more complicated. The main castes divided into hundreds of different groups, in which each person had the same occupation. Since people could not leave their caste, they did the same work that their parents and other group members did.

The caste system still exists in present-day India, but it is much less rigid. For example, people of different castes interact more freely. Also, many modern professions have no caste ranking.

✓ **Reading Check** How was Aryan society organized?

Indian Society
In the caste system, a weaver's son would be a weaver. A barber's daughter would marry a barber. The manuscript page above shows workmen building a royal city. **Summarize** *How did the caste system develop in India?*

Section 1 Assessment

Key Terms
Review the key terms at the beginning of this section. Use each term in a sentence that explains its meaning.

⟳ Target Reading Skill
What may have caused the decline of Indus valley civilizations around 2000 B.C.? What was the effect of this decline?

Comprehension and Critical Thinking
1. (a) Recall Describe the geography of the Indus and Ganges river valleys.

(b) Identify Effects How do the monsoons affect India and its climate?

2. (a) Explain How did geography influence the building of Mohenjo-Daro?
(b) Draw Conclusions How was Mohenjo-Daro similar to modern cities?

3. (a) Identify Who were the Aryans?
(b) Analyze Information How was it possible for the Aryans to spread their influence over the Indus and Ganges river valleys so successfully?

Writing Activity
List some words that describe the city and the people of Mohenjo-Daro. Use these words to write a paragraph about life in that city.

> **Writing Tip** Use vivid language when writing a description. Reread the text on Mohenjo-Daro to see what life was like in the ancient city. When you write your description, carefully choose adjectives that will bring Mohenjo-Daro to life.

Chapter 4 Section 1 **111**

Assess and Reteach

Assess Progress ▪L2▪
Have students complete the Section Assessment. Administer the *Section Quiz.*

▪All in One▪ **Unit 2 History of Our World Teaching Resources,** *Section Quiz,* p. 54

Reteach ▪L1▪
If students need more instruction, have them read this section in the Reading and Vocabulary Study Guide.

📖 Chapter 4, Section 1, **History of Our World World Reading and Vocabulary Study Guide,** pp. 48–50

Extend ▪L3▪
Have students complete the *Activity Shop Lab: Rivers That Flood* to learn more about the importance and dangers of rivers in Ancient India and other ancient civilizations.

▪All in One▪ **Unit 2 History of Our World Teaching Resources,** *Activity Shop Lab: Rivers That Flood,* pp. 78–79

Answers

Summarize Aryans introduced the caste system to India.

✓ **Reading Check** Aryan society was organized by a caste system in which people were grouped into different classes.

Writing Activity
Use the *Rubric for Assessing a Writing Assignment* to evaluate students' paragraphs.

▪All in One▪ **Unit 2 History of Our World Teaching Resources,** *Rubric for Assessing a Writing Assignment,* p. 86

Section 1 Assessment

Key Terms
Students' sentences should reflect knowledge of each key term.

⟳ Target Reading Skill
climate change, earthquakes; Aryans began to settle in the area.

Comprehension and Critical Thinking
1. (a) The Indus and Ganges rivers valleys were both created by rivers that start in the Himalayas and flow across rich plains.
(b) Summer monsoons produce wet summers and bring water to crops. They can also cause flooding. Winter monsoons produce dry winters.

2. (a) The city had to be built on high ground in order to avoid flooding from the Indus River. **(b)** Possible answer: Like Mohenjo-Daro, modern cities have waste drainage systems, shops, and busy streets.

3. (a) people who migrated from central Asia to the Indus valley between about 2000 and 1500 B.C. **(b)** The Aryans' horse-drawn chariots scared the local people and helped Aryans gain power.

Focus On Mohenjo-Daro

L2

Guided Instruction

- Read the paragraphs on pp. 112–113 and study the art, photo, and captions as a class.

- Ask **How were the homes in Mohenjo-Daro more advanced than those in ancient Egypt and Mesopotamia?** *(In Mohenjo-Daro, the homes were made of brick that kept them cool and many had indoor baths and well water, while in Egypt and Mesopotamia the homes were simple huts made of mud.)*

- Ask students **Why was Mohenjo-Daro built on mud-brick platforms?** *(to protect it from floods)*

- Have students work in pairs to answer the Assessment questions.

Focus On
Mohenjo-Daro

The advertisement shown below is fiction, of course, but the details are quite true. While villagers in ancient Mesopotamia and Egypt were living in mud huts, Indus valley dwellers lived in relatively high style—especially in the two large cities of Harappa and Mohenjo-Daro. Discovered by archaeologists in 1922, Mohenjo-Daro was a feat of engineering, architecture, design, mathematics, and social organization.

Homes available in fashionable Mohenjo-Daro! Houses feature from 1 to 24 rooms in cool, brick buildings, some with courtyards. Good security. Indoor baths and well water in most units. Close to the Indus River and to downtown area. Dogs, cats, chickens, pigs, goats, mules, and sheep welcome.

Corridor
A channel of the Indus River or a canal may have flowed between the lower city and the citadel.

A street scene from the lower city

Differentiated Instruction

For Gifted and Talented **L3**

Have students create their own travel advertisement encouraging people to come to Mohenjo-Daro. Tell them to use the information on these pages and in other parts of the section to help them create the ad. Encourage students to use illustrations and maps in their advertisements.

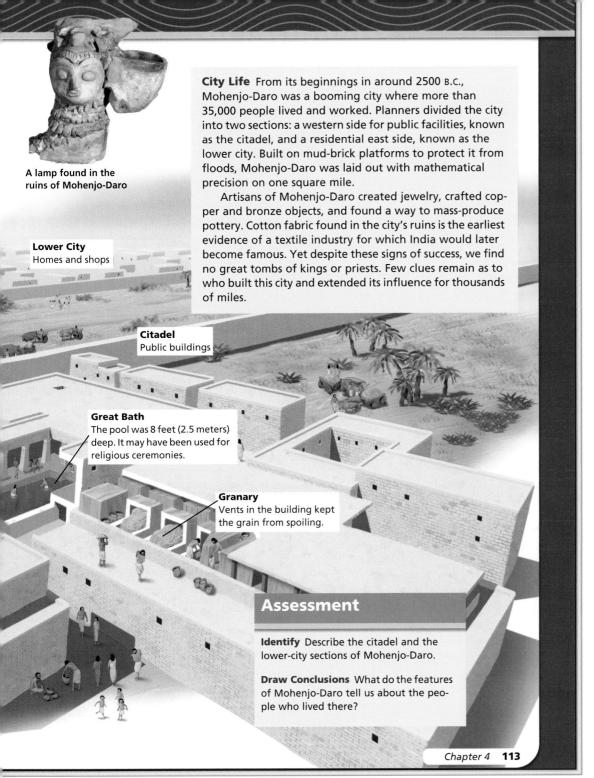

A lamp found in the ruins of Mohenjo-Daro

Lower City
Homes and shops

Citadel
Public buildings

Great Bath
The pool was 8 feet (2.5 meters) deep. It may have been used for religious ceremonies.

Granary
Vents in the building kept the grain from spoiling.

City Life From its beginnings in around 2500 B.C., Mohenjo-Daro was a booming city where more than 35,000 people lived and worked. Planners divided the city into two sections: a western side for public facilities, known as the citadel, and a residential east side, known as the lower city. Built on mud-brick platforms to protect it from floods, Mohenjo-Daro was laid out with mathematical precision on one square mile.

Artisans of Mohenjo-Daro created jewelry, crafted copper and bronze objects, and found a way to mass-produce pottery. Cotton fabric found in the city's ruins is the earliest evidence of a textile industry for which India would later become famous. Yet despite these signs of success, we find no great tombs of kings or priests. Few clues remain as to who built this city and extended its influence for thousands of miles.

Assessment

Identify Describe the citadel and the lower-city sections of Mohenjo-Daro.

Draw Conclusions What do the features of Mohenjo-Daro tell us about the people who lived there?

Independent Practice

Ask students to choose another ancient city they have learned about to compare with Mohenjo-Daro. Tell them to think about housing, use and storage of water, and products produced in the cities. Tell them to write a brief essay comparing and contrasting such aspects of the two cities.

Answers

Assessment

Identify Possible answers: The citadel and the lower city were separated by a large corridor. The citadel was made up of larger buildings than the homes and shops of the lower city, but they all seem to have been made out of similar material.

Draw Conclusions Possible answer: Some of the people were skilled architects and engineers; some were farmers who raised grain; some people of the city probably felt pride in their city and comfortable homes.

Objectives
Social Studies
1. Find out about the beginning of Hinduism.
2. Learn about the teachings of Hinduism.
3. Examine the many paths to truth in Hinduism.

Reading/Language Arts
Learn to identify cause-and-effect signal words.

Prepare to Read

Build Background Knowledge **L2**
In this section students will learn about the development and history of Hinduism. Have students preview the headings and visuals in this section with the following question in mind: **In what ways are Hinduism and ancient Egyptian religion similar and different?** Have students engage in a Give One, Get One activity (TE, p. T41) to share their answers.

Set a Purpose for Reading **L2**
- Preview the Objectives.
- Read each statement in the *Reading Readiness Guide* aloud. Ask students to mark the statements true or false.

  All in One **Unit 2 History of Our World Teaching Resources,** *Reading Readiness Guide,* p. 56

- Have students discuss the statements in pairs or groups of four, then mark their worksheets again. Use the Numbered Heads participation strategy (TE, p. T40) to call on students to share their group's perspectives.

Vocabulary Builder
Preview Key Terms **L2**
Pronounce each key term, then ask students to say the word with you. Provide a simple explanation such as, "Reincarnation is a belief that you can be reborn as a different living thing, such as an animal or another person."

Prepare to Read

Objectives
In this section you will
1. Find out about the beginning of Hinduism.
2. Learn about the teachings of Hinduism.
3. Examine the practice of Hinduism.

Taking Notes
As you read, find details about the basic beliefs of Hinduism. Copy the concept web below, and record your findings in it.

Target Reading Skill

Recognize Cause-and-Effect Signal Words
Sometimes certain words, such as *affect, from,* and *as a result,* signal a cause or an effect. In the following sentence, *from* signals both a cause and an effect: "*From* this blending of ideas and beliefs came one of the world's oldest living religions, Hinduism." The cause is a blend of ideas and beliefs, and the effect is Hinduism. As you read, look for signals announcing other causes and effects.

Key Terms
- **brahman** (BRAH mun) *n.* a single spiritual power that Hindus believe lives in everything
- **avatar** (av uh TAHR) *n.* a representation of a Hindu god or goddess in human or animal form
- **reincarnation** (ree in kahr NAY shun) *n.* the rebirth of the soul in the body of another living being
- **dharma** (DAHR muh) *n.* the religious and moral duties of Hindus
- **ahimsa** (uh HIM sah) *n.* the Hindu idea of non-violence

Shiva, one of the most important Hindu gods

The following prayer was part of one of the early Aryan Vedas:

“O Lord of the storm gods, . . . [d]o not hide the sun from our sight. O Rudra, protect our horseman from injury. . . . Your glory is unbounded, your strength unmatched among all living creatures, O Rudra, wielder [handler] of the thunderbolt. Guide us safely to the far shore of existence where there is no sorrow.”

—*Aryan Vedas*

The prayer praises Rudra and other gods of nature. What parts of the prayer ask the gods for their protection?

The Beginnings of Hinduism
Aryan prayers were passed down through generations. As Aryan culture mixed with India's existing cultures, new ideas and beliefs became part of the Vedas. From this blending of ideas and beliefs came one of the world's oldest living religions, Hinduism.

Target Reading Skill **L2**

Recognize Cause-and-Effect Signal Words
Point out the Target Reading Skill. Explain that some words and phrases, such as *from* and *as a result*, can signal cause and effect relationships.

Model the skill by identifying the signal word and the cause-and-effect relationship in the following sentence: From this blending of ideas and beliefs came one of the world's oldest living religions, Hinduism." (*Signal word: From; Cause: blending; Effect: Hinduism.*)

Give students *Recognize Cause-and-Effect Signal Words*. Have them complete the activity in groups.

All in One **Unit 2 History of Our World Teaching Resources,** *Recognize Cause-and-Effect Signal Words,* p. 68

A Blend of Religions As Hinduism developed over 3,500 years, it absorbed many beliefs from other religions. Hinduism became very complex over time, with many different practices existing side by side. Hindus believe that since people are different, they need many different ways of approaching god.

Hinduism is one of the world's major religions, and a way of life for more than 850 million people in India today. Its beliefs have influenced people of many other religions. Yet Hinduism is unlike other major world religions.

Hinduism has no one single founder, but Hindus have many great religious thinkers. Hindus worship many gods and goddesses. However, they believe in one single spiritual power called **brahman**, which lives in everything. Hindus believe that there is more than one path to the truth.

Hindu Gods and Goddesses The gods and goddesses of Hinduism stand for different parts of brahman. An ancient Hindu saying expresses this idea: "God is one, but wise people know it by many names." The most important Hindu gods are Brahma, the Creator; Vishnu, the Preserver; and Shiva, the Destroyer.

Hindu gods take many different forms, called avatars. An **avatar** is the representation of a Hindu god or goddess in human or animal form.

Hindu teachings say that the god Brahma was born from a golden egg. He created Earth and everything on it. However, he is not as widely worshiped as Vishnu and Shiva.

Bathing in the Ganges
People practice the ancient ritual of cleansing in the Ganges River. Hindus believe the waters of the Ganges to be sacred. **Infer** *Why do you think Hindus believe the Ganges to be sacred?*

The Beginnings of Hinduism L2

Guided Instruction

- **Vocabulary Builder** Clarify the high-use word **welfare** before reading.

- Have students read The Beginnings of Hinduism using the Structured Silent Reading technique (TE p. T38).

- Ask students **What two cultures blended to form the basis of Hinduism?** *(Aryan culture and India's preexisting culture.)*

- Discuss the differences between Hinduism and other major religions. *(There is no single founder of Hinduism. Hindus worship many gods and goddesses but believe in one spirit.)*

Independent Practice

Ask students to create the Taking Notes graphic organizer on a blank piece of paper. Help them fill in the details about the history of Hinduism to get them started. Then have them begin filling in the details about Hindu beliefs on their own.

Monitor Progress

As students fill in the details about beliefs in the graphic organizer, circulate to make sure students are choosing the appropriate details. Help students as needed.

Vocabulary Builder

Use the information below to teach students this section's high-use words.

High-Use Word	Definition and Sample Sentence
welfare, p. 116	*n.* well-being To protect the **welfare** of the team, the coach required that they wear face masks in practice.
fate, p. 117	*n.* a power that is believed to settle in advance how things will occur The two friends believed that they met by **fate**.

Answer

Infer Possible answer: They may have thought the river was associated with one of the Hindu gods or goddesses.

The Teachings of Hinduism
The Practice of Hinduism

L2

Guided Instruction

■ **Vocabulary Builder** Clarify the high-use word **fate** before reading.

■ Have students read more about the Hindu religion in The Teachings of Hinduism. Upon completion of the reading, make sure students can answer the Reading Check question.

■ Ask students to describe the Hindu idea of reincarnation. *(Hindus believe that when a person dies, the soul may be reborn into the body of another living thing. People who behave well will be reborn into higher positions or they will become one with brahman. If they behave badly, they will be reborn into lower positions or into animals.)*

■ Have students read about the different ways Hindus worship in The Practice of Hinduism.

■ Ask students to describe the various ways Hinduism allows its followers to search for truth. *(Followers can worship through various types of yoga which include physical activity, selfless deeds, and learning sacred writings. They may also worship by praying in temples and at home.)*

Answers

Synthesize There are many different Hindu gods that represent different parts of brahman.

✓ **Reading Check** Brahma, Vishnu, and Shiva

Hindu Temple
The Hindu temple of Kandarya Mahadeva was built in central India around A.D. 1000. The temple is covered with carvings of Hindu gods. **Synthesize** *In what ways are the gods of Hinduism complex, or many-sided?*

116 History of Our World

Hindus believe that Vishnu is a kindly god who is concerned with the welfare of human beings. Vishnu visits Earth from time to time in different forms. He does this to guide humans or to protect them from disaster.

Unlike Vishnu, Shiva is not concerned with human matters. He is very powerful. Shiva is responsible for both the creative and the destructive forces of the universe. Shiva developed from the god Rudra, the "wielder of the thunderbolt" in the prayer at the beginning of this section.

Hindu gods have their own families. Many Hindus, for example, worship Shiva's wife, the goddess Shakti. Hindus believe Shakti plays a role in human life. Like her husband, she is both a destroyer and a creator. She is both kind and cruel.

✓ **Reading Check** **What are the three main Hindu gods?**

Differentiated Instruction

For Less Proficient Readers L1
Have students pair up and create a chart listing the major Hindu gods and goddesses in one column and describing each god or goddess in a second column.

For Special Needs Students L1
Have students read this section in the Reading and Vocabulary Study Guide. Have students answer the questions in the side column to assess their understanding of the content.

📖 Chapter 4, Section 2, **History of Our World Reading and Vocabulary Study Guide**, pp. 51–53.

The Teachings of Hinduism

All Hindus share certain central beliefs that are contained in religious writings or sacred texts.

The Upanishads One of the Hindu religious texts is the Upanishads (oo PAN uh shadz). *Upanishad* means "sitting near a teacher." Much of the Upanishads is in the form of questions by pupils and responses by teachers. For example, a pupil asks, "Who created the world?" The teacher replies, "Brahman is the creator, the universal soul." When asked to describe brahman, the teacher explains that it is too complicated for humans to understand. Brahman has no physical form.

Reincarnation One important idea in the Upanishads is **reincarnation,** or rebirth of the soul. Hindus believe that when a person dies, the soul is reborn in the body of another living thing. Hindus believe that every living thing has a soul. This idea is an important part of other Asian beliefs as well.

According to Hindu belief, the actions of a person in this life affect his or her fate in the next. Good behavior is always rewarded. Bad behavior is always punished. Faithful followers of Hinduism will be reborn into a higher position. Those whose acts have been bad may be born into a lower caste, or may even return as animals. If a person leads a perfect life, he or she may be freed from this cycle of death and rebirth. As a result, the person's soul becomes one with brahman.

A Hindu's Duties To become united with the one spirit and escape the cycle of death and rebirth, a person must obey his or her dharma (DAHR muh). **Dharma** is the religious and moral duties of each person. These duties depend on such factors as a person's class, age, and occupation. In Hinduism, it is a man's duty to protect the women in his family, and it is a ruler's duty to protect his subjects. Another important idea of Hinduism is **ahimsa** (uh HIM sah), or nonviolence. To Hindus, people and living things are part of brahman and therefore must be treated with respect. For that reason, many Hindus do not eat meat and try to avoid harming living things.

✓ **Reading Check** According to Hindu belief, what happens to a person's soul after death?

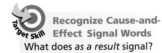

Recognize Cause-and-Effect Signal Words
What does *as a result* signal?

Independent Practice

Ask students to complete their graphic organizers by filling in the rest of the details about Hindu beliefs.

Monitor Progress

■ Show *Section Reading Support Transparency HOW 67* and ask students to check their graphic organizers individually. Go over key concepts and clarify key vocabulary as needed.

   History of Our World Transparencies, *Section Reading Support Transparency HOW 67*

■ Tell students to fill in the last column of their *Reading Readiness Guides.* Probe for what they learned that confirms or invalidates each statement.

   All in One Unit 2 History of Our World Teaching Resources, *Reading Readiness Guide,* p. 56

Target Reading Skill

Recognize Cause-and-Effect Signal Words
As a follow up, ask students to answer the Target Reading Skill question in the Student Edition. (*The phrase signals the effect of leading a perfect life.*)

Answer

✓ **Reading Check** According to Hindu beliefs, a person's soul is reborn into another living thing or it becomes one with brahman.

Assess and Reteach

Assess Progress `L2`

Have students complete the Section Assessment. Administer the *Section Quiz*.

All in One **Unit 2 History of Our World Teaching Resources,** *Section Quiz,* p. 58

Reteach `L1`

If students need more instruction, have them read this section in the Reading and Vocabulary Study Guide.

📖 Chapter 4, Section 2, **History of Our World World Reading and Vocabulary Study Guide,** pp. 51–53

Extend `L3`

Have students conduct library and Internet research about Hindu gods and goddesses and further explore one that interests them. Ask each student to prepare an oral presentation about the god or goddess researched and its importance to the Hindu religion. Then have students present their findings to the class. Use *Rubric for Assessing an Oral Presentation* to evaluate students' presentations.

All in One **Unit 2 History of Our World Teaching Resources,** *Rubric for Assessing an Oral Presentation,* p. 87

Answers

Contrast In private, Hindus offer gifts and food to their personal gods.

✓**Reading Check** Hindus who practice yoga use special exercises, breathing, and deep thinking to help free their souls and unite them with brahman.

Section 2 Assessment

Key Terms
Students' sentences should reflect knowledge of each Key Term.

🔄 **Target Reading Skill**
Good behavior (cause) leads to rewards (effect). Bad behavior (cause) leads to punishment (effect).

Comprehension and Critical Thinking
1. (a) As Aryan culture blended with India's preexisting cultures, new ideas and beliefs formed and led to the development of Hinduism. **(b)** Possible answers: Hinduism is different from Judaism because Hindus worship several gods and Jews worship one god. It is similar to the religion of ancient

Egypt because more than one god is worshipped in both religions.

2. (a) In Hinduism, good behavior results in reincarnation into higher status or unity with brahman; bad behavior results in being reincarnated into a lower class or into an animal. **(b)** To Hindus it means reuniting one's spirit with brahman.

3. (a) They practice various forms of yoga and worship in temples and at home.
(b) Possible answer: Practicing yoga helps

Hindus lead a more perfect life which may help their soul become one with brahman.

Writing Activity
Use the *Rubric for Assessing a Writing Assignment* to evaluate the students' dialogues.

All in One **Unit 2 History of Our World Teaching Resources,** *Rubric for Assessing a Writing Assignment,* p. 86

Home Altar
Many Hindus, like the woman shown above, worship before altars in their homes. **Contrast** *What are some differences between public and private worship for Hindus?*

The Practice of Hinduism

As you have read, Hinduism teaches that there is more than one path to the truth. Because of this view, Hinduism allows its followers to worship in various ways.

The Yogas Many non-Hindus know yoga (YOH guh) as a physical activity, a system of special exercises and breathing. Hindus believe yoga exercises help free the soul from the cares of the world. In this way, the soul may unite with brahman. In fact, the word *yoga* means "union." For Hindus, there are many yogas that may be used as paths to brahman. Physical activity is one yoga. Another is the yoga of selfless deeds, such as giving to the poor. By learning the sacred writings, a Hindu practices the yoga of knowledge. And by honoring a personal god, a Hindu follows the yoga of devotion.

Private Devotion Hindus worship in public by praying and performing rituals in temples. They also show devotion privately at home. It is common for Hindus to choose a personal god, and to honor that god by offering food, gifts, and prayers at a home altar. A Hindu's devotion to the god brings the soul closer to brahman.

✓ **Reading Check** **How is yoga practiced by Hindus?**

Section 2 Assessment

Key Terms
Review the key terms at the beginning of this section. Use each term in a sentence that explains its meaning.

🔄 **Target Reading Skill**
Return to the fourth paragraph on page 117 and find the signal word *affect*. What cause-and-effect relationships are described in the two sentences that follow?

Comprehension and Critical Thinking
1. (a) Explain How did the early Aryan religion grow into Hinduism?

(b) Compare and Contrast How is Hinduism different from other religions you have learned about? How is it similar?
2. (a) Analyze Information What is the relationship between good and bad behavior and the Hindu idea of reincarnation?
(b) Find the Main Idea What does "escaping the cycle of birth and death" mean to Hindus?
3. (a) Describe In what ways do Hindus practice their faith?
(b) Draw Conclusions How do you think the yogas bring Hindus closer to brahman?

Writing Activity
Hindu teachers often instruct their students through questions and answers. Write a dialogue in which a student asks questions about Hindu beliefs and the teacher responds.

Writing Tip A dialogue is similar to a script for a play. When you write your dialogue, make it clear that either the student or the teacher is speaking. Try to make the dialogue sound like a conversation.

Prepare to Read

Objectives
In this section you will
1. Learn about the Buddha and his teachings.
2. Find out how Buddhism was received inside and outside India.

Taking Notes
As you read, find details on the beginnings of Buddhism. Copy the flowchart below, and record your findings in it.

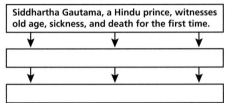

Beginnings of Buddhism

Siddhartha Gautama, a Hindu prince, witnesses old age, sickness, and death for the first time.

Target Reading Skill

Recognize Multiple Causes A cause is what makes something happen. An effect is what happens. Sometimes an effect can have more than one cause. For example, in the story that begins this section, Siddhartha Gautama witnesses three events that cause him to change the direction of his life. Can you identify the three causes? As you read, look for effects that have multiple causes.

Key Terms
- **meditate** (MED uh tayt) v. to focus the mind inward in order to find spiritual awareness or relaxation
- **nirvana** (nur VAH nuh) n. the lasting peace that Buddhists seek by giving up selfish desires
- **missionary** (MISH un ehr ee) n. a person who spreads his or her religious beliefs to others

According to Buddhist tradition, a young Hindu prince once lived a life of luxury in his palace in northern India. The prince was surrounded by beauty and youth. He had never witnessed old age, sickness, or death.

Then, around the age of 30, the prince traveled outside the palace walls. What he saw changed his life. He met a bent and tired old man. Then he saw a man who was very sick. Finally, he saw a corpse, or dead body, as it was carried to a funeral.

This suffering and death troubled the young man greatly. He wondered why there was so much misery and pain in the world. He decided he must change his life to find the answer. He gave up his wealth, his family, and his life of ease in order to find the causes of human suffering. The young man was named Siddhartha Gautama (sih DAHR tuh GOW tuh muh). What he discovered after seven years of wandering led to the beginnings of a major world religion: Buddhism.

Indian statue of the young Buddha

Chapter 4 Section 3 **119**

Target Reading Skill L2

Recognize Multiple Causes Point out the Target Reading Skill. Explain that sometimes an effect can have several causes.

Model the skill by identifying the multiple causes in the following passage: "Buddhism is practiced by many people in many countries. The Buddhist teaching that all people are equal and the work of Buddhist missionaries are just a few reasons for the spread of religion." *(Causes: Buddhism teaches that all people are equal, the work of Buddhist missionaries; Effect: Buddhism is practiced in many countries.)*

Give students *Recognize Multiple Causes.* Have them complete the activity in groups.

All in One Unit 2 History of Our World Teaching Resources, *Recognize Multiple Causes,* p. 69

Objectives
Social Studies
1. Learn about the Buddha and his teachings.
2. Find out how Buddhism was received inside and outside India.

Reading/Language Arts
Understand that an effect may have multiple causes.

Prepare to Read

Build Background Knowledge L2
Ask students to list five things that are important to them. Invite volunteers to share their lists with the class. Point out that the material things on their lists are things the Buddha would consider unimportant. Preview a few of the things Buddhism teaches are important in life, such as helping others and avoiding too much pleasure.

Set a Purpose for Reading L2
- Preview the Objectives.
- Read each statement in the *Reading Readiness Guide* aloud. Ask students to mark the statements true or false.

  All in One Unit 2 History of Our World Teaching Resources, *Reading Readiness Guide,* p. 60

- Have students discuss the statements in pairs or groups of four, then mark their worksheets again. Use the Numbered Head participation strategy (TE, p. T40) to call on students to share their group's perspectives.

Vocabulary Builder
Preview Key Terms L2
Pronounce each key term, then ask students to say the word with you. Provide a simple explanation such as, "Some people meditate in the morning to feel calm and relaxed during the rest of the day."

Instruct

The Buddha and His Teachings ㄴ2

Guided Instruction

- **Vocabulary Builder** Clarify the high-use words **fast, extreme,** and **appeal** before reading.

- Have students read The Buddha and His Teachings using the ReQuest Procedure reading technique (TE, p. T39).

- Ask students **Why did people call Siddhartha Gautama the Buddha, or "Enlightened One?"** (*He was able to explain things that troubled people.*)

- Ask **How did the teachings of Buddhism develop?** (*Buddha meditated to find the answer to why humans suffer. He then traveled across India teaching others what he learned.*)

- Ask students to explain what the Middle Way is and how Buddha thought one should go about finding it. (*The Middle Way avoids two extremes—too much pleasure and too much unhappiness. To find the Middle Way people should act unselfishly toward others, avoid harming living things, and always tell the truth.*)

The Buddha and His Teachings

As Gautama traveled in the 500s B.C., he sought answers to his questions about the meaning of life. At first, Gautama studied with Hindu philosophers, but their ideas did not satisfy him. He could not accept the Hindu belief that only priests could pass on knowledge.

The Search for Understanding Gautama decided to stop looking outwardly for the cause of suffering. Instead, he tried to find understanding within his own mind. To do this, he decided to **meditate,** to focus the mind inward in order to find spiritual awareness. Meditation was an ancient Hindu practice used by Indus valley civilizations. Buddhist tradition says that Gautama fasted and meditated under a fig tree. After 49 days, he found the answers he sought. He believed he finally understood the roots of suffering.

For the next 45 years, Gautama traveled across India and shared his knowledge. Over the years, he attracted many followers. His followers called him the Buddha (BOO duh), or "Enlightened One." His teachings became known as Buddhism.

The Middle Way Buddhism teaches people to follow the Eightfold Path, also called the Middle Way. By following this path, a person avoids a life of extreme pleasure or extreme unhappiness.

The Buddha believed that selfish desires for power, wealth, and pleasure cause humans to suffer. By giving up selfish pleasures, a person can become free from suffering. He taught that the way to end human suffering is by following the Eightfold Path. To overcome selfish desires, Buddhists must learn to be wise, to behave correctly, and to develop their minds.

The Practice of Buddhism: The Eightfold Path

1. Right Understanding
Having faith in the Buddhist view of the universe

2. Right Intention
Making a commitment to practice Buddhism

3. Right Speech
Avoiding lies and mean or abusive speech

4. Right Action
Not taking life, not stealing, and not hurting others

5. Right Livelihood
Rejecting jobs and occupations that conflict with Buddhist ideals

6. Right Effort
Avoiding bad attitudes and developing good ones

7. Right Mindfulness
Being aware of one's own body, feelings, and thoughts

8. Right Concentration
Thinking deeply to find answers to problems

SOURCE: *Encyclopaedia Britannica*

The Eightfold Path
The Eightfold Path outlines the steps a person should take to lead a balanced life.
Analyze *Which steps direct followers to lead a moral life?*

Vocabulary Builder

Use the information below to teach students this section's high-use words.

High-Use Word	Definition and Sample Sentence
fast, p. 120	*v.* to abstain from eating or eat sparingly Some people **fast** during religious holidays.
extreme, p. 121	*n.* the greatest or least amounts The **extreme** cold in Antarctica makes living there difficult.
appeal, p. 122	*v.* to be attractive or interesting The architectural design of the building made it **appealing** to the eye.
coexist, p. 122	*v.* to live together at the same time or in the same place The cat and dog **coexisted** in the house.

Answer

Chart Skills Analyze steps 3–6

Release From Reincarnation To find this Middle Way, the Buddha taught, people must act unselfishly toward others and treat people fairly. They must tell the truth at all times. People should also avoid violence and the killing of any living thing. If people follow the Buddha's path, their suffering will end. They will eventually find **nirvana,** or lasting peace. By reaching nirvana, people will be released from the cycle of reincarnation.

Followers of Buddhism Buddhism also taught that all people are equal. Anyone, the Buddha declared, could follow the path to nirvana, regardless of his or her social class. This idea appealed to many people living under the caste system.

Like other religions, Buddhism has priests. Although monastery life is difficult, people of any social class can work to become a Buddhist priest or monk. The Buddha encouraged his followers to establish monasteries. There they would learn, meditate, and teach. He also urged monks to become **missionaries,** or people who spread their religious beliefs to others.

✓ Reading Check **Why do Buddhists try to follow the Middle Way?**

Recognizing Multiple Causes
Which factors in the paragraph at the left affect a Buddhist's ability to reach nirvana?

Reclining Buddha
Like many statues of the Buddha, this sculpture in Vientiane, Laos, located in Southeast Asia, shows the Buddha lying down. The pose may be linked to one of the great events of the Buddha's life, his reaching nirvana. **Analyze** *Describe the importance of nirvana.*

Recognize Multiple Causes As a follow up, ask students to answer the Target Reading Skill question in the Student Edition. (*Acting unselfishly toward others, treating people fairly, telling the truth at all times, and avoiding violence will help lead Buddhists toward nirvana.*)

Independent Practice
Ask students to create the Taking Notes graphic organizer on a blank piece of paper. Have them fill in the sequences of Buddhism's beginnings. Briefly model how to identify which details to record.

Monitor Progress
As students fill in their graphic organizers, circulate to make sure students are choosing the appropriate details. Provide assistance as needed.

Skills for Life Skills Mini Lesson

Distinguishing Fact and Opinion L2

1. Teach the skill by explaining that facts are statements that can be proved or disproved, while opinions are statements that cannot be proved or disproved.

2. Help students practice the skill by writing the following sentences on the board: *Buddhism began in India* and *It is wrong to harm another living creature.* Ask students to identify which is fact, which is opinion, and why. (*The first sentence is factual because it is a statement that can be proven. The second is an opinion because it cannot be proven.*)

3. Have students apply the skill by recording other facts and opinions in the section as they read.

Answers

✓ Reading Check Buddhists try to follow the Middle Way so that they can avoid suffering.
Analyze By reaching nirvana, Buddhists escape the cycle of reincarnation and find everlasting peace.

Buddhism Inside and Outside India

L2

Guided Instruction

- **Vocabulary Builder** Clarify the high-use word **coexist** before reading.

- Have students read more about Buddhism in Buddhism Inside and Outside India. As students read, circulate and make sure students can answer the Reading Check questions.

- Ask students **What religion existed side by side with Buddhism in India?** *(Hinduism)*

- Ask students to describe some ways Buddhism spread through India and into other countries. Use an Idea Wave (TE, p. T39) to elicit students' responses. *(Possible answers: Missionaries traveled to other countries to spread Buddha's teachings; travelers who came to India learned the religion during their stay and brought it home with them.)*

Independent Practice

Ask students to finish their graphic organizers by filling in the remaining details on the sequence of the spread of Buddhism.

Monitor Progress

- Show *Section Reading Support Transparency HOW 68*. Go over key concept and clarify key vocabulary as needed.

  History of Our World Transparencies, *Section Reading Support Transparency HOW 68*

- Tell students to fill in the last column of their *Reading Readiness Guides*. Probe for what they learned that confirms or invalidates each statement.

  All in One Unit 2 History of Our World Teaching Resources, *Reading Readiness Guide*, p. 60

Answers

MAP MASTER Skills Activity **Identify** In the A.D. 500s
Conclude Possible answer: People had to travel a long way by land and sea to reach Japan, which may explain why it took hundreds of years for the religion to reach the country.

Go Online
PHSchool.com Students may practice their map skills using the interactive online version of this map.

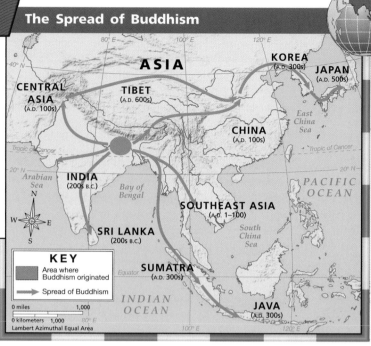

MAP MASTER Skills Activity
The Spread of Buddhism

Movement Missionaries and traders carried the Buddha's ideas and teachings throughout Asia. **Identify** When did the people of Japan learn about Buddhism? **Conclude** How might geography have affected the spread of Buddhism from India to Japan?

Go Online
PHSchool.com Use Web Code **lbp-2433** for step-by-step map skills practice.

KEY
- Area where Buddhism originated
- Spread of Buddhism

Some Hindus believed that the Buddha was the reincarnation of the god Vishnu, shown at the center of the bronze altar piece below.

122 History of Our World

Buddhism Inside and Outside India

After the Buddha's death, his teachings spread all over India. But the Buddha's teachings did not last in the land of his birth. Hinduism gradually regained favor among those in power. Meantime, Hinduism had developed in ways that made it more appealing to the lower castes. Over time, Buddhism died out almost completely in India. But for many years, Buddhism and Hinduism existed side by side.

Hindus and Buddhists: Shared Beliefs
When Hinduism and Buddhism coexisted in India, a number of basic ideas came to be shared by both. Both Hindus and Buddhists accept the idea that it is wrong to harm other living creatures. Both value nonviolence and believe in dharma and the cycle of rebirth. Some Hindus came to honor the Buddha as a reincarnation of the god Vishnu. But because Buddhists do not embrace the sacred texts of Hinduism, most Hindus do not worship the Buddha as an avatar.

Differentiated Instruction

For Advanced Readers
L3
Have students read *A Great Asian Thinker* individually to learn more about the teachings and philosophies of the Buddha.

Then ask students to answer the questions that follow the selection.

All in One Unit 2 History of Our World Teaching Resources, *A Great Asian Thinker*, p. 84

Buddhism Spreads to Other Countries Buddhism was accepted by millions of people in other lands. Missionaries and traders carried the Buddha's message throughout Asia. It took root first in China, where the ideas of the Buddha became mixed with those of earlier Chinese thinkers. Millions of Chinese became Buddhists, and Buddhist monastaries in China became centers of religious thought. From China, Buddhism spread to Korea and Japan. Today, Buddhism is part of the cultures of such countries as Japan, the Koreas, China, Tibet (part of China), and Vietnam.

✓ **Reading Check** What other countries has Buddhism spread to?

Boy Monks
Young novice monks study Buddhism in Sri Lanka, an island nation off the southeast coast of India. **Generalize** *How did Buddhism spread to Sri Lanka and other parts of Asia?*

Section 3 Assessment

Key Terms
Review the key terms at the beginning of this section. Use each term in a sentence that explains its meaning.

⊙ Target Reading Skill
What are the three events witnessed by Siddhartha Gautama that caused him to change his life?

Comprehension and Critical Thinking
1. (a) Identify Who was Siddhartha Gautama?

(b) Infer Why did Siddhartha Gautama look for the cause of human suffering?
(c) Identify Cause and Effect According to Buddhism, how is human suffering connected to human desires?
2. (a) Explain What happened to the Buddha's teachings in India after he died?
(b) Compare What is the relationship between Buddhist and Hindu beliefs?
(c) Analyze Why do you think that Buddhism was accepted in so many countries outside of India?

Writing Activity
Turn to page 119 and reread the passage about Siddhartha Gautama's journey outside the palace. Write a description of his journey from the point of view of a servant who has followed him from the palace.

Go Online
PHSchool.com

For: An activity on Buddhism
Visit: PHSchool.com
Web Code: lbd-2403

Chapter 4 Section 3 **123**

Objective

Learn how to read a table.

Prepare to Read

Build Background Knowledge L2

Ask students to turn back to p. 45 of their texts. Point out the table at the top of the page. Discuss what the table shows and ask the students if they think the information would be more or less clear if it were explained in the text rather than displayed in the table. (*Students should realize that the information is probably displayed more clearly in the table.*)

Instruct

Reading Tables L2

Guided Instruction

- Read the steps to reading a table as a class and write them on the board.

- Practice the skill by following the steps on p. 124 as a class.

- First, read the table title and headings together. Discuss what the table shows. (*where and when the world's major religions were founded*)

- Next, guide students through Step 2 to determine where Judaism was founded. Point out that they should read the Date Founded column head and the Judaism row head and find the cell where the two meet to find out where Judaism was founded. (*Southwest Asia*)

- Tell students to use the same method to find out which religion was founded most recently (*Islam*) and which religions were founded in India (*Buddhism and Hinduism*). Conduct the Idea Wave (TE, T39) to elicit student responses as to why it might be helpful to know that Buddhism and Hinduism were founded in India (*Possible answer: to help students analyze the spread of the religion*)

 **Reading Tables**

Ms. Bell's world studies class was working on a project. They had thought of a plan to help fight world hunger.

"We are going to sell candles and donate the money to a children's nutrition organization," said Indira.

"The group provides food and clean water for kids in poor countries," Troy explained.

"Look, Ms. Bell, we've already made a table to keep track of the orders we get," added Elizabeth.

A food relief program in Damana, India

A table displays information in vertical columns and horizontal rows. Look at the table on page 125 titled Candle Orders for Fundraiser. The numbers shown in the table are data, factual information collected and organized for a particular purpose. Making the table will help the class place an accurate order with the candle company.

Learn the Skill

To learn how to read a table, refer to the example of Ms. Bell's students and their fundraiser, as you follow the steps below.

1. **Read the title and then the column and row headings.** Reading the title and headings will help you determine the purpose of the table.

2. **Locate the information in the table.** Place one finger at the beginning of one row and another finger at the top of one column. Then look at the cell where the row and column meet. What does the number in each cell represent?

3. **Analyze information from the table.** Tables are helpful for summarizing and comparing data. The class can add the numbers in each column to find out how many of each color candle to buy from the manufacturer.

Independent Practice

Assign *Skills for Life* and have students complete it individually.

All in One **Unit 2 History of Our World Teaching Resources**, *Skills for Life*, p. 73

Monitor Progress

As students are analyzing the table, circulate and make sure individuals are applying the skill steps effectively. Check their questions to be sure they are answerable by reading the table. Provide assistance as needed.

Practice the Skill

In this text, you are learning about some of the world's major religions. Read the table at the right to find out more about those religions.

1 Study the kinds of information shown in the table.

2 Suppose you want to locate information on where Judaism was founded. Under which column heading would you look? Which row has the information you want?

3 Use the table to answer these questions: Which religion was founded most recently? Which religions were founded in India? How might this information be useful to you when reading about ancient history?

Major World Religions

Religion	Date Founded	Place of Origin
Buddhism	c. 525 B.C.	India
Christianity	c. A.D. 30	Southwest Asia
Hinduism	c. 1500 B.C.	India
Islam	c. A.D. 622	Southwest Asia
Judaism	c. 1800 B.C.	Southwest Asia

Candle Orders for Fundraiser

Seller	Green	Red	Blue
Katelyn			
Troy	2		5
Rashid			
Madelyn		3	
Indira	6		
Michael			
Elizabeth			

Apply the Skill

Now try making a table yourself. Interview at least four of your classmates to find out each person's favorite food, movie, and sport. Create a table to show the results.

Exchange tables with a classmate. Analyze the information in your classmate's table.

Assess Progress　L2

Ask students to do the Apply the Skill activity.

Reteach　L1

Ask students to use the skill steps to analyze the table on p. 45. Tell them to write three questions about the table. Then have them exchange their questions with a partner and have them answer each other's questions.

Extend　L3

Ask students to use the DK World Desk Reference Online to find out the percentage of people practicing each religion in India today. Tell them to display the information in a table. Remind them to give the table a title and use appropriate column and row labels.

Answers
Apply the Skill

Students' tables will vary, but should include column and row labels and an appropriate title.

Objectives

Social Studies

1. Learn about the rise of the Maurya Empire.
2. Understand the effects of Asoka's leadership on the Maurya Empire.

Reading/Language Arts

Understand that a cause may produce several effects.

Prepare to Read

Build Background Knowledge L2

Tell students that in this section they will learn about the rise and fall of the Maurya Empire. Have students preview the headings and visuals in this section with the following question in mind: **How would you describe the rulers of the Maurya empire?** Then use an Idea Wave (TE, p. T39) to have students come up with a list of qualities they think describe the Maurya rulers.

Set a Purpose for Reading L2

- Preview the Objectives.

- Read each statement in the *Reading Readiness Guide* aloud. Ask students to mark the statements true or false.

  All in One Unit 2 History of Our World Teaching Resources, *Reading Readiness Guide,* p. 64

- Have students discuss the statements in pairs or groups of four, then mark their worksheets again. Use the Numbered Heads participation strategy (TE, p. T40) to call on students to share their group's perspectives.

Vocabulary Builder
Preview Key Terms L2

Pronounce each key term, then ask students to say the word with you. Provide a simple explanation such as, "To convert means to change what you believe in, for example, a person may have once believed in the ideas of Hinduism but now believes in the teachings of the Buddha."

The Maurya Empire

Prepare to Read

Objectives

In this section you will
1. Learn about the rise of the Maurya Empire.
2. Understand the effects of Asoka's leadership on the Maurya Empire.

Taking Notes

As you read, compare and contrast the rulers of the Maurya Empire. Copy the Venn diagram below. Write similarities in the overlapping space and differences in the outside ovals.

Rulers of Maurya

Chandragupta   Asoka

⊙ Target Reading Skill

Understand Effects Sometimes one cause may produce several effects. Turn to page 127 and read the paragraph after the heading Chandragupta's Legacy. What were the effects of wealth on the Maurya Empire?

Key Terms

- **Maurya Empire** (MOWR yuh EM pyr) *n.* Indian empire founded by Chandragupta, beginning with his kingdom in northeastern India and spreading to most of northern and central India
- **convert** (kun VURT) *v.* to change one's beliefs; in particular, to change from one religion to another
- **tolerance** (TAHL ur uns) *n.* freedom from prejudice

Terra-cotta figure of a mother goddess worshiped in India, 200s B.C.

126 History of Our World

Around 321 B.C., a new ruler came to the throne of a kingdom in northeastern India. Within 35 years, the tiny kingdom had grown into the giant Maurya (MOWR yuh) Empire. Chandragupta (chun druh GUP tuh) Maurya founded India's **Maurya Empire**.

Chandragupta had been born to a poor family and sold into slavery at a young age. But later, when he became king, Chandragupta enjoyed luxuries from all parts of Asia. When he appeared before his subjects, he was often seated in a golden chair carried on his servants' shoulders. Sometimes he rode on an elephant covered with jewels.

The Rise of the Maurya Empire

India was made up of a number of warring states before Chandragupta came to power. Strong and ruthless, Chandragupta's armies overthrew kingdoms along the Ganges River. Turning west, the armies advanced into the Indus River valley. In only a few years, Chandragupta's power extended over most of northern and central India.

⊙ Target Reading Skill L2

Understand Effects Point out the Target Reading Skill. Explain that an effect is an event caused by another event. Sometimes causes result in several effects.

Model the skill by reading aloud the last paragraph under Absolute Rule on p. 127. Identify the multiple effects of Chandragup-ta's fear of being killed. (*He had servants taste his food, slept in a different room every night, and left the throne to become a monk.*)

Give students *Understand Effects.* Have them complete the activity in groups.

All in One Unit 2 History of Our World Teaching Resources, *Understand Effects,* p. 70

Absolute Rule Chandragupta was guided by the basic belief that a ruler must have absolute power. According to legend, one of Chandragupta's advisors gave him a book of advice called *Arthasastra*. The book urged kings to maintain control of their subjects and to establish an army of spies to inform on them.

Chandragupta commanded a huge army. Thousands of foot soldiers and mounted troops were ready to enforce the law and to crush any revolts. The army also had a herd of 9,000 war elephants, which struck fear into the hearts of opponents.

Under Chandragupta, the empire enjoyed great economic success. Most of its wealth came from farming. The Maurya Empire also built up trade with such faraway places as Greece, Rome, and China.

However, as his rule continued, Chandragupta became fearful for his life. Afraid of being poisoned, he made servants taste his food. He slept in a different room every night to ward off assassins, or people who murder rulers or political figures. One story says that near the end of his life, Chandragupta left the throne to his son and became a monk in southern India. Fasting and praying, he starved himself to death.

Chandragupta's Legacy Chandragupta did not gain wealth for himself only. Although his rule was harsh, he used his wealth to improve his empire. New irrigation systems brought water to farmers. Forests were cleared, and more food was produced. Government officials promoted crafts and mining. A vast network of roads made it easier for Maurya traders to exchange goods with foreign lands. Chandragupta's leadership brought order and peace to his people.

✓ **Reading Check** What kind of ruler was Chandragupta?

Fighting for Empire
Chandragupta's army rode elephants into war, causing fear and panic. This painting from the 1600s shows an elephant charging toward the enemy.
Evaluate How did Chandragupta use his army to create an empire?

Links to
Economics

The Emperor's Guidebook
Both Chandragupta and his grandson Asoka benefited from a book titled *Arthasastra*. *Artha* means "property and economics." Chandragupta used the book's advice on government as his guide to building an empire. Kautilya, the book's author, also served as an advisor to Chandragupta. Although Kautilya wrote about ways to achieve material success, he did not live in great luxury himself.

Vocabulary Builder

Use the information below to teach students this section's high-use words.

High-Use Word	Definition and Sample Sentence
promote, p. 127	*v.* to help the growth, success, or development of Practicing to write your letters **promotes** good penmanship.
humanely, p. 129	*adv.* with compassion, sympathy, or consideration for The king made sure all of his subjects had enough to eat and treated them **humanely**.

Instruct

The Rise of the Maurya Empire   L2

Guided Instruction

■ **Vocabulary Builder** Clarify the high-use word **promote** before reading.

■ Have students read The Rise of the Maurya Empire using the Oral Cloze reading strategy (TE, p. T37).

■ Ask **How did the Maurya empire arise?** *(Chandragupta conquered lands in north and central India with his strong armies, establishing the Maurya Empire.)*

■ Have students discuss why Chandragupta may have feared for his life. *(He may have been worried that because he ruled harshly, people disliked him and wanted to kill him.)*

■ Ask students **How was trade promoted during Chandragupta's rule?** *(A network of roads was built to make trade with distant lands easier.)*

Independent Practice
Assign *Guided Reading and Review.*

All in One Unit 2 History of Our World **Teaching Resources,** *Guided Reading and Review,* p. 65

Monitor Progress
Review the answers to the *Guided Reading and Review* questions that apply to The Rise of the Maurya Empire with students.

Links

Read the **Links to Language Arts** on this page. Ask students **What was the importance of *Arthasastra* to the Maurya Empire?** (*Arthasastra* influenced Chandragupta's rule by helping him to keep the order and peace of his people and build the empire's economy.)

Answers

✓ **Reading Check** Chandragupta was an absolute ruler who kept control over people using a large army. Though his rule was harsh, he used his wealth to improve the empire. His leadership brought order and peace to the people.
Evaluate He used his army to conquer kingdoms along the Ganges River and in the Indus River Valley and make them part of his empire.

Asoka's Leadership L2

Guided Instruction

- **Vocabulary Builder** Clarify the high-use word **humanely** before reading.

- Have students read about the Maurya Empire under a different ruler in Asoka's Leadership. As students read, circulate to make sure individuals can answer the Reading Check question.

- Ask students **How did Asoka's ruling style change when he became a Buddhist?** (*He stopped using force and violence to conquer people; he was more concerned about the welfare of his people; he promoted tolerance and discouraged the killing of living things.*)

- Have students discuss how they think the people of the Maurya Empire felt about the way Asoka ruled. (*They were probably grateful that he ruled mercifully and did many things to help their well-being, such as building hospitals. Overall, the people were probably pleased with the way Asoka ruled.*)

⤵ Target Reading Skill L2

Understand Effects As a follow up, ask students to answer the Target Reading Skill question in the Student Edition. (*They led him to give up war and violence, feed his prisoners and restore their land, and convert to Buddhism.*)

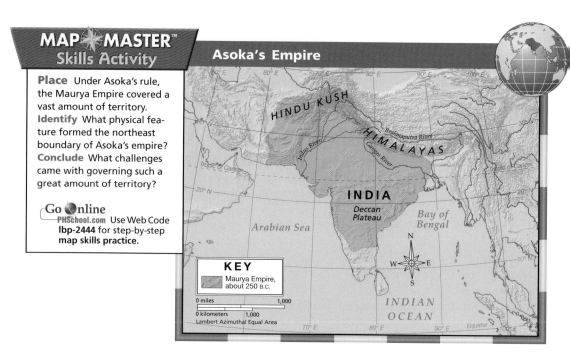

MAP MASTER™ Skills Activity

Asoka's Empire

Place Under Asoka's rule, the Maurya Empire covered a vast amount of territory. **Identify** What physical feature formed the northeast boundary of Asoka's empire? **Conclude** What challenges came with governing such a great amount of territory?

Go Online
PHSchool.com Use Web Code **lbp-2444** for step-by-step map skills practice.

KEY
Maurya Empire, about 250 B.C.

0 miles 1,000
0 kilometers 1,000
Lambert Azimuthal Equal Area

⤵ **Understand Effects** What effects did the Battle of Kalinga have on Asoka's life?

Asoka's Leadership

Chandragupta passed the leadership of the Maurya Empire on to his son. After the son died in 273 B.C., Chandragupta's grandson, Asoka, gained power. Asoka, whose name means "without sorrow," further expanded Chandragupta's empire. By the end of his lengthy rule in 232 B.C., Asoka had built the greatest empire India had ever seen.

The Battle of Kalinga For more than 35 years, Asoka ruled an empire that included much of the Indian subcontinent. During the first years of his rule, Asoka was as warlike as his grandfather had been. He conquered new territories which were not yet part of the empire.

Early in his rule, Asoka led his army south into the state of Kalinga. In about 261 B.C., he won a bloody battle in which thousands and thousands of people were injured or died. The great slaughter at Kalinga was a turning point in Asoka's life. He was filled with sorrow over the bloodshed. He gave up war and violence. He freed his prisoners and restored their land. Later, he chose to **convert**, or change his beliefs, to Buddhism. Asoka also spread the message of Buddhism to the people of his empire.

Answers

MAP MASTER Skills Activity **Identify** the Himalayas
Conclude Possible answer: It is difficult to maintain control and enforce laws over such a large territory.

Go Online
PHSchool.com Students can practice their map skills using the interactive online version of this map.

The Buddhist Ruler Asoka practiced and preached the teachings of the Buddha. He did not allow the use of animals for sacrifices. He gave up hunting, the traditional sport of Indian kings.

Asoka thought of his people as his children and was concerned about their welfare. He had hospitals built throughout his kingdom. He even had wells dug every mile beside the roads so that travelers and animals would not go thirsty.

Asoka was also concerned with his people's moral and spiritual life. To carry the Buddha's message throughout his vast empire, Asoka issued writings of moral advice. Some writings urged people to honor their parents. Others asked people not to kill animals. Still others encouraged people to behave with truthfulness and **tolerance,** or freedom from prejudice. Asoka also issued laws requiring that people be treated humanely. Throughout his empire, his advice and laws were carved on stone pillars about 40 feet (12 meters) high. One pillar bore these words:

Find out about Maurya's elephant army.

> **❝**Both this world and the other are hard to reach, except by great love of the law, great self-examination, great obedience, great respect, great energy.**❞**
>
> —*Asoka's laws*

Honoring the Buddha
This stupa, or Buddhist monument, was built sometime between 100 B.C. and A.D. 100, in Sanchi, India. The umbrella at the very top represents protection. **Transferring Information** *How did Asoka's rulings reflect the teachings of the Buddha?*

Show students *The Maurya Elephant Army.* Ask **How did elephants help Mauryan warriors?** (*Their thick skin and great strength made them well-suited for warriors to ride into battle. They were strong enough to carry several warriors into battle at once.*)

Independent Practice

Have students create the Taking Notes graphic organizer on a blank piece of paper. Then have them complete it by writing the similarities between Chandragupta and Asoka in the overlapping space of the ovals and their differences in the parts of the ovals that do not overlap. Model an example of each to get them started.

Monitor Progress

- Show *Section Reading Support Transparency HOW 69* and ask students to check their graphic organizers individually. Go over key concepts and clarify key vocabulary as needed.

  📖 **History of Our World Transparencies,** *Section Reading Support Transparency HOW 69*

- Tell students to fill in the last column of their *Reading Readiness Guides.* Probe for what they learned that confirms or invalidates each statement.

  All in One Unit 2 History of Our World Teaching Resources, *Reading Readiness Guide,* p. 64

Answers

Transferring Information He did not allow the use of animals for sacrifices; he did things to improve the welfare of his people, such as build hospitals and dig wells; he issued writings of moral advice; he passed laws requiring people be treated humanely.

Differentiated Instruction

For Advanced Readers   L3

Encourage students to conduct further research on Asoka and Chandragupta on the Internet, in encyclopedias, and in books on ancient India. Have them decide which leader they believe ruled ancient India best. Then have them prepare a brief argument as to why they chose that leader. Group the Asoka supporters and the Chandragupta supporters and alternate having one student from each team read their team's argument.

Assess and Reteach

Assess Progress L2

Have students complete the Section Assessment. Administer the *Section Quiz.*

All in One Unit 2 History of Our World Teaching Resources, *Section Quiz,* p. 66

Reteach L1

If Students need more instruction, have them read this section in the Reading and Vocabulary Study Guide.

Chapter 4, Section 4, **History of Our World Reading and Vocabulary Study Guide,** pp. 57–59

Extend L3

Students read that Chandragupta encouraged art. Have students conduct library and Internet research to find out more about the art created during this time period. Have them choose one piece of art that interests them and draw a copy of it or bring a picture of it to class, explaining what it is, the creator of the art (if known), and why the art interests them.

Answers

Predict Possible answer: People can communicate through dance even if they speak different languages.

✓ Reading Check Asoka became a Buddhist because he was filled with sorrow over the thousands of deaths in the Battle of Kalinga, which he initiated.

Section 4 Assessment

Key Terms

Students' sentences should reflect knowledge of each Key Term.

Target Reading Skill

Chandragupta was able to use the empire's wealth to improve the empire. For example, irrigation systems and roads were built.

Comprehension and Critical Thinking

1. (a) India consisted of separate warring states, each with its own rulers.
(b) Chandragupta used his powerful army to conquer kingdoms and build his empire.
(c) Answers will vary. Some students might think it is true because Chandragupta may have felt he needed to repent for the violence he caused. Others might think it is not true because he would not have wanted to give up all his power.

2. (a) Asoka issued writings of moral advice and he established laws that required people to treat each other with humanity. He spread Buddhism by sending out missionaries and united India. **(b)** The economy of the empire flourished and the people were united. **(c)** Asoka ruled using the teachings of Buddhism. He encouraged people to treat each other well, discouraged violence, and united the people of India.

Buddhism in Tibet
Monks dance in a colorful ceremony at the Ta Gong Monastery in Tibet, located on India's northern border.
Predict *How might ceremonies like this help spread Buddhism to peoples who speak different languages?*

Buddhism Outside of India

Asoka practiced religious tolerance toward the Hindus. During his rule, many of the Buddha's teachings became part of Hinduism. Buddhism grew under Asoka. He sent missionaries far and wide to spread its message. It was missionaries sent by Asoka who spread Buddhism to China. Asoka's sister and brother went to the island of Sri Lanka as Buddhist missionaries. He even sent teachers to Egypt, Greece, and North Africa.

At the time of Asoka's death, India was united as never before. After his death, however, the great Maurya Empire declined. Without his strong leadership, his territories became divided. Small states began fighting with one another. Several centuries of invasion and disorder followed. It took almost 600 years before India was united again.

✓ Reading Check Why did Asoka become a Buddhist?

✦ Section 4 Assessment

Key Terms

Review the key terms at the beginning of this section. Use each term in a sentence that explains its meaning.

Target Reading Skill

Reread Chandragupta's Legacy on page 127. What were the effects of wealth on the Maurya Empire?

Comprehension and Critical Thinking

1. (a) Recall How was India governed before the Maurya Empire?

(b) Describe How did Chandragupta build the Maurya Empire?
(c) Draw Conclusions Chandragupta ruled forcefully and with absolute power, but legend says he ended his life living in poverty as a monk. Do you think this story could be true? Explain.

2. (a) Describe What were some of Asoka's accomplishments?
(b) Explain Why is the time of the Maurya Empire considered a golden age in India?
(c) Identify Cause and Effect How did Buddhism influence Asoka's rule of the empire?

Writing Activity

Asoka wrote many rules of conduct for himself and for others to follow. Write a list of rules of conduct that you would like to see today's leaders follow.

Go Online PHSchool.com
For: An activity on Asoka
Visit: PHSchool.com
Web Code: lbd-2404

130 History of Our World

Writing Activity

Use *Rubric for Assessing a Writing Assignment* to evaluate students' rules of conduct.

All in One Unit 2 History of Our World Teaching Resources, *Rubric for Assessing a Writing Assignment,* p. 86

Go Online PHSchool.com Typing in the Web code when prompted will bring students directly to detailed instructions for this activity.

Review and Assessment

◆ Chapter Summary

Mohenjo-Daro seal

Section 1: The Indus and Ganges River Valleys

- India's geographic setting limited the contact the ancient peoples of the Indian subcontinent had with the rest of the world.
- Well-planned cities, such as Mohenjo-Daro, flourished along the banks of the Indus River.
- Aryans migrated in great waves from central Asia into India, influencing Indian life and culture.

Section 2: Hinduism in Ancient India

- Hinduism is a complex religion that developed over a span of about 3,500 years.
- Hindus believe in nonviolence, and that good behavior will be rewarded and bad behavior will be punished.
- Hindus take many paths in their search for truth.

Sanskrit

Sections 3: The Beginnings of Buddhism

- Buddhism was founded by a Hindu prince who preached nonviolence and unselfish behavior.
- Buddhism flourished in India, along with Hinduism, but it eventually declined there. Missionaries carried the Buddha's message to cultures throughout Asia.

Section 4: The Maurya Empire

- Chandragupta's Maurya Empire extended over northern and central India.
- Chandragupta's grandson, Asoka, made Maurya an even greater empire, one that included much of the Indian subcontinent.
- Asoka embraced Buddhism and sent missionaries to spread the Buddhist message to other regions.

Indian warriors

◆ Reviewing Key Terms

Circle the underlined key term that best completes the sentence.

1. A <u>citadel, subcontinent</u> is a large landmass that juts out from a continent.

2. <u>Dharma, Nirvana</u> is the religious and moral duties of a Hindu.

3. To <u>meditate, migrate</u> is to move from one place to settle in another area.

4. Hindus and Buddhists believe in <u>ahimsa, reincarnation</u>, which is the rebirth of the soul.

5. Under the <u>caste, avatar</u> system, a weaver's son always became a weaver and a barber's daughter always married a barber.

6. Buddhism spread to other countries with the help of <u>monsoons, missionaries</u>.

7. Asoka encouraged his people to behave with <u>tolerance, dharma</u>, or freedom from prejudice.

Chapter 4 **131**

Vocabulary Builder

Revisit this chapter's high-use words:

dominate	welfare	appeal
barrier	fate	coexist
flourish	extreme	promote
fashion	fast	humanely

Ask students to review the definitions they recorded on their *Word Knowledge* worksheet.

All in One Unit 2 History of Our World Teaching Resources, *Word Knowledge,* p. 71

Consider allowing students to earn extra credit if they use the words in their answers to the questions in the Chapter Review and Assessment. The words must be used correctly and in a natural context to win extra points.

Chapter 4

Review and Assessment

Review Chapter Content

- Review and revisit the major themes of the chapter by having students determine which Guiding Question is answered by each bulleted statement in the Chapter Summary. Have students work in groups to classify the statements. Use the Numbered Heads participation strategy (TE, p. T40) to have the groups share their answers in the group discussion. Refer to page 1 in the Student Edition for the text of the Guided Questions.

- Assign *Vocabulary Development* for students to review Key Terms.

All in One Unit 2 History of Our World Teaching Resources, *Vocabulary Development,* p. 85

Answers

Key Terms

1. subcontinent

2. Dharma

3. migrate

4. reincarnation

5. caste

6. missionaries

7. tolerance

Review and Assessment

Comprehension and Critical Thinking

8. (a) The Bay of Bengal, the Indian Ocean, and the Arabian Sea limited contact with lands to the east and west. India was separated from the rest of the continent by the Himalaya Mountains and the Hindu Kush range. India's climate was dominated by the summer and winter monsoons. **(b)** The monsoons helped create a fertile soil that allowed the people to grow a surplus of food. The surplus helped the population grow. The city of Mohenjo-Daro had to be built on higher ground to prevent flooding from the Indus River. **(c)** Scientists have studied the ruins of the ancient city.

9. (a) The Aryans were people from central Asia who moved into the Indus Valley. **(b)** Many Aryans were herders and warriors; the Aryans were always on the move. The Aryans organized their society in a caste system. **(c)** The Aryans spread their culture into the Indus valley. They also introduced their tools and the caste system to the people of the Indus valley.

10. (a) Aryan hymns and religious ideas mixed with those of India's preexisting cultures to form the beginnings of Hinduism. **(b)** The basic beliefs in Hinduism include the belief in reincarnation based on people's behavior, the belief that people must obey their dharmas, or religious and moral duties, and the belief in ahimsa, or nonviolence. **(c)** It is considered to be a complex religion because it absorbed the beliefs of many different religions and does not have one central god.

11. (a) The Buddha was Siddhartha Gautama, a young prince who gave up everything he had to find the cause of human suffering. **(b)** The central idea of Buddhism is that one must give up selfish desires in order to avoid human suffering. It appealed to many people because it taught that suffering would end if people followed the Buddha's path. **(c)** Possible answer: Hinduism and Buddhism were able to coexist because they shared many of the same beliefs.

12. (a) Asoka issued writings of moral advice, established laws that required people to treat each other with humanity, spread Buddhism by sending out missionaries, and united India. **(b)** Asoka encouraged nonviolence, posted laws and advice encouraging people to treat each other humanely, and

Review and Assessment (continued)

◆ Comprehension and Critical Thinking

8. (a) Describe What were the geography and climate of ancient India?
(b) Identify Effects How did India's geography and climate affect the people of Mohenjo-Daro?
(c) Infer How do we know that the people of Mohenjo-Daro created a highly organized civilization?

9. (a) Identify Who were the Aryans?
(b) Explain What were some characteristics of Aryan culture?
(c) Summarize What influence did the Aryans have on the people of the Indus valley?

10. (a) Recall Describe the beginnings of ancient Hinduism.
(b) Summarize What are some of the basic beliefs of Hinduism?
(c) Evaluate Information Why is Hinduism considered to be a complex religion?

11. (a) Identify Who was the Buddha?
(b) Explain What is the central idea of Buddhism, and why did the religion appeal to so many people?
(c) Draw Inferences Buddhism and Hinduism were able to coexist in India for some time. Why do you think this was possible?

12. (a) Recall List Asoka's achievements as ruler of the Maurya Empire.
(b) Explain How did Asoka's actions show that he was a Buddhist?
(c) Compare How did Siddhartha Gautama's life-changing experience with suffering compare to Asoka's?

◆ Skills Practice

Reading Tables In the Skills for Life activity, you learned how to read tables and how to create your own table.

Review the steps you follow to do this skill. Return to the concept web you created to take notes on Section 2 of this chapter. Organize that same information into a table. Then, write a brief explanation of how a table makes comparing information from the section easy.

◆ Writing Activity: Language Arts

Asoka helped spread the Buddha's message by having his teachings carved into stone pillars. Turn to page 129 and reread the quote from one of Asoka's pillars. Next, turn to page 117 and reread The Teachings of Hinduism. Finally, write similar messages that could teach people about Hinduism.

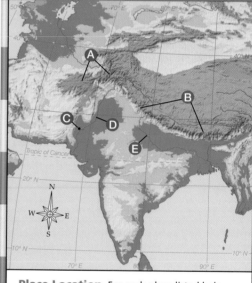

MAP✦MASTER™
Skills Activity

Ancient India

Place Location For each place listed below, write the letter from the map that shows its location.

1. Himalayas
2. Hindu Kush
3. Indus River
4. Ganges River
5. Mohenjo-Daro

Go Online
PHSchool.com Use Web Code lbp-2454 for an **interactive map**.

---

built hospitals and wells because he was concerned with the welfare of citizens. **(c)** Gautama and Asoka had similar experiences in that once they witnessed great suffering, they decided to change their lives to try and help eliminate it.

Skills Practice

Possible Table Details: Beliefs—Belief in more than one god; behavior determines how people will be reincarnated; people

should follow their dharma; people should not harm other living things. History—Aryan culture mixed with preexisting cultures, causing new beliefs to become part of the Vedas; Hinduism absorbed the beliefs of many different religions.

Possible explanation: The table allows you to separate information into smaller pieces that are organized and easy to read.

Standardized Test Prep

Test-Taking Tips

Some questions on standardized tests ask you to analyze a reading selection for the main ideas. Read the passage below. Then follow the tips to answer the sample question.

> Buddhist missionaries spread their religion throughout Asia. Buddhism took root in China and grew there. Millions of Chinese became Buddhists. Gradually, Buddhist ideas mixed with earlier Chinese teaching. Buddhism then spread from China to Korea and Japan.

Pick the letter that best answers the question.

Which topic sentence is missing from this paragraph?

A Buddhism died out in Turkey but took root in many parts of Asia.

B Buddhist monasteries became centers of thought in China.

C Buddhism died out in India but took root in many parts of Asia.

D Today, Buddhism is a part of many Asian cultures.

Think It Through Start with the main idea of the paragraph. Each sentence tells about the spread of Buddhism. You can rule out answer B because the paragraph is not about monasteries. Nor is the paragraph about Buddhism today, so you can rule out D. That leaves A and C. Did Buddhism spread from Turkey or from India? The answer is India. Even if you were not sure, you might guess that India is much closer to China and the eastern part of Asia. Therefore, the best answer is C.

TIP Some paragraphs have a topic sentence that states the main idea. All sentences in the paragraph support this idea.

TIP Read all of the answer choices before making a final pick. You can't be sure you have the best answer until you have read every one.

Practice Questions

Use the tips above and other tips in this book to help you answer the following questions.

1. The Vedas are
   A a mountain range in northern India.
   B Aryan religious books.
   C nomadic herders who moved into the Indus River valley.
   D early inhabitants of the Indus River valley.

Read the passage below, and then answer the questions that follow.

Under Chandragupta, the Maurya Empire prospered. Asoka expanded and strengthened the empire. He encouraged the spread of Buddhism and united the various Indian states.

2. Which of the following would serve as the best topic sentence for this passage?
   A Asoka was the "Father of Buddhism."
   B The Maurya Empire grew and prospered under two leaders, Chandragupta and Asoka.
   C Chandragupta believed in absolute power.
   D Asoka converted to Buddhism.

3. Unlike other major world religions, Hinduism
   A had no single founder.
   B has had no influence on other religions.
   C has no sacred texts.
   D has no great thinkers.

Use Web Code lba-2404 for a Chapter 4 self-test.

Chapter 4 **133**

Overview

Section **1**

The Geography of China's River Valleys
1. Examine the geography of ancient China.
2. Find out about early civilization in China.
3. Learn about the importance of family ties in early Chinese society.

Section **2**

Confucius and His Teachings
1. Learn about the life of Confucius.
2. Find out about the teachings of Confucius.
3. Understand the influence Confucianism had on Chinese society.

Section **3**

Warring Kingdoms Unite
1. Learn about the rise of the Qin dynasty.
2. Find out how Emperor Shi Huangdi attempted to unify the economy and culture of China.
3. Examine the actions of the Han dynasty's leaders.

Section **4**

Achievements of Ancient China
1. Learn about the Silk Road.
2. Find out about the Han dynasty's respect for tradition and learning.
3. Discover the important advances in technology that were made in China during the Han dynasty.

DISCOVERY
CHANNEL
SCHOOL
Video

The Great Wall of China
Length: 5 minutes, 58 seconds
Use with Section 3
This segment describes the story of the Great Wall of China, and includes information about its creation and its relationship to the struggles facing China during the hundreds of years it took to build.

 # Technology Resources

.PHSchool.com

Students use embedded Web codes to access Internet activities, chapter self-tests, and additional map practice. They may also access Dorling Kindersley's Online Desk Reference to learn more about each country they study.

Interactive Textbook

Use the Interactive Textbook to make content and concepts come alive through animations, videos, and activities that accompany the complete basal text—online and on CD-ROM.

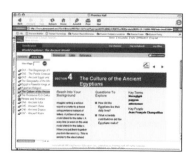

PRENTICE HALL
TeacherEXPRESS
Plan • Teach • Assess

Use this complete suite of powerful teaching tools to make planning lessons and administering tests quicker and easier.

Reading and Assessment

Reading and Vocabulary Instruction

🔊 Model the Target Reading Skill

Main Idea Tell students that identifying the main idea and supporting details in a passage is important because it can help them remember the most important ideas from their reading. The main idea is the most important point in a passage. It is supported by details that contain more specific information. Model identifying the main idea and supporting details by thinking aloud about the first paragraph with the heading *Effects on Civilization* on page 137 of the Student Edition.

I will read the paragraph to find the main idea. The last sentence seems to be the main idea: *They were so sure that they lived at the center of the world that they called themselves the Middle Kingdom.*

Now I will reread the other sentences in the paragraph to see if they are supporting details. Do they explain why the Chinese called themselves the Middle Kingdom? Each sentence seems to explain why the Chinese thought they lived in the center of the world.

Use the following worksheets from All-in-One Unit 2 History of Our World Teaching Resources (pp. 115–117) to support this chapter's Target Reading Skill.

Vocabulary Builder
High-Use Academic Words

Use these steps to teach this chapter's high-use words:

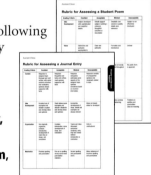

1. Have students rate how well they know each word on their Word Knowledge worksheets (All-in-One Unit 2 History of Our World Teaching Resources, p. 118).

2. Pronounce each word and ask students to repeat it.

3. Give students a brief definition and sample sentence (provided on TE pp. 137, 145, 150, and 157).

4. Work with students as they fill in the "Definition or Example" column of their Word Knowledge worksheets.

Assessment

Formal Assessment

Test students' understanding of core knowledge and skills.

Chapter Tests A and B, All-in-One Unit 2 History of Our World Teaching Resources, pp. 131–136

Customize the Chapter Tests to suit your needs.
Exam*View*® Test Bank CD-ROM

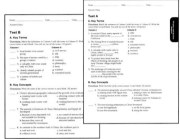

Skills Assessment

Assess geographic literacy.
MapMaster Skills, Student Edition, pp. 135, 152, 157, 162

Assess reading and comprehension.
Target Reading Skills, Student Edition, pp. 139, 145, 153, 158, and in Section Assessments

Chapter 5 Assessment, History of Our World Reading and Vocabulary Study Guide, p. 73

Performance Assessment

Assess students' performance on this chapter's Writing Activities using the following rubrics from All-in-One Unit 2 History of Our World Teaching Resources.

Rubric for Assessing a Writing Assignment, p. 128

Rubric for Assessing a Journal Entry, p. 129

Rubric for Assessing a Student Poem, p. 130

Assess students' work through performance tasks.

Small Group Activity: Making a Map of the Silk Road, All-in-One Unit 2 History of Our World Teaching Resources, pp. 121–124

Online Assessment

Have students check their own understanding.
Chapter Self-Test

Section 1 The Geography of China's River Valleys

 2 periods, 1 block (includes Skills for Life)

Social Studies Objectives

1. Examine the geography of ancient China.
2. Find out about early civilization in China.
3. Learn about the importance of family ties in early Chinese society.

Reading/Language Arts Objective

Learn how to find the main idea of a paragraph or section of text.

Prepare to Read	Instructional Resources	Differentiated Instruction
Build Background Knowledge Have students make comparisons between ancient India and ancient China. **Set a Purpose for Reading** Have students evaluate statements on the *Reading Readiness Guide*. **Preview Key Terms** Teach the section's Key Terms. **Target Reading Skill** Introduce the section's Target Reading Skill of **identifying main ideas**.	**All in One Unit 2 History of Our World Teaching Resources** L2 Reading Readiness Guide, p. 100 L2 Identify Main Ideas, p. 115	**Spanish Reading and Vocabulary Study Guide** L1 Chapter 5, Section 1, pp. 45–46 ELL

Instruct	Instructional Resources	Differentiated Instruction
The Geography of Ancient China Discuss the geography of ancient China. **Target Reading Skill** Review **identifying main ideas**. **Early Civilization in China** Ask questions about and discuss the Shang Dynasty. **Importance of the Family** Discuss the importance and living arrangements of families in ancient China.	**All in One Unit 2 History of Our World Teaching Resources** L2 Guided Reading and Review, p. 101 L2 Reading Readiness Guide, p. 100 **History of Our World Transparencies** L2 Section Reading Support Transparency HOW 70	**All in One Unit 2 History of Our World Teaching Resources** L2 Skills for Life, p. 120 AR, GT, LPR, SN **Spanish Support** L2 Guided Reading and Review (Spanish), p. 46 ELL

Assess and Reteach	Instructional Resources	Differentiated Instruction
Assess Progress Evaluate student comprehension with the section assessment and section quiz. **Reteach** Assign the Reading and Vocabulary Study Guide to help struggling students. **Extend** Extend the lesson by having students create posters about the Shang dynasty.	**All in One Unit 2 History of Our World Teaching Resources** L2 Section Quiz, p. 102 Rubric for Assessing a Writing Assignment, p. 128 **Reading and Vocabulary Study Guide** L1 Chapter 5, Section 1, pp. 61–63	**Spanish Support** L2 Section Quiz (Spanish), p. 47 ELL **Social Studies Skills Tutor CD-ROM** L1 Making Valid Generalizations ELL, LPR, SN **PHSchool.com** L3 **For:** Environmental and Global Issues: Local Water Use **Web code:** lbd-2501 AR, GT

Key

L1 Basic to Average   L3 Average to Advanced

L2 For All Students

LPR Less Proficient Readers
AR Advanced Readers
SN Special Needs Students

GT Gifted and Talented
ELL English Language Learners

Section 2 Confucius and His Teachings

 2 periods, 1 block

Social Studies Objectives
1. Learn about the life of Confucius.
2. Find out about the teachings of Confucius.
3. Understand the influence Confucianism had on Chinese society.

Reading/Language Arts Objective
Learn how to identify details that support a main idea.

Prepare to Read	Instructional Resources	Differentiated Instruction
Build Background Knowledge Ask students to preview the section and note facts about Confucius. **Set a Purpose for Reading** Have students evaluate statements on the *Reading Readiness Guide.* **Preview Key Terms** Teach the section's Key Terms. **Target Reading Skill** Introduce the section's Target Reading Skill of **identifying supporting details.**	**All in One Unit 2 History of Our World Teaching Resources** **L2** Reading Readiness Guide, p. 104 **L2** Identify Supporting Details, p. 116	**Spanish Reading and Vocabulary Study Guide** **L1** Chapter 5, Section 2, pp. 47–48 ELL

Instruct	Instructional Resources	Differentiated Instruction
The Life of Confucius Discuss the life of Confucius. **Target Reading Skill** Review **identifying supporting details.** **The Teachings of Confucius** Ask questions about Confucianism. **The Influence of Confucius** Discuss some of the teachings of Confucius and their impact.	**All in One Unit 2 History of Our World Teaching Resources** **L2** Guided Reading and Review, p. 105 **L2** Reading Readiness Guide, p. 104 **History of Our World Transparencies** **L2** Section Reading Support Transparency HOW 71	**Teacher's Edition** **L1** For Less Proficient Readers, TE p. 146 **L1** For English Language Learners, TE p. 146 **Reading and Vocabulary Study Guide** **L1** Chapter 5, Section 2, pp. 64–66 ELL, LPR, SN **Spanish Support** **L2** Guided Reading and Review (Spanish), p. 48 ELL

Assess and Reteach	Instructional Resources	Differentiated Instruction
Assess Progress Evaluate student comprehension with the section assessment and section quiz. **Reteach** Assign the Reading and Vocabulary Study Guide to help struggling students. **Extend** Extend the lesson by assigning the chapter's Enrichment activity.	**All in One Unit 2 History of Our World Teaching Resources** **L2** Section Quiz, p. 106 **L3** Enrichment, p. 119 Rubric for Assessing a Journal Entry, p. 129 **Reading and Vocabulary Study Guide** **L1** Chapter 5, Section 2, pp. 64–66	**Spanish Support** **L2** Section Quiz (Spanish), p. 49 ELL

Key
L1 Basic to Average   **L3** Average to Advanced
L2 For All Students

LPR Less Proficient Readers
AR Advanced Readers
SN Special Needs Students

GT Gifted and Talented
ELL English Language Learners

Section 3 **Warring Kingdoms Unite**

 2 periods, 1 block (includes Focus on China's Western Frontier)

Social Studies Objectives
1. Learn about the rise of the Qin dynasty.
2. Find out how Emperor Shi Huangdi attempted to unify the economy and culture of China.
3. Examine the actions of the Han dynasty's leaders.

Reading/Language Arts Objective
Learn how to identify main ideas when they are not stated directly.

Prepare to Read	**Instructional Resources**	**Differentiated Instruction**
Build Background Knowledge Help students create questions about the Qin and Han dynasties. **Set a Purpose for Reading** Have students evaluate statements on the *Reading Readiness Guide.* **Preview Key Terms** Teach the section's Key Terms. **Target Reading Skill** Introduce the section's Target Reading Skill of **identifying implied main ideas.**	**All in One Unit 2 History of Our World Teaching Resources** L2 Reading Readiness Guide, p. 108 L2 Identify Implied Main Ideas, p. 117	**Spanish Reading and Vocabulary Study Guide** L1 Chapter 5, Section 3, pp. 49–50 ELL

Instruct	**Instructional Resources**	**Differentiated Instruction**
The Qin Dynasty Discuss China's first emperor and his accomplishments. **Unifying Economy and Culture** Discuss how China's economy and culture were unified. **The Han Dynasty** Discuss the Han dynasty. **Target Reading Skill** Review **identifying implied main ideas.**	**All in One Unit 2 History of Our World Teaching Resources** L2 Guided Reading and Review, p. 109 L2 Reading Readiness Guide, p. 108 **History of Our World Transparencies** L2 Section Reading Support Transparency HOW 72 **World Studies Video Program** L2 The Great Wall of China	**All in One Unit 2 History of Our World Teaching Resources** L3 The Tale of a Frog, p. 126 Rubric for Assessing a Journal Entry, p. 129 **Teacher's Edition** L3 For Gifted and Talented, TE pp. 151, 154 L3 For Advanced Readers, TE p. 151 **Spanish Support** L2 Guided Reading and Review (Spanish), p. 40 ELL

Assess and Reteach	**Instructional Resources**	**Differentiated Instruction**
Assess Progress Evaluate student comprehension with the section assessment and section quiz. **Reteach** Assign the Reading and Vocabulary Study Guide to help struggling students. **Extend** Extend the lesson by assigning a map activity.	**All in One Unit 2 History of Our World Teaching Resources** L2 Section Quiz, p. 110 L3 Outline Map 29: East Asia, p. 125 Rubric for Assessing a Writing Assignment, p. 128 **Reading and Vocabulary Study Guide** L1 Chapter 5, Section 3, pp. 67–69	**Spanish Support** L2 Section Quiz (Spanish), p. 4 ELL

Key

L1 Basic to Average	L3 Average to Advanced	**LPR** Less Proficient Readers	**GT** Gifted and Talented
L2 For All Students		**AR** Advanced Readers	**ELL** English Language Learners
		SN Special Needs Students	

Section 4 Achievements of Ancient China

 2 periods, 1 block (includes Chapter Review and Assessment)

Social Studies Objectives

1. Learn about the Silk Road.
2. Find out about the Han dynasty's respect for tradition and learning.
3. Discover the important advances in technology that were made in China during the Han dynasty.

Reading/Language Arts Objective

Learn how to identify details that support the main idea.

Section Lesson Planner

Prepare to Read

Build Background Knowledge
Discuss what the achievements of ancient China say about the culture.

Set a Purpose for Reading
Have students evaluate statements on the *Reading Readiness Guide.*

Preview Key Terms
Teach the section's Key Terms.

Target Reading Skill
Introduce the section's Target Reading Skill of **identifying supporting details.**

Instructional Resources

All in One Unit 2 History of Our World Teaching Resources
L2 Reading Readiness Guide, p. 112
L2 Identify Supporting Details, p. 116

Differentiated Instruction

Spanish Reading and Vocabulary Study Guide
L1 Chapter 5, Section 4, pp. 51–52 ELL

Instruct

The Silk Road
Ask about how the Silk Road influenced the people of China.

Tradition and Learning
Ask a question about Confucius.

Target Reading Skill
Review **identifying supporting details.**

Han Technology
Ask about the invention of paper.

Instructional Resources

All in One Unit 2 History of Our World Teaching Resources
L2 Guided Reading and Review, p. 113
L2 Reading Readiness Guide, p. 112
History of Our World Transparencies
L2 Section Reading Support Transparency HOW 73

Differentiated Instruction

Teacher's Edition
L1 For Less Proficient Readers, TE p. 158
L1 For Special Needs Students, TE p. 158
Student Edition on Audio CD
L1 Chapter 5, Section 4 ELL, LPR, SN
Spanish Support
L2 Guided Reading and Review (Spanish), p. 52 ELL

Assess and Reteach

Assess Progress
Evaluate student comprehension with the section assessment and section quiz.

Reteach
Assign the Reading and Vocabulary Study Guide to help struggling students.

Extend
Extend the lesson by assigning a Small Group Activity.

Instructional Resources

All in One Unit 2 History of Our World Teaching Resources
L2 Section Quiz, p. 114
L3 Small Group Activity: Making a Map of the Silk Road, pp. 121–124
Rubric for Assessing a Student Poem, p. 130
Rubric for Assessing a Writing Assignment, p. 128
L2 Vocabulary Development, p. 127
L2 Word Knowledge, p. 118
L2 Chapter Tests A and B, pp. 131–136
Reading and Vocabulary Study Guide
L1 Chapter 5, Section 4, pp. 70–72

Differentiated Instruction

Spanish Support
L2 Section Quiz (Spanish), p. 53 ELL
L2 Chapter Summary (Spanish), p. 54 ELL
L2 Vocabulary Development (Spanish), p. 55 ELL

Key
L1 Basic to Average L3 Average to Advanced
L2 For All Students

LPR Less Proficient Readers
AR Advanced Readers
SN Special Needs Students

GT Gifted and Talented
ELL English Language Learners

Reading Background

Summarizing

The ability to summarize effectively can help improve students' abilities to comprehend and recall text. Good summarizers make notes on the text and reread as they write. Poor summarizers read the text once and begin writing. Share this information with your students, and then use the following steps to model how to create a useful summary.

1. Review structural aids, such as headings, Key Terms, Reading Checks, and visual information in the text.
2. Predict what you think you will learn from the selection.
3. Read the selection and sort through the main ideas and details. Reread and take notes on key words from topic sentences that express the main idea of each paragraph.
4. Organize the ideas in your notes. Cluster ideas that go together.
5. Write your summary. As you write, be sure to cross out any information that does not seem important.

Have students write a summary of Section 1 of this chapter, using the steps outlined above.

Question-Answer Relationships

Students who can ask the right questions will be better able to answer questions when asked. To help students improve their skills at asking the right questions, use activities that help them understand question-answer relationships.

Explain to students that there are many different types of questions. Understanding the types will help them write better answers. Ask students to write one example of each of the following types of questions, based on what they read in Section 2 of this chapter.

Questions with:

1. Answers that are found in one or two sentences in the book.
2. Answers that are found by looking at several different paragraphs in the book.
3. Answers that are not found directly in the book, but instead require you to think about what you've read in order to come up with an answer.
4. Answers that are not found directly in the book and which you can answer without having read the book.

Ask students to share their questions and ask the class to determine which type of question it is and to give an answer.

World Studies Background

Shang Culture

Although no significant pieces of literature have been found from the Shang Dynasty, historians have been able to tell a great deal about that society from artifacts. The dynasty had an extensive political system. The king appointed local governors to carry out his will. The Shang people also had a rich artistic culture. In addition to working with bronze, they made pottery out of clay and carved many items out of jade.

Confucianism: Religion or Philosophy?

People often dispute whether Confucianism is a religion or a philosophy. Traditionally, Confucianism is a philosophy meant to encompass all aspects of life. Whether that includes belief in a god is up to the individual. Today people follow Confucianism as both a religion and a philosophy.

Infoplease® provides a wealth of useful information for the classroom. You can use this resource to strengthen your background on the subjects covered in this chapter. Have students visit this advertising-free site as a starting point for projects requiring research.

Use Web code **lbd-2500** for **Infoplease®**.

Discussion Ideas

Students will be more willing and interested in engaging in discussion if they are discussing a topic of high interest that is well-suited to the discussion format.

As students read the chapter, ask them to write down one idea that could be used to conduct an interesting discussion. Ideas could relate to something they do not understand, something that seems interesting, or something that relates to something else they know, but should provoke interest and more ideas. Model the process by giving students both rich and poor ideas for a discussion.

Rich idea: What was the greatest achievement of ancient China?

Poor idea: What was the Silk Road used for?

Also ask students to suggest a discussion format for their ideas. If their discussion idea suits a quick whip around the class, they should suggest an Idea Wave (TE, p. T35) type of format. If the discussion idea prompts a longer, more thoughtful discussion, they may suggest a Give One, Get One (TE, p. T37) or Think-Write-Pair-Share (TE, p. T36) type of discussion. Have students take turns discussing their ideas.

Author's Craft

The ability to understand an author's approach to writing material can help students better understand the material when reading it.

Ask students to work in pairs to examine the text of the first paragraph on page 157, under the heading The Silk Road, and determine what organizational plan the author used to present the information. For example, is the organization of the text chronological, cause-and-effect, compare and contrast? *(cause-and-effect)* Ask students to write down what clues or signal words they used to determine the organization plan. *(in turn, gave rise to)*

Liu Bang as a Man of the People

Born a peasant, Chinese emperor Liu Bang had a special concern for the problems faced by peasants. As the first emperor of the Han Dynasty, Liu Bang put forth policies to help peasant farmers and to cut their taxes. He also had a reputation for treating people with compassion. However, he was very harsh with anyone who threatened his power. His use of brutal force helped him maintain his hold on the throne and set a pattern of leadership for the Han Dynasty.

The End of the Silk Road

The Silk Road was a major trade route in China for many centuries, but by about the early 900s A.D., changes in global power led to its decline. The route had a short-lived rebirth during the Mongol Empire in the 1200s and 1300s. European Marco Polo traveled the Silk Road when he visited China in the late 1200s. Today parts of the route still exist. The United Nations has discussed a plan to build a trans-Asian highway modeled after the Silk Road.

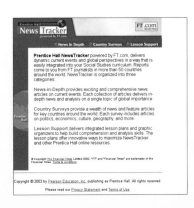

Get in-depth information on topics of global importance with **Prentice Hall Newstracker,** powered by FT.com.

Use web code **lbd-2506** for **Prentice Hall Newstracker.**

Guiding Questions

Remind students about the Guiding Questions introduced at the beginning of the book.

Section 1 relates to **Guiding Question** ①
How did physical geography affect the growth of ancient civilizations? *(Mountains and seas separated ancient China from other regions, and rivers such as the Huang deposited fertile soil suitable for growing crops.)*

Section 2 relates to **Guiding Question** ④
How did ancient peoples develop governments? *(A merit system based on the teachings of Confucius was instituted in which candidates for government jobs had to pass official examinations.)*

Section 3 relates to **Guiding Question** ②
What historical accomplishments is each civilization known for? *(Emperor Shi Huangdi united ancient China's warring kingdoms and implemented common weights and measurements, a common currency, an improved writing system, and a law code.)*

Section 4 relates to **Guiding Question** ②
What historical accomplishments is each civilization known for? *(During the Han dynasty, advancements were made in the arts, medicine, and technology.)*

⊙ Target Reading Skill

In this chapter, students will learn and apply the reading skill of identifying main ideas. Use the following worksheets to help students practice this skill:

All in One Unit 2 History of Our World Teaching Resources, *Identify Main Ideas* p. 115; *Identify Supporting Details,* p. 116; *Identify Implied Main Ideas,* p. 117

Differentiated Instruction

The following Teacher's Edition strategies are suitable for students of varying abilities.

Advanced Readers, p. 151
English Language Learners, p. 146
Gifted and Talented, pp. 143, 151, 154
Less Proficient Readers, pp. 146, 158
Special Needs Students, p. 158

Chapter Preview

This chapter will introduce you to the history of ancient China.

Section 1
The Geography of China's River Valleys

Section 2
Confucius and His Teachings

Section 3
Warring Kingdoms Unite

Section 4
Achievements of Ancient China

⊙ **Target Reading Skill**

Main Idea In this chapter you will focus on skills you can use to identify the main ideas as you read.

▶ The Great Wall of China

Bibliography

For the Teacher

Gascoigne, Bamber. *The Dynasties of China: A History.* Carroll & Graf, 2003.
D. C. Lau (Translator). *Confucius: The Analects.* Penguin USA, 1998.
Wood, Frances. *The Silk Road: Two Thousand Years in the Heart of Asia.* University of California Press, 2003.

For the Student

L1 Cotterell, Arthur. *Eyewitness: Ancient China (Eyewitness Books).* DK Publishing, 2000.
L2 Williams, Suzanne. *Made in China: Ideas and Inventions from Ancient China (Dragon Books).* Pacific View Press, 1997.
L3 Freedman, Russell. *Confucius: The Golden Rule.* Arthur A. Levine, 2002.

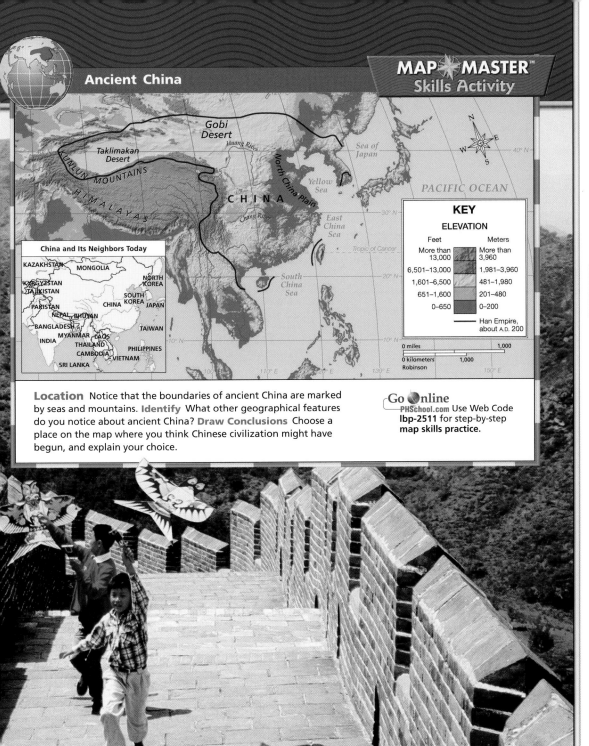

Ancient China

Gobi Desert

Taklimakan Desert

KUNLUN MOUNTAINS

HIMALAYAS

Huang River

North China Plain

C H I N A

Chang River

Sea of Japan

Yellow Sea

East China Sea

South China Sea

PACIFIC OCEAN

N
W E
S

40° N

30° N

Tropic of Cancer

20° N

10° N

China and Its Neighbors Today

KAZAKHSTAN
MONGOLIA
KYRGYZSTAN
TAJIKISTAN
NORTH KOREA
SOUTH KOREA
JAPAN
PAKISTAN
CHINA
NEPAL BHUTAN
BANGLADESH
INDIA
MYANMAR LAOS
THAILAND
CAMBODIA VIETNAM
TAIWAN
PHILIPPINES
SRI LANKA

90° E   110° E   130° E

KEY
ELEVATION

Feet	Meters
More than 13,000	More than 3,960
6,501–13,000	1,981–3,960
1,601–6,500	481–1,980
651–1,600	201–480
0–650	0–200

—— Han Empire, about A.D. 200

0 miles   1,000
0 kilometers   1,000
Robinson

Location Notice that the boundaries of ancient China are marked by seas and mountains. **Identify** What other geographical features do you notice about ancient China? **Draw Conclusions** Choose a place on the map where you think Chinese civilization might have begun, and explain your choice.

Go Online
PHSchool.com Use Web Code **lbp-2511** for step-by-step map skills practice.

Chapter 5 **135**

Ask students to look at the map on this page. Help students to understand that many early civilizations began near rivers, where there was often fertile soil and plenty of water to raise crops. Ask students where they think civilization may have begun in ancient China and why. (*Students may answer that civilization in ancient China probably began in the North China Plain near the Huang and Chang rivers where there is probably fertile soil for crops.*)

Go Online
PHSchool.com Students may practice their map skills using the interactive online version of this map.

Using the Visual   L2

Reach Into Your Background Draw students' attention to the caption accompanying the picture on pp. 134–135. Tell students that the Great Wall of China is over 4,000 miles long and thousands of years old. Ask students to think about fences or walls that they see in everyday life and what they are used for. Then have them study the photo of the Great Wall of China and brainstorm what it may have been used for. (*possible answers: protection from invaders, to show boundary*)

Answers

MAP MASTER™ Skills Activity **Identify** Other features in ancient China include the Gobi and Taklimakan deserts, the North China Plain, and the Huang and Chang rivers. **Draw Conclusions** Students may choose a place next to a river because rivers provide water for crops to feed many people.

Chapter Resources

Teaching Resources
L2 Vocabulary Development, p. 127
L2 Skills for Life, p. 120
L2 Chapter Tests A and B, pp. 131–136

Spanish Support
L2 Spanish Chapter Summary, p. 54
L2 Spanish Vocabulary Development, p. 55

Media and Technology
L1 Student Edition on Audio CD
L1 Guided Reading Audio CDs, English and Spanish
L2 Social Studies Skills Tutor CD-ROM
ExamView® Test Bank CD-ROM

DISCOVERY CHANNEL SCHOOL History of Our World Video Program

interactive Textbook

PRENTICE HALL
TeacherEXPRESS™
Plan · Teach · Assess

Section 1
Step-by-Step Instruction

Objectives
Social Studies
1. Examine the geography of ancient China.
2. Find out about early civilization in China.
3. Learn about the importance of family ties in early Chinese society.

Reading/Language Arts
Learn how to find the main idea of a paragraph or section of text.

Prepare to Read

Build Background Knowledge **L2**
Tell students that in this chapter their study of the Ancient World will move east from India to China. Ask students to preview the section with this question in mind: **How was ancient China different from ancient India?** Conduct an Idea Wave (TE, p. T39) to generate a class list on the board.

Set a Purpose for Reading **L2**
- Preview the Objectives.

- Read each statement in the *Reading Readiness Guide* aloud. Ask students to mark the statements true or false.

  All in One **Unit 2 History of Our World Teaching Resources,** *Reading Readiness Guide,* p. 100

- Have students discuss their statements in pairs or groups of four, and then mark their worksheets again. Use the Numbered Heads participation strategy (TE, p. T40) to call on students to share their group's perspectives.

Vocabulary Builder
Preview Key Terms **L2**
Pronounce each Key Term, and then ask students to say the word with you. Provide a simple explanation such as, "Loess is very good soil for growing plants."

Section 1

The Geography of China's River Valleys

Prepare to Read

Objectives
In this section you will
1. Examine the geography of ancient China.
2. Find out about early civilization in China.
3. Learn about the importance of family ties in early Chinese society.

Taking Notes
As you read, look for details about China's river valleys. Copy the chart below, and use it to record your findings.

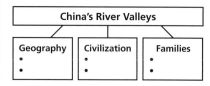

China's River Valleys
- Geography
- Civilization
- Families

Target Reading Skill

Identify Main Ideas
The main idea is the most important point in a section of text. On page 137, the main idea for the section titled The Geography of Ancient China is stated in this sentence: "The climate, soil, landforms, and waterways varied greatly, depending on the region."

As you read, look for the main idea stated after each red heading.

Key Terms
- **loess** (LOH es) *n.* yellow-brown soil
- **dike** (dyk) *n.* a protective wall that controls or holds back water
- **extended family** (ek STEN did FAM uh lee) *n.* closely related people of several generations

---

A sculpture of a Chinese dragon

136 History of Our World

What words would you use to describe dragons? You might think of these imaginary beasts as being fierce and scary. People of some cultures would agree with you. But to the ancient Chinese people, the dragon was a respected spirit, not a terrible monster. In ancient China, dragons were friendly beasts that brought good luck. Dragon gods were believed to be responsible for the rains that made the fields fertile. In China, dragon rain ceremonies date as far back as the 500s B.C.

The Chinese also used the image of this respected spirit to show the importance of their rivers. They traditionally described their rivers as dragons. The dragon's limbs were the smaller streams. They flowed into the dragon's body, or main river. The dragon's mouth was the delta, where the river flowed into the sea. Rivers were important to the development of civilization in China. Other landforms and climate played an important role as well.

Target Reading Skill **L2**
Identify Main Ideas Draw attention to the Target Reading Skill. Remind students that the main idea is the most important point in a section or paragraph. The other information in the section or paragraph gives them more information about the main idea.

Model identifying the main idea using the first paragraph under the heading Importance of the Family on p. 140. The main idea is the first sentence: "The family was the

center of early Chinese society." The rest of the paragraph gives examples of this: the family was more important than the individual or the nation, a person's first responsibility was to the family, and the family was the chief source of well-being.

Give students *Identify Main Ideas.* Have them complete the activity in groups.

All in One **Unit 2 History of Our World Teaching Resources,** *Identify Main Ideas,* p. 297

The Geography of Ancient China

Ancient China covered a large area. The climate, soil, landforms, and waterways varied greatly, depending on the region. Turn to the map on page 135 to study the geography of ancient China.

Contrasting Climate and Landforms   The North China Plain is located in East Asia. It is built up of soil deposits from the Huang (hwahng) River.

The North China Plain and its surrounding highlands, as well as far northern China, have only a brief, but intense, summer rainy season caused by monsoon winds. However, the region doesn't get much rain the rest of the year. As a result, the climate is very dry.

The climate in the south, in contrast, is warm and wet. Monsoons from the South China Sea bring heavy rains to southern China from March to September. Light rain falls the rest of the year.

A painting of a river voyage in China

Effects on Civilization   Geographic barriers such as mountains and seas separated China from other lands. As a result, the Chinese had little knowledge of the civilizations of Egypt, India, Greece, and Rome. They were so sure that they lived at the center of the world that they called themselves the Middle Kingdom.

China's rivers overflowed their banks each spring, bringing fresh, fertile topsoil to the land. For that reason, China's first farming villages developed along its rivers. Civilization began along the Huang River and later spread south to wetter land along the Chang, China's longest river.

Terrace Farming
A man grows a crop of millet in northern China. **Apply Information** *Why does it make sense to grow crops on terraces in this part of China?*

Vocabulary Builder

Use the information below to teach students this section's high-use words.

High-Use Word	Definition and Sample Sentence
intense, p. 137	*adj.* very strong or deep The **intense** heat of the sun made us very thirsty.
accomplishment, p. 139	*n.* an art or skill that has been learned Playing the guitar was just one of her **accomplishments.**
communication, p. 139	*n.* the spreading of information E-mail can be a good form of **communication.**

The Geography of Ancient China   L2

Guided Instruction

■ **Vocabulary Builder** Clarify the high-use word **intense** before reading.

■ Read The Geography of Ancient China, using the Choral Reading strategy (TE, p. T38). Circulate and make sure individuals can answer the Reading Check question.

■ Ask students **Why did China's geography cause the ancient Chinese to have little knowledge of other civilizations, such as those of Egypt, Greece, India, and Rome?** *(Geographic barriers, such as mountains and seas, separated China from other lands.)*

■ Ask students **Why do you think the Chinese continued to live along the Huang River, despite its dangers?** *(The Huang deposits loess on the surrounding land, making it excellent for growing crops and attracting people to the fertile farmland.)*

Answer

Apply Information Using terraces probably provides more land on which farmers can grow crops.

Independent Practice

Ask students to create the Taking Notes graphic organizer on a blank piece of paper. Then have them fill in the "Geography" portion with the information they have just learned. Briefly model how to identify which details to record.

Monitor Progress

As students fill in the graphic organizer, circulate and make sure individuals are choosing the correct details. Provide assistance as needed.

A woman collects water from the Huang River. ▶

Yellow River The Huang is the second-longest river in China. It is also the muddiest river in the world. In fact, it is called the Yellow River because of the **loess** (LOH es), or yellow-brown soil, that its waters carry along. When the Huang floods, it deposits loess on the surrounding plain. Over many years, the Huang has carpeted the North China Plain with a thick layer of fertile soil. There, the Chinese grow a grain called millet. Millet has been an important part of the Chinese diet for thousands of years.

Huang River The Chinese people also called the Huang China's Sorrow. It brought life to the land, but it also took life away. Destructive floods could come without warning, sometimes as often as every two years. Some floods drowned thousands of people. At times, the floodwaters ran with such force that they cut an entirely new path over the land. As a result, the course of the river could change by hundreds of miles.

Flood Control To help control the flooding, early Chinese people built dikes along the banks of the Huang. A **dike** is a protective wall that holds back the waters. As more loess settled to the bottom of the river, the level of the river rose. Eventually, the river rose high enough to overflow the dikes, causing even more deadly floods. Despite such dangers, the early Chinese people continued to settle along the banks of the Huang.

The Yellow River
You can see from this photograph why the Huang River is often called the Yellow River. **Analyze Images** *How is the land near the river used?*

✓ Reading Check **What did the Chinese do to control flooding?**

Skills Mini Lesson

Transferring Information from One Medium to Another L2

1. Teach the skill by outlining the steps to transfer written information to a visual format: state the main idea, identify the key information, choose an appropriate visual aid for the information, and put the information in the visual aid.

2. Have students practice the skill by going through the steps with the information about climate in Contrasting Climate and Landforms on p. 137 to create a table.

3. Have students apply the skill by creating a flow chart showing how the Huang River burst through dikes as described in the paragraph labeled Flood Control on p. 138.

Answers

Analyze Images to grow millet

✓ Reading Check They built dikes, or protective walls, along the Huang's banks.

Early Civilization in China

Early farmers of the North China Plain probably were once nomads who moved from place to place to hunt and gather food. Historians do not know exactly when the first farming settlements developed in the Huang Valley. Some think it was as early as 5000 B.C. These early farming societies grew into civilizations that controlled parts of the Huang Valley.

The Shang Dynasty The Shang dynasty was the first civilization in China. It probably arose sometime around 1760 B.C. The Shang people built China's first cities. Among their many accomplishments was the production of some of the finest bronze work of ancient China.

The Shang people also produced the first Chinese writing system. Like Mesopotamia's cuneiform and our own alphabet, the Chinese writing system could be used for different languages. This was helpful for communication, because China had many regional languages.

About 600 years after the founding of the Shang dynasty, a new group emerged. This group, known as the Zhou (joh) people, lived in the Wei Valley to the west of the Shang people.

The Zhou Dynasty The territory of the Zhou people partly bordered the Shang territory. Sometimes these two neighbors lived peacefully side by side. At other times, they fought over territory. Finally, the Zhou conquered the Shang in about 1122 B.C. The Zhou dynasty ruled over ancient China for almost 1,000 years. This long period is divided into two parts—the earlier Western Zhou dynasty and the later Eastern Zhou dynasty. It was near the end of the Eastern Zhou dynasty that a period known as the Warring States began. During that time, small kingdoms fought for control over one another until a new dynasty—the Qin (chin)— finally emerged.

Mandate of Heaven Sometimes Chinese rulers inherited the throne. At other times, they fought for the right to rule. In either instance, the Chinese believed that rulers came to power because it was their destiny, or fate. This idea was called the Mandate of Heaven. A mandate is a law, or an order. The Mandate of Heaven supported a leader's right to rule his people. It also gave a father authority over his family.

✓ Reading Check   What was the Mandate of Heaven?

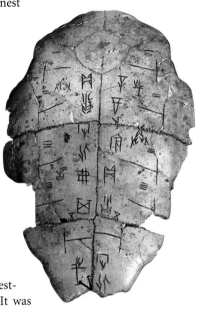

Identify Main Ideas
Which sentence states the main idea under the heading Early Civilization in China?

A Shang dynasty turtle shell shows one of the earliest examples of Chinese writing.

Target Reading Skill   L2

Identify Main Ideas As a follow up, ask students to answer the Target Reading Skill question on this page of the Student Edition. *(These early farming societies grew into civilizations that controlled parts of the Huang Valley.)*

Early Civilization in China   L2

Guided Instruction

- **Vocabulary Builder** Clarify the high-use words **accomplishment** and **communication** before reading.

- Ask students to read Early Civilization in China.

- Discuss with students the order of events leading up to and including China's first known civilization. *(First, people were probably nomads, then farming began around 5000 B.C.; finally the Shang Dynasty arose after 1700 B.C.)*

- Ask students **What were some of the accomplishments of the Shang Dynasty?** *(China's first cities, fine bronze work, the first Chinese writing system)*

Independent Practice

Ask students to fill in the "Early Civilization" portion of the Taking Notes graphic organizer with the information they have just learned.

Monitor Progress

As students fill in the graphic organizer, circulate and make sure individuals are choosing the correct details. Provide assistance as needed.

Background: Global Perspectives

Raging Rivers The people of China's Middle Kingdom were not alone in being at the mercy of a mighty river. People in Sumer in Mesopotamia also experienced the recurring destructiveness of floods. The Sumerians created a complex system of irrigation canals to control their floodwaters. Even so, stories of floods are found throughout Sumerian literature. Many believe that the biblical account of the great flood in the Book of Genesis is based in part on the Sumerians' experiences.

Answers

✓ Reading Check   The Mandate of Heaven was the idea that people came to power because it was their destiny.

Importance of the Family

L2

Guided Instruction

- Read Importance of the Family with students.

- Ask students to compare and contrast the living arrangements of rich and poor extended families in ancient China. (*In rich families, members might live in one large home, while in poor families, members might live in separate cottages within easy walking distance from one another.*)

- Ask students **In what ways did a traditional Chinese household illustrate the importance of family in Chinese culture?** (*Extended family lived together or close by; important decisions were made by the oldest male family member; family names came first.*)

Independent Practice

Have students complete the Taking Notes graphic organizer by filling in the "Families" portion with the information they have just learned.

Monitor Progress

- Show *Section Reading Support Transparency HOW 44* and ask students to check their graphic organizers individually. Go over key concepts and clarify key vocabulary as needed.

  History of Our World Transparencies, *Section Reading Support Transparency HOW 70*

- Tell students to fill in the last column of the *Reading Readiness Guide*. Probe for what they learned that confirms or invalidates each statement.

  All in One Unit 2 History of Our World Teaching Resources, *Reading Readiness Guide,* p. 100

Answer

Analyze Images The man in the light-colored robe seated in the center of the portrait is probably the family's center of authority. The people seated above him could be other older male family members, while the women's position seated below him shows their lower status.

A Chinese Family
Wealthy Chinese families could afford to have their portraits painted, like this one dating from the late 1700s. **Analyze Images** *How do we know that the family members in this portrait are probably part of an extended family?*

Bronze statue of a Chinese girl with a lamp, around 100 B.C. ▶

Importance of the Family

The family was the center of early Chinese society. It was considered to be of far more importance than the individual or the nation. A person's first responsibility was always to the family. The family, in turn, was each person's chief source of well-being.

Traditional Families A household in ancient China might contain as many as five generations living together. This meant that small children lived with their great-great-grandparents as well as their parents, uncles and aunts, cousins, brothers and sisters, and so on. These closely related people are called an **extended family.** In rich families, the members might live together in one big home. But most of China's people were poor. In farming villages, members of the extended family might live in separate one-room cottages. The cottages were within easy walking distance from one another.

Family Authority The status of each person in a Chinese extended family depended on his or her age and sex. The center of authority was usually the oldest man. He had the most privileges and the most power in the family. He decided who his children and grandchildren would marry. When children were disrespectful, he punished them severely. After the oldest male died, by tradition all his lands were divided among his sons. Each son then started his own household.

Women's Roles Women were considered to be of lower status than men. According to tradition, women were bound by what were called the three obediences: to obey their fathers in youth, their husbands after their marriage, and their sons in widowhood. Four virtues also guided women's behavior in ancient China: morality, modesty, proper speech, and domestic skills. When a woman married, she left her household and became part of her husband's family. In her new household, she was expected to obey her husband and respect the wishes of her mother-in-law.

Background: Links Across Time

The Family Extended Through the history of China, the family has continued to be a key feature of society. The Chinese emperors were known by the title "Son of Heaven," and each was expected to act as a father to his people. Magistrates, or local government leaders, have been called the "father-mother" officials right up to the present day. Even though Chinese government today has changed from being run by an emperor to being run by the Communist Party, the Chinese word for "state" still translates as "nation-family."

Family Names In the 300s B.C., Chinese established the practice of using inherited family names along with a personal name. The inherited name was passed down from father to child. The other was for the individual. Examples of present-day family names include Mao, Chan, and Lu. Of course, people in the United States also use two names. In Chinese society, however, the family name comes first. If this system were used in American society, you would know the first President of the United States as Washington George, not George Washington. Think of other famous people in American history. What would their names be in the Chinese naming style?

The tradition of using family names first dates back to China's earliest times. It showed how important the family was in China. Centuries later, a great philosopher, or thinker, named Confucius (kun FYOO shus) had ideas about the role of the family in Chinese society. These ideas would have a great effect on the Chinese people.

Royal Seals
Emperors used seals, like the decorated cube above, to mark their names in ink. The characters shown at the top left representing the emperor's name are carved into the bottom face of the cube. **Infer** *Why do you think the ancient Chinese began using family names in addition to personal names?*

√ **Reading Check** What factors determined a person's status within early Chinese families?

Section 1 Assessment

Key Terms
Review the key terms at the beginning of this section. Use each term in a sentence that explains its meaning.

Target Reading Skill
State the main ideas of each of the red headings in Section 1.

Comprehension and Critical Thinking
1. (a) Identify Effects How did the Huang River affect ancient Chinese civilization?
(b) Compare What do you think ancient China had in common with the ancient civilizations of Mesopotamia, Egypt, and India?

2. (a) Recall What was the first known civilization in China?
(b) Draw Conclusions Describe the importance of China's first civilization. What effect do you think it had on later civilizations in ancient China?

3. (a) Recall Describe the importance of family in early China.
(b) Apply Information In ancient China, members of an extended family often lived together in one home. How do you think the ancient Chinese benefited from their family structure?

Writing Activity
Suppose you were a member of an ancient Chinese family. Write a description of what your life would have been like.

Writing Tip Specific details will bring your description to life. First focus on one important aspect of life in ancient China that you want to describe. Then choose two or three interesting details to make your description more colorful.

Chapter 5 Section 1 **141**

Writing Activity
Use the *Rubric for Assessing a Writing Assignment* to evaluate students' descriptions.

All in One **Unit 2 History of Our World Teaching Resources,** *Rubric for Assessing a Writing Assignment,* p. 128

Assess Progress L2
Have students complete the Section Assessment. Administer the *Section Quiz.*

All in One **Unit 2 History of Our World Teaching Resources,** *Section Quiz,* p. 102

Reteach L1
If students need more instruction, have them read this section in the Reading and Vocabulary Study Guide.

Chapter 5, Section 1, **History of Our World Reading and Vocabulary Study Guide,** pp. 61–63

Extend L3
Ask students to create a poster on one aspect of the Shang dynasty such as kings, music, housing, or art. Encourage students to use Internet sources to find images for their posters. Display students' posters.

Answers
Infer to show how important the family is in Chinese society

√ **Reading Check** age and sex

Section 1 Assessment

Key Terms
Students' sentences should reflect knowledge of each Key Term.

Target Reading Skill
China's geography varied greatly, affecting life in the region. Early farming societies in the North China Plain grew into civilizations. Early Chinese society formed around the extended family.

Comprehension and Critical Thinking
1. (a) China's civilization began along the Huang. Its floods created excellent farmland, but also killed thousands of people and cut new paths over the land. **(b)** They all developed near rivers.

2. (a) the Shang dynasty **(b)** Its people built China's first cities, created fine bronze work, and created the first Chinese writing. Its system of writing enabled its people to pass down information to future generations.

3. (a) The family was the center of early Chinese society. **(b)** Possible answer: An older person might have been more knowledgeable and experienced.

Objectives

Learn how to make valid generalizations.

Prepare to Read

Build Background Knowledge **L2**

Give students a sample generalization based on something they may be familiar with, such as, "The school's lunches are nutritionally well-balanced." Using an Idea Wave (TE, p. T39), have students offer facts that support the generalization.

Instruct

Making Valid Generalizations **L2**

Guided Instruction

- Read the steps to making valid generalizations as a class and write them on the board.

- Practice the skill by following the steps on p. 142 and applying them to Practice the Skill on p. 143.

- Ask volunteers for facts given in the paragraph and write the list of facts on the board. If necessary, help students find similarities among the facts in step 2. *(Facts: Civilization began along the Huang River. It later spread to the wetter lands of the Chang River. Each spring, the rivers deposited fertile topsoil suitable for growing crops. China's first farming villages developed along its rivers.)*

- Divide students into small groups and ask each group to write a generalization for the practice paragraph. Offer help to groups whose generalizations do not seem valid. Ask each group to say their generalization aloud, and write each on the board, noting similarities and differences. *(Possible generalization: China's rivers were important to the growth of its ancient civilizations.)*

Skills for Life
Making Valid Generalizations

Sometimes people make broad generalizations that are not really true.

"People who like to read a lot are not interested in sports."

"Dog owners do not like cats."

A broad statement about a group of people is called a stereotype. A stereotype is not based on factual knowledge, and it is often untrue and unfair.

To avoid using stereotypes, be careful when you make a generalization. Some generalizations are valid—that is, they have value or worth. They are probably true, because they are based on specific facts. Other generalizations are not valid. They might be based on rumors or impressions instead of on facts. A stereotype is a generalization that may not be valid.

Learn the Skill

To make a valid generalization, follow these steps:

1 **Identify the specific facts that are contained within a source.** Become familiar with the facts in a piece of text, a table, or some other source.

2 **State what the facts have in common, and look for patterns.** Do any of the facts fit together in a way that makes a point about a broad subject? Do the data in a table or a graph point toward some kind of general statement?

3 **Make a generalization, or broad conclusion, about the facts.** Write your generalization as a sentence or paragraph.

4 **Test the generalization, and revise it if necessary.** You can test the validity of a generalization by using the guidelines in the box at left.

> **Testing a Generalization**
> - Are there enough facts in your source to support the generalization?
> - Do any other facts support the generalization?
> - Which are stronger, the examples of the generalization or the exceptions to it?
> - Does the statement generalize too broadly or stereotype a group of people? Look for words such as *all*, *always*, or *every*, which can make a generalization invalid.
> - Words such as *some*, *many*, *most*, and *often* help prevent a statement from being too general.

142 History of Our World

Independent Practice

Assign *Skills for Life* and have students complete it individually.

All in One **Unit 2 History of Our World Teaching Resources,** *Skills for Life,* p. 120

Monitor Progress

As students are completing *Skills for Life,* circulate and make sure individuals are applying the skill steps effectively. Provide assistance as needed.

Practice the Skill

Turn to page 137, and reread the second paragraph that follows the title Effects on Civilization.

1 The title of the text will help you understand the topic. Find and write down at least three facts that relate to that topic.

2 From reading these facts, what major ideas can you learn about the topic? Do the facts suggest any ideas about China's rivers that are not specifically stated in the text?

3 Make a generalization about China's rivers and how they affected the growth of Chinese civilization. Make sure the facts support your statement.

4 If your statement does not meet the test for a valid generalization, try making it valid by rewriting it so that it is more limited.

The Huang River, China

Apply the Skill

We generalize in everyday speech: "Everybody loves the summer." "Most kids I know are into sports." "Nobody rents videos anymore. They rent DVDs." Find and write down three valid generalizations, and explain why they are valid. You can use generalizations that you find in your textbook, or you can write your own based on facts you know. Write down the facts that support each generalization.

Assess and Reteach

Assess Progress L2
Ask students to do the Apply the Skill activity.

Reteach L1
If students are having trouble applying the skill steps, have them review the skill using the interactive Social Studies Skills Tutor CD-ROM.

⊙ *Making Valid Generalizations,* **Social Studies Skills Tutor CD-ROM**

Extend L3
To extend the lesson, divide students into pairs. Have the pairs choose one paragraph under the title Importance of the Family on pp. 140–141. One student will make a list of facts from the paragraph and the other will make a generalization based on the facts. Students can choose another paragraph from these two pages and switch roles.

Differentiated Instruction

For Gifted and Talented L3
To learn more about how water can affect how people live, have students work in groups to complete the activity *Local Water Use.* Have each group answer the Analyzing a Bar Graph questions and write a one-sentence generalization about water use based on the graph.

Go Online
PHSchool.com

For: Environmental and Global Issues, *Local Water Use*
Visit: PHSchool.com
Web Code: lbd-2501

Answers
Apply the Skill
Students' answers will vary but should include facts that support their generalizations.

Section 2
Step-by-Step Instruction

Objectives
1. Learn about the life of Confucius.
2. Find out about the teachings of Confucius.
3. Understand the influence Confucianism had on Chinese society.

Reading/Language Arts
Learn how to identify details that support a main idea.

Prepare to Read

Build Background Knowledge L2
In this section, students will learn about the wide impact of the teachings of one man, Confucius. Ask students to briefly preview the section and note one fact about Confucius. Use the Idea Wave participation strategy (TE, p. T39) to make a class list. Then, briefly discuss the facts the students have noted about Confucius, emphasizing that they will learn more about this remarkable person as they read.

Set a Purpose for Reading L2
■ Preview the Objectives.

■ Read each statement in the *Reading Readiness Guide* aloud. Ask students to mark the statements true or false.

All in One Unit 2 History of Our World Teaching Resources, *Reading Readiness Guide,* p. 104

■ Have students discuss the statements in pairs or groups of four, then mark their worksheets again. Use the Numbered Heads participation strategy (TE, p. T40) to call on students to share their group's perspectives.

Vocabulary Builder
Preview Key Terms L2
Pronounce each Key Term, and then ask the students to say the word with you. Provide a simple explanation such as, "Examples of people who work in the civil service are city clerks, police officers, and judges."

Section 2
Confucius and His Teachings

Prepare to Read

Objectives
In this section you will
1. Learn about the life of Confucius.
2. Find out about the teachings of Confucius.
3. Understand the influence Confucianism had on Chinese society.

Taking Notes
As you read, summarize the teachings of Confucius and the influence they had on China. Copy the chart below, and use it to record your findings.

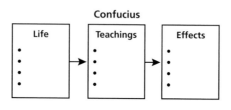

Confucius

Life → Teachings → Effects

Target Reading Skill

Identify Supporting Details The main idea of a section of text is supported by details. These details may explain the main idea or give examples. On page 147, the main idea for the text under the heading The Life of Confucius is stated in this sentence: "Confucius was the most famous—and important—of the early Chinese thinkers."

As you read, note the details following each of the blue headings that tell more about the life of Confucius.

Key Terms
• **Confucius** (kun FYOO shus) *n.* (551– 479 B.C.) a Chinese philosopher and teacher whose beliefs had a great influence on Chinese life
• **philosophy** (fih LAHS uh fee) *n.* a system of beliefs and values
• **civil service** (SIV ul SUR vis) *n.* the group of people whose job it is to carry out the work of the government

144 History of Our World

One day, the Chinese teacher and philosopher **Confucius** and his students were walking through the countryside. In the distance, they heard a woman crying. As they came around a bend in the road, they saw the woman kneeling at a grave. "Why are you crying?" they asked her. "Because," she answered, "a tiger killed my husband's father. Later, the tiger also killed my husband. Now, the tiger has killed my son as well."

They then asked the woman, "Why do you stay in this place after these terrible things have happened?" The woman answered, "Because there are no cruel rulers here." Confucius turned to his students and said, "Remember this. A cruel ruler is fiercer and more feared than a tiger."

After the death of Confucius, people told many stories about him. Like the story of the woman and the tiger, most stories contained an important lesson.

Confucius, c. 551– 479 B.C.

Target Reading Skill L2
Identify Supporting Details Point out the Target Reading Skill. Review with students what they learned about identifying the main idea in Section 1 of this chapter. Then explain that supporting details tell more about the main idea.

Model identifying a supporting detail by using the first paragraph on page 148. The main idea is that Confucius's teachings had a major effect on the Chinese government.

Point out that the following sentence supports this idea: "They became part of the basic training for members of the civil service." It tells readers more about how Confucius's teachings affected the government.

Give students *Identify Supporting Details*. Have them complete the activity in groups.

All in One Unit 2 History of Our World Teaching Resources, *Identify Supporting Details,* p. 116

The Life of Confucius

Confucius was the most famous—and important—of the early Chinese thinkers. The Chinese called him Kong Fu Zi (kong foo dzih), or "Master Kong." *Confucius* is the Latinized version of this name.

The Early Years Confucius was born in 551 B.C. to a noble but poor family of the North China Plain. He loved learning and was mostly self-taught. He hoped to advance to an important government office, but he never succeeded in that way. Instead, he decided to try teaching.

A Pioneer Teacher Many historians think that Confucius was China's first professional teacher. Confucius charged students a fee to take classes. He taught the students his views of life and government. He was a dedicated teacher:

> **❝**From the very poorest upward . . . none has ever come to me without receiving instruction. I instruct only a student who bursts with eagerness.**❞**
> —*Confucius*

Later in his life, Confucius searched for a ruler who would follow his teachings, but he could find no such ruler. He died in 479 B.C. at age 73. By the time of his death, he believed his life had been a failure. He had no way of knowing that his teachings would be followed for many centuries.

✔ **Reading Check** What kind of students did Confucius like to teach?

A Royal Welcome
A drawing shows Confucius meeting with leaders from various Chinese kingdoms. **Infer** *In what ways does the artist suggest the importance of Confucius?*

 **Identify Supporting Details** What detail in the paragraph at the left supports the idea that Confucius was an important Chinese thinker?

Vocabulary Builder

Use the information below to teach students this section's high-use words.

High-Use Word	Definition and Sample Sentence
professional, p. 145	*adj.* highly skilled and paid to provide a service The sink needs to be fixed by a **professional** plumber, not my father.
harmony, p. 147	*n.* agreement or cooperation My sister and I decided to live in **harmony** instead of fighting all the time.
generally, p. 148	*adv.* usually or normally I **generally** dislike washing the dishes, but today I didn't mind.

Instruct

The Life of Confucius ⌷L2

Guided Instruction

- **Vocabulary Builder** Clarify the high-use words **professional** and **harmony** before reading.

- Read The Life of Confucius, using the Structured Silent Reading strategy (TE, p. T38).

- Ask students **How did Confucius receive his education?** *(He was mostly self-taught.)*

- Ask students **Why do you think that Confucius thought that his life was a failure?** *(He never became an important government official, nor found a ruler willing to accept his teachings.)*

- Ask students **Do you think Confucius's life was a failure? Explain why or why not.** *(Yes—he did not accomplish what he set out to do. No—he became the first professional teacher in China, some of his students became important government officials, and he helped students from poor families.)*

Independent Practice

Ask students to create the Taking Notes graphic organizer on a blank piece of paper. Then have them fill in the "Life" portion with the information they have just learned. Briefly model how to identify which details to record.

Monitor Progress

As students fill in the graphic organizer, circulate and make sure individuals are choosing the correct details. Provide assistance as needed.

⟳ Target Reading Skill ⌷L2

Identify Supporting Details As a follow up, ask students to answer the Target Reading Skill question on this page of the Student Edition. *(His teachings would be studied in China for centuries.)*

Answers

Infer The group is gathered around him, and he is being fanned.

✔ **Reading Check** Confucius liked to teach students who were eager to learn.

The Teachings of Confucius L2

Guided Instruction

- Ask students to read The Teachings of Confucius. As students read, circulate and make sure individuals can answer the Reading Check question.

- Ask students **What is Confucianism?** (*A philosophy made up of the sayings of Confucius as recorded by his students. It is also a religion for some people.*)

- Ask students **Who did Confucius believe was responsible for setting a good example?** (*individuals in authority*) **What did he think would result from their good example?** (*the people would also behave well, order and peace would return, and society would prosper*)

Independent Practice

Ask students to fill in the "Teachings" portion of the Taking Notes graphic organizer with the information they have just learned.

Monitor Progress

As students fill in the graphic organizer, circulate and make sure individuals are choosing the correct details. Provide assistance as needed.

Answer

Conclude Confucius believed that people would follow a ruler's good example.

Relationships Based on the Teachings of Confucius

▼ Ruler and ruled

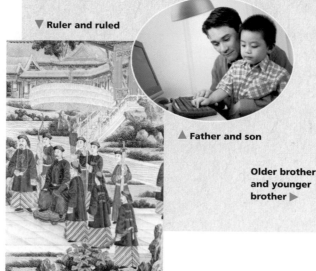

▲ Father and son

Husband and wife ▶

Older brother and younger brother ▶

Five Human Relationships
Confucius believed that Chinese society was built upon the five relationships shown above. **Conclude** *According to Confucius, how does a fair and just ruler benefit society?*

Confucius' ideas were studied in books like this one.

The Teachings of Confucius

Confucius did not claim to be an original thinker. He felt that his role was to pass on the forgotten teachings of wise people from an earlier age. In many of his teachings he tried to persuade rulers to reform. He also hoped to bring peace, stability, and prosperity to China's kingdoms.

Confucianism Confucius himself never wrote down his teachings. Instead, his students gathered a collection of his sayings after his death. Together, these writings made up a system of beliefs and values, or a **philosophy**. That philosophy became known as Confucianism. Confucianism was one of several important philosophies of ancient China. Over time, it began to govern many aspects of life there.

Bringing Order to Society Confucius lived during a time of frequent warfare in China. Powerful rulers of several Chinese states, or kingdoms, fought one another for the control of land. They seemed more interested in gaining power than in ruling wisely. Confucius hoped to persuade these rulers to change their ways and bring peace and order to China.

The goal of Confucius was to bring order to society. He believed that if people could be taught to behave properly toward one another, order and peace would result. Society would prosper.

Differentiated Instruction

For Less Proficient Readers L1

Have students read this section in the History of Our World Reading and Vocabulary Study Guide. This version provides basic-level instruction in an interactive format with questions and write-on lines.

📖 Chapter 5, Section 2, **History of Our World Reading and Vocabulary Study Guide,** pp. 64–66

For English Language Learners L1

Students may have difficulty pronouncing some of the words in this section, such as *persuading, prosperity, functioned, religious,* and *relationships*. Pair students with English speakers. Ask pairs to use a dictionary to find the pronunciations of unfamiliar words.

Respecting Others Confucius said that people should know their place in the family and in society. They ought to respect the people above and below them and treat others justly. He described five human relationships: ruler and ruled; father and son; husband and wife; older brother and younger brother; and friend and friend. Then he explained how people should behave in each of these relationships. Confucius said that people in authority—princes or parents—must set good examples. For example, if a ruler was fair, his people would follow his example and treat one another fairly, too. Confucius summarized his ideas about relationships in a simple way. It is similar to what Christians and Jews call the Golden Rule: "Do not do to others what you would not want done to yourself."

Religious Traditions Although Confucianism is a philosophy, it has also functioned as a religion for many people. Like Hindus or Buddhists, those who practice Confucianism are part of a moral community. The teachings of Confucius helped guide many of the ancient Chinese in how to behave. But many ancient Chinese also practiced Confucianism alongside their existing religious traditions.

Ancient China was home to many kinds of religious beliefs and practices: the worship of ancestors, the honoring of gods, and the belief in spirits. Most Chinese believed that life should be lived in harmony with nature. Happiness came from living a balanced life. A religious philosophy known as Taoism (DOW iz um) supported these ideas. Taoism was based on the writings of Laozi (LOW dzuh), a Chinese thinker who lived in the 500s B.C. The Taoists loved nature, and they believed in leading simple and selfless lives.

At times, Taoism would rival Confucianism for popularity in China. But overall, the teachings of Confucius would remain the most widely studied of Chinese philosophies.

A painting of Laozi riding a buffalo, attended by a servant

✓ Reading Check **Describe the religious traditions of ancient China.**

Background: Daily Life

Upward Mobility The Chinese civil service examination system, based on knowledge of the teachings of Confucius, became a way for some families without importance or political connections to rise in society. Passing the province-level exams would raise the social status, not just of the student who passed, but the student's entire family. The family became scholar gentry and received the prestige and privileges associated with their new status.

Guided Instruction

- **Vocabulary Builder** Clarify the high-use word **generally** before reading.

- Ask students to read The Influence of Confucius.

- Ask students **On which members of Chinese government did Confucius's teachings have an impact? How?** (*members of the civil service; an examination brought in more job candidates and the merit system was introduced*)

- Ask students **Do you agree with the idea of reward based on merit? Why or why not?** (*Agree: reward based on merit is a fair method of job promotion. Disagree: it is fair for the child of a businessperson to be rewarded with work in his or her parents' business or to take over the business even if he or she is not the most qualified.*)

Independent Practice

Ask students to complete the Taking Notes graphic organizer by filling in the "Effects" portion with the information they just learned.

Monitor Progress

- Show *Section Reading Support Transparency HOW 71* and ask students to check their graphic organizers individually. Go over key concepts and clarify key vocabulary as needed.

  📖 **History of Our World Transparencies,** *Section Reading Support Transparency HOW 71*

- Tell students to fill in the last column of the *Reading Readiness Guide*. Probe for what they learned that confirms or invalidates each statement.

  All in One **Unit 2 History of Our World Teaching Resources,** *Reading Readiness Guide,* p. 104

Answer

✓ Reading Check Ancient China was home to a variety of religious traditions, including ancestor worship, honoring gods, and belief in spirits. Most people believed that life should be lived in harmony with nature, including the members of Taoism, a religion based on the writings of a Chinese thinker named Laozi.

Assess and Reteach

Assess Progress L2

Have students complete the Section Assessment. Administer the *Section Quiz*.

All in One **Unit 2 History of Our World Teaching Resources,** *Section Quiz*, p. 106

Reteach L1

If students need more instruction, have them read this section in the Reading and Vocabulary Study Guide.

Chapter 5, Section 2, **History of Our World Reading and Vocabulary Study Guide,** pp. 64–66

Extend L3

Have students learn more about Confucius and his philosophies by completing the *Enrichment* activity.

All in One **Unit 2 History of Our World Teaching Resources,** *Enrichment,* p. 119

Answers

✓ Reading Check Civil servants had to know how to read. Many poor men did not possess that ability.

Section 2 Assessment

Key Terms
Students' sentences should reflect knowledge of each Key Term.

⊘ Target Reading Skill
Details will vary, but should support the main idea that Confucius was a famous and influential teacher and thinker in ancient China.

Comprehension and Critical Thinking
1. (a) He could not get a government post and decided to try teaching. **(b)** Possible answer: Students who did not want to learn would waste his time. Today, the law requires all children to go to school, whether they want to or not.

2. (a) Students' answers may include that people should: behave properly to one another so that order and peace return to society; know their place in society, respect those above and below them, and treat each other justly; behave in certain ways toward people to whom they have a particular relationship; set a good example if they are in a position of authority; not do unto others what they would not want done to themselves. **(b)** If a ruler was good, people would follow his example and be good.

A Chinese emperor oversees students at a civil service exam.

The Influence of Confucius

The teachings of Confucius came to have a major effect on Chinese government. They became part of the basic training for members of the civil service. The **civil service** is the group of people who carry out the work of government.

A Merit System Before the ideas of Confucius took hold, government posts were generally given to the sons of powerful people. Afterward, any man could hold a government post based on merit—that is, on how qualified he was or how well he did his job. Candidates for government jobs had to pass official examinations. These exams were based on the teachings of Confucius.

Rising to High Positions The examination system did not open government jobs to everyone. Candidates still had to know how to read. This rule made it difficult for a poor man to enter the government. But it was not impossible. Many talented but poor young men learned to read and rose to high government positions.

Confucius would have been surprised at the influence he had on China. He did not consider himself particularly wise or good. But he left a lasting mark on Chinese life.

✓ Reading Check Why was it difficult for poor men to work in the civil service?

✦ Section 2 Assessment

Key Terms
Review the key terms at the beginning of this section. Use each term in a sentence that explains its meaning.

⊘ Target Reading Skill
State the details that support the main idea on page 145.

Comprehension and Critical Thinking
1. (a) Recall How did Confucius become a teacher?
(b) Transfer Information Confucius would teach only those students who wanted to learn. How does his rule apply to your experience as a student?

2. (a) List What were the basic teachings of Confucius?
(b) Explain Why did Confucius think it was important to teach rulers how to behave?
3. (a) Describe How did the ideas of Confucius change the way civil servants were chosen in ancient China?
(b) Predict Confucius hoped to become a government worker, but he became a teacher instead. Do you think his influence on Chinese society would have been different if he had gotten his wish? Explain your answer.

Writing Activity
Suppose that you are a government official in a small state in northern China. One day, a wandering teacher named Confucius arrives. Write a journal entry that describes what Confucius says and how your ruler reacts to him.

For: An activity on Confucius
Visit: PHSchool.com
Web Code: lbd-2502

---

3. (a) Possible answer: Confucius taught that men should be chosen based on merit rather than their family connections. **(b)** Possible answer: No—He might have spread his ideas by example instead of by teaching. Yes—He might have been absorbed in his job and not had time to develop his philosophy.

Writing Activity
Use the *Rubric for Assessing a Journal Entry* to evaluate students' journal entries.

All in One **Unit 2 History of Our World Teaching Resources,** *Rubric for Assessing a Journal Entry*, p. 129

Go Online Typing in the Web code when prompted will bring students directly to detailed instructions for this activity.

Warring Kingdoms Unite

Prepare to Read

Objectives

In this section, you will

1. Learn about the rise of the Qin dynasty.
2. Find out how Emperor Shi Huangdi attempted to unify the economy and culture of China.
3. Examine the actions of the Han dynasty's leaders.

Taking Notes

As you read, find details about Chinese rulers and life in China during the Qin and the Han dynasties. Copy the table below, and use it to record your findings.

Qin Dynasty	Han Dynasty
•	•
•	•
•	•

🎯 Target Reading Skill

Identify Implied Main Ideas Sometimes main ideas are not stated directly. However, all the details in a section of text add up to a main idea. For example, after reading and adding up all the details on page 150 following the heading The Qin Dynasty, you could state the main idea this way: "China was unified and strengthened by its first emperor, Shi Huangdi."

Carefully read the details in the paragraphs below. Then state the main idea.

Key Terms

- **Shi Huangdi** (shur hwahng DEE) *n.* founder of the Qin dynasty and China's first emperor
- **currency** (KUR un see) *n.* the type of money used by a group or a nation
- **Liu Bang** (LYOH bahng) *n.* the founder of the Han dynasty
- **Wudi** (woo dee) *n.* Chinese emperor who brought the Han dynasty to its greatest strength
- **warlord** (WAWR lawrd) *n.* a local leader of an armed group

In 1974, several farmers were digging a well in a grove of trees in northern China. Six feet down, they found some terra cotta, a reddish type of pottery. Another five feet down, they unearthed the terra-cotta head of a man. Archaeologists took over and began digging. They discovered more than 6,000 life-sized statues of soldiers and horses, along with wood and bronze chariots and metal weapons. It was a terra-cotta army. For more than 2,000 years, these buried soldiers had kept watch at the tomb of China's first emperor, **Shi Huangdi** (shur hwahng DEE).

With his underground army, Shi Huangdi had planned to rule a second empire in the afterlife. He had also made grand plans for the real-life empire he created in China. His dynasty, he boasted, would last for 10,000 generations.

These terra-cotta warriors guarded Shi Huangdi's tomb in the ancient city of Chang'an, China.

Objectives

1. Learn about the rise of the Qin dynasty.
2. Find out how Emperor Shi Huangdi attempted to unify the economy and culture of China.
3. Examine the actions of the Han dynasty's leaders.

Reading/Language Arts

Learn how to identify main ideas when they are not stated directly.

Prepare to Read

Build Background Knowledge 〔L2〕

Tell students that they will learn about two dynasties that united China for hundreds of years. Ask them to quickly preview the section headings and form one question about the Qin dynasty and one about the Han dynasty. Use an Idea Wave (TE, p. T39) to get students to share their questions. Write a list on the board. Tell students to think about these questions as they read.

Set a Purpose for Reading 〔L2〕

- Preview the Objectives.

- Read each statement in the *Reading Readiness Guide* aloud. Ask students to mark the statements true or false.

  All in One Unit 2 History of Our World Teaching Resources, *Reading Readiness Guide,* p. 108

- Have students discuss the statements in pairs or groups of four, then mark their worksheets again. Use the Numbered Heads participation strategy (TE, p. T40) to call on students to share their group's perspectives.

Vocabulary Builder
Preview Key Terms 〔L2〕

Pronounce each Key Term, and then ask the students to say the word with you. Provide a simple explanation such as, "Coins and paper money are currency."

🎯 Target Reading Skill 〔L2〕

Identify Implied Main Ideas Point out the Target Reading Skill. Review with students what they learned about main ideas, and then explain that sometimes the main idea is not stated directly, but is implied by details in a passage. In this case, a reader must determine the main idea from the details.

Model identifying implied main ideas with this sentence about the last paragraph on p. 150: "Shi Huangdi developed plans to bring stability to his government." Point out the details in the paragraph that support this idea, even though it is not explicitly stated. *(He put thousands of farmers to work building roads so armies could rush to the scene of any uprisings, and divided his empire up into districts.)*

Give students *Identify Implied Main Ideas.* Have them complete the activity in groups.

All in One Unit 2 History of Our World Teaching Resources, *Identify Implied Main Ideas,* p. 117

Instruct

The Qin Dynasty L2

Guided Instruction

- **Vocabulary Builder** Clarify the high-use words **rebellion** and **enable** before reading.

- Have students read The Qin Dynasty, using the ReQuest procedure (TE, p. T39).

- Ask students **Who was Shi Huangdi?** *(the Qin dynasty and China's first emperor)* **What is he most noted for today?** *(the construction of the Great Wall of China)*

- Ask students **Why do you think that the wall created by Shi Huangdi is now called the "Great Wall of China"?** *(Possible answers: It was the largest construction project in Chinese history; it was built to protect China from invaders; it took years to build; it required hundreds of thousands of workers; it covered about 4,550 miles (7,300 kilometers); it still exists today.)*

Independent Practice

Ask students to create the Taking Notes graphic organizer on a blank piece of paper. Then have them fill in the "Qin Dynasty" column in the chart with the information they have just learned. Briefly model how to identify which details to record.

Show students *The Great Wall of China*. Ask **Do you think a wall would work today as a way to protect a country from invaders? Why or why not?** *(Yes—it would help to keep troops from invading by land; No—with airplanes and today's technology, a wall would not be of much use to keep invaders out.)*

Monitor Progress

As students fill in the graphic organizer, circulate and make sure individuals are choosing the correct details. Provide assistance as needed.

Answers

Infer They probably had large, powerful armies.

✓ **Reading Check** For about ten years, hundreds of thousands of farmers and merchants were ordered by Shi Huangdi to connect existing defensive walls.

The Great Wall of China
The Great Wall winds its way across the mountains and plains of northern China. **Infer** *What does the size of the wall tell you about Shi Huangdi's enemies?*

Explore the Great Wall of China.

The Qin Dynasty

Shi Huangdi's dynasty lasted only two generations, but that was still a huge accomplishment. Before that time, China was divided into seven warring kingdoms. Shi Huangdi conquered these kingdoms to unify China.

China's First Emperor Shi Huangdi's original name was Zhao Zheng (jow jeng). He ruled the Qin (chin) people, who lived along China's western border. By 221 B.C., Zheng had extended his rule over most of the land that makes up modern-day China. When Zheng established the Qin dynasty, he took the name Shi Huangdi, meaning "First Emperor." Because Qin is sometimes spelled *Chin*, the name China comes from the Qin dynasty.

Strengthening the Empire Shi Huangdi sought to strengthen China through strong and harsh rule. One of his first tasks was to protect the new empire from its enemies.

Throughout history, nomads had attacked China along its vast northern border. Shi Huangdi had a plan to end these border wars. He ordered what became the largest construction project in Chinese history. It is now called the Great Wall of China. Turn to page 152 and locate the wall on the map titled Qin and Han Empires.

Previous rulers had built walls along the border. Shi Huangdi decided to connect them. He ordered farmers from their fields and merchants from their stores to form an army of hundreds of thousands of workers. Shi Huangdi's wall took about ten years to construct. After Shi Huangdi died, the wall fell into disrepair. Over time, other emperors repaired the wall and added new sections to it. Today, the exact length of the Great Wall is unknown. However, some experts believe it may be about 1,500 miles (2,400 kilometers) long.

Organizing the Government To help put down rebellions within the empire, Shi Huangdi put thousands of farmers to work building roads. The new roads enabled his armies to rush to the scene of any uprisings. The emperor killed or imprisoned any local rulers who opposed him. Shi Huangdi divided all of China into areas called districts. Each district had a government run by the emperor's trusted officials.

✓ **Reading Check** How was China's Great Wall built?

Vocabulary Builder

Use the information below to teach students this section's high-use words.

High-Use Word	Definition and Sample Sentence
rebellion, p. 150	*n.* an armed fight against one's government. The **rebellion** lasted a year before the king's army put it down.
enable, p. 150	*v.* make something possible. The extra time **enabled** me to study more and do better on the test.

Unifying Economy and Culture

Shi Huangdi was not content to unify the government of China. He also wanted the many peoples of his united kingdom to have one economy and one culture.

Economic and Cultural Improvements   Shi Huangdi declared that one **currency,** or type of money, be used throughout China. The new currency was a round coin with a square hole in the middle. A common currency made it easier for one region of China to trade goods with another. Shi Huangdi also ordered the creation of common weights and measures, an improved system of writing, and a law code.

Restricting Freedoms   Shi Huangdi also tried to control the thoughts of his people. In 213 B.C., he outlawed the ideas of Confucius and other important thinkers. Instead, he required that people learn the philosophies of Qin scholars.

The Qin believed in legalism, the idea that people should be punished for bad behavior and rewarded for good behavior. Legalists thought that the people of China should work to serve the government and the emperor. The Qin dynasty practiced a strict and sometimes brutal form of legalism. Shi Huangdi commanded that all the books in China be burned except those about medicine, technology, and farming. Hundreds of scholars protested the order. Shi Huangdi had them all killed.

The End of a Dynasty   Shi Huangdi's death in 210 B.C. was followed by four years of chaos and civil war that ended in the murder of his son. Power then passed to Shi Huangdi's grandson, but he could not hold China together. Rebellions broke out. The dynasty that was supposed to last for 10,000 generations lasted for only 15 years.

√ **Reading Check**   How did Shi Huangdi try to limit his people's freedoms?

Bronze cooking pot, Shang dynasty

The Rise and Fall of Chinese Dynasties

A new dynasty rises.
• A strong ruler defeats other local rulers.
• The new dynasty expands China's borders.

The new dynasty rules.
• It restores peace.
• It chooses loyal officials.
• It makes reforms.

The dynasty grows weak.
• The large empire becomes difficult to govern.
• Leaders lose control of the provinces.

A period of violence follows. Local rulers fight for power.

Lady of the Emperor's court, statue, A.D. 600s

The dynasty falls. Rebellions destroy the weakened dynasty.

■ **Diagram Skills**

Although many different dynasties ruled China throughout its long history, each rose and fell in a similar pattern. **Describe** Why do dynasties fall? **Analyze Information** Why might a dynasty become weaker as it grows larger?

Guided Instruction

■ Ask students to read Unifying Economy and Culture. As they read, circulate and make sure individuals can answer the Reading Check question.

■ Ask students **How did using one currency throughout China help to unify the economy?** *(It made it easier for one region of China to trade with another.)*

■ Discuss with students how Shi Huangdi forced the people of China into having one culture. Ask students **Why do you think that Shi Huangdi ordered most books to be burned?** *(By burning books in most subjects, Shi Huandgi may have hoped to unify the culture by eliminating differing ideas. He may have decided that books in medicine, technology, and farming contained information that would not cause diversity in the culture.)*

Independent Practice

Have students continue to fill in the Qin Dynasty column in their Taking Notes chart.

Monitor Progress

As students fill in the graphic organizer, circulate and make sure individuals are choosing the correct details. Provide assistance as needed.

Answers

Diagram Skills **Describe** Their large empires become difficult to govern and leaders lose control of provinces, weakening the dynasty. **Analyze Information** It is more difficult to manage an empire as its land and population increase.

√ **Reading Check** by outlawing the ideas of Confucius and other thinkers, requiring that people learn the ideas of the Qin scholars, enforcing legalism, burning many books, and having scholars who protested killed

---

Differentiated Instruction

For Gifted and Talented   L3

Have students read more about Confucianism and legalism by researching the topics on the Internet, in reference books, or in other sources. Then organize students into groups. Have each group make charts that compare and contrast the two philosophies and have them present their findings to the class.

For Advanced Readers   L3

Have students read the poem *The Tale of a Frog* and answer the questions that follow. Then, ask them to write a brief paragraph on whether the ideas in the poem seem to relate more to Confucianism or legalism.

All in One Unit 2 History of Our World Teaching Resources, *The Tale of a Frog,* p. 126

The Han Dynasty

Guided Instruction

- **Vocabulary Builder** Clarify the high-use words **rebellion** before reading.

- Ask students to read The Han Dynasty. Then, review the Qin and Han Empires map with students.

- Ask students **Who was the first Han dynasty ruler? What was significant about his background?** (*Liu Bang; he was not royal by blood, but born a peasant.*)

- Discuss with students why they think the Han Dynasty lasted about 400 years. (*For most of its length, it had stable governments, prosperity, and an expanding empire.*)

Independent Practice

Ask students to complete the Taking Notes graphic organizer by filling in the "Han Dynasty" column in the chart with the information they have just learned.

Monitor Progress

- Show *Section Reading Support Transparency HOW 72* and ask students to check their graphic organizers individually. Go over key concepts and clarify key vocabulary as needed.

  📖 **History of Our World Transparencies,** *Section Reading Support Transparency HOW 72*

- Tell students to fill in the last column of the *Reading Readiness Guide*. Probe for what they learned that confirms or invalidates each statement.

  All in One Unit 2 History of Our World Teaching Resources, *Reading Readiness Guide,* p. 108

Links

Read **Links to Art** on this page. Ask students **Why were mirrors important in China?** (*They symbolized self-knowledge.*)

Answers

MAP MASTER Skills Activity **Identify** the Great Wall of China **Infer** the Himalayas

Go Online PHSchool.com Students may practice their map skills by using the interactive online version of this map.

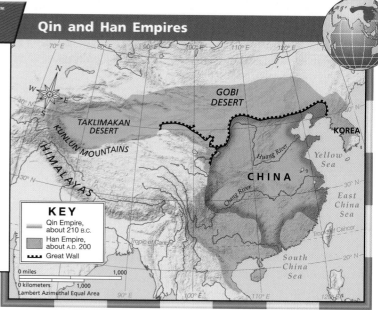

MAP MASTER Skills Activity

Qin and Han Empires

Human-Environment Interaction Both natural and human-made features shaped the borders of the Qin and Han empires. **Identify** What feature formed the northern border of the Qin Empire? **Infer** What geographical feature may have limited the expansion of the Han Empire to the southwest?

Go Online PHSchool.com Use Web Code lbp-2523 for step-by-step map skills practice.

KEY
- Qin Empire, about 210 B.C.
- Han Empire, about A.D. 200
- ▪▪▪ Great Wall

0 miles 1,000
0 kilometers 1,000
Lambert Azimuthal Equal Area

Map labels: GOBI DESERT, TAKLIMAKAN DESERT, KUNLUN MOUNTAINS, HIMALAYAS, KOREA, CHINA, Huang River, Chang River, Yellow Sea, East China Sea, South China Sea, Tropic of Cancer

The Han Dynasty

One of the rebels who helped overthrow the Qin dynasty was a talented ruler named Liu Bang (LYOH bahng). By 202 B.C., **Liu Bang** won out over his rivals and became emperor of China. Born a peasant, Liu Bang became the first emperor of a new dynasty: the Han (hahn). Liu Bang created a stable government, but one that was was less harsh than Shi Huangdi's.

Stable governments were a feature of the Han dynasty, which lasted for about 400 years. Han rulers realized that they needed educated people to work in the government. They set up the civil service system based on Confucianism to meet that need.

Wudi: The Warrior Emperor In 140 B.C., Liu Bang's great-grandson, Wudi, came to power. Under **Wudi** (woo dee), the Han dynasty reached its greatest power. About 15 years old when he took the throne, Wudi ruled for more than 50 years.

Wudi's main interests were war and military matters. In fact, his name means "Warrior Emperor." He made improvements to Shi Huangdi's Great Wall. He also strengthened the army. By the end of Wudi's reign, Chinese rule stretched west into Central Asia, east into present-day northern and central Korea, and south into present-day Vietnam. Locate the Han Empire on the map titled Qin and Han Empires.

Links to Art

Han Dynasty Bronze Work Han dynasty artisans created beautiful objects of bronze, including finely made mirrors. On one side of the mirror, the metal was polished enough to show a reflection. The back was decorated with gems, animal symbols, and writing. Mirrors were important in China because they symbolized self-knowledge. At the right is the decorated side of a bronze mirror.

152 History of Our World

Background: Biography

Lü Hou Lü Hou (also called Kao Hou), the wife of Liu Bang, was the first woman to rule China. She was an extremely ambitious woman and was instrumental in her husband's rise to power. When Liu Bang died, Lü Hou and Liu Bang's son ruled for a brief time. Lü Hou then appointed a child as emperor and seized power. She issued royal orders under her own name and hoped to begin her own dynasty by distributing important government jobs to members of her own family. Lü Hou was not ultimately successful—after her death in 180 B.C., power returned to her husband's family—but she did set a precedent. When an emperor died without an heir, the surviving empress (acting as a mouthpiece for senior statesmen) issued royal orders until a new ruler was chosen.

The End of the Han Empire   The great emperor Wudi died in 87 B.C. China's stability and prosperity continued under later Han emperors. Many new ideas and technologies developed. But over time, the empire began to weaken. A series of very young emperors—one was only 100 days old—ruled the empire. People within the government struggled for power over these young emperors. While they struggled, no one paid attention to running the empire. Roads and canals fell into disrepair.

As the rule of the emperors weakened, **warlords,** local leaders of armed groups, gained power. The last Han emperor was kept in power by one such warlord, named Cao Pei. At first Cao Pei tried to control the empire through the emperor. In A.D. 220, he declared an end to the Han dynasty. In its place, he set up his own Wei dynasty. However, the Wei dynasty had control only over parts of northern China. It ended after about 50 years, and China broke up into a number of smaller kingdoms.

✓ **Reading Check**   What happened in A.D. 220?

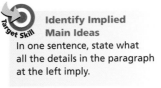

Identify Implied Main Ideas
In one sentence, state what all the details in the paragraph at the left imply.

This bronze statue of a man on horseback dates from the Han dynasty.

Section 3 Assessment

Key Terms
Review the key terms at the beginning of this section. Use each term in a sentence that explains its meaning.

Target Reading Skill
State the three main ideas in Section 3.

Comprehension and Critical Thinking
1. (a) Describe What measures did Shi Huangdi take to strengthen the empire and organize the government?
(b) Summarize Why is Shi Huangdi a major figure in Chinese history?

2. (a) Identify What measures did Shi Huangdi take to unite the economy and culture of China?
(b) Analyze Information How did all of Shi Huangdi's efforts strengthen the empire? How did his leadership hurt the empire?
3. (a) Recall What characterized the government of China during the Han dynasty?
(b) Compare and Contrast Compare the ways the emperors of the Qin dynasty and the emperors of the Han dynasty viewed the ideas of Confucius. How were their viewpoints similar or different?

Writing Activity
The farmers who discovered Shi Huangdi's terra-cotta army made one of the most important archaeological finds in history. Write a list of questions that you would like to ask them about their discovery.

> **Writing Tip** Write your questions in a logical order. For instance, you could begin with a few general questions. Later, narrow your focus with more specific questions.

Chapter 5 Section 3 **153**

⮌ **Target Reading Skill**   L2
Identify Implied Main Ideas   As a follow up, ask students to answer the Target Reading Skill question in the Student Edition. *(Although ancient China's prosperity continued after Wudi's death, the Han empire eventually declined.)*

Assess and Reteach

Assess Progress   L2
Have students complete the Section Assessment. Administer the *Section Quiz.*

All in One **Unit 2 History of Our World Teaching Resources,** *Section Quiz,* p. 110

Reteach   L1
If students need more instruction, have them read this section in the Reading and Vocabulary Study Guide.

📖 Chapter 5, Section 3, **History of Our World Reading and Vocabulary Study Guide,** pp. 67–69

Extend   L3
Ask students to compare the map on the previous page to *Outline Map 29: East Asia.* Have them add the borders of the Qin and Han Empires to the outline map.

All in One **Unit 2 History of Our World Teaching Resources,** *Outline Map 29: East Asia,* Physical p. 125

Answers

✓ **Reading Check**   Cao Pei declared an end to the Han dynasty and set up his own Wei dynasty.

Writing Activity
Use the *Rubric for Assessing a Writing Assignment* to evaluate students' questions.

All in One **Unit 2 History of Our World Teaching Resources,** *Rubric for Assessing a Writing Assignment,* p. 128

Section 3 Assessment

Key Terms
Students' sentences should reflect knowledge of each Key Term.

⮌ **Target Reading Skill**
Shi Huangdi sought to strengthen China through strong and harsh rule; Shi Huangdi wanted the many peoples of his united kingdom to have one economy and one culture; civil war and rebellion ended the Qin dynasty; the Han dynasty lasted for 400 years.

Comprehension and Critical Thinking
1. (a) He built the Great Wall and roads for the army to travel quickly, and divided China into districts and selected officials. **(b)** He was the first emperor of China and the Qin dynasty.
2. (a) He standardized currency, weights, measures, improved the system of writing, and created a law code. **(b)** He facilitated commerce and communication across the empire, but people ultimately rebelled, leading to chaos and civil war.

3. (a) stability and a Confucian civil service system **(b)** Qin—outlawed the ideas of Confucius, favored legalism; Han—based civil service system on Confucianism.

Focus on China's Western Frontier L2

Guided Instruction

- Ask students to read the text and study the art, photos, and captions on pages 154–155.

- Ask students **Who were the Xiongnu?** *(warriors from the Mongolian plain who attacked Chinese border towns, stealing Chinese silks and other luxuries)*

- Ask students **What happened to Zhang and his men during their first expedition?** *(They were captured by the Xiongnu and held for ten years until they managed to escape.)* **What was the ultimate outcome of the expeditions?** *(Wudi's warriors drove the Xiongnu from China's borders and opened a gateway to the west.)*

- As a class, answer the Assessment questions. Allow students to briefly discuss their responses with a partner before sharing their answers with the class.

Focus On
China's Western Frontier

Swooping down from the Mongolian plain, the legendary Xiongnu (shong noo) warriors came not to conquer, but to steal. They came on horseback, wild, dust-covered, and fierce. In attacks that terrorized Chinese border towns, the Xiongnu stole Chinese silks and other luxuries, galloping off with all they could carry. The great Han warrior emperor, Wudi, devoted his long half-century reign (140–87 B.C.) to taming China's frontier and exploring civilizations beyond the known world of his time.

The Expeditions Emperor Wudi chose Zhang Qian (jahng chyen) to lead a dangerous expedition to the western frontier. Zhang, an officer in Wudi's imperial guard, led the caravan (shown at the right) from the Han capital of Chang'an in 138 B.C. His mission was to befriend the Yuezhi (yooeh jur), enemies of the Xiongnu, and to rally them to war. Thirteen years later, Zhang returned—to tell Wudi not of war, but of unimagined wealth to be gained in trade with western societies. So Wudi sent him west again, in 119 B.C., to open government and economic ties with other lands.

During his travels, Zhang learned of swift horses owned by the people of the Fergana Valley. Wudi's forces later captured some of the Fergana horses (depicted in the bronze statue at the top of this page). Wudi's warriors ultimately drove the Xiongnu far from China's borders and opened a gateway to the west.

154 History of Our World

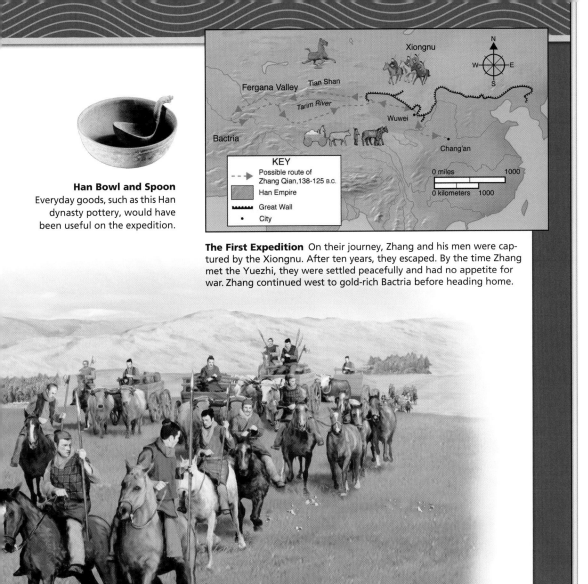

KEY

- - -→ Possible route of Zhang Qian, 138-125 B.C.
▨ Han Empire
▬▬▬ Great Wall
• City

0 miles 1000
0 kilometers 1000

Han Bowl and Spoon Everyday goods, such as this Han dynasty pottery, would have been useful on the expedition.

The First Expedition On their journey, Zhang and his men were captured by the Xiongnu. After ten years, they escaped. By the time Zhang met the Yuezhi, they were settled peacefully and had no appetite for war. Zhang continued west to gold-rich Bactria before heading home.

Assessment

Explain Why did Emperor Wudi send expeditions to China's western frontier?

Identify Effects How did these expeditions benefit China?

Independent Practice
Tell students to look at the map showing the Qin and Han empires on page 152. Have students locate the borders of the Han empire. Ask **What geographical features would Zhang Qian reach as he traveled west with his expedition?** (*Tarim River, Tianshan Mountains*) **How do you think these features might have affected the expedition?** (*Possible answer: They might have been dangerous and difficult to travel through.*)

Answers

Assessment

Explain He sent them to rally the Yuezhi to fight against the Xiongnu. **Identify Effects** These expeditions led to open government and economic ties with lands outside of China.

Section 4
Step-by-Step Instruction

Objectives

Social Studies
1. Learn about the Silk Road.
2. Find out about the Han dynasty's respect for tradition and learning.
3. Discover the important advances in technology that were made in China during the Han dynasty.

Reading/Language Arts
Learn how to identify details that support the main idea.

Prepare to Read

Build Background Knowledge **L2**
In this section, students will learn about the achievements of ancient Chinese society. Ask students to preview the section and write down one achievement. Then, ask them to think about how that achievement shows what was important to people in ancient China. Use the Think-Write-Pair-Share technique (TE, p. T40) to allow students to share and develop their ideas.

Set a Purpose for Reading **L2**
- Preview the Objectives.

- Read each statement in the *Reading Readiness Guide* aloud. Ask students to mark the statements true or false.

  All in One **Unit 2 History of Our World Teaching Resources,** *Reading Readiness Guide,* p. 112

- Have students discuss the statements in pairs or groups of four, then mark their worksheets again. Use the Numbered Heads participation strategy (TE, p. T40) to call on students to share their group's perspectives.

Vocabulary Builder
Preview Key Terms **L2**
Pronounce each Key Term, then ask the students to say the word with you. Provide a simple explanation such as, "The soft, smooth texture of silk makes it a good material to use for clothing."

Section 4
Achievements of Ancient China

Prepare to Read

Objectives
In this section you will
1. Learn about the Silk Road.
2. Find out about the Han dynasty's respect for tradition and learning.
3. Discover the important advances in technology that were made in China during the Han dynasty.

Taking Notes
As you read, create an outline of this section. Copy the outline below and use it to get started.

> I. The Silk Road
>   A. A series of routes
>   1.
>   2.
>   B.
> II. Tradition and learning

Target Reading Skill

Identify Supporting Details Details in a section of text may explain the main idea or give examples that support it. The main idea for the text on page 157 under the red heading The Silk Road, can be stated this way: "Both ideas and goods were exchanged along the Silk Road, a series of routes that connected the East to the West."

As you read, note the details following each of the blue headings that support the main idea.

Key Terms
- **Silk Road** (silk rohd) *n.* an ancient trade route between China and Europe
- **silk** (silk) *n.* a valuable cloth, originally made only in China from threads spun by caterpillars called silkworms
- **Sima Qian** (sih MAH chen) *n.* (c. 145–85 B.C.) a Chinese scholar, astronomer, and historian; author of the most important history of ancient China, *Historical Records*

A camel caravan in Gansu Province, western China

156 History of Our World

The caravan slowly plods across the hot sand of the Taklimakan Desert. Weary travelers wearing long robes sway on top of camels. Riderless camels are heaped high with heavy loads.

Suddenly the camels stop, huddle together, and snarl viciously. An old man riding the lead camel turns around and shouts. No one can hear him because the screaming wind drowns out his words. The man jumps from his camel and quickly wraps a strip of felt around his own nose and mouth. The other travelers rush to dismount and cover their faces, too. Just then, the sandstorm hits with full force. The fine desert sand flies at the caravan, stinging man and beast with needle-sharp grit.

Then, as quickly as it came, the sandstorm is gone. The travelers wipe sand from their eyes and tend to their camels. They have survived just one of the many challenges of traveling on the **Silk Road,** an ancient trade route between China and Europe.

Target Reading Skill **L2**
Identify Supporting Details Point out the Target Reading Skill. Review with students what they learned about identifying supporting details in Section 2 of this chapter. Remind them that supporting details tell more about the main idea.

Remind students about the skill of identifying a supporting detail with the first sentence under the heading A History of China on p. 159. The main idea is that Chinese people had little understanding of their history until the Han dynasty. Point out that the following sentence supports this idea: "No one was sure exactly when the various Chinese rulers had lived or what each accomplished." It tells readers more about how little the Chinese knew of their history.

Give students *Identify Supporting Details.* Have them complete the activity in groups.

All in One **Unit 2 History of Our World Teaching Resources,** *Identify Supporting Details,* p. 116

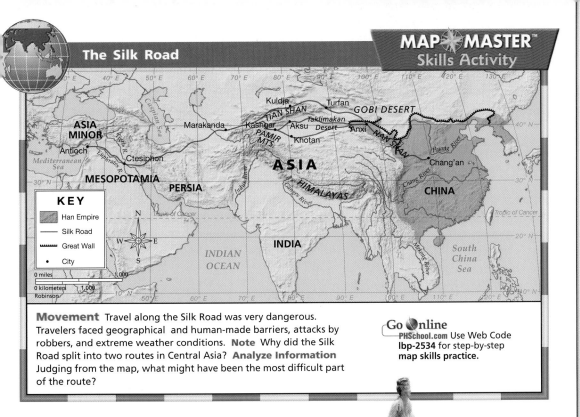

MAP MASTER™ Skills Activity

The Silk Road

Movement Travel along the Silk Road was very dangerous. Travelers faced geographical and human-made barriers, attacks by robbers, and extreme weather conditions. **Note** Why did the Silk Road split into two routes in Central Asia? **Analyze Information** Judging from the map, what might have been the most difficult part of the route?

Go Online
PHSchool.com Use Web Code lbp-2534 for step-by-step map skills practice.

KEY
Han Empire
Silk Road
Great Wall
• City

The Silk Road

The Emperor Wudi's conquests in the west brought the Chinese into contact with the people of Central Asia. Trade with these people introduced the Chinese to such new foods as grapes, walnuts, and garlic. In turn, Chinese goods and ideas passed to the peoples living to the West. This exchange of goods gave rise to a major trade route—the Silk Road. This ran all the way from China to the Mediterranean Sea.

Connecting Roads The Silk Road was a series of routes covering more than 4,000 miles (6,400 kilometers), a little less than the distance from present-day Chicago to Hawaii. Follow the routes on the map above titled The Silk Road.

The Silk Road followed a challenging route through mountainous country and desert land. The road passed through Persia and Mesopotamia. Finally, it turned north to the city of Antioch (AN tee ahk), in present-day Turkey. From there, traders shipped goods across the Mediterranean to Rome, Greece, Egypt, and other lands that bordered the Mediterranean.

A terra-cotta statue of a traveler on a camel, about A.D. 700

Chapter 5 Section 4 **157**

Vocabulary Builder

Use the information below to teach students this section's high-use words.

High-Use Word	Definition and Sample Sentence
contact, p. 157	*n.* the state of being in touch with I kept in **contact** with several friends after graduation.
reveal, p. 158	*v.* to make known A closer look **revealed** that much of the mess had been stuffed under the bed.
myth, p. 159	*n.* a traditional story, usually about a god or hero The **myth** told a story about the Greek goddess Athena.
availability, p. 160	*n.* the state of being ready for use The **availability** of books is a key factor in a library's success.

Instruct

The Silk Road [L2]

Guided Instruction
- **Vocabulary Builder** Clarify the high-use words **contact** and **reveal** before reading.

- Have students read The Silk Road, using the Paragraph Shrinking technique (TE, p. T38), and review The Silk Road map with students.

- Ask students **In what ways did the Silk Road influence the introduction of cultures between China and western peoples?** (*new foods, new fabrics, and new religious ideas were shared*)

Independent Practice
Ask students to create the Taking Notes graphic organizer on a blank piece of paper. Then have them complete The Silk Road portion of the organizer with the information they have just learned. Briefly model how to identify which details to record.

Monitor Progress
As students fill in the graphic organizer, circulate and make sure individuals are choosing the correct details. Provide assistance as needed.

Answers

MAP MASTER Skills Activity **Note** probably to avoid traveling through the Tian Shan mountain range **Analyze Information** probably where the route passes through mountain ranges or deserts

Go Online PHSchool.com Students may practice their map skills using the interactive online version of this map.

Tradition and Learning

L2

Guided Instruction

- **Vocabulary Builder** Clarify the high-use word **myth** before reading.

- Have students read Tradition and Learning. As students read, circulate and make sure individuals can answer the Reading Check question.

- Ask students **In what ways did the Han dynasty encourage the respect of tradition?** (*returning to the teachings of the past such as Confucius, appreciating Chinese culture through art and literature, learning from history*)

- Ask students **Why might Confucius have approved of Chinese scholars creating a dictionary?** (*He valued order, and a dictionary puts words into a useful order. He also valued education, and a dictionary is a valuable tool for students.*)

Independent Practice

Ask students to complete the Tradition and Learning portion of their graphic organizer with the information they have just learned.

Monitor Progress

As students fill in the graphic organizer, circulate and make sure individuals are choosing the correct details. Provide assistance as needed.

⟲ Target Reading Skill

L2

Identify Supporting Details As a follow up, ask students to answer the Target Reading Skill question on this page of the Student Edition. (*Han rulers wanted to bring back respect for tradition; they encouraged a return to Confucianism and required members of the civil service to know Confucian teachings. The arts and scholarship also flourished.*)

Answers

Infer probably because silk was often traded on the route

✓**Reading Check** Silkworms are caterpillars that make silk.

Making Silk
A scroll from the 1100s shows Chinese women beating silk fibers in a trough. Silk was used to make musical instruments, fishing line, and even paper. **Infer** *Why was the Silk Road named after this material?*

Identify Supporting Details
What details in the last paragraph on this page tell about tradition and learning during the Han dynasty?

A Route for Goods Few travelers ever journeyed the entire length of the Silk Road. Generally, goods were passed from trader to trader as they crossed Asia. With each trade along the route, the price of the goods went up. By the time the goods arrived at the end of their journey, they were very expensive.

The Silk Road got its name from **silk,** a valuable cloth originally made only in China. Han farmers had developed new methods for raising silkworms, the caterpillars that made the silk. Han workers found new ways to weave and dye the silk. These methods were closely guarded secrets. The penalty for revealing them was death.

The arrival of silk in Europe created great excitement. Wealthy Romans prized Chinese silk and were willing to pay high prices for it. And wealthy people in China would pay well for glass, horses, ivory, woolens, and linen cloth from Rome.

A Route for Ideas More than goods traveled the road. New ideas did, too. For example, missionaries from India traveled to China along a section of the road and brought the religion of Buddhism with them. By the time the Han dynasty ended, Buddhism was becoming a major religion in China.

✓ **Reading Check** **What are silkworms?**

Tradition and Learning

Traditional Chinese ideas flourished during the Han dynasty. People returned to the teachings of Confucius. A renewed interest in learning led one Han scholar to record the early history of China. His efforts helped the people of China understand their past.

Respect for Learning Han rulers found that during troubled times in the past, many people had lost respect for their traditions. As a way of bringing back this respect, rulers encouraged people to return to the teachings of Confucius. Rulers of the Han and later dynasties also required members of the civil service to be educated in Confucian teachings.

The arts and scholarship flourished under the Han dynasty. Expressive poetry reflected Chinese culture. Chinese scholars put together the first dictionary of the Chinese language. But the greatest advances happened in the field of history.

158 History of Our World

Differentiated Instruction

For Less Proficient Readers

L1

Ask students to suppose they are Chinese traders on the Silk Road. Have students write help-wanted ads for an assistant trader. As they read the section, encourage students to think about the skills and traits the assistant will need and the working conditions the assistant will encounter.

For Special Needs Students

L1

Have students read the section as they listen to the recorded version on the Student Edition on Audio CD. Pause the CD at the end of each paragraph and ask students to state the paragraph's main idea.

◉ Chapter 5, Section 4, **Student Edition on Audio CD**

A History of China Until the time of the Han dynasty, the Chinese people had little knowledge of their own history. They knew only myths that had been passed down from generation to generation. Often, these stories were in conflict with one another. No one was sure exactly when the various Chinese rulers had lived or what each had accomplished.

The scholar Sima Qian (sih MAH chen) decided to solve the problem. Sima Qian spent his life writing a history of China from mythical times to the reign of Wudi. Sima described his work:

> **"I wish to examine all that encircles heaven and man. I want to probe the changes of the past and present."**
>
> —Sima Qian

Sima Qian's work, called *Historical Records,* is a major source of information about ancient China.

✓ **Reading Check** What problem did Sima Qian solve?

Han Technology

Because the Han government was stable, the Chinese could turn their attention to improving their society. During the Han dynasty, China became the most advanced civilization in the world.

Advances in Technology The Chinese made significant advances in farming tools and other technologies. Some of these advances are shown in the chart at the right, titled Achievements in Ancient China. During the Han dynasty, the Chinese invented many practical devices that did not reach Europe until centuries later. Among these was paper—something the world still depends on every day.

Achievements in Ancient China

The Arts
- Silk weaving
- Bronze working
- Architecture (temples and palaces)
- Poetry and history
- Jade carving

Medicine
- Acupuncture—the treatment of disease using needles
- Herbal remedies—the use of plants in the practice of medicine
- Circulatory system—the discovery that blood travels through the body

Technology
- Paper made from wood pulp
- Iron plow for breaking up soil
- Rudder—a device used to steer ships
- Seismoscope—a device that registers the occurrence of earthquakes
- Compass
- Wheelbarrow

Arts, Medicine, and Technology
The Chinese made great advances during the Han dynasty. **Analyze** *Which two inventions were especially useful to farmers? Explain your answer.*

Guided Instruction

- **Vocabulary Builder** Clarify high-use word **availability** before reading.

- Ask students to read Han Technology and review the Achievements in Ancient China chart with students.

- Ask students **In what areas did the Han dynasty make technological advances in?** *(the arts, medicine, and technology)*

- Ask students **How did the invention of paper improve Chinese society?** *(Paper is lightweight, takes little space to store, and is easier to use than previous materials. Knowledge, art, and literature could be easily created, stored, shared, and carried on paper.)*

Independent Practice

Ask students to complete the Han Technology portion of their graphic organizer with the information they have just learned.

Monitor Progress

- Show *Section Reading Support Transparency HOW 73* and ask students to check their graphic organizers individually. Go over key concepts and clarify key vocabulary as needed.

  📖 **History of Our World Transparencies,** *Section Reading Support Transparency HOW 73*

Answer

✓ **Reading Check** Before his work, *Historical Records,* Chinese people knew little of their history.

Skills Mini Lesson

Analyzing Primary Sources L2

1. Teach the skill by listing the steps for analyzing primary sources: identify the source, identify the main idea, separate fact from opinion, look for evidence of bias, and evaluate the source's reliability.

2. Practice the skill by analyzing the quotation on page 145 for its main idea, bias, and reliability.

3. Have students apply the skill by analyzing the quotation on page 159. *(Source: historian Sima Qian during the Han dynasty; main idea: "My work is a complete record of Chinese history;" bias— sees China as the center of the universe; reliability—Sima Qian was an experienced historian, so this is probably an accurate description of his intentions.)*

Assess and Reteach

Assess Progress   L2

Have students complete the Section Assessment. Administer the *Section Quiz.*

 Unit 2 History of Our World Teaching Resources, *Section Quiz,* p. 114

Reteach   L1

If students need more instruction, have them read this section in the Reading and Vocabulary Study Guide.

Chapter 5, Section 4, **History of Our World Reading and Vocabulary Study Guide,** pp. 70–72

Extend   L3

Have students learn more about the Silk Road by completing the *Small Group Activity: Making a Map of the Silk Road.* Assign students to work in groups to complete the project.

 Unit 2 History of Our World Teaching Resources, *Small Group Activity: Making a Map of the Silk Road,* pp. 121–124

Answers

✔ Reading Check   wooden scrolls, bones, and silk

Section 4 Assessment

Key Terms
Students' sentences should reflect knowledge of each Key Term.

Target Reading Skill
Main idea: Sandstorms were one of the challenges faced by travelers on the Silk Road. Supporting details: screaming wind drowns out words; fine desert sand flies at the caravan, stinging man and beast with needle-sharp grit.

Comprehension and Critical Thinking
1. (a) began in Chang'an, went through Persia and Mesopotamia, and ended in Antioch **(b)** People would not be willing to pay high prices for silk cloth if they knew how to make it themselves.

2. (a) encouraged people to study Confucius' teachings, supported Chinese arts and scholarship **(b)** He helped the Chinese people to remember their past. His work may have been a model for historians of other civilizations.

A Chinese emperor's favorite horse, named Night-Shining White, is shown in this painting from the A.D. 700s.

The Invention of Paper   The Chinese first used wooden scrolls and bones to keep records. Later, they wrote messages and even whole books on silk. Then, around A.D. 105, the Chinese recorded one of their greatest achievements: the invention of paper. Archaeological evidence shows that paper may have already been in use before that time. Early paper was made from materials such as tree bark, hemp, and old rags. The materials were soaked in water, beaten into pulp, and dried flat on a screen mold.

The availability of paper greatly influenced learning and the arts in China. After several centuries, the use of paper spread across Asia and into Europe. Eventually, paper replaced papyrus from Egypt as the material for scrolls and books.

The Han dynasty came to an end in the A.D. 200s. But its accomplishments were not forgotten. Today, people in China still call themselves "the children of Han."

✔ **Reading Check**   **What did the Chinese write on before they invented paper?**

Section 4 Assessment

Key Terms
Review the key terms at the beginning of this section. Use each term in a sentence that explains its meaning.

Target Reading Skill
State the details that support the main idea on page 158.

Comprehension and Critical Thinking
1. (a) Locate Describe the route of the Silk Road.
(b) Infer Why were the secrets of silk-making so closely guarded?

2. (a) List In what ways did the Han dynasty show a respect for Chinese traditions?
(b) Draw Conclusions Describe the importance of Sima Qian's role in preserving Chinese traditions.
3. (a) Recall Name three important inventions or achievements during the Han dynasty.
(b) Predict How did the achievements of the Han dynasty affect later generations of Chinese people, as well as other peoples?

Writing Activity
Suppose that you are a poet living in ancient Chang'an, at one end of the Silk Road. Write a poem about what you have seen or heard about the Silk Road from living in Chang'an.

For: An activity on ancient Chinese technology
Visit: PHSchool.com
Web Code: lbd-2504

160 History of Our World

---

3. (a) Possible answers: paper, iron farming tools, rudder, wheelbarrow, collar and harness **(b)** They received the practical benefit of the inventions and achievements and also a sense of national pride.

Writing Activity
Use the *Rubric for Assessing a Student Poem* to evaluate students' poems.

Unit 2 History of Our World Teaching Resources, *Rubric for Assessing a Student Poem,* p. 130

Go Online PHSchool.com   Typing in the Web code when prompted will bring students directly to detailed instructions for this activity.

◆ Chapter Summary

Terra-cotta warriors

Section 1: The Geography of China's River Valleys

- Flooding rivers, monsoon rains, and mountain and ocean barriers greatly affected China's early peoples.
- China's first known civilization, the Shang dynasty, arose in the Huang Valley.
- The family, headed by the eldest man, was at the heart of early Chinese society.

Section 2: Confucius and His Teachings

- Confucius was a poor noble from the North China Plain who became a professional teacher.
- Confucius believed that a peaceful, orderly society was possible only when rulers treated others justly.
- Confucianism reformed Chinese government by requiring that civil service workers be hired based on merit.

Confucius

Section 3: Warring Kingdoms Unite

- Several warring states became one China under Shi Huangdi of the Qin dynasty.
- China's first emperor built the Great Wall to protect the empire. He also organized local governments by dividing China into districts.
- Under the Qin dynasty, some attempts to unify China's economy and culture benefited the people, while others caused unrest.
- China's second ruling dynasty, the Han, remained in power for about 400 years. China then broke into smaller kingdoms.

Section 4: Achievements of Ancient China

- The Silk Road opened China to trade with lands to the west.
- The Han dynasty embraced the ideas of Confucius.
- The Chinese made many advances in learning and technology under the Han dynasty.

◆ Key Terms

Match each definition in Column I with the correct key term in Column II.

Column I

1. a kind of money
2. a fine yellow soil
3. a protective wall built along a river to hold back the waters
4. several generations of closely related people
5. a system of beliefs and values
6. a valuable cloth first made in China
7. a group of people who carry out the government's work
8. a local leader of armed groups

Column II

A extended family
B dike
C civil service
D loess
E currency
F philosophy
G warlord
H silk

┌ Vocabulary Builder ─────

Revisit this chapter's high-use words:

intense	rebellion
accomplishment	enable
communication	contact
professional	myth
harmony	availability
generally	

Ask students to review the definitions they recorded on their *Word Knowledge* worksheets.

All in One Unit 2 History of Our World Teaching Resources, *Word Knowledge,* p. 118

Consider allowing students to earn extra credit if they use the words in their answers to the questions in the Chapter Review and Assessment. The words must be used correctly and in a natural context to earn the extra points.

Review Chapter Content

- Review and revisit the major themes of this chapter by asking students to classify which Guiding Question each bulleted statement in the Chapter Summary answers. Have students work in groups to classify the statements. Use the Numbered Heads participation strategy (TE, p. T40) to have the groups share their answers in a group discussion. Refer to page 1 in the Student Edition for the text of the Guiding Questions.

- Assign *Vocabulary Development* for students to review Key Terms.

  All in One Unit 2 History of Our World Teaching Resources, *Vocabulary Development,* p. 127

Answers

Key Terms

1. E
2. D
3. B
4. A
5. F
6. H
7. C
8. G

Review and Assessment

Comprehension and Critical Thinking

9. (a) in the north, along the Huang River **(b)** Deserts, mountains, and seas were barriers to contact with civilizations to the west. **(c)** Other civilizations may not have considered themselves to be the center of the world but might have been influenced more by other cultures.

10. (a) They should set good examples and be respectful and just. **(b)** He believed that if authority figures set a good example, the people would follow, resulting in a stable, peaceful society. **(c)** Some of the wealthy, important, and powerful felt threatened. They would have to treat others fairly, face more competition for government jobs, and possibly lose some of their power. The Han dynasty thought his ideas were useful and incorporated them into the civil service system.

11. (a) Possible answers: He built the Great Wall for defense, built new roads to connect the empire, organized China into districts run by his trusted officials, standardized currency, weights and measurements, improved the system of writing and created a law code. **(b)** He killed or imprisoned his opponents and attempted to control his people's thoughts and beliefs by burning books and killing scholars. **(c)** Because of the harshness of the Qin dynasty, Liu Bang became a leader of a rebellion and eventually emperor of a new dynasty.

12. (a) stable government; a Confucian civil service; growth of the Chinese empire; prosperity; contact with the west via the Silk Road; advances in the arts, scholarship, and technology **(b)** It was a time of many achievements. **(c)** They are proud of the Han legacy and hope to continue the Han tradition of achievement.

13. (a) began in Xi'an, went west along the Great Wall, between the Gobi Desert and the Nan Shan, around the edge of the Takla Makan Desert, over the Pamir Mountains, through Persia and Mesopotamia, and ended in Antioch **(b)** Goods and ideas passed from trader to trader along the road. **(c)** It was the route by which they learned of the Chinese achievements.

Review and Assessment (continued)

◆ Comprehension and Critical Thinking

9. (a) Recall Describe the geographic setting of China's first known civilization.
(b) Infer Why did the early Chinese have so little contact with other ancient civilizations?
(c) Compare and Contrast Think about the other ancient civilizations you have read about. How were the earliest Chinese civilizations similar? How were they different?

10. (a) Describe According to Confucius, how should rulers and other people in authority behave?
(b) Explain Why did Confucius think his ideas were necessary and important?
(c) Analyze Information Some Chinese people thought the ideas of Confucius were dangerous. Who felt most threatened by his ideas? Explain why. How do we know that others found his ideas useful?

11. (a) Name Identify three actions the emperor Shi Huangdi took to unite China.
(b) Draw Conclusions Why is the rule of Shi Huangdi judged as harsh?
(c) Identify Causes How did the harsh rule of Shi Huangdi help bring about Liu Bang's rise to power?

12. (a) Describe What characterized the rule of the Han dynasty?

(b) Make Generalizations Why is the Han dynasty considered to be an important part of Chinese history?
(c) Make Inferences Why do people in China today call themselves "the children of Han"?

13. (a) Identify What was the route of the Silk Road?
(b) Explain How was the Silk Road used?
(c) Apply Information What was the importance of the Silk Road to other civilizations?

◆ Writing Activity: Language Arts

Reread the story about Confucius and the grieving woman on page 144. Many legends about Confucius were written by scholars long after his death. Use what you know about Confucius and China to write a similar brief story. Use his ideas about family or government to write the moral, or lesson, of the story.

◆ Skills Practice

Making Valid Generalizations Review the steps you followed to learn this skill. Then reread Traditional Families on page 140. Using the skills you learned, make a generalization about traditional families in ancient China. Use the steps you have learned to make sure your generalization is valid.

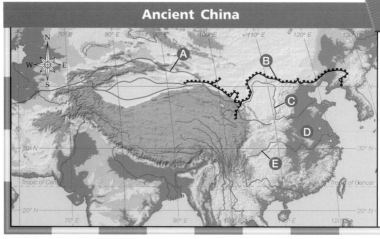

Ancient China

MAP MASTER™ Skills Activity

Place Location For each place listed below, write the letter from the map that shows its location.
1. Huang River
2. Chang River
3. North China Plain
4. Great Wall of China
5. Silk Road

Go Online
PHSchool.com Use Web Code **lbp-2544** for an **interactive map.**

Writing Activity: Language Arts
Student stories will vary but should include Confucius' ideas about respect, education, order, or proper behavior.
Use *Rubric for Assessing a Writing Assignment* to evaluate students' stories.

All in One Unit 2 History of Our World Teaching Resources, *Rubric for Assessing a Writing Assignment,* p. 128

Skills Practice
Students' answers will vary but should include a generalization and facts to support it. Sample answer: "Families in ancient China were very close." Facts that support this include: a household may have had as many as five generations living together, extended family members of rich families often lived in the same home, members of families living in farming villages lived within easy walking distance of one another.

Standardized Test Prep

Test-Taking Tips

Some questions on standardized tests ask you to analyze a graphic organizer. Study the concept web below. Then follow the tips to answer the sample question.

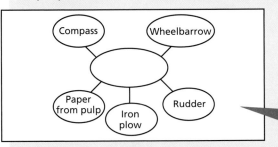

Choose the letter that best answers the question.

Which title should go in the center of the web?

A Gunpowder

B Inventions of Ancient Japan

C Inventions of Ancient China

D Technology

Think It Through The question asks for a title that describes all of the information in the smaller ovals. You can rule out A, because it does not describe all of the outer ovals. D could be a title, but it is not the *best* answer. To evaluate answers B and C, use your knowledge of history. Do you know where any of the items were first invented? If you recognize the origin of even one item shown in the web, then you know that the correct answer is C.

TIP When you study a chart or concept web, pay attention to the kind of information that goes in each part of it.

TIP Use what you already know about history, geography, government, and culture to help you answer the question.

Practice Questions

Use the tips above and other tips in this book to help you answer the following questions.

1. The Chinese called the Huang River China's Sorrow because
   A it was hard to navigate.
   B it flooded and destroyed property.
   C foreigners used it to invade China.
   D it carried no loess to use in farming.

2. What was the main goal of Confucianism?
   A to create original ideas
   B to produce written texts of philosophy
   C to bring order to society
   D to reward important people in society

3. Paper, the wheelbarrow, and iron farming tools were all invented during which dynasty?
   A the Qin   C the Shang
   B the Zheng   D the Han

Study the chart below and then answer the question that follows.

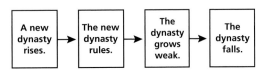

4. "Rulers lose control of the provinces" belongs under which of the headings above?
   A A new dynasty rises.
   B The new dynasty rules.
   C The dynasty grows weak.
   D The dynasty falls.

Use Web Code lba-2504 for **Chapter 5 self-test.**

Ancient Greece and Rome

Unit Overview

This unit covers classical civilizations in Greece and Rome. In Chapters 6 and 7, students will analyze the cultural contributions of classical Greece, including contributions in politics, science, arts and architecture, and intellectual life. They will also learn about daily life, culture, religion, government, and economy in ancient Greece. In Chapters 8 and 9, students will learn about key factors in the growth and expansion of the Roman Republic and trace the transformation of Rome from republic to empire. They will also learn about Roman cultural contributions, analyze the reasons for the decline and fall of the Roman Empire, and trace the beginnings of Christianity.

Monitoring Student Progress

After students have completed Chapter 9, administer Benchmark Test 3, the third of six benchmark tests provided to assess students' progress toward mastery of the National Geography Standards.

The Report Sheet for this test will identify which objectives or standards students have mastered and where they need additional work. It also correlates to the appropriate sections in the Reading and Vocabulary Study Guide, where students can get additional review as needed.

AYP Monitoring Assessment Resources

Determine students' progress toward mastery of the National Geography Standards.

📖 *Benchmark Test 3,* **AYP Monitoring Assessments,** pp. 93–98

Use the Report Sheet to identify which standards your students have mastered, where they need more work, and where they can get additional help.

📖 *Report Sheet, Benchmark Test 3,* **AYP Monitoring Assessments,** p. 127

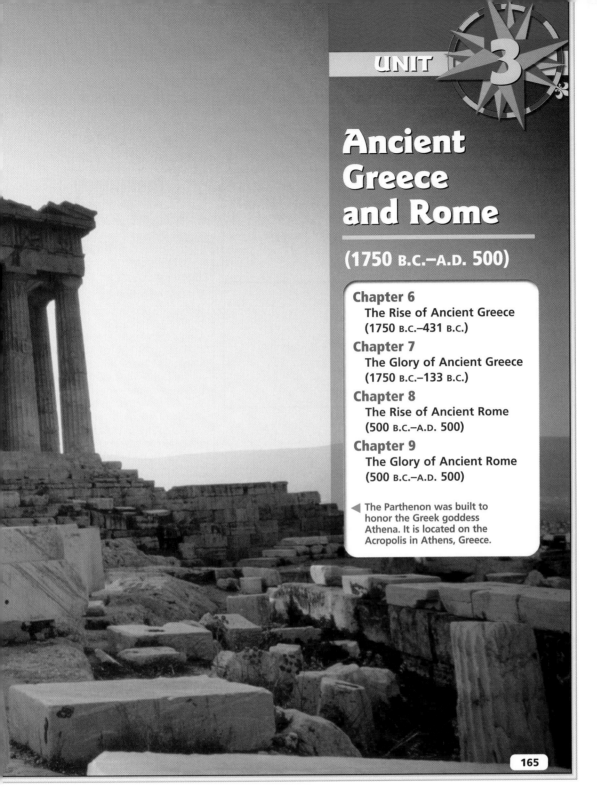

UNIT 3

Ancient Greece and Rome

(1750 B.C.–A.D. 500)

◄ The Parthenon was built to honor the Greek goddess Athena. It is located on the Acropolis in Athens, Greece.

165

Using the Visual

Ask students to study the picture on pp. 164–165. Have students read the caption on p. 165. Tell students that ancient Greeks made many lasting contributions to architecture. Point out the fluted columns of the Parthenon. Ancient Greek architects developed three kinds of columns: Doric, shown here, Ionic, and Corinthian. These columns have been used in Western architecture ever since. One of the most famous modern buildings to feature Doric columns is the Lincoln Memorial in Washington, D.C.

Overview

Section 1

The Rise of Greek Civilization

1. Understand how Greece's geographic setting influenced the development of Greek civilization.
2. Examine early Greek history.
3. Examine the development of democracy in Greece.

Section 2

Religion, Philosophy, and the Arts

1. Identify the religious beliefs of the ancient Greeks.
2. Explore how the Greeks searched for knowledge about the world.
3. Describe the relationship between the rise of democracy and the spread of new ideas in Greek city-states.

Discovery CHANNEL SCHOOL Video

Homer's Odyssey
Use with Section 1
Homer's 12,000-line epic tells the story of a mythical Greek warrior named Odysseus and his adventures as he struggles to return home to his kingdom of Ithaca. This segment relates part of the story of Odysseus' journey and how stories like these served an important purpose in ancient Greece. Such stories gave the Greeks an idea of what their gods were like and how their heroic mythical figures behaved.

Technology Resources

Go Online
PHSchool.com

Students use embedded web codes to access Internet activities, chapter self-tests, and additional map practice. They may also access Dorling Kindersley's Online Desk Reference to learn more about each country they study.

Interactive Textbook

Use the Interactive Textbook to make content and concepts come alive through animations, videos, and activities that accompany the complete basal text—online and on CD-Rom.

PRENTICE HALL
TeacherEXPRESS™
Plan • Teach • Assess

Use this complete suite of powerful teaching tools to make lesson planning and administering tests quicker and easier.

Reading and Assessment

Reading and Vocabulary Instruction

⟳ Model the Target Reading Skill

Sequence Tell students that the order in which significant events take place can help them understand and remember the events. Tell students that they can track the order of events by making a sequence chart.

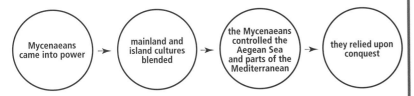

Model this skill aloud, showing students how to follow the sequenced steps. Point to the appropriate circle on the sequence chart as you model. Ask students to listen for the words or phrases that tell them a new event is coming.

Read aloud the paragraphs under The Mycenaneans.

Ask students what words or phrases let them know that a new event is coming and in what order the event comes. *(after, around 1400 B.C.)* Point out that these words are called Sequence Signal Words because they help you recognize sequence, or order in which events occur. Tell students that they can go through a similar process in their minds and use a similar chart when they are confronted with a confusing number of historical events.

Use the following worksheets from All-in-One Unit 3 Teaching Resources (pp. 13–14) to support this chapter's Target Reading Skill.

Vocabulary Builder
High-Use Academic Words
Use these steps to teach this chapter's high-use words.

1. Have students rate how well they know each word on their Word Knowledge worksheets (All-in-One Unit 3 Teaching Resources, p. 15).
2. Pronounce each word and ask students to repeat it.
3. Provide a brief definition or sample sentence (provided on TE pp. 169 and 181).
4. Work with students as they fill in the "Definition or Example" column of their Word Knowledge worksheets.

Assessment

Formal Assessment
Test students' understanding of core knowledge and skills.

Chapter Tests A and B, All-in-One Unit 3 History of Our World Teaching Resources, pp. 33–38

Customize the Chapter Tests to suit your needs.

Exam*View*® Test Bank CD-ROM

Skills Assessment
Assess geographic literacy.

MapMaster Skills, Student Edition, pp. 167, 190

Chart Skills, Student Edition, p. 183

Assess reading and comprehension.

Target Reading Skills, Student Edition, pp. 174 and 184

Chapter 6 Assessment, History of Our World Reading and Vocabulary Study Guide, p. 80

Performance Assessment
Assess students' performance on this chapter's Writing Activity using the following rubrics from All-in-One Unit 3 History of Our World Teaching Resources.

Rubric for Assessing a Student Poem, p. 31

Rubric for Assessing a Journal Entry, p. 32

Rubric for Assessing a Writing Assignment, p. 30

Rubric for Assessing a Letter to the Editor, p. 29

Assess students' work through performance tasks.

Small Group Activity: Write a Radio Play of a Greek Myth or Story, All-in-One Unit 3 History of Our World Teaching Resources, pp. 18–21

Online Assessment
Have students check their own understanding.

Chapter Self-Test

Section 1 The Rise of Greek Civilization

 3 periods, 1.5 blocks (includes Focus on Ancient Greek Theater and Skills for Life)

Social Studies Objectives

1. Understand how Greece's geographic setting influenced the development of Greek civilization.
2. Examine early Greek history.
3. Examine the development of democracy in Greece.

Reading/Language Arts Objective

Learn to identify sequence to make the order of events clear.

Prepare to Read	**Instructional Resources**	**Differentiated Instruction**
Build Background Knowledge Discuss photographs of Greece's geography. **Set a Purpose for Reading** Have students evaluate statements on the Reading Readiness Guide. **Preview Key Terms** Teach the section's Key Terms. **Target Reading Skill** Introduce the section's Target Reading Skill of identifying sequence.	**All in One Unit 3 History of Our World Teaching Resources** L2 Reading Readiness Guide, p. 6 L2 Word Knowledge, p. 15 L2 Identify Sequence, p. 13	**Spanish Reading and Vocabulary Guide** L1 Chapter 6, Section 1, pp. 54–55 ELL

Instruct	**Instructional Resources**	**Differentiated Instruction**
Greece's Geographic Setting Ask students questions that relate Greece's geography to its development as a country. **Greek Beginnings** Compare and contrast the Minoan and Mycenaean civilizations. **The Dark Ages of Greece** Discuss what happened during the Dark Ages and how Greece gradually began to change. **City-States Develop** Ask questions about how city-states developed. **Target Reading Skill** Review identifying sequence. **Democracy in Greece** Discuss democracy in Greece.	**All in One Unit 3 History of Our World Teaching Resources** L2 Guided Reading and Review, p. 7 L2 Reading Readiness Guide, p. 6 **History of Our World Transparencies** L2 Section Reading Support Transparency HOW 74	**Teacher's Edition** L1 For Special Needs Students, TE pp. 170, 179 L1 For English Language Learners, TE p. 171 L3 For Advanced Readers, TE p. 171 L3 For Gifted and Talented, p. 172 **Reading and Vocabulary Study Guide** L1 Chapter 6, Section 1, pp. 74–76 LPR, SN **Student Edition on Audio CD** L1 Chapter 6, Section 1 LPR, SN **Spanish Support** L2 Guided Reading and Review, p. 56 ELL

Assess and Reteach	**Instructional Resources**	**Differentiated Instruction**
Assess Progress Evaluate student comprehension with the section assessment and section quiz. **Reteach** Assign the Reading and Vocabulary Study Guide to help struggling students. **Extend** Extend the lesson by assigning students to write a journal entry.	**All in One Unit 3 History of Our World Teaching Resources** L2 Section Quiz, p. 8 L3 Enrichment, p. 16 **Reading and Vocabulary Study Guide** L1 Chapter 6, Section 1, pp. 74–76	**Spanish Support** L2 Section Quiz, p. 63 ELL

Key

L1 Basic to Average	L3 Average to Advanced	LPR Less Proficient Readers	GT Gifted and Talented
L2 For All Students		AR Advanced Readers	ELL English Language Learners
		SN Special Needs Students	

Section 2 Religion, Philosophy, and the Arts

 3 periods, 1.5 blocks

Social Studies Objectives

1. Identify the religious beliefs of the ancient Greeks.
2. Explore how the Greeks searched for knowledge about the world.
3. Describe the relationship between the rise of democracy and the spread of new ideas in Greek city-states.

Reading/Language Arts Objective

Learn to recognize and use sequence signal words to understand the order of events.

Prepare to Read	Instructional Resources	Differentiated Instruction
Build Background Knowledge Discuss the photographs of Greek works of art and talk about the headings in the section. **Set a Purpose for Reading** Have students evaluate statements on the Reading Readiness Guide. **Preview Key Terms** Teach the section's Key Terms. **Target Reading Skill** Introduce the section's Target Reading Skill of recognizing and using sequence signal words.	**All in One Unit 3 History of Our World Teaching Resources** **L2** Reading Readiness Guide, p. 10 **L2** Word Knowledge, p. 15 **L2** Recognize Sequence Signal Words, p. 14	**Spanish Reading and Vocabulary Guide** **L1** Chapter 6, Section 2, pp. 56–57 ELL

Instruct	Instructional Resources	Differentiated Instruction
The Golden Age of Athens Discuss what happened during Athens' Golden Age. **Ancient Greek Religious Beliefs** Discuss Greek religious beliefs. **The Search for Knowledge** Discuss how philosophers explained their world. **Target Reading Skill** Review how to recognize sequence signal words. **Visual and Dramatic Arts** Discuss why arts were important to the Greeks. **Many City-States, One People** Ask key questions about the rise of democracy.	**All in One Unit 3 History of Our World Teaching Resources** **L2** Guided Reading and Review, p. 11 **L2** Reading Readiness Guide, p. 10 **History of Our World Transparencies** **L2** Section Reading Support Transparency HOW 75 **History of Our World Video Program** Homer's Odyssey	**Teacher's Edition** **L1** For Less Proficient Readers, TE p. 180 **L1** For Special Needs Students, TE p. 183 **L3** For Advanced Readers, TE p. 185 **L3** For Gifted and Talented, TE p. 187 **Reading and Vocabulary Study Guide** **L1** Chapter 6, Section 2, pp. 77–79 LPR, SN **Student Edition on Audio CD** **L1** Chapter 6, Section 2 LPR, SN **Spanish Support** **L2** Guided Reading and Review, p. 58 ELL

Assess and Reteach	Instructional Resources	Differentiated Instruction
Assess Program Evaluate student comprehension with the section assessment and section quiz. **Reteach** Assign the Reading and Vocabulary Study Guide to help struggling students. **Extend** Extend the lesson by assigning the Enrichment.	**All in One Unit 3 History of Our World Teaching Resources** **L2** Section Quiz, p. 12 **L3** Enrichment, p. 16 **Reading and Vocabulary Study Guide** **L1** Chapter 6, Section 2, pp. 77–79	**Spanish Support** **L2** Section Quiz, p. 59 ELL **L2** Chapter Summary, p. 60 ELL **L2** Vocabulary Development, p. 61 ELL

Key

L1 Basic to Average   **L3** Average to Advanced

L2 For All Students

LPR Less Proficient Readers
AR Advanced Readers
SN Special Needs Students

GT Gifted and Talented
ELL English Language Learners

Professional Development

Reading Background

Geography Skills

Geography skills include the ability to ask geographic questions, acquire and analyze geographic information, and answer questions having to do with geography. To help students acquire these skills, make use of the map and MapMaster skills questions in this chapter.

Look at the map on page 167. The first question in the MapMaster Skills Activity asks students a lower-level question—to describe the geography of Greece. Point out the symbols on the map that indicate mountains. Ask students what other symbols on the map help them know about the geography of Greece.

The questions under **Draw Conclusions** in the MapMaster Skills Activity are higher-level questions that allow students to practice analyzing geographic information and to apply it to broader questions about a people. These questions—"What role did the sea have in their lives?" and "Why do you think some Greeks left ancient Greece to build cities elsewhere?"—ask students to draw conclusions based on their examinations of the map. Both questions also ask students to speculate. Tell students that when a question asks, "What do you think …?" it's an indicator that the student should make a guess based on what he or she already

knows or has learned from the material presented. For the second question, point out how little land the Greeks had—because of the mountains and sea—to grow food and raise animals. Knowing this fact will encourage students to consider why many of the Greeks found it necessary to emigrate.

Encourage Active Participation

In this chapter, students will use the Structured Silent Reading strategy to share their ideas. Pose a question such as "What was life like for people living in Greece 3,000 years ago?" Model how you would think while reading to find the answer to this question.

"Let's see. Did the geography of Greece affect what the people were like? The book says that most of the people in ancient Greece lived on islands or peninsulas. It also says that the land was mountainous. Probably the people were quite isolated, both from one another and from other countries. How would this isolation affect the people? I guess they wouldn't be counting on other people for much, so they'd have to learn to do everything themselves and in their own way. Relying only on themselves might make the people more independent and less willing to be told what to do by others. If they didn't have others telling them

World History Background

Theatrical Special Effects

Like their modern counterparts, Greek actors used special effects to make productions more exciting and dramatic. One technique was the use of two-faced masks that had a peaceful expression on one side and an angry or grotesque one on the other. Thus, with a sharp turn of the head, actors could get the attention of the audience with a sudden, and often terrifying, mood change. To create a "larger-than-life" look, performers wore boots with 10-inch soles and robes with flowing sleeves. Trap doors were used for dramatic exits, and various sound devices were used to re-create booms of thunder and cracks of lightning. With the aid of special cranes, actors playing gods were able to soar above the stage.

A Cynic's View

Today, people use the word *cynic* to describe someone who is jaded or distrustful. The Cynics, however, were not necessarily the ancient counterparts of today's curmudgeons. These Cynics belonged to a school of philosophy that developed in the 300s B.C. Cynics advocated moral virtue and a renunciation of worldly things, which were deemed to be the source of evil and unhappiness. To attain "freedom," Cynics reduced their possessions, their pleasures, and their relationships with other people as much as possible. Antisthenes, a founder of the Cynic school of philosophy and a student of Socrates, summarized the Cynic's goal when he said, "I would rather go mad than enjoy myself."

what to think, do, and believe, maybe they had to make up all those things by themselves—their own style of religion and government, as well as their own ways of protecting themselves.

On the other hand, because they were so close to the sea, maybe the people traveled to other places by ship. Maybe they traded with other countries in by sea and learned new ideas or spread their own ideas to other countries."

Point out that in this modeling you asked yourself questions and then answered them as you read. Challenge students to use this method when they are first learning about a new subject.

Numbered Heads Strategy

In this chapter, students will use the Numbered Heads strategy to devise and share their responses to questions. Numbered Heads allows students to become more confident of their individual responses by sharing them with a smaller group before facing the whole class. Because students are then called on at random to speak for the group, they alternate opportunities to take on a leadership role, and all students are responsible for paying attention to the team's ideas.

Remind students that it is a good idea to compare and contrast their responses with those of other teams. Below are sample language strategies to help students achieve this goal.

Our answer was (similar to/different from) that of team [blank] because [blank].
We agree with team [blank] that …
As team [blank] already mentioned, it seems that …
Team [blank] already mentioned…, but I would like to add that …

Using Oral Cloze

To ensure success with the Oral Close passage reading strategy, it is important to delete meaningful words that at least half of the class can read. Prepositions or connecting words don't work well with this technique. For example, in the first paragraph on page 184, try leaving out "responsible" (line 1), "disagreed," (line 2), and "understand" (line 4).

Plato

One of Socrates' most famous followers was Plato, an aristocrat from a powerful family. Plato founded a school called the Academy, which is considered by some to be the first university. Plato is best known for his philosophical works called *The Dialogues*. In many of the dialogues, Socrates appears as a character asking what other people's ideas of truth, justice, or beauty might be. In others, Plato seems to use Socrates as a spokesman for Platonian ideas, such as "living a virtuous life leads to happiness."

Socrates on Democracy

Socrates favored a system of government based on reasoning and knowledge, and he found Greek democracy to be seriously deficient. The men who served on the Council were chosen by lot. Socrates did not think that choosing officials by lot produced qualified leaders. Allowing everyone to vote on issues, whether or not they used proper reasoning, did not produce good laws. According to the Greek historian Xenophon, Socrates summed up the weakness of democracy this way:

"It is absurd to choose magistrates by lot where no one would dream of drawing lots for a pilot, a mason, a flute-player, or any craftsman at all, though the shortcomings of such men are far less harmful than those that disorder our government."

Infoplease© provides a wealth of useful information for the classroom. You can use this resource to strengthen your background on the subjects covered in this chapter. Have students visit this advertising-free site as a starting point for projects requiring research.

Use Web code **mud-0600** for **Infoplease©**.

Guiding Questions

Remind students about the Guiding Questions introduced at the beginning of the book.

Section 1 relates to **Guiding Question ❶** **How did physical geography affect the development and growth of societies around the world?** (*The location of Greece on mountainous islands and peninsulas led to the rise of independent Greek city-states that fostered fishing and trading rather than farming.*)

Section 2 relates to **Guiding Question ❸** **What were the beliefs and values of people in these societies?** (*The Greeks valued freedom, independence, beauty, and knowledge. These values led to their advancement in the arts, in democracy, in freedom of thought, and in philosophy.*)

⟳ Target Reading Skill

In this chapter, students will learn and apply the reading skill of identifying and using sequence. Use the following worksheets to help students practice this skill.

All in One Unit 3 History of Our World Teaching Resources, *Using Sequence,* Identify Sequence, p. 13; Recognize Sequence Signal Words, p. 14

Differentiated Instruction

The following Teacher's Edition strategies are suitable for students of varying abilities.
Advanced Readers, pp. 171, 185, 194
English Language Learners, pp. 171, 184
Gifted and Talented Students, pp. 172, 187
Less Proficient Readers, pp. 187, 194
Special Needs Students, pp. 170, 179, 183

Chapter 6 The Rise of Ancient Greece

Chapter Preview

This chapter will examine the rise of Ancient Greece and the development of democracy, philosophy, and the arts during the Golden Age of Athens.

Section 1
The Rise of Greek Civilization

Section 2
Religion, Philosophy, and the Arts

⟳ Target Reading Skill

Sequence In this chapter, you will focus on using sequencing to help you understand how events are related to one another. Sequencing helps you see the order in which events happened and can help you understand and remember them.

▶ The ruins of the Temple of Poseidon in Greece

166 History of Our World

— Bibliography —

For the Teacher

Moorehead, Caroline. *Lost and Found: The 9,000 Treasures of Troy: Heinrich Schliemann and the Gold that Got Away.* Viking, 1996.

Mee, Christopher, and Anthony Spanforth. *Greece: An Oxford Archaeological Guide.* Oxford University Press, 2001.

For the Student

L1 Middleton, Haydn. *Ancient Greek Jobs.* Heinemann Library, 2002.

L2 Sutcliff, Rosemary. *The Wanderings of Odysseus: The Story of the Odyssey.* Delacorte, 1996.

L3 Fleischman, Paul. *Dateline: Troy.* Candlewick Press, 1996.

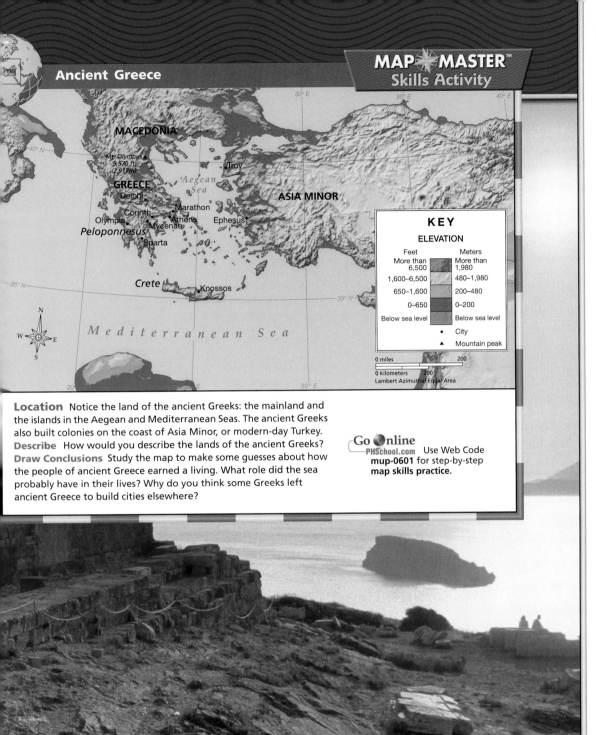

MAP MASTER™ Skills Activity

Ancient Greece

MACEDONIA

Mt. Olympus 9,570 ft (2,917m)

Troy

GREECE

Delphi

Aegean Sea

ASIA MINOR

Corinth
Marathon
Olympia • Athens
Mycenae • Ephesus
Peloponnesus
Sparta

Crete

Knossos

Mediterranean Sea

N
W E
S

KEY

ELEVATION

Feet		Meters
More than 6,500		More than 1,980
1,600–6,500		480–1,980
650–1,600		200–480
0–650		0–200
Below sea level		Below sea level

• City
▲ Mountain peak

0 miles 200
0 kilometers 200
Lambert Azimuthal Equal Area

Location Notice the land of the ancient Greeks: the mainland and the islands in the Aegean and Mediterranean Seas. The ancient Greeks also built colonies on the coast of Asia Minor, or modern-day Turkey.
Describe How would you describe the lands of the ancient Greeks?
Draw Conclusions Study the map to make some guesses about how the people of ancient Greece earned a living. What role did the sea probably have in their lives? Why do you think some Greeks left ancient Greece to build cities elsewhere?

Go Online PHSchool.com Use Web Code **mup-0601** for step-by-step map skills practice.

Chapter 6 **167**

MAP MASTER™ Skills Activity

■ Point out the shape of Greece and how it is made up of islands and peninsulas. Encourage students to trace its outline.

■ Ask students to look at a map to see on which continent Greece is located. *(Europe)* Ask if Greece is close to or far from most of the European countries that they know, such as France and Germany. *(It's quite far.)* Ask for the names of the seas close to Greece *(the Aegean and the Mediterranean Seas)* Ask students to speculate on how Greece's location might affect the country and its people. *(Greece is quite isolated, which perhaps makes it more independent; most Greek occupations had to do with the sea.)*

Go Online PHSchool.com Students may practice their map skills using the interactive online version of this map.

Using the Visual   L2

Reach Into Your Background Ask students to study the photograph on pages 166 and 167 and to read the caption on page 167. Ask them to note details about the image, then share their ideas with the class. Ask **Why do you think the ancient Greeks built a temple for Poseidon?** Point out that the ancient Greeks worshipped gods and goddesses and that Poseidon was the god of the sea. Ask students if they can relate this image to their own lives.

Answers

MAP MASTER™ Skills Activity **Describe** The Greek lands consisted of islands or peninsulas and were very mountainous. **Draw Conclusions** Possible answer: The sea figured largely in their lives for fishing, trade, and travel. Perhaps the Greeks left their land because it was too small.

Chapter Resources

Teaching Resources
L2 Vocabulary Development, p. 28
L2 Skills for Life, p. 17
L2 Chapter Tests A and B, pp. 33–38

Spanish Support
L2 Spanish Chapter Summary, p. 60
L2 Spanish Vocabulary Development, p. 61

Media and Technology
L1 Student Edition on Audio CD
L1 Guided Reading Audio CD, English and Spanish L2
L2 Social Studies Skills Tutor CD-ROM
Exam*View*® Test Bank CD-ROM

Discovery CHANNEL **SCHOOL** History of Our World Video Program

interactive Textbook
PRENTICE HALL

TeacherEXPRESS™
Plan • Teach • Assess

Objectives

Social Studies

1. Understand how Greece's geographic setting influenced the development of Greek civilization.
2. Examine early Greek history.
3. Examine the development of democracy in Greece.

Reading/Language Arts

Identify the order, or sequence, in which events take place in order to understand and remember them.

Prepare to Read

Build Background Knowledge L2

Tell students that in this section they will learn how Greece's geography affected its development as a civilization. Have them look at the photograph on page 169. Ask **What does this photograph reveal about Greece's geography?** Use the Idea Wave participation strategy (TE, p. T39) to generate responses. (*Possible answers: Greece is surrounded by water; therefore, the sea must be very important to its development. The land also looks very mountainous.*)

Set a Purpose for Reading L2

- Preview the Objectives.

- Read each statement in the *Reading Readiness Guide* aloud. Ask students to mark the statements true or false.

  All in One **Unit 3 History of Our World Teaching Resources,** *Reading Readiness Guide*, p. 6

- Have students discuss the statement in pairs or groups of four, and then mark their worksheets again. Use the Numbered Heads participation structure (TE, p. T40) to call on students to share each group's perspectives.

Vocabulary Builder
Preview Key Terms L2

Pronounce each Key Term, and then ask the students to say the word with you. Provide a simple explanation, such as "An epic might tell the story of a famous battle or hero in poetry rather than in prose."

Section 1 **The Rise of Greek Civilization**

Prepare to Read

Objectives

In this section you will
1. Understand how Greece's geographic setting influenced the development of Greek civilization.
2. Examine early Greek history.
3. Examine the development of democracy in Greece.

Taking Notes

As you read, find the main ideas and details concerning the rise of Greek civilization. Copy the chart below, and use it to record your findings.

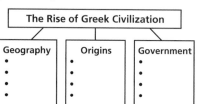

The Rise of Greek Civilization

Geography	Origins	Government
•	•	•
•	•	•
•	•	•
•	•	•

Target Reading Skill

Identify Sequence

Noting the order in which events take place can help you understand and remember them. You can track the order of events by making a sequence chart. In the first box, write the first event, or the development that sets the other events in motion. Then write each additional event in a box. Use arrows to show how one event leads to the next.

Key Terms

- **peninsula** (puh NIN suh luh) *n.* an area of land nearly surrounded by water
- **epic** (EP ik) *n.* a long poem that tells a story
- **acropolis** (uh KRAH puh lis) *n.* a high, rocky hill where early people built cities
- **city-state** (SIH tee stayt) *n.* a city with its own traditions, government, and laws; both a city and a separate independent state
- **aristocrat** (uh RIS tuh krat) *n.* a member of a rich and powerful family
- **tyrant** (TY runt) *n.* a ruler who takes power with the support of the middle and working classes
- **democracy** (dih MAHK ruh-see) *n.* a form of government in which citizens govern themselves

Following their defeat of the Titans, Zeus and his brothers and sisters battled the giants. The gods Apollo and Artemis, above left, confront a group of helmeted giants.

First there was nothing. Then came Mother Earth. The gods of Night and Day appeared next, and then the starry Sky. Earth and Sky created the Twelve Titans (TYT unz). These great gods rebelled against their father Sky and took away his power. The youngest of the Titans, Cronos (KROH nus), ruled in his father's place. In time, Cronos had six children. The youngest, mighty Zeus (zoos), toppled Cronos from his throne.

With such stories, the people of ancient Greece described the struggles of their gods. Like their gods, the people of Greece had to struggle for power and independence. Their struggles began with the land itself.

Target Reading Skill L2

Identify Sequence Point out the Target Reading Skill. Tell students that they can keep track of what happens in a story or non-fiction writing by paying attention to the sequence of events, or the order in which events happen.

Have students write the numbers 1–5 on a blank piece of paper and then list the sequence of events in A New Type of Ruler, p. 174: (*Sequence of events: 1. Greeks traded in foreign ports. 2. The city-states became richer. 3. A middle class of merchants developed. 4. Members of the middle class were able to arm themselves with weapons and armor. 5. Military strength shifted to the middle class.*)

Give students *Identify Sequence*. Have them complete the activity in groups.

All in One **Unit 3 History of Our World Teaching Resources,** *Identify Sequence*, p. 13

Greece's Geographic Setting

The land of Greece looks as if the sea had smashed it to pieces. Some pieces have drifted away to form small, rocky islands. Others barely cling to the mainland. Greece is a country made up of peninsulas. A **peninsula** is an area of land surrounded by water on three sides. Look at the map titled *Ancient Greece*. As you can see, no part of Greece is very far from the sea.

Mountains are the major landform of Greece. Greece's islands are mostly mountain peaks. Mountains wrinkle the mainland, so there are only small patches of farmland. Only about one fifth of Greece is good for growing crops. No wonder the Greeks became traders and sailors. At times, they left Greece to found colonies far away.

What was life like for people living in Greece 3,000 years ago? In a way, the ancient Greeks were all islanders. Some lived on real islands completely surrounded by water or on small peninsulas. Others lived on what could be thought of as land islands. Instead of water, mountains separated these small communities from one another. The geography of Greece made it hard for people from different communities to get together.

For this reason, it is no surprise that ancient Greek communities thought of themselves as separate countries. Each one developed its own customs and beliefs. Each believed its own land, traditions, and way of life were the best. And each was more than ready to go to war to protect itself. In fact, for most of their history, the Greeks were so busy fighting among themselves that it is easy to forget that they shared a common heritage, spoke the same language, and worshiped the same gods.

✓ **Reading Check** What do we mean when we say the ancient Greeks were all islanders?

Greece's Coastline
Several typical geographic features appear in this picture of the northwestern coast of Greece. These features include a rocky coastline and rugged mountains. **Critical Thinking** *How did the geographic features shown affect the way ancient people lived in this area?*

Chapter 6 Section 1 **169**

Vocabulary Builder

Use the information below to teach students this section's high-use words.

High-Use Word	Definition and Sample Sentence
heritage, p. 169	*n.* something transmitted by or acquired from a predecessor The Greeks' **heritage** includes a love of freedom and democracy.
impact, p. 170	*n.* a compelling effect Greece's geography has had a great **impact** on the way the society developed.
vibrant, p. 170	*adj.* lively The marketplace was a **vibrant** scene.

Greek Beginnings

Guided Instruction

- **Vocabulary Builder** Clarify the high-use words **impact** and **vibrant** before reading.

- Tell students to read Greek Beginnings. Ask them to look for the impact that the ancient Minoan and Mycenaean civilizations had on Greece. Ask students **Compare and contrast the Minoan and Mycenaean civilizations.** *(Possible answer: The Minoans, located on the island of Crete in the middle of the Mediterranean Sea, become a trading center. The Mycenaeans also used their location to control the seas. However, the Minoans gained power through trade, while the Mycenaeans did so through conquest. The Minoan culture encouraged beautiful artwork and worshipped goddesses. Both cultures made use of writing.)*

- Tell students that they will also learn about one of the most famous military tricks in history as they read the section The Trojan War. Ask them to pay close attention to how, centuries later, we know about this trick. Ask students **Explain how the story of the Trojan War survived until our day.** *(It was a legend that was passed down by word of mouth from one generation to another. Probably many poets helped compose it; however, the Greek poet Homer is credited with being the one to actually write it down.)*

Independent Practice

Have students continue to fill in the chart with details about Greek beginnings.

Monitor Progress

Allow students to continue filling in their charts. Circulate to make sure that students fill in the correct details.

Answers

Conclude Archaeological finds show it.

Greek Beginnings

Early Greek civilization arose on and off the Greek mainland. Two ancient peoples, the Minoans (mih NOH unz) and the Mycenaeans (my suh NEE unz), made an important impact on Greek history.

Early Greek Cultures
The fresco from the 1500s B.C., shown below, illustrates Minoan naval combat. A Mycenaean princess appears in the above photo. **Conclude** *How do we know that both the Minoans and the Mycenaeans developed advanced cultures?*

Minoan Civilization From about 3000 to about 1100 B.C., Bronze Age people called the Minoans lived on the island of Crete (kreet). Washed by the waters of the Aegean (ee JEE un) and Mediterranean Seas, Crete was an ideal place for the Minoans to develop a broad sea trade network. Mainland Greece and other Greek islands, as well as Egypt and Sicily, traded with the Minoans, who at one time dominated the Aegean. Archaeological finds show that the Minoans had developed a vibrant culture. Samples of Minoan writing have been found on thousands of clay tablets. A grand palace once stood in the ancient Crete city of Knossos (NAHS us). Palace ruins hint at rooms once covered with fanciful wall paintings. Various statues found within suggest that the Minoans worshiped goddesses. In the middle of the 1400s B.C., Knossos was destroyed, and Minoan civilization declined. People from mainland Greece, the Mycenaeans, were the likely invaders.

170 History of Our World

Differentiated Instruction

For Special Needs Students `L1`
Help students review the information about the Minoan and Mycenaean civilizations by drawing a chart on the chalkboard. Write "Minoan civilization" and "Mycenaean civilization" at the top of two columns. Ask students a question, such as "When did the Minoans live?" Direct them to find the answer in the text and then write the answer under the heading "Minoan civilization" on the chalkboard. Proceed in this manner until all the important facts about these two civilizations are listed on the board. Alternatively, students may draw their own charts and fill in the information as the class answers the questions.

The Mycenaeans After the Mycenaeans came into power, mainland and island cultures blended. However, the focus of these cultures moved to the mainland, where the city of Mycenae was located. At the height of their power, around 1400 B.C., the Mycenaeans controlled the Aegean Sea and parts of the Mediterranean. Like the Minoans, the Mycenaeans also used writing. Studies of the Mycenaeans' script show that they spoke an early form of modern Greek.

The Minoans had gained much of their power through trade. Although the Mycenaeans traded widely, they relied upon conquest to spread their power.

The Trojan War Greek myth tells the story of the Trojan War, a long struggle between Greece and the city of Troy on the west coast of Asia Minor, in present-day Turkey. It's possible that Mycenaean warriors inspired this legend.

According to the myths, the Greeks conquered Troy by using a trick—the Trojan Horse. Greek warriors hid inside a huge wooden horse. The horse was rolled to the city gates. Thinking it was a gift, the Trojans brought the horse into their city. During the night the Greek soldiers climbed out of the horse and let the rest of their army into Troy. The Greeks burned and looted Troy and then returned home.

Two **epics,** or long story-telling poems, about the Trojan War survive today. They are the *Iliad* (IL ee ud) and the *Odyssey* (AHD ih see). These epics may have been composed by many people, but they are credited to a poet called Homer. The poems were important to the Greeks. They taught them what their gods were like and how the noblest of their heroes behaved. Today, people think these poems came from stories memorized by several poets and passed down by word of mouth through many generations. Homer may have been the last and greatest in this line of poets who told about the Trojan War.

Most historians agree that the Trojan War did not happen exactly as Homer described it. Some believe that Homer's epics were inspired by a long battle between the Greeks and Trojans, but others argue that the epics were inspired by a series of minor battles. Troy was destroyed by a large fire in the mid-1200s B.C., an act that some historians believe may have been committed by invaders from Greece.

✓ Reading Check Contrast how Minoans and Mycenaeans spread their power.

Learn about two classic Greek epics.

Links to Science

Troy Discovered Over the years, people came to believe that Troy and the Trojan War were fiction. An amateur archaeologist, Heinrich Schliemann (HYNrik SHLEE mahn), disagreed. In the late 1800s he used clues in the *Iliad* to pinpoint the location of Troy. When he and later archaeologists dug there, they found nine layers of ruins from ancient cities. One was possibly the Troy of the *Iliad* and the *Odyssey*.

Show students *Homer's Odyssey*. Ask **What purpose did stories like the *Iliad* and the *Odyssey* serve in Ancient Greece?** (*They gave the Greeks an idea of what their gods were like and how their heroic mythical figures behaved.*)

Links

Read the **Links to Science** on this page. Ask students: **What did Heinrich Schliemann want to prove? What did his explorations uncover?** (*Schliemann wanted to prove that Troy was an actual place. He found nine layers of ruins from ancient cities.*)

Differentiated Instruction

For English Language Learners L1
Organize students into groups. Each group should have some proficient English speakers and some English learners. Have each group find a scene from either the *Iliad* or the *Odyssey* to read and present to the class. Give students various options for presentation. You may wish to videotape students' presentations.

For Advanced Readers L3
Provide copies of the *Odyssey* for students. Have them read a section and write questions about what they read. Then form them into groups and have them ask the questions they wrote. Ask each group: What was the purpose of the various stories about Odysseus? What does the *Odyssey* tell the Greeks?

Answers

✓ Reading Check Minoans gained their power through trade, while Mycenaeans gained it through conquest.

The Dark Ages of Greece

Guided Instruction

- Read the second paragraph of The Dark Ages of Greece with students using the Choral Reading Technique (TE, p. T38). Point out that the legends and history of Greece were kept alive during the Dark Ages by chanting in a way similar to their reading out loud.

- Discuss what life was like for the Greeks during their Dark Ages. (*The people were poor and no longer traded outside their own country. They forgot how to write and kept traditions alive by word of mouth. Some people moved to more fertile areas to be able to grow crops.*)

- Ask students to tell how and where Greek villages developed. Have them explain why they were built in these places. (*The villages developed from family farms. They were built near fortified hills, or acropolises, for safety.*)

Independent Practice

Assign *Guided Reading and Review*.

All in One **Unit 3 History of Our World Teaching Resources,** *Guided Reading and Review,* p. 7.

Monitor Progress

Circulate to see if students need any assistance with the *Guided Reading and Review* worksheet and provide help where needed.

Answers

Timeline Skills **Identify** About 3000 B.C. **Analyze** Mycenaen culture was located on mainland Greece; Minoan culture was located on an island.

✓ **Reading Check** Students' answers should mention that the people who remained in Greece during the Dark Ages became more isolated and poor and concentrated on survival. Writing was lost and traditions and history were passed down only by word of mouth. Many people relocated to be able to farm and eventually began to create villages from farms.

Beginnings of Ancient Greek Culture: 3000 B.C.–750 B.C.

about 1450 B.C. Fire destroys many towns and palaces on Crete.

Mid-1200s B.C. Troy is destroyed by fire.

3000 B.C. — 2500 B.C. — 2000 B.C. — 1500 B.C. — 1000 B.C. — 500 B.C.

about 3000 B.C. Minoan culture begins to flourish on the island of Crete.

about 1600 B.C. Mycenaean culture begins to flourish in Mycenae on mainland Greece.

about 1200 B.C. Mycenaean civilization collapses, possibly because of invasion.

1100s–750 B.C. Dark Ages in Greece.

■ Timeline Skills

Two ancient peoples, the Minoans and the Mycenaens, made an important impact on Greek history.
Identify Where and when did Minoan culture begin to flourish? **Analyze** How did the location of Mycenaean culture differ from the location of the Minoan culture?

Pottery painting of a Greek cobbler

The Dark Ages of Greece

Not long after the end of the Trojan War, civilization in Greece collapsed. No one knows exactly why. Life went on, but poverty was everywhere. People no longer traded for food and other goods beyond Greece. They had to depend on what they could raise themselves. Some were forced to move to islands and to the western part of Asia Minor. They were so concerned with survival that they forgot the art of writing.

These years, from the early 1100s B.C. to about 750 B.C., have been called Greece's Dark Ages. Without writing, people had to depend on word of mouth to keep their traditions and history alive. Old traditions were remembered only in the myths that were told and retold.

Greece's Dark Ages were not completely bleak. During this time, families gradually began to resettle in places where they could grow crops and raise animals. Some of these family farms may have developed into villages. When they chose where to build their farms, people favored places near rocky, protected hills. Here they built structures to protect them from attack. The name for such a fortified hill was **acropolis,** meaning "high city."

After 800 B.C., people in Greece began writing again. It was during this period that Homer is believed to have recorded in writing his epic about the Trojan War.

✓ **Reading Check** What happened during Greece's Dark Ages?

172 History of Our World

Differentiated Instruction

For Gifted and Talented Students **L3**
Some particularly artistic students may wish to re-create a model of an acropolis. Students may wish to discuss with the art teacher what materials to use for their model. Remind them that the hills were fortified with soldiers and fort-like structures and that farms or small villages were clustered at the bottom.

Temple of Artemis

The Temple of Artemis at Ephesus was the largest of all ancient Greek buildings. The temple was considered one of the seven wonders of the ancient world. In 1869 British archaeologist John Turtle Wood uncovered the remains of the temple. His discovery marked the first time an ancient Greek site had been excavated, or uncovered. Ancient Greeks worshipped Artemis as the goddess of wild animals and the hunt.

Ruins of the Temple
Fragments of marble are all that remain of the Temple of Artemis, located in present-day Turkey.

A triangular area called a pediment topped the two end walls of Greek temples. The Temple of Artemis had a pediment decorated with statues of female warriors called Amazons.

A giant statue of Artemis stood in an inner chamber of the temple.

A carving of the head of Medusa, a legendary monster with snakes for hair, decorated the front of the temple.

The columns stood more than 60 feet (18 meters) high. They numbered 127 in all.

ANALYZING IMAGES
How was the outside of the temple decorated?

Background: Links Across Time

The Lincoln Memorial Like the Temple of Artemis in Ephesus, the Lincoln Memorial in Washington, D.C., has impressive Greek-style architecture. Its 36 Doric columns soar to 44 feet. The Lincoln Memorial houses a huge statue. The seated white marble figure of Abraham Lincoln, carved by Daniel Chester French, is 19 feet tall and weighs around 120 tons. In 1963, Martin Luther King delivered his "I Have a Dream" speech from the steps of the Lincoln Memorial. Students can see a replica of the memorial on the back of a U.S. penny.

Temple of Artemis

Guided Instruction　L2
Have students study the diagram of the temple and read the callouts. Help students compare the photograph of the ruins with the diagram. Then put the size of the temple into a more easily understood context. For example, rooms in most modern homes have eight-foot ceilings, so each column in the temple was about as tall as 7 1/2 rooms stacked one on top of the other.

Independent Practice
Have students create a concept web with *Exploring Technology* written in the center. In each empty circle, students should write a topic for further exploration, based on information found as they read. For each topic, ask students to write one question for which they would like to find an answer. Model one example: "I wrote John Turtle Wood in one circle. My question is: What tools did Wood use to discover the temple ruins?" Encourage students to write questions related to technology. When students have finished their webs, ask them to share their questions with the class.

Extend　L3
Have volunteers each pick one of the topics from the web, conduct research to find the answer to the question, and report their findings to the class.

Answer
ANALYZING IMAGES Possible answers: Decorations include columns, carvings, and statues.

City-States Develop

Guided Instruction
- Have students read City-States Develop. Ask them to look for the two types of rulers in Greece as they read.

- Discuss how the Greek villages developed into powerful city-states. *(The villages that formed when farms joined together created cities when several of these villages joined together for protection near the fortified acropolises. The cities began to develop their own laws.)*

- Ask students to tell how and where Greek villages developed. Have them explain why they were built in these places. *(The villages developed from family farms. They were built near fortified hills, or acropolises, for safety.)*

Target Reading Skill

Identify Sequence As a follow up, ask students to answer the Target Reading Skill question in the Student Edition. (Make sure students list the sequence of events.)

Democracy in Greece

Guided Instruction
- Have students read how democracy developed in Democracy in Greece.

- Discuss what democracy was like in Greece. *(Possible answer: Free men over eighteen had the right to debate important laws and participate fully in government.)*

- Explain why democracy was more developed in Athens than in the other city-states. *(The Athenian leader Solon reformed laws that made government and economy more fair and democratic.)*

Answers

Analyze Aristocrats controlled most of the good land and could afford horses, chariots, and the best weapons.

√ **Reading Check** Tyrants

City-States Develop

Historians believe that sometime around 750 B.C., villages in a small area probably joined to form a city in the shadow of an acropolis. At that time, each city began to develop its own traditions and its own form of government and laws. Today, we call these tiny nations city-states. A **city-state** is not only a city, but also a separate independent state. Each city-state included a city and the villages and fields surrounding it. Hundreds of Greek city-states grew up, each more or less independent.

Identify Sequence What important changes led to the development of city-states in Greece?

Aristocracy: Nobles Rule The earliest rulers of city-states were probably chieftains or kings who were military leaders. By the end of Greece's Dark Ages, most city-states were ruled by **aristocrats,** members of the rich and powerful families. Aristocrats controlled most of the good land. They could afford horses, chariots, and the best weapons to make themselves stronger than others.

A New Type of Ruler As the Greeks sailed to foreign ports trading olive oil, marble, and other products, the city-states became richer. A middle class of merchants and artisans developed. They wanted some say in the government of their cities. These people could not afford to equip themselves with horses and chariots for war. However, they could afford armor, swords, and spears. With these weapons, large groups of soldiers could fight effectively on foot. Gradually, military strength in the cities shifted from aristocrats to merchants and artisans.

As a result of these changes, aristocratic governments were often overthrown and replaced by rulers called tyrants. A **tyrant** was a ruler who seized power by force. Tyrants were usually supported by the middle and working classes. Today, we think of tyrants as being cruel and violent. That was true of some Greek tyrants, but others ruled wisely and well.

√ **Reading Check** What kind of ruler often replaced aristocratic governments?

The Aristocrats
Some wealthy ancient Greeks owned chariots. **Analyze** *How did the aristocrats use their wealth to gain power?*

174 History of Our World

Background: Links Across Time

A Citizen's Lot In Athenian democracy, all male citizens voted in the Assembly. From this group, 500 were chosen by lot to serve for one year on the Council, a decision-making body. Jury members for court trials were also chosen by lot. But, as in modern democracies, some officials were elected. The 10 generals who formed the Board of Generals were elected by the Assembly.

Democracy in Greece

Eventually, the people of many city-states overthrew tyrants. Some of the cities adopted a form of government called democracy. In a **democracy**, citizens govern themselves. The city-state in which democracy was most fully expressed was Athens.

About 594 B.C., a wise Athenian leader called Solon (SOH lun) won the power to reform the laws. Solon was well known for his fairness. His laws reformed both the economy and the government of Athens. One of his first laws canceled all debts and freed citizens who had been enslaved for having debts. Another law allowed any male citizen of Athens aged 18 or older to have a say in debating important laws. These laws and others allowed Athens to become the leading democracy of the ancient world.

Not everyone living in ancient Athens benefited from democracy. Only about one in five Athenians was a citizen. To be a citizen, a man had to have an Athenian father and mother. Some of the people living in Athens were enslaved. These people did not take part in democracy, nor did women or foreigners. Men who were citizens of Athens were free and self-governing.

✓ **Reading Check** Why did some Athenians benefit more from democracy than others?

Tools of Democracy
Athenians used a machine to help select juries. A colored ball, top, dropped into an allotment machine, bottom, would fall at random next to the slots containing names of potential jurors. In the middle is a voting tablet used in Athens. **Infer** *How do you think voting helped to strengthen Athenian democracy?*

⬥ Section 1 Assessment

Key Terms
Review the key terms listed at the beginning of this section. Use each term in a sentence that explains its meaning.

Target Reading Skill
Place these events in the correct order: rise of the city-state, height of Minoan civilization, Greek Dark Ages.

Comprehension and Critical Thinking
1. (a) **Recall** Describe the geographic setting of ancient Greece.

(b) **Predict** What effect do you think the geography of Greece had on the kind of communities that developed there?
2. (a) **Recall** Describe early Greek civilization.
(b) **Make Generalizations** How were the Minoan and Mycenaean civilizations similar?
3. (a) **Identify** What two kinds of government first developed in the Greek city-states after the Greek Dark Ages?
(b) **Cause and Effect** How did the rise of the middle class help shape government in ancient Greece?

Writing Activity
Write a description of the conditions in Greece during the period between the 1100s B.C. and the 700s B.C. Why are these years referred to as Greece's Dark Ages?

For: An activity on the Trojan War
Visit: PHSchool.com
Web Code: mud-0610

Chapter 6 Section 1 **175**

Comprehension and Critical Thinking
1. (a) It was mountainous and surrounded by water. **(b)** Possible answer: They would develop the kind of livelihoods that had to do with the sea.

2. (a) Answers will vary. **(b)** Both developed trade networks and writing.

3. (a) city-states and tyranny **(b)** The people wanted a say in government.

Writing Activity
Use the *Rubric for Assessing a Writing Assignment* to evaluate students' stories.

All in One **Unit 3 History of Our World Teaching Resources,** *Rubric for Assessing a Writing Assignment,* p. 30

Go Online PHSchool.com Typing in the Web code will bring students directly to detailed instructions for this activity.

Ask students to complete the graphic organizer.

Monitor Progress
Show *Section Reading Support Transparency HOW 74.* Ask students to check their graphic organizers. Review key concepts and vocabulary.

📖 **History of Our World Transparencies,** *Section Reading Support HOW 74*

Tell students to complete the *Reading Readiness Guide.*

All in One **Unit 3 History of Our World Teaching Resources,** *Reading Readiness Guide,* p. 6

Answers

Infer Male citizens could in influence how Athens was governed.

✓ **Reading Check** Democracy did not apply to enslaved people, women, and foreigners.

Assess and Reteach

Assess Progress L2
Have students complete the Section Assessment. Administer the *Section Quiz.*

All in One **Unit 3 History of Our World Teaching Resources,** *Section Quiz,* p. 8

Reteach
If students need more instruction, have them read this section in the Reading and Vocabulary Study Guide.

📖 Chapter 6, Section 1, **History of Our World Reading and Vocabulary Study Guide,** pp. 74–76

Extend
Ask students to research and write a journal entry about life in ancient Athens.

All in One **Unit 3 History of Our World Teaching Resources,** *Rubric for Assessing a Journal Entry,* p. 32

Section 1 Assessment

Key Terms
Students' sentences should reflect knowledge of each Key Term.

⬥ **Target Reading Skill**
1) height of Minoan civilization, 2) Greek Dark Ages, 3) rise of city-states

Focus on Ancient Greek Theater

Guided Instruction

Hand out or have students create a three-column **K-W-L** chart. Tell students that the items on the board represent what the class **K**nows about modern drama. Tell students they will be reading about drama in ancient Greece, and ask them to fill in the **W**ant-to-know column on their charts. Then have students study the text and illustrations on these pages, filling in the **L**earn column as they read.

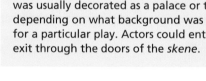

Focus On
Ancient Greek Theater

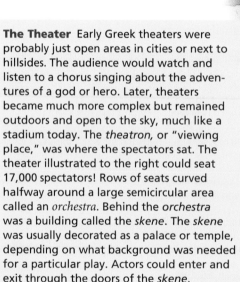

Drama was an important part of Greek culture. Many Greek plays were tragedies. These were often based on myth and were solemn and poetic. The main character was usually a good but imperfect person faced with a difficult choice. His or her struggles usually ended in death. Comedies dealt with well-known people and problems of the day. Greek plays were performed by only a few actors who played several roles. Instead of makeup, actors wore masks to indicate the kind of characters they played. A chorus danced, chanted, and commented on the action.

The Theater Early Greek theaters were probably just open areas in cities or next to hillsides. The audience would watch and listen to a chorus singing about the adventures of a god or hero. Later, theaters became much more complex but remained outdoors and open to the sky, much like a stadium today. The *theatron,* or "viewing place," was where the spectators sat. The theater illustrated to the right could seat 17,000 spectators! Rows of seats curved halfway around a large semicircular area called an *orchestra.* Behind the *orchestra* was a building called the *skene.* The *skene* was usually decorated as a palace or temple, depending on what background was needed for a particular play. Actors could enter and exit through the doors of the *skene.*

Differentiated Instruction

For English Language Learners 〔L1〕
Have students describe for the class how plays or festivals are presented in their native cultures. Encourage them to use the English terms in their description, such as *mask, chorus,* or *orchestra,* if appropriate.

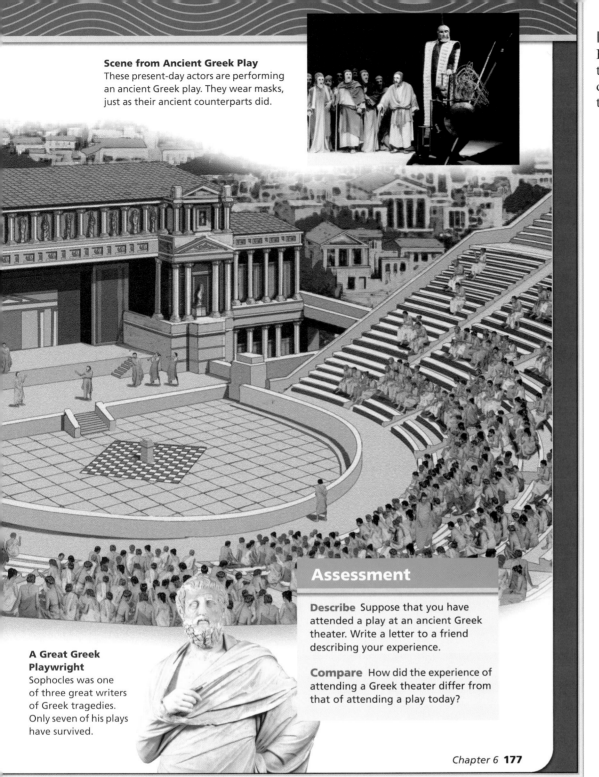

Scene from Ancient Greek Play
These present-day actors are performing an ancient Greek play. They wear masks, just as their ancient counterparts did.

A Great Greek Playwright
Sophocles was one of three great writers of Greek tragedies. Only seven of his plays have survived.

Assessment

Describe Suppose that you have attended a play at an ancient Greek theater. Write a letter to a friend describing your experience.

Compare How did the experience of attending a Greek theater differ from that of attending a play today?

Chapter 6 **177**

Background: Links Across Time

Projecting Sound Modern actors use electronic sound equipment to ensure that everyone in the audience can hear them. But how were actors in ancient Greece able to project their voices so that large audiences could hear them? Some scholars think actors' masks focused their voices much as megaphones do. Others say that the acoustics in existing ancient theaters are so good that even a whisper on stage can be heard in the last row of seats.

Independent Practice   L1
Have students locate unfamiliar words in the text and create a glossary of theater terms, defining the words by looking at their use in the text.

Answers

Assessment

Describe Descriptions will vary, but should accurately depict the experience of attending a Greek play, including the stage, the actors, the costumes, the chorus, and the seating for the audience.

Compare Remind students to use their descriptions and **KWL** charts as they discuss how modern plays have roots in ancient Greek theater.

Objective

Learn to draw conclusions from clues and experience.

Prepare to Read

Build Background Knowledge L2

Have students read the heading and look at the visuals. Then ask a volunteer to role-play the opening scene with you. Ask: **Can you recall experiences that were similar to Lisa's? How might this skill be used both in and out of school?** Have students use Lisa's experience to suggest the steps that drawing conclusions might require. Record these on the chalkboard.

Instruct

Drawing Conclusions L2

Guided Instruction

- Have students read the Learn the Skill, using the Oral Cloze technique (TE, p. T37). Then ask a volunteer to draw and complete the drawing conclusions graphic organizer on the board. Ask students to find each component in Lisa's efforts.

- Practice the skill by taking students through the Learn the Skill steps on page 178. Explain the importance of carefully examining one's personal knowledge for information that is relevant. You might model removing the specific context (Athens) from the sentence—*How did people feel about drama?*—is easier to check against students' own experiences.

- Have students complete diagrams about a possible event such as an upcoming test or project, noting clues and a conclusion.

Independent Practice

Assign the *Skills for Life* worksheet, and have students complete it individually.

All in One **Unit 3 History of Our World Teaching Resources,** *Skills for Life,* Drawing Conclusions, p. 17

Skills for Life — Drawing Conclusions

Greek actor's mask

> The teacher looked at Lisa and asked, "How did the people of Athens feel about drama?"
>
> Lisa had read the assignment, but there wasn't anything in the book about how Athenians felt about drama. She did remember a few facts, though. "They had a lot of theaters and put on a lot of plays. They had play-writing contests. So I guess if they had so many plays, drama must have been pretty important to them."

Like Lisa, when you draw a conclusion, you figure out something based on the information you have read or seen. Drawing conclusions is a skill that will help you benefit from your schoolwork and anything you read.

Learn the Skill

Use these steps to learn how to draw a conclusion:

1. **Gather factual information about the topic.** Find out as many factual details as you can by reading about your topic and then talking with people who know about the subject.

2. **Combine the facts with other information you already know.** Add the information you find in your research to what you already know.

3. **Write a conclusion that follows logically.** A conclusion is usually an educated guess.

178 History of Our World

Monitor Progress

Monitor students as they complete the *Skills for Life* worksheet, checking to make sure that they understand the skills steps.

Practice the Skill

Turn to page 171, and reread the first four paragraphs of text in the main column. Use this information to draw conclusions about the Trojan War.

1 The text tells you about the people who may have inspired the legend of the war. It tells where the war was fought, and it describes the heroes, how they fought, and how the story was handed down to us. Choose one of these topics. Write down facts about that topic.

2 Combine whatever facts you already know with the facts you have just read. You might know something about stories of other wars or about how people react to war stories.

3 Try to form an educated guess about your topic—something that is not specifically stated in the text. Your conclusion might answer a question starting with *why*. For instance: Why has the history of the Trojan War fascinated so many people through the centuries? Check your conclusion to make sure it is supported by the facts.

Apply the Skill

Turn to page 175, and reread the paragraphs titled Democracy in Greece. Use facts from that text plus facts you already know to draw conclusions about American democracy.

The Trojan horse inside the ancient city of Troy

Assess Progress L2
Ask students to do the Apply the Skill Activity, making sure they are able to answer the Apply the Skill questions.

Reteach L1
If students are having trouble applying the skill steps, have them review the skill using the Social Studies Skills Tutor CD-ROM.

 Drawing Conclusions, **Social Studies Skills Tutor CD-ROM**

Extend L3
Have each student find an article in a newspaper or magazine about current events and use the skill steps to draw conclusions from facts in the article.

Differentiated Instruction

For Special Needs Students L1
Pair special needs students with more proficient students. Have the pairs work together to complete Level 1 of the *Drawing Conclusions* lesson on the Social Studies Skills tutor CD-ROM. When special needs students feel more confident, they can move on to Level 2 by themselves.

 Drawing Conclusions, **Social Studies Skills Tutor CD-ROM**

Answers
Apply the Skill

Students' conclusions should be based on their prior knowledge of democracy, such as the fact that citizens elect people to govern. Students should demonstrate that they have used both prior knowledge and clues from their reading to draw other conclusions about democracy in America.

Section 2
Step-by-Step Instruction

Objectives

Social Studies

1. Identify the religious beliefs of the ancient Greeks.
2. Explore how the Greeks searched for knowledge about the world.
3. Describe the relationship between the rise of democracy and the spread of new ideas in Greek city-states.

Reading/Language Arts

Recognize sequence signal words to keep the relationships among ideas or events clear.

Prepare to Read

Build Background Knowledge **L2**

Have students look at the photographs in this section. Point out that the ancient Greeks' admiration for beauty is evident in their works of art. Tell them that this section will describe the Greeks' love of the arts, as well as for other things they admired. Have students look at the headings in this section. Ask them, based on the headings and the photographs and ideas they learned about Greece in Section 1, what other attributes the Greeks valued. Use the Think-Write-Pair-Share participation strategy (TE, p. T40).

Set a Purpose for Reading **L2**

■ Preview the Objectives.

■ Form students into pairs or groups of four. Distribute the *Reading Readiness Guide*. Ask students to fill in the first two columns of the chart. Use the Numbered Heads participation structure (TE, p. T40) to call on students to share one piece of information they already know and one piece of information they want to know.

All in One **Unit 3 History of Our World Teaching Resources,** *Reading Readiness Guide,* p. 10

Vocabulary Builder
Preview Key Terms **L2**

Pronounce each Key Term, and then ask the students to say the word with you. Provide a simple explanation such as "tribute is money that a powerful state makes a weaker state give to the powerful state."

Section 2
Religion, Philosophy, and the Arts

Prepare to Read

Objectives

In this section you will
1. Identify the religious beliefs of the ancient Greeks.
2. Explore how the Greeks searched for knowledge about the world.
3. Describe the relationship between the rise of democracy and the spread of new ideas in Greek city-states.

Taking Notes

As you read, look for details about the religion, philosophy, and the arts of the ancient Greeks. Use a copy of the outline below to record your findings.

> I. The Golden Age of Athens
>   A. Period from 479 to 431 B.C.
>   B. Sources of wealth
>   1.
>   2.
>   3.
> II. Ancient Greek religious beliefs

Target Reading Skill

Recognize Sequence Signal Words Signals point out relationships among ideas or events. This section discusses life in the Golden Age of Athens. To help keep the relationship between leaders, thinkers, and writers clear, look for words like *first, at that time,* and *in [date]* that signal the order in which these people were active.

Key Terms

• **tribute** (TRIB yoot) *n.* a payment made by a less powerful state or nation to a more powerful one

• **immortal** (ih MAWR tul) *n.* someone or something that lives forever
• **oracle** (AWH uh kul) *n.* in ancient Greece, a sacred site used to consult a god or goddess; any priest or priestess who spoke for the gods
• **philosopher** (fih LAHS uh fur) *n.* someone who used reason to understand the world; in Greece the earliest philosophers used reason to explain natural events
• **tragedy** (TRAJ uh dee) *n.* a type of serious drama that ends in disaster for the main character

Pericles led the Athenians in peace and war. The helmet he wears reminds us that he was a skilled general.

180 History of Our World

The Athenian leader Pericles (PEHR uh kleez) reminded the citizens that Athens was unique.

> **Our constitution does not copy the laws of neighboring states. We are a pattern to other cities rather than imitators. Our constitution favors the many instead of the few. That is why it is called a democracy. If we look at the laws, we see they give equal justice to all. . . . Poverty does not bar the way, if a man is able to serve the state. . . . In short, I say that as a city we are the school for all Greece.**
>
> — The History of the Peloponnesian War
> *Thucydides*

Pericles' words had special meaning: They were spoken during the first year of a war with Sparta, another Greek city-state. Eventually, it was conflict with Sparta that ended Athens' golden age of accomplishment.

Target Reading Skill **L2**

Recognize Sequence Signal Words Point out the Target Reading Skill. Tell students that they can keep clear the order in which events take place by looking for words, such as *first, later, next, still,* and *in (a certain date),* that signal time.

Have students list the signal words in The Parthenon, p. 186. *(Sequence Signal Words: Today, in 480 B.C., long ago, still)*

Give students *Recognize Sequence Signal Words.* Have them complete the activity in groups.

All in One **Unit 3 History of Our World Teaching Resources,** *Recognize Sequence Signal Words,* p. 14

The Golden Age of Athens

The years from 479 B.C. to 431 B.C. are called the Golden Age of Athens. During the Golden Age, Athens grew rich from trade and from silver mined by slaves in regions around the city. **Tribute,** or payments made to Athens by its allies, added to its wealth.

Athenians also made important achievements in the arts, philosophy, and literature, and democracy reached its high point. For about 30 years during the Golden Age, Pericles was the most powerful man in Athenian politics. This well-educated, intelligent man had the best interests of his city at heart. When he made speeches to the Athenians, he could move and persuade them.

Pericles was a member of an aristocratic family, but he supported democracy. Around 460 B.C., he became leader of a democratic group. He introduced reforms that strengthened democracy. The most important change was to have the city pay a salary to its officials. This meant that poor citizens could afford to hold public office.

One of the greatest accomplishments under the rule of Pericles was the construction of the Parthenon (PAHR thuh nahn) between 447 and 432 B.C. The construction of the Parthenon was part of the general reconstruction of the Acropolis at Athens. Many of the buildings there had been destroyed by invaders from Persia about three decades earlier. The Parthenon was a temple built to honor the patron, or protector, of Athens, the goddess Athena.

✔ **Reading Check** How did Pericles strengthen democracy?

An ancient Athenian silver coin bearing an owl, a symbol of the city

A vase depicting citizenship in Athens

Chapter 6 Section 2 **181**

Vocabulary Builder

Use the information below to teach students this section's high-use words.

High-Use Word	Definition and Sample Sentence
imitator, p. 180	*n.* one who is or appears to be similar The Romans have been **imitators** of Greek art.
shrine, p. 183	*n.* a place in which devotion is paid to a saint or god The temples were **shrines** to various gods.
influential, p. 185	*adj.* having the power to sway or affect based on position, ability, wealth, or prestige Socrates' ideas were very **influential** among the youth of Athens.

Instruct

The Golden Age of Athens

Guided Instruction

- **Vocabulary Builder** Clarify the high-use word **imitator** before reading.

- Have students read The Golden Age of Athens, using the Structured Silent Reading technique (TE, p. T38). Make sure students can answer the Reading Check after they read.

- Discuss what happened during the period of Athens' Golden Age. (*Athens grew rich from trade, silver, and tributes. It made great achievements in the arts, philosophy, and democracy.*)

- Ask students how they think Athens' wealth might be related to its achievements in the arts. Have them compare the art in the Golden Age to that of Greece's Dark Ages discussed in the last section. (*Possible answer: Wealth gave the Athenians more time to devote to the arts. During the Dark Ages, people spent time just trying to survive. They had no time for the arts.*)

Independent Practice

Ask students to create the Taking Notes outline on a blank piece of paper. Have them fill in the blanks under the heading "The Golden Age of Athens" with the information they have just learned. Briefly model how to identify which details to record.

Monitor Progress

As students fill in the outline, circulate and make sure individuals are choosing the correct details. Provide assistance as needed.

Answers

✔ **Reading Check** Pericles passed reforms that strengthened democracy, such as paying salaries to officials, which meant that even poor citizens could hold office.

Ancient Greek Religious Beliefs

Guided Instruction

- **Vocabulary Builder** Clarify the high-use word **shrine** before reading.

- Tell students to read Ancient Greek Religious Beliefs. Ask them to read to find out whom the Greeks worshipped and what these beings were like.

- Discuss with students the Greeks' religious beliefs. *(Possible answer: The Greeks worshipped twelve gods led by Zeus, the king of the gods. They also worshipped lesser gods and honored heroes in similar ways. They believed their gods showed them how to behave, and they visited oracles to receive advice from them.)*

- Ask students to describe the characteristics of the Greek gods. Have them explain how the gods differed from humans. *(The gods had human forms and human characteristics. Unlike humans, however, they were immortal and immensely powerful.)*

Ancient Greek Religious Beliefs

Greeks worshiped a family of gods and goddesses called the Twelve Olympians (oh LIM pea unz). Each ruled different areas of human life and the natural world. The chart titled "A Family of Gods" gives you more information about some of the Olympians.

The Greeks took great care when honoring their gods. They wished to give thanks and to receive blessings. They also tried to avoid angering the gods.

Gods and Goddesses Wherever the Greeks lived, they built temples to the gods. Because the gods had human forms, they also had many human characteristics. The main difference between gods and humans was that the gods were **immortal**, which meant they lived forever. They also had awesome power.

Mythology tells us that the Greeks worshiped gods led by Zeus, the king of the gods. From Mt. Olympus, Greece's highest mountain, Zeus ruled the gods and humanity. In addition to worshiping gods, the Greeks also honored mythical heroes like Achilles (uh KIL eez), whose great deeds are told in the *Iliad*.

Although the Greeks worshiped all their gods, each city-state honored one of the twelve gods, in part by building a temple to that god. Athena (uh THEE nuh), for example, was the patron goddess of Athens. The Greeks also honored their gods by holding festivals and by sacrificing animals and offering food to the gods. To honor Zeus, the city-states came together every four years for an Olympian festival and games. Modern Olympic Games are based on this tradition.

Poseidon, Athena, Apollo, and Artemis are shown in this relief.

 Skills Mini Lesson

Identifying Frame of Reference and Point of View L2

1. Teach the skill by explaining that point of view is an opinion or perspective on a topic and frame of reference is a person's background. Frame of reference often affects a person's perspective.

2. Help students practice the skill by asking them to identify the point of view of a slave visiting an oracle in ancient Greece.

3. Have students apply the skill by identifying an aristocrat's frame of reference when visiting the same oracle.

Delphi
The Tholos Temple at the Sanctuary of Athena Pronaia was once the gateway to Delphi. In the vase painting, Aegeus, a legendary Athenian king, consults a priestess at Apollo's oracle in Delphi. **Conclude** *Why did the ancient Greeks visit oracles?*

The Oracles In ancient cultures, people often looked to their gods for signs or advice. They wanted the gods to show them how to live or how to behave. The Greeks visited **oracles,** sacred sites where it was believed the gods spoke. At these shrines, the people would ask the gods to give them advice or to reveal the future. Sometimes the advice came through dreams. Often a response would come in the form of a riddle, delivered by priests or priestesses thought to be capable of hearing the voice of the gods. Oracles of various gods were located throughout Greece. Heads of state often sought advice on governing and wars from the oracle of the god Apollo at Delphi (DEL fy), an ancient town in central Greece. Because such advice was taken very seriously, the oracles had a great impact on Greek history.

✓ **Reading Check** How did the Greeks honor their gods?

■ Chart Skills

The Greeks believed the world was ruled by gods and goddesses. Ten of them are listed in the table below. **Identify** Who was considered to be the leader of all gods and goddesses? **Analyze** Why do you think this chart is titled "A Family of Gods?"

A Family of Gods

Zeus (zoos)	Ruler of all gods and humanity
Hera (HIHR uh)	Goddess of marriage and childbirth
Apollo (uh PAHL oh)	God of music, poetry
Artemis (AHR tuh mis)	Goddess of hunting
Athena (uh THEE nuh)	Goddess of wisdom and war
Ares (EHR eez)	God of war
Aphrodite (af ruh DY tee)	Goddess of love
Hermes (HUR meez)	Messenger of the gods
Poseidon (poh SY dun)	God of earthquakes and the ocean
Demeter (dih MEE tur)	Goddess of fertility

- Ask students what the purpose of the oracles was. (*The oracles were places where the people could communicate with their gods. People sought advice or asked to have the future revealed.*)

Independent Practice

- Ask students to continue filling in the Taking Notes outline that they began in The Golden Age of Athens. Have them fill in the blanks under the heading Ancient Greek Religious Beliefs with the information they have learned.

Monitor Progress

As students fill in the outline, circulate and make sure individuals are choosing the correct details.

Answers

Conclude to ask their gods for signs or advice

✓ **Reading Check** Possible answer: The Greeks honored their gods by building temples to them, by holding festivals in their names, by sacrificing animals to them, and by offering them food. For the god Zeus, the Greeks banded together and celebrated with the Olympic Games.

Chart Skills **Identify** Zeus
Analyze The gods and goddesses are all related.

Differentiated Instruction

For Special Needs Students ▪ L1

Organize students in small groups that contain both special needs students and more proficient students. Have more proficient students from each group research a Greek myth. Then have them assign parts to all members of the group and practice acting out the myth. It is not necessary for all students to have speaking parts. Have them dress in costumes such as those pictured in the text. When students are ready, have each group present the myth for the whole class.

The Search for Knowledge

Guided Instruction

- **Vocabulary Builder** Clarify the high-use words **influential** before reading.

- Read the first two paragraphs of The Search for Knowledge with students using the Oral Cloze technique (TE, p. T37).

- Discuss how the Greeks searched for knowledge about their world. *(The Greek philosophers were good observers and thinkers. They had ideas about the world that they taught to other people.)*

- Have students identify the system of explaining natural events that philosophy challenged. *(Philosophy challenged the mythological belief that the gods controlled everything in nature.)*

Target Reading Skill

Recognize Sequence Signal Words As a follow up, ask students to answer the Target Reading Skill question in the Student Edition. *(The words that signal that Democritus lived in the same century as Pericles are "who lived in the 400s B.C.")*

Answers

Conclude They distrusted Socrates because he encouraged Athenian youth to question beliefs.

Recognize Sequence and Signal Words
What words signal that Democritus lived in the same century as Pericles?

The Search for Knowledge

Most Greeks believed that their gods were responsible for all natural events. But a few thinkers disagreed. About 150 years before the Golden Age of Athens, some people thought about new ways to understand the world.

Greek Science and Philosophy You learned earlier about philosophy, which is a system of beliefs or values. **Philosophers** believed that people could use the powers of the mind and reason to understand natural events. One of the first philosophers, Thales (THAY leez), believed that water was the basic material of the world. Everything was made from it. Over the years, various philosophers had other ideas about the universe. They did not do experiments. But they were careful observers and good thinkers. Democritus (dih MAHK ruh tus), who lived in the 400s B.C., thought that everything was made of tiny particles he called atoms. More than 2,000 years later, modern science showed that he had been correct.

Socrates During the Golden Age and later, several important philosophers taught in Athens. One was a man called Socrates (SAHK ruh teez). People in the marketplace of Athens could not help but notice this sturdy, round-faced man. He was there at all hours of the day, eagerly discussing wisdom and goodness.

Socrates wanted people to consider the true meaning of qualities such as justice and courage. To do this, he asked questions that made others think about their beliefs. Sometimes they became angry because Socrates often showed them that they didn't know what they were talking about. "Know thyself" was his most important lesson.

Death of Socrates
Socrates urged his students to question and critically examine all around them. For "corrupting the youth" in this way, an Athenian jury sentenced him to death. **Conclude** *Why do you think some people believed Socrates corrupted the youth of Athens?*

Differentiated Instruction

For English Language Learners L2
Have students support the target reading skill by reading the following passage.

"Jack and Francesca wanted to write a report on Socrates. First, they found information on Socrates on the Internet and in the library. Next, they narrowed down their topic by asking each other questions and deciding which part of Socrates' life to cover. Then, they took notes on the subject. Finally, they were ready to present their report in class. Last Thursday, they gave the report and earned a good grade." Have students identify words that are sequence signal words. *(Sequence signal words: First, Next, Then, Finally, Last Thursday)*

In 399 B.C., Socrates was brought to trial. The authorities accused him of dishonoring the gods and misleading young people. He was sentenced to death by forced suicide, a common sentence in Athens at the time. Socrates drank a cup of hemlock, a poison, and died.

Plato and Aristotle Much of what is known about Socrates comes from the writings of Plato (PLAY toh), one of his students. Socrates' death caused Plato to mistrust democracy. In *The Republic,* Plato wrote that society should be made up of three groups: workers, soldiers, and philosopher-rulers. Plato founded a school in Athens called the Academy, where he taught a student named Aristotle (AR uh staht ul). Aristotle believed that reason should guide the pursuit of knowledge. He later founded his own school, the Lyceum.

✓ **Reading Check** How did Socrates challenge the values of the people of Athens?

■ Ask **What was the significance of Plato's contribution to the search for knowledge?** *(Plato founded a school in which astronomy, mathematics, biology, and other subjects were taught. It was probably the first university.)*

Independent Practice

Ask students to continue their outlines by creating the next heading: III. The Search for Knowledge. Have them write beneath that heading the information they have just learned.

Monitor Progress

As students fill in the outline, circulate and make sure individuals are choosing the correct details.

Differentiated Instruction

For Advanced Readers   L3
Have students discuss what they think "know thyself" means. Remind them to use what they have just read about Socrates as well as their own experiences to draw a conclusion about what "know thyself" means. After the discussion, have each student write an essay in which he or she tells why knowing oneself is an important goal.

Answers

✓ **Reading Check** Possible answer: Socrates made people think about important values and beliefs. His method was to use questions that often showed that people didn't know what they were talking about. Some thought this questioning showed a lack of belief in the gods and worried that his teachings would cause the young men who listened to him to stop believing in the gods.

Visual and Dramatic Arts

Guided Instruction

- Have students read the Visual and Dramatic Arts section. Tell them to look for the kinds of visual and dramatic arts for which the Greeks are famous.

- Discuss why the arts were important to the Greeks and what kind of arts flourished during Greece's Golden Age. *(The Greeks used the arts to honor their gods. The Greeks are especially known for their sculpture, architecture, and drama.)*

- Ask students to explain how Greek comedies differed from Greek tragedies. *(Tragedies told of humans faced with dilemmas that eventually destroyed them. A chorus was used to sing or chant background information. Comedies made fun of Greek customs and famous people.)*

Independent Practice

Ask students to continue their outlines by creating item IV. Visual and Dramatic Arts. Have them write beneath that heading the information they have just learned.

Monitor Progress

As students fill in the ouline, circulate and make sure individuals are choosing the correct details.

Links

Read the **Links to Math** on this page. Ask **Why did the Greeks use the Golden Rectangle in designing their buildings?** *(They thought Golden Rectangles made the buildings more pleasing to the eye.)*

Links to Math

The Golden Rectangle
Greek architects based the design of their buildings on a figure called the Golden Rectangle. A Golden Rectangle is one with the long sides about one and two-thirds times the length of the short sides. The Greeks thought Golden Rectangles made buildings more pleasing to look at. Modern architects have also used the Golden Rectangle.

The Acropolis
Once the religious center of Athens, the Acropolis now serves as a monument to Greek architecture.
① The Propylaia, the entrance to the Acropolis, was completed in 432 B.C.
② The Odeion (theater) of Herodes Atticus was built in A.D. 161.
③ The Erechtheion, named after a legendary king of Athens, was completed in 406 B.C.
④ Completed in 438 B.C., the Parthenon served as a temple to Athena, the patron goddess of Athens.
Predict *Why do you think the Athenians built the Acropolis?*

Visual and Dramatic Arts

The ancient Greeks devoted great attention to their arts. The Greeks used visual arts, such as architecture and sculpture, to glorify and honor their gods. The ancient Greeks are also known as the first playwrights, people who write dramas.

The Parthenon Today, the Athenian leader Pericles is probably best known for making Athens a beautiful city. The Acropolis, the religious center of Athens, had been destroyed in 480 B.C., during one of the city's many wars. Pericles decided to rebuild the Acropolis and create new buildings to glorify the city.

The builders of the new Acropolis brought Greek architecture to its highest point. Their most magnificent work was the Parthenon, a temple to the goddess Athena. The temple was made of fine marble. Rows of columns surrounded it on all four sides. Within the columns was a room that held the statue of Athena, made of wood, ivory, and gold. The statue rose 40 feet (12 m), as high as a four-story building.

The great statue of Athena disappeared long ago. However, much of the sculpture on the inside and outside of the temple still exists. Many of the scenes that decorate the Parthenon have three important characteristics. First, they are full of action. Second, the artist carefully arranged the figures to show balance and order. Third, the sculptures are lifelike and accurate. However, they are ideal, or perfect, views of humans and animals. These characteristics reflect the goal of Greek art. This goal was to present images of perfection in a balanced and orderly way.

Background: Links Across Time

Influence of Greek Art Greek art had a strong influence on both Roman and Hellenistic art. But by the Middle Ages, the Greek influence was no longer apparent in European painting and sculpture. Art during the Middle Ages was almost exclusively devoted to Christian religious themes. Portrayals of human figures were stiff, stylized, and unrealistic. This style of art remained the norm until the 1300s, when the works of the Italian painter Giotto heralded a return to classical ideals. In Giotto's paintings, human beings look more lifelike and are shown as expressive and emotional.

Answers

Predict They wanted a showcase of Greek architecture.

Dramas In addition to their achievements in architecture and sculpture, Athenians were the first people known to write dramas. Among the city's greatest achievements were the plays written and produced in the 400s B.C., during the Golden Age.

Some of the most famous Greek plays were tragedies. A **tragedy** is a serious story that usually ends in disaster for the main character. Often, tragedies told of fictional humans who were destroyed when forced to make impossible choices. A Greek tragedy consisted of several scenes that featured the characters of the story. Between the scenes, a chorus chanted or sang poems. In most plays, the author used the chorus to give background information, comment on the events, or praise the gods.

Comedies During the 400s B.C. in Athens, poets wrote comedies that made fun of well-known citizens and politicians and also made jokes about the customs of the day. Because of the freedom in Athens, people accepted the humor and jokes.

Greek actors performed in outdoor theaters, such as the one shown above at Epidauros. By using different masks, such as the one at top, actors could play a variety of roles.

✓ **Reading Check** What was the role of the chorus in Greek drama?

Many City-States, One People

Guided Instruction

- Have students read Many City-States, One People using the Structured Silent Reading technique. (TE, p. T38).

- Discuss how the rise of democracy contributed to the development of new ideas in Greece. (*The value Greeks placed on their freedom extended to freedom to explore new ideas.*)

- Ask students to explain how the Greek city-states could be so independent and compete against one another and yet have so much in common. (*They thought of themselves as the same people—they were the Hellenes, they spoke the same language, and they had many customs in common.*)

Independent Practice

Have students create an item V. on their outline titled "Greek City-States" and fill it in with information they have just learned to complete their graphic organizers.

Monitor Progress

Show *Section Reading Support Transparency HOW 75*, and ask students to check their outlines individually. Review key concepts and clarify key vocabulary as needed.

📖 **History of Our World Transparencies,** *Section Reading Support Transparency HOW 75*

Tell students to fill in the last column of the *Reading Readiness Guide*. Ask them to decide whether they learned what they had expected to learn.

All in One **Unit 3 History of Our World Teaching Resources,** *Reading Readiness Guide,* p. 10

Answers

✓ **Reading Check** The chorus chanted or sang poems between scenes. The chorus commented on events in the play, praised the gods, or gave background information.

Differentiated Instruction

For Less Proficient Readers L1

Assign small groups of students to read one paragraph on this page. Have groups select four words in the paragraph that they think are difficult. Have students discuss the words to see if they can acquire clues to their meaning from context clues or prior experience with each word. Then have group members teach their words to the other groups.

For Gifted and Talented L3

Point out that many American structures have been influenced by the architecture of the ancient Greeks. Have students locate pictures of ancient Greek theaters, temples, and other structures. Ask students to discuss why they think people still use the styles of architecture of a civilization that is more than 2,000 years old.

Assess and Reteach

Assess Progress

L2

Have students complete the Section Assessment. Administer the *Section Quiz*.

All in One **Unit 3 History of Our World Teaching Resources**, *Section Quiz*, p. 12

Reteach

If students need more instruction, have them read this section in the Reading and Vocabulary Study Guide.

Chapter 6, Section 2, **History of Our World Reading and Vocabulary Study Guide**, pp. 77–79

Extend

Have students learn more about ancient Greece by completing *Enrichment*.

All in One **Unit 3 History of Our World Teaching Resources**, *Enrichment*, p. 16

Answers

✓ **Reading Check** Education and wealth gave ancient Greeks freedom to explore new ideas.

Section 2 Assessment

Key Terms
Students' sentences should reflect knowledge of each Key Term.

Target Reading Skill
The words that signal time are "about 150 years before the Golden Age of Athens," "lived in the 400s B.C.," and "in 399 B.C."

Comprehension and Critical Thinking
1. (a) Answers will vary, but students should show their understanding that Athens made important contributions to arts, science, and philosophy. It was also a time that democracy was strengthened in Athens. **(b)** Possible answer: Athens was the center of intellectual activity.

2. (a) Possible answer: At first, the Greeks explained the world through myths. Then philosophers began questioning the old explanations and came up with their own ideas about the universe, based on their observations. **(b)** Socrates meant that people should understand themselves and what they think and believe before they try to influence others.

Many City-States, One People

The citizens of Greek city-states such as Athens had strong patriotic feelings and valued their freedoms. For these reasons, they took a very active role in their government. They were able to develop new ideas in philosophy, religion, government, and the arts in part because of the value they placed on free thinking. The spread of education and growing wealth through trade with Egypt, Sicily, and other places gave the Greeks the freedom to explore new ideas.

Though Athens was the most important city-state, it was not the only one in Greece at this time. City-states in Greece competed against one another, but their citizens spoke the same language and had many of the same customs. They thought of themselves as part of the same people, calling themselves Hellenes.

One example of the common culture of the city-states was the Olympic Games, which were held every four years throughout ancient Greece. The first recorded Olympic Games were held in 776 B.C. Other Olympic Games were held fairly regularly over the next thousand years. Athletes from city-states around Greece competed for prizes in competitions in running, horse racing, boxing, and many other events.

Aristides, a general at the Battle of Marathon, writes his name for someone who wants him banished from Athens. Inset photo is of a voting tablet used in Aristides' trial.

✓ **Reading Check** What role did education and growing wealth play in the development of philosophy and the arts in ancient Greece?

Section 2 Assessment

Key Terms
Review the key terms listed at the beginning of this section. Use each term in a sentence that explains its meaning.

Target Reading Skill
Review the section "The Search for Knowledge" on pages 184–185. Find the words that signal time related to the lives of the philosophers.

Comprehension and Critical Thinking
1. (a) Define What was the Golden Age of Athens?
(b) Draw Conclusions Why do you think Pericles called Athens "the school of all Greece"?
2. (a) Explain How did the Greeks attempt to understand the world?
(b) Explore Details What did Socrates mean when he said, "Know thyself"?
3. (a) Explain What characteristics did people in city-states throughout Greece share?
(b) Infer How did the growth of wealth through trade contribute to the spread of new ideas in Greece?

Writing Activity
Write a brief essay describing the achievements of Athenians during the Golden Age.

For: An activity on Greek architecture
Visit: PHSchool.com
Web Code: mud-0620

---

3. (a) The people spoke the same language and shared customs. They valued freedom and took active part in government. They contributed to developments in the arts, sciences, government, and religion.
(b) Possible answer: Trade brought citizens of city-states in contact with ideas from other places.

Writing Activity
Use the *Rubric for Assessing a Writing Assignment* to evaluate students' essays.

All in One **Unit 3 History of Our World Teaching Resources**, *Rubric for Assessing a Writing Assignment*, p. 30

Go Online PHSchool.com Typing in the Web code will bring students directly to detailed instructions for this activity.

Review and Assessment

◆ Chapter Summary

Section 1: Early Greek Civilization

- The geography of Greece encouraged the growth of independent communities that shared a common culture.
- The dominance of the Minoans and then of the Mycenaeans was followed by a collapse of these Greek civilizations.
- Greeks lost the art of writing and other advancements during Greece's Dark Ages, and people began living in villages.
- Greece's traditionally independent cities provided the foundation for government rule by the people.

Section 2: Religion, Philosophy and the Arts

- During the 400s B.C., Athens enjoyed a golden age of achievement in philosophy and the arts.
- Greeks worshiped many different gods and goddesses and sought their advice at oracles.
- Greek philosophers introduced new ways to think about the world.
- Visual arts, such as architecture and sculpture, and literary arts, such as drama, flourished during the Golden Age of Athens.
- Although city-states in Greece competed against one another, their citizens shared a common culture.

Minoan naval battle

The Golden Age of Athens

◆ Key Terms

Write a definition for each of the key terms listed below.

1. peninsula
2. epic
3. acropolis
4. city-state
5. aristocrat

6. tyrant
7. democracy
8. tribute
9. philosopher
10. tragedy

┌ Vocabulary Builder ─

High-Use Academic Words

Revisit this chapter's high-use academic words:

| heritage | impact | shrine |
| vibrant | imitator | influential |

Ask students to review the definitions they recorded on their *Word Knowledge* worksheets.

All in One **Unit 3 History of Our World Teaching Resources,** *Word Knowledge,* p. 15

Consider allowing students to earn extra credit if they use the words in their answers to the questions in the Chapter Review and Assessment. The words must be used correctly and in a natural context to win the extra points.

Review and Assessment

Review Chapter Content

- Review and revisit the major themes of this chapter by asking students to classify which Guiding Question each bulleted statement in the Chapter Summary answers. Have students work together in groups to classify the sentences. Refer to page 1 in the Student Edition for the text of the Guiding Questions.

- Assign *Vocabulary Development* for students to review Key Terms.

   All in One **Unit 3 History of Our World Teaching Resources,** *Vocabulary Development,* p. 28

Answers

Key Terms

Student definitions may vary.

1. A peninsula is land surrounded by water except for one connection to the land.
2. An epic is a long poem that tells a story about a country's origins or heroes.
3. An acropolis is a hill around which the early Greeks built their cities.
4. A city-state is a city that functions as a state with its own government and customs.
5. An aristocrat is a member of a rich and powerful family.
6. In Greece, a tyrant was a ruler who took power with the support of the middle class.
7. Democracy is a form of government in which the citizens have a say in the laws.
8. Tribute is a forced payment that a less powerful nation makes to a more power nation.
9. A philosopher is a person who uses reason to speculate on how the world was made and to help understand the world.
10. In Greek literature, a tragedy is a drama in which the fatal flaw of the main character leads to his downfall.

Review and Assessment

Comprehension and Critical Thinking

11. (a) The Minoans and the Mycenaeans were ancient people who were the ancestors of the Greeks. **(b)** Possible answer: The period after the Minoans and Mycenaeans is full of myth and legend. This period also included the Dark Ages of Greece. **(c)** Possible answer: Because the people could no longer write, history was only told by word of mouth through legends and myths. The legends praised their ancestors for their valor and bravery in battle.

12. (a) During the Dark Ages, villages combined to form cities, which acted as states with their own laws and government. **(b)** The middle class wanted a say in their own government. **(c)** The people of many city-states eventually overthrew the tyrants. Because they wanted to have a part in governing, the people helped develop democracy.

13. (a) The Greek religion was characterized by a belief in a whole family of gods, who helped explain the natural world to the Greeks. The Greek gods had human forms and were quite human-like in their attitudes. However, they were also immortal and had great powers. **(b)** The people believed that their gods would give them advice, foretell their future, and tell them how to behave through the oracles. **(c)** The philosophers thought that people could use reason to understand natural events.

14. (a) Architecture, sculpture, poetry, and drama were important. **(b)** Possible answer: The Greeks developed tragedies, which told of people destroyed by fate and bad choices, and comedies, which made fun of politicians and customs. **(c)** Possible answer: The comedies were an outcome of freedom of speech and thought in Greece. Also, this freedom encouraged more ideas to be expressed.

Skills Practice

Make sure students' conclusions reflect an understanding of both Socrates' ideas and of how to draw conclusions.

Chapter 6 Review and Assessment (continued)

◆ Comprehension and Critical Thinking

11. (a) Identify Who were the Minoans and the Mycenaeans?
(b) Generalize Describe the period in Greek history that followed the dominance of the Minoans and the Mycenaeans.
(c) Infer How did the story of the Trojan War help the ancient Greeks understand their history?

12. (a) Recall How did city-states arise in ancient Greece?
(b) Explain Why did tyrants replace aristocrats as rulers of the city-states?
(c) Identify Effects How did rule by tyrants affect the city-states?

13. (a) List Identify two characteristics that describe Greek religion.
(b) Describe What was the importance of the oracles to the Greeks?
(c) Apply Information According to Greek philosophers, how could people understand natural events?

14. (a) Generalize What arts were important in ancient Greece?
(b) Compare Describe the two types of dramas developed by ancient Greeks.
(c) Draw Conclusions How did the comedies affect the free exchange of ideas in ancient Greece?

◆ Skills Practice

Drawing Conclusions In the Skills for Life Activity, you learned how to draw conclusions from information that is not specifically stated in the text.

Review the steps you follow to apply this skill. Reread the passage in Section 2 titled Socrates. Use what you have read and your own observations of human nature to draw conclusions about Socrates and the impact of his ideas on future civilizations.

◆ Writing Activity Language Arts

Choose at least five terms from the Key Terms list on the previous page. Write a brief poem, essay, or dialogue about ancient Greece that uses the terms you have chosen.

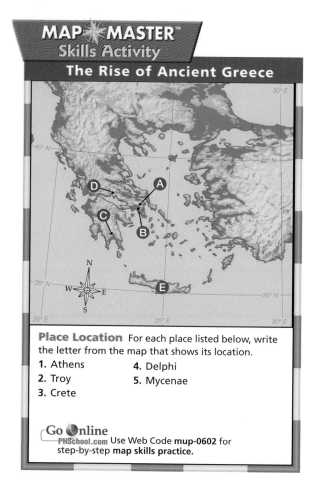

MAP★MASTER™ Skills Activity

The Rise of Ancient Greece

Place Location For each place listed below, write the letter from the map that shows its location.
1. Athens
2. Troy
3. Crete
4. Delphi
5. Mycenae

Go Online
PHSchool.com Use Web Code mup-0602 for step-by-step **map skills practice**.

Writing Activity: Language Arts
Check to see that students' work includes five Key Terms. Use the *Rubric for Assessing A Writing Assignment* to evaluate students' work.

All in One Unit 3 History of Our World Teaching Resources, *Rubric for Assessing A Writing Assignment,* p. 30.

Standardized Test Prep

Test-Taking Tips

Some questions on standardized tests ask you to analyze an outline. Study the outline below. Then follow the tips to answer the sample question.

TIP Use key words in the text to help you.

I Solon's Reforms
  A Outlawed slavery based on debt
  B Opened high offices to more citizens
  C _____
  D Gave the assembly more power
II Limited Rights
  A Allowed only male citizens to participate
  B Restricted citizenship
  C Left many slaves without rights

TIP Think about how the text is organized. Use that information to help you answer the question.

Pick the letter that best answers the question.

Which of the following belongs in I-C?
  A Later reforms under another ruler
  B Allowed male citizens to debate important laws
  C Life in Athens
  D Did not allow women to share in public life

Think It Through This outline is organized by major topics and subtopics. The question asks you to find a subtopic under Solon's Reforms. Answer C is too general; it could be the subject of an entire outline. Answer A is also general; it could be the subject of another topic in this outline. Answer D does not fit under Solon's Reforms. The key word *reforms* means "changes" or "improvements." Therefore, answer B is correct.

Practice Questions

Use the tips above and other tips in this book to help you answer the following questions.

1. Why did the ancient Greeks think of their communities as separate countries?
  A A different language was spoken in each community.
  B Each community's people came from a different country.
  C Each community practiced a different religion.
  D Geographical features cut communities off from one another.

2. Philosophers believed that they could understand the world around them by
  A using the powers of reason.
  B building shrines to the gods.
  C seeking answers at the oracle at Delphi.
  D paying tribute to their allies.

Study the outline below, and then answer the following question.

I Greek Beginnings
  A Minoan Civilization
    1. Lived on the island of Crete
    2.
  B Mycenaean Civilization

3. Which answer belongs in the space numbered 2 in the outline above?
  A Spoke an early form of modern Greek
  B Spread their power through conquest
  C Fought in the Trojan War
  D Dominated the Aegean Sea through trade

Use Web Code **mua-0603** for **Chapter 6 self-test.**

MAP ★ MASTER
Skills Activity

1. B
2. C
3. E
4. A
5. D

Go Online *PHSchool.com* Students may practice their map skills using the interactive online version of this map.

Standardized Test Prep

Answers

1. D
2. A
3. D

Go Online *PHSchool.com* Students may use the Chapter 6 self-test on PHSchool.com to prepare for the Chapter Test.

Assessment Resources

Use Chapter Tests A and B to assess students' mastery of chapter content.

All in One **Unit 3 History of Our World Teaching Resources,** *Chapter Tests A and B,* pp. 33–38

Tests are also available on the **Exam***View* **Test Bank CD-ROM.**

⊙ **Exam***View*® **Test Bank CD-ROM**

Objectives

- Learn about the Greek ideas of leadership and heroism.

- Think about the roles temptation and danger play in this story and in the lives of heroic people.

- Analyze the effectiveness of complex elements of plot, such as setting and conflicts.

Prepare to Read

Build Background Knowledge   L2

Lead the class in a discussion about whether or not television commercials make you want to buy the things they advertise. Talk about the feeling of being torn between better judgments and buying something for pleasure or beauty. Use the Numbered Heads participation strategy (TE, p. T40) to call on students to share their group's perspective.

Instruct

The Sirens   L2

Guided Instruction

- Read through the vocabulary words and definitions in the margin with students before reading.

- Partner students and have them use the Structured Silent Reading strategy (TE, p. T38) to read each section of the selection, writing the answers to each Reading Check as they read.

- Ask **What problem do Ulysses and his men face at the beginning of the story?** *(They must get through the narrow strait guarded by the Sirens.)*

- Ask **What is the setting for the story?** *(Ulysses and his men are at sea and they must reach the island of Thrinacia to get more provisions. To do so, they must pass through a narrow strait full of obstacles.)* **How does the setting affect the story?** *(The setting helps to create the conflict and tension in the story.)*

The Sirens
A Greek Myth From *The Adventures of Ulysses*
Retold by Bernard Evslin

Prepare to Read

Background Information
Have you ever been persuaded to go somewhere, do something, or buy something because someone made it sound fun or exciting? Messages like these can sometimes lead people in the wrong direction.

The Sirens (SY runz) in this myth are creatures who use their songs to lead sailors to destruction. The hero, Ulysses (yoo LIS eez), is warned about the Sirens as he tries to sail home to Greece after the Trojan War.

Ulysses is the name the Roman people gave to the Greek hero Odysseus (oh DIS ee us). The tale of Ulysses and the Sirens comes from a series of tales told in Homer's *Odyssey*. The clever Ulysses had expected an easy journey home. Instead, he was delayed by adventures that tested his body and spirit.

Like Homer himself and other storytellers, Bernard Evslin has retold the ancient story of the Sirens in his own words. The events are the same as those in the Odyssey myth. But the author has added many details to make the story his own.

Objectives
In this selection you will
1. Learn about the Greek ideas of leadership and heroism.
2. Think about the roles temptation and danger play in this story and in people's lives.

Sculpture of a Siren

In the first light of morning Ulysses awoke and called his crew about him.

"Men," he said. "Listen well, for your lives today hang upon what I am about to tell you. That large island to the west is <u>Thrinacia</u>, where we must make a landfall, for our provisions run low. But to get to the island we must pass through a narrow strait. And at the head of this <u>strait</u> is a rocky <u>islet</u> where dwell two sisters called Sirens, whose voices you must not hear. Now I shall guard you against their singing, which would lure you to shipwreck, but first you must bind me to the mast. Tie me tightly, as though I were a dangerous captive. And no matter how I struggle, no matter what signals I make to you, do not release me, lest I follow their voices to destruction, taking you with me."

Thereupon Ulysses took a large lump of the beeswax that was used by the sail mender to slick his heavy thread and kneaded it in his powerful hands until it became soft. Then he went to each man of the crew and plugged his ears with soft wax; he <u>caulked</u> their ears so tightly that they could hear nothing but the thin pulsing of their own blood.

Thrinacia (thrih NAY shee uh) *n.* mythological island that might have been Sicily

strait (strayt) *n.* narrow water passage between two pieces of land

islet (EYE lit) *n.* small island

caulk (kawk) *v.* to stop up and make tight

192 History of Our World

Read Fluently

Form the class into partners. Choose a paragraph from the selection. Have students take turns reading the paragraph aloud. Ask them to underline words that give them trouble as they read. Then, have them decode the problem words with their partner. Provide assistance as needed. Have them reread the paragraph two more times to improve their reading speed. Remind them to stop at the commas and periods and to read with expression.

Then he stood himself against the mast, and the men bound him about with rawhide, winding it tightly around his body, lashing him to the thick mast.

They had lowered the sail because ships cannot sail through a narrow strait unless there is a following wind, and now each man of the crew took his place at the great oars. The polished blades whipped the sea into a froth of white water and the ship nosed toward the strait.

Ulysses had left his own ears unplugged because he had to remain in command of the ship and had need of his hearing. Every sound means something upon the sea. But when they drew near the rocky islet and he heard the first faint <u>strains</u> of the Sirens' singing, then he wished he, too, had stopped his own ears with wax. All his strength suddenly <u>surged</u> toward the sound of those magical voices. The very hair of his head seemed to be tugging at his scalp, trying to fly away. His eyeballs started out of his head.

For in those voices were the sounds that men love:
Happy sounds like birds <u>railing</u>, sleet hailing, milk pailing....
Sad sounds like rain leaking, trees creaking, wind seeking....
Autumn sounds like leaves tapping, fire snapping, river <u>lapping</u>....
Quiet sounds like snow flaking, spider waking, heart breaking....

strain (strayn) *n.* tune

surge (surj) *v.* to rise or swell suddenly

rail (rayl) *v.* to cry, complain

lap (lap) *v.* to splash in little waves

✓ **Reading Check**

What does Ulysses do to keep his men from hearing the voices of the Sirens?

A Greek jar showing Ulysses and his men as they encounter the Sirens

■ Ask **Why did Ulysses command his crew to put beeswax in their ears as they passed through the narrow straits?** *(so they would not be tempted by the Sirens' sounds)* **Why did he not plug his own ears?** *(He needed to hear to guide the ship effectively.)*

■ Ask **Why might Ulysses find tempting the sounds that are described?** *(Students may speculate that anyone confined to a ship for a long period would find tempting sounds like "birds railing" or "milk pailing.")*

■ Ask **How does the author of the story make the Sirens' song seem appealing?** *(Lead students to see that the author uses rhyme and vivid imagery to set the Sirens' song apart in the text.)*

■ Ask **Why did Ulysses force himself to keep his eyes open once he had actually seen the Sirens?** *(The Sirens had the faces and sounds of young girls but were shaped like huge birds with claws instead of hands and feathers instead of hair. Ulysses realized that if he kept his eyes open he would see how ugly they were and not be tempted.)*

■ Ask **How did his men know when to unbind Ulysess?** *(when they saw Ulysses' face lose its look of madness)*

Answer

✓ Reading Check   He plugs their ears with wax.

Guided Instruction (continued)

- Ask **How does Ulysses show that he is a good leader?** *(He devises a plan to get him and his men through a dangerous situation; he takes on the responsibility of being the only one to not have his ears plugged; he trusts his men not to untie him.)*

- Ask students to discuss why Ulysses might have been considered a hero in Greek and Roman mythology. *(Possible answer: because he survived a difficult journey home after the Trojan War that tested his body and spirit.)*

Independent Practice

Invite students to write a journal entry about a time when they felt torn between their better judgment and the attraction of something very enticing. Did they resist, and, if so, how? Remind students that journal writings are private and they will not be shared with others. Give them *Structuring Paragraphs* and *Creating a Paragraph Outline* to help them get started.

All in One Unit 3 History of Our World **Teaching Resources,** *Structuring, Paragraphs p. 356; Creating Paragraph Outlines,* p. 25

Monitor Progress

As students construct their paragraphs, assess whether individuals need help in creating outlines or organizing their paragraphs.

---

purl (purl) *v.* to make a soft murmuring sound like a flowing stream

spume (spyoom) *n.* foam

hawser (HAW zur) *n.* a large rope

About the Selection

Homer's tale of Ulysses and the Sirens is only a few dozen verses long. This version of the tale, "The Sirens," as well as many other tales from Homer's *Odyssey,* can be found in *The Adventures of Ulysses,* by Bernard Evslin. The book was published in 1969.

It seemed to him then that the sun was burning him to a cinder as he stood. And the voices of the Sirens <u>purled</u> in a cool crystal pool upon their rock past the blue-hot flatness of the sea and its lacings of white-hot <u>spume</u>. It seemed to him he could actually see their voices deepening into a silvery, cool pool and must plunge into that pool or die a flaming death.

He was filled with such a fury of desire that he swelled his mighty muscles, burst the rawhide bonds like thread, and dashed for the rail.

But he had warned two of his strongest men—Perimedes (pehr ih MEE deez) and Eurylochus (yoo RIHL uh kus)—to guard him close. They seized him before he could plunge into the water. He swept them aside as if they had been children. But they had held him long enough to give the crew time to swarm about him. He was overpowered—crushed by their numbers—and dragged back to the mast. This time he was bound with the mighty <u>hawser</u> that held the anchor.

The men returned to their rowing seats, unable to hear the voices because of the wax corking their ears. The ship swung about and headed for the strait again.

Louder now, and clearer, the tormenting voices came to Ulysses. Again he was aflame with a fury of desire. But try as he might he could not break the thick anchor line. He strained against it until he bled, but the line held.

The men bent to their oars and rowed more swiftly, for they saw the mast bending like a tall tree in a heavy wind, and they feared that Ulysses, in his fury, might snap it off short and dive, mast and all, into the water to get at the Sirens.

Now they were passing the rock, and Ulysses could see the singers. There were two of them. They sat on a heap of white bones—the bones of shipwrecked sailors— and sang more beautifully than senses could bear. But their appearance did not match their voices, for they were shaped like birds, huge birds, larger than eagles.

A Siren

Differentiated Instruction

For Less Proficient Readers L1

Ask students to make a sensory detail chart. Have students copy *Transparency B4: Flow Chart* and label the columns *Sight, Sound, Taste, Touch,* and *Smell,* adding details from the story in the appropriate categories.

📖 **History of Our World Transparencies,** *Transparency B4: Flow Chart*

For Advanced Readers L3

Have students draw up a list of characteristics that Ulysses displays *(bravery, willpower, sensitivity to beauty, concern for others).* Then ask students to suppose that Ulysses can no longer serve as the captain. Have students develop and write a job description that describes the personal and professional qualifications required of the new captain.

They had feathers instead of hair, and their hands and feet were claws. But their faces were the faces of young girls.

When Ulysses saw them he was able to forget the sweetness of their voices because their look was so fearsome. He closed his eyes against the terrible sight of these bird-women perched on their heap of bones. But when he closed his eyes he could not see their ugliness, then their voices maddened him once again, and he felt himself straining against the bloody ropes. He forced himself to open his eyes and look upon the monsters, so that the terror of their bodies would blot the beauty of their voices.

But the men, who could only see, not hear the Sirens, were so <u>appalled</u> by their <u>aspect</u> that they swept their oars faster and faster, and the black ship scuttled past the rock. The Sirens' voices sounded fainter and fainter and finally died away.

When Perimedes and Eurylochus saw their captain's face lose its madness, they unbound him, and he signaled to the men to unstop their ears. For now he heard the whistling gurgle of a whirlpool, and he knew that they were approaching the narrowest part of the strait, and must pass between <u>Scylla</u> and <u>Charybdis</u>.

◀ **The Eastern coast of Sicily, Italy**

appall (uh PAWL) *v.* horrify
aspect (AS pekt) *n.* the way something looks
Scylla (SIL uh) *n.* a monster who ate sailors passing through the Straits of Messina, between Italy and Sicily
Charybdis (kuh RIB dis) *n.* a monster in the form of a deadly whirlpool near Scylla

✔ **Reading Check**

What are the Sirens doing on their rocky islet?

Review and Assessment

Thinking About the Selection

1. (a) Identify What are the Sirens?
(b) Apply Information Why do you think temptation is sometimes described as a "siren song"?
2. (a) Recall What fears does Ulysses have about the voyage?
(b) Infer Give two reasons Ulysses leaves his own ears unplugged during the voyage.
(c) Draw Conclusions Do you think Ulysses is a good leader? Explain why or why not.

Writing Activity

Retell the Story in a Different Form "The Sirens" is in the form of a short story. Use another form of writing to retell it. You might choose to make it into a poem. You could retell it as a movie script with dialog and scene descriptions. Or, you might write an instruction manual for sailors to follow when they have to travel near the Sirens.

About the Author

Homer Although "The Sirens" is retold here by Bernard Evslin, the tale was made famous by Homer. Homer was a Greek poet who lived around 700 B.C. Scholars believe that he wrote the epic poems the *Odyssey* and the *Iliad* for the educated upper class of ancient Greek society.

Chapter 6 **195**

Assess and Reteach

Assess Progress L2
Have students answer the assessment questions.

Reteach L1
If students need more instruction, have them create illustrations of the major scenes of the story and write a caption that summarizes the scene in their own words.

Extend L3
Have students write a journal entry from the perspective of one of Ulysses' sailors. Then group students and have them exchange and comment on each other's work, using the *Rubric for Assessing a Journal Entry*. Have groups select one or two works to be read aloud or performed before the class.

All in One History of Our World Teaching Resources, *Rubric for Assessing a Journal Entry,* p. 32

Answers

✔ **Reading Check** They are singing and luring sailors to their shore.

Review and Assessment

Thinking About the Selection

1. (a) creatures who use their songs to lead sailors to destruction **(b)** The Sirens' singing causes sailors to steer their ships into the shore. Because the Sirens' song was a powerful temptation to Ulysses, people compare other temptations to the one in this story.
2. (a) He was afraid he and his men would be lured to shipwreck by the Sirens' song. **(b)** He had to remain in command of the ship, and needed his hearing. **(c)** Answers will vary, but should be explained using evidence from the text.

Writing Activity

Use the *Rubric for Assessing a Student Poem* or the *Rubric for Assessing a Writing Assignment* to evaluate students' work.

All in One History of Our World Teaching Resources, *Rubric for Assessing a Writing Assignment,* p. 30, *Rubric for Assessing a Student Poem,* p. 31

Overview

Daily Life in Athens
Section 1
1. Learn about public life in Athens.
2. Find out how Athenians spent their time when they were at home.
3. Understand how slavery operated in ancient Greece.

Athens and Sparta
Section 2
1. Learn how people lived in ancient Sparta.
2. Discover some results of the Persian invasion of Greece.
3. Understand the conflicts that the Athenian empire faced.

The Spread of Greek Culture
Section 3
1. Learn how King Philip of Macedonia came to power and how Alexander the Great built his empire.
2. Understand what role the conquests of Alexander the Great played in spreading Greek culture.

Video

Spartan Warriors
Length: 4 minutes, 55 seconds
Use with Section 2
Around the eighth century B.C., a region in southern Greece known as the Peloponnesus was invaded by soldiers from the north. The invaders established a new city called Sparta. Sparta's neighbors would come to fear them. Spartans had a single-minded devotion to war and could out-drill, out-march, and out-fight anyone. This segment explores the Spartan system of training soldiers and tells of their ultimate demise.

Technology Resources

Go Online
PHSchool.com

Interactive Textbook

PRENTICE HALL
TeacherEXPRESS™
Plan • Teach • Assess

Students use embedded web codes to access Internet activities, chapter self-tests, and additional map practice. They may also access Dorling Kindersley's Online Desk Reference to learn more about each country they study.

Use the Interactive Textbook to make content and concepts come alive through animations, videos, and activities that accompany the complete basal text—online and on CD-Rom.

Use this complete suite of powerful teaching tools to make lesson planning and administering tests quicker and easier.

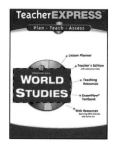

Reading and Assessment

Reading and Vocabulary Instruction

🔊 Model the Target Reading Skill

Compare and Contrast Tell students that comparing and contrasting can help them sort out and analyze information. Explain that when they contrast, they will look at the differences in two peoples, cultures, landforms, situations, or any other item whose relationship they want to understand. When they compare, they will try to see what these two peoples, cultures, landforms, situations, and so forth have in common.

Model this skill in the following manner: Tell students that if you were going to compare and contrast Athens and Sparta, you would ask yourself aloud: "How do Athens and Sparta differ? What did Athens and Sparta have in common? Examples from these questions help me conclude that the two city-states may have had a lot of differences, but they were also very similar."

Use the following worksheets from All-in-One Unit 3 Teaching Resources (pp. 55–57) to support this chapter's Target Reading Skill.

Vocabulary Builder
High-Use Academic Words

Use these steps to teach this chapter's high-use words.

1. Have students rate how well they know each word on their Word Knowledge worksheets. (All-in-One Unit 3 History of Our World Teaching Resources, p. 58)

2. Pronounce each word and ask students to repeat it.

3. Provide a brief definition or sample sentence (provided on TE pp. 199, 207, and 217).

4. Work with students as they fill in the "Definition or Example" column of their Word Knowledge worksheets.

Assessment

Formal Assessment

Test student's understanding of core knowledge and skills.

Chapter Tests A and B, All-in-One Unit 3 History of Our World Teaching Resources, pp. 71–76

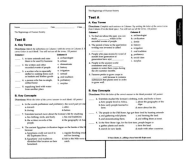

Customize the Chapter Tests to suit your needs.

Exam View® Test Bank CD-ROM

Skills Assessment

Assess geographic literacy.

MapMaster Skills, Student Edition, pp. 197, 212, 219

Timeline Skills, Student Edition, p. 221

Assess reading and comprehension.

Target Reading Skills, Student Edition, pp. 200, 209, 217 and in Section Assessments

Chapter 7 Assessment, All-in-One Unit 3 History of Our World Reading and Vocabulary Study Guide, p. 90

Performance Assessment

Assess students' performance on this chapter's Writing Activity using the following rubrics from All-in-One Unit 3 History of Our World Teaching Resources.

Rubric for Assessing a Journal Entry, p. 67

Rubric for Assessing a Writing Assignment, p. 68

Rubric for Assessing a Report, p. 69

Rubric for Assessing a Writing Assignment, p. 70

Assess students' work through performance tasks.

Small Group Activities, All-in-One Unit 3 History of Our World Teaching Resources, pp. 61–64

Online Assessment

Have students check their own understanding.

Chapter Self-Test

Section 1 Daily Life in Athens

 3 periods, 1.5 blocks (includes Focus on the Agora of Athens)

Social Studies Objectives
1. Learn about public life in Athens.
2. Find out how Athenians spent their time when they were at home.
3. Understand how slavery operated in ancient Greece.

Reading/Language Arts Objective
Learn to compare and contrast to understand the similarities and differences between items.

Prepare to Read	Instructional Resources	Differentiated Instruction
Build Background Knowledge Discuss section headings and have students speculate about Greek life. **Set a Purpose** Have students evaluate statements on the *Set a Purpose* worksheet. **Preview Key Terms** Teach the section's Key Terms. **Target Reading Skill** Introduce the section's Target Reading Skill of making comparisons.	**All in One Unit 3 History of Our World Teaching Resources** L2 Reading Readiness Guide, p. 44 L2 Word Knowledge, p. 58 L2 Compare and Contrast, p. 55	**Spanish Reading and Vocabulary Study Guide** L1 Chapter 7, Section 1, pp. 59–60 ELL

Instruct	Instructional Resources	Differentiated Instruction
Public Life Discuss public life for men in the agoras. **At Home in Athens** Discuss how Athenian women spent their time at home. **Target Reading Skill** Review making comparisons. **Slavery in Ancient Greece** Discuss what it meant to be a slave in Ancient Greece.	**All in One Unit 3 History of Our World Teaching Resources** L2 Guided Reading and Review, p. 45 L2 Reading Readiness Guide, p. 44 **History of Our World Transparencies** L2 Section Reading Support Transparency HOW 76	**All in One Unit 3 History of Our World Teaching Resources** L3 Enrichment, p. 59 GT, AR **Teacher's Edition** L1 English Language Learners, p. 200 L3 Gifted and Talented, p. 200 **Reading and Vocabulary Study Guide** L1 Chapter 7, Section 1, pp. 81–83 LPR **Spanish Support** L2 Guided Reading and Review , p. 62 ELL

Assess and Reteach	Instructional Resources	Differentiated Instruction
Assess Program Have students reevaluate the statements in Set a Purpose for reading. Evaluate student comprehension with the section assessment and section quiz. **Reteach** Assign the Reading and Vocabulary Study Guide to help struggling students. **Extend** Have students learn more about ancient Greece by completing the *Enrichment.* Assign students to work in groups to complete the project.	**All in One Unit 3 History of Our World Teaching Resources** L2 Section Quiz, p. 46 **Reading and Vocabulary Study Guide** L1 Chapter 7, Section 1, pp. 81–83	**Spanish Support** L1 Chapter 7, Section 1, pp. 81–83 ELL L2 Section Quiz, p. 63 ELL

Key
L1 Below Average	L3 Above Average	LPR Less Proficient Readers	GT Gifted and Talented
L2 Average		AR Advanced Readers	ELL English Language Learners
		SN Special Needs Students	

196c

Section 2 Athens and Sparta

 3 periods, 1.5 blocks (includes Skills for Life)

Social Studies Objectives
1. Learn how people lived in ancient Sparta.
2. Discover some results of the Persian invasion of Greece.
3. Understand the conflicts that the Athenian empire faced.

Reading/Language Arts Objective
Learn to identify contrasts between peoples, cultures, or other items to see how they differ.

Prepare to Read	**Instructional Resources**	**Differentiated Instruction**
Build Background Knowledge Compare the life of Spartan boys with what students know about the life of Athenian boys from Section 1. **Set a Purpose** Have students evaluate statements on the *Set a Purpose* worksheet. **Preview Key Terms** Teach the section's Key Terms. **Target Reading Skill** Introduce the section's Target Reading Skill of identifying contrasts.	**All in One Unit 3 History of Our World Teaching Resources** L2 Reading Readiness Guide, p. 48 L2 Word Knowledge, p. 58 L2 Identify Contrasts, p. 56	**Spanish Reading and Vocabulary Study Guide** L1 Chapter 7, Section 2, pp. 61–62 ELL

Instruct	**Instructional Resources**	**Differentiated Instruction**
Living in Sparta Discuss what life in Sparta was like. **Growing Up in Sparta** Ask students key questions about how Spartan boys and girls were raised and about the rights they had as adults. **Target Reading Skill** Review identifying contrasts. **The Persians Invade** Ask students key questions about the Persian invasion and the Battle of Marathon.	**All in One Unit 3 History of Our World Teaching Resources** L2 Guided Reading and Review, p. 49 L2 Reading Readiness, Guide, p. 48 **History of Our World Transparencies** L2 Section Reading Support Transparency HOW 77	**All in One Unit 3 History of Our World Teaching Resources** L3 Enrichment, p. 59 GT, AR **Teacher's Edition** L1 For Less Proficient Readers, TE pp. 209, 211 L3 For Advanced Readers, TE p. 211 L3 Gifted and Talented Students, TE p. 209 **Reading and Vocabulary Study Guide** L1 Chapter 7, Section 2, pp. 84–86 LPR **Spanish Support** L1 Guided Reading and Review, p. 64 ELL

Assess and Reteach	**Instructional Resources**	**Differentiated Instruction**
Assess Program Have students reevaluate the statements in Set a Purpose for reading. Evaluate student comprehension with the section assessment and section quiz. **Reteach** Assign the Reading and Vocabulary Study Guide to help struggling students. **Extend** Extend the lesson by assigning the Enrichment.	**All in One Unit 3 History of Our World Teaching Resources** L2 Section Quiz, p. 50 **Reading and Vocabulary Study Guide** L1 Chapter 7, Section 2, pp. 84–86	**Spanish Support** L2 Section Quiz, p. 65 ELL

Key

L1 Below Average   L3 Above Average
L2 Average

LPR Less Proficient Readers
AR Advanced Readers
SN Special Needs Students

GT Gifted and Talented
ELL English Language Learners

Section 3 The Spread of Greek Culture

 3 periods, 1.5 blocks

Social Studies Objectives

1. Learn how King Philip of Macedonia came to power and how Alexander the Great built his empire.
2. Understand what role the conquests of Alexander the Great played in spreading Greek culture.

Reading/Language Arts Objective

Learn to make comparisons between situations, people, or other items to see how they are alike.

Prepare to Read	Instructional Resources	Differentiated Instruction
Build Background Knowledge Discuss section headings and visuals and ask students what they already know about Greece to speculate what Alexander the Great accomplished. **Set a Purpose** Have students evaluate statements on the *Set a Purpose* worksheet. **Preview Key Terms** Teach the section's Key Terms. **Target Reading Skill** Introduce the section's Target Reading Skill of making comparisons.	**All in One Unit 3 History of Our World Teaching Resources** L2 Reading Readiness Guide, p. 52 L2 Word Knowledge, p. 58 L2 Make Comparisons p. 57	**Spanish Reading and Vocabulary Study Guide** L1 Chapter 7, Section 3, pp. 63–64 ELL

Instruct	Instructional Resources	Differentiated Instruction
Philip Comes to Power Ask key questions about what Macedonia was like before and after Philip came to power. **Target Reading Skill** Review making comparisons. **Alexander Builds an Empire** Discuss how Alexander was prepared to take over his father's legacy at such a young age and what his accomplishments were. **Greek Culture Spreads** Discuss how Greek culture spread after Alexander's death.	**All in One Unit 3 History of Our World Teaching Resources** L2 Guided Reading and Review, p. 53 L2 Reading Readiness Guide, p. 52 **History of Our World Transparencies** L2 Section Reading Support Transparency HOW 78	**All in One Unit 3 History of Our World Teaching Resources** L3 Enrichment, p. 59 GT, AR **Teacher's Edition** L1 For Special Needs Students, TE p. 219 L3 For Advanced Readers, TE p. 219 **Reading and Vocabulary Study Guide** L1 Chapter 7, Section 3, pp. 87–89 LPR **Spanish Support** L2 Guided Reading and Review, p. 66 ELL

Assess and Reteach	Instructional Resources	Differentiated Instruction
Assess Program Have students reevaluate the statements in Set a Purpose for reading. Evaluate student comprehension with the section assessment and section quiz. **Reteach** Assign the Reading and Vocabulary Study Guide to help struggling students. **Extend** Extend the lesson by assigning the Enrichment activity.	**All in One Unit 3 History of Our World Teaching Resources** L2 Section Quiz, p. 54 L3 Enrichment, p. 59 **Reading and Vocabulary Study Guide** L1 Chapter 7, Section 3, pp. 87–89	**Spanish Support** L2 Section Quiz, p. 67 ELL L2 Chapter Summary, p. 68 ELL L2 Vocabulary Development, p. 69 ELL

Key
L1 Below Average   L3 Above Average
L2 Average

LPR Less Proficient Readers
AR Advanced Readers
SN Special Needs Students

GT Gifted and Talented
ELL English Language Learners

Reading Background

Prepare to Read

Many secondary students do not have solid reading skills. Even students quite skilled in reading novels, short stories, and magazines often come to middle school ill-equipped for reading informational texts. They tend to dive right into a social studies chapter as if reading a story. That's why it is important that the teacher guide them before they begin to read.

The Build Background Knowledge slows students down by allowing them to look ahead at the visuals and headings so they know what they are going to be reading about before they begin. It also builds on what they have already read in previous sections or chapters or on what they already know from prior experience with a concept or a part of history.

It is also important for students to create a mental outline of what they are going to be reading by reading the objectives and establishing a reading purpose. It is also helpful for them to use other strategies, such as taking notes (especially helpful if the note taking involves something visual like a graphic organizer), reading to answer specific questions, and re-reading passages that have tricky sequence issues or other difficulties.

Encourage Active Participation

In Section 2, students will use the ReQuest strategy to share their ideas about Living in Sparta. After going through the Build Background Knowledge, Set a Purpose for Reading, and Preview Key Terms, read the first paragraph aloud.

Ask questions of yourself aloud: "How was life in Sparta different from life in Athens?" Then answer your own question: "Life was free and open in Athens but just the opposite in Sparta." Continue by asking yourself, "If the two armies were about the same—probably in size, experience, and equipment—why didn't Sparta ever equal Athens' other achievements?" Note that this second question is a higher level question than the first one you asked yourself. Your answer can speculate on why this might be so: "From what I already know from reading about Athens' Golden Age in the last chapter, I can guess that Athens never devoted itself wholly to its army and its protection the way that Sparta did. Its people were more interested in art and thought and science. So, maybe Sparta was just stuck on one idea of what to do and couldn't get beyond it."

After modeling this question and response pattern, ask students to read the next section of the text. Have them take turns asking you questions about what they read and answer the questions. Then switch so that you will be the one asking the questions and they will be the ones answering.

World History Background

Slavery in Ancient Times

Most slaves in ancient times were people captured in war, but others were criminals or people in debt. The ancient Egyptians, Sumerians, Babylonians, and Persians all had slaves. The Aztecs of ancient Mexico also enslaved prisoners of war; some were sacrificed in religious ceremonies.

A Citizen's Lot

In Athenian democracy, all male citizens voted in the Assembly. From this group, 500 were chosen by lot to serve for one year on the Council, a decision-making body. Jury members for court trials were also chosen by lot. But, as in modern democracies, some officials were elected.

The ten citizens who formed the Board of Generals were elected by the Assembly.

Spartan Personalities

Young children of Sparta were often cared for by helot nurses who were instructed not to hold or comfort the children when they were upset. Not surprisingly, many Spartan children grew up to be grim, stern, and silent. One story tells of a foreign king who threatened the Spartan city: "If I enter … I will level it to the ground." The Spartans replied with one word: "If."

Infoplease© provides a wealth of useful information for the classroom. You can use this resource to strengthen your background on the subjects covered in this chapter. Have students visit this advertising-free site as a starting point for projects requiring research.

Go Online
PHSchool.com

Use Web Code **1fa-0700** for Infoplease©.

Guiding Questions

Remind students about the Guiding Questions introduced at the beginning of the book.

Section 1 relates to **Guiding Question** **5** **How did each society develop and organize its economic activities?** *(Greece developed from family farms that united under the protection of fortified hills to form first villages and then city-states from combined villages. Its economy was influenced largely by its geography due to its location on islands and peninsulas. This location fostered trade. The Greeks owned slaves, who made a huge economic difference to the Greeks, allowing them to pursue activities other than manual labor.)*

Section 2 relates to **Guiding Question** **4** **What types of governments were formed in these societies and how did they develop?** *(Athens and the rest of Greece developed democracies that allowed citizens—free males—to have a say in their government. Sparta developed a grim, militaristic state that was always at war with Athens and other city-states.)*

Section 3 relates to **Guiding Question** **4** **What types of governments were formed in these societies and how did they develop?** *(Alexander conquered a huge empire that included Asia Minor, Persia, Palestine, and Egypt. Cities in these areas were modeled after Greek cities and culture and ruled by Greek kings.)*

Target Reading Skill
In this chapter, use the following worksheets:

All in One Unit 3 History of Our World Teaching Resources, *Compare and Contrast,* p. 55; *Identify Contrasts,* p. 56; *Make Comparisons,* p. 57

Differentiated Instruction

The following Teacher's Edition strategies are suitable for students of varying abilities.

Advanced Readers, pp. 211, 219
English Language Learners, pp. 200, 208
Gifted and Talented, pp. 200, 209
Less Proficient Readers, pp. 209, 211
Special Needs Students, pp. 215, 219

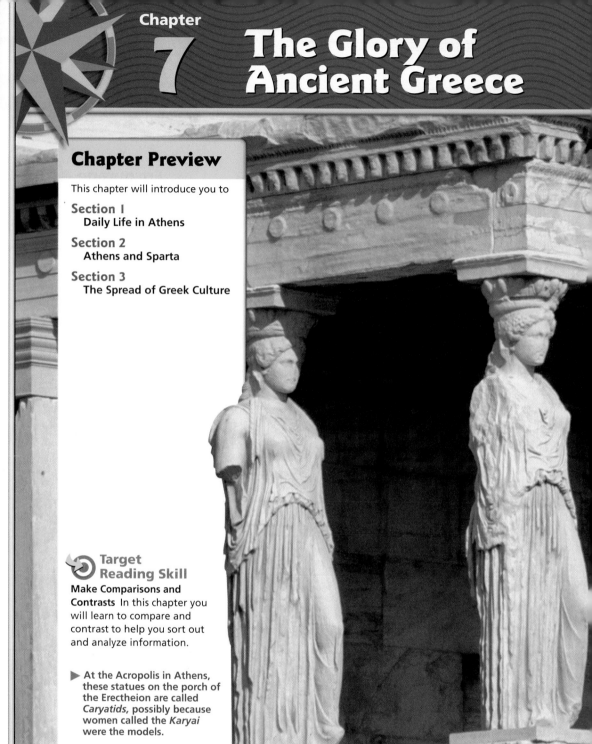

The Glory of Ancient Greece

Chapter Preview

This chapter will introduce you to

Section 1
Daily Life in Athens

Section 2
Athens and Sparta

Section 3
The Spread of Greek Culture

Target Reading Skill

Make Comparisons and Contrasts In this chapter you will learn to compare and contrast to help you sort out and analyze information.

▶ At the Acropolis in Athens, these statues on the porch of the Erectheion are called *Caryatids*, possibly because women called the *Karyai* were the models.

196 History of Our World

Bibliography

For the Teacher
Carledge, Paul. *The Spartans: The World of the Warrior Heroes of Ancient Greece.* Overlook Press, 2003 (accompanies the PBS series *The Spartans*).
Kagan, Donald. *The Peloponnesian War.* Viking, 2003.
Doherty, Paul C. *The Gates of Hell: A Mystery of Alexander the Great.* Carroll and Graf, 2003.

For the Student
ELL **L1** Tames, Richard. *Ancient Greek Children.* Heinemann Library, 2003.
L2 Nardo, Don. *Leaders of Ancient Greece.* Lucent Books, 1999.
L3 Wood, Michael. *In the Footsteps of Alexander the Great.*

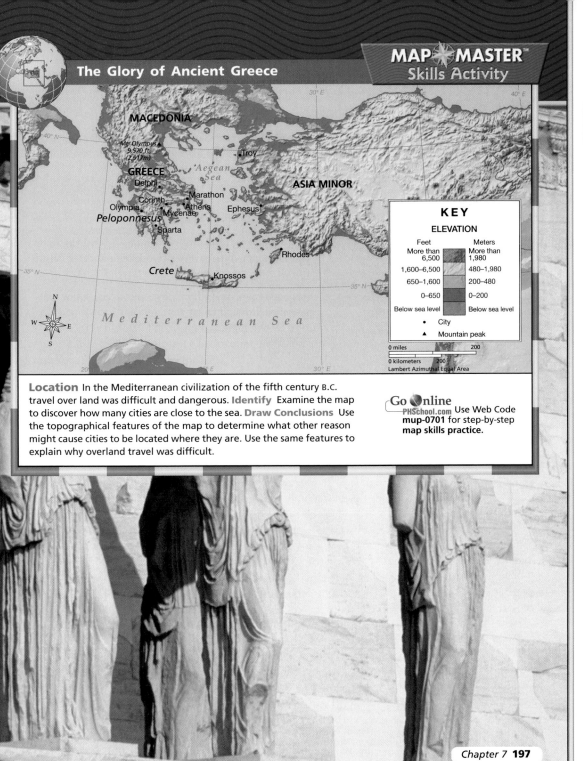

The Glory of Ancient Greece

MAP MASTER™ Skills Activity

MACEDONIA

Mt. Olympus
9,570 ft.
(2,917m)

GREECE

Delphi

Aegean Sea

Troy

Olympia
Corinth
Marathon
Athens
Mycenae
Ephesus

Peloponnesus

Sparta

ASIA MINOR

Rhodes

Crete
Knossos

Mediterranean Sea

N
W   E
S

KEY

ELEVATION

Feet		Meters
More than 6,500		More than 1,980
1,600–6,500		480–1,980
650–1,600		200–480
0–650		0–200
Below sea level		Below sea level

• City
▲ Mountain peak

0 miles   200
0 kilometers 200
Lambert Azimuthal Equal Area

Location In the Mediterranean civilization of the fifth century B.C. travel over land was difficult and dangerous. **Identify** Examine the map to discover how many cities are close to the sea. **Draw Conclusions** Use the topographical features of the map to determine what other reason might cause cities to be located where they are. Use the same features to explain why overland travel was difficult.

Go Online
PHSchool.com Use Web Code **mup-0701** for step-by-step **map skills practice.**

Chapter 7 **197**

MAP MASTER™ Skills Activity

Go Online
PHSchool.com Students may practice their map skills using the interactive online version of this map.

Using the Visual   L2

Reach Into Your Background Draw students' attention to the caption accompanying the photograph on pages 196–197. Discuss the photograph with students. From what they know about Greece from their reading of Chapter 6, have them guess what this building might be. Ask them to point out the structural features of the building and any geometrical shapes that they see. Point out that the Greeks were known to be master architects. Based on this building, ask students if they agree with this assessment. Have them explain why.

Answers

MAP MASTER Skills Activity **Identify** Most cities are close to the sea. **Draw Conclusions** Mountains separated the cities. It would be hard to travel far over mountainous terrain.

Chapter Resources

Teaching Resources
L2 Vocabulary Development, p. 66
L2 Chapter Tests A and B, pp. 71–76

Spanish Support
L2 Spanish Chapter Summary, p. 68
L2 Spanish Vocabulary Development, p. 69

Media and Technology
L1 Student Edition on Audio CD
L1 Guiding Reading Audio CD, English and Spanish
L2 Social Studies Skills Tutor CD-ROM
Exam*View* Test Bank CD-ROM

Discovery CHANNEL SCHOOL History of Our World Videos

Interactive Textbook

PRENTICE HALL
TeacherEXPRESS™
Plan · Teach · Assess

Section 1
Step-by-Step Instruction

Objectives

Social Studies
1. Learn about public life in Athens.
2. Find out how Athenians spent their time when they were at home.
3. Understand how slavery operated in ancient Greece.

Reading/Language Arts
Learn to compare and contrast items and use those similarities and differences to analyze information.

Prepare to Read

Build Background Knowledge [L2]

Point out to students that in Chapter 6 they learned about the history, art, philosophy, and religion of ancient Greece. Tell students that in this section they will learn about the everyday lives of the Greeks. Have students read the headings in this section. Use the Numbered Heads strategy (TE, p. T40) to have students speculate on how the life of the early Greeks might be similar to and different from their own. *(Possible response: Similarities: school, exercise, or sports, politics. Difference: housing, shopping, goods for sale, clothing)*

Set a Purpose for Reading [L2]

■ Preview the Objectives

■ Read each statement in the *Reading Readiness Guide* aloud. Ask students to mark the statements true or false.

All in One **Unit 3 History of Our World Teaching Resources,** *Reading Readiness Guide,* p. 44

■ Have students discuss the statements in pairs or groups of four, and then mark their worksheets again. Use the Numbered Heads strategy (TE, p. T40) to call on students to share their group's perspectives.

Vocabulary Builder
Preview Key Terms [L2]

Pronounce each Key Term, and then ask the students to say the word with you. Provide a simple explanation such as "a vendor is someone who sells items for people to buy."

Section 1 Daily Life in Athens

Prepare to Read

Objectives
In this section you will
1. Learn about public life in Athens.
2. Find out how Athenians spent their time when they were at home.
3. Understand how slavery operated in ancient Greece.

Taking Notes
As you read, look for ways that life is similar and different for various people in Ancient Greece. Copy the Venn diagram below. Write the differences in the outside areas and the similarities where the circles overlap.

Life in Ancient Greece

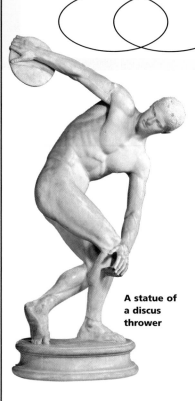

A statue of a discus thrower

Target Reading Skill

Compare and Contrast
Comparing and contrasting can help you sort out and analyze information. When you compare, you examine the similarities between things. When you contrast, you look at the differences. As you read this section, compare and contrast the daily life of Athenians. Write the information in your Taking Notes diagram.

Key Terms
- **Athens** (ATH unz) *n.* a city-state in ancient Greece; the capital of modern-day Greece
- **agora** (AG uh ruh) *n.* a public market and meeting place in an ancient Greek city; the Agora, spelled with a capital a, refers to the agora of Athens
- **vendor** (VEN dur) *n.* a seller of goods
- **slavery** (SLAY vur ee) *n.* condition of being owned by, and forced to work for, someone else

The light from the courtyard was still gray when the young boy awoke. He sat up on his hard bed and felt the morning air on his face. It was time to get up for school. The boy swallowed his breakfast, pulled his cloak around him, and left the house.

On the way to school, the boy met other students. All were carrying wooden tablets covered with wax. They would write their lessons on the tablets. They talked about their lesson, a long passage of history that they had to memorize.

The best part of the day came after school. Then, the boy spent the afternoon at the training ground. All the boys exercised and practiced wrestling and throwing a flat plate called a discus. Sometimes they watched older athletes training to compete in the Olympic Games, held in honor of Zeus.

This story shows how a boy might have spent his day in Athens, a city-state in ancient Greece. A look at daily life in ancient Athens will help you understand how many people lived in the early days of Greece.

198 History of Our World

🎯 Target Reading Skill [L2]

Compare and Contrast Point out the Target Reading Skill. Tell students that the ability to compare and contrast peoples, ideas, countries, and other items can help them analyze and understand information.

Have students compare the lives of Greek men to the lives of Greek women by reading the first paragraph on p. 201. *(Greek men could vote, take part in politics, and own property. Greek women had none of these freedoms.)*

Give students *Compare and Contrast.* Have them complete the activity in groups.

All in One **Unit 3 History of Our World Teaching Resources,** *Compare and Contrast,* p. 55

Public Life

Boys growing up in Athens needed only to look around to understand that it was the men who were active in politics, in society, and in other aspects of Athenian public life. The boys knew that they could look forward to assuming an important role in Athenian public life as they became adults.

The Marketplace On their way to school, the boys passed through the Agora of Athens. The Acropolis was the center of Athens' religious life, and the Agora was the center of its public life. The Agora was near the Acropolis, which rose in splendor above it. All Greek cities had **agoras,** or public markets and meeting places. The Agora in Athens was probably the busiest and most interesting of them all. The mild climate of Athens made it possible to carry on business in the open.

The Business of Men In the morning, many Athenian men made their way to the Agora. In the Agora, the men talked of politics, philosophy, or events in their community.

As they talked, they heard the cries of **vendors,** or sellers of goods. Buyers and vendors commonly haggled, or bargained, for the best prices. The streets were lined with shops. Farmers and artisans also sold their wares from stands set up under shady trees. Just about any food an Athenian would want could be found in the Agora. Other goods were also for sale—sheep's wool, pottery, hardware, cloth, and books.

Public Buildings Temples and government buildings lined the Agora. The buildings were often beautiful structures, for Athenians greatly admired beauty in architecture. The Greek classical style of architecture continues to influence how buildings are built in our time. Many government buildings in Europe and the United States were patterned after Greek architecture.

✓ **Reading Check** What business did Athenian men conduct in the Agora?

Community Life
The ruins of an agora are shown above. Greeks used agoras as public markets and meeting places. A vase from the 400s shows two Greeks discussing philosophy. **Analyze** *Why do you think the Agora was the center of public life in Athens?*

Vocabulary Builder

Use the information and sample sentences below to teach students this section's high-use words.

High-Use Word	Definition and Sample Sentence
splendor, p. 199	*n.* greatness or richness The **splendor** of Athens' architecture was breathtaking.
secluded, p. 200	*adj.* screened or hidden from view The wild animals lived in the most **secluded** areas of the park.
estimate, p. 202	*v.* to form a fairly accurate opinion We **estimate** that about 200 students from the school will attend the track meet.

Public Life

Guided Instruction

- **Vocabulary Builder** Clarify the high-use word **splendor** before reading.

- Have students read Public Life, using the Structured Silent Reading technique (TE, p. T38).

- Ask students **What was public life like for Greek men?** *(Greek men spent much of their day in the Agora, discussing politics, philosophy, or events.)*

- Have students describe a typical scene in the Agora. *(Possible response: The Agora was near the Acropolis. Beautiful temples and government buildings surrounded the Agora. Men would be busy talking together. Vendors would be selling their goods. The Agora was a very busy place.)*

Independent Practice

Assign *Guided Reading and Review*.

AII in One **Unit 3 History of Our World Teaching Resources,** *Guided Reading and Review,* p. 45

Monitor Progress

As students work on their *Guided Reading and Review* worksheet, circulate and make sure individuals are choosing the correct details. Provide assistance as needed.

Answers

✓ **Reading Check** The men discussed important events, politics, and philosophy. They also bought and sold goods.

Analyze Possible responses: The Agora was a public place located in the center of Athens. Athenians would know to meet others there for business or discussion. The Agora was like being downtown in a modern city.

At Home in Athens

Guided Instruction

- **Vocabulary Builder** Clarify the high-use word **secluded** before reading.

- Read At Home in Athens, using the Structured Silent Reading strategy (TE, p. T38). Challenge students to find out how Greek homes and meals differed from their own.

- Ask students **How did Athenians spend time in their homes?** *(Possible response: The Athenians ate simple meals. The men's and women's living quarters were often separate. The women spent their days running the household—caring for the children, organizing spinning and weaving, training and directing slaves, and keeping track of money.)*

- Ask students **How did poor women spend their time?** *(Poor women often worked outside the home making cloth, pottery, or tending sheep.)*

⟳ Target Reading Skill

Compare and Contrast As a follow up, ask students to answer the Target Reading Skill question in the Student Edition. *(Athenian men spent most of their time in the Agora, discussing business and socializing. Athenian women spent most of their time secluded at home. Athenian men and women lived together in the same house and ate the same food.)*

Answers

Predict Possible responses: The girls might gather to play games in the courtyard, which was outside but was hidden from the street.

Ancient Greek wine vessel

⟳ **Compare and Contrast** Where did Athenian men spend most of their time? Where did Athenian women spend most of their time? What was similar about their daily lives?

At Home in Athens

The splendor of public buildings in Athens contrasted with the simplicity of people's houses, even in the Golden Age.

Private Life Throughout Greece, private homes were plain. Made of mud bricks, Greek houses consisted of rooms set around an open courtyard that was hidden from the street. The courtyard was the center of the household. Other rooms might include a kitchen, storerooms, a dining room, and bedrooms. Some homes even had bathrooms. Water had to be carried from a public fountain.

The ancient Greeks ate simple foods. Breakfast might be just bread. For midday meals, Athenians might add cheese or olives to the bread. Dinner would be a hot meal that was more filling. It might consist of fish and vegetables followed by cheese, fruit, and even cakes sweetened with honey. Most Athenians ate little meat. Even wealthy families ate meat only during religious festivals.

Women of Athens If you had walked through the Agora, you would have noticed that most of the people there were men. If you had asked where the women were, an Athenian man might have replied, "At home."

Home was where most Athenian women spent their days. Women led secluded lives. Athenian men thought that women needed to be protected. Keeping them out of the public eye, men thought, gave women the most protection.

Greek Women
The women of ancient Greece making bread, as shown in the figure at right. **Predict** *Use what you know about the lives of ancient Greeks to predict where girls might gather to play games.*

Differentiated Instruction

For English Language Learners `L1`
Form small groups of English language learners and native speakers. Explain that ancient Greeks eagerly awaited festivals. Activities at the festival included grand processions, athletic contests, banquets, poetry readings, and plays. Have groups research ancient Greek festivals and then present their findings to the class.

For Gifted and Talented `L3`
Ask students to write a journal entry about a day in the life of a family in ancient Greece. Encourage them to use vivid details to make their entries come to life.

All in One **Unit 3 History of Our World Teaching Resources,** *Rubric for Assessing a Journal Entry*, p. 67

Most Greeks thought that women needed to be guided by men. Women had almost none of the freedom their husbands, sons, and fathers took for granted. They could not take any part in politics. Nor could they vote. They could not own property. About the only official activity allowed them was to be priestesses in religious groups.

Running the home and family was the job of women. In some wealthy families, men and women had completely separate quarters. Women organized the spinning and weaving, looked after supplies of food and wine, and cared for young children. They also kept track of the family finances. If a family was wealthy enough to have slaves, they were the woman's responsibility as well. She directed them, trained them, and cared for them when they were sick.

If a woman lived in a poor household, she often worked outside of the home. Women who had little money found jobs making pottery, tending sheep, or manufacturing cloth from wool.

Although women throughout Greece did important work, they were expected to be almost invisible. As Pericles once said: "The greatest glory belong to the woman who is least talked about by men, either they praise her or find fault with her."

✓ **Reading Check** What kinds of foods did Athenians eat?

Links to Art

Painting Their Lives
Athenians were known for their beautiful pottery. They decorated vases, jars, and cups with black or reddish-tan figures. Many scenes were mythological, but others showed Athenian daily life. Some of the pottery was used in religious ceremonies. However, much of it was used in Athenian households to carry water, serve food, and hold flowers.

Background: Links Across Time

Valuable Oil Ancient Greeks valued olive oil highly. They used it as cooking oil and as a fuel oil in lamps. They anointed people with it in religious rituals. They also traded it for grain and other foods.

Today, health-conscious people value olive oil for another reason. In recent years, scientists noted that people from Mediterranean countries have a relatively low incidence of heart disease despite a relatively high intake of fats and oils. Scientists theorize that when olive oil is substituted for saturated fats in the diet, it may help reduce the risk of heart disease.

Guided Instruction (continued)
■ Ask students **What did Athenian men think the role of women should be?** (*Men thought women should be guided by men and that they should be protected from the outside world.*)

■ Have students compare and contrast the lives of Athenian women with the lives of women today. (*Possible responses: Women today work outside the home. Women do not spin and weave fabric for clothing. Most women today do not spend their lives secluded in their homes. Some women then and now take care of the finances in the home*)

Independent Practice
Ask students to create the Venn diagram described in Taking Notes on blank pieces of paper. Have them write the differences between the lives of Greek men and women in the outside areas and the similarities in their lives in the inside area. Briefly model how to identify which details to record.

Monitor Progress
As students fill in their graphic organizers, circulate and make sure individuals are choosing the correct details. Provide assistance as needed.

Links

Read the **Links to Art** on this page. Ask students what uses the Greeks had for their beautiful pottery. (*Greeks used their pottery to carry water, serve food, and hold flowers.*)

Answers

✓ **Reading Check** Athenians ate simple meals of bread, cheese, olives, fish, vegetables, and sweet cakes. They seldom ate meat.

Slavery in Ancient Greece

Guided Instruction

- **Vocabulary Builder** Clarify the high-use word **estimate** before reading.

- Read the first two paragraphs of Slavery in Ancient Greece, using the Choral Reading technique (TE, p. T38). Before you begin, encourage students to think about how the ancient Greeks' attitudes toward slavery compare to what we think about slavery today.

- Ask students **How did people become slaves in ancient Greece?** *(Many slaves were captured by pirates or by armies during wars. Others were born into slavery.)*

- Discuss what it meant to be a slave in ancient Greece. *(Slaves did not have any political rights or personal freedom. They received no education. They could only become free if they bought their freedom or if their master freed them.)*

- Ask students **How did slave labor affect Greek society?** *(Possible answer: Slaves made it possible for Athenian men to spend time participating in government and in the arts. Slaves helped in the households so that the women did not have so much to do. Ancient Greek society probably could not have functioned without slaves.)*

Independent Practice

Ask students to fill in another Venn diagram. In the outer areas, have students write the ways in which slaves' lives were different from the lives of non-slaves. In the center, write the ways in which their lives were similar.

Monitor Progress

- Show *Section Reading Support Transparency HOW 76* and ask students to check their graphic organizers individually. Go over key concepts and clarify key vocabulary as needed.

  📖 **History of Our World Transparencies,** *Section Reading Support Transparency HOW 76.*

- Tell students to fill in the last column of the *Reading Readiness Guide.* Probe for what they learned that confirms or invalidates each statement.

  All in One Unit 3 History of Our World Teaching Resources, *Reading Readiness Guide,* p. 44.

Slavery in Ancient Greece

Slaves did a great deal of work throughout the city-states of Greece. It was the labor of the slaves that gave Athenian men the leisure time to go to the Agora, participate in government, and develop a love of the arts.

Slavery, the condition of being owned by someone else, was common in Athens. Historians estimate that as many as 100,000 slaves may have lived in Athens. This would mean that almost one third of the city's population were slaves. Today, we consider slavery a crime. However, in ancient times free people rarely questioned slavery, even in democratic Athens.

Who Were the Slaves? Many free people became enslaved when they were captured by armies during war or by pirates while traveling on ships. Children born into slave families automatically became slaves.

Some Greeks were uncomfortable owning other Greeks. Greeks with such scruples, or ethical objections to a situation, solved this problem by owning foreign slaves. A large number of slaves in Greece were foreigners.

The Slaves of Athens
In this detail from a vase, a servant attends to a seated woman. **Draw Conclusions** *Based on what you have read, draw a conclusion about the ancient Greek's attitudes toward slavery.*

Answers

Draw Conclusions Most Greeks preferred to have slaves who were non-Greeks. Ancient Greeks' attitudes toward slavery were different from those today because nearly one-third of the population were slaves.

The Lives of Slaves Slaves did not have any of the privileges taken for granted by the rest of Greek society. Citizenship in Greece was very restricted, so it follows that slaves, on the lowest rung of Greek society, were not citizens. They had no political rights or personal freedom and they received no formal education. Slaves could only become free if they bought their own freedom or if their master freed them.

Remember that without the labor of the slaves, Greek citizens—that is, Greek men—would not have had the leisure to participate in government and the arts. Slaves did many kinds of work. Some provided labor on farms. Others dug silver and other metals in mines. Still others assisted artisans by making pottery and other decorative items. Some slaves helped construct buildings. Others helped forge weapons and armor. Most Greek households could not have operated without slaves. They cooked and served food, tended children, cleaned, and wove cloth.

✓ **Reading Check** What kinds of labor did slaves perform?

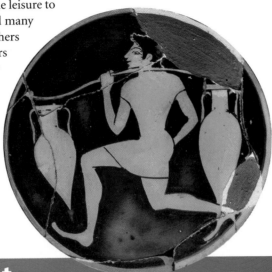
A painting from a cup shows a male slave balancing two vessels.

Section 1 Assessment

Key Terms
Review the key terms at the beginning of this section. Use each term in a sentence that explains its meaning.

Target Reading Skill
Name two ways in which the lives of Athenian men and women were similar. Name two ways in which they differed.

Comprehension and Critical Thinking
1. (a) Describe What activities took place in the Agora of Athens?
(b) Explore Main Ideas and Details What does the Agora tell us about the culture of Athens?

2. (a) Recall Describe the home life of the Athenians.
(b) Compare What were the responsibilities of men compared to those of women in ancient Athens?
(c) Draw Conclusions Considering your answer to the previous question, what conclusions can you make about society in ancient Athens?

3. (a) Recall Describe the various roles of slaves in Athens and of those in the rest of ancient Greece.
(b) Draw Inferences Free people rarely questioned slavery in ancient Greece. Why do you think this was so?

Writing Activity
Write a description of your school-day routine. How does your day compare with that of the Greek boy you read about at the beginning of this section?

For: An activity on the women of ancient Greece
Visit: PHSchool.com
Web Code: mud-0710

Chapter 7 Section 1 **203**

women lived almost separate lives and that democracy only applied to men.

3. (a) Possible answer: Slaves provided labor on farms, in mines, in artisans' shops, and in households. **(b)** Possible answer: The Greeks were so used to slavery that it did not occur to them to question it.

Writing Activity
Use the *Rubric for Assessing a Writing Assignment* to evaluate students' responses.

All in One **Unit 3 History of Our World Teaching Resources,** *Rubric for Assessing a Writing Assignment,* p. 68

Assess Progress L2
Have students complete the Section Assessment. Administer the *Section Quiz.*

All in One **Unit 3 History of Our World Teaching Resources,** *Section Quiz,* p. 46

Reteach L1
If students need more instruction, have them read this section in the *Reading and Vocabulary Study Guide.*

Chapter 7, Section 1, **History of Our World Reading and Vocabulary Study Guide,** pp. 81–83

Extend L3
Have students learn more about ancient Greece by completing the *Enrichment.* Assign students to work in groups to work on the project.

All in One **Unit 3 History of Our World Teaching Resources,** *Enrichment,* p. 59

Answers

✓ **Reading Check** Slaves worked in mines, on farms, as laborers assisting artisans, and in households.

Section 1 Assessment

Key Terms
Students' sentences should reflect knowledge of each Key Term.

Target Reading Skill
Possible responses: Athenian men and women ate the same food and lived in the same kind of houses. The men lived a more public life, attending to business in the Agora and socializing with each other. The women stayed at home, attending to the household. Men could participate in politics and vote, whereas women could not.

Comprehension and Critical Thinking
1. (a) Men discussed politics, philosophy, religion, and local events. Goods were sold.
(b) Possible response: Men led public lives and women led more private lives.
2. (a) Answers may vary, but should reflect some knowledge of Athenian women in the home. **(b)** Possible answer: Men conducted business in public, while women ran the households. **(c)** Student answers should show an understanding that men and

Focus On The Agora of Athens

L2

Guided Instruction

- Read the paragraphs on pp. 186–187 and study the art, photos, and captions as a class.

- Ask **Which building in the agora would Athenians probably have gone to for a religious ceremony?** *(Possible answer: Athenians would have probably gone to the Hephaeisteion for a religious ceremony because it was a temple that honored a god.)* **Where would Athenians probably have gone to conduct government business?** *(Possible answer: Athenians would have probably gone to the Bouleuterion to conduct government business because it was where the council met.)*

- Ask students **How was the layout of the agora of Athens different from some others? What do you think accounted for this difference?** *(Buildings in the Athenian agora were laid out in a rambling style, rather than as squares or rectangles. Possible answer: With the square or rectangle style, city dwellers probably planned the layout of the city before constructing the buildings. The agora of Athens probably developed without such planning).*

- Ask students **What are some historic events that took place in the Athenian agora?** *(Pericles spoke there, Socrates taught and was sentenced to death, and citizens participated in government.)*

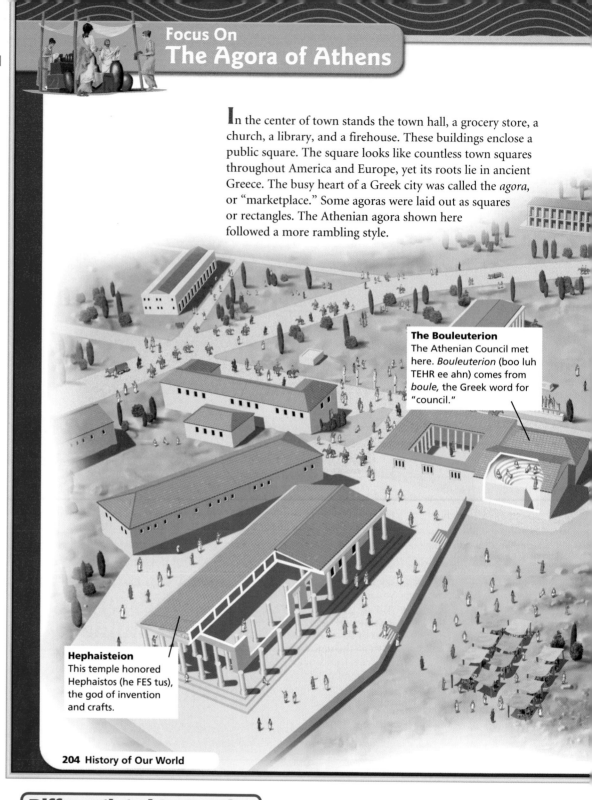

Focus On The Agora of Athens

In the center of town stands the town hall, a grocery store, a church, a library, and a firehouse. These buildings enclose a public square. The square looks like countless town squares throughout America and Europe, yet its roots lie in ancient Greece. The busy heart of a Greek city was called the *agora*, or "marketplace." Some agoras were laid out as squares or rectangles. The Athenian agora shown here followed a more rambling style.

The Bouleuterion
The Athenian Council met here. *Bouleuterion* (boo luh TEHR ee ahn) comes from *boule*, the Greek word for "council."

Hephaisteion
This temple honored Hephaistos (he FES tus), the god of invention and crafts.

Differentiated Instruction

For English Language Learners L1

Some of the words in the captions may be unfamiliar to students learning English. Share the following definitions with English language learners:

- *concil—n.* a group of people that makes laws or governs a city or town
- *rambling—adj.* extended over an irregular area; not orderly
- *temple— n.* any building used in the worship of gods or goddesses

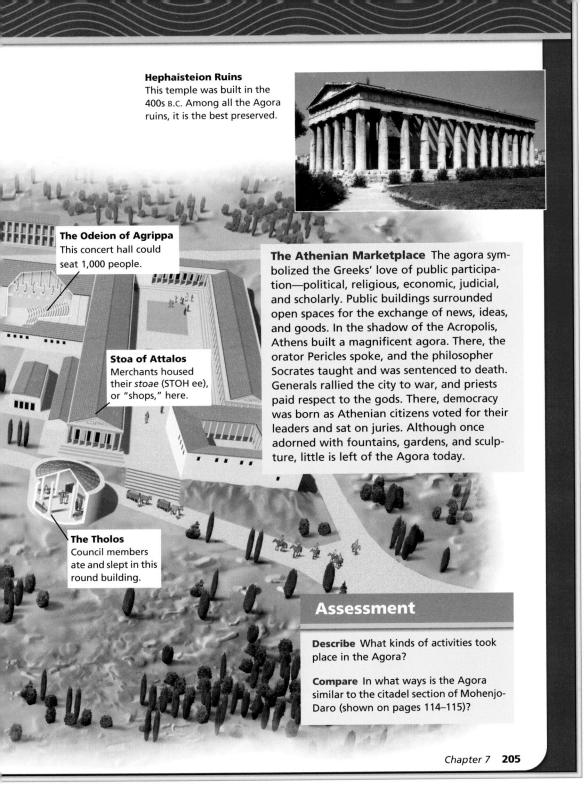

Hephaisteion Ruins
This temple was built in the 400s B.C. Among all the Agora ruins, it is the best preserved.

The Odeion of Agrippa
This concert hall could seat 1,000 people.

Stoa of Attalos
Merchants housed their *stoae* (STOH ee), or "shops," here.

The Tholos
Council members ate and slept in this round building.

The Athenian Marketplace The agora symbolized the Greeks' love of public participation—political, religious, economic, judicial, and scholarly. Public buildings surrounded open spaces for the exchange of news, ideas, and goods. In the shadow of the Acropolis, Athens built a magnificent agora. There, the orator Pericles spoke, and the philosopher Socrates taught and was sentenced to death. Generals rallied the city to war, and priests paid respect to the gods. There, democracy was born as Athenian citizens voted for their leaders and sat on juries. Although once adorned with fountains, gardens, and sculpture, little is left of the Agora today.

Assessment

Describe What kinds of activities took place in the Agora?

Compare In what ways is the Agora similar to the citadel section of Mohenjo-Daro (shown on pages 114–115)?

Independent Practice

Have students work in small groups to create a layout of their own community, town, or city and compare it to the illustration of the agora. Have groups draw a sketch of their community that shows the major public buildings. Captions should describe the major buildings and explain their function. Then ask the groups to write a list of differences and similarities between the agora and their own town, such as types of buildings or distances between major buildings.

Answers

Assessment

Describe People gathered to hear speeches or lessons, buy or sell goods, worship gods, vote and sit on juries.
Compare The agora and the Mohenjo-Daro citadel are both public spaces used for gatherings. Both include public buildings such as places of worship, and are separated in some way from the rest of the city.

Section 2 Athens and Sparta

Objectives

Social Studies
1. Learn how people lived in ancient Sparta.
2. Discover some results of the Persian invasion of Greece.
3. Understand the conflicts that the Athenian empire faced.

Reading/Language Arts
Identify contrasts between peoples, cultures, or other items to see how they differ.

Prepare to Read

Build Background Knowledge `L2`

Ask volunteers to read the first three paragraphs of this lesson. Then, using the Idea Wave strategy (TE, p. T39), ask students how the life of the young Spartan boy contrasts to that of the young Athenian boy they read about in the preceding section. Ask students to predict, based on what they know about Athenian life and what they have just read, what this conflict between Athens and Sparta might be. *(Possible response: The conflict probably has a lot to do with the different ways the two city-states approach life.)*

Set a Purpose for Reading `L2`

- Preview the Objectives.

- Form students into pairs or groups of four. Distribute the *Reading Readiness Guide.* Ask students to fill in the first two columns of the chart. Use the Numbered Heads strategy (TE, p. T40) to call on students to share one piece of information they already know and one piece of information they want to know.

All in One Unit 3 History of Our World Teaching Resources, *Reading Readiness Guide,* p. 48

Vocabulary Builder
Preview Key Terms `L2`

Pronounce each Key Term, and then ask the students to say the word with you. Provide a simple explanation such as "a plague is a disease that is spread easily and quickly to other people."

Prepare to Read

Objectives
In this section you will
1. Learn how people lived in ancient Sparta.
2. Discover some results of the Persian invasion of Greece.
3. Understand the conflicts that the Athenian empire faced.

Taking Notes
As you read, look for ways in which Spartans differed from Athenians. Copy the chart below, and use it to record those differences.

Differences Between Spartans and Athenians

Spartans	Athenians
• Boys trained in military arts	• Boys educated in arts, history, and physical training
•	•
•	•

⟳ Target Reading Skill

Identify Contrasts When you contrast two peoples or cultures, you examine how they differ. In this section, you will read about the Spartan people. Although they had many of the same elements of Greek culture that the Athenians did, they differed in other ways. As you read, list the differences between Athens and Sparta. Record your findings in your Taking Notes chart.

Key Terms
- **Sparta** (SPAHR tuh) *n.* a city-state in ancient Greece
- **helots** (HEL uts) *n.* In ancient Sparta, the term for slaves who were owned by the state
- **Peloponnesian War** (pel uh puh NEE shun wawr) *n.* (431–404 B.C.), war fought between Athens and Sparta in ancient Greece; almost every other Greek city-state was involved in the war
- **plague** (playg) *n.* a widespread disease
- **blockade** (blah KAYD) *n.* an action taken to isolate the enemy and cut off its supplies

A Spartan warrior

The boy stood still and straight beside his companions as their trainer approached. "You," the trainer barked, "Are you sick? Don't think you'll get out of sword practice—and why are you holding your belly? Hiding something?"

The trainer gave the boy's cloak a sharp tug. It fell to the ground, freeing a fox that streaked off into the underbrush. The boy fell to the ground. His cloak was blood red. His side was shredded with deep cuts and bites. The boy had stolen the fox and hidden it beneath his cloak.

Later, the boy died from his wounds. He had endured terrible pain without giving any sign of his distress. To the Spartans, this was the sign of true character.

This Spartan story of the boy and the fox may be true, or it might be just a legend. However, it tells us much about the people of **Sparta**, a city-state in southern Greece.

⟳ Target Reading Skill `L2`

Identify Contrasts Point out the Target Reading Skill. Explain to students that they can learn about peoples, cultures, or other items by understanding their differences as well as their similarities.

Model identifying contrasts by having students read the first paragraph on p. 207 and contrast it to what they already know about life in Athens. *(Life in Athens was free and open. The men spent time discussing ideas in the Agora. Life in Sparta was the opposite of life in Athens. It was harsh and cruel.)*

Give students *Identify Contrasts.* Have them complete the activity in their groups.

All in One Unit 3 History of Our World Teaching Resources, *Identify Contrasts,* p. 56

Living in Sparta

Life in Athens was free and open, but life for the citizens of Sparta was just the opposite. Life in Sparta was harsh and even cruel. The Spartans themselves were tough, silent, and grim. Sparta's army easily equaled that of Athens' in the 400s B.C. However, Sparta never came close to equaling Athens' other achievements.

In its early days, Sparta was similar to other Greek cities. Then, in the 600s B.C., wars inside and outside the city led to changes in the government and the way people lived. The changes turned Sparta into a powerful war machine. The city-state established one basic rule: Always put the city's needs above your own.

Early in its history, the Spartans conquered the land around their city. They turned the conquered people into **helots**, or slaves owned by the city-state of Sparta. Helots did all the farm work on the land owned by Spartan citizens. This system left the Spartans free to wage war. However, the helots far outnumbered the Spartans. Living in fear of a helot revolt, the Spartans turned their city into an armed camp. They treated the helots very harshly.

✓ **Reading Check** What type of people were the Spartans?

Sparta lies in a fertile valley with mountains on three sides. Sparta spent its money and energy on its army instead of fine buildings. Today, few ruins remain to tell us about this important city-state.

Chapter 7 Section 2 **207**

Vocabulary Builder

Use the information below to teach students this section's high-use words.

High-Use Word	Definition and Sample Sentence
revolt, p. 207	*n.* a rebellion The slaves planned a **revolt** when they could stand the hard conditions of their lives no more.
exaggerated, p. 210	*v.* to have enlarged beyond the truth; overstated In legends, people have often **exaggerated** the deeds of Greek heroes.
resent, p. 212	*v.* to feel or express ill will or annoyance The slaves began to **resent** the easy life of their masters.

Growing Up in Sparta

Guided Instruction

- Have students read Growing Up in Sparta. Tell them to keep in mind the differences between a Spartan upbringing and an Athenian one.

- Discuss what it was like for a boy to grow up in Sparta. (*Boys' training was very strict. They left home at age seven to live in a barracks where they were trained in the military arts. They were given little food and bedding to make them tough. Boys were expected to bear pain in silence.*)

- Ask students what the following statement means: "The life of every Spartan was in the hands of the government from birth." (*Possible response: The government decided if they would live or die at birth and controlled their education.*)

- Ask students **How would you feel living this way?** (*The government dictated that they would be soldiers for forty years.*)

- Ask students **What rights did Spartan men have?** (*At age 30, they could join the council, which approved decisions made by the king's advisors.*)

Helmet worn by Greek soldiers

Spartan soldiers were trained to be excellent warriors. Many armies suffered defeat at the hands of Spartan fighting forces.

Growing Up in Sparta

The life of every Spartan was in the hands of the government from birth. Only the healthiest children were raised because the Spartans wanted only the healthiest people in their city.

Growing Up Male Training began early. At seven, a Spartan boy left his home to live in barracks with other boys. His training continued for the next 13 years.

By the age of 12, a boy had spent long hours practicing with swords and spears. He had only one cloak and a thin mat to sleep on. He could hardly live on the small amount of food he was given, so he was urged to steal. The Spartans thought that a boy who learned to steal would know how to live off the land during a war. However, if the boy were caught stealing, he was severely punished. Boys were expected to bear pain, hardship, and punishment in silence. Through this rigid discipline, Spartan youths became excellent soldiers.

When he became 20, a young man officially became a soldier. Men remained soldiers until their sixtieth birthdays. At the age of 30, a man was able to take his place in the assembly, a council consisting of all the male citizens born in Sparta. As in Athens, only non-slave males were considered citizens in Sparta. The council approved the decisions made by the council of elders who, in turn, acted as advisors to the king.

Differentiated Instruction

For English Language Learners
Explain that many English words have Greek origins. Provide copies of the following examples of Greek roots and their meanings:

photo-	light	-scope	viewing, observing
micro-	small	-meter	measure
phono-	sound	-nomy	knowledge

L1 Show students how familiar words such as *microscope* are formed from Greek roots. Challenge students to use the list to form other familiar words. Have students consult a dictionary to verify unfamiliar words and to check definitions.

Growing Up Female Like the boys, girls also trained and competed in wrestling and spear throwing. No one expected girls to become soldiers. However, Spartans did believe that girls who grew up strong and healthy would have strong, healthy children. Therefore, unlike other Greek women, Spartan women were trained to exercise and build up their bodies.

Spartan women had a somewhat better life than women in other Greek city-states. They were allowed to own land and even take some part in business. However, like their Athenian sisters, they had to obey the males—the fathers, husbands, or brothers—in their lives. Because the men were so involved in military matters, some Spartan women took on larger responsibilities, such as the running of their farms or estates.

Spartan Attitudes The Spartans did not mingle with other Greeks. They were not allowed to travel. They looked down on the desire for wealth and on those engaged in trade. They lacked the interest in the arts that the Athenians and some other Greeks cultivated. However, Spartan warriors were known for their skill and bravery. The Spartan fighting force played a key role in the Greek wars against the Persians, a people who lived across the Aegean Sea, east of Greece.

Identify Contrasts Contrast the life of Spartan women to that of Athenian women. Enter your findings on your Taking Notes chart.

✓ **Reading Check** What was the Spartan attitude about trade?

Chapter 7 Section 2 **209**

Guided Instruction (continued)
■ Ask students **What did the Spartans think the place of women was in their society?** *(Women were trained to exercise and build up their bodies not for warfare but in order to have strong, healthy children.)*

Target Reading Skill

Identify Contrasts As a follow up, ask students to answer the Target Reading Skill question in the Student Edition. *(Spartan women had more rights than Athenian women. They could own land and run businesses. They learned to exercise and build up their bodies. They often had to take over the running of farms or estates because the men were so involved in war.)*

Independent Practice
Ask students to use the Taking Notes graphic organizer that they began in Living in Sparta. Have them fill in the blanks with the information they have just learned.

Monitor Progress
As students fill in the graphic organizer, circulate and make sure individuals are choosing the correct details.

Differentiated Instruction

For Less Proficient Readers　　**L1**
Tell students that the frieze was an important art form of ancient Greece. A frieze could depict historical or mythological events. Provide books that have Greek art so that students can look at and read about friezes. Then have students work together to create a frieze showing daily life in ancient Greece.

For Gifted and Talented　　**L3**
Have students divide into two teams, one representing Sparta and the other Athens. Have them conduct research on their respective city-states. Then have the two teams stage a debate on the question of which city offered a better way of life.

Answers

✓ **Reading Check** The Spartans were not interested in wealth and looked down on people who were involved in trade

The Persians Invade

Guided Instruction

- **Vocabulary Builder** Clarify the high-use word **exaggerate** before reading.

- Read The Persians Invade, using the Choral Reading strategy (TE, p. T38). Tell them to read to see how Persia came to attack Greece.

- Discuss the Persian invasion. Have students explain what happened to the individual Greek city-states when they knew Persia would attack. (*The Greeks put aside their differences and joined forces.*)

- Ask students **Why do you think the Athenians were able to defeat the Persians at Marathon?** (*Possible responses: The Athenians fought more fiercely, because they were defending their homeland. The Athenians valued their independence and freedom strongly and did not want to lose that to the Persians.*)

Independent Practice

Assign *Guided Reading and Review.*

All in One **Unit 3 History of Our World Teaching Resources,** *Guided Reading and Review,* p. 49

Monitor Progress

As students fill in the *Guided Reading and Review*, circulate and make sure individuals are choosing the correct details. Provide assistance as needed.

Links

Read **Links Across Time** on this page. Ask students **Why do you think that people honored the man who ran the first marathon?** (*Possible response: People then and now marvel and celebrate great feats of athleticism and endurance. Also, this young man was extremely valiant in performing what he considered a very important task.*)

Answers

✓ **Reading Check** The small Athenian army defeated the Persian army that outnumbered them 2 to 1.
Timeline Skills **Identify** The Persians burned the Acropolis. **Analyze** after the Peloponnesian War

---

Links Across Time

The Legend of the Marathon Stories say that after the battle at Marathon, the Athenians sent their fastest runner to tell the people of Athens of the victory. His chest heaving, the runner covered the distance to the city and shouted to the people "Rejoice! We have won." Then he dropped dead. The actual distance from Marathon to Athens is about 25 miles (40 km). Today's marathon races of 26.2 miles (42 km) honor this legend.

■ **Timeline Skills**

The timeline below covers events that occured during Classical Greece, an era that lasted from about 500 B.C. to 323 B.C. **Identify** What event occured near the end of the Persian Wars? **Analyze** After which war did Athens surrender to Sparta?

The Persians Invade

Much of Greek history tells of wars the Greeks fought among themselves. Near the beginning of the 400s B.C., a new threat loomed—the growing might of Persia. The Greeks put aside their differences and joined forces to defend their peninsula.

The Expanding Persian Empire Cyrus the Great had founded the Persian Empire in the mid-500s B.C. Cyrus and the rulers who followed him extended the original empire. By 520 B.C., the Persians had gained control of the Greek colonies on the west coast of Asia Minor.

Battle at Marathon In the fall of 490 B.C., a force including thousands of Persians landed in Greece. The Persian soldiers gathered at Marathon (MAR uh thahn), about 25 miles (40 km) north of Athens. The Athenians hastily put together a small army. However, the Persians outnumbered them by at least two to one. For several days, the armies stared tensely at each other across the plain of Marathon.

Then, without warning, the Athenians rushed the Persians, who were overwhelmed by the furious attack. By one account, at the end of the battle the Athenians had killed 6,400 Persians but had lost only 192 soldiers themselves. The Persian losses may have been exaggerated. However, it is true that in a short time this tiny state had defeated the giant that had come to destroy it.

✓ **Reading Check** What happened during the battle at Marathon?

Classical Greece

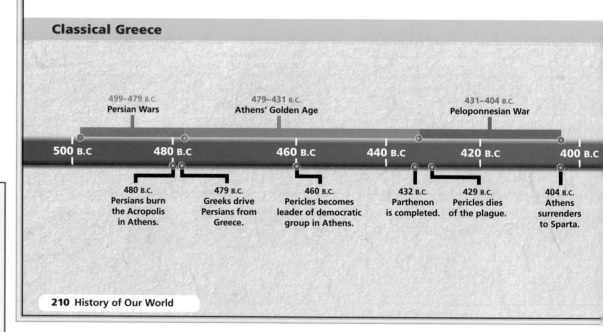

| 499–479 B.C. Persian Wars | 479–431 B.C. Athens' Golden Age | 431–404 B.C. Peloponnesian War |

500 B.C — 480 B.C — 460 B.C — 440 B.C — 420 B.C — 400 B.C

480 B.C. Persians burn the Acropolis in Athens.

479 B.C. Greeks drive Persians from Greece.

460 B.C. Pericles becomes leader of democratic group in Athens.

432 B.C. Parthenon is completed.

429 B.C. Pericles dies of the plague.

404 B.C. Athens surrenders to Sparta.

Background: Links Across Time

Most of what we know about the Persian Wars comes to us from the Greek historian, Herodotus. During the wars, according to Herodotus, some Greek deserters informed King Xerxes that the Greeks were holding their Olympic games. Xerxes asked about the prize for which the athletes were contending. Hearing that the prize was not money but a wreath of olives, Xerxes exclaimed aloud, "Good heavens, what manner of men are these against whom you have brought us to fight—men who contend with one another not for money but for honor!"

These warriors decorate a vase from the 500s B.C. The background is the natural color of the baked clay. The black figures were made by using a glossy black pigment.

Guided Instruction

- Have students read Conflict and the Athenian Empire to see what happened as a result of the Persian invasion.

- Ask students **What happened to the Greek city-states as a result of the Persian invasions?** *(The Greek city-states stopped fighting one another and united to fight Persia.)*

- Have students explain what happened to Athens after the Persian war. *(Possible response: Athens became the most powerful city-state after the war. Athens controlled the Delian League and treated the other city-states as subjects. Athens also fostered democracy at home.)*

Independent Practice

Assign *Guided Reading and Review*.

All in One **Unit 3 History of Our World Teaching Resources,** *Guided Reading and Review,* p. 49

Monitor Progress

As students are filling in the *Guided Reading and Review* sheet, circulate to see if they are doing so accurately. Provide assistance as needed.

Conflict and the Athenian Empire

More battles with Persia followed. As a common enemy, Persia distracted the Greek city-states from fighting one another. Briefly united, Greece drove away the Persians.

Their victory over the Persians increased the Greeks' sense of their own importance. They believed that the gods had favored them and had therefore influenced the outcome of the wars.

Athens emerged from the war as the most powerful city-state in Greece. Its influence spread over much of eastern Greece. Athens joined other city-states in the Delian League (DEE lee un leeg), named after the island of Delos (DEE lahs), where the league's treasury was kept. In time, however, these cities were treated more like subjects of Athens and less like allies. Athens came to dominate the league and used it to create its own empire.

Ironically, while Athens was expanding its empire and forcing other city-states to bow to its will, Athens came to champion political freedom at home. Athens did support democratic groups within the other city-states, but its focus was on freedom for its own people. The years following the Persian Wars were the Golden Age of Athens that you read about in Chapter 6.

✓ **Reading Check** Why did Greeks believe they had won their wars with Persia?

Citizen Heroes ★

Working Together

In one of the wars against the Persians, some 6,000 Greeks had to defend a mountain pass leading into southern Greece. They faced nearly 200,000 Persians. Most of the Greeks retreated, but 300 Spartan soldiers stood their ground. All of them died in the battle. They didn't hold back the Persians, but they earned undying praise for their brave sacrifice.

Citizen Heroes ★

Read the **Citizen Heroes** on this page. Ask students **What does the battle described here tell about the character of the Greeks?** *(Possible response: The fierceness and endurance of the fighters indicates just how important freedom and sacrifice were to the ancient Greeks.)*

Chapter 7 Section 2 **211**

Differentiated Instruction

For Less Proficient Readers **L1**

Have students discuss the events on the timeline on p. 210. Ask them to think of these questions during their discussion: **Why was the Greek victory against the Persians important? Why did Sparta go to war against Athens? Could Athens have prevented its own destruction?**

For Advanced Readers **L3**

Tell students that the marathon is a standard event in the Olympic Games, which originated from the ancient games. Encourage students to research the ancient Olympic Games. After they complete their research, have students present their findings.

Answer

✓ **Reading Check** They believed that the gods had favored them.

Sparta and Athens at War

Guided Instruction

- **Vocabulary Builder** Clarify the high-use word **resent** before reading.

- Have students read Sparta and Athens at War to see why the two city-states began fighting.

- Ask students **Why did Sparta form the Peloponnesian League?** Then have them tell who joined the league and why. (*Sparta was not part of the Delian League. Sparta wanted a league of its own. City-states who feared the power of Athens joined with Sparta.*)

- Ask students **What advantages and disadvantages did Athens have in fighting the war?** (*Athens had great wealth and a strong navy, but a geographic disadvantage.*)

- **What was Sparta's main advantage in the war?** (*Sparta was located inland so it could not be attacked by sea.*)

- Ask students **What other factors led to Athens' defeat?** (*A plague occurred when people from the country moved inside the walls. After Pericles' death, power struggles also weakened the city. Using the Persian navy, the Spartans blockaded Athens so they could not receive any food.*)

Show students Spartan Warriors. Ask students **What were the steps to becoming a Spartan Soldier? Would you have chosen to be one? Why or why not?** (*A boy was trained militarily from an early age to out-march and outfight everyone. Answers will vary.*)

Independent Practice
Have students add the information about the differences between Sparta and Athens to complete their graphic organizers.

Monitor Progress

- Show *Section Reading Support Transparency HOW 77* and ask students to check their graphic organizers individually. Go over key concepts and clarify key vocabulary as needed.

  History of Our World Transparencies, *Section Reading Support Transparency HOW 77*

- Tell students to fill in the last column of the *Reading Readiness Guide.* Ask them to evaluate whether what they learned was what they had expected to learn.

  All in One Unit 3 History of Our World Teaching Resources, *Reading Readiness Guide,* p. 48

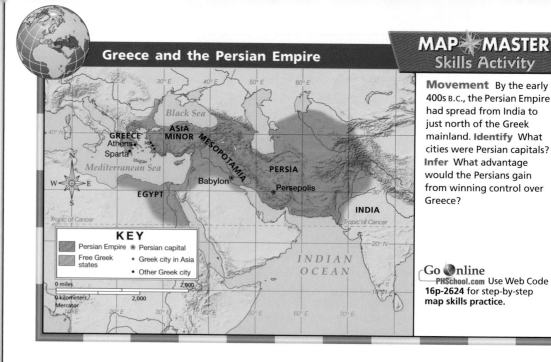

Greece and the Persian Empire

MAP MASTER™ Skills Activity

Movement By the early 400s B.C., the Persian Empire had spread from India to just north of the Greek mainland. **Identify** What cities were Persian capitals? **Infer** What advantage would the Persians gain from winning control over Greece?

Go Online PHSchool.com Use Web Code **16p-2624** for step-by-step map skills practice.

KEY
- Persian Empire
- Free Greek states
- ⊛ Persian capital
- ★ Greek city in Asia
- • Other Greek city

0 miles 2,000
0 kilometers 2,000
Mercator

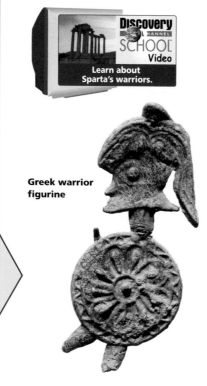

Learn about Sparta's warriors.

Greek warrior figurine

212 History of Our World

Sparta and Athens at War

Athens may have been a democracy at home, but it began to act unfairly toward other city-states. At first, allies of Athens had paid tribute to the city-state for protection, in case the Persians caused more trouble. Later, Athens moved the treasury from Delos to Athens and used the money that was supposed to help defend its allies to build the Parthenon and to finance other projects.

The Peloponnesian War The people of these city-states began to fear and resent Athens' power. They looked to Sparta, which had not joined the alliance, to protect them. To counter the Delian League, Sparta formed the Peloponnesian League, named after Peloponnesus, the southern Greek peninsula where Sparta was located. In 431 B.C., Sparta and its allies fought against Athens and its allies. Thus began the **Peloponnesian War**, a conflict between Athens and Sparta that lasted for 27 years.

Even though Athens had a fine navy and more wealth than the other city-states, its geography was a great disadvantage in the war. Sparta, located inland, could not be attacked from the sea. However, Sparta had only to march north to attack Athens by land.

Answers

MAP MASTER™ Skills Activity **Identify** Babylon, Persepolis **Infer** The Persians would rule more ports on the Black and Mediterranean Seas and also extend their empire into Europe.

When Sparta invaded Athens, the statesman Pericles, whom you read about in Chapter 6, let the people from the surrounding countryside move inside the city walls. The overcrowded conditions led to a **plague**, or widespread disease. By the time the plague ended five years later, about one third of the people of Athens had died from it. Among the dead was Pericles. The power struggles of those who sought to take Pericles' place also undermined the city's government.

The Fall of Athens Athens never recovered from its losses during the plague. To make matters worse, Sparta allied itself to its former common enemy to have the advantage of the Persian navy. In 405 B.C., with their new allies, the Spartans staged a **blockade**, an action taken to isolate the enemy and cut off its supplies. The Spartans surrounded and closed the harbor where Athens received food shipments. Starving and beaten, the Athenians surrendered in 404 B.C.

The victorious Spartans knocked down the walls of Athens. They destroyed its navy and decimated its empire. Athens never again dominated the Greek world.

✓ **Reading Check** What did Greek city-states do to overcome oppression by Athens?

Athens Defeated
Shields and spears, such as those carried by the warriors below, could not spare the Athenians from the plague. **Analyze** *What factors contributed to the fall of Athens?*

⭐ **Section 2 Assessment**

Key Terms
Review the key terms listed at the beginning of this section. Use each term in a sentence that explains its meaning.

⊙ **Target Reading Skill**
Look at the chart you made of the differences between the Spartans and the Athenians. Name one of the differences that led to the outcome of the Peloponnesian War.

Comprehension and Critical Thinking
1. (a) **Recall** Describe what life was like for boys living in Sparta.
(b) **Explain** What was the Spartan attitude toward wealth?

(c) **Draw Inferences** How did the Spartans' attitude toward wealth affect their trade and travel?
2. (a) **Describe** How did the Greeks overcome the Persian invasion?
(b) **Evaluate Information** What was at stake for the people of Athens at the Battle of Marathon?
(c) **Predict** How might the history of Greece have changed if the Persians had succeeded at Marathon?
3. (a) **Recall** What happened to the Greeks' attitude about themselves after defeating the Persians?
(b) **Summarize** How did the Athenian empire develop after its victory over Persia?

(c) **Synthesize Information** How did Athens play a part in its own downfall?

Writing Activity
Reread the story that begins this section. From a trainer's point of view, write a report that explains the event to other Spartan officers.

For: An activity on politics in Sparta
Visit: PHSchool.com
Web Code: mud-0720

---

3. (a) Greeks were impressed by their own importance. (b) Possible response: The empire formed the Delian League. Wealth gave the Athenians the time and freedom to explore ideas, which led to the Golden Age of Athens. (c) Possible response: Athens treated the other city-states unfairly and eventually turned them against Athens. Overcrowding of the city led to a plague, which killed one-third of the population.

Writing Activity
Use the *Rubric for Assessing a Report* to evaluate students' reports.

All in One **Unit 3 History of Our World Teaching Resources,** *Rubric for Assessing a Report*, p. 69

Assess Progress L2
Have students complete the Section Assessment and administer the *Section Quiz*.

All in One **Unit 3 History of Our World Teaching Resources,** *Section Quiz*, p. 50

Reteach L1
If students need more instruction, have them read this section in the *Reading and Vocabulary Study Guide*.

📖 Chapter 7, Section 2, **History of Our World Reading and Vocabulary Study Guide**, pp. 84–86

Extend L3
Have students learn more about ancient Greece by reading a primary source. Then have students write a brief description of what a typical day in the life of the Spartan might have been.

Answers

Analyze Athens lost many people during the plague; Sparta and the Peloponnesian League opposed Athens after the victory at Marathon; Sparta joined the Persian naval forces and staged a blockade against Athens, cutting off their food supplies and forcing Athens to surrender.

✓ **Reading Check** Some of the city-states joined the Peloponnesian League led by Sparta and eventually went to war against Athens.

Section 2 Assessment

Key Terms
Students' sentences should reflect knowledge of each Key Term.

⊙ **Target Reading Skill**
Answers will vary. Students' responses should indicate their understanding of the differences between the two city-states.

Comprehension and Critical Thinking
1. (a) Spartan boys lived a strict life of military training. (b) They looked down on wealth. (c) Possible response: The Spartans did not like people aspiring to wealth, which included traders.
2. (a) The Greek city-states united against the Persians. (b) Freedom. (c) Possible response: Persia might have absorbed Greece into its empire.

Objective

Learn how to analyze primary sources.

Prepare to Read

Build Background Knowledge   L2

Ask volunteers to read aloud the dialogue between Mary and Kevin. Have students use what they already know to explain what an eyewitness account is. Then have a volunteer explain why it would be difficult for Kevin and Mary to talk to an eyewitness for their report. Ask volunteers to speculate about what a primary source is. Then read aloud the paragraph that explains primary sources.

Instruct

Analyzing Primary Resources

Guided Instruction   L2

- Read the steps to learn how to analyze primary sources together as a class.

- Practice the skill by going through the steps on p. 214. Ask students to describe the difference between Atticus' and Demetrius' attitudes. Direct them to point to the clue words that helped them determine this difference. Ask them to guess what positions Atticus and Demetrius had in the army. Ask them what clues led them to this information. Then ask them to explain how the third passage differs from the other two. Ask them to speculate about who wrote the passage and how the passage indicates this information. *(Possible responses: Atticus reveres Alexander; Demetrius thinks Alexander is a great leader but is annoyed with him. Clue words: Atticus—"faithfully," "glorious commander"; Demetrius—"tired of," "how much farther," "but do we really need," "bit greedy," "wish I'd never joined"; Atticus is a commander— he talks about his regiment following his every command; Demetrius is a foot soldier— "marching," "walking"; third passage— written by a modern-day scholar; he writes in third person, "present-day vantage point")*

Mary and Kevin were writing a report on the Peloponnesian War.

"Where should we look for information?" Mary asked.

"You can find anything on the Internet," replied Kevin. "Here's a report that an eighth grader named Tracy wrote."

"It seems as though we ought to have something a little more official than a report written by another student."

"Well, there isn't anyone around to give us a firsthand account," retorted Kevin.

"It can't be a firsthand account," chimed in Kevin's mom, who overheard their conversation. "But you can use something written during a time much closer to the Peloponnesian Wars. You should try to use a primary source."

A primary source is a book, a document, an artifact, or another record that supplies firsthand information about a subject. When you do research, it is important to look carefully at the sources you are using to see how much you can rely on what the author is reporting.

Learn the Skill

Use these steps to learn how to analyze written primary sources:

1. **Look carefully at the material or object.** Who created it? Why?

2. **Find out when the source was written.** Was the information witnessed firsthand?

3. **Determine whether the author is a neutral source.** Does the author show a bias?

4. **Determine why the author created the source.** Is the material meant to persuade or inform?

214 History of Our World

- Discuss what biases Atticus and Demetrius may have had and what clue words let students know this information. Then ask what audience each of the three authors was writing to and what their purpose was. *(Atticus was probably writing home to relatives; he exaggerates by saying none of his soldiers were killed, the number of elephants, his regiment was the most fierce, his troops followed his every command; he wants both Alexander and himself to be honored. Demetrius was probably writing in a journal or to a friend, someone he can trust with his complaints. His purpose is to share his grievances. The historian was writing for a modern-day audience who would not know much about Alexander; his purpose is to inform.)*

> "I, Atticus, take care to write faithfully everything my glorious commander, Alexander, has done on the field of battle. Yesterday, Alexander led us into battle near the Indus River against a hundred thousand soldiers all riding atop gigantic elephants. My regiment was the most fierce of all and followed my every command. Not one of our soldiers died. We routed the enemy by midday."

> "My name is Demetrius. I am a soldier in Alexander's army. We have been marching for ten years now. I'm tired of walking and fighting. I'm cold and hungry all the time. I don't think I'll ever return to Macedonia and my family. How much farther can Alexander make us go? He's a great leader, but do we really need to go all the way to India? Isn't he just a bit greedy for land and power? I wish I'd never joined this army."

> "From our present-day vantage point, we can recognize both positive and negative things about Alexander's campaign to build an empire in the known world at that time. He was a great warrior, and his men were only too happy to follow him into battle. However, by the time they had reached the Indus River, his men began to rebel. They had fought with Alexander for thirteen years, extending the empire from Macedonia to Asia. But now it seemed time to go home."

Practice the Skill

If you were to come across the three quotations above while doing research, how would you evaluate them as historical sources? Ask yourself the following questions:

1. Who is Atticus? Who is Demetrius? Who could be the author of the third quote?

2. When is it likely that Atticus and Demetrius lived? What clues let you know when the third author wrote his or her statement?

3. Do you think that either Atticus or Demetrius is a neutral source? What bias might Demetrius have had? What might Atticus' bias have been? For whom were they writing? Provide evidence for your answers.

4. What purpose does Atticus have for writing? Demetrius? The third writer?

Apply the Skill

Research an aspect of Greek culture discussed in this chapter, such as the life of women in Athens contrasted with the life of women in Sparta. Examine two sources on the same subject, and evaluate the sources as to their bias and reliability.

Chapter 7 **215**

Independent Practice

Assign the *Skills for Life* worksheet, *Analyzing Primary Sources*, and have students complete it individually.

All in One **Unit 3 History of Our World Teaching Resources,** *Analyzing Primary Sources,* p. 60

Monitor Progress

Monitor the students while they are completing the *Skills for Life* worksheet, checking to make sure they understand the skills steps.

Assess and Reteach

Assess Progress L2
Ask students to complete the Apply the Skill Activity.

Reteach L1
If students are having trouble applying the skill steps, have them review the skill using the interactive Social Studies Skills Tutor CD-ROM.

⊙ *Analyzing Primary Sources,* Social Studies Skills Tutor CD-ROM

Extend L3
- Direct students to find examples of bias and prejudice in newspapers or magazines. Explain that a television or magazine advertiser who thinks his or her product is the best is one form of bias. Have them bring their findings to class to share.

- Discuss why some people are biased against others. (*Some points of discussion: Some people feel superior if other people are put down; people are afraid of things/people they do not know or are not comfortable with; some people have been taught a certain way and can not let go of their misinformation*)

Answers
Apply the Skill

Students' evaluations should reflect an understanding of the steps to learn how to analyze primary sources delineated in Learn the Skill.

Chapter 7 **215**

Section 3
Step-by-Step Instruction

Objectives

Social Studies

1. Learn how King Philip of Macedonia came to power and how Alexander the Great built his empire.
2. Understand what role the conquests of Alexander the Great played in spreading Greek culture.

Reading/Language Arts

Analyze information by comparing situations, people, or other items to see how they are alike.

Prepare to Read

Build Background Knowledge [L2]

In this section, students will learn about Alexander the Great, one of the most famous figures in the ancient world, and his father, King Philip. Have volunteers read the headings and look at the visuals on pages 216–219. Ask students what names and whose images appear in the headings and photographs. Then use the Idea Wave strategy (TE, p. T39) to ask students what they know from the visuals and what they have already read about ancient Greece that might help them predict what actions Alexander the Great will take. *(Possible response: The photographs show men at war; the map shows the empire that Alexander built. Section 3 must be about the wars that Alexander fought to gain his empire.)*

Set a Purpose for Reading [L2]

■ Preview the Objectives.

■ Read each statement in the *Reading Readiness Guide* aloud. Ask students to mark the statements true or false.

All in One Unit 3 History of Our World Teaching Resources, *Reading Readiness Guide,* p. 52

■ Have students discuss the statements in pairs or groups of four, and then mark their worksheets again. Use the Numbered Heads strategy (TE, p. T40) to call on students to share their group's perspectives.

Section 3
The Spread of Greek Culture

Prepare to Read

Objectives

In this section you will
1. Learn how King Philip of Macedonia came to power and how Alexander the Great built his empire.
2. Understand what role the conquests of Alexander the Great played in spreading Greek culture.

Taking Notes

As you read, look for details about the spread of Greek culture. Copy the chart below, and use it to record your findings.

The Spread of Greek Culture	
Alexander's Empire	**The Hellenistic Age**
•	•
•	•
•	•

Target Reading Skill

Make Comparisons Comparing two or more situations, people, or items enables you to see how they are alike. As you read this section, compare the ideas of Alexander the Great to those of his predecessors.

Key Terms

• **barbarian** (bahr BEHR eeun) *n.* a person who belongs to a group that others consider wild, or uncivilized

• **assassinate** (uh SAS uh nayt) *v.* to murder for political reasons
• **Alexander the Great** (alig ZAN dur thuh grayt) *n.* king of Macedonia (356–323 B.C.); conquered Persia and Egypt and invaded India
• **Hellenistic** (hel uh NIS tik) *adj.* describing Greek history or culture after the death of Alexander the Great, including the three main kingdoms formed by the breakup of Alexander's empire

A sculpture of King Philip of Macedonia

216 History of Our World

King Philip of Macedonia (mas uh DOH nee uh) had not wasted the money he spent on Greek tutors for his son. Young Alexander was a fine and eager student. The boy wanted to learn as much as he could, especially about the ideas and deeds of the Greeks.

The kingdom of Macedonia lay just north of Greece. Alexander thought of himself as Greek and spoke the Greek language. However, people who lived to the south did not accept the Macedonians as Greeks. They thought the Macedonians were **barbarians**, or wild, uncivilized people.

Alexander's tutor was the Greek philosopher Aristotle (AIR uh STAHT ul). Aristotle taught the boy Greek literature, philosophy, and science. Aristotle also passed on his strong feelings that the Greeks were a superior people and, therefore, deserved to rule.

Alexander loved his tutor, but his role model was Achilles, the warrior hero of the *Iliad*. Alexander vowed to visit the site of ancient Troy and lay a wreath at the tomb of his hero.

Vocabulary Builder
Preview Key Terms [L2]

Pronounce each Key Term, and then ask the students to say the word with you. Provide a simple explanation such as "to assassinate someone means to kill that person for political reasons."

Target Reading Skill [L2]

Make Comparisons Point out the Target Reading Skill. Explain to students that they can learn about different peoples, cultures, and other things by understanding their similarities.

Model making comparisons by having students read the second paragraph p. 217. Ask students **From your reading of Section 2 of this chapter, what other country had similar ideas about Greece?** *(Persia had similar ideas about conquering the Greek city-states.)*

Give students *Make Comparisons*. Have them complete the activity in their groups.

All in One Unit 3 History of Our World Teaching Resources, *Make Comparisons,* p. 57

Philip Comes to Power

Like his predecessors, the other Macedonian rulers before him, Philip had Greek ancestors and thought of himself as Greek. Also like his predecessors, Philip had maintained ties to his Greek neighbors. When he was young, Philip had studied in Greece. His experience of studying there led to his hiring of Aristotle to tutor Alexander.

When Philip came to power, he dreamed of conquering the rich city-states of Greece. He would accomplish this by using diplomacy as well as military force.

Before King Philip seized power in 359 B.C., Macedonia was poor and divided. Philip united Macedonia and then formed alliances with many of the Greek city-states by threatening or bribing them. He built an army even stronger than Sparta's. With this army and his talent for waging war, Philip captured one Greek city-state after another.

Demosthenes (dih MAHS thuh neez), who was a master of elocution (eluh KYOO shun), or the art of public speaking, tried to warn his fellow Athenians of the danger to the north:

“He is always taking in more, everywhere casting his net round us, while we sit idle and do nothing. When, Athenians, will you take the necessary action? What are you waiting for?”

In 338 B.C., Athens and another city-state, Thebes (theebz), at last joined to try to stop Philip. However, they were unsuccessful. Philip gained control of all of Greece.

✓ **Reading Check** Why did King Philip think Greece would be easy to conquer?

Make Comparisons How were Philip's attitudes about Greece similar to those of his predecessors'? What clue word helps you recognize the similarities?

In an effort to unite the people of his country and preserve Greek freedom, Demosthenes issued powerful speeches against King Philip of Macedonia. These speeches came to be known as Philipics. This term is still used today to describe strong appeals against someone or something.

Chapter 7 Section 3 **217**

Vocabulary Builder

Use the information below to teach students this section's high-use words.

High-Use Word	Definition and Sample Sentence
predecessor, p. 217	*n.* someone who comes before another person King Philip was Alexander's **predecessor** as king of Macedonia.
alliance, p. 217	*n.* an association to further the common interests of members The Athenians made **alliances** with other city-states.
conquer, p. 218	*v.* to gain or acquire by force of arms The poorly fortified city was easy for the Greeks to **conquer**.

Alexander Builds an Empire

Guided Instruction

- Have students read Alexander Builds an Empire. Tell them to read to see how Alexander built an empire in such a short amount of time.

- Discuss with students how Alexander came to power at such a young age. Ask them how Alexander was prepared for such a job despite his age. (*Alexander's father was assassinated when Alexander was just 20 years old. Alexander had been tutored by one of the greatest teachers of all time—Plato. He was also an experienced soldier at age 20.*)

- Ask students how Alexander's hero Achilles may have motivated him. Have them compare Alexander to Achilles as they answer. (*Possible response: Achilles was Alexander's role model. He was a warrior, so it is likely that Alexander wanted to model his life on that of the hero warrior. Comparison: Achilles and Alexander were both good warriors and heroes.*)

- Discuss with students how Alexander conquered the countries that made up his empire. (*He first invaded the Persian Empire, marched through Asia Minor, and then went on to Palestine, Egypt, Babylon, and into India.*)

Answers

Infer Alexander was called "Alexander the Great" because he conquered Persia, Egypt, and the other lands beyond the Indus River in the east in 11 short years.

Alexander Builds an Empire

After he had conquered all of Greece, Philip then planned to attack Persia. But in 336 B.C., before he could carry out his plan, Philip was **assassinated,** or murdered for political reasons, by a rival. At just 20 years old, Alexander became king. He now had a chance to be as great as his hero Achilles.

Alexander's Conquests Although he was young, Alexander was already an experienced soldier. One of his first actions was to invade the Persian Empire. The empire was much weaker than it had been in the days when Persia had attempted to conquer Greece. However, it was still huge, stretching from Egypt to India. In 334 B.C., Alexander won his first battle in the vast empire. He then led his army through Asia Minor, where together they won battle after battle. He then led them on to Palestine, Egypt, and Babylon, the Persian capital. Alexander's forces crossed the Indus River into India, taking extensive territory wherever they fought.

Within 11 short years, the Macedonian king had conquered Persia, Egypt, and lands extending beyond the Indus River in the east. He had earned the right to be called **Alexander the Great**.

Wherever Alexander went, he established cities. Many of them he named after himself. Even today, there are numerous cities named Alexandria or Alexandroupolis (ah lek sahn DROO puh lis) throughout western Asia.

Fighting the Persian Empire
The mosaic, at right, shows the Battle of Issus, in which Alexander the Great, above, defeated an army of Persians in 333 B.C. **Infer** *Why do you think Alexander is called "Alexander the Great?"*

 Skills Mini Lesson

Recognizing Bias and Propoganda

1. Teach the skill by explaining to students the importance of recognizing bias, or prejudice, in what they read and hear. Point out bias in Greeks calling the Macedonians "barbarians."

2. Help students practice the skill by brainstorming with students the words or phrases that come to mind when they hear the term *barbarian* and writing a list on the board.

3. Have students apply the skill by discussing why the Greeks wanted to belittle the Macedonians. Ask them to relate this reasoning to other reasons that people use name-calling and other forms of bias.

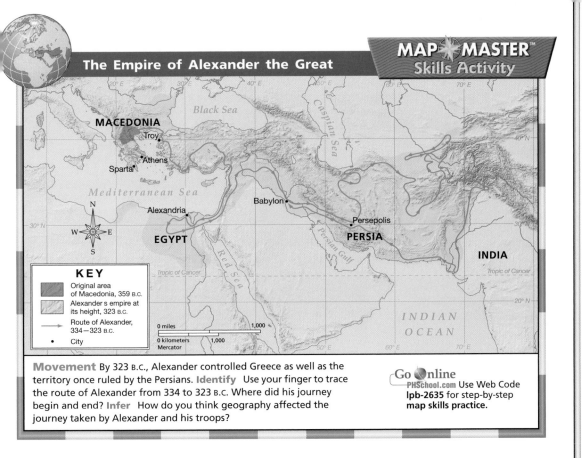

The Empire of Alexander the Great

MAP MASTER™ Skills Activity

MACEDONIA
Troy
Athens
Sparta

Mediterranean Sea

Alexandria
Babylon
Persepolis

EGYPT

PERSIA

INDIA

KEY

Original area of Macedonia, 359 B.C.

Alexander's empire at its height, 323 B.C.

Route of Alexander, 334–323 B.C.

City

0 miles 1,000
0 kilometers 1,000
Mercator

Movement By 323 B.C., Alexander controlled Greece as well as the territory once ruled by the Persians. **Identify** Use your finger to trace the route of Alexander from 334 to 323 B.C. Where did his journey begin and end? **Infer** How do you think geography affected the journey taken by Alexander and his troops?

Go Online
PHSchool.com Use Web Code **lpb-2635** for step-by-step map skills practice.

Alexander's Last Battle Alexander's energy and military genius helped him succeed. This leader drove himself and his army hard, advancing across vast lands at lightning speed. His soldiers grumbled, but they obeyed him. He traveled far into the east, never losing a battle.

At last, not far beyond the Indus River, his weary troops refused to go another step east. Alexander was angry, but he turned back. Alexander got as far as Babylon (BAB uh lahn), where he came down with a fever. In 323 B.C., only 13 years after he had come to the throne, Alexander died. Like the legendary warrior Achilles, Alexander had died young. However, he had gone far beyond the deeds of his hero. His conquests spread Greek culture throughout a vast area.

√ **Reading Check** Why was Alexander so successful as a military leader?

■ Ask students **How was Alexander like his hero Achilles in his death?** *(He died young, just as Achilles had, when he was still a warrior and a hero.)*

Answers

MAP MASTER Skills Activity **Identify** Students should trace the path marked by the arrow line from the starting point in Macedonia to the end point in Babylon. **Infer** The long distances they covered, many of which were in very hot climates and crossed difficult landscapes, must have exhausted them.

Independent Practice

Ask students to create the Taking Notes graphic organizer in the section opener. Have them fill in the blanks under "Alexander's Empire" with the information they have just learned. Briefly model how to identify which details to record.

Monitor Progress

As students fill in the graphic organizer, circulate and make sure individuals are choosing the correct details. Provide assistance as needed.

Differentiated Instruction

For Special Needs Students L1

List Spain, Egypt, Italy, Greece, Libya, Portugal, Lebanon, Tunisia, France, Israel, Turkey, Algeria, Albania, Syria, Yugoslavia, and Morocco on the board. Have students look at a map of the Mediterranean region. Then have students indicate the areas on the map that Alexander conquered.

For Advanced Readers L3

Have students make a map that illustrates Alexander's route of conquest, the lands that he conquered, the towns that he founded, and the division of his empire after his death. Students will need to do outside research to learn about the geographic division of Alexander's empire after his death.

Answers

√ **Reading Check** Alexander had a lot of energy and marched quickly from one place to another, winning battles wherever he went.

Greek Culture Spreads

Guided Instruction

- Have student read Greek Culture Spreads. Tell them to read to see what happened to Alexander's kingdom after his death.

- Discuss with students how Greek culture spread in cities after Alexander's death. *(Possible response: Alexander and his generals created new cities in the new lands. Many Greek soldiers remained in the new kingdoms after the wars.)*

- Ask students **What was the importance of emigrants to the spread of Greek culture?** *(Many artisan and merchant emigrants came from Greece to settle in the new cities. These settlers helped ensure the dominance of Greek culture in the new cities.)*

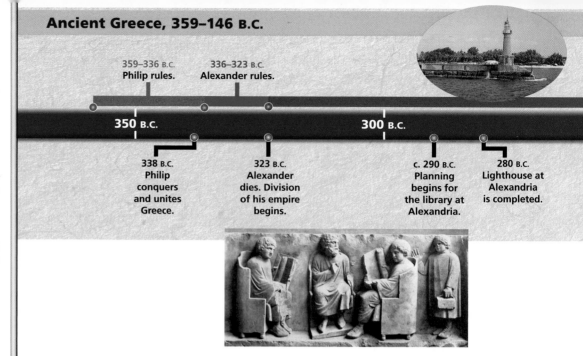

Ancient Greece, 359–146 B.C.

359–336 B.C. **Philip rules.**

336–323 B.C. **Alexander rules.**

350 B.C.

300 B.C.

338 B.C. **Philip conquers and unites Greece.**

323 B.C. **Alexander dies. Division of his empire begins.**

c. 290 B.C. **Planning begins for the library at Alexandria.**

280 B.C. **Lighthouse at Alexandria is completed.**

Use Context Clues Look at the word *Hellenistic* in this paragraph. If the word were not defined for you, what context clues would help you guess what it means?

Greek Culture Spreads

Alexander's death spelled death for his empire. After 50 years of confusion and disorder, the empire was split into three kingdoms, with each kingdom ruled by one of Alexander's former commanders. One commander ruled Greece and Macedonia, which were combined into one kingdom. The other two commanders ruled the kingdoms of Egypt and Persia. For the next three hundred years, the descendants of these commanders fought over the lands that Alexander had conquered.

As Alexander had done before them, his successors created new cities throughout the new kingdoms. Many Greek soldiers remained in the new kingdoms after Alexander's death and settled in those cities. Soon thousands of Greek traders and artisans followed. These emigrants, or people who leave their country to settle in another, ensured that Greek culture would remain alive and well in these Hellenistic kingdoms, as they came to be called. The word **Hellenistic** describes Greek history and culture after the death of Alexander the Great. *Hellenistic* comes from the word *Hellas*—the name Greeks gave their land.

Background: Links Across Time

Alexandria Since 1993, archaeologists have been searching the harbor of Alexandria for remnants of the ancient city. They have found many artifacts, including a sculpture from the Pharos, and have located the site of Cleopatra's palace.

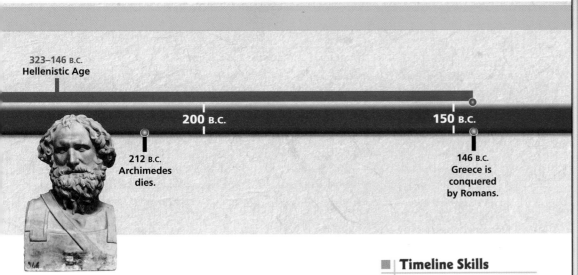

323–146 B.C.
Hellenistic Age

200 B.C.

150 B.C.

212 B.C.
Archimedes
dies.

146 B.C.
Greece is
conquered
by Romans.

The Hellenistic Kingdoms When Alexander took control of lands, he tried not to destroy the cultures of the defeated people. Instead, he hoped that the local cultures would mix with Greek culture in his new cities. Unfortunately, this mixing did not happen in the three Hellenistic kingdoms.

The cities of the Hellenistic world were modeled after Greek cities. Greek kings ruled, and Greeks held the most important jobs. The cities were designed with Greek temples and agoras. Citizens gathered at large theaters for performances of Greek tragedies. The Greek language was spoken in the cities for hundreds of years, even though people in the countryside continued to speak their local languages.

Greek Culture in Egypt The greatest of all Hellenistic cities was Alexandria in Egypt. Alexander had founded this city in 332 B.C. at the edge of the Nile delta. Alexandria became the capital of Egypt. Over the years, it grew famous as a center for business and trade. Its double harbor was dominated by a huge lighthouse that rose about 350 feet (106 m) in the air. The tower was topped by a flame that guided ships safely into port.

The important Hellenistic cities were centers of learning, but Alexandria outdid them all. It boasted the largest library in the world, with half a million scrolls. It was the learning capital of the Greek world. Scholars and writers from all over came to use the huge library.

✓ **Reading Check** Why was Alexandria in Egypt such an important city?

■ **Timeline Skills**

The Hellenistic Age began with the death of Alexander. **Identify** How long did the Hellenistic Age last? **Predict** Why do you think historians mark the end of the Hellenistic Age as 146 B.C.?

Guided Instruction (continued)

■ Ask students to explain Alexander's idea about combining Greek culture with the new cultures they conquered. Then ask what actually happened when the cultures were combined. (*Possible response: Alexander wanted to retain the cultures of the people he conquered. However, after his death the cultures of the conquered lands were assimilated into Greek culture.*)

■ Have students explain what the term *Hellenistic* means and what the word is derived from. Then have them describe what the Hellenistic cities were like. (*Hellenistic refers to Greek history and culture after the death of Alexander the Great. The word* Hellenistic *comes from the word* Hellas, *the Greek name for Greece. Greek kings ruled in the Hellenistic cities. The cities were designed with Greek temples, agoras, and theatres. Greek was the official language.*)

Independent Practice

Have students take out the graphic organizer they began. Have them complete the organizer by filling in the blanks under "Alexander's Empire" and "The Hellenistic Age" with the information they have just learned.

Monitor Progress

■ Show *Section Reading Support Transparency HOW 78* and ask students to check their graphic organizers individually. Go over key concepts and clarify key vocabulary as needed.

■ Tell students to fill in the last column of the *Reading Readiness Guide.* Probe for what they learned that confirms or invalidates each statement.

All in One **Unit 3 History of Our World Teaching Resources,** *Reading Readiness Guide,* p. 52

Answers

Timeline Skills Identify Over 175 years. **Predict** That is when Greece was conquered by the Romans.

✓ **Reading Check** Alexandria was a center of learning, business, and trade.

Math and Science

Guided Instruction

■ Have students read Math and Science to see what contributions Hellenistic scientists and mathematicians made to their fields.

Assess and Reteach

Assess Progress   L2

Have students complete the Section Assessment and administer the *Section Quiz.*

All in One Unit 3 History of Our World Teaching Resources, *Section Quiz,* p. 54

Reteach

If students need more instruction, have them read this section in the *Reading and Vocabulary Study Guide.*

📖 Chapter 7, Section 3, **History of Our World Reading and Vocabulary Study Guide,** pp. 87–89

Extend

Have students learn more about the glory of ancient Rome by completing the *Enrichment* activity.

All in One Unit 3 History of Our World Teaching Resources, *Enrichment,* p. 59

Section 3 Assessment

Key Terms

Students' sentences should reflect knowledge of each Key Term.

🎯 Target Reading Skill

Both Alexander and King Philip wanted to conquer Greece and Persia.

Answers

✓**Reading Check** Many Hellenistic scientists thought the Earth was round. The people in Columbus's time thought the world was flat.

222 *History of Our World*

Links to Science

The Earth and the Sun One scientist of the 200s B.C. rejected the idea that the Earth was the center of the universe. Aristarchus (AIR uh STAHR kus) of Samos believed that the sun is at the center and that the Earth revolves around it. His idea did not catch on. Astronomers continued to base their work on an Earth-centered universe until the A.D. 1500s.

Math and Science

Mathematics and science also flourished in Alexandria. Around 300 B.C., a mathematician named Euclid (YOO klid) developed the branch of mathematics called geometry. He started with accepted mathematical laws. Then, he wrote step-by-step proofs of mathematical principles. The proofs helped explain the qualities of such figures as squares, cubes, angles, triangles, and cones. Mathematicians today still use Euclid's system.

Unlike the people who lived at the time of Columbus, many scientists in Hellenistic times knew that the Earth was round. A scientist named Eratosthenes (ehr uh TAHS thuh neez) even calculated the distance around the Earth. His answer, 24,662,000 miles (39,679,000 km), was very close to the correct distance, which we now know is 24,900,000 miles (40,075,000 km).

Probably the greatest scientist of the times was Archimedes (ar kuh MEE deez). Archimedes studied in Alexandria. He discovered that people can use pulleys and levers to lift very heavy objects. One story says that he hoisted up a loaded ship with these devices. Once he boasted: "Give me a lever long enough and a place to stand on, and I will move the Earth."

✓ **Reading Check** How did scientists of Hellenistic times differ from scientists of Columbus's time in their thinking about the Earth?

★ Section 3 Assessment

Key Terms
Review the key terms listed at the beginning of this section. Use each term in a sentence that explains its meaning.

🎯 Target Reading Skill
What goals did Alexander and his father King Philip have in common?

Comprehension and Critical Thinking
1. (a) Recall Who was Alexander's tutor when he was young?
(b) Identify Cause and Effect How did Alexander's upbringing affect his attitudes about Greek culture?

(c) Draw Conclusions Alexander the Great wanted the cultures of his defeated cities to survive and mix with Greek culture. What happened instead? Why?
2. (a) Describe What features of Greek culture were carried over to the Hellenistic kingdoms?
(b) Make Inferences Name one way that the domination of Greek culture in the Hellenistic countries might have been an advantage. Name one way that it might have been a disadvantage.
(c) Evaluate Describe the importance of the contributions made by Euclid, Eratosthenes, and Archimedes.

Writing Activity
What do you think of Alexander's education? Write a short paragraph that supports your opinion.

For: An activity on Greek culture
Visit: PHSchool.com
Web Code: mud-0730

222 History of Our World

Comprehension and Critical Thinking

1. (a) Aristotle. **(b)** Aristotle taught Alexander about Achilles, whom Alexander wanted to emulate. **(c)** Possible response: The cities became models of Greek cities with Greek rulers.

2. (a) The temples, agoras, and theaters. Greek was the official language. **(b)** Possible response: one common language and the proliferation of science, math, and art throughout the empire. The suppression of the local culture's arts and language.
(c) Euclid's proofs of mathematical principles led to geometry. Eratosthenes the Earth's circumference. Archimedes discovered the principles behind using pulleys and levers.

Writing Activity: Science
Use the *Rubric for Assessing a Writing Assignment* to evaluate students' laws.

All in One Unit 3 History of Our World Teaching Resources, *Rubric for Assessing a Writing Assignment,* p. 70

Review and Assessment

Review Chapter Content

- Review and revisit the major themes of this chapter by asking students to classify what Guiding Question each bulleted statement in the Chapter Summary answers. Have students work together in groups to classify the sentences. Refer to p. 1 in the Student Edition for the text of the Guiding Questions.

- Assign *Vocabulary Development* for students to review Key Terms.

  All in One **Unit 3 History of Our World Teaching Resources,** *Vocabulary Development,* p. 66

◆ Chapter Summary

Section 1: Daily Life in Athens
- Greek men conducted business and social activities in the marketplace.
- Greek women stayed at home, tending to the running of the household.
- Slavery, especially of foreigners, was common in ancient Greece.

Women kneading dough

Section 2: Athens and Sparta
- Life in ancient Sparta was strictly ruled by the state in order to create a powerful army.
- Although outnumbered, the army of Athens fought back a force of invading Persians that threatened to take over all of Greece.
- Athens grew into an empire, but eventually it was destroyed by the forces of Sparta.

Spartans in battle

Section 3: The Spread of Greek Culture
- King Philip of Macedonia conquered all of Greece before he was killed in 336 B.C.
- Philip's son, Alexander the Great, conquered Persia, Palestine, Egypt, and lands extending beyond the Indus River in the East.
- After Alexander's death, Greek culture spread to the areas he had conquered.

Alexander the Great

◆ Key Terms

Each of the statements below contains a key term from the chapter. If the statement is true, write true. If it is false, rewrite the statement to make it true.

1. Athenian women lived in agoras, where they supervised spinning and other household activities.

2. The term Hellenistic refers to the period of Greek history after the death of Alexander the Great.

3. Helots were marketplaces where Greek men conducted business.

4. A plague is a disease that kills many people.

5. A barbarian is a person thought to be wild and savage by a group that considers itself to be more civilized.

6. Slavery is the owning of human beings.

7. If you were to assassinate someone, you would be worshiping that person as a god.

8. A vendor is someone who trains boys in the skill of military arts.

Chapter 7 **223**

Vocabulary Builder

Revisit this chapter's High-Use Academic Words:

splendor   secluded   estimate
revolt   exaggerated resent
predecessor alliance   conquer

Ask students to review the definitions they recorded on their *Word Knowledge Rating Forms.*

All in One **Unit 3 History of Our World Teaching Resources,** *Word Knowledge Rating Form,* p. 58.

Consider allowing students to earn extra credit if they use the high-use words in their answers to the questions in the Chapter Review and Assessment. The words must be used correctly and in a natural context to earn the extra points.

Answers

Key Terms
1. False. The agoras were marketplaces where the men met to conduct business and socialize.

2. True.

3. False. The agoras were marketplaces; helots were slaves of Sparta.

4. True.

5. True.

6. True.

7. False. If you were to assassinate someone, you would kill him or her for political reasons.

8. False. A vendor is someone who sells goods in the marketplace.

Review and Assessment

Comprehension and Critical Thinking

9. (a) Students should describe the life of these three groups as explained in the book. **(b)** Possible response: The Athenian society would have been different without the labor of the slaves.

10. (a) Possible response: Spartan boys received military training for thirteen years. **(b)** The Athenians also taught their young men to fight with a sword and to become fit athletes, but they also learned about art, literature, and philosophy. **(c)** Possible response: Perhaps their early military training made the Spartans stronger fighters, but strength is not what overpowered the Athenians. It was the Athenians' treatment of its allies, their greed, and their lack of attention to the problems surrounding them that caused Athens' downfall.

11. (a) The threat from Persia. **(b)** The Athenians' victory saved the peninsula from Persian rule. The battle is also a symbol of the bravery of a few against many. **(c)** The run that the soldier made to give the news of victory at Marathon has been immortalized by naming the 26-mile race held at the Olympics and elsewhere "the marathon."

12. (a) After defeating the Persians, Athens formed allies with other city-states to protect them. Soon it treated its allies more like subjects, using their protection money for its own needs. Many of the allies joined with Sparta in the Peloponnesian League and eventually went to war with Athens and its allies. **(b)** Athens lost its dominance by losing the support of its allies, becoming greedy, and thinking it was better and more favored by the gods than other Greeks. It also lost because a plague killed one-third of the population.

13. (a) Alexander conquered a vast empire that stretched from Greece to Egypt. Shortly after his death, his empire was divided into three kingdoms, each one ruled by a former commander in Alexander's army. **(b)** Possible responses: Alexander died too soon to name a successor. No leader emerged who was as strong as Alexander had been. There was continuous fighting over who would rule after his death. **(c)** Possible responses: Alexander might have named a successor. Alexander might have set up local rulers who would all report to Macedonia.

◆ Comprehension and Critical Thinking

9. (a) Compare Describe the roles of free men, free women, and slaves in Athenian life. **(b) Predict** How would the daily lives of Athenians have been affected if slavery had not been common in Athens?

10. (a) Describe How did the Spartans become skilled warriors? **(b) Compare** How did the Spartan emphasis on military training differ from Athenian ideas on how to train young men? **(c) Evaluate Information** Do you think the basic differences in the way that Sparta and Athens trained their young men accounted for what eventually happened to the two city-states? Explain your answer.

11. (a) Recall What event caused the Greek city-states to put aside their differences? **(b) Analyze Information** Why was the Athenian victory in the Battle at Marathon significant? **(c) Link Past and Present** How has the Battle of Marathon been immortalized in the present time?

12. (a) Identify Sequence What events led to the Peloponnesian War? **(b) Draw Conclusions** How did Athens lose its dominance over the rest of Greece?

13. (a) Recall Describe the empire of Alexander the Great before and after his death. **(b) Explain** Why did the empire begin to fall apart after Alexander's death? **(c) Predict** What might Alexander have done to make sure that his empire would hold together?

◆ Skills Practice

Analyzing Primary Source In the Skills for Life Activity, you learned how to analyze primary sources to determine whether they are reliable. Explain how you would decide whether an article about the Egyptian city of Alexandria under Hellenistic rule did or did not show bias.

◆ Writing Activity: Science

Choose one achievement in science or math that was made by the Greeks. Write at least two paragraphs about the difference that achievement has made in the modern world.

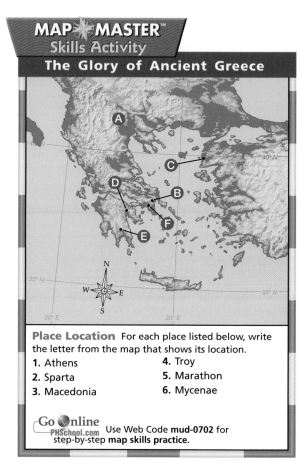

MAP MASTER™
Skills Activity
The Glory of Ancient Greece

Place Location For each place listed below, write the letter from the map that shows its location.
1. Athens
2. Sparta
3. Macedonia
4. Troy
5. Marathon
6. Mycenae

Go Online PHSchool.com Use Web Code **mud-0702** for step-by-step **map skills practice**.

Skills Practice

Students' explanations should reflect an understanding of how to analyze primary sources.

Writing Activity: Science

Students' paragraphs should discuss a legitimate achievement in science or math and give examples of how life is different today because of that achievement. Use the *Rubric for Assessing a Writing Assignment* to evaluate students' work.

All in One **Unit 3 History of Our World Teaching Resources,** *Rubric for Assessing a Writing Assignment,* p. 70

Standardized Test Prep

MAP★MASTER™
Skills Activity

1. F
2. E
3. A
4. C
5. B
6. D

Test-Taking Tips

Some questions on standardized tests ask you to analyze an outline. Study the outline below. Then follow the tips to answer the sample question.

> I Alexander's Conquests
>   A Invaded Persia
>   B Marched through Asia Minor
>   C Invaded Egypt
>   D Took territory across Indus River
> II Alexander's Legacy
>   A Invaded Persia
>   B Created centers of learning
>   C _____

TIP Use key words in the text to help you.

TIP Think about how the text is organized. Use that information to help you answer the question.

Choose the letter of the response that best answers the question.
Which of the following belongs in II-C?

  A Taught by Aristotle
  B Spread Greek culture throughout empire
  C Died in Babylon from a fever
  D Wanted to mix Greek culture and local cultures

Think It Through This outline is organized by major topics and subtopics. The question asks you to find a subtopic under Alexander's Legacy. Answers A and C introduce subtopics not covered in the outline. Answer D is something that Alexander wanted, but it did not happen. The correct answer is B.

Practice Questions

Use the tips above and other tips in this book to help you answer the following questions.

1. What was the role of women in ancient Greece?
   A Greek women sat on the councils that made all the decisions in Greece.
   B Greek women worked like slaves.
   C Greek women were protected and isolated in their homes.
   D Greek women went to war along with the men.

2. Most of the work in ancient Greece was performed by
   A slaves.
   B philosophers.
   C women.
   D boys.

3. For which of the following were Spartans well known?
   A art and architecture
   B war skills
   C philosophy
   D an open society

Study the partial outline below, and then answer the following question.

> II The Aftermath of the Persian Wars
>   A The Athenians feel favored by the gods.
>   B _____
>   C Athens' allies become more like subjects.

4. Which answer belongs in the space following letter B?
   A Sparta and its allies fight against Athens.
   B A plague kills one-third of the Athenians.
   C Athens becomes the most powerful city-state in Greece.
   D Sparta puts a blockade around the city.

Use Web Code **mua-0704** for Chapter 7 self-test.

Chapter 7 **225**

Standardized Test Prep

Answers

1. C
2. A
3. B
4. C

Go Online PHSchool.com Students may use the Chapter 7 self-test on PHSchool.com to prepare for the Chapter Test.

Go Online PHSchool.com Students may practice their map skills using the interactive online version of this map.

Chapter Overview

Overview

Section 1

The Roman Republic
1. Learn about the geography and early settlement of ancient Rome.
2. Understand how Romans formed a republic.
3. Identify the reasons that the Roman republic went into decline.

Section 2

The Roman Empire
1. Learn how Rome ruled an empire.
2. Understand the Greek influence on Rome.
3. Identify key aspects of Roman architecture and technology.
4. Learn about key aspects of Roman law.

Video

The Rise of the Roman Empire
Length: 4 minutes, 11 seconds
Use with Section 2
This video segment describes the daily life and scientific achievements of the Romans, who built one of the world's greatest empires.

 # Technology Resources

PRENTICE HALL

Students use embedded web codes to access Internet activities, chapter self-tests, and additional map practice. They may also access Dorling Kindersley's Online Desk Reference to learn more about each country they study.

Use the Interactive Textbook to make content and concepts come alive through animations, videos, and activities that accompany the complete basal text—online and on CD-ROM.

Use this complete suite of powerful teaching tools to make lesson planning and administering tests quicker and easier.

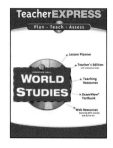

Reading and Assessment

Reading and Vocabulary Instruction

🔁 Model the Target Reading Skill

Word Analysis Using word parts and recognizing word origins helps students understand unfamiliar words as they read.

Many words in English can be broken into word parts. Word parts are roots, prefixes, and suffixes.

Model how to use prefixes and roots to figure out the meaning of an unfamiliar word by analyzing aloud the word *unjust* in Section 1 of this chapter (p. 228).

I come across the word unjust *as I read. I am not sure of its meaning so I break it into a prefix and a root. The prefix is* un-. *The root is* just. *I know that* un- *means "not." Just has something to do with justice. I think it could mean "fair." That would make the meaning of* unjust *"not fair."*

	Prefix +	Root	= Word
Word Parts	un-	just	unjust
Meaning	not	fair	not fair

Use the following worksheets from All-in-One Unit 3 History of Our World Teaching Resources (pp. 89–91) to support this chapter's Target Reading Skill.

Vocabulary Builder
High-Use Academic Words
Use these steps to teach this chapter's high-use words:

1. Have students rate how well they know each word on their Word Knowledge worksheets (All-in-One Unit 3 History of Our World Teaching Resources, p. 92).

2. Pronounce each word and ask students to repeat it.

3. Give students a brief definition and sample sentence (provided on TE pp. 229, 241).

4. Work with students as they fill in the "Definition or Example" column of their Word Knowledge worksheets.

Assessment

Formal Assessment

Test students' understanding of core knowledge and skills.

> **Chapter Tests A and B,** All-in-One Unit 3 History of Our World Teaching Resources, pp. 104–109

Customize the Chapter Tests to suit your needs.

> **Exam*View*® Test Bank CD-ROM**

Skills Assessment

Assess geographic literacy.

> **MapMaster Skills,** Student Edition, pp. 227, 231, 248

Assess reading and comprehension.

> **Target Reading Skills,** Student Edition, pp. 234, 243, and in Section Assessments

> **Chapter 8 Assessment,** History of Our World Reading and Vocabulary Study Guide, p. 97

Performance Assessment

Assess students' performance on this chapter's Writing Activities using the following rubrics from All-in-One Unit 3 History of Our World Teaching Resources.

> **Rubric for Assessing a Timeline,** p. 100

> **Rubric for Assessing a Writing Assignment,** p. 101

> **Rubric for Assessing a Journal Entry,** p. 102

> **Rubric for Assessing a Newspaper Article,** p. 103

Assess students' work through performance tasks.

> **Small Group Activity:** All-in-One Unit 3 History of Our World Teaching Resources, pp. 95–98

Online Assessment

Have students check their own understanding.

> **Chapter Self-Test**

Section 1 **The Roman Republic**

 3 periods, 1.5 blocks (includes Focus on the Roman Senate and Skills for Life)

Social Studies Objectives

1. Learn about the geography and early settlement of ancient Rome.
2. Understand how Romans formed a republic.
3. Identify the reasons that the Roman republic went into decline.

Reading/Language Arts Objective

Use word parts to understand the meaning of unfamiliar words.

Prepare to Read	**Instructional Resources**	**Differentiated Instruction**
Build Background Knowledge Discuss the settlement of ancient Rome and its development into a republic. **Set a Purpose for Reading** Have students evaluate statements on the *Reading Readiness Guide*. **Preview Key Terms** Teach the section's Key Terms. **Target Reading Skill** Introduce the section's Target Reading Skill of **using word parts**.	**All in One Unit 3 History of Our World Teaching Resources** **L2** Reading Readiness Guide, p. 82 **L2** Use Prefixes and Roots, p. 89	**Spanish Reading and Vocabulary Study Guide** **L2** Chapter 8, Section 1, pp. 66–67 ELL

Instruct	**Instructional Resources**	**Differentiated Instruction**
Rome's Geography and Early Settlement Discuss Rome's physical geography. **Romans Form a Republic** Discuss the organization of the Roman Republic. **The Decline of the Republic** Discuss reasons for the decline of the Republic. **Target Reading Skill** Review using prefixes and roots.	**All in One Unit 3 History of Our World Teaching Resources** **L2** Guided Reading and Review, p. 83 **L2** Reading Readiness Guide, p. 82 **History of Our World Transparencies** **L2** Section Reading Support Transparency HOW 79	**All in One Unit 3 History of Our World Teaching Resources** **L3** Small Group Activity, pp. 95–98 GT, AR **L2** Skills for Life, p. 94 AR, GT, LPR, SN **Teacher's Edition** **L1** For Special Needs Students, TE, pp. 231, 239 **L3** For Advanced Readers, TE, p. 233 **L3** For Gifted and Talented Students, p. 234 **Student Edition on Audio CD** **L1** Chapter 8, Section 1 ELL, LPR, SN **Spanish Support** **L2** Guided Reading and Review, p. 70

Assess and Reteach	**Instructional Resources**	**Differentiated Instruction**
Assess Progress Evaluate student comprehension with the section assessment and section quiz. **Reteach** Assign the Reading and Vocabulary Study Guide to help struggling students. **Extend** Extend the lesson by working with word parts.	**All in One Unit 3 History of Our World Teaching Resources** **L2** Section Quiz, p. 84 **L2** Rubric for Assessing a Writing Assignment, p. 101 **Reading and Vocabulary Study Guide** **L1** Chapter 8, Section 1, pp. 91–93	**Spanish Support** **L2** Section Quiz (Spanish), p. 71 ELL **Social Studies Skills Tutor CD-ROM** **L1** Synthesizing Information ELL, LPR, SN

Key

L1 Basic to Average   **L3** Average to Advanced

L2 For All Students

LPR Less Proficient Readers

AR Advanced Readers

SN Special Needs Students

GT Gifted and Talented

ELL English Language Learners

Section 2 The Roman Empire

 3 periods, 1.5 blocks

Social Studies Objectives

1. Learn how Rome ruled an empire.
2. Understand the Greek influence on Rome.
3. Identify key aspects of Roman architecture and technology.
4. Learn about key aspects of Roman law.

Reading/Language Arts Objective

Use word origins to understand the meaning of unfamiliar words.

Prepare to Read	Instructional Resources	Differentiated Instruction
Build Background Knowledge Discuss the expansion of the Roman Empire. **Set a Purpose for Reading** Have students begin to fill out the *Reading Readiness Guide.* **Preview Key Terms** Teach the section's Key Terms. **Target Reading Skill** Introduce the section's Target Reading Skill of recognizing word origins.	**All in One Unit 3 History of Our World Teaching Resources** L2 Reading Readiness Guide, p. 86 L2 Recognize Word Origins, p. 91	**Spanish Reading and Vocabulary Study Guide** L2 Chapter 8, Section 2, pp. 68–69 ELL

Instruct	Instructional Resources	Differentiated Instruction
Ruling an Empire Discuss how the Romans governed their empire. **Target Reading Skill** Review recognizing word origins. **The Greek Influence on Rome** Discuss how the Greeks influenced the Romans. **Architecture and Technology** Discuss Roman advances in architecture and technology. **Roman Law** Discuss Roman ideas of justice.	**All in One Unit 3 History of Our World Teaching Resources** L2 Guided Reading and Review, p. 87 L2 Reading Readiness Guide, p. 86 **History of Our World Transparencies** L2 Section Reading Support Transparency HOW 80 **History of Our World Video Program** L1 The Rise of the Roman Empire	**Teacher's Edition** L1 For English Language Learners, TE, p. 244 L1 For Less Proficient Readers, TE, p. 245 **Student Edition on Audio CD** L1 Chapter 8, Section 2 ELL, LPR, SN **Spanish Support** L2 Guided Reading and Review, p. 72

Assess and Reteach	Instructional Resources	Differentiated Instruction
Assess Progress Evaluate student comprehension with the section assessment and section quiz. **Reteach** Assign the Reading and Vocabulary Study Guide to help struggling students. **Extend** Extend the lesson by using the color transparency with overlays to examine the expansion of the Roman Empire.	**All in One Unit 3 History of Our World Teaching Resources** L2 Section Quiz, p. 88 L2 Rubric for Assessing a Writing Assignment, p. 101 L2 Vocabulary Development, p. 99 L2 Word Knowledge, p. 92 L2 Chapter Test A and B, pp. 104–109 **Reading and Vocabulary Study Guide** L1 Chapter 8, Section 2, pp. 94–96 **History of Our World Transparencies** L2 Roman Expansion HOW Set 1	**Spanish Support** L2 Section Quiz (Spanish), p. 73 ELL L2 Chapter Summary (Spanish), p. 74 ELL L2 Vocabulary Development (Spanish), p. 75 ELL

Key

L1 Basic to Average   L3 Average to Advanced

L2 For All Students

LPR Less Proficient Readers
AR Advanced Readers
SN Special Needs Students

GT Gifted and Talented
ELL English Language Learners

Reading Background

Structuring Paragraphs

Students can learn how to form logically organized and well-written paragraphs by arranging sentences in the correct order in a paragraph.

Write each sentence in a paragraph on a separate slip of paper. Mix up the strips and ask students to rearrange them in a well-ordered paragraph. Remind students to look for main ideas, supporting details, and transition words.

Try this exercise with this paragraph from page 231.

In the Roman Republic, the most powerful part of the government was the senate. The senate mirrors our own legislative branch of government—the branch that proposes and votes on new laws. At first, the senate was made up only of 300 upper-class men called patricians. A patrician was a member of a wealthy family in the ancient Roman Republic. Ordinary citizens were known as plebeians. In the early republic, plebeians could not hold office or be senators.

World Studies Background

Master of the Mediterranean

Rome had to fight and win three wars with Carthage to establish itself as the greatest power in the Mediterranean. These wars in the second and third centuries B.C. are known as the Punic Wars. The term Punic comes from the Latin and Greek words for Phoenician. The Phoenicians founded Carthage in 814 B.C. The First Punic War (246–241 B.C.) lasted 23 years. Another 23 years passed before the Second Punic War (218–201 B.C.), which lasted 17 years. Rome and Carthage went to war again 52 years later in the Third Punic War (149–146 B.C.). The last war was the shortest. Over the span of the three wars, Rome and Carthage were bitter enemies. Rome built a strong army and navy to fight Carthage. In the First Punic War, Rome became master of the sea. Carthage reacted by building a base of operations in Spain. Rome crushed the military power of Carthage once and for all in the Second Punic War. But Carthage remained an important commercial power. In the Third Punic War the Romans laid siege to the city of Carthage and then destroyed it. The area became a Roman province.

Roman Roads

Roman roads were rugged and strong. Snugly fitted flat stones provided a smooth surface for swift travel. Although some horse-drawn chariots carried loads of up to 725 pounds (330 kg) over Roman roads, the superior condition of the roads allowed vehicles to travel anywhere from 15 miles (24 km) to 75 miles (120 km) a day. The Romans used the same basic techniques to build more than 50,000 miles (80,000 km) of roads throughout Italy as well as in Greece, Spain, Asia Minor, North Africa, Gaul, and Britain. After the decline of the Roman Empire, the roads in these far-flung former provinces suffered neglect but remained in good enough repair to serve as transportation routes throughout the Middle Ages. Some even survive today.

Using the Structured Silent Reading Technique

In this chapter, students will use the Structured Silent Reading Technique to read a part of a section. As part of this activity, you may have students ask and answer their own questions as they read. Tell students to pause very briefly but frequently in their reading to ask and answer questions about what they have read. Students can either reread or read ahead to look for answers to their questions.

Model this technique by reading the text below aloud and asking and answering questions as you read.

While patricians and plebeians fought for power in Rome, Roman armies were conquering new territories. **Where were the new territories?** *(Roman armies invaded territories controlled by Carthage, a North African city in what is now the country of Tunisia. Carthage controlled some of these territories, so they were probably around the Mediterranean.)*

Augustus, Rome's First Emperor

After Julius Caesar's assassination, his adopted son Octavian hurried home to Rome from Illyria in the east, where he had been living. Octavian was just 18, but he quickly won the support of Caesar's soldiers in the intense struggle for power at Rome. The Roman senate also rallied behind Octavian. For a time Octavian shared power with his main rival, Mark Antony. The two divided the Roman world between them. Octavian ruled in Italy and western lands, and Antony took the east. When Antony joined forces with Cleopatra, queen of Egypt, Octavian declared war against Egypt. He soon returned to Rome as triumphant ruler of both east and west. In 27 B.C. the senate honored him with the title Augustus, meaning "sacred or high one." In the senate's eyes and now in the eyes of all Roman citizens, Augustus was superhuman, nearly a god. Under its first emperor, Rome entered a golden age of peace, prosperity, and achievement in the arts.

Infoplease® provides a wealth of useful information for the classroom. You can use this resource to strengthen your background on the subjects covered in this chapter. Have students visit this advertising-free site as a starting point for projects requiring research.

Use Web Code **mud-0800** for **Infoplease**®

Guiding Questions

Remind students about the Guiding questions introduced at the beginning of the book.

Section 1 relates to **Guiding Question** ❹ **What types of governments were formed in these societies and how did they develop?** *(After being ruled by kings, the Romans formed a republic in which the people elected leaders and no leader held all the power.)*

Section 2 relates to **Guiding Question** ❶ **How did physical geography affect the development and growth of societies around the world?** *(Located at the center of the Mediterranean world, Rome became the capital of a huge empire that included diverse peoples.)*

⟳ Target Reading Skill

In this chapter, students will learn and apply the reading skill of using word analysis. Use the following worksheets to help students practice this skill.

All in One **Unit 3 History of Our World Teaching Resources,** *Use Prefixes and Roots,* p. 89, *Use Roots and Suffixes,* p. 90, *Recognize Word Origins,* p. 91

The Rise of Ancient Rome

Chapter Preview

This chapter will examine the rise of the Roman Republic and the Roman Empire.

Section 1
The Roman Republic

Section 2
The Roman Empire

⟳ Target Reading Skill

Word Analysis In this section you will learn how to recognize and pronounce unfamiliar words by recognizing word origins and by breaking down words into prefixes, suffixes, and roots.

▶ The ruins of Ephesus (EF ih sus), a Roman city in Asia Minor

226 History of Our World

Differentiated Instruction

The following Teacher Edition strategies are suitable for students of varying abilities.

Special Needs Students, pp. 231, 239
Less Proficient Readers, p. 245
English Language Learners, p. 244
Gifted and Talented Students, p. 234
Advanced Readers, p. 233

Bibliography

For the Teacher
Brown, Dale, ed. *Rome: Echoes of Imperial Glory.* Time-Life, 1994.
Lintott, Andrew. *The Roman Republic.* Sutton, 2001.
Staccioli, Romolo A. *Ancient Rome: Monuments Past and Present.* Getty Trust, 2000.
What Life Was Like: When Rome Ruled the World: The Roman Empire 100 B.C.– A.D. 200. Time-Life, 1999.

For the Student
ELL **L1** Steele, Philip. *Antigua Rome.* Silver Dolphin, 2003.
L2 Platt, Richard, and Melanie Rice. *Julius Caesar: Great Dictator of Rome.* Dorling Kindersley, 2001.
L2 Rees, Rosemary. *The Ancient Romans.* Heinemann, 2001.
L3 Nardo, Don, ed. *The Collapse of the Roman Republic.* Lucent, 1997.

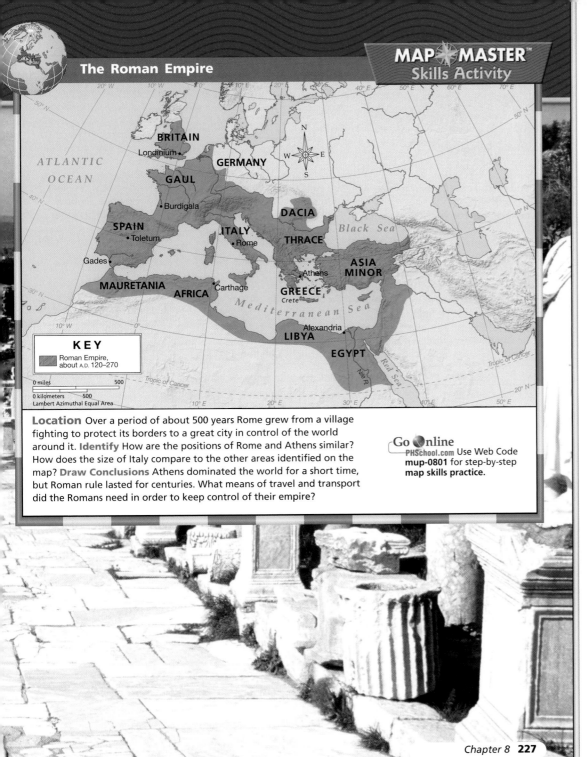

The Roman Empire

BRITAIN
Londinium
ATLANTIC OCEAN
GERMANY
GAUL
Burdigala
SPAIN
Toletum
DACIA
Black Sea
ITALY
Rome
THRACE
Gades
ASIA MINOR
MAURETANIA
AFRICA
Carthage
GREECE
Crete
Athens
Mediterranean Sea
LIBYA
Alexandria
EGYPT
Nile R.
Red Sea
Tropic of Cancer

KEY
Roman Empire, about A.D. 120–270

0 miles 500
0 kilometers 500
Lambert Azimuthal Equal Area

Location Over a period of about 500 years Rome grew from a village fighting to protect its borders to a great city in control of the world around it. **Identify** How are the positions of Rome and Athens similar? How does the size of Italy compare to the other areas identified on the map? **Draw Conclusions** Athens dominated the world for a short time, but Roman rule lasted for centuries. What means of travel and transport did the Romans need in order to keep control of their empire?

Go Online
PHSchool.com Use Web Code **mup-0801** for step-by-step map skills practice.

Chapter 8 **227**

- Point out to students the location of Athens and ask them to think about why Athens' rule was so much shorter than Rome's rule? *(Possible responses: Romans were better soldiers; Romans had a better government system; Athens was farther from western Europe)*

- Discuss with students a main benefit and challenge presented by living in an area surrounded by water on three sides. *(Benefit: protected by water on three sides, so no one can approach by horseback or on foot; Challenge: An army with ships could attack from three sides at once)*

Go Online
PHSchool.com Students may practice their map skills using the interactive online version of this map.

Using the Visual   L2

Reach Into Your Background   Draw students' attention to the caption and photo on pp. 226–227. Discuss the visual with students, and have them describe the visual. Ask **What kinds of items do you see in the picture?** *(stone walkway or road, pillars, columns, rubble)* **What does this ruin tell you about the Romans?** *(Parts of their buildings still exist today, so they must have been good builders.)*

Answers

MAP MASTER Skills Activity **Identify** Both locations are near the Mediterranean Sea; Italy is small when compared to other areas such as Germany **Draw Conclusions** Possible responses: Romans needed roads across the mountains; ships to cross the seas

Chapter Resources

Teaching Resources
- L2 Vocabulary Development, p. 99
- L2 Skills for Life, p. 94
- L2 Chapter Tests A and B, pp. 104–109

Spanish Support
- L2 Spanish Chapter Summary, p. 74
- L2 Spanish Vocabulary Development, p. 75

Media and Technology
- L1 Student Edition on Audio CD
- L1 Guided Reading Audio CD, English and Spanish
- L2 Social Studies Skills Tutor CD-ROM ExamView® Test Bank CD-ROM

Discovery History of Our ††World CHANNEL SCHOOL Video Program

interactive Textbook

PRENTICE HALL
TeacherEXPRESS™
Plan · Teach · Assess

Objectives

Social Studies

1. Learn about the geography and early settlement of ancient Rome.
2. Understand how Romans formed a republic.
3. Identify the reasons that the Roman republic went into decline.

Reading/Language Arts

Use word parts to understand the meaning of unfamiliar words.

Prepare to Read

Build Background Knowledge

Tell students that in this section they will learn about the settlement of ancient Rome and its development into a republic. Have students preview the section to form some preliminary ideas about early Rome and the Roman Republic. Use the Idea Wave participation structure (TE, p. T39) to elicit ideas from students.

Set a Purpose for Reading

- Preview the Objectives.

- Read each statement in the *Reading Readiness Guide* aloud. Ask students to mark the statements true or false.

  All in One Unit 3 History of Our World Teaching Resources, *Reading Readiness Guide,* p. 82

- Have students discuss the statement in pairs or groups of four, then mark their worksheets again. Use the Numbered Heads participation structure (TE, p. T40) to call on students to share their group's perspectives.

Vocabulary Builder
Preview Key Terms L2

Pronounce each Key Term, then ask students to say the word with you. Provide a simple explanation such as "a dictator does not share power with others."

Prepare to Read

Objectives

In this section you will
1. Learn about the geography and early settlement of ancient Rome.
2. Understand how Romans formed a republic.
3. Identify the reasons that the Roman Republic went into decline.

Taking Notes

As you read the section, look for details about the rise and collapse of the Roman Republic. Copy the chart below, and use it to record your findings.

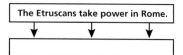

The Etruscans take power in Rome.
↓   ↓   ↓

🔄 Target Reading Skill

Use Word Parts In this section you will read the word *reorganized.* Break it into a prefix and root to try to learn its meaning. The prefix *re-* means "again." The root "organized" means "to put in order."

Key Terms

- **republic** (rih PUB lik) *n.* a type of government in which citizens select their leaders
- **patrician** (puh TRISH un) *n.* a member of a wealthy family in the ancient Roman Republic
- **plebeian** (plih BEE un) *n.* an ordinary citizen in the ancient Roman Republic
- **consul** (KAHN sul) *n.* an elected official who led the Roman Republic
- **veto** (VEE toh) *n.* the power of one branch of government to reject bills or proposals passed by another branch of government
- **dictator** (DIK tay tur) *n.* a person in the ancient Roman Republic appointed to rule for six months in times of emergency, with all the powers of a king

In ancient times, young Romans learned about the founding of their state. But it was a story that mixed a little fact with a great deal of legend. The main characters in the story were twin brothers, Romulus (RAHM yuh lus) and Remus (REE mus). They were the children of a princess and Mars, the Roman god of war. A jealous king feared that the twins would someday seize power from him. He ordered them to be drowned. But the gods protected the infants. A female wolf rescued them. Then a shepherd found the twins and raised them as his own. The twins grew up, killed the unjust king, and went off to build their own city. At a place where seven hills rise above the Tiber River, the twins founded the city of Rome.

The Tiber River in Rome

228 History of Our World

🔄 Target Reading Skill L2

Use Word Parts Point out the Target Reading Skill. Tell students that roots, prefixes, and suffixes are word parts.

Model using prefixes and roots to understand the meaning of unfamiliar words by breaking the word *proposes* on p. 231 into the prefix *pro-* and the root *poses.* Tell students that *pro-* means "forward or in front of" and *pose* means "place or put." Explain that the meaning of *proposes* becomes clear when the meaning of the prefix is added to the meaning of the root.

Give students *Use Prefixes and Roots.* Have them complete the activity in their groups.

All in One Unit 3 History of Our World Teaching Resources, *Use Prefixes and Roots,* p. 89

Rome's Geography and Early Settlement

We can learn much from the story of Rome's founding—even if the tale is mostly legend. We learn that the Romans valued loyalty and justice. People who broke the law were severely punished, just as Romulus and Remus punished the king. We also learn that the Romans highly valued the favor of the gods.

Geographical Advantages The first settlers on Rome's seven hills were not thinking about building a great empire. They chose that site because it seemed to be a good place to live. The hills made the area easy to defend. The soil was fertile, and the site had a river. From the mountains of central Italy, the Tiber River flowed through Rome before emptying into the Tyrrhenian (tih REE nee un) Sea. As centuries passed, Romans discovered that the location of their city gave them other advantages. Rome was at the center of a long, narrow peninsula we now call Italy. Italy juts out into the Mediterranean Sea, and the Mediterranean Sea was at the center of the known Western world.

The Dolomite Mountains are part of the Italian Alps. This mountain range stood as a great divide between Italy and the rest of Europe.

Instruct

Rome's Geography and Early Settlement L2

Guided Instruction

- **Vocabulary Builder** Clarify the meaning of the high-use words **found** and **attitude** before reading.

- Read Rome's Geography and Early Settlement on pp. 229–230, using the Oral Cloze technique (TE, p. T37).

- Discuss why the site chosen for Rome was a good place to live. *(The area had seven hills, which made it easy to defend; the soil was fertile; it was by a river.)*

- Ask students **How was the Tiber River important to the development of Rome?** *(Possible responses: The Tiber provided a way of transportation; it connected Rome to the Tyrrhenian Sea and the Mediterranean Sea, which was the center of the known Western world.)*

- Discuss the different groups associated with the early settlement of Rome. *(Little is known about the people who founded Rome except that their first settlements date to 900 B.C.; the Etruscans took power in Rome around 600 B.C.)*

- Ask students **Why do you think little is known about the people who founded Rome?** *(Possible response: They did not leave written records.)*

Vocabulary Builder

Use the information below to teach students this section's high-use words.

High-Use Word	Definition and Sample Sentence
found, p. 230	*v.* to begin to build or organize The students **founded** an academic team.
attitude, p. 233	*n.* a feeling or belief about something The students had friendly **attitudes** toward everyone they met.
decline, p. 234	*n.* movement toward a weaker condition The town went into a **decline** as stores on Main Street shut down.
uproot, p. 234	*v.* to displace The fire **uprooted** them from their old neighborhood.

Independent Practice

Ask students to create the Taking Notes graphic organizer on a blank sheet of paper. Then have them fill in the two boxes with details about the geography of Rome and its early civilization. Briefly model what kinds of information to include.

Monitor Progress

As students fill in the graphic organizer, circulate and make sure individuals are correctly identifying details about the geography and early civilization of ancient Rome. Provide assistance as needed.

Links

Read the **Links to Science** on this page. Ask students **How do we know that the Etruscans practiced dentistry?** (*Archaeologists have found evidence of the Etruscans' work on teeth, such as gold bands and replaced teeth.*)

Links to Science

Etruscan Dentistry The Etruscans were among the first people to use human-made substitutes for lost teeth. Evidence of ancient Etruscan dentistry has been found by archaeologists and can be seen today in museums. One notable example comes from the 600s B.C.: The Etruscan dentist placed soldered gold bands over the patient's remaining teeth, and in the empty bands the lost teeth were replaced by human teeth and, in one spot, the tooth of an ox!

The Etruscans We know very little about the people who actually founded Rome. We do know, however, that their first settlements date from about 900 B.C. Rome grew slowly as the Romans fought their neighbors for land.

About 600 B.C., a mysterious people, the Etruscans (ih TRUS kunz), took power in Rome. They spoke a language unlike any other in Italy. Although we have many examples of their writing, we can read very little of it.

Where did the Etruscans come from? Even today, no one is sure. For a time, Etruscans ruled as kings of Rome, but many Romans did not like being ruled by an all-powerful king and having no say in how they were governed. Some ancient Roman historians claimed that in 509 B.C. the Romans revolted against the harsh reign of Tarquinius Superbus (tahr KWIN ee us soo PUR bus) and drove the Etruscans from power. Many modern historians doubt the truth of this story and are not sure exactly how and when the rule of the Etruscan kings ended and the Roman Republic began.

Although the Romans defeated the Etruscans, the victors adopted Etruscan ideas. For example, many of the Roman gods were originally Etruscan gods. The Romans also borrowed the Greek alphabet that the Etruscans used. The Roman garment called the toga came from the Etruscans as well.

✓ **Reading Check** What is known about the Etruscans?

Etruscan Art
This Etruscan sarcophagus dates from about 510 B.C. Like many ancient peoples, the Etruscans used sarcophagi as coffins. This one was made for a married couple.
Analyze Images *How can you tell that this sarcophagus was found in pieces and then reassembled?*

230 History of Our World

Background: Links Across Place

The Etruscan Mystery Archaeologists and linguists think that the Etruscans may have come from the northern part of Asia Minor. Etruscans also seem to have lived on the island of Lemnos in the Aegean Sea. They probably settled in Italy between 1100 B.C. and 900 B.C. Although the Etruscans used the Greek alphabet to represent words in their language, the Etruscan language was in no way related to Greek. There has been limited success in deciphering the language of the Etruscans. Perhaps their language was spoken in parts of Asia Minor before the arrival of early Greeks migrating from central Europe.

Answers

✓ **Reading Check** The Etruscans spoke an unusual language, they left examples of their writing, they ruled as kings, and the Romans borrowed many ideas from them, including gods, an alphabet, and the toga.

Analyze Images Cracks are visible throughout the piece, with the most obvious one in the middle.

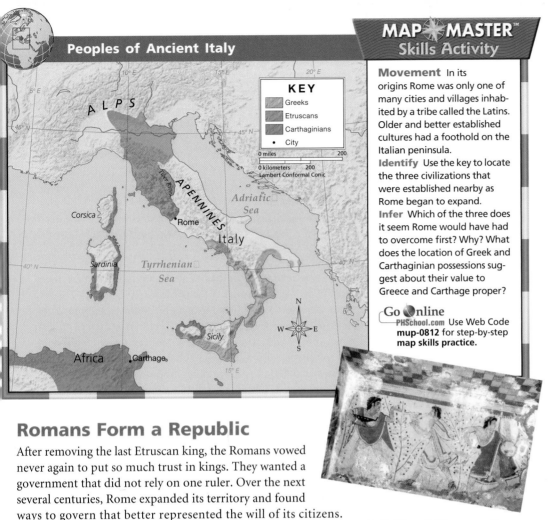

Peoples of Ancient Italy

MAP MASTER™ Skills Activity

KEY
- Greeks
- Etruscans
- Carthaginians
- • City

0 miles 200
0 kilometers 200
Lambert Conformal Conic

Movement In its origins Rome was only one of many cities and villages inhabited by a tribe called the Latins. Older and better established cultures had a foothold on the Italian peninsula.

Identify Use the key to locate the three civilizations that were established nearby as Rome began to expand.

Infer Which of the three does it seem Rome would have had to overcome first? Why? What does the location of Greek and Carthaginian possessions suggest about their value to Greece and Carthage proper?

Go Online
PHSchool.com Use Web Code **mup-0812** for step-by-step map skills practice.

Romans Form a Republic

After removing the last Etruscan king, the Romans vowed never again to put so much trust in kings. They wanted a government that did not rely on one ruler. Over the next several centuries, Rome expanded its territory and found ways to govern that better represented the will of its citizens.

By 264 B.C., the Romans had gained control of the entire Italian peninsula (the area that makes up present-day Italy) and had firmly established a new form of government—a republic. In a **republic,** citizens who have the right to vote select their leaders. The leaders rule in the name of the people.

The Roman Senate In the Roman Republic, the most powerful part of the government was the senate. The senate mirrors our own legislative branch of government—the branch that proposes and votes on new laws. At first, the senate was made up only of 300 upper-class men called patricians. A **patrician** was a member of a wealthy family in the ancient Roman Republic. Ordinary citizens were known as **plebeians.** In the early republic, plebeians could not hold office or be senators.

Daily life activities were often the subjects of Roman art.

Romans Form a Republic L2

Guided Instruction
- Have students read Romans Form a Republic using the Structured Silent Reading strategy (TE, p. 38). As students read, circulate and make sure individuals can answer the Reading Check question on p. 233.

- Ask students **What is a republic?** (*A republic is a form of government in which citizens elect their leaders and the leaders serve in the name of the people.*)

- Ask students **How did the Romans organize their republic?** (*The Roman Republic had a senate, two consuls as chief executives, an assembly of citizens, and praetors who served as judges.*)

- Examine the limitation of certain institutions and offices in the Roman Republic to certain classes of society. (*In the early republic the senate and various offices were open only to the patricians; plebeians could not be senators or consuls.*)

Differentiated Instruction

For Special Needs Students L1

On the board, draw a simple graphic organizer to help students understand the basic structure of the government. Show the senate, consuls, and praetors in three boxes as representing three branches of government. Then include information about the assembly and dictator above and below the consuls box to indicate that the assembly of citizens elected the consuls. The dictator could be appointed if the consuls did not agree. Use the graphic organizer as a prompt for discussion.

Answers

MAP MASTER Skills Activity **Identify** Greeks, Etruscans, and Carthaginians **Infer** Greeks. They were the closest in proximity. Their locations next to the sea suggest ports used in trade.

- Ask students **What was the purpose of a dictator in the Roman Republic?** *(A dictator could be appointed to handle an emergency, such as a situation in which the two consuls disagreed.)*

- Ask **Why do you think the Romans limited the dictator's term of office to six months?** *(Possible response: The dictator had all the powers of a king, and the Romans did not want one official to have that much power for long, after their experience with the Etruscan kings; the Romans had also set up their government so that it would not rely on one ruler.)*

The Roman Consuls Two chief officials called **consuls** led the government. The consuls, like our U.S. President, were the chief executives of the government. They were responsible for enforcing the Republic's laws and policies. The consuls were elected by the assembly of citizens. Before 367 B.C., plebeians could not be consuls. The senate advised the consuls on foreign affairs, laws, and finances, among other things.

Consuls ruled for one year only. They almost always did what the senate wanted them to do. Power was divided equally between the consuls. Both had to agree before the government could take any action. If only one consul said, "Veto" ("I forbid"), the matter was dropped. A **veto** is the rejection of any planned action by a person in power. Today, we use "veto" to mean the rejection of a proposed law by the President of the United States.

Other Important Officials The Romans knew that their government might not work if the two consuls disagreed. For this reason, Roman law held that a dictator could be appointed to handle an emergency. In the Roman Republic, a **dictator** was a Roman official who had all the powers of a king but could hold office for only six months.

Praetors (PREE turz) were other important officials. At first they functioned as junior consuls, but later, they served as judges in civil-law trials—trials that settled disputes about money, business matters, contracts, and so on. Thus, the *praetors* helped to develop some of the first rules for Roman courts of law.

■ Timeline Skills

The Roman Republic lasted for almost 500 years. **Identify** By what year did Rome control the Italian peninsula? **Analyze** About how long did the republic's main period of conquests around the Mediterranean Sea last? What event occured near the end of that period?

The Roman Republic

| 265–146 B.C. Roman conquests around the Mediterranean Sea | 120–44 B.C. Breakdown of the Roman Republic |

| 500 B.C. | 400 B.C. | 300 B.C. | 200 B.C. | 100 B.C. | A.D. 1 |

509 B.C. Roman Republic is founded.

450 B.C. Laws of the Twelve Tables are adopted.

367 B.C. Plebeians are allowed to be consuls.

264 B.C. Rome controls all of the Italian peninsula.

146 B.C. Carthage is destroyed.

44 B.C. Caesar rules Rome and is assassinated.

27 B.C. Octavian becomes the first Roman emperor.

Background: Links Across Time

Roman Law The legal systems of the United States, Canada, and many European countries have been influenced by Roman law. In fact, many common legal terms have Latin origins. The Latin root *leg-*, meaning "law," is the foundation of such English words as *legal, legislation,* and *legitimate.* Other law-related English words with Latin origins include *judicial* and *judgment,* which are derived from the Latin word *judex,* meaning "judge."

Answers

Identify by 264 B.C.

Analyze about 100 years; Carthage was destroyed near the end of that period

Patricians Versus Plebeians The expansion of Rome's influence throughout Italy caused growing troubles between patricians and plebeians. Patricians and plebeians had different attitudes and interests. Patricians thought of themselves as leaders. They fought hard to keep control of the government. Plebeians believed that they had a right to be respected and treated fairly. Plebeians did not trust the actions of the patrician senate. They believed that the senate was often unfair to the plebeians. Therefore, plebeians formed their own groups to protect their interests.

Many patricians grew wealthy because of Rome's conquests. They took riches from those they had defeated in war. Then they bought land from small farmers and created huge farms for themselves. Plebeians did not work on these farms. Rather, the work was done by slaves brought back from conquests. Many plebeian farmers found themselves without work. The cities, especially Rome, were filled with jobless plebeians.

Eventually, angry plebeians refused to fight in the Roman army. It was then that the patricians gave in to one of the main demands of the plebeians. This demand was for a written code of laws which was called the Laws of the Twelve Tables. The Twelve Tables applied equally to all citizens. They were hung in marketplaces so that everyone could know what the laws were. Despite this victory, the plebeians never managed to gain power equal to that of the patricians.

Master of the Mediterranean While patricians and plebeians fought for power in Rome, Roman armies were conquering new territories. Roman armies invaded territories controlled by Carthage, a North African city in what is now the country of Tunisia. The Romans drove Carthage from Spain and seized control there in 20 B.C. By 146 B.C., after a long series of bloody wars, the Romans had completely destroyed Carthage and its empire. Other Roman armies finished the job of conquering Macedonia in that same year. Then the Romans turned their attention to the land of Gaul, most of which is present-day France.

✓ **Reading Check** What complaints did the plebeians have against the patricians?

The Sack of Carthage
The artist Tiepolo portrays the final destruction of Carthage by the Roman Empire in his painting. At the final surrender, the city that once had a population of more than a quarter million people was left with only 50,000 survivors.
Analyze Images *What other titles might be appropriate for Tiepolo's depiction of the war with Carthage?*

- Point out Carthage on the map on p. 231. Have students describe its location. (*Like Rome, Carthage was at the center of the Mediterranean.*)

- Ask students **Why might the Romans have wanted to conquer Carthage?** (*Possible responses: The Romans might have wanted to conquer Carthage to establish their control of the Mediterranean region.*)

Independent Practice
Have students add two additional boxes to the Taking Notes graphic organizer. Then have students complete the boxes with details about the Republic and the conflict between patricians and plebeians in Rome.

Monitor Progress
As students fill in the graphic organizer, circulate and make sure individuals are choosing details related to the two topics. Provide assistance as needed.

Differentiated Instruction

For Advanced Readers **L3**
Have students conduct Internet or library research to learn more about ancient Carthage. Students may work in groups to find answers to these questions: How did Carthage benefit from its geographic location? How did Carthage expand its empire? How big was its empire? How was Carthage governed? Why did Rome and Carthage go to war with each other? Ask groups to present their findings to the class.

Answers

✓ **Reading Check** The plebeians did not like the fact that the patricians had control of the government; they did not think that the patricians gave them respect or treated them fairly; plebeians had no jobs while slaves worked on patrician farms; they also wanted a written code of laws.

Analyze Images The Destruction of Carthage or The Death of Carthage

The Decline of the Republic

Guided Instruction

- **Vocabulary Builder** Clarify the meaning of the high-use words **decline** and **uproot** before reading.

- Discuss reasons for the decline of the Roman Republic. (*Reasons include fighting between patricians and plebeians, civil war between generals and private armies, disagreements between consuls, and the rise of Julius Caesar.*)

- Ask students **How did Julius Caesar contribute to the decline of the Republic?** (*Possible response: Julius Caesar changed many elements of the government to make himself an all-powerful ruler; he took over important offices; he took much of the senate's power; he made himself dictator for life.*)

↻ Target Reading Skill ㋛

Prefixes and Roots As a follow up, ask students to answer the Target Reading Skill question on this page in the Student Edition. (*The meaning of* reorganize *is "to put in order again."*)

Independent Practice

Have students add and complete two additional boxes in the Taking Notes graphic organizer with topics and details related to the decline of the Republic.

Monitor Progress

- Show *Section Reading Support Transparency HOW 79* and ask students to check their graphic organizers individually. Go over key concepts and clarify key vocabulary as needed.

  📖 **History of Our World Transparencies,** *Section Reading Support Transparency HOW 79*

- Tell students to fill in the last column of the *Reading Readiness Guide.* Encourage students to evaluate what they have learned that confirms or invalidates each statement.

  ᴬˡˡ ⁱⁿ ᴼⁿᵉ **Unit 3 History of Our World Teaching Resources,** *Reading Readiness Guide,* p. 82

Julius Caesar was a powerful dictator of the Roman Empire. Later Roman leaders adopted his name as a title. In time, *Caesar* **came to mean "emperor."**

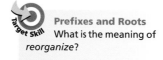

Prefixes and Roots
What is the meaning of *reorganize*?

The Decline of the Republic

Even though it ruled a large area, Rome was in trouble by 120 B.C. Some leaders tried to break up estates and give land to the plebeians. The patricians fought back, and plebeian leaders were murdered.

Over the next seventy-five years, a number of the most successful Roman generals gathered private armies around them and fought for power. Consuls no longer respected each other's veto power. Rome dissolved into civil war, with private armies roaming the streets and murdering enemies. As Rome seemed about to break up, Julius Caesar (JOOL yus SEE zur) arose as a strong leader.

The Rise of Julius Caesar Caesar was a smart leader, eager for power. From 58 to 51 B.C., he led the army that conquered Gaul. He killed, enslaved, and uprooted millions of Gauls. He captured huge amounts of gold. His strong leadership won him the loyalty of his troops. They would follow him anywhere—even back to Rome to seize power. In 49 B.C., Caesar returned to Italy. War broke out between Caesar and the senate. Caesar won the war and became dictator of the Roman world in 48 B.C. Recall that under Roman law, a dictator could rule for only six months. Caesar's rule, however, lasted far longer than that. Although some elements of the republic remained, Caesar ruled with great power, taking much of the power that had once belonged to the senate.

The Death of a Dictator For four years, Caesar took over important public offices. In 45 B.C., he became the only consul. In 44 B.C., he became dictator for life. Caesar took many useful steps to reorganize the government. But it seemed to many senators that Rome once again had a king. They hated this idea.

On March 15, 44 B.C., Caesar had plans to attend a meeting of the senate. His wife sensed danger and urged him not to go, but Caesar insisted. At the meeting, a group of senators gathered around Caesar. Suddenly, they pulled out knives and stabbed him. He fell to the ground, dead. Caesar had been a strong leader. However, many Romans felt that he had gone too far and too fast in gathering power.

Differentiated Instruction

For Gifted and Talented ㋡
Assign students selections from Julius Caesar's *Civil War.* Have students prepare oral readings of their selections. In addition to reading their selections to the class, students should present brief summaries of selections outlining their main points. Tell students to practice reading their selections aloud using correct pronunciation of names and clear enunciation. Then have students present their selections to the class.

From Republic to Empire Civil war followed Caesar's death. When the war ended after thirteen years, Caesar's adopted son, Octavian (ahk TAY vee un), held power. In 27 B.C., the senate awarded Octavian the title of Augustus (aw GUS tus), which means "highly respected." He was the first emperor of Rome. The rule of Augustus marked the beginning of the Roman Empire and the end of the Roman Republic.

The Roman Republic had lasted nearly 500 years. The government worked well for much of that time. As a republic, Rome grew from a city-state to a holder of vast territories. It developed the largest elected government the world had seen up to that time. But civil war and the ambition of powerful political figures ate away at Rome's republican forms of rule. For the next 500 years, the great Roman civilization would be ruled, not by the people, but by an all-powerful emperor.

In the next section, you will read about how the Roman emperors ruled their vast empires and about some of the innovations in technology and law that developed during the Roman Empire.

✓ **Reading Check** What did Julius Caesar do to become dictator of Rome?

In addition to receiving the title Augustus, Octavian was later honored as *Pater Patriae,* or father of his country.

Section 1 Assessment

Key Terms
Review the key terms listed at the beginning of this section. Use each term in a sentence that explains the term's meaning.

Target Reading Skill
Apply your knowledge of the prefix *re-*. What does re-create mean?

Comprehension and Critical Thinking
1. (a) Recall Describe the geography and early settlement of Rome.

(b) Explain Why did the Romans overthrow the Etruscans?
2. (a) List What were the important features of the Roman Republic?
(b) Analyze Why did the Romans want the republic to have two consuls rather than one?
3. (a) Identify Describe the features of the rule of Julius Caesar.
(b) Draw Conclusions Why would the Roman senate be likely to lead the opposition to Caesar's growing power?

Writing Activity
Julius Caesar was a strong leader, but his leadership angered the Roman senate. Write a list of pros and cons about Julius Caesar's leadership.

Go Online
PHSchool.com

For: An activity on the geography of Rome
Visit: PHSchool.com
Web Code: mud-0810

---

3. (a) Julius Caesar ruled as a dictator for life; he took over important offices such as consul and took away much of the senate's power; he also reorganized the government.
(b) Julius Caesar had taken away much of the senate's power.

Writing Activity
Use the *Rubric for Assessing a Writing Assignment* to evaluate students' work.

All in One Unit 3 History of Our World Teaching Resources, *Rubric for Assessing a Writing Assignment,* p. 101

Go Online
PHSchool.com Typing in the Web Code when prompted will bring students directly to detailed instructions for this activity.

Assess and Reteach

Assess Progress   L2
Have students complete the Section Assessment. Administer the *Section Quiz.*

All in One Unit 3 History of Our World Teaching Resources, *Section Quiz,* p. 84

Reteach   L1
If students need more instruction, have them read the section in the *Reading and Vocabulary Study Guide.*

History of Our World Reading and Vocabulary Study Guide, pp. 91–93

Extend   L3
Have students learn more about using word parts to understand word meanings. Many prefixes, roots, and suffixes in English words come from the Latin language. Give students a list of common Latin prefixes (for example: *co-, inter-, non-, post-, pre-, sub-, super-, trans-*) and suffixes (for example: *-able, -al, -ion, -ity, -ment*). Ask students to find the meaning of each affix in a dictionary. Then have students provide examples of words containing the prefixes and suffixes.

Answer

✓ **Reading Check** Julius Caesar fought and won a war with the senate to become dictator; then he took over important offices and made himself dictator for life.

Section 1 Assessment

Key Terms
Students' sentences should reflect knowledge of each Key Term.

Target Reading Skill
Recreate means "to create or make again."

Comprehension and Critical Thinking
1. (a) Rome was founded in a fertile valley surrounded by seven hills near the Tiber River at the center of a long, narrow peninsula, the first settlements date to about 900 B.C. **(b)** The Romans were not allowed to participate in government and were ruled by an all-powerful king.

2. (a) The government represented the will of the people, and citizens could vote to elect their leaders. **(b)** They did not want one person to have too much power.

Focus on The Roman Senate

Guided Instruction L2

- Have students read the paragraphs on pp. 236–237 and study the art, photo, and captions as a class.
- Have students answer the Assessment questions in groups of two or three.

Focus On
The Roman Senate

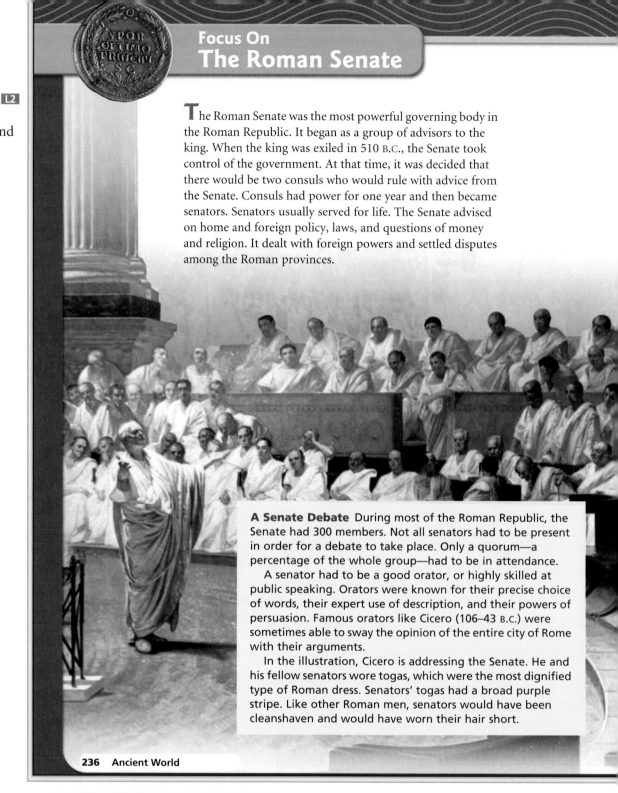

The Roman Senate was the most powerful governing body in the Roman Republic. It began as a group of advisors to the king. When the king was exiled in 510 B.C., the Senate took control of the government. At that time, it was decided that there would be two consuls who would rule with advice from the Senate. Consuls had power for one year and then became senators. Senators usually served for life. The Senate advised on home and foreign policy, laws, and questions of money and religion. It dealt with foreign powers and settled disputes among the Roman provinces.

A Senate Debate During most of the Roman Republic, the Senate had 300 members. Not all senators had to be present in order for a debate to take place. Only a quorum—a percentage of the whole group—had to be in attendance.

A senator had to be a good orator, or highly skilled at public speaking. Orators were known for their precise choice of words, their expert use of description, and their powers of persuasion. Famous orators like Cicero (106–43 B.C.) were sometimes able to sway the opinion of the entire city of Rome with their arguments.

In the illustration, Cicero is addressing the Senate. He and his fellow senators wore togas, which were the most dignified type of Roman dress. Senators' togas had a broad purple stripe. Like other Roman men, senators would have been cleanshaven and would have worn their hair short.

236 Ancient World

Differentiated Instruction

For Less Proficient Readers L1

Remind students that a word's meaning can often be found by looking at how it is used. Then model the process using the word *exile:* "The sentence says that the Senate took control after the king was exiled. The words *was exiled* indicate that being exiled was not something the king did or chose. If the Senate took control, that must mean that the king was no longer there. I think *exiled* means he was sent away."

Cicero
In the scene below, Cicero is shown making a speech shortly after becoming consul. His forceful speaking skills helped him win office.

A Senator's Toga
Roman senators wore togas edged with a broad purple stripe, as shown in the present-day photo.

Assessment

Explain What was the role of the Roman Senate?

Infer The United States also has a Senate. Why might the Founding Fathers have chosen this name for the American governing body?

Chapter 8 **237**

Background: Links Across Time

Cicero's Letters More than 900 of Cicero's letters survive. The letters are an especially important primary source because they mention dates and events that happened during Cicero's lifetime.

Primary sources such as Cicero's letters link modern historians with times past in a way that other, more formal writings, cannot.

Independent Practice
Have students write a paragraph explaining why Rome is called the Roman Republic during this time period. Remind students to use information from the feature to support their conclusions

Answers

Assessment

Explain Possible answers: The Roman Senate controlled the government. It advised the consuls on home and foreign policy, suggested laws, and advised the government on questions of money and religion. It settled disputes among Roman provinces.
Infer Possible answer: The United States Senate represents the people and so did the Roman Senate. The Roman Senate was the most powerful governing body in the Roman Republic, and the U.S. Senate is also very powerful. The U.S. Congress, including the Senate, gives advice and consent to the president of the United States about laws and policy.

Chapter 8 **237**

Objectives

Learn how to synthesize information.

Prepare to Read

Build Background Knowledge L2

Write the word *synthesize* on the board. Then write it again, this time separating its parts: *syn-* (prefix), *-thes-* (root), and *-ize* (suffix). Explain that the word *synthesize* comes from Greek. Its prefix means "together," its root means "to put," and its suffix makes it a verb. Tell students that when you synthesize pieces of information, you put them together or reorganize them to draw conclusions.

Instruct

Synthesizing Information L2

Guided Instruction

- Read the steps to Synthesizing Information as a class and write the instructions on the board.

- Practice the skill by following the steps on pp. 238–239 as a class. Model each step in the activity by identifying main ideas (*executive officials, senate, other important officials*), identifying details that support the main ideas (*consuls, dictator, consuls chosen by assembly of people; most powerful, patricians only; praetors, served as judges*), looking for connections between pieces of information (*shared power, chosen by the people*), and drawing a conclusion based on the connections (*Before the first emperor took over, ancient Rome had a government with three branches and elected leaders*).

- Ask students to identify other topics from the chapter that have information they might synthesize in a paragraph.

Independent Practice

Assign *Skills for Life* and have students complete it individually.

All in One **Unit 3 History of Our World,** *Skills for Life,* p. 94

> During his trip to Rome with his family, William was most impressed by the ancient ruins in the center of the city. It was here that government business of the Roman Republic had been conducted. The tour guide pointed out that many of America's present-day methods of government are borrowed from the ancient Roman Republic: an elected chief executive, a senate, and a court system based on laws designed to protect all citizens.
>
> William told his parents, "When we return from vacation, I would like to make a report to my class on the government of the Roman Republic. What should my first step be?"
>
> William's mother replied, "You will have to synthesize all the information you learned while in Rome."
>
> William gulped, "Synthesize information? How do I do that?"

When you are asked to synthesize information, you should find the main ideas and weave them into a conclusion. Synthesizing information is a skill that can help you in all of your subjects in school.

Learn the Skill

When you synthesize information, you summarize. Use the following steps to synthesize:

1. **Identify the main idea of each piece of information.** Main ideas are broad, major ideas that are supported by details.

2. **Identify details that support your main ideas.** You may want to make notes or create a chart. The details will give information about your main ideas.

3. **Look for connections between pieces of information.** These connections may be similarities, differences, causes, effects, or examples.

4. **Draw conclusions based on the connections you found.** Do not think about details at this point, but of the main ideas and the general, overall statements you can make to tie these together.

238 History of Our World

Monitor Progress

Monitor students as they complete the *Skills for Life* worksheet, checking to make sure they understand the skills steps.

Government of the Roman Republic	
Main Ideas	**Supporting Details**
1. Executive official	• Consul
	• dictator
2. Senate	

Practice the Skill

Use the steps above to synthesize information about the government of the Roman Republic. Rely mainly on Section 1 of this chapter, especially the material under the heading Romans Form a Republic.

1 Study the information about the government of the Roman Republic, and add one or two main ideas in the first column of the chart. Two are already supplied.

2 Now write details that support each main idea. Do this for other main ideas that you have identified.

3 Do the main ideas show contrasts or similarities among the branches of the government of the Roman Republic? Jot down any connections.

4 Your main ideas should help you write a one- or two-sentence conclusion that answers questions such as "What kind of government did ancient Rome have before the first emperor took over?"

Apply the Skill

Use the steps on this page to synthesize information about the government of the Roman Empire in a brief, well-organized paragraph. Refer to the main text of Section 2 of this chapter, but you may also use maps, photographs, captions, and other sources. Do not summarize everything you read about the Roman Empire. Concentrate on the form of government.

Chapter 8 **239**

Assess and Reteach

Assess Progress L2
Ask students to do the Apply the Skill activity.

Reteach L1
If students are having trouble applying the skill steps, have them review the skill using the interactive Social Studies Skills Tutor CD-ROM.

⊙ *Synthesizing Information*, Social Studies Skills Tutor CD-ROM

Extend L3

■ To extend the lesson, have students work in groups to synthesize information about the decline of the Roman Republic.

■ Tell students to create a chart of main ideas and supporting details, look for connections among the main ideas, and then formulate a conclusion based on the main ideas.

■ Direct the groups to write a brief paragraph synthesizing the information they have identified. Groups' paragraphs should end with conclusions they have drawn from the information.

■ Allow time for the groups to share their paragraphs with the rest of the class. Compare the paragraphs presented.

Answer
Apply the Skill

Students' paragraphs will vary somewhat but should synthesize information about the government of the Roman Empire from Section 2 under the headings The Power of Augustus and Governing Conquered Peoples. Possible conclusion: The emperor ruled the Roman Empire as a whole but needed others to help control and run it.

Section 2
Step-by-Step Instruction

Objectives

Social Studies
1. Learn how Rome ruled an empire.
2. Understand the Greek influence on Rome.
3. Identify key aspects of Roman architecture and technology.
4. Learn about key aspects of Roman law.

Reading/Language Arts
Use word origins to understand the meaning of unfamiliar words.

Prepare to Read

Build Background Knowledge L2

Tell students that in this section they will learn about the expansion of the Roman Empire. Ask students to preview the section and write two questions about the growth of the empire. Write students' questions on the board. Allow them to use these questions to fill in the second column of their charts in the Set a Purpose for Reading activity below.

Set a Purpose for Reading L2

- Preview the Objectives.

- Form students into pairs or groups of four. Distribute the *Reading Readiness Guide*. Ask students to fill in the first two columns of the chart. Use the Numbered Heads participation structure (TE, p. T40) to call on students to share one piece of information they already know and one piece of information they want to know.

> **All in One Unit 3 History of Our World Teaching Resources,** *Reading Readiness Guide,* p. 86

Vocabulary Builder
Preview Key Terms L2

Pronounce each Key Term, then ask students to say the word with you. Provide a simple explanation such as "Roman building projects included the Colosseum and many aqueducts."

Section 2
The Roman Empire

Prepare to Read

Objectives

In this section you will
1. Learn how Rome ruled an empire.
2. Understand the Greek influence on Rome.
3. Identify key aspects of Roman architecture and technology.
4. Learn about key aspects of Roman law.

Taking Notes

As you read, find main ideas and details about the Roman Empire. Copy the outline below, and use it to record your findings. Expand the outline as needed.

> **I. Governing the empire**
>   **A. Boundaries and territory**
>   **1.**
>   **2.**
>   **B. Augustus**

Target Reading Skill

Recognize Word Origins
You can decode an unfamiliar word by knowing the word's origin. For instance, you might not know the key term aqueduct, but you can uncover the meaning if you know that it comes from the Latin words *aqua* (water) + *ductus* (act of leading).

Key Terms

- **province** (PRAH vins) *n.* a unit of an empire
- **Colosseum** (kahl uh SEE um) a large amphitheater built in Rome around A.D. 70; site of contests and combats
- **aqueduct** (AK wuh dukt) *n.* a structure that carries water over long distances
- **polytheism** (PAHL ih thee iz um) *n.* a belief in more than one god
- **arch** (ahrch) *n.* a curved structure used as a support over an open space, as in a doorway

Located on the grounds of the Colosseum, the arches were built in honor of Constantine's victory over Maxentius. The arches are inscribed with the saying, "Constantine overcame his enemies by divine inspiration."

240 History of Our World

In his epic poem the *Aeneid* (ee NEE id), Virgil challenges Romans to play to their strengths. The following passage expresses his beliefs and hopes for Rome:

> **"There will be others to beat the breathing bronze with greater skill and grace. So others too will draw out living faces from the marble. Argue legal cases better, better trace the motions of the sky, And so pronounce the cycles of the stars. For you, O Roman, it is due to rule the peoples of your Empire. These are your arts: to impose peace and morality, To spare the subject [powerless] and subdue [control] the proud."**
>
> —from the *Aeneid*

Virgil says that other cultures may produce beautiful art or fine philosophers and astronomers. But Romans are most fit to govern, he says, and will do so wisely and fairly. Virgil was not alone in his hopes for just rule under Augustus, the first Roman emperor.

Target Reading Skill L2

Recognize Word Origins Model using word origins to understand the meaning of the word *philosophers* on this page. Tell students that the word comes from Greek. It contains the Greek root *phil-*, which means "love." It also contains the root *soph-* from the Greek word meaning "wisdom." Explain that this information suggests that philosophers are people who love wisdom or ideas.

Give students *Recognize Word Origins*. Have them complete the activity in groups.

> **All in One Unit 3 History of Our World Teaching Resources,** *Recognize Word Origins,* p. 91

Ruling an Empire

When Augustus came to power, Roman control had already spread far beyond Italy. Under Augustus and the emperors who followed him, Rome gained even more territory. Look at the map titled The Roman Empire at the beginning of this chapter. The Roman Empire stretched from Britain to Egypt. Rome controlled all the lands around the Mediterranean. With pride, Romans called the Mediterranean *mare nostrum* (MAH ray NAWS trum), or "our sea."

The Power of Augustus Augustus was an intelligent ruler. When he was struggling for power, he often ignored the senate and its laws. But after he won control, he changed his manner. He showed great respect for the senate and was careful to avoid acting like a king. He did not want to suffer the same fate as Julius Caesar. Augustus often said that he wanted to share power with the senate. He even said that he wanted to restore the republic.

What really happened was quite different. Romans were so grateful for Rome's peace and prosperity that they gave Augustus as much power as he wanted.

Governing Conquered Peoples The Romans took some slaves after a conquest, but most of the conquered people remained free. To govern, the Romans divided their empire into provinces. Each **province,** or area of the empire, had a Roman governor supported by an army. Often, the Romans built a city in a new province to serve as its capital.

Wisely, the Romans did not usually force their way of life on conquered peoples. They allowed these people to follow their own religions. Local rulers ran the daily affairs of government. As long as there was peace, Roman governors did not interfere in conquered peoples' lives. Rather, they kept watch over them. Rome wanted peaceful provinces that would supply the empire with the raw materials it needed. Rome also wanted the conquered people to buy Roman goods and to pay taxes. Many of the conquered people adopted Roman ways. Many learned to speak Latin, the language of the Romans, and worshiped Roman gods.

Augustus, First Emperor of Rome
With the rule of Augustus, a period of stability and prosperity known as the Pax Romana, or "Roman peace," began.
Generalize Use what you have read in the text to describe the kind of ruler Augustus was.

Ruling an Empire L2

Guided Instruction

■ **Vocabulary Builder** Clarify the meaning of the high-use words **brutality** before reading.

■ Read Ruling an Empire, using the Structured Silent Reading technique (TE, p. T38).

■ Discuss how the Romans governed their empire. *(The Romans divided the empire into provinces; each province had a Roman governor supported by an army; local rulers ran the daily affairs of government.)*

■ Ask students **How did the Romans benefit from not forcing their way of life on conquered peoples?** *(The provinces were generally peaceful, the Romans could get the raw materials they needed from the provinces, and conquered people bought Roman goods and paid taxes to Rome.)*

Vocabulary Builder

Use the information below to teach students this section's high-use words.

High-Use Word	Definition and Sample Sentence
despised, p. 242	*v.* to look down on with scorn. The cruel king **despised** everyone.
brutality, p. 242	*n.* the act of being cruel or ruthless He was punished for his **brutality** toward animals.
engineering, p. 243	*n.* the application of science and math in which the properties of matter and the sources of energy in nature are made useful to people Building projects involve knowledge of **engineering.**
network, p. 244	*n.* a system of things that are connected like the strands of a net The Internet is a worldwide **network.**

Answer

Generalize Answers will vary. Students should understand that Augustus was a powerful leader who was careful to avoid acting like a king.

Independent Practice

Ask students to create the Taking Notes outline on a blank sheet of paper. Then have them fill in and expand the outline with main ideas and details about how the Romans ruled their empire. Briefly model what kinds of information to include in the outline.

Monitor Progress

As students fill in the outline, circulate and make sure individuals are correctly identifying main ideas and details. Provide assistance as needed.

Marcus Aurelius was the last of the five "good emperors." In this stone sculpture, he pardons the barbarians whose attacks weakened the Roman Empire.

The Five "Good Emperors" Augustus died in A.D. 14. For eighty-two years after his death, Roman history was a story of good, bad, and terrible emperors. Two of the worst were Caligula (kuh LIG yuh luh) and Nero. Both may have been insane. Caligula proclaimed himself a god and was a cruel, unfair ruler. Nero murdered his half-brother, his mother, and his wife. In fact, Caligula and Nero were so despised that Romans later tried to forget them by removing mention of their reigns from official records.

In A.D. 96, Rome entered what is called the age of the five "good emperors." Only the last of these emperors had a son. Each of the others adopted the best young man he could find to be the next emperor.

Perhaps the greatest of the five "good emperors" was Hadrian (HAY dree un). He worked hard to build a good government. His laws protected women, children, and slaves. He issued a code of laws so that all laws were the same throughout the empire. Hadrian reorganized the army so that soldiers were allowed to defend their home provinces. This gave them a greater sense of responsibility. Hadrian traveled throughout his empire, commissioning many buildings and other structures. He even traveled to the British Isles, where he commissioned a great wall to be built, parts of which still stand today. Hadrian also encouraged learning.

The last of the "good emperors," Marcus Aurelius (MAHR kus aw REE lee uhs), chose his son Commodus (KAHM uh dus) to follow him. Commodus was a terrible leader who ruled with great brutality. His reign ended the age of peace and prosperity that Rome had enjoyed under its five previous emperors.

The Empire in Decline During the reign of Commodus, things started going badly for the Roman Empire. In Chapter 9, you will learn how bad government, economic problems, and foreign invaders all helped contribute to the fall of the Roman Empire.

✓ Reading Check **Why was Hadrian considered one of the five "good emperors"?**

Answer

✓ Reading Check Hadrian worked hard to build a good government. Laws made during his rule protected women, children, and slaves. He also issued a code of laws for the entire empire. He reorganized the army so that soldiers were responsible for the defense of their home provinces.

Skills Mini Lesson

Sequencing

1. Teach the skill by pointing out that a timeline is a tool for sequencing events.

2. Help students practice the skill by making a timeline. Tell students that the topic will be Rome under the five good emperors. Write the emperors' names and dates on the board. Then model

making a timeline by dividing a line into equal sections with a beginning date and an end date. With students' help, place the dates of the emperors' reigns on the timeline.

3. Ask students **How long was Rome ruled by the five "good emperors"?** (*84 years*)

The Greek Influence on Rome

The Romans had long admired Greek achievements. People said that Hadrian spoke Greek better than he spoke Latin. Marcus Aurelius wrote a famous book of philosophy in Greek. Many Romans visited Greece to study Greek art, architecture, and ideas about government.

Religion Greek religion influenced Roman religion. Like the Greeks, Romans practiced **polytheism**—the belief in more than one god—and offered prayers and sacrifices to their gods. Many Roman gods and goddesses had Greek counterparts. For example, the Roman god of the sky, Jupiter, shared characteristics with the Greek god Zeus. The Roman goddess of arts and trades, Minerva, is similar to the Greeks' Athena. The Romans also adopted heroes from Greek mythology, such as Heracles—known as Hercules to the Romans. As their empire spread, Romans appealed to and adopted other foreign gods as well.

Word Origins
The word *polytheism* comes from the Greek words *poly* and *theos*. If theos means "god," what does *poly* mean?

Building on Ideas Both the Greeks and the Romans valued learning, but in different ways. The Greeks were interested in ideas. They sought to learn truths about the world through reason. They developed studies such as mathematics, philosophy, and astronomy, or the study of the stars and planets. The Romans benefited from the study of these subjects, but they were more interested in using these studies to build and organize their world. Under the Romans, architecture and engineering blossomed. With these skills, the Romans built their empire.

✓ **Reading Check** In what ways did the Greeks and Romans value learning?

Zeus, the god of sky and weather, was the most important Greek god. He was a protector of peace and political order and hurled thunderbolts at those who angered him. He is shown here with Ganymede, his cup-bearer. His Roman counterpart, Jupiter, is shown above.

The Greek Influence on Rome ▣

Guided Instruction

■ **Vocabulary Builder** Clarify the meaning of the high-use word **engineering** before reading.

■ Read The Greek Influence on Rome. As students read, circulate and make sure individuals can answer the Reading Check question.

■ Identify areas in which the Greeks influenced the Romans. (*The Greeks influenced the Romans in art, architecture, government, religion, and areas of study such as mathematics, philosophy, and astronomy.*)

■ Ask students **How did the Romans know about Greek ideas and culture?** (*They visited Greece and made Greece part of the Roman Empire.*)

Independent Practice

Ask students to add main ideas and details about Greek influence on Rome to their Taking Notes outlines.

Monitor Progress

As students add to the outline, circulate and make sure individuals are correctly identifying main ideas and details. Provide assistance as needed.

Answers

✓ **Reading Check** The Greeks were interested in ideas and sought to learn about the world through reason in the study of mathematics, philosophy, and astronomy. The Romans were interested in using these studies to build and organize their world with architecture and engineering.

Background: Global Perspectives

A Multicultural Society By the time Hadrian came to power, Rome had a large population of immigrants from the provinces. In fact, both Hadrian and his predecessor, Trajan, were from Spain. In addition, many of the slaves who had been brought to Rome from conquered lands had bought their freedom. The former slaves and new immigrants represented nearly all of the ethnicities of the Roman Empire. They included ancestors of people from modern Greece, Turkey, Syria, Israel, Egypt, Tunisia, Algeria, Libya, Morocco, Britain, Spain, France, Germany, Austria, Switzerland, Bosnia, Serbia, Romania, and Russia.

Architecture and Technology L2

Guided Instruction

- **Vocabulary Builder** Clarify the meaning of the high-use word **network** before reading.

- Ask students to read Architecture and Technology and review images of buildings in Section 2.

- Discuss improvements that the Romans made in architecture and the construction of buildings. *(The Romans made advances in the use of the arch and developed concrete.)* Ask students **How did the use of technology benefit the empire?** *(The Romans built a network of roads that connected places across the empire and allowed the military to reach places quickly; they also built aqueducts to deliver water from the countryside to cities.)*

Independent Practice

Ask students to add main ideas and details about Roman architecture and technology to their Taking Notes outlines.

Monitor Progress

As students add to the outline, circulate and make sure individuals are correctly identifying main ideas and details. Provide assistance as needed.

Show *The Rise of the Roman Empire.* Ask **What does life in Ancient Rome tell you about people's values?** *(Answers will vary.)*

Links

Read the **Links to Science** on this page. Ask students **Why would arches be especially important in bridges?** *(Arches help a bridge bear the weight of people, animals, and vehicles such as chariots and wagons that passed over it.)*

Answer

✓ **Reading Check** Roman buildings were large with large open spaces inside.

Architecture and Technology

Early Roman art and architecture copied the Etruscan style. Then, the Romans studied and copied Greek sculpture and architecture. Later, they developed their own art and architecture styles.

The Roman Style Roman statues and buildings were heavier and stronger in style than those of the Greeks. The Romans made advances in the use of the **arch**—a curved structure used as a support over an open space, as in a doorway. Romans used arches to build larger structures. They used wide arched ceilings to create large open spaces inside buildings.

In earlier times, most large buildings had been built of bricks and then covered with thin slabs of marble. However, Romans developed an important new building material—concrete. Concrete was a mix of stone, sand, cement, and water that dried as hard as rock. Concrete helped the Romans construct buildings that were taller than any previously built.

The Colosseum Possibly the greatest Roman building was the **Colosseum,** the site of contests and combats between people and between people and animals. This giant arena held 50,000 spectators. Its walls were so well built that the floor of the arena could be flooded for mock naval battles in real boats. Stairways and ramps ran through the building. There were even elevators to carry wild animals from dens below up to the arena.

Roads and Aqueducts Roman engineers built roads from Rome to every part of the empire. Do you know the saying "All roads lead to Rome"? In Roman times all of the major roads did lead to Rome, so no matter what road travelers started out on, they could get to Rome. These roads allowed the Roman military to maintain firm control by traveling quickly to all parts of the empire. The map in the Regional Overview titled Ancient Roads of the Roman Empire shows this network of roads.

Romans were famous for their **aqueducts,** structures that carried water over long distances. The aqueducts were huge lines of arches, often many miles long. A channel along the top carried water from the countryside to the cities. Roman aqueducts tunneled through mountains and spanned valleys. Some are still being used today. To learn more, see the Eyewitness Technology feature titled The Roman Aqueduct.

✓ **Reading Check** What are some characteristics of Roman buildings?

Links to

Science

The Roman Arch Roman architects made great use of the curved structure called the arch. Arches span openings in buildings. An arch can hold great weight above it. The Romans probably learned about arches from the Etruscans. Beginning in the 300s B.C., Romans used arches for aqueducts (water channels), bridges, and monuments.

Learn about the rise of the Roman Empire.

Differentiated Instruction

For English Language Learners L1

Students may benefit from making a picture dictionary of words connected with Roman architecture and technology. Have students start with the following words: *arch, concrete, Colosseum, aqueduct.* If interested, they may then add these words: *arena, ramp, elevator, den, channel.* Have students draw a picture illustrating each word and then write a brief caption for the drawing that includes the word and either a simple definition or a sample sentence using the word.

The Roman Aqueduct

The Romans built aqueducts to bring fresh water to the city. Sources of water had to be at elevations higher than the city, as pumping was not a practical way of moving water. Engineers tunneled through mountains and bridged valleys to create a gradual, even slope. Follow the numbers to see how the water flowed from the mountains to the city.

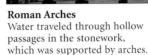

Roman Arches
Water traveled through hollow passages in the stonework, which was supported by arches.

2 Water pressure carries water across the valley and up the other side, to a pool at a lower elevation.

3 To maintain a gentle slope, arches carry the water high above the ground.

1 Water from mountain springs flows into a collecting pool. Mud and gravel settle out.

4 The water runs underground in tunnels and trenches.

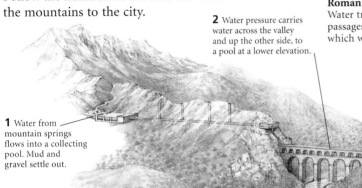

5 Aqueducts bound for different parts of the city cross at this tower.

6 The water runs into a settling pool. From there, smaller channels carry it to public baths and fountains.

Keeping the Water Fresh
Around four out of every five miles of aqueduct ran underground. Underground tunnels kept the water fresh, by keeping out dirt and animals. The Roman government did not allow anyone to damage an aqueduct, pollute the water, or use it for private consumption.

Fountain

ANALYZING IMAGES
Why were the arches built high above the land?

Differentiated Instruction

For Less Proficient Readers **L1**

Some students may need help identifying and understanding important content in this section. Pair these students with more proficient readers. Have the less proficient readers read passages of text aloud and then summarize them orally. Their partners should provide feedback as needed for each summary.

The Roman Aqueduct **L2**

Guided Instruction

Ask students to examine the illustration of the Roman aqueduct on this page. Tell students to follow the numbers and read the captions to understand how technology is used to move water from the mountains to the city. As a class, answer the question at the bottom of the page.

Independent Practice

Ask students to suppose that they are Roman engineers who have designed an aqueduct to bring water to a new city in one of the provinces. Have students write a one-page description of how the aqueduct moves water.

Answer

Analyzing Images Arches were built high above the land to maintain a gentle slope for the water.

Roman Law **L2**

Guided Instruction

- Discuss Roman ideas of justice basic to our own system of laws. (*Persons accused of crimes have the right to face their accusers; if reasonable doubt exists about a person's guilt, the person would be considered innocent.*)

- Ask students **How do you think Roman ideas about justice were passed on to our culture?** (*Possible response: Roman ideas about justice came to our country through England and English settlers.*)

Independent Practice

Ask students to complete their Taking Notes outlines with main ideas and details about Roman law.

Monitor Progress

- Show *Section Reading Support Transparency HOW 80* and ask students to check their graphic organizers individually.

  History of Our World, *Section Reading Support HOW 80*

- Tell students to fill in the last column of the *Reading Readiness Guide.*

  History of Our World Transparencies, *Reading Readiness Guide,* p. 86

Assess and Reteach

Assess Progress L2

Have students complete the Section Assessment. Administer the *Section Quiz.*

All in One Unit 3 History of Our World Teaching Resources, *Section Quiz,* p. 88

Reteach L1

If students need more instruction, have them read the section in the *Reading and Vocabulary Study Guide.*

Chapter 8, Section 1, **History of Our World Reading and Vocabulary Study Guide,** pp. 94–96

Extend L3

Use Transparency Set 1 to help students learn more about the expansion of the Roman Empire. Discuss the borders of the empire as students view each overlay.

Roman Expansion, Color Transparencies, HOW Set 1

Answers

✓ Reading Check Students may explain any two laws listed in the quotation from Justinian's code; they may explain that the code said that no one could be punished for his or her ideas and that the age and experience of the guilty person need to be considered when deciding the person's punishment.

Section 2 Assessment

Key Terms
Students' sentences should reflect knowledge of each Key Term.

Target Reading Skill
Possible response: The Colosseum is a very large structure.

Comprehension and Critical Thinking
1. (a) It stretched from Britain to Egypt and included all the lands around the Mediterranean. **(b)** The Romans divided the empire into provinces.

2. (a) The Romans learned mathematics, philosophy, and astronomy. **(b)** The Romans used technology to build roads and aqueducts.

3. (a) The Justinian code of law was a set of laws created by the emperor Justinian for the Roman Empire. **(b)** Possible response: No one is above the law.

Roman Law

Like Roman roads, Roman law spread throughout the empire. The great Roman senator Cicero (SIS uh roh) expressed Roman feeling about law when he said, "What sort of thing is the law? It is the kind that cannot be bent by influence, or broken by power, or spoiled by money."

A later ruler named Justinian (juh STIN ee un) created a code of justice from Roman law. That code includes these laws:

> **No one suffers a penalty for what he thinks. No one may be forcibly removed from his own house. The burden of proof is upon the person who accuses. In inflicting penalties, the age and inexperience of the guilty party must be taken into account.**
>
> —*Code of Justinian*

Roman law was passed on to other cultures, including our own. In fact, Roman ideas of justice are basic to our system of laws. For example, under Roman law, persons accused of crimes had the right to face their accusers. If reasonable doubt existed about a person's guilt, that person would be considered innocent.

Knowledge of the laws and legal procedures of Rome was helpful in pursuing a government career. Many Roman officials, such as the Senators depicted in this sculpture, argued cases in court and served as judges.

✓ Reading Check Recall two features of Justinian's code, and explain their meaning.

Section 2 Assessment

Key Terms
Review the key terms listed at the beginning of this section. Use each term in a sentence that explains the terms meaning.

Target Reading Skill
If the Latin word *colosseus* means "colossal" or "very large," what might you guess about the Colosseum?

Comprehension and Critical Thinking
1. (a) Describe At its height, what area did the Roman Empire cover?

(b) Explain How did Rome handle the difficulties of governing its large empire?
2. (a) List What did the Romans learn from the Greeks?
(b) Explore the Main Idea How did the Roman's technological achievements help them strengthen their empire?
3. (a) Name What was the Justinian code of law?
(b) Draw Conclusions What did Cicero mean when he said that the law "cannot be bent by influence, or broken by power, or spoiled by money"?

Writing Activity
Write down a few ideas for guidelines that you would give to every new governor of a Roman province. For example, how should the governor treat the people of the province?

For: An activity on the Roman Empire
Visit: PHSchool.com
Web Code: mud-0820

Writing Activity

Use the *Rubric for Assessing a Writing Assignment* to evaluate students' work.

All in One Unit 3 History of Our World Teaching Resources, *Rubric for Assessing a Writing Assignment,* p. 101

Go Online PHSchool.com Typing in the Web Code when prompted will bring students directly to detailed instructions for this activity.

Chapter 8 Review and Assessment

◆ Chapter Summary

Section 1: The Roman Republic

- Rome's geographic setting helped the city grow into an important civilization.
- Rome's early ruling people, the Etruscans, were overthrown by the Romans who established a Republic.
- Julius Caesar took over the weakened republic and became Rome's dictator.
- After Caesar's murder and a long civil war, Augustus emerged as the first emperor of Rome.

Section 2: The Roman Empire

- The expanding Roman Empire was a challenge for Augustus and other emperors who ruled it.
- The Greeks influenced Roman learning and religion.
- The Romans were masters at creating large public buildings and road networks.
- Roman law spread throughout the empire and continues to influence civilizations today.

Sarcophagus of the Spouses

The Arch of Constantine

◆ Key Terms

Choose the correct word(s) for each of the definitions below.

1. an ordinary citizen in the ancient Roman Republic
   - A patrician
   - B dictator
   - C plebeian
   - D consul

2. an arena in ancient Rome
   - A villa
   - B Colosseum
   - C aqueduct
   - D province

3. an elected official who led the ancient Roman Republic
   - A consul
   - B dictator
   - C plebeian
   - D patrician

4. a unit of an empire
   - A emperor
   - B province
   - C plebeian
   - D citizen

5. a structure that carries water over a long distances
   - A arch
   - B dictator
   - C patrician
   - D aqueduct

Chapter 8 **247**

─ Vocabulary Builder ─

High-Use Academic Words

Revisit this chapter's high-use words:

found	uproot	engineering
attitude	despised	network
decline	brutality	

Ask students to review the definitions they recorded on their *Word Knowledge* worksheet.

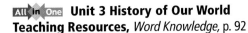 **Unit 3 History of Our World Teaching Resources,** *Word Knowledge,* p. 92

Consider allowing students to earn extra credit if they use the words in their answers to the questions in the Chapter Review and Assessment. The words must be used correctly and in a natural context to win the extra points.

Chapter 8

Review and Assessment

Review Chapter Content

- Review and revisit the major themes of this chapter by asking students to classify what Guiding Questions each bulleted statement in the Chapter Summary answers. Have students work together in groups to classify the sentences. Refer to p. 1 in the Student Edition for the text of the Guiding Questions.

- Assign *Vocabulary Development* to help students review the Key Terms.

All in One Unit 3 History of Our World Teaching Resources, *Vocabulary Development,* p. 99

Answers

Key Terms

1. C
2. B
3. A
4. B
5. D

Review and Assessment

Comprehension and Critical Thinking

6. (a) The Etruscans had kings. **(b)** Leaders were elected by the people and served in the name of the people.

7. (a) The consul had veto power. **(b)** A dictator could be appointed if the consuls did not agree with each other.

8. (a) The patricians were members of the upper class; the plebeians were ordinary citizens. **(b)** A written code of laws called the Twelve Tables was created.

9. (a) Conflict between patricians and plebeians, civil war between generals with private armies, disagreements between consuls, and the rise of Julius Caesar as dictator led to the decline of the Republic. **(b)** The government began to rely on the rule of one person.

10. (a) Augustus came to power at the end of the civil war that followed the assassination of Julius Caesar (Augustus was Julius Caesar's adopted son). **(b)** The Senate struck down Julius Caesar because he took much of its power and ruled like a king; Augustus showed great respect for the senate, said he wanted to share power with it, and was careful not to act like a king.

11. (a) The Colosseum was a giant arena where contests and combats were held for the entertainment of the people of Rome. **(b)** Possible responses: The Romans built a large network of roads, that connected Rome to its many outposts.

12. (a) The Romans contributed a code of laws that contained ideas of justice that form the basis of systems of laws in many cultures; Roman contributions to technology include an improved arch, concrete, and aqueducts. **(b)** Possible response: Better arches allowed the Romans to build larger structures and create large open spaces inside buildings; concrete made taller buildings possible; aqueducts moved water over long distances.

Skills Practice
Students' outlines will vary.

Writing Activity: Government
Students' speeches will vary, but should include accurate information in support of their argument for or against giving more power to Augustus.

◆ Comprehension and Critical Thinking

6. (a) Recall How were the Etruscans governed? **(b) Explain** How was the Roman republican form of government different from Etruscan rule?

7. (a) Identify What power allowed the consul to reject any proposed government policy? **(b) Draw Inferences** During the Republic, what problem in the two-consul setup was addressed by appointing a dictator?

8. (a) Contrast What were the main differences between the patricians and the plebeians? **(b) Identify Effects** What measure was taken to address the complaints of the plebeians?

9. (a) Identify Causes What led to the decline of the Roman Republic? **(b) Identify Effects** How did the decline of the Roman Republic affect the governing of Rome?

10. (a) Recall How did Augustus come to power? **(b) Compare and Contrast** Why did the Roman Senate strike down Caesar, but hand more power to Augustus?

11. (a) Identify What was the Colosseum? **(b) Explain** What does the saying "all roads lead to Rome" mean?

12. (a) Identify What contributions did Romans make to law? To technology? **(b) Generalize** What was the importance of these contributions?

◆ Skills Practice

Synthesizing Information In the Skills Activity in this chapter, you learned about the importance of synthesizing information. When synthesizing information, find the main ideas and use them to formulate a conclusion.

Reread the section on Architecture and Technology from Section 2 of this chapter. Create an outline in which you synthesize the most important information from this section.

◆ Writing Activity: Government

Suppose that you are a speechwriter for a Roman senator around the time that Augustus becomes the first emperor of Rome. Write a speech addressed to the senate that argues either for or against giving Augustus more power.

MAP MASTER™ Skills Activity
The Rise of the Roman Empire

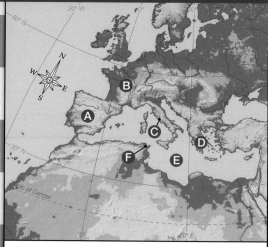

Place Location For each place listed below, write the letter from the map that shows its location.

1. Rome
2. Mediterranean Sea
3. Gaul
4. Spain
5. Greece
6. Carthage

Go Online
PHSchool.com Use Web Code **mup-0803** for step-by-step **map skills practice**.

Standardized Test Prep

Test-Taking Tips

Some questions on standardized tests ask you to analyze a timeline. Study the timeline below. Then follow the tips to answer the sample question.

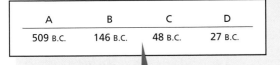

A	B	C	D
509 B.C.	146 B.C.	48 B.C.	27 B.C.

TIP When you read a timeline, line up each date with the significant event that occurred on that date. Place as many events as you know above the proper dates to help you eliminate wrong answers.

Choose the letter that best answers the question.

Where would "the first Roman emperor" go on the timeline?

A point A
B point B
C point C
D point D

TIP Carelessness costs points on multiple-choice tests. Think carefully about each date and event on the timeline.

Think It Through As you look over the timeline, ask yourself, When did the first emperor take office? It must have happened after all the trouble and turmoil surrounding the rule of the dictator Julius Caesar and his murder by a group of senators. If you know that, then you know that the first emperor took office after Caesar was murdered in 44 B.C. The only possible answer, then, is D.

Practice Questions

Use the tips above and other tips in this book to help you answer the following questions.

1. In the Roman Republic, what happened if the two consuls disagreed in an emergency?
   A A dictator was appointed.
   B A third consul was appointed.
   C The senate made the final decision.
   D All citizens voted.

2. The Romans were heavily influenced by
   A the Greeks.
   B the Chinese.
   C the Persians.
   D the plebeians.

3. Which of the following is a key feature of a republican government?
   A rule by a king
   B dictatorship
   C polytheism
   D elected officials

Use the timeline below to answer Question 4.

A	B	C	D
509 B.C.	146 B.C.	48 B.C.	27 B.C.

4. At which point on the timeline did the Romans overthrow the last Etruscan king?
   A point A
   B point B
   C point C
   D point D

Use Web Code **mua-0800** for **Chapter 8 self-test.**

Assessment Resources

Use Chapter Tests A and B to assess students' mastery of chapter content.

All in One **Unit 3 History of Our World Teaching Resources,** *Chapter Tests A and B,* pp. 104–109

Tests are also available on the ExamView® Test Bank CD-ROM.

⊙ Exam*View*® **Test Bank CD-ROM**

The Glory of Ancient Rome

Overview

Section 1
Roman Daily Life
1. Discover who could be a Roman citizen.
2. Find out how Romans of different social classes lived.
3. Understand the importance of family life in Roman society.
4. Learn about slavery in ancient Rome.

Section 2
Christianity and the Roman Empire
1. Learn about the rise of Christianity in the Roman Empire.
2. Discover how Christianity spread throughout the empire.
3. Understand the Roman government's reaction to the growth of Christianity.

Section 3
The Fall of Rome
1. Explore how bad government contributed to the decline of the empire.
2. Understand the fall of the Roman Empire.
3. Discuss Constantine's role in support of Christianity.
4. Learn how northern invaders brought about the collapse of the Roman Empire.

DISCOVERY CHANNEL
SCHOOL Video

Daily Life in Ancient Rome
Length: 4 minutes, 11 seconds
Use with Section 1
The Roman Empire was a place of grand cities, magnificent buildings, and riches of every kind. This video segment explores what Roman citizens wore, their dwellings, their meals, and other aspects of daily life.

Technology Resources

Go Online
PHSchool.com

interactive
Textbook

PRENTICE HALL
TeacherEXPRESS
Plan • Teach • Assess

Students use embedded web codes to access Internet activities, chapter self-tests, and additional map practice. They may also access Dorling Kindersley's Online Desk Reference to learn more about each country they study.

Use the Interactive Textbook to make content and concepts come alive through animations, videos, and activities that accompany the complete basal text—online and on CD-ROM.

Use this complete suite of powerful teaching tools to make lesson planning and administering tests quicker and easier.

Reading and Assessment

Reading and Vocabulary Instruction

⟳ Model the Target Reading Skill

Identify Main Ideas Being able to identify main ideas is essential to reading comprehension. Writers often state main ideas directly. Sometimes, however, main ideas are only implied, or hinted at, by details in the text.

Model how to identify an implied main idea by thinking aloud about the details in this paragraph:

After Commodus, emperors were almost always successful generals, not politicians. They often stole money from the treasury. They used the money to enrich themselves and to pay for the loyalty of their soldiers. The government and the economy became weak, and the senate lost power. Would-be rulers gained the throne by violence. Between A.D. 180 and A.D. 284, Rome had 27 emperors. Most were assassinated.

This paragraph gives details about emperors who came after Commodus, but it does not state a main idea. I can use the details to figure out the main idea. What main idea do details add up to? I think the main idea of the paragraph is that later Roman emperors were weak and corrupt rulers.

Use the following worksheets from All-In-One Unit 3 History of Our World Teaching Resources (pp. 125–127) to support this chapter's Target Reading Skill.

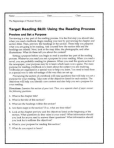 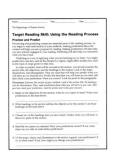

Vocabulary Builder
High-Use Academic Words

Use these steps to teach this chapter's high-use words:

1. Have students rate how well they know each word on their Word Knowledge worksheets (All-In-One Unit 3 History of Our World Teaching Resources, p. 128).

2. Pronounce each word and ask students to repeat it.

3. Give students a brief definition and sample sentence (provided on TE pp. 253, 260, and 271).

4. Work with students as they fill in the "Definition or Example" column of their Word Knowledge worksheets.

Assessment

Formal Assessment

Test students' understanding of core knowledge and skills.

Chapter Tests A and B, Unit 3 History of Our World Teaching Resources, pp. 144–149

Customize the Chapter Tests to suit your needs.

Exam*View*® Test Bank CD-ROM

Skills Assessment

Assess geographic literacy.

MapMaster Skills, Student Edition, pp. 251, 262, 272, 278

Assess reading and comprehension.

Target Reading Skills, Student Edition, pp. 255, 261, 271 and in Section Assessments

Chapter 9 Assessment, All-In-One Unit 3 History of Our World Reading and Vocabulary Study Guide, p. 107

Performance Assessment

Assess students' performance on this chapter's Writing Activities using the following rubric from All-In-One Unit 3 History of Our World Teaching Resources.

Rubric for Assessing a Writing Assignment, p. 143

Assess students' work through performance tasks.

Small Group Activity: Researching Hadrian's Wall, All-In-One Unit 3 History of Our World Teaching Resources, pp. 131–134

Online Assessment

Have students check their own understanding.

Chapter Self-Test

Section 1 Roman Daily Life

 3 periods, 1.5 blocks

Social Studies Objectives

1. Discover who could be a Roman citizen.
2. Find out how Romans of different social classes lived.
3. Understand the importance of family life in Roman society.
4. Learn about slavery in ancient Rome.

Reading/Language Arts Objective

Learn to identify the main idea of a paragraph or section.

Prepare to Read	Instructional Resources	Differentiated Instruction
Build Background Knowledge Discuss daily life in ancient Rome. **Set a Purpose for Reading** Have students evaluate statements on the *Reading Readiness Guide*. **Preview Key Terms** Teach the section's Key Terms. **Target Reading Skill** Introduce the section's Target Reading Skill of identifying main ideas.	**All in One Unit 3 History of Our World Teaching Resources** L2 Reading Readiness Guide, p. 114 L2 Identify Main Ideas, p. 125	**Spanish Reading and Vocabulary Study Guide** L2 Chapter 9, Section 1, pp. 71–72 ELL

Instruct	Instructional Resources	Differentiated Instruction
Roman Citizens Discuss who could be a Roman citizen. **Roman Social Classes** Compare and contrast the lives of rich and poor Romans. **Target Reading Skill** Review identifying main ideas. **Roman Family Life** Discuss the structure of the Roman household. **Slavery in Rome** Discuss slavery in Rome.	**All in One Unit 3 History of Our World Teaching Resources** L2 Guided Reading and Review, p. 115 L2 Reading Readiness Guide, p. 114 **History of Our World Video Program** L2 Daily Life in Ancient Rome **History of Our World Transparencies** L2 Section Reading Support Transparency HOW 81	**All in One Unit 3 History of Our World Teaching Resources** L3 Small Group Activity: Researching Hadrian's Wall, pp. 131–134 GT, AR **Teacher's Edition** L1 For Less Proficient Readers, TE, p. 254 L1 For Special Needs Students, TE, p. 254 L3 For Gifted and Talented Students, TE, p. 256 L3 For Advanced Readers, p. 256 **PHSchool.com** L3 **For:** An activity on daily Roman life **Web Code:** mud-0910 **Student Edition on Audio CD** L1 Chapter 9, Section 1 ELL **Spanish Support** L2 Guided Reading and Review, p. 76 ELL

Assess and Reteach	Instructional Resources	Differentiated Instruction
Assess Progress Evaluate student comprehension with the section assessment and section quiz. **Reteach** Assign the Reading and Vocabulary Study Guide to help struggling students. **Extend** Extend the lesson by assigning the Enrichment worksheet.	**All in One Unit 3 History of Our World Teaching Resources** L2 Section Quiz, p. 116 L2 Rubric for Assessing a Writing Assignment, p. 143 L3 Enrichment, p. 129 **Reading and Vocabulary Study Guide** L1 Chapter 9, Section 1, pp. 98–100	**Spanish Support** L2 Section Quiz (Spanish), p. 77 ELL

Key

L1 Basic to Average	L3 Average to Advanced	LPR Less Proficient Readers	GT Gifted and Talented
L2 For All Students		AR Advanced Readers	ELL English Language Learners
		SN Special Needs Students	

Section 2 Christianity and the Roman Empire

 3 periods, 1.5 blocks (includes Focus on the Roman Soldier and Skills for Life)

Social Studies Objectives

1. Learn about the rise of Christianity in the Roman Empire.
2. Discover how Christianity spread throughout the empire.
3. Understand the Roman government's reaction to the growth of Christianity.

Reading/Language Arts Objective

Learn to identify details that support the main idea of a paragraph or section.

Prepare to Read	**Instructional Resources**	**Differentiated Instruction**

Build Background Knowledge
Discuss the development and spread of Christianity in the Roman Empire.

Set a Purpose for Reading
Have students evaluate statements on the *Reading Readiness Guide.*

Preview Key Terms
Teach the section's Key Terms.

Target Reading Skill
Introduce the section's Target Reading Skill of identifying supporting details.

All in One Unit 3 History of Our World Teaching Resources
- **L2** Reading Readiness Guide, p. 118
- **L2** Identify Supporting Details, p. 126

Spanish Reading and Vocabulary Study Guide
- **L2** Chapter 9, Section 2, pp. 73–74 ELL

Instruct	**Instructional Resources**	**Differentiated Instruction**

The Rise of Christianity
Discuss the teachings of Jesus and their appeal to people in the empire.

Target Reading Skill
Review identifying supporting details.

Christianity Spreads
Examine the spread of Christianity after Jesus' death.

Rome Reacts
Discuss how Roman officials reacted to the spread of Christianity.

All in One Unit 3 History of Our World Teaching Resources
- **L2** Guided Reading and Review, p. 119
- **L2** Reading Readiness Guide, p. 118

History of Our World Transparencies
- **L2** Section Reading Support Transparency HOW 82

All in One Unit 3 History of Our World Teaching Resources
- **L2** Skills for Life, p. 130 AR, GT, LPR, SN

Teacher's Edition
- **L1** For Less Proficient Readers, TE, p. 261
- **L2** For English Language Learners, TE, p. 261
- **L3** For Gifted and Talented Students, TE, p. 263
- **L3** For Advanced Readers, TE, p. 263

Student Edition on Audio CD
- **L1** Chapter 9, Section 2 ELL

Spanish Support
- **L2** Guided Reading and Review, p. 78 ELL

Assess and Reteach	**Instructional Resources**	**Differentiated Instruction**

Assess Progress
Evaluate student comprehension with the section assessment and section quiz.

Reteach
Assign the Reading and Vocabulary Study Guide to help struggling students.

Extend
Extend the lesson by having students write biographies of figures of the period.

All in One Unit 3 History of Our World Teaching Resources
- **L2** Section Quiz, p. 120
- **L2** Rubric for Assessing a Writing Assignment, p. 143

Reading and Vocabulary Study Guide
- **L1** Chapter 9, Section 2, pp. 101–103

Spanish Support
- **L2** Section Quiz (Spanish), p. 79 ELL

Social Studies Skills Tutor CD-ROM
- **L1** Comparing and Contrasting ELL

Key

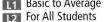

L1 Basic to Average	**L3** Average to Advanced
L2 For All Students	

LPR Less Proficient Readers
AR Advanced Readers
SN Special Needs Students

GT Gifted and Talented
ELL English Language Learners

Section 3 The Fall of Rome

 3 periods, 1.5 blocks

Social Studies Objectives

1. Explore how bad government contributed to the decline of the empire.
2. Understand the fall of the Roman Empire.
3. Discuss Constantine's role in support of Christianity.
4. Learn how northern invaders brought about the collapse of the Roman Empire.

Reading/Language Arts Objective

Learn to identify the implied main idea of a paragraph or section.

Prepare to Read	**Instructional Resources**	**Differentiated Instruction**
Build Background Knowledge Discuss the fall of the Roman Empire. **Set a Purpose for Reading** Have students begin to fill out the *Reading Readiness Guide*. **Preview Key Terms** Teach the section's Key Terms. **Target Reading Skill** Introduce the section's Target Reading Skill of identifying implied main ideas.	**All in One Unit 3 History of Our World Teaching Resources** L2 Reading Readiness Guide, p. 122 L2 Identify Implied Main Ideas, p. 127	**Spanish Reading and Vocabulary Study Guide** L2 Chapter 9, Section 3, pp. 75–76 ELL

Instruct	**Instructional Resources**	**Differentiated Instruction**
From Good Rule to Bad Discuss the rule of the emperor Commodus. **Target Reading Skill** Review identifying implied main ideas. **The Empire Crumbles** Discuss problems that led to the fall of Rome. **Constantine and Christianity** Discuss how Constantine supported Christianity. **Invasions and Collapse** Discuss invaders who overwhelmed the Roman Empire.	**All in One Unit 3 History of Our World Teaching Resources** L2 Guided Reading and Review, p. 123 L2 Reading Readiness Guide, p. 122 **History of Our World Transparencies** L2 Section Reading Support Transparency HOW 83	**Teacher's Edition** L1 For Less Proficient Readers, TE, p. 274 L3 For Advanced Readers, TE, p. 274 **PHSchool.com** L3 For: An activity on the fall of the Roman Empire Web Code: mud-0930 **Student Edition on Audio CD** L1 Chapter 9, Section 3 ELL **Spanish Support** L2 Guided Reading and Review, p. 80 ELL

Assess and Reteach	**Instructional Resources**	**Differentiated Instruction**
Assess Progress Evaluate student comprehension with the section assessment and section quiz. **Reteach** Assign the Reading and Vocabulary Study Guide to help struggling students. **Extend** Extend the lesson by assigning a problem-and-solution essay.	**All in One Unit 3 History of Our World Teaching Resources** L2 Section Quiz, p. 124 L2 Rubric for Assessing a Writing Assignment, p. 143 L2 Vocabulary Development, p. 135 L2 Word Knowledge, p. 128 L2 Chapter Tests A and B, pp. 144–149 **Reading and Vocabulary Study Guide** L1 Chapter 9, Section 3, pp. 104–106	**Spanish Support** L2 Section Quiz (Spanish), p. 81 ELL L2 Chapter Summary (Spanish), p. 82 ELL L2 Vocabulary Development (Spanish), p. 83 ELL

Key

L1 Basic to Average   L3 Average to Advanced   LPR Less Proficient Readers   GT Gifted and Talented
L2 For All Students   AR Advanced Readers   ELL English Language Learners
                                               SN Special Needs Students

Reading Background

Asking Questions and Finding Answers

Asking questions before, during, and after reading helps students monitor and increase their comprehension of the text. There are many types of questions. Understanding different types of questions will help students formulate better questions and find or arrive at the answers they are looking for.

List the following types of questions on the board:

1. Questions with answers that are found in one or two sentences in the text
2. Questions with answers that are found by looking at different paragraphs in the text
3. Questions with answers that are not found directly in the text but require you to think about what you have read
4. Questions with answers that are not found directly in the text but which you can answer without reading the text

Have students write one example of each type of question based on Section 2 of the chapter text. Ask students to share their questions. Have the rest of the class determine which type of question it is and then give an answer.

Taking an Active Part by Sharing Ideas

In this chapter, students will use the Give One, Get One strategy to participate in class discussion. This strategy has three stages: independent reflection, peer interaction, and class discussion. The independent reflection stage requires students to generate and evaluate their own ideas. The peer interaction and class discussion stages have them exchange ideas and then present each other's ideas.

Encourage students to consider their own ideas carefully to determine which are strongest and best to share with others. Remind students that accurately copying a partner's idea and then identifying it with the partner's name is an important step in the idea exchange that not only records the source of the idea but makes sure that the idea is presented correctly in the class discussion. Suggest that students use a simple chart to record their own and others' ideas.

World Studies Background

Roman Dining

The Romans made eating a social occasion. Every Roman looked forward to the *cena,* or evening meal, as a time to share food with family and sometimes a few guests. A *convivium,* or banquet, was a larger affair that might include friends and clients as well as relatives. Both *cena* and *convivium* were a time to relax and enjoy food and company. For most Romans, the *cena* was the only meal of the day. Family members gathered for the meal in the dining room of the house. The men would recline on couches, usually three to a couch, and eat with their right hands while propped up on their left elbows. Women and children ate at a table in the center of the room. This daily meal often included bread with oil, garlic, salt and herbs, and some dry cheese. Vegetable soup or bean puree might also be on the menu. If guests were invited, the host might offer a *gustatio,* or before-meal treat of olives, boiled eggs, or fresh greens. Bacon, chicken, goat, or lamb might also be part of the feast. Walnuts, figs, candied fruits, and wine were common accompaniments.

Get in-depth information on topics of global importance with **Prentice Hall Newstracker,** powered by FT.com.

Use Web Code mud-0900 for **Prentice Hall Newstracker.**

Chapter 9

Guiding Questions

Remind students about the Guiding questions introduced at the beginning of the book.

Section 1 relates to **Guiding Question** ❸ **What were the beliefs and values of people in these societies?** (*The Romans had a strong sense of traditional values and valued family life most of all.*)

Section 2 relates to **Guiding Question** ❷ **How did each society's belief system affect its historical accomplishments?** (*Roman rulers tried to stamp out Christianity, but over time the new religion spread throughout the Roman Empire.*)

Section 3 relates to **Guiding Question** ❹ **What types of governments were formed in these societies and how did they develop?** (*Weak, corrupt rulers and the huge size of the Roman Empire contributed to its fall.*)

⊙ Target Reading Skill

In this chapter, students will learn and apply the reading skill of identifying the main idea. Use the following worksheets to help students practice this skill.

All in One **Unit 3 History of Our World Teaching Resources,** *Identify Main Ideas,* p. 125; *Identify Supporting Details,* p. 126; *Identify Implied Main Ideas,* p. 127

Chapter Preview

In this chapter you will discover how people lived in ancient Rome. You will also learn about the birth of Christianity, its effect on Rome, and the collapse of the Roman Empire.

Section I
Roman Daily Life

Section 2
Christianity and the Roman Empire

Section 3
The Fall of Rome

 Target Reading Skill

Main Idea In this chapter you will identify the main idea of a paragraph or section. Identifying main ideas will help you better understand what you read. This skill also includes identifying supporting details and implied main ideas, or ideas that are not stated directly.

▶ Romans knew the Colosseum as the Flavian Amphitheatre. In use for almost 500 years, it held audiences of more than 45,000 for its bloody spectacles.

250 History of Our World

Differentiated Instruction

The following Teacher Edition strategies are suitable for students of varying abilities.

Less Proficient Readers, pp. 254, 261, 274

Special Needs Students, pp. 254, 269

Advanced Readers, pp. 256, 263, 274

English Language Learners, p. 261

Gifted and Talented, pp. 256, 263

Bibliography

For the Teacher

Brown, Dale, ed. *Rome: Echoes of Imperial Glory.* Time-Life, 1994.

Kohne, Eckart, and Cornelia Ewigleben, eds. *Gladiators and Caesars: The Power of Spectacle in Ancient Rome.* University of California, 2000.

Matz, David. *Daily Life of the Ancient Romans.* Greenwood, 2001.

For the Student

L1 Steele, Philip. *The Roman Empire.* Southwater, 2000.

L2 Connolly, Peter. *Ancient Rome.* Oxford, 2001.

L2 Watkins, Richard. *Gladiator.* Reprint. Houghton Mifflin, 2000.

L3 Nardo, Don, ed. *The Fall of the Roman Empire.* Greenhaven, 1998.

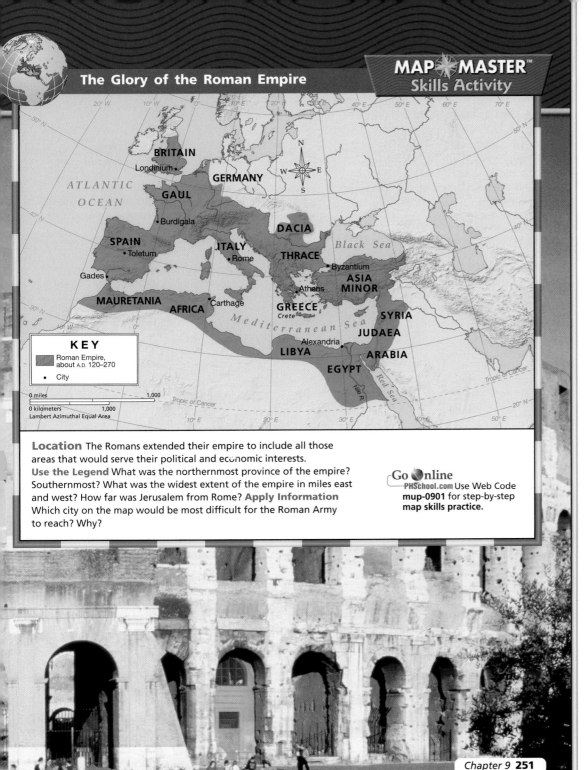

The Glory of the Roman Empire

MAP MASTER™ Skills Activity

KEY
- Roman Empire, about A.D. 120–270
- • City

0 miles 1,000
0 kilometers 1,000
Lambert Azimuthal Equal Area

Location The Romans extended their empire to include all those areas that would serve their political and economic interests.
Use the Legend What was the northernmost province of the empire? Southernmost? What was the widest extent of the empire in miles east and west? How far was Jerusalem from Rome? **Apply Information** Which city on the map would be most difficult for the Roman Army to reach? Why?

Go Online
PHSchool.com Use Web Code **mup-0901** for step-by-step map skills practice.

MAP MASTER™ Skills Activity

- **Location** Use the map to emphasize the vast area covered by the Roman Empire. Point to Rome on the map. Then have students point to the labeled provinces that are northernmost and southernmost in the empire. **L1**

- **Use the Legend** Have students use the map key to measure the widest extent of the empire both east and west. Then have them determine the distance from Jerusalem to Rome in miles. **L2**

- **Apply Information** Have students use the location and distance information to determine which city would be the most difficult one for the Roman Army to reach. Ask students to explain their answers. **L3**

Go Online
PHSchool.com Students may practice their map skills using the interactive online version of this map.

Using the Visual

Reach Into Your Background Discuss the photograph on these two pages. Tell students that the Colosseum was a giant arena that held 50,000 spectators. Point out that its walls were so well built that the floor of the arena could be flooded for mock naval battles using real people in real boats.

Answers

MAP MASTER™ Skills Activity **Use the Legend** Britain; 2,000 miles (3,250 km); 1,000 miles (1,625 km). **Apply Information** London. They would have to cross the English Channel.

Chapter Resources

Teaching Resources
- **L2** Vocabulary Development, p. 135
- **L2** Skills for Life, p. 130
- **L2** Chapter Tests A and B, pp. 144–149

Spanish Support
- **L2** Spanish Chapter Summary, p. 82
- **L2** Spanish Vocabulary Development, p. 83

Media and Technology
- **L1** Student Edition on Audio CD
- **L1** Guided Reading Audio CDs, English and Spanish
- **L2** Social Studies Skills Tutor CD-ROM
- **ExamView® Test Bank CD-ROM**

Discovery CHANNEL SCHOOL History of Our World Videos

interactive Textbook

PRENTICE HALL
TeacherEXPRESS™
Plan · Teach · Assess

Section 1
Step-by-Step Instruction

Objectives

Social Studies
1. Discover who could be a Roman citizen.
2. Find out how Romans of different social classes lived.
3. Understand the importance of family life in Roman society.
4. Learn about slavery in ancient Rome.

Reading/Language Arts
Learn to identify the main idea of a paragraph or section.

Prepare to Read

Build Background Knowledge **L2**

Tell students that in this section they will learn about daily life in ancient Rome. Read the opening paragraph on p. 252 to set the scene. Then have students look at the images on pp. 252–253. Ask students what the images tell them about the daily life in ancient Rome. Use the Idea Wave strategy (TE, p. T39) to elicit responses to the images.

Set a Purpose for Reading **L2**
- Preview the Objectives.

- Read aloud each statement in the *Reading Readiness Guide*. Ask students to mark the statements true or false.

  All in One **Unit 3 History of Our World Teaching Resources**, *Reading Readiness Guide*, p. 114

- Have students discuss the statement in pairs or groups of four, then mark their worksheets again. Use the Numbered Heads participation structure (TE, p. T40) to call on students to share their group's perspectives.

Vocabulary Builder
Preview Key Terms **L2**
Pronounce each Key Term, then ask the students to say the word with you. Provide a simple explanation such as, "a circus was not a traveling show in Roman times but a place where Romans went to watch shows and other events."

Section 1
Roman Daily Life

Prepare to Read

Objectives
In this section you will
1. Discover who could be a Roman citizen.
2. Find out how Romans of different social classes lived.
3. Understand the importance of family life in Roman society.
4. Learn about slavery in ancient Rome.

Taking Notes
As you read, note the most important points about the daily life of the ancient Romans. Copy the diagram. Then fill it in with the main idea of each section.

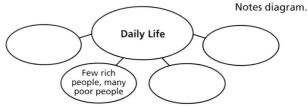

Target Reading Skill

Identify Main Ideas To remember information, good readers identify main ideas as they read. The main idea is the most important point in a text. Sometimes the main idea is stated directly. As you read, identify the main idea stated in each section. Write the main ideas in your Taking Notes diagram.

Key Terms
- **census** (SEN sus) *n.* an official count of people living in a place
- **villa** (VIL uh) *n.* a country estate
- **circus** (SUR kus) *n.* an arena in ancient Rome or the show held there
- **gladiator** (GLAD ee ayt ur) *n.* a person who fought to the death as entertainment for the Roman public

At the height of its glory, Rome had perhaps the most beautiful monuments and public buildings in the world. Wealth and goods flowed into Rome from all parts of the empire. Tourists and merchants flocked to the city. Its marketplaces and shops had more goods than any other city. Not everyone was thrilled with the excitement. One Roman complained of narrow streets "jammed with carts and their swearing drivers." Another, the poet Martial (MAHR shul), grumbled about the noise:

> **Before it gets light, we have the bakers. Then it's the hammering of the artisans all day. There's no peace or quiet in this city.**

An ancient wall painting from Pompeii, Italy

252 History of Our World

Target Reading Skill **L2**
Identify Main Ideas Point out the Target Reading Skill. Tell students that the main idea is the most important idea in a paragraph or section of the text.

Model how to identify the main idea of a paragraph by reading Support From the Government on p. 256. Point out that the main idea of the paragraph is stated in this sentence: "The Roman government provided family support, usually to the upper classes, in various ways." Explain that all the other information in the paragraph supports this main point.

Give students *Identify Main Ideas*. Have them complete the activity in their groups.

All in One **Unit 3 History of Our World Teaching Resources**, *Identify Main Ideas*, p. 125

Roman Citizens

Rome was a huge city, teeming with people. As the capital of an immense empire, it was first among the cities of its time. The poet Martial also used poetry to celebrate Rome's size and importance:

Take a look at life in ancient Rome.

> **"Goddess of continents and peoples, O Rome, whom nothing can equal and nothing approach."**

In its day, ancient Rome had no equal. In terms of its population, however, it was actually the size of some cities today. Rome actually had too many people. A million or more people lived within its limits by the time of Augustus. The citizens of Rome had to put up with noise and crowding every day.

Being Counted as a Citizen
Despite the problems caused by over-population, being a Roman citizen was a matter of great pride. In the republic and during the early years of the empire, only residents of the city of Rome itself enjoyed citizenship. Every five years Roman men registered for the **census**, or official count of people living in Rome. Registering for the census was the only way to claim citizenship. Roman men declared their families, slaves, and wealth to authorities at census time. If a man did not register, he ran the risk of losing his property. Worse yet, he could be sold into slavery. Women, girls, slaves, and those who had been freed from slavery were not counted as citizens. Their place in Roman society was determined only by their relationship to citizens.

An official Roman document, bronzed and written in hieroglyphics, grants Roman citizenship to provincials.

Citizens and City As the Roman Empire expanded, people beyond Rome gained Roman citizenship. But this expanded citizenship did not change the special love that residents of Rome felt for their city. Rome was everything to them. Its buildings and monuments were a constant reminder that their city was the center of religion, politics, and culture. Lively banquets and other gatherings made Rome the scene of all social life.

✓ **Reading Check** How did a person claim Roman citizenship?

Vocabulary Builder

Use the information below to teach students this section's high-use words.

High-Use Word	Definition or Sample Sentence
teeming, p. 253	*v.* to be full The sports arena was **teeming** with fans.
game, p. 254	*n.* wild animals hunted for sport or for use as food They went to Africa to hunt big **game**.
disarmed, p. 255	*v.* to take away weapons The soldier was **disarmed** and could no longer fight.

Show students *Daily Life in Ancient Rome.* Ask **What cultural and economic habits of the Romans have continued to be important in today's daily life?** *(Possible responses: Today's cultural and economic habits include the importance of family life, gatherings for special occasions, and government support for families and the poor.)*

Instruct

Roman Citizens   L2

Guided Instruction
■ **Vocabulary Builder** Clarify the meaning of the high-use word **teeming** before reading.

■ Read Roman Citizens, using the Choral Reading technique (TE, p. T38).

■ Discuss who could be a Roman citizen. *(At first, only men living in Rome could be citizens; later, people in other parts of the empire gained citizenship.)*

■ Ask students **Why do you think citizenship was extended to people outside Rome as the empire expanded?** *(Possible responses: To unify the people of the empire, to get tax money from more people, or to get more people to perform military service and other duties for Rome)*

Independent Practice
Ask students to create the Taking Notes graphic organizer (p. 252) on a blank sheet of paper. Have students use their own words to write the main idea of Roman Citizens in the first oval. Model how to complete the first oval with the main idea of this part of the section.

Monitor Progress
As students fill in the graphic organizer, circulate and make sure individuals are correctly identifying the main idea of Roman Citizens. Provide assistance as needed.

Answer
✓ **Reading Check** Roman men claimed Roman citizenship by registering for the census every five years.

Roman Social Classes ▪L2

Guided Instruction

- **Vocabulary Builder** Clarify the meaning of the high-use words **game** and **disarmed** before reading.

- Read the description of Roman society in Roman Social Classes on pp. 254–255. As students read, circulate and make sure individuals can answer the Reading Check question on p. 255.

- Ask students **How did the poor people of Rome survive without jobs?** *(They received handouts from the government.)*

- Compare and contrast the lives of rich and poor Romans. *(Wealthy Romans had elegant homes in the city and villas in the country; they had feasts with special dishes and entertainment; the poor lived in poorly built, rundown houses with few comforts or conveniences; the poor depended on wheat to survive and suffered when harvests were bad or shipments were late.)*

An ancient Roman glass flask shaped like a bunch of grapes

Roman Villas
Wealthy Roman families lived in villas, such as the one shown below. In this drawing, the roof is cut out to show the inside. **Analyze Images** *How did wealthy Romans eat their meals?*

1. Atrium
2. Study
3. Bedroom
4. Dining Room
5. Kitchen
6. Open Courtyard

Roman Social Classes

Roman society was made up of a small number of rich people and many poor free people and slaves. Most Romans had nothing like the luxuries of the wealthy. In fact, there was a huge difference between the lives of the rich and the poor. The majority of poor Romans were either slaves or without jobs. Most of Rome's jobless survived only by handouts from the government.

A Life of Luxury The rich often had elegant homes in the city. Many also had country estates called **villas.**

Wealthy Romans were famous for overdoing things. A Roman historian describes the eating habits of Aulus Vitellius (OH lus vuh TEL ee us), emperor for only six months in A.D. 69:

> **❝**He used to have three, or four, heavy meals a day. . . . He had himself invited to a different house for each meal. The cost to the host was never less than 400,000 coins a time.**❞**

Of course, few Romans could afford to eat as this emperor did. Still, the wealthy were known for their feasts. Often they served game, perhaps partridge or wild boar. For very special occasions, they might also serve exotic dishes such as flamingo or ostrich. Roman feasts often had entertainment, including musicians, dancers, and performers reciting poems.

254 History of Our World

Differentiated Instruction

For Less Proficient Readers ▪L1
Have students read the section in the Reading and Vocabulary Study Guide. This version provides basic-level instruction in an interactive format with questions and write-on lines.

📖 Chapter 9, Section 1, **History of Our World Reading and Vocabulary Study Guide,** pp. 98–100

For Special Needs Students ▪L1
Have students read pp. 254–255 as they listen to the recorded version. Check for comprehension by pausing the CD between each heading in the text and asking students to summarize the preceding passage.

◉ Chapter 9, Section 1, **Student Edition on Audio CD**

Answer

Analyze Images Their food was prepared and served by either servants or slaves. They ate their meals while seated on the floor.

Another Way of Life for the Poor The world of the poor stood in stark contrast to the feasts of the wealthy. In Rome, most people lived in poorly built, rundown housing. Many lived in tall apartment houses with no running water, toilets, or kitchens. All food and drink had to be carried up the stairs. Rubbish and human waste were carried down to the street or—as often happened—dumped out of a window. Because most houses were made of wood, fires were frequent and often fatal. The worst, in A.D. 64, destroyed most of the city.

Bread and Circuses The poor of Rome needed wheat to survive. When wheat harvests were bad or when grain shipments from overseas were late, the poor often rioted. To prevent these riots, the emperors supplied free grain and provided spectacular shows. These were held in the Colosseum or in arenas called circuses, so the shows came to be called circuses, too.

The circuses could be violent. Romans, rich and poor, packed the arenas to watch the events, which included animals fighting other animals, animals fighting humans, and humans fighting humans. Clowns might also entertain, or a criminal might be publicly executed. The highlights of the day were the fights between **gladiators**, people who fought to the death. Most gladiators were slaves who had been captured in battle. However, a few were free men—and some women—who enjoyed the fame and fortune they could gain from their success as gladiators.

Before the battles, the gladiators paraded onto the floor of the arena. Approaching the emperor's box, they raised their arms in salute and shouted "Hail, Caesar! We who are about to die salute you." Then the battles began. The end came when one gladiator was dead or dying, or disarmed and on the ground. A wounded gladiator's life might be spared if he had fought well. It is commonly thought that the crowd waved handkerchiefs to spare the loser. Thumbs pointed down signaled death.

Not all Romans approved of these violent sports. The writer Seneca noted:

> ❝It's sheer murder. In the morning, men are thrown to the lions or bears. At noon, they are thrown to the spectators.❞

✔ **Reading Check** What conditions often led the poor people of ancient Rome to riot?

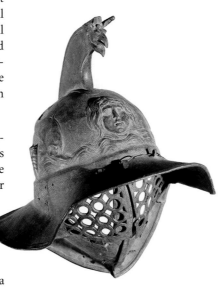
Gladiators wore helmets for protection.

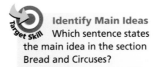
Identify Main Ideas Which sentence states the main idea in the section Bread and Circuses?

Independent Practice
Have students use their own words to write the main idea of Roman Social Classes in the second oval of their graphic organizers.

Monitor Progress
As students fill in the graphic organizer, circulate and make sure individuals are correctly identifying the main idea of Roman Social Classes. Provide assistance as needed.

Background

Job Security in Ancient Rome
Although the emperor officially provided each Roman family with a monthly ration of grain, in reality only about one third of the families received the ration. In addition, there was a severe job shortage because much of the unskilled and skilled labor was provided by slaves. The Roman workers who did have jobs set up guilds to keep their jobs secure. These guilds established set salaries and protected members from some forms of competition. Even workers in the lowliest occupations, such as sewer cleaners and public bath attendants, had their own guilds.

Answer

✔ **Reading Check** The poor often rioted when wheat harvests were bad or when grain shipments from overseas were late.

Roman Family Life L2

Guided Instruction

- Discuss the structure of the Roman house-hold. (*The head of the Roman household was the* paterfamilias. *The family included everyone below the* paterfamilias—*women, children, and slaves.*)

- Ask students **How do you know that family was important to Romans?** (*Several generations of men and their wives and children often lived together, no matter how small the house.*)

Independent Practice

Direct students to write the main idea of Roman Family Life in their own words in the third oval of their graphic organizers.

Monitor Progress

As students fill in the graphic organizer, circulate and make sure individuals are correctly identifying the main idea of Roman Family Life. Provide assistance as needed.

Links

Read the **Links to Language Arts** on this page. Ask students: **How did Latin words become part of the English language?** (*Some Latin words came into the English language directly; others came into English from French, after the French conquered England in 1066.*)

Breadmaking was one of a slave's daily tasks.

Links to
Language Arts

The Latin Language The Latin language was the source of today's French, Italian, Spanish, Portuguese, and Romanian languages. About half of all English words have a Latin history. Some, such as *legal, computer,* and *library,* came directly from the Latin language. Others came into the English language from the French, after French invaders conquered England in 1066.

Roman Family Life

Despite their taste for brutal sports, many Romans had a strong sense of traditional values. Most of all, they valued family life. Roman writings are filled with stories of happy families, dedication, and love.

Support from the Government

The Roman government provided family support, usually to the upper classes, in various ways. Under Julius Caesar, for example, fathers of three or more children received land from the government. Freeborn mothers of three children and freed slaves who had four children were given certain privileges. At the same time, unmarried men and couples with no children did not receive financial benefits provided by Roman law. These measures were designed to encourage the upper classes to increase the size of their families and to continue their family names.

The Roman Household The head of a Roman household was known as the *paterfamilias* (pay tur fuh MIL ee us). This Latin term means "father of the family." The family included everyone in the household below the rank of *paterfamilias*—women, children, and slaves. The *paterfamilias* could be the father, grandfather, or great-grandfather of the household. Three generations of men, and their wives and children, often lived together under the same roof. Romans of all social classes lived in large extended families. The lower classes gladly shared small houses or farms with many relatives.

Under Roman law, the *paterfamilias* had absolute power over the entire household. He owned everything in it—women, children, slaves, and furniture. To do business or to own property, a son had to be emancipated, or freed, by the father of the family. In the early days, the *paterfamilias* could sell a son or daughter into slavery. Later, this power was reduced.

Differentiated Instruction

For Advanced Readers
Have students research information about children in ancient Rome. Tell students to look for details about the daily life of children, including their education and activities in the household. Suggest that students present their findings in a brief oral report to the class.

For Gifted and Talented
Have students research information about food in ancient Rome. Encourage students to form two groups and have each group create two typical daily menus—one for a poor Roman family and one for a wealthy Roman family. Have groups share their menus with the class as brief oral reports.

The Roles of Women in Roman Society The Romans thought of property and genealogy in terms of households. A household passed among the men in the family. Women married into it from outside. A woman's place in the household depended on the kind of marriage she made. Sometimes a woman formally left the house of her father to live in the house of her husband. The new wife took on the role of a daughter under the *paterfamilias* in her new home. Depending on circumstances, a woman might keep ties with the family into which she was born. Her only role in her husband's family would be to produce children.

The amount of freedom a woman in ancient Rome enjoyed depended on her husband's wealth and status. Wealthy women had a great deal of independence. Women had a strong influence on their families, and some wives of famous men became famous themselves. The mothers or wives of some Roman emperors also gained great political power.

A few Roman women shaped roles for themselves outside the family. Some trained to be doctors and worked in women's medicine. Others became involved in business and even controlled their own money. Women are known to have owned ships, although it is unclear whether they engaged in trade. Lower-class women took on various kinds of work. They were cooks, dressmakers, and hairdressers. Some did jobs more commonly done by men, such as shoemaking. Others danced, sang, or acted for people's entertainment.

✓ **Reading Check** What rights did men and women have in ancient Rome?

Citizen Heroes

Cornelia

To many, Cornelia (kawr NEEL yuh) was the perfect daughter, wife, and mother. The daughter of Scipio Africanus (SIP ee oh af rih KAHN us), Cornelia married her father's rival, Tiberius Sempronius (ty BIHR ee us sem PROH nee us), to bring an end to their disagreements. Cornelia had twelve children. Three survived—a daughter and two sons. After her husband's death, Cornelia raised these children on her own. Her daughter married a Roman military hero. Her sons, Tiberius and Gaius (GY us), became two of Rome's greatest statesmen.

The Roman diet included the foods, herbs, and spices shown below.

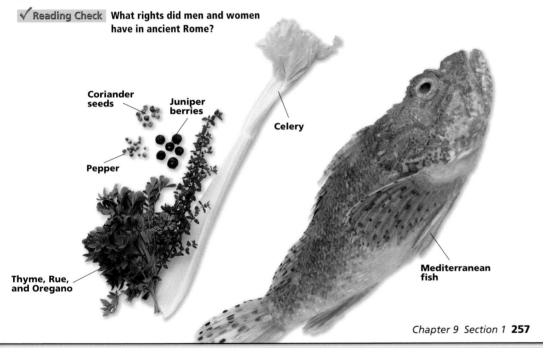

Coriander seeds

Juniper berries

Celery

Pepper

Thyme, Rue, and Oregano

Mediterranean fish

Citizen Heroes

Read aloud the **Citizen Heroes** text. Ask students **What hardships did Cornelia bear during her life?** *(Most of her children died; her husband died, leaving her to raise her children on her own; her two sons were assassinated.)*

Answer

✓ **Reading Check** Men had more freedom than women; the amount of freedom a woman had depended on her husband's wealth and status.

Slavery in Rome

Guided Instruction

■ Discuss slavery in Rome. *(Slavery was common.)*

■ Ask students **Why did most household slaves have better lives than other kinds of slaves?** *(Possible answer: Household slaves developed relationships with the family.)*

Independent Practice

Have students complete their Taking Notes graphic organizers by writing the main idea of Slavery in Rome in the fourth oval.

Monitor Progress

■ Show *Section Reading Support Transparency HOW 81* and ask students to check their graphic organizers individually. Go over key concepts and clarify key vocabulary as needed.

📖 **History of Our World Transparencies,** *Section Reading Support Transparency* p. HOW 81

■ Tell students to fill in the last column of the *Reading Readiness Guide.* Probe for what they learned that confirms or invalidates each statement.

All in One **Unit 3 History of Our World Teaching Resources,** *Reading Readiness Guide,* p. 114

Assess and Reteach

Assess Progress

Have students complete the Section Assessment. Administer the *Section Quiz.*

All in One **Unit 3 History of Our World Teaching Resources,** *Section Quiz,* p. 116

Reteach L1

If students need more instruction, have them read this section in the *Reading and Vocabulary Study Guide.*

History of Our World Reading and Vocabulary Study Guide, pp. 98–100

Extend L3

Have students learn more about daily life in ancient Rome by completing the *Enrichment* activity. Assign students to work groups to work on the project.

All in One **Unit 3 History of Our World Teaching Resources,** *Enrichment,* p. 129

Answer

✓ **Reading Check** Almost every wealthy family and some poor families owned slaves.
Analyze Slaves did much of the work that supported Roman society.

Section 1 Assessment

Key Terms
Students' sentences should reflect knowledge of each Key Term.

Target Reading Skill
Roman men registered for the census to be counted as Roman citizens; Roman society was made up of a few rich people and many poor people; the Romans valued family life; slavery was common in ancient Rome.

Comprehension and Critical Thinking
1. (a) In the republic and early years of the empire, only residents of the city of Rome could claim citizenship; later, people beyond Rome gained citizenship. **(b)** Possible response: So officials would have a record of the population.

2. (a) The rich had luxuries, while the poor often had very little. **(b)** Possible response: In order to keep them under control.

3. (a) The Romans lived in large extended families headed by a *paterfamilias.* **(b)** Possible response: It honored the emperor and its empire.

4. (a) Slaves performed as gladiators, or helped raise a family's children, worked on farms, in mines, or on ships. **(b)** Possible response: The number of wealthy people probably would have decreased, and the number of poor people would have increased.

Writing Activity
Use the *Rubric for Assessing a Writing Assignment* to evaluate students' journal entries.

Slavery in Rome

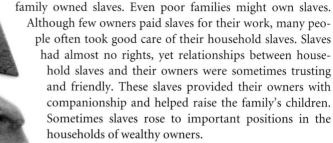

Slavery was common in ancient Rome. Almost every wealthy family owned slaves. Even poor families might own slaves. Although few owners paid slaves for their work, many people often took good care of their household slaves. Slaves had almost no rights, yet relationships between household slaves and their owners were sometimes trusting and friendly. These slaves provided their owners with companionship and helped raise the family's children. Sometimes slaves rose to important positions in the households of wealthy owners.

Household slaves were more fortunate than other kinds of slaves. Some slaves led short, hard lives. Those who worked on farms were sometimes chained together as they worked during the day and slept in chains at night. Slaves in copper, tin, and iron mines worked in terrible conditions. Gladiators, who were also slaves, risked death every time they fought. Slaves trained as rowers powered Roman warships.

Some slaves were able to save tips or wages and buy their freedom. These might be slaves with very special skills, such as gladiators and chariot racers. These sports heroes sometimes became famous and wealthy.

Artifacts of Slavery ▲
At top right is a bronze plaque naming a freed slave, Hedone, her former master, Marcus Crassus, and Feronia, a goddess popular with freed slaves. Beneath it is a figure of a weeping kitchen slave holding a mortar. **Analyze** *What was the importance of slaves in Roman society?*

✓ **Reading Check** **Who owned slaves in ancient Rome?**

Section 1 Assessment

Key Terms
Review the key terms listed at the beginning of this section. Use each term in a sentence that explains the term's meaning.

Target Reading Skill
What are the four main ideas in Section 1?

Comprehension and Critical Thinking
1. (a) Identify Who could claim Roman citizenship?
(b) Analyze Information Why do you think Roman men were required to register their families, slaves, and wealth at census time?

2. (a) Recall Describe how rich and poor Romans lived.
(b) Draw Inferences Why did the Roman government feed and entertain its people?

3. (a) Describe What was family life like for the ancient Romans?
(b) Evaluate Information Why do you think Romans valued peaceful family life but also enjoyed watching violent combat in Roman arenas?

4. (a) Name What kinds of jobs did slaves perform in ancient Rome?

(b) Predict How would abolishing slavery have affected Roman lifestyles?

Writing Activity
In this section you read Seneca's reaction to a circus. Write a journal entry that describes your reaction to a Roman circus.

For: An activity on daily Roman life
Visit: PHSchool.com
Web Code: mud-0910

All in One **Unit 3 History of Our World Resources,** *Rubric for Assessing a Writing Assignment,* p. 143

Go Online PHSchool.com Typing in the Web Code when prompted will bring students directly to detailed instructions for this activity.

Christianity and the Roman Empire

Prepare to Read

Objectives
In this section you will
1. Learn about the rise of Christianity in the Roman Empire.
2. Discover how Christianity spread throughout the empire.
3. Understand the Roman government's reaction to the growth of Christianity.

Taking Notes
As you read, look for details about the early history of Christianity. Copy the diagram. Fill it in with details that support this section's main ideas about Christianity.

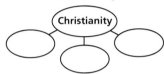

⊙ Target Reading Skill

Identify Supporting Details Details support the main idea of a paragraph or section by giving more information about it. Supporting details help explain the main idea and may also give examples or reasons for it. As you read, record in your Taking Notes diagram details that support the main idea of each section.

Key Terms
• **Jesus** (JEE zus) *n.* (C. 6 B.C. – A.D. 30) founder of Christianity; believed by Christians to be the Messiah
• **messiah** (muh SY uh) *n.* a savior in Judaism and Christianity
• **disciple** (dih SY pul) *n.* a follower of a person or belief
• **epistle** (ee PIS ul) *n.* in the Christian Bible, letters written by disciples
• **martyr** (MAHR tur) *n.* a person who dies for a cause

According to the Bible, a Jewish religious teacher named Jesus spoke the words below to his followers in the first century A.D.:

❝Blessed are the poor in spirit, for theirs is the kingdom of heaven. Blessed are those who mourn, for they shall be comforted. Blessed are the lowly, for they shall inherit the earth. Blessed are those who hunger and thirst for what is right, for they shall be satisfied. Blessed are the merciful, for they shall be treated with mercy. Blessed are the pure in heart, for they shall see God. Blessed are the peacemakers, for they shall be called children of God. Blessed are those who are persecuted in the cause of right, for theirs is the kingdom of heaven.❞

—*The Sermon on the Mount, Matthew 5:1–10*

This sermon and its meaning are an important part of a religion called Christianity. **Jesus** founded Christianity. In the beginning, its followers were mainly the poor and slaves. Over time, Christianity spread throughout the Roman Empire.

In this painting, Jesus heals a paralyzed man who had been lowered through the roof of the building.

⊙ Target Reading Skill L2
Identify Supporting Details Point out the Target Reading Skill. Explain that details in a paragraph or section of the text give information that supports the main idea.

Model how to identify supporting details by reading the last paragraph on this page. Point out that the main idea of the paragraph is stated in the sentence "Jesus founded Christianity." The sentences that follow provide details about the beginnings of Christianity. These details support the main point of the paragraph.

Give students *Identify Supporting Details.* Have them complete the activity in their groups.

All in One Unit 3 History of Our World Teaching Resources, *Identify Supporting Details,* p. 126

Objectives
Social Studies
1. Learn about the rise of Christianity in the Roman Empire.
2. Discover how Christianity spread throughout the empire.
3. Understand the Roman government's reaction to the growth of Christianity.

Reading/Language Arts
Learn to identify details that support the main idea of a paragraph or section.

Prepare to Read

Build Background Knowledge L2
In this section, students will learn about how Christianity developed and spread in the Roman Empire. Have students preview the headings and images in the section. Then ask this question **How do you think the Romans reacted to the growth of Christianity?** Use the Give One and Get One participation structure (TE, p. T41) to generate ideas.

Set a Purpose for Reading L2
■ Preview the Objectives.

■ Read each statement in the *Reading Readiness Guide* aloud. Ask students to mark the statements true or false.

All in One Unit 3 History of Our World Teaching Resources, *Reading Readiness Guide,* p. 118

■ Have students discuss the statement in pairs or groups of four, then mark their worksheets again. Use the Numbered Heads participation structure (TE, p. T40) to call on students to share their group's perspectives.

Vocabulary Builder
Preview Key Terms L2
Pronounce each Key Term, then ask the students to say the word with you. Provide a simple explanation such as "a Roman soldier serving in a faraway part of the empire might write an epistle to his family in Rome."

Instruct

The Rise of Christianity

Guided Instruction   L2

- **Vocabulary Builder** Clarify the high-use words **tolerant** and **reign** before reading.

- Read The Rise of Christianity, using the Oral Cloze technique (TE, p. T37).

- Ask students **How did Jesus spread his teachings?** *(He traveled and taught people.)*

- Prompt students to describe the teachings of Jesus. Then explore why these teachings appealed to many people in the Roman Empire. *(Answers may vary but should include that Jesus taught that God was loving and forgiving; that people should love God with all their hearts and their neighbors as themselves; and that if they followed these teachings they would have everlasting life; students may conjecture that people found these teachings appealing because their lives in the Roman Empire were difficult and without hope.)*

Links

Read the **Links to Language Arts** on this page. Ask **What special meaning did the Greek word for fish have for Christians?** *(Each letter of the Greek word for fish was the first letter of a word in a Greek phrase that meant "Jesus Christ, Son of God, Savior.")*

Links to Language Arts

Sign of the Fish A secret sign that Christians used to identify one another was a simple image of a fish. How did a fish come to be an early Christian symbol? Each letter of the Greek word for fish, ichthys (IK thoos), was the first letter of a word in a Greek phrase. The phrase meant "Jesus Christ, Son of God, Savior."

The Rise of Christianity

Christianity was one of many religions in the vast Roman Empire. The empire included many lands with different languages, customs, and religions. The Romans were tolerant toward the people in these lands. They allowed them to follow their own religions. But the conquered people had to show loyalty to Roman gods and to the emperor.

Unrest in Judaea The Romans conquered the Jewish homeland of Judaea (joo DEE uh) in 63 B.C. At first, they respected the Jews' right to worship their God. But many Jews resented foreign rule. Some believed that a messiah, or savior, would come to bring justice and freedom to the land. As opposition to Roman rule grew, the Romans struck back with harsh punishment. In 37 B.C., the Roman senate appointed a new ruler of Judaea named Herod (HEHR ud). It was during Herod's reign that Jesus was born in the Judaean town of Bethlehem.

Stories about what Jesus taught and how he lived are found in the New Testament, a part of the Christian Bible. After Jesus died, his disciples, or followers, told stories about his life and teachings. Between 40 and 70 years after Jesus' death, four stories of his life were written from these oral traditions. People came to believe that four disciples—Matthew, Mark, Luke, and John—had each written one story. These writings are called the Gospels.

Vocabulary Builder

Use the information below to teach students this section's high-use words.

High-Use Word	Definition and Sample Sentence
tolerant, p. 260	*adj.* understanding, allowing the practice of beliefs other than one's own They were **tolerant** of the heavy traffic because it brought business to town.
reign, p. 260	*n.* the period during which a particular leader rules Her **reign** lasted longer than her father's.

Christian Beliefs According to the New Testament, Jesus grew up in Nazareth (NAZ uh ruth). He learned to be a carpenter and began teaching when he was about 30 years old. Christian tradition holds that for three years Jesus traveled from place to place, preaching to Jews who lived in the countryside. Much of what he taught was part of the Jewish tradition he learned as he was growing up. Like all Jewish teachers, Jesus preached that there was only one true God. As you will read on the next page, the teachings of Jesus became known as Christianity.

Reread the excerpt that begins this section. The ideas expressed in this excerpt are important Christian beliefs. According to the Gospels, Jesus taught that God was loving and forgiving. He said that people must love God with all their hearts. He also taught that people had a responsibility to love their neighbors as they loved themselves. Jesus promised that people who followed his teachings would have everlasting life. His followers believed that Jesus was their messiah.

Fears About Christianity Jesus' teachings alarmed many people. Some people complained to the Romans that Jesus was teaching that God was greater than the emperor. The Romans feared that Jesus would lead an armed revolt against the government, so the Roman governor condemned Jesus to death. Jesus was crucified (KROO suh fyd), or put to death by being nailed to a large wooden cross. According to the Gospels, Jesus rose from the dead and spoke to his disciples, telling them to spread his teachings.

✓ **Reading Check** Why did the Romans fear Jesus?

Identifying Supporting Details
What details in the paragraphs under the heading Christian Beliefs tell about the rise of Christianity?

Jesus and His Disciples
This scene is painted on the wall of a Roman catacomb, an underground passageway. Many early Christians —and people of other faiths— buried their dead in catacombs. **Analyze Images** *Use what you know about the life of Jesus to identify him and his disciples in the painting. Explain your reasoning.*

Identify Supporting Details As a follow up, ask students to answer the Target Reading Skill question on this page in the Student Edition. (*The following details under the heading* Christian Beliefs *tell about the rise of Christianity: Jesus traveled for three years and preached to Jews in the countryside; much of what he taught was part of the Jewish tradition; Jesus promised that people who followed his teachings would have everlasting life; his followers believed that he was their messiah.*)

Independent Practice
Ask students to copy the Taking Notes graphic organizer on a blank piece of paper. Then have students fill in the first oval with a detail about the early history of Christianity. Briefly model details that students might include in the organizer.

Monitor Progress
As students fill in the graphic organizer, circulate and make sure individuals are choosing details about how Christianity developed in the Roman Empire. Provide assistance as needed.

Answer
✓ **Reading Check** Jesus had many followers and was said to teach that God was greater than the emperor, and the Romans feared that he might lead an armed revolt against the government.

Analyze Images Possible answers: Jesus is probably the fifth figure from the left because he is holding a book and appears to be teaching. Also, everyone in the painting is watching him and we know Jesus was the leader and teacher of the disciples. He is also the largest figure in the image.

Differentiated Instruction

For Less Proficient Readers 🄛1
Have students create a sequence of events timeline about the rise of Christianity in ancient Rome. For example, have them start with an early event, such as Herod's rise to power and then add Jesus' birth in Nazareth, and so on. Encourage students to update the timeline as they read the chapter.

For English Language Learners 🄛2
Have students create flash cards of unfamiliar words that they encounter frequently as they read. Model how to write a word on one side of a card and its definition on the other side.

Christianity Spreads L2

Guided Instruction

- Ask students **What new idea of Paul's helped spread Christian beliefs?** *(Paul persuaded other followers of Jesus to spread Jesus' teachings not just among Jews but among Greeks and Romans.)*

- Discuss how Paul's epistles helped make the Christian faith an organized religion. *(Possible response: Paul's letters helped unify, or bring together, people in distant cities who followed Christian beliefs.)*

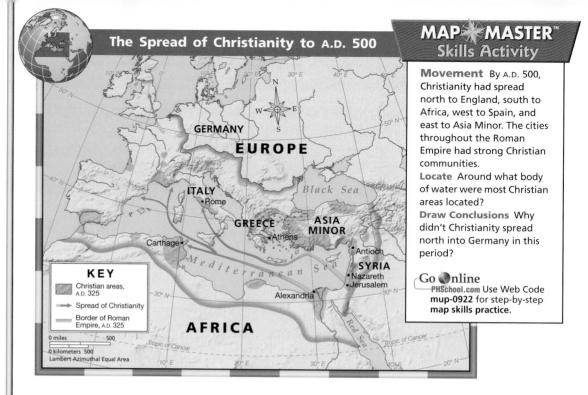

MAP MASTER™
Skills Activity

The Spread of Christianity to A.D. 500

GERMANY

EUROPE

ITALY
• Rome

Black Sea

GREECE
• Athens

ASIA
MINOR

Carthage •

Mediterranean Sea

• Antioch

SYRIA
• Nazareth
• Jerusalem

Alexandria •

AFRICA

Red Sea

KEY
- Christian areas, A.D. 325
- → Spread of Christianity
- Border of Roman Empire, A.D. 325

0 miles   500
0 kilometers 500
Lambert-Azimuthal Equal Area

Movement By A.D. 500, Christianity had spread north to England, south to Africa, west to Spain, and east to Asia Minor. The cities throughout the Roman Empire had strong Christian communities.

Locate Around what body of water were most Christian areas located?

Draw Conclusions Why didn't Christianity spread north into Germany in this period?

Go Online
PHSchool.com Use Web Code **mup-0922** for step-by-step **map skills practice**.

Christianity Spreads

The Greek equivalent of the word *messiah* was *christos* (KRIS tohs). Many educated people of Jesus' time spoke Greek. As these people accepted the teachings of Jesus, they began calling him Christ. After his death, Jesus' followers, called Christians, spread the new religion from Jerusalem across the empire, and finally to Rome itself.

The Letters of Paul One of the most devoted followers of Jesus' teachings was a Jew whose original name was Saul. Saul was well educated and spoke Greek, the common language of the eastern Roman Empire. According to the New Testament, Saul at first rejected the Christian message. One day, however, he believed he had a vision in which Jesus spoke to him. After this experience, Saul changed his name to Paul and carried Christianity to the cities around the Mediterranean, spreading Jesus' teachings as he traveled.

Paul's writings also helped turn the Christian faith into an organized religion. Paul wrote many **epistles**, or letters, to Christian groups in distant cities. Some of these epistles became a part of the Christian Bible.

The Apostle St. Paul by Marco Pino.

Answers

MAP MASTER Skills Activity **Locate** the Mediterranean Sea **Draw Conclusions** Possible responses: The border of the Roman Empire at this time stopped at Germany's border. The mountains north of Italy may have been a physical barrier to the spread of Christianity.

Skills for Life **Skills Mini Lesson**

Using Cartographer's Tools

1. Teach the skill by pointing out to students that most maps have certain elements in common. These elements include a compass rose, a key, and a scale, for example.

2. Help students practice the skill by looking at the map on page 262 and noting the cities included in Christian areas in A.D. 325. *(Athens, Antioch, Nazareth, Jerusalem, Alexandria, Carthage, and Rome)*

3. Have students apply the skill by answering this question. **In what directions did Christianity spread from Jerusalem?** *(west, northwest, northeast)*

Christianity Moves to the Cities Others also helped spread Christian beliefs throughout the Roman world. By A.D. 100, groups of Christians were gathering for worship in Alexandria, Antioch (AN tee ahk), Corinth (KAWR inth), Ephesus (EF ih sus), Thessalonica (thes uh LAHN ih kuh), and even Rome. The new religion gained many followers in cities. Many poor city dwellers welcomed the message of Christianity as good news. These early Christians used the word *paganus* (pah GAH nus) for anyone who did not share their beliefs. *Paganus* means "country dweller" in Latin. It is the root of the English word *pagan*. Today, *pagan* is used to describe someone who is not a Christian, a Jew, or a Muslim.

Ways of Worship Early Christians shared a common faith in the teachings of Jesus and a common way of worship. Over time, their scattered communities organized under a structured Church. Christians borrowed some practices from Jewish worship. They prayed and sang. They also read from the scripture or from one of Paul's letters. Often someone interpreted these readings for those gathered. Christians set aside Sunday, the day they believed Jesus had risen from the dead, as their day of worship.

The Baptism of Constantine is a painting by Raphael and is displayed at the Vatican palace in Rome.

As Jesus had instructed, Christians also practiced two rites, or holy acts. In the rite of baptism, a believer was dipped in water to wash away his or her sin. Baptism made the person a member of the church. In the rite of the Lord's Supper, Christians shared bread and wine in a sacred meal called the Eucharist. They did this in memory of Jesus, whose last supper was described in the Gospels. Christians believed that through the Eucharist they were receiving the body and blood of Jesus.

✓ **Reading Check** Why did Christianity find many followers in the cities of the Roman Empire?

Guided Instruction (continued)

■ Examine the spread of Christianity after Jesus' death. (*Christianity gained followers throughout the Roman world, and by the year A.D. 100 groups of Christians were gathering in the cities of Alexandria, Antioch, Corinth, Ephesus, Thessalonica, and Rome.*)

■ Ask students **What besides shared beliefs helped set Christians apart as members of an organized religion?** (*Possible responses: Practices such as worshipping on Sunday, rites such as baptism and the Lord's Supper indicated Christianity was an organized religion.*)

Independent Practice

Ask students to fill in another oval in the Taking Notes graphic organizer with a supporting detail they have just identified about the spread of Christianity.

Monitor Progress

As students fill in the graphic organizer, circulate and make sure individuals are choosing details about how Christianity developed in the Roman Empire. Provide assistance as needed.

Answer

✓ **Reading Check** Many city dwellers were poor people who welcomed the message of Christianity as good news.

Rome Reacts

L2

Guided Instruction

- Read Rome Reacts. As students read, circulate and make sure individuals can answer the Reading Check question.

- Discuss how Roman officials reacted to the spread of Christianity. (*Many officials saw Christians as enemies of the empire; the Romans began to persecute the Christians in various ways and later tried to stamp out the new religion.*)

- Ask students **Why do you think the Romans were unable to stop the spread of Christianity?** (*Answers may vary but should include observations about the strength of many people's devotion to Christian beliefs and the example set by Christians who faced punishment or death.*)

Independent Practice

Have students fill in the last oval in the Taking Notes graphic organizer with an additional detail about the growth of Christianity.

Monitor Progress

- Show *Section Reading Support Transparency HOW 82* and ask students to check their graphic organizers individually. Go over key concepts and clarify key vocabulary as needed.

  📖 **History of Our World Transparencies,** *Section Reading Support Transparency* HOW 82

- Tell students to fill in the last column of the *Reading Readiness Guide.* Probe for what they learned that confirms or invalidates each statement.

  All in One Unit 3 History of Our World Teaching Resources, *Reading Readiness Guide,* p. 118

Answer

Infer Nero blamed the fire on Christians, because he thought that they were a threat to the current political system. Nero could get rid of the Christians if people blamed them for the fire.

Rome Reacts

The fast-growing new religion alarmed the Roman government. Christians refused to worship the Roman gods and did not show the emperor the respect that was required. Some Christians turned away from their responsibilities as Roman citizens, such as serving in the army. Many Roman officials began to view Christians as enemies of the empire.

The Burning of Rome
After the fire, rumors placed the blame on Nero for the fire that destroyed the city. Legend suggests that in his glee for the ruin of Rome, Nero played his lyre while standing atop the Palatine. The legend is depicted above. **Infer** *Why was Nero so quick to blame Christians?*

Rome Burns Under the emperor Nero, the first official campaign against the Christians began in A.D. 64. One night, a fire started in some shops in Rome. The fire spread and burned for nine days, and it left much of the city in ruins.

According to some accounts, Nero blamed the Christians. He ordered the arrest of Christians, who were sent to their deaths. Some were forced to fight wild animals in the Colosseum. Others were soaked with oil and burned alive; others were crucified. Paul was imprisoned for two years and then killed.

Treatment of Christians The Romans persecuted Christians at various times for another 250 years. To *persecute* means to treat repeatedly in a cruel or an unjust way. During these years, the Roman Empire began to lose its power. To explain the decline, Romans looked for people to blame. They found them among the followers of the new religion. As one Roman wrote:

> "If the Tiber River reaches the walls, if the Nile fails to rise to the fields, if the sky doesn't move or the Earth does, if there is famine or plague, the cry is at once: 'The Christians to the Lions.'"

In the Roman world it had become a crime just to be a Christian. As you have read, the punishment for following the new religion was death.

Background

Martyrdom Martyrs are not unique to Christianity. The Jews' long history of persecution includes many instances of martyrdom. One of the earliest examples is Akiba, a Jewish teacher and leader who was killed by the Romans around the year 135. The millions of Jews murdered by German Nazis during World War II are regarded as martyrs by Jewish authorities.

The Appeal of Christianity Despite the persecution of its followers, Christianity continued to spread throughout the empire. The help that Christian communities gave to widows, orphans, and the poor drew people to the new religion. Its messages of love, forgiveness, and a better life after death appealed to many. The figure of Jesus also attracted followers. Jesus was not a hero from myth. He had actually lived among people of the empire. The writings known as the Gospels helped spread Jesus' teachings. The simple style of the Gospels also made Jesus' teachings easy to grasp. They were written in the language that ordinary people used.

As the Christian religion gained more followers, emperor after emperor tried to halt its spread. Actions against Christians were especially severe under Domitian (duh MISH un), Marcus Aurelius, Decius (DEE shus), and Valerian (vuh LIHR ee un). The emperor Diocletian (dy uh KLEE shuhn) was determined to stamp out the new religion, but not even he could stop the growth of Christianity. He outlawed Christian services, imprisoned Christian priests, and put many believers to death. Diocletian's actions accomplished the opposite of what he wanted, however. Many Romans admired the Christians. They saw them as martyrs and heroes. A **martyr** is someone who dies for a cause. By the A.D. 300s, about one in every ten Romans had accepted the Christian faith.

✓ **Reading Check** How did the Romans persecute Christians?

According to tradition, Saint Agnes, shown above, died for her beliefs under the persecution of Christians by Diocletian.

Section 2 Assessment

Key Terms
Review the key terms listed at the beginning of this section. Use each term in a sentence that explains the term's meaning.

Target Reading Skill
List three details that support the main idea of the section under the heading Rome Reacts.

Comprehension and Critical Thinking
1. (a) Describe What ideas did Jesus teach?

(b) Draw Conclusions Why do you think the Roman governor had Jesus put to death?
2. (a) Recall To what new groups did Paul want to spread the teachings of Jesus?
(b) Draw Inferences Why might Christians have borrowed ways of worship from the Jewish religion?
3. (a) Explain Why did Roman officials consider Christians enemies of the empire?
(b) Identify Cause and Effect What effect did Diocletian's actions have on the growth of Christianity? Explain.

Writing Activity
You are a Roman citizen who has just learned about Christianity. Write a paragraph describing what you now know about it.

For: An activity on the spread of Christianity
Visit: PHSchool.com
Web Code: mud-0920

Comprehension and Critical Thinking
1. (a) Jesus taught that people should love God and their neighbors. **(b)** The governor thought that Jesus was becoming too powerful.

2. (a) Greeks and Romans **(b)** Many early followers of Jesus were Jews.

3. (a) Christians refused to worship the Roman gods and did not show the Roman emperor the respect that was required. **(b)** Diocletian's actions helped Christianity gain more followers.

Writing Activity
Use the *Rubric for Assessing a Writing Assignment* to evaluate students' paragraphs.

All in One **Unit 3 History of Our World Teaching Resources,** *Rubric for Assessing a Writing Assignment*, p. 143

Go Online PHSchool.com Typing in the Web Code when prompted will bring students directly to detailed instructions for this activity.

Assess and Reteach

Assess Progress L2
Have students complete the Section Assessment. Administer the *Section Quiz*.

All in One **Unit 3 History of Our World Teaching Resources,** *Section Quiz*, p. 120

Reteach L1
If students need more instruction, have them read this section in the *Reading and Vocabulary Study Guide.*

📖 Chapter 9, Section 2, **History of Our World Reading and Vocabulary Study Guide,** pp. 101–103

Extend L3
Ask students to write a short biography (two or three sentences) of each person mentioned in the section describing each person's efforts to promote or stop the spread of Christianity.

Answer

✓ **Reading Check** The Romans persecuted Christians by imprisoning them or putting them to death.

Section 2 Assessment

Key Terms
Students' sentences should reflect knowledge of each Key Term.

Target Reading Skill
Possible supporting details include the following: Under the emperor Nero, the first official campaign against the Christians began in A.D. 64; the Romans persecuted Christians at various times for another 250 years; Diocletian outlawed Christian services, imprisoned Christian priests, and put many believers to death.

Focus on The Roman Soldier

L2

Guided Instruction

- Read the introductory paragraph and study the art, photos, and captions as a class.

- Discuss the job of the scouts. *(They traveled ahead of the legion to choose a site for a temporary camp.)* **What did the scouts consider when choosing a site?** *(They looked for level land and tried to choose land located near a water source.)*

- Ask **What was the purpose of trenches and ramparts?** *(to protect the soldiers from attack)*

- Ask students **Why do you think the soldiers were forbidden to marry during their service?** *(Possible answer: to ensure that they remained loyal to the army.)*

- Have students work in pairs to answer the Assessment questions.

The Roman soldier was a citizen and a professional, committed to serving on the battlefield for at least 25 years. Away from his homeland for years at a time and forbidden to marry during his service, he formed strong bonds of loyalty to his commander and his comrades. If he survived to complete his dangerous service, he could expect to be well rewarded with land or money.

Pocket Sundial
This travel-sized Roman sundial was used to keep time.

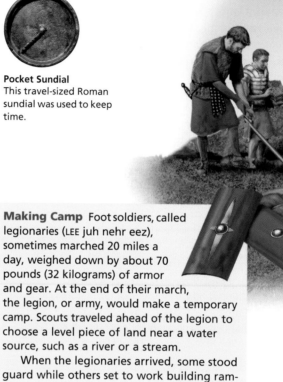

Making Camp Foot soldiers, called legionaries (LEE juh nehr eez), sometimes marched 20 miles a day, weighed down by about 70 pounds (32 kilograms) of armor and gear. At the end of their march, the legion, or army, would make a temporary camp. Scouts traveled ahead of the legion to choose a level piece of land near a water source, such as a river or a stream.

When the legionaries arrived, some stood guard while others set to work building ramparts—banks of earth to protect them from attack. First they cut strips of turf from the ground. Then they dug trenches about 10 feet (3 meters) deep. The earth piled up from the trenches formed the ramparts, which were then covered with turf. Finally, stakes driven into the ramparts created a fence. Inside the camp, tents were pitched in orderly rows. The entire job probably took about two hours.

Ruins of a Roman military camp built near the Dead Sea in Israel

266 History of Our World

Differentiated Instruction

For Less Proficient Readers L1
Pair less proficient readers with more proficient students and have them write step-by-step instructions detailing how to make a temporary camp. Tell them to use the sequence signal words in the Making Camp paragraph on p. 216 to help them identify the order of the steps. Remind them to number each step.

Armor
Various styles of armor were introduced throughout the army's history.

Tools
The men used pickaxes and turf cutters to build the camp's defenses.

Centurions
These officers led the legionaries into battle and directed them in their duties.

Iron Tools
Roman soldiers used many different kinds of tools. The axe (left) and a hook (right) used to lift cauldrons from a fire date from the A.D. 100s.

Assessment

Describe What types of challenges did legionaries face during their service in the Roman army?

Generalize Why do you think Roman soldiers developed a strong sense of loyalty to the army during their service?

Chapter 9 **267**

Objective

Learn how to compare and contrast two or more events, people, ideas, or things.

Prepare to Read

Build Background Knowledge **L2**

Explain that when you compare two or more things you look at how they are alike. Sometimes you may also look at how they are different. When you contrast two or more things you look only at how they are different. Have students brainstorm things in their own lives or experience that they might compare and contrast.

Instruct

Comparing and Contrasting **L2**

Guided Instruction

- Read the steps to Comparing and Contrasting as a class and write the instructions on the board.

- Practice the skill by following the steps on pp. 268–269 as a class. Model each step in the activity.

- Read step 1 on p. 269 aloud and ask students what the chart headings tell them about this activity. *(They are comparing the Roman Empire and the Qin Dynasty for ways in which they are similar or different)*

- Read aloud the first question in step 2. Then ask volunteers to name the categories of comparison. *(Length of empire, Major Characteristics, Religion or Philosophy)* Ask the second question in step 2. *(The rows provide categories of information and the information in each row, under each heading provide information about the category)*

- As a class, compare and contrast the information in each column and row and write S or D in the last column.

- Model how to draw a conclusion from the comparison and then write a sentence on the board that tells whether the two items

---

Suppose your teacher gave you this extra-credit project: Write a paper comparing and contrasting the ancient empire of Rome with China during the Qin dynasty.

To compare means to find similarities. (Sometimes people use *to compare* to mean to find similarities *and* differences. Be sure to ask your teachers what they mean when they ask you to compare.) You also know that *to contrast* means to find differences. For this project, you need to find out how Rome and China were alike and how they were different.

Learn the Skill

Whenever you are asked to compare and contrast, follow these steps:

1 **Identify a topic and purpose.** What do you want to compare, and for what purpose? For example, you may want to:
- make a choice
- understand a topic
- discover patterns
- show that items are more alike or more different

2 **Identify categories of comparison, and fill in details for each category.** You will need to take notes. You may want to organize your notes in a chart. Make a column for each item you want to compare, and make a row for each category of comparison. Then fill in specific information under each of your categories.

3 **Identify similarities and differences.** If you make a chart, you can mark an *S* for similar or a *D* for different items.

4 **Draw conclusions.** Write a sentence telling whether the items you're comparing have more similarities or more differences.

---

have more similarities or contrasts. *(The Roman Empire was more similar to the Qin Dynasty than it was different from it.)*

- Ask students to identify topics from the chapter that might make good subjects for comparing and contrasting. *(Possible responses: comparing the early Roman republic with the later years of the Roman Empire; contrasting the lives of the Roman rich and poor)*

Independent Practice

Assign *Skills for Life* and have students complete it individually.

All in One **Unit 3 History of Our World Teaching Resources,** *Skills for Life,* p. 130

Monitor Progress

Teacher should monitor the students doing the *Skills for Life* worksheet, checking to make sure they understand the skills steps.

Practice the Skill

Use the chart below to practice comparing and contrasting.

① Examine the headings in the chart below to identify the chart's topic and its purpose.

② What are the main categories of comparison in the chart? How do the details shown support each category?

③ Fill in S or D in the last column of the chart to identify the similarities and the differences between the two empires.

④ As you write your conclusion, keep in mind the topic and the purpose of the chart.

The remains of an ancient Roman road in Sicily

The Roman Empire and the Qin Dynasty

Characteristic	Roman Empire	Qin Dynasty	Similar or Different
Length of empire	About 520 years (44 B.C.–A.D. 476)	About 15 years (221–206 B.C.)	
Major characteristics	• Built a network of roads • Created local governments • Established code of laws • Created a money system (currency) • Supported literature and the arts	• Built a network of roads • Created local governments • Established code of laws • Created a money system (currency) • Restricted the freedoms of scholars	
Religion or philosophy	Roman religion; later Christianity	Philosophy of legalism	

An ancient Chinese road

Apply the Skill

Use the steps on this page to compare and contrast features of Roman life with life in the United States today. Take notes or put your comparisons in a chart. Write a sentence that draws a conclusion about your findings.

Differentiated Instruction

For Special Needs Students **L1**

Partner special needs students with more proficient students to do Level 1 of the Comparing and Contrasting lesson on the Social Studies Skills Tutor CD-ROM together. When the students feel more confident, they can move on to Level 2 alone.

⊙ *Comparing and Contrasting,* **Social Studies Skills Tutor CD-ROM**

Assess and Reteach

Assess Progress **L2**

Ask students to do the Apply the Skill activity.

Reteach **L1**

If students are having trouble applying the skill steps, have them review the skill using the interactive Social Studies Skills Tutor CD-ROM.

⊙ *Comparing and Contrasting,* **Social Studies Skills Tutor CD-ROM**

Extend **L3**

■ To extend the lesson, show students how a Venn diagram can be used to show how two things are alike and different. Draw a Venn diagram on the board. Model where to list similarities and differences between two things in the diagram.

■ Have students create their own Venn diagrams to show the similarities and differences between life in ancient Rome and life in the United States today.

■ For extra credit, students may compare and contrast items of their choice from the chapter. Students may explain their completed Venn diagrams in a brief oral presentation.

Answers
Apply the Skill

Ancient Rome: most people had to rely on the government for food; women could not be citizens; many Romans had slaves; entertainment was violent and deadly;
United States today: most people do not rely on the government for food; women can be citizens and own property; US Citizens do not own slaves; entertainment is mostly safe.
Summary: There are more differences between the daily life of ancient Romans and modern United States citizens than there are similarities.

Objectives

Social Studies

1. Explore how bad government contributed to the decline of the empire.
2. Understand the fall of the Roman Empire.
3. Discuss Constantine's role in support of Christianity.
4. Learn how northern invaders brought about the collapse of the Roman Empire.

Reading/Language Arts

Learn to identify the implied main idea of a paragraph or section.

Prepare to Read

Build Background Knowledge **L2**

In this section, students will learn about the fall of the Roman Empire. Ask students to preview the section and write two questions about the empire's collapse. Write students' questions on the board. Allow them to use these questions to fill in the second column of their charts in the Set a Purpose for Reading activity below.

Set a Purpose for Reading **L2**

■ Preview the Objectives.

■ Form students into pairs or groups of four. Distribute the *Reading Readiness Guide*. Ask each student to fill in the first two columns of the chart. Use the Numbered Heads participation structure (TE, p. T40) to call on students to share one piece of information they already know and one piece of information they want to know.

All in One **Unit 3 History of Our World Teaching Resources,** *Reading Readiness Guide*, p. 122

Vocabulary Builder
Preview Key Terms **L2**

Pronounce each Key Term, then ask students to say the word with you. Provide a simple explanation such as "because of inflation, Roman money had almost no value in the later years of the empire."

Prepare to Read

Objectives

In this section you will

1. Explore how bad government contributed to the decline of the empire.
2. Understand the fall of the Roman Empire.
3. Discuss Constantine's role in support for Christianity.
4. Learn how northern invaders brought about the collapse of the Roman Empire.

Taking Notes

As you read, identify each section's main idea and details. For each section, copy the diagram below. Fill in each main idea and details.

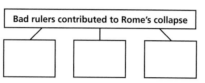

Bad rulers contributed to Rome's collapse

⊙ Target Reading Skill

Identify Implied Main Ideas Sometimes main ideas are not stated directly. The details in a section or paragraph hint at a main idea, but you must state it yourself. As you read, study the details in each section. Then write the section's main idea and supporting details in your Taking Notes diagram.

Key Terms

- **Constantine** (KAHN stun teen) (C. A.D. 278–337) emperor of Rome from A.D. 312 to 337; encouraged the spread of Christianity
- **mercenary** (MUR suh neh ree) *n.* a soldier who serves for pay in a foreign army
- **inflation** (in FLAY shun) *n.* an economic situation in which the government issues more money with lower value

---

This statue of Emperor Constantine originally towered over 30 feet (9m). Today, only the head remains.

270 History of Our World

Emperor Constantine (KAHN stun teen) stood with his troops near a bridge spanning the Tiber River. On that day in A.D. 312, the sky was full of clouds and Constantine was filled with doubts. His enemies were waiting on the other side of the river.

As Constantine stood, hoping for victory, the sun broke through the clouds. According to one story, Constantine saw a cross in the sky. Above the cross was written in Latin: "Under this sign you will conquer!"

A different story claims that Constantine had a dream. Because of this dream, Constantine had his soldiers' shields marked with a Christian symbol. In the battle, Constantine's army won an overwhelming victory. Constantine believed that the victory had come from the Christian God. Constantine vowed to become a Christian.

Historians today debate whether Constantine had these religious experiences. But **Constantine**, Rome's emperor from A.D. 312 to 337, strongly encouraged the spread of Christianity.

⊙ Target Reading Skill **L2**

Identify Implied Main Ideas Point out the Target Reading Skill. Explain that the main idea of a paragraph or section of the text is not always stated directly. Instead, details in the text hint at the main idea, and you must state it yourself.

Model identifying the implied main idea of The Empire Crumbles on p. 272. Point out that the text under this heading provides details about why the Roman Empire fell apart. Tell students that based on these details the main idea of the section could be stated as follows: The Roman Empire fell apart for a variety of reasons.

Give students *Identify Implied Main Ideas*. Have them complete the activity in groups.

All in One **Unit 3 History of Our World Teaching Resources,** *Identify Implied Main Ideas*, p. 127

The Roman Empire, A.D. 180–476

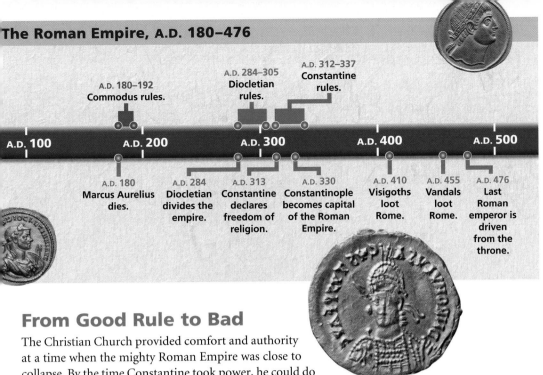

A.D. 180–192 Commodus rules.

A.D. 284–305 Diocletian rules.

A.D. 312–337 Constantine rules.

A.D. 100 — A.D. 200 — A.D. 300 — A.D. 400 — A.D. 500

A.D. 180 Marcus Aurelius dies.

A.D. 284 Diocletian divides the empire.

A.D. 313 Constantine declares freedom of religion.

A.D. 330 Constantinople becomes capital of the Roman Empire.

A.D. 410 Visigoths loot Rome.

A.D. 455 Vandals loot Rome.

A.D. 476 Last Roman emperor is driven from the throne.

From Good Rule to Bad

The Christian Church provided comfort and authority at a time when the mighty Roman Empire was close to collapse. By the time Constantine took power, he could do little to stop the empire's fall. The trouble had started 125 years earlier, when Marcus Aurelius died. The emperor left his son Commodus in power in A.D. 180.

Commodus was only eighteen when he became emperor. Marcus Aurelius was aware that his son was not qualified to rule the empire. But Commodus was in line to inherit power. Marcus Aurelius may have believed that Commodus would grow to be a good emperor as time went by.

Commodus allowed others to help him run the empire, but he made poor choices. He stood by as others worked to destroy the power and prestige of the senate. Commodus himself showed little use for the senate by not seeking its approval before he acted. He kept a grip on power by bribing the army to support him.

His bold, extravagant, and savage ways were his downfall. He loved the bloodshed of the gladiators. He took part in the games himself, dressed as the hero Hercules as well as in other costumes. Commodus had planned to appear as a gladiator on the first day of 193, but he was assassinated on New Year's Eve in 192.

√ Reading Check What happened to the Roman senate under the emperor Commodus?

■ Timeline Skills

These timeline entries show the decline and collapse of the Roman Empire. **Identify** When did Diocletian divide the Roman Empire? **Summarize** Summarize the important events from the timeline.

Identify Implied Main Ideas
In one sentence, state the main idea that all the details in this section support.

Chapter 9 Section 3 **271**

Chapter 9 Section 3 **271**

The Empire Crumbles L2

Guided Instruction

- Read The Empire Crumbles on pp. 272–273. Use the Structured Silent Reading strategy (TE, p. T38).

- Identify problems that led to the fall of Rome. (*Possible response: There were several reasons for fall of Rome: weak, corrupt rulers, a mercenary army, the size of the empire, and serious economic problems.*)

- Ask students **Why was the size of the empire a problem?** (*Possible responses: The Roman Empire was so large that it was difficult to control and govern and it was constantly under attack. Many conquered territories regained their independence. The Roman army spent more time defending the empire than it did extending its authority and helping govern Roman lands.*)

- Discuss how the size of the Roman Empire created economic problems. (*The Roman Empire was shrinking. Without new lands, Rome did not have the new sources of wealth it needed to pay its army. In order to raise money, the government raised taxes.*)

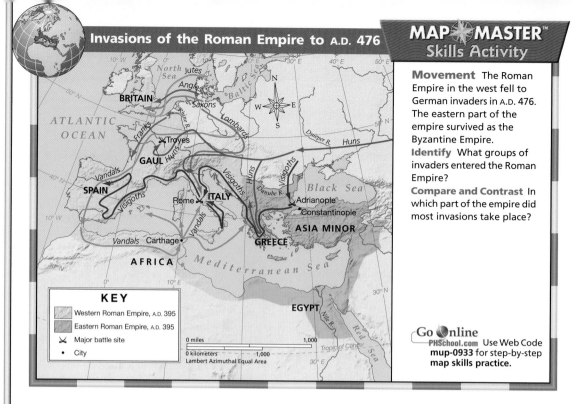

MAP MASTER™ Skills Activity

Movement The Roman Empire in the west fell to German invaders in A.D. 476. The eastern part of the empire survived as the Byzantine Empire.
Identify What groups of invaders entered the Roman Empire?
Compare and Contrast In which part of the empire did most invasions take place?

KEY
- Western Roman Empire, A.D. 395
- Eastern Roman Empire, A.D. 395
- Major battle site
- City

0 miles 1,000
0 kilometers 1,000
Lambert Azimuthal Equal Area

Go Online
PHSchool.com Use Web Code
mup-0933 for step-by-step
map skills practice.

The Empire Crumbles

The decline of the Roman Empire began under Commodus. Historians do not agree on any one cause for this decline. They believe that several problems led to the fall of Rome.

Weak, Corrupt Rulers After Commodus, emperors were almost always successful generals, not politicians. They often stole money from the treasury. They used the money to enrich themselves and pay for the loyalty of their soldiers. The government and the economy became weak and the senate lost power. Would-be rulers gained the throne by violence. Between A.D. 180 and A.D. 284, Rome had 29 emperors. Most were assassinated.

A Mercenary Army In earlier times, the Roman army had been made up of citizen soldiers ready to defend their land. Now the army was filled with **mercenaries**, foreign soldiers who serve for pay. Mercenaries were motivated by money, not by loyalty to any cause. They often switched sides if doing so could work to their personal advantage. Rome's strength depended on a strong army that was loyal to the nation in which was now a memory.

Relief showing a barbarian fighting a Roman soldier

272 History of Our World

Background

Elagabalus the Eccentric Elagabalus became emperor in A.D. 218, when he was only 14. He had no real qualifications to be emperor and is chiefly remembered for his eccentricities. He amused himself by concocting outlandishly labor-intensive tasks for those beneath him. Elagabalus's most bizarre antic may have been his establishment of a competition among slaves to collect spider webs. When 10,000 pounds had been collected, he exclaimed, "That proves how big Rome is!" After four purposeless years on the throne, Elagabalus was murdered by his own guards.

Answers

MAP MASTER Skills Activity **Identify** The Jutes, Angles, Saxons, Franks, Vandals, Visigoths, Lombards, and Huns entered the Roman Empire.
Compare and Contrast Western Roman Empire

The Size of the Empire The Roman Empire had grown too large. Enemies launched attacks all over the empire. Many conquered territories regained their independence. The Roman army spent its time defending the empire instead of extending its authority. Consequently, the empire shrank.

Serious Economic Problems When Rome stopped conquering new lands, new sources of wealth were no longer available. The empire struggled to pay its army. To raise money, the government raised taxes. Meanwhile, the people of the empire suffered severe unemployment.

Food was scarce, so its price went up. To pay for food, the government produced more coins. The value of those coins was dependent upon the amount of silver in them. But because the government did not have much silver, less of this metal was put in each coin. This change resulted in **inflation,** an economic situation in which more money circulates, but the money has less value. When inflation is not controlled, money buys less and less. Roman coins soon became worthless.

Efforts to Stop the Decline Some emperors tried to stop the empire's decline. Diocletian worked to strengthen Rome. He enlarged the army, built new forts at the borders, and improved the tax system. Diocletian also divided the empire into two parts to make it easier to rule. He ruled the wealthier eastern part of the empire, and appointed a co-emperor to rule the western part.

√ Reading Check **What problems did having a mercenary army cause for the empire?**

Roman warship

Independent Practice
Have students copy the Taking Notes graphic organizer on a blank sheet of paper for this section. Tell them to fill in the organizer with the main idea and details of The Empire Crumbles.

Monitor Progress
As students fill in the graphic organizer, circulate and make sure individuals are correctly identifying the main idea of the section and the details that support it. Provide assistance as needed.

Answers

√ Reading Check The empire's army was not as strong as it had been, because mercenary soldiers were motivated by money rather than loyalty and would switch sides if that worked to their advantage.

Constantine and Christianity

L2

Guided Instruction

- Ask students to read Constantine and Christianity on pp. 274–275. Circulate to make sure that students can answer the Reading Check question.

- Discuss how Constantine supported Christianity. (*Constantine and Licinius proclaimed freedom of worship for people across the empire. Constantine strengthened the church by helping to solve a religious crisis that would have led to a split in the church; Constantine also supported the construction of Christian places of worship.*)

- Ask students **Why do you think Constantine wanted to keep the Christian church from splitting into a western part and an eastern part?** (*Possible response: Constantine may have believed that keeping the church from splitting into eastern and western parts might also keep the people of the empire unified, which in turn might strengthen the empire.*)

Independent Practice

Have students copy the Taking Notes graphic organizer on a blank sheet of paper for this section. Then have them fill in the organizer with the main idea and details of this section. If necessary, briefly model again how to identify the main idea based on details from the section.

Monitor Progress

As students fill in the graphic organizer, circulate and make sure individuals are correctly identifying the main idea and supporting details. Provide assistance as needed.

Answer

Summarize He won control of the eastern half of the Roman Empire and ended persecution of Christians there.

Christianity in the Roman Empire
Above is the church of St. John the Theologian in Ephesus, an ancient city whose ruins are located in present-day Turkey. Ephesus was an early base of Christianity within the Roman Empire. **Summarize** *How did Constantine encourage the spread of Christianity?*

Constantine and Christianity

Diocletian and his co-emperor stepped down in A.D. 305. A struggle for power followed. For seven years, generals fought one another for power until one—Constantine—became the winner. As you read earlier, Constantine reported that the Christian God had helped his army win the battle for control of Rome. The victory at the bridge over the Tiber made Constantine sole ruler of the Roman Empire in the West. In the East, rule of the Roman Empire was shared by Licinius (ly SIN ee us) and Maximinus (mak suh MEE nus). In 313 Licinius took complete control of the eastern parts of the empire.

Freedom of Religion Also in 313, Constantine and Licinius proclaimed freedom of worship for people across the empire. Under Diocletian and others, Christians had been tortured and punished for their beliefs. Now Rome would no longer persecute the Christians. They were free to practice their religion openly. They could organize churches. Property that had been taken from them was returned. Christianity would soon became the official religion of the Roman Empire.

Another Christian Victory In 324 Constantine won several battles against Licinius for control of the eastern half of the Roman Empire. Now Constantine was emperor of both East and West. Although Licinius and Constantine had agreed to tolerate all religions when they began sharing power in 313, Licinius had continued to allow the persecution of Christians in the East. Constantine saw his victory over Licinius as further proof that the Christian God was working through him.

Differentiated Instruction

For Less Proficient Readers   L1

Have students outline the section to help them remember key points in their reading. Use the *Outline Transparency* to model creating an outline.

📖 **History of Our World Transparencies,** *Transparency B15: Outline*

For Advanced Readers   L3

Have students research one key point from their reading. Guide them to select a person, place, or event of interest and examine the topic more closely. Invite them to present a brief oral report on their findings to the class.

Building a Faith During his 25 years as emperor, Constantine worked to strengthen the Christian church. In 325 he stepped in to help solve a religious crisis. The church almost split apart when eastern and western church leaders disagreed on certain issues of faith. Constantine led a meeting in Nicaea (ny SEE uh) that brought the two sides together and kept the church whole.

Constantine was a leading force behind the construction of important Christian places of worship. He helped plan and pay for the construction of a church in Jerusalem on the spot where Jesus was crucified, buried, and is said to have risen from the dead. The church of St. Peter in Rome was also built with his help. Constantine also supported the building of churches in the city that would become the empire's new capital.

A New Capital In 330, Constantine moved the capital of the Roman Empire east to the city of Byzantium (bih ZAN tee um), in what is now Turkey. It was a natural move for the emperor. He had grown up in the East and had lived in the eastern Roman city of Nicomedia (ni kuh MEED ee uh) at the court of the emperor Diocletian. The move east also made sense for the empire. Rome had not been its political center for some time.

Constantine spared no expense in enlarging Byzantium and filling it with riches. When he dedicated the city as the new capital of the empire, he called it New Rome. Soon, however, the capital was known by a different name, Constantinople (kahn stan tuh NOH pul), "the city of Constantine." With the emperor and the empire's capital in Constantinople, the power of the Roman Empire was now firmly in the East.

This shows the Hagia Sophia in Sultan Ahmet Square in Constantinople, the capital of the eastern Roman Empire. Today, Constantinople is known as Istanbul, Turkey.

✓ **Reading Check** What city became the new capital of the Roman Empire?

Chapter 9 Section 3 **275**

Background

The Visigoths The Visigoths, who had settled in what is now Romania, were one of the largest Germanic tribes that invaded the Roman Empire. Though deemed "barbaric" by the Romans, the Visigoths farmed and herded cattle, had their own language, and were fairly skilled metal workers. Threatened by other invaders, the Visigoths asked Rome for protection. The Romans allowed them to settle in the empire but treated them cruelly. The Visigoths revolted in 378 and defeated the Roman army in battle. In 410, they captured and sacked Rome.

Invasions and Collapse 🔢

Guided Instruction

- Ask students to read Invasions and Collapse on p. 276. Circulate to make sure that students can answer the Reading Check question.

- Ask students to identify some of the northern invaders who overwhelmed the empire. (*The northern invaders included the Visigoths, Vandals, and other Germanic tribes.*)

- Ask students **Why were groups of invaders from the north able to overwhelm the Roman Empire in the 400s?** (*The Roman army was very weak and the Roman emperor was almost powerless by the 400s.*)

> **Links**
>
> Read the **Links Across Time** on p. 276. Ask students **Why is someone who destroys or steals property called a vandal?** (*The Vandals looted Rome and their name has become connected with destructive behavior.*)

Independent Practice

Have students copy the Taking Notes graphic organizer on a blank piece of paper for this section. Students should fill in the organizer with the main idea and details of Invasions and Collapse.

Monitor Progress

- Show *Section Reading Support Transparency HOW 83* and ask students to check their graphic organizers individually. Go over key concepts and clarify key vocabulary as needed.

  📖 **History of Our World Transparencies,** *Section Reading Support Transparency* HOW 83

- Tell students to fill in the last column of the *Reading Readiness Guide.*

  All in One **Unit 3 History of Our World Teaching Resources,** *Reading Readiness Guide,* p. 122

Answer

✓ **Reading Check** Byzantium became the new capital of the Roman Empire and soon became known as Constantinople.

Assess and Reteach

Assess Progress L2

Have students complete the Section Assessment. Administer the *Section Quiz*.

All in One Unit 3 History of Our World **Teaching Resources**, *Section Quiz*, p. 124

Reteach L1

If students need more instruction, have them read the section in the *Reading and Vocabulary Study Guide*.

History of Our World, Reading and Vocabulary Study Guide, pp. 104–106

Extend L3

Ask students to work in groups to prepare a plan to rescue the Roman Empire from collapse. Tell students to list the problems Rome faced and suggest a solution for each. Then have each student in the group write an essay describing one problem and a possible solution.

Answer

✓**Reading Check** Romulus Augustulus was the last emperor; a German general removed Romulus Augustulus from power in 476 and sent him to work on a farm.

Section 3 Assessment

Key Terms

Students' sentences should reflect knowledge of each Key Term.

Target Reading Skill

The implied main idea can be stated as follows: Constantine helped strengthen Christianity in the Roman Empire in many ways.

Comprehension and Critical Thinking

1. (a) as a writer and philosopher **(b)** No; Commodus was not qualified.

2. a. Weak, corrupt rulers, a mercenary army, the size of the empire, and economic problems. **(b)** Weak, corrupt rulers weakened the empire's government. The mercenary army were motivated by pay instead of loyalty to Rome. The large size of the empire made it difficult to control. The empire suffered from high taxes, severe unemployment, and inflation.

3. (a) He allowed Christians to practice their religion openly. **(b)** He believed that the Christian God was working through him.

Links Across Time

Vandals Today, we call someone who destroys property and valuable things a vandal. The Vandals were one of the Germanic tribes that invaded the Roman Empire. They looted Rome in A.D. 455, stealing artwork and other highly prized items. Their name came to be connected with this kind of destructive behavior.

The Anglo-Saxons who invaded Roman England buried their kings in ships. At a site discovered in England in 1939, the ancient ship had rotted. Yet many items, including this helmet remained.

Invasions and Collapse

Constantine struggled to keep the empire together, but the forces pulling it apart were too great. After his death, invaders swept across Rome's borders and overwhelmed the empire. The invaders belonged to northern tribes. Today, we call them Germanic tribes. The Romans called them barbarians. In the past, the Roman army had been able to defeat these tribes. Now, however, they could not stop the intruders. In the 400s, the Germanic tribes overran the empire. One tribe, the Visigoths (VIZ ee gahths), captured and looted Rome in 410. The Vandals (VAN dulz), another Germanic tribe, took Rome in 455. The Roman emperor was almost powerless.

The last Roman emperor was 14-year-old Romulus Augustulus (RAHM yuh lus oh GUS chuh lus). His name recalled more than 1,000 years of Roman glory. But the boy emperor did not win glory for himself. In 476, a German general took power and sent the emperor to work on a farm. After Romulus Augustulus, no emperor ruled over Rome and the western part of the empire.

However, even after Rome fell, the eastern part of the empire remained strong. Its capital, Constantinople, remained the center of another empire, the Byzantine Empire, for a thousand years.

✓**Reading Check** Who was Romulus Augustulus, and what was his fate?

Section 3 Assessment

Key Terms

Review the key terms listed at the beginning of this section. Use each term in a sentence that explains the term's meaning.

Target Reading Skill

State the main idea of the section Constantine and Christianity.

Comprehension and Critical Thinking

1. (a) Recall How is Marcus Aurelius remembered?
(b) Analyze Was Commodus a good choice for emperor?

2. (a) Identify What factors contributed to the Roman Empire's decline?
(b) Identify Cause and Effect How did each cause you listed affect the empire's stability?

3. (a) Describe What did Constantine do to show that he accepted Christianity?
(b) Draw Conclusions Why did Constantine take steps to strengthen the Christian church?

4. (a) Recall What events led to the fall of Rome?
(b) Analyze Information Why was the Roman army unable to resist the invading armies?

Writing Activity

The fall of the western Roman Empire was a turning point in history, but many people in those days may not have noticed any change. Why might this be true?

For: An activity on the fall of the Roman Empire
Visit: PHSchool.com
Web Code: mud-0930

---

4. (a) Invasions by the Germanic tribes.
(b) By the time invading armies overran the empire, the Roman army was very weak.

Writing Activity

Use the *Rubric for Assessing a Writing Assignment* to evaluate students' writing.

All in One Unit 3 History of Our World **Teaching Resources**, *Rubric for Assessing a Writing Assignment*, p. 143

Go Online PHSchool.com Typing in the Web code when prompted will bring students directly to detailed instructions for this activity.

Chapter 9 Review and Assessment

◆ Chapter Summary

Section 1: Roman Daily Life

- As the Roman Empire expanded, people beyond Rome gained Roman citizenship.
- A small number of people in ancient Rome were wealthy, but many people were poor.
- Men held a great deal of power compared with that of women and children in the Roman family.
- Slavery was common in ancient Rome.

Section 2: Christianity and the Roman Empire

- According to the Christian Bible, Jesus' followers thought he was their savior.
- After Jesus' death, Christianity spread throughout the Roman Empire.
- Roman officials viewed Christians as enemies of the empire and persecuted them.

Section 3: The Fall of Rome

- Political and economic problems brought about the decline of the Roman Empire.
- The emperor Constantine strengthened the Christian church and made Constantinople the empire's capital.
- Germanic tribes invaded the empire, and Rome's last emperor stepped down in 476.

Roman soldier's helmet

Symbols of Christianity

Present-day Constantinople

◆ Key Terms

Match each definition with the correct term.

1. an official count of people living in a place
   - A circus
   - B census
   - C inflation
   - D martyr
2. an arena in ancient Rome
   - A villa
   - B circus
   - C gladiator
   - D census
3. a follower of a person or belief
   - A epistle
   - B disciple
   - C gladiator
   - D martyr
4. an economic situation in which there is more money with lower value
   - A circus
   - B inflation
   - C census
   - D epistle

Chapter 9 **277**

⌐ Vocabulary Builder

High-Use Academic Words

Revisit this chapter's high-use words:

teeming	tolerant	prestige
game	reign	appointed
disarmed	authority	

Ask students to review the definitions they recorded on their *Word Knowledge* worksheet.

All in One **Unit 3 History of Our World Teaching Resources,** *Word Knowledge,* p. 128

Consider allowing students to earn extra credit if they use the words in their answers to the questions in the Chapter Review and Assessment. The words must be used correctly and in a natural context to win the extra points.

Review Chapter Content

- Review and revisit the major themes of this chapter by asking students to classify the Guiding Questions for each bulleted statement in the Chapter Summary. Have students work together in groups to classify the sentences. Refer to p. 1 in the Student Edition for the text of the Guiding Questions.

- Assign *Vocabulary Development* for students to review the Key Terms.

All in One **Unit 3 History of Our World Teaching Resources,** *Vocabulary Development,* p. 135

Answers

Key Terms

1. B

2. B

3. B

4. B

Review and Assessment

Comprehension and Critical Thinking

5. (a) Roman men claimed citizenship by registering for the census every five years. **(b)** Roman citizens in the later empire included people who lived outside of the city of Rome. In the republic and early empire, only residents of the city of Rome could claim citizenship. **(c)** Possible response: A person might be proud to be part of a huge and powerful empire whose capital was the center of religion, politics, and culture.

6. (a) The rich had elegant homes in Rome, villas in the country, and enjoyed many banquets and other luxuries. The poor lived in poorly built, rundown housing with few conveniences and comforts, and many needed government handouts to live. Slaves in wealthy households lived fairly well and sometimes had important positions, but other slaves had hard lives and worked in terrible conditions without pay. **(b)** Circuses, which were held in the Coliseum or another arena, were often violent shows in which humans fought humans or animals, costing criminals or Christians their lives. **(c)** Rich, poor, and enslaved people came together at circuses to be entertained.

7. (a) Jesus taught that God was loving and forgiving, that people should love God with all their hearts, and love their neighbors as themselves. If people followed these teachings they would have everlasting life. **(b)** Poor Romans and slaves had hard lives and were drawn to Christianity's messages of love, forgiveness, and a better life after death, which gave them hope for the future.

8. (a) Christians would not worship the Roman gods, did not show the emperor respect, and did not carry out their responsibilities as citizens, such as serving in the army. **(b)** Nero blamed the Christians for the fire at Rome in A.D. 64. **(c)** The Romans continued to persecute the Christians because they wanted someone to blame for the decline of the empire.

9. (a) Commodus was a weak and corrupt Roman emperor. **(b)** Commodus contributed to the decline of the empire by letting the senate's power and prestige be destroyed, by not asking for senate approval for actions, by bribing the army to support him, and by supporting bloodshed at the games.

◆ Comprehension and Critical Thinking

5. **(a) Explain** Why was it important for Roman men to register in the census?
   (b) Compare and Contrast How did Roman citizens in the later empire differ from citizens in the republic and early empire?
   (c) Draw Inferences Why might someone be proud to be a Roman citizen?

6. **(a) List** Give examples of ways the rich, the poor, and slaves lived in ancient Rome.
   (b) Identify Describe the circuses of ancient Rome.
   (c) Summarize In what ways did the Roman circuses bring the rich, poor, and slaves together?

MAP MASTER™ Skills Activity
The Glory of the Roman Empire

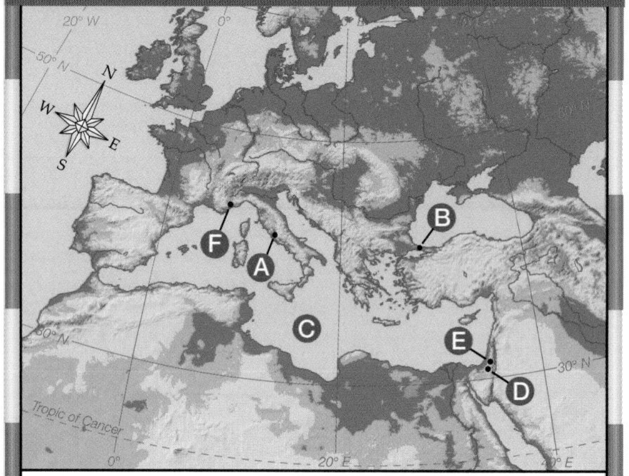

[map showing locations labeled A–F]

Place Location For each place listed below, write the letter from the map that shows its location.
1. Rome
2. Mediterranean Sea
3. Bethlehem
4. Jerusalem
5. Nicaea
6. Constantinople

Go Online
PHSchool.com Use Web Code **mud-0902** for step-by-step map skills practice.

7. **(a) Recall** What were some of the teachings of Jesus?
   (b) Draw Conclusions Why did poor Romans and slaves find Christianity appealing?

8. **(a) Explain** Why did the Roman government view Christians as enemies of the empire?
   (b) Identify Causes Why did Nero start a campaign against Christians?
   (c) Identify Effects How did the decline of the Roman Empire affect Christians?

9. **(a) Identify** Name a weak and corrupt Roman ruler.
   (b) Explore the Main Idea Explain how this ruler contributed to the decline of the empire.

10. **(a) Recall** What happened to the western part of the empire after Romulus Augustulus was removed from power?
    (b) Predict How do you think life in the West changed after the fall of Rome?

◆ Skills Practice

Comparing and Contrasting In the Skills Activity in this chapter, you learned how to compare and contrast. You learned to identify how different ideas, objects, historical figures, or situations are alike or different.

Review the steps you followed to learn this skill. Reread the part of Section 1 in Chapter 8 describing the decline of the Roman Republic. Then reread the part of Section 3 in this chapter describing the fall of the Roman Empire. Create a chart to help identify the similarities and differences between the two events. Finally, use your findings to draw conclusions about the events.

◆ Writing Activity History

Suppose you were a resident of Rome in A.D. 476, when northern invaders entered the city. Write a letter about the experience to a relative who lives in Constantinople. Also discuss your hopes and fears for the future

10. (a) After Romulus Augustulus was overthrown, the western part of the empire was no longer under a Roman Emperor's rule. **(b)** Possible response: Rome was no longer a center of culture and politics, and many people still had hard lives.

Skills Practice

Similarities and differences listed in students' charts should reflect information about the events as presented in Chapters 8 and 9.

Students' conclusions will vary but should be based on the similarities and differences they have identified.

Writing Activity: History

Students' letters will vary but should reflect accurate information about conditions at Rome in A.D. 476 and demonstrate some imagination about people's reactions to developments of the period and their hopes and fears for the future.

Standardized Test Prep

Test-Taking Tips

Some questions on standardized tests ask you to analyze a timeline. Study the timeline below. Then follow the tips to answer the sample question.

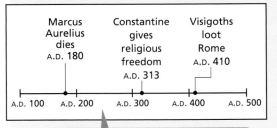

TIP When you read a timeline, align each event with the nearest date. Make sure you can read a date for each point on the timeline.

Pick the letter that best answers the question.

Where would the event "Last Roman emperor driven from power" go on the timeline?

A between A.D. 100 and A.D. 200

B between A.D. 200 and A.D. 300

C between A.D. 300 and A.D. 400

D between A.D. 400 and A.D. 500

TIP Carelessness costs points on multiple-choice tests. Think carefully about each date and event on the timeline.

Think It Through Review the timeline. Ask yourself, "When did the last emperor rule Rome?" It must have happened near the end of the Roman Empire; that means you can rule out A and B. Even if you don't know the exact date, make a thoughtful guess. The last emperor ruled after the Visigoths looted Rome. The correct answer is D.

Practice Questions

Use the tips above and other tips in this book to help you answer the following questions.

1. The Roman government gave family support to the upper classes to
   A reduce their power over their households.
   B encourage them to increase their families.
   C allow wealthy women more independence.
   D gain political power for the emperor.

2. Followers of Jesus believe that he was the
   A messiah.
   B emperor.
   C disciple.
   D ruler.

3. Paul's epistles became part of
   A the Torah.
   B the Gospels.
   C the Greek language.
   D the Christian Bible.

Use the timeline below to answer Question 4.

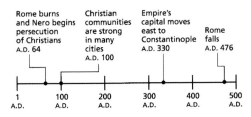

4. How many years passed between the capital's move to Constantinople and the fall of Rome?
   A 142
   B 100
   C 146
   D 64

Use Web Code **mua-0904** for Chapter 9 self-test.

Standardized Test Prep

Answers

1. B
2. A
3. D
4. C

Go Online PHSchool.com Students may use the Chapter 9 self-test on PHSchool.com to prepare for the Chapter Test.

Assessment Resources

Use Chapter Tests A and B to assess students' mastery of chapter content.

All in One Unit 3 History of Our World Teaching Resources, *Chapter Tests A and B,* pp. 144–149

Tests are also available on the Exam-*View*® Test Bank CD-ROM.

⊙ **Exam*View*® Test Bank CD-ROM**

Unit 4

Regional Civilizations

Unit Overview

In Unit 4, students will learn about civilizations that developed in the regions of North Africa and Southwest Asia, sub-Saharan Africa, South Asia, East Asia, and the Americas. Beginning with Chapter 10, they will learn about the rise of the Byzantine Empire and its institutions and legacy. They will also learn about the characteristics and spread of Islamic civilizations. In Chapter 11, the focus shifts to sub-Saharan Africa. Students will learn about the West African kingdoms of Mali, Ghana, and Songhai, and the East African kingdoms of Ethiopia and Aksum. Chapter 12 covers early civilizations of the Americas, including the Mayas, Aztecs, and Incas. Chapter 13 concludes the unit with a study of civilizations that thrived in China, Japan, and India.

Monitoring Student Progress

After students have completed Chapter 13, administer Benchmark Test 4, the fourth of six benchmark tests provided to assess students' progress toward mastery of the National Geography Standards.

The Report Sheet for this test will identify which objectives or standards students have mastered and where they need additional work. It also correlates to the appropriate sections in the Reading and Vocabulary Study Guide, where students can get additional review as needed.

AYP Monitoring Assessment Resources

Determine students' progress toward mastery of the National Geography Standards.

📖 *Benchmark Test 4,* **AYP Monitoring Assessments,** pp. 99–104

Use the Report Sheet to identify which standards your students have mastered, where they need more work, and where they can get additional help.

📖 *Report Sheet, Benchmark Test 4,* **AYP Monitoring Assessments,** p. 128

UNIT 4

Regional Civilizations

(1400 B.C.–A.D. 1650)

◄ These Incan ruins are located at Machu Picchu, Peru.

281

Using the Visual

Ask students to study the picture on pp. 280–281. Have students read the caption on p. 281. Machu Picchu is an Incan city built in the Andes Mountains in present-day Peru. Ask students to find such details as stairs, windows, and terraces. Machu Picchu was probably built and inhabited from the mid-1400s to the early 1500s. Although Spain conquered the Incan Empire in 1532, the Spanish invaders did not come across Machu Picchu. The ruins of Machu Picchu were rediscovered in 1911 by American archaeologist Hiram Bingham.

Overview

  Section 1

The Byzantine Empire

1. Find out how Constantinople and the Byzantine Empire became powerful.

2. Discover the achievements of the Age of Justinian.

3. Learn about the later years of the Byzantine Empire.

  Section 2

The Beginnings of Islam

1. Learn about the Arabian Peninsula, its nomadic people, and its centers of trade.

2. Find out about the life and mission of the Muslim prophet Muhammad.

3. Learn about Muslim beliefs.

Section 3

The Golden Age of Muslim Civilization

1. Find out how the religion of Islam spread.

2. Learn about the golden age of Islam under the rule of the caliphs.

3. Discover the achievements of Islamic culture.

Video

Constantinople, Capital of the Byzantine Empire
Length: 4 minutes, 44 seconds
Use with Section 1
This segment explores the city of Constantinople, which the Roman emperor Constantine named after himself in A.D. 330. The segment will show how the city's location made it important to many different cultures throughout history.

Technology Resources

Students use embedded Web codes to access Internet activities, chapter self-tests, and additional map practice. They may also access Dorling Kindersley's Online Desk Reference to learn more about each country they study.

Use the Interactive Textbook to make content and concepts come alive through animations, videos, and activities that accompany the complete basal text—online and on CD-ROM.

PRENTICE HALL

Use this complete suite of powerful teaching tools to make planning lessons and administering tests quicker and easier.

Reading and Assessment

Reading and Vocabulary Instruction

⟳ Model the Target Reading Skill

Reading Process Explain to students that reading actively will help them retain knowledge and become better readers. To read actively, students should preview the text before reading and determine a purpose for their reading. Two ways to set a purpose for reading are to predict what they will learn about, and to ask themselves questions to answer while reading. Model this skill by thinking about the chapter aloud:

"This chapter's title is *Byzantine and Muslim Civilizations*. I will be learning about two civilizations. I know that the word *civilization* contains the word *civilize*, but I'm not sure what it means. I think it has to do with societies. I'm not sure what *Byzantine* and *Muslim* mean, either. I will scan the chapter to get a better idea of their meanings before reading. Section 1 is titled *The Byzantine Empire*. From scanning the section, it seems as though this empire is related to the Roman Empire. I predict that I will learn the differences between the Byzantine and Roman Empires in this section. Section 2 is titled *The Beginnings of Islam*. I know that *Islam* is a religion. Could *Islam* and *Muslim* be related? I will keep that question in mind while I read the chapter."

Use the following worksheets from All-in-One Unit 4 History of Our World Teaching Resources (pp. 19–21) to support the chapter's Target Reading Skill.

Vocabulary Builder
High-Use Academic Words

Use these steps to teach this chapter's high-use words:

1. Have students rate how well they know each word on their Word Knowledge worksheets (All-in-One Unit 4 History of Our World Teaching Resources, p. 22).

2. Pronounce each word and ask students to repeat it.

3. Give students a brief definition and sample sentence (provided on TE pp. 285, 293, and 301).

4. Work with students as they fill in the "Definition or Example" column of their Word Knowledge worksheets.

Assessment

Formal Assessment

Test students' understanding of core knowledge and skills.

Chapter Tests A and B, All-in-One Unit 4 History of Our World Teaching Resources, pp. 35–40

Customize the Chapter Tests to suit your needs.

Exam*View*® Test Bank CD-ROM

Skills Assessment

Assess geographic literacy.

MapMaster Skills, Student Edition, pp. 283, 301, and 306

Assess reading and comprehension.

Target Reading Skills, Student Edition, pp. 288, 296, 302, and in Section Assessments

Chapter 1 Assessment, History of Our World Reading and Vocabulary Study Guide, p. 117

Performance Assessment

Assess students' performance on this chapter's Writing Activities using the following rubrics from All-in-One Unit 4 History of Our World Teaching Resources.

Rubric for Assessing a Writing Assignment, p. 33

Rubric for Assessing a Newspaper Article, p. 34

Assess students' work through performance tasks.

Small Group Activity: Writing Articles About the Art of Islam, All-in-One Unit 4 History of Our World Teaching Resources, pp. 25–28

Online Assessment

Have students check their own understanding.

Chapter Self-Test

Section 1 **The Byzantine Empire**

 3 periods, 1.5 blocks (includes Focus on)

Social Studies Objectives

1. Find out how Constantinople and the Byzantine Empire grew powerful.
2. Discover the achievements of the Age of Justinian.
3. Learn about the later years of the Byzantine Empire.

Reading/Language Arts Objective

Learn how to preview and set a purpose for reading.

Prepare to Read	**Instructional Resources**	**Differentiated Instruction**

Build Background Knowledge
Show a video about Constantinople and ask students to take notes on the important details.

Set a Purpose for Reading
Have students evaluate statements on the Reading Readiness Guide.

Preview Key Terms
Teach the section's Key Terms.

Target Reading Skill
Introduce the section's Target Reading Skill of **previewing and setting a purpose.**

All in One Unit 4 History of Our World Teaching Resources
L2 Reading Readiness Guide, p. 8
L2 Preview and Set a Purpose, p. 19

Spanish Reading and Vocabulary Study Guide
L1 Chapter 10, Section 1, pp. 78–79 ELL

Instruct	**Instructional Resources**	**Differentiated Instruction**

Constantinople at a Crossroads
Discuss Constantinople during the reign of Constantine.

The Age of Justinian
Ask questions about the early Byzantine Empire and the Justinian Code.

Target Reading Skill
Review **previewing and setting a purpose.**

The Empire's Later Years
Discuss the events that led to the decline of the Byzantine Empire and the fall of Constantinople.

All in One Unit 4 History of Our World Teaching Resources
L2 Guided Reading and Review, p. 9
L2 Reading Readiness Guide, p. 8

History of Our World Transparencies
L2 Section Reading Support HOW 84

History of Our World Video Program
L2 Constantinople, Capital of the Byzantine Empire

All in One History of Our World Teaching Resources
L3 Small Group Activity: Writing Articles About the Art of Islam, pp. 25–28 AR, GT
L3 Byzantine Empress Theodora, p. 29 AR, GT
L2 Skills for Life, p. 24 AR, GT, LPR, SN

Teacher's Edition
L3 For Gifted and Talented, TE pp. 286, 290
L1 For Less Proficient Readers, TE p. 286
L1 For English Language Learners, TE p. 288
L3 For Advanced Readers, TE p. 288

Reading and Vocabulary Study Guide
L1 Chapter 10, Section 1, pp. 108–110 ELL, LPR, SN

Spanish Support
L2 Guided Reading and Review (Spanish), p. 84 ELL

Assess and Reteach	**Instructional Resources**	**Differentiated Instruction**

Assess Progress
Evaluate student comprehension with the section assessment and section quiz.

Reteach
Assign the Reading and Vocabulary Study Guide to help struggling students.

Extend
Extend the lesson by assigning a Book Project.

All in One Unit 4 History of Our World Teaching Resources
L2 Section Quiz, p. 10
L3 Book Project: Two Tales of One City, pp. 16–18 Rubric for Assessing a Writing Assignment, p. 33

Reading and Vocabulary Study Guide
L1 Chapter 10, Section 1, pp. 108–110

Spanish Support
L2 Section Quiz (Spanish), p. 85 ELL

Social Studies Skills Tutor CD-ROM
L1 Transferring Information from One Medium to Another ELL, LPR, SN

Key

L1 Basic to Average   L3 Average to Advanced   LPR Less Proficient Readers   GT Gifted and Talented

L2 For All Students   AR Advanced Readers   ELL English Language Learners

SN Special Needs Students

Section 2 The Beginnings of Islam

 2 periods, 1 block (includes Skills for Life)

Social Studies Objectives

1. Learn about the Arabian Peninsula, its nomadic people, and its centers of trade.
2. Find out about the life and mission of the Muslim prophet Muhammad.
3. Learn about Muslim beliefs.

Reading/Language Arts Objective

Preview and make predictions about the text to help set a purpose for reading.

Prepare to Read

Build Background Knowledge
Have students preview the section and think about the beliefs and origins of Islam, and write down a question they have about the religion.

Set a Purpose for Reading
Have students evaluate statements on the Reading Readiness Guide.

Preview Key Terms
Teach the section's Key Terms.

Target Reading Skill
Introduce the section's Target Reading Skill of **previewing and predicting.**

Instructional Resources

All in One Unit 4 History of Our World Teaching Resources
- **L2** Reading Readiness Guide, p. 12
- **L2** Preview and Predict, p. 20

Differentiated Instruction

Spanish Reading and Vocabulary Study Guide
- **L1** Chapter 10, Section 2, pp. 80–81 ELL

Instruct

The Arabian Peninsula
Ask questions about the geography and people of the Arabian Peninsula.

The Prophet Muhammad
Discuss how Muhammad founded Islam.

Muslim Belief
Discuss different aspects of the Islam religion.

Target Reading Skill
Review **previewing and predicting.**

Instructional Resources

All in One Unit 4 History of Our World Teaching Resources
- **L2** Guided Reading and Review, p. 13
- **L2** Reading Readiness Guide, p. 12

History of Our World Transparencies
- **L2** Transparency B15: Outline
- **L2** Section Reading Support Transparency HOW 85

Differentiated Instruction

History of Our World Transparencies
- **L1** Transparency HOW 27: South Asia: Physical-Political ELL, LPR, SN

Teacher's Edition
- **L1** For Less Proficient Readers, TE p. 294
- **L3** For Advanced Readers, TE p. 296
- **L1** For Special Needs Students, TE pp. 296, 299

Spanish Support
- **L2** Guided Reading and Review (Spanish), p. 86 ELL

PHSchool.com
- **L3** **For:** Long-Term Integrated Project: Building Models of Housing Around the World
  Web Code: lgd-8104

Assess and Reteach

Assess Progress
Evaluate student comprehension with the section assessment and section quiz.

Reteach
Assign the Reading and Vocabulary Study Guide to help struggling students.

Extend
Extend the lesson by assigning an Enrichment activity.

Instructional Resources

All in One Unit 4 History of Our World Teaching Resources
- **L2** Section Quiz, p. 14
- **L3** Enrichment, p. 23
  Rubric for Assessing a Writing Assignment, p. 33

Reading and Vocabulary Study Guide
- **L1** Chapter 10, Section 2, pp. 111–113

Differentiated Instruction

Spanish Support
- **L2** Section Quiz (Spanish), p. 87 ELL

Key

L1 Basic to Average	**L3** Average to Advanced
L2 For All Students	

- **LPR** Less Proficient Readers
- **AR** Advanced Readers
- **SN** Special Needs Students
- **GT** Gifted and Talented
- **ELL** English Language Learners

Section 3 The Golden Age of Muslim Civilization

 2 periods, 1 block (includes Chapter Review and Assessment)

Social Studies Objectives

1. Find out how the religion of Islam spread.
2. Learn about the golden age of Islam under the rule of the caliphs.
3. Discover the achievements of Islamic culture.

Reading/Language Arts Objective

Preview and ask questions to help understand or remember important parts of the text.

Prepare to Read	**Instructional Resources**	**Differentiated Instruction**
Build Background Knowledge Use a concept web to list words and ideas that relate to the term "Golden Age." **Set a Purpose for Reading** Have students evaluate statements on the Reading Readiness Guide. **Preview Key Terms** Teach the section's Key Terms. **Target Reading Skill** Introduce the section's Target Reading Skill of **previewing and asking questions**.	**All in One Unit 4 History of Our World Teaching Resources** **L2** Reading Readiness Guide, p. 16 **L2** Preview and Ask Questions, p. 21	**Spanish Reading and Vocabulary Study Guide** **L1** Chapter 10, Section 3, pp. 82–83 ELL

Instruct	**Instructional Resources**	**Differentiated Instruction**
The Spread of Islam Discuss the success of Islam. **Target Reading Skill** Review **previewing and asking questions**. **The Golden Age** Discuss how the caliphs and Muslim attitudes contributed to the advancements of the Golden Age.	**All in One Unit 4 History of Our World Teaching Resources** **L2** Guided Reading and Review, p. 17 **L2** Reading Readiness Guide, p. 16 **History of Our World Transparencies** **L1** Transparency B20: Timeline **L2** Section Reading Support Transparency HOW 86	**History of Our World Transparencies** **L3** Transparency HOW Set 2: Spread of Islam AR, GT **Teacher's Edition** **L3** For Gifted and Talented, TE p. 302 **L1** For Special Needs Students, TE p. 303 **Student Edition on Audio CD** **L1** Chapter 10, Section 3 ELL, LPR, SN **Spanish Support** **L2** Guided Reading and Review (Spanish), p. 88 ELL

Assess and Reteach	**Instructional Resources**	**Differentiated Instruction**
Assess Progress Evaluate student comprehension with the section assessment and section quiz. **Reteach** Assign the Reading and Vocabulary Study Guide to help struggling students. **Extend** Extend the lesson by assigning a literature reading.	**All in One Unit 4 History of Our World Teaching Resources** **L2** Section Quiz, p. 18 **L3** The King's Wealth, pp. 30–31 Rubric for Assessing a Newspaper Article, p. 34 **L2** Word Knowledge, p. 22 **L2** Vocabulary Development, p. 32 **L2** Chapter Tests A and B, pp. 35–40 **Reading and Vocabulary Study Guide** **L1** Chapter 10, Section 3, pp. 114–116	**Spanish Support** **L2** Section Quiz (Spanish), p. 89 ELL **L2** Chapter Summary (Spanish), p. 90 ELL **L2** Vocabulary Development (Spanish), p. 91 ELL

Key

L1 Basic to Average	**L3** Average to Advanced
L2 For All Students	

LPR Less Proficient Readers
AR Advanced Readers
SN Special Needs Students

GT Gifted and Talented
ELL English Language Learners

Reading Background

Previewing and Prereading

This chapter's Target Reading Skill asks students to preview each section and set a purpose for reading. Students who do a brief, preliminary reading of complex material are in a strategic position to take control of their learning and comprehension. Previewing helps students consider what they already know about a topic they will be studying and gives some idea of what a text selection is about before they read it. Previewing also helps students identify the text structure and develop a mental framework for ideas to be encountered in the text. This can help them in formulating a more realistic reading and study plan.

Follow the steps below to teach students how to preview and preread.

1. Tell students that previewing will help them identify the text structure and develop a mental outline of ideas they will encounter in the text.

2. List the various text features you will be previewing in the order in which you would like students to examine them: section title, text headings, introduction, list of Key Terms, questions or tasks in the reading selection, photographs, drawings, maps, charts and other visuals in the text. Focus students' attention on some of these items, or ask them to look at all of them.

3. Prompt students to reflect after examining various text features. They may ask themselves questions such as: What is this reading selection about? What are some key words I will learn? How should I tackle this reading and divide up the task?

Applying New Words Outside the Classroom

Tell students that the vocabulary words in Chapter 1, such as *Muslim, mosque,* and *revealed,* often appear in books, newspapers, magazines, and on television. Challenge students to find real-life uses of at least three Key Terms or high-use words from the chapter. As "evidence," have students bring in a newspaper clipping with the word or write down the sentence in which the word was used during a radio or television broadcast, and include the time and date of the broadcast.

World Studies Background

Hagia Sophia

Hagia Sophia, built in Constantinople under the direction of Emperor Justinian, was the first monument with a central dome supported by pendentives, a device that enables a circular dome to be built above a square room. Originally a church, Hagia Sophia became a mosque after the Turks conquered the city in 1453. Today it is a museum and a lasting tribute to the achievements of Byzantine architecture.

Hadith

After the Quran, the most important document in Islam is Hadith, the recorded sayings and experiences of the prophet Muhammad, which together form a sort of biography. The role of Hadith in Islam is to provide authoritative rules and examples for Islamic religious and moral behavior.

Islamic Art

Although not stated in the Quran, by the mid-eighth century a formal prohibition had been made against depictions of living things—humans or animals—in Islamic art. This restriction is thought to be based on the idea that only God was believed to create life and that images of living things could become a focus for idolatry, or the worship of images other than God.

Infoplease® provides a wealth of useful information for the classroom. You can use this resource to strengthen your background on the subjects covered in this chapter. Have students visit this advertising-free site as a starting point for projects requiring research.

 Use Web code **lgd-8100** for **Infoplease®.**

Guiding Questions

Remind students about the Guiding Questions introduced at the beginning of the book.

Section 1 relates to **Guiding Question** ④
What types of government were formed in these societies? *(Constantine became the first Christian ruler of the Roman Empire. He moved the imperial capital to Byzantium, which was renamed Constantinople. Later, Justinian, one of the greatest Byzantine emperors, collected and summarized centuries of Roman Laws to form Justinian's Code. Justinian's Code became the basis for the legal systems of most modern European countries.)*

Section 2 relates to **Guiding Question** ②
How did each society's belief system affect its history? *(Muhammad was the founder of the religion of Islam and became its prophet. His followers became known as Muslims. In 656, Islam split into two groups, Shiites and Sunnis.)*

Section 3 relates to **Guiding Question** ③
What was the pattern of day-to-day life in these societies? *(After Muhammad's death, Islam spread west. From about 800 to 110 there was a golden age of Muslim culture. Traders from all over the world brought goods to the caliph's court at Baghdad. The work of Muslim mathematicians enabled later scientists to make discoveries in astronomy, physics, and chemistry, and Muslim writers created lasting works of literature.)*

🎯 Target Reading Skill

In this chapter, students will learn and apply the reading skill of previewing. Use the following worksheets to help students practice this skill:

> **All in One Unit 4 History of Our World Teaching Resources,** *Preview and Set a Purpose,* p. 19; *Preview and Predict,* p. 20; *Preview and Ask Questions,* p. 21

⌐ Differentiated Instruction ¬

The following Teacher Edition strategies are suitable for students of varying abilities.

Advanced Readers, pp. 288, 296
English Language Learners, p. 288
Gifted and Talented, pp. 286, 290, 302
Less Proficient Readers, pp. 286, 294
Special Needs Students, pp. 296, 299, 303

Chapter
10 Byzantine and Muslim Civilizations

Chapter Preview

This chapter will introduce you to the Byzantine Empire, the religion of Islam, and the golden age of Muslim civilization.

Section 1
The Byzantine Empire

Section 2
The Beginnings of Islam

Section 3
The Golden Age of Muslim Civilization

🎯 Target Reading Skill

Reading Process In this chapter, you will focus on the reading process by using previewing to help you understand and remember what you read.

▶ Interior of a Byzantine church in present-day Turkey

⌐ Bibliography

For the Teacher
Armstrong, Karen. *Islam: A Short History.* Modern Library, 2002.
Evans, James Allan. *The Empress Theodora: Partner of Justinian.* University of Texas Press, 2002.
Mango, Cyril A. *The Oxford History of Byzantium.* Oxford Press, 2003.

For the Student
L1 Demi, Margaret K. *Muhammad.* McElderry, 2003.
L2 Macaulay, David. *Mosque.* Houghton Mifflin/Walter Lorraine Books, 2003.
L3 Barrett, Tracy. *Anna of Byzantium.* Laurel Leaf, 2000.

The Byzantine Empire and Islamic World

MAP MASTER™ Skills Activity

KEY
- Byzantine Empire, about A.D. 1000
- Islamic rule, about A.D. 1000
- Roman Empire, about A.D. 120
- • City

ATLANTIC OCEAN

Kiev · Venice · Rome · Córdoba · Constantinople · *Asia Minor* · Antioch · Baghdad · Crete · Cyprus · *Mediterranean Sea* · Jerusalem · Alexandria · Medina · Mecca · *Arabian Peninsula* · *Arabian Sea* · *INDIAN OCEAN*

Black Sea · *Bosporus* · *Caspian Sea* · *Danube R.* · *Dnieper R.* · *Volga R.* · *Tigris R.* · *Euphrates R.* · *Indus R.* · *Persian Gulf* · *Red Sea* · *Nile R.*

0 miles 1,000
0 kilometers 1,000
Lambert Azimuthal Equal Area

Regions Notice the three political regions on this map. **Identify** Which empire was the earliest? The largest? **Conclude** Find Constantinople. How do you think its location contributed to its growth and importance?

Go Online
PHSchool.com Use Web Code **lgp-8111** for step-by-step **map skills practice.**

MAP MASTER™ Skills Activity

- Tell students to look at the map and use their fingers to trace the borders of each empire. Ask them to name the empires in order of size, from smallest to largest.

- On the board, list all of the cities found on the map. Working in pairs, have students identify which empire or empires these cities were a part of. Then have students make a table with the information.

Using the Visual   L2

Reach Into Your Background Draw students' attention to the photo and its caption on pp. 282–283. Ask them to describe the church. *(It is made of stone, and decorated with carvings and paintings.)* How does this church compare with other buildings of worship they have seen? Conduct an Idea Wave (TE, p. T39) to elicit student responses.

Answers

MAP MASTER™ Skills Activity **Identify** the Roman Empire; Islamic rule **Conclude** Its location on the Bosporus, between the Black Sea and the Mediterranean Sea, meant that many people would have traveled through the city, eventually causing it to grow and become important.

Chapter 10 **283**

Chapter Resources

Teaching Resources
Letter Home, p. 107
L2 Vocabulary Development, p. 32
L2 Skills for Life, p. 24
L2 Chapter Tests A and B, pp. 35–40

Spanish Support
L2 Spanish Chapter Summary, p. 90
L2 Spanish Vocabulary Development, p. 91

Media and Technology
L1 Student Edition on Audio CD
L1 Guided Reading Audio, English and Spanish
L2 Social Studies Skills Tutor CD-ROM
ExamView® Test Bank CD-ROM

DISCOVERY History of Our World
CHANNEL Video Program
SCHOOL

PRENTICE HALL
TeacherEXPRESS™
Plan · Teach · Assess

Objectives

Social Studies

1. Find out how Constantinople and the Byzantine Empire became powerful.
2. Discover the achievements of the Age of Justinian.
3. Learn about the later years of the Byzantine Empire.

Reading/Language Arts

Learn how to preview and set a purpose for reading.

Prepare to Read

Build Background Knowledge L2

Tell students that they will start their study of the Byzantine Empire by learning about the capital city of Constantinople. Show *Constantinople: Capital of the Byzantine Empire.* As students watch the video, ask them to write down details about the city that contributed to its success. Then conduct an Idea Wave (TE, p. T35) to have students share their responses.

Set a Purpose for Reading L2

■ Preview the Objectives.

■ Read each statement in the *Reading Readiness Guide* aloud. Ask students to mark the statements true or false.

All in One Unit 4 History of Our World Teaching Resources, *Reading Readiness Guide,* p. 8

■ Have students discuss the statements in pairs or groups of four, then mark their worksheets again. Use the Numbered Heads participation strategy (TE, p. T40) to call on students to share their group's perspectives.

Vocabulary Builder
Preview Key Terms

Pronounce each Key Term, and then ask students to say the word with you. Provide a simple explanation such as, "A schism occurs when a group splits, or breaks away, from its main group."

Prepare to Read

Objectives

In this section you will

1. Find out how Constantinople and the Byzantine Empire became powerful.
2. Discover the achievements of the Age of Justinian.
3. Learn about the later years of the Byzantine Empire.

Taking Notes

As you read this section, take notes about the Byzantine Empire's capital and rulers. Copy the concept web below and record your data in it.

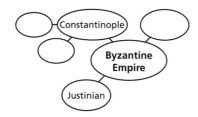

Target Reading Skill

Preview and Set a Purpose When you set a purpose for reading, you give yourself a focus. Before you read this section, look at the headings, photos, and illustrations to see what the section is about. Then set a purpose for reading, such as finding out about the city of Constantinople or the Byzantine Empire. Now read to meet your purpose.

Key Terms

- **Constantinople** (kahn stan tuh NOH pul) *n.* the capital of the eastern Roman Empire and later of the Byzantine Empire
- **Constantine** (KAHN stun teen) *n.* an emperor of the Roman Empire and the founder of Constantinople
- **Justinian** (jus TIN ee un) *n.* one of the greatest Byzantine emperors
- **Justinian's Code** (jus TIN ee unz kohd) *n.* an organized collection and explanation of Roman laws for use by the Byzantine Empire
- **schism** (SIZ um) *n.* a split, particularly in a church or religion

Greek fire being used in battle, as shown in a Byzantine manuscript

Prince Igor (EE gawr) of Kiev, which was then an important city in Russia, watched as a large force of his warships sailed across the Black Sea in A.D. 941. The prince was sure that **Constantinople,** capital of the Byzantine (BIZ un teen) Empire, would soon be his.

As his fleet drew close to the city, the prince's excitement turned to horror. Byzantine ships shot "Greek fire" at the invaders. Anything this "fire" touched burst into flames. Soon, most of Igor's fleet was ablaze. Water could not put out the flames.

Greek fire was made from a formula so secret that it was never written down. Even today, no one knows exactly how it was made, except that it contained petroleum. But this deadly weapon gave the Byzantines tremendous power throughout the Mediterranean area.

284 History of Our World

Target Reading Skill L2

Preview and Set a Purpose Point out the Target Reading Skill. Tell students that previewing the text helps them see what the text will be about, and setting a purpose helps give them a focus while reading.

Model previewing and setting a purpose by thinking aloud: "Previewing this section tells me that the text will be about the history of the Byzantine Empire and its rulers. My purpose for reading will be to find out who these rulers were and what contributions they made to the empire."

Give students *Preview and Set a Purpose.* Have them complete the activity in their groups.

All in One Unit 4 History of Our World Teaching Resources, *Preview and Set a Purpose,* p. 19

Constantinople at a Crossroads

At its height, the ancient Roman Empire controlled the lands surrounding the Mediterranean Sea. It also ruled parts of northern Europe and the region we now call the Middle East. In the centuries after Rome's power faded, these lands went through a tug of war. Two groups—the Christian Byzantines and the Muslim Arabs and Turks—developed powerful civilizations at this time. These two groups sometimes shared control and sometimes fought over the region.

Constantine and His Capital The emperor **Constantine** began his rule of the enormous Roman Empire in A.D. 306. His reign was marked by two important changes. First, Constantine became a Christian and stopped the persecution of Christians in the empire. Second, after 20 years of ruling from the city of Rome, Constantine decided to build a new imperial capital.

Constantine chose Byzantium, an ancient city founded by the Greeks, at the eastern end of the empire. He spared no expense building and fortifying his capital. In A.D. 330, Byzantium was renamed Constantinople (kahn stan tuh NOH pul), the "city of Constantine." By the early 500s, Constantinople had large markets, forums or public squares, paved roads, a cathedral, a palace, public baths, and a hippodrome or circus. An estimated half a million people lived there. Although the name of their city had changed, the people who lived there were still called Byzantines.

Fortress City
Notice the walls that protect Constantinople in the medieval painting and in the diagram of the city. The photo shows ruins of a city wall.
Infer *Why would the aqueduct, which carried water, and the cisterns, which stored water, also be important if the city were attacked?*

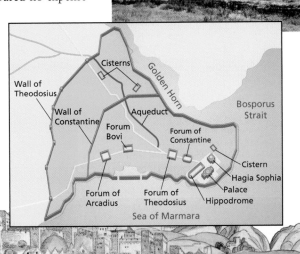

Vocabulary Builder

Use the information below to teach students this section's high-use words.

High-Use Word	Definition and Sample Sentence
reign, p. 285	*n.* period of power of a ruler During the **reign** of Constantine, the Roman capital moved to Byzantium.
imperial, p. 285	*adj.* of or related to an empire The emperor and his family lived in the **imperial** palace.
distinct, p. 288	*adj.* not alike; different The two sweaters had **distinct** styles.
regain, p. 288	*v.* to have again After resting for a while, she **regained** some of her strength.

Guided Instruction (continued)

- Discuss with students how and why Constantinople became such a powerful city. *(The city was located right at a crossroads of major land and sea trade routes. Duties on trade goods gave the city great wealth, and the diversity of people and ideas that entered the city made it an international center of trade and culture.)*

- Ask students **What factors contributed to the fall of the western Roman Empire?** *(By A.D. 350 the western Roman Empire was already in decline; Roman armies had difficulty holding back invaders from Europe; Germanic groups were coming closer to Rome.)*

Independent Practice

Have students create the Taking Notes graphic organizer on a blank piece of paper. Then have them fill in the ovals in with information they have just learned.

Monitor Progress

As students fill in the graphic organizer, circulate and make sure that individuals are choosing the correct details. Provide assistance as needed.

Gold coin from Constantinople ▶

Justinian and His Court
This work of art is a mosaic made of ceramic tiles fitted closely together.
Analyze Images *How does the artist indicate that Justinian (center) is the most important person?*

286 History of Our World

The emperors who followed Constantine continued to rule from Constantinople, in the eastern part of the empire. Over time, the Roman Empire split in two. The eastern half was by far the stronger. One reason for its strength was military. The Byzantines had the strongest army in the world. Another reason for the Byzantines' strength was trade.

Trade Constantinople was built at a major crossroads of land and sea trade routes. Find it on the map on page 283. Notice that it is located on the Bosporus. The Bosporus is a strait, or narrow passage that links two bodies of water. It connects the Black Sea and the Sea of Marmara, which flows into the Mediterranean Sea. The Bosporus also links two continents, Europe and Asia.

Goods came to Constantinople from Kiev in the north, from Egypt in the south, and across Central Asia from as far away as China. The Byzantines charged taxes on all goods that went through the city. The diverse people, goods, and ideas that poured into Constantinople made it a major center of international trade. And over time, the Byzantine Empire grew rich.

The Fall of the Western Empire Meanwhile, by A.D. 350, the western Roman Empire was already in decline. Roman armies were having difficulty holding back invaders from Europe. Germanic groups were coming closer and closer to Rome itself. In 476, a Germanic leader ousted the emperor. Historians call that event the fall of the Roman Empire.

✓ **Reading Check** **Why did Constantinople become rich and powerful?**

The Age of Justinian

As Rome was falling to invaders, strong fortifications and an excellent army protected Constantinople. But these were not the city's only strengths. The early Byzantine Empire had many excellent rulers who were wise as well as popular. They encouraged education and made reforms to laws and government. This kind of leadership also contributed to the strength of their empire.

The Emperor Justinian One of the greatest Byzantine emperors was **Justinian** (jus TIN ee un), whose rule began in 527. Justinian was an energetic ruler who rarely gave up on a task until it was completed. He had been born into a poor family, and he listened to the ideas of all his subjects—whether they were wealthy nobles or poor peasants.

Answers

✓ **Reading Check** The city was located at a major crossroads of trade.

Analyze Images He is in the center of the painting, in front of the other people, and is wearing a jeweled crown.

Justinian's Code One of Justinian's most lasting contributions was a system of laws. When he became emperor, the empire was using a disorganized system of old Roman laws. Some laws even contradicted others. It was difficult to make sense of them—or to enforce them. Justinian appointed a team to collect and summarize centuries of Roman laws. The result was **Justinian's Code,** an organized collection and explanation of Roman laws for use by the Byzantine Empire. Eventually, this code became the basis for the legal systems of most modern European countries.

Byzantine Culture In addition to preserving the principles of Roman law, Byzantine scholars also kept and copied the works of the ancient Greeks. At its peak, Byzantine civilization blended Greek, Roman, and Christian influences. Later, when the empire was in decline, scholars took the ancient manuscripts and their knowledge of the rich Byzantine culture to the newly powerful city-states of Italy. In Chapter 6 you will read how these influences helped to spark the Renaissance.

✓ **Reading Check** What cultures influenced Byzantine civilization?

Hagia Sophia
It took 10,000 workers five years to build the Hagia Sophia cathedral in Constantinople. Since the fall of the empire, it has been used as a mosque. **Infer** Why do you think Justinian built such a majestic church?

Citizen Heroes

Read **Citizen Heroes** on this page. Ask students **How did Theodora use the power she gained when she married Justinian?** (*Many of Justinian's decisions were made with her advice, and she worked to improve women's rights and change divorce laws to protect women.*)

The Age of Justinian L2

Guided Instruction
- Have students read The Age of Justinian to learn about developments in the Byzantine Empire under the emperor Justinian. As students read, circulate to make sure they can answer the Reading Check question.

- Ask students **What qualities made the early Byzantine Empire strong?** (*The Byzantine Empire had a strong army and excellent rulers who were both popular and wise.*)

- Ask students **What was Justinian's code?** (*an organized collection and explanation of Roman laws used by the Byzantine Empire*) **Why do you think it was an important part of the Byzantine Empire?** (*Answers will vary, but should include that it was necessary to have laws that were easy to make sense of and enforce to keep order in the empire.*)

Independent Practice
Have students continue to fill in their graphic organizers with details about Emperor Justinian.

Monitor Progress
As students fill in their graphic organizers, circulate to make sure they are adding circles as needed. Provide assistance as needed.

Answers
✓ **Reading Check** Greek, Roman, and Christian cultures influenced Byzantine culture.

Infer Possible answer: He wanted to show the wealth and strength of his empire and show his devotion to God.

Skills for Life **Skills Mini Lesson**

Making Valid Generalizations

1. Teach the skill by telling students that valid generalizations can be made about a group if the statements are supported by facts that relate to the vast majority of the group.

2. Help students practice the skill by identifying a generalization in the first paragraph under The Age of Justinian on page 286. Ask them to note if this statement can be supported by facts in the paragraph. (*Generalization: The early Byzantine Empire had excellent rulers. Facts: rulers were popular, wise; encouraged education, made reforms.*)

3. Have students apply the skill by asking them to identify a generalization and the facts that support it in the last paragraph on page 288.

Target Reading Skill

Preview and Set a Purpose As a follow up, have students answer the Target Reading Skill question in the Student Edition. (*The paragraph gives information about the decline of the Byzantine Empire.*)

The Empire's Later Years

Guided Instruction

- **Vocabulary Builder** Clarify the high-use words **distinct** and **regain** before reading.

- Have students read The Empire's Later Years.

- Discuss with students the events that led to the decline of the Byzantine Empire. (*After the death of Justinian, a series of wars with neighboring enemies caused a decline in trade. Also, the splitting of the Christian church further weakened the empire.*)

- Ask students to list some of the differences that led to the schism in the Christian church in 1054. (*The Byzantine emperor outlawed the use of icons; the pope disagreed with this decision and banished the emperor from the church. Many Byzantines argued that the pope did not have authority over the emperor.*)

Independent Practice

Have students complete their graphic organizers.

Monitor Progress

- Show *Section Reading Support Transparency HOW 84* and ask students to check their work individually. Go over key concepts and clarify key vocabulary as needed.

   Unit 4 History of Our World Transparencies, *Section Reading Support Transparency HOW 84*

- Tell students to fill in the last column of the *Reading Readiness Guide.* Probe for what they learned that confirms or invalidates each statement.

   All in One Unit 4 History of Our World Teaching Resources, *Reading Readiness Guide,* p. 8

Answer

Identify Frame of Reference Viewing icons might have helped them feel a stronger connection to their religious beliefs.

The Importance of Icons
This icon shows the Virgin Mary and the baby Jesus. The ban on icons was finally lifted in A.D. 843, and they are important in Eastern Orthodox Christianity to this day. **Identify Frame of Reference** *Why might medieval Christians have valued icons?*

288 History of Our World

The Empire's Later Years

After Justinian's death in 565, the Byzantine Empire began to decline. Later emperors had to fight wars against many neighboring enemies—including Persians and Turks to the east, Arabs to the south, and Germanic peoples to the north and west. The Byzantine Empire was shrinking in both size and power. As the Byzantines struggled to keep nearby enemies from invading Constantinople, religious and political arguments were weakening the empire from within.

A Religious Dispute Although most Byzantines were Christians, they did not practice Christianity the same way as the people in Western Europe did. Byzantine Christians rejected the authority of the pope, the leader of the church in Rome. The Byzantine emperor had to approve the choice of the patriarch, or highest church official in Constantinople. Greek was the language of the Byzantine church, while Latin was the language of the Roman church. The two branches of Christianity began to grow apart.

At that time, many Christians prayed to saints or holy people, represented by icons, or paintings of these people. In the 700s, a Byzantine emperor outlawed the use of icons, saying that they violated God's commandments. The pope disagreed, and banished the emperor from the church.

Byzantines felt that the pope did not have the authority to banish the emperor from the church. These disputes led to a **schism,** or split, in the Christian church in 1054. Now there were two distinct forms of Christianity: the Roman Catholic Church in the west and the Eastern (Greek) Orthodox Church in the east.

A Second Golden Age From about 900 until the mid-1000s, the Byzantine Empire experienced a final period of greatness. Trade increased and merchants came to Constantinople from as far away as Venice and Russia. Once again the population of the city grew in size and diversity.

As the economy grew in strength, so did the government. The long reign of Basil II—from 976 until 1025—was the most exceptional period of Byzantine history since the rule of Justinian. The empire regained some of the land it had lost. There was a burst of creativity in the arts.

Differentiated Instruction

For English Language Learners To help students with unfamiliar vocabulary, ask them to preview the section before they read and choose five to seven words that are unfamiliar to them. Have students write each word with its part of speech and definition, and then write a sentence using the word correctly. Partner them with native English speakers to review their sentences.

For Advanced Readers Encourage students to do research to learn more about Justinian's wife, Theodora. As a starting point, have students read the primary source *Byzantine Empress Theodora.*

All in One Unit 4 History of Our World Teaching Resources, *Byzantine Empress Theodora,* p. 29

The Fall of Constantinople During the 1000s, however, Muslim peoples to the east were also gaining power. By the late 1100s, Turks had taken the inland areas of Asia Minor away from the weakening Byzantine Empire.

The Byzantines were also threatened by Europeans. In 1171, disagreements over trade led to a war with Venice. And in the early 1200s, Constantinople was attacked by Christian crusaders. Western Christians ruled the city for 50 years. In 1261, the Byzantines regained their capital, but little was left of their empire.

In 1453, a force of about 70,000 Turks surrounded Constantinople. They came both by sea and by land, and they brought cannons to attack the city's walls. The defending force, which numbered about 7,000, held out for two months. Then the Byzantine capital—which had been a defensive fortress for more than 1,000 years—finally fell.

However, like Constantine before them, the new rulers would rebuild the city and make it an imperial capital. Renamed Istanbul, the city at the crossroads became a great center of Muslim culture and the capital of the Ottoman Empire.

✓ **Reading Check** Why did Constantinople finally fall?

The Turks Take Constantinople
The Turks dragged some of their ships overland and launched them into Constantinople's harbor. **Synthesize** *From what you know about the city's fortifications, why was this a good strategy?*

Section 1 Assessment

Key Terms
Review the key terms at the beginning of this section. Use each term in a sentence that explains its meaning.

Target Reading Skill
What was your purpose for reading this section? Did you accomplish it? If not, what might have been a better purpose?

Comprehension and Critical Thinking
1. (a) Locate Where was Constantinople located?

(b) Identify Effects How did its location contribute to its growth and to the strength of the Byzantine Empire?

2. (a) Recall What qualities made Justinian a good and successful ruler?

(b) Draw Conclusions Why was Justinian's Code so important?

3. (a) Explain What was the dispute that split the medieval Christian church?

(b) Draw Conclusions Why might that split have weakened the empire?

Writing Activity
Write a letter to a friend or family member from the point of view of a foreign merchant traveling to Constantinople during the reign of Justinian. Describe the city and its location as well as what you have heard about the emperor.

For: An activity on the Byzantines
Visit: PHSchool.com
Web Code: lgd-8101

Assess and Reteach

Assess Progress L2
Have students complete the Section Assessment. Administer the *Section Quiz.*

All in One Unit 4 History of Our World Teaching Resources, *Section Quiz,* p. 10

Reteach L1
If students need more instruction, have them read this section in the *Reading and Vocabulary Study Guide.*

Chapter 1, Section 1, **Unit 4 History of Our World Reading and Vocabulary Study Guide,** pp. 108–110

Extend L3
Have students further explore the history of Constantinople, which was later renamed Istanbul, by completing the book project, *Two Tales of One City.*

All in One Unit 4 History of Our World Teaching Resources, *Book Project: Two Tales of One City,* pp. 16–18

Answers

✓**Reading Check** The city was weakened by attacks from Muslim peoples from the east and Christian crusaders from the west. It finally fell to the Turks in 1453.

Synthesize Attacking this way gave them access to the inside of the city.

Writing Activity

All in One Unit 4 History of Our World Teaching Resources, *Rubric for Assessing a Writing Assignment,* p. 33

Go Online PHSchool.com Typing in the Web code when prompted will bring students directly to detailed instructions for this activity.

Section 1 Assessment

Key Terms
Students' sentences should reflect knowledge of each Key Term.

Target Reading Skill
Answers will vary, but students should indicate what their purpose was, and whether or not they achieved it. If they did not achieve their purpose, they should indicate a better purpose.

Comprehension and Critical Thinking
1. (a) at the eastern end of the Roman Empire, on the Bosporus **(b)** It was at a crossroads of land and sea trade routes between Asia and Europe. Goods passing through the city enriched it through duties and the diversity of people made it an important center of ideas.

2. (a) He was energetic, did not give up on a task until it was finished, and listened to everyone's ideas. **(b)** It organized a collection of disorganized Roman laws and became the basis for later legal systems.

3. (a) During an argument over whether or not icons should be worshipped, the pope banished the Byzantine emperor from the Christian church. **(b)** Possible answers: Fighting may have broken out between supporters of the two churches; Roman Catholics may not have wanted to trade in Constantinople.

Objective

Learn how to transfer information from one medium to another by using a table to write a paragraph.

Prepare to Read

Build Background Knowledge **L2**

Explain to students that the skill Using a Table to Write a Paragraph is an example of transferring information from one medium to another, or taking information presented one way and expressing it in another way that better suits your purpose. Using the Idea Wave participation strategy (TE, p. T39), have students think of situations where they would use this skill. *(Possible answers: writing a report, giving an oral presentation, creating a flowchart)*

Instruct

Using a Table to Write a Paragraph **L2**

Guided Instruction

- Read the steps to using a table to write a paragraph as a class, and write them on the board.

- Practice the skill by following the steps on p. 298 as a class. Model each step in the activity: identify what the table is about *(The table contrasts the same data for Istanbul in the past and today.)*; identify the headings *(Characteristic, Constantinople in A.D. 540, Istanbul Today, Importance, Population, Major Religion, Sources of Wealth, Language, Challenges)*; look for similarities and differences in the data *(Similarities—largest city; faced challenges of overpopulation and earthquakes; Differences—population is larger today, major religion is Islam rather than Christianity, sources of wealth are textiles, manufacturing and tourism rather than trade, people speak Turkish rather than Greek, and the challenges of disease and attack by foreigners have been replaced by pollution)*; analyze the most important information, and state the conclusions. *(The differences seem more important. Possible conclusion: Although Istanbul*

today has some similarity to Constantinople in A.D. 540, the city has changed greatly, particularly its size, culture, and economic activities.)

Independent Practice

Assign *Skills for Life* and have students complete it individually.

All in One **Unit 4 History of Our World Teaching Resources,** *Skills for Life,* p. 24

Mr. Perez's students have just finished studying the Byzantine Empire. Now they are studying modern Turkey, which occupies some of the same land. They have learned that Istanbul is the modern name of Constantinople. Mr. Perez has asked the students to use a table of information about Istanbul and Constantinople to write a paragraph that compares the two cities.

I nformation—words or numbers—presented in graphs, charts, or tables is called data. When you use this type of data to write a paragraph, you are transferring information from one medium to another.

Byzantine cup

Learn the Skill

Follow these steps to write a paragraph based on data from a table.

1 **Identify the topic of the table.** First read the title. Then look at the table to get a general idea of its purpose.

2 **Identify the key pieces of information.** Headings tell the main topics. Read both across and down to understand how the data relate to the headings.

Modern Istanbul

290 History of Our World

3 **Look for similarities and differences in data.** The columns of a table often compare and contrast information.

4 **Analyze the meaning of the information.** What information seems most important? List several conclusions you can draw from the data.

5 **Write a paragraph that states and supports your conclusions.** Your main conclusion can be your topic sentence. Support it with examples from the data.

Monitor Progress

As students are completing *Skills for Life,* circulate to make sure individuals are applying the skill steps effectively. Provide assistance as needed.

Istanbul Past and Present

Characteristic	Constantinople in A.D. 540	Istanbul Today
Importance	Capital of Byzantine Empire, largest city in Byzantine Empire	Turkey's largest city
Population	About 500,000	About 10 million
Major Religion	Christianity	Islam
Sources of Wealth	Trade	Textiles, manufacturing, tourism
Language	Greek	Turkish
Challenges	Overpopulation, disease, earthquakes, attacks by foreigners	Overpopulation, earthquakes, pollution

Practice the Skill

Use the steps in Learn the Skill to transfer the information in the table above into a paragraph.

1. What is the title of the table? In your own words, state what the table is about.

2. What are the important headings? How do you find key information, such as the major religion of present-day Istanbul?

3. Note how Istanbul is similar to Constantinople and how it is different.

4. Which headings or topics represent the most important information? Are the similarities or the differences more important?

5. What is the most important thing you've learned about the two cities? Use your conclusion as the topic sentence, and support it with data from the table.

Apply the Skill

Study the table at the right, and draw a conclusion about the information in it. Write a paragraph that uses data from the table to support your conclusion.

The Christian Church Divides, A.D. 1054

Characteristic	Eastern Orthodox	Roman Catholic
Head of Church	Patriarch	Pope
Had Most Power Over Church	Emperor	Pope
Main Location	Eastern Europe	Western Europe
Language	Greek	Latin
Practices	• Priests could marry • Pope's authority was not recognized	• Priests could not marry • Pope had supreme authority

Assess and Reteach

Assess Progress L2
Ask students to do the Apply the Skill activity.

Reteach L1
If students are having trouble applying the skill steps, have them review the skill using the interactive Social Studies Skills Tutor CD-ROM.

 Transferring Information from One Medium to Another, **Social Studies Skills Tutor CD-ROM**

Extend L3
Have students read pp. 302–304, beginning with the text under the heading The Golden Age. Working in pairs, have students create a table with information about the achievements of the Golden Age. Tables should include information about achievements in mathematics, science, and literature. Tell students to also include the key figures involved in these achievements in their tables.

Answer
Apply the Skill

Answers will vary, but students should draw a conclusion about the information in the table, and their paragraphs should include data from the table that supports their conclusions. *(Possible conclusion: There are major differences between the Eastern Orthodox and the Roman Catholic churches.)*

Objectives

Social Studies

1. Learn about the Arabian Peninsula, its nomadic people, and its centers of trade.
2. Find out about the life and mission of the Muslim prophet Muhammad.
3. Learn about Muslim beliefs.

Reading/Language Arts

Preview and make predictions about the text to help set a purpose for reading.

Prepare to Read

Build Background Knowledge **L2**

Explain to students that in this section they will learn about the religion of Islam. Ask students to preview the section with this question in mind: **What are the beliefs of Islam and how did the religion start?** Conduct a Give One, Get One participation strategy (TE, p. T41) to elicit responses and record them on the board. Then ask students to write one question that they hope to be able to answer after they have read the section. Be sure to revisit students' questions when reading is complete.

Set a Purpose for Reading **L2**

- Preview the Objectives.

- Read each statement in the *Reading Readiness Guide* aloud. Ask students to mark the statements true or false.

  All in One **Unit 4 History of Our World Teaching Resources,** *Reading Readiness Guide,* p. 12

- Have students discuss the statements in pairs or groups of four, then mark their worksheets again. Use the Numbered Heads participation strategy (TE, p. T40) to call on students to share their group's perspectives.

Vocabulary Builder

Preview Key Terms **L2**

Pronounce each Key Term, and then ask students to say the word with you. Provide a simple explanation such as, "Many Muslims say their daily prayers in a mosque."

The Beginnings of Islam

Prepare to Read

Objectives

In this section you will
1. Learn about the Arabian Peninsula, its nomadic people, and its centers of trade.
2. Find out about the life and mission of the Muslim prophet Muhammad.
3. Learn about Muslim beliefs.

Taking Notes

As you read this section, keep track of the most important ideas about the beginnings of Islam. Copy the outline started below, and add to it as you read.

> I. The Arabian Peninsula
>   A. Nomadic Bedouins
>   1.
>   2.
>   B. Mecca: A center of trade

 Target Reading Skill

Preview and Predict
Making predictions about your text helps you set a purpose for reading and remember what you read. Before you begin, look at the headings, photos, and anything else that stands out. Then predict what the text might be about. For example, you might predict that this section will tell about the origins of Muslim beliefs. As you read, if what you learn doesn't support your prediction, revise your prediction.

Key Terms

- **Muhammad** (muh HAM ud) *n.* the prophet and founder of Islam
- **nomads** (NOH madz) *n.* people with no permanent home, who move from place to place in search of food, water, or pasture
- **caravan** (KA ruh van) *n.* a group of traders traveling together for safety
- **Mecca** (MEK uh) *n.* an Arabian trading center and Muhammad's birthplace
- **Muslim** (MUZ lum) *n.* a follower of Islam
- **mosque** (mahsk) *n.* a Muslim house of worship
- **Quran** (koo RAHN) *n.* the holy book of Islam

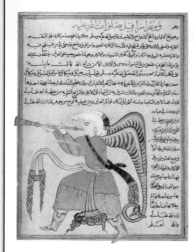

In this miniature painting, an angel's announcement is symbolized by the blowing of a horn.

The religion of Islam (IS lahm) teaches that in about 610, the prophet **Muhammad** (muh HAM ud) went into a cave in the Arabian mountains to pray. (A prophet is a person who is regarded as speaking for God.) It is said that while Muhammad was inside the cave, he heard the voice of an angel. God told Muhammad through the angel that people had abandoned the true faith. Instead of worshiping only God, they worshiped many false gods. Muhammad was to share this message.

According to Islamic teaching, Muhammad was frightened and unsure that he was worthy of such an important mission. But he obeyed. God continued to send Muhammad messages, which Muhammad shared with the people of the Arabian Peninsula. These teachings became a religion that brought great changes to the region. And in the centuries after Muhammad's death, the new religion spread to many parts of the world.

 Target Reading Skill **L2**

Preview and Predict Point out the Target Reading Skill. Tell students that making predictions about the text they are about to read will help them set a purpose for reading and remember what they read.

Model previewing and predicting by thinking aloud, using the text on p. 293 under the heading The Arabian Peninsula. "From the headings, photos, and captions on these pages, I predict that I will learn about the geography, people, and one important city of the Arabian Peninsula."

Give students *Preview and Predict.* Have them complete the activity in their groups.

All in One **Unit 4 History of Our World Teaching Resources,** *Preview and Predict,* p. 20

The Arabian Peninsula

In Muhammad's time, as today, much of the Arabian Peninsula was covered by desert. Although surrounded by water, the peninsula has no major rivers and receives little rainfall. Trade with neighboring peoples supported the growth of towns along trade routes. And many groups of Bedouins (BED oo inz) made their homes among the shifting sand dunes of the desert.

Nomadic Bedouins The Bedouins were **nomads,** or people who have no permanent home but move from place to place in search of food, water, and pasture. The Arabian desert yielded little food for the Bedouins or for their herds of sheep, camels, and goats. Water was also scarce—for people as well as for animals.

To make their way across the desert, the Bedouins followed traditional routes from one oasis to another. An oasis is a green area within a desert, fed by underground water. These all-important oases provided plenty of water for the nomads and their animals.

Because of their knowledge of the desert and its oases, the Bedouins also worked as guides for traders. They helped traders travel across the desert in large groups called **caravans.** These desert caravans depended on camels, which carried both people and their goods. Camels are sturdy animals with a special ability to store water for long periods.

Bedouins Today
These Bedouins in the Sinai desert of Egypt are still nomads like their ancestors. **Predict** What kinds of events and conditions might prevent the Bedouins from continuing their traditional way of life?

Vocabulary Builder

Use the information below to teach students this section's high-use words.

High-Use Word	Definition and Sample Sentence
abandon, p. 294	*v.* to give up or leave Ariella did not want to **abandon** her old toys when she moved.
foundation, p. 295	*n.* basis or support for something Protecting the environment is the **foundation** of most recycling laws.
descendant, p. 297	*n.* a person who is related to an ancestor Jessica is a **descendant** of her grandmother.

Instruct

The Arabian Peninsula L2

Guided Instruction

- With students, read The Arabian Peninsula using the Oral Cloze reading strategy (TE, p. T37).

- Have students describe the physical characteristics of the Arabian Peninsula. *(Much of it is covered by desert, it has no major rivers and receives little rainfall; there is water at oases.)*

- Ask students **What was the purpose of the caravans?** *(to move trade goods across the desert)* **What role did the Bedouins play in the movement of goods?** *(Because of their knowledge of the desert and its oases, they probably established the caravan routes. They also became guides for the caravans.)*

- Ask students **How did Mecca become an important trading center?** *(It was an oasis on a caravan route. Goods traveled in caravans between Mecca and the Mediterranean, and eventually to Europe and what is now Iraq.)*

Independent Practice

Have students create the Taking Notes graphic organizer on a blank piece of paper. Then have them fill in the outline with information they have just learned. Using *Transparency B15: Outline,* briefly model how to label and fill in the outline.

📖 **Unit 4 History of Our World,** *Transparency B15: Outline*

Monitor Progress

As students work on their outlines, circulate and provide assistance as needed.

Answer

Predict Possible answer: Development of the land or severe drought might prevent the Bedouins from continuing their traditional way of life.

Read **Links To Economics** on this page. Ask **Why do you think merchants wanted to avoid carrying large sums of cash across thousands of miles?** *(They might have been worried that it would get lost or stolen.)*

The Prophet Muhammad

L2

Guided Instruction

- **Vocabulary Builder** Clarify the high-use word **abandon** before reading.

- With students, read about how Muhammad founded the religion of Islam in The Prophet Muhammad.

- Ask students **Who was Muhammad?** *(Muhammad was an Arab who was born in Mecca in about 570. He became the founder of the religion of Islam and its prophet.)*

- Ask students **What happened to Muhammad in 622?** *(He and his followers were invited to Yathrib, now Medina, where he was regarded as a prophet. This movement was called the* hijra, *or "migration," and 622 became year 1 on the Muslim calendar.)*

- Ask students **Based on what you have learned about Mecca, why do you think the religion of Islam spread so quickly?** *(Because Mecca was a busy trading center, religious ideas, as well as goods, could travel quickly and over great distances.)*

Independent Practice

Have students continue filling in their outlines with details about Muhammad's life.

Monitor Progress

As students continue to fill in their outlines, circulate to make sure they are placing details in the same order as they appear in the text. Provide assistance as necessary.

Answer

✔ **Reading Check** The Bedouins had knowledge of the desert and its oases.

Links to Economics

New Business Methods
From 750 to 1350, Muslims like the Arab traders shown above dominated the trade routes in Arabia and far beyond. They not only found new goods to trade, they also developed new *ways* to trade. Muslim merchants bought and sold goods on credit and set up locations for exchanging currency. To avoid carrying large sums of cash across thousands of miles, they developed a way to transfer money from one location to another—a forerunner to today's checks. Merchants could deposit funds at one location and use a letter of credit to withdraw those funds at a different location.

Mecca: A Center of Trade The oases on the Arabian Peninsula became busy trading centers. One of the most important was **Mecca** (MEK uh). From Mecca, great caravans traveled northwest to markets in what is now Syria. From Syria, goods could be shipped across the Mediterranean Sea to Europe. Other caravans traveled northeast from Mecca. They made a dangerous journey across the desert to markets in the area now known as Iraq. Trade was also conducted with Yemen to the south. Precious goods traded along these routes included perfume and spices, incense, expensive cloth, elephant tusks, and gold.

✔ **Reading Check** **Why did Bedouins make good guides for traders?**

The Prophet Muhammad

Muhammad was born and grew up in the trading center of Mecca. His great-grandfather had been a wealthy merchant. However, by the time Muhammad was born in about 570, his family was poor. As a young man, Muhammad worked on caravans. His job took him to distant places, including Syria, which was then part of the Byzantine Empire.

Muhammad's Mission Muhammad liked to walk in the mountains outside Mecca. Troubled by problems he saw in society, he liked to be alone to pray and think. When Muhammad was 40 years old, he first heard God speak to him through the angel in the cave. God told him that people would submit to, or agree to obey, the one true God. In time, a person who accepted the teachings of Muhammad came to be known as a **Muslim** (MUZ lum), "a person who submits." The religion of Muslims is called Islam.

Muhammad preached God's message—that all people were brothers and sisters in a community established by God—but few people in Mecca listened. They thought Muhammad's teachings threatened their old gods. They feared that abandoning their old gods would end Mecca's importance as a religious center. Many Arabs traveled to Mecca in order to pray at an ancient shrine called the Kaaba (KAH buh). People in Mecca also feared that Muhammad might gain political power.

Differentiated Instruction

For Less Proficient Readers **L1**
Help students visualize the routes traveled by trade caravans from Mecca by displaying *Color Transparency MT 14: South Asia: Physical-Political*. Select students to come up and trace the routes with their fingers, identifying the physical features, countries, and cities along the way.

📖 **History of Our World Transparencies,** *Color Transparency HOW 27: South Asia: Physical-Political*

Muhammad in Medina In 622, Muhammad and his followers were invited to Yathrib (yah THREEB), a city north of Mecca. The people there regarded Muhammad as a prophet. This movement of early Muslims is known as the hijra (hih JY ruh), or "the migration." The year of the hijra—622 in the calendar used in the United States—became year 1 on the Muslim calendar.

After the hijra, the name of Yathrib was changed to Medina. This name means "city" and is short for "city of the prophet." Medina quickly became an important Islamic center. But Islam did not remain limited to Medina. In 630, Muhammad returned to Mecca—this time in triumph. By the time Muhammad died two years later, the new religion of Islam had spread all across the Arabian Peninsula.

✓ **Reading Check** Why did Muhammad go to Yathrib?

Muslim Belief

A muezzin (myoo EZ in), a man who calls Muslims to worship, looks out over the city and begins his loud call. The muezzin's voice echoes in all directions: "There is no god but God, and Muhammad is the messenger of God." In Arabic, the word for God is *Allah.* Five times each day, Muslims are called to worship in this way. And five times a day, every faithful Muslim stops whatever he or she is doing to pray.

Some Muslims gather in a house of worship called a **mosque** (mahsk). Others kneel outside. Wherever Muslims are in the world—in the Arabian Peninsula, in North Africa, or in the United States—they kneel in a direction that faces toward Mecca. "There is no god but God," the faithful respond, "and Muhammad is the messenger of God."

The Five Pillars of Islam Basic Muslim beliefs are expressed in the Five Pillars of Islam. These practices, shown in the table above, are the foundations of Islam. Muslims regard these pillars as sacred duties. The fifth pillar—the hajj (haj), or pilgrimage to the Kaaba—is required only of those who are able to travel to Mecca.

The Five Pillars of Islam

Pillar	Description
Declaration of Faith	Muslims must regularly declare the belief that there is only one God and Muhammad is God's messenger.
Prayer	Muslims must pray five times each day, facing in the direction of the holy city of Mecca.
Almsgiving	Muslims must give alms, or money that goes to the needy.
Fasting	Muslims must fast during daylight hours in the month of Ramadan.
Pilgrimage	Muslims must make a pilgrimage to Mecca at least one time in their lives if they are able.

■ **Chart Skills**

The photo above shows Muslim men and boys worshiping at a mosque in Brunei, in Southeast Asia. **Identify** Which pillar of Islam are they fulfilling? **Analyze Information** Which one of the five pillars would it be most difficult to fulfill? Explain why.

Muslim Belief

Guided Instruction

■ **Vocabulary Builder** Clarify the high-use words **foundation** and **descendant** before reading.

■ With students, read Muslim Belief and have them study the chart. As students read, circulate to make sure they can answer the Reading Check question.

■ Have students describe some of the aspects of Muslim prayer. (*A muezzin calls Muslims to worship with the words "There is no god but God, and Muhammad is His prophet." Muslims pray five times a day, sometimes in a mosque, but always kneeling in the direction of Mecca.*)

■ Direct students' attention to the chart on this page and discuss the Five Pillars of Islam. Ask **What are they and what do they say?** (*The Five Pillars of Islam state the basic beliefs and practices of the religion. They include declaring the belief that there is only one God and Muhammad is God's messenger, praying five times a day in the direction of Mecca, giving money to the needy, fasting during the daylight hours in the month of Ramadan, and making at least one pilgrimage to Mecca if possible.*)

Background: Daily Life

Ramadan Ramadan, the ninth month on the Islamic calendar, is also one of the holiest months for Muslims. During Ramadan, Muslims recall the revealing of the Quran to Muhammad, and atone for their sins through fasting and prayer. All able adults and older children fast from sunrise to sunset, and spend extra hours praying. In the mornings, before the sun rises, Muslims eat a meal called a *suhoor.* In the evenings, Muslims break their fast with an *iftar,* or festive meal. This meal includes many courses of different kinds of food, and is usually shared with friends or family. Ramadan officially ends when the new moon is sighted. The end of Ramadan, is marked with a festival called *Id al-Fitr.* Muslims observe this three-day festival with feasting and celebration.

Answers

✓ **Reading Check** Muhammad and his followers were invited to go there by the people who regarded him as a prophet.

Chart Skills Identify prayer **Analyze Information** Answers will vary, but most students will probably identify the pilgrimage to Mecca as the most difficult of the five pillars to fulfill because it involves a long and expensive journey.

- Ask students: **What is the name of the holy book of Islam?** *(the Quran)* **How is it similar to holy books in other religions?** *(It contains many kinds of writings, including stories, promises, warnings, and instructions, similar to the Torah, or Jewish holy book, and the Christian Bible.)*

- Ask students **How did Islam change the status of women in Arab society?** *(Islam taught that men and women were spiritually equal and gave women more rights.)*

- Ask students **What caused the split in Islam after the assassination of Uthman in 656?** *(One group, the Shiites, believed that the leader of Islam should be a descendant of Muhammad and the other group, the Sunnis, believed that any truly religious Muslim could lead.)*

Independent Practice

Have students complete their outlines with details from the section.

Monitor Progress

- Show *Section Reading Support Transparency HOW 85* and ask students to check their graphic organizers individually. Go over key concepts and clarify key vocabulary as needed.

    History of Our World Transparencies, *Section Reading Support Transparency HOW 85*

- Tell students to fill in the last column of the *Reading Readiness Guide.* Probe for what they learned that confirms or invalidates each statement.

    All in One Unit 4 History of Our World Teaching Resources, *Reading Readiness Guide,* p. 12

Answer

Compare that the tradition has not changed much over time

Target Reading Skill L2

Preview and Predict As a follow up, have students perform the Target Reading Skill activity in the Student Edition. *(Answers will vary, but students should determine if their prediction is on target, and if it is not, revise it accordingly.)*

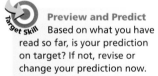

The Hajj
Muslims making a hajj to the Kaaba wear special white, seamless garments. The large photo shows a modern hajj. The small painting is from a 1410 manuscript. **Compare** *What can you conclude about this tradition by comparing the two pictures?*

Preview and Predict Based on what you have read so far, is your prediction on target? If not, revise or change your prediction now.

The Quran The holy book of Islam is called the **Quran** (koo RAHN). It contains the messages God revealed to Muhammad, including the rules of Islam. Many Muslims have memorized the Quran. Muslims believe that the meaning and beauty of the Quran are best appreciated in its original language. Therefore, many converts to Islam learn Arabic. This shared language has helped unite Muslims from many regions.

Like the Torah (TOH ruh), the Jewish holy book, and the Christian Bible, the Quran contains many kinds of writing, including stories, promises, warnings, and instructions. There is a reason for the similarity of the Quran to Jewish and Christian holy books. Muslims, like Jews and Christians, believe in one God. They regard Adam, Noah, Abraham, and Moses as important people in their religious history. Muhammad saw himself as the last prophet in a long line of prophets that included all these men. Muhammad felt respect for Jews and Christians, whom he called "people of the Book."

The Role of Women Before Islam, in most of Arab society, women were not regarded as equal to men, and female children were not valued. The Quran, however, taught that men and women were spiritually equal. It also gave women more rights under the law, such as the right to inherit property and to get an education. Muslim women could not be forced to marry against their will, and they had the right to divorce.

296 History of Our World

Differentiated Instruction

For Advanced Readers L3
Working in pairs or groups, have students use the section content to create a time line that lists important dates in Muhammad's life and in the development of Islam. Encourage students to add maps to their time lines. You may wish to display students' work in the classroom.

For Special Needs Students L1
Have students read the Key Terms and their definitions, and then find each word in the text. Ask students to note how the context, or the surrounding text, helps them to better understand each word.

A Split Among Muslims You have already read about a schism that split the Christian church at the time of the Byzantine Empire. A schism, or split, also occurred among followers of Islam.

In 656, Uthman (OOTH mahn), the leader of the Muslim community, was assassinated. His death split the Muslim world in two. Muslims disagreed over who should be their rightful leader. Over the next several decades, two main groups gradually emerged on opposite sides of this disagreement.

The smaller group, called Shiites (SHEE yts), argued that the ruler should be a man who was a direct descendant of Muhammad. They believed that Muhammad's descendants would be inspired by God, just as Muhammad had been. They felt that their leader should explain the meanings of the messages Muhammad received from God, which are found in the Quran.

The larger group, called Sunnis (SOO neez), argued that any truly religious Muslim man of Muhammad's tribe could lead the community. They believed that no one man, not even the leader of Islam, should tell Muslims what God's messages meant. The Sunnis argued that a group of Muslim scholars could best explain the Quran. Today, about 85 percent of all Muslims are Sunnis.

Illustrated manuscript pages from a 1500s Quran

✓ **Reading Check** What issues split the Shiites and Sunnis?

Section 2 Assessment

Key Terms

Review the key terms at the beginning of this section. Use each term in a sentence that explains its meaning.

Target Reading Skill

What did you predict about this section? How did your prediction guide your reading?

Comprehension and Critical Thinking

1. (a) Note What geographic feature covers most of the Arabian Peninsula?

(b) Identify Effects How did geography affect trade and settlement there?
(c) Conclude Why do you think the Bedouins became nomads?
2. (a) Recall What were the main events of Muhammad's life?
(b) Synthesize What are the main beliefs of Islam?
(c) Compare and Contrast What beliefs do Sunnis and Shiites share? Which beliefs separate them?

Writing Activity

Write a poem or a paragraph describing what it might have been like to travel in a caravan. How would it feel to ride a camel? To cross the desert? To stop for a rest at an oasis?

> **Writing Tip** Review the illustrations in this section. Then think about the sights, sounds, and smells you would expect to experience as part of caravan life. Use vivid descriptive words and phrases to describe what you see and feel.

Muhammad went back to Mecca, where he died in 632. **(b)** Muslims believe that there is one God and Muhammad is his prophet. Muslims pray five times a day in the direction of Mecca, must give money to the needy, fast during the daylight hours of the month of Ramadan, make a pilgrimage to Mecca at least once in their lives if they are able. **(c)** Both groups follow the Five Pillars. However, the Shiites believe that only a direct descendant of Muhammad's should

lead Islam, while Sunnis believe that any truly religious Muslim can lead Islam.

Writing Activity

Use the *Rubric for Assessing a Writing Assignment* to evaluate students' poems or paragraphs.

All in One **Unit 4 History of Our World Teaching Resources,** *Rubric for Assessing a Writing Assignment,* p. 33

Assess and Reteach

Assess Progress

Have students complete the Section Assessment. Administer the *Section Quiz.*

All in One **Unit 4 History of Our World Teaching Resources,** *Section Quiz,* p. 14

Reteach

If students need more instruction, have them read this section in the *Reading and Vocabulary Study Guide.*

Chapter 1, Section 2, **History of Our World Reading and Vocabulary Study Guide,** pp. 111–113

Extend

To learn more about Islamic art, have students complete the *Enrichment* activity.

All in One **Unit 4 History of Our World Teaching Resources,** *Enrichment,* p. 23

Answer

✓ **Reading Check** After the assassination of Uthman, the Shiites wanted the new leader to be a direct descendant of Muhammad. Another group, who became the Sunnis, thought any truly religious Muslim could lead Islam.

Section 2 Assessment

Key Terms

Students' sentences should reflect an understanding of each Key Term.

Target Reading Skill

Answers will vary, but students should indicate what they predicted about the section and how their prediction helped guide their reading.

Comprehension and Critical Thinking

1. (a) desert **(b)** Most of the population was settled along the coast. One group of nomads, called the Bedouins, lived in the desert areas, herding animals and leading trade caravans. Desert oases also developed into trade centers. **(c)** Possible answer: Because they herded animals, the Bedouins had to search constantly for enough food and water for their herds.

2. (a) He was born in about 570 in Mecca. At age 40 he believed he heard God speak to him and began to preach God's message. In 622, Muhammad and his followers moved to the city that is now called Medina. In 630,

Focus on Bedouin Life

Guided Instruction

- Ask students to read the text and study the art, photos, and captions on these pages.

- Ask students **What animals were important to the Bedouins and how were they used?** (*Camels provided transportation, milk, meat, hides and camel dung provided fuel for fires; the hair from goats was used to make tent panels, and goatskin was used to make bags to carry water.*)

- Have students describe some of the different responsibilities of Bedouin women and men. (*Women were responsible for making the tents and putting them up and taking them down at campsites; men herded camels and other livestock.*)

- As a class, answer the Assessment questions. Allow students to briefly discuss their responses with a partner before sharing their answers with the class.

Focus On
Bedouin Life

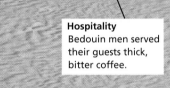

The air is hot and dry. A blinding, bright sun scorches the sand. At times, a screaming wind sweeps across the land, blowing clouds of sand that block the sun. These are the desert lands of the Arabian Peninsula. By the time of the prophet Muhammad in the A.D. 600s, the Bedouins of Arabia had been thriving in the desert for hundreds of years. These nomadic peoples lived in tents and moved camp frequently in their search for water. Some of their descendants still live in the desert today.

Surviving in the Desert The ancient Bedouins depended upon the desert, the camel, their fellow tribe members, and the family tent. Plants gathered from the desert were used for food and medicine. Camels provided transportation, as well as milk, meat, and hides. Family members worked together to search for water and to herd their camels, goats, and sheep. The family tent sheltered the Bedouins in the harsh desert climate.

Women were responsible for the tents. They spun goats' hair into yarn to make the tent panels. When it was time to move their camp, the women took down the tents and then pitched them at the new campsite.

It was the men's job to herd camels and other livestock. Sometimes Bedouin men would raid villages or other tribes for goats, sheep, camels, and other goods.

The illustration at the right shows a Bedouin family in their tent. Bedouin women created jewelry, like the necklace shown at the top of this page.

Hospitality
Bedouin men served their guests thick, bitter coffee.

Goatskin Bag
Bags made from goatskin carried precious water.

Differentiated Instruction

For Gifted and Talented   L3

Have students learn more about the way Bedouins live in the desert by completing the *Long Term Integrated Project: Building Models of Housing Around the World*. Assign students to work in groups for the project.

Go Online
PHSchool.com

For: Long Term Integrated Project: *Building Models of Housing Around the World*
Visit: PHSchool.com
Web Code: lgd-8104

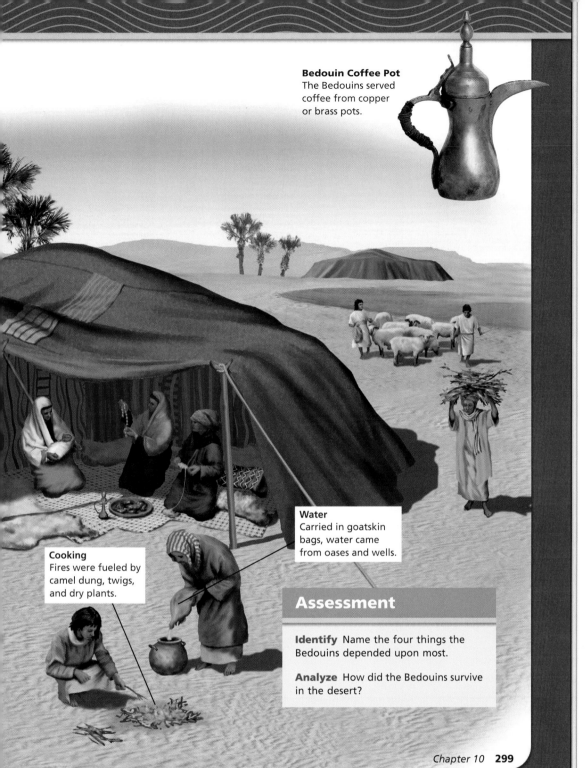

Bedouin Coffee Pot
The Bedouins served coffee from copper or brass pots.

Cooking
Fires were fueled by camel dung, twigs, and dry plants.

Water
Carried in goatskin bags, water came from oases and wells.

Assessment

Identify Name the four things the Bedouins depended upon most.

Analyze How did the Bedouins survive in the desert?

Independent Practice

Tell students to suppose they are a Bedouin boy or girl living in the desert of the Arabian Peninsula. Using the information from the text, art, photos, and captions on these pages, have students write a journal entry, describing what a typical day would be like. Tell students that they may also add drawings to their entries if they wish.

Answers

Assessment

Identify the desert, the camel, their fellow tribe members, the family tent
Analyze They gathered plants to use for food and medicine, raised camels, sheep and goats for a variety of uses, used tents to shelter them from the harsh climate, and obtained water from oases and wells.

Objectives

Social Studies

1. Find out how the religion of Islam spread.
2. Learn about the golden age of Islam under the rule of the caliphs.
3. Discover the achievements of Islamic culture.

Reading/Language Arts

Preview and ask questions to help understand or remember important parts of the text.

Prepare to Read

Build Background Knowledge L2

Explain that in this section students will learn about the development of Islam and the golden age of its culture. Ask students to quickly preview the headings and visuals in the section with this question in mind: **What aspects of a culture contribute to a "golden age?"** Draw a concept web on the board with "Golden Age" in the center. Conduct an Idea Wave (TE, p. T39) to generate ideas or words related to that term to fill in the concept web. Examples might include works of art or advances in science.

Set a Purpose for Reading L2

■ Preview the Objectives.

■ Read each statement in the *Reading Readiness Guide* aloud. Ask students to mark the statements true or false.

> **All in One Unit 4 History of Our World Teaching Resources**, *Reading Readiness Guide*, p. 16

■ Have students discuss the statements in pairs or groups of four, then mark their worksheets again. Use the Numbered Heads participation strategy (TE, p. T40) to call on students to share their group's perspectives.

Vocabulary Builder
Preview Key Terms L2

Pronounce the Key Terms, and then ask students to say the words with you. Provide a simple explanation such as, "A caliph was a Muslim ruler, similar to a king."

Prepare to Read

Objectives

In this section you will

1. Find out how the religion of Islam spread.
2. Learn about the golden age of Islam under the rule of the caliphs.

Taking Notes

As you read this section, jot down key events of early Muslim history and when they occurred. Copy the timeline below and use your data to complete it.

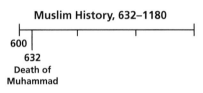

Muslim History, 632–1180

600 |
632
Death of Muhammad

🎯 Target Reading Skill

Preview and Ask Questions Before you read this section, preview the headings and illustrations to see what the section is about. Then write two questions that will help you understand or remember something important in the section. For example, you might ask, "How did Islam spread beyond the Arabian Peninsula?" Then read to answer your question.

Key Terms

- **Omar Khayyam** (OH mahr ky AHM) *n.* a Muslim poet, mathematician, and astronomer
- **caliph** (KAY lif) *n.* a Muslim ruler
- **Sufis** (SOO feez) *n.* a mystical Muslim group that believed they could draw closer to God through prayer, fasting, and a simple life

The cover of a book of verses by Omar Khayyam

Almost one thousand years ago, Persia boasted great scientists, mathematicians, and poets. One man was all three. **Omar Khayyam** (OH mahr ky AHM) was a skilled Muslim astronomer, one of the most famous mathematicians in the world, and a great poet. The poems he wrote in the Persian language are still read today. This is one of his poems:

> ❝When I was a child, I sometimes went to a teacher.
> And sometimes I taught myself, but eventually I learned
> The limits to all knowledge: we come into this world upon
> the waters, we leave it on the wind. ❞
>
> —Omar Khayyam

Although Khayyam writes of limits to knowledge, his was a time when mathematics, science, and poetry were all making new breakthroughs and expanding the boundaries of knowledge. It was called the golden age of Muslim civilization, and it took place across a wide geographic area.

300 History of Our World

🎯 Target Reading Skill L2

Preview and Ask Questions Point out the Target Reading Skill. Tell students that previewing and asking questions about the text they are about to read will help them see what the section is about and understand and remember important ideas in the text.

Model previewing and asking questions using the text on pp. 302–304 under the heading The Golden Age. Think aloud: "Previewing the subheadings, photographs, and captions tell me that the text is about the golden age of Muslim culture. Two questions I can ask are: What was the golden age of Muslim culture? What were some Arab contributions to mathematics and science? I will read the text to answer these questions."

Give students *Preview and Ask Questions*. Have them complete the activity in their groups.

> **All in One Unit 4 History of Our World Teaching Resources**, *Preview and Ask Questions*, p. 21

The Spread of Islam

Within 150 years after Muhammad's death in 632, Islam spread west to North Africa, and into present-day Spain. It also spread north into Persia and east to the borders of northern India and China.

Many New Converts Arab merchants traveled to many parts of Asia and North Africa and along the Mediterranean coast. Many of these traders were Muslims, and they helped to spread their new religious beliefs. Arab armies also conquered neighboring regions. This was another way that Islam spread.

In 717, the Arabs attacked Constantinople, but they were unable to take the great fortress. Even so, most Christians who lived along the eastern and southern Mediterranean converted to Islam in the 700s and 800s. By the 700s, Muslims had also crossed from North Africa into Spain. In 732, Arab forces were defeated by European soldiers at the Battle of Tours, in present-day France. This battle halted the Muslim advance into Christian Europe.

The Battle of Tours

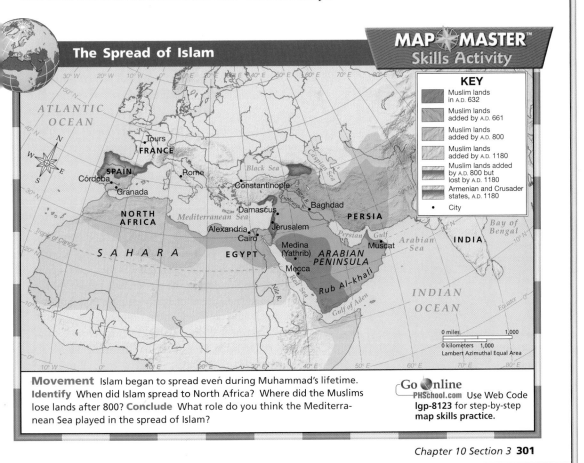

The Spread of Islam

MAP MASTER™ Skills Activity

KEY
- Muslim lands in A.D. 632
- Muslim lands added by A.D. 661
- Muslim lands added by A.D. 800
- Muslim lands added by A.D. 1180
- Muslim lands added by A.D. 800 but lost by A.D. 1180
- Armenian and Crusader states, A.D. 1180
- • City

Movement Islam began to spread even during Muhammad's lifetime. **Identify** When did Islam spread to North Africa? Where did the Muslims lose lands after 800? **Conclude** What role do you think the Mediterranean Sea played in the spread of Islam?

Go Online PHSchool.com Use Web Code lgp-8123 for step-by-step map skills practice.

0 miles 1,000
0 kilometers 1,000
Lambert Azimuthal Equal Area

Chapter 10 Section 3 **301**

Vocabulary Builder

Use the information below to teach students this section's high-use words.

High-Use Word	Definition and Sample Sentence
advance, p. 301	*n.* a movement forward The invention of computers formed a major **advance** in technology.
tolerate, p. 302	*v.* to allow My grandmother **tolerated** my drum playing, even though she did not like it.
prosperity, p. 303	*n.* wealth; success The wealthy king's followers enjoyed a time of great **prosperity.**
scholar, p. 303	*n.* learned person Professor Jones' knowledge of history made him a great **scholar** in his field.

Instruct

The Spread of Islam L2

Guided Instruction

- **Vocabulary Builder** Clarify the high-use words **advance** and **tolerate** before reading.

- Read The Spread of Islam using the ReQuest Procedure (TE, p. T39).

- Ask students **Where did Islam spread after Muhammad's death?** *(west to North Africa and then to present-day Spain; north into Persia; east to northern India and China)* **How did this religion gain converts so quickly?** *(Muslim merchants traveled great distances, bringing Islamic ideas with them. Islam was also spread through Arab conquests of neighboring regions.)*

- Ask students **What was significant about the Battle of Tours?** *(European Christians defeated Arab Muslims, which stopped the advance of Islam into Europe, beyond Spain.)*

- Discuss with students how Arab Muslims were able to grow so powerful. *(Possible answer: Islam had united and organized the Arab peoples. Also, Islamic leaders were tolerant of other religions in their territories. After they conquered an area, there was not much resistance since people were not forced to give up their own religions.)*

Independent Practice

Have students create the Taking Notes graphic organizer on a blank sheet of paper. Then have them fill in the time line with details they learn as they read. Briefly model how to add details using *Transparency B20: Timeline.*

📖 **History of Our World Transparencies,** *Transparency B20: Timeline*

Monitor Progress

As students fill in the timeline, circulate and make sure that individuals are placing events in chronological order. Provide assistance as necessary.

Answers

MAP MASTER Skills Activity **Identify** by A.D. 662; Spain and Syria **Conclude** Possible answer: It provided a method of transportation for reaching other areas such as Europe and North Africa.

Go Online PHSchool.com Students may practice their map skills using the interactive online version of this map.

Preview and Ask Questions As a follow up, ask students to perform the Target Reading Skill activity in the Student Edition. *(Answers will vary, but students should ask a question, and then read the paragraph to answer their question.)*

The Golden Age L2

Guided Instruction

■ **Vocabulary Builder** Clarify the high-use words **prosperity** and **scholar** before reading.

■ With students, read about some of the important Arab contributions to math and science during the rule of the caliphs in The Golden Age. As they read, circulate and make sure individuals can answer the Reading Check question.

■ Ask students **Who were the caliphs?** *(a series of Muslim rulers who were Muhammad's successors)* **Why did a golden age of Islamic culture develop under their rule?** *(Under their rule, an empire developed and grew rich from trade. Traders from many parts of the world brought goods to the caliph's court at Baghdad. The caliphs were supporters of the arts.)*

■ Ask students **How did the work of Arab mathematicians influence later scientists?** *(It enabled later scientists to make discoveries in astronomy, physics, and chemistry.)*

Answers

✓ **Reading Check** Muslim rulers tolerated other faiths, while Byzantine rulers did not.

Infer He was very wealthy and wanted to impress Charlemagne.

Preview and Ask Questions Ask a question that will help you learn something important from the paragraph at the right. Now read the paragraph, and answer your question.

Reasons for Success In the centuries before Muhammad, Arab peoples had not been able to conquer neighboring regions. The strong Roman Empire made invasions of these lands nearly impossible. And the later Byzantine and Persian empires successfully blocked Arabs from advancing north. So why were the Muslims successful after Muhammad's death?

By that time, the three empires that might have stopped the Arab expansion north and east were either defeated or weakened. Also, a shared religion now united the Arab peoples into one community. And once they began to work together, the Muslims quickly grew powerful.

Under Muslim Rule Unlike Byzantine leaders of the time—who did not accept different religions—Muslims tolerated other faiths. Muslim rulers allowed Christians and Jews to practice their own religions and pursue their own business affairs. Non-Muslim citizens did have fewer rights than Muslims, however. For example, they were forbidden to carry weapons and could not serve in the military. They also paid a special tax, which helped support the government.

✓ **Reading Check** Compare Muslim rulers and Byzantine rulers.

A Royal Gift
The caliph Harun ar-Rashid presented this water jug to Charlemagne, the ruler of a Christian empire in Europe. He hoped to form an alliance with Charlemagne. **Infer** *What can you infer about Harun from this gift?*

302 History of Our World

The Golden Age

The golden age of Muslim culture from about 800 to 1100 was a brilliant period of history. Great advances were made in mathematics and science, and lasting works of literature and architecture were created. Why did so much happen at that time?

The Age of the Caliphs One reason was the great wealth of the Arab world. Under Muslim rulers called **caliphs** (KAY lifs), an empire developed and grew rich. Its wealth came both from the many lands it controlled and from trade. Baghdad was the capital of the Muslim empire during the golden age. Find it on the map titled The Spread of Islam on page 301. You can see that Baghdad, like Constantinople, was a natural center for trade. With your finger, trace a route from India to Baghdad. Now trace a route from the Mediterranean Sea to Baghdad. Traders from all over the world brought their goods to the caliph's court. The caliph was considered to be Muhammad's successor, or the next person who had the right to rule.

Differentiated Instruction

For Gifted and Talented L3
Show students *Transparency HOW Set 2: Spread of Islam*. Have them work in small groups to answer the following questions: Where did the Muslim Empire begin? *(Arabia)* Where did it spread? *(Europe, Africa, and other parts of Asia)* During which period did it spread into Western Europe? *(under the Umayyad caliphs, 661–750)*

Describe the area that became part of the Muslim empire under the first four caliphs. *(much of Southwest Asia, including part of Persia, and the northern part of Egypt)*

📖 **Unit 4 History of Our World,** *Transparency HOW Set 2: Spread of Islam*

Harun ar-Rashid: A Powerful Caliph

Harun ar-Rashid (hah ROON ar rah SHEED) became caliph of Baghdad in 786. His rule was a time of prosperity. For 23 years, Harun ruled the world's most glamorous court. He and his favorite subjects ate off gold plates and drank from goblets studded with jewels.

Harun did not use the riches of Baghdad just for his own pleasure. He was also a great patron, or supporter, of the arts. Harun paid many skilled writers, musicians, dancers, and artists to live in Baghdad. And he lavishly rewarded those whose works pleased him. One musician is said to have received a gift of 100,000 silver pieces for a single song.

Achievements of the Golden Age

Arab scholars not only created new works but also studied history and ideas from other cultures. One scholar wrote,

> ❝We should not be ashamed to acknowledge truth from whatever source it comes to us, even if it is brought to us by former generations and foreign peoples. ❞
>
> —al-Kindi

This approach led Muslim scholars to make great advances in mathematics, in science, and in literature.

Mathematics and Science

Arab scholars studied both Greek and Indian mathematics. They learned about the idea of zero from Indian scholars. And they borrowed the use of the so-called Arabic numerals that we use today from India, too. The Muslim mathematician al-Khwarizme (al KWAHR iz mee) wrote a book explaining Indian arithmetic. He also made significant contributions to the development of algebra. The word *algebra* comes from the Arabic word "al-jabr." These contributions enabled later scientists to make great discoveries in astronomy, physics, and chemistry.

The famous Islamic scientist and philosopher Ibn Sina (IB un SEE nah) lived from 980 to 1037. Also known as Avicenna (ahv ih SEN uh), he organized the medical knowledge of the Greeks and Arabs into the *Canon of Medicine*.

Arab Contributions to Mathematics and Science

Medicine
The Arabs were the first to organize separate pharmacies, which sold spices, herbs, and other medicines to the public.

Mathematics
Arab mathematicians made important contributions to algebra. They studied formulas like this one. It explains how to find the length of one side of a right triangle when you know the length of the other sides.

Machines
Water-driven machines fascinated Arab scientists. Here, water falling into the cups causes the globe at the top to turn.

Guided Instruction (continued)

- Ask students **Who were the Sufis?** *(a group of Muslim poets who used poetry to teach ideas and beliefs)* **What did they teach?** *(They taught that prayer, fasting, and a simple life would draw people closer to God.)*

- Ask students **How do you think Muslim attitudes contributed to the achievements of the Golden Age?** *(Answers will vary, but should include that Muslims, unlike Byzantines, tolerated other faiths and allowed people to practice their own religions and pursue their own affairs; Arab scholars were also free to study ideas from past history and other cultures.)*

Independent Practice

Have students complete their graphic organizers with dates and details from the section.

Monitor Progress

- Show *Section Reading Support Transparency HOW 86*, and ask students to check their work individually. Go over key concepts and clarify key vocabulary as needed.

  📖 **Unit 4 History of Our World,** *Section Reading Support Transparency HOW 86*

- Tell students to fill in the last column of the *Reading Readiness Guide*. Probe for what they learned that confirms or invalidates each statement.

  All in One **Unit 4 History of Our World Teaching Resources,** *Reading Readiness Guide,* p. 16

Differentiated Instruction

For Special Needs Students　L1

Have students read the section as they listen to the recording on the Student Edition on Audio CD. Check for comprehension by pausing the CD and asking students to share their answers to the Reading Check questions.

🔘 Chapter 1, Section 3, **Student Edition on Audio CD**

Have students read **Links Across the World.** Ask **Why do you think Maimonides felt it was important to write a book about the laws of Judaism?** (*Possible answer: Because he lived in a Muslim-controlled land, he might have felt it was important to explain the laws of his own religion.*)

Assess and Reteach

Assess Progress   L2

Have students complete the Section Assessment. Then administer the *Section Quiz.*

All in One Unit 4 History of Our World Teaching Resources, *Section Quiz,* p. 18

Reteach   L1

If students need more instruction, have them read this section in the *Reading and Vocabulary Study Guide.*

Chapter 1, Section 3, **History of Our World, Reading and Vocabulary Study Guide,** pp. 114–116

Extend   L3

To learn more about the wealth and possessions of Harun ar-Rashid, have students read *The King's Wealth* and then answer the questions that follow.

All in One Unit 4 History of Our World Teaching Resources, *The King's Wealth,* pp. 30–31

Answer

√ **Reading Check** They taught that the world will reveal its mysteries to careful observers, and that people could get closer to God through prayer, fasting, and a simple life.

Section 3 Assessment

Key Terms

Students' sentences should reflect an understanding of each Key Term.

Target Reading Skill

Answers will vary, but students should identify which questions helped them and what the answers to their questions were.

Comprehension and Critical Thinking

1. (a) through trade and conquest **(b)** Possible answer: All of Europe might be Muslim or under Muslim control and Europeans might also speak and write Arabic.

304 *History of Our World*

Explorations of Faith Moses Maimonides (my MAHN uh deez) was a Jewish scholar, doctor, and philosopher. He lived in the Muslim-controlled lands of Spain, North Africa, and Southwest Asia. In 1180, he completed *The Torah Reviewed,* which classified and explained all the laws of Judaism. His *Guide for the Perplexed,* written in Arabic, tried to resolve reason and faith by exploring how people could believe in both science and religion at the same time. The Latin translation of the *Guide* influenced the Christian writers of the Scholastic movement of medieval Europe.

Literature Muslim writers created many lasting works of literature. Poetry was particularly important in the Islamic world. Poets were treated as popular musicians are today. One group of Muslims used poetry to teach their ideas and beliefs.

This group, called the **Sufis** (soo feez), were mystics who believed that they could draw close to God through prayer, fasting, and a simple life. They taught that the world will reveal its mysteries to careful observers. Sufi missionaries also helped spread Islam to Central Asia, India, and Africa south of the Sahara.

The most famous Sufi poet, Rumi (ROO mee), founded a religious group known to Europeans as the Whirling Dervishes. This group used music and dance to communicate with God. Rumi composed these verses:

> **"Never think the earth [empty] or dead—**
> **It's a hare, awake with shut eyes:**
> **It's a saucepan, simmering with broth—**
> **One clear look, you'll see it's in [motion]. "**
>
> —*Rumi*

√ **Reading Check** **What did the Sufis teach?**

Section 3 Assessment

Key Terms

Review the key terms at the beginning of this section. Use each term in a sentence that explains its meaning.

Target Reading Skill

What questions helped you learn something important from this section? What are the answers to your questions?

Comprehension and Critical Thinking

1. (a) Recall Describe the two main ways that Islam spread beyond the Arabian Peninsula.

(b) Predict How might the culture of Europe be different today if the Arabs had won the Battle of Tours in 732?

2. (a) Locate Where is Baghdad located?

(b) Synthesize Information What made it a good choice for the capital of an empire?

(c) Generalize How do geography and trade contribute to a city's prosperity and power?

3. (a) Identify Name three Arab contributions to mathematics and science.

(b) Analyze How do these contributions combine borrowed knowledge and new ideas?

Writing Activity

Write a newspaper editorial either for or against the use of government money to support the arts. Use Harun ar-Rashid as one example in your argument. Begin with a statement of your position and then support it with reasons and facts.

For: An activity on Islam's golden age
Visit: PHSchool.com
Web Code: lgd-8103

304 History of Our World

---

2. (a) on the Tigris River **(b)** It was located at a major trade route crossroads. **(c)** Possible answer: A city can make money from duties or other taxes on trade goods or tolls. Trade routes bring in diverse people and new ideas, which enriches a city's culture.

3. (a) Possible answers: algebra, the "Canon of Medicine," the use of hospitals and pharmacies **(b)** Arab mathematicians and scientists expanded on existing ideas, such as Greek medical knowledge and the existing concept of zero.

Writing Activity

Use the *Rubric for Assessing a Newspaper Article* to evaluate students' editorials.

All in One Unit 4 History of Our World Teaching Resources, *Rubric for Assessing a Newspaper Article,* p. 34

Go Online PHSchool.com Typing in the Web code when prompted will bring students directly to detailed instructions for this activity.

 **10** Review and Assessment

◆ Chapter Summary

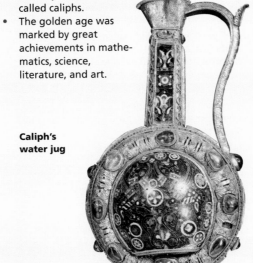

Justinian

Section 1: The Byzantine Empire

- The Roman emperor Constantine established a new capital in the eastern part of the Roman Empire. Later, Constantinople became the capital of the rich and powerful Byzantine Empire.
- Justinian, one of the greatest Byzantine emperors, organized a system of laws called Justinian's code.
- After Justinian's death, the Byzantine Empire shrank in size and power. It later enjoyed a second golden age. A schism split the Christian church into eastern and western branches.

Section 2: The Beginnings of Islam

- Although much of the Arabian Peninsula is covered by desert, important cities, such as Mecca, grew up on trade routes.
- The Muslim prophet Muhammad preached in Mecca and Medina. His teachings became the religion of Islam.
- The Five Pillars of Islam and the Quran are the basis of Muslim beliefs. A dispute among Muslims led to the split between Shiites and Sunnis.

Section 3: The Golden Age of Muslim Civilization

- After the death of Muhammad, the religion of Islam spread to many neighboring regions by both trade and conquest.
- The golden age of Islam occurred under wealthy Muslim rulers called caliphs.
- The golden age was marked by great achievements in mathematics, science, literature, and art.

Caliph's water jug

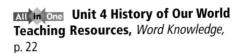

◆ Key Terms

Match each key term with its definition from the list at the right.

1. mosque
2. Constantine
3. nomads
4. caliph
5. Justinian
6. caravan
7. schism
8. Omar Khayyam

A a Muslim ruler
B a group of traders traveling together for safety
C emperor of the Byzantine Empire
D emperor of the Roman Empire
E Muslim house of worship
F a Muslim astronomer, mathematician, and poet
G people with no permanent home, who move from place to place
H a split, particularly in a church or religion

Vocabulary Builder

High-Use Academic Words

Revisit this chapter's high-use words:

reign   abandon   tolerate
imperial   foundation   prosperity
distinct   descendant   scholar
regain   advance

Ask students to review the definitions they recorded on their *Word Knowledge* worksheets.

AlL in One Unit 4 History of Our World Teaching Resources, *Word Knowledge*, p. 22

Consider allowing students to earn extra credit if they use the words in their answers to the questions in the Chapter Review and Assessment. The words must be used correctly and in a natural context to win the extra points.

Review Chapter Content

- Review and revisit the major themes of this chapter by asking students to classify what Guiding Question each bulleted statement in the Chapter Summary answers. Form students into groups and ask them to complete the activity together. Refer to page 1 in the Student Edition for the text of the Guiding Questions.

- Assign *Vocabulary Development* for students to review Key Terms.

  AlL in One Unit 4 History of Our World Teaching Resources, *Vocabulary Development,* p. 32

Answers

Key Terms

1. E
2. D
3. G
4. A
5. C
6. B
7. H
8. F

Review and Assessment

Comprehension and Critical Thinking

9. (a) the eastern end **(b)** Because it was at a major crossroads of trade, it was constantly filled with diverse people, goods, and ideas, and it grew very rich. **(c)** It had the strongest army in the world and was a major center for trade.

10. (a) an organized collection and explanation of Roman laws for use by the Byzantine Empire **(b)** It helped people make sense of the laws and allowed the government to enforce them.

11. (a) when he went into a cave in the Arabian mountains to pray **(b)** Possible answer: he believed that he had been commanded by God to share his message with all people, even if some did not listen.

12. (a) holy books, the belief in one God, and many of the same important figures in their religious history **(b)** After the assassination of Uthman in 656, one group, the Shiites, believed that the leader of Islam should be a descendant of Muhammad and the other group, the Sunnis, believed that any truly religious Muslim could lead.

13. (a) in Baghdad, from about 800 to 1100 **(b)** These years produced a wealth of mathematical and scientific knowledge, inventions, and literature that were extremely valuable. It could be said that these contributions were as valuable as gold, an expensive metal.

Skills Practice

Students' paragraphs will vary, but should include a conclusion and supporting details from the table The Five Pillars of Islam on page 295.

Writing Activity: Language and Arts

Students' monologues will vary, but should be written from the point of view of one of the rulers in this chapter, and should include information about that person's life or an important event.

Use *Rubric for Assessing a Writing Assignment* to evaluate students' monologues.

All in One Unit 4 History of Our World Teaching Resources, *Rubric for Assessing a Writing Assignment,* p. 33

Review and Assessment (continued)

◆ Comprehension and Critical Thinking

9. (a) Recall In what part of the old Roman Empire was Constantinople located?
(b) Identify Cause and Effect How did Constantinople's location affect the culture that developed there?
(c) Compare and Contrast What enabled the eastern part of the Roman Empire to survive after the western Roman Empire "fell"?

10. (a) Define What was Justinian's Code?
(b) Infer How did Justinian's Code help make the Byzantine Empire strong and successful?

11. (a) Describe How did Muhammad first receive God's message?
(b) Infer Why do you think Muhammad did not give up preaching when few people listened?

12. (a) Recall What do Muslims, Jews, and Christians have in common?
(b) Contrast How do the beliefs of Sunni and Shiite Muslims differ?

13. (a) Recall When and where did the golden age of Muslim civilization occur?
(b) Synthesize Explain in your own words why these years are called a golden age.

◆ Skills Practice

Using a Table to Write a Paragraph In the Skills for Life activity in this chapter, you learned how to use the data in a table to write a paragraph. Review the steps you followed to learn the skill.

Now review the table The Five Pillars of Islam on page 295. Use the data in the table to draw a conclusion about the topic. Write a paragraph that states your conclusion and that uses data from the table as supporting details.

◆ Writing Activity: Language Arts

A monologue is a speech by one person. In drama, a monologue is spoken directly to the audience. Choose one of the rulers you have read about in this chapter. Write a monologue that this ruler might speak in a theatrical performance. It can be about the person's whole life or about one important event. Do further research on the ruler if you wish. You may want to perform your monologue for your class.

MAP MASTER™ Skills Activity

The Byzantine Empire and the Spread of Islam

Place Location For each place or feature listed below, write the letter from the map that shows its location.
1. Rome
2. Mecca
3. Constantinople
4. Mediterranean Sea
5. Bosporus
6. Baghdad
7. Arabian Peninsula

Go Online PHSchool.com Use Web Code lgp-8133 for an interactive map.

Standardized Test Prep

Test-Taking Tips

Some questions on standardized tests ask you to evaluate a source for a research assignment. Read the passage below. Then use the tip to help you answer the sample question.

> Vera is writing a research paper about Justinian's Code. At the school library, she found four books that she might use.

Think It Through Even if you don't know about Justinian's Code, you can eliminate A because it is fiction—an invented story. You can also rule out C because it is about a merchant's travels, not about Justinian's Code. That leaves B and D. Justinian's Code refers to laws, not to copying Roman and Greek books. The correct answer is B.

Pick the letter that best answers the question.

Which one of the following books would be best for Vera's topic?

A ~~Justinian's Bride—a novel about the Empress Theodora~~

B *The Birth of Law*—a nonfiction book about the Byzantine legal system

C ~~The Journal of Ignatius—a firsthand account of a merchant's travels during the time of Justinian~~

D *The Rescue of Knowledge*—the story of how Byzantine scholars copied and cared for books of ancient Rome and Greece

TIP Rule out choices that don't make sense. Then choose the best answer from the remaining choices.

Practice Questions

Use the tip above and other tips in this book to help you answer the following questions.

1. Miguel's history class has been studying the Byzantine Empire. Miguel has decided to write a research paper about the empire's capital, Constantinople. He would like to find out the population of Constantinople at the time of Justinian's rule.

   Which one of the following would be the best choice for this information?

   A *An Atlas of Modern Turkey*—a nonfiction book that includes maps and factual data

   B *Our Trip to Istanbul*—a new Web site that tells about a family's vacation to the city formerly called Constantinople

   C *An Atlas of the Ancient World*—a nonfiction book that includes historical maps and other historical data

   D *Population Growth of Major U.S. Cities*—a nonfiction book that includes charts and maps

Pick the letter of the word or phrase that best completes each sentence.

2. Muslims are called to worship _____.

   A once a day   **B** four times a month

   C five times a day   **D** once a year

3. Constantine was the first _____ to rule the Roman Empire.

   A Muslim   **B** Jew

   C Sufi   **D** Christian

4. The _____ links the Black Sea and the Sea of Marmara, which flows into the Mediterranean Sea.

   A Bosporus   **B** Arabian Peninsula

   C Mecca   **D** hijra

Use Web Code lga-8103 for a **Chapter 10 self-test.**

MAP★MASTER
Skills Activity

1. B   **2.** E
3. C   **4.** A
5. G   **6.** D
7. F

Go Online *PHSchool.com* Students may practice their map skills using the interactive online version of this map.

Standardized Test Prep

Answers

1. C

2. C

3. D

4. A

Go Online *PHSchool.com* Students may use the Chapter 10 self-test on PHSchool.com to prepare for the Chapter Test.

⌐ Assessment Resources

Use *Chapter Tests A and B* to assess students' mastery of the chapter content.

All in One **Unit 4 History of Our World Teaching Resources,** *Chapter Tests A and B,* pp. 35–40

Tests are also available on the **ExamView**® **Test Bank CD-ROM.**

◉ **ExamView® Test Bank CD-ROM**

Overview

 1 **Africa and the Bantu**
1. Learn about the physical geography of Africa.
2. Find out about the Bantu and their movement across the continent.

Section 1

 2 **Kingdoms of West Africa**
1. Learn about the trading kingdoms of the West African savanna.
2. Investigate the kingdoms of the West African rain forests.

Section 2

 3 **East Africa's Great Trading Centers**
1. Learn about powerful East African civilizations whose cities included Aksum and Lalibela.
2. Find out why the coastal cities of East Africa were important.

Section 3

Great Zimbabwe: The Lost City
Length: 3 minutes, 30 seconds
Use with Section 3
This segment describes how cattle trade brought wealth to Great Zimbabwe, and gives possible reasons for the kingdom's decline. The segment also explores the ruins of the monument the Great Enclosure.

 **Technology Resources**

Students use embedded Web codes to access Internet activities, chapter self-tests, and additional map practice. They may also access Dorling Kindersley's Online Desk Reference to learn more about each country they study.

Use the Interactive Textbook to make content and concepts come alive through animations, videos, and activities that accompany the complete basal text—online and on CD-ROM.

Use this complete suite of powerful teaching tools to make planning lessons and administering tests quicker and easier.

Reading and Assessment

Reading and Vocabulary Instruction

⏩ Model the Target Reading Skill

Clarifying Meaning When rereading and reading ahead, students look within the text for the meaning of unfamiliar words and terms. Paraphrasing helps students restate ideas in words they better understand and remember. When summarizing, students state the main points of the passage. Model techniques for clarifying meaning by thinking aloud about this selection from page 315:

As the Bantu migrated, they also carried a knowledge of metalworking with them. Iron tools gave the Bantu more control over their environment than older cultures had. With strong axes, they could cut down trees and clear the land. Their sharp, iron-headed spears and arrows were powerful weapons for hunting and for warfare.

The first sentence mentions metalworking. I'm not sure what that means. By reading ahead, I see that the next sentence clarifies the meaning. Metalworking is the creation of iron tools. I will restate the first two sentences and summarize the passage to make sure I remember the information: *As they traveled from place to place, the Bantu had an advantage over older cultures because they used iron tools to clear land, to hunt, and to control other tribes.*

Use the following worksheets from All-in-One Unit 4 History of Our World Teaching Resources (pp. 56, 57, and 58) to support the chapter's Target Reading Skill.

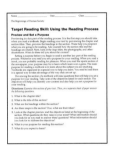

Vocabulary Builder
High-Use Academic Words

Use these steps to teach this chapter's high-use words:

1. Have students rate how well they know each word on their Word Knowledge worksheets (All-in-One Unit 4 History of Our World Teaching Resources, p. 59).

2. Pronounce each word and ask students to repeat it.

3. Give students a brief definition or sample sentence (provided on TE pp. 311, 319, and 327).

4. Work with students as they fill in the "Definition or Example" column of their Word Knowledge worksheets.

Assessment

Formal Assessment

Test students' understanding of core knowledge and skills.

Chapter Tests A and B, All-in-One History of Our World Teaching Resources, pp. 73–78

Customize the Chapter Tests to suit your needs.
Exam*View*® Test Bank CD-ROM

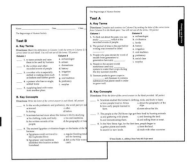

Skills Assessment

Assess geographic literacy.
MapMaster Skills, Student Edition pp. 309, 311, 313, and 332

Assess reading and comprehension.
Target Reading Skills, Student Edition, pp. 312, 320, 329 and in Section Assessments

Chapter 11 Assessment, History of Our World Reading and Vocabulary Study Guide, p. 127

Performance Assessment

Assess students' performance on this chapter's Writing Activities using the following rubrics from All-in-One Unit 4 History of Our World Teaching Resources.

Rubric for Assessing a Writing Assignment, p. 71
Rubric for Assessing a Report, p. 72

Assess students' work through performance tasks.

Small Group Activity: Simulation: Trading Items With Silent Barter, All-in-One History of Our World Teaching Resources, pp. 62–65

Online Assessment

Have students check their own understanding.

Chapter Self-Test

Section 1 Africa and the Bantu

 2 periods, 1 block (includes Skills for Life)

Social Studies Objectives
1. Learn about the physical geography of Africa.
2. Find out about the Bantu and their movement across the continent.

Reading/Language Arts Objective
Reread and read ahead to find connections among words and sentences and to clarify unfamiliar words and ideas.

Prepare to Read	Instructional Resources	Differentiated Instruction
Build Background Knowledge Ask students to think about how geography affects travel. **Set a Purpose for Reading** Have students evaluate statements on the Reading Readiness Guide. **Preview Key Terms** Teach the section's Key Terms. **Target Reading Skill** Introduce the section's Target Reading Skill of **rereading or reading ahead.**	**All in One Unit 4 History of Our World Teaching Resources** **L2** Reading Readiness Guide, p. 45 **L2** Reread or Read Ahead, p. 56	**Spanish Reading and Vocabulary Study Guide** **L1** Chapter 11, Section 1, pp. 85–86 ELL

Instruct	Instructional Resources	Differentiated Instruction
Africa's Physical Geography Discuss Africa's tropical rain forests and savannas. **Target Reading Skill** Review **rereading or reading ahead.** **The Bantu Migrations** Discuss how scientists have researched sub-Saharan Africa and ask about their discoveries. Ask questions about the Bantu people.	**All in One Unit 4 History of Our World Teaching Resources** **L2** Guided Reading and Review, p. 46 **L2** Reading Readiness Guide, p. 45 **History of Our World Transparencies** **L2** Section Reading Support Transparency HOW 87	**All in One Unit 4 History of Our World Teaching Resources** **L1** Reading a Historical Map, p. 66 ELL, LPR, SN **L2** Skills for Life, p. 61 AR, GT, LPR, SN **Teacher's Edition** **L1** For Special Needs Students, TE p. 312 **L1** For Less Proficient Readers, TE p. 312 **Student Edition on Audio CD** **L1** Chapter 11, Section 1 ELL, LPR, SN **Spanish Support** **L2** Guided Reading and Review (Spanish), p. 92 ELL

Assess and Reteach	Instructional Resources	Differentiated Instruction
Assess Progress Evaluate student comprehension with the section assessment and section quiz. **Reteach** Assign the Reading and Vocabulary Study Guide to help struggling students. **Extend** Extend the lesson by assigning a Book Project.	**All in One Unit 4 History of Our World Teaching Resources** **L2** Section Quiz, p. 47 **L3** Book Project: Major Migrations, pp. 22–24 Rubric for Assessing a Writing Assignment, p. 71 **Reading and Vocabulary Study Guide** **L1** Chapter 11, Section 1, pp. 118–120	**Spanish Support** **L2** Section Quiz (Spanish), p. 93 ELL **Social Studies Skills Tutor CD-ROM** **L1** Using Reliable Information ELL, LPR, SN

Key

L1 Basic to Average   **L3** Average to Advanced
L2 For All Students

LPR Less Proficient Readers
AR Advanced Readers
SN Special Needs Students

GT Gifted and Talented
ELL English Language Learners

Section 2 Kingdoms of West Africa

 2 periods, 1 block (include Focus On Tomboctou)

Social Studies Objectives
1. Learn about the trading kingdoms of the West African savanna.
2. Investigate the kingdoms of the West African rain forests.

Reading/Language Arts Objective
Learn how to paraphrase to remember information.

Prepare to Read	**Instructional Resources**	**Differentiated Instruction**
Build Background Knowledge Have students generate a list of items that come from another country and think about how their lives would be different without those items. **Set a Purpose for Reading** Have students evaluate statements on the Reading Readiness Guide. **Preview Key Terms** Teach the section's Key Terms. **Target Reading Skill** Introduce the section's Target Reading Skill of **paraphrasing.**	**All in One Unit 4 History of Our World Teaching Resources** **L2** Reading Readiness Guide, p. 49 **L2** Paraphrase, p. 57	**Spanish Reading and Vocabulary Study Guide** **L1** Chapter 11, Section 2, pp. 87–88 ELL

Instruct	**Instructional Resources**	**Differentiated Instruction**
Kingdoms of the Savanna Discuss trading centers in the Savanna. **Target Reading Skill** Review **paraphrasing.** **Kingdoms of the Forest** Discuss Ile-Ife and Benin.	**All in One Unit 4 History of Our World Teaching Resources** **L2** Guided Reading and Review, p. 50 **L2** Reading Readiness Guide, p. 49 **History of Our World Transparencies** **L2** Section Reading Support Transparency HOW 88	**All in One Unit 4 History of Our World Teaching Resources** **L3** Al-Bakri Describes the Court of Ghana, Ibn Battuta Praises the Fairness of Mali's People, Leo Africanus Describes Tombouctou, pp. 67–69 AR, GT **History of Our World Transparencies** **L2** Transparency HOW 17: Africa: Political AR, GT, LPR, SN **Teacher's Edition** **L3** For Gifted and Talented, TE p. 321 **Spanish Support** **L2** Guided Reading and Review (Spanish) ELL

Assess and Reteach	**Instructional Resources**	**Differentiated Instruction**
Assess Progress Evaluate student comprehension with the section assessment and section quiz. **Reteach** Assign the Reading and Vocabulary Study Guide to help struggling students. **Extend** Extend the lesson by assigning this chapter's Enrichment activity.	**All in One Unit 4 History of Our World Teaching Resources** **L2** Section Quiz, p. 51 **L3** Enrichment, p. 60 Rubric for Assessing a Writing Assignment, p. 71 **Reading and Vocabulary Study Guide** **L1** Chapter 11, Section 2, pp. 121–123	**Spanish Support** **L2** Section Quiz (Spanish), p. 95 ELL

Key
L1 Basic to Average **L3** Average to Advanced
L2 For All Students

LPR Less Proficient Readers
AR Advanced Readers
SN Special Needs Students

GT Gifted and Talented
ELL English Language Learners

Section 3 East Africa's Great Trading Centers

 2 periods, 1 block (includes Chapter Review and Assessment)

Social Studies Objectives
1. Learn about powerful East African civilizations whose cities included Aksum and Lalibela.
2. Find out why the coastal cities of East Africa were important.

Reading/Language Arts Objective
Learn to summarize to help you remember and study what you read.

Prepare to Read	Instructional Resources	Differentiated Instruction
Build Background Knowledge Show a video about Great Zimbabwe, then lead a discussion. **Set a Purpose for Reading** Have students evaluate statements on the Reading Readiness Guide. **Preview Key Terms** Teach the section's Key Terms. **Target Reading Skill** Introduce the section's Target Reading Skill of **summarizing.**	**All in One Unit 4 History of Our World Teaching Resources** L2 Reading Readiness Guide, p. 53 L2 Summarize, p. 58 **World Studies Video Program** L2 Great Zimbabwe: The Lost City	**Spanish Reading and Vocabulary Study Guide** L1 Chapter 11, Section 3, pp. 89–90 ELL

Instruct	Instructional Resources	Differentiated Instruction
Ancient Ethiopia Discuss the rise and fall of Aksum and ask about the customs and traditions of East Africa's churches. **Target Reading Skill** Review **summarizing.** **Rich Centers of Trade** Discuss how trade centers on the southeast coast influenced the people of Africa.	**All in One Unit 4 History of Our World Teaching Resources** L2 Guided Reading and Review, p. 54 L2 Reading Readiness Guide, p. 53 **History of Our World Transparencies** L2 Section Reading Support Transparency HOW 89	**Teacher's Edition** L3 For Advanced Readers, TE p. 329 **PHSchool.com** L3 **For:** Long-Term Integrated Projects: Mapping World Trade **Web Code:** lgd-8204 AR, GT **Spanish Support** L2 Guided Reading and Review (Spanish), p. 96 ELL

Assess and Reteach	Instructional Resources	Differentiated Instruction
Assess Progress Evaluate student comprehension with the section assessment and section quiz. **Reteach** Assign the Reading and Vocabulary Study Guide to help struggling students. **Extend** Extend the lesson by assigning a Small Group Activity.	**All in One Unit 4 History of Our World Teaching Resources** L2 Section Quiz, p. 55 L3 Small Group Activity: Simulation: Trading Items With Silent Barter, pp. 62–65 Rubric for Assessing a Writing Assignment, p. 71 Rubric for Assessing a Report, p. 72 L2 Word Knowledge, p. 59 L2 Vocabulary Development, p. 70 L2 Chapter Tests A and B, pp. 73–78 **Reading and Vocabulary Study Guide** L1 Chapter 11, Section 3, pp. 124–126	**Spanish Support** L2 Section Quiz (Spanish), p. 97 ELL L2 Chapter Summary (Spanish), p. 98 ELL L2 Vocabulary Development (Spanish), p. 99 ELL

Key
L1 Basic to Average   L3 Average to Advanced   LPR Less Proficient Readers   GT Gifted and Talented
L2 For All Students   AR Advanced Readers   ELL English Language Learners
                                            SN Special Needs Students

Reading Background

Pre-Teaching Vocabulary

Research literature on academic vocabulary instruction indicates that effective strategies require students to go beyond simply looking up dictionary definitions or examining the context of a word. Vocabulary learning must be based on the learner's dynamic engagement in constructing understanding.

If students are not retaining the meaning of the Key Terms or high-use words, use this extended vocabulary sequence to engage them in learning new words.

1. Present the word in writing and point out the part of speech.
2. Pronounce the word and have students pronounce the word.
3. Provide a range of familiar synonyms (or "it's like" words) before offering definitions.
4. Provide an accessible definition and concrete examples, or "showing sentences."
5. Rephrase the simple definition or example sentence, asking students to complete the statement by substituting the word aloud.
6. Check for understanding by providing an application task/ question requiring critical thinking.

Sample instructional sequence:

1. Our first word is *unique*. It is an adjective, a word that describes something.
2. Say the word *unique* after me. (Students repeat.)
3. Something *unique* is *unparalleled* or *one-of-a-kind*.
4. The word *unique* means *without an equal*; Your handwriting is *unique* because it like no one else's.
5. Many families have _____ customs and traditions for different holidays.
6. Would a product created on an assembly line be considered *unique*? Yes-No-Why? (Students answer the question.)

Simplified Outlining

In this simplified approach to outlining, students will learn to differentiate between main ideas and details. Model simplified outlining using the paragraphs under the heading *Africa's Physical Geography* on page 311 of the Student Edition. Main ideas should be assigned to Level 1. Details should be Level 2, 3, or 4.

Level 1 (Main idea): Africa's vegetation
   Level 2: (detail or support for Level 1): savanna
   Level 2: (detail or support for Level 1): Sahara
      Level 3: (detail or support for Level 2): oasis
      Level 3: (detail or support for Level 2): desert

World Studies Background

Ivory Trade

In the mid-1800s, prosperity in Europe and North America increased the demand for ivory products. This meant that traders from the north would have to travel through the Sahara to the upper Congo basin, where elephants were still abundant. This resulting upsurge in ivory trade in Central Africa greatly disrupted its people. As traders crossed the area, they raided villages and kidnapped local people to serve as workers in ivory camps or slaves in Constantinople and Cairo.

Lingua Francas

Multilingualism, the ability to speak more than one language, is important in Africa, where there are more than 800 languages spoken. However, this can make it difficult to create newspapers, radio broadcasts, and textbooks that address the various language groups. To alleviate this problem, Africans have adopted lingua francas, or "official" languages, such as Swahili, Yoruba, and even English, in distinct regions. This allows for more widespread communication between the people of Africa.

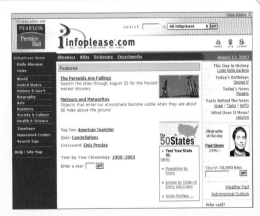

Get in-depth information on topics of global importance with **Prentice Hall Newstracker,** powered by FT.com.

Use Web code lgd-8204 for **Prentice Hall Newstracker.**

Guiding Questions

Remind students about the Guiding Questions introduced at the beginning of the book.

Section 1 relates to **Guiding Question** ❶ How did physical geography affect the development of societies around the world? (*Africa's physical geography has affected how its people make a living; for example, there is little farming in the deserts because of the lack of water.*)

Section 2 relates to **Guiding Question** ❺ How did each society organize its economic activities? (*West African kingdoms became rich by controlling important trade routes across the Sahara.*)

Section 3 relates to **Guiding Question** ❷ How did each society's belief system affect its history? (*Many people in Aksum, a city in ancient Ethiopia, converted to Christianity during the A.D. 300s. In the 600s, the rulers of Aksum fought with Muslims over trade routes and religious differences. Christianity in Ethiopia produced unique traditions and unusual churches that are still used today.*)

🔄 Target Reading Skill

In this chapter, students will learn and apply the reading skill of clarifying meaning to understand and remember what they read. Use the following worksheets to help students practice this skill:

All in One **Unit 4 History of Our World Teaching Resources,** *Reread or Read Ahead,* p. 56, *Paraphrase,* p. 57, *Summarize,* p. 58

Differentiated Instruction

The following Teacher Edition strategies are suitable for students of varying abilities.

Advanced Readers, p. 329
English Language Learners, p. 321
Gifted and Talented, p. 321
Less Proficient Readers, pp. 312, 325
Special Needs Students, p. 312

Chapter

11 Civilizations of Africa

Chapter Preview

This chapter will introduce you to the early history of Africa and to some of its great civilizations.

Section 1
Africa and the Bantu

Section 2
Kingdoms of West Africa

Section 3
East Africa's Great Trading Centers

🔄 Target Reading Skill

Clarifying Meaning In this chapter, you will focus on clarifying meaning by learning how to reread, how to paraphrase, and how to summarize.

▶ Ruins of the Great Mosque of Kilwa, in present-day Tanzania, East Africa

308 History of Our World

Bibliography

For the Teacher

Davidson, Basil. *Africa in History.* Touchstone Books, 1995.

Oliver, R. A. and Anthony Atmore. *Medieval Africa, 1250–1800.* Cambridge University Press, 2001.

Marcus, Harold G. *A History of Ethiopia: Updated Edition.* University of California Press, 2002.

For the Student

L1 Burns, Khephra. *Mansa Musa: The Lion of Mali.* Harcourt, 2001.

L2 McKissack, Frederick L. *The Royal Kingdoms of Ghana, Mali, and Songhay: Life in Medieval Africa.* Henry Holt & Company, 1995.

L3 Bessire, Mark H. C. *Great Zimbabwe (First Book).* Orchard Books, 1999.

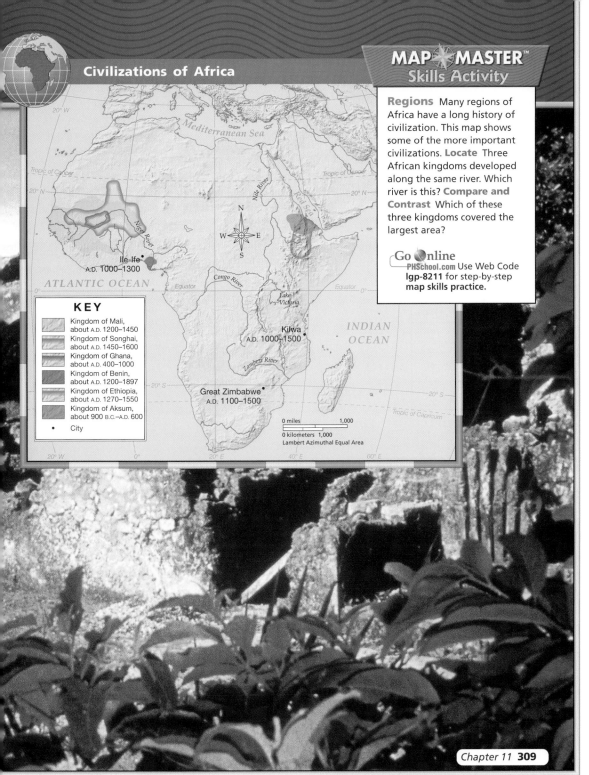

Civilizations of Africa

MAP MASTER™
Skills Activity

Regions Many regions of Africa have a long history of civilization. This map shows some of the more important civilizations. **Locate** Three African kingdoms developed along the same river. Which river is this? **Compare and Contrast** Which of these three kingdoms covered the largest area?

Go Online
PHSchool.com Use Web Code lgp-8211 for step-by-step **map skills practice.**

KEY

	Kingdom of Mali, about A.D. 1200–1450
	Kingdom of Songhai, about A.D. 1450–1600
	Kingdom of Ghana, about A.D. 400–1000
	Kingdom of Benin, about A.D. 1200–1897
	Kingdom of Ethiopia, about A.D. 1270–1550
	Kingdom of Aksum, about 900 B.C.–A.D. 600
•	City

Mediterranean Sea
Nile River
Red Sea
Niger River
Ile-Ife A.D. 1000–1300
ATLANTIC OCEAN
Congo River
Lake Victoria
INDIAN OCEAN
Kilwa A.D. 1000–1500
Zambezi River
Great Zimbabwe A.D. 1100–1500

0 miles 1,000
0 kilometers 1,000
Lambert Azimuthal Equal Area

Chapter 11 **309**

MAP MASTER™
Skills Activity

■ Have students study the map, paying particular attention to the key. Point out to students that though all of the civilizations are shown on one map, they did not exist at the same time.

■ Have students copy the names of each kingdom and the dates they thrived onto a separate sheet of paper. Then have students list the kingdoms in order of the date they were founded.

Go Online
PHSchool.com Students may practice their map skills using the interactive online version of this map.

Using the Visual L2

Reach Into Your Background Draw students' attention to the caption accompanying the photograph on pp. 34–35. Ask students to list any historic ruins they have visited or read about. Then have them think about why it is important to preserve these kinds of sites. Use an Idea Wave (TE, p. T39) to help students share their thoughts.

Answers

MAP MASTER
Skills Activity **Locate** the Niger River
Compare and Contrast the Kingdom of Mali

Chapter Resources

Teaching Resources
L2 Vocabulary Development, p. 70
L2 Skills for Life, p. 61
L2 Chapter Tests A and B, pp. 73–78

Spanish Support
L2 Spanish Chapter Summary, p. 98
L2 Spanish Vocabulary Development, p. 99

Media and Technology
L1 Student Edition on Audio CD
L1 Guided Reading Audio CDs, English and Spanish
L2 Social Studies Skills Tutor CD-ROM
Exam*View*® Test Bank CD-ROM

DISCOVERY History of Our World
CHANNEL Video Program
SCHOOL

interactive Textbook
PRENTICE HALL
Teacher*EXPRESS*™
Plan • Teach • Assess

Objectives

Social Studies

1. Learn about the physical geography of Africa.
2. Find out about the Bantu and their movement across the continent.

Reading/Language Arts

Reread and read ahead to find connections among words and sentences and to clarify unfamiliar words and ideas.

Prepare to Read

Build Background Knowledge **L2**

In this section students will learn about Africa's physical geography and how landforms affected the Bantu people. Pose the question: **How does geography affect travel?** then have students use the Think-Write-Pair-Share participation strategy (TE, p. T40) to work together to brainstorm answers to the questions. Provide a simple example to get students started.

Set a Purpose for Reading **L2**

■ Preview the Objectives.

■ Read each statement in the *Reading Readiness Guide* aloud. Ask students to mark the statements true or false.

All in One Unit 4 History of Our World Teaching Resources, *Reading Readiness Guide,* p. 45

■ Have students discuss the statements in pairs or groups of four, then mark their worksheets again. Use the Numbered Heads participation strategy (TE, p. T40) to call on students to share their group's perspectives.

Vocabulary Builder
Preview Key Terms **L2**

Pronounce each Key Term, and then ask students to say the word with you. Provide a simple explanation such as, "The migration of geese during autumn takes them from the northern to the southern region of the country."

Prepare to Read

Objectives

In this section, you will
1. Learn about the physical geography of Africa.
2. Find out about the Bantu and their movement across the continent.

Taking Notes

As you read this section, look for information about the major physical features of Africa. Copy the table below, and record your findings in it.

Physical Features of Africa	
Deserts	• •
Savannas	• •
Rain Forests	• •

Target Reading Skill

Reread or Read Ahead If you do not understand a passage, reread it to look for connections among the words and sentences. Reading ahead can also help. Words and ideas may be clarified further on.

Key Terms

- **migration** (my GRAY shun) *n.* the movement from one country or region to settle in another
- **Bantu** (BAN too) *n.* a large group of central and southern Africans who speak related languages
- **savanna** (suh VAN uh) *n.* an area of grassland with scattered trees and bushes
- **Sahara** (suh HA ruh) *n.* a huge desert stretching across most of North Africa
- **oral history** (AWR ul HIS tuh ree) *n.* accounts of the past that people pass down by word of mouth
- **clan** (klan) *n.* a group of families who trace their roots to the same ancestor

Zulu women in traditional dress in South Africa

About 4,000 years ago, many families left the places where they lived in West Africa. They would never return to their homeland. Some families had to climb over rocky hills. Others journeyed through forests or across lands baked by the sun. Mothers, fathers, and children carried everything they owned with them. After traveling for many miles, these people settled somewhere new.

No one knows exactly why they first moved. The population may have grown very quickly. If so, there may not have been enough land and resources to support all of the people. Over many years, later generations moved farther away from their original homes. They kept searching for better land for farming. Over time, their **migration** (my GRAY shun), or movement from one region to settle in another, took them across most of Africa south of the Equator. Today, their descendants number more than 200 million. The name **Bantu** (BAN too) describes both this large group of Africans and the related languages they speak.

Target Reading Skill **L2**

Reread or Read Ahead Point out the Target Reading Skill. Tell students that rereading and reading ahead may help them to figure out the meaning of an unfamiliar word or idea in the passage.

Model reading ahead using the last paragraph on p. 311 and the first paragraph on p. 314, in which students learn that until modern times, historians knew little about sub-Saharan Africa. By reading ahead, they learn that the lack of information was caused by the disintegration of artifacts. Students also learn that researchers are beginning to uncover new information about this area.

Give students *Reread or Read Ahead.* Have them complete the activity in groups.

All in One Unit 4 History of Our World Teaching Resources, *Reread or Read Ahead,* p. 56

Africa's Physical Geography

Look at the map titled Africa: Natural Vegetation. Notice the tropical rain forests that are located on either side of the Equator. They have hot, moist climates.

Surrounding these forests are bands of **savanna**, areas of grassland with scattered trees and bushes. Much of Africa is savanna. Africa's lions, zebras, and elephants live mainly on the savannas. Deserts stretch north and south of the savannas. The **Sahara** (suh HA ruh) is a desert stretching across most of North Africa. It is the world's largest desert. The Sahara is a hot, dry place of sand dunes and rocky mountains. A band of lakes, deep valleys, and rugged mountains runs north to south through East Africa.

Africa's physical geography has affected its people's ways of life. For example, there is little farming in Africa's deserts, because there is too little water. People herd cattle on the savannas, but cattle cannot survive in the rain forests. Flies and other pests in the rain forests carry diseases that are deadly for cattle.

An Oasis in the Sahara
An oasis (oh AY sis) is an area of vegetation within a desert, fed by springs and underground water.
Infer How might oases help travelers crossing a desert?

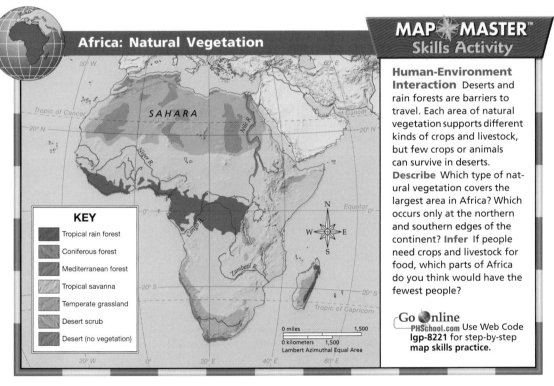

Africa: Natural Vegetation

SAHARA

Niger R.
Nile R.
Congo R.
Zambezi R.

KEY
- Tropical rain forest
- Coniferous forest
- Mediterranean forest
- Tropical savanna
- Temperate grassland
- Desert scrub
- Desert (no vegetation)

Tropic of Cancer
Equator
Tropic of Capricorn

0 miles 1,500
0 kilometers 1,500
Lambert Azimuthal Equal Area

MAP MASTER™ Skills Activity

Human-Environment Interaction Deserts and rain forests are barriers to travel. Each area of natural vegetation supports different kinds of crops and livestock, but few crops or animals can survive in deserts. **Describe** Which type of natural vegetation covers the largest area in Africa? Which occurs only at the northern and southern edges of the continent? **Infer** If people need crops and livestock for food, which parts of Africa do you think would have the fewest people?

Go Online
PHSchool.com Use Web Code lgp-8221 for step-by-step map skills practice.

Chapter 11 Section 1 **311**

Instruct

Africa's Physical Geography L2

Guided Instruction

- **Vocabulary Builder** Clarify the high-use word **environment** before reading.

- Read Africa's Physical Geography using the Oral Cloze reading strategy (TE, p. T37) and have students study the vegetation map on this page.

- Ask students **Where are Africa's tropical rain forests located?** (*on either side of the Equator*)

- Ask students **What vegetation region is north and south of the savanna?** (*desert areas, including the Sahara*)

- Ask students **How are Africa's people affected by geography?** (*There is little farming in the deserts because of the lack of water; people herd cattle on the savanna, but not in the rain forest.*)

Independent Practice

Ask students to create the Taking Notes graphic organizer on a blank piece of paper. Then have them complete the organizer. Briefly model how to identify which details to record.

Monitor Progress

- As students fill in and complete the graphic organizer, circulate and make sure individuals are choosing the correct details.

- Show *Section Reading Support Transparency HOW 87* and ask students to check their graphic organizers individually. Go over key concepts and clarify key vocabulary as needed.

📖 **History of Our World Transparencies,** *Section Reading Support Transparency HOW 87*

Answers

Infer An oasis would provide travelers with water and shelter from the sun.

MAP MASTER Skills Activity **Describe** tropical savanna; Mediterranean forest **Infer** the desert

Go Online PHSchool.com Students may practice their map skills using the interactive online version of this map.

Vocabulary Builder

Use the information below to teach students this section's high-use words.

High Use Word	Definition and Sample Sentence
environment, p. 312	*n.* natural surroundings Many people recycle to help keep the **environment** clean.
technique, p. 314	*n.* a way of doing something The painter's **technique** includes a special paintbrush.
traditional, p. 314	*adj.* coming from customs handed down through time She wore the **traditional** wedding dress of her culture.
adapt, p. 315	*v.* to become accustomed to a new situation He **adapted** quickly to city life after moving from a small town.

Target Reading Skill L2

Reread As a follow up, ask students to answer the Target Reading Skill question on this page. *(Because each area of natural vegetation supports different kinds of crops and livestock, it is difficult for groups to move from one area to another.)*

The Bantu Migrations L2

Guided Instruction

■ **Vocabulary Builder** Clarify the high-use words **technique, traditional,** and **adapt** before reading.

■ Read The Bantu Migrations with students. As students read, circulate and make sure individuals can answer the Reading Check question.

■ Discuss with students why it has been difficult for scientists and historians to piece together the history of sub-Saharan Africa. *(The Sahara cut off this area from Europe for more than 2,000 years and materials Africans used for buildings and tools have disintegrated.)*

■ Ask students **How have scientists recently uncovered new information?** *(They have gathered stories about people's past from African storytellers and modern techniques have helped scientists uncover new information.)*

Answer

✓ Reading Check It affects how they make their living; for example, there is little farming in the deserts because of the lack of water.

Reread
Reread the last four paragraphs, under the heading Africa's Physical Geography, to understand how Africa's physical features might have been a barrier to movement.

The Zambezi River plunges over Victoria Falls, on the Zambia-Zimbabwe border.

Groups that share the same environment may live differently. For example, Mbuti (em BOO tee) people of Africa's rain forest live mainly by hunting animals and gathering plants, but neighboring peoples live mainly by farming.

✓ Reading Check How do Africa's physical features affect people's ways of life?

The Bantu Migrations

The physical barriers formed by lakes, forests, mountains, and rivers did not stop the movement of people across Africa. The map titled Bantu Migrations, on page 313, traces the major routes of the Bantu people. These migrations continued for more than 1,000 years. They are among the largest population movements in all of human history.

The History of Sub-Saharan Africa Historians know a great deal about North Africa's history. But they have only a sketchy knowledge of the history of Africa south of the Sahara. That area is called sub-Saharan Africa. Until modern times, the Sahara cut off this larger part of Africa from Europe. European historians have found it difficult to study sub-Saharan Africa. Today, scientists and historians are working to piece together the history of this area. In many ways, it is like solving a puzzle.

Differentiated Instruction

For Special Needs Students L1
Have students read the section as they listen to the recorded version on the Student Edition on Audio CD. Check for comprehension by pausing the CD and asking students to share their answers to the Reading Checks.

  ◉ Chapter 11, Section 1, **Student Edition on Audio CD**

For Less Proficient Readers L2
Some students may have difficulty reading the historical map on p. 313. To help them develop their map skills, ask students to complete *Reading a Historical Map.*

  All in One **Unit 4 History of Our World Teaching Resources,** *Reading a Historical Map,* p. 66

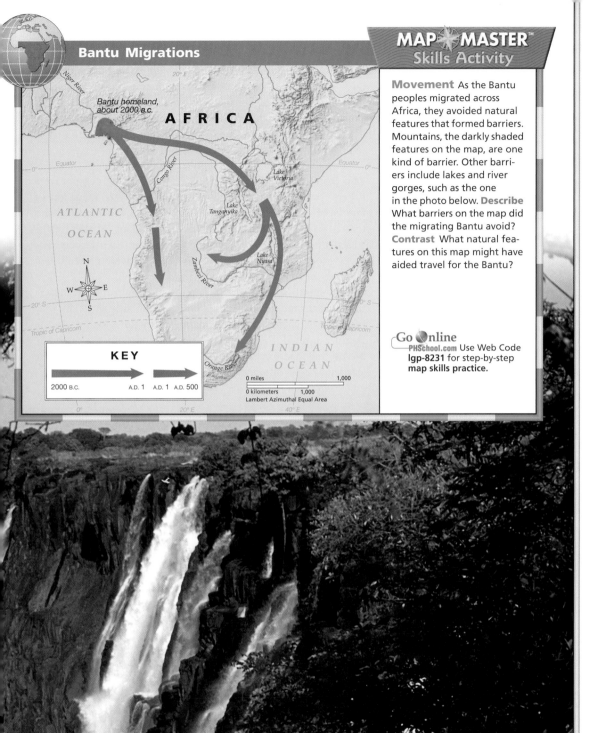

Bantu Migrations

AFRICA

Bantu homeland, about 2000 B.C.

Niger River

ATLANTIC OCEAN

Equator

Congo River

Lake Victoria

Lake Tanganyika

Zambezi River

Lake Nyasa

Tropic of Capricorn

Orange River

INDIAN OCEAN

KEY

2000 B.C. — A.D. 1   A.D. 1 — A.D. 500

0 miles 1,000
0 kilometers 1,000
Lambert Azimuthal Equal Area

Movement As the Bantu peoples migrated across Africa, they avoided natural features that formed barriers. Mountains, the darkly shaded features on the map, are one kind of barrier. Other barriers include lakes and river gorges, such as the one in the photo below. **Describe** What barriers on the map did the migrating Bantu avoid? **Contrast** What natural features on this map might have aided travel for the Bantu?

Go Online
PHSchool.com Use Web Code **lgp-8231** for step-by-step **map skills practice.**

Guided Instruction (continued)

■ Ask students **How did Bantu-speaking people meet their needs in early times?** (*They were fishers, farmers, and herders.*)

■ Ask students **Why were property and positions of power passed down through the mother's side of the family in Bantu culture?** (*Many clans traced their ancestry through the mother.*)

■ Ask students **Why might the Bantu have moved from their traditional homelands?** (*to search for better farmland and grazing*)

■ Discuss with students how the Bantu had to change their way of living when they migrated to different environments. (*They had to learn new ways of farming and caring for livestock.*)

Skills Mini Lesson

Using Cartographer's Tools

1. Teach the skill by pointing out to students that maps have features that make them easier to read. These may include a compass rose, a scale, and a map key.

2. Help students practice the skill by identifying the information that appears in the map key on p. 313. (*Bantu migration routes are shown with arrows.*)

3. Have students apply the skill by using the compass rose on p. 313 to determine in which directions the Bantu migrated. (*south, west, and east*)

Answers

MAP MASTER™ Skills Activity **Describe** mountains, lakes, and river gorges **Contrast** rivers and mountains

Go Online
PHSchool.com Students may practice their map skills using the interactive online version of this map.

Read the **Links Across Time** on this page. Ask students **How have the Bantu migrations affected Africans today?** (*Today more than 200 million Africans speak Bantu languages.*)

Guided Instruction (continued)

- Ask students **What did the Bantu do when they encountered other people as they moved?** (*Sometimes they joined with the group and introduced Bantu culture to them, and other times they drove away the people they met.*)

- Ask students **Why was the metalworking that the Bantu taught to others a valuable skill?** (*Iron weapons and tools could be used for hunting, defense, clearing land, and cutting trees.*)

- Ask students **What would happen when an area in which the Bantu lived became too crowded?** (*The Bantu would migrate to a new area.*)

Independent Practice

Assign *Guided Reading and Review*.

All in One **Unit 4 History of Our World Teaching Resources,** *Guided Reading and Review*, p. 46

Monitor Progress

Tell students to fill in the last column of the *Reading Readiness Guide*. Probe for what they learned that confirms or invalidates each statement.

All in One **Unit 4 History of Our World Teaching Resources,** *Reading Readiness Guide*, p. 45

Bantu Languages As the Bantu speakers moved through Africa, they also spread their languages. Today, more than 200 million Africans speak Bantu languages. In fact, about 500 of the languages spoken in Africa south of the Sahara belong to the Bantu language family.

One reason this puzzle is difficult is that the wood and clay that many African peoples used for building have disintegrated. Even iron tools and weapons have not lasted, because iron rusts fairly quickly. However, modern techniques and inventions have helped scientists uncover new information. Stories told by traditional African storytellers have led to new areas of exploration. That is because these stories are often **oral history,** accounts of the past that people pass down by word of mouth.

The Bantu In early times, most Bantu-speaking peoples were fishers, farmers, and herders. Their villages were made up of families from the same **clan** (klan), or group of families who traced their roots to the same ancestor. Many of these clans traced their ancestry through mothers rather than fathers. For this reason, property and positions of power were passed down through the mother's side of the family.

The Bantu-speaking peoples moved slowly from their traditional homelands. Each generation moved a fairly short distance in their search for better farmland and better grazing. As the Bantu migrated, they entered different environments. In many places, they had to change the way they lived. For example, they learned to raise different crops or different kinds of animals.

These women in Windhoek, Namibia, belong to a present-day Bantu group, the Herero.

314 History of Our World

Background: Global Perspectives

The Columbian Exchange Just as the Bantu introduced their culture to other groups, Europeans and Native Americans exchanged many products in the late 1400s. This is called the Columbian Exchange, after Christopher Columbus, the first European to establish lasting contact between the two hemispheres. Native Americans had never before seen the horse, pig, cow, sheep, wheat, peaches, sugar, bananas, or dandelions. Similarly, maize, tomatoes, potatoes, cocoa, pineapples, tobacco, and turkeys were brought to the Eastern hemisphere for the first time. Europeans also unknowingly introduced many diseases that Native Americans had never been exposed to; many American Indians died as a result.

The Spread of Bantu Culture Often, Bantu people moved into areas where other people already lived. When this happened, they sometimes joined the groups living there. The older cultures then usually adapted to Bantu culture. For example, the Bantu introduced crops such as yams to other parts of Africa. At other times, however, the Bantu forced the people already living there to leave their homes.

As the Bantu migrated, they also carried a knowledge of metalworking with them. Iron tools gave the Bantu more control over their environment than older cultures had. With hard axes, they could cut down trees and clear the land. Their sharp, iron-headed spears and arrows were powerful weapons for hunting and for warfare.

These migrations continued over many generations, with groups moving whenever an area became crowded. In time, the Bantu had settled throughout Central and Southern Africa.

✓ Reading Check What kinds of skills did the Bantu carry with them?

Making Iron Tools
Bantu peoples heated rocks containing iron in furnaces to produce a lump of iron, shown above at the far left. They then gradually hammered it to shape a useful tool, such as the hoe above at the right. *Draw Conclusions How might iron tools have given the Bantu an advantage over people who lacked metal tools?*

Section 1 Assessment

Key Terms
Review the key terms at the beginning of this section. Use each term in a sentence that explains its meaning.

⟳ Target Reading Skill
What were you able to clarify about Africa's physical features by rereading?

Comprehension and Critical Thinking
1. (a) Identify Describe the main physical features of Africa.

(b) Synthesize Information How do Africa's physical features affect people's ways of life?
2. (a) Recall Over how many years did the Bantu migrations occur?
(b) Summarize Tell what happened when the Bantu met other African peoples.
(c) Conclude Why are the Bantu migrations an important part of African history?

Writing Activity
Consider the Bantu people's long history of migration and adaptation to new environments. Write a paragraph to answer the following question: What does this history suggest about the kind of people the Bantu were?

For: An activity on the Bantu migration
Visit: PHSchool.com
Web Code: lgd-8201

Assess Progress [L2]
Have students complete the Section Assessment. Administer the *Section Quiz.*

All in One Unit 4 History of Our World Teaching Resources, *Section Quiz,* p. 47

Reteach [L1]
If students need more instruction, have them read this section in the Reading and Vocabulary Study Guide.

📄 Chapter 11, Section 1, **History of Our World Reading and Vocabulary Study Guide,** pp. 121–123

Extend [L3]
Have students learn more about migrations by completing the book project *Major Migrations.*

All in One Unit 4 History of Our World Teaching Resources, *Book Project: Major Migrations,* pp. 22–24

Answers

Draw Conclusions Iron tools gave them an advantage in hunting and warfare.

✓ Reading Check They carried knowledge of how to farm crops such as yams, and taught metalworking.

Writing Activity
Use the *Rubric for Assessing a Writing Assignment* to assess students' paragraphs.

All in One Unit 4 History of Our World Teaching Resources, *Rubric for Assessing a Writing Assignment,* p. 71

Go Online PHSchool.com Typing in the Web code when prompted will bring students to detailed instructions for this activity.

Section 1 Assessment

Key Terms
Students' sentences should reflect knowledge of each Key Term.

⟳ Target Reading Skill
Answers will vary, but students should demonstrate their understanding of the skill with examples from the text.

Comprehension and Critical Thinking
1. (a) Tropical rain forests with thick vegetation and plenty of rainfall are located on either side of the Equator; the savanna is located farther from the Equator and may include lush, tall grass or short, sparse grass with some trees and bushes; desert areas, with sand dunes, rocky mountains, oases, and high temperatures, are located north and south of the savanna. **(b)** tropical rain forest

2. (a) more than 1,000 years **(b)** Sometimes the Bantu joined other cultures and introduced aspects of their culture, such as raising certain crops and metalworking to the new groups. Other times the Bantu drove other groups away. **(c)** Possible answers: they are among the largest population movements in all of human history; their culture has affected large parts of Africa.

Objective

Learn to determine the reliability of a source.

Prepare to Read

Build Background Knowledge L2

Define the word *reliable* for any students who are unsure of its definition, explaining that it means "trustworthy or dependable." Then ask students why it is important to be able to determine how reliable a piece of writing is. Use the Numbered Heads participation strategy (TE, p. T40) to conduct a class discussion.

Instruct

Using Reliable Information L2

Guided Instruction

■ Read the steps to using reliable information as a class and write them on the board.

■ Practice the skill by following the steps on p. 316 as a class using the selection from *Travels in Asia and Africa 1325–1354* on p. 317. Model each step in the activity with students. They should identify when the passage was written *(the 1300s)*, decide whether more recent information would be more reliable *(it is an eyewitness account of the Sahara in the 1300s; more current sources would be needed to study the Sahara as it is today)*, examine the author's qualifications *(he saw the Sahara firsthand)*, identify any loaded language *("bitter" and "plagued with flies;" these impressions could be proved true or false for the present-day Sahara)* and determine whether they think the source is reliable *(the source is probably reliable for information about Ibn Battuta's journey in the 1300s. The passage would be a good source of information if one was writing a report about travel in the 1300s. If one was writing about the present-day Sahara, a newer source of information would be better)*.

Skills for Life Using Reliable Information

Grace was writing a paper about the Nok culture, the earliest known Iron Age culture in West Africa. She found this passage in a book called *Great Civilizations of Ancient Africa,* published in 1971. It was written by the historian Lester Brooks. Was this passage a good source for Grace's paper?

"The Nok peoples are known to have had a sophisticated agricultural society and . . . the ability to produce weapons of iron at this early time. They undoubtedly must have had relations—peaceful or otherwise—with other peoples over a wide expanse of the African interior. . . .

"But the truth . . . is that we just do not know who the Nok peoples were or how they lived. We have no written records, we have no legends or myths that explain them."

All books are not equally reliable. Use the skill below to help you determine how reliable a piece of writing is.

Nok statue

Learn the Skill

To decide whether a piece of writing is reliable, use the following steps:

1 **Look at the date of the source.** A source might have been written near the time of an event or many years later. Eyewitness accounts can tell you how an event was understood at the time it happened. Later writing may be based on respected research. New discoveries might have been made since the passage above was written.

2 **Identify the author's qualifications and purpose.** A "historian" should be a reliable source. But think about the sentence beginning, "The Nok peoples are known to have had a . . ." Who is it who *knows*? Where might this author have gotten his information?

3 **Decide whether the author has a bias.** Look for opinions, beliefs that cannot be proved. "They undoubtedly must have had relations . . ." is an opinion, not a fact. Also look for loaded words and phrases. The word *sophisticated* gives a positive impression that may or may not be accurate. Sometimes biased writers leave out information that does not support their bias.

4 **Decide how reliable the source is and why.** Consider your purpose: Are you writing about how an event seemed to the people who experienced it? Or, do you need the latest research to support your conclusions about the event?

Independent Practice

Assign *Skills for Life* and have students complete it individually.

All in One **Unit 4 History of Our World Teaching Resources,** *Skills for Life,* p. 61

Monitor Progress

As students are completing *Skills for Life,* circulate to make sure individuals are applying the skill steps effectively. Provide assistance as needed.

The following passage is from *Travels in Asia and Africa 1325–1354*, written by a North African merchant named Ibn Battutah. He describes a journey through the Sahara.

"[W]e passed ten days of discomfort because the water there is bitter and the place is plagued with flies. . . . We passed a caravan on the way and they told us that some of their party had become separated from them. We found one of them dead under a shrub of the sort that grows in the sand. . . ."

Practice the Skill

Read the passage above. Then follow the steps in Learn the Skill to decide if it is a reliable source.

1. When was the passage written? Would this information be more reliable if it had been written more recently? Explain why or why not.

2. What qualifies the author to describe the Sahara? Do you think he was an accurate observer?

3. Identify an example of loaded language in the passage. Could this statement be proved true or false? Is it possible that the writer has left important information out of his account?

4. Do you consider this passage a reliable source? How might your purpose in using the passage affect your decision?

Sand dunes in the Sahara

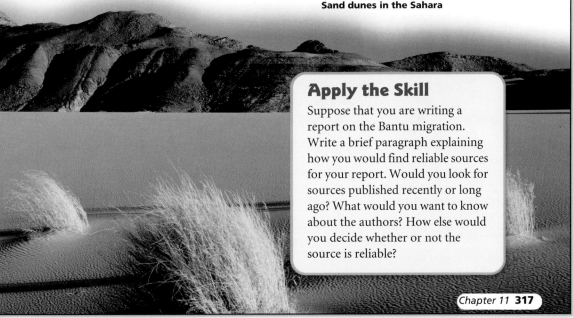

Apply the Skill

Suppose that you are writing a report on the Bantu migration. Write a brief paragraph explaining how you would find reliable sources for your report. Would you look for sources published recently or long ago? What would you want to know about the authors? How else would you decide whether or not the source is reliable?

Assess and Reteach

Assess Progress   L2
Ask students to do the Apply the Skill activity.

Reteach   L1
If students are having trouble applying the skill steps, have them review the skill using the interactive Social Studies Skills Tutor CD-ROM.

⊙ *Using Reliable Information,* **Social Studies Skills Tutor CD-ROM**

Extend   L3
Have students choose a topic that interests them, such as a historical figure or a country. Have them collect a wide variety of sources, such as books from the library, articles from the Internet, and encyclopedia entries. Then have them assess the reliability of each source and write a short paper on their topic. Students may read their papers to the class and explain what kinds of sources they decided to use and why.

Answer
Apply the Skill
Students' paragraphs will vary, but should show an understanding of the skill steps.

Section 2
Step-by-Step Instruction

Objectives
Social Studies
1. Learn about the trading kingdoms of the West African savanna.
2. Investigate the kingdoms of the West African rain forests.

Reading/Language Arts
Learn how to paraphrase to remember information.

Prepare to Read

Build Background Knowledge   L2
Explain to students that in this section they will learn about trading kingdoms of the West African savanna and rain forests. Using the Idea Wave participation strategy (TE, p. T39), have students generate a list of items, such as foods, which come from other countries. Ask students to discuss how their lives would be different without these items, and what they can conclude about the importance of trade.

Set a Purpose for Reading   L2
■ Preview the Objectives.

■ Read each statement in the *Reading Readiness Guide* aloud. Ask students to mark the statements true or false.

All in One Unit 4 History of Our World Teaching Resources, *Reading Readiness Guide,* p. 49

■ Have students discuss the statements in pairs or groups of four, then mark their worksheets again. Use the Numbered Heads participation strategy (TE, p. T40) to call on students to share their group's perspectives.

Vocabulary Builder
Preview Key Terms   L2
Pronounce each Key Term, then ask the students to say the word with you. Provide a simple explanation such as, "Mansa Musa ruled the kingdom of Mali in the 1300s and built it into a great trading empire."

Section 2 — Kingdoms of West Africa

Prepare to Read

Objectives
In this section, you will
1. Learn about the trading kingdoms of the West African savanna.
2. Investigate the kingdoms of the West African rain forests.

Taking Notes
As you read this section, look for the main ideas and details about different African cultures. Create an outline of the section using the example below as a model.

```
I. Kingdoms of the savanna
   A. Ghana
      1.
      2.
   B.
II.
```

 **Target Reading Skill**

Paraphrase When you paraphrase, you restate what you have read in your own words. For example, you could paraphrase the first paragraph below this way: "Thousands of people and dozens of camels carrying gold marched in a group."

As you read this section, paraphrase the information after each red or blue heading.

Key Terms
• **Mansa Musa** (MAHN sah MOO sah) *n.* a king of Mali in the 1300s
• **Mali** (MAH lee) *n.* a rich kingdom of the West African savanna
• **Ghana** (GAH nuh) *n.* the first West African kingdom based on the gold and salt trade
• **Songhai** (SAWNG hy) *n.* a powerful kingdom of the West African savanna
• **Ile-Ife** (EE lay EE fay) *n.* the capital of a kingdom of the West African rain forest
• **Benin** (beh NEEN) *n.* a kingdom of the West African rain forest

Mansa Musa, the king of Mali

318 History of Our World

Soldiers whose swords hung from gold chains rode horses decorated with gold. Hundreds of government officials marched along with the soldiers. Thousands of slaves, each one dressed in silk and carrying a staff made of gold, also accompanied the marchers. The procession included more than 60,000 people and dozens of camels, each camel loaded with many pounds of gold.

This sight greeted the astonished people of Cairo, Egypt, one day in July 1324. It was the caravan of **Mansa Musa** (MAHN sah MOO sah), the powerful king of Mali, in West Africa. The caravan was traveling from Mali across North Africa. Mansa Musa was performing his duty as a Muslim by traveling to the Southwest Asian city of Mecca, the holiest city of Islam. Many years later, people in Egypt were still talking about Mansa Musa's amazing visit—and about the amount of gold that he and his officials had spent.

Target Reading Skill   L2

Paraphrase Point out the Target Reading Skill. Tell students that paraphrasing can help them organize information and better understand what they read.

Model paraphrasing using the text on p. 323. (*The city of Benin flourished from the 1200s to the 1600s. The mining industry, slave trade, and control of trade routes all contributed to the city's growth. The city was also a center of art, and its artists may have influenced modern western artists.*)

Give students *Paraphrase.* Have them complete the activity in their groups.

All in One Unit 4 History of Our World Teaching Resources, *Paraphrase,* p. 57

Kingdoms of the Savanna

Mansa Musa ruled **Mali** (MAH lee), a rich kingdom of the West African savanna. The kingdoms of the savanna controlled important trade routes across the Sahara. The Niger River, which flows through the region, was another important trade route. Traders traveling through these lands had to pay taxes on all their goods. This made the kingdoms rich. In return, the rulers kept peace and order throughout the land. Thus, merchants—and their caravans of valuable goods—could travel safely from one place to another.

Ghana, a Kingdom Built on Trade Salt and gold were the basis of West African trade. Most of the salt came from mines in the central Sahara. Salt was very valuable. People needed it to flavor food, to preserve meat, and to maintain good health. Salt was scarce in the rain forest region. So people from the forest region of West Africa sold gold in exchange for salt. Some gold was sold to traders on their way to North Africa. These traders returned with glass and other precious North African goods. Traders could travel hundreds of miles across the dry Sahara because their camels could travel for days without water.

The first West African kingdom to be based on the wealth of the salt and gold trade was **Ghana** (GAH nuh). By about A.D. 400, the people of Ghana took control of the trade routes across the Sahara. Ghana's location was ideal. Find Ghana on the map titled Civilizations of Africa, on page 309. Ghana was just north of the rich gold fields. Land routes south from the Sahara went through Ghana. By about A.D 800, Ghana was a major trading kingdom.

The Salt Trade in Africa
Camel caravans like the one shown at the bottom of the page carried slabs of salt from salt mines in the Sahara. Slabs of salt were traded in markets like the one below, in Mopti, Mali.
Apply Information *When traders from the forest region bought salt, what might they have offered in exchange?*

Instruct

Kingdoms of the Savanna L2

Guided Instruction

- **Vocabulary Builder** Clarify the high-use words **independent, conquer,** and **province** before reading.

- Read Kingdoms of the Savanna, using the Choral Reading strategy (TE, p. T38).

- Have students name the three kingdoms of the West African savanna. *(Mali, Ghana, Songhai)* **How did they become wealthy?** *(They controlled important trade routes across the Sahara.)*

- Ask students **What resources were at the heart of West African trade?** *(salt and gold)* **Where was most of Africa's salt and gold found?** *(Salt came from mines in the central Sahara, and gold came from the forest region of West Africa.)*

- Discuss with students how Ghana became a major trading kingdom. *(Ghana began to conquer neighboring peoples and took control of trade routes across the Sahara.)*

- Ask students **Why did Ghana's power begin to fade?** *(Northern invaders overran the capital and other cities, and people fled the area. By the 1200s Ghana had broken up into a number of small states.)*

Vocabulary Builder

Use the information below to teach students this section's high-use words.

High-Use Word	Definition and Sample Sentence
independent, p. 320	*adj.* not under the control of another The United States became **independent** from Great Britain.
conquer, p. 320	*v.* to get possession of by force The ruler **conquered** all the lands south of his kingdom.
province, p. 321	*n.* a political region of a country She was born in the Canadian **province** of Manitoba.
stability, p. 322	*n.* the condition of being solid and steady This kind of sailboat is known for its strength and **stability**.

Answer
Apply Information gold

Paraphrase As a follow up, ask students to answer the Target Reading Skill question on this page. *(Ghana was a powerful kingdom until about A.D. 1000. By the 1200s, it had broken into independent states. The area was then controlled by Mali.)*

Guided Instruction (continued)

- Discuss with students how Sundiata helped Mali become the most powerful kingdom in West Africa. *(He took control of the salt and gold trade, and conquered surrounding areas.)*

- Ask students **What was a result of Mansa Musa's trip to Mecca?** *(It created ties between Mali and the Muslim peoples of North Africa and Southwest Asia.)*

- Have students list ways in which Mansa Musa helped make Mali a center of learning. *(Possible answers: Muslims built mosques and religious leaders moved to Mali; scholars came to teach religion, arithmetic, medicine, and law.)*

- Ask students **Why do you think Mali's power began to fade after Mansa Musa died?** *(Possible answer: No strong ruler was able to take his place and hold the kingdom together.)*

Answer

Analyze Images This large mosque suggests that Islam is very important in the region.

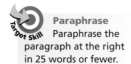

Paraphrase Paraphrase the paragraph at the right in 25 words or fewer.

The Great Mosque at Djenné The mosque below is in the city of Djenné, an important trading center in the kingdoms of Mali and Songhai. A mosque is a Muslim place of worship. **Analyze Images** *What does the scale of this mosque suggest about the importance of Islam to people in this region?*

Ghana's capital, Kumbi Saleh, was divided into two cities. One was the center of trade. The other was the royal city, where the king had his court and handed down his decisions. Around A.D. 1000, the power of Ghana began to weaken. Invaders from the north overran the capital and other cities. By the 1200s, Ghana had broken into small, independent states. Soon, most of the trade in the area was controlled by a powerful new kingdom, the kingdom of Mali.

The Powerful Kingdom of Mali Mali was centered in the Upper Niger Valley. Under the leadership of Sundiata (sun JAH tah), who united the kingdom about 1230, Mali took control of the salt and gold trade. Sundiata conquered surrounding areas and increased the size of the kingdom. By 1255, when Sundiata died, Mali had grown rich from trade. It had become the most powerful kingdom in West Africa. Mali continued to grow in the years after Sundiata's death.

In 1312, Mansa Musa became ruler of Mali. By this time, traders from North Africa had brought a new religion, Islam, to West Africa. Muslims, or people who practice Islam, worship one god. Mansa Musa greatly expanded his kingdom and made Islam the official religion. Mansa Musa's trip to the holy city of Mecca created new ties between Mali and the Muslim peoples of North Africa and Southwest Asia.

Background: Links Across Time

The Gold Coast The Kingdom of Ghana disappeared as a major trading empire in the 1200s. Europeans made first contact with what is now Ghana in 1471 and named the area the "Gold Coast" because of the quantities of gold found there. Great Britain later made the Gold Coast one of its colonies. In 1957, the Gold Coast achieved independence as the modern nation of Ghana. Today gold remains a major export of Ghana.

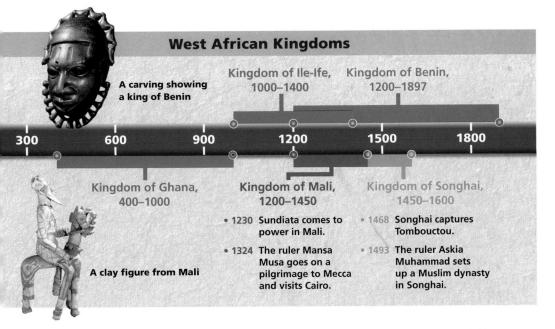

West African Kingdoms

A carving showing a king of Benin

Kingdom of Ile-Ife, 1000–1400

Kingdom of Benin, 1200–1897

300   600   900   1200   1500   1800

Kingdom of Ghana, 400–1000

Kingdom of Mali, 1200–1450

- 1230 Sundiata comes to power in Mali.
- 1324 The ruler Mansa Musa goes on a pilgrimage to Mecca and visits Cairo.

Kingdom of Songhai, 1450–1600

- 1468 Songhai captures Tombouctou.
- 1493 The ruler Askia Muhammad sets up a Muslim dynasty in Songhai.

A clay figure from Mali

During his 25-year rule, Mansa Musa used his new ties to these Muslim peoples to make Mali a center of learning. Scholars came to teach religion, mathematics, medicine, and law. In the late 1300s, however—about 50 years after Mansa Musa died— Mali's power began to fade. Raiders attacked from the north, and fighting broke out within the kingdom. Several provinces broke away and became independent. One of these former provinces became an empire in its own right. It was called Songhai (SAWNG hy).

The Rise and Fall of Songhai Songhai became the leading kingdom of the West African savanna during the 1400s. Like the rulers of Ghana and Mali, Songhai's leaders controlled trade routes and the sources of salt and gold. Songhai's wealth and power grew when it conquered the rich trading city of Tombouctou in 1468. Find Songhai on the map titled Civilizations of Africa on page 309.

In less than 100 years, however, the kingdom of Songhai began to lose power. In the late 1500s, the people of Songhai began fighting among themselves. The kingdom became weaker. And it easily fell to the guns and cannons of an army from Morocco, in North Africa. The era of the rich and powerful trading empires of West Africa was at an end.

✓ **Reading Check** Name the two most important trade items in West Africa.

■ **Timeline Skills**

This timeline shows five West African kingdoms. Vertical lines mark specific dates. Horizontal bars show periods of time. The kingdoms of the savanna are at the bottom of the timeline. The forest kingdoms are at the top. **Identify** Which kingdom lasted the longest? Which lasted the shortest time? **Analyze** Which forest kingdoms overlapped in time with the kingdom of Mali?

Guided Instruction (continued)
■ Ask students **How was Songhai's rise as an empire similar to Ghana's and Mali's?** (*All three grew from conquests and controlled trade routes.*)

■ Ask students to list the events that led to the fall of Songhai. (*The people of Songhai began fighting among themselves; the kingdom became weaker and fell to an army from North Africa.*)

Independent Practice
Ask students to create the Taking Notes graphic organizer on a blank piece of paper. Then have them fill in the outline with main ideas and details about Africa's savanna kingdoms. Briefly model how to identify which main ideas and details to record.

Monitor Progress
As students fill in the graphic organizer, circulate and make sure individuals are organizing the information correctly. Provide assistance as needed.

Differentiated Instruction

For Gifted and Talented L3
Have students read the three primary sources listed below and answer the questions that follow.

All in One Unit 4 History of Our World Teaching Resources, *Al-Bakri Describes the Court of Ghana, Ibn Battuta Praises the Fairness of Mali's People, Leo Africanus Describes Tombouctou,* pp. 67–69

For English Language Learners L1
Help English language learners use pictures to visualize the meaning of words. Pair them with more advanced students in the class and assign several words—such as *salt, agriculture,* and *journey*—from the sub-heading The Powerful Kingdom of Mali to the pairs. Have each pair draw pictures that depict the assigned words.

Answers

✓ **Reading Check** Salt and gold were the most important trade items in West Africa.

Timeline Skills Identify Benin lasted the longest—697 years; Songhai the briefest— 150 years **Analyze** Ile-Ife and Benin both overlapped with the kingdom of Mali.

Kingdoms of the Forest

L2

Guided Instruction

- **Vocabulary Builder** Clarify the high-use word **stability** before reading.

- Read Kingdoms of the Forest with students. As students read, circulate and make sure individuals can answer the Reading Check question.

- Discuss with students why there is little information about Ile-Ife and what scientists have been able to find. (*The modern town of Ife is located on top of the earlier city, trees cover sites outside of the town, rains have washed away mud buildings, and dampness has rusted iron and rotted wood and fabrics. However, scientists have discovered sculptures believed to represent powerful onis.*)

- Ask students to describe Benin's slave trade. (*Enslaved people were sold along the traditional trade routes; some worked for families in the savannah, others joined slaves from Europe and Asia in North Africa.*)

- Ask students **How was Benin a center of art?** (*Obas hired artists to make objects from bronze, brass, ivory, and copper.*)

Independent Practice

Have students complete the graphic organizer by filling in main ideas and details about Ile-Ife and Benin, in the correct order.

Monitor Progress

- Show *Section Support Transparency HOW 88* and ask students to check their graphic organizers individually. Go over key concepts and clarify key vocabulary as needed.

    History of Our World Transparencies, *Section Reading Support Transparency HOW 88*

- Tell students to fill in the last column of the *Reading Readiness Guide*. Probe for what they learned that confirms or invalidates each statement.

     Unit 4 History of Our World Teaching Resources, *Reading Readiness Guide*, p. 49

322 History of Our World

Kingdoms of the Forest

Ghana, Mali, and Songhai developed on West Africa's savanna. At the same time, other kingdoms arose in the rain forests to the south of these grasslands. The peoples of the rain forests were not Muslim. They practiced religions with hundreds of different gods.

Two of the most important kingdoms of the West African forests were centered around the cities of **Ile-Ife** (EE lay EE fay) and **Benin** (beh NEEN). Both of these cities were located in the present-day nation of Nigeria. As with the kingdoms of the savanna, trade made these forest kingdoms powerful and wealthy. With their wealth and stability, these kingdoms supported larger populations than other African rain forest regions could support.

Ile-Ife: A Center of Culture and Trade

About A.D. 1000, Ile-Ife became a major cultural and trading center. The powerful leaders of this kingdom were called onis (OH neez). Traditional stories told by these people described Ile-Ife as "the place where the world was created," but historians know little about the early city or the people who lived there.

One of the reasons that we know little about Ile-Ife is that the modern town of Ife is located on top of the earlier city. Also, the region is thickly forested and damp. Trees have covered old sites outside the town, and rains have washed away old mud buildings. Dampness has also rusted iron and long since rotted wood and fabrics.

Among the most important artifacts that have survived are sculptures. Many were discovered only in the last 100 years. Scientists have dated these works of art to the years between the 1100s and the 1300s. Many of these sculptures are lifelike and may be portraits of the powerful onis of Ile-Ife.

The rain forests of West Africa have a damp climate and lush vegetation.

Skills Mini Lesson

Comparing and Contrasting

1. Tell students that comparing means finding similarities, and contrasting means finding differences. The steps for comparing and contrasting are (1) identify what you are comparing (2) notice words that compare, such as *both*, and words that contrast, such as *but*, and (3) draw conclusions.

2. Help students compare the cities of Ile-Ife and Benin as described on pp. 322–323. (*Both were located in present-day Nigeria, both were centers of art and trade, and they shared a language and religion.*)

3. Have students contrast Ile-Ife and Benin. (*They reached the peak of their power at different times—Ile-Ife around A.D. 1000, and Benin by the 1400s.*)

Benin Rules an Empire The city of Benin dates to the 1200s. At that time, workers in the region mined copper, iron, and gold. Benin's leaders, called obas (OH buz), also sold slaves to African traders. Many of these slaves were forced to work as servants for rich families on the savanna. Others joined slaves from Europe and Asia to work in North Africa.

By the 1500s, Benin reached its greatest strength and size. The oba controlled a large army, priests, government workers, and less important local chiefs. The city of Benin ruled the trade routes along the rivers to the north and south. It became immensely rich. It ruled much of present-day southern Nigeria. Benin remained strong until the late 1600s, when the kingdom began to lose its power over the region.

Like Ile-Ife, the city of Benin also became a center of art. The obas hired skilled artists to make many beautiful objects from bronze, brass, ivory, and copper. These artists may have borrowed some cultural traditions from Ile-Ife, but the exact relationship between the two kingdoms is unclear. The artists of Benin and other West African kingdoms have in turn influenced modern artists in Europe and the Americas.

✓ **Reading Check** What were the leaders of Ile-Ife and Benin called?

Section 2 Assessment

Key Terms
Review the key terms at the beginning of this section. Use each term in a sentence that explains its meaning.

Target Reading Skill
Find the second paragraph under the heading Kingdoms of the Forest, on page 322. Paraphrase this paragraph by rewriting it in your own words.

Comprehension and Critical Thinking
1. (a) List What were the names of the three major kingdoms of the West African savanna?

(b) Identify Causes What made each of the three kingdoms rich?
(c) Apply Information What do the powerful countries of today have in common with these kingdoms?
2. (a) Recall Describe some of the art objects that the people of Ile-Ife and Benin left behind.
(b) Identify Cause and Effect Why are these objects among the few things that have survived from these cultures?

Writing Activity
Suppose that you are a foreign visitor who has traveled to the kingdom of Benin in the late 1500s. You will be allowed to meet briefly with the current oba. Write a list of five or six questions that you would like to ask him about his daily life, his kingdom, and the people he rules.

Writing Tip Be sure that your questions are worded in a way that shows respect for the powerful ruler and his kingdom. Also be sure to include a brief introduction identifying yourself and the purpose of your visit.

Assess and Reteach

Assess Progress L2
Have students complete the Section Assessment. Administer the *Section Quiz.*

All in One **Unit 4 History of Our World Teaching Resources,** *Section Quiz,* p. 51

Reteach L1
If students need more instruction, have them read this section in the Reading and Vocabulary Study Guide.

Chapter 11, Section 2, **History of Our World Reading and Vocabulary Study Guide,** pp. 121–123

Extend L3
Have students learn more about West African culture by completing the *Enrichment* activity about folk tales.

All in One **Unit 4 History of Our World Teaching Resources,** *Enrichment,* p. 60

Answer

✓ **Reading Check** The leaders of Ile-Ife were called onis and the leaders of Benin were called obas.

Writing Activity
Use the *Rubric for Assessing a Writing Assignment.*

All in One **Unit 4 History of Our World Teaching Resources,** *Rubric for Assessing a Writing Assignment,* p. 71

Section 2 Assessment

Key Terms
Students' sentences should reflect knowledge of each Key Term.

Target Reading Skill
Student should be able to accurately paraphrase the information from the text.

Comprehension and Critical Thinking
1. (a) Ghana, Mali, and Songhai **(b)** trade in salt and gold **(c)** Possible answer: they have economies that depend on trade with other regions.

2. (a) Ile-Ife—life-like sculptures that may be portraits of the onis; Benin—bronze, brass, ivory, and copper objects that may be influenced by Ile-Ife traditions **(b)** Possible answer: The objects may have survived because some metals can stay intact over time better than other materials, and the cultures that followed the kingdoms may have appreciated and preserved the art.

Focus on Tombouctou L2

Guided Instruction

- Ask students to read the text and study the art, photos, and captions on these pages.

- Ask students **What items were traded in Tombouctou's markets?** *(metal wares, wood, grains, nuts, fish, camel meat, milk, water, dates, rugs, linen, precious ivory, gold, salt, and slaves)*

- Have students study the map p. 325. Ask Students **Which journey do you think would be the most difficult—traveling fom Tangier to Ife, or from Taghaza to Taoudenni?** *(probably the traveling from Tangier to Ife, because it is a much longer distance)*

- As a class, answer the Assessment questions. Allow students to briefly discuss their responses with a partner before sharing their answers with the class.

Focus On
Tombouctou

From the salt mines of the Sahara, caravan leaders drove their camels through the hot desert sand. Heavily weighted with slabs of salt, the camel train headed south. Meantime, trade caravans from West Africa's gold mines traveled north. They met in the West African city of Tombouctou (tohm book TOO). In the 1500s, salt was as valuable as gold in the city's markets.

A Marketplace of Goods and Ideas Business was brisk in Tombouctou's markets. Buyers and sellers traded for metal wares and wood; grains and nuts; fish, camel meat, milk, water, and dates; rugs and linen; precious ivory, gold, salt, and even slaves.

By the mid-1500s, about 60,000 people lived in Tombouctou. Artisans such as weavers, dyers, and metalsmiths had shops in the busy city.

More than just a marketplace, this city drew scholars from all over the Islamic world to study and exchange ideas. Many people within the city spoke Arabic. Muslims could pray at three impressive dried-mud mosques.

The illustration at the right shows a market scene in Tombouctou with a mosque in the background. The illustration at the top of the page is of an ancient manuscript that was found in the city.

Background: Links Across Time

The Value of Salt In ancient times, salt was so valuable that it was traded for gold. In Ethiopia and elsewhere in Africa, salt cakes were actually used as money. But it was not necessarily the taste of salt that made it so valuable. Salt can be used as a condiment and a preservative, and could therefore preserve meat and other food items for long journeys. Also, although excessive amounts of salt can be dangerous, salt is necessary for human survival. The consequences of salt deprivation in humans can range from nausea and weakness to a coma and even death.

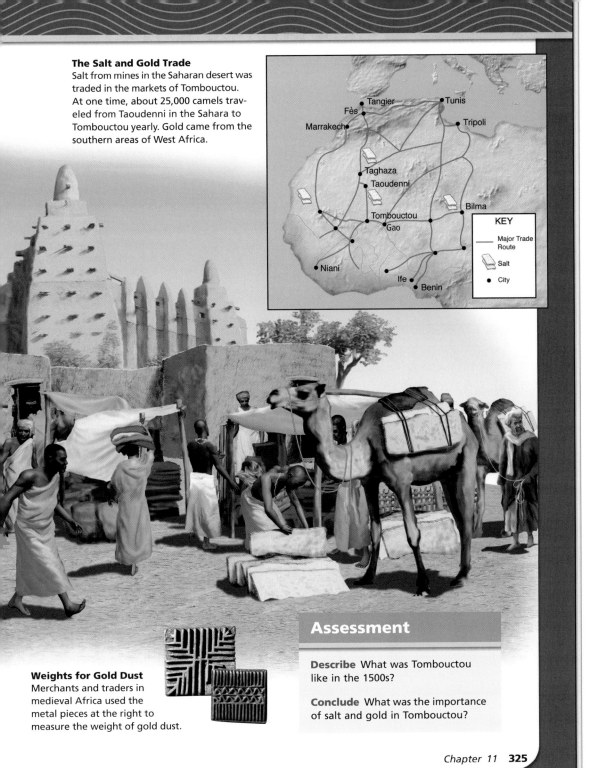

The Salt and Gold Trade
Salt from mines in the Saharan desert was traded in the markets of Tombouctou. At one time, about 25,000 camels traveled from Taoudenni in the Sahara to Tombouctou yearly. Gold came from the southern areas of West Africa.

KEY
Major Trade Route
Salt
City

Weights for Gold Dust
Merchants and traders in medieval Africa used the metal pieces at the right to measure the weight of gold dust.

Assessment

Describe What was Tombouctou like in the 1500s?

Conclude What was the importance of salt and gold in Tombouctou?

Independent Practice
Show students *Transparency HOW 17: Africa: Political.* As a class, have students compare the map on page 325 with the transparency, and identify in which present-day countries the cities on the map in the Student Edition are located. Then, create a two-column table on the board, labeling one column *City* and the other *Present-day country where located.* Have students take turns coming up to the board and filling in parts of the chart.

📖 **History of Our World Transparencies,** *Transparency HOW 17: Africa: Political*

Answers

Assessment

Describe By the mid-1500s, about 60,000 people lived in Tombouctou; in addition to being a marketplace, the city was filled with Islamic scholars from all over the world; many people spoke Arabic; and the city had three impressive dried-mud mosques.
Conclude The trade of salt and gold made Tombouctou an important city with a large population; this in turn attracted scholars from all over the Islamic world.

Objectives

Social Studies

1. Learn about powerful East African civilizations whose cities included Aksum and Lalibela.
2. Find out why the coastal cities of East Africa were important.

Reading/Language Arts

Learn to summarize to help you remember and study what you read.

Prepare to Read

Build Background Knowledge ▪L2

Tell students that in this section they will learn about East Africa's trading centers, including one called Great Zimbabwe. Show the video *Great Zimbabwe: The Lost City.* Ask students to note possible reasons for the decline of Great Zimbabwe. Have students decide which theory they believe best answers the mystery and why. Use the Numbered Head participation strategy (TE, p. T36) to get students to share their opinion.

📼 *Great Zimbabwe: The Lost City,*
World Studies Video Program

Set a Purpose for Reading ▪L2

- Preview the Objectives.

- Read each statement in the *Reading Readiness Guide* aloud. Ask students to mark the statements true or false.

  All in One Unit 4 History of Our World Teaching Resources, *Reading Readiness Guide,* p. 53

- Have students discuss the statements in pairs or groups of four, then mark their worksheets again. Use the Numbered Heads participation strategy (TE, p. T40) to call on students to share their group's perspectives.

Vocabulary Builder
Preview Key Terms ▪L2

Pronounce each Key Term, then ask students to say the word with you. Provide a simple explanation such as, "Swahili is one of the most important languages of East Africa today."

Prepare to Read

Objectives

In this section, you will

1. Learn about powerful East African civilizations whose cities included Aksum and Lalibela.
2. Find out why the coastal cities of East Africa were important.

Taking Notes

As you read this section, look for the major events in this period of East Africa's history. Copy the timeline below, and add events and dates in the proper places on it.

A.D. **100** ————————————— A.D. **1600**

 **Target Reading Skill**

Summarize When you summarize, you review and state, in the correct order, the main points you have read. Summarizing can help you understand and study. As you read, pause occasionally to summarize what you have read.

Key Terms

- **Kilwa** (KEEL wah) *n.* one of many trading cities on the East African coast
- **Aksum** (AHK soom) *n.* an important East African center of trade

- **city-state** (SIH tee stayt) *n.* a city that is also a separate, independent state
- **Swahili** (swah HEE lee) *n.* a Bantu language with Arabic words, spoken along the East African coast
- **Great Zimbabwe** (grayt zim BAHB way) *n.* a powerful southeast African city

The ruins of the Great Mosque of Kilwa in Tanzania

326 History of Our World

The port was full of hurrying people, bobbing ships, and bundles of goods. The bright sun reflected off the water. Some traders were unloading glass beads, rice, spices, and expensive jewels carried from India. Others were bringing honey and wheat from Southwest Asia. Rich silks and fragile porcelains were also arriving after the long voyage from faraway China.

This was the bustling scene at **Kilwa** (KEEL wah), one of many trading cities along the coast of East Africa. Find Kilwa on the map titled Civilizations of Africa on page 309. Located in present-day Tanzania, Kilwa was an Islamic city with a royal palace and lush orchards and gardens. Kilwa's rulers charged taxes on all goods that entered their port. These taxes made Kilwa rich. Ibn Battutah (IB un bat TOO tah)—a famous Muslim traveler from North Africa—visited in the 1330s. He wrote that Kilwa was "one of the most beautiful and best-constructed towns in the world."

🔄 Target Reading Skill ▪L2

Summarize Point out the Target Reading Skill. Tell students that summarizing the text will help them remember what they read.

Model the skill by reading and summarizing the last paragraph on p. 329. (*Like many medieval African kingdoms, Great Zimbabwe grew strong by trading goods such as the gold mined between two rivers of the region.*)

Give students *Summarize.* Have them complete the activity in their groups.

All in One Unit 4 History of Our World Teaching Resources, *Summarize,* p. 58

Ancient Ethiopia

Thousands of years ago, rich civilizations began to develop in southern Arabia and northeastern Africa along the Red Sea. By A.D. 1, the city of **Aksum** (AHK soom), located in present-day Ethiopia, was an important East African center of trade.

Aksum, a Center of Trade and Christianity Although the city of Aksum was located in the mountains about 100 miles (160 kilometers) inland, it controlled a trading port at Adulis (AD oo lis) on the Red Sea. Over time, Aksum conquered much of modern Ethiopia and southwestern Arabia. It grew steadily in strength and wealth.

The merchants of Aksum traded goods at ports as far away as India. One of the main trade goods they controlled was ivory. Ivory, the white material from elephant tusks, was highly valued for carving. As they traded goods with foreign merchants, the people of Aksum also exchanged ideas and beliefs with them.

During the A.D. 300s, King Ezana (ay ZAH nuh) of Aksum learned about a new religion—Christianity. Soon, the king became a Christian himself and made Christianity the official religion of his kingdom. Over time, most people under Aksum's rule converted to Christianity.

For several hundred years, Aksum kept its control of the major trade routes linking Africa with Europe and Asia. Then in the A.D. 600s, Muslims fought with the rulers of Aksum for control of the Red Sea trade routes. Eventually, the Muslims conquered the coastal ports. The Muslim conquest of the coast ended the trade that had given Aksum its power and wealth.

Christianity in Ethiopia
The city of Aksum, at top, remains an important religious center today. The St. Mary of Zion Church is at the right. The young priest above is holding a Coptic cross, a symbol of Ethiopian Christianity. **Compare and Contrast** *How do these images of Christianity compare to Christian imagery in the United States?*

Vocabulary Builder

Use the information below to teach students this section's high-use words.

High Use Word	Definition and Sample Sentence
convert, p. 327	*v.* to cause someone to change a belief The preacher hoped to **convert** people to his religion.
contact, p. 328	*n.* communication or connection While on vacation, she had no **contact** with her friends.
unique, p. 328	*adj.* one of a kind He bought the painting because he liked its **unique** designs.

Instruct

Ancient Ethiopia L2

Guided Instruction

- **Vocabulary Builder** Clarify the high-use words **convert, contact,** and **unique** before reading.

- Read Ancient Ethiopia using the Structured Silent Reading strategy (TE, p. T38).

- Ask students **Where was the city of Aksum?** *(in the mountains about 100 miles from the coast of the Red Sea, in what is now Ethiopia)* **How did it become a center of trade even though it was located 100 miles inland?** *(Possible answers: It controlled the trading port Adulis on the Red Sea; it conquered lands in southwestern Arabia; it controlled major trade routes linking Africa with Europe and Asia.)*

- Have students discuss how Aksum became a center of Christianity. *(King Azana learned about Christianity and made it the official religion of the kingdom during the A.D. 300s.)*

- Ask students **What was the cause of Aksum's fall from power and wealth?** *(In the A.D. 600s, Muslims fought with the Christian rulers of Aksum and gained control of the trade from the coastal ports.)*

Answer

Compare and Contrast The St. Mary of Zion Church has a different architectural style from many churches in the United States. Also, the Coptic cross, which has four arms that are all the same length, is not traditionally used in the United States.

Guided Instruction (continued)

■ Ask students **Why do you think the churches of East Africa have unique customs and traditions?** (*Possible answer: Many neighboring lands had converted to Islam and mountains separated political and religious leaders from other Christians, so they developed their own customs and traditions.*)

■ Ask students **What is unusual about the churches built during the rule of King Lalibela?** (*The flat rooftops of the churches are level with surrounding land.*)

Independent Practice

Ask students to create the Taking Notes graphic organizer on a blank piece of paper. Then have them add major events about ancient Ethiopia's history on the timeline, along with the corresponding dates for each event.

Monitor Progress

As students fill in the graphic organizer, circulate and make sure individuals are choosing the correct facts and dates. Provide assistance as needed.

St. George's Church, Lalibela
At top, worshipers surround St. George's Church, one of the churches that King Lalibela had carved into the rock about A.D. 1200. Above, a priest at the church's entrance.
Apply Information *How long has this church been in use?*

Lalibela and the Spread of Christianity

After Aksum had lost power, the Christian kings of the region built churches and monasteries. But these kings did not build a new capital. Instead, they moved from place to place around the kingdom. They lived in royal tents and were accompanied by thousands of citizens and servants.

Many neighboring lands converted to Islam, but present-day Ethiopia remained Christian. Cut off in their mountainous home, the Ethiopians had little direct contact with other Christian peoples. In time, their churches developed unique customs and traditions. In one such tradition, churchgoers rest their foreheads against the outside wall of a church and kiss it to show respect.

Another unique feature of the region's Christianity is a group of churches built about A.D. 1200 under King Lalibela (lah lee BAY lah). The king had his people build new churches—but not from the ground up. Instead, the people were to carve the churches down into the solid red rock. The flat rooftops of the buildings are level with the surrounding land. The churches are in a town named Lalibela in honor of the king. These fascinating churches are still used today by the Christians of Ethiopia.

✓ **Reading Check** Describe the churches of Lalibela.

⌐ Background: Links Across Time

Religion in Ethiopia Today Today, between 35 to 40 percent of Ethiopians practice the Ethiopian Orthodox religion, one of the world's oldest Christian churches. Islam is practiced by 45 to 50 percent of Ethiopians, while the remaining Ethiopians practice other religions, including traditional African religions. A small number of Ethiopians practice Judaism, but most of the country's Jews emigrated to Israel in the 1980s and early 1990s when Ethiopia was affected by war and drought.

Answers

Apply Information for about 800 years

✓ **Reading Check** The churches, built almost one thousand years ago during the rule of King Lalibela, are carved from the region's solid red stone. Instead of being built from the ground up, their flat rooftops are level with the surrounding land. The churches are still used today by Ethiopia's Christians.

Rich Centers of Trade

After Muslims gained control of Indian Ocean trade, trade centers developed along the east coast of Africa. Each of these ports was a **city-state** (SIH tee stayt), a city with its own government that controls much of the surrounding land. By 1400, there were about 30 such city-states along Africa's Indian Ocean coast.

Trade thrived in East Africa because the region supplied goods such as gold and ivory that were very scarce outside Africa. In return, Muslim traders brought luxury goods that could not be found in Africa. Muslim traders from Arabia also brought their religion and language to these African city-states.

The City-State of Kilwa The merchants of Kilwa traded goods from inland regions of Africa for the foreign goods that traders brought to the port by sea. Contact between Africans and Arabs in Kilwa and other coastal city-states led to a new culture and language. Called **Swahili** (swah HEE lee), this Bantu language has words borrowed from Arabic. Swahili was spoken all along the East African coast. Most people on this coast converted to Islam.

In the 1500s, Portuguese troops sailing from Europe captured and looted Kilwa and the other coastal city-states. Portugal took over the prosperous trade routes. But the influence of Swahili culture remained. Today, Swahili is an official language in Kenya and Tanzania, and most East Africans use Swahili for business. Islam is still an important religion in the region.

Great Zimbabwe Much of the gold traded at Kilwa was mined in an inland area to the south, between the Zambezi and Limpopo rivers. This was the region controlled by the powerful southeastern African city of **Great Zimbabwe** (grayt zim BAHB way). Like other medieval African centers that you have read about, Great Zimbabwe grew rich and powerful through trade.

Summarize Summarize the two paragraphs under the red heading at the left. Give two reasons why trade developed in this region.

Video

Learn about Great Zimbabwe and explore its ruins.

Mombasa Harbor, Kenya
Like Kilwa, the port of Mombasa on the Indian Ocean has a long history of trade. Wooden sailing ships like the ones below carried the trade of these city-states. **Infer** *Why were the East African city-states located along the coast?*

Differentiated Instruction

For Advanced Readers L3
Students can learn more about the importance of trade with the project *Mapping World Trade*. Have them work in small groups to complete the project.

Go Online
PHSchool.com

For: Long-Term Integrated Projects: *Mapping World Trade*
Visit: PHSchool.com
Web Code: lgd-8104

Target Reading Skill L2

Summarize As a follow up, ask students to complete the Target Reading Skill activity on this page. (*East Africa's location on the Indian Ocean and demand for the area's natural resources encouraged trade in the region. By 1400, there were about 30 city-states along Africa's east coast. Muslim traders brought luxury goods and elements of their culture to these areas.*)

Video

Show *Great Zimbabwe: The Lost City*. Ask students **Why did Great Zimbabwe become a large urban center?** (*because of its control of trade*)

Rich Centers of Trade L2

Guided Instruction
- Read Rich Centers of Trade with students.

- Ask students **What happened as Muslims gained control of the east coast of Africa?** (*Trade centers developed along the southeast coast of Africa.*)

- Ask students **What was Great Zimbabwe?** (*a medieval African trading kingdom*) **What signs of Great Zimbabwe remain today?** (*Its stone ruins remain and its name lives on in the nation of Zimbabwe.*)

Independent Practice
Have students complete the graphic organizer with main events from the section.

Monitor Progress
- Show *Section Reading Support Transparency HOW 89* and ask students to check their graphic organizers. Go over key concepts and clarify key vocabulary as needed.

   History of Our World Transparencies, *Section Reading Support Transparency HOW 89*

- Tell students to fill in the last column of the *Reading Readiness Guide*. Probe for what they learned that confirms or invalidates each statement.

  All in One Unit 4 History of Our World Teaching Resources, *Reading Readiness Guide*, p. 53

Answers

Infer because trade developed there

Assess and Reteach

Assess Progress L2
Have students complete the Section Assessment. Administer the *Section Quiz*.

All in One Unit 4 History of Our World Teaching Resources, *Section Quiz*, p. 55

Reteach L1
If students need more instruction, have them read this section in the Reading and Vocabulary Study Guide.

Chapter 11, Section 3, **History of Our World Reading and Vocabulary Study Guide,** pp. 124–126

Extend L3
Have students learn more about how trade is conducted by completing the small group activity *Trading Items With Silent Barter*. Ask them to write a short report about the result of the barter and how they managed to communicate without talking.

All in One Unit 4 History of Our World Teaching Resources, *Small Group Activity: Trading Items With Silent Barter,* pp. 62–65

Answer

✓ Reading Check Trade routes may have moved, with other centers becoming more important; farmers may have overused the soil.

Section 3 Assessment

Key Terms
Students' sentences should reflect knowledge of each Key Term.

Target Reading Skill
Answers will vary, but summaries should focus on the most important ideas from the text and place them in the correct order.

Comprehension and Critical Thinking
1. (a) He became a Christian and made Christianity the official religion of the kingdom. **(b)** a group of Christian churches carved from solid red stone and built about one thousand years ago during the rule of King Lalibela **(c)** Possible answer: The churches might not have been built if King Ezana had not made Christianity the official religion of the kingdom.

2. (a) The gold traded at Kilwa was mined in Great Zimbabwe. **(b)** Possible answer: Kilwa's location as a port city along the southeast

---

Stone-walled ruins at Great Zimbabwe, in the present-day nation of Zimbabwe

Historians believe that the city of Great Zimbabwe had been founded by about 1100. Its Bantu-speaking people were the ancestors of today's Shona (SHOHN uh) people. Most people in this area were poor farmers. For those who were better off, large herds of cattle were an important form of wealth. Richest of all were the leaders who controlled the gold trade. These powerful leaders and their families lived among impressive stone-walled structures.

Great Zimbabwe thrived for hundreds of years. Historians believe that the city reached its peak before the early 1400s. By 1500, the city had fallen. Trade routes may have moved to favor other centers. Farmers also may have worn out the soil. In either case, the glory of Great Zimbabwe was not entirely lost. Its stone ruins still stand, and its history is a source of pride for the present-day nation of Zimbabwe.

✓ Reading Check **What were two possible causes for the collapse of Great Zimbabwe?**

Section 3 Assessment

Key Terms
Review the key terms at the beginning of this section. Use each term in a sentence that explains its meaning.

Target Reading Skill
Write a summary of the two paragraphs at the top of this page.

Comprehension and Critical Thinking
1. (a) Recall What change did King Ezana of Aksum make in the A.D. 300s?

(b) Identify What are some of the most famous sites in Ethiopia today?
(c) Synthesize Information How are these famous sites related to the changes made by King Ezana?
2. (a) Explain What connection was there between Great Zimbabwe and Kilwa?
(b) Analyze Information How did the locations of Kilwa and Great Zimbabwe make them powerful and rich?

Writing Activity
Study the photo of the rock-cut church of Lalibela on page 328. Write a description of this unusual church to a friend or relative. Where is it located? What does the building look like? How was it built? In what ways is it similar to or different from other buildings?

Go Online PHSchool.com
For: An activity on historic Ethiopia
Visit: PHSchool.com
Web Code: lgd-8203

---

coast of Africa made it a prosperous trading center; the kingdom of Great Zimbabwe ruled an inland area between two rivers where gold was mined and then traded.

Writing Activity
Use the *Rubric for Assessing a Writing Assignment*.

All in One Unit 4 History of Our World Teaching Resources, *Rubric for Assessing a Writing Assignment,* p. 71

Go Online PHSchool.com Typing in the Web code when prompted will bring students directly to detailed instructions for this activity.

Review and Assessment

Review Chapter Content

- Review and revisit the major themes of this chapter by asking students to classify what Guiding Questions each bulleted statement in the Chapter Summary answers. Have students work in groups to match the statements with the appropriate questions. Conduct an Idea Wave (TE, p. T39) to share their answers. Refer to p. 1 of the Student Edition for the text of the Guiding Questions.

- Assign Vocabulary Development for students to review Key Terms.

  All in One **Unit 4 History of Our World Teaching Resources,** *Vocabulary Development*, p. 70

◆ Chapter Summary

Section 1: Africa and the Bantu

- The physical geography and natural vegetation of Africa are diverse, from tropical rain forests along the Equator to the world's largest desert.
- More than 2,000 years ago, the Bantu-speaking people of West Africa began migrating across central and southern Africa, carrying their culture wherever they went.

Section 2: Kingdoms of West Africa

- Powerful trading kingdoms, including Ghana, Mali, and Songhai, controlled the savannas of West Africa for hundreds of years.
- The cities of Ile-Ife and Benin were important centers of trade and art in the West African rain forests.

Section 3: East Africa's Great Trading Centers

- Strong kings built lasting monuments and brought changes to the lands they ruled in present-day Ethiopia.
- City-states along the East African coast and the inland city of Great Zimbabwe grew rich from trade.

A bronze plaque from Benin

◆ Key Terms

Each statement below includes a key term from this chapter. If the statement is true, write *true*. If it is false, rewrite the statement to make it true.

1. Swahili is a language based on Portuguese, with Bantu words, that is spoken in West Africa.

2. Movement from one country or region to settle in another is called migration.

3. Mansa Musa ruled the kingdom of Mali.

4. A city-state is a city with its own government that controls much of the surrounding land.

5. The Sahara is the world's longest river.

6. Oral history is an account of the past that is passed down from generation to generation by word of mouth.

Vocabulary Builder

High-Use Academic Words

Revisit this chapter's high-use words:

environment	conquer	convert
technique	independent	contact
traditional	province	unique
adapt	stability	

Ask students to review the definitions they recorded on their *Word Knowledge* worksheets.

All in One **Unit 4 History of Our World Teaching Resources,** *Word Knowledge*, p. 59

Consider allowing students to earn extra credit if they use the words in their answers to the questions in the Chapter Review and Assessment. The words must be used correctly and in a natural context to win the extra points.

Answers

Key Terms

1. False. Swahili is a Bantu language, with Arabic words, spoken along the East African coast.

2. True

3. True

4. True

5. False. The Sahara is the world's largest desert.

6. True

Review and Assessment

Comprehension and Critical Thinking

7. (a) on either side of the Equator
(b) Savannas are grassland with scattered trees and bushes. **(c)** Africa's rain forests are hot and moist, while its savannas are drier and cooler. The two climates are both capable of sustaining vegetation.

8. (a) modern techniques and oral history
(b) because historians often must piece together clues to find the whole story

9. (a) African Muslims fought the rulers of Aksum in the A.D. 600s for control of the Red Sea trade routes. **(b)** It led to further development of trade on the eastern coast of Africa.

10. (a) Ile-Ife and Benin **(b)** Possible answer: to pay tribute to the king

11. (a) Cairo **(b)** Possible answer: to rest, to trade for food and supplies

Skills Practice
Students' sentences should determine that the source is not reliable, using the skill steps they have learned.

Review and Assessment (continued)

◆ **Comprehension and Critical Thinking**

7. (a) Locate Where are Africa's tropical rain forests located?
(b) Describe What are some important features of Africa's savannas?
(c) Compare and Contrast In what ways are Africa's rain forests and savannas alike? In what ways are they different?

8. (a) List Name two things that have helped modern historians study the history of Africa south of the Sahara.
(b) Explain Why is studying this history "like solving a puzzle"?

9. (a) Summarize When and why did African Muslims fight the rulers of Aksum?
(b) Analyze Why was this fight important?

10. (a) Recall In which two rain forest kingdoms did artists make bronze sculptures?
(b) Generalize Why might an artist depict a powerful king in his or her work?

11. (a) Identify Where did Mansa Musa and his caravan stop in July 1324?
(b) Infer Why might a large caravan need to stop in the middle of a very long journey?

◆ **Skills Practice**

Using Reliable Information In the Skills for Life activity in this chapter, you learned how to judge whether information is reliable. Review the steps for this skill. Suppose you found the text below in a recent travel guide to Africa. Use the steps for this skill to decide whether the information is reliable. Write a sentence that explains why or why not.

"The mosque at Djenné is the most magnificent building in all of Africa. It must have been built by a powerful ruler with a strong religious faith. Every traveler to Africa should visit this mosque."

◆ **Writing Activity: Science**

You have read about the importance of iron tools and weapons to early peoples. Do research, using reliable sources, to find out how Africans made these early iron tools. What were the different steps in the process? What equipment did they use? What kind of tools did they make? Write a short report on your findings.

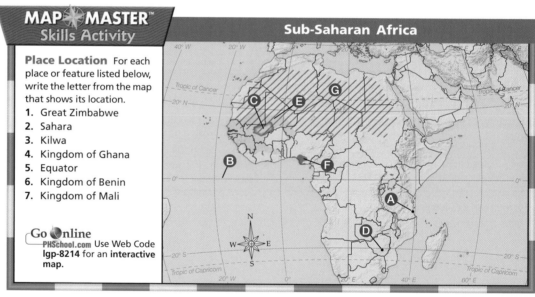

MAP MASTER™
Skills Activity

Place Location For each place or feature listed below, write the letter from the map that shows its location.
1. Great Zimbabwe
2. Sahara
3. Kilwa
4. Kingdom of Ghana
5. Equator
6. Kingdom of Benin
7. Kingdom of Mali

Go Online
PHSchool.com Use Web Code lgp-8214 for an **interactive map.**

Sub-Saharan Africa

Writing Activity: Science
Reports will vary, but should use reliable sources of information to explain how early tools and weapons were made and used. Use *Rubric for Assessing a Report,* to evaluate students' reports.

All in One Unit 4 History of Our World Teaching Resources, *Rubric for Assessing a Writing Assignment,* p. 72

MAP MASTER™
Skills Activity

1. D	**2.** G
3. A	**4.** C
5. B	**6.** F
7. E	

Go Online
PHSchool.com Students may practice their map skills using the interactive online version of this map.

Standardized Test Prep

Test-Taking Tips

Some questions on standardized tests ask you to find main ideas. Read the paragraph below. Then follow the tips to answer the sample question.

> Imagine trading a pound of salt for a pound of gold. At today's prices, a pound of salt costs only about 50 cents, but a pound of gold is worth thousands of dollars. That has not always been true everywhere. In parts of Africa, <u>salt was as scarce as gold in medieval times</u>. People needed <u>salt</u> to preserve their food. They needed it to stay healthy, too. So they <u>traded their gold for nearly the same weight of salt</u>.

TIP As you read the paragraph, try to identify its main idea, or most important point. In some cases, the main idea may be stated. In other cases, such as this one, you have to add up the details to find the main idea.

Pick the letter that best answers the question.

The main idea of this paragraph is that

A today, a pound of <u>salt</u> costs only about 50 cents.

B in medieval Africa, <u>salt</u> was nearly as valuable as <u>gold</u> because it was needed and scarce.

C people need <u>salt</u> to stay healthy.

D in medieval Africa, <u>gold</u> was easier for traders to carry than <u>salt</u>.

TIP Look for key words in the answer choices or question that connect to the paragraph. In this case, two key words are *salt* and *gold*.

Think It Through The paragraph's main idea is that Africans traded gold for salt long ago, when salt was hard to get. Look at all four choices. A and C both just give details about salt. They do not compare the values of salt and gold. That leaves B and D. D gives information that is not in the paragraph. So, the correct answer is B, which is the main idea of the paragraph.

Practice Questions

Use the tips above and other tips in this book to help you answer the following questions.

1. In Africa, tropical rain forests lie along
   A Madagascar.
   B the Equator.
   C an oasis.
   D the Nile.

2. The kingdom of Mali rose to power after this West African kingdom weakened.
   A Songhai
   B Benin
   C Ghana
   D Nigeria

3. Which Christian king of East Africa had his people carve underground churches?
   A Sundiata
   B Ezana
   C Mansa Musa
   D Lalibela

Read the paragraph below, and answer the question that follows.

Medieval traders sold East African ivory in India. Ivory comes from elephant tusks. India has its own elephants, so why did Indians buy East African ivory? East African elephants have softer tusks. East African ivory is better for carving.

4. The main idea of this paragraph is that
   A ivory comes from elephant tusks.
   B Indians bought East African ivory because it was good for carving.
   C trading elephant tusks is illegal today.
   D East African elephants have softer tusks than Indian elephants.

Use Web Code **lga-8201** for a **Chapter 11 self-test.**

Chapter 11 **333**

Standardized Test Prep

Answers

1. B
2. C
3. D
4. B

Go Online PHSchool.com Students may use the Chapter 11 self-test on PH.School.com to prepare for the Chapter Test.

Overview

Section 1 — South America and the Incas
1. Find out about the geography of the Americas.
2. Learn about the empire established by the Incas of South America.

Section 2 — Cultures of Middle America
1. Learn about the Mayan culture of Middle America.
2. Find out about the powerful Aztec empire.

Section 3 — Cultures of North America
1. Find out about the Mound Builders who lived in eastern North America.
2. Learn about the cultures of the Southwest and Great Plains.
3. Find out about the Woodland peoples of North America.

DISCOVERY CHANNEL SCHOOL Video

Cortés and the Aztec Empire
Length: 2 minutes, 57 seconds
Use with Section 2
This video segment describes how Cortés defeated the mighty Aztec empire.

Technology Resources

Go Online
PHSchool.com

Students use embedded Web codes to access Internet activities, chapter self-tests, and additional map practice. They may also access Dorling Kindersley's Online Desk Reference to learn more about each country they study.

Interactive Textbook

Use the Interactive Textbook to make content and concepts come alive through animations, videos, and activities that accompany the complete basal text—online and on CD-ROM.

PRENTICE HALL
TeacherEXPRESS
Plan • Teach • Assess

Use this complete suite of powerful teaching tools to make planning lessons and administering tests quicker and easier.

Reading and Assessment

Reading and Vocabulary Instruction

⟲ Model the Target Reading Skill

Main Idea Tell students that the main idea is the most important idea in a section. All of the details in a well-written paragraph should support the main idea. Write the paragraph below, from page 347 of the Student Edition, on the board. Point out that the main idea is that Tenochtitlan was a grand city. With students, identify and underline each supporting detail.

In spite of its swampy origins, Tenochtitlán became a magnificent capital city. At its center were an open plaza and one or more towering pyramid-temples. There were schools for the sons of the nobles and large stone palaces. Raised streets of hard earth, called causeways, connected the city to the surrounding land. To supply the city with enough fresh water, the Aztecs also built aqueducts. These special channels carried spring water from distant sources to storage areas in the city.

Ask yourself aloud: What do these details have in common? *(They all support the main idea that Tenochtitlan was magnificent because of its grand structures, roads, and aqueducts.)*

Use the following worksheets from Unit 4 All-in-One History of Our World Teaching Resources (pp. 94, 95, and 96) to support the chapter's Target Reading Skill.

Vocabulary Builder
High-Use Academic Words

Use these steps to teach this chapter's high-use words:

1. Have students rate how well they know each word on their Word Knowledge worksheets (All-in-One History of Our World Teaching Resources, p. 97).
2. Pronounce each word and ask students to repeat it.
3. Give students a brief definition or sample sentence (provided on TE pp. 337, 345, and 353).
4. Work with students as they fill in the "Definition or Example" column of their Word Knowledge worksheets.

Assessment

Formal Assessment

Test students' understanding of core knowledge and skills.

Chapter Tests A and B, All-in-One Unit 4 History of Our World Teaching Resources, pp. 110–115

Customize the Chapter Tests to suit your needs.

Exam*View*® Test Bank CD-ROM

Skills Assessment

Assess geographic literacy.

MapMaster Skills, Student Edition, pp. 335, 354, 360

Assess reading and comprehension.

Target Reading Skills, Student Edition, pp. 340, 346, 355, and in Section Assessments

Chapter 12 Assessment, History of Our World Reading and Vocabulary Study Guide, p. 137

Performance Assessment

Assess students' performance on this chapter's Writing Activities using the following rubric from All-in-One Unit 4 History of Our World Teaching Resources.

Rubric for Assessing a Writing Assignment, p. 108

Assess students' work through performance tasks.

Small Group Activity: Writing a Message Using Your Own Hieroglyphics, All-in-One Unit 4 History of Our World Teaching Resources, pp. 100–103

Online Assessment

Have students check their own understanding.

Chapter Self-Test

Section 1 South America and the Incas

 2 periods, 1 block (includes Skills for Life)

Social Studies Objectives
1. Find out about the geography of the Americas.
2. Learn about the empire established by the Incas of South America.

Reading/Language Arts Objective
Learn how to identify main ideas while you read.

Prepare to Read	Instructional Resources	Differentiated Instruction
Build Background Knowledge Have students scan the visuals in the section to determine what some of the accomplishments of ancient South American civilizations may have been. **Set a Purpose for Reading** Have students evaluate statements on the Reading Readiness Guide. **Preview Key Terms** Teach the section's Key Terms. **Target Reading Skill** Introduce the section's Target Reading Skill of **identifying main ideas.**	**All in One Unit 4 History of Our World Teaching Resources** L2 Reading Readiness Guide, p. 83 L2 Identify Main Ideas, p. 94	**Spanish Reading and Vocabulary Study Guide** L1 Chapter 12, Section 1, pp. 92–93 ELL

Instruct	Instructional Resources	Differentiated Instruction
Geography of the Americas Discuss how geography and climate affected ancient peoples who lived in the Americas. **The Mountain Empire of the Incas** Discuss the accomplishments of the Incan empire and ask about the events preceding its collapse. **Target Reading Skill** Review **identifying main ideas.**	**All in One Unit 4 History of Our World Teaching Resources** L2 Guided Reading and Review, p. 84 L2 Reading Readiness Guide, p. 83 **History of Our World Transparencies** L2 Section Reading Support Transparency HOW 90	**All in One Unit 4 History of Our World Teaching Resources** L2 Skills for Life, p. 99 AR, GT, LPR, SN **Teacher's Edition** L1 For Special Needs Students, TE p. 339 L1 For Less Proficient Readers, TE p. 339 **History of Our World Transparencies** L1 Section Reading Support Transparency HOW 90 ELL, LPR, SN **Spanish Support** L2 Guided Reading and Review (Spanish), p. 100 ELL

Assess and Reteach	Instructional Resources	Differentiated Instruction
Assess Progress Evaluate student comprehension with the section assessment and section quiz. **Reteach** Assign the Reading and Vocabulary Study Guide to help struggling students. **Extend** Extend the lesson by assigning a Book Project.	**All in One Unit 4 History of Our World Teaching Resources** L2 Section Quiz, p. 85 L3 Book Project: One Job Through the Ages, pp. 13–15 Rubric for Assessing a Writing Assignment, p. 108 **Reading and Vocabulary Study Guide** L1 Chapter 12, Section 1, pp. 128–130	**Spanish Support** L2 Section Quiz (Spanish), p. 101 ELL **Social Studies Skills Tutor CD-ROM** L1 Identifying Cause and Effect ELL, LPR, SN

Key

L1 Basic to Average   L3 Average to Advanced   LPR Less Proficient Readers   GT Gifted and Talented

L2 For All Students   AR Advanced Readers   ELL English Language Learners

                                             SN Special Needs Students

Section 2 Cultures of Middle America

 *2 periods, 1 block*

Social Studies Objectives
1. Learn about the Mayan culture of Middle America.
2. Find out about the powerful Aztec empire.

Reading/Language Arts Objective
Learn how to identify details that support a main idea.

Prepare to Read

Build Background Knowledge
Show a video and have students compare the reasons for the fall of the Aztec and Incan empires.

Set a Purpose for Reading
Have students begin to fill out the Reading Readiness Guide.

Preview Key Terms
Teach the section's Key Terms.

Target Reading Skill
Introduce the section's Target Reading Skill of **identifying supporting details.**

Instructional Resources

All in One Unit 4 History of Our World Teaching Resources
- L2 Reading Readiness Guide, p. 87
- L2 Identify Supporting Details, p. 95

World Studies Video Program
- L2 Cortés and the Aztec Empire

Differentiated Instruction

Spanish Reading and Vocabulary Study Guide
- L1 Chapter 12, Section 2, pp. 94–95 ELL

Instruct

The Culture of the Maya
Discuss the Maya's farming techniques, religion, and cities.

Target Reading Skill
Review **identifying supporting details.**

The Aztec Empire
Ask about the characteristics of the Aztec empire and discuss how the Aztecs dealt with challenges.

Instructional Resources

All in One Unit 4 History of Our World Teaching Resources
- L2 Guided Reading and Review, p. 88
- L2 Reading Readiness Guide, p. 87

History of Our World Transparencies
- L2 Section Reading Support Transparency HOW 91

Differentiated Instruction

All in One History of Our World Teaching Resources
- L3 The Talking Stone, pp. 104–106 AR, GT

Teacher's Edition
- L1 For Special Needs Students, TE pp. 346, 351
- L3 For Advanced Readers, TE p. 347
- L2 For English Language Learners, TE p. 347

Spanish Support
- L2 Guided Reading and Review (Spanish), p. 102 ELL

Assess and Reteach

Assess Progress
Evaluate student comprehension with the section assessment and section quiz.

Reteach
Assign the Reading and Vocabulary Study Guide to help struggling students.

Extend
Extend the lesson by assigning a Small Group Activity.

Instructional Resources

All in One Unit 4 History of Our World Teaching Resources
- L2 Section Quiz, p. 89
- L3 Small Group Activity: Writing a Message Using Your Own Hieroglyphics, pp. 100–103
  Rubric for Assessing a Writing Assignment, p. 108

Reading and Vocabulary Study Guide
- L1 Chapter 12, Section 2, pp. 131–135

Differentiated Instruction

Spanish Support
- L2 Section Quiz (Spanish), p. 103 ELL

Key
- L1 Basic to Average
- L3 Average to Advanced
- L2 For All Students
- LPR Less Proficient Readers
- AR Advanced Readers
- SN Special Needs Students
- GT Gifted and Talented
- ELL English Language Learners

Section 3 Cultures of North America

 2 periods, 1 block (includes Chapter Review and Assessment)

Social Studies Objectives

1. Find out about the Mound Builders who lived in eastern North America.
2. Learn about the cultures of the Southwest and Great Plains.
3. Find out about the Woodland peoples of North America.

Reading/Language Arts Objective

Learn how to identify details that add up to the main idea in a paragraph.

Prepare to Read	Instructional Resources	Differentiated Instruction
Build Background Knowledge Ask students preview the headings, maps, and photographs in the section to predict what they will be learning about. **Set a Purpose for Reading** Have students begin to fill out the Reading Readiness Guide. **Preview Key Terms** Teach the section's Key Terms. **Target Reading Skill** Introduce the section's Target Reading Skill of **identifying implied main ideas.**	**All in One Unit 4 History of Our World Teaching Resources** L2 Reading Readiness Guide, p. 91 L2 Identify Implied Main Ideas, p. 96	**Spanish Reading and Vocabulary Study Guide** L1 Chapter 12, Section 3, pp. 96–97 ELL

Instruct	Instructional Resources	Differentiated Instruction
The Eastern Mound Builders Ask questions about and discuss the characteristics of the North American mound building societies. **Target Reading Skill** Review **identify implied main ideas.** **Peoples of the Southwest and Great Plains** Discuss the lives of the Anasazi, Pueblo peoples, and Plains Indians. **Peoples of the Woodlands** Ask about how Native American groups in the Northwest showed their wealth and obtained food, and discuss the Iroquois political system.	**All in One Unit 4 History of Our World Teaching Resources** L2 Guided Reading and Review, p. 92 L2 Reading Readiness Guide, p. 91 **History of Our World Transparencies** L2 Transparency B12: Chart/Table L2 Section Reading Support Transparency HOW 92	**Teacher's Edition** L1 For English Language Learners, TE p. 356 L3 For Gifted and Talented, TE p. 356 L1 For Less Proficient Readers, TE p. 357 **Spanish Support** L2 Guided Reading and Review (Spanish), p. 104 ELL

Assess and Reteach	Instructional Resources	Differentiated Instruction
Assess Progress Evaluate student comprehension with the section assessment and section quiz. **Reteach** Assign the Reading and Vocabulary Study Guide to help struggling students. **Extend** Extend the lesson by assigning an Enrichment activity.	**All in One Unit 4 History of Our World Teaching Resources** L2 Section Quiz, p. 93 L3 Enrichment, p. 98 Rubric for Assessing a Writing Assignment, p. 108 L2 Word Knowledge, p. 97 L2 Vocabulary Development, p.107 L2 Chapter Tests A and B, pp. 110–115 **Reading and Vocabulary Study Guide** L1 Chapter 12, Section 3, pp. 134–136	**Spanish Support** L2 Section Quiz (Spanish), p. 105 ELL L2 Chapter Summary (Spanish), p. 106 ELL L2 Vocabulary Development (Spanish), p. 107 ELL

Key

L1 Basic to Average   L3 Average to Advanced   LPR Less Proficient Readers   GT Gifted and Talented

L2 For All Students   AR Advanced Readers   ELL English Language Learners

                                        SN Special Needs Students

Reading Background

Passage Reading Strategies

In this chapter, students will use the ReQuest strategy to read the text in Section 1. This strategy calls for students to ask their own questions while reading. Answering their own questions gives students a specific purpose for reading and helps them to monitor their own success. Model the strategy using the following passage from page 338 of the Student Edition. Read the selection aloud, and then ask and answer your own questions. Questions should progress from recall to interpretive or applied thinking.

The Incas extended their control over nearby lands through conquests, or the conquering of other peoples. Over time, many different groups came under its rule. By the 1400s, lands ruled by the Incas had grown into an empire. At its height, the Incan Empire included as many as 12 million people.

Questions:

1. How many people lived in the Incan Empire by the 1400s? *(about 12 million people)*

2. How did the Incas expand their empire? *(by conquering other peoples)*

3. Why would an empire grow through conquests? *(Once a ruling group has conquered another people, it can take over the land and establish power there, thus expanding their control and their empire.)*

Continue in this fashion, alternating between student- and teacher-proposed questions.

Mapping Word Definitions

Research shows that mapping word definitions helps students develop the ability to investigate word meanings independently and provide elaborated definitions (as opposed to simple one or two word definitions).

Model mapping word definitions by developing a graphic organizer similar to the one below for the high-use word *diverse*.

the definition (in their own words)	*different from one another*
a synonym	*different, varied*
a sentence using the word	*The people who live in North America today are diverse because they come from all over the world.*

World Studies Background

Tikal

Located in the tropical rain forests of what is now northern Guatemala, Tikal was once a major center of Mayan civilization. At its height, between 600 and 700 A.D., the city had a population of 60,000 people. Today, tourists flock to the ruins of Tikal's ceremonial center to see the remains of Mayan religious and artistic achievements, such as pyramids, temples, palaces, and plazas.

Aztec Education

For most Aztec youngsters, education began at home. Boys were taught by their fathers until they were about ten years old. After that, they were usually sent to schools either run by family groups called *calpolli* or connected with a temple. Calpolli schools gave boys general education and military training. Temple schools prepared them for the priesthood or offices of the state.

Kachinas

Kachinas play an important role in the Hopi culture. According to Hopi belief, kachinas are spirits of the dead. During the winter, the Hopi dedicate special dances and services to these spirits to ensure good harvests. Boys and girls are given carved wooden dolls to help them learn about the real kachinas.

Infoplease® provides a wealth of useful information for the classroom. You can use this resource to strengthen your background on the subjects covered in this chapter. Have students visit this advertising-free site as a starting point for projects requiring research.

Use Web Code **lgd-8300** for **Infoplease®**.

Guiding Questions

Remind students about the Guiding Questions introduced at the beginning of the book.

Section 1 relates to **Guiding Question** ④
What types of governments were formed in these civilizations? *(The Sapa Inca, or emperor, owned all the land in the Incan Empire and divided it among those under his rule. He relied on government officials to help him run the empire smoothly.)*

Section 2 relates to **Guiding Question** ③
What was the pattern of day-to-day life in these societies? *(Mayan life was based on farming. The Mayas grew a variety of crops including beans, pepper, and their most important crop—maize. The Mayas held religious festivals throughout the year and played games such as pok-ta-tok. Aztecs also relied on farming and built chinampas so they would have more farmland. They held religious festivals. War was a part of life in the Aztec Empire.)*

Section 3 relates to **Guiding Question** ⑤
How did each society organize its economic activities? *(The Adena, Hopewell, Mississippians, Anasazi, and Plains Indians all traded with distant civilizations to acquire the goods they needed.)*

◐ Target Reading Skill

In this chapter, students will learn and apply the reading skill of identifying main ideas and supporting details. Use the following worksheets to help students practice this skill:

All in One Unit 4 History of Our World Teaching Resources, *Identify Main Ideas,* p. 94; *Identify Supporting Details,* p. 95; *Identify Implied Main Ideas,* p. 96

Differentiated Instruction

The following Teacher Edition strategies are suitable for students of varying abilities.

Advanced Readers, pp. 342, 347
English Language Learners, pp. 347, 356
Gifted and Talented, pp. 342, 356
Less Proficient Readers, pp. 339, 357
Special Needs Students, pp. 339, 346, 351

Chapter **12** Early Civilizations of the Americas

Chapter Preview

This chapter will introduce you to the civilizations that existed in the Americas before the arrival of Europeans.

Section 1
South America and the Incas

Section 2
Cultures of Middle America

Section 3
Cultures of North America

◐ **Target Reading Skill**

Main Idea In this chapter you will focus on finding and remembering the main idea, or the most important point, of sections and paragraphs.

▶ Temple of the Cross, Palenque, Mexico

334 History of Our World

Bibliography

For the Teacher
Bakewell, Peter. *A History of Latin America.* Blackwell Publishers, 2003.
Soustelle, Jacques. *Daily Life of the Aztecs.* Dover Publications, 2002.
Zimmerman, Larry J. *American Indians: The First Nations: Native North American Life, Myth, and Art.* Duncan Baird Publishers, 2003.

For the Student
L1 Mann, Elizabeth. *Machu Picchu.* Mikaya Press, 2000.
L2 Baquedano, Elizabeth. *Aztec, Inca & Maya.* Eyewitness Books, DK Publishing, 2000.
L3 Hall, Eleanor. *Life Among the Aztec.* Lucent Books, 2004.

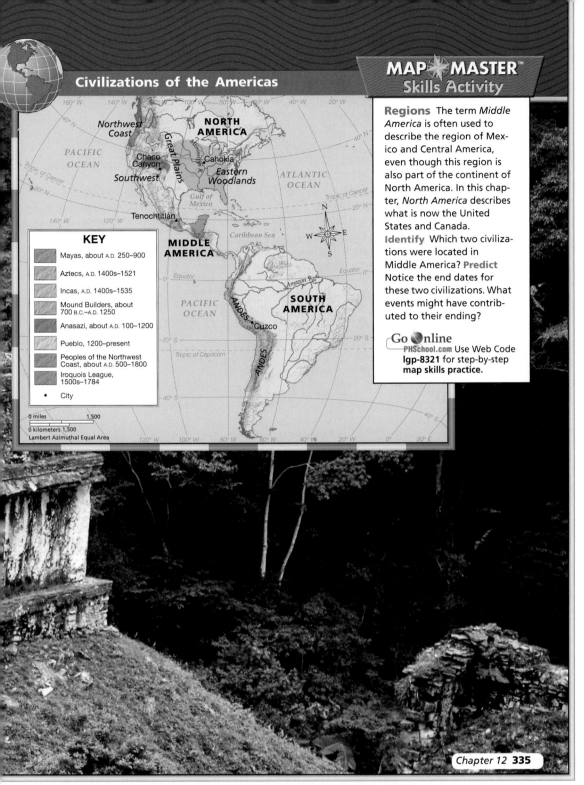

Civilizations of the Americas

NORTH AMERICA

Northwest Coast

PACIFIC OCEAN

Chaco Canyon

Cahokia

Southwest

Great Plains

Eastern Woodlands

ATLANTIC OCEAN

Gulf of Mexico

Tenochtitlán

Caribbean Sea

MIDDLE AMERICA

Equator

PACIFIC OCEAN

Amazon R.

SOUTH AMERICA

ANDES

Cuzco

Tropic of Cancer

Tropic of Capricorn

Equator

N
W   E
S

KEY

- Mayas, about A.D. 250–900
- Aztecs, A.D. 1400s–1521
- Incas, A.D. 1400s–1535
- Mound Builders, about 700 B.C.–A.D. 1250
- Anasazi, about A.D. 100–1200
- Pueblo, 1200–present
- Peoples of the Northwest Coast, about A.D. 500–1800
- Iroquois League, 1500s–1784
- • City

0 miles 1,500
0 kilometers 1,500
Lambert Azimuthal Equal Area

Regions The term *Middle America* is often used to describe the region of Mexico and Central America, even though this region is also part of the continent of North America. In this chapter, *North America* describes what is now the United States and Canada. **Identify** Which two civilizations were located in Middle America? **Predict** Notice the end dates for these two civilizations. What events might have contributed to their ending?

Go Online
PHSchool.com Use Web Code lgp-8321 for step-by-step map skills practice.

■ Ask students to create a table that shows which region each civilization is located in—North America, Middle America, or South America. Remind them to give the table a title.

Go Online
PHSchool.com Students may practice their map skills using the interactive online version of this map.

Using the Visual   L2

Reach Into Your Background Point out the photograph on pp. 334–335 and the caption. Ask **What does the structure in the photograph tell about the past?** Ask students to think about monuments or buildings in their area that might tell about the past.

Answers

 **Identify** Aztecs and Mayas
Predict Possible answer: conquests by Europeans

Chapter Resources

Teaching Resources
L2 Vocabulary Development, p. 107
L2 Skills for Life, p. 99
L2 Chapter Tests A and B, pp. 110–115

Spanish Support
L2 Spanish Chapter Summary, p. 106
L2 Spanish Vocabulary Development, p. 107

Media and Technology
L1 Student Edition on Audio CD
L1 Guided Reading Audio CDs, English and Spanish
L2 Social Studies Skills Tutor CD-ROM
Exam*View*® Test Bank CD-ROM

DISCOVERY History of Our World
CHANNEL Video Program
SCHOOL

interactive Textbook
PRENTICE HALL

TeacherEXPRESS™
Plan · Teach · Assess

Section 1
Step-by-Step Instruction

Objectives

Social Studies

1. Find out about the geography of the Americas.
2. Learn about the empire established by the Incas of South America.

Reading/Language Arts

Learn how to identify main ideas while you read.

Prepare to Read

Build Background Knowledge **L2**

Remind students that they have learned about ancient civilizations in several parts of the world. In this section, they will learn about an ancient civilization in South America. Ask students to quickly survey the visuals in the section with this question in mind: **What might some of the accomplishments of this civilization have been?** Conduct an Idea Wave (TE, p. T39) to generate a list.

Set a Purpose for Reading **L2**

- Preview the Objectives.

- Read each statement in the *Reading Readiness Guide* aloud. Ask students to mark the statements true or false.

- Have students discuss the statements in pairs or groups of four, then mark their worksheets again. Use the Numbered Heads participation strategy (TE, p. T40) to call on students to share their group's perspectives.

All in One Unit 4 History of Our World Teaching Resources, *Reading Readiness Guide*, p. 83

Vocabulary Builder
Preview Key Terms **L2**

Pronounce each Key Term, then ask students to say the word with you. Provide a simple explanation such as, "Every ten years the United States government conducts a census to count its people and learn more about them."

Section 1
South America and the Incas

Prepare to Read

Objectives

In this section, you will
1. Find out about the geography of the Americas.
2. Learn about the empire established by the Incas of South America.

Taking Notes

As you read this section, record key points about the Incan Empire. Copy the start of the outline below, and then add more information to complete it.

> I. The mountain empire of the Incas
>   A. Growth of an empire
>   1.
>   2.
>   B.
> II.

Target Reading Skill

Identify Main Ideas Good readers identify the main idea in every written passage. The main idea is the most important, or the biggest, point of the section. It includes all of the other points made in the section. As you read, note the main idea of each paragraph or written passage.

Key Terms

- **Incas** (ING kuhz) *n.* people of a powerful South American empire during the 1400s and 1500s
- **Andes** (AN deez) *n.* a mountain chain of western South America
- **Cuzco** (KOOS koh) *n.* the capital city of the Incan Empire, located in present-day Peru
- **census** (SEN sus) *n.* an official count of people in a certain place at a certain time
- **quipu** (KEE poo) *n.* a group of knotted strings used by the Incas to record information
- **terraces** (TEHR us iz) *n.* steplike ledges cut into mountains to make land suitable for farming

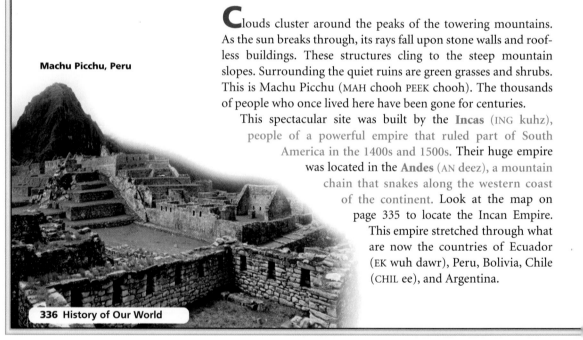

Machu Picchu, Peru

Clouds cluster around the peaks of the towering mountains. As the sun breaks through, its rays fall upon stone walls and roofless buildings. These structures cling to the steep mountain slopes. Surrounding the quiet ruins are green grasses and shrubs. This is Machu Picchu (MAH chooh PEEK chooh). The thousands of people who once lived here have been gone for centuries.

This spectacular site was built by the **Incas** (ING kuhz), people of a powerful empire that ruled part of South America in the 1400s and 1500s. Their huge empire was located in the **Andes** (AN deez), a mountain chain that snakes along the western coast of the continent. Look at the map on page 335 to locate the Incan Empire. This empire stretched through what are now the countries of Ecuador (EK wuh dawr), Peru, Bolivia, Chile (CHIL ee), and Argentina.

Target Reading Skill **L2**

Identify Main Ideas Point out the Target Reading Skill. Tell students that the main idea of a section is the most important point in the section.

Model the skill by identifying the main idea of the Lasting Achievements section on p. 340. Explain that much of the main idea is stated in the introductory paragraph, and the supporting details are provided in the paragraphs that follow. *(Main idea: The Incas were amazing builders and many of their achievements still stand today.)*

Give students *Identify Main Ideas*. Have them complete the activity in groups.

All in One Unit 4 History of Our World Teaching Resources, *Identify Main Ideas*, p. 94

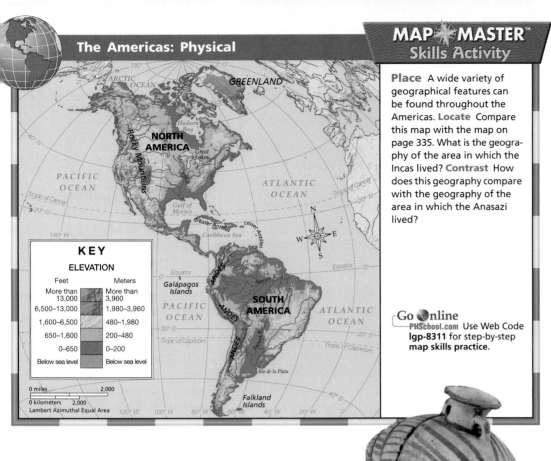

The Americas: Physical

Place A wide variety of geographical features can be found throughout the Americas. **Locate** Compare this map with the map on page 335. What is the geography of the area in which the Incas lived? **Contrast** How does this geography compare with the geography of the area in which the Anasazi lived?

KEY

ELEVATION

Feet	Meters
More than 13,000	More than 3,960
6,500–13,000	1,980–3,960
1,600–6,500	480–1,980
650–1,600	200–480
0–650	0–200
Below sea level	Below sea level

0 miles 2,000
0 kilometers 2,000
Lambert Azimuthal Equal Area

Go Online
PHSchool.com Use Web Code lgp-8311 for step-by-step map skills practice.

Geography of the Americas

The Incas were not the first culture to develop in the Americas. Many groups had lived in the region for thousands of years. Individual cultures developed different ways of life to fit their geographic settings. Some peoples made their homes in dense forests or fertile river valleys. Other peoples lived among rocky cliffs in areas that were dry for much of the year.

Locate the mountain ranges on the map above. See which parts of the Americas are covered by plains, highland plateaus, and deserts. Also, locate the Mississippi and Amazon rivers, two of the largest river systems in the world. In North America, temperatures range from extreme cold in the far north to hot and tropical in the southern region. In South America, mountain regions are cold. Areas near sea level are hot near the Equator but much cooler in the far south.

✓ **Reading Check** Which two river systems in the Americas are among the largest in the world?

This earthenware vessel was designed to be carried on the back of a llama.

Chapter 12 Section 1 **337**

Vocabulary Builder

Use the information below to teach students this section's high-use words.

High-Use Word	Definition and Sample Sentence
dense, p. 337	*adj.* crowded closely together The **dense** fog made it hard to see the road.
complex, p. 339	*adj.* complicated; sophisticated The class invented a new game with **complex** rules.
unify, p. 339	*v.* to link together The border around the page helped to **unify** the pictures.

Instruct

Geography of the Americas L2

Guided Instruction

- **Vocabulary Builder** Clarify the high-use word **dense** before reading.

- Read Geography of the Americas with students using the ReQuest reading strategy (TE, p. T39).

- Ask **Were the Incas the first culture to develop in the Americas?** (*No.*) **How long had other groups lived in the region before the Incan culture developed?** (*for thousands of years*)

- Have students give an example of how geography could affect the kinds of homes people build. (*Possible answer: People in forests might build homes with wood while those on rocky cliffs might use stone.*)

- Ask students to describe the climates of the Americas. (*In North America temperatures range from very cold in the north to hot and tropical in the south. In South America, mountain regions are cold, and areas near sea level are hot near the Equator but cooler farther south.*)

Independent Practice

Assign *Guided Reading and Review*.

All in One Unit 4 History of Our World Teaching Resources, *Guided Reading and Review,* p. 84

Monitor Progress

Circulate and make sure students are correctly answering the questions. Provide assistance as needed.

Answers

MAP MASTER™ Skills Activity **Locate** The Incas lived near the Andes Mountains, down South America's Pacific coast. **Contrast** The Anasazi lived inland near the Rocky Mountains, which have lower elevations than the Andes Mountains.

Go Online
PHSchool.com Students may practice their map skills using the interactive online version of this map.

✓ **Reading Check** the Mississippi and Amazon river systems

The Mountain Empire of the Incas L2

Guided Instruction

- **Vocabulary Builder** Clarify the high-use words **complex** and **unify** before reading.

- Invite students to read about the Incan empire with you. As students read, circulate and make sure individuals can answer the Reading Check question.

- Ask students **What was the capital of the Incan empire?** *(Cuzco)* **How did the Incas extend their control?** *(by conquering other peoples)*

- Discuss the role of the Inca emperor. *(He owned all the land and divided it among those he ruled. He hired government officials to help him run the empire smoothly.)*

338 History of Our World

The Mountain Empire of the Incas

At its peak, the powerful South American empire of the Incas measured 2,500 miles (4,020 kilometers) from one end to the other. This great empire grew from small beginnings over many years.

Growth of an Empire About the year A.D. 1200, the Incas settled in a small village on a high plateau in the Andes. This village, named **Cuzco** (KOOS koh), became the Incas' capital city and a center of both government and religion. In fact, the word *cuzco* means "center" in the Incan language.

The Incas extended their control over nearby lands through conquests, or the conquering of other peoples. Over time, many different groups came under their rule. By the 1400s, the lands ruled by the Incas had grown into an empire. At its height, the Incan Empire included as many as 12 million people.

Even when the empire included millions of people, it was run in an orderly way. Incan rulers had a complex system of gathering knowledge about events that happened hundreds of miles away from their capital city.

Festival of the Sun
Thousands of people gather at the ruins of an Incan fortress in Cuzco for the yearly Festival of the Sun, which celebrates the winter solstice.
Infer *How can you tell which people are part of the festival and which are just watching?*

Answer

Infer The people watching the festival are dressed in street clothes and seated in chairs. Those who are taking part in the festival are dressed in bright clothing and are moving around.

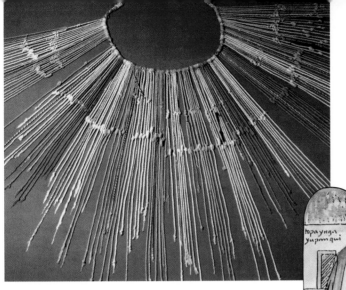

Quipus in Incan Life
In the drawing below, dating from the 1500s, an official gives a noble a quipu like the one at left. The quipu may have been created hundreds of miles away. **Analyze Images** *What details in the drawing tell which person is the noble?*

Incan Government The Incan ruler was called Sapa Inca, or "the emperor." The people believed that their emperor was related to the sun-god. The emperor, and only he, owned all the land and divided it among those under his rule. Under the Sapa Inca was the noble class. Nobles oversaw government officials, who made sure the empire ran smoothly.

Officials used a **census,** or an official count of the people, to keep track of everyone's responsibilities. The census helped to make sure that everyone paid taxes. It recorded which men worked as soldiers or on public projects such as gold mining and road building. Farmers had to give the government part of their crops, while women had to weave cloth. In return, the empire took care of the poor, the sick, and the elderly.

The official spoken language of the empire was Quechua (KECH wuh), but the Incas did not have a written language. Instead, they invented a complex system for keeping detailed records. Information such as births, deaths, and harvests was recorded on a group of knotted strings called a **quipu** (KEE poo). Each quipu had a main cord with several colored strings attached. The colors represented different items, and knots of varying sizes recorded numbers.

Incan relay runners carried quipus across vast networks of roads and bridges to keep the government informed about distant parts of the empire. These roads also carried the Incan armies and trade caravans, both of which helped to unify the vast empire.

Guided Instruction (continued)

- Ask students **What was the purpose of the census?** (*It was a way to keep track of everyone's responsibilities. It helped ensure that everyone paid taxes and recorded which men worked as soldiers or on public projects.*)

- Discuss the use of quipus. (*Incas created quipus to keep track of important information such as births, deaths, and harvests.*) Ask students **How do you think quipus helped to unify the Incan empire?** (*Possible answer: They were used to record statistics that were important for running the empire. The quipus were carried all over the empire and helped keep the government informed about distant parts of the empire.*)

- Ask students **How did the Incas use stone to increase farm production?** (*They used stone to create terraces on steep mountainsides, to hold the soil in place, and to build channels to carry water to farms.*)

Differentiated Instruction

For Special Needs Students L1
Ask students to demonstrate that they are listening and following along by having them use a piece of cardboard to underline each line of text as it is read.

For Less Proficient Readers L1
Show *Section Reading Support Transparency HOW 90* before students begin reading the section. Point out the section's key concepts to help focus students' reading.

📖 **History of Our World Transparencies,** *Section Reading Support Transparency HOW 90*

Answer

Analyze Images Possible answer: The person on the right is kneeling and holding a quipu, and the person on the left is standing and seems to be wearing gold jewelry. These details would indicate that the person on the left is the noble.

Read the **Links Across Time** on this page. Ask students **How do you think bridges helped spread information across the Incan empire?** (*Bridges were part of the huge network of roads that linked all parts of the empire. People traveled along this system to carry information to and from the government.*)

Guided Instruction (continued)

- Ask **What two problems helped trigger the fall of the Incan empire before the Spanish had even arrived?** (*Members of the ruling family began to fight among themselves for control, and workers started to rebel against the strict government.*)

Independent Practice

Have students create the Taking Notes graphic organizer on a separate piece of paper. As they read about the Incan empire, have them fill in important headings and details on their outlines.

Monitor Progress

- Show *Section Reading Support Transparency HOW 90* and ask students to check their graphic organizers individually. Go over key concepts and clarify key vocabulary as needed.

    📖 **History of Our World,** *Section Reading Support Transparency HOW 90*

- Tell students to fill in the last column of their *Reading Readiness Guides.* Probe for what they learned that confirms or invalidates each statement.

    All in One **Unit 4 History of Our World Teaching Resources,** *Reading Readiness Guide,* p. 83

🎯 Target Reading Skill

Identify Main Ideas As a follow-up, ask students to answer the Target Reading Skill question in the Student Edition. (*The Incas were amazing uilders and many of their achievements still stand today.*)

Rope Bridges This rope bridge, strung across a gorge in the Andes, is similar to those used by the Incas. A gorge is a narrow pass between steep cliffs or walls. Incan bridges were made with strong cords of braided vines and reeds. Some peoples in the Andes still make bridges from vines and reeds today. Modern steel suspension bridges in other parts of the world use the engineering principles developed by the Incas hundreds of years ago when they built their rope-and-vine bridges.

🎯 **Identify Main Ideas** Which sentence states the main idea under the blue heading Lasting Achievements?

Lasting Achievements The achievements of the Incas still amaze people today. They constructed thousands of miles of paved roads, massive walls, and mountaintop buildings. And they did all this with only stone hammers and bronze chisels. Remarkably, much of what the Incas built hundreds of years ago with only primitive tools still stands today.

The Incas took advantage of their environment. They used stone—plentiful in the Andes—for many purposes. Sometimes they used enormous stones whole. At other times, they carefully broke stones into smaller blocks. First they cut a long groove into a rock's surface. Then they drove stone or wooden wedges into the groove until the rock split.

When Incan stonemasons made a wall, they made sure its large, many-sided stones fit together perfectly. After a wall was complete, the fit was so tight that not even a very thin knife blade could be slipped between two blocks. Construction without mortar, or cement, also allowed the massive stones to move and resettle during earthquakes without damaging the wall.

Among their many ingenious uses of stone was a method to increase farm production. The Andes are steep, dry, and rocky. There is little natural farmland. By building **terraces,** or steplike ledges cut into the mountains, the Incas could farm on slopes that would otherwise have been too steep. Stone terraces held the soil in place so it would not be washed away by rain. A complex system of aqueducts, or stone-lined channels, carried water to these farms. One of these aqueducts was 360 miles (579 kilometers) long.

340 History of Our World

⌐ Background: Daily Life ——

Incan Agriculture Despite the steep terrain of the Andes, the Incan empire was primarily agrarian. In addition to the use of terraces and irrigation systems, the Incas used fertilizers to enrich the soil. Their main food crops were potatoes, corn, quinoa (a grain), and oca (an edible root). The Incas developed a way of freeze-drying potatoes to preserve them. The Incas had no draft animals, wheels, or plows. They did have some domesticated animals including ducks, llamas, vicuña, alpacas, and dogs. In addition to food, the Incas grew cotton and used the wool of vicuña and alpacas for textiles.

The Decline of the Incan Empire The power of the Incan Empire peaked in the 1400s. After that, it lasted for less than 100 years. A number of factors contributed to the fall of the empire. Members of the ruling family began to fight among themselves for control. Also, many workers started to rebel against the strict government.

Then, in the 1530s, a Spanish conquistador (kahn KEES tuh dawr), or conqueror, named Francisco Pizarro arrived in South America. Pizarro had heard of the wealthy Incan Empire. He wanted to explore the region and conquer its peoples. The Incan emperor welcomed Pizarro. But when he and his unarmed men met the conquistador, they walked into a trap. Pizarro captured the emperor and killed his men.

The Spanish had superior weapons. They also carried diseases, such as smallpox and measles, to which the Incas had never been exposed. These diseases killed much of the Incan population. The Spanish quickly gained control of the vast Incan Empire. For decades, the Incas tried to regain rule of their land, but they never succeeded.

A wooden cup made for Pizarro shows Spanish and Incan figures.

✓ **Reading Check** Which Spanish conquistador conquered the Incas?

Section 1 Assessment

Key Terms
Review the key terms at the beginning of this section. Use each term in a sentence that explains its meaning.

Target Reading Skill
State the main idea of the first paragraph on this page.

Comprehension and Critical Thinking
1. (a) **Identify** Name two geographic settings in which peoples of the Americas lived.
(b) **Synthesize Information** What are the climates of those two regions?

(c) **Infer** How might the people who lived in these regions have adapted to their geography and climate?
2. (a) **Recall** How much land did the Incan Empire cover at its greatest extent?
(b) **Explain** How did the government in Cuzco keep track of distant parts of the empire?
(c) **Draw Conclusions** What do you think were the major problems of keeping such a large empire running smoothly? Explain your answer.

Writing Activity
If you could interview a stonemason from the Incan Empire, what would you ask? Make a list of questions you would ask in order to learn how these skilled workers accomplished so much so long ago. Then write a paragraph explaining why you want to ask the questions.

Go Online
PHSchool.com

For: An activity on the Incas
Visit: PHSchool.com
Web Code: lgd-8301

Chapter 12 Section 1 **341**

Objective

Learn how to understand cause-and-effect relationships.

Prepare to Read

Build Background Knowledge L2

Tell students to suppose that their school decided to cancel all school vacations. Instead, students would have to attend school year-round without any vacations. Ask students what they think the effects of such a policy would be. Conduct an Idea Wave (TE p. T39) to elicit student responses.

Instruct

Identifying Cause and Effect L2

Guided Instruction

■ Read the steps to understanding cause-and-effect relationships as a class and write them on the board.

■ Practice the skill by reading the passage and following the steps on p. 342 as a class. Model each step in the activity by choosing a condition (*Every Incan village sent a few young men and women away to work for the empire.*) and looking for possible causes. (*Villages had to pay taxes on their harvest and herds; villages could pay their taxes by having their people do special work.*)

■ Then, look for clue words (*For this reason*). Finally, make a cause-and-effect diagram on the board, and summarize the cause-and-effect relationships. (*Incan villages had to pay taxes on their harvest and herds; because villages could pay their taxes by having their people do special work, every village sent a few men and women to work for the empire; in return, the Incan government gave help to the poor, the old, and the sick villagers.*)

Independent Practice

Assign *Skills for Life* and have students complete it individually.

All in One **Unit 4 History of Our World Teaching Resources,** *Skills for Life,* p. 99

Identifying Cause and Effect

Wondering why things happen is something every human being does. Why does the sun rise in the east? Why does the United States have a president and not a king? Why did the Incas build Machu Picchu? This curiosity has driven people to ask how history has shaped our world. When we ask "why" about something, we are really trying to figure out causes and effects.

 cause is something that makes an event or a situation happen. An effect is a result of a cause. When you identify cause and effect, you understand how an action or several actions led to a particular result. Causes and effects can be short term or long term.

CAUSES		EVENT		EFFECTS
• • •	→	•	→	• • •

Learn the Skill

Use these steps to understand cause-and-effect relationships.

1 **Choose one event or condition as a starting point.** Determine whether in this case it is a cause or an effect.

2 **Look at earlier events or conditions for possible causes.** Also look for clue words that signal cause, such as *because, so,* and *since.* Words such as *therefore, then, reason,* and *as a result* signal effects.

3 **Make a cause-and-effect diagram.** A diagram like the one above can help you understand cause-and-effect relationships. Remember that sometimes an effect becomes a cause for another effect.

4 **Summarize the cause-and-effect relationships.** Be sure to include all of the causes and effects.

Monitor Progress

As students are completing *Skills for Life*, circulate to make sure individuals are applying the skill steps effectively. Provide assistance as needed.

An Incan woman weaving

Incan Taxes

The Incas did not use money. Even so, villages had to pay taxes on their harvest and herds. To do so, they gave one third of their crops and animals to the empire. Villages could also pay their taxes by having their people do special work.

For this reason, every village sent a few young men and women to work for the empire. Some made jewelry, textiles, or pottery for nobles. Many men worked as soldiers or miners. Others built buildings or inspected roads or bridges.

In return, the government gave something back to the villages. The poor, the old, and the sick received government help.

Practice the Skill

Follow the steps in Learn the Skill to look for causes and effects in the passage above.

1. Read the passage. Find one event or condition that can serve as your starting point. Decide if it is a cause or an effect. How might the title help you?

2. What facts or conditions led to the way Incas paid taxes? What clue words in the second paragraph signal cause and effect?

3. Make a cause-and-effect diagram. Check for effects that in turn become causes for other effects. Expand your diagram if you need to.

4. Summarize the cause-and-effect relationships you have discovered.

Incan men building a fortress

Apply the Skill

Reread the two paragraphs under the heading The Decline of the Incan Empire on page 341. Use the steps in this skill to identify the causes and effects described in the passage. Make a cause-and-effect diagram or write a paragraph explaining the cause-and-effect relationships you find.

Assess Progress　L2

Ask students to do the Apply the Skill activity.

Reteach　L1

If students are having trouble applying the skill steps, have them review the skill using the interactive Social Studies Skills Tutor CD-ROM.

　 Identifying Cause and Effect, **Social Studies Skills Tutor CD-ROM**

Extend　L3

Have students turn to p. 357 and read the last paragraph under the heading The Plains Indians. Then, working in pairs, have them create a cause-and-effect diagram using the information in the text.

Answer
Apply the Skill

Answers will vary, but students should create a cause-and-effect diagram or write a paragraph explaining the cause-and-effect relationships they found in the text.

Differentiated Instruction

For Special Needs Students　L1
Partner special needs students with more proficient students to do Level 1 of the *Identifying Cause and Effect* lesson on the Social Studies Skill Tutor CD-ROM

together. When students feel more confident, they can move onto Level 2 alone.

　 Identifying Cause and Effect, **Social Studies Skill Tutor CD-ROM**

Objectives

Social Studies

1. Learn about the Mayan culture of Middle America.
2. Find out about the powerful Aztec empire.

Reading/Language Arts

Learn how to identify details that support a main idea.

Prepare to Read

Build Background Knowledge   L2

Tell students that they will learn about two more ancient civilizations in Middle America. Show the video *Great Zimbabwe: The Lost City*. Ask students to note the reasons the Aztec empire ended and to compare them to the demise of the Incan empire. Have students engage in a Give One, Get One activity (TE, p. T41) to share their ideas.

📼 *Great Zimbabwe: The Lost City*, **World Studies Video Program**

Set a Purpose for Reading   L2

■ Preview the Objectives.

■ Form students into pairs or groups of four. Distribute the *Reading Readiness Guide*. Ask students to fill in the first two columns of the chart. Use the Numbered Heads participation strategy (TE, p. T40) to call on students to share one piece of information they already know and one piece of information they want to know.

All in One Unit 4 History of Our World Teaching Resources, *Reading Readiness Guide*, p. 87

Vocabulary Builder
Preview Key Terms   L2

Pronounce each Key Term, then ask students to say the word with you. Provide a simple explanation such as, "Maize, a type of corn, has been grown for thousands of years in North America."

Prepare to Read

Objectives

In this section, you will
1. Learn about the Mayan culture of Middle America.
2. Find out about the powerful Aztec Empire.

Taking Notes

As you read this section, look for the characteristics of the Mayan and Aztec civilizations. Copy the web diagram below and record your findings for the Mayas. Then make a similar diagram for the Aztecs.

🎯 Target Reading Skill

Identify Supporting Details Sentences in a paragraph may give further details that support the main idea. These details may give examples, explanations, or reasons. In the first paragraph on page 345, this sentence states the main idea: "Thousands of years before the Aztecs built Tenochtitlán, other cultures thrived in Middle America." Note three details that support this main idea.

Key Terms

- **Aztecs** (AZ teks) *n.* a people who lived in the Valley of Mexico
- **Tenochtitlán** (teh nawch tee TLAHN) *n.* capital city of the Aztecs
- **Mayas** (MAH yuhz) *n.* a people who established a great civilization in Middle America
- **slash-and-burn agriculture** (slash and burn AG rih kul chur) *n.* a farming technique in which trees are cut down and burned to clear and fertilize the land
- **maize** (mayz) *n.* corn
- **hieroglyphics** (hy ur oh GLIF iks) *n.* the signs and symbols that made up the Mayan writing system

This page dating from the 1500s illustrates the Aztec legend. A version of it forms part of the Mexican flag today.

In about 1325, the **Aztecs** (AZ teks), a people who lived in the Valley of Mexico, began looking for a place to build a new capital. According to legend, the Aztecs asked their god of war where they should build this capital. He replied, "Build at the place where you see an eagle perched on a cactus and holding a snake in its beak."

When the Aztecs found the sign their god had described, they were surprised. The cactus on which the eagle perched was growing on a swampy island in the center of Lake Texcoco. It was an unlikely setting for an important city. But they believed their god had given them this sign, and so this was the place where the Aztecs built **Tenochtitlán** (teh nawch tee TLAHN), their capital. It would become one of the largest and finest cities of its time.

🎯 Target Reading Skill   L2

Identify Supporting Details Call attention to the Target Reading Skill. Point out that supporting details provide more information about the main idea.

Model the skill by reading the first two paragraphs under The Culture of the Mayas on p. 345 and identifying the main idea and its supporting details: "The first sentence gives the main idea, that other cultures thrived in Middle America before the Aztecs did." Then read each of the following sentences and ask students if the sentences supply supporting details. *(yes)*

Give students *Identify Supporting Details*. Have them complete the activity in groups.

All in One Unit 4 History of Our World Teaching Resources, *Identify Supporting Details*, p. 95

The Culture of the Mayas

Thousands of years before the Aztecs built Tenochtitlán, other cultures thrived in Middle America. One of these ancient peoples, called the Olmec (AHL mek), lived along the Gulf Coast from about 1200 B.C. until about 600 B.C. The Olmec are known for their pyramid-shaped temples and huge carved stone heads.

Somewhat later, an important culture developed in parts of Central America and the Yucatán Peninsula to the north. The Yucatán Peninsula is located at Mexico's southeastern tip. These people, called the **Mayas** (MAH yuhz), established a great civilization and built many cities in this region of Middle America. The Mayas may have been influenced by Olmec culture. The Mayan way of life lasted for many centuries. Its greatest period was from about A.D. 250 until 900.

A Farming Culture Mayan life was based on farming. To grow crops, Mayan farmers used a technique called **slash-and-burn agriculture.** They first cleared the land by cutting down trees. They then burned the tree stumps, saving the ash to use as fertilizer. Finally, they planted seeds. After a few years, however, the soil would be worn out. The farmers would then have to clear and plant a new area.

Mayan farmers grew a variety of crops, including beans, squash, peppers, papayas (puh PY uz), and avocados. But their most common crop was **maize** (mayz), or corn. In fact, maize was so important to the Mayas that one of the gods they worshiped was a god of corn. And since the corn needed the sun and rain to grow, it is not surprising that the Mayas also worshipped a rain god and a sun god.

Olmec statues like this one were usually several feet tall.

Tikal—Ruins of a Great City
Tikal, located in Guatemala, was once a thriving Mayan city. The city and its surrounding areas had a population of nearly 100,000. **Infer** *Judging from the photo, what challenge probably faced Mayan farmers who lived in this region?*

Instruct

The Culture of the Mayas L2

Guided Instruction

■ **Vocabulary Builder** Clarify the high-use words **thrive, decline,** and **establish** before reading.

■ Read about Mayan culture with students using the Choral Reading strategy (TE, p. T38).

■ Ask students **What were two cultures that thrived in Middle America long before the Aztecs?** *(the Olmec and Mayan cultures)*

■ Have students describe the technique of slash-and-burn agriculture. *(First, farmers cut down trees Then they burned the tree stumps and saved the ash to use as fertilizer. Finally, they planted seeds.)* Ask **What was a disadvantage to this way of farming?** *(It wore out the soil after a few years, forcing farmers to clear new areas for planting.)*

■ Have students discuss why the Mayas worshipped a god of corn, a god of rain, and a god of sun. *(Corn was their most common and important crop. The Mayas worshipped gods of the sun and rain because these elements were important for growing corn.)*

Answer

Infer Possible answer: Mayan farmers faced the challenge of clearing the trees that grew thickly in their region.

Vocabulary Builder

Use the information below to teach students this section's high-use words.

High-Use Word	Definition and Sample Sentence
thrive, p. 345	*v.* to flourish; to gain in wealth and possessions The city **thrived** under new leadership.
establish, p. 345	*v.* to set up on a permanent basis Our club met to **establish** some rules for the coming year.
decline, p. 346	*v.* to weaken Business in the town **declined** after the factory closed.
equip, p. 348	*v.* to provide with the appropriate supplies for action Ty **equipped** himself with the proper pads in preparation for the football game.

Read the **Links to Math** on this page. Ask students **What did dots and bars stand for in the Mayan number system?** *(Dots stood for single numbers and bars stood for groups of five.)*

Guided Instruction (continued)

- Discuss the role of religion in Mayan culture. *(Religion was an important part of Mayan culture. Cities held religious festivals and ceremonies, including human sacrifices, to honor Mayan gods. Mayan priests developed a calendar to plan when to hold religious festivals.)*

- Have students describe common structures found in a Mayan city. *(Large palaces where religious and governmental leaders lived and religious temple-pyramids were located within the city. Outdoor courts where games were played could also be found in the city.)*

- Ask students to list the possible reasons that Mayans abandoned their cities. *(crop failures, war, disease, overuse of natural resources, rebellion)*

Independent Practice

Assign *Guided Reading and Review.*

All in One Unit 4 History of Our World Teaching Resources, p. 88

Monitor Progress

As students work on *Guided Reading and Review,* circulate and make sure that individuals are completing the worksheet correctly.

Target Reading Skill   L2

Identify Supporting Details As a follow-up, ask students to answer the Target Reading Skill question in the Student Edition. *(Today, descendants of the Mayas still live in Middle America. Many continue some of the cultural traditions of their Mayan ancestors.)*

Links to
Math

Mayan Counting The Mayas created a number system to count and record information. Dots stood for single numbers. For example, three dots in a row represented the number three. Bars stood for groups of five. Unlike our number system, which is based on 10, the Mayas' number system was based on 20. So, to record a number larger than 19, they used one large dot standing alone to represent the number 20, and more large dots for larger numbers divisible by 20. Dots and bars were used to make up the rest of the number. In the Mayan book at left, the number 29 is circled in white.

Centers of Religion and Government Mayan cities were religious and governmental centers. A different ruler commanded each city. Priests and nobles were also important community leaders. These leaders lived in large palaces within the city. Ordinary people lived on the edges of the city. Each city held great festivals to honor the many Mayan gods. The most important religious events took place at large temple-pyramids. Some of the ceremonies included human sacrifice.

Skilled mathematicians, Mayan priests developed a calendar to plan when to hold religious celebrations. The Mayas also created a system of writing using signs and symbols called **hieroglyphics.** They used these hieroglyphics to record information in books made from the bark of fig trees.

A Mayan Game Cities also had outdoor courts where a special ball game called pok-ta-tok was played. A court was about the size of a football field, and the game was a bit like soccer and basketball combined. The ball was made of hard rubber. Players tried to knock it through a stone hoop set on a wall. They could hit the ball with their elbows, knees, or hips—but not with their hands or feet. The ball could not touch the ground.

The Mayas Abandon Their Cities Around A.D. 900, the Mayas abandoned their cities, and their civilization declined. No one knows the exact reason they left. Crop failures, war, disease, or overuse of natural resources may have altered the Mayan way of life. Or people may have rebelled against their leaders. Today, descendants of the Mayas still live in Middle America. Many continue some of the cultural traditions of their Mayan ancestors.

✓ **Reading Check** What did Mayan priests do?

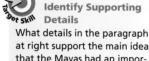
Identify Supporting Details
What details in the paragraph at right support the main idea that the Mayas had an important culture?

346 History of Our World

Differentiated Instruction

For Special Needs Students L1
Have students make a list of the Key Terms and other new words defined within the section, such as *tributes.* Then have them create flashcards with the word on one side and its definition on the other. Pair students with a partner and have them quiz each other on the definitions of the words using the flash cards.

Answer

✓ **Reading Check** They were important community leaders who developed a calendar to plan when to hold celebrations.

The Aztec Empire

You have already read that the Aztecs built their new capital, Tenochtitlán, in the middle of a lake in about 1325. They had first settled in the Valley of Mexico in the 1100s. By the 1470s, the Aztecs had conquered the surrounding lands. Their large empire stretched from the Gulf of Mexico in the east to the Pacific Ocean in the west. A single powerful leader, the Aztec emperor, ruled these lands. All the people he conquered were forced to pay him tribute, or heavy taxes, in the form of food, gold, or slaves.

Waterways and Gardens In spite of its swampy origins, Tenochtitlán became a magnificent capital city. At its center were an open plaza and one or more towering pyramid-temples. There were schools for the sons of the nobles and large stone palaces. Raised streets of hard earth, called causeways, connected the city to the surrounding land. To supply the city with enough fresh water, the Aztecs also built aqueducts. These special channels carried spring water from distant sources to storage areas in the city.

As the population of Tenochtitlán grew, the Aztecs realized they needed more farmland. Their solution was to build many island gardens in the shallow lakes around the capital. These raised fields, called chinampas (chih NAM puz), were made from rich soil dredged up from the lake bottom. Trees planted along the edges prevented soil from washing away. Between the fields were canals. Farmers used the canals to transport produce by boats to a huge marketplace near the capital.

Video
Find out how Cortés defeated the Aztecs.

Floating Gardens Today
A man poles a boat among the chinampas on the outskirts of Mexico City. **Draw Conclusions** List some advantages and disadvantages of growing crops on chinampas.

Differentiated Instruction

For Advanced Readers [L3]

Ask students to read *The Talking Stone* to learn more about the Aztec Empire. Have students work individually to answer the questions at the end of the selection.

All in One Unit 4 History of Our World Teaching Resources, *The Talking Stone,* pp. 104–106

For English Language Learners [L2]

Pair English language learners with more proficient readers to read *The Talking Stone* together. Encourage students to work together to answer and discuss the questions at the end of the selection.

All in One Unit 4 History of Our World Teaching Resources, *The Talking Stone,* pp. 104–106

Show students *Cortéz and the Aztec Empire.* Ask **Who and what helped Cortéz defeat the Aztecs?** *(other Native Americans and diseases unknowingly carried by the Spanish to which the Aztecs had no immunity)*

The Aztec Empire [L2]

Guided Instruction

- **Vocabulary Builder** Clarify the high-use word **equip** before reading.

- Ask students to read The Aztec Empire. As students read, circulate to make sure individuals can answer the Reading Check question.

- Discuss the extent of the Aztec Empire. *(It stretched from the Gulf of Mexico in the east to the Pacific Ocean in the west.)* Ask **How did the Aztec emperor benefit from his conquests?** *(People he conquered were forced to pay him tributes in the form of food, slaves, and gold.)*

- Ask students to name two challenges that faced the Aztecs in Tenochtitlán. *(getting fresh water and having enough farmland)* Then ask students to describe how the Aztecs met these challenges. *(They built aqueducts to carry water from the mainland to storage areas in the city. They built chinampas, or raised fields, using rich soil from the bottom of the lake for farmland.)*

Answer

Draw Conclusions Advantages: difficult for wild animals to destroy crops, soil from the lake is very fertile; Disadvantages: farmers have to travel by boat to get to the crops, concern about soil washing away.

Guided Instruction (continued)

- Ask students **Why might the Aztec civilization be described as war-like?** (*War was a constant part of life; most young men served as soldiers; their religion included prayers for victories; prisoners became either slaves or sacrificial victims.*)

- Ask **What was the largest class in Aztec society?** (*farmers*) **Why do you think this was so?** (*Possible answer: Since the empire was very large, a lot of food was needed to feed all the people.*)

- Ask students **Why do you think diseases brought by the Spanish killed so many Aztecs?** (*Possible answer: These diseases were new to the Aztecs so they had no immunity to them.*)

Independent Practice
Ask students to create the concept web graphic organizer on a blank piece of paper. Then have them fill in the circles with information about the Aztecs.

Monitor Progress
- Show *Section Reading Support Transparency HOW 91* and ask students to check their graphic organizers individually. Go over key concepts and clarify key vocabulary as needed.

  📖 **History of Our World Transparencies,** *Section Reading Support Transparency HOW 91*

- Tell students to fill in the last column of the *Reading Readiness Guide*. Ask them to evaluate if what they learned was what they had expected to learn.

  All in One **Unit 4 History of Our World Teaching Resources,** *Reading Readiness Guide,* p. 87

Answer

Make Generalizations Aztecs valued their priests and, like the Mayas, relied on maize for food.

Aztec Gods and Goddesses
The Aztec God Quetzalcoatl (top) was the god of priests, and was believed to have invented the Aztec calendar. Above is the Aztec maize goddess. Both figures appear often in Aztec art.
Make Generalizations *What does the worship of gods and goddesses such as these tell you about Aztec society?*

Religion and Learning To bring about good harvests, Aztec priests held ceremonies that would win the favor of their gods. Their most important god was the sun god. Aztec religion taught that the sun would not have the strength to rise and cross the sky every day without human blood. Of course, if the sun did not rise, crops could not grow, and the people would starve. Therefore, Aztec religious ceremonies included human sacrifice. The Aztecs also prayed to their gods for victory in war. Prisoners captured in war often served as human sacrifices.

To schedule their religious festivals and farming cycles, Aztec priests created a calendar based on the Mayan calendar and their own knowledge of astronomy. The calendar had 13 periods, like months, of 20 days each. The Aztecs also kept records using hieroglyphs similar to those used by the Mayas.

Tenochtitlán had schools and a university. Boys from noble families attended these schools. They studied to be government officials, teachers, or scribes.

Aztec Society Aztec society had a strict class structure. The emperor, of course, was most important. Next were members of the royal family, nobles, priests, and military leaders. Soldiers were next in importance. Below soldiers came artisans—skilled creators of jewelry, pottery, sculpture, and other goods—and merchants. Then came the farmers. They made up the largest class of people. The lowest position in Aztec society was held by slaves, most of whom were prisoners captured in battle.

War was a part of life in the Aztec Empire, as new territory was conquered. Most young men over the age of 15 served as soldiers for a period of time. They were well trained and well equipped. Soldiers had swords and bows and arrows. For protection, they had special armor made from heavy quilted cotton. Priests and government officials did not serve in the military.

348 History of Our World

Background: Biography

Moctezuma (c. 1480–1520) Moctezuma ruled as emperor of the Aztec empire from about 1502 to 1520. During his reign there was constant warfare and unrest. When the Spanish arrived in 1519, Moctezuma believed that they were descendants of Quetzalcoatl, a legendary Aztec god.

Moctezuma received the Spanish, led by Hernán Cortéz, into his court. Soon, Cortéz had seized Moctezuma and taken over Tenochtitlán. Moctezuma was killed in 1520. No one is sure whether he was killed by the Spanish or his subjects.

Aztec women were not allowed to work as soldiers or military leaders, though they could train to be priestesses. Most women—even women from noble families—had to be skilled at weaving. Some of the cloth they wove was used for trade. Some was used to decorate temples. The finest cloth was used to make clothing for the Aztec royal family and nobles. Before teenage girls learned to weave, they were expected to grind flour, make tortillas, and cook meals.

The End of an Empire In 1519, Spanish conquistadors invaded the Aztec Empire. Some of the peoples whose lands the Aztecs had conquered joined forces with the Spanish. Together, they fought the Aztecs and tried to overthrow the Aztec emperor, Moctezuma. The two sides waged fierce battles. Diseases carried by the Spanish spread to the Aztecs and killed many of them. In 1521, the Aztecs surrendered to the Spanish. The once-powerful Aztec Empire was at an end.

Aztec Feather Headdress
Moctezuma's head covering was decorated with feathers—an important symbol in the Aztec religion.

✓ **Reading Check** Describe the levels of Aztec society.

Section 2 Assessment

Key Terms
Review the key terms at the beginning of this section. Use each term in a sentence that explains its meaning.

Target Reading Skill
State three details that support the main idea of the first paragraph under the heading Aztec Society.

Comprehension and Critical Thinking
1. (a) Recall What activity was the basis of Mayan life?

(b) Explain How did Mayan religion reflect the importance of this activity?
(c) Infer What do you think is the most likely reason the Mayas abandoned their cities? Explain your choice.
2. (a) Describe How did the Aztec Empire expand?
(b) Synthesize How did the Aztecs treat the peoples they conquered in war?
(c) Draw Conclusions Why might some of the peoples conquered by the Aztecs have wanted to overthrow the emperor?

Writing Activity
The Mayas and the Aztecs created great civilizations. How were their cultures alike? How were they different? Write a paragraph comparing and contrasting the two civilizations.

> **Writing Tip** First take notes on the similarities and differences. You may want to use a chart to help you organize. Be sure to write a topic sentence for your paragraph, and then support it with details from your notes.

Assess Progress [L2]
Have students complete the Section Assessment. Administer the *Section Quiz*.

 Unit 4 History of Our World Teaching Resources, *Section Quiz,* p. 89

Reteach [L1]
If students need more instruction, have them read this section in the Reading and Vocabulary Study Guide.

📖 Chapter 12, Section 2, **History of Our World Reading and Vocabulary Study Guide,** pp. 131–133

Extend [L3]
To help students appreciate the accomplishments of ancient civilizations, have them complete *Writing a Message Using Your Own Hieroglyphics.*

 Unit 4 History of Our World Teaching Resources, *Small Group Activity: Writing a Message Using Your Own Hieroglyphics,* pp. 100–103

Answer

✓ **Reading Check** At the top was the emperor. Next were the priests, nobles, royal family members, and military leaders. Soldiers were next, followed by artisans. Next came traders, and then farmers. Slaves were in the lowest position.

Writing Activity
Use the *Rubric for Assessing a Writing Assignment* to evaluate students' paragraphs.

 Unit 4 History of Our World Teaching Resources, *Rubric for Assessing a Writing Assignment,* p. 108

Section 2 Assessment

Key Terms
Students' sentences should reflect knowledge of each Key Term.

Target Reading Skill
Students may cite any of the appropriate details in the paragraph.

Comprehension and Critical Thinking
1. (a) farming **(b)** The Mayan rain-god and sun-god were important because rain and sun were needed for growing maize.
(c) Reasons might include crop failure, war, disease, overuse of natural resources, or rebellion against leaders. Students should provide an adequate explanation for their choice.

2. (a) The Aztecs conquered other peoples.
(b) Conquered peoples had to pay tributes to the emperor. Some people captured in war were used as human sacrifices. **(c)** Possible answer: They resented their treatment and having to pay tributes.

Focus on The Great Temple

Guided Instruction

- Ask students to read the text and study the art, photos, and captions on these pages.

- Ask students **Why was the Great Temple rebuilt so many times?** (*Because it was a solid, earth-filled temple, it began to sink into the soft soil of Tenochtitlán; in order to save the Great Temple, the Aztecs rebuilt it six times.*)

- Ask students **Why do you think the Aztecs rebuilt the Great Temple instead of building a new one in a different place?** (*Possible answers: It was easier and faster to rebuild the temple instead of building a new one; the area where the temple was built might have been special in some way for the Aztecs and their gods.*)

- As a class, answer the Assessment questions. Allow students to briefly discuss their responses with a partner before sharing their answers with the class.

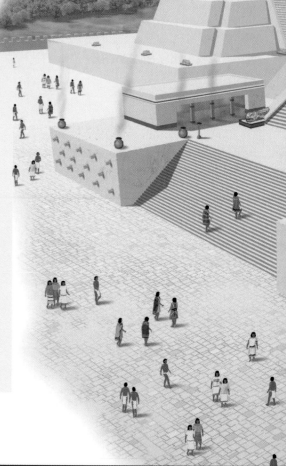

Focus On
The Great Temple

In 1521, the Spanish conquered the Aztecs and began to destroy the Aztec capital of Tenochtitlán. On the site of the ruined Aztec city, they built a new capital: Mexico City. For many years, an important piece of Mexico's past—the Great Temple of the Aztecs—remained buried under this new city. Scholars were not sure where the site of the Great Temple lay. Then in 1978, electrical workers dug up an old stone carving. Experts who studied the carving knew that it had been made by the Aztecs. The site of the Great Temple had been found.

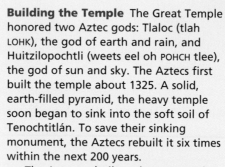

Building the Temple The Great Temple honored two Aztec gods: Tlaloc (tlah LOHK), the god of earth and rain, and Huitzilopochtli (weets eel oh POHCH tlee), the god of sun and sky. The Aztecs first built the temple about 1325. A solid, earth-filled pyramid, the heavy temple soon began to sink into the soft soil of Tenochtitlán. To save their sinking monument, the Aztecs rebuilt it six times within the next 200 years.

The Aztecs rebuilt each new temple over the previous temple. After rebuilding, they honored their gods with human sacrifices in the temple's shrines. A figure called a chacmool, at the top left, was used to hold offerings to the gods.

The illustration at the right shows some of the temple layers. By the time the Spanish began to destroy Tenochtitlán in 1521, the Great Temple had been built seven times.

Differentiated Instruction

For Gifted and Talented   L3

Working in pairs, have students do research to learn more about other Aztec gods, such as Chalchiuhtlicue, Huix-tocíhuatl, or Quetzalcóatl. Have students give a short presentation on the Aztec god they chose. Encourage students to be creative and include drawings or photos of artifacts in their presentations.

For Advanced Readers   L3

Have students do research on the Internet or in the library to learn more about the Aztec gods Tlaloc and Huitzilopochtli. Using the information they find, have students write a short essay about either of the two gods. Encourage students to be creative and include drawings or photos of artifacts related to the gods with their essays.

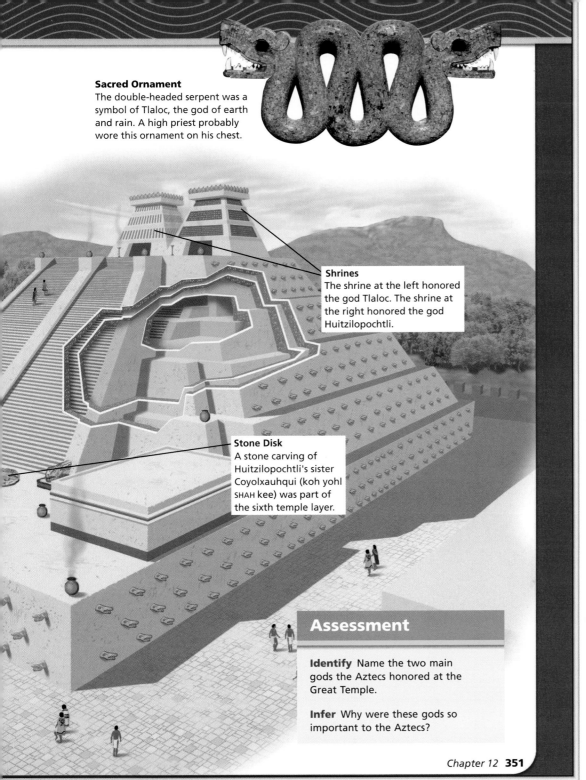

Sacred Ornament
The double-headed serpent was a symbol of Tlaloc, the god of earth and rain. A high priest probably wore this ornament on his chest.

Shrines
The shrine at the left honored the god Tlaloc. The shrine at the right honored the god Huitzilopochtli.

Stone Disk
A stone carving of Huitzilopochtli's sister Coyolxauhqui (koh yohl SHAH kee) was part of the sixth temple layer.

Assessment

Identify Name the two main gods the Aztecs honored at the Great Temple.

Infer Why were these gods so important to the Aztecs?

Chapter 12 **351**

Independent Practice

Have students do research in the library or on the Internet to learn more about other well-known religious sites in the region, such as the Temple of the Sun at Machu Picchu in Peru, built by the Incas. Working in pairs, have students create a brochure in which they list some of the history of their chosen site, as well as other important information, such as age and location.

Answers

Assessment

Identify Tlaloc, Huitzilopochtli
Infer Possible answer: The Aztecs depended on agriculture for survival, therefore they would have believed that Tlaloc, the god of earth and rain, and Huitzilopochtli, the god of sun and sky would be important to their survival. They probably believed that these gods were responsible for helping their crops grow.

Section 3
Step-by-Step Instruction

Objectives

Social Studies

1. Find out about the Mound Builders who lived in eastern North America.
2. Learn about the cultures of the Southwest and Great Plains.
3. Find out about the Woodland peoples of North America.

Reading/Language Arts

Learn how to identify details that add up to the main idea in a paragraph.

Prepare to Read

Build Background Knowledge L2

Review with students the ancient civilizations in Middle America they read about in earlier sections. Have students preview the headings, maps, and photographs in this section to predict what they will be learning about. Write students' predictions on the board and return to them after reading the section to assess their accuracy and make revisions as needed.

Set a Purpose for Reading L2

■ Preview the Objectives.

■ Form students into pairs or groups of four. Distribute the *Reading Readiness Guide*. Ask students to fill in the first two columns of the chart. Use the Numbered Heads participation strategy (TE, p. T40) to call on students to share one piece of information they already know and one piece of information they want to know.

All in One Unit 4 History of Our World Teaching Resources, *Reading Readiness Guide*, p. 91

Vocabulary Builder
Preview Key Terms L2

Pronounce each Key Term, then ask students to say the word with you. Provide a simple explanation such as, "The flat land east of the Rocky Mountains makes up the Great Plains."

Section 3
Cultures of North America

Prepare to Read

Objectives
In this section, you will
1. Find out about the Mound Builders who lived in eastern North America.
2. Learn about the cultures of the Southwest and the Great Plains.
3. Find out about the Woodland peoples of North America.

Taking Notes
As you read this section, look for information about three major Native American cultures. Copy the table below and record your findings in it. Add categories as needed.

Culture	Location	Source of Food	Type of Dwelling

Target Reading Skill

Identify Implied Main Ideas Identifying main ideas can help you remember what you read. Even if a main idea is not stated directly, the details in a paragraph add up to the main idea. For example, the details in the paragraph under the heading The Eastern Mound Builders add up to this main idea: The Mound Builders, hunters and gatherers who relied on the land's resources, became settled farmers over time.

Key Terms

• **Mound Builders** (mownd BIL durz) *n.* Native American groups who built earthen mounds
• **Anasazi** (ah nuh SAH zee) *n.* one of the ancient Native American peoples of the Southwest
• **pueblo** (PWEB loh) *n.* a Native American stone or adobe dwelling, part of a cluster of dwellings built close together
• **kiva** (KEE vuh) *n.* a round room used by the pueblo people for religious ceremonies
• **Great Plains** (grayt playnz) *n.* a mostly flat and grassy region of western North America

A Mississippian copper sculpture dating from the 1000s

Seen from above, a huge snake seems to twist and turn across the landscape. A mysterious shape—perhaps an egg?—is at its mouth. This enormous earthwork was created hundreds of years ago in what is now Ohio. Called the Great Serpent Mound, it is the largest image of a snake anywhere in the world. Uncoiled, the serpent would be about 1,349 feet (411 meters) long.

Archaeologists have found more than 1,000 earthen mounds across eastern North America. They were made by thousands of workers moving baskets of earth by hand. There are small mounds and large ones. Some contain graves, but others—like the Great Serpent Mound—do not. Most were constructed between around 700 B.C. and A.D. 1250. Today, we call the different Native American groups who built these curious and long-lasting mounds the **Mound Builders**.

Target Reading Skill L2

Identify Implied Main Ideas Point out the Target Reading Skill. Tell students that when a main idea is not specifically expressed, readers can combine important details to express the main idea themselves.

Model the skill by pointing out that the details in the first paragraph under The Hopewell Culture on p. 354 can be combined to express the main idea. (*The Hopewell were mound builders who lived along the Ohio and upper Mississippi rivers, appearing there about 100 years before the Adena disappeared.*)

Give students *Identify Implied Main Ideas*. Have them complete the activity in groups.

All in One Unit 4 History of Our World Teaching Resources, *Identify Implied Main Ideas*, p. 96

The Eastern Mound Builders

The Mound Builders lived in eastern North America. They occupied the region roughly between Minnesota and Louisiana, and between the Mississippi River and the Atlantic Ocean. The Mound Builders lived along the area's many rivers, which provided them with plenty of fish and fresh water. They hunted wild animals for food, including deer, turkeys, bears, and even squirrels. They also gathered nuts such as acorns, pecans, and walnuts to supplement their diet. Over time, these communities began to grow their own food. This meant they did not have to move as much in search of food and could form settlements.

Early Mound Builders: The Adena Archaeologists have discovered evidence of early Mound Builders who lived about 600 B.C. in the Ohio Valley. Called the Adena (uh DEE nuh), these people constructed mounds that are usually less than 20 feet high. Certain mounds were tombs that contained weapons, tools, and decorative objects in addition to bodies. Some items were made from materials not found locally, such as copper and seashells. Thus, historians believe that the Adena must have taken part in long-distance trade. Little is known about the daily life of the Adena, but they seem to have declined about 100 B.C.

Great Serpent Mound
The Great Serpent Mound snakes across Ohio's countryside.
Infer *What about the mound suggests that it may have had religious importance?*

Chapter 12 Section 3 **353**

Chapter 12 Section 3 **353**

Guided Instruction (continued)

- Ask students **Where did the Hopewell live?** *(in North America along the Ohio and upper Mississippi rivers)*

- Have students use the map on p. 354 to locate the different mound sites they have read about. Ask **Why do you think so many early cultures settled along rivers?** *(Rivers were a source of water for farming and drinking and a means of transportation.)*

- Ask **Why were maize and beans so important to the Mississippians?** *(These crops could be easily dried and stored, which ensured food during times of drought or bad harvests.)*

Independent Practice

Ask students to create the Taking Notes graphic organizer on a blank piece of paper. Tell students to write the names of Native American cultures they have learned about in the first column. Then have them fill out the information in each culture's row. Display the *Chart/Table* transparency and briefly model how to choose details to complete the chart.

📖 **History of Our World Transparencies,** *Transparency B12: Chart/Table*

Monitor Progress

As students work on their organizers, circulate and make sure individuals are using the correct information. Provide assistance as needed.

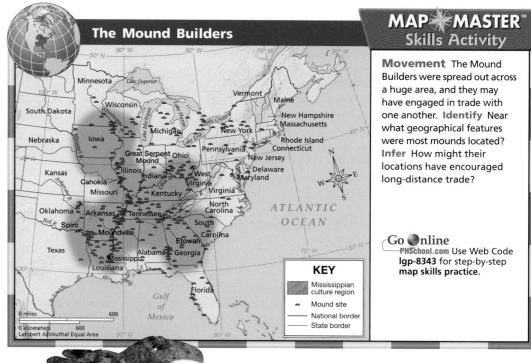

The Mound Builders

MAP MASTER™ Skills Activity

Movement The Mound Builders were spread out across a huge area, and they may have engaged in trade with one another. **Identify** Near what geographical features were most mounds located? **Infer** How might their locations have encouraged long-distance trade?

Go Online
PHSchool.com Use Web Code lgp-8343 for step-by-step map skills practice.

KEY
- Mississippian culture region
- Mound site
- National border
- State border

0 miles 600
0 kilometers 600
Lambert Azimuthal Equal Area

The Hopewell made figures like the copper raven (above) and the hand (bottom right), which is made of mica, a soft mineral.

The Hopewell Culture About 100 years before the Adena disappeared, another culture appeared along the Ohio and upper Mississippi rivers. Called the Hopewell, these peoples built larger mounds. The Hopewell did not have a highly organized society with a single ruler. Instead, they lived in many small communities with local leaders.

The Hopewell peoples grew a greater variety of crops than did the Adena. They also seem to have traded over a wider area. There is evidence that goods were traded from the Gulf of Mexico to present-day Canada and from the Rocky Mountains to the Atlantic Ocean. Hopewell sites have silver from the Great Lakes region and alligator teeth from present-day Florida.

About A.D. 400, the long-distance trade across eastern North America seems to have faded out. Also, the Hopewell stopped building new mounds. Historians are not sure why. The climate may have turned colder and hurt agriculture. The Hopewell may have suffered a severe drought or been invaded. Overpopulation is also a possible reason for their decline.

Background: Global Perspectives

Burial Mounds The practice of burying people in tombs covered with mounds dates to prehistoric times. These mounds are also called *barrows* or *stupa*. The Romans, Sax- ons, and Vikings all used barrows for the burial of important people. Stupa, used in Buddhist regions, can be found in India, Sri Lanka, Myanmar, and other Asian countries.

Answers

MAP MASTER™ Skills Activity **Identify** rivers **Infer** Mound Builders could travel along the river to trade goods with other civilizations.

The Mississippians By about A.D. 700, a new and important culture called Mississippian (mis uh SIP ee un) began to flower in eastern North America. These peoples inhabited both small and large communities. Like the earlier Mound Builders, the Mississippians lived along rivers and built mounds. They, too, grew new kinds of crops. Maize and beans became important parts of their diet. Both foods are easily dried and stored in large amounts. This helped the Mississippians protect themselves against years of drought and bad harvests.

The Mississippian culture spread over a wide area in the present-day South and Midwest. During this period, long-distance trade revived. Populations increased over time, and major centers of government and religion developed. These include Moundville in present-day Alabama, and Etowah (ET uh wah) in present-day Georgia. The largest center was Cahokia (kuh HOH kee uh), located in what is now Illinois. One of Cahokia's mounds, around 100 feet tall, was the largest mound in North America.

Cahokia was a large city for its day. Historians estimate that it reached its peak about A.D. 1100. At that time, as many as 20,000 to 30,000 people may have lived there. But by 1250, the population dropped. The disappearance of the last of the Mound Builders is as mystifying as the many earthworks they left behind.

✓ **Reading Check** How did the Mississippians live?

Peoples of the Southwest and the Great Plains

The mounds of the Mound Builders are not the only amazing structures built by early Native American cultures. Other peoples in North America adapted to different landscapes and climates to create distinctive structures. One of these groups created remarkable multistory homes from the available materials of the Southwest.

The Ancient Ones The **Anasazi** (ah nuh SAH zee) were an ancient Native American peoples of the Southwest. Their name can be translated as "the ancient ones." Anasazi culture began about A.D. 100. Historians think that Chaco Canyon, in present-day New Mexico, was a trading center for the region. A network of roads connected distant Anasazi villages to Chaco Canyon. Archaeologists have found tens of thousands of turquoise pieces as well as baskets, pottery, shells, and feathers in Chaco Canyon.

Identify Implied Main Ideas
List several details from the paragraphs under the heading The Mississippians. What implied main idea do these details support?

An archaeologist digs at Chaco Canyon, New Mexico.

Chapter 12 Section 3 **355**

➲ Target Reading Skill L2

Identify Implied Main Ideas As a follow-up, ask students to answer the Target Reading Skill question in the Student Edition. *(Students may list any of the details in these three paragraphs. Possible main idea: The Mississippian culture was an important culture of Mound Builders who lived along rivers in what is now the South and Midwest from about A.D. 700–1250.)*

Peoples of the Southwest and the Great Plains L2

Guided Instruction

■ **Vocabulary Builder** Clarify the high-use words **diverse, alter,** and **revive** before reading.

■ Read about the Anasazi, Pueblo, and Plains Indians in Peoples of the Southwest and the Great Plains.

■ Ask students **Who were the Anasazi?** *(an early Native America people who lived in the Southwest)* **What does their name mean?** *("the ancient ones")*

■ Discuss the geography and climate of the Southwest. *(The soil is poor and there is little water. The winters are harsh and the summers are hot and dry.)* Ask **How were the Anasazi able to grow crops in their dry land?** *(They created a system of canals and dams.)*

■ Ask **How did the Anasazi create homes that were adapted to their environment?** *(They built pueblos from adobe and stone; these dwellings stayed warm in the winter and cool in the summer.)*

■ Ask **Why did the Anasazi abandon their pueblos?** *(A severe drought hit the region.)*

⟲ Skills for Life **Skills Mini Lesson**

Sequencing L2

1. Teach the skill by explaining that sequencing means putting things in the order in which they occurred. Tell students that making a timeline to show events in time order makes it easier to see relationships between events.

2. Help students practice the skill by putting these events in time order:

(a) Pueblo people follow Anasazi customs; (b) Anasazi culture begins in A.D. 900; (c) Anasazi abandon pueblos by A.D. 1300 *(b, c, a)*

3. Have students apply the skill by identifying a relationship between the Anasazi and the Pueblo. *(The Pueblo people modeled their culture after the Anasazi culture.)*

Answer

✓ **Reading Check** They lived along rivers as farmers. They conducted long-distance trade with other groups.

- Ask **How were the Pueblo people like the Anasazi?** *(They built similar dwellings and had similar crafts; both were skilled farmers; both developed irrigation systems.)*

- Ask students **Why was sign language important to the Plains Indians?** *(Since it was understood across the region, it allowed different groups to communicate and trade.)*

- Ask students **How did the Europeans change the ways of life of the Plains Indians?** *(Europeans settled on Indian land; introduced guns, horses, railroads; brought disease; forced Native American groups from the east to move west and coexist with the groups already living there.)*

Independent Practice

Tell students to continue filling in their charts with information about the Anasazi, Pueblo, and Plains Indians.

Monitor Progress

As students work on their charts, circulate to make sure they are filling in each row with the correct information. Provide assistance as needed.

Anasazi Cliff Village
Entire villages of Anasazi people lived under the shelter of massive stone cliffs like this one in Colorado. Anasazi craftspeople decorated pottery like the jar above with black and white patterns.
Analyze Images *What might be some advantages to living under cliffs like these?*

Southwestern North America has harsh winters in some areas and hot, dry summers. The soil is mostly poor, and there is little water. To capture rainwater for their fields, the Anasazi created a system of canals and dams. This system allowed them to grow maize, beans, and squash for food. They also grew cotton for cloth.

For their homes, the Anasazi constructed **pueblos** (PWEB lohz). These stone and adobe dwellings, built next to one another, helped to keep people warm in the winter and cool in the summer. Pueblos had thick walls, and many had high ceilings. Round rooms called **kivas** (KEE vuz) were used for special religious ceremonies. As the population grew, so did the pueblos. Some pueblos were five stories tall and had hundreds of rooms. Between 1275 and 1300, however, severe droughts hit the region. The Anasazi abandoned all their major pueblos, never to return.

Later Pueblo Peoples Anasazi customs survived among later groups who lived to the south of the Anasazi sites. They are called Pueblo peoples, or simply Pueblos. These groups also built apartment-style stone and adobe dwellings with kivas. Like the Anasazi, their crafts included weaving, basket-making, and pottery. They were also skilled farmers.

The region of New Mexico where the Pueblos lived receives only 8 to 13 inches of rain a year, but it does have rivers. The Pueblos planted corn, squash, beans, and other crops in the river bottoms near their dwellings. They relied on intensive irrigation to raise these crops. Hunting and gathering provided the Pueblos with the food they could not grow.

356 History of Our World

Differentiated Instruction

For English Language Learners L1
Students whose native language is Spanish may benefit from studying this section in the Spanish Reading and Vocabulary Study Guide.

📖 Chapter 12, Section 3, **History of Our World Spanish Reading and Vocabulary Study Guide,** pp. 96–97

For Gifted and Talented L3
Invite students to visit the past by researching Mesa Verde National Park in the library or on the Internet. Have students use their information to plan a trip to these cliff dwellings built along canyon walls in what is now southwestern Colorado. Have students share their findings and travel plans with the class.

Answer

Analyze Images Possible answers: shaded from the hot sun, protected from invaders

The Pueblos believed in many spirits, called kachinas (kuh CHEE nuz). They wanted to please these spirits, who they believed controlled the rain, wild animals, and harvests. Many times a year, the Pueblos gathered for ceremonies that involved prayer, dancing, and singing. They also appealed to their ancestors, another type of kachina. Today the modern descendants of the Pueblo peoples, including the Hopi and the Zuni, keep many of these traditions alive.

The Plains Indians West of the Mississippi River and east of the Rocky Mountains is a mostly flat and grassy region called the **Great Plains.** For centuries, this land was home to diverse groups of Native Americans called Plains Indians. Individual groups had their own languages and traditions. They used a form of sign language to trade with one another.

Some groups, such as the Mandan, were farmers. They lived in fenced villages along the Missouri River, in lodges made of earth and wood. Others, such as the Sioux (soo), followed herds of bison that roamed the plains. Dwellings such as tipis (TEE peaz)—easy to take apart, carry, and set up again—were ideal for such a lifestyle.

After the arrival of Europeans, the lives of Plains Indians changed rapidly. They had to share their land with eastern Native Americans, such as the Omaha, who had been forced west by white settlers. Newly introduced horses, guns, and railroads altered their traditions. Most groups suffered from diseases brought by Europeans and lost their land to European settlement. Many Native American cultures began to break down. Today, there is a strong effort to revive these traditional cultures.

✓ **Reading Check** How did the Sioux live?

Links Across
The World

The Arrival of the Horse
The arrival of the horse in the Americas brought major changes to the lives of many Plains Indians. Native Americans on horseback became expert buffalo hunters. They came to depend more and more on the buffalo for their existence, using the animal for food, clothing, and shelter. Many previously settled Indian groups became nomadic. They rode their horses across the plains, following the great herds of buffalo.

Differentiated Instruction

For Less Proficient Readers [L1]
Students who are less proficient readers may have difficulty absorbing the information in this section. Pair students with more proficient readers and have them create an outline of the material. Tell students to use the headings in the section as guidelines for their outlines.

Peoples of the Woodlands [L2]

Guided Instruction

- Read Peoples of the Woodlands with students. As students read, circulate to make sure individuals can answer the Reading Check question.

- Ask students **What were distinguishing symbols of wealth among Native Americans of the Northwest?** *(totem poles and potlatch ceremonies)*

- Ask **How did the people of the Northwest get food?** *(by hunting and fishing)* **In the Eastern Woodlands?** *(by hunting and farming)*

- Have students explain the Iroquois political system. *(Five nations formed a peace alliance. Each nation governed its own villages, but they all met in council to discuss issues that affected the entire group.)*

Independent Progress
Have students complete the table.

Monitor Progress

- Show *Section Reading Support Transparency HOW 92* and ask students to check their graphic organizers individually.

  📖 **History of Our World Transparencies,** *Section Reading Support Transparency HOW 92*

- Tell students to fill in the last column of the *Reading Readiness Guide.* Ask them to evaluate if what they learned was what they had expected to learn.

  All in One **Unit 4 History of Our World Teaching Resources,** *Reading Readiness Guide,* p. 91

Links
Read the **Links Across the World** on this page. Ask students **How did the introduction of the horse change the lives of many Plains Indians?** *(Plains Indians used the horse to hunt buffalo, which caused them to become more dependent on the buffalo for their survival.)*

Answer

✓ Reading Check They followed bison herds across the plains.

Assess and Reteach

Assess Progress L2

Have students complete the Section Assessment. Administer the *Section Quiz*.

All in One **Unit 4 History of Our World Teaching Resources,** *Section Quiz,* p. 93

Reteach L1

If students need more instruction, have them read this section in the Reading and Vocabulary Study Guide.

📖 Chapter 12, Section 3, **History of Our World Reading and Vocabulary Study Guide,** pp. 134–136

Extend L3

Have students complete the *Enrichment* activity to learn more about the Iroquois.

All in One **Unit 4 History of Our World Teaching Resources,** *Enrichment,* p. 98

Answer

✓ **Reading Check** It was an alliance of five Iroquois nations designed to keep the peace.

Section 3 Assessment

Key Terms

Students' sentences should reflect knowledge of each Key Term.

🔁 **Target Reading Skill**

See the main ideas as stated in the Chapter Summary on p. 359.

Comprehension and Critical Thinking

1. (a) Adena, Hopewell, Mississippians **(b)** They built mounds, carried on long-distance trade, and grew a variety of crops.

2. (a) It has harsh winters and hot, dry summers. **(b)** They used available materials, such as sun dried adobe bricks or stone cliffs.

3. (a) totem pole—a carved, painted log stood on end that typically had images of animals carved into and painted on it; potlatch—a ceremony held by a person of high rank to show wealth **(b)** Possible answer: An elaborate totem pole with intricate carvings and paintings might signify wealth because it indicated that the owner might have had more free time to create it or could afford to pay a good artist to create it. At potlatches, people were able to show how wealthy they were by giving guests expensive gifts.

Peoples of the Woodlands

Native American groups lived in woodlands in different parts of present-day Canada and the United States. The peoples of the Northwest Coast hunted in the forests and fished in rivers full of salmon as well as in the Pacific Ocean. They lived in settlements of wooden homes. Like the Mound Builders and the Pueblos, early Native Americans of the Northwest Coast created remarkable structures. They were called totem poles.

Totem poles were carved and painted logs stood on end. They typically had images of real or mythical animals. Often the animals were identified with the owner's family line, much as a family crest is used in European cultures. Totem poles were a symbol of the owner's wealth, as were ceremonies called potlatches. At a potlatch, a person of high rank invited many guests and gave them generous gifts.

In the eastern woodlands, Native American groups such as the Iroquois (IHR uh kwoy) not only hunted in the forests but also cleared land for farms. Because the men were often at war, the women were the farmers. In the 1500s, five Iroquois nations—Mohawk, Onondaga, Cayuga, Seneca, and Oneida—formed a peace alliance. Nations of the Iroquois League governed their own villages, but they met to decide issues that affected the group as a whole. This was the best-organized political system in the Americas when Europeans arrived.

✓ **Reading Check** What was the Iroquois League?

Totem pole in Vancouver, Canada

Section 3 Assessment

Key Terms
Review the key terms at the beginning of this section. Use each term in a sentence that explains its meaning.

🔁 **Target Reading Skill**
State the main ideas in Section 3.

Comprehension and Critical Thinking
1. (a) Sequence List the three groups of Mound Builders, from earliest to latest.

(b) Compare In what ways were the three groups alike?
2. (a) Identify What is the climate of southwestern North America?
(b) Identify Cause and Effect Why did peoples of this region build pueblos rather than other types of structures?
3. (a) Define What are totem poles and potlatches?
(b) Infer Why were totem poles and potlatches symbols of a family's wealth?

Writing Activity
Study the photograph of the Anasazi cliff dwellings on pages 356–357. Write a paragraph describing the site. What are the buildings like? Where are they located? What might it be like there at night or during a storm?

> **Writing Tip** Use descriptive adjectives for colors, textures, and shapes. Also include any sounds and smells you might experience there at different times of the day or year.

Writing Activity

Use the *Rubric for Assessing a Writing Assignment* to evaluate students' paragraphs.

All in One **Unit 4 History of Our World Teaching Resources,** *Rubric for Assessing a Writing Assignment,* p. 108

12 Review and Assessment

◆ Chapter Summary

Section 1: South America and the Incas

- The varied geography and climate of the Americas produced a diversity of Native American peoples and cultures.
- The Incas ruled a large, highly organized mountain empire in South America. Their accomplishments included long-lasting stone structures.

Section 2: Cultures of Middle America

- Mayan civilization was based on farming, which supported cities throughout the Yucatán Peninsula of Middle America.
- The Aztecs ruled a rich and powerful empire of diverse peoples in Middle America, from a magnificent capital called Tenochtitlán.

Aztec feather headdress

Section 3: Cultures of North America

- The Mound Builders lived along the rivers of eastern North America and built thousands of earthen mounds across the region.
- The Anasazi, and later the Pueblo peoples, adapted to the dry environment of the Southwest, while the Plains Indians farmed or followed herds of buffalo.
- Woodlands peoples of the Northwest Coast were hunters and fishers. In eastern forests, the Iroquois League was formed to bring peace to the region.

Anasazi clay vessel

◆ Key Terms

Match each term with its definition.

1. quipu
2. kivas
3. hieroglyphics
4. census
5. pueblos
6. maize
7. terraces

A corn
B an official count of people
C steplike ledges cut into mountains
D stone dwellings, built next to one another
E group of knotted strings used to record information
F round rooms used for religious ceremonies
G signs and symbols that made up the Mayan writing system

Chapter 12 **359**

Vocabulary Builder

Revisit this chapter's high-use words:

dense	establish	diverse
complex	decline	alter
unify	equip	revive
thrive	supplement	

Ask students to review the definitions they recorded on their *Word Knowledge* worksheets.

All in One **Unit 4 History of Our World Teaching Resources,** *Word Knowledge,* p. 97

Consider allowing students to earn extra credit if they use the words in their answers to the questions in the Chapter Review and Assessment. The words must be used correctly and in a natural context to win the extra points.

Review and Assessment
Review Chapter Content

- Review and revisit the major themes of this chapter by asking students to identify which Guiding Question each bulleted statement in the Chapter Summary answers. Have students write each statement down and work in groups to determine which statement applies to which Guiding Question. Refer to page 1 in the Student Edition for the text of Guiding Questions.

- Assign *Vocabulary Development* for students to review Key Terms.

All in One **Unit 4 History of Our World Teaching Resources,** *Vocabulary Development,* p. 107

Answers

Key Terms

1. E
2. F
3. G
4. B
5. D
6. A
7. C

Review and Assessment

Comprehension and Critical Thinking

8. (a) Incas—farming on terraces, steplike ledges cut into mountains; Aztecs—raised fields for farming in lakes, called chinampas **(b)** Both methods were based on alterations of the natural landscape. **(c)** By building terraces, Incan farmers made use of the mountainous landscape. Stone terraces prevented the soil from being washed away by rain. The Aztecs used the shallow lakes around Tenochtitlán to form their chinampas.

9. (a) Each city had its own ruler and community leaders. **(b)** The Mayas did not seek control over other peoples. **(c)** Because a civilization like the Mayas was not organized around war and conquest, the people might find their land hard to defend against a more war-like people.

10. (a) Tenochtitlán **(b)** It was built in the middle of a lake and was connected to the mainland by causeways. It had an open plaza, towering pyramid-temples, stone palaces, aqueducts, and a huge marketplace. **(c)** Many modern capital cities have imposing structures like the Aztec pyramid-temples and stone palaces. They also have water systems that carry water from outlying sources into the city.

11. (a) in the region roughly between Michigan and Alabama, and between the Mississippi River and the Atlantic Ocean **(b)** They have learned about the Mound Builders' weapons, tools, and decorative objects, and that the Mound Builders probably engaged in long-distance trade. **(c)** The Mound Builders left no written records.

12. (a) The Great Plains are a flat and grassy region located between the Mississippi River and the Rocky Mountains. **(b)** Europeans arrived and settled on Indian land; introduced guns, horses, and railroads; brought disease; and forced Native American groups from the east to move west and coexist with the groups already living there. **(c)** They were trying to keep their land and preserve their way of life.

Skills Practice

Answers will vary.

Possible event Native American cultures began to break down (effect).

◆ Comprehension and Critical Thinking

8. (a) Describe What special farming methods were developed by the Incas and the Aztecs?
(b) Compare How were these methods similar?
(c) Analyze Information How did each method suit the geography of the region where it was used?

9. (a) Recall What type of government did Mayan cities have?
(b) Analyze Why is it not correct to call Mayan civilization an "empire"?
(c) Make Generalizations If a civilization like that of the Mayas came under attack, would it be easy or hard to defend? Explain your answer.

10. (a) Identify What city was the capital of the Aztec Empire?
(b) Describe What was this capital city like?
(c) Generalize In what ways are modern capital cities like the Aztec capital?

11. (a) Locate Where in North America are human-built mounds located?
(b) Synthesize What have archaeologists learned from studying these mounds?
(c) Analyze Why is it difficult to determine the exact use of some mounds?

12. (a) Describe Where are the Great Plains, and what are they like?
(b) Identify Cause and Effect What changes to their way of life did many Plains Indians experience, and why?
(c) Infer Why do you think some Plains Indians battled with European settlers?

◆ Skills Practice

Identifying Cause and Effect Review the steps to identify causes and effects that you learned in the Skills for Life activity in this chapter. Then reread the part of Section 3 titled The Plains Indians. Choose an event from this section, and decide if it is a cause or an effect. Look for earlier or later events that might be causes or effects. Then summarize the cause-and-effect relationships you have identified.

◆ Writing Activity: Science

Review this chapter to find out which crops were grown or collected for food by early Native Americans. Choose three crops. Do research to find out why each one might be important to a healthful diet. To which food group does it belong? What is its nutritional value? How is it different from or similar to other foods eaten by these people? Write a brief report on what you learn.

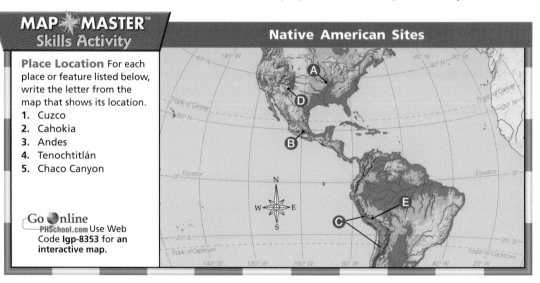

MAP MASTER™ Skills Activity

Place Location For each place or feature listed below, write the letter from the map that shows its location.
1. Cuzco
2. Cahokia
3. Andes
4. Tenochtitlán
5. Chaco Canyon

Go Online
PHSchool.com Use Web Code **lgp-8353** for an interactive map.

Native American Sites

Possible causes European diseases killed many Native Americans; they lost their land to Europeans; they died in battles with Europeans.

Possible effect Today, there is a strong effort to revive Native American cultures.

Writing Activity: Science
Reports will vary but possible crops include maize, beans, squash, peppers, papayas, and avocados.

Use *Rubric for Assessing a Writing Assignment* to assess students' reports.

All in One Unit 4 History of Our World Teaching Resources, *Rubric for Assessing a Writing Assignment,* p. 108

Standardized Test Prep

Test-Taking Tips

Some questions on standardized tests ask you to analyze a timeline. Study the timeline below. Then follow the tips to answer the sample question.

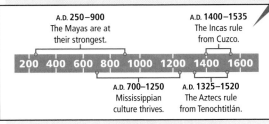

A.D. 250–900
The Mayas are at their strongest.

A.D. 1400–1535
The Incas rule from Cuzco.

200 400 600 800 1000 1200 1400 1600

A.D. 700–1250
Mississippian culture thrives.

A.D. 1325–1520
The Aztecs rule from Tenochtitlán.

Choose the letter of the best answer.

Based on the timeline, which statement is true?

- **A** Mississippian culture ended at A.D. 1100.
- **B** The Incas ruled from Cuzco for more than 400 years.
- **C** The Aztecs and the Incas did not live at the same time.
- **D** Mississippian culture began to thrive about A.D. 700.

TIP Use the lines at the beginning and end of each civilization bracket to calculate how long each civilization lasted.

Think It Through You can see that the line marking the end of Mississippian culture falls after 1200. Therefore A is incorrect. "The Incas rule from Cuzco" starts at 1400 and ends before 1600, so you can rule out B, too. The brackets on the timeline show that the Incas and the Aztecs did live at the same time. And the dates for the Aztecs, 1325–1520, overlap with the dates for the Incas, 1400–1535. So C is incorrect. That leaves only D. You can see that the line marking the start of Mississippian culture does indeed fall halfway between 600 and 800. D is the correct answer.

TIP Preview the question and skim over the answer choices before you look at the timeline. Keep the questions and possible answers in mind as you study the timeline.

Practice Questions

Use the timeline above to help you choose the letter of the best answer.

1. Based on the timeline, which statement is true?
   - **A** The Incas began to rule from Cuzco about A.D. 1000.
   - **B** The Aztecs and the Incas did not live at the same time.
   - **C** The Mayas were at their strongest for more than 600 years.
   - **D** Mississippian culture lasted for only 200 years.

Choose the letter of the best answer to complete each sentence.

2. The _____ built stone and adobe dwellings close together.
   - **A** Incas
   - **B** Hopewell peoples
   - **C** Anasazi
   - **D** Adena

3. The spectacular site of Machu Picchu is located in
   - **A** the Great Plains.
   - **B** South America.
   - **C** North America.
   - **D** Lake Texcoco.

4. The _____ lived along rivers in eastern North America.
   - **A** Mound Builders
   - **B** Aztecs
   - **C** Mayas
   - **D** Pueblo peoples

Go Online PHSchool.com

Use Web Code lga-8303 for a **Chapter 12 self-test.**

Chapter 12 **361**

Civilizations of Asia

Overview

Section 1

Golden Ages of China
1. Learn about the Golden Age of the Tang dynasty.
2. Discover the achievements of the Song dynasty, which ruled China after the Tang.
3. Find out about Mongol rule of China.

Section 2

Medieval Japan
1. Learn about the geography of Japan.
2. Discover the changes that occurred during the Heian period of Japanese history.
3. Find out about feudalism and the rule of the shoguns in Japan.

Section 3

The Great Mughal Empire in India
1. Find out about the geography of the Indian subcontinent.
2. Learn about the Delhi Sultanate, a period of Muslim rule.
3. Learn about the founding and achievements of the Mughal Empire.

DISCOVERY CHANNEL
SCHOOL Video

Kung Fu and the Shaolin Monks
Length: 5 minutes, 18 seconds
Use with Section 1
This video segment describes the origins of Kung Fu and explains how Chinese monks used Kung Fu to combat injustice and evil.

Technology Resources

Go Online
PHSchool.com

Students use embedded Web codes to access Internet activities, chapter self-tests, and additional map practice. They may also access Dorling Kindersley's Online Desk Reference to learn more about each country they study.

Interactive Textbook

Use the Interactive Textbook to make content and concepts come alive through animations, videos, and activities that accompany the complete basal text—online and on CD-ROM.

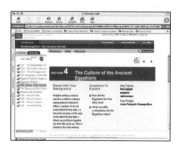

PRENTICE HALL

TeacherEXPRESS
Plan • Teach • Assess

Use this complete suite of powerful teaching tools to planning lessons and administering tests quicker and easier.

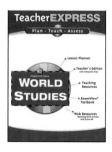

Reading and Assessment

Reading and Vocabulary Instruction

🔄 Model the Target Reading Skill

Cause and Effect Explain to students that understanding cause and effect will help them increase their understanding of the events that they read about. By identifying causes and effects, understanding that some effects are the results of multiple causes, and analyzing effects in context, students become more adept at seeing patterns both within and beyond the reading. Model this skill by thinking aloud about these statements about the Silk Road in China:

People traveling along the Silk Road introduced new ideas and goods to China.

China became a major center of trade and culture.

One of these sentences states a cause, and the other one states an effect. How will I decide which is which? Let me set up the statements in two ways, using a connection word like "because," to see which makes more sense. 1) "Because people traveling along the Silk Road introduced new ideas and goods to China, China became a major center of trade and culture." 2) "Because China became a major center of trade and culture, people traveling along the Silk Road introduced new ideas and goods to China."

My first statement makes more sense. People introducing new ideas and goods to China happened first, and caused China to become a major center of trade and culture, which is the effect.

Use the following worksheets from All-in-One Unit 4 History of Our World Teaching Resources (pp. 131–133) to support the chapter's Target Reading Skill.

Vocabulary Builder
High-Use Academic Words

Use these steps to teach this chapter's high-use words:

1. Have students rate how well they know each word on their Word Knowledge worksheets (All-in-One Unit 4 History of Our World Teaching Resources, p. 134).
2. Pronounce each word and ask students to repeat it.
3. Give students a brief definition or sample sentence (provided on TE pp. 365, 375, and 383).
4. Work with students as they fill in the "Definition or Example" column of their Word Knowledge worksheets.

Assessment

Formal Assessment

Test students' understanding of core knowledge and skills.

Chapter Tests A and B, All-in-One Unit 4 History of Our World Teaching Resources, pp. 152–157

Customize the Chapter Tests to suit your needs.
**Exam*View*®
Test Bank CD-ROM**

Skills Assessment

Assess geographic literacy.

MapMaster Skills, Student Edition, pp. 363, 366, 375, 385, 388

Assess reading and comprehension.

Target Reading Skills, Student Edition, pp. 369, 376, 384, and in Section Assessments

Chapter 13 Assessment, History of Our World Reading and Vocabulary Study Guide, p. 147

Performance Assessment

Assess students' performance on this chapter's Writing Activities using the following rubrics from All-in-One Unit 4 History of Our World Teaching Resources.

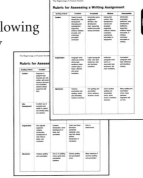

Rubric for Assessing a Journal Entry, p. 148

Rubric for Assessing a Student Poster, p. 149

Rubric for Assessing an Oral Presentation, p. 150

Rubric for Assessing a Writing Assignment, p. 151

Assess students' work through performance tasks.

Small Group Activity: Create a Museum Exhibit About Feudalism in Japan, All-in-One Unit 4 History of Our World Teaching Resources, pp. 137–140

Online Assessment

Have students check their own knowledge.

Chapter Self-Test

Test Preparation

Benchmark Test 4, AYP Monitoring Assessments, pp. 99–104

Section 1 Golden Ages of China

 2 periods, 1 block (includes Skills for Life)

Social Studies Objectives
1. Learn about the Golden Age of the Tang dynasty.
2. Discover the achievements of the Song dynasty, which ruled China after the Tang.
3. Find out about Mongol rule of China.

Reading/Language Arts Objective
Learn how to identify causes and effects.

Prepare to Read

Build Background Knowledge
Have students preview the section and discuss the inventions of the Tang and Song Dynasties.

Set a Purpose for Reading
Have students evaluate statements on the Reading Readiness Guide.

Preview Key Terms
Teach the section's Key Terms.

Target Reading Skill
Introduce the section's Target Reading Skill of **identifying causes and effects.**

Instructional Resources

All in One Unit 4 History of Our World Teaching Resources
- **L2** Reading Readiness Guide, p. 120
- **L2** Identify Causes and Effects, p. 131

Differentiated Instruction

Spanish Reading and Vocabulary Study Guide
- **L1** Chapter 13, Section 1, pp. 99–100 ELL

Instruct

The Tang Dynasty
Discuss achievements of the Tang Dynasty and how they affected China.

The Song Dynasty
Discuss new developments that arose in China during the Song Dynasty.

Target Reading Skill
Review **identifying causes and effects.**

The Mongols Conquer China
Discuss the Mongol Empire and contrast Mongol rule of China with rule under the Song Dynasty.

Instructional Resources

All in One Unit 4 History of Our World Teaching Resources
- **L2** Guided Reading and Review, p. 121
- **L2** Reading Readiness Guide, p. 120

History of Our World Transparencies
- **L2** Transparency B16: Venn Diagram
- **L2** Section Reading Support Transparency HOW 93

History of Our World Video Program
Kung Fu and the Shaolin Monks

Differentiated Instruction

All in One Unit 4 History of Our World Teaching Resources
- **L3** Writing to Inform and Explain, p. 146 AR, GT
- **L2** Skills for Life, p. 136 AR, GT, LPR, SN

Teacher's Edition
- **L3** For Gifted and Talented, TE p. 366
- **L3** For Advanced Readers, TE p. 368
- **L1** For Less Proficient Readers, TE p. 368
- **L2** For English Language Learners, TE p. 370
- **L1** For Special Needs Students, TE p. 370

Spanish Support
- **L2** Guided Reading and Review (Spanish), p. 108 ELL

Student Edition on Audio CD
- **L1** Chapter 13, Section 1 ELL, LPR, SN

Assess and Reteach

Assess Progress
Evaluate student comprehension with the section assessment and section quiz.

Reteach
Assign the Reading and Vocabulary Study Guide to help struggling students.

Extend
Extend the lesson by assigning an Enrichment activity.

Instructional Resources

All in One Unit 4 History of Our World Teaching Resources
- **L2** Section Quiz, p. 122
- **L3** Enrichment, p. 135
  Rubric for Assessing a Journal Entry, p. 148

Reading and Vocabulary Study Guide
- **L1** Chapter 13, Section 1, pp. 138–140

Differentiated Instruction

Spanish Support
- **L2** Section Quiz (Spanish), p. 109 ELL

History of Our World Transparencies
- **L2** Transparency B15: Outline ELL, LPR, SN

Key
- **L1** Basic to Average
- **L3** Average to Advanced
- **L2** For All Students
- **LPR** Less Proficient Readers
- **AR** Advanced Readers
- **SN** Special Needs Students
- **GT** Gifted and Talented
- **ELL** English Language Learners

Section 2 Medieval Japan

 2 periods, 1 block (includes Focus On A Japanese Home)

Social Studies Objectives
1. Learn about the geography of Japan.
2. Discover the changes that occurred during the Heian period of Japanese history.
3. Find out about feudalism and the rule of the shoguns in Japan.

Reading/Language Arts Objective
Learn how to understand effects.

Prepare to Read

Build Background Knowledge
Ask students to study a map and answer questions about Japan's geography.

Set a Purpose for Reading
Have students evaluate statements on the Reading Readiness Guide.

Preview Key Terms
Teach the section's Key Terms.

Target Reading Skill
Introduce the section's Target Reading Skill of **understanding effects**.

Instructional Resources

All in One Unit 4 History of Our World Teaching Resources
- **L2** Reading Readiness Guide, p. 124
- **L2** Understand Effects, p. 132

Differentiated Instruction

Spanish Reading and Vocabulary Study Guide
- **L1** Chapter 13, Section 1, pp. 101–102 ELL

Instruct

A Country of Islands
Discuss Japan's location and how its geography influences the people who live there.

The Heian Empire
Discuss the city of Kyoto and the people of the Heian Empire.

Target Reading Skill
Review **understanding effects**.

Feudalism in Japan
Ask questions about samurai and the Kamakura shogunate.

Japan and the Outside World
Discuss European influence on Japan and how the Tokugawa shogunate affected Japan's relationship with Europeans.

Instructional Resources

All in One Unit 4 History of Our World Teaching Resources
- **L2** Guided Reading and Review, p. 125
- **L2** Reading Readiness Guide, p. 124

History of Our World Transparencies
- **L2** Section Reading Support Transparency HOW 94

Differentiated Instruction

All in One Unit 4 History of Our World Teaching Resources
- Rubric for Assessing a Student Poster, p. 149 AR, GT
- **L3** Small Group Activity: Create a Museum Exhibit About Feudalism in Japan, pp. 137–140 AR, GT

Teacher's Edition
- **L3** For Gifted and Talented, TE p. 376
- **L1** For English Language Learners, TE p. 376
- **L3** For Advanced Readers, TE p. 377

Spanish Support
- **L2** Guided Reading and Review (Spanish), p. 110 ELL

Assess and Reteach

Assess Progress
Evaluate student comprehension with the section assessment and section quiz.

Reteach
Assign the Reading and Vocabulary Study Guide to help struggling students.

Extend
Extend the lesson by asking students to research samurai warriors.

Instructional Resources

All in One Unit 4 History of Our World Teaching Resources
- **L2** Section Quiz, p. 126
  - Rubric for Assessing an Oral Presentation, p. 150
  - Rubric for Assessing a Writing Assignment, p. 151

Reading and Vocabulary Study Guide
- **L1** Chapter 13, Section 1, pp. 141–143

Differentiated Instruction

Spanish Support
- **L2** Section Quiz (Spanish), p. 111 ELL

Key
- **L1** Basic to Average
- **L2** For All Students
- **L3** Average to Advanced
- LPR Less Proficient Readers
- AR Advanced Readers
- SN Special Needs Students
- GT Gifted and Talented
- ELL English Language Learners

Section 3 The Great Mughal Empire in India

 2 periods, 1 block (includes Chapter Review and Assessment)

Social Studies Objectives

1. Find out about the geography of the Indian subcontinent.
2. Learn about the Delhi Sultanate, a period of Muslim rule.
3. Learn about the founding and achievements of the Mughal Empire.

Reading/Language Arts Objective

Learn how to recognize cause-and-effect signal words.

Prepare to Read	Instructional Resources	Differentiated Instruction
Build Background Knowledge Ask students to preview the section and think about the qualities a great ruler should have. **Set a Purpose for Reading** Have students evaluate statements on the Reading Readiness Guide. **Preview Key Terms** Teach the section's Key Terms. **Target Reading Skill** Introduce the section's Target Reading Skill of **recognizing cause and effect signal words.**	**All in One Unit 4 History of Our World Teaching Resources** L2 Reading Readiness Guide, p. 128 L2 Recognize Cause-and-Effect Signal Words, p. 133	**Spanish Reading and Vocabulary Study Guide** L1 Chapter 13, Section 3, pp. 103–104 ELL

Instruct	Instructional Resources	Differentiated Instruction
India's Geography **The Delhi Sultanate** Discuss the Himalayas, Muslim rule of India, and the Hindu caste system. **Target Reading Skill** Review **recognizing cause and effect signal words.** **The Mughal Empire** Ask questions about Akbar the Great and how extravagant buildings may have led to the downfall of the Mughal Empire.	**All in One Unit 4 History of Our World Teaching Resources** L2 Guided Reading and Review, p. 129 L2 Reading Readiness Guide, p. 128 **History of Our World Transparencies** L2 Transparency B20: Timeline L2 Section Reading Support Transparency HOW 95	**All in One Unit 4 History of Our World Teaching Resources** L1 Using a Map Key, p. 141 **Teacher's Edition** L1 For Less Proficient Readers, TE p. 385 L1 For Special Needs Students, TE p. 385 **Spanish Support** L2 Guided Reading and Review (Spanish), p. 112 ELL

Assess and Reteach	Instructional Resources	Differentiated Instruction
Assess Progress Evaluate student comprehension with the section assessment and section quiz. **Reteach** Assign the Reading and Vocabulary Study Guide to help struggling students. **Extend** Extend the lesson by assigning a literature reading.	**All in One Unit 4 History of Our World Teaching Resources** L2 Section Quiz, p. 130 L3 Savitri: A Tale of Ancient India, pp. 142–145 Rubric for Assessing a Writing Assignment, p. 151 L2 Word Knowledge, p. 134 L2 Vocabulary Development, p. 147 L2 Chapter Tests A and B, pp. 152–157 **Reading and Vocabulary Study Guide** L1 Chapter 13, Section 3, pp. 144–146	**Spanish Support** L2 Section Quiz (Spanish), p. 113 ELL L2 Chapter Summary (Spanish), p. 114 ELL L2 Vocabulary Development (Spanish), p. 115 ELL

Key

L1 Basic to Average   L3 Average to Advanced   **LPR** Less Proficient Readers   **GT** Gifted and Talented

L2 For All Students   **AR** Advanced Readers   **ELL** English Language Learners

                                                        SN Special Needs Students

Professional Development

Reading Background

Discussion Ideas

One way to enrich a lesson is to encourage students to discuss the material from the chapter. Ideas for discussion must be complex enough to spark an interesting dialogue. They can relate to something students don't understand, something that seems interesting, or information students already know.

Read aloud the selection *The Song Dynasty* on page 367 of the Student Edition and model the difference between strong and weak discussion ideas.

For example, a strong discussion idea for what you have just read might be:
I think it is more fair to hire officials based on their abilities rather than their social position or wealth.

A weak discussion idea might be:
The Song Dynasty ruled from 960 to 1276.

As students read the chapter, ask them to write down one idea that could be used to conduct an interesting discussion. Begin the class discussion by having one student present his or her idea. Monitor the discussion to ensure that an adequate number of students have had a chance to respond before you introduce another idea.

Encourage Active Participation

In this chapter, students will use an Idea Wave to share their ideas. Remind students that if their idea is closely related to another person's idea, they should acknowledge the other person's ideas when they share theirs. Below are some language strategies for active classroom participation:

> *My idea is similar to _____'s idea.*
> *As _____ already pointed out, it seems like....*
> *I don't agree with _____ because.....*

Be sure students understand that it is acceptable and desirable for them to build on their classmates' ideas, using these strategies.

World Studies Background

Jing Hao

Jing Hao, one of the most significant landscape artists in China, created most of his paintings from 910–950 A.D. Jing Hao's bold manner of using brush and ink to paint crisp lines differed from the softer techniques of other Chinese painters. In addition to his paintings, Jing Hao is thought to have written an essay describing the principles and techniques necessary for a landscape painter to work in harmony with nature.

Kyoto's Many Names

Kyoto, Japan's capital from 794 to 1868, has been known by a number of different names. *Kyoto* means *Capital City*. The city has also been called *Heian-kyo*, which means *Capital of Peace and Tranquility*, and *Miyako*, meaning *The Capital*. When Tokyo became Japan's capital in 1868, Kyoto was called *Saikyo*, or *Western Capital*.

Taj Mahal

The Taj Mahal is known as one of the finest examples of Mughal architecture. One of the main decorative features repeated throughout the complex is *pietra dura*, or inlaid semiprecious stones. These form colorful geometric and floral designs on the walls and archways of the Taj Mahal. Also, verses from the Quran are inscribed in some of the marble structures in the complex.

Get in-depth information on topics of global importance with **Prentice Hall Newstracker,** powered by FT.com.

 Use Web code **lgd-8400** for **Prentice Hall Newstracker.**

Guiding Questions

Remind students about the Guiding Questions introduced at the beginning of the book.

Section 1 relates to **Guiding Question ④**
What types of government were formed in these societies? (*China has been ruled by various dynasties. Mongols ruled China from 1259 to 1368.*)

Section 2 relates to **Guiding Question ①**
How did physical geography affect the development of societies around the world? (*because of Japan's mountainous terrain, the sea became an important transportation route for the Japanese; it protected them from invaders but also isolated them from the outside world.*)

Section 3 relates to **Guiding Question ④**
What types of government were formed in these societies? (*The Muslim Delhi Sultanate and Mughal Empire ruled India for hundreds of years. Religious differences still divide Hindus and Muslims in India today.*)

⟳ Target Reading Skill

In this chapter, students will learn and apply the reading skill of determining cause and effect. Use the following worksheets to help students practice this skill:

All in One Unit 4 History of Our World Teaching Resources, *Identify Causes and Effects*, p. 131; *Understand Effects*, p. 132; *Recognize Cause-and-Effect Signal Words*, p. 133

Chapter 13 Civilizations of Asia

Chapter Preview

This chapter will introduce you to the civilizations that thrived in China, Japan, and India during the medieval period.

Section 1
Golden Ages of China

Section 2
Medieval Japan

Section 3
The Great Mughal Empire in India

⟳ **Target Reading Skill**

Cause and Effect In this chapter you will focus on determining cause and effect in order to help you understand relationships among situations and events.

► A large stone statue of the Buddha in the Qian Qi Temple Cave, China, carved during the Tang dynasty

---

Differentiated Instruction

The following Teacher Edition strategies are suitable for students of varying abilities.

Advanced Readers, pp. 368, 377
English Language Learners, pp. 370, 376
Gifted and Talented, pp. 366, 373, 376
Less Proficient Readers, pp. 368, 385
Special Needs Students, pp. 370, 385

Bibliography

For the Teacher
Benn, Charles. *Daily Life in Traditional China: The Tang Dynasty.* Greenwood Publishing Group, 2002.
Jackson, Peter. *The Delhi Sultanate: A Political and Military History.* Cambridge University Press, 2004
Kure, Mitsuo. *Samurai: An Illustrated History.* Charles E. Tuttle, 2002.

For the Student
L1 Kimmel, Eric A. *Sword of the Samurai: Adventure Stories from Japan.* HarperTrophy, 2000.
L2 Dutemple, Lesley A. *The Taj Mahal.* Lerner Publications Company, 2003.
L3 Freedman, Russell. *Confucius: The Golden Rule.* Arthur A. Levine, 2002.

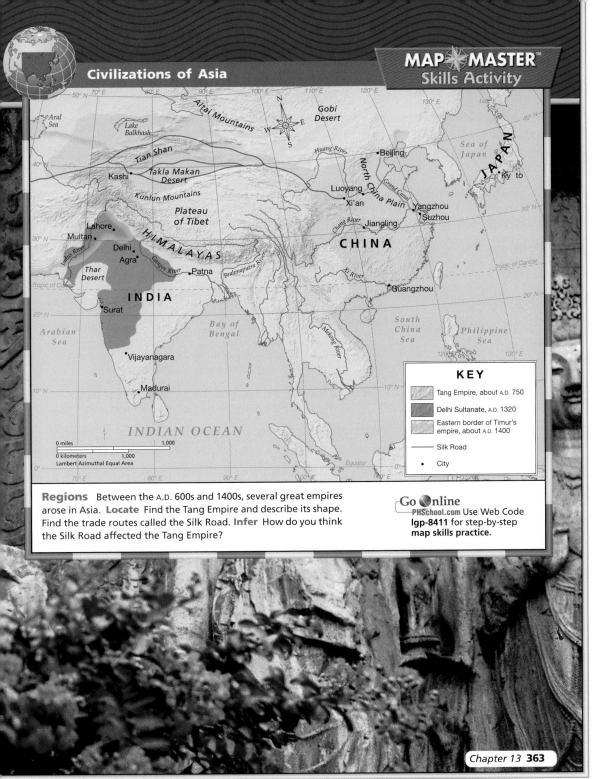

MAP MASTER™ Skills Activity

Regions Between the A.D. 600s and 1400s, several great empires arose in Asia. **Locate** Find the Tang Empire and describe its shape. Find the trade routes called the Silk Road. **Infer** How do you think the Silk Road affected the Tang Empire?

Go **Online**
PHSchool.com Use Web Code
lgp-8411 for step-by-step
map skills practice.

KEY

Tang Empire, about A.D. 750
Delhi Sultanate, A.D. 1320
Eastern border of Timur's empire, about A.D. 1400
— Silk Road
• City

Chapter 13 **363**

MAP MASTER™ Skills Activity

- Tell students to look at the map and find the following: borders of the Tang Empire, borders of the Delhi Sultanate, eastern border of Timur's empire, and the Silk Road. Have students use their finger to trace these locations on the map.

- On the board, list all of the cities found on the map. Working in pairs, have students identify which empire or empires these cities were a part of. Then have students make a table with the information.

Go **Online**
PHSchool.com Students may practice their map skills using the interactive online version of this map.

Using the Visual L2

Reach Into Your Background Draw students' attention to the photo and caption on p. 362. Lead a discussion about the challenges of carving such a large statue without the use of modern technology. Then ask students why it is important to study the art and artifacts of ancient civilizations.

Answers

MAP MASTER™ Skills Activity **Locate** The Tang Empire stretched from western and central China to the eastern coast. **Infer** It helped the Tang Empire expand by opening trade with the west.

Chapter Resources

Teaching Resources
- L2 Vocabulary Development, p. 147
- L2 Skills for Life, p. 136
- L2 Chapter Tests A and B, pp. 152–157

Spanish Support
- L2 Spanish Chapter Summary, p. 114
- L2 Spanish Vocabulary Development, p. 115

Media and Technology
- L1 Student Edition on Audio CD
- L1 Guided Reading Audio CDs, English and Spanish
- L2 Social Studies Skills Tutor CD-ROM
- **Exam*View*® Test Bank CD-ROM**

Discovery CHANNEL SCHOOL History of Our World Video Program

Interactive Textbook
PRENTICE HALL

Teacher EXPRESS™
Plan • Teach • Assess

Objectives

Social Studies

1. Learn about the Golden Age of the Tang dynasty.
2. Discover the achievements of the Song dynasty, which ruled China after the Tang.
3. Find out about Mongol rule of China.

Reading/Language Arts

Learn how to identify causes and effects.

Prepare to Read

Build Background Knowledge [L2]

Tell students that in this section they will learn about the Tang and Song dynasties and some of their achievements. Have students preview the photos and captions showing inventions of the Tang and Song dynasties on page 369. Using the Think-Write-Pair-Share strategy (TE, p. T40) have students identify the inventions and note whether they are still used today and where.

Set a Purpose for Reading [L2]

■ Preview the Objectives.

■ Read each statement in the *Reading Readiness Guide* aloud. Ask students to mark the statements true or false.

> **All in One** **Unit 4 History of Our World Teaching Resources,** *Reading Readiness Guide,* p. 120

■ Have students discuss the statements in pairs or groups of four, then mark their worksheets again. Use the Numbered Heads participation strategy (TE, p. T40) to call on students to share their group's perspectives.

Vocabulary Builder
Preview Key Terms [L2]

Pronounce each Key Term, and then ask students to say the word with you. Provide a simple explanation such as, "In a merit system, people are hired for a job based on their ability to do a job well."

Section 1 Golden Ages of China

Prepare to Read

Objectives

In this section you will

1. Learn about the Golden Age of the Tang dynasty.
2. Discover the achievements of the Song dynasty, which ruled China after the Tang.
3. Find out about Mongol rule of China.

Taking Notes

As you read this section, look for similarities and differences between the Tang and Song dynasties. Copy the diagram below and record your findings in it.

Two Dynasties of China

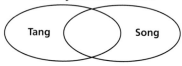

Tang   Song

Target Reading Skill

Identify Causes and Effects A cause makes something happen. An effect is what happens. Determining causes and effects helps you understand relationships among situations and events. As you read this section, think of the cultures of the Tang and Song dynasties as effects. Write their characteristics in your Taking Notes diagram. Then look for the causes of these effects.

Key Terms

- **Silk Road** (silk rohd) *n.* a chain of trade routes stretching from China to the Mediterranean Sea
- **dynasty** (DY nus tee) *n.* a series of rulers from the same family
- **Tang** (tahng) *n.* a dynasty that ruled China for almost 300 years
- **Song** (sawng) *n.* a dynasty that ruled China after the Tang
- **merit system** (MEHR it SIS tum) *n.* a system of hiring people based on their abilities
- **Kublai Khan** (KOO bly kahn) *n.* a Mongol emperor of China

Silk from the Tang dynasty

A Chinese traveler wrote, "You see nothing in any direction but the sky and the sands, without the slightest trace of a road; and travelers find nothing to guide them but the bones of men and beasts." He was describing crossing the Gobi Desert along the Silk Road. In spite of its name, the **Silk Road** was not a single road. It was a long chain of connecting trade routes across Central Asia. These routes stretched about 4,000 miles (6,400 kilometers), all the way from China to the eastern Mediterranean Sea.

For centuries, camels, horses, and donkeys carried traders and their precious goods along the Silk Road. Travelers braved blowing desert sands, cold and rocky mountain passes, and even robbers. Most of the goods they carried were small and very valuable. One—a beautiful, lightweight fabric called silk—was so important that it gave the route its name.

Target Reading Skill [L2]

Identify Causes and Effects Point out the Target Reading Skill. Tell students that a cause makes something happen, and an effect results from a cause.

Model identifying causes and effects using the second paragraph under the head The Tang Dynasty on p. 365. (*Causes—People and traders traveling along the Silk Road introduced new ideas and new goods to China;* *Chinese ideas and inventions also spread to other nations. Effect—China became an important center of trade and culture.*)

Give students *Identify Causes and Effects.* Have them complete the activity in groups.

> **All in One** **Unit 4 History of Our World Teaching Resources,** *Identify Causes and Effects,* p. 131

The Tang Dynasty

China covers much of East Asia. It is an immense land with a varied landscape. In the east are low-land and coastal regions. Fertile valleys lie along the Chang and the Huang (hwahng) rivers. To the north and west of these farmlands are great deserts and mountainous regions, including the Gobi Desert in the north and the Plateau of Tibet in the west.

Look at the map titled Tang and Song Empires on page 366. Notice that under the Tang, the land under Chinese control stretched westward into Central Asia. Peoples from these distant areas and traders traveling along the Silk Road introduced new ideas—as well as new goods—to China. In return, the Chinese traded their tea, jade, ivory, ceramics, and silk. Chinese ideas and inventions also spread to other nations. Such exchanges helped China become an important center of trade and culture.

Guarding the Silk Road
This beacon tower along the Silk Road is in western China. **Infer** Why do you think towers like this were built along the Silk Road?

Dynasties Rule China Throughout its long history, China has been ruled by many different dynasties. A **dynasty** is a series of rulers from the same family. For example, the Han dynasty ruled China from 206 B.C to A.D. 220. After the collapse of the Han dynasty, China broke up into several kingdoms, but Chinese culture survived. Buddhism spread throughout China, and the arts and learning continued to develop. In 581, the Sui (swee) dynasty came to power. The Sui ruled only until 618, but they united the north and south of China for the first time in centuries.

A Golden Age Begins In 618, the Sui dynasty was overthrown. The **Tang** came to power and ruled China for almost 300 years. The Tang dynasty was a golden age of political and cultural achievement. Under Tang rule, China grew in both area and population. Its capital, Chang'an (chahng ahn), was the world's largest city at that time. Historians estimate that it was home to about one million people. Chang'an was shaped like a rectangle and surrounded by tall walls for protection. A variety of foods, entertainment, and fine goods were available to those who lived there.

Vocabulary Builder

Use the information below to teach students this section's high-use words.

High-Use Word	Definition and Sample Sentence
fertile, p. 365	*adj.* able to produce much In order to have a good crop of vegetables, Sally planted her seeds in **fertile** soil.
estimate, p. 365	*v.* to make a general, but careful, guess We **estimated** that it would be a ten minute walk to the park.
reform, p. 367	*v.* change, improve Steve promised to try and do better in school by **reforming** his study habits.
adopt, p. 370	*v.* to choose and follow an idea or practice I **adopted** her way of exercising because it was the most effective.

The Tang Dynasty L2

Guided Instruction

■ **Vocabulary Builder** Clarify the high-use words **fertile**, **estimate**, and **reform** before reading.

■ Have students read The Tang Dynasty using the Structured Silent Reading strategy (TE, p. T38). As they read, circulate to make sure individuals can answer the Reading Check question.

■ Ask students **What were the effects of the Silk Road on China and other countries?** (*Traders traveling along the Silk Road introduced new ideas and goods to China, and also spread Chinese ideas and inventions to other nations.*)

■ Have students describe China under the Tang Dynasty. (*Under the Tang Dynasty, China entered a golden age of political and cultural achievement; China grew in area and population; the capital of Chang'an was the world's largest city, and a variety of foods, entertainment, and goods were available to those that lived there.*)

Answer

Infer Possible answers: Guards stationed in towers could serve as lookouts and protect people traveling on the Silk Road from thieves or bandits; people might also be able to use the towers for shelter.

Guided Instruction (continued)

- Ask students **What was the Grand Canal?** (*a waterway that linked the Huang and Chiang River*) **How did it unite the country of China?** (*It joined northern and southern China and made it possible to transport large amounts of grain grown in the south.*)

- Have students describe the teachings of Confucius. (*He wanted to bring peace and stability to China, and taught that society would be peaceful and stable if all people treated one another with respect.*) Ask students **How did his teachings affect China under the Tang Dynasty?** (*Tang Taizong, one of the rulers of the Tang Dynasty, began to reform the government according to Confucian ideas; he hired officials trained in Confucian philosophy and began giving more land to the peasants who farmed it.*)

Independent Practice

Have students create the Taking Notes graphic organizer on a blank piece of paper. Then have them fill in the "Tang" circle with details from the section they have just read. Using *Transparency B16: Venn Diagram*, briefly model how to label and fill in the Venn diagram.

📖 **History of Our World Transparencies,** *Transparency B16: Venn Diagram*

Monitor Progress

As students fill in the graphic organizer, circulate and make sure that individuals are choosing the correct details and placing them in the appropriate circle. Provide assistance as needed.

Tang Taizong

The Grand Canal Tang leaders continued projects that had been started under the Sui. One of the largest of these projects was the creation of a huge canal.

The Grand Canal was a waterway that linked the Huang River and the Chang River. Millions of workers took part in the construction of the canal. At more than 1,000 miles (1,600 kilometers) long, it is still the longest canal ever built. The Grand Canal helped join northern and southern China and made it possible to supply the capital with large amounts of grain grown in the south.

A Great Ruler The greatest ruler of the Tang dynasty was Tang Taizong (tahng ty ZAWNG). He began his military career at the age of 16, and helped his father establish the Tang dynasty. During his rule, from 626 to 649, he was not only a successful general, but also a scholar and historian. In addition, Tang Taizong was a master of calligraphy, the art of beautiful handwriting.

MAP MASTER™ Skills Activity

Regions Notice the difference in the areas controlled by the Tang and the Song dynasties. **Identify** Under which dynasty did China lose control of much of the Silk Road? **Infer** How might that have affected China's trade with lands to the west?

Go Online
PHSchool.com Use Web Code lgp-8421 for step-by-step map skills practice.

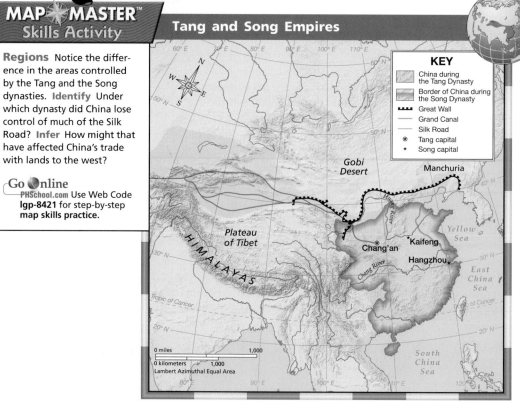

Tang and Song Empires

KEY
- China during the Tang Dynasty
- Border of China during the Song Dynasty
- Great Wall
- Grand Canal
- Silk Road
- ⊛ Tang capital
- ✷ Song capital

Gobi Desert
Manchuria
Plateau of Tibet
HIMALAYAS
Yellow Sea
Chang'an
Kaifeng
Hangzhou
East China Sea
Huang River
Chang River
Tropic of Cancer
South China Sea

0 miles 1,000
0 kilometers 1,000
Lambert Azimuthal Equal Area

Answers

MAP MASTER Skills Activity **Identify** the Song dynasty **Infer** It may have hurt China's ability to travel on the Silk Road as it would have been controlled by other groups.

Go Online
PHSchool.com Students may practice their map skills using the interactive online version of this map.

Differentiated Instruction

For Gifted and Talented L3

Have students do research in the library or on the Internet to find out more about the life and teachings of Confucius. Then have them write a short essay about Confucius with the information they have found. Tell them to make sure to include at least two of Confucius' teachings and explain what they mean. Give them *Writing to Inform and Explain* to help get them started.

All in One **Unit 4 History of Our World Teaching Resources,** *Writing to Inform and Explain,* p. 146

Late in his reign, Tang Taizong grew tired of war. He had been studying the teachings of Confucius (kun FYOO shus), an ancient Chinese teacher who had taught that all people had duties and responsibilities. Confucius had wanted to bring peace and stability to China. To create this kind of society, Confucius said, all people must treat one another with respect.

Tang Taizong began to reform the government according to Confucius's ideas. The Tang government hired officials trained in Confucian philosophy. It also began land reform, giving more land to the peasants who farmed it.

✓ **Reading Check** What are some achievements of Tang Taizong?

The Song Dynasty

After 850, China's control of its westernmost lands weakened. Then fighting among different groups within China ended the Tang dynasty. Order was restored about 50 years later by the **Song** (sawng), the dynasty that ruled China from 960 to 1279.

Changes in Government At the beginning of the Song dynasty, the Chinese capital was located at Kaifeng (KY fung), along the Grand Canal. After the Song lost control of regions to the north, they moved the capital to Hangzhou (hahn JOH), near the coast.

The Song rulers made many advances in government. They expanded the **merit system** of hiring government officials. Under this system, officials had to pass tests and prove their ability to do the work. Before the Song, officials came from rich and powerful families. They were allowed to keep their positions for life even if they did not do a good job. Hiring people based on their abilities, rather than on their wealth or social position, greatly improved the Chinese government.

Improvements in Agriculture During the Song dynasty, new strains of rice and better irrigation methods helped peasants grow more rice. These two improvements allowed farmers to produce two crops a year instead of one. Food surpluses meant that more people could follow other trades or pursue the arts.

Links to Language Arts

Poems and Legends Poetry was popular and respected during the Tang dynasty. Li Bo and Tu Fu were two of the greatest poets of the era. Li Bo was also famous for his adventurous life—once he was even accused of treason. His poems, however, dealt with quieter subjects, such as nature and friendship. After Li Bo died, this legend spread about his death: Li Bo was in a boat at night. The moon's reflection was so beautiful that he reached out to seize it, fell overboard, and drowned. This painting shows Li Bo at a waterfall.

Links
Read the **Links to Language Arts** on this page. Ask students **Do you think the legend of Li Bo's death is true? Why or why not?** (*Possible answer: The legend is probably untrue but may have been created to reflect the idea that Li Bo was a poet who wrote about nature and had an adventurous life.*)

The Song Dynasty L2

Guided Instruction

■ Have students learn about the achievements of the Song dynasty in The Song Dynasty.

■ Ask students **What events led to the rule of the Song Dynasty?** (*After 850, China's control of its land in the west weakened, and fighting broke out among different. The Song dynasty restored order in China and ruled from 960 to 1279.*)

■ Ask students **What is a merit system?** (*A system that hires people based on their abilities rather than their wealth or social position.*)

■ Ask students **Do you think people in China agreed with the use of the merit system in hiring people? Why or why not?** (*Possible answer: People who were not from rich and powerful families probably agreed with the use of the merit system because it made it possible for them to get jobs in the government.*)

Background: Biography

Wu Hou Wu Hou (625–705) was one of the most remarkable members of the Tang Dynasty. Once a low-ranking concubine of the emperor T'ai-tsung, Wu used her position, personality, and ruthlessness to secure her position as empress. In spite of her dubious path to power, Wu Hou instituted policies that reformed Chinese society. One of these was her choice of associates without regard to their social standing. This led to a replacement of the military and political aristocracy with a more scholarly administration. The overall effect was to establish a more unified empire, paving the way for change in the governments of later Chinese dynasties.

Answer

✓ **Reading Check** Tang Taizong began to reform the government according to the ideas of Confucius; this meant that the government began hiring officials trained in Confucian philosophy. He also began land reform, giving more land to the peasants who farmed it.

Read the **Links to Economics** on this page. Ask students **Based on your reading, what do you think was one way that tea drinking spread from China to other areas?** *(through trade along the Silk Road)*

Guided Instruction (continued)

■ Ask students **What were the Chinese landscape paintings of the Song dynasty?** *(paintings on silk that featured peaceful scenes of water, rocks, and plants; the Chinese believed that these paintings helped both the painter and the viewer meditate)*

■ Have students name art objects made during the Song dynasty. *(Chinese landscape paintings, porcelain, and silk)* Ask students **Why were people in Asia and Europe willing to pay high prices for Chinese silk?** *(It was the best quality in the world.)*

Answer

Analyze Images Students' answers will vary, but should indicate which object they would buy and why.

The Arts and Trade Chinese rulers supported many different forms of art, including music and poetry. During the Song dynasty, artists created the earliest known Chinese landscape paintings. They were painted on silk and featured peaceful scenes of water, rocks, and plants. The Chinese believed that such scenes helped both the painter and the viewer think about important forces in the natural world.

Song rulers also prized graceful art objects, such as those made from porcelain (PAWR suh lin), a white and very hard type of ceramic. Because it was first made in China, porcelain is often called *china*. For hundreds of years, Chinese craftspeople produced the finest ceramics. Because the Chinese produced the best porcelain in the world, it became an important item for trade.

Another item of great beauty and value was silk. It was so beautiful that it was called the queen of fibers. Silk comes from the cocoons of caterpillars called silkworms. For a long time, only the Chinese knew how to make silk. Even after others learned the method, Chinese silk was still the highest quality in the world. People in southwest Asia and Europe were willing to pay high prices for Chinese silk.

Chinese Ceramics
Europeans paid dearly for Song dynasty wares, such as these beautiful ceramics. **Analyze Images** *If you were a European trader, which of these objects would you buy? Explain your answer.*

368 History of Our World

Differentiated Instruction

For Advanced Readers L3
In order to help students understand the chronological order of the dynasties in this section, have them work in pairs to create a timeline showing the dynasties and the periods in which they ruled China. Encourage students to add drawings and photos to their timelines. When students have completed their timelines, have them present their work to the class.

For Less Proficient Readers L1
Have students read the section in the Reading and Vocabulary Study Guide. This version provides basic level instruction in an interactive format with questions and write-on lines.

Chapter 13, Section 1, **History of Our World Reading and Vocabulary Study Guide,** pp. 138–140

Inventions of the Tang and Song Dynasties

◀ Gunpowder
The Chinese invented gunpowder in the 800s. At first, they used it to make fireworks. By about 1000, however, it was being used in weapons.

◀ Compass
In the 1000s, Chinese sailors were using the magnetic compass for navigation on long voyages. At the left is a replica of a compass from the Song dynasty.

▼ Movable Type
By 1045, Chinese printers used individual characters carved on small blocks to create a page of text. The blocks could be reused in a different order to produce various pieces of writing.

Smallpox Vaccine
As early as the 900s, the Chinese fought smallpox with a vaccine. They gave tiny doses of smallpox to healthy people so that they would develop an immunity to the deadly disease.

Printing, Books, and Learning One of the historic Song inventions was a new way to print books. For centuries, the Chinese had carved the characters of each page onto a wood block. They brushed ink over the carving and laid a piece of paper on it to print the page. Printers could make many copies of a book using these blocks, but carving the block for each page took a long time. Around 1045, Bi Sheng (bee sheng) developed a printing method that used movable type. He made many separate characters out of clay and rearranged them to make each page.

During the Song dynasty, books became less expensive. In earlier times, only the rich could buy them. With more people able to afford books, the number and kinds of books increased. More people, including women, also learned to read and write. By the 1200s, books about farming, medicine, religion, and poetry were in print. They helped to spread knowledge throughout China. This Song saying reflects the new importance of books:

Identify Causes and Effects
What made it easier for people to buy books? List that as a cause. What resulted from the increase in books? List those effects.

> **❝To enrich your family, no need to buy good land: Books hold a thousand measures of grain. For an easy life, no need to build a mansion: In books are found houses of gold. ❞**
>
> — *A Song emperor*

✓ **Reading Check** What does the Song emperor's saying mean?

Skills Mini Lesson

Analyzing Primary Sources

1. Tell students that when they analyze primary sources they should: identify the source and main idea, separate fact from opinion, look for bias, and evaluate the source's reliability.

2. Have students practice the skill by analyzing the quotation from the Chinese traveler on page 364.

3. Apply the skill by analyzing the quotation on page 369. *(source: a Song emperor; main idea: books are worth more than material wealth; opinions: books will enrich one's life; bias: the emperor is wealthy, therefore he might say that books are more important than wealth; reliability: the speaker lived when books became more available in China)*

Guided Instruction (continued)

■ Have students list the inventions of the Tang and Song dynasties in chronological order. *(gunpowder–800s; smallpox vaccine–900s, compass–1000s; moveable type–1045)*

■ Ask students **How did the widespread availability of books change life in China?** *(As books became less expensive, the numbers and kinds of books increased. Also, more people, including women, learned to read and write; and books about farming, medicine, religion, and poetry spread knowledge throughout China.)*

Independent Practice
Have students complete their graphic organizers with details about the Song dynasty.

Monitor Progress
Show *Section Reading Support Transparency HOW 93* and ask students to check their graphic organizers individually. Go over key concepts and clarify key vocabulary as needed.

History of Our World Transparencies, *Section Reading Support Transparency HOW 93*

Target Reading Skill
Identify Causes and Effects As a follow up, ask students to answer the Target Reading Skill questions in the Student Edition. *(Cause: Moveable type made books less expensive. Effects: More people learned to read and write, the number and kinds of books increased, and knowledge spread throughout China.)*

Answer
✓ **Reading Check** Possible answer: that the knowledge in books is more valuable than material wealth

The Mongols Conquer China

L2

Guided Instruction

- **Vocabulary Builder** Clarify the high-use word **adopt** before reading.

- Have students read The Mongols Conquer China to learn about the Mongols and their leaders.

- Ask students **Who were the Mongols?** (*nomads from Central Asia, who were fierce warriors*) **How far did their empire eventually extend?** (*across China and Korea in the east, into Russia and Eastern Europe in the west, and into the Persian Gulf*)

- Ask students **How was the Chinese government run under the Mongols?** (*The government became centralized; Mongols did not allow the old Chinese ruling class to govern, and high government positions were reserved for Mongols and even foreigners instead of Chinese.*) **How was this different from the Song Dynasty?** (*Under the Song Dynasty, people were hired based on their ability rather than their social position.*)

Independent Practice

Assign *Guided Reading and Review*.

All in One **Unit 4 History of Our World Teaching Resources,** *Guided Reading and Review,* p. 121

Monitor Progress

Tell students to fill in the last column of the *Reading Readiness Guide.* Probe for what they learned that confirms or invalidates each statement.

All in One **Unit 4 History of Our World Teaching Resources,** *Reading Readiness Guide,* p. 120

Answer

Conclude They wore armor; used swords, shields, bows and arrows; and attacked on horseback.

The Mongols Attack China
This illustration from the 1400s shows Kublai Khan's armies crossing a bridge to attack a Chinese fortress. **Conclude** *Use details in the illustration to draw conclusions about the dress, equipment, and methods of Kublai Khan's armies.*

The Mongols Conquer China

The Mongols were nomads from the plains of Central Asia, north of China. They were fierce warriors, said to "live in the saddle" because they spent so much time on horseback. By the 1200s, they were a tough military force. Under the leadership of Genghis Khan, they began forging an empire that eventually included China and Korea in the east, stretched into Russia and Eastern Europe in the west, and extended to the southwest as far as the Persian Gulf.

Kublai Khan, Mongol Ruler of China

Genghis Khan had conquered all of northern China by 1215. But the southern Song empire continued to resist. It was left to Genghis Khan's grandson **Kublai Khan** to complete the conquest of China and to rule it.

Kublai Khan came to power in 1259. Within 20 years, he had toppled the last Song emperor. From his capital at the present-day city of Beijing, Kublai Khan declared himself emperor of China. He named his new dynasty *Yuan*, which means "beginning," because he intended that Mongol rule of China would last for centuries.

China Under Mongol Rule

The Mongols centralized government in China. They did not allow the old Chinese ruling class to govern. High government positions were reserved for Mongols and were even given to foreigners rather than to Chinese. The Mongols also kept their own language and customs rather than adopting Chinese culture. They did, however, allow the practice of many religions.

Differentiated Instruction

For English Language Learners **L2**

As they read, have students identify any unfamiliar words and write them down. Divide students into pairs, and give each pair a dictionary to use. Then have the students create flashcards with the words on one side, and the part of speech and definition on the other. Students may then quiz each other on the words.

For Special Needs Students **L1**

Have students read the section as they listen to the recorded version on the Student Edition on Audio CD. Check for comprehension by pausing the CD and asking students to share their answers to the Reading Checks.

⊙ Chapter 13, Section 1, **Student Edition on Audio CD**

Marco Polo at Kublai Khan's Court
The Italian Marco Polo, shown kneeling before Kublai Khan, worked for the khan for 17 years. **Analyze Images** *What detail in the painting indicates that Polo is reporting to Kublai Khan?*

Visitors from all lands were welcome at Kublai Khan's court. One of these was Ibn Battutah, an African Muslim. Another was a Christian from Europe, Marco Polo. He came from Venice in present-day Italy in 1271. After returning to Europe, Polo wrote about his travels. He described the riches of Kublai Khan's palace, China's efficient mail system, and its well-maintained roads.

Marco Polo's writings sparked increased trade between Europe and China. China prospered under Kublai Khan, but not under the khans, or emperors, who followed him. In 1368, a Chinese peasant led an uprising that overthrew the foreign rulers and ended Mongol rule of China.

Explore the history of kung fu.

✔ **Reading Check** Describe Mongol rule of China.

Section 1 Assessment

Key Terms
Review the key terms at the beginning of this section. Use each term in a sentence that explains its meaning.

⊙ **Target Reading Skill**
What were two effects of the Mongol rule of China?

Comprehension and Critical Thinking
1. (a) **Recall** What is the Grand Canal?

(b) **Synthesize** Why was it important?
2. (a) **Identify** Describe one important change in government made by the Song.
(b) **Identify Effects** How did this change affect China?
3. (a) **Summarize** How did the Mongols conquer China?
(b) **Identify Frame of Reference** Why do you think the Mongols did not adopt Chinese customs?

Writing Activity
During the Song dynasty, printed materials became available to many more people. What would life be like today without books and other printed materials? Write a journal entry to express your thoughts.

For: An activity on Chinese inventions
Visit: PHSchool.com
Web Code: lgd-8401

Chapter 13 Section 1 **371**

Objective

Learn how to make an outline.

Prepare to Read

Build Background Knowledge   L2

Use the Numbered Heads participation strategy (TE p. T40) to elicit student responses to the following question: **What do you think is the best way to study for a test?** Tell students that creating an outline is one way of organizing information that they can use when they study for a test, read, or research a topic. When they create an outline, they are organizing information in an easy-to-read format.

Instruct

Making an Outline   L2

Guided Instruction

- Read the steps to making an outline as a class and write them on the board.

- Practice the skill by following the steps on p. 373 as a class. Model each step in the activity by working with students to create the following outline on the board:

Title: Chinese Silk Making

I. How and when the Chinese made silk
   A. How silk is made
      1. Made by unwinding the cocoons of silkworms
      2. Process is done by hand and is long and difficult
      3. Silk strands are twisted to form yarn, and then woven into fabric
   B. History of silk making
      1. Dates back more than 3,000 years
      2. Empress His Ling Shi is said to have invented the loom to weave silk
      3. silk was expensive, only royalty and nobles could afford it
      4. because silk was so valuable, the Chinese kept the process secret

Making an Outline

An outline is a way to organize information. It identifies the main ideas and supporting details. You can use an outline to take notes on what you read or to plan a report that you will write.

Learn the Skill

1. **Identify the most important points or main ideas, and list them with Roman numerals.** If you are outlining a text, look for headings stating these ideas.

2. **Decide on important subtopics for each main idea, and list them with capital letters.** Indent these entries under the main ideas, as shown in the sample outline below.

3. **Use Arabic numerals to list supporting ideas or details under each subtopic.** Indent these entries. Because an outline is a type of summary, you don't have to be as detailed or complete as your source. See the sample outline below.

4. **Check your outline for balance.** Make sure that the entries with Roman numerals are the most important ideas. Check that the ideas and information listed under the main ideas support those ideas. Make sure that main topics have at least two supporting subtopics or details.

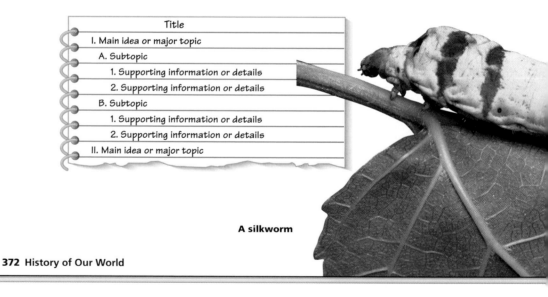

Title
I. Main idea or major topic
   A. Subtopic
      1. Supporting information or details
      2. Supporting information or details
   B. Subtopic
      1. Supporting information or details
      2. Supporting information or details
II. Main idea or major topic

A silkworm

372 History of Our World

Independent Practice

Assign *Skills for Life* and have students complete it individually.

All in One **Unit 4 History of Our World Teaching Resources,** *Skills for Life*, p. 136

Monitor Progress

As students are completing *Skills for Life*, circulate to make sure individuals are applying the skill steps effectively. Provide assistance as needed.

Women preparing newly woven silk

Practice the Skill

Suppose you are outlining an article on silk making. You want to cover two main ideas: The Chinese were the first to make silk, and silk became an important trade product for China. Use the passage at the right as the source for the beginning of your outline. Then follow the steps below to outline it.

1 What is the main idea of the passage? Make it Roman numeral I of your outline.

2 Identify at least two important subtopics, and list them with capital letters.

3 Which details support the important topics or ideas? List those with Arabic numerals under the appropriate subtopics.

4 Reread your outline to be sure you have included all the important ideas and details. Make sure your outline correctly indicates which ideas are the most important and how other ideas and details support the main ideas.

Chinese Silk Making The fabric known as silk is made from the cocoons of caterpillars called silkworms. The cocoons are unwound very carefully, to avoid breaking the fibers. This process is long and difficult if done by hand—as it was in ancient China. The silk strands are then twisted together to form yarn, which is woven into fabric on a loom.

Silk making in China dates back more than 3,000 years. It is said that the empress Hsi Ling Shi, called the Goddess of Silk, invented the loom to weave this valuable fabric. She was a patron of the silk industry, which involved tending silkworms and cultivating the mulberry trees on which the caterpillars fed. This laborious work was done by women.

Silk was so beautiful and expensive that only royalty and nobles could afford to wear it. Because the fabric was so valuable and desirable, the Chinese kept the silk-making process a secret.

Apply the Skill

Reread the portion of text titled Achievements of the Song Dynasty on pages 367–369. Make an outline of that text.

Assess Progress   L2

Ask students to do the Apply the Skill activity.

Reteach   L1

If students are having trouble applying the skill steps, use the Outline transparency to walk through making an outline of the subsection titled The Tang Dynasty on pages 365–367. Title the outline "The Tang Dynasty," and use the blue heads as Roman numeral entries. Model how to draw information for the subtopics and the supporting details from the text.

Extend   L3

- Help students prepare to study the material in Section 2 by dividing the class into four groups. Each group should be assigned one of the following subsections of information from Section 2: A Country of Islands, The Heian Empire, Feudalism in Japan, Japan and the Outside World. Each group should create an outline of the information in the subsection, and share their outline with the rest of the class by writing it on the board.

Differentiated Instruction

For Gifted and Talented   L3

Tell students that making an outline of a report or essay before writing would help them clarify their ideas before they start to write. Ask students to create an outline for an essay titled "The Wonders of the Song Dynasty." Their outlines should include the main point they wish to make, and what details they will use to support it.

Answers
Apply the Skill

Answers will vary, but students' outlines should include appropriate information about the achievements of the Song Dynasty.

Objectives

Social Studies
1. Learn about the geography of Japan.
2. Discover the changes that occurred during the Heian period of Japanese history.
3. Find out about feudalism and the rule of the shoguns in Japan.

Reading/Language Arts
Learn how to understand effects.

Prepare to Read

Build Background Knowledge **L2**

Tell students that in this chapter they will read about the geography and history of Japan. Have students look at the map of Japan on page 375, and think about the following questions: **What are some of the advantages and disadvantages a nation might have if it is completely surrounded by water? How might living on an island influence the way of life for people there?** Using the Idea Wave participation strategy (TE p. T39), have students share their responses with the class.

Set a Purpose for Reading **L2**

- Preview the Objectives.

- Read each statement in the *Reading Readiness Guide* aloud. Ask students to mark the statements true or false.

    All in One Unit 4 History of Our World Teaching Resources, *Reading Readiness Guide,* p. 124

- Have students discuss the statements in pairs or groups of four, then mark their worksheets again. Use the Numbered Heads participation strategy (TE, p. T40) to call on students to share their group's perspectives.

Vocabulary Builder
Preview Key Terms **L2**

Pronounce each Key Term, and then ask students to say the word with you. Provide a simple explanation such as, "The many islands of Japan form an archipelago."

Medieval Japan

Prepare to Read

Objectives

In this section you will
1. Learn about the geography of Japan.
2. Discover the changes that occurred during the Heian period of Japanese history.
3. Find out about feudalism and the rule of the shoguns in Japan.

Taking Notes

As you read this section, look for details about the major periods of Japan's history. Copy the table below and record your findings in it.

Japan, 794–1867	
Period	**Characteristics**
Heian period	
Rise of the samurai	
Kamakura shogunate	
Tokugawa shogunate	

Target Reading Skill

Understand Effects An effect is what happens as the result of a specific cause or factor. For example, you can see in the paragraphs on the next page that the geography of Japan has had several effects on that nation. This section also discusses how contact with the outside world affected Japan. As you read, note the effects on Japan of the contact with the Mongols and with Europeans.

Key Terms

- **archipelago** (ahr kuh PEL uh goh) *n.* a group or chain of many islands
- **Kyoto** (kee OH toh) *n.* the capital city of medieval Japan
- **feudalism** (FYOOD ul iz um) *n.* a system in which poor people are legally bound to work for wealthy landowners
- **samurai** (SAM uh ry) *n.* Japanese warriors
- **shogun** (SHOH gun) *n.* the supreme military commander of Japan

Japanese woodcut of Mount Fuji

374 History of Our World

In A.D. 882, a group of more than 100 officials sailed across the sea to Japan. They were from a kingdom in Manchuria, north of China. They carried greetings for the Japanese emperor, as well as gifts of tiger skins and honey. When the emperor heard the news, he was pleased. This visit would give the Japanese a chance to display their achievements. The emperor's name was Yozei (yoh zay ee). At the time, he was only 14 years old.

Yozei sent expensive gifts of food and clothing to the visitors. He also sent people to escort them to his capital. The officials from Manchuria had landed in the north, and the capital was far to the south. The journey over land would take five months. The Japanese quickly fixed roads and bridges along the way. When the visitors arrived, there was a celebration. Japan's nobles, government leaders, and best poets were invited. Horse races, archery, and a poetry contest took place. A great feast was held, too, with much music and dancing.

Target Reading Skill **L2**

Understand Effects Point out the Target Reading Skill. Tell students that effects are the result of an event or some other cause.

Model understanding effects by having students read the second paragraph on page 375. Point out the effect of Japan's geography on they way people traveled there. (*The sea became an important highway for the Japanese.*)

Give students *Understand Effects.* Have them complete the activity in their groups.

All in One Unit 4 History of Our World Teaching Resources, *Understand Effects,* p. 132

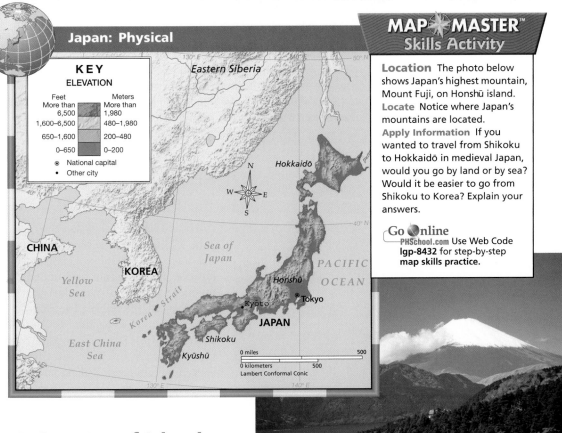

KEY
ELEVATION

Feet	Meters
More than 6,500	More than 1,980
1,600–6,500	480–1,980
650–1,600	200–480
0–650	0–200

⊛ National capital
• Other city

Eastern Siberia

Hokkaidō

CHINA

Sea of Japan

KOREA

Yellow Sea

Honshū

PACIFIC OCEAN

Kyoto • ⊛ Tokyo

JAPAN

East China Sea

Korea Strait

Shikoku

Kyūshū

0 miles 500
0 kilometers 500
Lambert Conformal Conic

MAP ✦ MASTER™
Skills Activity

Location The photo below shows Japan's highest mountain, Mount Fuji, on Honshū island. **Locate** Notice where Japan's mountains are located. **Apply Information** If you wanted to travel from Shikoku to Hokkaidō in medieval Japan, would you go by land or by sea? Would it be easier to go from Shikoku to Korea? Explain your answers.

Go Online
PHSchool.com Use Web Code **lgp-8432** for step-by-step **map skills practice**.

A Country of Islands

The visitors from Manchuria had a long trip over both land and sea to Japan. Japan is an **archipelago** (ahr kuh PEL uh goh), or chain of many islands, in the Pacific Ocean off the coast of the Asian mainland. It is about 500 miles (800 kilometers) from the coast of China but it is only 100 miles (160 kilometers) from Korea. The islands of Japan were formed by volcanoes, and earthquakes are common in the region.

Look at the map above. Notice that the islands of Japan are mountainous. The mountains make traveling by land difficult. As a result, the sea became an important highway for the Japanese—even for those traveling from place to place on the same island. On the other hand, for centuries, the sea helped to protect Japan from invaders. Over time, this isolation also led the Japanese to develop a distinctive way of life.

✓ **Reading Check** **Describe Japan's geography.**

Chapter 13 Section 2 **375**

Vocabulary Builder

Use the information below to teach students this section's high-use words.

High-Use Word	Definition and Sample Sentence
isolation, p. 375	*n.* a state of separation Mary did not like the **isolation** of living alone.
distinctive, p. 375	*adj.* showing a difference from others Postal workers wear **distinctive** uniforms.
related, p. 376	*adj.* connected to in some manner The fans at the football game wore shirts **related** to their favorite team.
supreme, p. 378	*adj.* highest in rank The president of the United States is the country's **supreme** leader.

Instruct

A Country of Islands L2

Guided Instruction

■ **Vocabulary Builder** Clarify the high-use words **isolation** and **distinctive** before reading.

■ With students, read A Country of Islands using the Oral Cloze strategy (TE, p. T37).

■ Have students describe the location of Japan in relation to mainland Asia. (*It is in the Pacific Ocean off the coast of mainland Asia, about 500 miles from the coast of China.*)

■ Ask students **How do the mountains of Japan influence the lives of the people who live there?** (*The mountains make travel difficult; as a result, the sea is an important highway for those traveling from place to place.*)

Independent Practice

Assign *Guided Reading and Review*.

All in One Unit 4 History of Our World Teaching Resources, *Guided Reading and Review,* p. 125

Monitor Progress

As students work on the worksheets, circulate and provide assistance as needed.

Answers

✓ **Reading Check** Japan is an archipelago in the Pacific Ocean, off the coast of mainland Asia, about 500 miles from the coast of China. The mountainous islands were formed by volcanoes, and earthquakes are common.

MAP ✦ MASTER™ **Locate** They are located in the center of the islands. **Apply Information** Possible answers: To travel from Shikoku to Hokkaidō in medieval Japan it would have been easier to travel by sea, since the mountains would have made travel difficult; It would be easier to travel from Shikoku to Korea, since the distance is shorter and Korea is just across the Korea strait.

Instruct

The Heian Empire   L2

Guided Instruction

- **Vocabulary Builder** Clarify the high-use word **related** before reading.

- Together with students, learn about Japan during the years A.D. 794 to 1185 in The Heian Empire.

- Have students describe the city of Kyoto. (*It was the capital of Japan, modeled after the city of Chang'an in Tang China; it was surrounded by walls and had mansions, marketplaces, and a palace. Most of the buildings were wooden, and fires were common; canals ran through the capital to provide water.*)

- Ask students **How did the majority of the population, aside from the nobles, live during the Heian period?** (*They were poor and had to work hard.*) **What kind of attitude do you think they had toward the nobles?** (*Students may suggest attitudes such as fear, respect, loyalty, or resentment. Encourage them to provide reasoning to support their views.*)

Independent Practice

Ask students to create the Taking Notes graphic organizer on a blank piece of paper. Then have them fill in the "Heian Period" column with details from the section.

Monitor Progress

As students fill in their tables, circulate to make sure they are putting details in the appropriate column. Provide assistance as needed.

⟳ Target Reading Skill   L2

Understand Effects As a follow up, ask students to answer the Target Reading Skill question in the Student Edition. (*The feeling of superiority set them apart from the rest of the population.*)

Answers

Infer It suggests that modern Japanese culture is a blend of old and new traditions.

√ **Reading Check** Nobles lived in mansions and enjoyed fine architecture, literature, and beautiful gardens.

376 *History of Our World*

Modern Kyoto
The traditional Japanese pagoda, or shrine, in the foreground is still an important part of the modern, bustling city. **Infer** *What does this blend of architecture suggest about modern Japanese culture?*

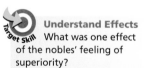 **Understand Effects** What was one effect of the nobles' feeling of superiority?

The Heian Empire

The emperor Yozei ruled Japan during the Heian (HAY ahn) period, which lasted from 794 to 1185. Before this time, Japan's culture—including its literature, laws, and religion—was similar to China's. But during the 800s, Japan began to develop its own traditions. In fact, official relations between the Japanese and Chinese governments ended in 894. The split would last for more than 500 years.

An Impressive Capital: Kyoto

Heian emperors ruled from a new capital, **Kyoto** (kee OH toh). Modeled after Chang'an, the great city of Tang China, it was a rectangle of tree-lined streets. Unlike Chang'an, however, Kyoto was not surrounded by high walls. The city boasted mansions for the nobles, two marketplaces, and a palace for the emperor. Most Japanese buildings were wooden at the time, and fires were common. Kyoto's main street was very wide—to keep fires on one side from spreading to the other. Canals running through the capital also provided water to help put out any fires.

The Japanese Nobility The Heian period was a mostly peaceful time, during which Japanese culture thrived. Fine architecture, literature, and beautiful gardens all became a part of life for the nobility. Life for most of the population, however, was very different. Farmers, fishers, traders, and builders were usually poor and spent their time doing hard work.

The nobles believed that the importance of their families and their positions within the government set them apart from others. But even among the nobles, people belonged to different ranks, or classes. In fact, noblemen wore specially colored robes related to their position in society. Noblewomen were not affected by such rules because they could not hold official positions in the government.

√ **Reading Check** How did nobles live during the Heian period?

376 History of Our World

Differentiated Instruction

For Gifted and Talented   L3

Have students research a major city in Japan today. Then have students create a poster identifying vital facts about the city. *Use Rubric for Assessing a Student Poster* to evaluate students' work.

 Unit 4 History of Our World Teaching Resources, *Rubric for Assessing a Student Poster,* p. 149

For English Language Learners   L1

Students may have difficulty pronouncing some of the words in this section, such as *emperor, official, surrounded, and mansions.* Encourage students to break down these words into smaller parts to help them sound out the pronunciations.

Feudalism in Japan

During the 1000s, the Japanese emperor began to lose power. He continued to rule the capital, but he had less control over the rest of Japan. At the same time, the nobles gained greater power and wealth. They owned estates, or large tracts of land, outside the capital. The work on these estates was done by peasants. This kind of economic system, in which poor people are legally bound to work for wealthy landowners, is called **feudalism.**

Samurai Warriors Rich estate owners became so independent that they often disobeyed the emperor. They even hired private armies. The nobles paid these armies to defend them, their estates, and the peasants who worked for them. The armies were made up of warriors called **samurai** (SAM uh ry).

Samurai warriors followed a strict set of rules for behavior, called *bushido* (BOO shee doh). They swore an oath to follow these rules without question. According to bushido, honor meant more than wealth or even life itself. This code said that a samurai must never show weakness or surrender to an enemy. The true samurai had no fear of death, and would rather die than shame himself. He was expected to commit ritual suicide rather than betray the code of bushido.

Prepared for War
Samurai armor was made of small scales tied with silk and leather. The painting below shows the charge of a samurai on horseback. **Analyze Images** What do these two images suggest about samurai warriors?

Instruct

Feudalism in Japan　　L2

Guided Instruction

- **Vocabulary Builder** Clarify the high-use word **supreme** before reading.

- Read Feudalism in Japan to learn about the feudal system and samurai of Japan. As students read, circulate to make sure they can answer the Reading Check question.

- Ask students **Who were the samurai?** (*Private warriors hired by nobles to defend their estates and peasants*) **How do you think the hiring of samurai further weakened the power of the Japanese emperor?** (*Possible answer: The nobles did not have to depend on the emperor for protection; also a noble could become more powerful as he acquired a stronger samurai army.*)

- Have students discuss the idea of Bushido. Ask **How did samurai warriors think about the relationship of honor and death?** (*According to Bushido, honor means more to a Samurai than anything else. Therefore, a samurai would rather die than dishonor himself.*)

- Ask students **Who was Minamoto Yoritomo?** (*the leader of the Minamoto clan in 1192*) **How was he important to Japan?** (*He was made shogun by the emperor and set up the Kamakura shogunate.*)

Independent Practice

Have students continue filling in their tables with details about the rise of the samurai and the Kamakura shogunate.

Monitor Progress

As students continue to fill in their tables, circulate and make sure they are including all of the details in the section. Provide assistance as necessary.

Answer

Analyze Images That the Samurai were brave and skilled in creating armor to protect themselves.

Japan and the Outside World

L2

Guided Instruction

- Learn how Japan was influenced by Europeans in Japan and the Outside World.

- Ask students **How did Europeans influence life in Japan?** *(They traded many items with the Japanese; European missionaries converted many Japanese to Christianity.)*

- Have students describe what life was like in Japan under the Tokugawa shogunate. *(It was a period of peace and prosperity; the population increased; trade increased and a merchant class developed; the arts flourished.)*

Independent Practice

Have students complete their tables with details from the section.

Monitor Progress

- Show *Section Reading Support Transparency HOW 94* and ask students to check their graphic organizers individually. Go over key concepts and clarify key vocabulary as needed.

   📖 **History of Our World Transparencies,** *Section Reading Support Transparency HOW 94*

- Tell students to fill in the last column of the *Reading Readiness Guide.* Probe for what they learned that confirms or invalidates each statement.

   All in One **Unit 4 History of Our World Teaching Resources,** *Reading Readiness Guide,* p. 124

Answer

✓ **Reading Check** The samurai became powerful as nobles relied upon them for protection rather than the emperor. Over time, the samurai grew in number and banded together under daimyos.

Citizen Heroes

A Peasant Warrior

Toyotomi Hideyoshi (toh yoh TOH mee hee duh YOH shee) started life as a peasant. Through hard work, he became a respected warrior. Because of his great military skills, he became a chief lieutenant in the army of a powerful daimyo. When the daimyo was assassinated in 1582, Hideyoshi took his place. A skillful leader, he went on to unite Japan. He then tried, but failed, to conquer Korea and China. Nevertheless, Hideyoshi, shown below, became one of the most admired heroes in Japan.

378 History of Our World

A New Class Gains Power Over time, the samurai warriors grew in number and formed their own clans. Each clan promised loyalty to a powerful warlord, or daimyo (DY myoh). The daimyo expected his samurai warriors to be willing to give their lives for him. As the different warlords grew in power, small wars broke out among them. Eventually the Minamoto clan became the most powerful.

In 1192, the emperor gave the title of **shogun** (SHOH gun), or supreme military commander, to the leader of the Minamoto clan. Minamoto Yoritomo (mee nah MOH toh yoh ree TOH moh) became the supreme ruler of all Japan. He set up the Kamakura (kah mah KUR ah) shogunate, a series of military dynasties.

✓ **Reading Check** How did the samurai become powerful?

Japan and the Outside World

Within a century after shogun rule began, Japan was threatened by outsiders. One group came from Mongolia, north of China. Under their fierce and brilliant leader Kublai Khan, the Mongols had already conquered China and Korea. Kublai Khan tried to invade Japan twice, and failed both times. For nearly 300 years after the Mongols were defeated in the 1200s, few foreigners came to Japan.

The Arrival of Europeans In 1543, several Portuguese ships were blown off course and landed on Japan's coast. The Japanese showed great interest in these foreigners—especially in their guns. In the years that followed, a lively trade developed between East and West. Many European traders and missionaries made the long voyage to these islands in the Pacific. And thousands of Japanese converted to Christianity. The European influence in Japan did not last long, however.

The Tokugawas Unify Japan In 1603, Tokugawa Ieyasu (toh koo GAH wah ee yay AH soo) became shogun. Ieyasu was determined to bring order to the country. To end the fighting among warring samurai bands, Ieyasu divided Japan into about 250 regions. The daimyo of each region promised to serve the shogun and swore loyalty to him. To control these local leaders, the Tokugawas required each daimyo to live in the shogun's capital Edo (now called Tokyo) for several months every other year.

Skills for Life · Skills Mini Lesson

Problem-Solving

1. Tell students that to solve a problem, they should identify the problem, evaluate its impact, identify possible solutions, choose a solution, and determine its effectiveness.

2. Have students read The Tokugawas Unify Japan, identify the problem faced by Tokugawa Ieyasu when he became shogun, and use the skill steps to determine how the problem was solved. *(Problem: a lack of order in the country; impact: fighting among samurai bands; solution: divide Japan into regions led by a daimyo who would swear loyalty to Ieyasu. The solution was effective.)*

3. Have students apply the skill by identifying another problem faced by Tokugawa Ieyasu, and the steps he took to solve it.

The Tokugawa shogunate ruled Japan until 1867. It was a period of peace. The economy thrived. Food was plentiful, the population increased, trade flourished inside Japan, and a merchant class developed. Cities grew, and the arts flourished. A type of Buddhism called Zen became popular in Japan. It emphasized meditation, the practice of good deeds, and reverence for nature.

Theater and poetry also thrived under the Tokugawas. Haiku—three-line poems that express a feeling or picture in only 17 syllables—were greatly admired. Plays featuring life-size puppets were popular. So was the Kabuki theater. Kabuki combines drama, dance, and music.

Japan Becomes Isolated Again At the same time, the Tokugawa shogunate was isolating Japan from foreign influences. Even Tokugawa Ieyasu had worried that Europeans might try to conquer Japan. He and the shoguns who ruled after him decided that Japan should remain isolated from Westerners. They outlawed Christianity and forced Europeans to leave. By 1638, they had closed Japan's ports, banning most foreign travel and trade. The shoguns also stopped the building of large ships that could travel long distances. For more than 200 years, the Japanese would remain cut off from the outside world.

✓ **Reading Check** How did the Tokugawas change Japan?

Kabuki Theater
Even today, men play women's roles in Kabuki theater, and many of the plays recount tales of feudal Japan. **Analyze Images** *What do the elaborate makeup, costumes, and gestures suggest about Kabuki performances?*

Section 2 Assessment

Key Terms
Review the key terms at the beginning of this section. Use each term in a sentence that explains its meaning.

◑ Target Reading Skill
What were two effects of the growing power of the daimyo?

Comprehension and Critical Thinking
1. (a) **Describe** What are the geographical features of Japan?

(b) **Identify** When did Japan start to develop its own traditions?
(c) **Identify Causes** What led to Japan's isolation?
2. (a) **Recall** What happened to the emperor and the nobles during the 1000s?
(b) **Identify Causes** What led to the establishment of shoguns?
3. (a) **Recall** How did trade develop between Japan and Europe in the 1500s?
(b) **Synthesize** How and why did the Tokugawas isolate Japan?

Writing Activity
Suppose you could interview a samurai. Write five questions that you would ask him. Then write a paragraph to introduce your interview.

For: An activity about the samurai
Visit: PHSchool.com
Web Code: lgd-8402

Focus on A Japanese Home

Guided Instruction

- Ask students to read the text and study the art, photos, and captions on these pages.

- Have students describe the rules of the Tokugawa government's decree. *(Peasant men and women were not allowed to buy tea; men had to work in the fields and women at the loom; both men and women had to work at night; if a woman neglected her household duties, she must be divorced; peasants could only wear cotton or hemp.)*

- Ask students **Do you think these rules were fair? Why or why not?** *(Students' answers will vary, but most will indicate that the rules were unfair because the government prevented people from buying certain goods, and told them what to wear and how to live their lives.)*

- As a class, answer the Assessment questions. Allow students to briefly discuss their responses with a partner before sharing their answers with the class.

Focus On
A Japanese Home

In 1649, authorities of the Tokugawa government sent a decree to Japanese villages: "[Peasants] must not buy tea . . . to drink, nor must their wives. . . . The husband must work in the fields, [and] the wife must work at the loom. Both must do night work. However good-looking a wife may be, if she neglects her household duties, she must be divorced. Peasants must wear only cotton or hemp—no silk." This decree shows how the Tokugawa government tried to maintain a firm grip on Japanese society. Both outside and inside the home, the lives of the Japanese were guided by tradition and by law.

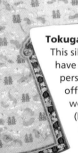

Tokugawa Fashions
This silk kimono, or robe, would have been worn by a wealthy person. Townspeople kept mud off their feet by wearing raised wooden clogs called geta (below). Peasants usually wore straw sandals.

Inside a Japanese Farmhouse The illustration at the right shows a typical farmhouse during the Tokugawa shogunate. In Tokugawa Japan, most houses had a main room with a sunken fire pit. The family gathered around the fire pit, and sat according to rank. At night, they slept on the floor on thin mattresses, which had been stored away in cupboards during the day.

Not shown are the two back rooms. One of these was the zashiki, a formal room used for receiving guests. Inside it was a butsudan, a Buddhist altar, and a tokonoma, a recessed space decorated with a flower vase, candlestick, and incense burner. The other back room was the nando, used for sleeping and for storage. In some farmhouses, women raised silkworms on a second floor.

The illustration shows raised wood floors covered with straw mats called tatami. It was customary to remove one's shoes before stepping onto the tatami. This custom is still practiced in Japan today.

Hiroma
This was the family's living and dining room.

Doma
This earthen-floored area was used for cooking and working, and sometimes, for sheltering farm animals.

Assessment

Describe Identify the features of a Japanese farmhouse during the Tokugawa shogunate.

Compare and Contrast Compare the Japanese farmhouse with the Bedouin tent on pages 298–299. How are they similar? How are they different?

Chapter 13 **381**

Have students reread the book and study the art, photos, and captions on these pages. Then have them compare their homes to the Japanese farmhouse. What things are the same? What things are different? Use the Think-Write-Pair-Share strategy (TE, p. T40) to elicit student responses.

Answers

Assessment

Describe Farmhouses had a hiroma, which was the family's living and dining room; a doma, which was an earthen-floored area used for cooking, working, and sometimes for sheltering farm animals; a zashiki, which was a formal room for receiving guests and contained a butsudan, or Buddhist altar, and a tokonoma, a recessed space with a flower vase, candlestick, and incense burner; a hando, used for sleeping and for storage. Some farmhouses had second floors where women raised silkworms. Most houses had a main room with a sunken fire pit, cupboards for storing mattresses, and raised wooden floors covered with straw mats called tatami.
Compare and Contrast Similar: both houses have large open areas for sleeping, and cooking is done outside the home but near it; different: the Bedouin tent is made of animal hair and is a temporary structure, while the Japanese farmhouse is made of wood and is a permanent structure.

Section 3
Step-by-Step Instruction

Objectives

Social Studies

1. Find out about the geography of the Indian subcontinent.
2. Learn about the Delhi Sultanate, a period of Muslim rule.
3. Learn about the founding and achievements of the Mughal Empire.

Reading/Language Arts

Learn how to recognize cause-and-effect signal words.

Prepare to Read

Build Background Knowledge `L2`

Have students preview the headings and visuals in this section. Tell them that they will be reading about some of India's great rulers. Ask students what qualities they think a good ruler should have. For example, should he or she be intelligent, compassionate, or courageous? Use the Give One, Get One strategy (TE, p. T41) to elicit answers from the class. Remind them to keep the qualities they chose in mind as they read through the section.

Set a Purpose for Reading `L2`

■ Preview the Objectives.

■ Read each statement in the *Reading Readiness Guide* aloud. Ask students to mark the statements true or false.

   All in One Unit 4 History of Our World Teaching Resources, *Reading Readiness Guide,* p. 128

■ Have students discuss the statements in pairs or groups of four, then mark their worksheets again. Use the Numbered Heads participation strategy (TE, p. T40) to call on students to share their group's perspectives.

Vocabulary Builder
Preview Key Terms `L2`

Pronounce the Key Terms, and then ask students to say the words with you. Provide a simple explanation such as, "A sultan is a Muslim ruler, similar to a king."

Section 3 The Great Mughal Empire in India

Prepare to Read

Objectives

In this section you will

1. Find out about the geography of the Indian subcontinent.
2. Learn about the Delhi Sultanate, a period of Muslim rule.
3. Learn about the founding and achievements of the Mughal Empire.

Taking Notes

As you read this section, look for important events in India's history, and note when they occurred. Copy the timeline below and record your findings on it.

India's History, 600–1707

```
|--------|--------|--------|
600
Hindu revival begins.
```

Target Reading Skill

Recognize Cause-and-Effect Signal Words

Sometimes certain words, such as *because, affect,* or *as a result,* signal a cause or an effect. In this section, you will learn about invasions of India and the rise and fall of two Indian empires. Look for signal words to help you understand the causes and effects of these events.

Key Terms

- **sultan** (SUL tun) *n.* a Muslim ruler
- **caste system** (kast SIS tum) *n.* a Hindu social class system that controlled every aspect of daily life
- **Mughal Empire** (MOO gul EM pyr) *n.* a period of Muslim rule of India from the 1500s to the 1700s
- **Akbar** (AK bahr) *n.* the greatest Mughal leader of India
- **Taj Mahal** (tahzh muh HAHL) *n.* a tomb built by Shah Jahan for his wife

Timur, from an Indian manuscript

Even before Timur (tee MOOR) invaded India, people there had heard of this Mongol conqueror. He had destroyed entire cities and their populations in other parts of Asia. In 1398, he and his troops marched into northern India, in search of fabled riches. They ruined fields of crops and quickly captured Delhi (DEL ee), the capital city. Timur and his troops killed many people and took hundreds of slaves. They also carried away great treasures—pearls, golden dishes, rubies, and diamonds.

For a brief time, Delhi became part of the huge empire that Timur controlled from his capital, Samarkand (sam ur KAND). But Timur was more interested in conquering new lands than in governing those he had defeated. Not long after the Mongols invaded Delhi, they departed. Once again, a **sultan,** or Muslim ruler, took control of the city. But Delhi did not regain its command over the region, as you will see.

382 History of Our World

Target Reading Skill `L2`

Recognize Cause-and-Effect Signal Words Point out the Target Reading Skill. Ask students to be aware of the signal words listed here.

Model recognizing cause-and-effect signal words using this sentence: *As a result, the prince defeated the sultan and went on to control the capital city, Delhi.* Identify the cause-and-effect signal words. *(as a result)*

Give students *Recognize Cause-and-Effect Signal Words.* Have the complete the activity in groups.

   All in One Unit 4 History of Our World Teaching Resources, *Recognize Cause-and-Effect Signal Words,* p. 133

India's Geography

The triangular Indian subcontinent forms the southernmost part of Central Asia. A mountain range called the Himalayas stretches across the north of India. Although these mountains have helped to isolate India from lands to the north, the passes through the Himalayas have allowed some conquerors from the north to enter the subcontinent. To the west of India is the Arabian Sea, and to the east is the Bay of Bengal.

A large plain lies to the south of the Himalayas. It is dominated by major river systems, including the Indus and Ganges rivers. These rivers are fed by melting mountain snows, and much of the land here is well suited to farming. Farther to the south are highlands and plains.

✓ **Reading Check** Describe India's geography.

The Delhi Sultanate

The Mongols led by Timur were not the first people to invade India. Long before they came, India's riches had tempted others. Muslim invaders began raiding the Indian subcontinent around A.D. 1000. From 1206 to 1526, a series of sultans controlled northern India as well as parts of present-day Bangladesh and Pakistan. This period of India's history is called the Delhi Sultanate—after the capital city, Delhi.

A Hindu Revival At the time of the Muslim invasion, the region was experiencing a revival of the ancient Hindu religion. This revival had begun about A.D. 600. Hindus accept many gods, but they believe that all of these gods are just different aspects of one supreme being. Hindus also believe that social classes are part of the natural order of the universe.

In India at this time, the Hindu **caste system**—a strict system of social classes—controlled everyday life. Caste determined a person's job and status. At the top of the caste system were priests, teachers, and judges. Warriors were second. Then came farmers and merchants. The fourth class included craftspeople and laborers. Finally, there was a group of poor and powerless people who were called untouchables.

A Himalayan Mountain Pass
Even today, it is difficult to cross the Himalayas. **Infer** Why do you think modern travelers are still using pack animals rather than trucks or automobiles to cross these mountains?

Chapter 13 Section 3 **383**

Vocabulary Builder

Use the information below to teach students this section's high-use words.

High-Use Word	Definition and Sample Sentence
conflict, p. 384	*n.* a fight or struggle My brother and I avoided a **conflict** by sharing the computer game.
expand, p. 385	*v.* to make larger; spread out Judy **expanded** her chain by opening three new stores.
extravagant, p. 386	*adj.* too showy; beyond reasonable limits The gown, covered with jewels, was very **extravagant**.
rebel, p. 386	*v.* to resist or fight against The American colonists **rebelled** against Great Britain.

Instruct

India's Geography ▪️L2

The Delhi Sultanate ▪️L2

Guided Instruction

- **Vocabulary Builder** Clarify the high-use word **conflict** before reading.

- Read India's Geography and The Delhi Sultanate using the ReQuest Procedure (TE, p. T39).

- Ask students **What effects have the Himalayas had on India?** *(They have isolated India from lands to the north, but the mountain passes have allowed conquerors from the north to enter the country.)*

- Have students describe the invasion that began around A.D. 1000. *(Muslim invaders began raiding the Indian subcontinent around that time.)*

- Ask students **What was the Delhi Sultanate?** *(the period of history from 1206 to 1526 when Muslim rulers, or sultans, controlled northern India and parts of present-day Bangladesh and Pakistan)*

- Have students discuss Hindu religious beliefs. *(Hindus accept many gods, but believe that they are all aspects of one supreme being; Hindus also believe that social class is a part of the natural order of the universe.)*

Answers

✓ **Reading Check** India is shaped like a triangle and surrounded by water on the west, south, and east. The Himalaya mountains stretch across the north, and highlands and plains are in the south. India has two major river systems.

Infer Pack animals can travel on narrower roads than modern motor vehicles can navigate.

Chapter 13 Section 3 **383**

Recognize Cause-and-Effect Signal Word
As a follow up, have students answer the Target Reading Skill question in the Student Edition. (*The signal word is "caused."*)

Guided Instruction (continued)

- Ask students **What was the Hindu caste system?** (*a strict system of social classes*) **What were the different classes of the Hindu caste system?** (*Priests, teachers, and judges were at the top; warriors were second; farmers and merchants were third; craftsmen and laborers were fourth; and untouchables, who were poor and powerless, were at the bottom.*)

- Ask students **Why did conflicts occur between Hindus and Muslims?** (*Muslim culture is based on beliefs that are very different from Hindu beliefs. These beliefs led to conflicts that still exist today.*)

- Ask students **How was the Delhi Sultanate defeated?** (*A Mongol prince named Babur attacked and defeated the Sultan's army with the use of cannons and better fighters.*)

Independent Practice

Have students create the Taking Notes graphic organizer on a blank sheet of paper. Then have them fill in the time line with details they learn as they read. Briefly model how to add details using *Transparency B20: Timeline.*

📖 **History of Our World Transparencies,** *Transparency B20: Timeline*

Monitor Progress

As students fill in the time line, circulate and make sure that individuals are placing events in chronological order. Provide assistance as necessary.

Answers

✓ **Reading Check** The Mongols attacked the weakened Delhi Sultanate. They had cannons and were better fighters.

Conclude Akbar's court was made up of many men who supported him.

⮌ Target Skill **Recognize Cause-and-Effect Signal Words** What signal word in the paragraph at the right helped you understand the conflicts between Hindus and Muslims?

Akbar Holds Court
Akbar supported many kinds of artists, including those who made beautiful miniature paintings like this one. **Conclude** *What can you conclude about Akbar's court from this painting?*

The Muslims who controlled the Delhi Sultanate did not become part of Hindu society. As you read in Chapter 1, Muslim culture is based on beliefs that are very different from those of Hindu culture. These differences caused conflicts between the two groups. In fact, religious disagreements still divide the Hindus and Muslims who live in India today.

The Fall of the Delhi Sultanate   In 1526, a Mongol prince named Babur (BAH bur) took advantage of the weakened Delhi Sultanate. Babur was a Muslim descendant of the Mongol conqueror Timur. Even though Babur and his troops were outnumbered almost ten to one, they attacked the sultan's army.

The sultan's forces had 100 elephants to help them fight. Babur's troops had none. But the Mongols had cannons—and they were better fighters. The prince defeated the sultan and went on to control the capital city, Delhi. A new period of India's history would now begin.

✓ **Reading Check**   How was the Delhi Sultanate defeated?

The Mughal Empire

Babur founded the celebrated **Mughal Empire,** whose Muslim rulers controlled India until the 1700s. (*Mughal* is another word for "Mongol.") About 25 years after Babur's death, the empire came under the control of Babur's grandson. His name was **Akbar** (AK bahr), and he would become the greatest Mughal leader of India.

Akbar the Great   When Akbar came to power, he was only 13 years old. He grew up to become a talented soldier. Through conquest, treaties, and marriage, he greatly expanded the Mughal Empire.

Akbar also encouraged the arts. He set up studios for painters at his court. He supported poets, although he himself never learned to read or write. Akbar also brought together scholars from different religions for discussions. He consulted with Muslims, Hindus, Buddhists, and Christians.

Although he was a Muslim, Akbar gained the support of his Hindu subjects through his policy of toleration. He allowed Hindus to practice their religion freely, and he ended unfair taxes that had been required of non-Muslims.

┌─ **Background: Daily Life** ─────────────

Hinduism   Dating back more than 3,000 years, Hinduism is one of the world's oldest religions. Unlike Judaism, Islam, or Christianity, Hinduism has no single founder, holy book, or system of beliefs. Hindus may worship many different lesser gods; however they are all seen as part of one being called Brahman. Brahman is believed to have the form of three major gods: Brahma, the creator; Vishnu, the pre- server; and Shiva, the destroyer. Reincarnation, or rebirth, is an important belief in Hinduism. Hindus believe that after a person dies, his or her soul is reborn into another person or animal. What a person does in this life affects how he or she will be reborn in the next life. Eventually, Hindus hope to escape this cycle of death and rebirth and become part of Brahman.

MAP MASTER™
Skills Activity

KEY

Mughal Empire, A.D. 1605

Border of the Delhi Sultanate, A.D. 1320

Border of Timur's empire, about A.D. 1400

• City

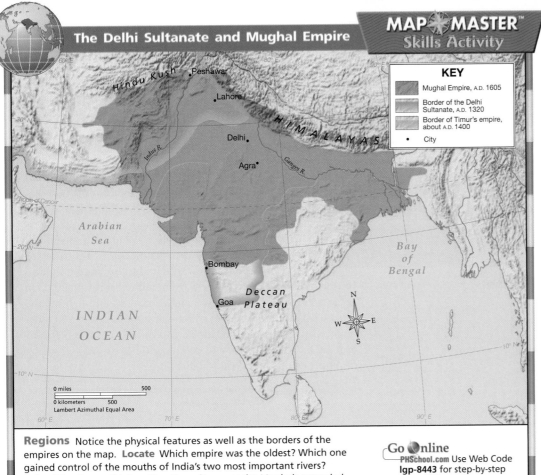

Hindu Kush
Peshawar
Lahore
HIMALAYAS
Delhi
Indus R.
Agra
Ganges R.
Arabian Sea
Bombay
Deccan Plateau
Goa
INDIAN OCEAN
Bay of Bengal
Tropic of Cancer

0 miles 500
0 kilometers 500
Lambert Azimuthal Equal Area

Regions Notice the physical features as well as the borders of the empires on the map. **Locate** Which empire was the oldest? Which one gained control of the mouths of India's two most important rivers? **Infer** Why do you think neither the sultans nor the Mughals extended their empires farther north?

Go Online
PHSchool.com Use Web Code lgp-8443 for step-by-step map skills practice.

Akbar created a strong central government, and he gave government jobs to qualified people, whatever their religion or caste. Hindus served as generals, governors, administrators, and clerks. These policies helped Hindus and Muslims live together more peacefully. They also strengthened Mughal power in India.

In 1605, when Akbar died, most of northern India was under his control. Akbar had ruled the Mughal Empire for 49 years, earning himself the nickname "the Great." During this long reign, his system of government had become firmly established in India. This system allowed the empire to continue developing and expanding for the next 100 years—even under rulers who were less capable than Akbar the Great.

Royal emblem from the Gujari Palace, India

Chapter 13 Section 3 **385**

The Mughal Empire L2

Guided Instruction

- **Vocabulary Builder** Clarify the high-use words **extravagant** and **rebel** before reading.

- Read The Mughal Empire to learn about Akbar the Great and other Mughal leaders.

- Ask students **How did Akbar improve relations between Hindus and Muslims?** *(He allowed Hindus to practice their religion freely and ended unfair taxes required of non-Muslims, which helped Hindus and Muslims to live together more peacefully.)*

- Ask students **What was the Taj Mahal?** *(a tomb built by Shah Jahan for his wife, Mumtaz Mahal)* **How do you think this and other extravagant buildings might have contributed to the decline of the Mughal Empire?** *(Possible answer: the buildings cost the empire a great deal of money and perhaps took too much time and money that could have been used in other areas of the empire.)*

Independent Practice

Have students complete their graphic organizers with dates from the section.

Monitor Progress

- Show *Section Reading Support Transparency HOW 95.* Go over key concepts and clarify key vocabulary as needed.

    📖 **History of Our World Teaching Resources,** *Section Reading Support Transparency HOW 95*

- Tell students to fill in the last column of the *Reading Readiness Guide.* Probe for what they learned that confirms or invalidates each statement.

    All in One Unit 4 History of Our World Teaching Resources, *Reading Readiness Guide,* p. 128

Answers

MAP MASTER™ Skills Activity **Locate** the Delhi Sultanate; the Mughal Empire; **Infer** The Himalayas were difficult to cross and would have prevented large armies from reaching lands to the north.

Go Online
PHSchool.com Students may practice their map skills using the interactive online version of this map.

Assess and Reteach

Assess Progress L2

Have students complete the Section Assessment. Then administer the *Section Quiz.*

 Unit 4 History of Our World Teaching Resources, *Section Quiz,* p. 130

Reteach L1

If students need more instruction, have them read this section in the Reading and Vocabulary Study Guide.

 Chapter 13, Section 3, **History of Our World Reading and Vocabulary Study Guide,** pp. 134–136

Extend L3

Have students read the story *Savitri: A Tale of Ancient India,* to see an example of Indian literature that contains Hindu gods as characters.

Unit 4 History of Our World Teaching Resources, *Savitri: A Tale of Ancient India,* pp. 142–145

Answer

✓ Reading Check He spent money on expensive wars, and reversed Akbar's policies toward Hindus, causing rebellions and wars.

Section 3 Assessment

Key Terms

Students' sentences should reflect an understanding of the Key Terms.

Target Reading Skill

The words *as a result* signal a cause-and-effect relationship in the last paragraph on this page.

Comprehension and Critical Thinking

1. (a) The Himalayas are in the north; south of the Himalayas is a large plain with two great river systems, the Indus and the Ganges; the Arabian Sea is in the west, and the Bay of Bengal is in the east. **(b)** Conquerors and invaders might not have reached India.

2. (a) the period of history from 1206 to 1526 when Muslim rulers, or sultans, controlled northern India and parts of present-day Bangladesh and Pakistan **(b)** Muslims did not become a part of Hindu society, and the two cultures had many conflicts.

The Taj Mahal

The Reign of Shah Jahan More than 100 years after Akbar's death, the Mughal Empire began to fall apart. Akbar's grandson, Shah Jahan (shah juh HAHN), became emperor in 1628. Jahan spent a fortune on extravagant buildings. The most famous of these is the **Taj Mahal** (tahzh muh HAHL), a tomb for the emperor's wife, Mumtaz Mahal (mum TAHZ muh HAHL).

When his wife died, Jahan was overcome with grief. The two had been constant companions, and Jahan had asked his wife's opinion on many issues. After she died, Jahan set out to build a tomb "as beautiful as she was beautiful."

Jahan's son, Aurangzeb (AWR ung zeb), spent still more money on expensive wars. He also reversed Akbar's policies toward Hindus. Aurangzeb tried to force Hindus to convert to the Muslim faith, and he began to tax them again. As a result, many Hindus rebelled, and fighting the rebels cost still more money. After Aurangzeb died in 1707, the empire split into small kingdoms. But to this day, people from around the globe journey to see his mother's tomb—a lasting reminder of the once great Mughal Empire.

 ✓ Reading Check How did Aurangzeb contribute to the decline of the Mughal Empire?

 Section 3 Assessment

Key Terms

Review the key terms at the beginning of this section. Use each term in a sentence that explains its meaning.

 Target Reading Skill

What words in the last paragraph on this page signal cause and effect?

Comprehension and Critical Thinking

1. (a) Identify What are the major geographic features of the Indian subcontinent?

(b) Predict How might India's history have been different if there had been no mountain passes in the north?

2. (a) Define What was the Delhi Sultanate?

(b) Synthesize How did Hindus and Muslims live together in India during this time?

3. (a) Explain Why was Akbar called "the Great"?

(b) Identify Causes What caused the decline of the Mughal Empire?

Writing Activity

Suppose that Akbar is a leader under a system of government like the United States government. He is running for reelection, and you are his campaign manager. Write a short speech stating why voters should reelect him.

> **Writing Tip** Remember to support your position with specific examples.

---

3. (a) He was a just ruler, who ruled the Mughal Empire successfully for 49 years. He encouraged the arts and persuaded Hindus and Muslims to live together more peacefully. When he died, most of northern India was under his control. **(b)** Rulers after Akbar spent money on extravagant buildings and expensive wars, and reversed Akbar's policies toward Hindus, which caused Hindus to rebel and cost the empire even more money.

Writing Activity

Use the *Rubric for Assessing a Writing Assignment* to evaluate students' speeches.

Unit 4 History of Our World Teaching Resources, *Rubric for Assessing a Writing Assignment,* p. 151

Review and Assessment

◆ Chapter Summary

Section 1: Golden Ages of China

Kublai Khan's court

- The Tang dynasty ruled China for almost 300 years. That period was the beginning of a golden age, during which China's territory increased, and Chinese culture and trade flourished.
- The Song dynasty, which ruled China after the Tang, expanded the merit system and promoted the spread of knowledge.
- The Mongols conquered China, and their leader, Kublai Khan, centralized China's government.

Section 2: Medieval Japan

- Japan is a mountainous island country of East Asia. The sea has provided both transportation and protection for the people of Japan.
- During the Heian period, the Japanese built a new capital and began to develop a distinctive culture.
- Warriors, called samurai, and powerful military leaders, called shoguns, took control away from the emperor. The shoguns eventually closed Japan to outsiders.

Section 3: The Great Mughal Empire in India

- The Indian subcontinent is shaped like a triangle, with mountains to the north and seas to the east and west.
- During the Delhi Sultanate, Muslim rulers called sultans ruled India.
- Mongols conquered India and established the Mughal Empire. Akbar the Great was the greatest Mughal leader.

Kabuki performer

◆ Key Terms

Define each of the following terms.

1. Silk Road
2. Tang
3. shogun
4. sultan
5. caste system
6. Kublai Khan
7. archipelago
8. samurai
9. Taj Mahal
10. dynasty

┌ Vocabulary Builder ────

fertile	isolation	conflict
estimate	distinctive	expand
reform	related	extravagant
adopt	supreme	rebel

Ask students to review the definitions they recorded on their *Word Knowledge* worksheets.

All in One **Unit 4 History of Our World Teaching Resources,** *Word Knowledge,* p. 134

Consider allowing students to earn extra credit if they use the words in their answers to the questions in the Chapter Review and Assessment. The words must be used correctly and in a natural context to win the extra points.

Chapter 13
Review and Assessment
Review Chapter Content

- Review and revisit the major themes of this chapter by asking students to classify what Guiding Question each bulleted statement in the Chapter Summary answers. Form students in groups and ask them to complete the activity together. Refer to page 1 in the Student Edition for the text of the Guiding Questions.

- Assign Vocabulary Development for students to review Key Terms.

    All in One **Unit 4 History of Our World Teaching Resources,** *Vocabulary Development,* p. 147

Answers

Key Terms

1. a chain of trade routes stretching from China to the Mediterranean Sea
2. a dynasty that ruled China for almost 300 years
3. the supreme military commander of Japan
4. a Muslim ruler
5. Hindu social class system that controlled every aspect of daily life
6. a Mongol emperor of China
7. a group or chain of islands
8. Japanese warriors
9. a tomb built by Shah Jahan for his wife
10. a series of rulers from the same family

Review and Assessment

Comprehension and Critical Thinking

11. (a) Students should list any two of the following: tea, jade, ivory, ceramics, silk **(b)** They were luxury goods that were new to the people of other countries. **(c)** Traders along the Silk Road introduced new ideas and goods to China, and China became an important center of trade and culture.

12. (a) The Song began using the merit system to hire government officials. The Mongols centralized government and stopped using the merit system; instead, high government positions were reserved only for Mongols. **(b)** The Song's use of the merit system benefited China since the hiring of people based on ability improved the Chinese government. Under the Mongols, only Mongols could be part of the government; which probably angered the Chinese who lived there and weakened the government's effectiveness.

13. (a) Japan is a mountainous archipelago in the Pacific Ocean off the coast of mainland Asia; India is a triangular subcontinent in the southernmost part of Central Asia, with the Himalayas stretching across northern India and a large plain to the south of the mountains. **(b)** Because of the mountainous terrain, the sea became an important transportation route for the Japanese. It protected Japan from outside invaders but it also isolated the country. The Himalayas isolated India from the north, but mountain passes allowed some invaders to enter India and conquer it.

14. (a) a series of Japanese military dynasties **(b)** Samurai warriors formed their own clans and promised loyalty to a powerful warlord and eventually the Minamoto clan became the most powerful; in 1192 the emperor of Japan gave the title of shogun to the leader of the Minamoto clan, Yoritomo, who set up the Kamakura shogunate. **(c)** They wanted to isolate Japan from foreign influences and prevent Europeans from conquering Japan.

15. (a) Aurangazeb **(b)** Akbar had allowed Hindus freedom to practice their religion while Aurangazeb tried to force Hindus to convert to Islam. During Akbar's reign, a system of governing became firmly established in India, but after Aurangazeb's death the empire split into small kingdoms. **(c)** Under the leaders who followed Akbar, great sums of money were spent on expensive wars. During Aurangazeb's reign many

Hindus rebelled, and money was spent on fighting them.

Skills Practice

Making an Outline Outlines will vary, but check to make sure students have created their outlines using the proper format and have included information from the text about the Mughal empire.

Review and Assessment (continued)

◆ **Comprehension and Critical Thinking**

11. (a) Identify Name two Chinese products that were important for trade.
(b) Explain Why were these products valued by other countries?
(c) Identify Effects How did trade in these products affect China?

12. (a) Recall How did the Song, and then the Mongols, change Chinese government?
(b) Evaluate Which changes benefited China? Which were harmful? Explain.

13. (a) Identify What are the major geographic features of Japan? Of India?
(b) Compare and Contrast How did the geography of these two places affect their history and culture?

14. (a) Define What is a shogunate?
(b) Summarize How did shoguns gain power in Japan?
(c) Identify Causes Why did shoguns ban most foreign travel and trade?

15. (a) Identify Who was the last ruler of India's Mughal Empire?
(b) Contrast How was his rule different from that of his great-grandfather, Akbar?
(c) Analyze What factors contributed to the downfall of the Mughal Empire?

◆ **Skills Practice**

Making an Outline In the Skills for Life activity in this chapter, you learned how to make an outline. Review the steps you followed to learn the skill. Then reread the text under the heading The Mughal Empire on pages 384–386. Make an outline of that text.

◆ **Writing Activity: Science**

Use encyclopedias, other reliable books, or reliable Internet sources to research one Chinese invention of the Tang or Song dynasty. Describe the invention, how it works, when and how it was invented, and why it was important. Write your findings as an essay or as an illustrated report that you can display in your classroom.

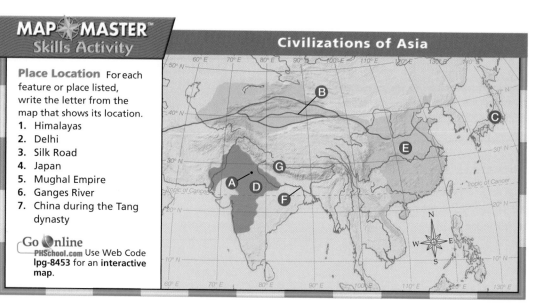

MAP MASTER™
Skills Activity

Civilizations of Asia

Place Location For each feature or place listed, write the letter from the map that shows its location.
1. Himalayas
2. Delhi
3. Silk Road
4. Japan
5. Mughal Empire
6. Ganges River
7. China during the Tang dynasty

Go Online
PHSchool.com Use Web Code **lpg-8453** for an **interactive map**.

Writing Activity: Science
Students' reports will vary, but should include information about a Chinese invention from the Tang or Song dynasty. *Use Rubric for Assessing a Writing Assignment* to evaluate student's reports.

All in One Unit 4 History of Our World Teaching Resources, *Rubric for Assessing a Writing Assignment,* p. 151

Standardized Test Prep

Test-Taking Tips

Some questions on standardized tests may ask you to identify the main topic or the topic sentence of a passage. Read the paragraph below. Then use the tip to help you answer the sample question.

> Beginning in the 1600s, the powerful shoguns of Japan outlawed Christianity. The shoguns forced Europeans to leave the country. They also closed Japanese ports to foreigners and banned foreign trade. Through their efforts to isolate Japan, the shoguns hoped to protect it from foreign invasion.

Think It Through Read all four choices. Answers A and D tell about specific actions, not broad ideas or main topics. Even though C is the first sentence of the passage, it also describes one particular action. Therefore, it is not more important than A or D. Because B summarizes the information of the other sentences, it is the correct answer.

Practice Questions

Pick the letter that best answers the question.

1. Read the passage below. Which of the sentences that follow states the main topic of the passage?

> Hideyoshi was born a poor peasant in Japan in the 1500s. Through hard work, he became a samurai warrior. Because of his military skills, Hideyoshi was promoted to an important position working for a powerful warlord. In 1582, the warlord was killed, and Hideyoshi took his place. A skillful leader from poor beginnings, Hideyoshi became ruler of Japan.

   A Through hard work, he became a samurai warrior.

   B Hideyoshi was born a poor peasant in Japan in the 1500s.

   C A skillful leader from poor beginnings, Hideyoshi became ruler of Japan.

   D In 1582, the warlord was killed, and Hideyoshi took his place.

Pick the letter that best answers the question.

Which of these sentences states the main topic of the passage?

   A They also closed Japanese ports to foreigners and banned foreign trade.

   B Through their efforts to isolate Japan, the shoguns hoped to protect it from foreign invasion.

   C Beginning in the 1600s, the powerful shoguns of Japan outlawed Christianity.

   D The shoguns forced Europeans to leave the country.

> **TIP** Many paragraphs have one sentence that states the main topic. The other sentences in the paragraph all support this topic sentence. The first and last sentences are the most likely to be the topic sentence.

Read each of the following statements. If the statement is true, write *true*. If it is false, write *false*.

2. The samurai warriors of Japan followed a set of strict rules for behavior.

3. Song rulers used the merit system in Chinese government.

4. The Indian subcontinent could not be invaded from the north.

5. Akbar was a great Mughal ruler of India.

6. Japan's islands are mostly flat, and traveling by land is easy.

Go Online PHSchool.com

Use Web Code **lga-8403** for a **Chapter 13 self-test.**

Chapter 13 **389**

MAP MASTER Skills Activity

1. G	**2.** A
3. B	**4.** C
5. D	**6.** F
7. E	

Go Online PHSchool.com Students may practice their map skills using the interactive online version of this map.

Standardized Test Prep

Answers

1. C
2. True
3. True
4. False
5. True
6. False

Go Online PHSchool.com Students may use the Chapter 13 self-test on PHSchool.com to prepare for the Chapter Test.

Assessment Resources

Use *Chapter Tests A and B* to assess students' mastery of the chapter content.

All in One Unit 4 History of Our World Teaching Resources, *Chapter Tests A and B,* pp. 152–157

Tests are also available on the *ExamView®* *Test Bank CD-ROM.*

ExamView® Test Bank CD-ROM

Use a benchmark test to evaluate students' cumulative understanding of what they have learned in Chapters 10 through 13.

History of Our World, Benchmark Test 4, **AYP Monitoring Assessments,** pp. 99–104

Age of Encounter

Unit Overview

Unit 5 examines the emergence of a global age during which Europeans launched the Crusades, experienced the Renaissance, reacted to the Reformation, and explored lands beyond their own territories. The unit begins by grounding students in the more inward-looking Europe of the Middle Ages and ends by introducing students to the causes and effects of the age of exploration and col-onization beyond Europe to the Americas, Africa, and Asia.

Monitoring Student Progress

After students have completed Chapter 17, administer Benchmark Test 5, the fifth of six benchmark tests provided to assess students' progress toward mastery of the National Geography Standards.

The Report Sheet for this test will identify which objectives or standards students have mastered and where they need additional work. It also correlates to the appropriate sections in the Reading and Vocabulary Study Guide, where students can get additional review as needed.

AYP Monitoring Assessment Resources

Determine students' progress toward mastery of the National Geography Standards.

📖 *Benchmark Test 5,* **AYP Monitoring Assessments,** pp. 105–110

Use the Report Sheet to identify which standards your students have mastered, where they need more work, and where they can get additional help.

📖 *Report Sheet, Benchmark Test 5,* **AYP Monitoring Assessments,** p. 129

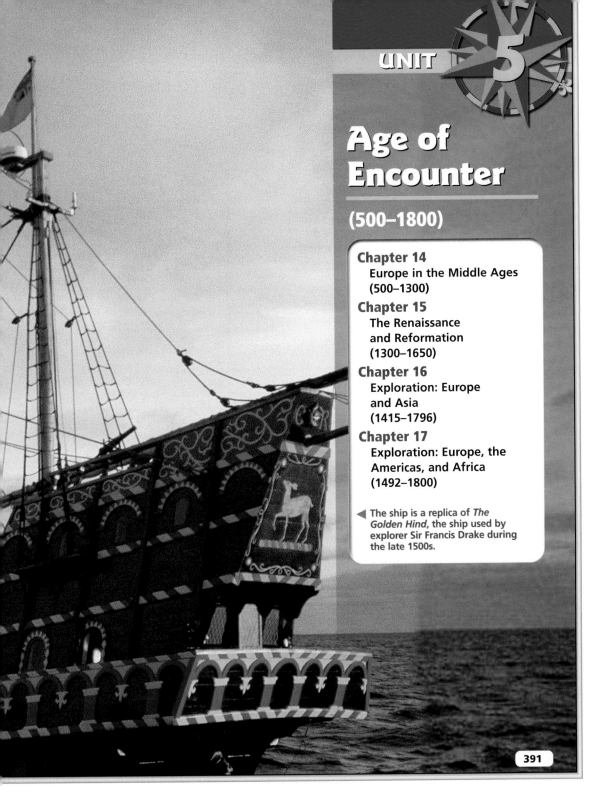

Age of Encounter

(500–1800)

◄ The ship is a replica of *The Golden Hind*, the ship used by explorer Sir Francis Drake during the late 1500s.

391

Using the Visual

Ask students to study the picture on pp. 390–391. Have students read the caption on p. 391. Tell students that Sir Francis Drake was an English explorer. He was the first English explorer to sail around the world. This voyage took place between 1577 and 1580. One of the ships in Drake's fleet was the *Golden Hind*, of which a working replica is pictured here. The ship was named for the golden hind, the golden-horned deer of Greek mythology. Visible in the photo is a painting of the golden hind on the stern of the ship.

Overview

Section 1 — Feudalism and the Manor System

1. Learn when the Middle Ages were and what they were like.
2. Find out how land and power were divided under feudalism.
3. Learn how the manor system worked.
4. Discover what life was like for peasants and serfs.

Section 2 — The Church and the Rise of Cities

1. Learn why the Roman Catholic Church was so important and powerful during the Middle Ages.
2. Discover the connection between an increase in trade and the growth of towns.
3. Find out what life was like in a medieval town.
4. Understand the role of culture and learning in the Middle Ages.

Section 3 — The Crusades

1. Learn about the causes of the Crusades.
2. Find out about the different Crusades and what they accomplished.
3. Discover the effects the Crusades had on life in Europe.

Section 4 — The Power of Kings

1. Learn about the forces that led to nation building in Europe.
2. Find out about nation building in England.
3. Discover how the Hundred Years' War affected England and France.

DISCOVERY CHANNEL SCHOOL Video

Feudal Life in the Middle Ages
Length: 5 minutes, 28 seconds
Use with Section 1
This video segment introduces the idea of feudalism and its effects on the relationships between lords and their servants. The segment also explores the castles and the knights who protected feudal life.

Technology Resources

Go Online PHSchool.com

Students use embedded Web codes to access Internet activities, chapter self-tests, and additional map practice. They may also access Dorling Kindersley's Online Desk Reference to learn more about each country they study.

Interactive Textbook

Use the Interactive Textbook to make content and concepts come alive through animations, videos, and activities that accompany the complete basal text—online and on CD-ROM.

PRENTICE HALL
TeacherEXPRESS
Plan · Teach · Assess

Use this complete suite of powerful teaching tools to make planning lessons and administering tests quicker and easier.

Reading and Assessment

Reading and Vocabulary Instruction

⟳ Model the Target Reading Skill

Sequence Explain to students that sequence is the order in which something occurs. Understanding sequence is important when reading because it allows students to recognize the order in which events in history occurred and how one event might influence another. Point out some words that are often used when describing sequence: *first, second, next, then, before, later.* You can teach this skill using the following selection from page 412 of the Student Edition:

After the capture of Jerusalem, most of the crusaders returned to Europe. Those who stayed in the Holy Land set up four Christian kingdoms. The Muslim Turks attacked these kingdoms repeatedly. European Christians then launched more Crusades to keep control of the region.

Write the selection on the board, and ask students to identify the sequence signal words as you underline them. *(after; then)* Point out that the word *after* in the first sentence refers to the fact that the return of the crusaders to Europe followed the capture of Jerusalem. Next, create a timeline on the board to show the order in which the events occurred. *(The timeline should show, in this order: capture of Jerusalem; four Christian kingdoms set up in Holy Land; Muslim Turks attack kingdoms; more crusades launched by European Christians.)*

Use the following worksheets from All-in-One Unit 5 History of Our World Teaching Resources (pp. 23–24) to support the chapter's Target Reading Skill.

Vocabulary Builder
High-Use Academic Words

Use these steps to teach this chapter's high-use words:

1. Have students rate how well they know each word on their Word Knowledge worksheets (All-in-One Unit 5 History of Our World Teaching Resources, p. 25).

2. Pronounce each word and ask students to repeat it.

3. Give students a brief definition or sample sentence (provided on TE pp. 395, 403, 410, and 417).

4. Work with students as they fill in the "Definition or Example" column of their Word Knowledge worksheets.

Assessment

Formal Assessment

Test students' understanding of core knowledge and skills.

Chapter Tests A and B, All-in-One Unit 5 History of Our World Teaching Resources, pp. 38–43

Customize the Chapter Tests to suit your needs.

Exam*View*® Test Bank CD-ROM

Skills Assessment

Assess geographic literacy.

MapMaster Skills, Student Edition, pp. 393, 395, 406, 411, 422

Assess reading and comprehension.

Target Reading Skills, Student Edition, pp. 396, 407, 412, 418, and in Section Assessments

Chapter 5 Assessment, History of Our World Reading and Vocabulary Study Guide, p. 160

Performance Assessment

Assess students' performance on this chapter's Writing Activities using the following rubrics from All-in-One Unit 5 History of Our World Teaching Resources.

Rubric for Assessing a Writing Assignment, p. 35

Rubric for Assessing a Newspaper Article, p. 36

Rubric for Assessing a Report, p. 37

Assess students' work through performance tasks.

Small Group Activity: Writing a Documentary, All-in-One Unit 5 History of Our World Teaching Resources, pp. 28–31

Online Assessment

Have students check their own understanding.

Chapter Self-Test

Section 1 Feudalism and the Manor System

 3 periods, 1.5 blocks (includes Focus On A Medieval Manor)

Social Studies Objectives

1. Learn when the Middle Ages were and what they were like.
2. Find out how land and power were divided under feudalism.
3. Learn how the manor system worked.
4. Discover what life was like for peasants and serfs.

Reading/Language Arts Objective

Recognize sequence signal words to help in understanding the relationships in time between ideas and events.

Prepare to Read	**Instructional Resources**	**Differentiated Instruction**
Build Background Knowledge Have students preview the headings and visuals to predict what they will learn. **Set a Purpose for Reading** Have students evaluate statements on the Reading Readiness Guide. **Preview Key Terms** Teach the section's Key Terms. **Target Reading Skill** Introduce the section's Target Reading Skill of **recognizing sequence signal words.**	**All in One Unit 5 History of Our World Teaching Resources** L2 Reading Readiness Guide, p. 8 L2 Recognize Sequence Signal Words, p. 23	**Spanish Reading and Vocabulary Study Guide** L1 Chapter 14, Section 1, pp. 106–107 ELL

Instruct	**Instructional Resources**	**Differentiated Instruction**
The Middle Ages Discuss the time span of the Middle Ages and the major empires that existed during that time. **Target Reading Skill** Review **recognizing sequence signal words.** **Feudalism: A Kind of Government** Ask about the people who held power in the feudal system, and discuss the role of lords and vassals. **The Manor System** **Peasants and Serfs** Discuss the differences between feudalism and the manor system.	**All in One Unit 5 History of Our World Teaching Resources** L2 Guided Reading and Review, p. 9 L2 Reading Readiness Guide, p. 8 **History of Our World Transparencies** L2 Section Reading Support Transparency HOW 96 **World Studies Video Program** L2 Feudal Life in the Middle Ages	**All in One Unit 5 History of Our World Teaching Resources** L1 Lords and Vassals, p. 32 AR, GT **Teacher's Edition** L1 For Less Proficient Readers, TE p. 396 L3 For Gifted and Talented, TE p. 396 L3 For Advanced Readers, TE p. 397 L1 For Special Needs Students, TE pp. 397, 400 **Student Edition on Audio CD** L1 Chapter 14, Section 1 ELL, LPR, SN **Spanish Support** L2 Guided Reading and Review (Spanish), p. 116 ELL

Assess and Reteach	**Instructional Resources**	**Differentiated Instruction**
Assess Progress Evaluate student comprehension with the section assessment and section quiz. **Reteach** Assign the Reading and Vocabulary Study Guide to help struggling students. **Extend** Extend the lesson by assigning a Small Group Activity.	**All in One Unit 5 History of Our World Teaching Resources** L2 Section Quiz, p. 10 L3 Small Group Activity: Writing a Documentary, pp. 28–31 Rubric for Assessing a Writing Assignment, p. 35 **Reading and Vocabulary Study Guide** L1 Chapter 14, Section 1, pp. 148–150	**Spanish Support** L2 Section Quiz (Spanish), p. 117 ELL

Key

L1 Basic to Average	L3 Average to Advanced	LPR Less Proficient Readers	GT Gifted and Talented
L2 For All Students		AR Advanced Readers	ELL English Language Learners
		SN Special Needs Students	

Section 2 The Church and the Rise of Cities

 2 periods, 1 block

Social Studies Objectives

1. Learn why the Roman Catholic Church was so important and powerful during the Middle Ages.
2. Discover the connection between an increase in trade and the growth of towns.
3. Find out what life was like in a medieval town.
4. Understand the role of culture and learning in the Middle Ages.

Reading/Language Arts Objective

Identify the sequence of events to help you understand and remember them.

Section Lesson Planner

Prepare to Read

Build Background Knowledge
Use transparencies to introduce a Cathedral.

Set a Purpose for Reading
Have students evaluate statements on the Reading Readiness Guide.

Preview Key Terms
Teach the section's Key Terms.

Target Reading Skill
Introduce the section's Target Reading Skill of **identifying sequence.**

Instructional Resources

All in One Unit 5 History of Our World Teaching Resources
- **L2** Reading Readiness Guide, p. 12
- **L2** Identify Sequence, p. 24

History of Our World Transparencies
- **L2** Color Transparency HOW 35: The Cathedral at Reims
- **L2** Color Transparency HOW 36: The Cathedral at Reims: Interior

Differentiated Instruction

Spanish Reading and Vocabulary Study Guide
- **L1** Chapter 14, Section 2, pp. 108–109 ELL

Instruct

The Church in the Middle Ages
Discuss the Roman Catholic Church and its influence on the people of the Middle Ages.

Eyewitness Technology
Study a diagram to learn about gothic cathedrals.

Trade Revives and Towns Grow
Discuss how the rise in travel and growth of towns led to an increase in trade.

Life in Towns and Cities Medieval Culture
Discuss the middle class and the role of guilds in the Middle Ages.

Target Reading Skill
Review **identifying sequence.**

Instructional Resources

All in One Unit 5 History of Our World Teaching Resources
- **L2** Guided Reading and Review, p. 13
- **L2** Reading Readiness Guide, p. 12

History of Our World Transparencies
- **L2** Section Reading Support Transparency HOW 97

Differentiated Instruction

Teacher's Edition
- **L3** For Gifted and Talented, TE p. 404
- **L1** For Less Proficient Readers, TE p. 405
- **L3** For Advanced Readers, TE p. 406

History of Our World Transparencies
- **L3** Color Transparency HOW 23: Western Europe: Physical-Political AR, GT

Spanish Support
- **L2** Guided Reading and Review (Spanish), p. 118 ELL

Assess and Reteach

Assess Progress
Evaluate student comprehension with the section assessment and section quiz.

Reteach
Assign the Reading and Vocabulary Study Guide to help struggling students.

Extend
Extend the lesson by assigning an Enrichment activity.

Instructional Resources

All in One Unit 5 History of Our World Teaching Resources
- **L2** Section Quiz, p. 14
- **L3** Enrichment, p. 26
  Rubric for Assessing a Writing Assignment, p. 35

Reading and Vocabulary Study Guide
- **L1** Chapter 14, Section 2, pp. 151–153

Differentiated Instruction

Spanish Support
- **L2** Section Quiz (Spanish), p. 119 ELL

Key

L1 Basic to Average	**L3** Average to Advanced	**LPR** Less Proficient Readers	**GT** Gifted and Talented
L2 For All Students		**AR** Advanced Readers	**ELL** English Language Learners
		SN Special Needs Students	

Section 3 The Crusades

 2 periods, 1 block (includes Skills for Life)

Social Studies Objectives
1. Learn about the causes of the Crusades.
2. Find out about the different Crusades and what they accomplished.
3. Discover the effects the Crusades had on life in Europe.

Reading/Language Arts Objective
Recognize sequence signal words to help build an understanding of the relationships between ideas and events.

Prepare to Read

Build Background Knowledge
Ask students to preview the section and write five questions to answer as they read.

Set a Purpose for Reading
Have students begin to fill out the Reading Readiness Guide.

Preview Key Terms
Teach the section's Key Terms.

Target Reading Skill
Introduce the section's Target Reading Skill of **recognizing sequence signal words.**

Instructional Resources
All in One Unit 5 History of Our World Teaching Resources
- L2 Reading Readiness Guide, p. 16
- L2 Recognize Sequence Signal Words, p. 23

Differentiated Instruction
Spanish Reading and Vocabulary Study Guide
- L1 Chapter 14, Section 3, pp. 110–111 ELL

Instruct

Causes of the Crusades
Discuss the Crusades and the Holy Land of Jerusalem.

Target Reading Skill
Review **recognizing sequence signal words.**

A Series of Crusades
The Results of the Crusades
Compare and contrast the First and Second Crusades and discuss effects of the Crusades.

Instructional Resources
All in One Unit 5 History of Our World Teaching Resources
- L2 Guided Reading and Review, p. 17
- L2 Reading Readiness Guide, p. 16

History of Our World Transparencies
- L2 Section Reading Support Transparency HOW 98

Differentiated Instruction
All in One Unit 5 History of Our World Teaching Resources
- L2 Skills for Life, p. 27 AR, GT, LPR, SN

Teacher's Edition
- L1 For Special Needs Students, TE pp. 411, 415

Social Studies Skills Tutor CD-ROM
- L1 Analyzing and Interpreting Special-Purpose Maps ELL, LPR, SN

Spanish Support
- L2 Guided Reading and Review (Spanish), p. 120 ELL

Assess and Reteach

Assess Progress
Evaluate student comprehension with the section assessment and section quiz.

Reteach
Assign the Reading and Vocabulary Study Guide to help struggling students.

Extend
Extend the lesson by assigning an Internet activity.

Instructional Resources
All in One Unit 5 History of Our World Teaching Resources
- L2 Section Quiz, p. 18
  Rubric for Assessing a Newspaper Article, p. 36

Reading and Vocabulary Study Guide
- L1 Chapter 14, Section 3, pp. 154–156

PHSchool.com
- L3 For: Environmental and Global Issues: Why Do Wars Begin?
  Web Code: lgd-8506

Differentiated Instruction
Spanish Support
- L2 Section Quiz (Spanish), p. 121 ELL

Social Studies Skills Tutor CD-ROM
- L1 Distinguishing Fact and Opinion ELL, LPR, SN

Key
- L1 Basic to Average
- L2 For All Students
- L3 Average to Advanced
- LPR Less Proficient Readers
- AR Advanced Readers
- SN Special Needs Students
- GT Gifted and Talented
- ELL English Language Learners

Section 4 The Power of Kings

 2 periods, 1 block (includes Chapter Review and Assessment and Literature)

Social Studies Objectives

1. Learn about the forces that led to nation building in Europe.
2. Find out about nation building in England.
3. Discover how the Hundred Years' War affected England and France.

Reading/Language Arts Objective

Identify the order of events to help in understanding and remembering them.

Section Lesson Planner

Prepare to Read

Build Background Knowledge
Discuss how the United States became a nation.

Set a Purpose for Reading
Have students begin to fill out the Reading Readiness Guide.

Preview Key Terms
Teach the section's Key Terms.

Target Reading Skill
Introduce the section's Target Reading Skill of **identifying sequence.**

Instructional Resources

All in One Unit 5 History of Our World Teaching Resources
- L2 Reading Readiness Guide, p. 20
- L2 Identify Sequence, p. 24

Differentiated Instruction

Spanish Reading and Vocabulary Study Guide
- L1 Chapter 14, Section 4, pp. 112–113 ELL

Instruct

Nation Building
Discuss how the decline of feudalism led to the building of nations and affected the Church's power.

Target Reading Skill
Review **identifying sequence.**

Changes in England
Discuss King John and the Magna Carta.

The Hundred Years' War
Discuss the causes and effects of the Hundred Years' War.

Instructional Resources

All in One Unit 5 History of Our World Teaching Resources
- L2 Guided Reading and Review, p. 21
- L2 Reading Readiness Guide, p. 20

History of Our World Transparencies
- L2 Transparency B11: Chart/Table
- L2 Section Reading Support Transparency HOW 99

Differentiated Instruction

All in One Unit 5 History of Our World Teaching Resources
- L2 Organizing Details, p. 33 AR, GT, LPR, SN
  Rubric for Assessing a Writing Assignment, p. 35

Teacher's Edition
- L2 For English Language Learners, TE pp. 418, 426

Spanish Support
- L2 Guided Reading and Review (Spanish), p. 122 ELL

Assess and Reteach

Assess Progress
Evaluate student comprehension with the section assessment and section quiz.

Reteach
Assign the Reading and Vocabulary Study Guide to help struggling students.

Extend
Extend the lesson by assigning a Book Project.

Instructional Resources

All in One Unit 5 History of Our World Teaching Resources
- L2 Section Quiz, p. 22
- L3 Book Project: Birth of a Nation, pp. 19–21
  Rubric for Assessing a Writing Assignment, p. 35
- L2 Word Knowledge, p. 25
- L2 Vocabulary Development, p. 34
  Rubric for Assessing a Report, p. 37
- L2 Chapter Tests A and B, pp. 38–43

Reading and Vocabulary Study Guide
- L1 Chapter 14, Section 4, pp. 157–159

Differentiated Instruction

Spanish Support
- L2 Section Quiz (Spanish), p. 123 ELL
- L2 Chapter Summary (Spanish), p. 124 ELL
- L2 Vocabulary Development (Spanish), p. 125 ELL

History of Our World Transparencies
- L1 Transparency B5: Flow Chart

Key

L1 Basic to Average	L3 Average to Advanced	
L2 For All Students		
	LPR Less Proficient Readers	GT Gifted and Talented
	AR Advanced Readers	ELL English Language Learners
	SN Special Needs Students	

Reading Background

Question-Answer Relationships

Explain to students that there are many different types of questions. Understanding question-answer relationships can help students answer questions correctly and develop appropriate questions for initiating discussions. Give students examples of the different types of questions, referring to this chapter in the Student Edition.

Questions with:

1. Answers that are found explicitly in one or two sentences in the book. *(Example: Who were the Vikings?)*
2. Answers that are found in several different paragraphs in the book. *(Example: What were the roles of different people, such as lords, vassals, and noblewomen, under feudalism?)*
3. Answers that are not found directly in the book, but instead require you to think about what you've read. *(Example: Why do you think the Vikings did not unite the lands they settled into an empire?)*
4. Answers that are not found directly in the book and which you can answer without having read the book. *(Example: Why might a pilgrimage, or travel to a sacred place, be important to some people?)*

Divide students into teams. Have each team create examples of each type of question. Invite the teams to present the questions to the class. Before answering each question, the other students in the class should name the type of question and justify it by finding the answer in the text. Once students are comfortable with question-answer relationships, they can develop their own questions for class discussion, keeping in mind that the more interpretive type 2, 3, and 4 questions usually lead to more complex discussions.

Pattern Puzzles

One way for students to become familiar with paragraph structure is to have them complete pattern puzzles. To do this, form students into groups or pairs. Write a paragraph from the textbook on a piece of paper. Next, cut each sentence into a separate strip of paper and put the strips into an envelope. Do this with enough paragraphs to distribute to all the groups. Each group should arrange the strips into a logical paragraph. Remind students that a paragraph consists of a main idea and supporting details. The first sentence usually introduces the information in the paragraph, and the last sentence is frequently a conclusion.

World Studies Background

Geoffrey Chaucer (c. 1342–1400)

Geoffrey Chaucer was an English poet best known for his work, *The Canterbury Tales,* a poem about 17,000 lines long. He was also a courtier, diplomat, and civil servant. Chaucer invaded France with Edward III's army in 1359. He later served as a messenger during peace negotiations between England and France. In the 1370s, Chaucer was sent on a number of diplomatic missions to France and Italy.

The Beginnings of a Postal Service

Although no regulated postal service existed in the Middle Ages, kings and vassals as well as religious orders and universities needed to correspond frequently. Therefore, they set up groups of messengers to transmit information. Messenger systems improved with the increase in trade in the later Middle Ages, and corporations and guilds employed messengers to contact their customers. The travel necessary for trading was often combined with the carrying of letters. The invention of the printing press in the late 1400s increased demand for written correspondence, and some powerful families in Europe developed postal organizations. Government regulation of the postal service began in 1477, when Louis XI established the Royal Postal Service in France.

Infoplease® provides a wealth of useful information for the classroom. You can use this resource to strengthen your background on the subjects covered in this chapter. Have students visit this advertising-free site as a starting point for projects requiring research.

Use Web code **lgd-8500** for **Infoplease®**.

Sharing Key Concepts

Students can learn and remember key concepts and vocabulary from the chapter through discussion with their classmates. One way for students to do this is to complete an activity in which they will be sharing information with other students. After students have read through the chapter at least once, ask each student to write an explanation for one Key Term, high-use word, or concept from the chapter on an index card. Then, have students form two concentric circles so that each student is facing another. The pairs should explain the concepts from their index cards to one another. Encourage students to ask each other to elaborate upon their ideas, or to explain concepts that may be unclear. Students then trade cards and the outside circle moves clockwise one person. Repeat the process until students end up with their original cards.

Identifying Author's Craft

Knowing the author's craft, or strategy for writing, can help students understand the text. Explain that authors often present information *chronologically*, using *cause-and-effect,* or by *comparing and contrasting.* Have students choose which of these strategies was used to write each of the following sentences from the chapter:

1. *After Charlemagne's death, his empire was divided among his three sons.* (chronology)
2. *Like the men in her family, a noblewoman was often sent to other noble families for training.* (compare and contrast)
3. *The Church also held that if people* didn't *obey those rules, they would be punished after death.* (cause-and-effect)

Challenge students to determine the author's craft in other paragraphs and sections throughout the chapter.

Roger Bacon (c. 1220–1292)

The increase in learning during the Middle Ages is reflected by Roger Bacon, a medieval philosopher, scholar, and advocate of experimental science. Trained in geometry, arithmetic, music, and astronomy, Bacon was the first European to thoroughly describe the process of making gunpowder. He also developed a description of spectacles, or eyeglasses. In the late thirteenth century, after the pope's suggestion, Bacon created two works that attempted to scientifically explain the natural world through direct study and experimentation. Unrelenting in his quest for knowledge, Bacon wrote a number of other works, most of which remained incomplete.

Stained Glass

Stained glass windows are possibly the most remarkable elements in medieval architecture. Early medieval windows were filled with sheets of wood or marble pierced with holes into which glass, colored by mixing with metal oxides in a molten state, was inserted. Later, pieces of colored glass were connected with lead to form rich designs and symbolic pictorial compositions.

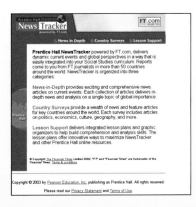

Get in-depth information on topics of global importance with **Prentice Hall Newstracker,** powered by FT.com.

 Use Web code **lgd-8505** for **Prentice Hall Newstracker.**

Guiding Questions

Remind students about the Guiding Questions introduced at the beginning of the book.

Section 1 relates to **Guiding Question 4**
What types of government were formed in these societies? *(Medieval Europeans developed a feudal system of government. Land was owned by kings or lords and held by vassals in return for their loyalty. Power belonged to those who controlled the land.)*

Section 2 relates to **Guiding Question 3**
What was the pattern of day-to-day life in these societies? *(Medieval towns and cities had a large middle class made up of merchants, traders, and crafts workers. Towns and cities were often overcrowded, and their lack of sanitation bred disease.)*

Section 3 relates to **Guiding Question 2**
How did each society's belief system affect its history? *(In 1096 European Christians launched the Crusades, which were military expeditions to bring Jerusalem—a city sacred to Christians as well as Muslims and Jews—under Christian control.)*

Section 4 relates to **Guiding Question 4**
What types of government were formed in these societies? *(By the late Middle Ages, large parts of Europe were unifying under a single king, instead of existing as a patchwork of fiefs ruled by many nobles. Gradually, these kingdoms evolved into nations.)*

🎯 Target Reading Skill

In this chapter, students will learn and apply the reading skill of sequence. Use the following worksheets to help students practice this skill:

All in One Unit 5 History of Our World Teaching Resources, *Recognize Sequence Signal Words,* p. 23; *Identify Sequence,* p. 24

Differentiated Instruction

The following Teacher's Edition strategies are suitable for students of varying abilities.

Advanced Readers, pp. 397, 406
English Language Learners, pp. 418, 426
Gifted and Talented , pp. 396, 404
Less Proficient Readers, pp. 396, 405
Special Needs Students, pp. 397, 411, 415

Chapter Preview

This chapter will introduce you to life in Europe during the Middle Ages.

Section 1
Feudalism and the Manor System

Section 2
The Church and the Rise of Cities

Section 3
The Crusades

Section 4
The Power of Kings

🎯 **Target Reading Skill**

Sequence In this chapter you will focus on using sequence to note the order in which events take place. This skill will help you understand and remember those events.

▶ The medieval castle at Carcassonne, France

392 History of Our World

Bibliography

For the Teacher

Seward, Desmond. *The Hundred Years' War: The English in France 1337–1453.* Penguin USA, 1999.

Vallejo, Yli Remo. *The Crusades.* AeroArt International Inc., 2003

Becher, Matthias. *Charlemagne.* Yale University Press, 2003.

For the Student

L1 McDonald, Fiona, and David Salariya. *How Would You Survive in the Middle Ages?* Scholastic Library Publishing, 1997.

L2 Woog, Adam. *Medieval Knight.* Gale Group, 2003.

L3 Platt, Richard, and Melanie Rice. *Crusades: The Battle for Jerusalem.* DK Publishing, 2001.

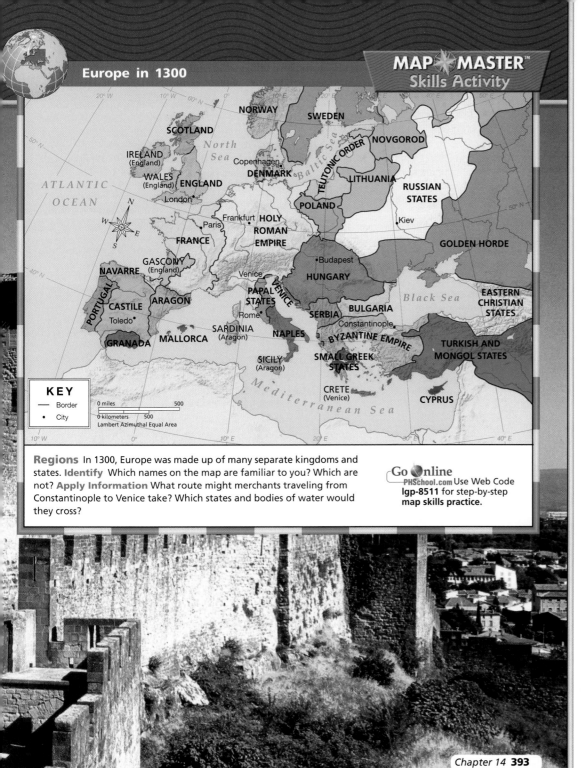

Europe in 1300

NORWAY
SWEDEN
SCOTLAND
North
Sea
IRELAND
(England)
Copenhagen•
NOVGOROD
TEUTONIC ORDER
WALES
(England) ENGLAND
DENMARK
LITHUANIA
London•
RUSSIAN
STATES
Frankfurt• HOLY
Paris•
ROMAN
POLAND
•Kiev
FRANCE
EMPIRE
GASCONY
(England)
•Budapest
GOLDEN HORDE
NAVARRE
Venice•
HUNGARY
Black Sea
PORTUGAL
CASTILE
ARAGON
PAPAL
STATES
VENICE
EASTERN
CHRISTIAN
STATES
Toledo•
Rome•
SERBIA
BULGARIA
Constantinople•
MALLORCA
SARDINIA
(Aragon)
NAPLES
BYZANTINE EMPIRE
TURKISH AND
MONGOL STATES
GRANADA
SICILY
(Aragon)
SMALL GREEK
STATES
Mediterranean Sea
CRETE
(Venice)
CYPRUS

ATLANTIC
OCEAN

KEY
— Border
• City

0 miles 500
0 kilometers 500
Lambert Azimuthal Equal Area

Regions In 1300, Europe was made up of many separate kingdoms and states. **Identify** Which names on the map are familiar to you? Which are not? **Apply Information** What route might merchants traveling from Constantinople to Venice take? Which states and bodies of water would they cross?

Go Online
PHSchool.com Use Web Code
lgp-8511 for step-by-step
map skills practice.

Chapter 14 **393**

■ Have students study the names of the various kingdoms shown on the map. Ask them to list the names of kingdoms that contain the names of countries that exist in Europe today.

Go Online
PHSchool.com Students may practice their map skills using the interactive online version of this map.

Using the Visual　L2

Reach Into Your Background
Have students study the photograph on pp. 392–393 and read the caption on p. 392. Discuss the location and architectural features of the castle with students. *(on top of a hill; high stone walls, small window openings)* Ask **Why do you think medieval castles would have had these features?** Conduct a Give One, Get One activity (TE, p. T41) to elicit student responses.

Answers

MAP MASTER™
Skills Activity
Identify Answers will vary: students may find England, Ireland, Scotland and France familiar, and Castile, Aragon, and Holy Roman Empire may be unfamiliar.
Apply Information Merchants traveling from Constantinople to Venice would travel down the coast of the small Greek States past Crete to the Mediterranean Sea, then northward past the coasts of the Byzantine Empire, Serbia, and Hungary to the east and Naples and the Papal States to the west.

Chapter Resources

Teaching Resources
L2 Vocabulary Development, p. 34
L2 Skills for Life, p. 27
L2 Chapter Tests A and B, pp. 38–43

Spanish Support
L2 Spanish Chapter Summary, p. 124
L2 Spanish Vocabulary Development, p. 125

Media and Technology
L1 Student Edition on Audio CD
L1 Guided Reading Audio CDs, English and Spanish
L2 Social Studies Skills Tutor CD-ROM
ExamView® Test Bank CD-ROM

DISCOVERY
CHANNEL
SCHOOL History of Our World
Video Program

Interactive
Textbook

PRENTICE HALL
TeacherEXPRESS™
Plan • Teach • Assess

Section 1
Step-by-Step Instruction

Objectives

Social Studies

1. Learn when the Middle Ages were and what they were like.
2. Find out how land and power were divided under feudalism.
3. Learn how the manor system worked.
4. Discover what life was like for peasants and serfs.

Reading/Language Arts

Recognize sequence signal words to help in understanding the relationships in time between ideas and events.

Prepare to Read

Build Background Knowledge L2

Ask students to preview the headings and visuals in this section. Tell them to make predictions about what they will learn. Provide a few examples to get students started. Have them engage in a Think-Write-Pair-Share activity (TE, p. T40) to generate a list of predictions. Write their responses on the chalkboard.

Set a Purpose for Reading L2

■ Preview the Objectives.

■ Read each statement in the *Reading Readiness Guide* aloud. Ask students to mark the statements true or false.

■ Have students discuss the statements in pairs or groups of four, then mark their guides again. Use the Numbered Heads participation strategy (TE, p. T40) to call on students to share their group's perspectives.

All in One Unit 5 History of Our World Teaching Resources, *Reading Readiness Guide,* p. 8

Vocabulary Builder
Preview Key Terms L2

Pronounce each Key Term, then ask the students to say the word with you. Provide a simple explanation such as, "The period known as the Middle Ages was given this title because it falls between ancient times and modern times."

Section 1
Feudalism and the Manor System

Prepare to Read

Objectives

In this section, you will
1. Learn when the Middle Ages were and what they were like.
2. Find out how land and power were divided under feudalism.
3. Learn how the manor system worked.
4. Discover what life was like for peasants and serfs.

Taking Notes

As you read this section, look for the major features of feudalism. Copy the web diagram below and record your findings in it.

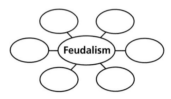

Target Reading Skill

Recognize Sequence Signal Words Noting the order in which important events take place can help you understand how the events relate to one another. Sequence signal words, such as *first, then, began,* and *in [date],* point out relationships in time. Look for such words in this section to help you understand the Middle Ages.

Key Terms

• **knight** (nyt) *n.* a man who received honor and land in exchange for serving a lord as a soldier

• **Middle Ages** (MID ul AY juz) *n.* the years between ancient and modern times
• **medieval** (mee dee EE vul) *adj.* referring to the Middle Ages
• **feudalism** (FYOOD ul iz um) *n.* a system in which land was owned by kings or lords but held by vassals in return for their loyalty
• **manor** (MAN ur) *n.* a large estate, often including farms and a village, ruled by a lord
• **serf** (surf) *n.* a farm worker considered part of the manor on which he or she worked

A knighting ceremony

As darkness fell, a young man put on a white tunic and red and black cloaks. Then he walked to the church, where he spent the long night alone, praying. Soon he would no longer be a mere squire, or knight-in-training. He would become a real **knight,** who would receive honor and land in exchange for serving his lord as a soldier.

The next morning, the squire entered the castle courtyard, where knights and ladies had gathered. His lord presented him with his sword, spurs, and shield. The squire knelt. Then he felt the lord's sword lightly tap him on each shoulder. "In the name of God, Saint Michael, and Saint George, I call you a knight," declared the lord. "Be loyal, brave, and true."

A knight was expected to be loyal to the lord who knighted him. His lord was loyal to a more powerful lord or king. Knights and lords protected the less powerful people loyal to them. This system held society together.

Target Reading Skill L2

Recognize Sequence Signal Words Point out the Target Reading Skill. Tell students that recognizing sequence signal words will help them find the relationship between events and ideas.

Model the skill by identifying the signal words in Charlemagne Reunites Western Europe on p. 396 *(in 768, at the time, soon, nearly 50 years, after Charlemagne's death).*

Give students *Recognize Sequence Signal Words.* Have them complete the activity in groups.

All in One Unit 5 History of Our World Teaching Resources, *Recognize Sequence Signal Words,* p. 23

The Middle Ages

A thousand years ago, scenes like the one you just read about took place throughout Western Europe. These were the times of knights in shining armor, lords and ladies, and castles and cathedrals. These were the **Middle Ages**, the years between ancient times and modern times.

Historians usually say that ancient times lasted until about A.D. 500 and that modern times started about 1500. The period in the middle, the Middle Ages, is also called the **medieval** period. *Medieval* comes from Latin words that mean "middle ages."

The Collapse of the Roman Empire The Middle Ages began with the collapse of the Roman Empire in Western Europe. For centuries, the Roman Empire had provided order and stability in the region. It had spread its culture, the Latin language, and Christianity across the continent. Over time, however, the Roman Empire grew weak. It suffered economic and social troubles. Worse, the Roman Empire also suffered from invasions by peoples from the north.

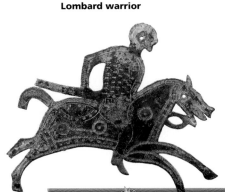

Bronze plaque of a Lombard warrior

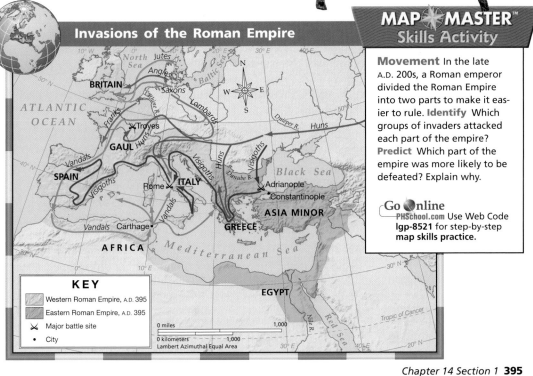

Invasions of the Roman Empire

MAP MASTER™ Skills Activity

Movement In the late A.D. 200s, a Roman emperor divided the Roman Empire into two parts to make it easier to rule. **Identify** Which groups of invaders attacked each part of the empire? **Predict** Which part of the empire was more likely to be defeated? Explain why.

Go Online
PHSchool.com Use Web Code lgp-8521 for step-by-step map skills practice.

KEY

Western Roman Empire, A.D. 395
Eastern Roman Empire, A.D. 395
✕ Major battle site
• City

0 miles 1,000
0 kilometers 1,000
Lambert Azimuthal Equal Area

Vocabulary Builder

Use the information below to teach students this section's high-use words.

High-Use Word	Definition and Sample Sentence
promote, p. 396	*v.* contribute to the growth of The students organized a pep rally to **promote** school pride.
majority, p. 398	*n.* a number greater than half of a total The **majority** of the students in the class enjoyed the extended recess.
interior, p. 399	*n.* the inner part of something The **interior** of the car was much cleaner than the outside of it.

Guided Instruction

- **Vocabulary Builder** Clarify the high-use word **promote** before reading.

- Read The Middle Ages using the Oral Cloze strategy (TE, p. T37).

- Ask students **When did the Middle Ages begin?** (*about* A.D. *500*) **When did they end?** (*about* A.D. *1500*)

- Discuss the reasons why the Roman Empire collapsed. (*It suffered economic and social troubles and was invaded by people from the north.*)

Answers

MAP MASTER Skills Activity **Identify** Visigoths and Huns attacked the Eastern Roman Empire; Visigoths, Huns, Vandals, Franks, Lombards, Saxons, Angles, and Jutes attacked the Western Empire. **Predict** The Western European Empire; according to the map, this region suffered more invasions than the Eastern Roman Empire.

Go Online
PHSchool.com Students may practice their map skills using the interactive online version of this map.

Guided Instruction (continued)

- Ask students **What did Charlemagne accomplish during his reign?** *(He kept Western Europe united, established schools, spread the Christian religion, issued money, and improved the economy.)*

- Ask **Who were the Vikings?** *(skilled sailors and tough warriors who came from northern Europe)*

- Have students compare the collapse of the Roman Empire with the collapse of Charlemagne's empire. *(Invasions by people from the north helped lead to the collapse of both empires.)*

Independent Practice

Assign *Guided Reading and Review.*

All in One Unit 5 History of Our World Teaching Resources, *Guided Reading and Review,* p. 9

Monitor Progress

Circulate and make sure students are correctly answering the questions. Provide assistance as needed.

⟳ Target Reading Skill

Recognize Sequence Signal Words As a follow up, ask students to answer the Target Reading Skill question in the Student Edition. *(began, continued)*

The Emperor Charlemagne
In return for Charlemagne's support of the Church, Pope Leo III crowned him emperor in 800. **Analyze Images** *How does this statue show Charlemagne's greatness and power?*

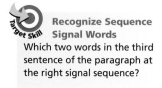

Recognize Sequence Signal Words
Which two words in the third sentence of the paragraph at the right signal sequence?

In wave after wave, the invaders destroyed Roman towns and cut off trade routes. They claimed parts of the empire for themselves. Because these peoples kept their own languages and laws, they broke the bonds that had held the Roman Empire together.

By about A.D. 500, the Roman Empire in Western Europe had completely collapsed. It was replaced by a patchwork of small kingdoms. Reading and writing were in danger of disappearing from Europe because many of the invading groups could not do either.

Charlemagne Reunites Western Europe One of the invading groups was the Franks. They claimed the area called Gaul, which is now France. In fact, the name *France* comes from the word "Franks." In 768, a skilled military leader named Charlemagne (SHAHR luh mayn) became king of the Franks.

At the time, the many small kingdoms of Western Europe were often at war with one another. Charlemagne expanded his kingdom by conquering these weaker kingdoms. Soon, he ruled an empire that stretched across most of Western Europe.

Charlemagne ruled his empire for nearly 50 years. During that time he worked hard to keep Western Europe united. He established schools throughout the land to promote learning and culture. He spread the Christian religion. He issued money and improved the economy. Western Europe had not been so prosperous or so united since the time of the Roman Empire.

After Charlemagne's death, his empire was divided among his three sons. They fought one another, weakening the empire. Other groups also attacked the weakened empire. Perhaps the fiercest attacks were made by the Vikings.

Attacks From the North The Vikings came from the far north of Europe—present-day Denmark, Sweden, and Norway. They were skilled sailors and tough warriors. Their attacks began around 800 and continued for about 300 years. Relying on surprise, the Vikings burned and looted European towns. But they also reopened trade routes to Mediterranean lands and beyond. And they settled in other parts of northern Europe, mixing with the local populations. Even so, the Vikings did not unite these lands into a lasting empire.

√ **Reading Check** Why did Charlemagne's empire fall apart?

Answers

Analyze Images Possible answer: The crown shows that Charlemagne was in power and the armor shows his strength.

√ **Reading Check** When Charlemagne died, the empire was divided among his three sons who fought one another and weakened the empire. Invasions from outsiders, such as the Vikings, also contributed to the empire's collapse.

Differentiated Instruction

For Less Proficient Readers **L1**

Have students read the section as they listen to the recorded version on the Student Edition on Audio CD. Check for comprehension by pausing the CD and asking students to share their answers to the Reading Checks.

⊙ Chapter 14, Section 1, **Student Edition on Audio CD**

Gifted and Talented **L3**

Ask students to do Internet or library research to find out more about Charlemagne. Tell them to use what they learn to write a short biography about him. Encourage them to include illustrations and other helpful visuals in their biographies.

Feudalism: A Kind of Government

Charlemagne's empire was gone. Western Europe was again divided into many small kingdoms. Viking attacks were a constant threat. Life was dangerous. The people of Europe had to find a way to defend themselves and to organize their communities. Slowly they worked out a new system of government.

The Feudal System The system that developed was called feudalism. Under **feudalism**, land was owned by kings or lords but held by vassals in return for their loyalty. By about 1000, feudalism was the way of life throughout Western Europe. It would last for hundreds of years.

In medieval Europe, power belonged to those who controlled the land. These landowners were nobles, such as barons and princes. They gave a share of land, called a fief (feef) to each of their vassals, who promised to follow the landowner's laws and to fight for him. A vassal could also be a lord.

Feudal Duties Lords promised to treat their vassals with honor. In addition, the chief duty of lords was to protect their vassals and their lands. If a vassal with young children died, for example, the lord became the children's protector. The lord also asked his vassals' advice before making laws or going to war.

Vassals were expected to raise and lead armies that would fight for their lord. Many of these vassals were knights—professional horse soldiers who led other men into battle. Vassals also appeared at the lord's court when commanded to do so. And they paid taxes, often in the form of crops, to their lords.

✓ **Reading Check** What did lords give vassals in exchange for the vassals' loyalty?

The Manor System

Feudalism was the way medieval Europeans organized power and government. Manorialism was the way they organized their economy. This system was based on the **manor,** a large estate that included farm fields, pastures, and often an entire village. It also included a large house, called the manor house, where the lord, or ruler, of the manor lived.

Vikings in America The Vikings did not limit their conquests to Europe. They went as far south as North Africa. Viking ships, such as the one shown below, also traveled westward to Greenland and beyond. An Icelandic saga, or story, gives clues about the location of Vinland, a Viking settlement in lands west of Greenland. Historians who have studied these clues and examined ruins in North America think that Vinland was probably in what is now Newfoundland, Canada.

A medieval knight in armor

Links

Read the **Links Across the World** on this page. Ask students **What has led some historians to suggest that Vinland was located in Newfoundland?** *(clues provided in an Icelandic saga and the study of ruins in North America)*

Feudalism: A Kind of Government L2

Guided Instruction

■ Read Feudalism: A Kind of Government with students. As students read, circulate and make sure individuals can answer the Reading Check question.

■ Ask students **Who held the power in the feudal system?** *(those who owned land, such as kings, barons, and princes)*

■ Ask **Why do you think lords believed it was important to give vassals land and treat them well?** *(Possible answer: They wanted vassals to remain loyal and fight hard for them when necessary.)*

Independent Practice

Ask students to create the Taking Notes graphic organizer on a separate piece of paper. Tell them to fill in the circles with details about feudalism. Briefly model how to choose the correct details.

Monitor Progress

As students fill in the graphic organizer, circulate and make sure individuals are choosing the correct details. Provide assistance as needed.

Differentiated Instruction

For Advanced Readers L3
Ask students to read *Lords and Vassals* to learn more about the duties of lords and vassals. Then have students answer the questions at the end of the selection.

All in One Unit 5 History of Our World Teaching Resources, *Lords and Vassals,* p. 32

For Special Needs Students L1
Pair special needs students with more proficient students and have them create flashcards to help them learn the roles of each type of person in the feudal system. Provide the title of the person on one side, such as vassal, and his or her role and duties on the opposite side. Invite students to quiz each other after they have studied the cards.

Answer

✓ **Reading Check** a share of their land

The Manor System L2

Peasants and Serfs L2

Guided Instruction

- Clarify the high-use academic words **majority** and **interior** before reading.

- Read The Manor System and Peasants and Serfs together as a class.

- Ask students to explain the difference between the manor system and feudalism. *(Feudalism was the way Medieval Europeans organized their government, while the manor system was the way they organized their economy.)*

- Discuss the role of noblewomen in feudal society. *(A noblewoman managed the household, provided medical care, and supervised servants.)*

Independent Practice

Ask students to complete their graphic organizers with the information they have just learned.

Monitor Progress

- Show *Section Reading Support Transparency HOW 96* and ask students to check their graphic organizers individually. Go over key concepts and clarify key vocabulary as needed.

  History of Our World Transparencies, *Section Reading Support Transparency HOW 96*

Show students *Feudal Life in the Middle Ages.* Ask **How was society divided under feudalism?** *(It was strictly divided into social classes, including lords and peasants.)*

- Tell students to fill in the last column of the *Reading Readiness Guide.* Probe for what they learned that confirms or invalidates each statement.

  All in One Unit 5 History of Our World Teaching Resources, *Reading Readiness Guide,* p. 8

Answers

Generalize Possible answer: Noblewomen were educated and were in charge of household functions.

✓ Reading Check They were far from towns, villages, or other manors.

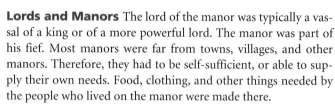

Noblewomen at Home
The larger illustration shows a lady in charge of a dinner where her guests are seated according to rank. A noblewoman sits at her desk in the smaller illustration. **Generalize** *What can you infer about the lives of noblewomen from these illustrations?*

Lords and Manors The lord of the manor was typically a vassal of a king or of a more powerful lord. The manor was part of his fief. Most manors were far from towns, villages, and other manors. Therefore, they had to be self-sufficient, or able to supply their own needs. Food, clothing, and other things needed by the people who lived on the manor were made there.

A lord depended on the wealth his manor provided. He ruled over his manor—and the poor people who lived there. He made the rules and acted as judge. He decided who would oversee the farming and other daily work. And he collected taxes from the peasants who lived on the manor.

The Role of Noblewomen Women of the noble classes also played an important part in feudal society. Like the men in her family, a noblewoman went to other noble families for training. Then, she took her place as lady of the household. She managed the household, performed necessary medical tasks, and supervised servants. When her husband or father was away fighting, she often served as "lord of the manor," making important decisions.

✓ Reading Check Why did manors have to be self-sufficient?

Peasants and Serfs

The majority of the people of medieval Europe were not lords, ladies, or knights. They were peasants, a group of people who made their living as farmers and laborers. Their lives were very different from the lives of the nobles.

Peasants were often very poor. They did all of the work on the manors of the Middle Ages. They farmed the lord's fields to raise food for his household. They were only allowed to farm a small strip of land for themselves. Even so, they had to give part of their own harvest to their lord.

Learn about the knights and castles of the Middle Ages.

Tied to the Manor Most peasants were also serfs. Serfs were peasants who were considered to be part of the manor. When a noble was given a manor as part of his fief, its serfs became his. They could not leave the manor, or even get married, without his permission.

Although serfs were property, they were not quite slaves. A serf who saved enough money to buy a plot of land could become a free peasant. A serf who escaped to a city and lived there for a year and a day without being caught also became free. Most serfs, however, remained serfs their whole lives.

A Hard Life Medieval peasants worked hard for most of their lives. They farmed their own fields and those of their lord. Men, women, and children were all required to work.

Peasants lived in one-room huts that often had only a single opening for a window. For heating and cooking, they built a fire on the dirt floor. Smoke filled the dark, cramped interior before drifting out of a hole in the roof. Peasants ate mostly simple foods such as black bread, cabbage, and turnips. They rarely ate meat, since the animals of the manor and surrounding land were reserved for their lord. Peasants even suffered when they slept: their mattresses were cloth sacks stuffed with straw.

Peasant Life
Peasant women worked in the fields along with the men. **Contrast** *Use this illustration and those on page 398 to contrast the lives of peasant women and noblewomen.*

✓ **Reading Check** What was life like for medieval peasants?

Section 1 Assessment

Key Terms
Review the key terms at the beginning of this section. Use each term in a sentence that explains its meaning.

Target Reading Skill
Review the text under the heading The Collapse of the Roman Empire. List the words that signal the order of events.

Comprehension and Critical Thinking
1. (a) Recall When were the Middle Ages?

(b) Identify Cause and Effect Why did the collapse of the Roman Empire lead to a new age in Western Europe?
2. (a) Define What was feudalism?
(b) Explain How did the system of feudalism work?
3. (a) Describe How was a manor organized?
(b) Conclude Why did a manor produce a wide variety of goods?
4. (a) Explain What was the relationship of a serf to his or her manor?
(b) Infer How and why might a serf become free?

Writing Activity
During the Middle Ages, most poor peasants remained poor their entire lives. Why do you think this was so? Write a paragraph explaining what you think the reason or reasons were.

For: An activity on feudalism
Visit: PHSchool.com
Web Code: lgd-8501

Assess and Reteach

Assess Progress L2
Have students complete the Section Assessment. Administer the *Section Quiz.*

 Unit 5 History of Our World Teaching Resources, *Section Quiz,* p. 10

Reteach L1
If students need more instruction, have them read this section in the Reading and Vocabulary Study Guide.

📖 Chapter 14, Section 1, **History of Our World Reading and Vocabulary Study Guide,** pp. 148–150

Extend L3
Assign the *Small Group Activity* in which students will write a documentary about knights in the Middle Ages.

 Unit 5 History of Our World Teaching Resources, *Small Group Activity: Writing a Documentary,* pp. 28–31

Answers
Contrast Possible answer: Both classes of women had responsibilities, but peasant women had to perform grueling physical labor.

✓ **Reading Check** Peasants worked almost every day, lived in one-room huts, slept on uncomfortable hay beds, and ate simple foods.

Writing Activity
Use the *Rubric for Assessing a Writing Assignment* to evaluate students' paragraphs.

 Unit 5 History of Our World *Rubric for Assessing a Writing Assignment,* p. 35

Typing in the Web code when prompted will bring students directly to detailed instructions for this activity.

Section 1 Assessment

Key Terms
Students' sentences should reflect knowledge of each Key Term.

Target Reading Skill
began, for centuries, over time, by about 500

Comprehension and Critical Thinking
1. (a) from about A.D. 500 to 1500, between ancient times and modern times **(b)** The

empire had broken into many small kingdoms, and other groups began moving into the region.

2. (a) the system of government that existed in Western Europe during the Middle Ages **(b)** Landowner nobles such as lords and kings held the power. Vassals held the land in return for their loyalty to the nobles. Vassals were expected to raise armies and fight for the nobles when necessary.

3. (a) Farmers, laborers, and any skilled craftspeople needed to keep the manor running on a self-sufficient basis. **(b)** Manors had to be self-sufficient.

4. (a) A serf was considered to be part of the manor. **(b)** A serf could become free by buying a plot of land or by running away to a city without being caught for a year and a day.

Focus on A Medieval Manor

L2

Guided Instruction

- Ask students to read the text and study the art, photos, and captions on these pages.

- Ask students **What kinds of goods were produced on manor estates?** *(grain, bread, fence posts, shingles, planks, linen cloth, shirts, honey, chickens, eggs, cheese, and butter.)* **What were many of these goods used for?** *(Nobles depended on what peasants produce to pay taxes to higher nobles and to the king.)*

- Ask students **How did the people in a medieval manor use the surrounding manor lands?** *(The lands and forests surrounding the peasant houses provided grain, fruits, and vegetables; peasants grazed cattle, sheep, and goats in the fields, and pigs roamed in the forests in search of food; woods provided timber and fuel; nobles hunted in the forests.)*

- As a class, answer the Assessment questions. Allow students to briefly discuss their responses with a partner before sharing their answers with the class.

Focus On A Medieval Manor

Although peasants and nobles led very different lives, their reliance on the lands of the manor estate bound them together. Peasants worked the land to pay what they owed to their lords. Nobles depended on what the peasants produced so that they could pay taxes to higher nobles and to the king. In addition to cash, taxes were paid in grain, bread, fence posts, shingles and planks, linen cloth, shirts, honey, chickens, eggs, cheese, and butter. All of these goods were produced on the manor estate.

A peasant's house

The Manor Estate Medieval manors included the lord's home, the homes of the peasants and serfs, a mill for grinding grain, and often a chapel or a church. Attached to the manor house, or in a separate building, was a bakery that peasants and serfs would use for baking bread.

Most people in medieval Europe were agricultural workers. The lands and forests surrounding the manor and peasant houses provided grain, fruits, and vegetables. Peasants grazed cattle, sheep, and goats in the manor fields. Their pigs roamed the manor's woodlands in search of food. Woodlands also provided timber for building and fuel. Hunting in the forests was reserved for the nobles.

The illustration on the facing page shows a manor estate of the Middle Ages. At the top of this page is a shield painted with a noble's coat of arms.

Differentiated Instruction

For Special Needs Students
L2
Help reinforce the different parts of a manor by having students draw and label their own picture of a medieval manor. Tell them to use the diagram on pp. 400–401 as a guide, and to label the different buildings in their drawings. Encourage students to be creative, and add animals and people to their drawings. Then have them present their drawings to the class.

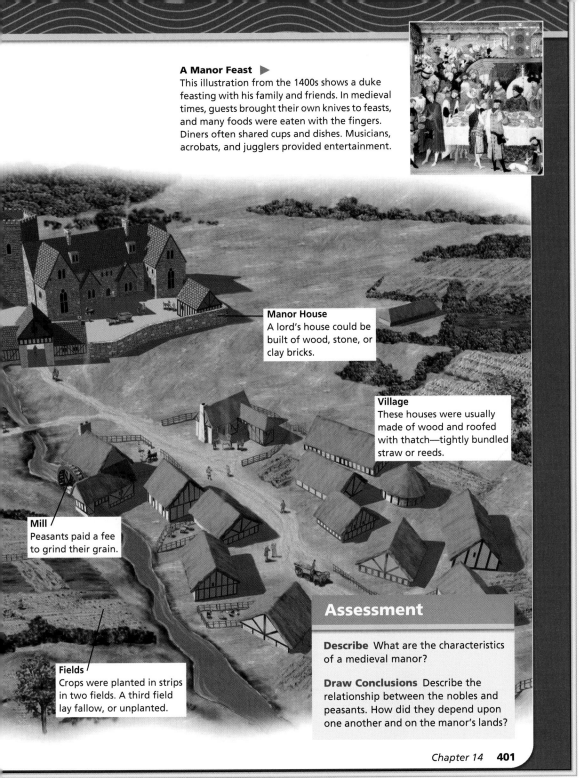

A Manor Feast ▶
This illustration from the 1400s shows a duke feasting with his family and friends. In medieval times, guests brought their own knives to feasts, and many foods were eaten with the fingers. Diners often shared cups and dishes. Musicians, acrobats, and jugglers provided entertainment.

Manor House
A lord's house could be built of wood, stone, or clay bricks.

Village
These houses were usually made of wood and roofed with thatch—tightly bundled straw or reeds.

Mill
Peasants paid a fee to grind their grain.

Fields
Crops were planted in strips in two fields. A third field lay fallow, or unplanted.

Assessment

Describe What are the characteristics of a medieval manor?

Draw Conclusions Describe the relationship between the nobles and peasants. How did they depend upon one another and on the manor's lands?

Chapter 14 **401**

Ask students to carefully examine the illustration of a manor feast on this page, and reread its accompanying caption. Then ask students to think about the ways in which meals in their homes today are similar or different. Conduct an Idea Wave (TE, p. T39) to elicit student responses, and then list them on the board.

Answers

Assessment

Describe Medieval manors included the lord's home and homes of the peasants and serfs, a mill, a chapel or church, a bakery, and usually surrounding fields for growing crops, and woodlands.
Drawing Conclusions Nobles depended on the peasants to produce goods so that the nobles could use them to pay taxes to higher nobles and the king. Peasants depended on the lands to produce goods that they used to pay what they owed to the nobles.

Section 2
Step-by-Step Instruction

Objectives
Social Studies
1. Learn why the Roman Catholic Church was so important and powerful during the Middle Ages.
2. Discover the connection between an increase in trade and the growth of towns.
3. Find out what life was like in a medieval town.
4. Understand the role of culture and learning in the Middle Ages.

Reading/Language Arts
Identify the sequence of events to help you understand and remember them.

Prepare to Read

Build Background Knowledge **L2**
Tell students that in this section they will learn about the role of the Roman Catholic Church in the Middle Ages. Display *Color Transparencies HOW 35 and 36*. Ask students to describe what they see and discuss the cathedral's features.

📖 **History of Our World Transparencies,** *Color Transparency HOW 35; Color Transparency HOW 36*

Set a Purpose for Reading **L2**
■ Preview the Objectives.

■ Read each statement in the *Reading Readiness Guide* aloud. Ask students to mark the statements true or false.

■ Have students discuss the statements in pairs or groups of four, then mark their guides again. Use the Numbered Heads participation strategy (TE, p. T40) to call on students to share their group's perspectives.

All in One Unit 5 History of Our World Teaching Resources, *Reading Readiness Guide,* p. 12

Vocabulary Builder
Preview Key Terms **L2**
Pronounce each Key Term, then ask the students to say the word with you. Provide a simple explanation such as, "An apprentice works for free in exchange for being trained to learn a certain trade."

Section 2
The Church and the Rise of Cities

Prepare to Read

Objectives
In this section you will
1. Learn why the Roman Catholic Church was so important and powerful during the Middle Ages.
2. Discover the connection between an increase in trade and the growth of towns.
3. Find out what life was like in a medieval town.
4. Understand the role of culture and learning in the Middle Ages.

Taking Notes
As you read this section, think about what caused towns to grow in the Middle Ages and the effects of this growth. Copy the diagram below and record your findings in it.

CAUSES		EVENT		EFFECTS
•	→	**TOWNS GROW**	→	•
•				•

🎯 Target Reading Skill
Identify Sequence
Noting the order in which significant events occur can help you understand and remember them. You can track the order of events by making a list. Then use signal words and dates in the text to make sure your events are listed in the correct order.

Key Terms
- **clergy** (KLUR jee) *n.* persons with authority to perform religious services
- **excommunication** (eks kuh myoo nih KAY shun) *n.* expelling someone from the Church
- **guild** (gild) *n.* a medieval organization of crafts workers or tradespeople
- **apprentice** (uh PREN tis) *n.* an unpaid person training in a craft or trade
- **chivalry** (SHIV ul ree) *n.* the code of honorable conduct for knights
- **troubadour** (TROO buh dawr) *n.* a traveling poet and musician of the Middle Ages

The cathedral at Chartres, France, still dominates the city.

402 History of Our World

Tall spires reach toward the heavens. Gorgeous stained-glass windows feature rich colors. Sculptures and carvings of people, plants, and animals seem to be everywhere. Amazing flying buttresses—masses of stonework or brickwork attached to the walls—help hold the building up. What is this building? It is a Gothic cathedral.

Even today, these huge medieval churches dominate towns in many parts of Europe. During the Middle Ages, cathedrals were built not only to glorify God but also to be a credit to their city. Entire communities worked for decades to build the biggest, tallest, most beautiful cathedral.

Once completed, a cathedral served as a house of worship, a gathering place, and even as a religious school. Its beautiful glass windows and sculptures told Bible stories and presented the lives of the saints to a population that could not read or write.

🎯 Target Reading Skill **L2**

Identify Sequence Point out the Target Reading Skill. Explain that identifying the sequence of events can help you understand and remember them.

Model the skill by reading The Revival of Trade on p. 406 and listing in order the events that led to the revival of trade. (*People felt safe; people traveled to distant places, such as Asia; they brought goods back from Asia;* *Europeans began wanting more of these goods; ancient trade routes came into use again; merchants traveled to trade for these goods.*)

Give students *Identify Sequence*. Have them complete the activity in groups.

All in One Unit 5 History of Our World Teaching Resources, *Identify Sequence,* p. 24

The Church in the Middle Ages

Most Gothic cathedrals were built in Western Europe between 1100 and 1400. *Gothic* refers to the style of architecture, as you can see in the Eyewitness Technology feature on page 404. A cathedral was the church of a bishop, an important leader of the Roman Catholic Church. During the Middle Ages, nearly all people in Western Europe were Roman Catholic. The Roman Catholic Church had so much influence that it was known simply as "the Church." Why was the Church so powerful? There were many reasons.

Religious and Economic Power During the Middle Ages, life was short and hard for most people. They were comforted by the Christian belief that they would enjoy the rewards of heaven after death if they lived according to Church teachings. The Church also held that if people *didn't* obey those rules, they would be punished after death. The promise of reward combined with the threat of punishment made most people follow the teachings of the Church.

The Church also had great economic power. It gained great wealth by collecting taxes. It also took fiefs from lords in exchange for services performed by **clergy**, or persons with authority to perform religious services. In fact, the Church was the single largest owner of land in Europe during the Middle Ages.

Political Power of the Church The combination of religious and economic power enabled the Church to take on many of the roles that government performs today. It even made laws and set up courts to enforce them. People who did not obey the Church were threatened with being excommunicated. **Excommunication** means being expelled from membership in the Church and participation in Church life. This was a very serious threat. Few people would associate with someone who had been excommunicated.

High Church officials were advisors to kings and lords. The ever-present threat of excommunication gave Church officials great influence in political matters. The Church used its authority to limit feudal warfare. It declared periods of truce, or temporary peace. That was one reason warfare began to decline during the 1100s.

Teaching Tool
This stained glass window in Canterbury Cathedral, England, shows the three kings following a star to the birth of Jesus. **Infer** *How might this window have helped medieval people understand Church teachings?*

The Church in the Middle Ages

L2

Guided Instruction

- **Vocabulary Builder** Clarify the high-use words **expel, authority,** and **dedicate** before reading.

- Read The Church in the Middle Ages, using the Request Procedure (TE, p. T39).

- Discuss the reasons why most Western Europeans followed the teachings of the Roman Catholic Church. *(Life for people in the Middle Ages was short and hard. They were comforted by the Roman Catholic belief that they would go to heaven if they followed the Church's teachings. They also feared punishment after death for not following the Church's teachings.)*

- Ask **What gave the Church so much political power?** *(the combination of its religious power and the economic power it obtained from collecting taxes and being the single largest landowner in Europe)*

- Ask students to make a prediction about the role of the Roman Catholic Church in daily life during the Middle Ages. *(Possible answer: The Roman Catholic Church probably affected most aspects of people's daily lives because the Church held religious, economic, and political power in Europe.)*

Vocabulary Builder

Use the information below to teach students this section's high-use words.

High-Use Word	Definition and Sample Sentence
expel, p. 403	*v.* to force to leave The principal warned that he would **expel** students who disobeyed school rules.
authority, p. 405	*n.* power, control The general had **authority** over the conquered region.
dedicate, 405	*v.* to devote to the worship of a divine being The priest vowed to **dedicate** his life to God.
prevent, p. 407	*v.* to keep from happening Jay put the food in the freezer to **prevent** it from spoiling.

Answer

Infer Possible answer: The window helped teach people who could not read about the story of Jesus' birth.

Gothic Cathedral

Guided Instruction

L2

Read the introductory paragraph aloud as a class and study the diagram and other images. Then have student volunteers take turns reading each caption aloud. Tell students to answer the Analyzing Images question individually. Then allow them to share their answers with their neighbor.

Independent Practice

Have students do Internet or library research to find photos and information about another Gothic cathedral built in the Middle Ages, such as those in Chartres, France, or Canterbury, England. Ask them to write a brief report about the cathedral, including why and when it was built and any other information unique to the cathedral. Tell them to include photos, illustrations, or tracings of the cathedral in their reports.

Gothic Cathedral

In the mid 1100s, Northern Europeans began to build large stone churches in a new style, called Gothic. This style allowed walls to be thinner and higher. The Gothic cathedral was an expression of medieval religion, and became a symbol of European medieval society.

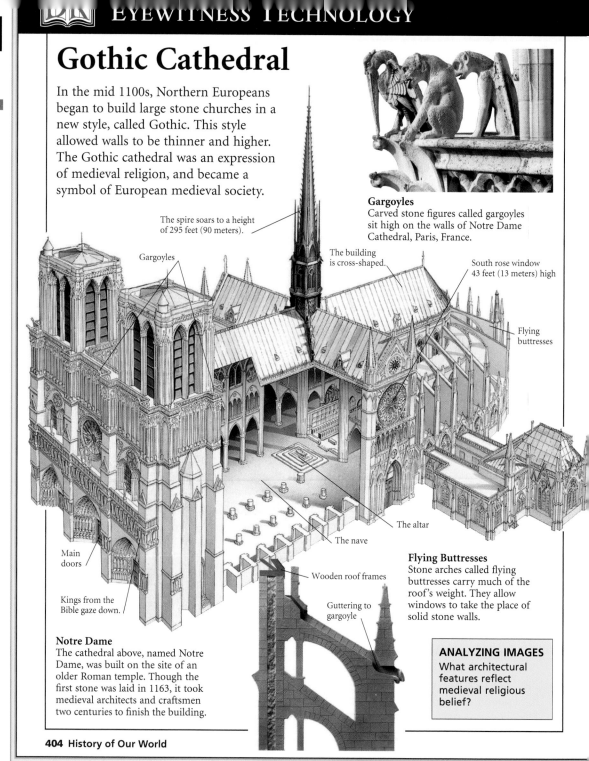

Gargoyles
Carved stone figures called gargoyles sit high on the walls of Notre Dame Cathedral, Paris, France.

The spire soars to a height of 295 feet (90 meters).

Gargoyles

The building is cross-shaped.

South rose window 43 feet (13 meters) high

Flying buttresses

The altar

The nave

Main doors

Wooden roof frames

Kings from the Bible gaze down.

Guttering to gargoyle

Flying Buttresses
Stone arches called flying buttresses carry much of the roof's weight. They allow windows to take the place of solid stone walls.

Notre Dame
The cathedral above, named Notre Dame, was built on the site of an older Roman temple. Though the first stone was laid in 1163, it took medieval architects and craftsmen two centuries to finish the building.

ANALYZING IMAGES
What architectural features reflect medieval religious belief?

404 History of Our World

Differentiated Instruction

For Gifted and Talented

L3

Challenge students to make a three-dimensional model of a cathedral using clay, cardboard, or another medium of their choice. Tell them to use the diagram on this page as a guide. Encourage students to research other cathedrals as well for further guidance.

Answer

Analyze Images features of the Gothic style of architecture, including soaring spires

Church Organization The Church was highly organized. Almost every village had a priest. A bishop supervised several priests and an archbishop supervised several bishops. Finally, the archbishops were under the authority of the pope. The papacy, or government of the Church, was based in Rome. These areas of Church authority overlapped and crossed the boundaries of kingdoms. Thus, the Church had power in every kingdom, every fief, and every village.

The Church in Everyday Life The medieval Church touched nearly all aspects of life. Think of any major event—the birth of a child, a serious illness, a marriage, or a death. During the Middle Ages, the clergy were almost always in attendance to offer a blessing or to perform a service.

The clergy helped people follow Church rules about how to live. They also listened when people came to church to confess their sins. In the name of God, the clergy then forgave them for the wrongs to which they had confessed.

Monasteries and Convents Some religious men felt that they should dedicate their lives to God by living together in religious communities called monasteries. Religious women, called nuns, lived in similar communities called convents. This form of religious life is called monasticism.

These religious communities developed better ways of growing crops and tending livestock. In this way, the Church helped improve the economy of the Middle Ages, which was based mostly on farming. Monks and nuns also looked after the sick and set up schools. Monks were more educated than most people. Because they copied books from ancient times, they preserved knowledge that otherwise would have been lost. Convents gave women a rare opportunity to become educated.

Scholasticism Some Christian scholars studied ancient Greek texts that said people should use reason to discover truth. However, the Church taught that many ideas must be accepted on faith. These medieval scholars worked out a system that tried to resolve the two philosophies. Called scholasticism, it used reason to support Christian beliefs.

✓ **Reading Check** What were monasteries and convents?

Medieval Wedding
In the Middle Ages, ceremonies such as weddings had to be performed by a priest. **Conclude** How did this requirement increase Church power?

This detail from a medieval manuscript shows a monk copying a manuscript.

- Ask **Which official had the most authority in the Church?** *(the pope)*

- Have students list the major events for which Roman Catholic clergy offered their services. *(births, deaths, illnesses, and marriages)*

- Ask students **What unique opportunity did convents offer to women?** *(the opportunity to receive an education)*

- Ask students to create a cause and effect chart similar to the one on p. 402 to help them see the relationship between the events explained in Scholasticism. *(Cause: Christian scholars respected Greek texts that said people should use reason to discover truth, while the Church taught that some ideas must be accepted on faith. Effect: Scholars worked out a system called scholasticism that used reason to support Christian beliefs.)*

Independent Practice
Assign *Guided Reading and Review.*

All in One **Unit 5 History of Our World Teaching Resources,** *Guided Reading and Review,* p. 13

Monitor Progress
Circulate and make sure students are correctly answering the questions. Provide assistance as needed.

Differentiated Instruction

For Less Proficient Readers **L1**
Pair less proficient readers with more proficient students and have them make a table showing the organization of the Roman Catholic Church. Tell them to place the highest ranking official at the top and the lowest ranking at the bottom. Remind them to include a title for their table.

Answers

Conclude It gave the Church power in more aspects of everyday life.

✓ **Reading Check** Monasteries and convents were religious communities where people who wanted to dedicate their lives to God lived and worked. Men lived in monasteries and women lived in convents.

Trade Revives and Towns Grow L2

Guided Instruction

- Have students read Trade Revives and Towns Grow.

- Ask **Why did people begin to travel more in Western Europe?** (*Feudalism and the Church had stabilized the region, making it a safer place.*) **Explain how this led to the revival of trade.** (*People brought back desirable goods from the places they visited and introduced them to their region. People then began to want more of these goods, leading to the revival of trade for them.*)

- **Discuss the two major reasons for the growth of towns.** (*An increase in trade and overcrowding of manors led to the growth of towns. Towns grew into busy trade meeting places, such as river crossings. As manors became crowded, it became difficult to provide food and clothing for everyone who lived there, so lords encouraged peasants to buy their freedom and move to the new towns.*)

- Draw students' attention to the map on p. 406. Point out that many of the major trade centers are located on the coast. Ask students to explain why they think this is so. (*Possible answer: It may have been easier for traders to travel by sea to reach meeting places rather than to travel over the often mountainous terrain of Western Europe.*)

Independent Practice

Ask students to create the Taking Notes graphic organizer on a separate piece of paper. Tell them to fill in the first box with the causes of town growth. Briefly model how to record information on the chart.

Monitor Progress

As students fill in the graphic organizer, circulate and make sure individuals are choosing the correct details. Provide assistance as needed.

Answers

MAP MASTER Skills Activity **Identify** inland; near the coast **Infer** Possible answer: Their locations on or near the coast of the Mediterranean Sea made them easily accessible by boat.

Go Online PHSchool.com Students may practice their map skills using the interactive online version of this map.

This beautiful bottle from Syria, made in the 1300s, would have been a valued trade item.

Trade Revives and Towns Grow

By about A.D. 1000—the middle of the Middle Ages—feudalism was well established in Europe and the Church was a stabilizing force. Europe was becoming a safer place, and the population was growing.

The Revival of Trade As people felt safer, they began to travel more and learn more about distant places. As you will read in Section 3, the crusaders brought many desirable goods back from Asia. Europeans began to demand such things as spices and cloth that they could get only from Africa and Asia. Ancient trade routes came into use again. European merchants traveled abroad to buy and sell valued goods.

The Growth of Towns At first, local goods were traded in the markets of small villages. As trade grew, so did these markets. Some developed into major trade fairs. You can find these market towns on the map below.

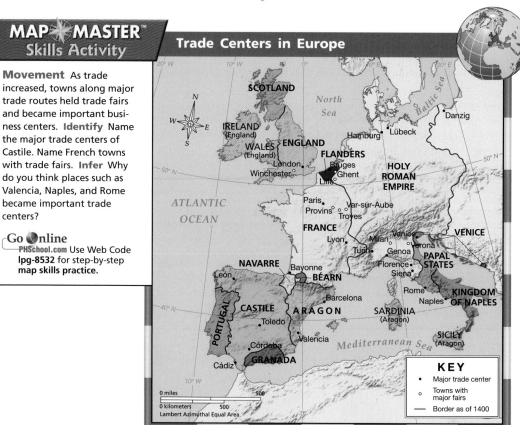

MAP MASTER Skills Activity

Trade Centers in Europe

Movement As trade increased, towns along major trade routes held trade fairs and became important business centers. **Identify** Name the major trade centers of Castile. Name French towns with trade fairs. **Infer** Why do you think places such as Valencia, Naples, and Rome became important trade centers?

Go Online PHSchool.com Use Web Code lpg-8532 for step-by-step map skills practice.

KEY
- Major trade center
- ○ Towns with major fairs
- — Border as of 1400

0 miles 500
0 kilometers 500
Lambert Azimuthal Equal Area

Differentiated Instruction

For Advanced Readers L3

Display *Color Transparency HOW 23: Western Europe: Physical-Political.* Ask students to compare the borders of today with the borders from the past shown on the map on p. 406. Tell them to write three quiz questions asking which kingdoms and empires made up modern-day countries.

For example, students could ask **In which modern-day country was the kingdom of Aragon located?** (*Spain*) Have students exchange their quizzes with a partner and answer each others' questions.

📖 **History of Our World Transparencies,** *Color Transparency HOW 23: Western Europe: Physical-Political*

Traders also gathered at convenient places for travelers, such as river crossings and along highways. They chose important monasteries and fortified places built by nobles. Before long, towns developed in these locations, too.

Also during this time, many manors were becoming overcrowded. Providing food and clothing for everyone on the manor became difficult. Many lords gladly allowed peasants to buy their freedom and move to the new, growing towns.

✓ **Reading Check** Why did towns begin to grow?

Life in Towns and Cities

By about 1300, many towns in Western Europe were growing into cities. Paris, with a population approaching 300,000, was the largest city in the world.

The Rise of a Middle Class Town life was not at all like farm or manor life. Towns and cities were not self-sufficient. Instead, their economies were based on the exchange of money for goods and services. A new class of people developed, made up of merchants, traders, and crafts workers. In status, it was between nobles and peasants, and so it was called the *middle class.*

The Role of Guilds In many towns and cities, the merchants, traders, and crafts workers began to form associations called guilds. A **guild** included all the people who practiced a certain trade or craft. Thus there was a guild of weavers, a guild of grocers, a guild of shoemakers, and so on.

Guilds set prices and prevented outsiders from selling goods in town. They set standards for the quality of their goods. Guild members paid dues. This money was used to help needy members or to support the families of members who had died.

It took a long time to become a member of a guild. Between the ages of 8 and 14, a boy who wanted to learn a certain trade became an **apprentice**, or unpaid worker being trained in a craft. He lived and worked in the home of a master of that trade for as long as seven years. Then he could become a journeyman, or salaried worker. In time, if guild officials judged that the journeyman's work met their standards, he could join the guild.

Shops in a Paris Street
Notice the many kinds of shops in Paris in the early 1500s. Merchants were becoming an important part of society at this time. **Generalize** *What types of goods were available in European cities in the 1500s?*

◄ **A shield representing the Guild of Notaries, who prepared and verified documents**

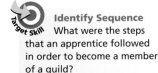

Identify Sequence What were the steps that an apprentice followed in order to become a member of a guild?

Background: Global Perspectives

Higher Learning The first university in Europe was founded in Bologna, Italy, during the 1000s. Universities had the right to explore all academic subjects without interference from the government or the Church. However, universities paid a price for their freedom—they received no funding from the government or the Church. As a result, university teachers had to charge fees for their services. They also had to be sure they satisfied their students so that they would not leave to attend another university.

Life in Towns and Cities ▣

Medieval Culture ▣

Guided Instruction

■ **Vocabulary Builder** Clarify the high-use word **prevent** before reading.

■ Read Life in Towns and Cities and Medieval Culture as a class.

■ Ask students to describe the middle class. *(the class of people who were between nobles and peasants that included merchants, traders, and crafts workers)*

■ Discuss the role of guilds in Medieval towns and cities. *(Guilds allowed people in the same business to work together for common goals. They helped support needy members, train new members, and standardized prices and the quality of goods.)*

Independent Practice

Ask students to complete their graphic organizer with the information they have just learned.

Monitor Progress

■ Show *Section Reading Support Transparency HOW 97* and ask students to check their graphic organizers individually. Go over key concepts and clarify key vocabulary as needed.

📖 **History of Our World Transparencies,** *Section Reading Support Transparency HOW 97*

■ Tell students to fill in the last column of the *Reading Readiness Guide.* Probe for what they learned that confirms or invalidates each statement.

All in One Unit 5 History of Our World Teaching Resources, *Reading Readiness Guide,* p. 12

↪ Target Reading Skill

Identify Sequence As a follow up, ask students to answer the Target Reading Skill question in the Student Edition. *(A boy became an apprentice for up to seven years. Then he became a salaried worker, or journeyman. If guild members thought his work met standards, he was then invited to join the guild.)*

Answer

Generalize A variety of items produced by crafts workers

Assess and Reteach

Assess Progress　L2

Have students complete the Section Assessment. Administer the *Section Quiz.*

All in One Unit 5 History of Our World Teaching Resources, *Section Quiz,* p. 14

Reteach　L1

If students need more instruction, have them read this section in the Reading and Vocabulary Study Guide.

Chapter 14, Section 2, **History of Our World Reading and Vocabulary Study Guide,** pp. 151–153

Extend　L3

Assign the *Enrichment* activity in which students will learn about the history of Vatican City.

All in One Unit 5 History of Our World Teaching Resources, *Enrichment,* p. 26

Answers

√ Reading Check a disease called the bubonic plague which was spread by fleas and killed one third of Europe's population

√ Reading Check Cities attracted traveling scholars and were centers for learning and art.

Section 2 Assessment

Key Terms
Students' sentences should reflect knowledge of each Key Term.

Target Reading Skill
growth of trade, gathering of traders at convenient places for travelers, overcrowding of manors

Comprehension and Critical Thinking
1. (a) The Church touched nearly all aspects of life, providing services for many major events including births and marriages.
(b) The influence of the Church in everyday life increased its power.
2. (a) The region became safer, leading to increased travel and exposure to new goods that people wanted. **(b)** Possible answer: An ordinary person might have access to a new variety of goods.

3. (a) associations formed by merchants, traders, and crafts workers **(b)** Possible answer: Since consumers knew that guild members' goods met quality standards, they might have preferred to buy goods from a member, increasing the member's business.

4. (a) the code of honorable conduct by which knights were supposed to live
(b) Possible answer: People probably considered stories of chivalry to be exciting and entertaining.

Troubadours provided entertainment and preserved traditional tales.

Overcrowding and Disease Medieval towns and cities were extremely crowded. Their lack of sanitation, or procedures for keeping the town clean, bred disease, and the overcrowded conditions meant that disease spread quickly. One disease, the bubonic plague, wiped out one third of Europe's population between 1347 and 1351. Called the Black Death, it was spread by fleas living on the rats that thrived in the unsanitary towns.

√ Reading Check **What was the Black Death?**

Medieval Culture

Despite its hardships, medieval life was not all a struggle for survival. The growing cities attracted traveling scholars, and young men flocked to cathedral schools. Many of these schools became great centers of learning. Much of the beautiful artwork of the Middle Ages was displayed in churches where many could enjoy it.

Stories, poems, and songs about chivalry were also very popular. **Chivalry** is the code of honorable conduct by which knights were supposed to live. Throughout Western Europe, traveling poets and musicians called **troubadours** went from place to place singing about the brave deeds performed by knights to win the love of a beautiful and worthy woman.

√ Reading Check **Describe some advantages of living in a medieval city.**

Section 2 Assessment

Key Terms
Review the key terms at the beginning of this section. Use each term in a sentence that explains its meaning.

Target Reading Skill
Identify and list in sequence three events or conditions that led to the growth of towns.

Comprehension and Critical Thinking
1. (a) Recall How was the Church important in everyday life?

(b) Identify Effects How did this importance contribute to the Church's power?
2. (a) List What factors led to the increase in trade in Western Europe?
(b) Infer How might the growth of trade have affected the life of an ordinary person?
3. (a) Define What were guilds?
(b) Draw Conclusions Why would someone join a guild?
4. (a) Explain What was chivalry?
(b) Infer Why was chivalry a popular topic for troubadours?

Writing Activity
During the Middle Ages, children began apprenticeships as early as the age of eight. Do you think that is too young an age to start such work? Write a paragraph that answers this question.

> **Writing Tip** Begin your paragraph with a topic sentence that tells whether or not you think eight years old is too young. Use supporting sentences to give reasons for your position.

408 History of Our World

Writing Activity
Use the *Rubric for Assessing a Writing Assignment* to evaluate students' paragraphs.

All in One Unit 5 History of Our World Teaching Resources, *Rubric for Assessing a Writing Assignment,* p. 35

The Crusades

Prepare to Read

Objectives
In this section you will
1. Learn about the causes of the Crusades.
2. Find out about the different Crusades and what they accomplished.
3. Discover the effects the Crusades had on life in Europe.

Taking Notes
As you read this section, look for the ways various people or groups contributed to the Crusades. Copy the table below and record your findings in it.

Person or Group	Contribution

Target Reading Skill
Recognize Sequence Signal Words Signal words point out relationships between ideas or events. This section discusses the Crusades, which took place over many years. To help keep the order of events clear, look for words such as *first, then, finally,* and *in [date]* that signal the order in which the events took place.

Key Terms
- **Holy Land** (HOH lee land) *n.* Jerusalem and parts of the surrounding area where Jesus lived and taught
- **Crusades** (kroo SAYDZ) *n.* a series of military expeditions launched by Christian Europeans to win the Holy Land back from Muslim control
- **Jerusalem** (juh ROOZ uh lum) *n.* a city in the Holy Land, regarded as sacred by Christians, Muslims, and Jews
- **pilgrim** (PIL grum) *n.* a person who journeys to a sacred place

On November 18, 1095, a crowd gathered in the town of Clermont, located in present-day France. They came to hear an urgent message from the pope:

> "You common people who have been miserable sinners, become soldiers of Christ! You nobles, do not [quarrel] with one another. Use your arms in a just war! Labor for everlasting reward."
>
> —*Pope Urban II*

The crowd roared its approval. They shouted, "God wills it!"

Pope Urban II was calling the people of Europe to war. The purpose of this war was to capture the **Holy Land,** a region sacred to Christians because Jesus had lived and taught there. It was a small region on the eastern shore of the Mediterranean Sea, in present-day Israel, Jordan, and Palestine. Now, said the pope, the Holy Land has fallen to an enemy. Christians must win it back.

Pope Urban II calling for a crusade to the Holy Land

Chapter 14 Section 3 **409**

Objectives
Social Studies
1. Learn about the causes of the Crusades.
2. Find out about the different Crusades and what they accomplished.
3. Discover the effects the Crusades had on life in Europe.

Reading/Language Arts
Recognize sequence signal words to help build an understanding of the relationships between ideas and events.

Prepare to Read

Build Background Knowledge L2
In this section, students will learn about the Crusades. Ask students to preview the headings, map, and other visuals in the section. Then tell them to write five questions they would like to have answered that will help them remember important information from the section. Students can use these questions to fill in the second columns of their *Reading Readiness Guides.* Ask students to answer the questions as they read the section.

Set a Purpose for Reading L2
- Preview the Objectives.
- Form students into pairs or groups of four. Distribute the *Reading Readiness Guide.* Ask the students to fill in the first two columns of the chart. Use the Numbered Heads participation strategy (TE, p. T40) to call on students to share one piece of information they already know and one piece of information they want to know.

All in One Unit 5 History of Our World Teaching Resources, *Reading Readiness Guide,* p. 16

Vocabulary Builder
Preview Key Terms L2
Pronounce each Key Term, then ask the students to say the word with you. Provide a simple explanation such as, "Pilgrims have traveled to Jerusalem for many centuries because it is considered to be a holy place."

Target Reading Skill L2
Recognize Sequence Signal Words Point out the Target Reading Skill. Tell students that recognizing sequence signal words will help them find the relationship between events or ideas.

Model the skill by identifying the signal words in Later Crusades on p. 412 *(then, by 1187).*

Give students *Recognize Sequence Signal Words.* Have them complete the activity in groups.

All in One Unit 5 History of Our World Teaching Resources, *Recognize Sequence Signal Words,* p. 23

Instruct

Causes of the Crusades L2

Guided Instruction

- **Vocabulary Builder** Clarify the high-use words **launch** and **prestige** before reading.

- Read Causes of the Crusades, using the Paragraph Shrinking strategy (TE, p. T38). As students read, circulate and make sure individuals can answer the Reading Check question.

- Ask **What were the Crusades?** *(eight military expeditions started by the Church to capture the Holy Land)* **What city in the Holy Land attracted religious pilgrims?** *(Jerusalem)*

- Ask students to identify the religious groups that considered Jerusalem sacred. *(Christians, Muslims, and Jews)*

- Have students contrast the ways Arab Muslims and Seljuk Turks treated Christian pilgrims. *(Arab Muslims allowed Christian pilgrims to visit Jerusalem, while the Seljuk Turks sometimes attacked pilgrims and eventually closed pilgrimage routes.)*

Answer

Conclude Possible answer: Many people had to work to load the boats with supplies the large army would need.

Embarking on a Crusade
Huge armies of crusader knights sailed to the Holy Land.
Conclude *What was involved in transporting these large armies?*

Causes of the Crusades

Over the next 200 years, the Church launched eight military expeditions, called the **Crusades**, to capture the Holy Land. The word comes from *crux*, the Latin word for "cross." People who carried the Christian cross into battle against the non-Christian enemy were called crusaders.

Pilgrims to the Holy Land Since about A.D. 200, European Christians had been traveling to **Jerusalem**, a city in the Holy Land regarded as sacred by Christians, Muslims, and Jews. These people were **pilgrims**—people who journey to a sacred place. Nobles and peasants alike made the long and difficult journey. They wanted to visit the places written about in the Bible.

The Rise of the Turks For centuries, Jerusalem had been controlled by Arab Muslims who generally welcomed Christian pilgrims. Then, in the 1000s, the Seljuk Turks (SEL jook turks) took control of the Holy Land. This Muslim group sometimes attacked the Christian pilgrims from Europe. Then they closed the pilgrimage routes to Jerusalem.

At the same time, the Turks were also conquering much of the Byzantine Empire. The Byzantine emperor in Constantinople asked Pope Urban II to send knights to defend his Christian empire. The pope agreed and called on the people of Europe to fight the Muslim Turks.

Many medieval Christians believed that Jerusalem was the center of the world, as this map from the 1200s shows.

410 History of Our World

Vocabulary Builder

Use the information below to teach students this section's high-use words.

High-Use Word	Definition and Sample Sentence
launch, p. 410	*v.* to set in motion The candidate **launched** a campaign to help her win the election.
prestige, p. 411	*n.* a commanding position in people's minds Pat gained **prestige** for himself by consistently earning the highest grades in the class.
advise, p. 412	*v.* to give a recommendation The coach **advised** Jim to swing at a fastball, not a curveball.

Why Go to War? Why did Pope Urban II agree to organize a war against the Muslim Turks? Mainly, he wanted the Holy Land to be under the control of Christians. He wanted Christian pilgrims to be able to visit Jerusalem and other religious sites.

But he also had other reasons. The pope thought a crusade would unite Europeans against a common enemy—the Muslim Turks—and they would stop fighting among themselves. He also hoped to gain power and prestige for himself and the Church.

Some Europeans had other reasons for encouraging the Crusades. They wanted to control not only the Holy Land but also key trade routes between Africa, Asia, and Europe.

✓ **Reading Check** Why did the pope want to conquer the Holy Land?

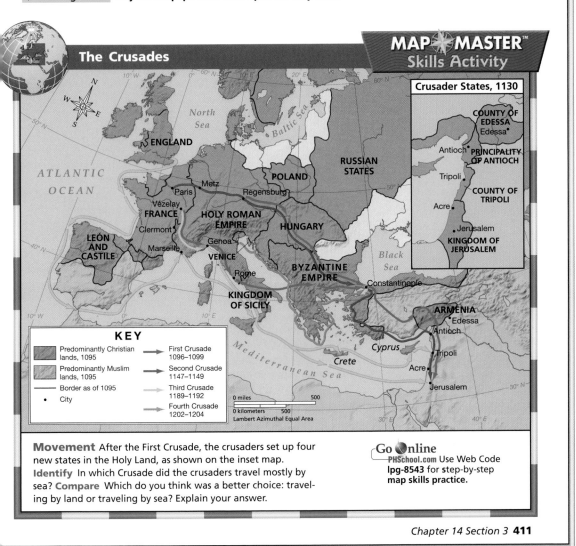

The Crusades

MAP MASTER™
Skills Activity

Crusader States, 1130

COUNTY OF EDESSA
Edessa•
Antioch• **PRINCIPALITY OF ANTIOCH**
Tripoli•
COUNTY OF TRIPOLI
Acre•
•Jerusalem
KINGDOM OF JERUSALEM

North Sea
Baltic Sea
ATLANTIC OCEAN
ENGLAND
RUSSIAN STATES
POLAND
Metz• Regensburg•
Paris•
Vézelay•
FRANCE
HOLY ROMAN EMPIRE
HUNGARY
Clermont•
Genoa•
LEÓN AND CASTILE
Marseille•
VENICE
•Rome
Black Sea
BYZANTINE EMPIRE
Constantinople•
KINGDOM OF SICILY
ARMENIA
•Edessa
Antioch•
Cyprus
Crete
Tripoli•
Mediterranean Sea
Acre•
Jerusalem•

KEY

Predominantly Christian lands, 1095
Predominantly Muslim lands, 1095
Border as of 1095
• City

→ First Crusade 1096–1099
→ Second Crusade 1147–1149
→ Third Crusade 1189–1192
→ Fourth Crusade 1202–1204

0 miles 500
0 kilometers 500
Lambert Azimuthal Equal Area

Movement After the First Crusade, the crusaders set up four new states in the Holy Land, as shown on the inset map. **Identify** In which Crusade did the crusaders travel mostly by sea? **Compare** Which do you think was a better choice: traveling by land or traveling by sea? Explain your answer.

Go Online
PHSchool.com Use Web Code lpg-8543 for step-by-step map skills practice.

Chapter 14 Section 3 **411**

Guided Instruction (continued)

■ Ask **How did the Turks' attack on the Byzantine Empire help trigger the Crusades?** *(The Byzantine emperor in Constantinople asked Pope Urban II to send knights to help Constantinople defend against an attack by Muslim Turks. Pope Urban II agreed to help and declared war against the Turks, who were also occupying the Holy Land.)*

■ Discuss the three reasons why Pope Urban II wanted to control the Holy Land. *(He wanted Christian pilgrims to be able to visit Jerusalem; he thought that if Europeans united against a common enemy, they would stop fighting each other; he wanted to gain power and prestige for himself and the Church.)*

Independent Practice

Ask students to create the Taking Notes graphic organizer on a blank piece of paper. Then have them fill in the table with information about the people and groups they have just read about. Briefly model how to identify which details to record.

Monitor Progress

As students fill in the graphic organizer, circulate and make sure individuals are filling in the appropriate information. Help students as needed.

Answers

✓ **Reading Check** The Pope wanted to conquer the Holy Land to enable Christian pilgrims to visit Jerusalem. He also hoped that Europeans would unite against a common enemy and stop fighting each other, and he hoped to gain power and prestige for himself and the Church.

MAP MASTER™ **Skills Activity** **Identify** the Third Crusade **Compare** Some students may think that traveling by sea was easier because at the time of the Crusades, people did not have modern means of transportation for travel by land. Others might suggest that traveling by land might be easier because Crusaders could sometimes take shorter routes.

Go Online PHSchool.com Students may practice their map skills using the interactive online version of this map.

Target Reading Skill

Recognize Sequence Signal Words As a follow up, ask students to answer the Target Reading Skill question in the Student Edition. *(before; Possible answer: It tells you that the events explained in the next paragraph happened before the events explained in the paragraphs that follow.)*

A Series of Crusades `L2`

The Results of the Crusades `L2`

Guided Instruction

- **Vocabulary Builder** Clarify the high-use word **advise** before reading.

- Read A Series of Crusades and The Results of the Crusades as a class.

- Ask students to compare and contrast the First and Second Crusades. *(Both Crusades were launched to gain control of Jerusalem. The First Crusade succeeded while the Second Crusade had little success.)*

- Have students choose one effect of the Crusades and explain why it was important to Europe. *(Effects include revival of trade, growth of cities, increased use of money, introduction of new ideas and technology.)*

Independent Practice

Ask students to complete their organizers with the information they have just learned.

Monitor Progress

- Show *Section Reading Support Transparency HOW 98* and ask students to check their graphic organizers individually. Go over key concepts and clarify key vocabulary as needed.

  📖 **History of Our World Transparencies,** *Section Reading Support Transparency HOW 98*

- Tell students to fill in the last column of the *Reading Readiness Guide*. Ask them to evaluate if what they learned was what they had expected to learn.

  AllinOne **Unit 5 History of Our World Teaching Resources,** *Reading Readiness Guide,* p. 16

Answer

✓ **Reading Check** He said that Jerusalem was as important to Muslims as it was to Christians.

Recognize Sequence Signal Words What word in the paragraph at the right signals sequence? How does this clue help you understand the next few paragraphs?

A Series of Crusades

The pope's best hope for capturing the Holy Land rested with European lords and their knights. But before these armies could assemble, a band of common people set out for Jerusalem.

Peter the Hermit and the People's Crusade Peter, a small man who wore monk's robes, gathered an "army" of common people. They set out in 1096. When they got to Constantinople, the Byzantine emperor advised them to wait for help from an army of knights from Europe. Peter agreed, but his followers rebelled. His soldiers attacked the Turks, who easily defeated them. Only a small part of his army survived.

Crusaders led by Louis IX of France retake the city of Damietta, near Jerusalem.

The First Crusade At last, the European armies sent by Pope Urban II reached Constantinople. Joined by what remained of Peter's army, the knights fought their way to Jerusalem and captured it in 1099. While taking control of the city, the crusaders killed about 10,000 of its Muslim, Christian, and Jewish inhabitants.

After the capture of Jerusalem, most of the crusaders returned to Europe. Those who stayed in the Holy Land set up four Christian kingdoms. The Muslim Turks attacked these kingdoms repeatedly. European Christians then launched more Crusades to keep control of the region.

Later Crusades The Second Crusade had little success. Then a strong Arab Muslim leader rose to power. He was known to the Europeans as Saladin (SAL uh din). By 1187, Saladin had retaken Jerusalem. King Richard I of England tried to persuade Saladin to return the Holy City to the Christians. Saladin refused, saying,

> "To us Jerusalem is as precious . . . as it is to you, because it is the place from where our Prophet [Muhammad] made his journey by night to heaven. . . . Do not dream that we will give it up to you. "
>
> —*Saladin*

Even so, Saladin negotiated a treaty with King Richard. He agreed to reopen Jerusalem to Christian pilgrims.

✓ **Reading Check** Why did Saladin refuse to give up Jerusalem?

Skills for Life ## Skills Mini Lesson

Identifying Frame of Reference and Point of View

1. Teach the skill by explaining that point of view is an opinion or perspective on a topic and frame of reference is a person's background. Frame of reference often affects point of view.

2. Help students practice the skill by identifying the topic of the Saladin quote on p. 412 *(control of Jerusalem)* and his point of view on the topic *(He felt that Muslims should control Jerusalem.)*

3. Have students apply the skill by identifying Saladin's frame of reference and how it might have affected his point of view.

The Results of the Crusades

Although crusaders did capture the Holy Land for a while, they were never able to gain firm control of it. Still, the Crusades brought important and lasting changes to Europe.

Increased Trade The European ships that carried crusaders and their supplies to the Holy Land returned with rugs, jewelry, glass, and spices. Soon, these goods were in great demand in Europe. Thus, the Crusades helped revive trade, which in turn led to the growth of towns and cities.

The Crusades also encouraged the use of money in Europe. For much of the Middle Ages, most people bartered, or traded goods for other goods or for land or protection. But the crusaders went far from home, where they needed to *buy* supplies. In that case, it was easier to use money than it was to barter.

New Ideas Returning crusaders also brought new ideas and technology back to Europe. You have read about the advances made by Arabs in medicine, mathematics, and technology. The crusaders helped increase European knowledge of these techniques. Europeans learned how to make better ships and maps—skills that would help them become worldwide explorers.

✓ **Reading Check** Describe two effects of the Crusades.

Medieval Banking
A man deposits gold in a bank.
Synthesize *Why did banking increase after the Crusades?*

★ Section 3 Assessment

Key Terms
Review the key terms at the beginning of this section. Use each term in a sentence that explains its meaning.

◉ Target Reading Skill
Reread the text on page 410 under the heading The Rise of the Turks. What signal words helped you understand the sequence of these events?

Comprehension and Critical Thinking
1. (a) Find Main Ideas What was the chief goal of the crusaders?

(b) Infer Why do you think Pope Urban II called the First Crusade a "just," or honorable, war?
2. (a) Sequence List the events of the First Crusade in order.
(b) Identify Frame of Reference How do you think European Christians viewed the Muslim Turks? How do you think Muslims living in the Holy Land viewed the crusaders?
3. (a) Identify Effects What were the main effects of the Crusades on life in Europe?
(b) Predict What might have happened in Europe if the Crusades had never taken place?

Writing Activity
Suppose that there were European newspapers that published editorials at the time of the Crusades. Write an editorial either in support of or against the First Crusade.

> **Writing Tip** Remember that editorials are persuasive writing. State your position. Then use reasons and facts to convince readers that your opinion is the right one.

Section 3 Assessment

Key Terms
Students' sentences should reflect knowledge of each Key Term.

◉ Target Reading Skill
for centuries, then, in the 1000s, at the same time

Comprehension and Critical Thinking
1. (a) to capture the Holy Land **(b)** Possible answer: He believed that Christians should control the Holy Land and felt that going to war to gain control of it was just.

2. (a) Peter and his army set out in 1096 to go to Constantinople; the Byzantine emperor suggested they wait for more knights to arrive before they attacked; Peter agreed but his followers rebelled and attacked the Turks; many died; remaining troops joined with the army of Pope Urban II and captured the Holy Land in 1099. **(b)** Possible answer:

Assess and Reteach

Assess Progress [L2]
Have students complete the Section Assessment. Administer the *Section Quiz*.

📘 **Unit 5 History of Our World Teaching Resources,** *Section Quiz*, p. 18

Reteach [L1]
If students need more instruction, have them read this section in the Reading and Vocabulary Study Guide.

📖 Chapter 14, Section 3, **History of Our World Reading and Vocabulary Study Guide,** pp. 154–156

Extend [L3]
Have students work with a partner to complete the *Why Do Wars Begin?*

> Go **Online**
> PHSchool.com **For:** Environmental and Global Issues: *Why Do Wars Begin?*
> **Visit:** PHSchool.com
> **Web Code:** lgd-8506

Answers

Synthesize It was easier to use money than to trade goods. This increased the use of money and the need for banking.

✓ **Reading Check** Students should describe two of the following: revival of trade, growth of cities, use of money, and introduction of new ideas and technology.

Writing Activity
Use the *Rubric for Assessing a Newspaper Article* to evaluate students' editorials.

📘 **Unit 5 History of Our World Teaching Resources,** *Rubric for Assessing a Newspaper Article*, p. 36

European Christians probably viewed the Muslim Turks as enemies who were trying to control something that was more important to Christians. Muslim Turks probably viewed European Christians as enemies who were trying to take something that was more important to Muslims.

3. (a) revival of trade, growth of cities, increased use of money, introduction of new ideas and technology **(b)** Possible answers: European cities might not have grown as quickly. Europeans may not have started explorations when they did.

Objective

Learn how to distinguish fact and opinion.

Prepare to Read

Build Background Knowledge `L2`

Write the following statements on the board: *Geography is the study of people and places.* *Geography is the best subject.*

Ask students which statement is a fact and which is an opinion. Poll students by asking for a show of hands. Explain that sometimes it is difficult to distinguish facts from opinions, but they will learn the steps for this skill in this lesson.

Instruct

Distinguishing Fact and Opinion `L2`

Guided Instruction

- Read the steps to distinguishing fact and opinion. Summarize each step and write it on the board.

- Practice the skill by using the steps on p. 415 to distinguish the facts and opinions in the passage about Richard I on p. 414. Identify one fact that tells how much (*He spent most of his reign fighting in the Crusades.*), one that tells what (*He made peace with Saladin.*), one that tells where (*He spent only six months of his reign in England.*), and one that tells when (*Richard died in 1199.*).

- Explain that students can check these facts in an encyclopedia or other reliable reference book or website.

- Help students find two words in the passage that show personal feelings (*loved, admired*). Point out that the statements containing these words cannot be proven true or false. Identify a word that judges (*bravely, great, courage*) and explain that the statements containing these words cannot be proven true or false either.

- Explain that some people could make the argument that the passage helps prove that Richard was a good king, but the passage does not provide enough information to prove that he was a kind king.

> Richard I was born on September 8, 1157. He became king of England in 1189 but spent most of his reign fighting in the Crusades. He led his armies to free the Holy Land. Richard loved to be in the midst of battle and always fought bravely. He spent only six months of his reign in England, but his people loved him anyway. They admired his great courage and called him Richard the Lion-Hearted.
>
> Richard won many battles, but he failed to free the Holy Land. He did make peace with the Muslim leader Saladin, who allowed Christians to visit the holy city of Jerusalem. That was a great accomplishment. Richard died in 1199. He was a good and kind king.

King Richard I of England

Facts are statements that can be proved true. Opinions are personal beliefs or value judgments. You will often need to make your own judgments or decisions based on facts, so you must be able to recognize them.

Learn the Skill

To distinguish fact from opinion, use the following steps:

1. **Look for facts by asking what can be proved true or false.** A fact usually tells who, what, when, where, or how much. A fact can be proved true.

2. **Ask how you could check whether each fact is true.** Could you do your own test by measuring or counting? Could you find information in an encyclopedia or in another reliable reference book?

3. **Look for opinions by identifying personal beliefs or value judgments.** Look for words that signal personal feelings, such as *I think* or *I believe*. Look for words that judge, such as *great* or *brave*, or *should* or *ought to*. An opinion cannot be proved true or false.

4. **Decide whether facts or good reasons support each opinion.** A well-supported opinion can help you make up your own mind—as long as you recognize it as an opinion and not a fact.

414 History of Our World

Independent Practice

Assign *Skills for Life* and have students complete it individually.

All in One **Unit 5 History of Our World Teaching Resources,** *Skills for Life,* p. 27

Monitor Progress

As students are completing *Skills for Life,* circulate to make sure students are correctly applying the skill steps. Provide assistance as needed.

Practice the Skill

Read the passage about Richard the Lion-Hearted until you are sure that you understand it. Then reread it for facts and opinions.

1 Identify facts in the paragraph that tell who, what, when, where, and how much.

2 Explain how each fact could be proved true or false.

3 (a) Identify two examples of words that show personal feelings. Can these statements be proved true or false? (b) Now identify one word that signals judgment. Can the statement containing this word be proved true or false?

4 The last sentence in the passage expresses an opinion. Is the opinion well supported with facts and reasons? Explain your answer.

Richard I riding into battle

Burying victims of the plague, 1349

Apply the Skill

Read the passage at the right. List two facts and two opinions from the passage. If you found this passage in a book, how useful would it be as a source for a research paper? Explain your answer.

> The Black Death was the worst thing that happened in medieval Europe. The disease struck quickly. It caused horrible spots and almost certain death. The Black Death eventually killed so many people—more than 25 million—that normal life broke down. There was a labor shortage, and those workers who survived the disease unfairly demanded higher wages. Farmers turned from growing crops to grazing sheep, which required fewer workers. Fear of the disease and economic disruption caused riots all over Europe. That kind of reaction would never happen today.

Chapter 14 **415**

Assess and Reteach

Assess Progress L2
Ask students to do the Apply the Skill activity.

Reteach L1
If students are having trouble applying the skill steps, have them review the skill using the Social Studies Skills Tutor CD-ROM.

⊙ *Distinguishing Fact and Opinion,* **Social Studies Skills Tutor CD-ROM**

Extend L3
Ask students to write a brief essay about any subject they have studied in this text. Tell them to include three facts and three opinions. Ask them to underline the facts and circle the opinions.

Answer
Apply the Skill

Possible facts: The Black Death struck in Europe during medieval times. The disease struck quickly. It caused spots and almost certain death. It killed more than 25 million people. The disease caused labor shortages, and workers who survived demanded higher wages. Farmers turned from growing crops to grazing sheep. Fear of the disease and economic disruption caused riots all over Europe.

Possible opinions: The Black Death was the worst thing that happened in medieval Europe. Workers' demands for higher wages were unfair. That kind of reaction would never happen today.

Students should explain that they could use some of the facts for a research paper but should take care to not include the opinions. It might also he helpful to check the facts against another source.

Objectives

Social Studies

1. Learn about the forces that led to nation building in Europe.
2. Find out about nation building in England.
3. Discover how the Hundred Years' War affected England and France.

Reading/Language Arts

Identify the order of events to help in understanding and remembering them.

Prepare to Read

Build Background Knowledge L2

Ask students to share what they know about how the United States became a nation. Use the Give One, Get One participation strategy (TE, p. T41) to lead a discussion on the causes and effects of the American Revolution and the creation of the United States government. Explain that the building of the United States began hundreds of years after the building of European nations. Ask students to think about the similarities and differences between the building of the United States and the building of European nations as they read.

Set a Purpose for Reading L2

■ Preview the Objectives.

■ Form students into pairs or groups of four. Distribute the *Reading Readiness Guide*. Ask the students to fill in the first two columns of the chart. Use the Numbered Heads participation structure (TE, p. T40) to call on students to share one piece of information they already know and one piece of information they want to know.

All in One Unit 5 History of Our World Teaching Resources, *Reading Readiness Guide,* p. 20

Vocabulary Builder
Preview Key Terms L2

Pronounce each Key Term, then ask the students to say the word with you. Provide a simple explanation such as, "France is considered to be a nation because the people living there share territory, a government, a language, and a culture."

Prepare to Read

Objectives

In this section you will
1. Learn about the forces that led to nation building in Europe.
2. Find out about nation building in England.
3. Discover how the Hundred Years' War affected England and France.

Taking Notes

As you read this section, think about what factors led to nation building in England and France. Copy the table below and record your findings in it.

Nation Building	
England	France
•	•
•	•

Target Reading Skill

Identify Sequence Noting the order of events can help you understand and remember them. Make a sequence chart of events that led to nation building in England. Write the first event in the first box. Then write each additional event in a box. Use arrows to show how one event led to the next.

Key Terms

• **nation** (NAY shun) *n.* a community of people that shares territory and a government

• **Magna Carta** (MAG nuh KAHR tuh) *n.* the "Great Charter," in which the king's power over his nobles was limited, agreed to by King John of England in 1215
• **Model Parliament** (MAHD ul PAHR luh munt) *n.* a council of lords, clergy, and common people that advised the English king on government matters
• **Hundred Years' War** (HUN drud yeerz wawr) *n.* a series of conflicts between England and France, 1337–1453

Pope Gregory VII forgiving King Henry IV

416 History of Our World

For three days, the king waited outside the castle where Pope Gregory VII was staying. Barefoot in the winter cold, the king begged forgiveness. Would the pope forgive King Henry IV?

During the Middle Ages, kings and popes quarreled over who should select bishops. Because bishops were Church officials, popes claimed the right to choose them. Kings wanted this right because bishops often controlled large areas of their kingdoms. They also wanted to play a role in the Church.

In 1077, Henry IV of Germany ruled much of Europe. He had been choosing bishops even though Pope Gregory had ordered him not to. In response, the pope had excommunicated the king and declared that his people no longer had to obey him. However, after putting Henry off for three long, cold days, the pope gave in. He allowed Henry to rejoin the Church.

Pope Gregory had made a serious mistake. In 1081, King Henry invaded Italy, where the pope lived. By 1084, Henry had replaced Pope Gregory with a new pope, who crowned Henry emperor of the Holy Roman Empire. Gregory was sent into exile.

Target Reading Skill L2

Identify Sequence Point out the Target Reading Skill. Explain that identifying the sequence of events can help you understand and remember them.

Model the skill by reading the last two paragraphs on p. 416 and listing in order the events that led to Henry becoming emperor of the Holy Roman Empire. (*In 1077 King Henry ruled much of Europe; he appointed bishops against Pope Gregory's will; the pope excommunicated Henry; the pope allowed Henry to rejoin the Church; in 1081, Henry attacked Italy; by 1084 he replaced Pope Gregory with a new pope; the new pope crowned Henry emperor.*)

Give students *Identify Sequence*. Have them complete the activity in groups.

All in One Unit 5 History of Our World Teaching Resources, *Identify Sequence,* p. 24

Nation Building

Henry's success in overthrowing the pope was a hint of things to come. As later kings gained power, they often dared to put their own wishes before those of the Church. They would soon increase their power in other ways as well.

Castle Stronghold
This English castle is protected by walls and water. **Infer** *What would be involved in defending this castle from attack?*

The Power of Nobles When the 1200s began, Europe was still a feudal society. While kings reigned over kingdoms, the wealthiest lords also had great power. Many saw themselves as nearly the king's equal. In fact, it was not unusual for a noble to have more land, vassals, and knights than his king. But the nobles' power was based on the feudal system. If the feudal system began to decline, so would the nobles' power.

The Decline of Feudalism One reason for the decline of the feudal system was the growth of trade and towns. Kings began to support the new towns in exchange for money. They agreed to protect towns and made laws to help towns grow rich. Then, with the money paid by townspeople, kings hired armies and used them to attack troublesome nobles.

The Crusades also weakened the nobles. Many gave up land to raise money so they could join the Crusades. Other nobles were killed in the Crusades, and kings claimed their land.

The Birth of Nations Over time, kings became more and more powerful. Instead of a patchwork of fiefs ruled by many nobles, large areas of Europe became united under a single king. The kings became strong enough to challenge the Church.

Gradually, these larger kingdoms began to turn into nations. A **nation** is a community of people that shares territory and a government. A common language and culture also often unite the people of a nation. The process of combining smaller communities into a single nation with a national identity and a national government is called nation building.

In the late Middle Ages, the idea of nationhood was taking hold in Europe. A royal marriage united the two largest kingdoms in Spain. In Russia, rulers called tsars were expanding their territory and their power over other nobles. In France, a long line of kings slowly but surely increased royal power. Louis IX, who ruled from 1226 to 1270, was a deeply religious king. He strengthened both Christianity and the central government in his kingdom.

✓ **Reading Check** What is nation building?

Vocabulary Builder

Use the information below to teach students this section's high-use words.

High-Use Word	Definition and Sample Sentence
object, p. 418	*v.* to oppose actively Jill **objects** to the use of animals for medical research.
inspire, p. 419	*v.* to fill with an emotion or attitude that encourages someone to do something The beauty of the Grand Canyon **inspired** Alex to draw a picture of it.

Target Reading Skill

Identify Sequence As a follow up, ask students to answer the Target Reading Skill question in the Student Edition. *(William of Normandy conquered England in 1066. As king, he was a strong ruler who made sure to keep more power than the nobles. Kings who followed William—especially Henry I and Henry II—further increased the power of the king.)*

Changes in England **L2**

Guided Instruction

- **Vocabulary Builder** Clarify the high-use word **object** before reading.

- Read Changes in England as a class. As students read, circulate and make sure individuals can answer the Reading Check question.

- Ask **How did King John anger the people of England?** *(He taxed people heavily, and jailed enemies unjustly.)* **How did he anger the Church?** *(He objected to the appointment of a bishop, and seized Church property.)*

- Ask students to make a generalization about the effect of the Magna Carta on the people of England. *(Possible answer: The Magna Carta gave people more voice in government and protected some of their basic rights.)*

Independent Practice

Ask students to continue to fill in their tables with the information they have just learned.

Monitor Progress

Circulate and make sure students are correctly filling in the graphic organizer. Provide assistance as needed.

Answers

Synthesize nobles and clergy

✓ **Reading Check** It gave more power to the Great Council. This later became the Model Parliament, which was made up of all types of people, from common people to lords and clergy.

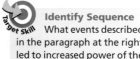
Identify Sequence What events described in the paragraph at the right led to increased power of the king? Write these events in a sequence chart.

King John at Runnymede
The Magna Carta marked the beginning of limitations on the power of the king. **Synthesize** Which groups of English society are shown with King John in this engraving? How did they benefit from the Magna Carta?

Changes in England

By the 1200s, England was already well on its way to becoming a unified nation. In 1066, William of Normandy, a duke from France, had conquered England in what came to be called the Norman Conquest. As king of England, William the Conqueror was a strong ruler who made sure to keep more power than his nobles. The kings who followed William—especially Henry I and Henry II—further increased the power of the king. Of course, the nobles began to resent this power. King John, a son of Henry II, would soon face their anger.

King John Angers the Nobles When John became king of England in 1199, he quickly moved to increase his wealth and power. He taxed people heavily. He jailed his enemies unjustly and without trial. Even the most powerful nobles were hurt by John's unfair actions.

John also clashed with the pope by objecting to the appointment of a bishop he did not like. The king seized Church property. The pope struck back by excommunicating John and declaring that he was no longer king.

The Magna Carta John was now at the mercy of the nobles and clergy whom he had angered. With the backing of the bishops, English nobles demanded a meeting with the king. On June 15, 1215, about 2,000 English nobles gathered at Runnymede, a meadow along the Thames River. They presented John with a list of their demands. John was forced to place the royal seal on the document, and it became law. Called the **Magna Carta** (MAG nuh KAHR tuh), or the "Great Charter," it limited the king's power over the nobles. The king could no longer jail any freeman without just cause, and he could not raise taxes without consulting his Great Council of lords and clergy.

This council later became the **Model Parliament,** which included common people as well as lords and clergy. Eventually, Parliament evolved into a powerful legislature. As it gained power, Parliament also helped unify England. At the same time, however, the Magna Carta also strengthened the power of the king. Because nobles now had a say in government, they were more likely to support what the king did.

✓ **Reading Check** How did the Magna Carta help unite England?

418 History of Our World

Differentiated Instruction

For English Language Learners **L2**
Pair English language learners with native English speakers to complete the *Guided Reading and Review*. If appropriate, give English language learners *Guided Reading and Review (Spanish)* and ask them to work with their partners to answer the questions in English.

 **Unit 5 History of Our World Teaching Resources,** *Guided Reading Review,* p. 21

History of Our World Spanish Support, *Guided Reading and Review (Spanish),* p. 122

The Hundred Years' War

Despite the growth of nations, Western Europe was not at peace. Now, instead of nobles fighting each other, the emerging nations went to war. One long series of clashes between England and France was called the **Hundred Years' War.** It lasted from 1337 to 1453.

Causes of the War In the 1300s, the borders of England and France were not the ones we know today. As a result of marriage and inheritance, the English king had come to be the lord of many counties in present-day France.

You have read that William the Conqueror, who became king of England in 1066, was also Duke of Normandy in France. The 1152 marriage of King Henry II of England and the French noblewoman Eleanor of Aquitaine brought more French land under English control.

Then, in 1328, the French king died. King Edward III of England, whose mother had been a French princess, claimed to be king of France under feudal law. The French nobles did not agree. Determined to get his way, Edward III invaded France—and began the Hundred Years' War.

There were other causes of the war. Both England and France wanted to control the English Channel, the waterway that separates their countries. Each nation also wanted to control trade in the region and the wealth it brought.

Joan of Arc's Victory The Hundred Years' War dragged on, fought by one king after another. England won most of the battles, but the French continued to fight. However, the tide turned in 1429 when a peasant girl called Joan of Arc took charge of the French forces at the battle of Orléans (awr lay AHN). French troops at Orléans greeted her with hope and curiosity.

Under Joan's command, the French defeated the English at Orléans. She then led her forces to victory in other battles. In 1430, Joan was taken prisoner by allies of the English. England tried Joan for witchcraft. She was convicted and burned at the stake.

The French saw Joan of Arc as a martyr, and her death inspired them to many victories. By 1453, the English had been driven from most of France. With the English troops in retreat, France was on its way to becoming a strong and united nation.

Citizen Heroes

Joan of Arc

The young girl who would become one of France's greatest heroes was the daughter of a tenant farmer. Joan was very religious and believed that she saw heavenly visions. In 1429, when she was only 17, she journeyed to the court of Charles, the heir to the French throne. She convinced him that God had called her to lead the French forces at the battle of Orléans. Charles finally agreed. He gave Joan armor, attendants, horses, and a special banner to carry into battle. You can see that banner in this statue of Joan, which stands in Paris.

Background: Links Across Time

Wars of the Roses From 1455 to 1485 descendants of Edward III fought each other for control of England. The descendants from Lancaster, England, used the white rose as their emblem while the descendants from York, England, used the red rose, causing the civil wars to later be named the Wars of the Roses. Power seesawed between the two families until 1485 when Lancastrian Henry Tudor defeated the last Yorkist ruler and married a York descendant, uniting the two families' claims to the throne. He became Henry VII, founder of the Tudor dynasty which later included the rulers Henry VIII and Elizabeth I.

Citizen Heroes

Read the **Citizen Heroes** text on this page. Ask **Why did Joan of Arc travel to see the heir to the French Throne?** *(She believed that God had told her to lead the French forces at the battle of Orléans, so she went to ask the heir for permission to do so and for the supplies and army she needed.)*

The Hundred Years' War L2

Guided Instruction

- **Vocabulary Builder** Clarify the high-use word **inspire** before reading.

- Read about the causes and effects of the Hundred Years' War.

- Discuss the causes of the Hundred Years' War. *(Edward III claimed to be king of France, but French nobles did not agree. Edward III invaded France to get his way. Also, both England and France wanted to control the English Channel and trade in the region.)*

- Ask students to draw a conclusion about how the Hundred Years' War helped lead to the colonization of North America. *(After the war, the English realized that they must give up their dream for an empire in Europe and eventually began to look toward other lands for trade and conquest.)*

Independent Practice

Ask students to complete the table with information about nation building in France.

Monitor Progress

- Show *Section Reading Support Transparency HOW 99* and ask students to check their graphic organizers individually. Go over key concepts and clarify key vocabulary as needed.

  History of Our World Transparencies, *Section Reading Support Transparency HOW 99*

- Tell students to fill in the last column of the *Reading Readiness Guide.* Ask them to evaluate if what they learned was what they had expected to learn.

  All in One Unit 5 History of Our World Teaching Resources, *Reading Readiness Guide,* p. 20

Assess Progress L2

Have students complete the Section Assessment. Administer the *Section Quiz*.

All in One Unit 5 History of Our World Teaching Resources, *Section Quiz*, p. 22

Reteach L1

If students need more instruction, have them read this section in the Reading and Vocabulary Study Guide.

📖 Chapter 14, Section 4, **History of Our World Reading and Vocabulary Study Guide**, pp. 157–159

Extend L3

Have students begin to work on the *Book Project: The Birth of a Nation.* Tell them that they can choose to research and write about England, France, or another nation they have learned about.

All in One Unit 5 History of Our World Teaching Resources, *Book Project: The Birth of a Nation* pp. 19–21

Answers

Analyze Images Possible answer: His stance and ornate clothes suggest that he is a confident and powerful man.

✓**Reading Check** Students should explain any two of the following: New weapons that were developed during the war increased the importance of soldiers and decreased the importance of knights. The war inspired national feeling. It gave kings more power, but also gave Parliament more power. It helped set the modern boundaries for England and France. It ultimately led England to explore and colonize distant lands.

Section 4 Assessment

Key Terms
Students' sentences should reflect knowledge of each Key Term.

🎯 **Target Reading Skill**
grew up on a farm; had a vision that she should lead the French at Orléans; visited Charles VII in 1429 to get permission to do so; defeated the English; taken prisoner in 1430; was burned at the stake.

Comprehension and Critical Thinking
1. (a) They reigned over kingdoms but often had the same power as wealthy lords. **(b)** the growth of trade and towns and the weakening of nobles; kings gained more power

2. (a) The king could no longer jail freemen without a trial or raise taxes without consulting the Great Council. **(b)** It gave more power to the Great Council.

3. (a) England and France **(b)** Possible answer: It stirred national pride and helped define the borders of the two countries.

King Henry VIII
The Tudor monarchs of England, 1485–1603, were very powerful. Yet Henry VIII consulted with Parliament on important issues. **Analyze Images** *How does this portrait show Henry's power and personality?*

The Growing Power of Kings The Hundred Years' War affected the balance of power in England and France. On the battlefield, new weapons such as the longbow and cannon increased the importance of footsoldiers. Armored knights, on the other hand, became less valuable in battle. Feudal castles could not stand up to the firepower of the new cannons. Kings now needed large armies, not small bands of knights, to fight for them.

The Hundred Years' War also led to national feeling. People began to think of themselves as citizens of England or of France, not simply as loyal to their local lords. Kings who had led their nations in battle became more powerful as the influence of nobles declined. On the other hand, the English king had been forced to ask Parliament for more and more money to fund the war. This helped Parliament win "the power of the purse" and increased its power in relation to the king. These two developments helped unify England.

The Hundred Years' War helped set the modern boundaries of England and France. Forced to give up their dream of an empire in Europe, the English began to look to more distant lands for trade and conquest. Leaving feudalism behind, Europe was becoming a continent of nations. And some of these nations, as you will read in Chapter 15, would soon rule much of the world.

✓**Reading Check** **Explain two effects of the Hundred Years' War.**

⭐ Section 4 Assessment

Key Terms
Review the key terms at the beginning of this section. Use each term in a sentence that explains its meaning.

🎯 **Target Reading Skill**
Reread page 419. Write the events of Joan of Arc's life in a sequence chart.

Comprehension and Critical Thinking
1. (a) Recall How much power did kings have under feudalism?

(b) Identify Cause and Effect Why did feudalism decline, and how did this affect the power of kings?

2. (a) Identify What are two limits on the king's power established by the Magna Carta?

(b) Identify Effects How did the Magna Carta help unify England as a nation?

3. (a) Name Who fought the Hundred Years' War?

(b) Identify Effects How did this war help unify two nations?

Writing Activity
Suppose that you are a French soldier preparing for the battle of Orléans. Describe your reaction to the news that a young peasant girl is your new commander.

For: An activity on the Hundred Years' War
Visit: PHSchool.com
Web Code: lgd-8504

420 History of Our World

Writing Activity
Use the *Rubric for Assessing a Writing Assignment* to evaluate students' reactions.

All in One Unit 5 History of Our World Teaching Resources, *Rubric for Assessing a Writing Assignment,* p. 35

Go Online
PHSchool.com Typing in the Web code when prompted will bring students directly to detailed instructions for this activity.

Review and Assessment

Lombard warrior

◆ Chapter Summary

Section 1: Feudalism and the Manor System

- The Middle Ages was the period from about A.D. 500 to 1500.
- Feudalism, in which land was owned by nobles but held by vassals in return for loyalty, was the medieval government system.
- The manor system, in which many people lived and worked on large estates owned by lords, was the medieval economic system.
- Most people of the Middle Ages were peasants. Serfs were peasants who were considered part of the manors on which they worked.

Section 2: The Church and the Rise of Cities

- During the Middle Ages, the Roman Catholic Church was a powerful force that touched nearly every aspect of people's lives.
- An increase in trade led to the growth of towns and cities.
- The new middle class organized craft and trade guilds. Medieval towns and cities were crowded and unsanitary.
- Culture and learning were limited to only a few people. Troubadours brought stories of chivalry from place to place.

Section 3: The Crusades

- The Crusades were a series of wars launched by European Christians to capture the Holy Land from Muslim Turks.
- The First Crusade succeeded in capturing the holy city of Jerusalem.
- Later Crusades were launched to defend the Christian kingdoms in the Holy Land from Muslim Turk attacks.
- The Crusades changed life in Europe: trade increased, towns grew, the use of money increased, and the learning of the Arab world came to Europe.

Section 4: The Power of Kings

- Nation building in Europe began as feudalism declined and kings increased their power.
- The Magna Carta limited the power of the English king but also helped unify England into a nation.
- The Hundred Years' War helped unify both England and France into nations.

◆ Key Terms

Write one or two paragraphs about life in the Middle Ages. Use all of the following terms correctly in your paragraphs.

1. Middle Ages
2. feudalism
3. vassals
4. fief
5. manor
6. serfs
7. clergy
8. apprentice
9. troubadour
10. Crusades

Chapter 14 **421**

Vocabulary Builder

Revisit this chapter's high-use words:

promote	authority	prestige
majority	dedicate	advise
interior	prevent	object
expel	launch	inspire

Ask students to review the definitions they recorded on their *Word Knowledge* worksheets.

All in One **Unit 5 History of Our World Teaching Resources,** *Word Knowledge,* p. 25

Consider allowing students to earn extra credit if they use the words in their answers to the questions in the Chapter Review and Assessment. The words must be used correctly and in a natural context to win the extra points.

Review and Assessment

Review Chapter Content

- Review and revisit the major themes of this chapter by asking students to classify which Guiding Question each bulleted statement in the Chapter Summary answers. Form students into groups and ask them to complete the activity together. Refer to page 1 in the Student Edition for text of Guiding Questions.

- Assign *Vocabulary Development* for students to review Key Terms.

All in One **Unit 5 History of Our World Teaching Resources,** *Vocabulary Development,* p. 34

Answers

Key Terms

1–10. Students' paragraphs should use each Key Term correctly and in the appropriate context.

Comprehension and Critical Thinking

11. (a) Lords were powerful landowners. A vassal was given a share of the lord's land in return for the vassal's promise to follow the lord's laws and fight for him. **(b)** Possible answer: A lord might be another lord's vassal.

12. (a) A manor was a large estate that included farms, pastures, the manor house where the lord or ruler lived, and often an entire village. Everything needed by the workers and other people living on a manor was produced on the manor. **(b)** Serfs were people who were considered possessions of the manor. **(c)** Possible answer: The manor system helped keep lords powerful and wealthy. This made it possible for lords to serve as vassals for more powerful lords or kings.

13. (a) the Roman Catholic Church **(b)** Most people followed the Church's teachings; the Church had economic power through collecting taxes and controlling large plots of land; the Church's religious and economic power enabled it to perform many governmental roles.

14. (a) at crossroads for trade, such as river crossings and along roads **(b)** Possible answer: By preventing outsiders from selling goods in their towns, guild members encouraged the production and sale of goods within the town, thus helping it to grow.

15. (a) military expeditions organized for the purpose of capturing the Holy Land **(b)** Possible answer: The Crusades helped Europe because they revived trade, helped the growth of cities, encouraged the use of money, and introduced new ideas and technology to Europe.

16. (a) the combining of communities into a single nation with a national identity and government **(b)** the decline of feudalism and the increase in national pride stirred by the Hundred Years' War

17. (a) a French peasant who led the French to victory over the English at Orléans **(b)** She led the French to military victories over the English. After she was captured and executed, the French saw her as a martyr and her death inspired them to many victories.

Skills Practice
Students should identify the following phrases as opinions: gorgeous stained-glass windows; amazing flying buttresses; beautiful glass windows. Students might suggest that

◆ Comprehension and Critical Thinking

11. (a) Recall In the feudal system, what was the role of a lord? Of a vassal?
(b) Synthesize How could one person be both a lord and a vassal at the same time?

12. (a) Describe What was a manor, and how did it meet people's needs?
(b) Explain What was the relationship of serfs to the manor?
(c) Draw Conclusions How did manorialism help support feudalism?

13. (a) Identify What was "the Church" in the Middle Ages?
(b) Draw Conclusions Why was the Church so powerful in the Middle Ages?

14. (a) Recall Where did towns spring up during the Middle Ages?
(b) Synthesize Information How was the growth of medieval towns related to the growth of guilds?

15. (a) Define What were the Crusades?
(b) Draw Conclusions Do you think the Crusades helped or hurt Europe? Explain.

16. (a) Define What is nation building?
(b) Identify Causes What factors led to nation building in Europe in the later Middle Ages?

17. (a) Recall Who was Joan of Arc?
(b) Identify Effects How did she influence the outcome of the Hundred Years' War?

◆ Skills Practice

Distinguishing Fact and Opinion In the Skills for Life activity in this chapter, you learned how to distinguish fact from opinion. Review the steps you followed to learn the skill. Then reread the opening paragraphs of Section 2 of this chapter on page 402. List the facts and opinions in this text. For each opinion, note whether or not you think the opinion is well supported and reliable.

◆ Writing Activity: Science

The bubonic plague—the Black Death that killed so many Europeans during the Middle Ages—still exists today. However, it is not nearly so common or deadly as it once was. Use an encyclopedia and other reliable sources to learn how modern medicine and sanitation prevent and control the disease. Write a brief report titled "The Bubonic Plague in Modern Times."

MAP MASTER™ Skills Activity

Europe and the Holy Land

Place Location For each place listed below, write the letter from the map that shows its location.
1. England
2. France
3. Jerusalem
4. Mediterranean Sea
5. Rome
6. Constantinople

Go Online
PHSchool.com Use Web Code lgd-8554 for an **interactive** map.

photographs throughout the section support these opinions.

All of the remaining sentences on p. 126 are facts.

Writing Activity: Science
Students' answers will vary, but should reflect what they have learned about the bubonic plague in this section and should reflect the completion of outside research.

Use *Rubric for Assessing a Report* to evaluate students' reports.

All in One Unit 5 History of Our World Teaching Resources, *Rubric for Assessing a Report,* p. 37

Standardized Test Prep

Test-Taking Tips

Some questions on standardized tests ask you to identify cause and effect. Study the graphic organizer below. Then use the tip to help you answer the sample question.

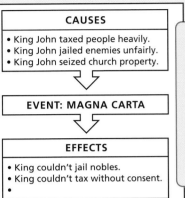

CAUSES
• King John taxed people heavily.
• King John jailed enemies unfairly.
• King John seized church property.

↓

EVENT: MAGNA CARTA

↓

EFFECTS
• King couldn't jail nobles.
• King couldn't tax without consent.
•

TIP Remember that a *cause* is what makes something happen. An *effect* is what happens as a result of something else. Is the question asking for a cause or an effect?

Pick the letter that best answers the question.

What information belongs with the last bullet (•) in the graphic organizer?

A King John clashed with the pope.

B It became law with King John's seal.

C It helped unite England.

D King John seized Church property.

Think It Through The question is asking for an effect: What else happened as a result of the Magna Carta? You can eliminate A and D because both were causes, or events leading up to the Magna Carta. That leaves B and C. The Magna Carta did become law with King John's seal, but that was not an *effect* of the law. The answer is C: the Magna Carta had the effect of helping to unite England.

Practice Questions

Choose the letter of the best answer.

1. Which of the following was a major cause of the growth of towns during the Middle Ages?

   A a decrease in the power of the Church

   B an increase in trade

   C a decrease in Europe's population

   D an increase in the number of manors

2. Which of the following was NOT an effect of the Crusades?

   A The demand for foreign goods increased.

   B Europeans learned new shipbuilding techniques.

   C The use of money became more common.

   D The Holy Land came under permanent European control.

3. The decline of _____ helped the growth of _____.

   A trade, towns

   B feudalism, manorialism

   C Charlemagne's empire, feudalism

   D the Roman Empire, trade

Study the diagram. Then use it to answer the question that follows.

1 Factors	→	2 Nation Building	→	3 Changes in England

4. In the diagram,

   A **1** represents a single effect of nation building, and **2** and **3** represent several causes.

   B **1** represents a single cause of **2**, and **2** is a cause of **3**.

   C **2** is a cause of both **1** and **3**.

   D **1** represents several causes of **2**, and **3** represents how nation building affected England.

Go Online
PHSchool.com

Use Web Code lga-8504 for a **Chapter 14 self-test.**

Standardized Test Prep

Answers

1. B

2. D

3. C

4. D

Go Online
PHSchool.com Students may use the Chapter 14 self-test on PHSchool.com to prepare for the Chapter Test.

Assessment Resources

Use *Chapter Tests A and B* to assess students' mastery of chapter content.

All in One Unit 5 History of Our World Teaching Resources, *Chapter Tests A and B,* pp. 38–43

Tests are also available on the **ExamView®** **Test Bank CD-ROM.**

⊙ Exam*View®* **Test Bank CD-ROM**

Objectives

- Understand why King Arthur's subjects loved him.

- Learn about some of the rules of honor in battle that were part of the code of chivalry.

- Analyze the effectiveness of plot elements such as setting and conflicts.

Prepare to Read

Build Background Knowledge L2

Have students read the title of the story and the text on p. 424 under the heading Background Information. Ask students to recall any stories they have read or movies they have seen about King Arthur, Merlin, or Camelot. Use the Numbered Heads participation strategy (TE, p. T40) to help students share what they know with the rest of the class.

Instruct

Of Swords and Sorcerers L2

Guided Instruction

- Point out that some potentially unfamiliar words are defined for students in the margin. Clarify the meanings of the words before reading.

- Have students read the selection using the Structured Silent Reading strategy (TE, p. T38).

- Ask **Who did Arthur defeat in order to unite his land?** *(twelve kings, including his brother-in-law, King Lot)*

- Ask **Who are Gawain and Mordred?** *(They are Lot's sons; they both become knights at Camelot. Gawain is handsome, strong, and courteous, while Mordred is insincere and thirsts for power.)*

- Ask students to scan the first two paragraphs of the story. Then ask students to describe Arthur based on his actions, information that the author gives about him, and vivid words that the author uses to describe him. *(Answers may include that Arthur is an able leader, courageous in battle, and loved by his people.)*

Of Swords and Sorcerers:
The Adventures of King Arthur and His Knights
By Margaret Hodges and Margery Evernden

Prepare to Read

Background Information
How should a good and just ruler behave? What traits should a king or queen have? What do you admire in people who lead others?

People have read and enjoyed the stories of King Arthur for hundreds of years. To many, he symbolizes the virtue and justice of a good ruler. According to legend, he was loved and respected by all of his people.

Legends about King Arthur exist in many forms, and stories about him have been written and rewritten in several languages. The following selection is one tale of how Arthur met his friend Pellinore and found his sword, which was named Excalibur.

Objectives
As you read this selection, you will
1. Understand why King Arthur's subjects loved him.
2. Learn about some of the rules of honor in battle that were part of the code of chivalry.

petty (PET ee) *adj.* unimportant; of low rank

fealty (FEE ul tee) *n.* loyalty to a feudal lord

No king before Arthur had been able to unite the realm and rule it. This Arthur did. Lightnings and thunders surrounded him as he fought. In twelve great battles he defeated <u>petty</u> kings who had been constantly at war, laying waste all the land. The last to surrender was Arthur's own brother-in-law, King Lot of Orkney. When Lot laid down his arms and swore <u>fealty</u> to Arthur, he sent his sons to become knights at Camelot.

King Arthur standing with the crowns of 30 kingdoms, in an illustration from 1325

One son was Gawain, handsome and strong, whom Arthur called Gawain the Courteous. Another was Mordred, whose foxy smile and <u>gimlet eyes</u> concealed <u>malice</u> and a thirst for power. Gawain took the vows of knighthood in good faith, but Mordred's vows were insincere, and he soon began listening at the castle doors in hope of ferreting out secrets that might damage the court and someday play into his own hands. He saw that the time to strike had not yet come. The powers of heaven and earth all seemed to be on Arthur's side. The people loved him, and Camelot was in its glory.

Now there came a day when Arthur rode with Merlin seeking adventure, and in a forest they found a knight named Pellinore, seated in a chair, blocking their path.

"Sir, will you let us pass?" said Arthur.

"Not without a fight," replied Pellinore. "Such is my custom."

"I will change your custom," said Arthur.

"I will defend it," said Pellinore. He mounted his horse and took his shield on his arm. Then the two knights rode against each other, and each splintered his spear on the other's shield.

"I have no more spears," said Arthur. "Let us fight with swords."

"Not so," said Pellinore. "I have enough spears. I will lend you one."

Then a squire brought two good spears, and the two knights rode against each other again until those spears were broken.

"You are as good a fighter as ever I met," said Pellinore. "Let us try again."

Two great spears were brought, and this time Pellinore struck Arthur's shield so hard that the king and his horse fell to the earth.

Then Arthur pulled out his sword and said, "I have lost the battle on horseback. Let me try you on foot."

Pellinore thought it unfair to attack from his horse, so he dismounted and came toward Arthur with his sword drawn. Then began such a battle that both were covered with blood. After a while they sat down to rest and fought again until both fell to the ground. Again they fought, and the fight was even. But at last Pellinore struck such a blow that Arthur's sword broke into two pieces. Thereupon the king leaped at Pellinore. He threw him down and pulled off his helmet. But Pellinore was a very big man and strong enough to wrestle Arthur under him and pull off the

gimlet eyes (GIM lit eyez) *n.* eyes having a piercing quality

malice (MAL is) *n.* spite; a desire to damage or hurt someone

Knights in battle, in an illustration by N. C. Wyeth

✓ **Reading Check**

Why did Arthur and Pellinore fight?

Chapter 14 **425**

Read Fluently

Partner students and have them choose a paragraph from the selection. Have students take turns reading the paragraph aloud. Ask them to underline words that give them trouble as they read. Then, have them decode the problem words with their partner. Provide assistance as needed. Have them reread the paragraph two more times to improve their reading speed. Remind them to stop at the commas and periods and to read with expression.

Guided Instruction (continued)

■ Ask students to reread pp. 425–426, paying careful attention to the fight between Arthur and Pellinore. Ask **How do Arthur and Pellinore show respect for one another?** *(Pellinore lends Arthur a spear, compliments Arthur's fighting, dismounts his horse to make the battle fairer, and is fearful when he finds that he is fighting the king. Arthur calls Pellinore "Sir" when they first meet, and says Pellinore is the best knight he has ever fought. They allow each other a short rest during the fight.)*

■ Ask **How does Arthur lose his sword?** *(It is destroyed in his fight with Pellinore.)* **How does Merlin help Arthur after the fight?** *(Merlin brings Arthur to a hermit to treat his wound, and takes him to the Lady of the Lake, who gives Arthur a new sword with special powers.)*

■ Ask students to discuss how the setting, or the time and place of the story, is important to the story's plot. *(The story takes place sometime in the Middle Ages in a feudal society. The characters travel on horses; Arthur and Pellinore fight with swords and spears and observe codes of chivalry during their battle. Many of the characters are knights, a type of soldier. A story with similar events would have a very different meaning if it was set in the present.)*

Answer

✓ **Reading Check** It was Pellinore's custom not to let anyone pass without fighting him.

Independent Practice

Partner students and have them review Arthur's qualities as a leader. *(bravery, fairness, being a great warrior)* Then ask students to suppose that Arthur can no longer serve as the king of Camelot. Have students write a job description that explains the personal and professional qualifications required of the new king. If students are having trouble organizing their thoughts, give them *Organizing Details* to help them.

All in One **Unit 5 History of Our World Teaching Resources,** *Organizing Details,* p. 33

Monitor Progress

Circulate to make sure students are communicating their ideas effectively to their partners. Provide assistance as needed.

---

wrath (rath) *n.* great anger or rage

hermit (HUR mit) *n.* a person who lives alone and away from others
salve (sahv) *n.* an oily substance used as medicine on the skin

---

king's helmet. All this time Merlin had watched, silent, but when he saw that Pellinore was about to cut off Arthur's head, he interfered.

"Do not kill this man," he said to Pellinore. "You do not know who he is."

"Why, who is he?" said the knight.

"It is King Arthur," said Merlin.

When he heard this, Pellinore trembled with fear of the royal <u>wrath</u>, for he would not knowingly have fought against the king. Then Merlin cast a spell of sleep on Pellinore so that he fell to the earth as if dead.

"Alas," said Arthur, "you have killed the best knight I ever fought."

"Have no fear," said Merlin. "He will awake in three hours as well as ever he was."

Then he mounted Pellinore's horse and led Arthur to a <u>hermit</u>, who bound up the king's wounds and healed them with good <u>salves</u>, so that he might ride again and go on his way.

But Arthur said, "I have no sword."

"Never fear," said Merlin. "Not far away is a sword that can be yours." So they rode on until they came to a broad lake of clear water. Far out in the middle of the lake Arthur saw an arm clothed in shining white and holding a noble sword, its golden hilt richly set with jewels.

"Lo," said Merlin, "yonder is the sword Excalibur."

King Arthur claiming Excalibur, in an illustration by N. C. Wyeth

426 History of Our World

Differentiated Instruction

For English Language Learners **L2**
Have students create flashcards of the words defined in the margin. Students can also include any other words from the story that are unfamiliar to them, using a classroom dictionary to find definitions. Then partner students and have them take turns quizzing each other using their flashcards.

Then they saw a lady floating toward them as if she walked on the water. Her garments were like a mist around her.

"That is the Lady of the Lake," said Merlin. "Within the lake is a rock, and within the rock is a palace, and within the palace lives this lady with many other ladies who serve her. She is called Vivien. Speak to her as a friend, and she will give you that sword."

So, when she had come close, Arthur said to her, "Lady, I wish that sword were mine, for I have no sword."

"It shall be yours," said the lady, and she showed Arthur a little boat lying at the edge of the lake. "Row out to the sword," she said. "Take it with its <u>scabbard</u>." Then she disappeared. Arthur and Merlin rowed out into the lake, and Arthur took the sword from the hand that held it. And the arm and the hand vanished under the water.

Arthur and Merlin rowed to shore and went on their way, and whenever Arthur looked on the sword, he liked it well.

"Which do you like better? asked Merlin. "The sword or the scabbard?"

"I like the sword better," said Arthur.

"The scabbard is worth ten such swords," said Merlin, "for while you wear the scabbard, you will never lose blood, no matter how sorely you are wounded."

So they rode back to Arthur's court, and all his knights marveled when they heard that the king risked his life in single combat as his poor knights did. They said it was merry to be under such a <u>chieftain</u>.

About the Selection

Of Swords and Sorcerers: The Adventures of King Arthur and His Knights was published in 1993. It includes nine episodes in the life of King Arthur.

scabbard (SKAB urd) *n.* a case or cover for a sword or dagger
chieftain (CHEEF tun) *n.* the head of a clan; leader of many people

✓ **Reading Check**

Which did Arthur like better, the sword or the scabbard?

About the Authors

Margaret Hodges (b.1911), above, was a children's librarian and a storyteller for a children's radio program. She believes that myths are still important in our modern world. **Margery Evernden** has written children's books, biographies, and plays.

Review and Assessment

Thinking About the Selection

1. (a) Describe How did Arthur and Pellinore fight?
(b) Predict How do you think the fight would have ended if Merlin had not interfered? Why do you think so?
2. (a) Note What did Arthur's knights think when they heard about his fight with Pellinore?
(b) Draw Conclusions What qualities does Arthur demonstrate in this episode that would make him a good ruler?

(c) Predict What kind of a ruler do you think Arthur would be in today's world? Explain your answer.

Writing Activity

Write a Poem or a Story Many characters in myths and legends have objects that protect them or give them special powers, as Arthur's sword and scabbard did for him. Write a poem or a story about a character who receives one such tool. What are its powers? How does it help the character?

Assess and Reteach

Assess and Progress [L2]

Have students answer the assessment questions.

Reteach [L1]

If students are having difficulty remembering the plotline of the selection, have them create a chart of the story's major events. Show the blank *Flow Chart Transparency* to help students structure their charts.

📖 **History of Our World Transparencies,** *Transparency B5: Flow Chart*

Extend [L3]

To extend the lesson, have students create a short play based on the selection. Have students form groups and assign each group a responsibility such as creating simple props, writing the story in script form, or playing the roles of the characters. If possible, have students perform their play for another class.

Answers

✓ **Reading Check** Arthur liked the sword better than the scabbard.

Review and Assessment

Thinking About the Selection

1. (a) They fought on horseback with spears and on foot with swords. **(b)** Pellinore probably would have killed Arthur, because Arthur no longer had his sword.

2. (a) They were amazed that Arthur risked his life just as they themselves did, and were happy to have a leader who fought in the same manner they did. **(b)** He is fair-minded, even when facing an enemy in battle. **(c)** Answers will vary, but should be supported from the text. Most students will probably think that Arthur has leadership qualities, such as being courageous and just, that would make him a good ruler in today's world.

Writing Activity

Use the *Rubric for Assessing a Writing Assignment* to evaluate students' poems or stories.

All in One **Unit 5 History of Our World Teaching Resources,** *Rubric for Assessing a Writing Assignment,* p. 35

15 The Renaissance and Reformation

Chapter Overview

Overview

1 The Renaissance Begins

Section **1**

1. Find out why Italy was the birthplace of the Renaissance.
2. Understand how literature and art were transformed during the Renaissance.

2 The Renaissance Moves North

Section **2**

1. Understand how the Renaissance spread from Italy to Northern Europe.
2. Identify key literary figures and ideas of the Northern Renaissance.
3. Identify key artists and artistic ideas of the Northern Renaissance.

3 Martin Luther and the Reformation

Section **3**

1. Understand the developments that led to the Reformation.
2. Learn about Luther's criticism of the Church.
3. Understand the immediate effects of Luther's ideas in Europe.

4 Reformation Ideas Spread

Section **4**

1. Learn that Luther was the first of several religious reformers.
2. Identify other religious movements of the 1500s in Europe.
3. Understand how the Catholic Church responded to the Reformation.

DISCOVERY CHANNEL **SCHOOL** Video

Leonardo da Vinci: A Renaissance Man
Length: 5 minutes, 7 seconds
Use with Section 1
Leonardo da Vinci was a painter, sculptor, architect, engineer, and scientist. He had one of the finest minds of his century. This video segment honors da Vinci as the ultimate Renaissance man.

Technology Resources

Go Online PHSchool.com

Students use embedded web codes to access Internet activities, chapter self-tests, and additional map practice. They may also access Dorling Kindersley's Online Desk Reference to learn more about each country they study.

Interactive Textbook

Use the Interactive Textbook to make content and concepts come alive through animations, videos, and activities that accompany the complete basal text—online and on CD-ROM.

PRENTICE HALL

TeacherEXPRESS
Plan • Teach • Assess

Use this complete suite of powerful teaching tools to make planning lessons and administering tests quicker and easier.

Reading and Assessment

Reading and Vocabulary Instruction

🔊 Model the Target Reading Skill

Compare and Contrast Comparing and contrasting is an effective method for sorting and analyzing events, people, places, and ideas. When you compare two or more things, you examine their similarities. When you contrast them, you study their differences.

Model this skill by thinking aloud about similarities between art of the Italian Renaissance and art of the Northern Renaissance:

I think the art of the Italian Renaissance and the art of the Northern Renaissance are good topics for comparison. From what I recall from my reading, they are similar in more ways than they are different.

First, both focused not only on religious scenes but also on nature and the human form.

Second, both used realism. Italian artists showed the human body with great accuracy and detail. Northern artists painted realistic portraits of people.

Third, artists in both Italy and the north used new techniques such as oil paints.

Finally, artists in Italy and artists in northern and western Europe often had wide interests. Two examples are Leonardo da Vinci in Italy and Albrecht Dürer in Germany.

Use the following worksheets from All-in-One Unit 4 History of Our World Teaching Resources (pp. 63–66) to support this chapter's Target Reading Skill.

Vocabulary Builder
High-Use Academic Words

Use these steps to teach this chapter's high-use words:

1. Have students rate how well they know each word on their Word Knowledge worskheets (All-in-One Unit 5 History of Our World Teaching Resources, p. 67).

2. Pronounce each word and ask students to repeat it.

3. Give students a brief definition and sample sentence (provided on TE pp. 431, 435, 441, and 447).

4. Work with students as they fill in the "Definition or Example" column of their Word Knowledge worksheets.

Assessment

Formal Assessment

Test students' understanding of core knowledge and skills.

Chapter Tests A and B, All-in-One Unit 5 **History of Our World** Teaching Resources, pp. 80–85

Customize the Chapter Tests to suit your needs.

Exam*View*® Test Bank CD-ROM

Skills Assessment

Assess geographic literacy.

MapMaster Skills, Student Edition, pp. 429, 431, 447, and 450

Assess reading and comprehension.

Target Reading Skills, Student Edition, pp. 431, 435, 442, 448, and in Section Assessments

Chapter 15 Assessment, All-in-One Unit 5 History of Our World Reading and Vocabulary Study Guide, p. 173

Performance Assessment

Assess students' performance on this chapter's Writing Activities using the following rubric from All-in-One Unit 5 History of Our World Teaching Resources.

Rubric for Assessing a Writing Assignment, p. 78

Rubric for Assessing a Report, p. 78

Assess students' work through performance tasks.

Small Group Activity: Creating a Guild Advertisement, All-in-One History of Our World Teaching Resources, pp. 70–73

Online Assessment

Have students check their own understanding.

Chapter Self-Test

Section 1 The Renaissance Begins

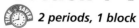 *2 periods, 1 block*

Social Studies Objectives

1. Find out why Italy was the birthplace of the Renaissance.
2. Understand how literature and art were transformed during the Renaissance.

Reading/Language Arts Objective

Learn to identify causes and effects to better understand the relationships among situations and events.

Prepare to Read

Build Background Knowledge
Discuss the beginnings of the Renaissance.

Set a Purpose for Reading
Have students evaluate statements on the Reading Readiness Guide.

Preview Key Terms
Teach the section's Key Terms.

Target Reading Skill
Introduce the section's Target Reading Skill of identifying causes and effects.

Instructional Resources

All in One Unit 5 History of Our World Teaching Resources
L2 Reading Readiness Guide, p. 48
L2 Identify Causes and Effects, p. 63

Differentiated Instruction

Spanish Reading and Vocabulary Study Guide
L2 Chapter 15, Section 1, pp. 115–116 ELL

Instruct

The Renaissance Begins in Italy
Discuss conditions that explain why the Renaissance began in Italy.

Target Reading Skill
Review identifying causes and effects.

Art in the Italian Renaissance
Examine how literature and art changed during the Renaissance.

Instructional Resources

All in One Unit 5 History of Our World Teaching Resources
L2 Guided Reading and Review, p. 49
L2 Reading Readiness Guide, p. 48

History of Our World Video Program
L2 Leonardo da Vinci: A Renaissance Man

History of Our World Transparencies
L2 Section Reading Support Transparency HOW 100

Differentiated Instruction

All in One Unit 5 History of Our World Teaching Resources
L3 Small Group Activity: Creating a Guild Advertisement, pp. 70–73 GT, AR

Spanish Support
L2 Guided Reading and Review (Spanish), p. 126 ELL

Teacher's Edition
L3 For Gifted and Talented, TE, p. 432

Student Edition on Audio CD
L1 Chapter 15, Section 1 ELL, LPR, SN

Assess and Reteach

Assess Progress
Evaluate student comprehension with the section assessment and section quiz.

Reteach
Assign the Reading and Vocabulary Study Guide to help struggling students.

Extend
Extend the lesson by viewing examples of Italian Renaissance art.

Instructional Resources

All in One Unit 5 History of Our World Teaching Resources
L2 Section Quiz, p. 50
L2 Rubric for Assessing a Writing Assignment, p. 78

Reading and Vocabulary Study Guide
L1 Chapter 15, Section 1, pp. 161–163

Differentiated Instruction

Spanish Support
L2 Section Quiz (Spanish), p. 127 ELL

Key

L1 Basic to Average   L3 Average to Advanced
L2 For All Students

LPR Less Proficient Readers
AR Advanced Readers
SN Special Needs Students

GT Gifted and Talented
ELL English Language Learners

Section 2 The Renaissance Moves North

 4 periods, 2 blocks

Social Studies Objectives
1. Understand how the Renaissance spread from Italy to the north.
2. Identify key literary figures and ideas of the Northern Renaissance.
3. Identify key artists and artistic ideas of the Northern Renaissance.

Reading/Language Arts Objective
Learn to recognize multiple causes to understand the development of complex events.

Prepare to Read	**Instructional Resources**	**Differentiated Instruction**
Build Background Knowledge Discuss the spread of Renaissance ideas to the north. **Set a Purpose for Reading** Have students evaluate statements on the Reading Readiness Guide. **Preview Key Terms** Teach the section's Key Terms. **Target Reading Skill** Introduce the section's Target Reading Skill of recognizing multiple causes.	**All in One Unit 5 History of Our World Teaching Resources** **L2** Reading Readiness Guide, p. 52 **L2** Recognize Multiple Causes, p. 64	**Spanish Reading and Vocabulary Study Guide** **L2** Chapter 15, Section 2, pp. 117–118 ELL

Instruct	**Instructional Resources**	**Differentiated Instruction**
Renaissance Thought and Literature Spread Discuss changes in life in western and northern Europe that allowed the spread of Renaissance ideas. **Target Reading Skill** Review recognizing multiple causes. **Literature of the Northern Renaissance** Discuss key literary figures and ideas of the northern Renaissance. **Art of the Northern Renaissance** Discuss artists of northern and western Europe and their techniques.	**All in One Unit 5 History of Our World Teaching Resources** **L2** Guided Reading and Review, p. 53 **L2** Reading Readiness Guide, p. 52 **History of Our World Transparencies** **L2** Section Reading Support Transparency HOW 101	**Spanish Support** **L2** Guided Reading and Review (Spanish) p. 128 ELL **Teacher's Edition** **L1** For English Language Learners, pp. 436, 438 **Student Edition on Audio CD** **L1** Chapter 15, Section 2 ELL, LPR, SN

Assess and Reteach	**Instructional Resources**	**Differentiated Instruction**
Assess Progress Evaluate student comprehension with the section assessment and section quiz. **Reteach** Assign the Reading and Vocabulary Study Guide to help struggling students. **Extend** Extend the lesson by having students write a biography of a Renaissance figure.	**All in One Unit 5 History of Our World Teaching Resources** **L2** Section Quiz, p. 54 **L2** Rubric for Assessing a Writing Assignment, p. 78 **Reading and Vocabulary Study Guide** **L1** Chapter 15, Section 2, pp. 164–166	**Spanish Support** **L2** Section Quiz (Spanish), p. 129 ELL

Key
L1 Basic to Average **L3** Average to Advanced   LPR Less Proficient Readers   GT Gifted and Talented
L2 For All Students   AR Advanced Readers   ELL English Language Learners
                                                     SN Special Needs Students

Section 3 Martin Luther and the Reformation

 2 periods, 1 block (includes Skills for Life)

Social Studies Objectives
1. Understand the developments that led to the Reformation.
2. Learn about Luther's criticism of the Church.
3. Understand the immediate effects of Luther's ideas in Europe.

Reading/Language Arts Objective
Learn how to understand how one cause can bring about multiple effects.

Prepare to Read	**Instructional Resources**	**Differentiated Instruction**
Build Background Knowledge Discuss the movement known as the Reformation. **Set a Purpose for Reading** Have students evaluate statements on the Reading Readiness Guide. **Preview Key Terms** Teach the section's Key Terms. **Target Reading Skill** Introduce the section's Target Reading Skill of understanding how one cause can bring about effects.	**All in One Unit 5 History of Our World Teaching Resources** L2 Reading Readiness Guide, p. 56 L2 Understand Effects p. 65	**Spanish Reading and Vocabulary Study Guide** L2 Chapter 15, Section 3, pp. 119–120 ELL

Instruct	**Instructional Resources**	**Differentiated Instruction**
The Church at the Time of Luther Discuss the power of the Church by the time of the Renaissance. **Luther Starts the Reformation** Discuss Martin Luther's criticisms of the Church and the Church's reaction. **Target Reading Skill** Review understanding effects. **The Reformation Succeeds** Examine reasons for the success of the Reformation.	**All in One Unit 5 History of Our World Teaching Resources** L2 Guided Reading and Review, p. 57 L2 Reading Readiness Guide, p. 56 **History of Our World Transparencies** L2 Section Reading Support Transparency HOW 102	**All in One Unit 5 History of Our World Teaching Resources** L2 Skills for Life, p. 69 AR, GT, LPR, SN **Teacher's Edition** L1 For Less Proficient Readers, p. 443 **Student Edition on Audio CD** L1 Chapter 15, Section 3 ELL, LPR, SN **Spanish Support** L2 Guided Reading and Review (Spanish), p. 130 ELL

Assess and Reteach	**Instructional Resources**	**Differentiated Instruction**
Assess Progress Evaluate student comprehension with the section assessment and section quiz. **Reteach** Assign the Reading and Vocabulary Study Guide to help struggling students. **Extend** Extend the lesson by having students write a script for a scene from a play about the Reformation.	**All in One Unit 5 History of Our World Teaching Resources** L2 Section Quiz, p. 58 L2 Rubric for Assessing a Writing Assignment, p. 78 **Reading and Vocabulary Study Guide** L1 Chapter 15, Section 2, pp. 167–169	**Spanish Support** L2 Section Quiz (Spanish), p. 131 ELL **Social Studies Skills Tutor CD-ROM** L1 Identifying Point of View ELL, LPR, SN

Key

L1 Basic to Average	L3 Average to Advanced	LPR Less Proficient Readers	SN Special Needs Students
L2 For All Students		AR Advanced Readers	GT Gifted and Talented
			ELL English Language Learners

Section 4 Reformation Ideas Spread

 *2 periods, 1 block*

Social Studies Objectives
1. Learn that Luther was the first of several religious reformers.
2. Identify other religious movements of the 1500s in Europe.
3. Understand how the Catholic Church responded to the Reformation.

Reading/Language Arts Objective
Learn how to recognize cause-and-effect signal words.

Section Lesson Planner

Prepare to Read	Instructional Resources	Differentiated Instruction
Build Background Knowledge Discuss how the Reformation spread to other parts of Europe. **Set a Purpose for Reading** Have students begin to fill out the Reading Readiness Guide. **Preview Key Terms** Teach the section's Key Terms. **Target Reading Skill** Introduce the section's Target Reading Skill of recognizing cause-and-effect signal words.	**All in One Unit 5 History of Our World Teaching Resources** **L2** Reading Readiness Guide, p. 60 **L2** Recognize Cause-and-Effect Signal Words, p. 66	**Spanish Reading and Vocabulary Study Guide** **L2** Chapter 15, Section 4, pp. 121–122 ELL

Instruct	Instructional Resources	Differentiated Instruction
The Reformation After Luther Discuss Protestant religious reformers after Luther. **The Catholic Church Reforms** Discuss developments that were part of the Catholic Reformation. **Target Reading Skill** Review recognizing cause-and-effect signal words.	**All in One Unit 5 History of Our World Teaching Resources** **L2** Guided Reading and Review, p. 61 **L2** Reading Readiness Guide, p. 60 **History of Our World Transparencies** **L2** Section Reading Support Transparency HOW 103	**Teacher's Edition** **L3** For Advanced Readers, p. 448 **Spanish Support** **L2** Guided Reading and Review (Spanish), p. 132 ELL **Student Edition on Audio CD** **L1** Chapter 15, Section 4 ELL, LPR, SN

Assess and Reteach	Instructional Resources	Differentiated Instruction
Assess Progress Evaluate student comprehension with the section assessment and section quiz. **Reteach** Assign the Reading and Vocabulary Study Guide to help struggling students. **Extend** Extend the lesson by having students make a timeline of events of the Protestant Reformation and the Catholic Reformation.	**All in One Unit 5 History of Our World Teaching Resources** **L2** Section Quiz, p. 62 **L2** Rubric for Assessing a Writing Assignment, p. 78 **L2** Vocabulary Development, p. 77 **L2** Word Knowledge, p. 67 **L2** Chapter Tests A and B, pp. 80–85 **Reading and Vocabulary Study Guide** **L1** Chapter 15, Section 4, pp. 170–172	**Spanish Support** **L2** Section Quiz (Spanish), p. 133 ELL **L2** Chapter Summary (Spanish), p. 134 ELL **L2** Vocabulary Development (Spanish), p. 135 ELL

Key

L1 Basic to Average	**L3** Average to Advanced	**LPR** Less Proficient Readers	**GT** Gifted and Talented
L2 For All Students		**AR** Advanced Readers	**ELL** English Language Learners
		SN Special Needs Students	

Professional Development

Reading Background

Sharing Key Concepts and Terms

The identification of key concepts and terms is itself the key to comprehension of the text. Students benefit from reviewing significant content and vocabulary with partners or groups.

Use the following activity to help students identify and process key ideas and words for enhanced understanding of what they have read.

1. Distribute note cards to students. Have each student write an explanation of a key concept or term from the chapter on a note card.
2. Ask students to arrange themselves in two concentric circles. Students in the inside circle should face out; students in the outside circle should face in. Tell students to sit opposite a partner in the other circle.
3. Direct student partners to explain their concepts or terms to each other using the notes on their cards. Tell students to ask each other questions as necessary to make sure they understand the concepts or terms being presented.
4. Have student partners trade cards. Then have the outside circle of students move one person clockwise.
5. Repeat the process until students receive their original cards in trade.

Structuring Paragraphs

Learning to structure a paragraph gives students insights that will improve their reading comprehension. Students learn to distinguish between main ideas and details, recognize transitions, and identify topic and summary statements.

Model how to structure a paragraph with these steps.

1. Write a topic sentence that states the main idea.
   Other reformers were active outside of Germany.
2. Add three to five examples of the main idea. Connect them as necessary with transition words.
   Ulrich Zwingli and John Calvin formed churches in Switzerland. Lefèvre d'Étaples worked for church reform in France. In England, John Colet pushed for changes within the church.
3. End with a summary sentence that restates the main idea.
   All were important contributors to the Reformation in the rest of Europe.

Have students write a paragraph following the same steps. Remind students to vary sentence length and structure to hold the reader's attention.

World Studies Background

Humanists and the Renaissance

The Renaissance was a period of rediscovery of classical literature and renewed interest in Greek and Roman culture. Some of the writings of the ancient Greeks and Romans were known to medieval scholars. But much of classical literature had been lost to the general populace during the Middle Ages. Copyists in monasteries had been the keepers of the classics, transcribing plays, poems, and other ancient works over the centuries. At the dawn of the Renaissance, the humanists brought the works of the ancients out of monastery libraries for study. The poet and scholar Francesco Petrarch led this quest for classical literature and learning.

Renaissance Art

The artists of the Renaissance turned to ancient Greek and Roman models for inspiration. Classical art taught them the role of harmony and beauty in art. Renaissance artists became concerned with perspective, experimented with oils for painting, and used living models as their subjects. Great Italian Renaissance artists included Leonardo da Vinci, Michelangelo, and Raphael. Titian, Tintoretto, and Coreggio were other Italian Renaissance artists of note. To the north, Van Eyck took oil painting to new levels. Albrecht Dürer and Hans Holbein helped introduce printed engraving.

Working with Capsule Vocabulary

When students work with capsule vocabulary, or a variety of words related to a topic, they reinforce their understanding of all the words. They also increase their comprehension of the text.

Engage students with capsule vocabulary by following these steps.

1. On the board, write a list of words related to a topic in the chapter. Here is a list of capsule words related to the Reformation.
   indulgence
   theses
   reform
   authority
   salvation
   outlaw
   predestination
   Protestant

2. With students, discuss the Reformation for ten minutes using as many of the capsule words as possible.
3. Have students form groups and have a conversation about the Reformation in their group. Tell students to record each time they use a capsule word in the group conversation.
4. Have students write a brief paragraph about the Reformation using all of the capsule words.

The Reformation and Protestants

Martin Luther's attack on the Catholic Church in his *Ninety-Five Theses* marks the beginning of the Reformation. People were clamoring for change. They identified with Luther's challenges to the Church. By the late 1520s groups for religious reform had formed in many places in Europe. The term *Protestant* was first used in 1529. That year it was decreed in Germany that religious reforms must be halted and the Church's authority must be reestablished. A group of Lutherans signed a protest against the decree. The term came to be used widely for church groups outside of the Catholic Church.

Infoplease® provides a wealth of useful information for the classroom. You can use this resource to strengthen your background on the subjects covered in this chapter. Have students visit this advertising-free site as a starting point for projects requiring research.

 Use Web Code **mud-1500** for **Infoplease®**.

Guiding Questions

Remind students about the Guiding Questions introduced at the beginning of the book.

Section 1 relates to **Guiding Question 3** **What were the beliefs and values of people in these societies?** *(Renaissance writers and artists showed a new interest in the classics and explored nature, beauty, and the human form.)*

Section 2 relates to **Guiding Question 1** **How did physical geography affect the development and growth of societies around the world?** *(Renaissance ideas spread to northern and western Europe as industry and trade expanded.)*

Section 3 relates to **Guiding Question 2** **How did each society's belief system affect its historical accomplishments?** *(Martin Luther challenged beliefs and practices of the Church, starting the Reformation.)*

Section 4 relates to **Guiding Question 2** **How did each society's belief system affect its historical accomplishments?** *(Other reformers used Luther's ideas to form Protestant groups, and the Catholic Church made reforms that helped it survive and grow strong.)*

⊙ Target Reading Skill

In this chapter, students will learn and apply the reading skill of using cause and effect. Use the following worksheets to help students practice this skill.

All in One Unit 5 History of Our World Teaching Resources, *Identify Causes and Effects*, p. 63, *Recognize Multiple Causes*, p. 64, *Understand Effects*, p. 65, *Recognize Cause-and-Effect Signal Words*, p. 66

Differentiated Instruction

The following Teacher Edition strategies are suitable for students of varying abilities.

Less Proficient Readers, p. 443
Special Needs Students, p. 445
Advanced Readers, pp. 439, 448
English Language Learners, pp. 436, 438
Gifted and Talented, p. 432

The Renaissance and Reformation

Chapter Preview

This chapter will explore the sweeping cultural changes in Europe known as the Renaissance and the Reformation.

Section 1
The Renaissance Begins

Section 2
The Renaissance Moves North

Section 3
Martin Luther and the Reformation

Section 4
Reformation Ideas Spread

 Target Reading Skill

Cause and Effect Determining causes and effects helps you understand the relationship between events. A cause makes something happen. An effect is something that results from another event or change. In this chapter you will focus on identifying and understanding historical causes and events.

▶ A gondolier rows along a canal lined by old weathered buildings and spanned by a narrow arched bridge near Piazza San Maria Formosa, Venice, Italy.

428 History of Our World

Bibliography

For the Teacher

Belloc, Hilaire. *How the Reformation Happened.* Kessinger Publishing Company, 2002.

Johnson, Paul. *The Renaissance: A Short History.* Modern Library, 2000.

Rabb, Theodore K. *Renaissance Lives: Portraits of an Age.* Basic Books, 2001.

For the Student

L1 Langley, Andrew. *Eyewitness: Leonardo & His Times.* Dorling Kindersley, 2000.

L2 January, Brendan. *Science in the Renaissance.* Franklin Watts, 1999.

L2 MacDonald, Fiona. *The Reformation.* Raintree/Steck Vaughn, 2002.

L3 *What Life Was Like at the Rebirth of Genius: Renaissance Italy, A.D. 1400–1550.* Time-Life, 1999.

MAP★MASTER™ Skills Activity

Renaissance Italy, 1510

Regions Before the modern idea of nations existed, what we know as Italy was made up of regions, each controlled by a powerful city.

Use the Key Who controlled Corsica? Sicily and Sardinia? Which states had little or no access to the sea?

Draw Conclusions Venice was a great European trading and commercial power during the Renaissance. What information does the map provide that would support that fact?

Milan
Venice
Genoa
Pisa
Florence
Adriatic Sea
Corsica
Rome
NAPLES
Naples
SARDINIA
Mediterranean Sea
SICILY

KEY
Duchy of Milan
Papal States
Other Italian states
Republic of Genoa
Republic of Venice
• City
Republic of Florence
Kingdoms under Spanish sovereignty

0 miles 200
0 kilometers 200
Lambert Azimuthal Equal Area

Go Online
PHSchool.com Use Web Code **mup-1501** for step-by-step map skills practice.

Chapter 15 **429**

MAP★MASTER™ Skills Activity

- Point out to students the shape of Italy. Encourage students to trace the outline of the region, while describing its shape.

- Ask students to use the map's scale to measure the approximate length of the territories held by each duchy, republic, state, or kingdom, and compare them. Ask **Which had the most area?** *(Spain)* **Which had the smallest?** *(Florence)*

Go Online
PHSchool.com Students may practice their map skills using the interactive online version of this map.

Using the Visual

Reach Into Your Background Ask students to study the photograph on pages 428 and 429 and to read the caption on page 428. Discuss the visual with students and have them note details about the image. Ask them to reach into their own background: Have they ever seen buildings similar to those shown in the photograph? If so, where? Encourage students to discuss their ideas.

Answers

MAP★MASTER Skills Activity Use the Key Genoa; Spain; Milan. **Draw Conclusions** Milan, because it is inland; there is no way to approach this city by sea.

Chapter Resources

Teaching Resources
L2 Vocabulary Development, p. 77
L2 Skills for Life, p. 69
L2 Chapter Tests A and B, pp. 80–85

Spanish Support
L2 Spanish Chapter Summary, p. 134
L2 Spanish Vocabulary Development, p. 135

Media and Technology
L1 Student Edition on Audio CD
L1 Guided Reading Audio CDs, English and Spanish
L2 Social Studies Skills Tutor CD-ROM
ExamView© **Test Bank CD-ROM**

Discovery CHANNEL **SCHOOL** History of Our World Video Program

interactive **Textbook**
PRENTICE HALL
TeacherEXPRESS™
Plan • Teach • Assess

Objectives

Social Studies

1. Find out why Italy was the birthplace of the Renaissance.

2. Understand how literature and art were transformed during the Renaissance.

Reading/Language Arts

Learn to identify causes and effects to better understand the relationships among situations and events.

Prepare to Read

Build Background Knowledge [L2]

Tell students that in this section they will learn about the beginnings of the period known as the Renaissance. Read the paragraphs on page 432 aloud. Ask students **What words or phrases would you use to describe Renaissance art and literature?** Use the Idea Wave participation structure (TE, p. T39) to generate responses. *(Possible responses: change, new, wide interests, new ideas, art, new skills, nature, humanism, human form)*

Set a Purpose for Reading [L2]

■ Preview the Objectives.

■ Read each statement in the *Reading Readiness Guide* aloud. Ask students to mark the statements true or false.

All in One Unit 5 History of Our World Teaching Resources, *Reading Readiness Guide,* p. 48

■ Have students discuss the statement in pairs or groups of four, then mark their worksheets again. Use the Numbered Heads participation structure (TE, p. T40) to call on students to share their group's perspectives.

Vocabulary Builder
Preview Key Terms [L2]

Pronounce each Key Term, then ask students to say the word with you. Provide a simple explanation such as "the word *renaissance* means 'rebirth,' and during the Renaissance ideas from the ancient world were born again when people began to look at them in new ways."

Prepare to Read

Objectives

In this section you will

1. Find out why Italy was the birthplace of the Renaissance.

2. Understand how literature and art were transformed during the Renaissance.

Taking Notes

As you read, look for reasons why the Renaissance began in Italy and how literature and art changed during this period. Copy the outline below, and record your findings in it.

> I. Why the Renaissance started in Italy
>   A.
>   B.
> II. The effects of the Renaissance
>   A.
>   B.

 Target Reading Skill

Identify Causes and Effects To understand a historical period or event, it is helpful to know what caused it to happen and what effects it had. As you read this section, identify the causes of the Renaissance in Italy, as well as the effects. Write the causes and effects in your Taking Notes diagram.

Key Terms

- **Renaissance** (REN uh sahns) *n.* a widespread change in culture that took place in Europe, beginning with the 1300s
- **humanism** (HYOO muh niz um) *n.* an interest in the classics

La Gioconda (lah joh KAHN duh) is another name for the *Mona Lisa.*

430 History of Our World

The *Mona Lisa* is perhaps the most famous piece of art in the world. It is one of the masterpieces created by the great Italian artist, Leonardo da Vinci (lee uh NAHR doh duh VIN chee). Like many of da Vinci's works, however, the *Mona Lisa* may have never been finished. It is possible that da Vinci was drawn to another project without finishing the painting, as he had done on other projects. Da Vinci was not only a painter. He was also one of the world's greatest inventors and scientists.

The story of da Vinci and the *Mona Lisa* reveals much about the Renaissance. This is the term historians use for the period between 1300 and 1650 in Europe. During that time, the culture of Europe changed dramatically. Artists used new skills and techniques to create works of great beauty and charm. Scholars began looking at the world and its people in new ways. The spirit of the Renaissance is clearly seen in the life of Leonardo da Vinci. His great skills and wide interests reflect much of the spirit and character of the era.

 Target Reading Skill [L2]

Identify Causes and Effects Point out the Target Reading Skill. Tell students that being able to identify causes and effects will help them to understand how and why events occur or why situations develop.

Model identifying the cause and effect in the paragraph on p. 432 that begins with this sentence: "The first great humanist was Francesco Petrarch (1304–1374)." Explain that Petrarch loved the works of Cicero and other Latin classics is a cause. This love is seen in the poetry for which he is known is an effect of this cause.

Give students *Identify Causes and Effects.* Have them complete the activity in their groups.

All in One Unit 5 History of Our World Teaching Resources, *Identify Causes and Effects,* p. 63

The Renaissance Begins in Italy

The **Renaissance** was a widespread change in culture that took place in Europe beginning with the 1300s. The movement began in Italy.

Look at the map on this page, and notice Italy's place on the Mediterranean Sea. Because of this location, Italy became a center of European trade with the rich lands of the East during the late Middle Ages. While feudalism still dominated the rest of Europe, Italy's merchants were building great fortunes.

Italy's trade was based in its cities. Over time, these cities became centers of power and wealth. Successful merchants bought up feudal lands, and many nobles moved to the cities to seek their fortunes. The most powerful Italian cities became independent city-states. They were not under the control of a king or a noble. Even the Roman Catholic Church held little power in these cities.

✓ Reading Check Why did the Renaissance begin in Italy?

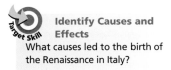

Identify Causes and Effects
What causes led to the birth of the Renaissance in Italy?

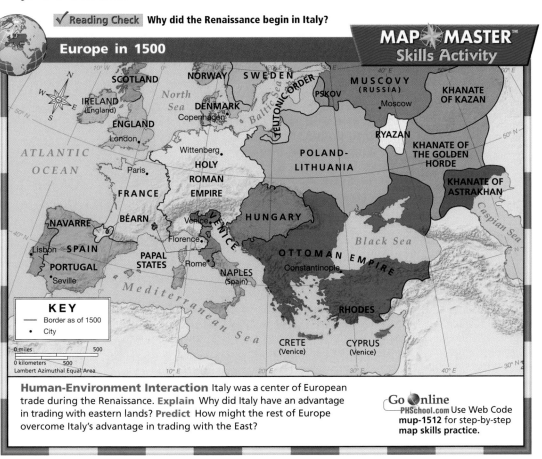

Europe in 1500

MAP MASTER™ Skills Activity

KEY
— Border as of 1500
• City

0 miles 500
0 kilometers 500
Lambert Azimuthal Equal Area

Human-Environment Interaction Italy was a center of European trade during the Renaissance. **Explain** Why did Italy have an advantage in trading with eastern lands? **Predict** How might the rest of Europe overcome Italy's advantage in trading with the East?

Go Online
PHSchool.com Use Web Code **mup-1512** for step-by-step map skills practice.

Chapter 15 Section 1 **431**

Vocabulary Builder

Use the information below to teach students this section's high-use words.

High-Use Word	Definition and Sample Sentence
nobles, p. 431	*n.* people of high birth or exalted rank The **nobles** formed the upper class of society.

The Renaissance Begins in Italy [L2]

Guided Instruction

■ **Vocabulary Builder** Clarify the meaning of the high-use word **nobles** before reading.

■ Read The Renaissance Begins in Italy, using the Choral Reading technique (TE, p. T38).

■ Discuss conditions that help explain why the Renaissance began in Italy. *(Italy was at the center of the Mediterranean; it was a center of trade with the East; its merchants and cities became powerful and wealthy.)*

■ Ask students **How did the wealth and independence of Italian city-states encourage cultural changes?** *(Wealthy merchants had time to pursue art, reading, and writing; artists and writers could work in the city-states, free from the control of kings, nobles, and the Church.)*

Independent Practice

Ask students to create the Taking Notes outline on a blank piece of paper. Then have them fill in details about why the Renaissance began in Italy. Briefly model the kinds of information to include.

Monitor Progress

As students fill in the outline, circulate and make sure individuals are choosing correct details. Provide assistance as needed.

⊙ Target Reading Skill

Identify Causes and Effects As a follow up, ask students to answer the Target Reading Skill question in the Student Edition. *(Italy became a center of European trade. Merchants and ordinary people could earn fame and fortune. Italy's trade was based in its cities, which became centers of power and wealth. The most powerful Italian cities became independent city-states.)*

Answers

MAP MASTER™ Skills Activity **Explain** It was closer to Eastern lands and had access to important waterways. **Predict** They would develop new trade routes that were shorter or more efficient.

✓ Reading Check Its location helped Italian cities grow in power and wealth.

Renaissance Art and Literature

Guided Instruction

- Read Renaissance Art and Literature. As students read, circulate and make sure individuals can answer the Reading Check question.

- Examine how literature and art changed during the Renaissance. (*Writers turned to the writings of the ancient Greeks and Romans and explored ideas such as nature and beauty; artists began to focus on nature and the human form.*)

- Ask students **Why do you think classical works were largely ignored during the Middle Ages?** (*Possible answer: The Church had great influence during the Middle Ages, and it wanted people to turn away from the worship of many gods.*)

Independent Practice

Have students complete the Taking Notes outline with details about the effects of the Renaissance.

Show *Leonardo da Vinci: A Renaissance Man.* Ask **In what ways did Leonardo da Vinci demonstrate Renaissance ideals?** (*Leonardo had great skills and wide interests in art, science, architecture, and engineering and produced paintings, sculptures, sketches, and inventions.*)

Monitor Practice

- Show *Section Reading Support Transparency HOW 100* and ask students to check their graphic organizers individually. Review key concepts and clarify key vocabulary as needed.

  History of Our World Transparencies, *Section Reading Support Transparency HOW 100*

- Tell students to fill in the last column of the *Reading Readiness Guide.* Probe for what they learned that confirms or invalidates each statement.

  All in One Unit 5 History of Our World Teaching Resources, *Reading Readiness Guide,* p. 48

Answer

Analyze Possible answer: Renaissance artists were influenced by the ideas and writings of the ancient Greeks.

Renaissance Art
Raphael depicts the great thinkers of Ancient Greece.
Analyze *Why do you think Raphael included the Greek philosophers in this painting?*

Explore the art and science of Leonardo da Vinci.

Renaissance Art and Literature

The Renaissance is celebrated today as a time of great artistic achievement. Artists in all fields created stunning works. These efforts marked a sharp change from the art of the Middle Ages. During that period, art had focused on the Church. That focus began to change in the 1300s.

Literature As you have read, a new social system was taking shape in Italy's cities. Life no longer centered on feudalism and the Church. Many writers began to turn their attention to something new—or, rather, to something very old. These were the ideas and writings of the ancient Romans and Greeks. The classical works focused on worldly issues, not religious matters. They explored nature, beauty, and other concepts long ignored in medieval life. This new interest in the classics is known as **humanism.**

The first great humanist was Francesco Petrarch (frahn CHES koh PEA trahrk) (1304–1374). Even as a child, he had loved the works of Cicero (SIS uh roh) and other Latin writers. Petrarch's father disapproved of his son's tastes. He once became so angry that he threw Petrarch's books into a fire. Yet Petrarch continued to study the ancient Romans. His love of the classics is clearly seen in the flawless poetry for which he is known. Petrarch's sonnets reveal a view of love and nature that is far different from medieval sonnets. He also collected the works of many Latin authors.

432 History of Our World

Differentiated Instruction

For Gifted and Talented L3
Have students present a reading of some of Petrarch's sonnets. Assign appropriate and representative poems to students. Students should practice reading their poems aloud and should prepare brief comments on how the poems reflect Renaissance views of the world.

Visual Art Medieval art had dealt mostly with religious topics. Like Renaissance writers, however, artists of the Renaissance began to focus on nature and the human form. Painters and sculptors still created religious scenes. These works, however, showed the human body with great accuracy and detail.

You have read about Leonardo da Vinci and his great works. Da Vinci also became famous for the more than 4,000 notebook pages that he filled with sketches and notes about the world around him. The Italian Renaissance also produced such masters as Michelangelo (my kul AN juh loh). His greatest work may be the famous ceiling of the Sistene Chapel. Like da Vinci's *Mona Lisa*, this work is among the most beloved and recognized paintings in history.

In the early to mid-1400s, the sculptor Donatello (doh nuh TEL oh) worked in the city of Florence, creating life-like sculptures of the human body. He was inspired by the Greeks and Romans of antiquity. Some of Donatello's most famous works are a series of sculptures of the Biblical figure David. Donatello was a master of many techniques, using a variety of materials, including marble and bronze, for his sculptures.

✓ **Reading Check** What was the main focus of Renaissance visual artists?

Section 1 Assessment

Key Terms
Review the key terms at the beginning of this section. Use each term in a sentence that explains its meaning.

Target Reading Skill
Explain the causes that brought about the Renaissance in Italy.

Comprehension and Critical Thinking
1. (a) Recall What activity helped transform life in Italy in the late Middle Ages?

(b) Identify Cause and Effect What affect did the rise of cities have on feudal life in Italy?
2. (a) Identify What was the major influence on writers of the Renaissance?
(b) Summarize How did the interest in Greek and Roman classical literature affect Renaissance authors?
3. (a) Explain How did the focus of Italian artists change during the Renaissance?
(b) Analyze Images What details from Raphael's painting on page 432 illustrate the key features of Renaissance art?

Writing Activity
From the perspective of a person living in an Italian city-state at the start of the Renaissance, write a letter to a relative living somewhere in feudal Europe. Describe some of the changes you see taking place in the world around you.

For: An activity on the Renaissance in Northern Italy
Visit: PHSchool.com
Web Code: mud-1510

---

2. (a) Greek and Roman ideas and writing
(b) Renaissance authors focused on ideas such as nature and beauty, which were the focus of classical literature.

3. (a) It began to focus more on nature and the human form. **(b)** Answers will vary.

Writing Activity
Use the *Rubric for Assessing a Writing Assignment* to evaluate students' work.

All in One Unit 5 History of Our World Teaching Resources, *Rubric for Assessing a Writing Assignment,* p. 78

Go Online PHSchool.com Typing in the Web Code when prompted will bring students directly to detailed instructions for this activity.

Citizen Heroes

Read the **Citizen Heroes** text on page 433. Ask students **Why did Cosimo de Medici promote study of the Greek language?** (*He wanted people to be able to read Greek classical works in their original language.*)

Assess and Reteach

Assess Progress   L2
Have students complete the Section Assessment. Administer the *Section Quiz.*

All in One Unit 5 History of Our World Teaching Resources, *Section Quiz,* p. 50

Reteach   L1
If students need more instruction, have them read the section in the Reading and Vocabulary Study Guide.

History of Our World Reading and Vocabulary Study Guide, Chapter 15, Section 1, pp. 161–163

Extend   L3
Show students images of the works of art mentioned in the section. Discuss how each represents Renaissance ideas. Then have students use the Internet or library resources to find other examples of the visual art of the Italian Renaissance. Students should write a paragraph about how one of the images they have found represents Renaissance ideas.

Answer

✓ **Reading Check** Renaissance visual artists focused on nature and the human form.

Section 1 Assessment

Key Terms
Students' sentences should reflect knowledge of each Key Term.

Target Reading Skill
Wealth passed into the hands of people other than nobles and clergy. More money was spent on the arts. As trade grew, goods and services, ideas, and art were exchanged.

Comprehension and Critical Thinking
1. (a) Trade **(b)** The Church and nobles lost power; merchants bought land, and nobles had to move to the cities to make their fortunes.

Section 2
Step-by-Step Instruction

Objectives

Social Studies

1. Understand how the Renaissance spread from Italy to the north.
2. Identify key literary figures and ideas of the Northern Renaissance.
3. Identify key artists and artistic ideas of the Northern Renaissance.

Reading/Language Arts

Learn to recognize multiple causes to understand the development of complex events.

Prepare to Read

Build Background Knowledge L2

In this section, students will learn about the spread of Renaissance ideas from Italy to the north. Ask students to preview the section, noting headings, images, and anything else that stands out. Then have them predict how the Renaissance in the north was similar to and different from the Renaissance in Italy. Use the Give One, Get One participation structure (TE, p. T41) to generate predictions. Students may then read to check their predictions.

Set a Purpose for Reading L2

■ Preview the Objectives.

■ Read each statement in the *Reading Readiness Guide* aloud. Ask students to mark the statements true or false.

All in One Unit 5 History of Our World Teaching Resources, *Reading Readiness Guide,* p. 52

■ Have students discuss the statement in pairs or groups of four, then mark their worksheets again. Use the Numbered Heads participation structure (TE, p. T40) to call on students to share their group's perspectives.

Vocabulary Builder
Preview Key Terms L2

Pronounce each Key Term. Then ask students to say the word with you. Provide a simple explanation, such as "Type can mean using a keyboard to write something, but it also is the letters and marks that you see on the pages of your book."

Section 2 The Renaissance Moves North

Prepare to Read

Objectives
In this section you will

1. Understand how the Renaissance spread from Italy to the north.
2. Identify key literary figures and ideas of the Northern Renaissance.
3. Identify key artists and artistic ideas of the Northern Renaissance.

Taking Notes
As you read, look for material that explains how Renaissance ideas spread and developed throughout Europe. Copy the graphic organizer below. Record your findings in it.

Renaissance North of Italy		
Renaissance Spreads North	Literature of the Northern Renaissance	Art of the Northern Renaissance
•	•	•
•	•	•

Target Reading Skill

Recognize Multiple Causes Historical events can be complicated; sometimes several factors cause an event to happen. As you read this section, identify the multiple reasons why the Renaissance spread to the North.

Key Terms
• **movable type** (MOO vuh bul typ) *n.* individual letters and marks that can be arranged and rearranged quickly

The artisan's work was painstaking. At his bench was a block of wood. With great care, he carved away the surface. His task was to create a raised surface that could then be smeared with ink and pressed onto a flat material. What was the result of all this effort? It was a single page of a book.

In the mid-1400s, a German printer named Johannes Gutenberg (yoh HAHN us GOOT un burg) began work on a project that would create a new way of printing books. He would develop a system of **movable type**—individual letters and marks that could be arranged and rearranged quickly. Gutenberg also developed a printing press, a machine that used movable type to print pages. The availability of books would change the way information and ideas traveled in Europe and the world.

Movable type allowed printers to use the same letters for different pages.

434 History of Our World

Target Reading Skill L2

Recognize Multiple Causes Point out the Target Reading Skill. Tell students that often an event or problem has more than one cause. To understand a complex situation, it is important to recognize if it has various causes and what they might be.

Model recognizing multiple causes by looking at the first paragraph on p. 435. (*Causes—northern industry and trade* expanded and the feudal and religious base of medieval society weakened. Effects—changes in literature, art, and culture*)

Give students *Recognize Multiple Causes.* Have them complete the activity in their groups.

All in One Unit 5 History of Our World Teaching Resources, *Recognize Multiple Causes,* p. 64

Renaissance Thought and Literature Spreads

Over time, the changes that supported the birth of the Renaissance in Italy moved northward into western and northern Europe. Northern industry and trade expanded. The feudal and religious base of medieval society weakened. These changes were followed by changes in literature, art, and culture. Renaissance ideas, along with developments such as Gutenberg's printing methods, helped bring great change to the entire European continent.

As had happened in Italy, many scholars in northern and western Europe became interested in humanism. Renaissance thinkers throughout Europe applied the ideas of humanism to religious thinking, a movement called Christian humanism. These thinkers were concerned with the study of Christianity, rather than with the study of Greek and Roman texts. The leading figure of Christian humanism was Dutch-born Desiderius Erasmus (des uh DIHR ee us ih RAZ mus) (1466–1536).

Erasmus was a Roman Catholic priest. However, in one of his most famous works, *In Praise of Folly*, he mocked certain Church practices. These practices, he believed, had little to do with true faith. In fact, Erasmus thought that such practices often covered up corruption. Erasmus was also a leading scholar of Greek and Latin. His efforts had a powerful impact on education in Europe.

One of Erasmus's close friends was England's Sir Thomas More (sur TAHM us mawr). More was a lawyer. He may have been influenced by Greek thinkers such as Plato and Aristotle. His famous work *Utopia* (yoo TOH pea uh) describes an ideal world that is based on Greek philosophy. By writing about this perfect place, More was actually pointing out problems he saw in his own world, such as divisions between people who were politically weak and others who were politically powerful.

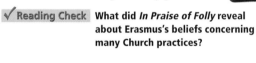 **Reading Check** What did *In Praise of Folly* reveal about Erasmus's beliefs concerning many Church practices?

Target Skill **Recognize Multiple Causes**
What are some of the causes that allowed Renaissance ideas to spread northward?

Gutenberg built this printing press to produce the Bible.

Chapter 15 Section 2 **435**

Vocabulary Builder

Use the information below to teach students this section's high-use words.

High-Use Word	Definition and Sample Sentence
painstaking, p. 434	*adj.* involving diligent care and effort Her research on the subject was **painstaking.**
immortality, p. 436	*n.* unending existence The idea of **immortality** has interested philosophers through the ages.
realism, p. 437	*n.* accurate representation without idealization The **realism** of the painting made it seem almost like a photograph.

Literature of the Northern Renaissance L2

Guided Instruction

- **Vocabulary Builder** Clarify the meaning of the high-use word **immortality**.

- Read Literature of the Northern Renaissance. Circulate to make sure students can answer the Reading Check question.

- Discuss key literary figures and ideas of the Northern Renaissance.

Links

Read the **Links to Art** Ask students **How were medieval and Renaissance churches different?** *(Renaissance churches were circular and medieval churches were cross-shaped.)*

Art of the Northern Renaissance L2

Guided Instruction

- **Vocabulary Builder** Clarify the meaning of the high-use word **realism**.

- Read Art of the Northern Renaissance.

- Identify artists of northern and western Europe and discuss their techniques. *(Van Eyck used layers of oil paints and bright colors; Dürer painted but also made woodcuts and engravings.)*

Independent Practice

Have students complete the Taking Notes graphic organizer.

Monitor Practice

- Show *Section Reading Support Transparency HOW 101.* Ask students to check their graphic organizers. Review key concepts and key vocabulary.

  History of Our World Transparencies, *Section Reading Support Transparency HOW 101*

- Tell students to complete the *Reading Readiness Guide.* Probe for what they learned that confirms or invalidates each statement

  All in One Unit 5 History of Our World Teaching Resources, *Reading Readiness Guide,* p. 52

Answers

Name Answers will vary.

✓ **Reading Check** love and patriotism

Links to Art

Renaissance Architecture
The Renaissance also affected architecture in Europe. Like artists and writers of the period, Renaissance architects drew ideas and forms from ancient Greece and Rome. For instance, medieval churches had been built in the shape of a cross. Now, architects designed buildings in a circular shape. In the ancient world, the circle—a simple, clean figure—represented the perfect shape.

The Globe Theater
The Globe, one of the public theaters in London during the Renaissance, saw the production of many of Shakespeare's plays. A modern staging of *A Midsummer Night's Dream* is pictured at right. **Name** *What other Shakespeare plays do you know?*

436 History of Our World

Literature of the Northern Renaissance

Many writers in northern and western Europe were influenced by new literary ideas developed during the Italian Renaissance. Like Petrarch and other Italian writers, these authors experimented with new ideas and unfamiliar literary forms.

François Rabelais (frahn SWAH rab uh LAY) of France was a devoted follower of Erasmus. Rabelais's best-known work is *Gargantua and Pantagruel* (gahr GAN choo uh and pan tuh groo EL), a tale that uses comedy to express the ideas of humanism.

A group of seven French poets known as the Pleiade (play YAD) applied ancient Greek and Roman forms to create new poetry in French. These poems focused on common themes, such as love and patriotism.

The spread of Renaissance ideas also brought new energy to poets in England. Sir Thomas Wyatt and the Earl of Surrey helped introduce a popular Italian form of poetry, the sonnet, to English audiences in the early 1500s.

England's best-known poet, William Shakespeare (WIL yum SHAYK spihr) (1564–1616), wrote at least 37 verse plays, many of them based on plots borrowed from ancient works. Shakespeare changed details of these ancient stories to appeal to the audiences of his day, and he created many memorable characters, including Romeo and Juliet. Shakespeare's interest in the human character was a key feature of the Renaissance.

✓ **Reading Check** **What common theme was shared by many Renaissance writers in France and England?**

Differentiated Instruction

English Language Learners L1

Pair English language learners and English-proficient readers. Have English language learners read the section as they listen to the recorded version on the Student Edition on Audio CD. Have their partners check their comprehension by pausing the CD after several paragraphs and asking questions about the content. Students should discuss answers to questions and any content that is not clear before resuming listening.

History of Our World Chapter 15, Section 2, **Student Edition on Audio CD**

Art of the Northern Renaissance

Several artists in northern and western Europe distinguished themselves during the Renaissance. Flemish painter Jan van Eyck (yahn van yk), who lived in the early 1400s, was a master of realistic portraits. Van Eyck used multiple layers of oil paints to create rich visual effects. His bright colors and eye for realism show the details of everyday life in the region that is now part of Belgium and the Netherlands. He was only one of several well-known Renaissance painters from the Netherlands.

Germany's Albrecht Dürer (AHL brekt DYOOR ur) (1471–1528) was a painter as well as a master of woodcuts and engravings. In the late 1400s, Dürer visited Italy to see firsthand the work of Italian Renaissance masters. This visit had a deep impact on the young artist, whose work began to reflect the Italian style.

Dürer was a person of wide interests. In the early 1500s, his work began to reflect events that were just then shaking the religious foundation of Europe. In the next lesson you will read about these events, which are known collectively as the Reformation.

One of Van Eyck's most famous paintings, *The Marriage of Giovanni Arnolfini and Giovanna Cenami*

 Reading Check From which country did Jan Van Eyck come?

Section 2 Assessment

Key Terms
Review the key terms listed at the beginning of this section. Use each term in a sentence that explains its meaning.

Target Reading Skill
What caused the Renaissance to spread beyond Italy?

Comprehension and Critical Thinking
1. (a) Explain What developments in Europe help explain why the Renaissance spread north from Italy?
(b) Synthesize Information Why did Renaissance developments in northern and eastern Europe lag behind those of Italy?
2. (a) List Identify two literary figures of the Renaissance in western and northern Europe.
(b) Summarize How would you summarize the spread of Renaissance literary ideas in western and northern Europe?
3. (a) List Identify two artists who were part of the Northern Renaissance.
(b) Make Generalizations What features did the art of Dürer and Van Eyck share with Italian Renaissance art?

Writing Activity
With a classmate, write a debate about whether the Renaissance in Italy was more spectacular than the Renaissance in northern and western Europe. Have one student argue in favor of Italy and the other argue in favor of northern and western Europe.

For: An activity on the Renaissance in the North
Visit: PHSchool.com
Web Code: mud-1520

Writing Activity
Use the *Rubric for Assessing a Writing Assignment* to evaluate students' work.

All in One Unit 5 History of Our World Teaching Resources, *Rubric for Assessing a Writing Assignment,* p. 78

Go Online PHSchool.com Typing in the Web Code when prompted will bring students directly to detailed instructions for this activity.

Assess and Reteach

Assess Progress L2
Have students complete the Section Assessment. Administer the *Section Quiz.*

All in One Unit 5 History of Our World Teaching Resources, p. 54

Reteach L1
If students need more instruction, have them read the section in the Reading and Vocabulary Study Guide.

History of Our World Reading and Vocabulary Study Guide, Chapter 15, Section 2, pp. 164–166

Extend L3
Have students research a figure of the Northern Renaissance discussed in the section. Ask students to write a two-page biography of the person that includes basic information about the person's life and explains the person's significance as a Renaissance figure.

Answer

Reading Check the Netherlands

Section 2 Assessment

Key Terms
Students' sentences should reflect knowledge of each Key Term.

Target Reading Skill
The Renaissance moved into western and northern Europe because industry and trade expanded, and feudal and religious bases weakened. These changes were followed by changes in literature, art, and culture. Renaissance ideas, along with developments such as Gutenberg's printing methods, helped bring change to Europe.

Comprehension and Critical Thinking
1. (a) Industry and trade expanded, and the feudal and religious base of society weakened. **(b)** Trade with the East brought new wealth and ideas to Italy before other parts of Europe.

2. (a) Rabelais and Shakespeare **(b)** Writers in northern and western Europe used new ideas and new literary forms that had developed during the Italian Renaissance.

3. (a) Jan Van Eyck and Albrecht Dürer **(b)** Both were influenced by Italian Renaissance art.

Focus on Renaissance Printing

Guided Instruction

Ask students how long they think it would take them to copy their textbook by hand. Remind students that before the printing press was invented, all books were copied by hand. Explain that students will learn about the development of the printing press. Then ask students to predict what effects printing books by hand had on the books and the readers, using the Idea Wave. *(high cost and low availability, easier to make errors; fewer people who could read; new ideas and new inventions developed slowly; most people were uninformed so political power rested with an elite.)*

Focus On
Renaissance Printing

Suppose that in order to create a new book, you had to copy every word by hand. Or you had to brush ink on individual letters and stamp each one on paper. Either process would be enormously time-consuming. There would be very few books in existence and limited ways for people to share knowledge and discoveries. The invention of the printing press around 1450 solved this problem. The printing press helped satisfy the great desire for learning and books fueled by the Renaissance.

The Printing Press Johannes Gutenberg, a German inventor, is credited with inventing the printing press. His press was adapted from machines used to press grapes. It used movable type—separate pieces of raised metal type that could be used again and again.

As he prepared to print, the printer took pieces of type, letter-by-letter, from a box, or type case. He then arranged the letters and screwed or tied them in place. He inked the type. Then he placed paper on the type. By turning a huge screw on the press, he brought down a wooden block against the paper to create a printed page.

If you entered a Renaissance print shop like the one shown in this illustration, you might see a highly skilled master printer and an apprentice, or student printer. A journeyman who had completed his apprenticeship and was qualified to work as a printer might also be there. The first books were literary and scientific works, as well as religious texts. Therefore, a scholar might also be present. His job was to advise on the accuracy of the texts.

An Early Bible
Artists decorated printed pages with bright colors and elaborate paintings and designs.

Differentiated Instruction

For English Language Learners L1
The distinctions among the terms *apprentice*, *journeyman*, and *master printer* may be confusing for some students. Clarify the meaning of the terms as they are encountered.

Background: Global Perspectives

Gutenberg Bible Online Just as Gutenberg's new technology made books more accessible, computer technology is allowing people around the world to view his original books online. The British Library has cooperated with experts from Keio University in Tokyo, Japan, to create digital images of the two copies owned by The British Library. Librarians hope the digitized copies will make comparing the versions easier. The copies are not identical. One copy, the King's copy donated by King George III, is more highly decorated than the Grenville copy, which was printed on vellum.

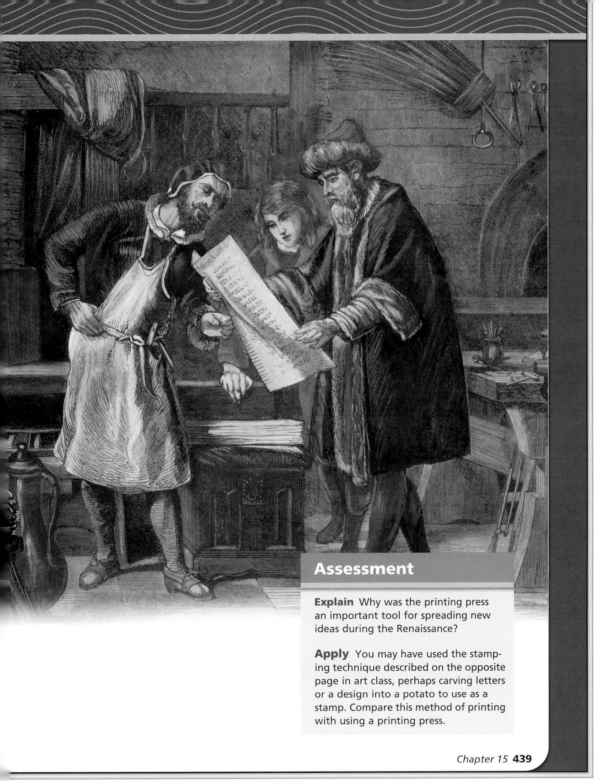

Ask students to take notes on The Printing Press on page 438. Then organize students in pairs. Instruct partners to create a flow chart that shows the sequence of the printing process.

Assessment

Explain Why was the printing press an important tool for spreading new ideas during the Renaissance?

Apply You may have used the stamping technique described on the opposite page in art class, perhaps carving letters or a design into a potato to use as a stamp. Compare this method of printing with using a printing press.

Differentiated Instruction

For Advanced Readers **L3**
Have students read more about the techniques used to preserve old books, such as the Gutenberg Bible, which is now more than 500 years old. Suggest that students look for information on the kinds of paper and inks used in old printing, and how old texts are protected and stored. Working in pairs or small groups, students may find information on the Internet or at a library. Then students can present the information to the class in a short oral report.

Answer

Assessment

Explain Possible answer: The printing press made publishing less expensive and more timely. People learned about new ideas more quickly, and more people learned to read because they could afford books.

Apply Answers will vary, but should include references to speed, accuracy, and difficulty.

Section 3 Martin Luther and the Reformation

Objectives

Social Studies
1. Understand the developments that led to the Reformation.
2. Learn about Luther's criticism of the Church.
3. Understand the immediate effects of Luther's ideas in Europe.

Reading/Language Arts
Learn how to understand how one cause can bring about multiple effects.

Prepare to Read

Build Background Knowledge L2

Tell students that in this section they will learn about the movement known as the Reformation. Have students skim the text of the section and preview the images to find answers to these questions: **What kind of movement was the Reformation? Who started the movement? What was the main effect of the Reformation?** Have students use the Think-Pair-Share participation structure (TE, p. T40) to share answers. (*Possible answers: The Reformation was a religious movement; Martin Luther started it; its main effect was the creation of a faith that was different from the Church of Rome.*)

Set a Purpose for Reading L2

■ Preview the Objectives.

■ Read each statement in the *Reading Readiness Guide* aloud. Ask students to mark the statements true or false.

All in One Unit 5 History of Our World Teaching Resources, *Reading Readiness Guide,* p. 56

■ Have students discuss the statement in pairs or groups of four, then mark their worksheets again. Use the Numbered Heads participation structure (TE, p. T40) to call on students to share their group's perspectives.

Vocabulary Builder
Preview Key Terms L2

Pronounce each Key Term. Then ask students to say the word with you. Provide a simple explanation such as "The Reformation was a movement that wanted changes in practices of the Church of Rome."

440 *History of Our World*

Prepare to Read

Objectives
In this section you will
1. Understand the developments that led to the Reformation.
2. Learn about Luther's criticism of the Church.
3. Understand the immediate effects of Luther's ideas in Europe.

Taking Notes

As you read, look for the effects of the Church's behavior. Copy the diagram below, and record your findings in it.

```
┌─────────────────────────────┐
│          CAUSES             │
│                             │
└─────────────────────────────┘
              │
              ▼
┌─────────────────────────────┐
│ EVENT: Luther posts his     │
│ "95 Theses"                 │
└─────────────────────────────┘
              │
              ▼
┌─────────────────────────────┐
│          EFFECTS            │
│                             │
└─────────────────────────────┘
```

Target Reading Skill

Understand Effects
A cause makes an effect happen. Sometimes a cause creates several effects. As you read this section, think of the behavior of the Church as a cause. What was the effect of this cause? Write the effects in your Taking Notes diagram.

Key Terms
• **indulgence** (in DUL juns) *n.* an official pardon for a sin given by the pope in return for money
• **salvation** (sal VAY shun) *n.* to go to heaven, in religious terms
• **Reformation** (ref ur MAY shun) *n.* the term used to describe Luther's break with the Church and the movement it inspired

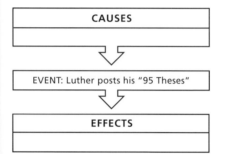

Reformers tried to stop Church abuses by distributing leaflets such as the one above.

440 History of Our World

The preacher was Johann Tetzel (YOH hahn Tet sul), and in return for a contribution to the Church, Tetzel said, a person could receive an indulgence. An **indulgence** allowed the buyer to escape punishment for sins. Moreover, Tetzel said, an indulgence could be used to help a loved one who had died. In vivid language, Tetzel told of the torment of the dead as they suffered for their sins. This suffering could be avoided, Tetzel suggested, for a small sum.

The granting of indulgences was not new in the Church. It had been taking place for centuries. In the early 1500s, the Church was trying to raise money for a glorious new church to be built in Rome. Tetzel was selling indulgences as part of this effort. However, attitudes towards this and other Church practices were changing. For a German monk named Martin Luther (MAHRT un LOO thur), Johann Tetzel's actions went too far.

Target Reading Skill L2

Understand Effects Point out the Target Reading Skill. Tell students that it is important to understand what the effects of different causes are, and how those effects change and shape the world.

Model understanding effects by writing these two events on the board: Johann Tetzel began selling indulgences. Martin Luther issued a challenge to the Church. Connect the two with an arrow. Explain that Tetzel's act was a cause of what Luther did, and Luther's act was an effect of Tetzel's action.

Give students *Understand Effects*. Have them complete the activity in their groups.

All in One Unit 5 History of Our World Teaching Resources, *Understand Effects,* p. 65

Differences Between Catholics and Protestants
This German woodcut from the Reformation visually expresses religious conflicts. **Critical Thinking** *Note the details in the two halves of the woodcut. Which half represents Protestants and which represents Catholics?*

The Church at the Time of Luther

As you have read, the Church had been at the very heart of medieval European life. In fact, during the medieval period, the Church had become one of the most powerful political institutions in Europe. It carried out wars and made alliances with other states. Its leader, the Pope, was a major public figure. His power was very like that of a king. Often, it seemed that the Church was involved as much in the affairs of the world as in questions of faith.

You have read about Erasmus and other humanist writers of the Renaissance. Many of these thinkers called attention to the changes in the Church. They observed that Church leaders had, in some cases, lost sight of the Church's main purpose—to guide people's religious life.

In the early 1500s, one of those who was dissatisfied with the Church was a monk named Martin Luther. For several years, Luther had struggled with his belief in Church teachings. For example, he was troubled by the Church's belief in the importance of doing good works as a way to get to heaven.

It was while Luther was struggling with these questions that Johann Tetzel began his campaign to sell indulgences. When Luther heard of Tetzel's efforts, he became angry. He decided to issue an official criticism to the Church.

✓ **Reading Check** How did the Church's great power lead to criticism of the Church during the Renaissance?

Vocabulary Builder

Use the information below to teach students this section's high-use words.

High-Use Word	Definition and Sample Sentence
torment, p. 440	*n.* extreme pain or anguish of body or mind He suffered great **torment** about what had happened.

Instruct

The Church at the Time of Luther

Guided Instruction

- **Vocabulary Builder** Clarify the meaning of the high-use word **torment** before reading.

- Read The Church at the Time of Luther, using the Structured Silent Reading technique (TE, p. T38). Discuss the power of the Church by the time of the Renaissance. *(The Church had become one of the most powerful political institutions in Europe, and its leader, the pope, had power like that of a king.)* Ask students **Why were thinkers and others disturbed by the power of the Church?** *(Possible answers: They thought that the Church was more focused on world affairs and having political power than on questions of faith and guiding people's religious lives.)*

Independent Practice

Ask students to create the Taking Notes graphic organizer on a blank piece of paper. Then have them add to the causes listed. Briefly model what kinds of information to include.

Monitor Progress

As students fill in the graphic organizer, circulate and make sure individuals are correctly identifying causes. Provide assistance as needed.

Answers

Critical Thinking The depiction on the left is of Protestants and the one on the right is of Catholics.

✓ **Reading Check** Some people felt that the Church was more interested in affairs of the world than in matters of faith.

Luther Starts the Reformation L2

Guided Instruction

- Read Luther Starts the Reformation. Circulate to make sure students can answer the Reading Check question.

- Discuss Luther's criticisms of the Church and the Church's reaction. *(Luther challenged the idea that salvation was based on good works, the role of priests, and the authority of the pope; the Church labelled Luther an outlaw.)*

- Ask students **Why didn't the Church punish Luther?** *(Possible answer: Luther's popularity was growing and the Church feared people would revolt if Luther were punished.)*

Target Reading Skill L2

Understand Effects Luther and his followers broke with the Church. Church officials were outraged and labeled Luther an outlaw.

The Reformation Succeeds L2

Guided Instruction

- Read The Reformation Succeeds to identify some effects of the movement.

- Examine reasons for the Reformation's success. *(Many were attracted to Luther's teachings, some nobles resented the pope and the power of Rome, and the poor liked Luther's message of equality.)* Ask students **What event marked the success of the Reformation?** *(the Peace of Augsburg)*

Independent Practice

Have students add to the effects in the Taking Notes graphic organizer.

Monitor Practice

- Show *Section Reading Support Transparency HOW 102.* Ask students to check their graphic organizers. Review key concepts and vocabulary.

  📄 **History of Our World Transparencies,** *Section Reading Support Transparency HOW 102*

- Tell students to complete the *Reading Readiness Guide.* Probe for what they learned that confirms or invalidates each statement

  All in One Unit 5 History of Our World Teaching Resources, *Reading Readiness Guide,* p. 56

Answer

✓ Reading Check the Bible

In October 1517, Luther wrote a document in which he challenged the Church on the issue of indulgences. This document featured 95 *theses,* or arguments. Luther posted his Ninety-Fives Theses on the Church door at Wittenberg, Germany.

Church officials tried to silence Luther. Luther responded by widening his criticism of the Church. For example, he argued that people could achieve salvation through faith alone. **Salvation,** in religious terms, means to go to heaven. This differed from Church teachings on the importance of doing good works. Luther also challenged the role of priests. In Church teachings, only a priest could perform certain Church rituals. Wrote Luther, "A priest . . . is nothing else than an officeholder."

Luther also challenged the authority of the pope to rule on religious matters. He said that the Bible was the only true authority. If the pope's teachings did not follow the Bible, Luther said, people could disobey the pope.

Luther's ideas outraged Church officials. They tried to force German officials to have Luther punished. Luther refused to take back what he had said and written. "Here I stand, may God help me. Amen," he said.

In 1521 the Church succeeded in having Luther labeled an outlaw in Germany. However, Luther's popularity was growing, and his ideas were spreading quickly. The judgment against him was never enforced.

✓ Reading Check **What did Luther say was the final authority in religious matters?**

 Understand Effects In this section, you have read about Luther's criticisms of the Church. What effects did Luther's criticisms have on the Church? How did Church leaders respond to his actions and statements?

The portrait above shows a quiet Martin Luther, but in the illustration to the right, members of the upper class look on as Luther posts his Ninety-Five Theses.

Skills for Life Skills Mini Lesson

Analyzing Images

1. Teach the skill by pointing out that analyzing images involves asking these questions: Who or what does the image show? When and where does the scene take place? What general feeling do you get from the image? Who created the image and why?

2. Help students practice the skill by analyzing the image on page 440. Ask **Who is the person on the donkey, and what is he doing?** *(Johann Tetzel, selling indulgences)* **How do you know?** *(The writing gives his name in Latin; he is holding something out as if selling it.)*

3. Have students apply the skill by explaining what the chest in the center of the image represents. *(the money the Church was collecting from indulgences)*

The Reformation Succeeds

The **Reformation** is the term used to describe Luther's break with the Church and the movement it inspired. This movement continued in the 1520s.

There are many reasons for the Reformation's success. Many Germans were attracted to Luther's teachings. Some nobles resented the pope and the power of Rome. They welcomed a break with the Church. The poor were encouraged by what they saw as Luther's message of equality. In the 1520s, German peasants rose in revolt. They were disappointed when Luther spoke out against them. He believed that people should respect authority in nonreligious matters.

Still, Lutheranism (LOO thur un iz um), as the movement was called, took hold in many parts of Germany. It also spread to other parts of Europe, including Sweden and Norway. In 1555 the Church of Rome finally gave in. With the Peace of Augsburg (peas uv AWGS burg), Lutherans won the right to practice their religion.

The Peace of Augsburg did not end the Reformation. In the next section, you will read about how Reformation ideas affected other parts of Europe.

©The delivery of the Augsburg Confession, 25th June 1530, 1617 (oil on panel) German School (17th Century) Georgenkirche, Eisenach, Germany/Bridgeman Art Library

In the painting above, German princes in 1530 present Emperor Charles V with the Augsburg Confession, in which Philip Melanchthon tried to present Lutheran theology in a form that Roman Catholics could accept. His attempt failed.

✓ **Reading Check** Why were peasants drawn to Luther's teachings?

Section 3 Assessment

Key Terms
Review the key terms at the beginning of this section. Use each term in a sentence that explains its meaning.

Target Reading Skill
What effect did Martin Luther's teachings have on religion in Europe?

Comprehension and Critical Thinking
1. (a) Explain What was the role of the Church in European life in the Renaissance?

(b) Draw Inferences Why do you think the political power of the pope and Church officials troubled many people in Europe?

2. (a) Identify What action by Johann Tetzel upset Luther and led to the Ninety-Five Theses?

(b) Synthesize Information Which of Luther's key complaints against the Church did the selling of indulgences represent?

3. (a) Recall What happened to Luther after he was declared an outlaw in Germany?

(b) Analyze Information Why do you think the movement started by Martin Luther is known as the Reformation?

Writing Activity
The year is 1520. Write a memo to the pope, summarizing the events taking place in Germany. Briefly trace the story behind Martin Luther and his ideas. Explain how these ideas differ from Church teachings.

Go Online PHSchool.com

For: An activity on the Reformation
Visit: PHSchool.com
Web Code: mud-1530

Writing Activity
Use the *Rubric for Assessing a Writing Assignment* to evaluate students' work.

All in One Unit 5 History of Our World Teaching Resources, *Rubric for Assessing a Writing Assignment,* p. 78

Go Online PHSchool.com Typing in the Web Code when prompted will bring students directly to detailed instructions for this activity.

Differentiated Instruction

For Less Proficient Readers ▪L1▪
To increase comprehension during reading of the section, pair students with proficient readers. Have the pairs use the Paragraph Shrinking technique (TE, p. T38) to exchange main ideas and details and to summarize as they read.

Assess and Reteach

Assess Progress ▪L2▪
Have students complete the Section Assessment. Administer the *Section Quiz*.

All in One Unit 5 History of Our World Teaching Resources, *Section Quiz,* p. 58

Reteach ▪L1▪
If students need more instruction, have them read the section in the Reading and Vocabulary Study Guide.

📖 **History of Our World Reading and Vocabulary Study Guide,** Chapter 15, Section 3, pp. 167–169

Extend ▪L3▪
Have students work in groups to write a one-page script for a scene from a play about Martin Luther and the Reformation. Tell them the image on page 442 shows the scene they will create. Students should write dialogue for both the monks and the bystanders. If students wish, they may use their script to present the scene to the class.

Answer

✓ **Reading Check** They were encouraged by Luther's message of equality.

Section 3 Assessment

Key Terms
Students' sentences should reflect knowledge of each Key Term.

Target Reading Skill
Lutheranism grew, and the Church finally had to give Lutherans the right to practice their religion.

Comprehension and Critical Thinking
1. (a) The Church was a powerful political and social force in the Renaissance. **(b)** It seemed to many people that the Church had lost sight of its religious purpose and was too focused on worldly matters.

2. (a) Tetzel's selling of indulgences upset Luther. **(b)** The selling of indulgences went against Luther's idea that faith alone could bring salvation.

3. (a) Luther was never punished because there was widespread support for him. **(b)** The term *Reformation* suggests reform, or fixing something that is not working properly. The Reformation was an attempt to fix problems in the Church.

Objective

Learn how to identify point of view.

Prepare to Read

Build Background Knowledge **L2**

Ask students to name current issues on which people have different points of view. Point out that being able to identify point of view is a skill that students can use when reading newspaper or magazine articles or watching television news about current issues.

Instruct

Identifying Point of View **L2**

Guided Instruction

- Read the steps to Identifying Point of View as a class and write the instructions on the board.

- Practice the skill by following the steps on pages 444 as a class. Model each step in the activity by identifying the backgrounds of the speakers (*Karen, is leader of the school chorus; Jason, has an interest in acting; Sandra, is chairperson of the school theater committee*), considering facts and evidence given about the points of view (*Karen believes the attendance will be good since the holiday musical's attendance was good; Jason believes there is a lot of students who would rather act than sing*), and identifying and explaining the speakers' points of view based on the facts and evidence.

- Ask students to identify people or groups in the chapter who might have different points of view.

 **Identifying Point of View**

Karen, the leader of the student chorus, got right to the point during the planning meeting. "A lot of people would come out to see a spring musical," she said. "We have a number of strong singers, and we had very good attendance at our holiday musical."

"I don't know," replied Jason. "Some of the students who want to be in a spring play aren't involved in chorus, and some of us who are in chorus would rather act than sing."

Sandra, chairperson of the school theater committee, had to decide whether their class should put on a musical or a play in the spring.

After thinking all afternoon about what Karen and Jason had said, Sandra realized that Karen really wanted to do a spring musical, but that Jason preferred to put on a play. She would have to decide between their points of view.

Identifying point of view helps you understand different viewpoints and make judgments about them.

Learn the skill

Use the steps below to identify point of view.

1 **Consider what you know about the background of each speaker and how that background might affect the speaker's viewpoint.** Sandra knew that Karen wanted to do another musical in the spring, but she also knew that Jason and other students would rather act than sing.

2 **Consider facts and other evidence that the speakers give to support their points of view.** Karen used the attendance at the holiday musical as a reason for a spring musical. Jason gave the example of students who would rather act than sing.

3 **Identify and explain each speaker's point of view, basing your conclusions on what you know about the speaker and the evidence that the speaker gives.** Sandra knew that Karen supported a spring musical because Karen enjoyed singing and that Jason preferred a spring play because he wanted to include students who weren't involved in chorus.

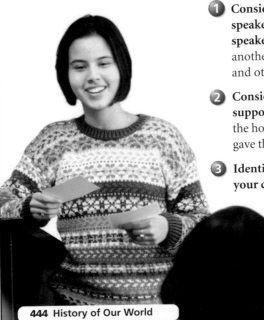

444 History of Our World

Independent Practice

Assign *Skills for Life* and have students complete it individually.

All in One **Unit 5 History of Our World Teaching Resources**, *Skills for Life*, p. 69

Monitor Progress

Monitor the students doing the *Skills for Life* worksheet, checking to make sure they understand the skills steps.

In this painting, Martin Luther is shown defending himself to Charles V at the Diet of Worms.

Practice the Skill

Reread The Church at the Time of Luther and Luther Starts the Reformation in Section 3 of this chapter. Then use the steps above to identify different points of view.

1 Answer these questions to help you identify the backgrounds of speakers: Who was Martin Luther? How did Catholic Church leaders live at this time?

2 Consider the facts and other evidence given about the points of view expressed. State your ideas in this form: "X said he believed Y because . . . " For example, "Church officials believed that Martin Luther should be declared an outlaw because he challenged their power."

3 From the questions you have answered and the statements you have written, what is each side's point of view?

Apply the Skill

Turn to Section 4 of this chapter and read the passage titled The Reformation After Luther. Use the steps in this skill to identify the points of view of various Protestant groups, such as the Calvinists, Zwinglians, and Anabaptists.

Assess and Reteach

Assess Progress [L2]

Ask students to do the Apply the Skill activity.

Reteach [L1]

If students are having trouble applying the skill steps, have them review the skill using the interactive Social Studies Skills Tutor CD-ROM.

 Identifying Point of View, Social Studies Skills Tutor CD-ROM

Extend [L3]

Give students a newspaper editorial on a current issue. Have them read the editorial and follow the skill steps to identify the point of view expressed in the editorial. Ask students to write a sentence that states the point of view expressed. Students may share their statements using the Idea Wave participation structure (TE, p. 39).

Differentiated Instruction

For Special Needs Students [L1]

Partner special needs students with more proficient students to do Level 1 of the Identifying Point of View lesson on the Social Studies Skills Tutor CD-ROM.

When the students feel more confident, they can move on to Level 2 alone.

 Identifying Point of View, Social Studies Skills Tutor CD-ROM

Answer

Apply the Skill

Calvinists believed that faith alone could win salvation and that God had already decided who would be saved; the Zwinglians believed that the Bible contained all religious truth; the Anabaptists believed that only older people should receive baptism.

Objectives

Social Studies

1. Learn that Luther was the first of several religious reformers.
2. Identify other religious movements of the 1500s in Europe.
3. Understand how the Catholic Church responded to the Reformation.

Reading/Language Arts

Learn how to recognize cause-and-effect signal words.

Prepare to Read

Build Background Knowledge L2

In this section, students will learn how the Reformation spread into other parts of Europe. Have students preview the images in this section and predict where Reformation ideas took hold after Luther. Use the Give One, Get One participation structure (TE, p. 41) to generate predictions. *(Reformation ideas took hold throughout Europe in places such as England, Ireland, Scotland, and Switzerland.)*

Set a Purpose for Reading L2

■ Preview the Objectives.

■ Read each statement in the *Reading Readiness Guide* aloud. Ask students to mark the statements true or false.

   All in One Unit 5 History of Our World Teaching Resources, *Reading Readiness Guide,* p. 60

■ Have students discuss the statement in pairs or groups of four, then mark their worksheets again. Use the Numbered Heads participation structure (TE, p. T40) to call on students to share their group's perspectives.

Vocabulary Builder
Preview Key Terms L2

Pronounce each Key Term, then ask students to say the word with you. Provide a simple explanation, such as "Protestant groups protested or questioned beliefs and practices of the Catholic Church."

Prepare to Read

Objectives

In this section you will

1. Learn that Luther was the first of several religious reformers.
2. Identify other religious movements of the 1500s in Europe.
3. Understand how the Catholic Church responded to the Reformation.

Taking Notes

As you read, look for ways that the Reformation inspired new religious groups and changed the Catholic Church. Copy the diagram below, and record your findings in it.

Spread of Reformation Ideas	
Other Religious Movements	**Changes in the Catholic Church**
• • •	• • •

Target Reading Skill

Recognize Cause-and-Effect Signal Words
Causes and effects follow one another in a certain sequence. This section contains information about the spread of Reformation ideas. To help keep the order of events clear, look for words and phrases like *so, suddenly, finally, for this reason,* and *as a result.* These terms signal the relationship between a cause and its effects.

Key Terms

• **Protestant** (PRAHT us tunt) *adj.* refers to Christian groups that separated from the Catholic church

A portrait of Henry VIII by Dutch painter Hans Hobein the Younger

© Hans the Younger Holbein (1497/8–1543), Dutch, *"Portrait of Henry VIII"*, 16th Century / Bridgeman Art Library

446 History of Our World

Henry VIII, King of England, was unhappy. He wanted very much to have a male child to inherit his throne. He and his wife, Catherine, had only one surviving child, a girl. So Henry decided that it was time to marry another woman. First, however, he needed the Church of Rome to officially end his marriage to Catherine. The pope refused Henry's request.

Henry had always been a strong supporter of the Church. In 1521 he had written an attack on Martin Luther's ideas. In response, the pope had given Henry the title of Defender of the Faith. Now, however, Henry attacked the Church and its practices. Still, the Church would not end his marriage. Finally, in 1534, Henry officially broke from the Catholic Church and became the head of a new church—the Church of England. Suddenly, the people of England were part of the Reformation.

Target Reading Skill L2

Recognize Cause-and-Effect Signal Words Point out the Target Reading Skill. Tell students that recognizing cause-and-effect signal words point out relationships among ideas or events. This section discusses events related to the Reformation over many years. To help keep the order of events clear, look for words like *first, at that time, in [date]* that signal the order in which the events took place.

Model recognizing cause-and-effect signal words by looking at the text under the heading The Catholic Church Reforms on p. 448. Tell students to look for signal words. *(as a result, in the mid-1500s)*

Give students *Recognize Cause-and-Effect Signal Words.* Have them complete the activity in their groups.

All in One Unit 5 History of Our World Teaching Resources, *Recognize Cause-and-Effect Signal Words,* p. 66

The Reformation After Luther

Many people in Europe adopted Martin Luther's ideas in the mid-1500s and several other Protestant groups appeared. **Protestant** refers to Christians who separated from the Catholic Church.

John Calvin began his preaching in the 1530s in Switzerland. He believed that faith alone could win salvation and that God had determined long ago who would be saved, a belief known as predestination.

Also from Switzerland came Ulrich Zwingli (ool rik ZWING lee). His church was formed in the 1520s. Zwinglians (ZWING lee unz) believed that the Bible contained all religious truth.

The Anabaptists (an uh BAP tists) also formed at this time. They did not believe in the baptism of infants. Only older people, they argued, could have the faith that this religious practice required.

✓ **Reading Check** Where did the Zwinglians first appear?

John Calvin

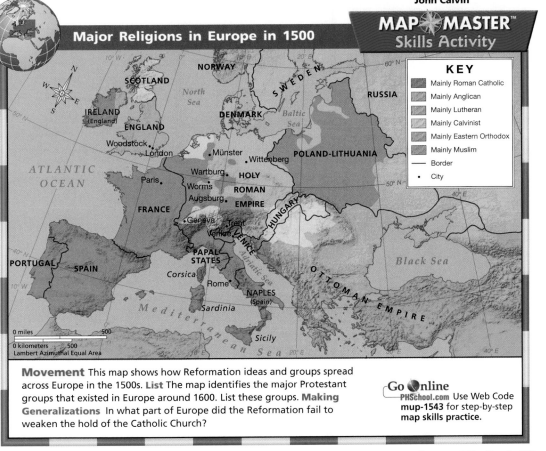

MAP★MASTER™ Skills Activity

Major Religions in Europe in 1500

KEY

- Mainly Roman Catholic
- Mainly Anglican
- Mainly Lutheran
- Mainly Calvinist
- Mainly Eastern Orthodox
- Mainly Muslim
- — Border
- • City

Movement This map shows how Reformation ideas and groups spread across Europe in the 1500s. **List** The map identifies the major Protestant groups that existed in Europe around 1600. List these groups. **Making Generalizations** In what part of Europe did the Reformation fail to weaken the hold of the Catholic Church?

Go Online
PHSchool.com Use Web Code **mup-1543** for step-by-step map skills practice.

Vocabulary Builder

Use the information below to teach students this section's high-use words.

High-Use Word	Definition and Sample Sentence
corrupt, p. 448	*adj.* characterized by improper conduct The **corrupt** salesman cheated people of their money.
clergy, p. 448	*n.* a group ordained to perform pastoral functions in a Christian church Members of the church turned to the **clergy** for leadership.

The Reformation After Luther L2

Guided Instruction

- Read The Reformation After Luther, using the Choral Reading technique (TE, p. T38).

- Discuss religious reformers after Luther. Ask students **What belief did Calvin share with Luther?** (*Both believed that faith alone could win salvation.*)

The Catholic Church Reforms L2

Guided Instruction

- **Vocabulary Builder** Clarify the meaning of the high-use words **corrupt** and **clergy**.

- Read The Catholic Church Reforms. Circulate to make sure students can answer the Reading Check question.

- Discuss developments that were part of the Catholic Reformation. Ask students **How did Renaissance thinkers such as Erasmus play a part in bringing about the Council of Trent?** (*Erasmus and others criticized the Church for focusing on worldly matters instead of matters of religion.*)

Independent Practice

Ask students to create the Taking Notes graphic organizer. Then have them fill in details about religious movements and changes in the Catholic Church. Model what kinds of information to include.

Monitor Practice

- Show *Section Reading Support Transparency HOW 103*. Have students check their graphic organizers for key concepts and vocabulary.

  📄 **History of Our World Transparencies,** *Section Reading Support Transparency HOW 103*

- Tell students to complete the *Reading Readiness Guide*. Probe for what they learned that confirms or invalidates each statement

  All in One **Unit 5 History of Our World Teaching Resources,** *Reading Readiness Guide,* p. 60

Answers

MAP★MASTER Skills Activity **List** Anglican, Lutheran, Calvinist, Eastern Orthodox, Muslim **Making Generalizations** Southwestern Europe

✓ **Reading Check** Switzerland

⊘ **Target Reading Skill** 〖L2〗

Recognize Cause-and-Effect Signal Words As a follow up, ask students to answer the Target Reading Skill question on this page in the Student Edition. *(As a result)*

Assess and Reteach

Assess Progress 〖L2〗

Have students complete the Section Assessment. Administer the *Section Quiz.*

All in One Unit 5 History of Our World Teaching Resources, *Section Quiz,* p. 62

Reteach 〖L1〗

If students need more instruction, have them read the section in the Reading and Vocabulary Study Guide.

History of Our World Reading and Vocabulary Study Guide, Chapter 15, Section 4, pp. 170–172

Extend 〖L3〗

Have students make a time line that shows significant events in the Protestant and Catholic Reformations. Tell students to draw events and dates from this section.

Answer

✓Reading Check The Jesuits worked to educate people and to spread the Catholic faith.

Section 4 Assessment

Key Terms

Students' sentences should reflect knowledge of each Key Term.

⊘ **Target Reading Skill**

The words *first, in response, now, finally,* and *suddenly* signal the cause and effect.

Comprehension and Critical Thinking

1. (a) Other Europeans adopted Luther's ideas. **(b)** Many were unhappy with the Catholic Church and had their own ideas about reforms.

2. (a) Calvin, Zwingli, and the Anabaptists **(b)** Possible answer: The Bible was the source of all truth.

3. (a) The Catholic Church carried out its own reforms. **(b)** The Jesuits educated people and spread the Catholic faith.

 Recognize Cause-and-Effect Signal Words Which words signal the effect of the Reformation on the Church?

The Council of Trent addressed the abuses that prompted the Reformation, but it did not reunite the Church.

The Catholic Church Reforms

The Reformation was a significant challenge to the Church of Rome. As you have read, much of Europe was swept up in the Reformation. As a result, the Church carried out its own reforms in the mid-1500s. These helped the Church survive and regain strength in much of Europe. The initial reforms of Luther and others became known as the Protestant Reformation. The Catholic Church's reforms were called the Catholic Reformation.

One key development of the Catholic Reformation was the establishment of the Society of Jesus in 1540. This was a religious order, or group, led by Ignatius Loyola (ig NAY shus loy OH luh). The Jesuits (JEZH oo its), as they came to be called, worked tirelessly to educate people and spread the Catholic faith. Their efforts helped build Church strength in southern Europe.

The Catholic Church was also strengthened by Paul III, who became pope in 1534. Paul III helped focus the Church on many of the abuses that had led to the Reformation. These included corrupt practices among the clergy. In 1542 Paul III called for a meeting now known as the Council of Trent. This meeting helped return the Church's focus to matters of religion and spirituality.

✓Reading Check **What was the function of the Jesuits?**

Section 4 Assessment

Key Terms

Review the key terms at the beginning of this section. Use each term in a sentence that explains its meaning.

⊘ **Target Reading Skill**

Reread the description of Henry VIII's break with the Church of Rome. Which words signal the cause-and-effect relationship that led to the founding of the Church of England?

Comprehension and Critical Thinking

1. (a) Explain How did the Reformation develop following Luther's break with the Church? **(b) Draw Conclusions** Why did other reformers follow Luther?

2. (a) List Name three religious reformers who established a Protestant faith in Europe. **(b) Compare** What basic idea did the Protestant reformers share?

3. (a) Explain How did the Catholic Church respond to the Reformation? **(b) Summarize** How did the Jesuits help the Catholic Church?

Writing Activity

Summarize the Reformation in Europe in the mid-1500s. Explain key features of the groups, and identify the places in which the new movements were strongest.

For: An activity on the spread of the Reformation
Visit: PHSchool.com
Web Code: mud-1540

Writing Activity

Use the *Rubric for Assessing a Writing Assignment* to evaluate students' work.

All in One Unit 5 History of Our World Teaching Resources, *Rubric for Assessing a Writing Assignment,* p. 78

Go Online PHSchool.com Typing in the Web Code when prompted will bring students directly to detailed instructions for this activity.

Differentiated Instruction

For Advanced Readers 〖L3〗

Have students research and write a report on the Scotsman and Protestant reformer John Knox, who adapted Calvinist ideas and founded what became known as the Presbyterian Church. Students may use the Internet or library resources.

Review and Assessment

◆ Chapter Summary

Section 1: The Renaissance Begins

- The Renaissance began in Italy because Italy's geography encouraged trade and the development of large trade cities.
- Ancient ideas inspired humanism and helped transform the literature of Italy.
- Renaissance art flourished as new techniques helped artists produce works of great beauty.

Section 2: The Renaissance Moves North

- Renaissance ideas spread northward from Italy into the rest of Europe.
- Key literary figures of the Renaissance in northern and western Europe included François Rabelais and William Shakespeare.

A Shakespeare Play

- Renaissance art in northern Europe was led by masters such as Jan van Eyck and Albrecht Dürer.

Luther

Section 3: Martin Luther and the Reformation

- Martin Luther opposed such Roman Catholic Church practices as the selling of indulgences.
- Luther's challenge to Church authority and teaching touched off the Reformation.
- In spite of Church opposition, Lutheran ideas spread to many parts of Europe.

Section 4: Reformation Ideas Spread

- Other Protestant reformers followed Martin Luther in breaking with the Roman Catholic Church.
- The Catholic Church responded to the Reformation with reforms of its own.

John Calvin

- Review and revisit the major themes of this chapter by asking students to classify what Guiding Questions each bulleted statement in the Chapter Summary answers. Have students work together in groups to classify the sentences. Refer to page 1 in the Student Edition for the text of the Guiding Questions.

- Assign *Vocabulary Development* to help students review the Key Terms.

  All in One **Unit 5 History of Our World Teaching Resources,** *Vocabulary Development,* p. 77

◆ Key Terms

Each of the statements below contains a key term from the chapter. If the statement is true, write "true." If it is false, rewrite the statement to make it true.

1. The **Reformation** began in Italy, which was a center of commerce

2. All **Protestants** were alike in that they opposed certain beliefs and practices of the Catholic Church

3. **Humanists** believed that the ideas and values of the ancient world were corrupt.

4. Martin Luther believed that a person could achieve **salvation** through faith alone.

5. Erasmus was best known for his development of **movable type,** which helped make possible the large-scale printing of books.

6. Luther was a firm believer in the practice of selling **indulgences.**

7. **Renaissance** art featured an interest in realistic depiction of the human form.

Chapter 15 **449**

Vocabulary Builder

Revisit this chapter's high-use words:

nobles	realism	clergy
painstaking	torment	
immortality	corrupt	

Ask students to review the definitions they recorded on their *Word Knowledge* worksheet.

All in One **Unit 5 History of Our World Teaching Resources,** *Word Knowledge,* p. 67

Consider allowing students to earn extra credit if they use the words in their answers to the questions in the Chapter Review and Assessment. The words must be used correctly and in a natural context to win the extra points.

Answers

Key Terms

1. True

2. True

3. False. Possible answer: Humanists were drawn to the ideas and values of the ancient world.

4. True

5. False. Johannes Gutenberg is known for his development of movable type.

6. False. The selling of indulgences angered Luther.

7. True

Review and Assessment

Comprehension and Critical Thinking

8. (a) Da Vinci was an artist, scientist, and inventor. **(b)** Da Vinci had great skills in many areas and wide interests.

9. (a) The Renaissance was a period of widespread cultural change in Europe beginning in the 1300s. **(b)** Italy became a center of trade between Europe and the East.

10. (a) Rabelais and Shakespeare **(b)** Shakespeare's work reflected an interest in the human character. His work also borrowed plots from ancient works.

11. (a) Luther began to question Catholic teachings and practices as a monk in the early 1500s. **(b)** His belief in scripture as the final authority questioned the authority of the pope.

12. (a) The Church tried to get German officials to punish Luther and labeled him an outlaw. **(b)** His popularity grew, and his ideas spread quickly.

13. (a) Henry VIII broke from the Church because it did not allow him to end his marriage to Catherine. **(b)** Henry VIII was only willing to support Church teachings if they benefited him.

Skills Practice

Possible answer: Cosimo de Medici believed that the changes that Renaissance ideas brought were positive, exciting, and worth supporting.

Review and Assessment (continued)

◆ Comprehension and Critical Thinking

8. (a) List List some of the accomplishments of Leonardo da Vinci.
(b) Synthesize Information Why is da Vinci considered a true example of a Renaissance artist and thinker?

9. (a) Recall What was the Renaissance?
(b) Identify Cause and Effect How did Italy's location help shape its economic life at the start of the Renaissance?

10. (a) List Name two Renaissance writers from northern or western Europe.
(b) Identify Frame of Reference How did William Shakespeare's work reflect Renaissance ideas?

11. (a) Recall When did Luther first begin to question Catholic teachings and practices?
(b) Draw Inferences Why was Luther's idea that scriptures were the final authority in religious matters so radical?

12. (a) Recall How did the Church respond to Luther's challenges?
(b) Identify Cause and Effect How did Luther's popularity in Germany change after his challenge of the Roman Catholic Church?

13. (a) Explain What was Henry VIII's reason for breaking with the Church?
(b) Draw Inferences What can you infer about Henry VIII's views of Church teachings?

◆ Skills Practice

Identifying Point of View In the Skills for Life activity, you learned how to identify point of view. Review the steps you follow to use this skill. Reread the Citizen Heroes passage in Section 1 about Cosimo de Medici. Use what you read and your own thinking to identify de Medici's view of the changes that Renaissance ideas brought to Italy.

◆ Writing Activity: Art

You are an art critic in Italy during the Renaissance. Artists of the day are painting pictures that are amazingly realistic; for example, round objects look round. The technique these artists use is called *perspective*. Research and write a brief report on this technique. Explain how an artist can make a flat surface look "deep."

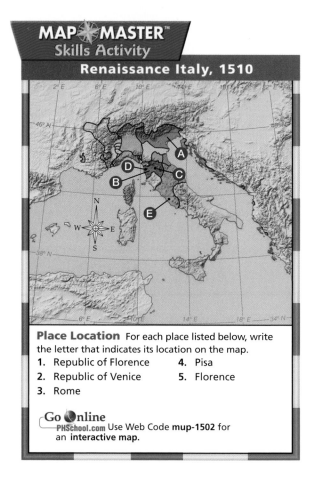

MAP MASTER™ Skills Activity

Renaissance Italy, 1510

Place Location For each place listed below, write the letter that indicates its location on the map.
1. Republic of Florence
2. Republic of Venice
3. Rome
4. Pisa
5. Florence

Go Online PHSchool.com Use Web Code **mup-1502** for an **interactive map.**

Writing Activity: Art
Students' reports will vary but should contain accurate information about the technique of perspective.

MAP MASTER™ Skills Activity

1. B	**2.** A
3. E	**4.** D
5. C	

Go Online PHSchool.com Students may practice their map skills using the interactive online version of this map.

Standardized Test Prep

Test-Taking Tips

Some questions on standardized tests ask you to find main ideas. Read the paragraph below. Then follow the tips to answer the sample question.

> The Renaissance supported a spirit of adventure and a wide-ranging curiosity that led people to explore new worlds. The Italian navigator Christopher Columbus represented that spirit. So did Nicolaus Copernicus, a Polish scientist who revolutionized the way people viewed the universe. Renaissance writers and artists, eager to experiment with new forms, also demonstrated that adventurous spirit.

TIP As you read the passage, identify its main ideas, or most important points.

Choose the statement that best reflects the main idea.

This passage shows that—
A art influenced science
B curiosity led to new ways of thinking and exploration.
C exploration inspired curiosity.
D exploration led to adventure.

TIP Look for a key word in the question or answer choices that connects to the paragraph. In this case, the word is *curiosity*.

Think It Through Start with the main idea—the curious nature of Renaissance thinkers encouraged changes in science, art, and exploration. You can link this idea to the key word, *curiosity*. You can rule out A and D, which do not discuss curiosity. C is a statement linking exploration to curiosity, but the statement does not reflect main point of the passage. The correct answer is B.

Practice Questions

Use the tips above and other tips in this book to help you answer the following questions.

1. How did the growth of Italian cities at the dawn of the Renaissance affect the feudal system?
   A The growth of cities strengthened feudal power.
   B The growth of cities weakened feudal power.
   C The growth of cities forced nobles to fight one another.
   D The growth of cities expanded the feudal system into a city environment.

2. Which of the following was one of Luther's central Reformation ideas?
   A The Jesuits should spread religious faith.
   B Infants should not be baptized.
   C Women should be allowed into the priesthood.
   D Faith, not good works, was the key to salvation.

Use the passage below to answer question 3.

> "Dare we believe, my brothers, that St. Benedict had such expensive horses and mules as we now see many a [Church official] possess? Certainly not!"

3. Which of the following best summarizes the main idea of this passage?
   A St. Benedict should have had better horses.
   B The Church is much better off today than it was during the Renaissance.
   C Church officials live too well and should follow the example of St. Benedict.
   D Expensive horses are better than expensive mules

Use Web Code **mua-1505** for **Chapter 15 self-test.**

Chapter 15 **451**

Standardized Test Prep

Answers

1. B
2. D
3. C

Go Online PHSchool.com Students may use the Chapter 15 self-test on PHSchool.com to prepare for the Chapter Test.

┌─ **Assessment Resources** ─

Use Chapter Tests A and B to assess students' mastery of chapter content.

All in One **Unit 5 History of Our World Teaching Resources,** *Chapter Tests A and B,* pp. 80–85

Tests are also available on the Exam-View Test Bank CD-ROM.

💿 **Exam*View*® Test Bank CD-ROM**

16 Exploration: Europe and Asia

Chapter Overview

Overview

Section 1 — European Explorations Begin
1. Learn why Europeans began exploring the world in the 1400s.
2. Identify the early achievements of Portuguese exploration under Prince Henry the Navigator.
3. Understand how Portugal's efforts inspired early Spanish exploration.

Section 2 — Europeans in India and Southeast Asia
1. Learn how Portugal traded in India.
2. Understand how Portuguese trade expanded into India and the Spice Islands.
3. Identify the English and the Dutch as challengers to Portugal's power in Asia.

Section 3 — Europe Explores East Asia
1. Learn about European efforts to expand trade in East Asia.
2. Understand European encounters with China and Japan, 1600–1700.

Discovery CHANNEL SCHOOL Video

China and the West: The Struggle Over Trade
Length: 5 minutes, 27 seconds
Use with Section 3
This video segment explores Lord George Macartney's diplomatic mission to China to negotiate trading rights for Britain and describes the mission's repercussions.

Technology Resources

 **Go Online**
PHSchool.com

Students use embedded web codes to access Internet activities, chapter self-tests, and additional map practice. They may also access Dorling Kindersley's Online Desk Reference to learn more about each country they study.

 **Interactive Textbook**

Use Interactive Textbook to make content and concepts come alive through animations, videos, and activities that accompany the complete basal text—online and on CD-ROM.

PRENTICE HALL
 **TeacherEXPRESS**
Plan • Teach • Assess

Use this complete suite of powerful teaching tools to make lesson planning and administering tests quicker and easier.

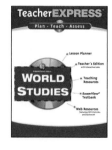

Reading and Assessment

Reading and Vocabulary Instruction

🔊 Model the Target Reading Skill

Clarifying Meaning Reading involves more than just learning what the words mean. Students can become better, more active readers by learning how to clarify the meaning of what they read. One way of clarifying meaning is to read ahead, quickly skimming to see what's coming up *before you start to read*.

Model this skill by thinking about this chapter aloud: This chapter's title is Exploration: Europe and Asia. I wonder if I'll be learning about the explorers who traveled to these lands? I'm going to read ahead and see what's coming in each section. Section 1's title is European Explorations Begin. I see that in this section is the title, Prince Henry the Navigator and Portuguese Exploration. So, I'll be reading about the Portuguese. The titles of Sections 2 and 3 both mention European exploration. Section 2 is about India and Southeast Asia and Section 3 is about East Asia. There must be a difference between explorations to Southeast Asia and those to East Asia. I'll make sure to watch for that when I read those sections. I also see several titles and pictures here that have to do with trade. So, not only will I be reading about explorers, it looks like I'll be learning about trade between the Europeans and Asians. I think that by reading ahead, I'm better able to understand the meaning of what I'm going to read in this chapter.

Use the following worksheets from All-in-One Unit 5 History of Our World Teaching Resources (pp. 101–103) to support this chapter's Target Reading Skill.

Vocabulary Builder
High-Use Academic Words

Use these steps to teach this chapter's high-use words:

1. Have students rate how well they know each word on their World Knowledge worksheets (All-in-One Unit 5 History of Our World Teaching Resources, p. 105).
2. Pronounce each word and ask students to repeat it.
3. Provide a brief definition or sample sentence (provided on TE pp. 455, 467, and 472).
4. Work with students as they fill in the "Definition or Example" column of their World Knowledge worksheets.

Assessment

Formal Assessment

Test students' understanding of core knowledge and skills.

Chapter Tests A and B, All-in-One Unit 5 History of Our World Teaching Resources, pp. 116–121

Customize the Chapter Tests to suit your needs.
Exam*View*® Test Bank CD-ROM

Skills Assessment

Assess geographic literacy.

MapMaster Skills, Student Edition, pp. 453 and 458

Assess reading and comprehension.

Target Reading Skills, Student Edition, pp. 456, 469, 473 and in Section Assessments

Chapter 16 Assessment, History of Our World Reading and Vocabulary Study Guide, p. 183

Performance Assessment

Assess students' performance on this chapter's Writing Activities using the rubrics from All-in-One Unit 5 History of Our World Teaching Resources.

Rubric for Assessing a Writing Assignment, p. 114

Rubric for Assessing a Student Poster, p. 115

Assess students' work through performance tasks.

Small Group Activities, All-in-One Unit 5 History of Our World Teaching Resources, pp. 108–111

Online Assessment

Have students check their own understanding.

Chapter Self Test

Section 1 European Explorations Begin

 2 periods, 1 block (includes Focus on a Sailor's Life at Sea and Skills for Life)

Social Studies Objectives

1. Learn why Europeans began exploring the world in the 1400s.
2. Identify the early achievements of Portuguese exploration under Prince Henry the Navigator.
3. Understand how Portugal's efforts inspired early Spanish exploration.

Reading/Language Arts Objective

Paraphrase or restate what you have read in your own words, to strengthen reading comprehension.

Prepare to Read	Instructional Resources	Differentiated Instruction
Build Background Knowledge Discuss the impact of Portuguese exploration. **Set a Purpose for Reading** Have students evaluate statements on the Reading Readiness Guide. **Preview Key Terms** Model use of key terms. **Target Reading Skill** Introduce the section's Target Reading Skill of paraphrasing.	**All in One Unit 5 History of Our World Teaching Resources** L2 Reading Readiness Guide, p. 90 L2 Word Knowledge, p. 105 L2 Paraphrase, p. 101	**Spanish Reading and Vocabulary Study Guide** L2 Chapter 16, Section 1, pp. 124–125 ELL

Instruct	Instructional Resources	Differentiated Instruction
Why Europe Looked to the East Discuss the spread of Christianity. **Portuguese Exploration** Discuss Prince Henry and other explorers. **Target Reading Skill** Review how to paraphrase a paragraph. **Columbus Sales Under Spanish Flag** Discuss Columbus's plan to find the East. **Eyewitness: The Santa Maria** Discuss the layout of the Santa Maria. **Other Explorers Look West** Discuss the naming of America, Balboa's reaching the Pacific Ocean, and Magellan's circumnavigation.	**All in One Unit 5 History of Our World Teaching Resources** L2 Guided Reading and Review, p. 91 L2 Reading Readiness Guide, p. 90 **History of World Transparencies** L2 Section Reading Support Transparency HOW 104	**All in One Unit 5 History of Our World Teaching Resources** L2 Skills for Life, p. 107 AR, GT, LPR, SN **Teacher's Edition** L1 For Special Needs Students, TE p. 465 LPR, SN L2 For English Language Learners, TE p. 465 **Spanish Support** L2 Guided Reading and Review (Spanish), p. 136 ELL

Assess and Reteach	Instructional Resources	Differentiated Instruction
Assess Progress Evaluate student comprehension with the section assessment and section quiz. **Reteach** Assign the Reading and Vocabulary Study Guide to help struggling students. **Extend** Extend the lesson by assigning the MapMaster Skills Handbook.	**All in One Unit 5 History of Our World Teaching Resources** L2 Section Quiz, p. 92 **Reading and Vocabulary Study Guide** L1 Chapter 16, Section 1, pp. 174–176	**Spanish Support** L2 Section Quiz (Spanish), p. 137 ELL **Student Edition on Audio CD** L1 Chapter 16, Section 1 ELL, LPR, SN

Key

L1 Basic to Average L3 Average to Advanced LPR Less Proficient Readers GT Gifted and Talented
L2 For All Students AR Advanced Readers ELL English Language Learners
  SN Special Needs Students

Section 2 Europeans in India and Southeast Asia

 *2 periods, 1 block*

Social Studies Objectives
1. Learn how Portugal traded in India.
2. Understand how Portuguese trade expanded into India and the Spice Islands.
3. Identify the English and the Dutch as challengers to Portugal's power in Asia.

Reading/Language Arts Objective
Summarize important details and events to help build understanding.

Section Lesson Planner

Prepare to Read	**Instructional Resources**	**Differentiated Instruction**
Build Background Knowledge Discuss Portugal's expanding empire and growing interest in trade. **Set a Purpose for Reading** Have students begin to follow Reading Readiness Guide. **Preview Key Terms** Model use of key terms. **Target Reading Skill** Introduce the section's Target Reading Skill of summarizing.	**All in One Unit 5 History of Our World Teaching Resources** L2 Reading Readiness Guide, p. 94 L2 Summarize, p. 102	**Spanish Reading and Vocabulary Study Guide** L2 Chapter 16, Section 2, pp. 126–127

Instruct	**Instructional Resources**	**Differentiated Instruction**
Portugal Gains a Foothold in India Discuss Cabral's journey to Brazil and Calicut. **The Portuguese Empire Expands** Discuss Portuguese conquests of India and the Spice Islands. **Target Reading Skill** Review summarizing. **Challengers to Portugal** Discuss Dutch and English battles to control trading posts in Asia.	**All in One Unit 5 History of Our World Teaching Resources** L2 Guided Reading and Review, p. 95 L2 Reading Readiness Guide, p. 94 **History of Our World Transparencies** L2 Section Reading Support Transparency HOW 105	**Teacher's Edition** L2 For Advanced Readers, TE p. 468 GT L1 For Less Proficient Readers, TE p. 469 LPR, SN, ELL **Spanish Support** L2 Guided Reading and Review (Spanish), p. 138 ELL

Assess and Reteach	**Instructional Resources**	**Differentiated Instruction**
Assess Progress Evaluate student comprehension with the section assessment and section quiz. **Reteach** Assign the Reading and Vocabulary Study Guide **Extend** Extend the lesson by having students research spices and their history.	**All in One Unit 5 History of Our World Teaching Resources** L2 Section Quiz, p. 96 **Reading and Vocabulary Study Guide** L1 Chapter 16, Section 2, pp. 177–179 L2 Rubric for Assessing a Writing Assignment, p. 114	**Spanish Support** L2 Section Quiz (Spanish), p. 139 ELL

Key

L1 Basic to Average	L3 Average to Advanced	LPR Less Proficient Readers	GT Gifted and Talented
L2 For All Students		AR Advanced Readers	ELL English Language Learners
		SN Special Needs Students	

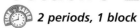
Section 3 Europe Explores East Asia

2 periods, 1 block

Social Studies Objectives

1. Learn about European efforts to expand trade in East Asia.
2. Understand European encounters with China and Japan, 1600–1700.

Reading/Language Arts Objective

Reread or read ahead to clarify words and ideas in text.

Prepare to Read

Build Background Knowledge
Discuss the expanding European trade in China and Japan.

Set a Purpose for Reading
Have students complete the Reading Readiness Guide.

Preview Key Terms
Model use of key terms.

Target Reading Skill
Discuss how to reread or read ahead.

Instructional Resources

All in One Unit 5 History of Our World Teaching Resources
- L2 Reading Readiness Guide, p. 98
- L2 Reread or Read Ahead, p. 103

Differentiated Instruction

Spanish Reading and Vocabulary Study Guide
- L2 Chapter 16, Section 2, pp. 128–129

Instruct

Expanding European Trade
Discuss Portuguese and Spanish attempts to trade with China.

European Contacts with China and Japan
Discuss China's dislike of European trade goods.

Target Reading Skill
Introduce students to the Target Reading Skill of reading ahead to clarify meaning

Instructional Resources

All in One Unit 5 History of Our World Teaching Resources
- L2 Guided Reading and Review, p. 99
- L2 Reading Readiness Guide, p. 98

History of Our World Transparencies
- L2 Section Reading Support Transparency HOW 106
- L2 Terra Cotta Soldiers HOW 33

History of Our World Video Program
China and the West: the Struggle Over Trade

Differentiated Instruction

History of Our World Transparencies
- L2 Transparency HOW 33

Teacher's Edition
- L3 For Gifted and Talented, TE p. 473 GT
- L3 For English Language Learners, TE p. 473 ELL

Spanish Support
- L2 Guided Reading and Review (Spanish), p. 140 ELL

Assess and Reteach

Assess Progress
Evaluate student comprehension with the section assessment and section quiz.

Reteach
Assign the Reading and Vocabulary Study Guide to help struggling students.

Extend
Extend the lesson by assigning students to read the primary sources and literature selection.

Instructional Resources

All in One Unit 5 History of Our World Teaching Resources
- L2 Section Quiz, p. 100

Reading and Vocabulary Study Guide
- L1 Chapter 16, Section 3, pp. 180–182
- L2 Primary Sources and Literature Readings, p. 112

Differentiated Instruction

Spanish Support
- L2 Section Quiz (Spanish), p. 141 ELL
- L2 Chapter Summary (Spanish), TE p. 142
- L2 Vocabulary Development (Spanish) p. 143 ELL

Key

L1 Basic to Average L3 Average to Advanced
L2 For All Students

LPR Less Proficient Readers
AR Advanced Readers
SN Special Needs Students

GT Gifted and Talented
ELL English Language Learners

Reading Background

Paraphrasing

Because it is difficult to paraphrase something you do not understand, learning to paraphrase encourages students to take an active role in clarifying what they read. Paraphrasing asks students to examine a passage closely and interpret the author's views. If you asked five students to paraphrase the same passage, you'd probably get five different paraphrases. This is true because paraphrasing requires the student to convey his or her own viewpoint about what the author is saying.

Follow these steps to teach students how to paraphrase:

1. Explain that paraphrasing demands more than simply substituting one word with another. It also involves changing sentence structure and combining or reorganizing ideas.
2. Write this passage on the board: **Dias explored a total of about 1,260 miles of previously unknown African coast. He sailed on an expedition led by Pedro Cabral and participated in the exploration of Brazil.**
3. Show students that in addition to replacing some words with others, you can eliminate unnecessary words and combine sentences. Write the paraphrased sentence next to the original passage: **Dias explored more than a thousand miles of the African coast and sailed with Pedro Cabral to explore Brazil.**
4. Explain to students that you pinpointed the author's main ideas when you paraphrased.

Learning to Paraphrase

One active way of helping students learn to paraphrase is to show them how to analyze a passage. Have students follow these steps:

1. Select a passage from the text that is 2–3 sentences long. Read and reread the passage.
2. Find in a dictionary the meaning of any words that may be confusing.
3. Replace some of the words in the passage or combine several words into one idea.
4. Combine the sentences in a way that does not alter the main idea of the passage.
5. Ask yourself if the paraphrased sentence conveys the same meaning as the original.
6. List the words that you have left out of the original sentence. If any are important to the meaning of the passage, replace them in the paraphrased sentence.

World Studies Background

The Importance of Spices

Most of the spices we use today were discovered by primitive humans who were attracted to the aromas and the oils produced by spice plants. Spices have always played an important role in trade because of their use in preserving foods, enhancing the flavor of foods, and for their medicinal qualities.

Life Aboard Ship

Life for the crew on an early sailing vessel was far from glamorous and exciting. A sailor's life was filled with hard work, and many died from disease, hunger, and thirst. On Christopher Columbus' voyages, the crew's duties included cleaning the deck and checking the sails, ropes, and cargo.

Each man got one hot meal a day, usually a biscuit, meat, fish, dried peas, cheese, and wine. Only the ship's captain had a private room, while the crew slept anywhere they could find space.

Infoplease® provides a wealth of useful information for the classroom. You can use this resource to strengthen your background on the subjects covered in this chapter. Have students visit this advertising-free site as a starting point for projects requiring research.

 Use Web Code **mud-1600** for **Infoplease®**.

Guiding Questions

Remind students about the Guiding Questions introduced at the beginning of the book.

Section 1 relates to **Guiding Question** ❸ **What were the beliefs and values of Europeans during the 1400s?** *(Europeans were interested in exploring new lands, expanding trade, and spreading their belief in Christianity.)*

Section 2 relates to **Guiding Question** ❺ **How did the Europeans develop and organize trade with India and Southeast Asia?** *(They sought to control trade by establishing trading centers and posts in these lands and by sending armed forces to battle for control of the land and its people.)*

Section 3 relates to **Guiding Question** ❸ **What shared belief caused conflicts over trade between the Chinese and the Europeans?** *(Conflicts arose because each believed it was the more advanced culture and possessed superior trade goods.)*

⟳ Target Reading Skill

In this chapter, students will learn and apply the reading skill of clarifying meaning. Use the following worksheets to help students practice this skill.

All in One **Unit 5 History of Our World Teaching Resources,** *Paraphrase*, p. 101; *Summarize*, p. 102; *Reread or Read Ahead*, p. 103

Chapter

16 Exploration: Europe and Asia

Chapter Preview

This chapter will examine European exploration in Africa between the 1400s and 1700s.

Section 1
European Exploration Begins

Section 2
Europeans in India and Southeast Asia

Section 3
Europe Explores East Asia

⟳ **Target Reading Skill**

Clarifying Meaning In this chapter you will focus on clarifying, or better understanding, the meaning of what you read.

▶ In Lisbon, Portugal, the Monument to the Discoveries honors Prince Henry, the first in Europe to run a school for navigators. It includes statues of Magellan and Vasco da Gama.

452 History of Our World

Differentiated Instruction

The following Teacher Edition strategies are suitable for students of varying abilities.

For Special Needs Students, p. 465
For Advanced Readers, p. 468
For Less Proficient Readers, p. 469
For Gifted and Talented Students, p. 473
For English Learners, pp. 465, 473

Bibliography

For the Teacher

Curtin, Philip D. *The World and the West: The European Challenge and the Overseas Response in the Age of Empire.* Cambridge University Press, 2000.

Friedman, John Block, Kristen Mossler Figg, et al., eds. *Trade, Travel and Exploration in the Middle Ages: An Encyclopedia.* New York: Garland, 2000.

For the Student

L2 Fritz, Jean, and Anthony Bacon Venti. *Around the World in a Hundred Years: From Henry the Navigator to Magellan.* Puffin, 1998.

L2 Haywood, John. *Age of Discovery 1492–1815: World Atlas of the Past.* Oxford University Press, 2000.

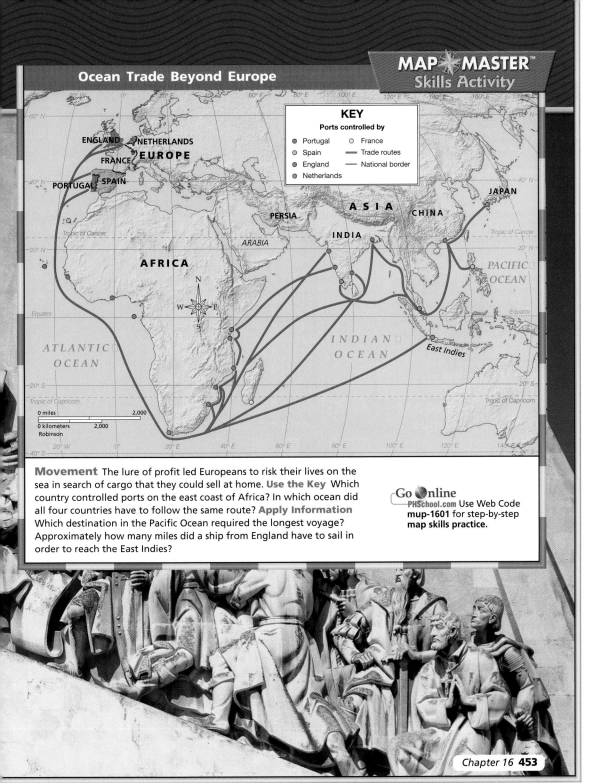

Ocean Trade Beyond Europe

KEY

Ports controlled by
- Portugal
- Spain
- England
- Netherlands
- France
— Trade routes
— National border

ENGLAND NETHERLANDS
EUROPE
FRANCE
PORTUGAL SPAIN

JAPAN

PERSIA **ASIA** CHINA

INDIA

ARABIA

AFRICA

PACIFIC OCEAN

Tropic of Cancer

Equator

INDIAN OCEAN

East Indies

ATLANTIC OCEAN

Tropic of Capricorn

0 miles 2,000
0 kilometers 2,000
Robinson

Movement The lure of profit led Europeans to risk their lives on the sea in search of cargo that they could sell at home. **Use the Key** Which country controlled ports on the east coast of Africa? In which ocean did all four countries have to follow the same route? **Apply Information** Which destination in the Pacific Ocean required the longest voyage? Approximately how many miles did a ship from England have to sail in order to reach the East Indies?

Go Online
PHSchool.com Use Web Code
mup-1601 for step-by-step
map skills practice.

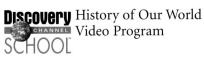

Chapter 16 **453**

■ Have students describe how a compass rose helps readers understand a map. Have students identify the farthest point south that a ship following a trade route needed to travel. Ask **If you flew from Portugal to Japan, in which direction would you travel?** (*Northeast*)

Go Online
PHSchool.com Students may practice their map skills using the interactive online version of this map.

Using the Visual L2

Reach into Your Background Have students look at the images on page 454 of the telescope and sextant used by Antarctic explorer Robert Falcon. Explain that these instruments helped guide him on his journey through uncharted lands. Ask students **What tools do modern scientists and astronomers use to learn about planets, moons, and galaxies?** Have students describe the tools they might use to help them learn about the world they live in, such as their city or state. (*Possible answers: Students might note that scientists and researchers today learn about space using telescopes, satellites, computers, space stations, and spaceships. Possible answers for how students can learn about their environment: using maps, compasses, binoculars, and the Internet.*)

Answers

MAP MASTER™ Skills Activity **Use the Key** England; Atlantic Ocean. **Apply Information** Japan; approximately 14,000 miles (21,000 kilometers)

Chapter Resources

Teaching Resources
- L2 Vocabulary Development, p. 113
- L2 Skills for Life, p. 107
- L2 Chapter Tests A and B, pp. 116–121

Spanish Support
- L2 Spanish Chapter Summary, p. 142
- L2 Spanish Vocabulary Development, p. 143

Media and Technology
- L1 Student Edition on Audio CD
- L1 Guided Reading Audio CDs, English and Spanish
- L2 Social Studies Skills Tutor CD-ROM
- *ExamView®* **Test Bank CD-ROM**

Discovery CHANNEL **SCHOOL** History of Our World Video Program

interactive Textbook PRENTICE HALL

TeacherEXPRESS™ Plan • Teach • Assess

Section 1
Step-by-Step Instruction

Objectives
Social Studies
1. Learn why Europeans began exploring the world in the 1400s.
2. Identify the early achievements of Portuguese exploration under Prince Henry the Navigator.
3. Understand how Portugal's efforts inspired early Spanish exploration.

Reading/Language Arts
Learn to paraphrase what you read.

Prepare to Read

Build Background Knowledge L2

Tell students that in this section, they will learn about the people who were the driving force behind Europe's exploration of the East. Have students look at the picture of Prince Henry on page 456. Then read aloud the first two paragraphs on that page. Ask students this question: **How did the capture of Ceuta affect Portuguese exploration?** Have students engage in a Give One, Get One activity to share their answers (TE, p. T41). *(Possible responses: The Portuguese became excited about the wealth to be found in other lands, they learned of the riches that could be had from trade, and they realized the need to sail around Muslim areas in the region.)*

Set a Purpose for Reading L2
■ Preview the Objectives.

■ Read each statement in the *Reading Readiness Guide* aloud. Ask students to mark the statements true or false.

> **All in One** **Unit 5 History of Our World Teaching Resources,** *Reading Readiness Guide,* p. 90

■ Have students discuss the statement in pairs or groups of four, then mark their worksheets again. Use the Numbered Heads participation structure (TE, p. T40) to call on students to share each group's perspectives.

Vocabulary Builder
Preview Key Terms L2
Pronounce each Key Term, and then ask the students to say the word with you. Provide a simple explanation.

Section 1
European Exploration Begins

Prepare to Read

Objectives
In this section you will
1. Learn why Europeans began exploring the world in the 1400s.
2. Identify the early achievements of Portuguese exploration under Prince Henry the Navigator.
3. Understand how Portugal's efforts inspired early Spanish exploration.

Taking Notes
As you read, look for information about the earliest oceangoing explorations of the land beyond Europe. Copy the graphic organizer below, and record your findings in it.

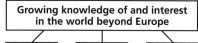
Growing knowledge of and interest in the world beyond Europe

Target Reading Skill
Paraphrase Paraphrasing can help you understand what you read. When you paraphrase, you restate what you have read in your own words. You could paraphrase the first paragraph of this section this way: "European sailors in the 1300s did not know what to expect, so they were afraid to sail their ships very far into the ocean."
As you read, paraphrase or "say back" the information following each red or blue heading.

Key Terms
• **circumnavigation** (sur kum nav ih GAY shun) *n.* going completely around the Earth, especially by water
• **isthmus** (IS mis) *n.* a narrow strip of land connecting two larger areas of land

The use of the sun and moon to determine latitude and longitude led to the creation of navigational tools. Early tools gave way to the sextant, as shown above.

What was out there in the ocean, beyond the horizon? In the 1300s, no European knew for sure. Were there monsters that could gobble ships whole? Did the waters of the sea reach the boiling point if you sailed too far to the south? Some European sailors actually held such fears. In fact, there was little firsthand knowledge of the open ocean. European vessels did not sail there.

That was about to change, however. As you learned in Chapter 15, Europe was emerging from the Middle Ages. Europeans were growing more interested in faraway lands and were learning more about them. Merchants were looking for ways to expand their trade and wealth. Kings and queens were looking for power and glory—for themselves and their God.

These were some of the reasons that ships from Europe first sailed out into the deep and mysterious sea. With those first ocean journeys, Europe's age of exploration began.

Target Reading Skill L2

Paraphrase Point out the Target Reading Skill.

Model how to paraphrase by reading aloud the sentence on page 458 that begins "Columbus believed that by sailing . . ." Write a new sentence on the board in your own words that helps clarify the meaning of the original sentence: "Columbus thought he could find the lands of the East by going west."

Give students the *Paraphrase* worksheet. Have them complete the activity in groups.

> **All in One** **Unit 5 History of Our World Teaching Resources,** *Paraphrase,* p. 101

Why Europe Looked to the East

You have already read about the journey of Marco Polo and about the Crusades. These events helped increase European awareness of the wonders of the East. In the last chapter you also read about the successful merchants of the Italian city-states. These merchants made fortunes bringing spices and other goods from Asia and northern Africa. In fact, Italians controlled this trade when the Renaissance began. But other Europeans also were interested in expanded trade.

The Crusades also drove Europe's explorations. The spirit of the Crusades lived on in some parts of Europe. The desire to defeat the Muslims and spread Christianity remained strong, especially on the Iberian Peninsula. This is the peninsula on which Portugal and Spain are located. Here Christians had been fighting to remove the Moors, Muslims who had arrived on the Iberian Peninsula in the 700s.

✓ **Reading Check** What two factors caused Europeans to look to the East during the Renaissance?

The Spice Trade
Europeans traded with merchants in the East for spices. **Explain** Why were spices considered prize trade items?

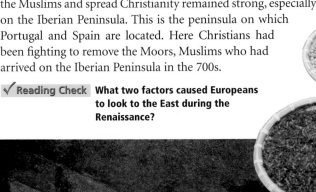

Chapter 16 Section 1 **455**

Vocabulary Builder

Use the information below to teach students this section's high-use words.

High-Use Word	Definition and Sample Sentence
domination, p. 456	*n.* supremacy over another Our basketball team's **domination** of the other team was exciting to watch.
scholars, p. 458	*n.* a learned person The **scholars** studied hard for their science exam.
expedition, p. 460	*n.* a journey undertaken for a specific purpose The explorers discovered an old path across the Bitterroot Mountains on their **expedition** in America's West.

Portuguese Exploration

L2

Guided Instruction

- **Vocabulary Builder** Clarify the high-use word **domination** before reading.

- Read aloud the section heading Portuguese Exploration.

- After students read this section, make sure they can answer the Reading Check question on page 457.

- Discuss with students how Prince Henry's voyages down Africa's west coast negatively affected some of the African people. (*Some African people were captured and enslaved.*)

- Have students discuss the impact of Prince Henry's conquest of Africa for people who traveled to the continent after him. (*The Portuguese were able to create maps of Africa, which aided later travelers.*)

Independent Practice

Have students fill in the second empty box with an example from the material they have just learned about Europe's growing interest in and knowledge of the world. Briefly model the kinds of information to record.

Monitor Progress

As students fill in the graphic organizer, circulate to make sure that individuals are choosing the correct details. Provide assistance as needed.

Target Reading Skill L2

Paraphrase As a follow up, ask students to answer the Target Reading Skill question in the Student Edition. (*In 1419, Prince Henry of Portugal paid scientists, mapmakers, and shipbuilders to continue exploring the African coast.*)

Prince Henry the Navigator at the conquest of Ceuta in 1415

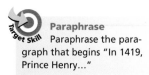

Paraphrase
Paraphrase the paragraph that begins "In 1419, Prince Henry..."

Portuguese Exploration

Prince Henry the Navigator was born in 1394. The third son of Portugal's King João I (king zhoo OW), Henry became a driving force behind Portuguese exploration. Under Henry's guidance, Portuguese navigation and trade advanced significantly.

As a young man, Henry took part in the conquest of Ceuta (say OO tah), in North Africa. Ceuta was a rich Muslim trading city. For several years after Ceuta's capture, Henry served as its governor. The capture of this city gave the prince and his country a taste for the wealth that was available in trade. First, however, Portugal would have to break through—or sail around—Muslim domination of the region.

Exploring the African Coast The conquest of Ceuta also helped the Portuguese learn more about the continent of Africa. Before taking Ceuta, they knew little about this land and the riches it held. The conquest of Ceuta allowed the Portuguese to have access to excellent maps of North Africa.

In 1419, Prince Henry decided to press Portugal's exploration of the African coast. He hired many of Europe's best navigators, scientists, mapmakers, and shipbuilders. He also provided money for these journeys of discovery.

Soon Prince Henry's ships were sailing into the unknown. Over several decades, these voyages pushed farther and farther down Africa's western coast, establishing trade with the newly discovered areas. Many historians believe that Henry's ships sailed as far south as modern-day Sierra Leone. Unfortunately, these journeys also began the terrible practice of the European trade in slaves. In the mid-1400s, Portuguese ships were returning to port with African captives. It was a practice that grew rapidly in the centuries ahead.

Prince Henry died in 1460. He left behind a strong tradition of Portuguese exploration.

Bartolomeu Dias The Portuguese continued their quest of exploration. Bartolomeu Dias (bahr too loo MEE oo DEE us) had taken part in explorations of Africa's western coast. In 1487, he left Portugal to find the southern tip of Africa. In spite of a terrible storm, he succeeded in traveling around Africa's southern tip in 1488. He named the tip the Cape of Storms. The name was later changed to the Cape of Good Hope.

Vasco da Gama Dias's journey led the way for another Portuguese explorer. In November 1497, Vasco da Gama (VAHS koh duh GAM uh) sailed around the Cape of Good Hope and into the Indian Ocean. In 1498, da Gama sailed into the port of Calicut (KAL uh kut) in India. Da Gama was celebrated as a hero at home. A Portuguese poet wrote of da Gama's rank at the top of history's brave explorers:

> "Cease All, whose Actions ancient Bards [poets] exprest: 'A brighter Valour rises in the West'"
>
> —The Lusiad, *Luis de Camões*

As you will read in the next section, the European presence in Asia continued to expand in the coming years.

✓ Reading Check What two Portuguese voyages took place after Prince Henry's death?

Links to Science

Navigation The astrolabe (AS troh layb) was one of the devices that helped make possible the exploits of European ocean explorers. The mariner's astrolabe made it possible for sailors to figure out their latitude. Sailors did this by taking measurements of the sun or stars.

Astrolabes were developed by the ancient Greeks. Muslim scholars helped perfect astrolabe technology. They also introduced the astrolabe to Europe.

Links

Read the **Links to Science** on this page. Ask students **What problems may have been presented by using an astrolabe to navigate on a long ocean voyage?** (*Because one had to see the sun and stars when using an astrolabe, bad weather, cloud cover, and the darkness of night would have limited the ability to navigate well all the time.*)

A King's Blessing
Below, King Manuel I of Portugal blesses da Gama and his expedition to Asia. Da Gama was later hailed a hero for successfully sailing around the Cape of Good Hope, as visible in the map on the left. **Compare and Contrast** Compare this map with the one on page 453. How are the maps similar? How are they different?

Background

The expeditions that Prince Henry sent down the west coast of Africa went very slowly as the ships got closer to the Equator. Early sailors believed that the waters near the Equator were boiling hot and that their skin would turn black from the heat. They also feared that sea monsters would attack their ships. None of Henry's crews were brave enough to venture as far south as the Cape of Good Hope.

Answers

✓ Reading Check Bartolomeu Dias's journey to the Cape of Good Hope and Vasco da Gama's journey to India

Compare and Contrast The maps are similar in that they both have labels and a compass rose and they both show mountains. The maps are different because the map on page 453 shows all of Africa, while the map on page 457 shows only the southeastern coast.

Columbus Sails Under Spanish Flag L2

Guided Instruction

- **Vocabulary Builder** Clarify the high-use word **scholars** before reading.

- Have students read the section heading Columbus Sails Under Spanish Flag.

- Ask students **What nationality was Christopher Columbus?** *(Italian)* Then ask **What country eventually agreed to support his plan to reach Asia?** *(Spain)*

- Ask students to explain why it took Columbus so long to gain financial support for his plan to sail west. *(He believed Earth was round and that he could reach India and lands in the East by sailing to the west. Most people at the time believed Earth was flat, so they assumed that Columbus would fail.)*

Independent Practice

Assign *Guided Reading and Review*

All in One **Unit 5 History of Our World Teaching Resources,** *Guided Reading and Review,* p. 91

Monitor Progress

Have students fill in the third empty box on their graphic organizer. Circulate to make sure that individuals are choosing the correct details. Provide assistance as needed.

Citizen Heroes

Read the **Citizen Heroes** on this page. Ask students why Isabella agreed to support Columbus's voyage. *(Spain had finally achieved their long struggle to push the Moors from the land.)*

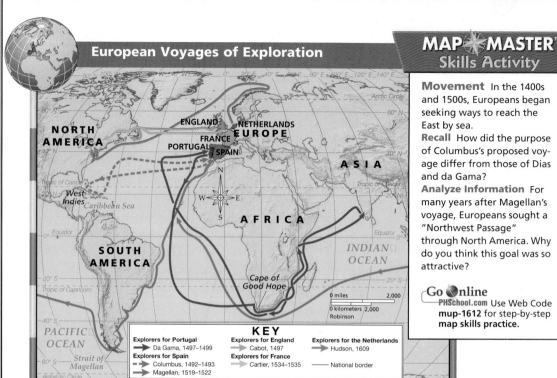

European Voyages of Exploration

MAP MASTER™ Skills Activity

Movement In the 1400s and 1500s, Europeans began seeking ways to reach the East by sea.
Recall How did the purpose of Columbus's proposed voyage differ from those of Dias and da Gama?
Analyze Information For many years after Magellan's voyage, Europeans sought a "Northwest Passage" through North America. Why do you think this goal was so attractive?

Go Online
PHSchool.com Use Web Code **mup-1612** for step-by-step map skills practice.

KEY

Explorers for Portugal	Explorers for England	Explorers for the Netherlands
Da Gama, 1497–1499	Cabot, 1497	Hudson, 1609
Explorers for Spain	**Explorers for France**	
Columbus, 1492–1493	Cartier, 1534–1535	National border
Magellan, 1519–1522		

Citizen Heroes

Queen Isabella

In 1492, Spain had just completed its centuries-old struggle to push the Moors from the land. With this battle won, Isabella was willing to take on a challenge that had seemed hopeless to other European leaders: supporting Columbus's idea for a voyage to the West. Thanks to Isabella's backing, Columbus was able to set sail on his fateful journey.

Columbus Sails Under Spanish Flag

Christopher Columbus was born in or around Genoa, Italy, in 1451. Like many Genoese, he became a skilled sailor. He traveled to Portugal and, later, Spain. He also developed a plan to reach the rich lands of India and the East by sailing to the West.

Little was known about the globe at this time. Even though most people thought the Earth was flat, many scholars knew that it was round. Columbus believed that by sailing far enough to the west, a sailor would eventually arrive at the lands of the East.

Columbus tried unsuccessfully for several years to win support for his plan. But in 1492, Queen Isabella of Spain finally agreed to pay for the voyage. That year, Columbus led three ships, the *Niña,* the *Pinta,* and the *Santa Maria.* After ten weeks, Columbus and his weary crew reached an island in the area now known as the Caribbean. The date was October 12, 1492.

Columbus's journey changed history. Instead of reaching Asia, he had reached the Americas. In Chapter 17, you will read more about the results of Columbus's voyage.

✓ **Reading Check** How did Columbus believe one could reach Asia?

Answers

MAP MASTER Skills Activity **Recall** Columbus proposed reaching the East by sailing west. **Analyze Information** The trip around the southern tip of South America was very long and difficult, as was the trip around the southern tip of Africa. A northwest passage would make their travels easier.

✓ **Reading Check** He believed that one could reach Asia by sailing west.

The *Santa Maria*

After years of preparation, Christopher Columbus sailed from Spain on August 3, 1492, on what would be his first voyage to the Americas. The *Santa Maria* was the flagship, or lead ship of Columbus's fleet of three ships. The *Santa Maria* was the biggest of the three. It was also the slowest and the hardest to handle. Thirty-three days of clear sailing brought the fleet across the Atlantic Ocean to a small island in the Bahamas, where Columbus landed on October 12, 1492.

Christopher Columbus
After successfully completing his voyage in 1492, Columbus was honored with the title Admiral of the Ocean Sea.

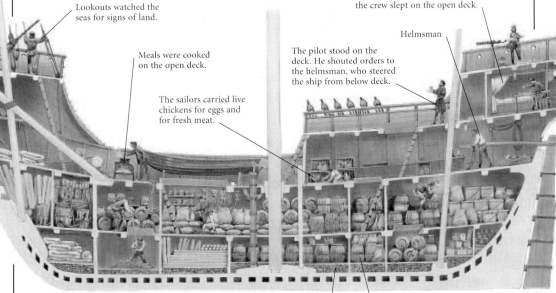

Lookouts watched the seas for signs of land.

Meals were cooked on the open deck.

The sailors carried live chickens for eggs and for fresh meat.

The pilot stood on the deck. He shouted orders to the helmsman, who steered the ship from below deck.

Columbus had his own cabin on board the *Santa Maria*. The rest of the crew slept on the open deck.

Helmsman

Stones were used as ballast, making the ship stable.

Wooden barrels held water, vinegar, salted fish, pork, and beef. Sacks held flour, rice, and beans.

Life-Sized Replicas
In this photo of life-sized replicas of Columbus's first fleet, the *Santa Maria* is in the lead. The *Pinta* and the *Niña* follow behind.

> **ANALYZING IMAGES**
> Why did the crew, except for Columbus, sleep on the open deck of the *Santa Maria*?

Chapter 16 Section 1 **459**

Guided Instruction
Have students read the paragraph on this page. As a class, look at the diagram and read the labels. Help students see that the diagram shows a cross-section of the ship so the viewer can see the interior. Have students discuss their answers to the Analyzing Images question. Then direct students' attention to the photos and captions.

Independent Practice
Have students work in pairs to plan a voyage of exploration on a sailing ship. Tell students their voyage will be six months. Have students decide on a destination and make a list of supplies and equipment, including navigational tools such items as maps and compasses.

Answer
ANALYZING IMAGES Students should see that the areas below deck were packed with supplies and equipment and had no room for sleeping areas.

Other Explorers Look West

L2

Guided Instruction

- **Vocabulary Builder** Clarify the high-use word **expedition** before reading.

- Read aloud the section heading: Other Explorers Look West.

- Discuss how Spanish explorer Balboa came to discover the Pacific Ocean. *(He arrived at the Isthmus of Panama, which connects North and South America, and he organized an expedition that reached the Pacific Ocean.)*

Independent Practice

Ask students to create the Taking Notes graphic organizer on a blank piece of paper. Then have them fill in the three empty circles with examples from what they have just learned about other explorers' growing interest in and knowledge of the world. *(The lands of South America are explored and given their name by explorer Amerigo Vespucci; Balboa's expedition finds the Pacific Ocean, which he calls the South Sea; Balboa claims the South Sea and the lands it touches for Spain.)*

Monitor Progress

- Show *Section Reading Support Transparency HOW 104,* and ask students to check their graphic organizers individually. Go over key concepts and clarify key vocabulary as needed.

    History of Our World Transparencies, Section Reading Support HOW 104

- Tell students to fill in the last column of the *Reading Readiness Guide.* Probe for what they learned that confirms or invalidates each statement.

    All in One Unit 5 History of Our World Teaching Resources, *Reading Readiness Guide,* p. 90

Answers

Chart Skills Identify Nũno Tristão
Infer Possible response: The Gambia may be a difficult river to navigate and it took a few years before someone was able to sail it.

Other Explorers Look West

Europeans came to know the western lands Columbus had reached as America. The name can be traced to an Italian trader known as Amerigo Vespucci (ah meh REE goh ves POOT chee). In a letter to a government official in Florence, Italy, Vespucci claimed to have taken part in four voyages across the Atlantic Ocean. He wrote that in 1497 he explored the coast of what is now South America. The name America soon appeared on a map and came into common use.

For his part, Columbus never gave up the idea that the lands he had reached were part of Asia. By the early 1500s, however, Europeans knew that the Americas were not lands of the East.

Balboa Sees the Pacific In 1511, a Spanish explorer named Vasco Núñez de Balboa (VAHS koh NOO nyeth theh bal BOH uh) arrived on the Isthmus of Panama (IS mis uv PAN uh mah). An **isthmus** is a narrow strip of land connecting two larger areas of land. The Isthmus of Panama connects the continents of North America and South America. Balboa had heard stories about a huge ocean and gold treasure to the south. He organized an expedition to find both. After nearly a month, his expedition reached the shores of a sea that stretched far into the distance. This great body of water was the Pacific Ocean. Balboa called it the South Sea. Then he claimed it and all the lands it touched for Spain. Asia still lay beyond.

Chart Skills

Even before Magellan's historic voyages, Portuguese explorers and navigators of the 1400s made many important discoveries. **Identify** Name the navigator who rounded Cape Blanco in 1443.
Infer What can you infer from the fact that the Gambia River was spotted in 1446 but was not sailed upon until 1456?

Other Portuguese Navigators and Explorers

Names	Accomplishments
João Gonçalves Zarco (zhoo OW gohn SAHL veezh ZAHR koo) and Tristão Vaz Teixeira (treesh TOW vahsh tay SHAY ruh)	Rediscovered the islands of Porto Santo (PAWR toh SAHN toh) and Madeira (muh DIHR uh) (1418)
Gil Eanes (zhil YAH neesh)	Sailed around Cape Bojador (BOH juh dohr) (1434)
Dinís Dias (dee NEESH DEE us)	Reached the mouth of the Senegal River (SEN ih gawl RIV ur) (1445)
Nuño Tristão (NOO nyoo treesh TOW)	Rounded Cape Blanco (kayp BLANG koh) (1443), spotted the Gambia River (GAM bee uh RIV ur) (1446)
Diogo Gomes (DYOH goo GOH mish)	Explored the West African coast and sailed up the Gambia River (1456), landed on the Cape Verde Islands (kayp vurd EYE lundz) (1460)
Diogo Cão (DYOH goo kow)	Found the Congo River (1482), reached Cape Cross in present-day Namibia (nuh MIB ee uh) (1485–86)

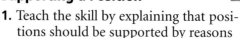 **Skills Mini Lesson**

Supporting a Position

L2

1. Teach the skill by explaining that positions should be supported by reasons and evidence.

2. Have students suppose they live in one of the countries discussed in Chapter 16. Have students brainstorm whether their country should or should not trade with China. Then have them write their position in one sentence.

3. Students can apply the skill by writing a letter to the country's leader, explaining why the country should or should not trade with China.

Magellan's Voyage In 1519, the Portuguese navigator Ferdinand Magellan (FUR duh nand muh JEL un) set out to achieve Columbus's unfulfilled goal of reaching Asia by sailing west. With great difficulty, Magellan and three of his ships managed to reach the Pacific in 1520. In 1521 Magellan landed in the Philippines, where he was killed by native people. The crew pressed on, and the one remaining ship reached Spain in 1522. The voyage of nearly three years was the first circumnavigation of the globe. **Circumnavigation** means going completely around the earth, especially by water.

Quest for the Northwest Passage Magellan's voyage showed just how hard it was to circle the globe. For this reason, many Europeans sought a shortcut through North America. This hoped-for shortcut was referred to as the Northwest Passage. European explorers, including England's Henry Hudson, looked for such a shortcut for hundreds of years. It was not until the 1900s that a ship successfully traveled from the Atlantic Ocean to the Pacific Ocean by sailing north of Canada.

Ferdinand Magellan

✓ **Reading Check** What did Magellan's voyage have to do with the search for the Northwest Passage?

Section 1 Assessment

Key Terms
Review the key term at the beginning of this section. Use each term in a sentence that explains its meaning.

Target Reading Skill
Paraphrase the achievements of early Portuguese explorers.

Comprehension and Critical Thinking
1. (a) Recall Which part of Europe dominated Asian trade at the start of the Renaissance?

(b) Synthesize Information What did the quests to expand trade and to spread Christianity have in common?

2. (a) Identify Why was the crusading spirit strong in Portugal?

(b) Summarize How did the conquest of Ceuta affect the Portuguese?

3. (a) Identify Where did Christopher Columbus first learn to be a sailor?

(b) Draw Inferences What can you infer from the fact that Columbus did not know about the existence of North and South America?

Writing Activity
Sailors in the 1400s and 1500s often did not know what they would find when they started their journeys. Write a diary entry from the point of view of a sailor leaving for his or her first voyage. Be sure to talk about both your hopes and your fears about what will happen to you.

For: An activity on the explorers of Portugal and Spain
Visit: PHSchool.com
Web Code: mud-1610

Chapter 16 Section 1 **461**

Writing Activity
Use the Rubric for *Assessing a Writing Assignment* to evaluate students' diary entries.

All in One Unit 5 History of Our World Teaching Resources, *Rubric for Assessing a Writing Assignment,* p. 114

Go Online
PHSchool.com Typing in the Web Code when prompted will bring students to detailed instructions for this activity.

Focus On A Sailor's Life at Sea

L2

Guided Instruction

- Have students study the text, visuals and captions on pp. 462–463 as a class.

- Ask students to list the different jobs people had on ships. *(pages, sailor's apprentices, sailors, ship's pilot, master of a ship)*

- Ask students to discuss why they think so few men became the master of a ship. *(Possible answers: Very few jobs as ship masters were available; it was a difficult job that many men competed for.)*

- Have students answer the Assessment questions in groups of two or three.

Focus On
A Sailor's Life at Sea

In the 1500s, a life at sea was a hard life. During lengthy voyages of exploration, sailors performed tiring physical labor, suffered from poor nutrition, and endured long stretches of boredom. They were often lonely, surrounded by vast and sometimes violent seas, far from home and family. They ate dried and salted food that was often infested with insects or gnawed by rats. They suffered injuries from their work or from fights with other sailors. Sailors' registries often identified men by their injuries, including crushed fingers and splinters embedded in the flesh.

Onboard a Ship Sailing was often the best job available for poor, uneducated men and orphaned boys who lived near busy ports. Boys as young as seven or eight served as ship's pages until they were about fifteen. A page's duties included scrubbing the ship and turning the sand clocks every half hour to mark the time. Unless they were assigned to specific officers, pages took orders from everyone on board. When they were old enough, pages became sailor's apprentices.

Apprentices were young men training to become sailors. They climbed the rigging in their bare feet to furl, or gather, the sails. They served as lookouts at the top of the masts, rowed smaller boats, and carried heavy cargo.

Sailors might work their way up to other positions, including that of ship's pilot, whose job it was to navigate. A very few men became the master of a ship. The master commanded the ship and was usually part owner of the vessel. The illustration at the right shows a vessel from the 1500s that sailed with about 45 crew members.

Sunken Treasures
This decorated plate and the pottery jug above were recovered from a Venetian shipwreck in the Adriatic Sea. The shipwreck probably occurred in the late 1500s.

Master's or Captain's Cabin
Common sailors slept on deck on straw-filled sacks.

Differentiated Instruction

For Gifted and Talented **L3**

Have students conduct Internet and library research on a topic that interests them related to the life of sailors in the 1500s, such as the technology that allowed ships to travel long distances or the voyages of a particular explorer. Students should create a poster with visuals and text on their topic to present to the class.

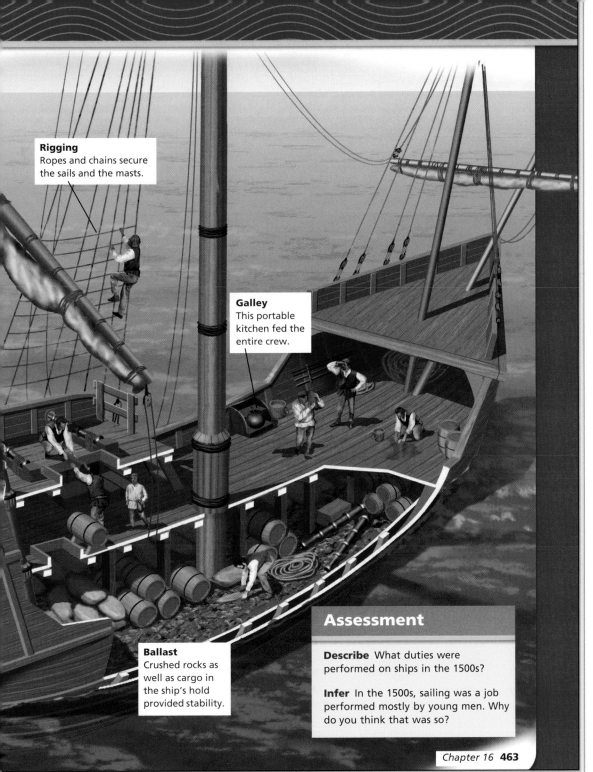

Rigging
Ropes and chains secure the sails and the masts.

Galley
This portable kitchen fed the entire crew.

Ballast
Crushed rocks as well as cargo in the ship's hold provided stability.

Assessment

Describe What duties were performed on ships in the 1500s?

Infer In the 1500s, sailing was a job performed mostly by young men. Why do you think that was so?

Have students write a short story from the perspective of a page, sailor, or master of a ship using the information on pp. 462–463 as a guide. Students may conduct library or Internet research if they require further information in order to write their stories. Use the *Rubric for Assessing a Writing Assignment* to evaluate students' work.

All in One Unit 5 Teaching Resources, *Rubric for Assessing a Writing Assignment,* p. 114

Answers

Assessment

Describe Pages cleaned the ship, turned the sand clocks every half hour, and took orders from everyone on board unless they were assigned to specific officers; sailor's apprentices and sailors climbed the rigging to furl the sails, served as lookouts, rowed smaller boats, and carried cargo; ship's pilots navigated the ship; the master of a ship commanded the ship and usually owned part of the vessel.

Infer Possible answer: Women were probably not allowed to become sailors at that time.

Objective L2

Learn to recognize an author's bias.

Prepare to Read

Build Background Knowledge L2

Ask students to define the word *bias*. (*a partial or narrow view of a fact or situation*) Then ask them how bias in television commercials, such as those for fast food, video games, or toys, might affect what the viewer thinks about a product.

Instruct

Recognizing Author's Bias L2

Guided Practice

- Read the steps to recognizing an author's bias as a class, and write the steps on the board.

- Practice the skill by following the steps on page 464. Model the activity steps by choosing a sample product (*a video game*), and have students visualize a commercial for the product. Ask them what words would be used in the commercial to describe the game favorably. Then have students say who would be a good spokesperson for the commercial (*Possible answers: a young person who is an expert at playing the game; the person who designed the game; a celebrity*).

- Ask students to say how the commercial might reflect bias. (*Possible answers: The words to describe the product are favorable ones meant to sell the product. They don't use any negative words or mention what might be wrong with the game. The spokesperson is biased because he or she wants to sell the product and might benefit from product sales.*)

Independent Practice

Assign *Skills for Life* and have students complete it individually.

All in One Unit 5 History of Our World Teaching Resources, *Skills for Life,* p. 107

Recognizing Author's Bias

(a) "Christopher Columbus discovered America in 1492."

(b) "Native Indians discovered America."

Each of these statements is true in a way. Yet each reflects a different bias, a partial or narrow view of a fact or situation. Statement (a) might reflect the view of the Europeans who were discovering an area that was new to them when they arrived in the Americas. Statement (b) might reflect the view of the native people who had already been there a long time when Columbus arrived. Some of the authors you read may have an open or a hidden bias. Recognizing an author's bias can help you become a more careful and alert reader.

This painting is an artist's representation of Captain Christopher Newport and his followers landing in Jamestown.

Learn the skill

Use the following guidelines for becoming more alert to an author's possible bias.

1. **Look for one-sided language and evidence.** Look for words or information that seems to favor only one side of a situation or an argument.

2. **Ask what kind of sources the writer relies on.** Is the writing based on a balanced variety of sources, or does the writer rely only on sources that favor one side or viewpoint?

3. **Look for bias names and titles.** For example, one author might describe a historical figure as an "explorer"; another might describe the same person as a "conqueror."

4. **Look for information about the author.** Look at the author's background to see whether that could influence his or her outlook.

464 History of Our World

Monitor Progress

As students work on the *Skills for Life* worksheet, circulate and check to make sure they understand the skill steps. Provide assistance as needed.

Practice the Skill

Read the numbered sentences in the boxed advertisement at the right. Then answer the following questions.

1. Analyze the choice of words and use of language in sentence 1. Which words or phrases show bias?

2. Does sentence 2 use a balanced variety of sources? Explain.

3. How might the use of the word "Captain" influence the readers of this advertisement?

4. What does the author's background say about the possible bias of the ad? Would the preferred means of travel be the same if a flight attendant had written the advertisement?

1. Many people planning a trip around the world prefer ocean liners to airplanes.
2. A recent survey of ocean-liner travelers found that they place a high value on a leisurely pace of travel.
3. Captain Oswald Harris, a long-time skipper of big ocean liners, points out that the food and service are much better on cruise ships than on airplanes.
4. For more reasons to travel around the world by boat, come see me, Abe Fenster, represenative for Worldwide Ocean Cruises.

Apply the Skill

Reread the story of the encounter between Sir George Macartney and Qianlong in Section 3 of this chapter. Then write a biased version of the story, relating the events from the viewpoint of either Sir George Macartney or Qianlong. Use your imagination to invent new details or dialogue that will make your version persuasive and lively.

Assess and Reteach

Assess Progress   L2
Ask students to do the Apply the Skill activity.

Reteach   L1
If students are having trouble applying the skill steps, have them review the skill using the interactive Social Studies Skills Tutor CD-ROM.

 Recognizing Author's Bias, **Social Studies Skills Tutor CD-ROM**

Extend   L3
Have students learn more about recognizing bias by asking them to write a speech for Christopher Columbus. The speech should announce that he has succeeded in reaching Asia. Students can perform their speeches for the class.

Differentiated Instruction

For Special Needs Students   L1
Have students create flash cards of words that they encounter frequently as they read. Model how to write a word on one side of a card and its definition on the other side. Encourage students to use a dictionary if they need help defining the words.

For English Language Learners   L2
Have students read the section as they listen to the recorded version on the Student Edition on Audio CD. Check for comprehension by pausing the CD and asking students to share their answers to the Reading Checks.

◉ Chapter 16, Section 1, **Student Edition on Audio CD**

Section 2
Step-by-Step Instruction

Objectives

Social Studies

1. Learn how Portugal traded in India.
2. Understand how Portuguese trade expanded into India and the Spice Islands.
3. Identify the English and the Dutch as challengers to Portugal's power in Asia.

Reading/Language Arts

Learn to summarize what you read.

Prepare to Read

Build Background Knowledge L2

Tell students that in this section, they will study Portugal's expanding empire and growing interest in trade with India and the Spice Islands. Remind students of how eager the Portuguese were to explore North Africa and the African coast. Have students look at the images in this section. Then ask them to predict why the Portuguese and others may have been interested in India and Southeast Asia. Use the Idea Wave participation strategy (TE, p. T39) to generate responses. *(Answers will vary, but should explain that interest in trade and the riches available in new lands drove exploration to these lands.)*

Set a Purpose for Reading L2

- Preview the Objectives.

- Read each statement in the *Reading Readiness Guide* aloud. Ask students to mark the statements true or false.

  All in One **Unit 5 History of Our World Teaching Resources,** *Reading Readiness Guide,* p. 94

- Have students discuss the statement in pairs or groups of four, then mark their worksheets again. Use the Numbered Heads participation structure (TE, p. T40) to call on students to share their group's perspectives.

Preview Key Terms L2

Pronounce each Key Term, and then ask the students to say the word with you. Provide a simple explanation such as "When Sophie discovered a hidden box of trading cards, she had a monopoly and could charge higher prices for each card."

Section 2 Europeans in India and Southeast Asia

Prepare to Read

Objectives

In this section you will
1. Learn how Portugal traded in India.
2. Understand how Portuguese trade expanded into India and the Spice Islands.
3. Identify the English and the Dutch as challengers to Portugal's power in Asia.

Taking Notes

As you read, look for information about European trading in Asia. Copy the graphic organizer below. Record your findings in it.

Portuguese seek to control India and Moluccas
↓   ↓   ↓
↓   ↓   ↓

Target Reading Skill

Summarize You can better understand a text if you pause to restate the key points briefly in your own words. A good summary includes important events and details, notes the order in which the events occurred, and makes connections. Use the graphic organizer at the left to summarize what you have read.

Key Terms

- **monopoly** (muh NAHP uh lee) *n.* the exclusive control of goods or services in a market
- **colony** (KAHL uh nee) *n.* a territory ruled over by a distant state

Ducats were gold coins used as currency in various European countries.

It was horrifying to think about: In 1519, Ferdinand Magellan had set out from Spain with a crew of more than 250 men on five ships. Nearly three years later—on September 6, 1522—the single remaining vessel from that voyage sailed into port under a different commander and with a ragged crew of eighteen.

The journey, however, was far from a total loss. The ship carried a valuable cargo: tons of cloves. The ship had picked up the cloves in the Moluccas (moh LUK uz)—islands in the East Indies also known as the Spice Islands. The value of these spices was 41,000 ducats (DUK utz). The entire voyage had cost a mere 20,000 ducats.

The people of Europe greatly prized spices. The spices you can now buy at your supermarket for just a few dollars were worth a small fortune hundreds of years ago.

At the beginning of the 1500s, even before Magellan's voyage, the Portuguese were the first Europeans to take advantage of these riches. They were followed, however, by other nations.

Target Reading Skill L2

Summarize Point out the Target Reading Skill. Tell students that a summary briefly restates key information and helps clarify meaning.

Model how to summarize by reading aloud the first page of this section. Write on the board the key points on this page. *(Magellan had a difficult voyage; Many of his men died; Those who returned brought with them valuable cloves; The Portuguese were first* to discover the cloves; Other nations would follow the Portuguese)

Have students create a summary using this information.

Give students the *Summarize* worksheet. Have them complete the activity in groups.

All in One **Unit 5 History of Our World Teaching Resources,** *Summarize,* p. 102

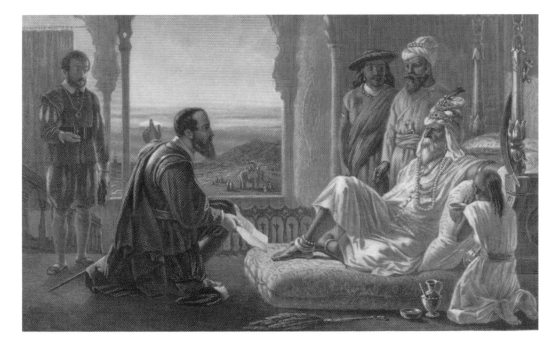

At the palace of the Zamorin, da Gama negotiated for trade rights and spices.

Portugal Gains a Foothold in India

As you have read, Portugal was the first European country to reach the rich ports of Asia. Vasco da Gama's voyage had reached the trading center of Calicut, India, in 1498 but da Gama left India empty-handed. Calicut traders had rejected the humble cloth, honey, and other trade goods he brought from Europe. The Portuguese soon returned, however. The next time, they were not disappointed in their quest for riches.

In 1500, Pedro Alvarez Cabral (PAY droh AL vuh rez kuh BRAHL) set out for India. This long journey included the first Portuguese landing in an area that is now southeastern Brazil. Cabral claimed this land for Portugal. The journey also included a shipwreck that took the life of Bartolomeu Dias, who was part of Cabral's crew.

Cabral eventually did reach Calicut. There, his efforts to trade for spices went slowly. A frustrated Cabral got into an armed conflict with Arab traders that left many people dead. In spite of the bloodshed, Cabral was able to establish a trading post in India. In 1501, he returned to Portugal with a load of spices. But this Portuguese show of force abroad was not to be the last.

√ **Reading Check** Why did da Gama come home empty-handed on his first voyage to Calicut?

Links to
Math

Profits Magellan's voyage cost 20,000 ducats. It brought back a cargo worth 41,000 ducats. This means the profit on the voyage was 21,000 ducats.

Vocabulary Builder

Use the information below to teach students this section's high-use words.

High-Use Word	Definition and Sample Sentence
humble, p. 467	*adj.* not proud or haughty The young prince showed what a **humble** man he was by offering his seat to the lady.
enterprise, p. 469	*n.* a business organization Mr. Thompson's **enterprise** to clean up the sidewalks along Main Street took more time than he intended.
emerged, p. 470	*v.* to come forth Two students in my class **emerged** from the game as contestants in our state spelling bee.

The Portuguese Empire Expands L2

Guided Instruction

- Read aloud the section heading The Portuguese Empire Expands.

- Ask students **What did the Portuguese lack that may have led to the empire's downfall?** *(Although they controlled trade, they held very little territory.)*

- Have students explain the manner in which the Portuguese gained control of trade in India and the Spice Islands. *(The Portuguese gained control of trading centers after bloody conquests against others by their armed forces.)*

Independent Practice

Ask students to create the Taking Notes graphic organizer on a blank piece of paper. Then have them fill in the two empty squares with examples from what they have just read about how Portugal sought to control trade in India and the Spice Islands. *(Portugal sends many ships and armed forces to Asia; Portugal seizes control of the Spice Islands)*

Monitor Progress

Show *Section Reading Support Transparency HOW 105*, and ask students to check their graphic organizers individually. Go over key concepts and clarify key vocabulary as needed.

The Portuguese Empire Expands

Cabral's voyage was considered a great success. Soon Portugal was sending more ships to trade in Asia. They were also sending armed forces. With these forces, Portugal was able to gain control of many trading centers between the east coast of Africa and the west coast of India. These conquests were sometimes accomplished with bloodshed. Despite the cost in lives, Portugal succeeded in controlling the trade in the region.

Next Portugal looked further to the East. There lay the Moluccas—the Spice Islands, which lie in the northeastern part of present-day Indonesia. As you have read, these lands were the major source of cloves, a highly prized spice. In 1511, Afonso de Albuquerque (ah FAHN soh duh AL buh kur kee) led a mission to Malacca, located near these islands, which helped establish the Portuguese spice trade.

Portugal's hold on the East was vast. However, its control was limited mainly to trade. Portugal held very little territory. This Portuguese empire did not last very long, as you will read.

✓ **Reading Check** What was Portugal's response to the success of Cabral's voyage?

Troubles at Sea
Expeditions to the Spice Islands faced many challenges—storms at sea, tropical heat, sickness, and mutiny. **Link Past and Present** *What types of challenges do modern-day crews and their ships encounter?*

Differentiated Instruction

For Advanced Readers L3

Have students do Internet or library research to learn more about the large sailing ships that carried trade goods during the 1500s and 1600s. Have students summarize their findings in a short essay. Encourage them to illustrate their essay with drawings or photographs.

Answers

Link Past and Present storms at sea, tropical heat, equipment failure

✓ **Reading Check** Portugal sent more trading vessels and military forces

Challengers to Portugal

The Portuguese empire brought wealth to Portugal in the 1500s. Soon other powerful European nations became interested in the region.

The Rise of the Dutch The Dutch, the people from Holland (what we now call the Netherlands), soon challenged Portugal's leading role in the East. During the 1500s, the Dutch were growing into an economic and military power in Europe. As the century ended, they sought to control Portugal's empire of Asian trading posts. Portugal was unable to defend these posts against the more powerful Dutch.

In 1602, the Dutch East India Company was founded in Holland. The Dutch government gave this company a trade monopoly in Asia. A **monopoly** is complete control of the trade in a market or product.

The Dutch East India Company became a powerful force in Southeast Asia. From its base in modern-day Indonesia, it established many new trading posts and relationships. The company developed close ties with other Asian nations. It even had its own armies, which it used to seize land and people to serve its enterprise.

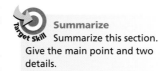

Summarize
Summarize this section. Give the main point and two details.

Differentiated Instruction

For Less Proficient Readers L1
Tell students to use looping to help them focus on a topic in this section to write about. Have them follow these steps: Write freely on your topic for about five minutes. Read what you have written, and circle the most important idea. Write for five minutes on the circled idea. Repeat the process until you isolate a topic narrow enough to cover well in a short essay.

Challengers to Portugal L2

Guided Instruction

- **Vocabulary Builder** Clarify the high-use words **enterprise** and **emerged** before reading.

- Have students read the section heading Challengers to Portugal.

- Ask students **Why were the Portuguese unable to maintain control of their trading posts in the East?** (*The strength of the Dutch economy and military had grown, so the Dutch were able to overpower the Portuguese and take control of trade.*)

- Discuss with students how both the Dutch and the English treated the inhabitants of Southeastern Asia. (*Both the Dutch and the English seized the land and ruled over its people.*)

Independent Practice
Assign *Guided Reading and Review*.

All in One **Unit 5 History of Our World Teaching Resources,** *Guided Reading and Review,* p. 95

Monitor Progress

- Show *Section Reading Support Transparency* HOW 105 and ask students to check their graphic organizers individually. Review key concepts and clarify key vocabulary as needed.

- Tell students to fill in the last column of the *Reading Readiness Guide.* Probe for what they learned that confirms or invalidates each statement.

All in One **Unit 5 History of Our World Teaching Resources,** *Reading Readiness Guide,* p. 94

Target Reading Skill L2

As a follow up, ask students to answer the Target Reading Skill question in the Student Edition. (*Portugal was a trading power in the 1600s, but other nations eventually gained control of their lands and trade. The Dutch overpowered the Portuguese's Asian empire, establishing the Dutch East India Company. The English became the leading power in India, driving out the Portuguese and then winning control from the Mughal Empire. In the 1800s, India became a colony of Great Britain.*)

Assess and Reteach

Assess Progress **L2**

Have students complete the Section Assessment. Administer the *Section Quiz.*

All in One **Unit 5 History of Our World Teaching Resources,** *Section Quiz,* p. 96

Reteach **L1**

If students need more instruction, have them read this section in the Reading and Vocabulary Study Guide.

📖 Chapter 16, Section 2, **History of Our World Reading and Vocabulary Study Guide,** pp. 177–179

Extend **L3**

Have students work in the library to learn about the spices found on the Spice Islands. Ask students to research the types of spices that were traded as well as how they were used. Students may want to prepare a treat made with one of these spices to share with the class.

Answer

✓**Reading Check** The English focused on India, and the Dutch focused on the East Indies.

Section 2 Assessment

Key Terms
Students' sentences should reflect knowledge of each key term.

🎯 **Target Reading Skill**
Answers will vary, but should demonstrate the ability to summarize.

Comprehension and Critical Thinking
1. (a) There was great wealth to be made in the Asian trade. **(b)** Possible answer: The Portuguese were not always interested in conducting fair trade or allowing for competition; the native populations may have resented the power of the Portuguese outsiders.

2. (a) a Dutch monopoly for Asian trade **(b)** Possible answer: The Dutch sought to control some of the same markets that the Portuguese did. The Dutch, however, did more than set up trading posts, as the Portuguese had. They took over lands and conquered people.

3. (a) Netherlands and France **(b)** Possible answer: The Mughal power that had controlled India began to decline, and the

---

The English in Asia England was also interested in Asian trade. The East India Company, established in England in 1600, led this effort.

For a time, the British East India Company competed with the Dutch East India Company in the East Indies. The English soon moved their focus to India. First the English drove out the Portuguese. Then they expanded their own trading operations. Throughout the 1600s, they enjoyed great success, replacing the Portuguese as the area's leading trading power.

As the English made headway, the main power in India, the Mughal Empire, began to lose control of the country. Groups in India began to fight for power. The French East India Company, which was also trying to establish itself there, was among the groups battling for control. In the mid-1700s, the British emerged from these struggles as the leading power in India. Over the next hundred years, Britain tightened its hold. Eventually, in the mid-1800s, India became a colony of Great Britain. A **colony** is a territory ruled over by a faraway country.

European interest in Asia did not stop with India and the East Indies. In the next section, you will read about European involvement elsewhere in the region.

✓ **Reading Check** In what parts of Asia did the English and Dutch focus their efforts?

Trading port established by the British East India Company in Surat, India

Section 2 Assessment

Key Terms
Review the key terms at the beginning of this section. Use each term in a sentence that explains its meaning.

🎯 **Target Reading Skill**
Summarize the information in the last page of this section.

Comprehension and Critical Thinking
1. (a) Recall Why were the Portuguese interested in Asian trade?

(b) Draw Inferences What can you infer from the fact that the Portuguese sometimes used force in order to set up trading posts?
2. (a) Explain What was the Dutch East India company?
(b) Compare and Contrast How was the Dutch expansion into Asia similar to and different from the Portuguese expansion into Asia?
3. (a) Identify Which countries were England's main rivals for control of India?
(b) Cause and Effect Why were the English eventually able to gain total control over India?

Writing Activity
You are a Dutch businessperson in the late 1500s. Write a letter to colleagues in your business about possible business opportunities in Asia. Be sure to discuss the role of the Portuguese and other European rivals, such as the British.

Go Online
PHSchool.com
For: An activity on the explorers of Portugal and Spain
Visit: PHSchool.com
Web Code: mud-1620

470 History of Our World

English took advantage of the power struggle to gain control; also, the English forces proved stronger than those of their Dutch and French rivals.

Writing Activity
Use the Rubric for *Assessing a Writing Assignment* to evaluate students' letters.

All in One **Unit 5 History of Our World Teaching Resources,** *Assessing a Writing Assignment,* p. 114

Go Online PHSchool.com Typing in the Web Code when prompted will bring students to detailed instructions for this activity.

Section 3
Europe Explores East Asia

Prepare to Read

Objectives
In this section you will
1. Learn about European efforts to expand trade in East Asia.
2. Understand European encounters with China and Japan, 1600–1700.

Taking Notes
As you read, look for information about European efforts to expand trade in East Asia. Copy the graphic organizer below and record your findings in it.

> I. Europeans seek trade in East Asia: 1500s and 1600s
>   A. Portuguese
>   B.
>   C.
> II. China and the Europeans
>   A.
>   B.
> III. Japan and the Europeans
>   A.
>   B.

🎯 Target Reading Skill

Reread or Read Ahead Rereading and reading ahead are strategies that can help you understand words and ideas in the text. If you do not understand a certain passage, reread it to look for connections among the words and sentences. It might also help to read ahead, because a word or idea may become clearer later on in the text.

Key Terms
- **missionary** (MISH un ehr ee) *n.* a person who is sent to do religious or charitable work in a foreign country
- **persecution** (pur sih KYOO shun) *n.* the causing of injury or distress to others because of their religion, race, or political beliefs

I n 1793, the British government sent Sir George Macartney (sur jawrg muh KAHRT nee) to ask for greater British trading rights in China. He presented Qianlong (CHYAHN lawng), the Chinese emperor, with samples of fine British manufactured goods. The Chinese, however, were not moved. "We possess all things," wrote the emperor in his official response to George III. "I set no value on things strange or ingenious, and have no use for your country's manufactures." With that, the Chinese rejected the British requests.

Great Britain was not alone in seeking greater trade in East Asia from the 1500s through the 1700s. Nor was it the only country to come away disappointed. As you will read, the Portuguese, the Dutch, and the Spanish also tried to tap the riches of the region during this era. Few of them returned home with much to show for their efforts.

A Chinese export teapot from the Qianlong dynasty decorated with a river landscape.

🎯 Target Reading Skill   L2

Reread or Read Ahead Point out the Target Reading Skill.

Model how reading ahead can help clarify meaning. Read aloud the first paragraph on page 471. Students may not understand the meaning of the quotation. Have students turn to page 473 and read aloud the first paragraph of The China Trade. After they have read this informa-

tion, have students reread the first passage. They should have a clearer understanding of the emperor's words.

Give students the *Reread or Read Ahead* worksheet. Have them complete the activity in groups.

All in One Unit 5 History of Our World Teaching Resources, *Reread or Read Ahead,* p. 103

Objectives

Social Studies
1. Learn about European efforts to expand trade in East Asia.
2. Understand European encounters with China and Japan, 1600–1700.

Reading/Language Arts
Learn how to reread and read ahead.

Prepare to Read

Build Background Knowledge   L2
Tell students that in this section, they will learn about the growing interest in expanding European trade in East Asia, particularly in China and Japan. Have students look at the pictures in this section of Chinese and Japanese trade items. Then discuss why Europeans may have been interested in trade with China and Japan. Have students compare Chinese and Japanese trade items to what they have learned about trade goods from other Asian lands. Use the Think-Write-Pair-Share Strategy to engage students in responding to your questions (TE, p. T40) *(Possible answer: Spices were prized trade goods in some Asian lands, such as the Spice Islands and India. China and Japan traded finely detailed goods such as porcelain, jade carvings, jewelry, and silks, which were highly valued by Europeans.)*

Set a Purpose for Reading   L2
- Preview the Objectives.

- Read each statement in the *Reading Readiness Guide* aloud. Ask students to mark the statements true or false.

    All in One Unit 5 History of Our World Teaching Resources, *Reading Readiness Guide,* p. 98

- Have students discuss the statement in pairs or groups of four, then mark their worksheets again. Use the Numbered Heads participation structure (TE, p. T40) to call on students to share their group's perspectives.

Preview Key Terms   L2
Pronounce each Key Term, and then ask the students to say the word with you. Provide a simple explanation.

Expanding European Trade
L2

Guided Instruction

■ **Vocabulary Builder** Clarify the high-use words **ingenious** and **porcelain** before reading.

■ Read aloud the section heading Expanding European Trade. To help students read actively, read a passage of this section and use the Oral Cloze Strategy (TE, p. T37).

■ Ask students **Why did Spain have more success than Portugal in efforts to trade with China?** (*Spain traded silver, which the Chinese valued. The Chinese viewed the Portuguese as little more than pirates and limited their trade.*)

Independent Practice

Ask students to create the Taking Notes graphic organizer on a blank piece of paper. Then have them fill in the organizer with information from what they have just read about trade with China and Japan.

Monitor Progress

As students fill in the outline, circulate to make sure that individuals are choosing correct details. Provide assistance as needed.

Answer

✓ **Reading Check** the Portuguese

Links

Read the **Links Across Time** on this page. Ask **Name other ethnic or minority groups that currently live in places where their ancestors settled.** (*Possible answers include: Native Americans in the West; Mormons in Utah; Asians on the west coast; Hispanics in Florida and Texas*)

Expanding European Trade

European powers established trade and acquired some territory in India and Southeast Asia in the 1500s. Yet they were aware that another valuable prize existed nearby: the great riches of China. This land was famed for its porcelain, jade, and silk.

Even as Portugal seized control of Southeast Asia in the early 1500s, the country was beginning to explore trade in China. At first, the Chinese saw little reason to deal with the Portuguese, whom they viewed as little more than pirates. The Portuguese would not be denied, however; by 1557 they had secured a trading post at Macao (muh KOU). Yet China strictly limited and controlled this trade and did not formally recognize Portuguese control of Macao.

The Spanish also traded with China during this time. They operated from their colony of the Philippines. Recall that Magellan had landed—and died—in the Philippines during his ill-fated voyage. Spain later gained control of the entire chain of islands. Spain's trade with China was active. Spain used silver mined in Mexico to pay for fine silks and other goods from China.

It was also in the mid-1500s that Europeans first learned about Japan. In the 1540s, a Portuguese vessel landed there after being blown off course. More Europeans later returned to trade and to spread Christianity.

✓ **Reading Check** Who were the first Europeans to make contact with China in the early 1500s?

Links Across
Time

The Philippines The Spanish colony of the Philippines was a center for Chinese trade. However, the Spanish also came to Asia to spread religion. In fact, they did convert many Filipinos to Christianity. Today, the Philippines remains largely Christian.

Jade and silk were two of the riches that attracted European powers to East Asia.

472 History of Our World

Vocabulary Builder

Use the information below to teach students this section's high-use words.

High-Use Word	Definition and Sample Sentence
ingenious, p. 471	*adj.* resourceful; clever Tara's **ingenious** plan to have students work with partners in their homeroom solved the study hall seating problem.
porcelain, p. 472	*n.* hard, fine-grained, white ceramic ware I could see tiny cracks in the old doll's **porcelain** face.
charitable, p. 474	*adj.* full of love for and goodwill toward others We decided to give an award to the class that had been the most **charitable** to the homeless during the holidays.

European Contacts with China and Japan

Learn about a trading mission to China.

As you have read, the Dutch and the British replaced the Portuguese as the main trading powers in Asia in the 1600s. Like the Portuguese, they hoped to tap China's riches.

The China Trade Trade with China was difficult for Europeans in this era. The Chinese viewed themselves as the greatest empire in the world. They held little regard for "foreign devils," as they called the Europeans. The Europeans also tended to think of themselves as superior. This attitude sometimes caused conflict with the Chinese. When the Chinese did trade, they usually accepted silver for their goods. Some Europeans, such as the British, would have preferred trading their own manufactured goods.

Still, Europeans pressed for trade. The Dutch seized the southern part of the island of Taiwan in 1624. Their goal was to use Taiwan as a base for trade with China and Japan. However, the Chinese drove the Dutch from this base in 1661.

The British were also frustrated in their efforts. Chinese rulers allowed only tightly controlled trade. Sir George Macartney's unsuccessful mission of 1793 aimed at opening up this trade. For now, China was able to resist the British.

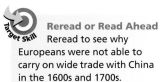

Target Skill

Reread or Read Ahead Reread to see why Europeans were not able to carry on wide trade with China in the 1600s and 1700s.

These workers are dyeing silk fabric.

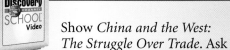

Show *China and the West: The Struggle Over Trade.* Ask **Why did the Chinese emperors reject trade with European nations?** *(Possible answers: The Chinese did not value European trade goods; The Chinese believed their goods were superior to European goods.)*

European Contacts with China and Japan [L2]

Guided Instruction

- **Vocabulary Builder** Clarify the high-use word **charitable** before reading.

- Have students recall **What major cause of conflict-hampered trade between the Chinese and Europeans?** *(Each country thought it was the most superior and possessed the finest trade goods.)*

- Discuss with students how the relationship between the Japanese and the Portuguese deteriorated by the late 1500s. *(The Japanese did not trust the Portuguese missionaries.)*

Independent Practice
Assign *Guided Reading and Review.*

All in One **Unit 5 History of Our World Teaching Resources,** *Guided Reading and Review,* p. 99

Monitor Progress

- Show *Section Reading Support Transparency HOW 106,* and ask students to check their graphic organizers individually.

- Tell students to fill in the last column of the *Reading Readiness Guide.*

All in One **Unit 5 History of Our World Teaching Resources,** *Reading Readiness Guide,* p. 98

Target Reading Skill [L2]

Reread or Read Ahead As a follow up, ask students to discuss the Target Reading Skill in the Student Edition.

Differentiated Instruction

For English Language Learners [L2]
To help students understand the tasks you have given them, provide them with an example of a well-executed essay from a different class or a previous year. The example essay should be well written and organized, but not above grade level.

For Gifted and Talented [L3]
Show students Transparency HOW 33. Have students do Internet or library research to learn more about the warriors and why they were buried. Then have students write an essay explaining what Chinese rulers valued during this period of time.

Assess and Reteach

Assess Progress   L2
Have students complete the Section Assessment. Administer the *Section Quiz*.

All in One **Unit 5 History of Our World Teaching Resources,** p. 100

Reteach   L1
If students need more instruction, have them read this section in the Reading and Vocabulary Study Guide.

Chapter 16, Section 3, **History of Our World** *Reading and Vocabulary Study Guide,* pp. 180–182

Extend   L3
Have students learn more about how items, such as trade goods, were used to build a country's power and wealth. Have students read *The King's Wealth*. Then, have them write a paragraph describing what types of things made a Chinese emperor feel powerful.

All in One **Unit 5 Primary Sources and Literature Readings,** p. 112

Answer

✓ **Reading Check**   the Netherlands

Section 3 Assessment

Key Terms
Students' sentences should reflect knowledge of each key term.

Target Reading Skill
Answers will vary, but should demonstrate the ability to reread or read ahead.

Comprehension and Critical Thinking
1. (a) The Chinese did not feel a need for European manufactured products and would accept only gold or silver as payment for Chinese goods. **(b)** The Portuguese did establish a trading post in China, just as they had in other parts of Asia. However, they were not very successful in their China trade.

2. (a) The Chinese regarded the Europeans as foreign devils or pirates with whom they did not need to do business. **(b)** Possible answers: The Chinese had an advanced and prosperous society. Or, the Chinese had a false sense of pride about their accomplishments.

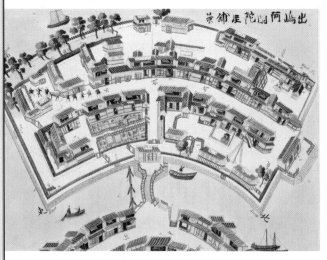

Isaac Titsingh was the director of the Dutch East India Company. Titsingh illustrated his plan for a Dutch factory on the island of Deshima at Nagasaki.

Europeans in Japan   Earlier you read about the first Portuguese to reach Japan in the 1540s. Soon Portuguese traders and missionaries returned to Japan. A **missionary** is someone who travels to a foreign country to spread a religion or do charitable work. By the late 1500s, however, Japanese rulers had come to distrust the Portuguese. Religion was a major cause of this distrust. The missionaries and Japanese Christians were persecuted. **Persecution** is threatening or hurting someone because of his or her religion, race, or political beliefs. The Portuguese soon left Japan altogether.

In the early 1600s, the Dutch came to Japan seeking trade. They were allowed to build a trading post. This post was eventually moved to a human-made island called Deshima (DAY shee mah), near the city of Nagasaki (nah guh SAH kee). The Japanese closely controlled this trade. The Dutch remained the only Europeans to trade with Japan until the 1800s.

✓ **Reading Check**   Which country dominated trade with Japan starting in the 1600s?

Section 3 Assessment

Key Terms
Review the key terms at the beginning of this section. Use each term in a sentence that explains its meaning.

Target Reading Skill
What idea from this section were you able to clarify by reading ahead?

Comprehension and Critical Thinking
1. (a) Recall What were Chinese attitudes toward trade in the 1500s?
(b) Compare and Contrast Compare and contrast Portugal's experience in China with its experience in Southeast Asia and India.
2. (a) Explain How did the Chinese regard the Europeans who arrived to trade with them?
(b) Draw Inferences What can you infer about China based on its leader's beliefs that it was superior to European countries?
3. (a) Identify Which countries succeeded in trading with Japan?
(b) Cause and Effect What was the effect of Portuguese efforts to spread Christianity in Japan?

Writing Activity
The year is 1550. You are a merchant for a major European firm. Create and label a map of Asia. Labels should provide information about the major competitor countries in the region. It should also identify the trade climate in different areas.

For: An activity on the explorers of Portugal and Spain
Visit: PHSchool.com
Web Code: mud-1630

---

3. (a) Portugal and the Netherlands traded with Japan. **(b)** Possible answer: The missionary efforts upset Japanese officials, and they persecuted the missionaries and Christians.

Writing Activity
Make sure students' maps accurately reflect a map of the period.

Go Online PHSchool.com   Typing in the Web Code when prompted will bring students to detailed instructions for this activity.

16 Review and Assessment

Review and Assessment
Review Chapter Content

- Review and revisit the major themes of this chapter by asking students to classify what Guiding Question each bulleted statement in the Chapter Summary answers. Have students work together in groups to classify the sentences. Refer to page 1 in the Student Edition for the text of the Guiding Questions.

- Assign *Vocabulary Development* to help students review the Key Terms.

  All in One **Unit 5 History of Our World Teaching Resources,** *Vocabulary Development,* p. 113

◆ Chapter Summary

Section 1: European Exploration Begins
- At the start of the Renaissance, several European countries began to expand their interest and involvement in the wider world.
- Portugal led the way in ocean exploration.
- Spain was also a leader in seeking new ocean routes to the East.

Section 2: Europeans in India and Southeast Asia
- The Portuguese became the first European country to establish trade in the East.
- The Dutch followed the Portuguese and built an extensive trading network in Southeast Asia.
- The British dominated trade with India and eventually took direct control of the entire area.

Section 3: Europe Explores East Asia
- European nations sought trade in East Asia.
- China permitted trade, but only under strict Chinese controls.
- Japan also strictly limited trade with European powers.

The sextant

Vasco da Gama negotiates trade rights

Teapot from Qianlong dynasty

◆ Key Terms

Match each of the following terms with its definition.

1. missionary
2. circumnavigation
3. persecution
4. monopoly
5. colony

A Causing injury or distress to others because of religion, race, or political beliefs

B One who is sent to do religious or charitable work in a foreign country

C Traveling completely around the Earth, especially by water.

D A territory ruled by a distant state

E Exclusive control of goods or services in a market

Chapter 16 **475**

┌ Vocabulary Builder ─

Revisit this chapter's high-use words:

domination	humble	ingenious
scholars	enterprise	porcelain
expedition	emerged	charitable

Use these steps to teach this chapter's high-use words:

Ask students to review the definitions they recorded on their Word Knowledge worksheets.

All in One **Unit 5 History of Our World Teaching Resources,** *Word Knowledge,* p. 105.

Consider allowing students extra credit if they use the words in their answers to the questions in the Chapter Review and Assessment. The words must be used correctly and in a natural context to earn the extra points.

Answers

Key Terms

1. B
2. C
3. A
4. E
5. D

Review and Assessment

Comprehension and Critical Thinking

6. (a) Sailors knew very little about what they would find on the open ocean, and some believed it was terribly dangerous. **(b)** Possible answer: Sailors believed that rewards would be great if they took the risk of an ocean voyage and survived.

7. (a) The Northwest Passage was the name given to the hoped-for shortcut that would lead through North America to Asia. **(b)** Possible answer: The Northwest Passage was not a practical route for reaching Asia for sailing vessels of the Renaissance era.

8. (a) The Netherlands replaced Portugal as a major trading power in Asia. **(b)** Possible answer: The Portuguese military was not strong enough to defend its interests in the region.

9. (a) India **(b)** Possible answer: The British established trading relationships in India. The Government of India became unstable. The British won the struggle for power that resulted.

10. (a) Spain **(b)** The Spanish were able to convert many Filipinos to Christianity.

11. (a) Macartney hoped to open China to trade with Great Britain. **(b)** Qianlong said that China was not impressed with British goods and that China did not need any imports from foreign countries.

Skills Practice

Make sure students' conclusions reflect an understanding of both the topic and of how to recognize author bias.

Writing Activity: History

Check to see that students' work includes five Key Terms. Use the *Rubric for Assessing a Writing Assignment*, depending on which students have written, to evaluate students' work.

All in One Unit 5 History of Our World Teaching Resources, *Rubric for Assessing a Writing Assignment*, p. 114

Review and Assessment (continued)

◆ Comprehension and Critical Thinking

6. (a) Explain What kind of knowledge did sailors in the 1300s have of the open ocean?
(b) Draw Conclusions Why do you think sailors were willing to make the journey into the unknown in the early 1400s?

7. (a) Identify What is the Northwest Passage?
(b) Make Predictions How would trade have been affected if European explorers had discovered the Northwest Passage?

8. (a) Identify Which nation replaced Portugal as a trading power in Asia?
(b) Draw Conclusions Basing your conclusion on Portugal's experience with this country, what can you infer about Portuguese military strength?

9. (a) Identify Over which country did Great Britain gain control in Asia?
(b) Sequence Describe the sequence of events that led to Britain's control of India.

10. (a) Recall Which European country colonized the Philippines?
(b) Evaluate Information In what area besides trade did the Spanish affect Philippine life?

11. (a) Explain What did Sir George Macartney hope to accomplish in China?
(b) Summarize Briefly summarize Qianlong's response to Macartney's presentation.

◆ Skills Practice

Recognizing Author's Bias In the Skills Activity in this chapter, you learned that authors sometimes show bias in their writing. You also learned that you can become a more informed and careful reader by learning to recognize an author's bias. Review the steps you followed to learn this skill. Then read an article on world trade or international affairs from an encyclopedia or from your local newspaper. Does the article show signs of bias? Explain your conclusions in a brief essay.

◆ Writing Activity: History

Using the library or the Internet, research the history of Korea in the era of the 1500s through the 1700s. Learn about Korea's relationships with China and Japan. Then write a brief report about what European traders of the era might find if they were to seek trading relationships with Korea.

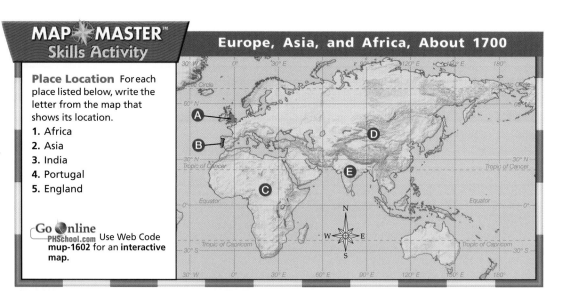

MAP MASTER™ Skills Activity

Place Location For each place listed below, write the letter from the map that shows its location.
1. Africa
2. Asia
3. India
4. Portugal
5. England

Go Online PHSchool.com Use Web Code **mup-1602** for an **interactive map.**

Europe, Asia, and Africa, About 1700

Standardized Test Prep

Test-Taking Tips

Some questions on standardized tests ask you to analyze a reading selection. Read the paragraph and follow the tips to answer the sample question.

In 1519, Ferdinand Magellan sailed for South America with five ships. From the beginning, the voyage had serious problems. A mutiny occurred during the Atlantic crossing, but Magellan was able to overcome it and continue the expedition. After reaching the coast of South America, the crews of these ships refused to sail on. Once again, Magellan stopped the mutiny, and the ships continued searching for a passage to the other side of the continent.

TIP When reading a paragraph, pay attention to the structure. Did the author order the paragraph by cause-and-effect, by topic, or by chronological order

Choose the letter that best answers the question.
What information would you expect to find in the next paragraph of an article about Ferdinand Magellan?

TIP Use what you already know to help you answer multiple-choice questions.

- **A** what Magellan's childhood was like
- **B** what happened after Magellan reached the Pacific Ocean
- **C** how Magellan's crew got through the Strait of Magellan
- **D** how Magellan died in the Philippines

Think It Through Start with the structure of the paragraph. It is in chronological order. You can rule out A, something that happened long before the voyage. You might also rule out D, which happened near the end of the voyage. You can use what you already know to determine that the passage through the Strait of Magellan would logically come before the crew reached the Pacific Ocean. The correct answer is C.

Practice Questions

Use the tips above and other tips in this book to help you answer the following questions.

1. Which of the following is linked to Prince Henry of Portugal?
   - **A** the Crusades
   - **B** the conquest of Cueta
   - **C** the East India Company
   - **D** the discovery of the Americas

2. Which of the following took place at Deshima?
   - **A** Sir George Macartney met Emperor Qianlong.
   - **B** The Spanish tried to convert the people of the Philippines to Christianity.
   - **C** The British established the headquarters of the East India Company.
   - **D** The Dutch based their trade with Japan.

Read the diary entry below, and then answer the question that follows.

"Wednesday, 10 October . . . Here the men lost all patience, and complained about the length of the voyage, but the Admiral encouraged them in the best manner he could, representing the profits they were about to acquire."

3. What might you find in the next diary entry?
   - **A** how many men were part of the crew.
   - **B** what caused the men to lose patience.
   - **C** the crew's reaction to the Admiral's reassurance.
   - **D** why the crew was sent on the expedition.

Use Web Code **mua-1604** for **Chapter 16 self-test.**

Chapter 16 **477**

Overview

 Section 1

Conquest in the Americas
1. Learn what attitudes and events led to the Spanish exploration of the Americas.
2. Find out how the Spanish conquered Mexico.
3. Learn how the Spanish conquered Peru.

 Section 2

Colonies in Central and South America
1. Learn how Spain and Portugal colonized the Americas.
2. Find out how the Spanish ruled their new colonies.
3. Understand the economic systems of the Spanish colonies.

 Section 3

Colonies in North America
1. Identify the European countries that sought colonies in North America.
2. Understand the impact of European colonization on Native Americans.
3. Find out how the rivalry between France and England led to the French and Indian War.

 Section 4

Africa and the Atlantic Slave Trade
1. Understand that the slave trade that began with the exploration of Africa and the colonization of South America and Central America also spread to North America.
2. Discover what the triangular trade was and how it expanded with the growth of the European colonization of North America.

The African Slave Trade
Length: 2 minutes, 52 Seconds
Use with Section 4
Exploring one of the darkest times in human history, this segment delves into the history and the horror of the African Slave Trade. It discusses the early practice of slavery in Africa and how the treatment of slaves changed when European traders began buying them from African kings in the fifteenth century.

Technology Resources

Students use embedded web codes to access Internet activities, chapter self-tests, and additional map practice. They may also access Dorling Kindersley's Online Desk Reference to learn more about each country they study.

Use the Interactive Textbook to make content and concepts come alive through animations, videos, and activities that accompany the complete basal text—online and on CD-ROM.

PRENTICE HALL

Use this complete suite of powerful teaching tools to make lesson planning and administering tests quicker and easier.

Reading and Assessment

Reading and Vocabulary Instruction

⟳ Model the Target Reading Skill

Main Idea Tell students that the main idea in a paragraph, section, or other kind of writing is the most important point. All of the details should explain, give more information about, give reasons for, or give examples of this main idea. In other words, these details support the main idea.

Write the first paragraph on p. 490 on the board.

Model the skill by thinking about this chapter aloud. Read the first two sentences aloud. Then ask yourself: Who are the "these people" mentioned in the second sentence? Perhaps the first sentence is the main idea of the paragraph. I'll see if the other sentences support it. Reread the rest of the paragraph. The second, third, and fourth sentences are supporting details for the main idea in the first sentence.

Use the following worksheets from All-in-One Unit 5 History of Our World Teacher Resources (pp. 141–143) to support this chapter's Target Reading Skill.

Vocabulary Builder
High-Use Academic Words

Use these steps to teach this chapter's High-Use Words.

1. Have students rate how well they know each word on their Word Knowledge Worksheets (All-in-One Unit 5 History of Our World Teaching Resources, p. 144).

2. Pronounce each word and ask students to repeat it.

3. Give students a brief definition and sample sentence (provided on TE pp. 481, 485, 489, 497).

4. Work with students as they fill in the "Definition or Example" column of their Word Knowledge Worksheets.

Assessment

Formal Assessment

Test students' understanding of core knowledge and skills.

Chapter Tests A and B, All-in-One Unit 5 History of Our World Teaching Resources pp. 158–163

Customize the Chapter Tests to suit your needs.

Exam*View*® **Test Bank CD-ROM**

Skills Assessment

Assess geographic literacy.

MapMaster Skills, Student Edition, pp. 479, 485, 500

Assess reading and comprehension.

Target Reading Skills, Student Edition, pp. 482 486, 490, 497, and in Section Assessments

Chapter 17 Assessment, History of Our World Reading and Vocabulary Study Guide, p. 196

Performance Assessment

Assess students' performance on this chapter's Writing Activity using the following rubrics from All-in-One Unit 5 History of Our World Teaching Resources.

Rubric for Assessing a Summary, p. 154

Rubric for Assessing a Newspaper Article, p. 155

Rubric for Assessing a Letter, p. 156

Rubric for Assessing a Journal Entry, p. 157

Assess students' work through performance tasks.

Small Group Activity, All-in-One Unit 5 History of Our World Teaching Resources pp. 147–150

Online Assessment

Have students check their own understanding.

Chapter Self-Test

Section 1 Conquest in the Americas

 *2 periods, 1 block*

Social Studies Objectives

1. Learn what attitudes and events led to the Spanish exploration of the Americas.
2. Find out how the Spanish conquered Mexico.
3. Learn how the Spanish conquered Peru.

Reading/Language Arts Objective

Identify the main idea of a paragraph or other kind of writing to help remember information.

Prepare to Read	**Instructional Resources**	**Differentiated Instruction**
Build Background Knowledge Discuss the visuals and ask students to speculate about what happens when a force with superior weapons meets a lesser force. **Set a Purpose** Have students share information from their Reading Readiness Guide worksheets. **Preview Key Terms** Teach the section's Key Terms. **Target Reading Skill** Introduce the section's Target Reading Skill of identifying main ideas.	**All in One Unit 5 History of Our World Teaching Resources** L2 Reading Readiness Guide, p. 126 L2 Word Knowledge, p. 144 L2 Identify Main Ideas, p. 141	**Spanish Reading and Vocabulary Study Guide** L1 Chapter 17, Section 1, pp. 131–132 ELL

Instruct	**Instructional Resources**	**Differentiated Instruction**
Spain's Explorations of the Americas Discuss the attitudes held by Spaniards that led them to want to explore. **The Spanish Conquest of Mexico** Discuss how Cortés was able to conquer the Aztecs. **Target Reading Skill** Review identifying main ideas. **The Spanish Conquest of Peru** Discuss Pizarro's conquest of the Incan empire in Peru.	**All in One Unit 5 History of Our World Teaching Resources** L2 Guided Reading and Review, p. 127 L2 Reading Readiness Guide, p. 126 **History of Our World Transparencies** L2 Section Reading Support Transparency HOW 107	**Spanish Support** L1 Guided Reading and Review (Spanish), p. 144 ELL **Teacher's Edition** L1 For Less Proficient Readers, TE p. 482 **Reading and Vocabulary Study Guide** L1 Chapter 17, Section 1, pp. 184–186 LPR, SN **Student Edition on Audio CD** L1 Chapter 17, Section 1 LPR, SN

Assess and Reteach	**Instructional Resources**	**Differentiated Instruction**
Assess Progress Have students compare what they learned with what they had predicted that they would learn in the Set a Purpose for Reading. Evaluate student comprehension with the section assessment and section quiz. **Reteach** Assign the Reading and Vocabulary Study Guide to help struggling students. **Extend** Extend the lesson by assigning a book project.	**All in One Unit 5 History of Our World Teaching Resources** L2 Section Quiz, p. 128 L3 Enrichment, p. 145 **Reading and Vocabulary Study Guide** L1 Chapter 17, Section 1, pp. 184–186 **Spanish Support**	L2 Section Quiz (Spanish), p. 145 ELL

Key

L1 Below Average L3 Above Average

L2 Average

LPR Less Proficient Readers
AR Advanced Readers
SN Special Needs Students

GT Gifted and Talented
ELL English Language Learners

Section 2 Colonies in Central and South America

 *2 periods, 1 block*

Social Studies Objectives
1. Learn how Spain and Portugal colonized the Americas.
2. Find out how the Spanish ruled their new colonies.
3. Understand the economic systems of the Spanish colonies.

Reading/Language Arts Objective
Identify supporting details that give further information about the main idea.

Prepare to Read

Build Background Knowledge
Discuss the headings and visuals and ask students what they know about the words *colonies* and *colonize.*

Set a Purpose
Have students share information from their Reading Readiness Guide worksheets.

Preview Key Terms
Teach the section's Key Terms.

Target Reading Skill
Introduce the section's Target Reading Skill of identifying supporting details.

Instructional Resources

All in One Unit 5 History of Our World Teaching Resources
- L2 Reading Readiness Guide, p. 130
- L2 Word Knowledge, p. 144
- L2 Identify Supporting Details, p. 142

Differentiated Instruction

All in One Unit 5 History of Our World Teaching Resources
- L1 Chapter 17, Section 2, pp. 133–134 ELL

Instruct

Spain and Portugal Colonize Central and South America
Discuss the colonization of Brazil and how it differed from colonization in Mexico and Peru.

Spanish Rule in the Colonies
Discuss the role of the viceroys and the Catholic Church in governing the Spanish colonies.

Target Reading Skill
Review identifying supporting details.

The Economy of the Colonies
Discuss the encomienda system and how the Spanish used it to form their labor force.

Instructional Resources

All in One Unit 5 History of Our World Teaching Resources
- L2 Guided Reading and Review, p. 131
- L2 Reading Readiness Guide, p. 130

History of Our World Transparencies
- L2 Section Reading Support Transparency HOW 108

Differentiated Instruction

Spanish Support
- L1 Guided Reading and Review (Spanish), p. 146 ELL

Teacher's Edition
- L3 For Gifted and Talented, TE p. 486

Reading and Vocabulary Study Guide
- L1 Chapter 17, Section 2, pp. 187–189 LPR, SN

Student Edition on Audio CD
- L1 Chapter 17, Section 2 LPR, SN

Assess and Reteach

Assess Progress
Have students compare what they learned with what they had predicted that they would learn in the Set a Purpose for Reading. Evaluate student comprehension with the section assessment and section quiz.

Reteach
Assign the Reading and Vocabulary Study Guide to help struggling students.

Extend
Extend the lesson by assigning a book project.

Instructional Resources

All in One Unit 5 History of Our World Teaching Resources
- L2 Section Quiz, p. 132
- L3 Enrichment, p. 145

Reading and Vocabulary Study Guide
- L1 Chapter 17, Section 2, pp. 187–189

Differentiated Instruction

Spanish Support
- L2 Section Quiz (Spanish), p. 147 ELL

Key
- L1 Below Average
- L2 Average
- L3 Above Average

- LPR Less Proficient Readers
- AR Advanced Readers
- SN Special Needs Students

- GT Gifted and Talented
- ELL English Language Learners

Section 3 Colonies in North America

2 periods, 1 block (includes Focus on Plymouth Colony and Skills for Life)

Social Studies Objectives

1. Identify the European countries that sought colonies in the Americas.
2. Understand the impact that European colonization had on Native Americans.
3. Find out how the rivalry between France and England led to the French and Indian War.

Reading/Language Arts Objective

Find the main idea of a paragraph or other writing when it is implied rather than directly stated in order to help you remember information.

Prepare to Read	Instructional Resources	Differentiated Instruction
Build Background Knowledge Discuss the visuals and the section headings, and ask students to speculate which countries were interested in settling North America. **Set a Purpose** Have students share information from their Reading Readiness Guide worksheets. **Preview Key Terms** Teach the section's Key Terms. **Target Reading Skill** Introduce the section's Target Reading Skill of identifying implied main ideas.	**All in One Unit 5 History of Our World Teaching Resources** L2 Reading Readiness Guide, p. 134 L2 Word Knowledge, p. 144 L2 Identify Implied Main Ideas, p. 143	**Spanish Reading and Vocabulary Study Guide** L1 Chapter 17, Section 3, pp. 135–136 ELL

Instruct	Instructional Resources	Differentiated Instruction
European Countries Seek Colonies in North America Ask key questions about the Dutch, French, and British interests in the New World. **The Effect of European Colonization on Native Americans** Discuss what happened to the Native Americans when the Europeans colonized North America. **Target Reading Skill** Review identifying implied main ideas.	**All in One Unit 5 History of Our World Teaching Resources** L2 Guided Reading and Review, p. 135 L2 Reading Readiness Guide, p. 134 **History of Our World Transparencies** L2 Section Reading Support Transparency HOW 109	**Spanish Support** L1 Guided Reading and Review (Spanish), p. 148 ELL **Teacher's Edition** L1 For Special Needs Students, pp. 490, 493, 495 **Reading and Vocabulary Study Guide** L1 Chapter 17, Section 3, pp. 193–195 LPR, SN **Student Edition on Audio CD** L1 Chapter 17, Section 3 LPR, SN

Assess and Reteach	Instructional Resources	Differentiated Instruction
Assess Progress Have students compare what they learned with what they had predicted that they would learn in the Set a Purpose for Reading. Evaluate student comprehension with the section assessment and section quiz. **Reteach** Assign the Reading and Vocabulary Study Guide to help struggling students. **Extend** Extend the lesson by assigning a Book Project.	**All in One Unit 5 History of Our World Teaching Resources** L2 Section Quiz, p. 136 L3 Enrichment, p. 145 **Reading and Vocabulary Study Guide** L1 Chapter 17, Section 3, pp. 190–192	**Spanish Support** L2 Section Quiz (Spanish), p. 149 ELL

Key

L1 Below Average
L2 Average
L3 Above Average

LPR Less Proficient Readers
AR Advanced Readers
SN Special Needs Students
GT Gifted and Talented
ELL English Language Learners

Section 4 Africa and the Atlantic Slave Trade

 *2 periods, 1 block*

Social Studies Objectives

1. Understand that the slave trade that began with the exploration of Africa and the colonization of South America and Central America also spread to North America.
2. Discover what the triangular trade was and how it expanded with the growth of the European colonization of North America.

Reading/Language Arts Objective

Identify main ideas stated in paragraphs or other writing to help remember information.

Prepare to Read	Instructional Resources	Differentiated Instruction
Build Background Knowledge Discuss what students already know about slavery. **Set a Purpose** Have students share information from their Reading Readiness Guide worksheets. **Preview Key Terms** Teach the section's Key Terms. **Target Reading Skill** Introduce the section's Target Reading Skill of identifying stated main ideas.	**All in One Unit 5 History of Our World Teaching Resources** **L2** Reading Readiness Guide, p. 138 **L2** Word Knowledge, p. 144 **L2** Use Identify Main Ideas, p. 141	**Spanish Reading and Vocabulary Study Guide** **L1** Chapter 17, Section 4, pp. 137–138 ELL

Instruct	Instructional Resources	Differentiated Instruction
Slavery in the Americas Discuss how the slave trade began and why the English colonies became dependent on slaves. **Target Reading Skill** Review stated main ideas. **The Triangular Trade** Discuss the triangular trade and how it expanded.	**All in One Unit 5 History of Our World Teaching Resources** **L2** Guided Reading and Review, p. 139 **L2** Reading Readiness Guide, p. 138 **History of Our World Transparencies** **L2** Section Reading Support Transparency HOW 110	**Spanish Support** **L1** Guided Reading and Review (Spanish), p. 150 ELL **Reading and Vocabulary Study Guide** **L1** Chapter 17, Section 4, pp. 196–198 LPR, SN **Student Edition on Audio CD** **L1** Chapter 17, Section 4 LPR, SN

Assess and Reteach	Instructional Resources	Differentiated Instruction
Assess Progress Have students compare what they learned with what they had predicted that they would learn in the Set a Purpose for Reading. Evaluate student comprehension with the section assessment and section quiz. **Reteach** Assign the Reading and Vocabulary Study Guide to help struggling students. **Extend** Extend the lesson by assigning a book project.	**All in One Unit 5 History of Our World Teaching Resources** **L2** Section Quiz, p. 140 **L3** Enrichment, p. 145 **Reading and Vocabulary Study Guide** **L1** Chapter 17, Section 4, pp. 193–195	**Spanish Support** **L2** Section Quiz, p. 151 **L2** Chapter Summary, p. 152 **L2** Vocabulary Development, p. 153

Key

L1 Below Average   **L3** Above Average

L2 Average

LPR Less Proficient Readers
AR Advanced Readers
SN Special Needs Students

GT Gifted and Talented
ELL English Language Learners

Reading Background

Understanding Word Origins

Knowing the origins of unfamiliar words, especially foreign ones, will help students understand and remember the words. A number of words in this chapter have Spanish origins or roots. One example is *conquistador*. After students have read the second paragraph on p. 481, write *conquistar* on the board and ask students to guess what it means. Point out that it is a verb. If necessary, turn to the dictionary for its definition. Point out that knowing that *conquistar* means "to conquer" in Spanish will help them remember that *conquistadors* are "ones who conquer" or "conquerors."

Using Context Clues

Explain to students that they can build their vocabularies and read more easily if they know how to look for context clues when they encounter unfamiliar words. Tell students that they can often figure out the meaning of a word from its context or the words that surround it. When they figure out what a word means from its context, they are using context clues.

Have students look at the word *resistance* on p. 483. Point out the words *unable* and *against*. Ask them what the Inca were trying to do. What do those two words suggest what, in fact, happened to the Inca? *(They did not win; they were conquered.)* From these negative words, it seems clear that the *resistance*, or defense, the Inca tried to mount did not work.

World History Background

Quetzalcóatl's Return

When Moctezuma, the Aztec leader, heard reports about Cortés and his army, he feared that Cortés was Quetzalcóatl, a powerful white Aztec god. According to Aztec traditions, Quetzalcóatl was the god of creation, wind, and civilization. In human form, Quetzalcóatl had discovered maize, arts, science, and the calendar. Defeated by an enemy king, Quetzalcóatl had sailed east, vowing to some day return to claim his earthly realm. When Cortés arrived from the east, some Aztecs believed him to be the returning Quetzalcóatl.

Lasting Divisions

In 1545, after securing the adoption of laws forbidding the enslavement of Native Americans, Bartolomé de Las Casas became the bishop of Chiapas in Mexico. The Spanish slave owners greeted him with open hostility. Some Spanish settlers even rioted. After many stormy months, Las Casas gave up and returned to Spain.

In 1994, almost 450 years later, rebels known as Zapatistas took up arms in the Mexican state of Chiapas to dramatize Native American grievances against the government. In the city of San Cristóbal de las Casas, Bishop Samuel Ruiz Garcia tried to mediate between the rebels and the government. Like Las Casas before him, Ruiz Garcia became a hero to many native people—and an enemy to local landowners, who saw him as a troublemaker.

French Influences

As the French explored and settled North American lands, they gave French names to forts, towns, and natural features. Many of these names remain familiar to us today and remind us of the extent of France's North American empire. Here are some French place names and their original meanings:

Detroit—strait
Des Moines—French version of Algonquin name
Baton Rouge—red stick
Vermont—green mountains
Terre Haute—high ground
Boise—wooded

Encourage Active Participation

In Section 4, students will use the Give One, Get One technique (TE, p. T41) to share their ideas. After going through the Build Background Knowledge, Reading Readiness Guide, and Preview Key Terms, read the first paragraph aloud. Ask students to think about what they already know about slavery and what they have just learned. Direct them to take a few minutes to jot down a number of responses. Then tell students to place a check mark next to the two or three ideas that seem to be their best answers.

Give students a set amount of time to move around the room to share ideas. Then have them find partners, exchange papers, and read each other's ideas. Partners should discuss the ideas briefly. Then have each student select one idea from the partner's list and add it to his or her own list. Students then move on to a new partner.

At the end of the exchange period, call on a volunteer to share one new idea acquired from a conversation partner. The student whose idea has just been reported then shares the next idea, which he or she got from another conversation partner. Continue in this manner until all of the students' ideas about slavery have been discussed.

The Middle Passage

The account that follows was published in 1788 by Alexander Falconbridge, a doctor who had served as ship's surgeon on a slave ship.

"They are commonly fed twice a day. . . . Their food is served up to them in tubs about the size of a small water bucket. They are placed round these tubs, in companies of ten to each tub, out of which they feed themselves with wooded spoons. These they soon lose, and when they are not allowed others they feed themselves with their hands. . . . Their allowance of water is about half a pint each at every meal. . . .

"Upon the Negroes refusing to take sustenance, I have seen coals of fire, glowing hot, put on a shovel and placed so near their lips as to scorch and burn them. And this has been accompanied with threats of forcing them to swallow the coals if they any longer persisted in refusing to eat. . . .

"Exercise being deemed necessary for the preservation of their health they are sometimes obliged to dance when the weather will permit their coming on deck. If they go about it reluctantly or do not move with agility, they are flogged; a person standing by them all the time with a cat-o'-nine-tails in his hands for the purpose."

Infoplease© provides a wealth of useful information for the classroom. You can use this resource to strengthen your background on the subjects covered in this chapter. Have students visit this advertising-free site as a starting point for projects requiring research.

 Use Web Code **mud-1700** for Infoplease©.

Chapter

17 Exploration: Europe, the Americas, and Africa

Guiding Questions

Remind students about the Guiding Questions introduced at the beginning of the book.

Section 1 relates to **Guiding Question** ❷ **How did each society's belief system affect its historical accomplishments?** *(The Spanish people admired warriors who fought for glory and for the faith.)*

Section 2 relates to **Guiding Question** ❹ **What types of governments were formed in these societies and how did they develop?** *(The Spanish set up viceroyalties. The clergy had a large role in local government.)*

Section 3 relates to **Guiding Question** ❺ **How did each society develop and organize its economic activities?** *(Most of the North American colonies were established to trade with the mother countries.)*

Section 4 relates to **Guiding Question** ❶ **How did physical geography affect the development and growth of societies around the world?** *(The climate and soil conditions favored growing crops like tobacco, sugar, and cotton, which led to the introduction of slave labor.)*

⊙ Target Reading Skill

In this chapter, students will learn and apply the reading skill of identifying main ideas. Use the following worksheets to help students practice this skill.

All in One Unit 5 History of Our World Teaching Resources, *Identify Main Ideas,* p. 141; *Supporting Details,* p. 142; *Identify Implied Main Ideas,* p. 143

Chapter Preview

This chapter will examine European exploration in North America, South America, and Africa.

Section 1
Conquest in the Americas

Section 2
Colonies in Central and South America

Section 3
Colonies in North America

Section 4
Africa and the Atlantic Slave Trade

 Target Reading Skill

Main Idea In this chapter you will focus on identifying the main idea of a paragraph or section. The main idea is the most important point—the one that includes all the other points in a paragraph or section. Identifying main ideas will help you better understand what you read.

▶ No other pyramid built before Columbus landed in the New World was as large as this, the Pyramid of the Sun in Teotihuacan, Mexico

Differentiated Instruction

The following Teacher's Edition strategy is suitable for students of varying abilities.

Less Proficient Readers, p. 482
Special Needs Students, pp. 490, 493, 495
English Language Learners, p. 497
Gifted and Talented Students, p. 486
Advanced Readers, p. 497

Bibliography

For the Teacher
Jacobs, William Jay. *Pizarro, Conqueror of Peru.* F. Watts, 2000.
Collier, Christopher and James Lincoln Collier. *The French and Indian War: 1660–1763.* Benchmark Books, 1998.
Schneider, Dorothy and Carl J. Schneider, *Slavery In America: From Colonial Times to the Civil War.* Facts on File, 2000.

For the Student
ELL L1 Manning, Ruth. *Francisco Pizarro.* Heinemann Library, 2001.
L1 De Angelis, Gina. *Hernando Cortés and the Conquest of Mexico.* Chelsea House, 2000.
L3 Wibberley, Leonard. *Red Pawns.* Farrar, Straus & Giroux, 1973.

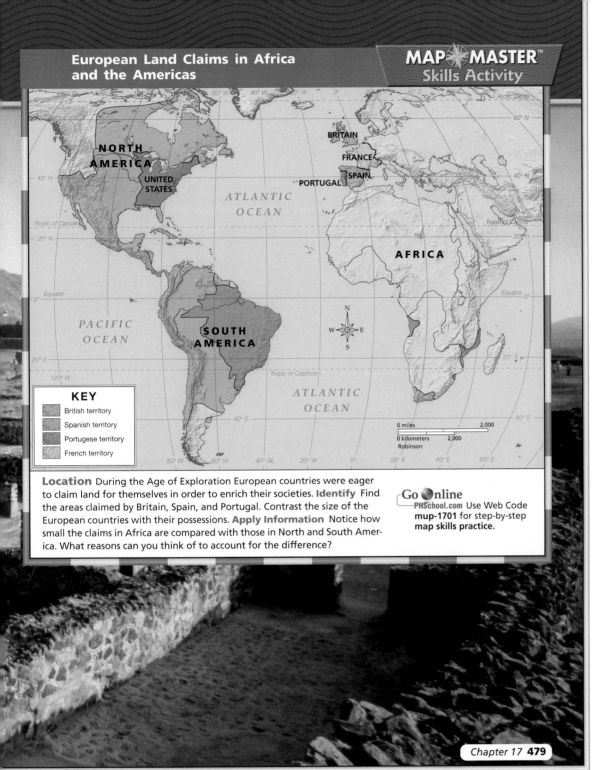

European Land Claims in Africa and the Americas

MAP MASTER™ Skills Activity

KEY

- British territory
- Spanish territory
- Portugese territory
- French territory

Location During the Age of Exploration European countries were eager to claim land for themselves in order to enrich their societies. **Identify** Find the areas claimed by Britain, Spain, and Portugal. Contrast the size of the European countries with their possessions. **Apply Information** Notice how small the claims in Africa are compared with those in North and South America. What reasons can you think of to account for the difference?

Go Online PHSchool.com Use Web Code **mup-1701** for step-by-step map skills practice.

Chapter 17 **479**

MAP MASTER™ Skills Activity

Ask volunteers to read the names of countries listed on the right-hand side of the map. Ask students **What continents are these countries on?** Ask volunteers to name the continents on the left-hand side of the map. Have students look at the title of the chapter. Then ask students what they think the European countries will have to do with the other countries. Point out the position of Africa relative to South and North America. Ask students **Which continent in the Americas is closer to Africa?** Have students speculate about how this closeness might affect the relationship of these two continents in this chapter.

Go Online PHSchool.com Students may practice their map skills using the interactive online version of this map.

Using the Visual L2

Reach Into Your Background Discuss the photograph on these two pages with students. Ask students what they think the purpose of the structure in the background might be. Point out that ancient people often built large structures as part of their religious beliefs.

Answers

MAP MASTER™ Skills Activity **Identify** Britain: parts of North, Central, and South America and Africa. Spain: parts of North, Central, and South America. Portugal: parts of South America and Africa. The areas of European countries were very small when compared to the lands they possessed. **Apply Information** The Europeans were interested in the coastal areas of Africa because these were transportation points for the slave trade.

Chapter Resources

Teaching Resources

- L2 Vocabulary Development, p. 153
- L2 Skills for Life, p. 146
- L2 Chapter Tests A and B, pp. 158–163

Spanish Support

- L2 Spanish Chapter Summary, p. 152
- L2 Spanish Vocabulary Development, p. 153

Media and Technology

- L1 Student Edition on Audio CD
- L1 Guiding Reading Audio CD, English and Spanish
- L2 Social Studies Skills Tutor CD-ROM

Exam*View*® Test Bank CD-ROM

Discovery CHANNEL SCHOOL History of Our World Videos

Interactive Textbook

PRENTICE HALL

TeacherEXPRESS™
Plan • Teach • Assess

Objectives

Social Studies

1. Learn what attitudes and events led to the Spanish exploration of the Americas.
2. Find out how the Spanish conquered Mexico.
3. Learn how the Spanish conquered Peru.

Reading/Language Arts

Identify the main idea of a paragraph or other kind of writing to remember information.

Prepare to Read

Build Background Knowledge **L2**

Have students read the headings and look at the visuals in this section. Refer them to the color photo on page 481. Use the Idea Wave strategy (TE, p.T39) to a) have them speculate what the photograph might depict and b) ask them what they think might happen when these two forces of warriors meet. Tell them to recall what they already know from their reading of history to speculate about what happens when a force with superior weapons meets one with less sophisticated weapons.

Set a Purpose for Reading **L2**

- Preview the Objectives.

- Form students into pairs or groups of four. Distribute the Reading Readiness Guide. Ask students to fill in the first two columns of the chart. Use the Numbered Heads participation structure (TE, p. T40) to call on students to share one piece of information they already know and one piece of information they want to know.

  All in One Unit 5 History of Our World Teaching Resources, *Reading Readiness Guide,* p. 126

Vocabulary Builder
Preview Key Terms **L2**

Pronounce each Key Term, and then ask the students to say the word with you. Provide a simple explanation, such as "a siege occurs when an army surrounds a town, blockading it so that it is unable to receive food and other supplies."

Section 1
Conquest in the Americas

Prepare to Read

Objectives

In this section you will

1. Learn what attitudes and events led to the Spanish exploration of the Americas.
2. Find out how the Spanish conquered Mexico.
3. Learn how the Spanish conquered Peru.

Taking Notes

As you read this section, look for information relating to Spanish attitudes about and aims for the Americas. Copy the graphic organizer below, and record your findings in it.

```
        Spanish Conquest in the Americas

    ┌──────────────────┐    ┌──────────────────┐
    │    Attitudes     │    │      Aims        │
    │ Towards the      │    │   for the        │
    │   Americas       │    │   Americas       │
    │ •                │    │ •                │
    │ •                │    │ •                │
    │ •                │    │ •                │
    └──────────────────┘    └──────────────────┘
```

🎯 Target Reading Skill

Identify Main Ideas It is impossible to remember every detail that you read. To help remember important information, good readers identify main ideas. The main idea is the most important point of a paragraph or section of text. Sometimes this idea is stated directly. As you read, identify the main idea stated in each section.

Key Terms

- **conquistador** (kahn KEES tuh dawr), *n.* a Spanish conqueror of the Americas in the sixteenth century
- **siege** (seej), *n.* the surrounding and blockading of a town by an army intent on capturing it
- **civil war** (SIV ul wawr), *n.* a war between different regions of one country

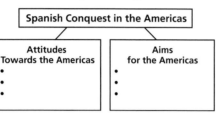

Columbus mistook the beautiful islands of the Caribbean for the Indies.

480 History of Our World

The land he had discovered offered gold and spices, Columbus wrote. "To these," Columbus added, "may be added slaves, as numerous as may be wished for."

Columbus was describing the Caribbean islands, which lie off the southeastern coast of North America. Columbus stumbled across these lands while searching for the Indies, a group of Southeast Asian islands. Native peoples, mainly a group called the Taínos (TY nohz), lived on the Carribean islands. Columbus thought that he was in the Indies, so he called these people Indians.

Columbus was mistaken about where he landed, but there was no mistaking the opportunities the Carribean presented. He claimed the islands and all their riches for Spain. As for the native people, Columbus believed that they posed no threat.

In this instance, Columbus was correct. Spain soon conquered the land of the Taíno. This was the first of many Spanish conquests in the Americas.

🎯 Target Reading Skill **L2**

Identify Main Ideas Point out the Target Reading Skill. Tell students that being able to identify the main idea of a paragraph or other piece of writing can help them remember information.

Model the skill by having students identify the main idea of the third paragraph on page 481: *(The main idea is "The Spanish set out to conquer the Americas.")*

Give students *Identify Main Ideas.* Have them complete the activity in groups.

All in One Unit 5 History of Our World Teaching Resources, *Identify Main Ideas,* p. 141

Aztec warriors attack Spanish conquistadors in the image on the left. A member of Moctezuma's army is shown below.

Duran, Diego (16th century), Codex Duran: Pedro de Alverado (c.1485-1541).

Spain's Exploration of the Americas

The Spanish completed their centuries-long quest to drive the Moors from the Iberian Peninsula in 1492, and now they were eager to explore and claim new territories. Late in that year, Queen Isabella and King Ferdinand sent Columbus on a voyage to the Indies. He returned to Spain with the exciting news of a new land.

The centuries of war with the Moors shaped Spanish culture. Spaniards admired the warriors who fought for glory and for their faith. The lands that Columbus discovered represented a new opportunity. The Americas were a place where the Spanish **conquistadors**, or conquerors, could seek glory for themselves, for Spain, and for their God, while winning great fortunes.

The Spanish set out to conquer the Americas. In the decades after Columbus's first voyage, conquistadors gained control of many islands in the Caribbean. They also conquered present-day Mexico, Central America, and parts of South America.

As you will discover in the next section, the Spanish also conquered two great civilizations. Some native groups put up resistance for a while. In general, however, the native people of the Americas were overwhelmed by the conquistadors' superior weapons. In addition, thousands of Native Americans died from diseases carried by the Spanish. Some peoples, such as the Taíno, disappeared entirely.

√ Reading Check   What effect did the long struggle with the Moors have on the Spanish people?

Links to Science

Imported Illnesses More Native Americans were killed by disease than by Spanish weapons. Europeans carried germs to which Native Americans had never been exposed. Therefore, the Native Americans had not built up immunity, or natural defenses, to these illnesses as the Europeans had. Diseases such as smallpox, measles, and influenza (in floo EN zuh) killed huge numbers of Native Americans.

Chapter 17 Section 1 **481**

Companion-at-Arms of Hernando Cortes (1485-1547) besieged by Aztec warriors (vellum)/Bridgeman Art Library

Instruct

Spain's Exploration of the Americas

Guided Instruction

- **Vocabulary Builder** Clarify the high-use word **quest** before reading.

- Read Spain's Exploration of the Americas, using the Paragraph Shrinking strategy (TE, p. T38).

- Ask students **What made Spain think about exploration?** *(Spain had driven the Moors from the Iberian Peninsula, and conquistadors wanted new opportunities.)*

- Have students explain what led the Spanish to want to explore and conquer new lands. *(Centuries of war had war produced a people who glorified war and warriors.)*

- Ask students **What islands did Columbus and other Spanish conquerors first control?** *(Columbus and other explorers conquered many islands in the Caribbean.)*

Independent Practice

Ask students to create the Taking Notes graphic organizer on a blank piece of paper. Then have them fill in the blanks under "Attitudes Toward Americas" and/or "Aims for Americas" with the information they have just learned. Briefly model how to identify which details to record.

Monitor Progress

As students fill in the graphic organizer, circulate to make sure students are choosing the correct details. Provide assistance as needed.

Links

Read **Links to Science** on this page. Ask students **Why were the Native Americans prone to catching European diseases?** *(The Native Americans had not been exposed to the new germs brought by the Europeans and therefore had not built up immunity against them.)*

Answer

√ Reading Check The war made many Spaniards look forward to a life of fighting for glory and for treasure.

Vocabulary Builder

Use the information below to teach students this section's high-use words.

High-Use Word	Definition and Sample Sentence
quest, p. 481	*n.* pursuit; search Cortés's **quest** for riches was realized when he conquered the Aztecs.
resistance, p. 483	*n.* the act of resisting, opposing or withstanding another The Native Americans' **resistance** to the Spanish invaders failed.

The Spanish Conquest of Mexico

Guided Instruction

- Have students read The Spanish Conquest of Mexico to see how Cortés was able to conquer the extensive Aztec empire with a relatively small force.

- Ask students to explain why Cortés went to Tenochtitlán and what he did there. *(Cortés went to Tenochtitlán because he had heard that the Aztec empire was wealthy. He conquered the Aztecs in the area that is now Mexico.)*

⟳ Target Reading Skill

Identify Main Idea Ask students to answer the Target Reading Skill question in the Student Edition. *(Cortés conquered the Aztecs by using Native American reinforcements and by blockading Tenochtitlán.)*

Answers

Conclude The location allowed the Aztecs to see Cortés approaching. Cortés could blockade Tenochtitlán from the mainland by using the passageways to the mainland.

✓ **Reading Check** Moctezuma thought Cortés was the Aztec god Quetzalcóatl.

The Spanish Conquest of Peru

Guided Instruction

- **Vocabulary Builder** Clarify the high-use word **resistance** before reading.

- Tell students to read The Spanish Conquest of Peru (p. 483) to see how civil war influenced the conquest of Peru.

- Discuss Pizarro's conquest of the Incas.

- Ask students to explain what mistake the Incan king made and what tricks Pizarro carried out that led to the Incan conquest. *(Atahualpa made the mistake of visiting the Spanish encampment. Pizarro demanded a ransom for Atahualpa but, after it was paid, had Atahualpa killed.)*

- Ask students to explain how the differences in weaponry affected the outcome of the war. *(The Inca had a large force of people, but the Spaniards' guns and horses made the difference in who won the war.)*

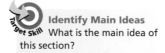

Identify Main Ideas What is the main idea of this section?

Island City
In the sixteenth century, the city of Tenochtitlán was the capital of the great Aztec empire. Notice that passageways cross the water to connect the city to the mainland. **Conclude** *When Cortés attacked, how did the city's location help the Aztecs? What advantage did the water provide for Cortés and his men?*

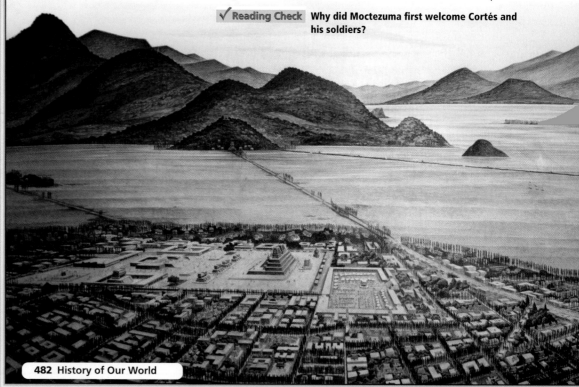

The Spanish Conquest of Mexico

In the sixteenth century, central Mexico was home to the great Aztec (AZ tek) empire. Its capital was Tenochtitlán (teh nawch tee TLAN), where the powerful Moctezuma (mahk tih ZOO muh) ruled. Moctezuma's empire was vast, and it included many conquered peoples.

In 1519, the conquistador Hernán Cortés (hur NAHN kohr TEZ) arrived in Mexico. Drawn by rumors of a wealthy Aztec empire, he journeyed to Tenochtitlán. With him traveled a force of several hundred soldiers. According to one legend, Moctezuma welcomed the Spanish because he feared that Cortés was a god named Quetzalcóatl (ket sahl koh AHT el). Aztec religious beliefs held that Quetzalcóatl, a pale-skinned god, would one day return to Mexico. Soon, however, the Aztec grew tired and suspicious of their visitors. Aztec soldiers surrounded Cortés and his men. The Spaniards fought their way out of the city.

Then Cortés gathered a large army, including reinforcements from Spain and thousands of Native Americans who resented Aztec rule. Cortés's army surrounded the city in a long siege. A **siege** is the surrounding and blockading of a town by an army. The battle ended in 1521 with Tenochtitlán in ruins. The Aztec empire that had controlled much of Mexico was utterly defeated.

✓ **Reading Check** **Why did Moctezuma first welcome Cortés and his soldiers?**

Differentiated Instruction

For Less Proficient Readers **L1**
Have students read the section in the Reading and Vocabulary Study Guide. This version provides basic-level instruction in an interactive format with questions and write-on lines.

📖 Chapter 17, Section 1, **Reading and Vocabulary Study Guide,** pp. 184–186

The Spanish Conquest of Peru

The story of Cortés's success inspired many conquistadors. Among them was Francisco Pizarro (frahn SEES koh pea SAHR oh). Pizarro's goal was the conquest of the great Incan empire of present-day Peru. Like the Aztec, the Inca (ING kuh) were a great civilization with vast treasures of gold.

Pizarro arrived in Peru in 1532. The Incan empire at this time had been weakened by a **civil war**, a war between people of the same country. Pizarro managed to lead a small force of under 200 soldiers into the heart of Peru. The Inca king Atahualpa (ah tuh WAHL puh) watched the Spaniards closely. However, he made the mistake of visiting the Spaniards' camp, where Pizarro captured him. Although the Spanish force was small, its guns and horses overwhelmed Atahualpa's much larger army. The Incan soldiers had only spears and small weapons.

Pizarro forced the Inca to pay a ransom, a large sum of money, for the release of their king. Pizarro demanded that the Inca fill a room with gold if they wanted their king back alive. The Inca paid the ransom, but Pizarro had Atahualpa killed anyway. Now leaderless, the Inca were unable to mount an effective resistance against the conquest of their once-great empire. Spain added Peru to its list of conquests in the Americas.

✓ **Reading Check** What inspired Francisco Pizarro's interest in Peru?

The Incan civilization had vast treasures of gold. Some of the gold was sculpted, such as this gold figurine.

Section 1 Assessment

Key Terms
Review the key terms at the beginning of this section. Use each term in a sentence that explains its meaning.

◉ Target Reading Skill
What are the three main ideas of Section 1?

Comprehension and Critical Thinking
1. (a) Explain Why was the year 1492 so important in Spanish history?

(b) Synthesize Information How did the struggle against the Moors prepare the Spanish for conquest in the Americas?

2. (a) Recall Who joined Cortés in his siege of Tenochtitlán?

(b) Draw Inferences Why do you think these people supported Cortés's attack of Tenochtitlán?

3. (a) Identify What conditions in the Inca empire favored Pizarro's conquest?

(b) Summarize How was Pizarro able to overcome the larger Incan force?

Writing Activity
Suppose that you are a Native American living in Central or South America in the 1500s. Write a brief summary of the history of your region from the point of view of Native American people.

Go Online PHSchool.com
For: An activity on Spanish conquests in the Americas
Visit: PHSchool.com
Web Code: mud-1710

Chapter 17 Section 1 **483**

Section 2
Step-by-Step Instruction

Objectives

Social Studies

1. Learn how Spain and Portugal colonized the Americas.
2. Find out how the Spanish ruled their new colonies.
3. Understand the economic systems of the Spanish colonies.

Reading/Language Arts

Identify supporting details that give further information about the main idea.

Prepare to Read

Build Background Knowledge L2

Have students read the headings and look at the visuals in this section. Point out the words *colonies* and *colonize*. Explain that other countries also colonized in the Americas. Have students look at the pictures on pages 486–487. Using the Idea Wave strategy (TE, p. T39), ask students how they think the colonization of South America might have differed from what they know of the colonization of North America. Ask how it might have been similar. (*Possible answer: The style of the houses looks different; the cross indicates a Christian influence. The picture looks similar to the plantations of the southern United States.*)

Set a Purpose for Reading L2

■ Preview the Objectives.

■ Form students into pairs or groups of four. Distribute the Reading Readiness Guide. Ask students to fill in the first two columns of the chart. Use the Numbered Heads participation structure (TE, p. T40) to call on students to share one piece of information they already know and one piece of information they want to know.

All in One Unit 5, History of Our World Teaching Resources, *Reading Readiness Guide,* p. 130

Vocabulary Builder
Preview Key Terms L2

Pronounce each Key Term, and then ask the students to say the word with you. Provide a simple explanation, such as "a viceroy is a person who rules a country or colony acting in the place of the king or queen of the country that sent him."

Section 2
Colonies in Central and South America

Prepare to Read

Objectives

In this section you will
1. Learn how Spain and Portugal colonized the Americas.
2. Find out how the Spanish ruled their new colonies.
3. Understand the economic systems of the Spanish colonies.

Taking Notes

As you read this section, look for information about European colonization of the Americas. Copy the graphic organizer below, and record your findings in it.

Spanish Colonization in the Americas		
Type of Government	Type of Economic System	Culture
•	•	•
•	•	•
•	•	•

Target Reading Skill

Identify Supporting Details The main idea of a paragraph or section is supported by details that give further information about it. These details may give examples or reasons to explain the main idea. As you read, look for details that support the main idea of each section.

Key Terms

- **viceroy** (VYS roy), *n.* a governor of a country or colony who rules as the representative of a king or queen
- **plantation** (plan TAY shun), *n.* a large estate or farm
- **encomienda** (en koh mee EN dah), *n.* the right granted by the king to certain Spanish colonists to force the Native Americans to work for them
- **encomenderos** (en koh men DAY rohz), *n.* Portuguese colonists who were granted encomiendas

Native American gods, such as Quetzalcóatl, sometimes merged with Christian saints in religious art.

484 History of Our World

Following the conquest of the Americas, Catholic monks and priests spread out across Spain's new empire. They sought to convert the Native Americans to the Christian faith. They undertook this conversion process with great enthusiasm and enjoyed great success. One man named Toribio de Benevente (toh ree BEE oh duh bay nay VEN teh) claimed to have brought 300,000 Native Americans into the faith.

Although Europeans taught the Native Americans Christianity, the faith practiced by these new converts had its own special character. It blended Christian ideas with the people's traditions. For example, in religious art, Native American gods such as Quetzalcóatl merged with Christian saints. Stones from old Native American temples were placed in new Christian churches. Old native ceremonial sites became Christian holy places. This blend of Spanish Christianity and Native American religion formed part of the new culture of the Spanish colonies of the Americas.

Target Reading Skill L2

Identify Supporting Details Point out the Target Reading Skill. Tell students that supporting details give more information about the main idea by explaining or giving examples.

Model the skill by having students find three supporting details in the following passage from p. 484. "*Although Europeans taught the Native Americans Christianity, the faith*

practiced by these new converts had its own special character. (It blended Christian ideas with the people's own traditions.)

Give students *Identify Supporting Details*. Have them complete the activity in groups.

All in One Unit 5 History of Our World Teaching Resources, *Identify Supporting Details*, p. 142

Spain and Portugal Colonize Central and South America

As you have read, the Spanish succeeded in conquering a large portion of the Americas in the 1500s. They eventually controlled territory that stretched from southern South America northward into the present-day United States. In some places, Native Americans, such as the Maya on Mexico's Yucatán Peninsula (yoo kah TAN puh NIN suh luh), resisted the invasion. Spain, however, eventually won control of the Mayan region.

In South America, Brazil escaped Spanish control. Recall from Chapter 16 that Portugal's Pedro Alvarez Cabral had landed in 1500. Portugal based its claim to Brazil on this event alone. Eventually, Portugal established a colony in Brazil. However, the area lacked the gold and other rich treasures of Mexico and Peru, and it had no major cities. Fortunately, the land was rich in valuable brazilwood, a dense and colorful wood. Colonists sent many shiploads of this wood to Portugal. Over time, Portuguese settlements spread along the coastal areas of Brazil.

√ Reading Check On what did Portugal base its claim to Brazil?

Links to Math

Brazilwood In 1506, Portugal's king charged a group of Portuguese citizens 4,000 ducats for the right to go to Brazil and harvest its brazilwood. The land produced 20,000 units of wood. Each unit brought a profit of 2.5 ducats.

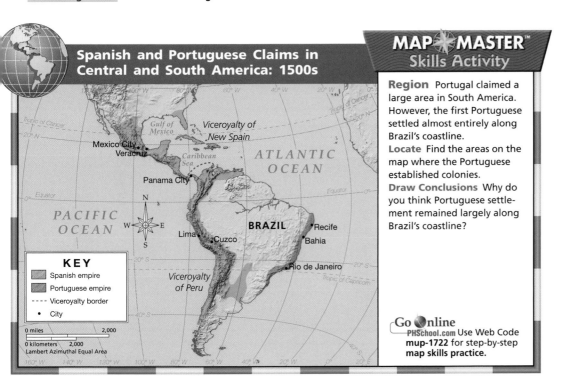

Spanish and Portuguese Claims in Central and South America: 1500s

KEY
- Spanish empire
- Portuguese empire
- - - - Viceroyalty border
- • City

0 miles 2,000
0 kilometers 2,000
Lambert Azimuthal Equal Area

MAP★MASTER Skills Activity

Region Portugal claimed a large area in South America. However, the first Portuguese settled almost entirely along Brazil's coastline.
Locate Find the areas on the map where the Portuguese established colonies.
Draw Conclusions Why do you think Portuguese settlement remained largely along Brazil's coastline?

Go Online
PHSchool.com Use Web Code mup-1722 for step-by-step map skills practice.

Vocabulary Builder

Use the information below to teach students this section's high-use words.

High-Use Word	Definition and Sample Sentence
conversion, p. 484	*n.* a change from lack of faith to religious belief; adoption of a religion The Catholic priests came to America for the **conversion** of Native Americans.
intervened, p. 486	*v.* came between, as in order to settle, or hinder an action, such as an argument. The teacher **intervened** when the two boys' argument turned into a fight.
enterprise, p. 487	*n.* an important undertaking The wealthy man set up a new business **enterprise** in every state.

Spain and Portugal Colonize Central and South America

Guided Instruction

- **Vocabulary Builder** Clarify the meaning of the high-use word **conversion** before reading.

- Read Spain and Portugal Colonize Central and South America, using the Structured Silent Reading technique (TE, p. T38).

- Have students describe the territory that Spain held in the Americas in the 1500s. (*Spain held territory from southern South America into the southern part of the present-day United States.*)

- Ask **How did the colony in Brazil differ from the colonies in Mexico and Peru?** (*Brazil lacked the gold of Mexico and Peru and had no large cities. However, it had a lot of valuable brazilwood.*)

Independent Practice

Assign *Guided Reading and Review.*

All in One Unit 5 History of Our World Teaching Resources, *Guided Reading and Review,* p. 131

Monitor Progress

As students work on the assigned *Guided Reading and Review* worksheet, circulate to make sure that they are filling in the information correctly.

Links

Read the **Links to Math** on this page. Ask students to calculate what the total profit of a Portuguese citizen's brazilwood harvest was. (*The profit from the brazilwood was 50,000 ducats minus the charge to use the land. Thus, the total profit for the Portuguese colonizer was 46,000 ducats.*)

Answers

MAP★MASTER Skills Activity **Locate** The Portuguese established colonies along the eastern edge of South America, along the Atlantic Ocean.
Draw Conclusions Possible answer: The Portuguese harvested brazilwood, which grew mostly along the coast.

√ Reading Check Portugal based its claim to Brazil on Cabral's landing there in 1500.

Spanish Rule in the Colonies

Guided Instruction

- **Vocabulary Builder** Clarify the high-use words **intervened** and **enterprise** before reading.

- Have students read Spanish Rule in the Colonies to find out how Spain governed its colonies.

- Discuss the role the Catholic Church assumed in governing the Spanish colonies.

Independent Practice

Have each student create the graphic organizer in Taking Notes. Have students fill in the blanks under Type of Government. Model how to identify which details to record.

Monitor Progress

As students fill in the graphic organizer, circulate to make sure students choose the correct details. Provide assistance as needed.

↻ Target Reading Skill

Identify Supporting Details As a follow-up, ask students to answer the Target Reading Skill question in the Student Edition. *(The Catholic Church built settlements, acted as a governing body, and helped protect Native Americans from Spanish abuse.)*

Answer

✓ **Reading Check** The Spanish set up viceroyalties ruled by viceroys.

The Economy of the Colonies

Guided Instruction

- Have students read The Economy of the Colonies.

- Discuss the encomienda system. *(An encomienda granted the right to control Native Americans in a certain area, which meant that holders of the encomiendas could force the Native Americans to work for them.)*

- Have students compare the encomienda system to slavery. *(Both African Americans and Native Americans were forced to work for the Spanish, both suffered under horrible conditions and neither had any rights.)*

Identify Supporting Details

What details in this section support the idea that the Catholic Church played a large role in governing the Spanish colonies?

Spanish Rule in the Colonies

To govern the Americas, Spain divided its lands into different units, called viceroyalties. Each viceroyalty was ruled by an official called a viceroy. A **viceroy** is a person who rules a colony in the name of the king or queen. Officials in Spain watched over the viceroys.

The Catholic Church also played a large role in governing the Spanish colonies. Although its main purpose for being in the Americas was to convert Native Americans to Christianity, the Church soon assumed a larger role. The clergy, men ordained for religious service, led the way in building Spanish-style settlements in the colonies. In many cases, the clergy acted as a sort of local government. Because becoming Christian meant accepting the clergy's rule and authority, the clergy enforced basic rules of behavior for both the Spanish and the Native Americans. Members of the clergy also intervened when they thought that the Spanish were abusing Native Americans.

Although the clergy forced Native Americans to adopt Spanish ways as well as beliefs, the priests also made it possible for some blending of the Native American and Spanish cultures. They allowed the Native Americans to keep some of their traditions and their art, which the Church then incorporated into its own culture. This blend created a new culture in the Americas.

✓ **Reading Check** How did the Spanish govern the people in the Americas?

In this painting, enslaved Africans work as the owners of the sugar cane plantation ride away from the main house.

⎡ Differentiated Instruction ⎤

For Gifted and Talented 🄻🄴

Have students research Native American and Spanish traditions in art and architecture. Instruct them to compare and contrast either an art form or a style of building and present their findings to the class. Encourage students to prepare visual aids to emphasize their points.

The Economy of the Colonies

The new colonies produced great wealth for Spain. Shiploads of gold, silver, and other treasure crossed the ocean. **Plantations**—large farming enterprises—grew such valuable crops as sugar cane.

The Spanish needed workers to mine the gold and work the land. For their work, the Spanish used enslaved Africans. The Spanish brought these slaves to the Americas by the thousands. The Spanish encomienda system provided another source of labor. An **encomienda** was a document that granted the right to control the Native American population in a given area. Spain granted encomiendas to conquistadors as rewards for their service. Native Americans could be forced to work for the Spanish **encomendero,** the colonist who had been given an encomienda. The encomendero was supposed to care for the Native Americans under his control. In reality, conditions were often terrible for the Native Americans. The encomienda system faded as Native American populations were reduced by disease. In place of encomiendas, Spaniards began to receive large grants of land. Therefore, the Spanish continued to depend on declining Native American labor.

The Pueblo church of San Defonso is an example of the blending of Native American culture with European culture; the building is Native American, the religion is European.

√ Reading Check Why did the encomienda system end?

Section 2 Assessment

Key Terms
Review the key terms at the beginning of this section. Use each term in a sentence that explains its meaning.

Target Reading Skill
List three details that support the main idea of the section entitled The Economy of the Colonies.

Comprehension and Critical Thinking
1. (a) Recall What European country claimed the territory of Brazil?

(b) Compare and Contrast How was the Portuguese colony in the Americas similar to and different from Spanish colonies?
2. (a) Explain What role did the Catholic Church play in the Spanish colonies?
(b) Synthesize Information How did the clergy affect the culture of the Native Americans?
3. (a) Define What was the encomienda system?
(b) Draw Inferences From your knowledge of the encomienda system, what can you infer about Spanish attitudes toward Native Americans?

Writing Activity
You are a newspaper reporter in the Spanish colonies. Write a report about the activities of Bartolomé de las Casas. Explain his complaints and relate proposed solutions.

Go Online PHSchool.com
For: An activity on Spanish conquests in the Americas
Visit: PHSchool.com
Web Code: mud-1720

Chapter 17 Section 2 **487**

Section 2 Assessment

Key Terms
Students' sentences should reflect knowledge of each Key Term.

Target Reading Skill
They used enslaved Africans. They developed the encomienda system. They received large land grants.

Comprehension and Critical Thinking
1. (a) Portugal **(b)** Both sent valuable materials from the colonies back to Europe, but the Portuguese did not require the conquest of Native American empires.

2. (a) The Church spread the Catholic faith. **(b)** Possible answer: The clergy helped retain some of the Native American culture.

3. (a) a grant given to conquistadors to force Native Americans to work for them **(b)** Possible answer: The Spanish treated Native Americans almost as slaves.

Independent Practice
Have students complete the Taking Notes graphic organizer.

Monitor Progress
■ Show *Section Reading Support Transparency HOW 109.*

 History of Our World Transparencies, *Section Reading Support Transparency, HOW 108*

■ Tell students to fill in the last column of the *Reading Readiness Guide.*

All in One Unit 5 History of Our World Teaching Resources, *Reading Readiness Guide,* p. 130

Assess and Reteach

Assess Progress L2
Have students complete the Section Assessment. Administer the *Section Quiz.*

All in One Unit 5 History of Our World Teaching Resources, *Section Quiz,* p. 132

Reteach L1
If students need more instruction, have them read this section in the *Reading and Vocabulary Study Guide.*

 Chapter 17, Section 2, **Reading and Vocabulary Study Guide,** pp. 187–189

Extend L3
Have students learn more about the Spanish colonies in South America by completing the *Enrichment.* Assign students to work in groups to complete the project.

All in One Unit 5 History of Our World Teaching Resources, *Enrichment,* p. 145

Answer

√ Reading Check When the Native American population began to fall, there were not enough people that could be forced to work.

Writing Activity
Use the *Rubric for Newspaper Writing* to evaluate students' reports.

All in One Unit 5 History of Our World Teaching Resources, *Rubric for Assessing a Newspaper Article,* p. 155

Go Online PHSchool.com Typing in the Web Code when prompted will bring students directly to detailed instructions for this activity.

Section 3
Step-by-Step Instruction

Objectives

Social Studies
1. Identify the European countries that sought colonies in the Americas.
2. Understand the impact of European colonization on Native Americans.
3. Find out how the rivalry between France and England led to the French and Indian War.

Reading/Language Arts
Find the main idea when it is implied rather than directly stated in order to help you remember information.

Prepare to Read

Build Background Knowledge **L2**

Have students look at the visuals in this section. Ask them to explain what the photograph on p. 490 depicts. Then have them read the section headings. Using the Idea Wave technique (TE, p. T39), ask them to predict which countries were interested in settling in North America.

Set a Purpose for Reading **L2**
- Preview the Objectives.
- Organize students in pairs or groups of four. Distribute the *Reading Readiness Guide*. Ask students to fill in the first two columns of the chart. Use the Numbered Heads participation structure (TE, p. T40) to call on students to share one piece of information they already know and one piece of information they want to know.

  All in One **Unit 5 History of Our World Teaching Resources,** *Reading Readiness Guide,* p. 134

Vocabulary Builder
Preview Key Terms **L2**

Pronounce each Key Term, and then ask the students to say the word with you. Provide a simple explanation, such as "to emigrate means to leave the country in which you were born in order to settle in a new country."

Section 3
Colonies in North America

Prepare to Read

Objectives
In this section you will
1. Identify the European countries that sought colonies in North America.
2. Understand the impact of European colonization on Native Americans.
3. Find out how the rivalry between France and England led to the French and Indian War.

Taking Notes
As you read this section, look for information about the European colonization of North America. Copy the graphic organizer below, and record your findings in it.

> I. Europeans in North America
>   A. Dutch Colonies
>   B.
>   C.
> II. European colonies affect Native Americans
>   A. Many Native Americans die from exposure to disease carried by the Europeans
>   B.

 ### Target Reading Skill

Identify Implied Main Ideas Identifying main ideas as you read can help you remember important information. Sometimes the main ideas are not stated directly. The details add up to a main idea, but the idea itself is not stated. You must state it yourself. Carefully read the details of each section. Then state the main idea of each section.

Key Terms
- **emigrate** (EM ih grayt), *v.* to leave one country or region to settle in another
- **ally** (AL eye), *n.* a country or group that is united with another for a common purpose

---

A pilgrim's hat from 1620

488 History of Our World

Francis I, the King of France, was upset. "I would like to see the [part] in Adam's will which excludes France from the division of the world," he said. In the Bible, Adam is the first human being created by God. Francis I was saying that Spain and Portugal should not be the only nations allowed to claim the Americas. Francis I wanted the French to gain territory as well.

France was not the only power there to challenge the right of Spain and Portugal to dominate the Americas. Starting in the 1500s, other countries sent explorers and settlers by the thousands across the Atlantic. Competition for North American colonies was fierce and sometimes bloody. Also fierce and bloody were the conflicts that colonists had with the Native Americans who had lived on the land before the Europeans arrived.

◎ Target Reading Skill **L2**

Identify Implied Main Ideas Point out the Target Reading Skill. Tell students that when the main idea is not stated directly, they need to read the details of the paragraph or other writing carefully because they will all relate to a common idea. After reading, they can then state in their own words the common idea—the main idea of the paragraph—that is implied by the details.

Have students read The Dutch Colonies on p. 489 and then state the implied main idea of the paragraph. *(Although the Dutch tried to establish a presence in the Americas, they were mostly unsuccessful.)*

Give students *Identify Implied Main Ideas.* Have them complete the activity in groups.

All in One **Unit 5 History of World Teaching Resources,** *Identify Implied Main Ideas,* p. 143

European Countries Seek Colonies in North America

In the 1600s, France, England, and the Netherlands tried to join Spain and Portugal in establishing colonies in the Americas.

The Dutch Colonies The Dutch established colonies in the Caribbean to take advantage of the trade in sugar cane, a product highly valued in Europe. They also established a colony on the North American Continent, which they named New Netherland. However, the English seized this colony in 1664 and renamed it New York.

The French in Canada Soon after Columbus's discovery of a new land, the French began crossing the Atlantic to fish for cod off the Canadian coast. In 1608, Samuel de Champlain (SAM yoo ul duh sham PLAYN) established the first French settlement in Quebec. As they had in South America, Catholic priests and monks soon followed, converting Native Americans and making their way farther into the Canadian interior. Local Native Americans helped the French trade in furs. The fur trade led to exploration and to the claiming of land from the Great Lakes down the Mississippi to Louisiana.

The British in North America The British were successful colonists. The first British settle-ment, established in 1607, was in Jamestown, Virginia. Despite early perils of disease and starvation, the settlement finally flourished when the Native Americans taught settlers to grow tobacco.

In 1620, other English settlers—the Pilgrims—traveled to the northeastern coast and established the Plymouth colony. Unlike most colonists, these people came seeking religious freedom rather than profit. Because of the success of that small settlement, more and more British emigrated to northern America. To **emigrate** is to leave one's country to settle in another. The British eventually established a string of thirteen colonies along the East Coast.

✓ **Reading Check** Which five European countries established colonies in the Americas?

The Mayflower Compact
By signing the Mayflower Compact, the Pilgrims pledged their obedience to the laws and government of their new colony. **Sequence** *When did the Pilgrims establish the Plymouth colony?*

Instruct

European Countries Seek Colonies in North America

Guided Instruction
- Read European Countries Seek Colonies in North America, using the Structured Silent Reading technique (TE, p. T38).

- Discuss where the Dutch established colonies in North America.

- Ask students to explain what first interested the French in the New World. Discuss with them how the French settlements expanded. (*The French first came to fish for cod. Catholic priests and monks established settlements in their efforts to convert Native Americans. Many Frenchmen were involved in the fur trade.*)

- Ask students to explain how the colony in Plymouth differed from the one in Jamestown. (*Plymouth was settled by Pilgrims seeking religious freedom rather than profit, the motive behind most other colonization.*)

Independent Practice
Ask students to create the Taking Notes graphic organizer. Have students fill in the blanks under "Europeans in North America." Model how to identify which details to record.

Monitor Progress
As students fill in the graphic organizer, circulate to make sure individuals are choosing the correct details. Provide assistance as needed.

> **Links**
>
> Read **Links to Economics** on this page. Ask students to explain the economic theory of mercantilism. (*The theory of mercantilism says that one way to build a country's strength is to expand its trade.*)

Answers
✓ **Reading Check** Spain, Portugal, France, England, and the Netherlands
Sequence in 1620

The Effect of European Colonization on Native Americans

Guided Instruction

- **Vocabulary Builder** Clarify the high-use words **rival** and **legacy** before reading.

- Have students read The Effect of European Colonization on Native Americans. Ask them to recall what happened to the Native Americans in the Spanish conquest of South America as they read.

- Ask students **Why did the French and English go to war in North America?** *(They were rivals and fought for dominance in North America.)*

- Discuss the French and Indian War and its outcome.

⊙ Target Reading Skill

Identify Implied Main Ideas Ask students to complete the Target Reading Skill activity in the Student Edition. *(Possible answer: Although the Native Americans in North America tried to resist the spread of the British colonists, they suffered from European diseases and were pushed westward as the colonies expanded.)*

Links

Read **Links to Science** on p. 491. Ask students **How did Native Americans use witch hazel as an herbal medicine?** *(Native Americans used the boiled leaves of the plant for bruised eyes and to increase blood circulation in the legs.)*

Independent Practice

Have each student fill in the blanks of the graphic organizers under the head "European colonies' affect on Native Americans" with information he or she have just learned.

Monitor Progress

Show Section Reading Support Transparency, How 109. Ask students to check their graphic organizers. Review key concepts and vocabulary.

📖 **History of Our World Transparencies,** *Section Reading Support Transparency, HOW 109*

Identify Implied Main Ideas

In one sentence, state the main idea that this section details.

This reenactment of the first Thanksgiving in 1971 at Plymouth Plantation brought together descendants of Pilgrims and Native Americans who took part in the first Thanksgiving 350 years ago.

The Effect of European Colonization on Native Americans

When Europeans arrived in North America, Native American groups lived throughout the land. For these people, the arrival of colonists brought great misfortune. European diseases hit these groups hard, just as they had the native people of South and Central America. Disease weakened or killed many native people. Those who survived faced the loss of their lands to the growing numbers of European colonists. Because the English colonies along the East Coast were growing the most rapidly, the Native Americans in this area faced the greatest problems.

In some cases, Native Americans tried to fight the colonists and slow the spread of their settlements. As colonists claimed more land, Native Americans resisted their advances. Bitter fighting resulted. Although they won some battles, Native Americans generally lost the wars. Year by year, group by group, they were steadily pushed westward as the British colonies expanded. This pattern of Native American defeat and removal would be repeated often as the British colonized and settled North America.

490 History of Our World

Differentiated Instruction

For Special Needs Students `L1`
If students are having difficulty using the outline style of the organizer, convert the outline style to a different graphic organizer. Draw a large box to represent items I and II. Under each large box, draw a series of smaller boxes to contain the information in items A. B. C. and so forth. Help students arrange information in chronological or logical order. Encourage students to transfer the information back to the outline.

Tell students to fill in the last column of the *Reading Readiness Guide.* Ask them to evaluate if what they learned was what they had expected to learn.

All in One Unit 5 History of Our World Teaching Resources, *Reading Readiness Guide,* p. 134

The French and Indian War As you have read, the English and the French were already rivals in India and Europe. They also regarded each other as rivals in the new lands. In 1754, they went to war in North America. This part of the conflict between the French and the English is known as the French and Indian War because the French were allies with several Native American groups. An **ally** is a person or group that joins with another to reach a common goal. The Native Americans had long served as guides for French fur traders and had become friendly with them. However, the French were defeated in the war and were eventually driven from most of North America.

Native American Legacy in America The Native American way of life contributed to the new culture that was developing in the new country. Native Americans helped both the Pilgrims and the settlers of Jamestown survive by teaching them how to grow crops. Native American trails formed the highways for westward movement. Hundreds of Native American names—of rivers, states, cities, and mountains—are preserved across the North American continent.

✓ **Reading Check** Why did the Native Americans become allies of the French during the French and Indian War?

Links to
Science

Herbal Medicine
European settlers brought their own plants to use as medicine to North America, but they also learned herbal remedies from Native Americans. For example, in the 1700s, the bark of a witch hazel plant was used by the Mohawks to treat bruised eyes. Other Native American groups used the boiled leaves of the witch hazel plant as a liniment for aching legs.

Section 3 Assessment

Key Terms
Review the key terms at the beginning of this section. Use each term in a sentence that explains its meaning.

Target Reading Skill
State the main ideas of this section.

Comprehension and Critical Thinking
1. (a) List What countries besides Spain and Portugal sought colonies in North America?
(b) Compare and Contrast How did the French and English colonies differ?

2. (a) Identify Name a place other than North America where England and France competed for influence and power.
(b) Draw Inferences What can you infer about the power of England and France in Europe, based on the outcome of their colonizing competition?
3. (a) Explain What was the general pattern of interaction between the English colonists and the Native Americans?
(b) Identify Point of View How do you think the English colonists viewed the misfortune suffered by the Native Americans in the years after colonization?

Writing Activity
You are an English settler on the East Coast of North America. Write a letter to relatives in England, describing your endeavor. Be sure to discuss the relationship of your colony with the Native Americans who live in the area.

For: An activity on Spanish conquests in the Americas
Visit: PHSchool.com
Web Code: mud-1730

Writing Activity
Use the *Rubric for Assessing Letters* to evaluate student's letters.

All in One Unit 5 History of Our World Teaching Resources, *Rubric for Assessing a Letter,* p. 156

Go Online PHSchool.com Typing in the Web Code when prompted will bring students directly to detailed instructions for this activity.

Assess and Reteach

Assess Progress
Have students complete the Section Assessment and administer the *Section Quiz*.

All in One Unit 5 History of Our World Teaching Resources, *Section Quiz,* p. 136

Reteach
If students need more instruction, have them read this section in the Reading and Vocabulary Study Guide.

📖 Chapter 17, Section 3, **Reading and Vocabulary Study Guide,** pp. 190–192

Extend
Have students learn more about the Effect of Colonization on Native Americans by completing the *Enrichment*. Assign students to groups to complete the project.

All in One Unit 5 History of Our World Teaching Resources, *Enrichment,* p. 145

Answer

✓ **Reading Check** Native Americans had served as guides for the French fur traders for years and were friendly with them.

Section 3 Assessment

Key Terms
Students' sentences should reflect knowledge of each Key Term.

Target Reading Skill
The Dutch, French, and British established colonies in North America, but after several battles, the British dominated the continent. Native Americans tried to resist the spread of the British colonists, but were weakened by European diseases and were pushed westward.

Comprehension and Critical Thinking
1. (a) England, France, and the Netherlands
(b) The British built colonies along the coast. The French had fewer, smaller colonies inland and carried on trade with Native Americans.

2. (a) They competed in India and in Europe. **(b)** England and France fought many battles in Europe, but England eventually won the North American colonies.

3. (a) Native Americans were forced to move west. **(b)** Possible answers: The English believed they had a right to claim land and benefited from the misfortune of the Native Americans since it gave the colonies more land for the colonies.

Focus on Plymouth Colony

L2

Guided Instruction

- Remind students of the diagram of the Santa Maria on page 459. Ask **How would the things that the people of Plymouth Colony brought with them be similar to the cargo of the Santa Maria and how would they be different?** *(Lead students to understand that the colonists not only had to provision their trip, but they also had to bring everything they needed for a new life, such as seeds, tools, cooking utensils, dishes, and so on.)*

- Have students study the photographs and read the captions. Then lead the class in a discussion of what life would be like in the places shown on these pages

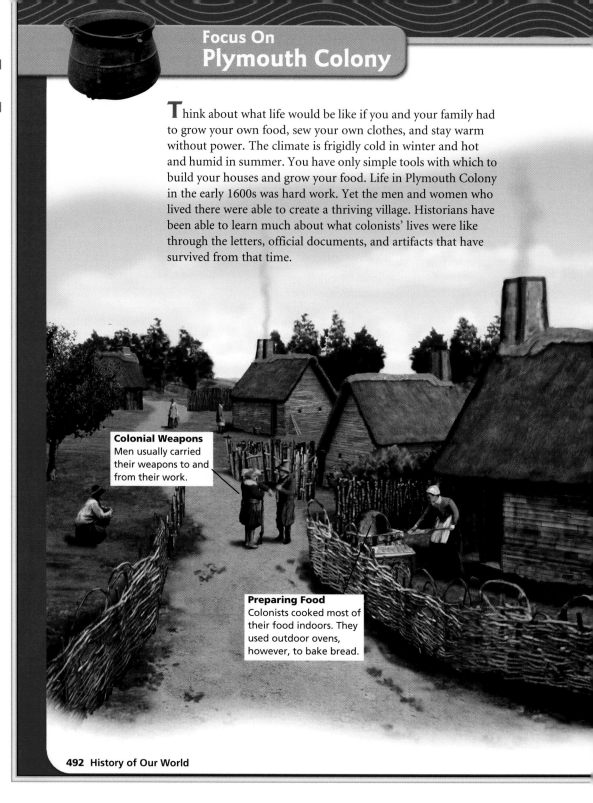

Focus On
Plymouth Colony

Think about what life would be like if you and your family had to grow your own food, sew your own clothes, and stay warm without power. The climate is frigidly cold in winter and hot and humid in summer. You have only simple tools with which to build your houses and grow your food. Life in Plymouth Colony in the early 1600s was hard work. Yet the men and women who lived there were able to create a thriving village. Historians have been able to learn much about what colonists' lives were like through the letters, official documents, and artifacts that have survived from that time.

Colonial Weapons
Men usually carried their weapons to and from their work.

Preparing Food
Colonists cooked most of their food indoors. They used outdoor ovens, however, to bake bread.

Background: Links Across Time

The Little Colony That Grew For 70 years, the Plymouth Colony was independent. It was unable to secure a charter and merged with the Massachusetts Bay Colony to become the Royal Colony of Massachusetts. Its identity changed again when the colony became the U.S. state of Massachusetts. Many of the colony's first 102 residents did not survive the first year in North America. But by 1640, about 3,000 people lived there. By 1765, the Massachusetts Bay Colony had almost 223,000 people, and by 2001, the Census Bureau placed the population of the state of Massachusetts at almost 6 1/2 million.

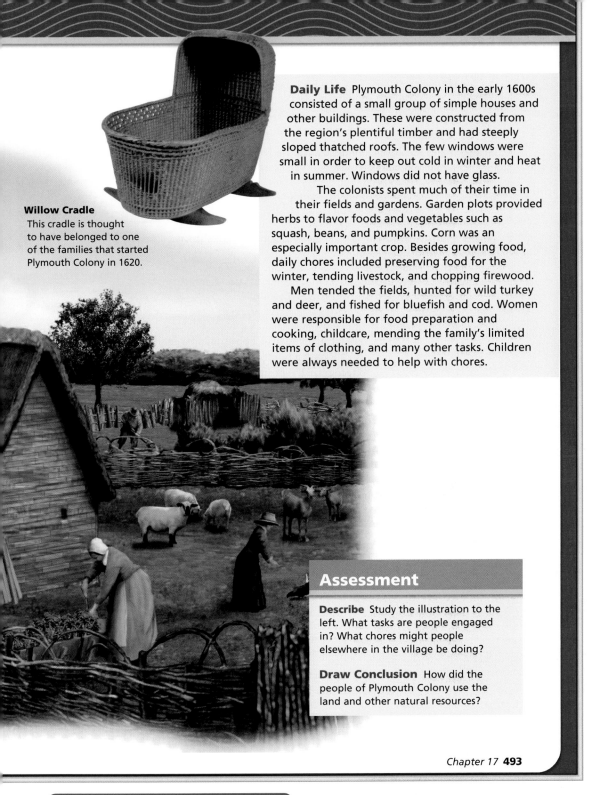

Willow Cradle
This cradle is thought to have belonged to one of the families that started Plymouth Colony in 1620.

Daily Life Plymouth Colony in the early 1600s consisted of a small group of simple houses and other buildings. These were constructed from the region's plentiful timber and had steeply sloped thatched roofs. The few windows were small in order to keep out cold in winter and heat in summer. Windows did not have glass.

The colonists spent much of their time in their fields and gardens. Garden plots provided herbs to flavor foods and vegetables such as squash, beans, and pumpkins. Corn was an especially important crop. Besides growing food, daily chores included preserving food for the winter, tending livestock, and chopping firewood.

Men tended the fields, hunted for wild turkey and deer, and fished for bluefish and cod. Women were responsible for food preparation and cooking, childcare, mending the family's limited items of clothing, and many other tasks. Children were always needed to help with chores.

Assessment

Describe Study the illustration to the left. What tasks are people engaged in? What chores might people elsewhere in the village be doing?

Draw Conclusion How did the people of Plymouth Colony use the land and other natural resources?

Independent Practice

Have students learn more about everyday life in the colony. Give students a list of topics and have them bring to class one interesting fact about their topic. Some possible topics include farming, building homes, clothing, shoes, food, keeping warm, planting a garden, raising animals, hunting for food, finding drinking water, fishing, furnishing a home, education, religion, and books, and letters home.

Differentiated Instruction

For Special Needs Students   L1
Partner special needs students with more proficient students to make a sequence chart. Have the partners infer how the events in Plymouth Colony came about and in what order. Then have the partners put them into order starting with the colonist's departure. Tell students that the text will not always tell them in what order the events happened, but that they should use their common sense to decide where information goes in their chart.

Answers

Assessment

Describe Working in the fields and gardens; preserving food, tending livestock, and chopping firewood
Draw Conclusions Possible answers: They used timber to build homes and for firewood. They used the land to grow herbs and vegetables. They hunted wild game in forests and fields and fished in local waters.

Objective

Learn to support a position.

Prepare to Read

Build Background Knowledge **L2**

Ask three volunteers to take the parts of Kayla, Melanie, and Ms. Murrow and read through the dialogue. (Read the non-dialogue parts when they occur.) Ask students whether they have been in similar discussions where they have disagreed with someone else's ideas on a particular topic. How well did they do in the discussion? Did they have good and persuasive reasons for their way of thinking? Were they able to use statistics or other information from outside sources to back up their ideas? Explain that the reasons and the informational and authoritative sources that students use to back up their reasons are the *support* for their position. Ask students to speculate about what a position is. Then read the first paragraph after the dialogue.

Instruct

Supporting a Position

Guided Instruction **L2**

- Read the steps to learn how to support a position together as a class.

- Practice the skill by going through the steps in the Practice the Skill on p. 495. Using the Idea Wave (TE, p. T39), have students tell what they already know about this topic. (*Possible answer: Students know from their reading that the Spanish were seeking riches and that the civil war did draw the people's attention from the invaders.*)

- Discuss what a counterargument is. Have volunteers suggest what the counterargument to the statement is. (*Possible answer: The Spanish weapons were, in fact, superior to those of the Native Americans. They had guns while the Native Americans only had spears. Other counterarguments to statements made: Other factors besides the civil war led to the Inca defeat, such as the capture of the king and the superior Spanish weapons. The statements about the Incan civilization have nothing to do with their vulnerability to attack.*)

 Skills for Life

Supporting a Position

> Kayla and Melanie were discussing the French and Indian War.
> "If France had won the war, we'd all be speaking French today," said Kayla excitedly.
> "No, we wouldn't," rejoined Melanie. "The French just wanted to make sure that they could still trade for furs. They didn't care about ruling the whole nation."
> Ms. Murrow overheard their conversation. "Girls," she said, "You need to support your position."
> "Position? I didn't know I had a position," said Kayla.
> "Support? How do I support what I think?" said Melanie.
> "I'll show you," said Ms. Murrow with a smile.

When you take a position on a subject or a question, you have a point of view or attitude about it. It is important to recognize the positions you have on various topics. It is just as important to be able to support, or back up, your position with solid arguments, information, and authoritative sources.

©Smithsonian American Art Museum, Washington, DC/Art Resource, NY

Learn the Skill

Use these steps to learn how to support your position.

1 **Look at the information you already know about your topic.** Write your ideas on a sheet of paper.

2 **Look at arguments that oppose your position.** Write these ideas next to those you've already written.

3 **Do further research on the subject. Learn more about the topic.** Take notes on the subject.

4 **Sort facts from opinions.** Facts can be proven true, whereas opinions cannot be proven true.

- Ask students to look for clues that show the author did more research on the topic. (*Possible answer: The introduction of an authoritative source is a clue that the author did outside research. For example, "Indeed, historian Frank Wright says …" and the introduction of new information, such as "They were wonderful architects and astronomers," show that the writer researched the topic.*)

- Explain that a statement loaded with an author's emotion usually indicates that it is an opinion rather than fact. (*Words or phrases that indicate emotion in this passage are "no way," "deplorable," "I think," "didn't deserve." Verifiable statements: "They were wonderful architects and astronomers"; "The civil war drew the people's attention from the threat of invasion"; and "They used trickery to capture the Incan king."*)

If the Inca hadn't just had a civil war, the Spanish invasion could not have happened. The Inca were an old, proud civilization. They were wonderful architects and astronomers. Indeed, historian Frank Wright says of them, "The Inca were ahead of their counterparts in Europe in their scientific knowledge." The Spanish invaders, by contrast, were just adventurers, out to become rich. The Spanish didn't have superior technology. I think that their behavior toward the Inca was deplorable, and they didn't deserve to rule the country. The civil war drew the Inca's attention away from the threat of invasion. The Spanish used trickery to capture the Incan king. If he had not been captured, the Inca would never have been overrun.

Practice the Skill

Read the above paragraph. Identify the position taken in the paragraph. Then reread the paragraph, taking note of the following:

1 What do you already know about this topic that would help you agree or disagree with the author's premise?

2 Identify the counterarguments to the claims made in the article. For example, what is the counterargument to the statement, "The Spanish didn't have superior technology?"

3 Point to a sentence that shows that the author did some additional research on the subject.

4 Identify two words that indicate that the author's opinion on the subject, rather than factual information, is being offered. Name one example of factual information, something that can be verified.

Apply the Skill

Choose another student as a partner. One partner should prepare arguments for the following statement; the other partner should prepare arguments against the statement. "The *encomienda* system was an important way of developing the economic growth of the Spanish colonies." Take turns presenting your arguments in class.

Independent Practice

Assign *Skills for Life*, and have students complete it individually.

All in One **Unit 5 History of Our World Teaching Resources**, *Skills for Life*, p. 146

Monitor Progress

Monitor students while they are complete the *Skills for Life* worksheet, checking to make sure they understand the skills steps.

Assess and Reteach

Assess Progress L2

Ask students to complete the Apply the Skill Activity.

Reteach L1

If students are having trouble applying the skill steps, have them review the skill using the interactive Social Studies Skills Tutor CD-ROM.

Supporting a Position, **Social Studies Skills Tutor CD-ROM**

Extend L3

To extend the lesson, form students into groups of four. Ask groups to consider the statement, "The Europeans could have treated the Native Americans more fairly and integrated them into their own culture." Have two members of the group do research that supports this statement and the other two find the counterarguments to the statement. Remind them to use the steps in the Learn the Skill while doing their research. Encourage them to discuss the question as they are doing research so that they might practice, or reaffirm, their arguments. Have groups present their positions to the class.

Differentiated Instruction

For Special Needs Students L1
Partner special needs students with more proficient students to do Level 1 of the *Supporting a Position* lesson on the Social Studies Skills CD-ROM together. When the students feel more confident, they can move on to Level 2 alone.

Supporting a Position, **Social Studies Skills Tutor CD-ROM**

Answer
Apply the Skill
Students' arguments will vary but should follow the steps in the Practice the Skill.

Objectives

Social Studies

1. Understand that the slave trade that began with the exploration of Africa and the colonization in South America and Central America also spread to North America.

2. Discover what the triangular trade was and how it expanded with the growth of the European colonization of North America.

Reading/Language Arts

Identify main ideas stated in paragraphs or other writing to help remember information.

Prepare to Read

Build Background Knowledge 〖L2〗

Using the Give One, Get One participation technique (TE, p. T41), ask students to share what they already know about slavery.

Set a Purpose for Reading 〖L2〗

- Preview the Objectives.

- Distribute the *Reading Readiness Guide.* Ask students to fill in the first two columns of the chart. Use the Numbered Heads participation structure (TE, p. T40) to call on students to share one piece of information they already know and one piece of information they want to know.

  〖All in One〗 **Unit 5 History of Our World Teaching Resources,** *Reading Readiness Guide,* p. 138

Vocabulary Builder

Preview Key Terms 〖L2〗

Pronounce each Key Term, and then ask the students to say the word with you. Provide a simple explanation, such as "to import means to bring in goods from another country."

Prepare to Read

Objectives

In this section you will

1. Understand that the slave trade that began with the exploration of Africa and the colonization of South America and Central America also spread to North America.

2. Discover what the triangular trade was and how it expanded with the growth of the European colonization of North America.

Taking Notes

As you read this section, look for information about the growth of slavery in the Americas. Copy the graphic organizer below, and record your findings in it.

Slavery in the Americas	
South America	**North America**
• Developed when population of Native Americans declined •	• •

🎯 Target Reading Skill

Identify Main Ideas To remember information, good readers identify main ideas as they read. The most important point in a paragraph or section is the main idea. As you read, identify the main idea stated in each section.

Key Terms

- **enslaved** (en SLAYVD), *v.* made into a slave and treated as property
- **import** (im PAWRT), *v.* to bring in goods from a foreign country

Leg shackles worn by enslaved Africans

The journey of the enslaved African was a living nightmare. One day he or she was living as a free person in an African village. The next, he or she was captured by slave traders, placed in chains, and forced to march for days. At the end of the march was the slave trading fort and a dungeon where captured Africans might sit for weeks or months. Eventually, people would be brought from the dungeon and then loaded onto a ship. A couple of months later, those who survived the voyage would arrive in the Americas. This destination was the end of the journey—but the beginning of a lifetime of slavery.

This bitter story is one that could have been told by millions of Africans from the 1500s to the 1800s. During those centuries, trade in human beings from Africa thrived. This trade helped enrich traders in Europe, Africa, and the Americas. It provided much of the labor that built European colonies in the Americas. It also changed the cultures of the Americas, as Africans brought with them their traditions and values, which helped them endure enslavement.

496 History of Our World

🎯 Target Reading Skill 〖L2〗

Identify Main Ideas Point out the Target Reading Skill. Tell students that it will help them remember information in a paragraph or other writing if they first identify the main idea stated in that paragraph.

Model the skill by reading the last paragraph on p. 497 and having students find the stated main idea in the paragraph.

Give students *Identify Main Ideas.* Have them complete the activity in groups.

〖All in One〗 **Unit 5 History of Our World Teaching Resources,** *Identify Main Ideas,* p. 141

Slavery in the Americas

In Chapter 16, you read about the Portuguese explorations under the leadership of Prince Henry the Navigator. In the 1400s, Portugal had explored the western coast of Africa. During that time, Portugal began capturing and trading enslaved human beings in Africa. **Enslaved** means held as the property of another person and to have no individual rights.

You have also read how the Spanish used enslaved Africans in their American colonies. The Spanish turned to this source of labor as vast numbers of Native Americans died from European diseases for which they had no immunity. The Portuguese also imported large numbers of enslaved Africans to Brazil. To **import** means to bring in products—in this case, people—from a foreign country.

The growing English colonies in North America also relied on enslaved Africans. This dependence on slaves was especially true in the southern regions, where climate and soil conditions favored crops such as tobacco and sugar. The raising of these crops required cheap labor if profits were to be made.

European colonists preferred enslaved Africans to other sources of labor. Africans came from very different cultures and were usually not Christian. This may have made it easier for the colonists to excuse their enslavement of human beings.

✓ **Reading Check** Which European country began the European trade in African slaves?

Learn what the African slave trade was like.

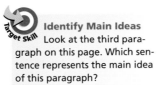
Identify Main Ideas Look at the third paragraph on this page. Which sentence represents the main idea of this paragraph?

Slavery
This drawing of a tobacco plantation was made by a European who lived at the time of slavery. **Analyze Images** What attitude do you think the artist had about slavery?

A TOBACCO PLANTATION

Vocabulary Builder

Use the information below to teach students this section's high-use words.

High-Use Word	Definition and Sample Sentence
thrived, p. 496	*v.* grew vigorously The hardy plants **thrived** in the plentiful sunshine and rain.
critic, p. 498	*n.* one who forms and expresses judgments of the merits, faults, value, or truth of a matter In the 1800s, there were many **critics** of the system of slavery that existed in this country.

Show *The African Slave Trade*. Ask **How did the slave trade affect African kingdoms?** *(African kingdoms decreased in size, and conflict developed as African kings sold members of their kingdoms)*

Instruct

Slavery in the Americas

Guided Instruction
- Read Slavery in the Americas, using the Structured Silent Reading technique (TE, p. T38).
- Ask students **How did the trade in enslaved human beings begin?** *(When Portugal began its exploration in Africa.)*

Independent Practice
Ask students to create the Taking Notes graphic organizer on a blank piece of paper. Have them fill in the blanks under "North America" with information they have just learned. Briefly model how to identify which details to record.

Monitor Progress
As students fill in the graphic organizer, circulate to make sure individuals are choosing the correct details. Provide assistance as needed.

⟳ Target Reading Skill

Identify Main Ideas As a follow up, ask students to answer the Target Reading Skill question in the Student Edition.

The Triangular Trade

Guided Instruction
- Have students read The Triangular Trade on p. 498. Have them draw a triangle on a piece of paper. As they read, tell them to label each corner and each side of the triangle with the information they learn.
- Discuss the triangular trade. Have students speculate about how the trade in human beings grew.

Answers

Analyze Images Possible response: That slavery was an acceptable source of labor.

✓ **Reading Check** Portugal

Independent Practice

Ask students to complete their graphic organizers and their triangular trade.

Monitor Progress

- As students fill in the graphic organizer and their triangular trade triangles, circulate and make sure individuals are choosing the correct details.

- Show *Section Reading Support Transparency HOW 110* and ask students to check their graphic organizers individually.

  History of Our World Transparencies
  Section Reading Support Transparency HOW 110

- Tell students to fill in the last column of the *Reading Readiness Guide.*

  All in One Unit 5 History of Our World Teaching Resources, *Reading Readiness Guide,* p. 138.

Assess and Reteach

Assess Progress
L2

Have students complete the Section Assessment and administer the *Section Quiz.*

All in One Unit 5 History of Our World Teaching Resources, *Section Quiz,* p. 140

Reteach
L1

If students need more instruction, have them read this section in the Reading and Vocabulary Study Guide.

Chapter 17, Section 4, **Reading and Vocabulary Study Guide,** pp. 193–195

Extend
L3

Have students learn more about the Effect of Colonization by having students research an aspect of colonization that interests them. Have each student present his or her research to the class.

Answer

√ Reading Check the term for the three-part trade between Europe, Africa, and the Americas

Section 4 Assessment

Key Terms
Students' sentences should reflect knowledge of each Key Term.

Target Reading Skill
Students' responses should reflect understanding of each section's main idea.

The Triangular Trade

The trade in enslaved Africans was part of a larger trade pattern called the triangular trade, so called because it had three "sides." The first corner of the triangle was in Europe, where ships were loaded with manufactured goods. These goods were shipped to Africa, the second point on the triangle. Here Europeans traded the manufactured goods for enslaved Africans. Slave traders then sent the slaves to the Americas, the third point of the triangle. In the Americas, enslaved Africans were traded for raw materials, which were then shipped back to Europe for manufacturing, completing the triangle.

The journey of enslaved Africans across the Atlantic Ocean was known as the Middle Passage. Wrote one British critic, "Never can so much misery be found condensed in so small a place as in a slave ship during the Middle Passage." The ships were extremely crowded. Death rates on the voyage may have averaged as much as 20 percent.

Slavery became critical to the economic stability of several American colonies. In the 1600s and 1700s, it formed an important part of trade between Europe and the American colonies.

√ Reading Check **What was the triangular trade?**

In the Goree Island "slave house" near Dakar, slave dealers had comfortable upstairs apartments while slaves were housed in overcrowded cells below. The door in the center was sometimes called "the door of no return" because slaves had to pass through it to go to the slave ships.

Section 4 Assessment

Key Terms
Review the key terms at the beginning of this section. Use each term in a sentence that explains its meaning.

Target Reading Skill
Identify the main idea in each heading in this section.

Comprehension and Critical Thinking
1. (a) Identify In which century did Europeans begin trading in African slaves?
(b) Identify Cause and Effect What event helped lead the Spanish turn to enslaved labor in their American colonies?
2. (a) Identify In what part of the English colonies was slavery most common?
(b) Draw Inferences Why do you think slavery was less common in the other colonies?
3. (a) Define What was the Middle Passage?
(b) Summarize Why did the Spanish turn to enslaved Africans as a source of labor for their American colonies?

Writing Activity
You are an enslaved African, waiting for shipment to the Americas from the dungeon of a coastal African trading fort. Write a journal entry about your feelings. Be sure to discuss what has happened to you and your thoughts about what the future may hold.

For: An activity on Spanish conquests in the Americas
Visit: PHSchool.com
Web Code: mud-1740

498 History of Our World

Comprehension and Critical Thinking
1. (a) the fifteenth **(b)** The population of Native Americans dropped sharply in the years after Spanish conquest.

2. (a) in the southern colonies **(b)** Possible answer: The northern colonies did not grow the kind of the crops that required a large labor force.

3. (a) the term used for the voyage by sea on which enslaved Africans were taken to the Americas **(b)** because enslaved Africans were a source of cheap labor

Writing Activity
Use the *Rubric for Assessing a Journal Entry.*

All in One Unit 5 History of Our World Teaching Resources, *Rubric for Assessing a Journal Entry,* p. 157

Go Online PHSchool.com Typing in the Web Code when prompted will bring students directly to detailed instructions for this activity.

Review and Assessment

Review Chapter Content

- Review and revisit the major themes of this chapter by asking students to classify which Guiding Question each bulleted statement in each Chapter Summary answers. Have students work together in groups to classify the sentences. Refer to p. 1 in the Student Edition for the text of the Guiding Questions.

- Assign *Vocabulary Development* for students to review Key Terms.

  All in One **Unit 5 History of Our World Teaching Resources,** *Vocabulary Development,* p. 153

◆ Chapter Summary

Section 1: Conquest in the Americas

- The Spanish conquered large areas in the Americas because the Native Americans had inferior weapons and many died from diseases carried by the Spanish.

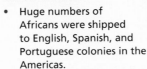

Aztec warriors

- Hernán Cortés led his Spanish soldiers and some Native American in the conquest of the Aztec empire in present-day Mexico.
- Francisco Pizarro led the Spanish conquest of the Incan Empire in present-day Peru.

Section 2: Colonies in Central and South Americas

- The Spanish and the Portuguese colonized South America and southern portions of North America.

Pueblo church

- Spanish colonies relied on the labor of Native Americans and some African Americans.
- The Catholic Church played a role in governing the colonies.

Section 3: Colonies in North America

- European powers such as England, France, and the Netherlands sought colonies in North America.

Pilgrim hat

- The rivalry between the French and the English resulted in the French and Indian War, which the English won.
- Native American groups were forced from their land by the advance of colonies in North America.

Section 4: Africa and the Atlantic Slave Trade

- Huge numbers of Africans were shipped to English, Spanish, and Portuguese colonies in the Americas.

Tobacco plantation

- The triangular trade in slaves was a central part of colonial and European trade.
- Africans suffered unspeakable horrors in their journey from their homes to lives of slavery in the Americas.

◆ Key Terms

Select the proper term to complete the sentence.

1. Africans were captured in their villages and _____.
2. The _____ ruled in the name of the Spanish king or queen.
3. The deaths of large numbers of Native Americans led the Spanish to _____ enslaved Africans.
4. Cortés finally conquered Tenochtitlán after a long _____.
5. A Spanish _____ wanted to earn glory for himself, his country, and his god.
6. In their war with the British, the French had an _____ in friendly Native American groups.
7. Operating a _____ required large numbers of workers.

A. conquistador
B. siege
C. viceroy
D. plantation
E. ally
F. enslaved
G. import

┌ Vocabulary Builder

Revisit this chapter's high-use academic words:

quest	intervened	legacy
resistance	enterprise	thrived
conversion	rival	critic

Ask students to review the definitions they recorded on their *Word Knowledge Rating Forms.*

All in One **Unit 5 History of Our World Teaching Resources,** *Word Knowledge Rating Form,* p. 144.

Consider allowing students to earn extra credit if they use the words in their answers to the questions in the Chapter Review and Assessment. The words must be used correctly and in a natural context to win the extra points.

Answers

Key Terms

1. F
2. B
3. G
4. B
5. A
6. E
7. D

Review and Assessment

Comprehension and Critical Thinking

8. (a) The Native Americans had never been exposed to the European diseases and had not developed any natural protection against them. **(b)** Large numbers of Native Americans died, making them unable to resist conquest by the Spanish. Some groups of Native Americans were totally wiped out.

9. (a) The Inca had engaged in a civil war. **(b)** Possible answer: The war probably left many Incan soldiers dead. It may have weakened support for the leader, Atahualpa. The war also probably took all of the combatants' attention, diverting them from the larger threat of Spanish invasion.

10. (a) Possible answer: The declining Native American population and opposition by the clergy helped stop the encomienda system. **(b)** Possible answer: The clergy felt that the encomienda system was unjust and sometimes abusive. They may have felt that more should have been done to support the Native Americans and help them become Christians. **(c)** When the population of the Native Americans dropped, the amount of labor the Spanish could rely on from them also dropped. The Spanish needed a way of replacing this cheap labor, so they started dealing with slave traders.

11. (a) The English colonies were along the east coast of North America. **(b)** Many Native Americans lost their lives to disease. They also lost their land.

12. (a) Europe sent goods to Africa for enslaved Africans; enslaved Africans were sent to the Americas for raw materials; raw materials were sent to Europe for manufacture.

13. (a) Possible answer: The exchange of enslaved Africans was a central part of trade between Europe and its American colonies.

14. (a) Enslaved Africans were used mainly on plantations to help raise the crops. **(b)** Possible answer: To the slave traders, enslaved Africans were like any other kind of cargo: The more slaves the ship could carry, the more money the traders could make.

Skills Practice

Answers will vary. 1) Sentence that uses a quotation from an authority: "Wrote one British critic of the slave trade, 'Never can so much misery be found condensed in so small a place as in a slave ship during the Middle

---

Chapter 17 Review and Assessment (continued)

◆ Comprehension and Critical Thinking

8. (a) Explain Why were many Native Americans vulnerable to European diseases?
(b) Cause and Effect What effect did disease have on many Native American groups after the arrival of the Spanish?

9. (a) Identify What important event had occurred in the Inca empire around the time of Pizarro's arrival?
(b) Cause and Effect Why might this event have made it easier for Pizarro to conquer the Inca?

10. (a) Identify What factors helped bring an end to the encomienda system?
(b) Identify Point of View Why did the Catholic missionaries resist the encomienda system?
(c) Draw Conclusions How did the end of the encomienda system lead to the use of slavery in the Spanish colonies?

11. (a) Recall In what part of North America did the English have their colonies?
(b) Cause and Effect Name two consequences of the European invasion for the Native Americans.

12. (a) Identify What were the three legs of the triangular trade?

13. (b) Analyze Information What role did the slave trade play in the colonial trading system?

14. (a) Explain What was the main use of enslaved Africans in the English colonies?
(b) Draw Conclusions Why do you think enslaved Africans were packed so tightly into ships on the Middle Passage?

◆ Skills Practice

Supporting a Position In the Skills Activity, you learned how to support your position. Review the steps you followed to learn this skill. Then reread the part of Section 3 called The Effect of European Colonization on Native Americans. Identify and support your position on Native Americans and colonization.

◆ Writing Activity: Geography

Using the library or the Internet, research the term Columbian Exchange. Write a brief report on how the European arrival in the Americas not only changed life for Native Americans but also for Europeans. Include specific examples of items that were "exchanged" as a part of the Columbian Exchange.

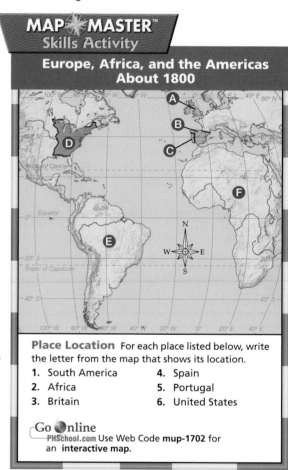

MAP MASTER™ Skills Activity

Europe, Africa, and the Americas About 1800

Place Location For each place listed below, write the letter from the map that shows its location.

1. South America
2. Africa
3. Britain
4. Spain
5. Portugal
6. United States

Go Online
PHSchool.com Use Web Code **mup-1702** for an **interactive map**.

Passage.'" 2) Verifiable facts: "Death rates may have averaged as much as 20 percent" and "By the late 1700s, enslaved Africans made up well over 30 percent of the population in several places." 3) A word that signals an emotional reaction: "terrible."

Writing Activity: Geography

Use the *Rubric for Assessing a Summary* to evaluate students' work.

All in One Unit 5 History of Our World Teaching Resources, *Rubric for Assessing a Summary*, p. 154

Standardized Test Prep

Test-Taking Tips

Some questions on standardized tests ask you to find main ideas. Read the paragraph below. Then follow the tips to answer the sample question.

Imagine trading a pound of salt for a pound of gold. At today's prices a pound of salt costs about 50 cents, but a pound of gold is worth thousands of dollars. However, that has not always been true. In some parts of West Africa, salt was scarce 1,200 years ago, but gold was not. People needed salt to flavor their food and preserve their meat, so they traded gold for salt.

TIP As you read the paragraph, try to identify its main ideas, or most important points.

Pick the letter that best answers the question.
This paragraph shows that—

A salt is scarce today.

B supply and demand determine value.

C the value of gold affects the value of salt.

D salt demand decreased as supply increased.

TIP Look for a key word that connects to the paragraph. In this case, the key word is *value*.

Think It Through Start with the main idea, people traded gold for salt when salt was scarce and gold was not. Link this idea to the key word: value, what something is worth. You can rule out A and D, which do not have to do with value. C is a statement linking the value of salt and gold; but the statement is not true. The answer is B.

Practice Questions

Use the tips above and other tips in this book to help you answer the following question:

1. Portugal's colony in the Americas was located in

 A Peru.

 B the Caribbean.

 C Brazil.

 D Mexico.

Use the graph below to answer questions 2 and 3.

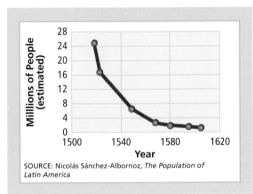

SOURCE: Nicolás Sánchez-Albornoz, *The Population of Latin America*

2. This graph most likely shows which of the following:

 A the change in the population of enslaved Africans in the Americas.

 B the change in the population of Native Americans in Mexico following the Spanish conquest.

 C the change in the numbers of British colonists following the French and Indian War.

 D the change in the number of Portuguese colonists after the establishment of Brazil.

3. Between which years was there the greatest decline in population?

 A between 1500 and 1540

 B between 1540 and 1580

 C between 1580 and 1620

 D decline was consistent for all years

Use Web Code **mua-1700** for **Chapter 17 self-test.**

MAP★MASTER
Skills Activity

1. E   2. F
3. A   4. B
5. C   6. D

Go Online PHSchool.com Students may practice their map skills using the interactive online version of this map.

Standardized Test Prep

Answers

1. C

2. B

3. A

4. B

Go Online PHSchool.com Students may use the Chapter 17 self-test on PHSchool.com to prepare for the Chapter Test.

Assessment Resources

Use *Chapter Tests A and B* to assess students' mastery of chapter content.

All in One **Unit 5 History of Our World Teaching Resources,** *Chapter Tests A and B,* pp. 158–163

Tests are also available on the **ExamView Test Bank CD-ROM**.

💿 **Exam***View*® **Test Bank CD-ROM**

Projects

- Students can further explore the Guiding Questions by completing hands-on projects.

- Eight projects are provided in the History of World Teaching Resources. Each project includes three pages of structured guidance for students.

  History of Our World Teaching Resources, Book Projects, *Ancient World Travel Guide,* p. 3; *The Hall of Ancient Heritage,* p. 4; *Ancient Civilizations Debate,* p. 7; *Life in the Ancient World,* p. 10; *One Job Through the Ages,* p. 13; *Two Tales of One City,* p. 16; *The Birth of a Nation,* p. 19; *and Major Migrations,* p. 22

- Review the project with the students.

- Have each student select one of the projects, or design his or her own. Work with students to create a project description and a schedule.

- Post project schedules and monitor student progress by asking for progress reports.

- Assess student projects by using rubrics from the History of Our World Teaching Resources.

  History of Our World Teaching Resources, Book Projects, *Rubric for Assessing Student Performance on a Project,* p. 25; *Rubric for Assess Performance of an Entire Group,* p. 26; *Rubric for Assessing Individual Performance in a Group,* p. 27

 Tell students they can add their completed Book Projects as the final item in their portfolios.

History of Our World Teaching Resources, Book Projects, *Rubric for Assessing a Student Portfolio,* p. 28

Projects

Create your own projects to learn more about world history. At the beginning of this book, you were introduced to these Guiding Questions for studying the chapters and special features. But you can also find answers to these questions by doing projects on your own or with a group.

1. **Geography** How did physical geography affect the development and growth of societies around the world?

2. **History** How did each society's belief system affect its historical accomplishments?

3. **Culture** What were the beliefs and values of people in these societies?

4. **Government** What types of governments were formed in these societies and how did they develop?

5. **Economics** How did each society develop and organize its economic activities?

Project
STAGE A DEBATE

Researching Modern Societies
Which of the modern societies in this book made the greatest contributions to the world? Stage a debate with representatives from each society. To support your argument, research your society's form of government, art, inventions, language, science, and literature. Visual aids such as pictures and posters could make your arguments more convincing.

Colossal statue of a seated Buddha at Kyaikpun Pagoda, Burma (Myanmar)

Project
CREATE A TRAVEL GUIDE

Travel the Ancient World
As you study each civilization in this book, write a chapter for a travel guide to the world of ancient times. Create a map for each place, and write about its geography and history. Include a picture of a special place or an interesting feature of each civilization that is a "must see" for travelers. When you have finished all of the chapters, combine them to make a travel guidebook.

Reference

Table of Contents

The World: Political

ARCTIC OCEAN

GREENLAND (Denmark)

RUSSIA

ALASKA (U.S.)

Arctic Circle

Reykjavík

C A N A D A

NORTH AMERICA

Ottawa

UNITED STATES

Washington, D.C.

ATLANTIC OCEAN

AZORES (Portugal)

Tropic of Cancer

HAWAII (U.S)

MEXICO

20° N

Mexico City

CENTRAL AMERICA AND THE CARIBBEAN
For detail, see map
North and South
America: Political.

CAPE VERDE

Praia

40° N

MARSHALL ISLANDS

Majuro

K I R I B A T I

NAURU

Bairiki

PALMYRA ATOLL (U.S.)

Equator

0°

GALÁPAGOS ISLANDS (Ecuador)

Caracas

VENEZUELA Georgetown

Bogotá

GUYANA

Paramaribo

SURINAME

FRENCH GUIANA (France)

COLOMBIA

ECUADOR

Quito

SOUTH AMERICA

TUVALU

Fongafale

SOLOMON ISLANDS

Honiara

COOK ISLANDS (New Zealand)

P A C I F I C

OCEAN

Lima

PERU

BRAZIL

Brasília

VANUATU

Port-Vila

FIJI

SAMOA

Apia

AMERICAN SAMOA (U.S.)

FRENCH POLYNESIA (France)

La Paz

BOLIVIA

Sucre

Suva

NIUE (New Zealand)

20° S

Nuku'alofa

TONGA

PITCAIRN ISLANDS (U.K.)

PARAGUAY

Asunción

NEW CALEDONIA (France)

Tropic of Capricorn

CHILE

ARGENTINA

NEW ZEALAND

URUGUAY

Santiago

Montevideo

Buenos Aires

40° S

Wellington

FALKLAND ISLANDS (U.K.)

SOUTH GEORGIA & SOUTH SANDWICH ISLANDS (U.K.)

60° S

S O U T H E R N   O C E A N

Antarctic Circle

80° S

ANTARCTICA

0 miles   2,000

0 kilometers   2,000

Robinson

504 Reference

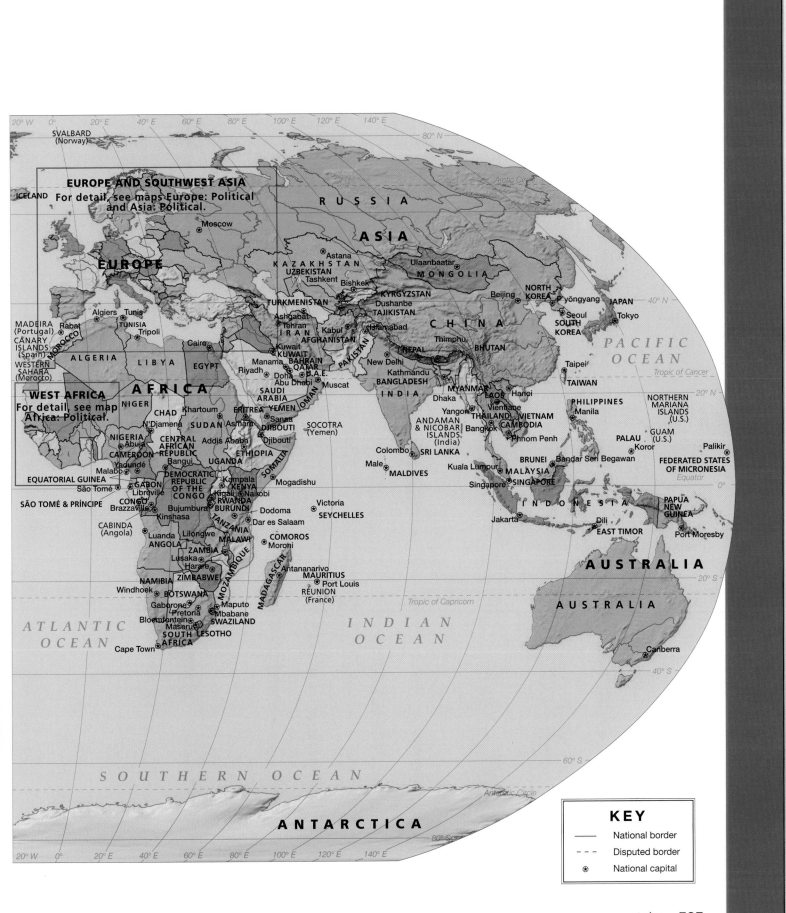

EUROPE AND SOUTHWEST ASIA
For detail, see maps Europe: Political
and Asia: Political.

WEST AFRICA
For detail, see map
Africa: Political.

SVALBARD
(Norway)

ICELAND

RUSSIA

ASIA

Moscow

EUROPE

Astana

KAZAKHSTAN

UZBEKISTAN
Tashkent

Bishkek

Ulaanbaatar

MONGOLIA

Beijing

NORTH
KOREA

P'yŏngyang

JAPAN

KYRGYZSTAN

Algiers Tunis

MADEIRA
(Portugal)
CANARY
ISLANDS
(Spain)

WESTERN
SAHARA
(Morocco)

TUNISIA

Rabat

MOROCCO

ALGERIA

TURKMENISTAN
Ashgabat

Tehran

IRAN

LIBYA

EGYPT

Cairo

Dushanbe
TAJIKISTAN

Kabul

AFGHANISTAN

Islamabad

Seoul
SOUTH
KOREA

Tokyo

CHINA

Thimphu

PACIFIC
OCEAN

Tropic of Cancer

Taipei

TAIWAN

Kuwait
KUWAIT
Manama BAHRAIN
QATAR
Doha
Abu Dhabi
Riyadh

SAUDI
ARABIA

Muscat

New Delhi
Kathmandu
NEPAL

BHUTAN

BANGLADESH

INDIA

Dhaka

MYANMAR

Hanoi

LAOS

PHILIPPINES

Manila

NORTHERN
MARIANA
ISLANDS
(U.S.)

AFRICA

NIGER

CHAD

Khartoum

ERITREA

YEMEN

SUDAN Asmara
N'Djamena

NIGERIA

Abuja

CENTRAL
AFRICAN
REPUBLIC

Sanaa
DJIBOUTI
Djibouti

SOCOTRA
(Yemen)

Yangon
ANDAMAN
& NICOBAR
ISLANDS
(India) Bangkok

THAILAND

Vientiane
CAMBODIA

VIETNAM

Phnom Penh

GUAM
(U.S.)

PALAU
Koror

Palikir

CAMEROON

Yaundé

Addis Ababa

ETHIOPIA

UGANDA

Bangui

Colombo

SRI LANKA

BRUNEI Bandar Seri Begawan

FEDERATED STATES
OF MICRONESIA

EQUATORIAL GUINEA

Malabo

São Tomé

GABON

SÃO TOMÉ & PRÍNCIPE

Libreville

DEMOCRATIC
REPUBLIC
OF THE
CONGO

Kampala
KENYA
Kigali
RWANDA Nairobi
BURUNDI

SOMALIA

Male

MALDIVES

Kuala Lumpur

MALAYSIA

Singapore SINGAPORE

CONGO
Brazzaville
Kinshasa

Bujumbura

Mogadishu

TANZANIA

Dodoma

Victoria

SEYCHELLES

INDONESIA

Jakarta

PAPUA
NEW
GUINEA

CABINDA
(Angola)

Luanda

Lilongwe
Lilongwe

ANGOLA

ZAMBIA

MALAWI

Dar es Salaam

COMOROS
Moroni

Dili
EAST TIMOR

Port Moresby

Lusaka

Harare

MOZAMBIQUE

NAMIBIA ZIMBABWE

Windhoek

BOTSWANA

MADAGASCAR

Antananarivo
MAURITIUS
Port Louis
RÉUNION
(France)

AUSTRALIA

Tropic of Capricorn

AUSTRALIA

Gaborone

Maputo

ATLANTIC
OCEAN

Pretoria
Bloemfontein Mbabane
Maseru SWAZILAND
SOUTH LESOTHO
AFRICA

Cape Town

INDIAN
OCEAN

Canberra

SOUTHERN OCEAN

Antarctic Circle

ANTARCTICA

KEY

— National border

- - - Disputed border

⊛ National capital

The World: Physical

0 miles 2,000
0 kilometers 2,000
Robinson

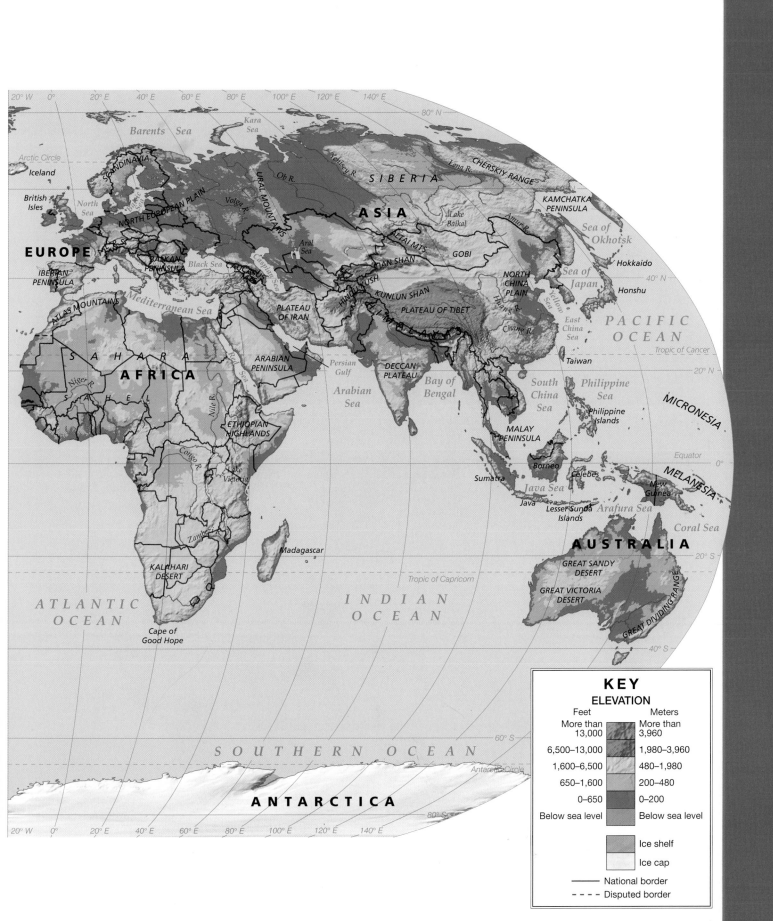

20° W   0°   20° E   40° E   60° E   80° E   100° E   120° E   140° E

80° N

Arctic Circle

Iceland

British Isles

North Sea

Barents Sea

Kara Sea

SCANDINAVIA

NORTH EUROPEAN PLAIN

Yenisey R.

Lena R.

SIBERIA

CHERSKIY RANGE

URAL MOUNTAINS

Ob R.

Volga R.

EUROPE

ASIA

KAMCHATKA PENINSULA

Lake Baikal

Amur R.

Sea of Okhotsk

IBERIAN PENINSULA

BALKAN PENINSULA

Black Sea

CAUCASUS

Caspian Sea

Aral Sea

ALTAI MTS.

TIAN SHAN

GOBI

NORTH CHINA PLAIN

Hokkaido

Sea of Japan

40° N

Honshu

ATLAS MOUNTAINS

Mediterranean Sea

PLATEAU OF IRAN

HINDU KUSH

KUNLUN SHAN

PLATEAU OF TIBET

HIMALAYAS

Huang R.

Yellow Sea

Chang R.

East China Sea

PACIFIC OCEAN

Tropic of Cancer

SAHARA

AFRICA

Red Sea

ARABIAN PENINSULA

Persian Gulf

DECCAN PLATEAU

Taiwan

20° N

Niger R.

SAHEL

Nile R.

Arabian Sea

Bay of Bengal

South China Sea

Philippine Sea

MICRONESIA

ETHIOPIAN HIGHLANDS

Philippine Islands

Congo R.

Lake Victoria

MALAY PENINSULA

Equator   0°

MELANESIA

Sumatra

Borneo

Celebes

New Guinea

Java Sea

Java

Lesser Sunda Islands

Arafura Sea

Zambezi R.

Madagascar

Coral Sea

AUSTRALIA

ATLANTIC OCEAN

KALAHARI DESERT

Tropic of Capricorn

INDIAN OCEAN

GREAT SANDY DESERT

20° S

GREAT VICTORIA DESERT

GREAT DIVIDING RANGE

Cape of Good Hope

40° S

60° S

SOUTHERN OCEAN

Antarctic Circle

ANTARCTICA

80° S

20° W   0°   20° E   40° E   60° E   80° E   100° E   120° E   140° E

KEY
ELEVATION

Feet	Meters
More than 13,000	More than 3,960
6,500–13,000	1,980–3,960
1,600–6,500	480–1,980
650–1,600	200–480
0–650	0–200
Below sea level	Below sea level

Ice shelf

Ice cap

——— National border

- - - Disputed border

North and South America: Political

KEY

— National border

⊛ National capital

• Other city

0 miles 2,000

0 kilometers 2,000

Lambert Azimuthal Equal Area

508 Reference

North and South America: Physical

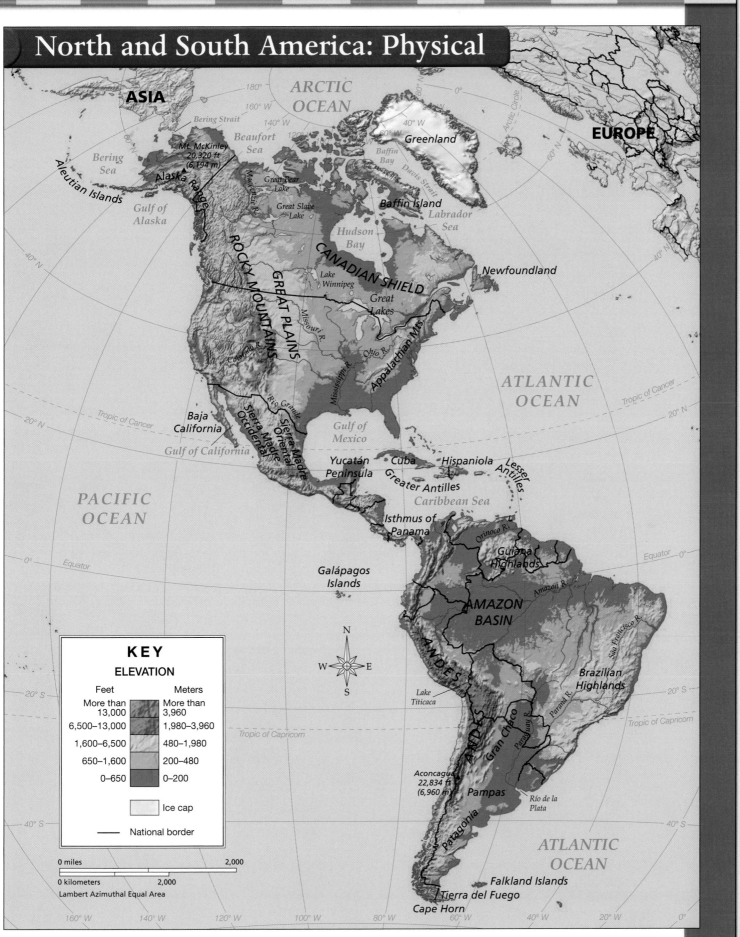

ASIA

ARCTIC OCEAN

EUROPE

Bering Strait

Mt. McKinley 20,320 ft (6,194 m)

Beaufort Sea

Greenland

40° W

60° W

Baffin Bay

Arctic Circle

Bering Sea

Aleutian Islands

Alaska Range

Gulf of Alaska

Mackenzie R.

Great Bear Lake

Great Slave Lake

Davis Strait

Baffin Island

Labrador Sea

Newfoundland

ROCKY MOUNTAINS

GREAT PLAINS

Hudson Bay

CANADIAN SHIELD

Lake Winnipeg

Great Lakes

60° N

40° N

Missouri R.

Colorado R.

Mississippi R.

Ohio R.

Appalachian Mts.

ATLANTIC OCEAN

Tropic of Cancer

20° N

Baja California

Sierra Madre Occidental

Río Grande

Sierra Madre Oriental

Gulf of Mexico

Gulf of California

Tropic of Cancer

20° N

PACIFIC OCEAN

Yucatán Peninsula

Cuba

Greater Antilles

Hispaniola

Lesser Antilles

Caribbean Sea

Isthmus of Panama

Orinoco R.

Guiana Highlands

Galápagos Islands

Equator

AMAZON BASIN

Amazon R.

Equator

ANDES

São Francisco R.

Brazilian Highlands

Lake Titicaca

Paraná R.

20° S

KEY

ELEVATION

Feet		Meters
More than 13,000		More than 3,960
6,500–13,000		1,980–3,960
1,600–6,500		480–1,980
650–1,600		200–480
0–650		0–200

Ice cap

National border

0 miles 2,000

0 kilometers 2,000

Lambert Azimuthal Equal Area

N
W E
S

Gran Chaco

Paraguay R.

Tropic of Capricorn

Aconcagua 22,834 ft (6,960 m)

Pampas

Río de la Plata

Patagonia

20° S

40° S

ATLANTIC OCEAN

Falkland Islands

Tierra del Fuego

Cape Horn

160° W 140° W 120° W 100° W 80° W 60° W 40° W 20° W 0°

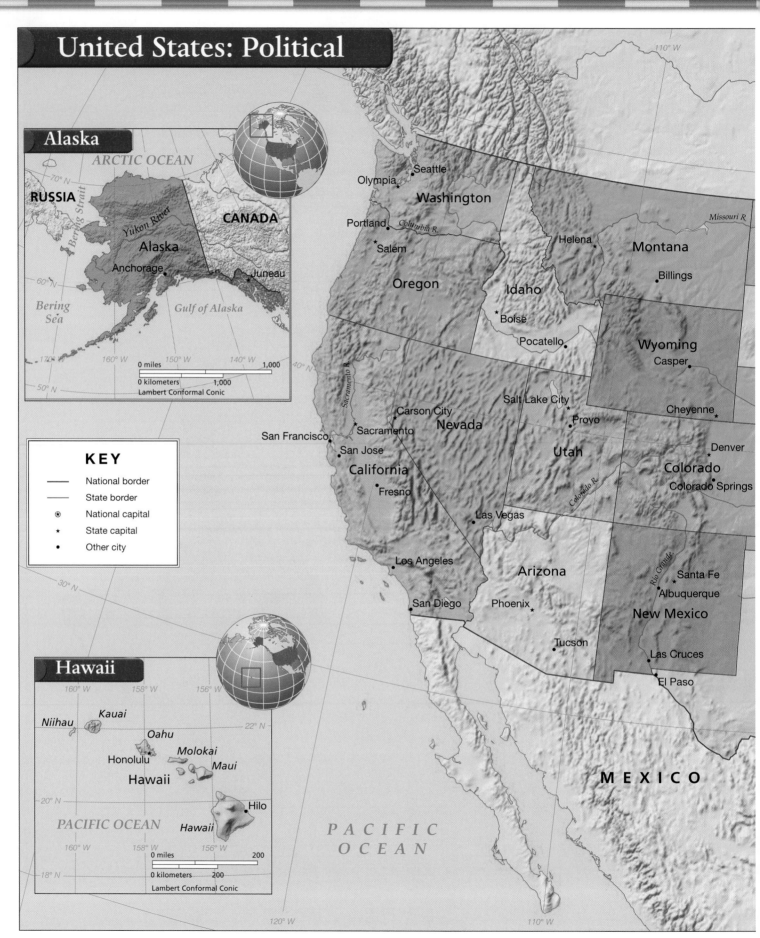

United States: Political

Alaska

ARCTIC OCEAN

RUSSIA

Bering Strait

Yukon River

CANADA

Alaska

Anchorage

Juneau

Bering Sea

Gulf of Alaska

70° N

60° N

50° N

170° W   160° W   150° W   140° W

0 miles 1,000
0 kilometers 1,000
Lambert Conformal Conic

KEY

——— National border
——— State border
⊛ National capital
★ State capital
• Other city

Hawaii

160° W   158° W   156° W

Niihau   Kauai

Oahu   22° N

Honolulu   Molokai

Hawaii   Maui

20° N

PACIFIC OCEAN   Hawaii   Hilo

160° W   158° W   156° W

18° N

0 miles 200
0 kilometers 200
Lambert Conformal Conic

Seattle
Olympia
Washington
Portland   Columbia R.
Salem
Helena
Montana
Missouri R.
Oregon   Idaho
Boise
Billings
Pocatello
Wyoming
Casper
Salt Lake City
Carson City   Nevada   Provo
Cheyenne
San Francisco   Sacramento   Utah   Denver
San Jose   Colorado
California   Colorado Springs
Fresno   Colorado R.
Las Vegas
Los Angeles   Santa Fe
Arizona   Rio Grande   Albuquerque
San Diego   Phoenix   New Mexico
Tucson   Las Cruces
El Paso

Sacramento R.

110° W

120° W   110° W

40° N

30° N

PACIFIC OCEAN

MEXICO

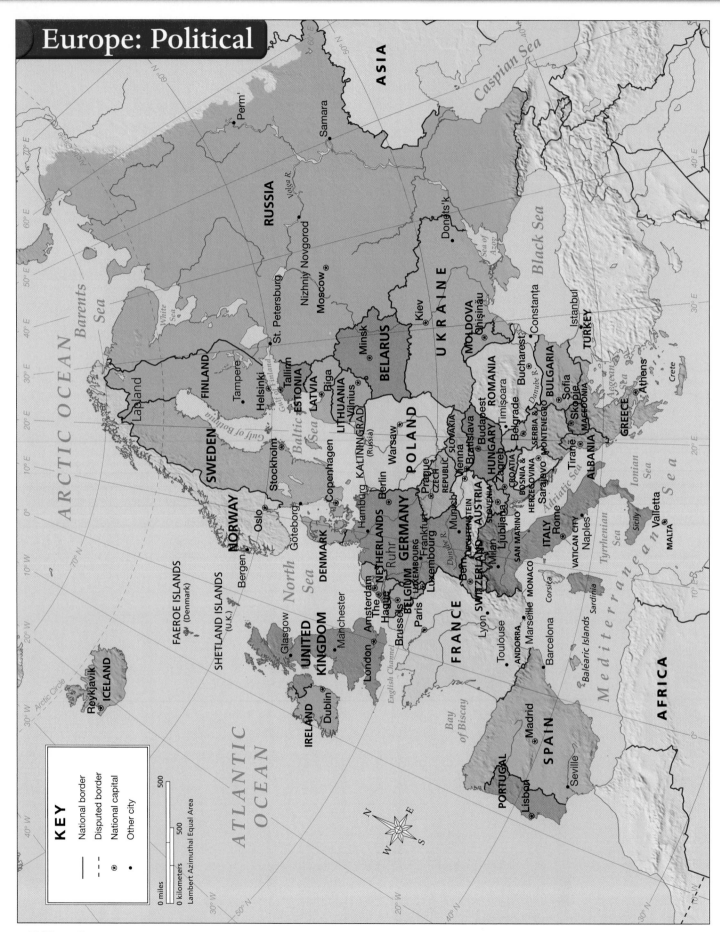

Europe: Political

ASIA

Caspian Sea

Perm'

Samara

RUSSIA

Volga R.

Barents Sea

Nizhniy Novgorod

Moscow

Black Sea

Donets'k

Sea of Azov

ARCTIC OCEAN

White Sea

St. Petersburg

Kiev

UKRAINE

MOLDOVA

Chişinău

Constanţa

Istanbul

TURKEY

FINLAND

Tampere

Helsinki

Tallinn

ESTONIA

Riga

LATVIA

Vilnius

LITHUANIA

Minsk

BELARUS

Danube R.

Bucharest

ROMANIA

Timişoara

BULGARIA

Sofia

Skopje

MACEDONIA

Athens

GREECE

Aegean Sea

Crete

Lapland

SWEDEN

Gulf of Bothnia

Baltic Sea

Stockholm

Copenhagen

KALININGRAD
(Russia)

Warsaw

POLAND

Berlin

SLOVAKIA

Bratislava

Budapest

HUNGARY

Belgrade

SERBIA &
MONTENEGRO

Sarajevo

Tiranë

ALBANIA

Adriatic Sea

Ionian Sea

NORWAY

Bergen

Oslo

Göteborg

DENMARK

Hamburg

GERMANY

Prague

CZECH
REPUBLIC

Vienna

SLOVENIA

AUSTRIA

LIECHTENSTEIN

Zagreb

CROATIA

BOSNIA &
HERZEGOVINA

Ljubljana

Danube R.

Munich

Milan

SAN MARINO

MONACO

ITALY

Rome

VATICAN CITY

Naples

Tyrrhenian Sea

Sicily

Valletta

MALTA

Mediterranean Sea

FAEROE ISLANDS
(Denmark)

SHETLAND ISLANDS
(U.K.)

North Sea

Amsterdam

NETHERLANDS

The
Hague

Ruhr

Brussels

BELGIUM

LUXEMBOURG

Luxembourg

Frankfurt

Bern

SWITZERLAND

Paris

FRANCE

Lyon

Corsica

Sardinia

Reykjavik

ICELAND

Arctic Circle

Glasgow

**UNITED
KINGDOM**

Manchester

London

English Channel

IRELAND

Dublin

*Bay
of Biscay*

Toulouse

ANDORRA

Marseille

Barcelona

Balearic Islands

**ATLANTIC
OCEAN**

Madrid

SPAIN

Seville

PORTUGAL

Lisbon

AFRICA

KEY

— National border

--- Disputed border

⊛ National capital

• Other city

0 miles   500

0 kilometers   500

Lambert Azimuthal Equal Area

N
W   E
S

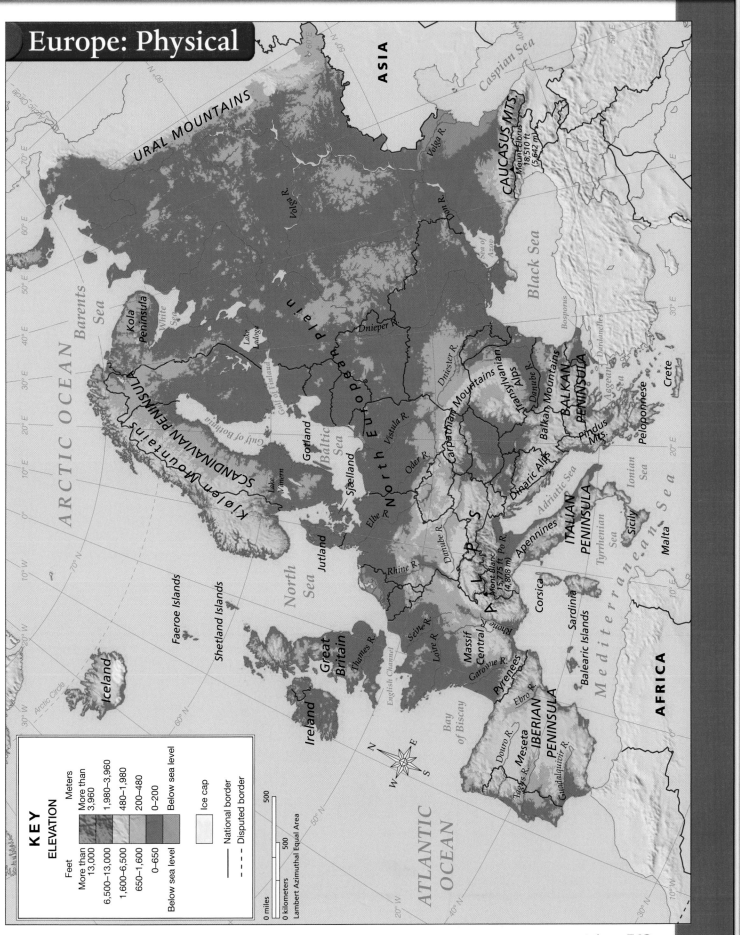

Europe: Physical

ASIA

URAL MOUNTAINS

CAUCASUS MTS.
Mount Elbrus
18,510 ft
(5,642 m)

Caspian Sea

Volga R.

Volga R.

Don R.

Sea of
Azov

Black Sea

Barents
Sea

Kola
Peninsula

White
Sea

Lake
Ladoga

Gulf of Finland

North European Plain

Dnieper R.

Bosporus

Dardanelles

Dniester R.

Carpathian Mountains

Transylvanian Alps

Danube R.

Balkan Mountains

BALKAN PENINSULA

Pindus Mts.

Aegean Sea

Crete

ARCTIC OCEAN

SCANDINAVIAN PENINSULA

Kjølen Mountains

Gulf of Bothnia

Lake
Vänern

Lake
Vättern

Gotland

Baltic
Sea

Sjælland

Vistula R.

Oder R.

Elbe R.

Dinaric Alps

Adriatic Sea

ITALIAN PENINSULA

Peloponnese

Ionian
Sea

Danube R.

A L P S

Mont Blanc
15,775 ft
(4,808 m)

Rhine R.

Apennines

Tyrrhenian
Sea

Sicily

Malta

Mediterranean Sea

Faeroe Islands

Shetland Islands

North
Sea

Jutland

Thames R.

English Channel

Great
Britain

Seine R.

Loire R.

Massif
Central

Rhône R.

Garonne R.

Corsica

Sardinia

Balearic Islands

Iceland

Arctic Circle

Ireland

Bay
of
Biscay

Pyrenees

Ebro R.

IBERIAN
PENINSULA

Douro R.

Meseta

Tagus R.

Guadalquivir R.

ATLANTIC
OCEAN

AFRICA

N
E
S
W

KEY

ELEVATION

Feet	Meters
More than 13,000	More than 3,960
6,500–13,000	1,980–3,960
1,600–6,500	480–1,980
650–1,600	200–480
0–650	0–200
Below sea level	Below sea level

Ice cap

—— National border
---- Disputed border

0 miles 500
0 kilometers 500
Lambert Azimuthal Equal Area

Africa: Political

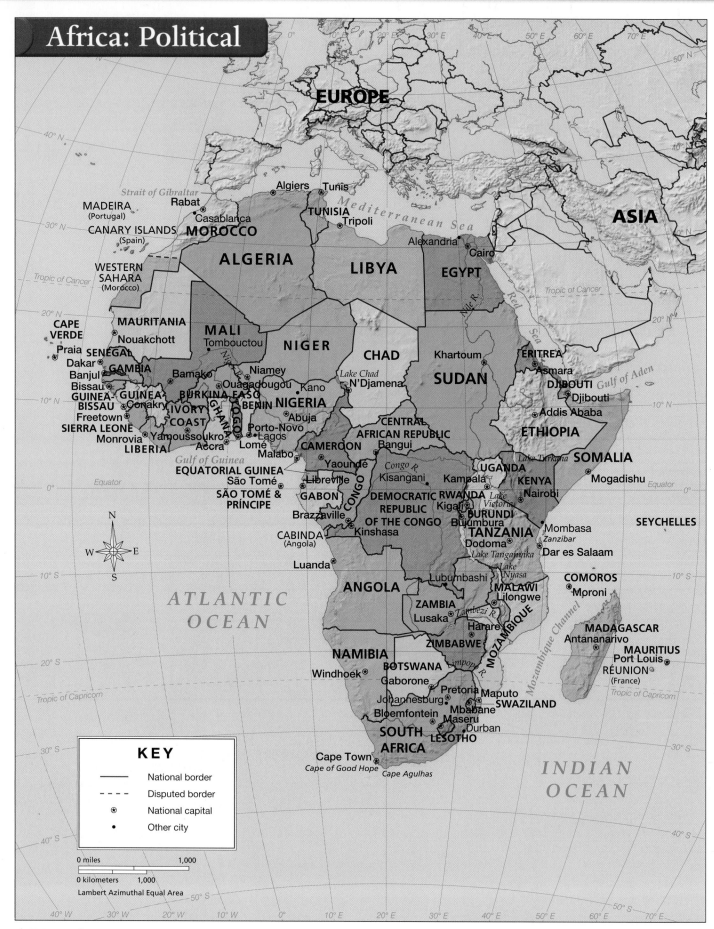

EUROPE

ASIA

Mediterranean Sea

Strait of Gibraltar
Algiers • Tunis
Rabat •
MADEIRA
(Portugal)
Casablanca
CANARY ISLANDS
(Spain)
MOROCCO
TUNISIA
• Tripoli

Alexandria ⊛ Cairo

Tropic of Cancer

WESTERN
SAHARA
(Morocco)

ALGERIA

LIBYA

EGYPT

Tropic of Cancer

20° N

MAURITANIA

CAPE
VERDE
Nouakchott ⊛
MALI
Tombouctou

NIGER

CHAD

Khartoum ⊛

ERITREA

Praia
•
Dakar ⊛
SENEGAL
Bamako
Niamey ⊛

Asmara •

Lake Chad

DJIBOUTI

Gulf of Aden

Banjul
GAMBIA
Bissau
GUINEA-
BISSAU
Freetown
SIERRA LEONE
Monrovia •
LIBERIA

Ouagadougou ⊛
BURKINA FASO
Conakry
GUINEA
IVORY
COAST
Yamoussoukro •
GHANA
Accra
TOGO
BENIN

• Kano
NIGERIA
⊛ Abuja
Porto-Novo
Lagos •
Lomé
Malabo ⊛

N'Djamena ⊛

SUDAN

• Djibouti

Addis Ababa •

CENTRAL
AFRICAN REPUBLIC
Bangui ⊛

ETHIOPIA

10° N

Gulf of Guinea

CAMEROON
Yaoundé ⊛
Libreville ⊛

Lake Turkana
SOMALIA

EQUATORIAL GUINEA
São Tomé •
SÃO TOMÉ &
PRÍNCIPE
GABON

Kisangani •
CONGO

UGANDA
Kampala ⊛
KENYA
Nairobi ⊛

Mogadishu ⊛

Equator

DEMOCRATIC
REPUBLIC
OF THE CONGO
Brazzaville ⊛
Kinshasa ⊛

Congo R.
RWANDA
Kigali ⊛
BURUNDI
Bujumbura ⊛

*Lake
Victoria*

SEYCHELLES

CABINDA
(Angola)

TANZANIA
Dodoma ⊛

Mombasa •
Zanzibar
Dar es Salaam •

Luanda ⊛

Lake Tanganyika

COMOROS
Moroni •

10° S

ANGOLA

ZAMBIA
Lusaka ⊛

Lubumbashi •

*Lake
Nyasa*
MALAWI
Lilongwe ⊛

MOZAMBIQUE

Mozambique Channel

MADAGASCAR
Antananarivo ⊛

MAURITIUS
Port Louis •
RÉUNION
(France)

*ATLANTIC
OCEAN*

NAMIBIA
Windhoek ⊛

Zambezi R.
Harare ⊛
ZIMBABWE

Limpopo R.

20° S

Tropic of Capricorn

BOTSWANA
Gaborone ⊛

Pretoria ⊛ Maputo
Johannesburg •
Mbabane ⊛ SWAZILAND
Bloemfontein • Maseru ⊛ Durban •
SOUTH
AFRICA
LESOTHO

*INDIAN
OCEAN*

30° S

KEY

——— National border

– – – Disputed border

⊛ National capital

• Other city

Cape Town •
Cape of Good Hope
Cape Agulhas

0 miles   1,000
0 kilometers   1,000
Lambert Azimuthal Equal Area

Africa: Physical

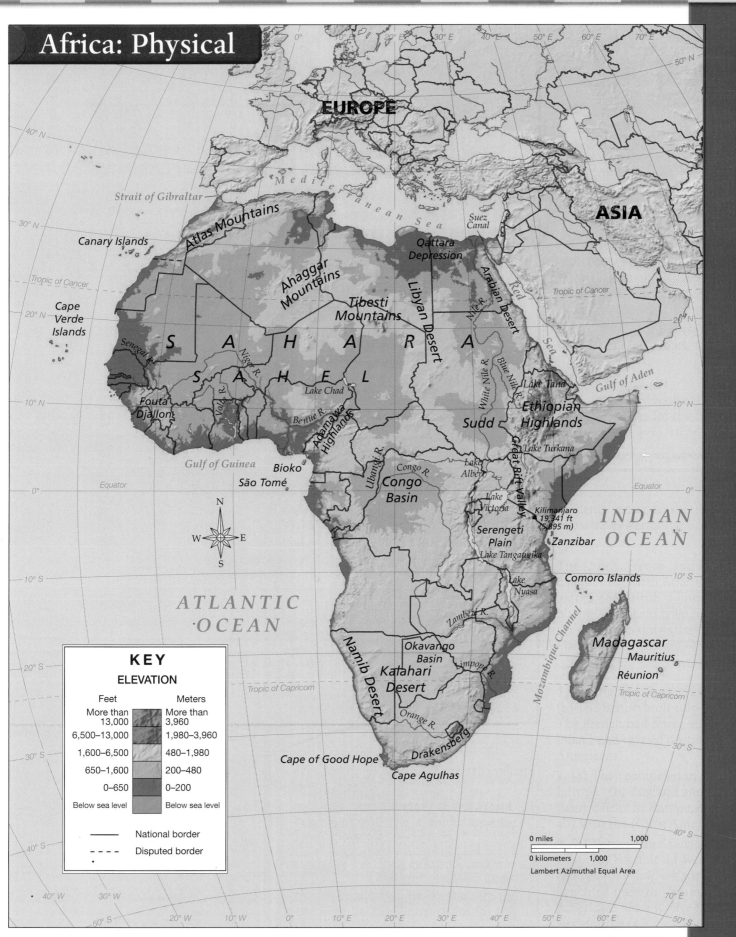

EUROPE

ASIA

Strait of Gibraltar

Mediterranean Sea

Suez Canal

Atlas Mountains

Canary Islands

Qattara Depression

Cape Verde Islands

Ahaggar Mountains

Tibesti Mountains

Libyan Desert

Arabian Desert

Red Sea

Tropic of Cancer

S A H A R A

Senegal R.

Niger R.

S A H E L

Lake Chad

White Nile R.

Blue Nile R.

Lake Tana

Gulf of Aden

Fouta Djallon

Volta R.

Benue R.

Adamawa Highlands

Sudd

Ethiopian Highlands

Lake Turkana

Gulf of Guinea

Bioko

São Tomé

Ubangi R.

Congo R.

Congo Basin

Lake Albert

Great Rift Valley

Equator

Lake Victoria

Kilimanjaro 19,341 ft (5,895 m)

INDIAN OCEAN

N
W   E
S

Serengeti Plain

Lake Tanganyika

Zanzibar

ATLANTIC OCEAN

Lake Nyasa

Comoro Islands

Mozambique Channel

Madagascar

Zambeze R.

Mauritius

Namib Desert

Okavango Basin

Kalahari Desert

Limpopo R.

Réunion

Tropic of Capricorn

Orange R.

Cape of Good Hope

Drakensberg

Cape Agulhas

KEY
ELEVATION

Feet	Meters
More than 13,000	More than 3,960
6,500–13,000	1,980–3,960
1,600–6,500	480–1,980
650–1,600	200–480
0–650	0–200
Below sea level	Below sea level

———— National border

- - - - Disputed border

0 miles 1,000
0 kilometers 1,000
Lambert Azimuthal Equal Area

Asia: Political

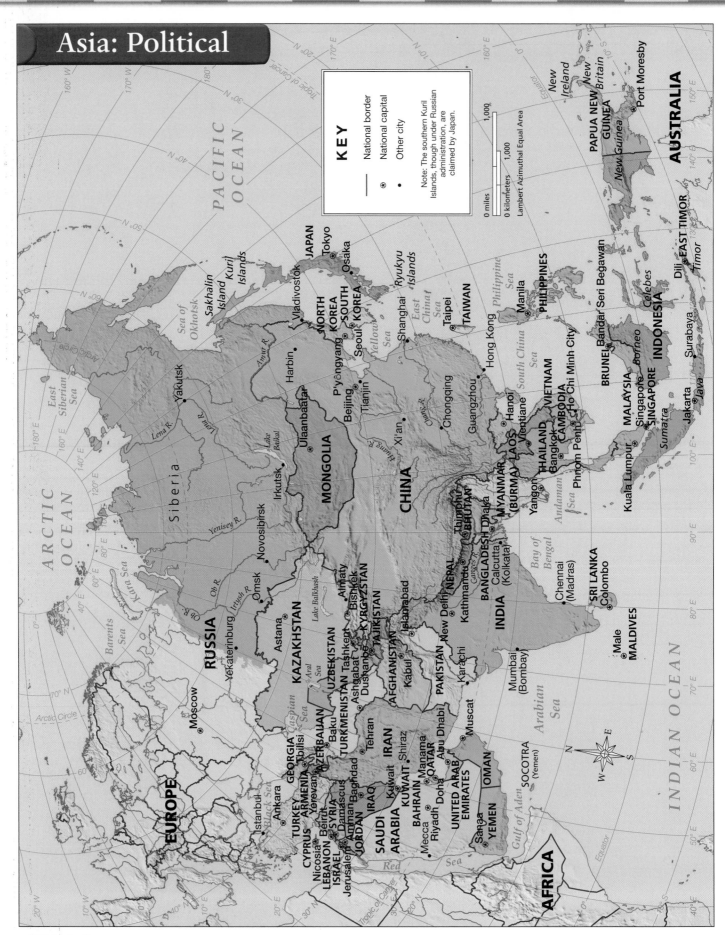

KEY

— National border
⊛ National capital
• Other city

Note: The southern Kuril Islands, though under Russian administration, are claimed by Japan.

0 miles   1,000
0 kilometers   1,000
Lambert Azimuthal Equal Area

ARCTIC OCEAN

PACIFIC OCEAN

EUROPE

AFRICA

AUSTRALIA

RUSSIA

Siberia

Sea of Okhotsk

Sakhalin Island
Kuril Islands

East Siberian Sea

Moscow ⊛

Yekaterinburg •

Yakutsk •

Vladivostok •

JAPAN
Tokyo ⊛
Osaka •

Barents Sea

Kara Sea

Ob R.
Irtysh R.

Lena R.

Amur R.

NORTH KOREA
P'yongyang ⊛
SOUTH KOREA
Seoul ⊛

Ryukyu Islands

Omsk •

Novosibirsk •

Irkutsk •

Lake Baikal

Harbin •

MONGOLIA
Ulaanbaatar ⊛

Beijing ⊛
Tianjin •

Shanghai •

East China Sea

Yellow Sea

Astana ⊛

KAZAKHSTAN

Aral Sea

Lake Balkhash

CHINA

Xi'an •

Huang R.

Chang R.

Chongqing •

Guangzhou •

Hong Kong •

TAIWAN
Taipei ⊛

Philippine Sea

Caspian Sea

GEORGIA
Tbilisi ⊛
ARMENIA
Yerevan ⊛
AZERBAIJAN
Baku ⊛

TURKMENISTAN
Ashgabat ⊛

UZBEKISTAN
Tashkent ⊛

Almaty •

KYRGYZSTAN
Bishkek ⊛

TAJIKISTAN
Dushanbe ⊛

AFGHANISTAN
Kabul ⊛

Islamabad ⊛

NEPAL
Kathmandu ⊛

New Delhi ⊛

BHUTAN
Thimphu ⊛

BANGLADESH
Dhaka ⊛

Ganges R.

MYANMAR (BURMA)
Yangon ⊛

LAOS
Vientiane ⊛

Hanoi ⊛
VIETNAM

THAILAND
Bangkok ⊛

CAMBODIA
Phnom Penh ⊛

Ho Chi Minh City •

South China Sea

PHILIPPINES
Manila ⊛

BRUNEI
Bandar Seri Begawan ⊛

MALAYSIA
Kuala Lumpur ⊛

SINGAPORE
Singapore ⊛

Borneo

Celebes

INDONESIA
Jakarta ⊛

Sumatra

Java

Surabaya •

EAST TIMOR
Dili ⊛
Timor

PAPUA NEW GUINEA
Port Moresby ⊛

New Britain
New Ireland

TURKEY
Ankara ⊛
Istanbul •

CYPRUS
Nicosia ⊛

LEBANON
Beirut ⊛
ISRAEL
Jerusalem ⊛
Amman ⊛
JORDAN

SYRIA
Damascus ⊛

IRAQ
Baghdad ⊛

IRAN
Tehran ⊛
Shiraz •

Kuwait ⊛
KUWAIT

BAHRAIN
Manama ⊛
QATAR
Doha ⊛

SAUDI ARABIA
Riyadh ⊛
Mecca •

UNITED ARAB EMIRATES
Abu Dhabi ⊛

OMAN
Muscat ⊛

YEMEN
Sanaa ⊛

SOCOTRA (Yemen)

Gulf of Aden

Red Sea

Arabian Sea

PAKISTAN
Karachi •

INDIA
Mumbai (Bombay) •

Calcutta (Kolkata) •

Chennai (Madras) •

Bay of Bengal

Andaman Sea

SRI LANKA
Colombo ⊛

Male ⊛
MALDIVES

INDIAN OCEAN

Black Sea

Arctic Circle

Tropic of Cancer

Equator

Asia: Physical

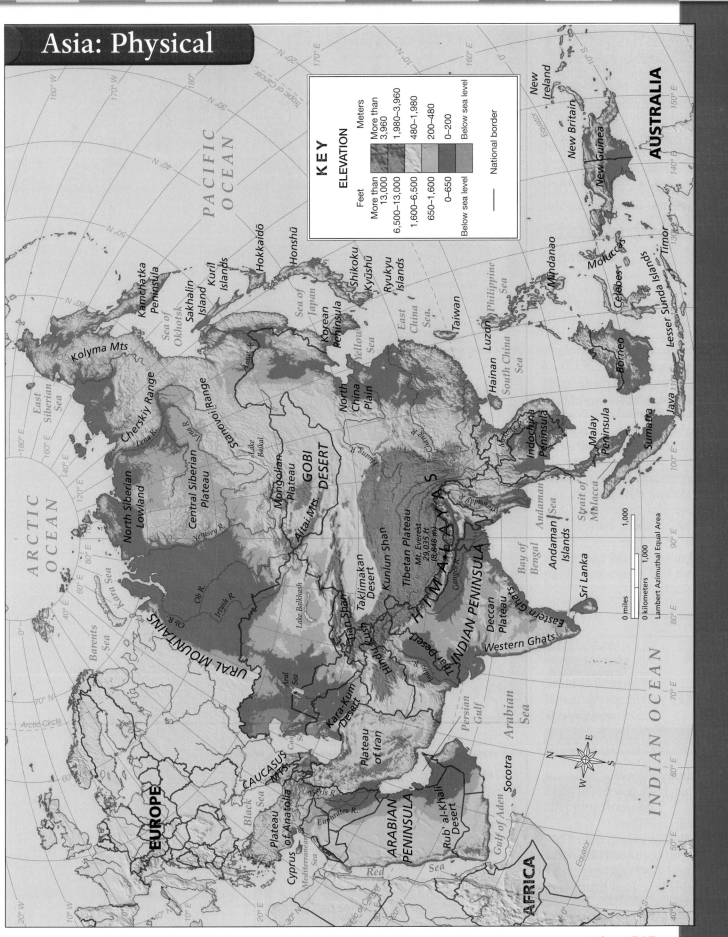

KEY

ELEVATION

Feet	Meters
More than 13,000	More than 3,960
6,500–13,000	1,980–3,960
1,600–6,500	480–1,980
650–1,600	200–480
0–650	0–200
Below sea level	Below sea level

——— National border

ARCTIC OCEAN

PACIFIC OCEAN

INDIAN OCEAN

EUROPE

AFRICA

AUSTRALIA

East Siberian Sea
Barents Sea
Kara Sea
Laptev Sea
Sea of Okhotsk
Sea of Japan
Yellow Sea
East China Sea
Philippine Sea
South China Sea
Andaman Sea
Bay of Bengal
Arabian Sea
Persian Gulf
Red Sea
Gulf of Aden
Black Sea
Mediterranean Sea
Caspian Sea
Aral Sea

Kolyma Mts
Kamchatka Peninsula
Cherskiy Range
Stanovoy Range
Sakhalin Island
Kuril Islands
Hokkaidō
Honshū
Shikoku
Kyūshū
Ryukyu Islands
Korean Peninsula
Taiwan
Hainan
Luzon
Mindanao
Moluccas
Celebes
Borneo
New Ireland
New Britain
New Guinea
Timor
Lesser Sunda Islands
Java
Sumatra
Malay Peninsula
Indochina Peninsula
Sri Lanka
Andaman Islands
Socotra

North Siberian Lowland
Central Siberian Plateau
Mongolian Plateau
GOBI DESERT
Altai Mts
Lake Baikal
Kunlun Shan
Taklimakan Desert
Tibetan Plateau
Tian Shan
HIMALAYAS
Mt. Everest 29,035 ft (8,848 m)
Hindu Kush
Deccan Plateau
Eastern Ghats
Western Ghats
INDIAN PENINSULA
Thar Desert
Kara-Kum Desert
Plateau of Iran
Lake Balkhash
CAUCASUS Mts
Plateau of Anatolia
Cyprus
URAL MOUNTAINS
ARABIAN PENINSULA
Rub' al-Khali Desert

North China Plain

Lena R.
Amur R.
Yenisey R.
Ob R.
Irtysh R.
Huang R.
Chang R.
Mekong R.
Irrawaddy R.
Ganges R.
Indus R.
Euphrates R.
Tigris R.

Strait of Malacca

Tropic of Cancer
Arctic Circle
Equator

N E S W

0 miles 1,000
0 kilometers 1,000
Lambert Azimuthal Equal Area

Oceania

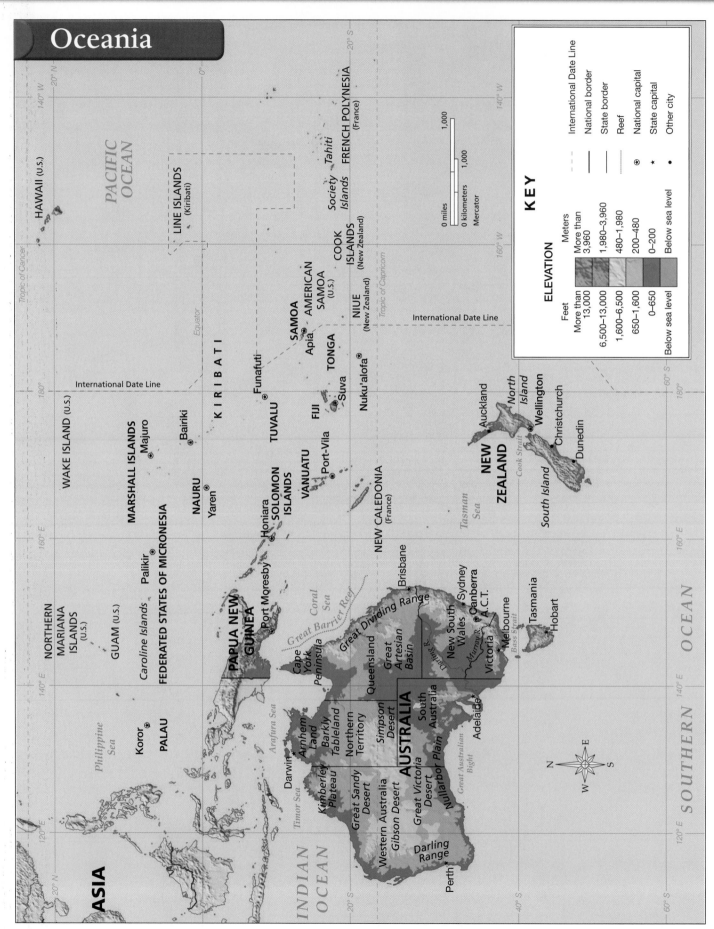

ASIA

INDIAN OCEAN

Philippine Sea

PACIFIC OCEAN

HAWAII (U.S.)

Tropic of Cancer

LINE ISLANDS (Kiribati)

WAKE ISLAND (U.S.)

NORTHERN MARIANA ISLANDS (U.S.)

GUAM (U.S.)

Koror ⊛
PALAU

Caroline Islands   Palikir ⊛
FEDERATED STATES OF MICRONESIA

MARSHALL ISLANDS
Majuro ⊛

NAURU ⊛
Yaren

Equator

K I R I B A T I

Bairiki ⊛

Funafuti ⊛
TUVALU

FRENCH POLYNESIA (France)

Tahiti
Society Islands

COOK ISLANDS (New Zealand)

SAMOA
Apia ⊛

AMERICAN SAMOA (U.S.)

NIUE (New Zealand)

TONGA
Nuku'alofa ⊛

Tropic of Capricorn

International Date Line

International Date Line

Suva ⊛
FIJI

VANUATU
Port-Vila ⊛

SOLOMON ISLANDS
Honiara ⊛

NEW CALEDONIA (France)

Tasman Sea

NEW ZEALAND

Auckland ●
North Island
Wellington ⊛
Christchurch ●
South Island
Dunedin ●

Cook Strait

PAPUA NEW GUINEA
Port Moresby ★

Coral Sea

Great Barrier Reef

Brisbane ●

Cape York Peninsula

Great Dividing Range

Queensland

Darwin ★
Arnhem Land
Barkly Tableland
Northern Territory

Kimberley Plateau

Simpson Desert

Great Artesian Basin

New South Wales
Sydney ●
Canberra ⊛
A.C.T.

Murray R.
Darling R.

Victoria
Melbourne ★

Tasmania
Hobart ★
Bass Strait

AUSTRALIA

South Australia
Adelaide ★

Great Sandy Desert
Gibson Desert
Western Australia
Great Victoria Desert
Great Australian Bight
Nullarbor Plain

Darling Range
Perth ★

Timor Sea

Arafura Sea

SOUTHERN OCEAN

N
W E
S

KEY

ELEVATION

Feet	Meters
More than 13,000	More than 3,960
6,500–13,000	1,980–3,960
1,600–6,500	480–1,980
650–1,600	200–480
0–650	0–200
Below sea level	Below sea level

- - - - International Date Line
——— National border
——— State border
········· Reef
⊛ National capital
★ State capital
● Other city

0 miles   1,000
0 kilometers   1,000
Mercator

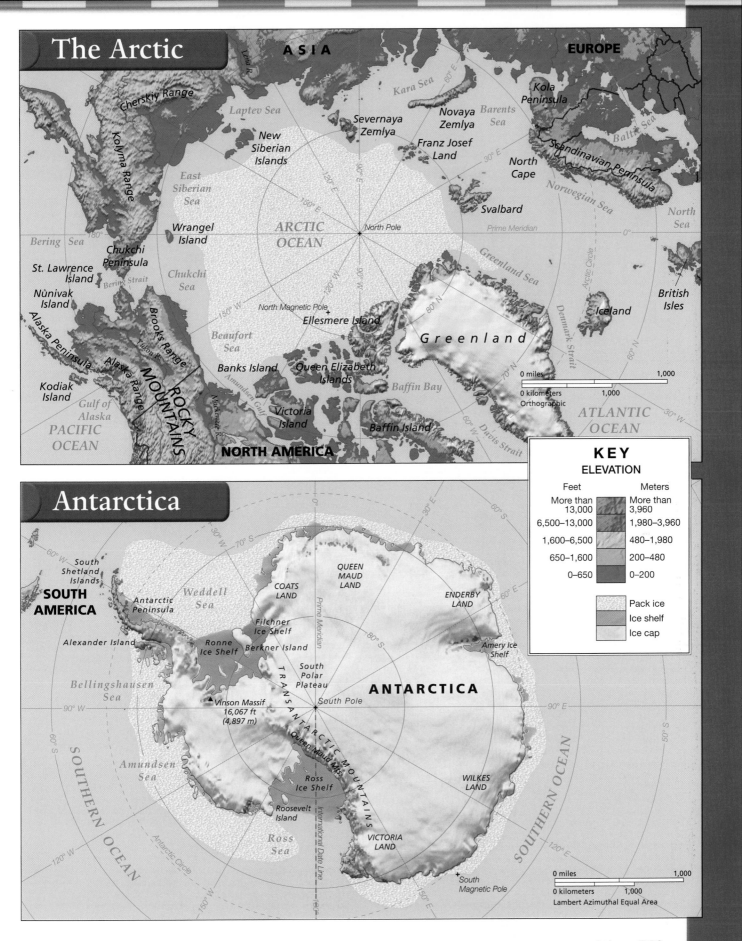

The Arctic

ASIA   EUROPE

Cherskiy Range
Kolyma Range
Laptev Sea
Lena R.
Kara Sea
60° E
Novaya Zemlya
Kola Peninsula
Barents Sea
Baltic Sea
New Siberian Islands
Severnaya Zemlya
Franz Josef Land
30° E
North Cape
Scandinavian Peninsula
East Siberian Sea
ARCTIC OCEAN
90° E
North Pole
Svalbard
Norwegian Sea
Prime Meridian
0°
North Sea
Wrangel Island
Chukchi Sea
120° W
150° E
Greenland Sea
Arctic Circle
Iceland
British Isles
Bering Sea
180°
Chukchi Peninsula
Bering Strait
North Magnetic Pole
Ellesmere Island
150° W
80° N
Denmark Strait
60° N
St. Lawrence Island
Nunivak Island
Beaufort Sea
G r e e n l a n d
70° N
Alaska Peninsula
Brooks Range
Yukon R.
Banks Island
Queen Elizabeth Islands
Baffin Bay
0 miles 1,000
0 kilometers 1,000
Orthographic
Kodiak Island
Gulf of Alaska
Alaska Range
ROCKY MOUNTAINS
Amundsen Gulf
Mackenzie R.
Victoria Island
Baffin Island
Davis Strait
30° W
ATLANTIC OCEAN
PACIFIC OCEAN
NORTH AMERICA

Antarctica

South Shetland Islands
60° W
SOUTH AMERICA
Antarctic Peninsula
Alexander Island
Weddell Sea
30° W
70° S
COATS LAND
QUEEN MAUD LAND
Prime Meridian
0°
ENDERBY LAND
60° E
Filchner Ice Shelf
Ronne Ice Shelf
Berkner Island
Amery Ice Shelf
Bellingshausen Sea
90° W
Vinson Massif 16,067 ft (4,897 m)
South Polar Plateau
TRANSANTARCTIC MOUNTAINS
ANTARCTICA
South Pole
90° E
Amundsen Sea
60° S
Queen Maud Mts.
Ross Ice Shelf
WILKES LAND
SOUTHERN OCEAN
50° S
Roosevelt Island
International Date Line
VICTORIA LAND
Ross Sea
120° W
SOUTHERN OCEAN
Antarctic Circle
150° W
South Magnetic Pole
0 miles 1,000
0 kilometers 1,000
Lambert Azimuthal Equal Area
120° E
150° E

KEY
ELEVATION

Feet	Meters
More than 13,000	More than 3,960
6,500–13,000	1,980–3,960
1,600–6,500	480–1,980
650–1,600	200–480
0–650	0–200

Pack ice
Ice shelf
Ice cap

Africa

Algeria
Capital: Algiers
Population: 32.3 million
Official Languages: Arabic and Tamazight
Land Area: 2,381,740 sq km; 919,590 sq mi
Leading Exports: petroleum, natural gas, petroleum products
Continent: Africa

Angola
Capital: Luanda
Population: 10.6 million
Official Language: Portuguese
Land Area: 1,246,700 sq km; 481,551 sq mi
Leading Exports: crude oil, diamonds, refined petroleum products, gas, coffee, sisal, fish and fish products, timber, cotton
Continent: Africa

Benin
Capital: Porto-Novo
Population: 6.9 million
Official Language: French
Land Area: 110,620 sq km; 42,710 sq mi
Leading Exports: cotton, crude oil, palm products, cocoa
Continent: Africa

Botswana
Capital: Gaborone
Population: 1.6 million
Official Language: English
Land Area: 585,370 sq km; 226,011 sq mi
Leading Exports: diamonds, copper, nickel, soda ash, meat, textiles
Continent: Africa

Burkina Faso
Capital: Ouagadougou
Population: 12.6 million
Official Language: French
Land Area: 273,800 sq km; 105,714 sq mi
Leading Exports: cotton, animal products, gold
Continent: Africa

Burundi
Capital: Bujumbura
Population: 6.4 million
Official Languages: Kirundi and French
Land Area: 25,650 sq km; 9,903 sq mi
Leading Exports: coffee, tea, sugar, cotton, hides
Continent: Africa

Cameroon
Capital: Yaoundé
Population: 16.1 million
Official Languages: English and French
Land Area: 469,440 sq km; 181,251 sqmi
Leading Exports: crude oil and petroleum products, lumber, cocoa, aluminum, coffee, cotton
Continent: Africa

Cape Verde
Capital: Praia
Population: 408,760
Official Language: Portuguese
Land Area: 4,033 sq km; 1,557 mi
Leading Exports: fuel, shoes, garments, fish, hides
Location: Atlantic Ocean

Central African Republic
Capital: Bangui
Population: 3.6 million
Official Language: French
Land Area: 622,984 sq km; 240,534 sq mi
Leading Exports: diamonds, timber, cotton, coffee, tobacco
Continent: Africa

Chad
Capital: N'Djamena
Population: 9 million
Official Languages: Arabic and French
Land Area: 1,259,200 sq km; 486,177 sq mi
Leading Exports: cotton, cattle, gum arabic
Continent: Africa

Comoros
Capital: Moroni
Population: 614,382
Official Languages: Arabic, Comoran, and French
Land Area: 2,170 sq km; 838 sq mi
Leading Exports: vanilla, ylang-ylang, cloves, perfume oil, copra
Location: Indian Ocean

Congo, Democratic Republic of the
Capital: Kinshasa
Population: 55.2 million
Official Language: French
Land Area: 2,267,600 sq km; 875,520 sq mi
Leading Exports: diamonds, copper, coffee, cobalt, crude oil
Continent: Africa

Congo, Republic of the
Capital: Brazzaville
Population: 3.3 million
Official Language: French
Land Area: 341,500 sq km; 131,853 sq mi
Leading Exports: petroleum, lumber, sugar, cocoa, coffee, diamonds
Continent: Africa

Djibouti
Capital: Djibouti
Population: 472,810
Official Languages: Arabic and French
Land Area: 22,980 sq km; 8,873 sq mi
Leading Exports: reexports, hides and skins, coffee (in transit)
Continent: Africa

Egypt
Capital: Cairo
Population: 70.7 million
Official Language: Arabic
Land Area: 995,450 sq km; 384,343 sq mi
Leading Exports: crude oil and petroleum products, cotton, textiles, metal products, chemicals
Continent: Africa

Equatorial Guinea
Capital: Malabo
Population: 498,144
Official Languages: Spanish and French
Land Area: 28,050 sq km; 10,830 sq mi
Leading Exports: petroleum, timber, cocoa
Continent: Africa

Eritrea
Capital: Asmara
Population: 4.5 million
Official Language: Tigrinya
Land Area: 121,320 sq km; 46,842 sq mi
Leading Exports: livestock, sorghum, textiles, food, small manufactured goods
Continent: Africa

Ethiopia
Capital: Addis Ababa
Population: 67.7 million
Official Language: Amharic
Land Area: 1,119,683 sq km; 432,310 sq mi
Leading Exports: coffee, qat, gold, leather products, oilseeds
Continent: Africa

Gabon
Capital: Libreville
Population: 1.2 million
Official Language: French
Land Area: 257,667 sq km; 99,489 sq mi
Leading Exports: crude oil, timber, manganese, uranium
Continent: Africa

Gambia
Capital: Banjul
Population: 1.5 million
Official Language: English
Land Area: 10,000 sq km; 3,861 sq mi
Leading Exports: peanuts and peanut products, fish, cotton lint, palm kernels
Continent: Africa

Ghana
Capital: Accra
Population: 20.2 million
Official Language: English
Land Area: 230,940 sq km; 89,166 sq mi
Leading Exports: gold, cocoa, timber, tuna, bauxite, aluminum, manganese ore, diamonds
Continent: Africa

Guinea
Capital: Conakry
Population: 7.8 million
Official Language: French
Land Area: 245,857 sq km; 94,925 sq mi
Leading Exports: bauxite, alumina, gold, diamonds, coffee, fish, agricultural products
Continent: Africa

Guinea-Bissau
Capital: Bissau
Population: 1.4 million
Official Language: Portuguese
Land Area: 28,000 sq km; 10,811 sq mi
Leading Exports: cashew nuts, shrimp, peanuts, palm kernels, lumber
Continent: Africa

Ivory Coast
Capital: Yamoussoukro
Population: 16.8 million
Official Language: French
Land Area: 318,000 sq km; 122,780 sq mi
Leading Exports: cocoa, coffee, timber, petroleum, cotton, bananas, pineapples, palm oil, cotton, fish
Continent: Africa

Kenya
Capital: Nairobi
Population: 31.3 million
Official Languages: Swahili and English
Land Area: 569,250 sq km; 219,787 sq mi
Leading Exports: tea, horticultural products, coffee, petroleum products, fish, cement
Continent: Africa

Lesotho
Capital: Maseru
Population: 2.2 million
Official Languages: Sesotho and English
Land Area: 30,355 sq km; 11,720 sq mi
Leading Exports: manufactured goods (clothing, footwear, road vehicles), wool and mohair, food and live animals
Continent: Africa

Liberia
Capital: Monrovia
Population: 3.3 million
Official Language: English
Land Area: 96,320 sq km; 37,189 sq mi
Leading Exports: rubber, timber, iron, diamonds, cocoa, coffee
Continent: Africa

Libya
Capital: Tripoli
Population: 5.4 million
Official Language: Arabic
Land Area: 1,759,540 sq km; 679,358 sq mi
Leading Exports: crude oil, refined petroleum products
Location: Indian

Madagascar
Capital: Antananarivo
Population: 16.5 million
Official Languages: French and Malagasy
Land Area: 581,540 sq km; 224,533 sq mi
Leading Exports: coffee, vanilla, shellfish, sugar, cotton cloth, chromite, petroleum products
Location: Indian Ocean

Malawi
Capital: Lilongwe
Population: 10.7 million
Official Languages: English and Chichewa
Land Area: 94,080 sq km; 36,324 sq mi
Leading Exports: tobacco, tea, sugar, cotton, coffee, peanuts, wood products, apparel
Continent: Africa

Mali
Capital: Bamako
Population: 11.3 million
Official Language: French
Land Area: 1,220,000 sq km; 471,042 sq mi
Leading Exports: cotton, gold, livestock
Continent: Africa

Mauritania
Capital: Nouakchott
Population: 2.8 million
Official Language: Arabic
Land Area: 1,030,400 sq km; 397,837 sq mi
Leading Exports: iron ore, fish and fish products, gold
Continent: Africa

Mauritius
Capital: Port Louis
Population: 1.2 million
Official Language: English
Land Area: 2,030 sq km; 784 sq mi
Leading Exports: clothing and textiles, sugar, cut flowers, molasses
Location: Indian Ocean

Morocco
Capital: Rabat
Population: 31.2 million
Official Language: Arabic
Land Area: 446,300 sq km; 172,316 sq mi
Leading Exports: phosphates and fertilizers, food and beverages, minerals
Continent: Africa

Mozambique
Capital: Maputo
Population: 19.6 million
Official Language: Portuguese
Land Area: 784,090 sq km; 302,737 sq mi
Leading Exports: prawns, cashews, cotton, sugar, citrus, timber, bulk electricity
Continent: Africa

Namibia
Capital: Windhoek
Population: 1.8 million
Official Language: English
Land Area: 825,418 sq km; 318,694 sq mi
Leading Exports: diamonds, copper, gold, zinc, lead, uranium, cattle, processed fish, karakul skins
Continent: Africa

Niger
Capital: Niamey
Population: 11.3 million
Official Language: French
Land Area: 1,226,700 sq km; 489,073 sq mi
Leading Exports: uranium ore, livestock products, cowpeas, onions
Continent: Africa

Nigeria
Capital: Abuja
Population: 129.9 million
Official Language: English
Land Area: 910,768 sq km; 351,648 sq mi
Leading Exports: petroleum and petroleum products, cocoa, rubber
Continent: Africa

Rwanda
Capital: Kigali
Population: 7.4 million
Official Languages: Kinyarwanda, French, and English
Land Area: 24,948 sq km; 9,632 sq mi
Leading Exports: coffee, tea, hides, tin ore
Continent: Africa

São Tomé and Príncipe
Capital: São Tomé
Population: 170,372
Official Language: Portuguese
Land Area: 1,001 sq km; 386 sq mi
Leading Exports: cocoa, copra, coffee, palm oil
Location: Atlantic Ocean

Senegal
Capital: Dakar
Population: 10.6 million
Official Language: French
Land Area: 192,000 sq km; 74,131 sq mi
Leading Exports: fish, groundnuts (peanuts), petroleum products, phosphates, cotton
Continent: Africa

Seychelles
Capital: Victoria
Population: 80,098
Official Languages: English and French
Land Area: 455 sq km; 176 sq mi
Leading Exports: canned tuna, cinnamon bark, copra, petroleum products (reexports)
Location: Indian Ocean

Sierra Leone
Capital: Freetown
Population: 5.6 million
Official Language: English
Land Area: 71,620 sq km; 27,652 sq mi
Leading Exports: diamonds, rutile, cocoa, coffee, fish
Continent: Africa

Somalia
Capital: Mogadishu
Population: 7.8 million
Official Languages: Somali and Arabic
Land Area: 627,337 sq km; 242,215 sq mi
Leading Exports: livestock, bananas, hides, fish, charcoal, scrap metal
Continent: Africa

South Africa
Capital: Cape Town, Pretoria, and Bloemfontein
Population: 43.6 million
Official Languages: Eleven official languages: Afrikaans, English, Ndebele, Pedi, Sotho, Swazi, Tsonga, Tswana, Venda, Xhosa, and Zulu
Land Area: 1,219,912 sq km; 471,008 sq mi
Leading Exports: gold, diamonds, platinum, other metals and minerals, machinery and equipment
Continent: Africa

Sudan
Capital: Khartoum
Population: 37.1 million
Official Language: Arabic
Land Area: 2,376,000 sq km; 917,374 sq mi
Leading Exports: oil and petroleum products, cotton, sesame, livestock, groundnuts, gum arabic, sugar
Continent: Africa

Swaziland
Capital: Mbabane
Population: 1.1 million
Official Languages: English and siSwati
Land Area: 17,20 sq km; 6,642 sq mi
Leading Exports: soft drink concentrates, sugar, wood pulp, cotton yarn, refrigerators, citrus and canned fruit
Continent: Africa

Tanzania
Capital: Dar es Salaam and Dodoma
Population: 37.2 million
Official Languages: Swahili and English
Land Area: 886,037 sq km; 342,099 sq mi
Leading Exports: gold, coffee, cashew nuts, manufactured goods, cotton
Continent: Africa

Togo
Capital: Lomé
Population: 5.2 million
Official Language: French
Land Area: 54,385 sq km; 20,998 sq mi
Leading Exports: cotton, phosphates, coffee, cocoa
Continent: Africa

Tunisia
Capital: Tunis
Population: 9.8 million
Official Language: Arabic
Land Area: 155,360 sq km; 59,984 sq mi
Leading Exports: textiles, mechanical goods, phosphates and chemicals, agricultural products, hydrocarbons
Continent: Africa

Uganda
Capital: Kampala
Population: 24.7 million
Official Language: English
Land Area: 199,710 sq km; 77,108 sq mi
Leading Exports: coffee, fish and fish products, tea, gold, cotton, flowers, horticultural products
Continent: Africa

Zambia
Capital: Lusaka
Population: 10.1 million
Official Language: English
Land Area: 740,724 sq km; 285,994 sq mi
Leading Exports: copper, cobalt, electricity, tobacco, flowers, cotton
Continent: Africa

Zimbabwe
Capital: Harare
Population: 11.3 million
Official Language: English
Land Area: 386,670 sq km; 149,293 sq mi
Leading Exports: tobacco, gold, iron alloys, textiles and clothing
Continent: Africa

Asia and the Pacific

Afghanistan
Capital: Kabul
Population: 27.8 million
Official Languages: Pashtu and Dari
Land Area: 647,500 sq km; 250,000 sq mi
Leading Exports: agricultural products, hand-woven carpets, wool, cotton, hides and pelts, precious and semiprecious gems
Continent: Asia

Armenia
Capital: Yerevan
Population: 3.3 million
Official Language: Armenian
Land Area: 29,400 sq km; 10,965 sq mi
Leading Exports: diamonds, scrap metal, machinery and equipment, brandy, copper ore
Continent: Asia

Australia
Capital: Canberra
Population: 19.6 million
Official Language: English
Land Area: 7,617,930 sq km; 2,941,283 sq mi
Leading Exports: coal, gold, meat, wool, alumina, iron ore, wheat, machinery and transport equipment
Continent: Australia

Azerbaijan
Capital: Baku
Population: 7.8 million
Official Language: Azerbaijani
Land Area: 86,100 sq km; 33,243 sq mi
Leading Exports: oil and gas, machinery, cotton, foodstuffs
Continent: Asia

Bahrain
Capital: Manama
Population: 656,397
Official Language: Arabic
Land Area: 665 sq km; 257 sq mi
Leading Exports: petroleum and petroleum products, aluminum, textiles
Continent: Asia

Bangladesh
Capital: Dhaka
Population: 133.4 million
Official Language: Bengali
Land Area: 133,910 sq km; 51,705 sq mi
Leading Exports: garments, jute and jute goods, leather, frozen fish and seafood
Continent: Asia

Bhutan
Capital: Thimphu
Population: 2.1 million
Official Language: Dzongkha
Land Area: 47,000 sq km; 18,147 sq mi
Leading Exports: electricity, cardamom, gypsum, timber, handicrafts, cement, fruit, precious stones, spices
Continent: Asia

Brunei
Capital: Bandar Seri Begawan
Population: 350,898
Official Language: Malay
Land Area: 5,270 sq km; 2,035 sq mi
Leading Exports: crude oil, natural gas, refined products
Continent: Asia

Cambodia
Capital: Phnom Penh
Population: 12.8 million
Official Language: Khmer
Land Area: 176,520 sq km; 68,154 sq mi
Leading Exports: timber, garments, rubber, rice, fish
Continent: Asia

China
Capital: Beijing
Population: 1.29 billion
Official Languages: Mandarin and Chinese
Land Area: 9,326,410 sq km; 3,600,927 sq mi
Leading Exports: machinery and equipment, textiles and clothing, footwear, toys and sports goods, mineral fuels
Continent: Asia

Cyprus
Capital: Nicosia
Population: 767,314
Official Languages: Greek and Turkish
Land Area: 9,240 sq km; 3,568 sq mi
Leading Exports: citrus, potatoes, grapes, wine, cement, clothing and shoes
Location: Mediterranean Sea

East Timor
Capital: Dili
Population: 952,618
Official Languages: Tetum and Portuguese
Land Area: 15,007 sq km; 5,794 sq mi
Leading Exports: coffee, sandalwood, marble
Continent: Asia

Fiji
Capital: Suva
Population: 856,346
Official Language: English
Land Area: 18,270 sq km; 7,054 sq mi
Leading Exports: sugar, garments, gold, timber, fish, molasses, cocnut oil
Location: Pacific Ocean

Georgia
Capital: Tbilisi
Population: 5 million
Official Languages: Georgian and Abkhazian
Land Area: 69,700 sq km; 26,911 sq mi
Leading Exports: scrap metal, machinery, chemicals, fuel reexports, citrus fruits, tea, wine, other agricultural products
Continent: Asia

India
Capital: New Delhi
Population: 1.05 billion
Official Languages: Hindi and English
Land Area: 2,973,190 sq km; 1,147,949 sq mi
Leading Exports: textile goods, gems and jewelry, engineering goods, chemicals, leather manufactured goods
Continent: Asia

Indonesia
Capital: Jakarta
Population: 231.3 million
Official Language: Bahasa Indonesia
Land Area: 1,826,440 sq km; 705,188 sq mi
Leading Exports: oil and gas, electrical appliances, plywood, textiles, rubber
Continent: Asia

Iran
Capital: Tehran
Population: 66.6 million
Official Language: Farsi
Land Area: 1,636,000 sq km; 631,660 sq mi
Leading Exports: petroleum, carpets, fruits and nuts, iron and steel, chemicals
Continent: Asia

Iraq
Capital: Baghdad
Population: 24.7 million
Official Language: Arabic
Land Area: 432,162 sq km; 166,858 sq mi
Leading Exports: crude oil
Continent: Asia

Israel
Capital: Jerusalem
Population: 6.0 million
Official Languages: Hebrew, Arabic
Land Area: 20,330 sq km; 7,849 sq mi
Leading Exports: machinery and equipment, software, cut diamonds, agricultural products, chemicals, textiles and apparel
Continent: Asia

Japan
Capital: Tokyo
Population: 127 million
Official Language: Japanese
Land Area: 374,744 sq km; 144,689 sq mi
Leading Exports: motor vehicles, semiconductors, office machinery, chemicals
Continent: Asia

Jordan
Capital: Amman
Population: 5.3 million
Official Language: Arabic
Land Area: 91,971 sq km; 35,510 sq mi
Leading Exports: phosphates, fertilizers, potash, agricultural products, manufactured goods, pharmaceuticals
Continent: Asia

Kazakhstan
Capital: Astana
Population: 16.7 million
Official Language: Kazakh
Land Area: 2,669,800 sq km; 1,030,810 sq mi
Leading Exports: oil and oil products, ferrous metals, machinery, chemicals, grain, wool, meat, coal
Continent: Asia

Kiribati
Capital: Bairiki (Tarawa Atoll)
Population: 96,335
Official Language: English
Land Area: 811 sq km; 313 sq mi
Leading Exports: copra, coconuts, seaweed, fish
Location: Pacific Ocean

Korea, North
Capital: Pyongyang
Population: 22.3 million
Official Language: Korean
Land Area: 120,410 sq km; 46,490 sq mi
Leading Exports: minerals, metallurgical products, manufactured goods (including armaments), agricultural and fishery products
Continent: Asia

Korea, South
Capital: Seoul
Population: 48.3 million
Official Language: Korean
Land Area: 98,190 sq km; 37,911 sq mi
Leading Exports: electronic products, machinery and equipment, motor vehicles, steel, ships, textiles, clothing, footwear, fish
Continent: Asia

Kuwait
Capital: Kuwait City
Population: 2.1 million
Official Language: Arabic
Land Area: 17,820 sq km; 6,880 sq mi
Leading Exports: oil and refined products, fertilizers
Continent: Asia

Kyrgyzstan
Capital: Bishkek
Population: 4.8 million
Official Languages: Kyrgyz and Russian
Land Area: 191,300 sq km; 73,861sq mi
Leading Exports: cotton, wool, meat, tobacco, gold, mercury, uranium, hydropower, machinery, shoes
Continent: Asia

Laos
Capital: Vientiane
Population: 5.8 million
Official Language: Lao
Land Area: 230,800 sq km; 89,112 sq mi
Leading Exports: wood products, garments, electricity, coffee, tin
Continent: Asia

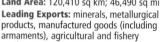

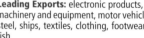

Lebanon
Capital: Beirut
Population: 3.7 million
Official Language: Arabic
Land Area: 10,230 sq km; 3,950 sq mi
Leading Exports: foodstuffs and tobacco, textile, chemicals, precious stones, metal and metal products, electrical equipment and products, jewelry, paper and paper products
Continent: Asia

Malaysia
Capital: Kuala Lumpur and Putrajaya
Population: 22.7 million
Official Language: Bahasa Malaysia
Land Area: 328,550 sq km; 126,853 sq mi
Leading Exports: electronic equipment, petroleum and liquefied natural gas, wood and wood products, palm oil, rubber, textiles, chemicals
Continent: Asia

Maldives
Capital: Malé
Population: 320,165
Official Language: Dhivehi (Maldivian)
Land Area: 300 sq km; 116 sq mi
Leading Exports: fish, clothing
Location: Indian Ocean

Marshall Islands
Capital: Majuro
Population: 73,360
Official Languages: Marshallese and English
Land Area: 181.3 sq km; 70 sq mi
Leading Exports: copra cake, coconut oil, handicrafts
Location: Pacific Ocean

Micronesia, Federated States of
Capital: Palikir (Pohnpei Island)
Population: 135,869
Official Language: English
Land Area: 702 sq km; 271 sq mi
Leading Exports: fish, garments, bananas, black pepper
Location: Pacific Ocean

Mongolia
Capital: Ulaanbaatar
Population: 2.6 million
Official Language: Khalkha Mongolian
Land Area: 1,555,400 sq km; 600,540 sq mi
Leading Exports: copper, livestock, animal products, cashmere, wool, hides, fluorspar, other nonferrous metals
Continent: Asia

Myanmar (Burma)
Capital: Rangoon (Yangon)
Population: 42.2 million
Official Language: Burmese (Myanmar)
Land Area: 657,740 sq km; 253,953 sq mi
Leading Exports: apparel, foodstuffs, wood products, precious stones
Continent: Asia

Nauru
Capital: Yaren District
Population: 12,329
Official Language: Nauruan
Land Area: 21 sq km; 8 sq mi
Leading Exports: phosphates
Location: Pacific Ocean

Nepal
Capital: Kathmandu
Population: 25.9 million
Official Language: Nepali
Land Area: 136,800 sq km; 52,818 sq mi
Leading Exports: carpets, clothing, leather goods, jute goods, grain
Continent: Asia

New Zealand
Capital: Wellington
Population: 3.8 million
Official Languages: English and Maori
Land Area: 268,680 sq km; 103,737 sq mi
Leading Exports: dairy products, meat, wood and wood products, fish, machinery
Location: Pacific Ocean

Oman
Capital: Muscat
Population: 2.7 million
Official Language: Arabic
Land Area: 212,460 sq km; 82,030 sq mi
Leading Exports: petroleum, reexports, fish, metals, textiles
Continent: Asia

Pakistan
Capital: Islamabad
Population: 147.7 million
Official Languages: Urdu and English
Land Area: 778,720 sq km; 300,664 sq mi
Leading Exports: textiles (garments, cotton cloth, and yarn), rice, other agricultural products
Continent: Asia

Palau
Capital: Koror
Population: 19,409
Official Languages: English and Palauan
Land Area: 458 sq km; 177 sq mi
Leading Exports: shellfish, tuna, copra, garments
Location: Pacific Ocean

Papua New Guinea
Capital: Port Moresby
Population: 5.2 million
Official Language: English
Land Area: 452,860 sq km; 174,849 sq mi
Leading Exports: oil, gold, copper ore, logs, palm oil, coffee, cocoa, crayfish, prawns
Location: Pacific Ocean

Philippines
Capital: Manila
Population: 84.5 million
Official Languages: Filipino and English
Land Area: 298,170 sq km; 115,123 sq mi
Leading Exports: electronic equipment, machinery and transport equipment, garments, coconut products
Continent: Asia

Qatar
Capital: Doha
Population: 793,341
Official Language: Arabic
Land Area: 11,437 sq km; 4,416 sq mi
Leading Exports: petroleum products, fertilizers, steel
Continent: Asia

Samoa
Capital: Apia
Population: 178,631
Official Languages: Samoan and English
Land Area: 2,934 sq km; 1,133 sq mi
Leading Exports: fish, coconut oil cream, copra, taro, garments, beer
Location: Pacific Ocean

Saudi Arabia
Capital: Riyadh and Jiddah
Population: 23.5 million
Official Language: Arabic
Land Area: 1,960,582 sq km; 756,981 sq mi
Leading Exports: petroleum and petroleum products
Continent: Asia

Singapore
Capital: Singapore
Population: 4.5 million
Official Languages: Malay, English, Mandarin, Chinese, and Tamil
Land Area: 683 sq km; 264 sq mi
Leading Exports: machinery and equipment (including electronics), consumer goods, chemicals, mineral fuels
Continent: Asia

Solomon Islands
Capital: Honiara
Population: 494,786
Official Language: English
Land Area: 27,540 sq km; 10,633 sq mi
Leading Exports: timber, fish, copra, palm oil, cocoa
Location: Pacific Ocean

Sri Lanka
Capital: Colombo
Population: 19.6 million
Official Language: Sinhala, Tamil, and English
Land Area: 64,740 sq km; 24,996 sq mi
Leading Exports: textiles and apparel, tea, diamonds, coconut products, petroleum products
Continent: Asia

Syria
Capital: Damascus
Population: 17.2 million
Official Language: Arabic
Land Area: 184,050 sq km; 71,062 sq mi
Leading Exports: crude oil, textiles, fruits and vegetables, raw cotton
Continent: Asia

Taiwan
Capital: Taipei
Population: 22.5 million
Official Language: Mandarin Chinese
Land Area: 32,260 sq km; 12,456 sq mi
Leading Exports: machinery and electrical equipment, metals, textiles, plastics, chemicals
Continent: Asia

Tajikistan
Capital: Dushanbe
Population: 6.7 million
Official Language: Tajik
Land Area: 142,700 sq km; 55,096 sq mi
Leading Exports: aluminum, electricity, cotton, fruits, vegetables, oil, textiles
Continent: Asia

Thailand
Capital: Bangkok
Population: 62.5 million
Official Language: Thai
Land Area: 511,770 sq km; 197,564 sq mi
Leading Exports: computers, transistors, seafood, clothing, rice
Continent: Asia

Tonga
Capital: Nuku'alofa
Population: 106,137
Official Languages: Tongan and English
Land Area: 718 sq km; 277 sq mi
Leading Exports: squash, fish, vanilla beans, root crops
Location: Pacific Ocean

Turkey
Capital: Ankara
Population: 67.3 million
Official Language: Turkish
Land Area: 770,760 sq km; 297,590 sq mi
Leading Exports: apparel, foodstuffs, textiles, metal manufactured goods, transport equipment
Continent: Asia

Turkmenistan
Capital: Ashgabat
Population: 4.7 million
Official Language: Turkmen
Land Area: 488,100 sq km; 188,455 sq mi
Leading Exports: gas, oil, cotton fiber, textiles
Continent: Asia

Asia and the Pacific (continued)

Tuvalu
Capital: Fongafale
Population: 10,800
Official Language: English
Land Area: 26 sq km; 10 sq mi
Leading Exports: copra, fish
Location: Pacific Ocean

United Arab Emirates
Capital: Abu Dhabi
Population: 2.4 million
Official Language: Arabic
Land Area: 82,880 sq km; 32,000 sq mi
Leading Exports: crude oil, natural gas, reexports, dried fish, dates
Continent: Asia

Uzbekistan
Capital: Tashkent
Population: 25.5 million
Official Language: Uzbek
Land Area: 425,400 sq km; 164,247 sq mi
Leading Exports: cotton, gold, energy products, mineral fertilizers, ferrous metals, textiles, food products, automobiles
Continent: Asia

Vanuatu
Capital: Port-Vila
Population: 196,178
Official Languages: English, French, and Bislama
Land Area: 12,200 sq km; 4,710 sq mi
Leading Exports: copra, kava, beef, cocoa, timber, coffee
Location: Pacific Ocean

Vietnam
Capital: Hanoi
Population: 81.1 million
Official Language: Vietnamese
Land Area: 325,320 sq km; 125,621 sq mi
Leading Exports: crude oil, marine products, rice, coffee, rubber, tea, garments, shoes
Continent: Asia

Yemen
Capital: Sanaa
Population: 18.7 million
Official Language: Arabic
Land Area: 527,970 sq km; 203,849 sq mi
Leading Exports: crude oil, coffee, dried and salted fish
Continent: Asia

Europe and Russia

Albania
Capital: Tiranë
Population: 3.5 million
Official Language: Albanian
Land Area: 27,398 sq km; 10,578 sq mi
Leading Exports: textiles and footwear, asphalt, metals and metallic ores, crude oil, vegetables, fruits, tobacco
Continent: Europe

Andorra
Capital: Andorra la Vella
Population: 68,403
Official Language: Catalan
Land Area: 468 sq km; 181 sq mi
Leading Exports: tobacco products, furniture
Continent: Europe

Austria
Capital: Vienna
Population: 8.2 million
Official Language: German
Land Area: 82,738 sq km; 31,945 sq mi
Leading Exports: machinery and equipment, motor vehicles and parts, paper and paperboard, metal goods, chemicals, iron and steel, textiles, foodstuffs
Continent: Europe

Belarus
Capital: Minsk
Population: 10.3 million
Official Languages: Belarussian and Russian
Land Area: 207,600 sq km; 80,154 sq mi
Leading Exports: machinery and equipment, mineral products, chemicals, textiles, food stuffs, metals
Continent: Europe

Belgium
Capital: Brussels
Population: 10.3 million
Official Languages: Dutch and French
Land Area: 30,230 sq km; 11,172 sq mi
Leading Exports: machinery and equipment, chemicals, metals and metal products
Continent: Europe

Bosnia and Herzegovina
Capital: Sarajevo
Population: 4.0 million
Official Language: Serbo-Croat
Land Area: 51,129 sq km; 19,741 sq mi
Leading Exports: miscellaneous manufactured goods, crude materials
Continent: Europe

Bulgaria
Capital: Sofía
Population: 7.6 million
Official Language: Bulgarian
Land Area: 110,550 sq km; 42,683 sq mi
Leading Exports: clothing, footwear, iron and steel, machinery and equipment, fuels
Continent: Europe

Croatia
Capital: Zagreb
Population: 4.4 million
Official Language: Croatian
Land Area: 56,414 km; 21,781 sq mi
Leading Exports: transport equipment, textiles, chemicals, foodstuffs, fuels
Continent: Europe

Czech Republic
Capital: Prague
Population: 10.3 million
Official Language: Czech
Land Area: 78,276 sq km; 29,836 sq mi
Leading Exports: machinery and transport equipment, intermediate manufactured goods, chemicals, raw materials and fuel
Continent: Europe

Denmark
Capital: Copenhagen
Population: 5.4 million
Official Language: Danish
Land Area: 42,394 sq km; 16,368 sq mi
Leading Exports: machinery and instruments, meat and meat products, dairy products, fish, chemicals, furniture, ships, windmills
Continent: Europe

Estonia
Capital: Tallinn
Population: 1.4 million
Official Language: Estonian
Land Area: 43,211 sq km; 16,684 sq mi
Leading Exports: machinery and equipment, wood products, textiles, food products, metals, chemical products
Continent: Europe

Finland
Capital: Helsinki
Population: 5.2 million
Official Languages: Finnish and Swedish
Land Area: 305,470 sq km; 117,942 sq mi
Leading Exports: machinery and equipment, chemicals, metals, timber, paper, pulp
Continent: Europe

France
Capital: Paris
Population: 59.8 million
Official Language: French
Land Area: 545,630 sq km; 310,668 sq mi
Leading Exports: machinery and transportation equipment, aircraft, plastics, chemicals, pharmaceutical products, iron and steel, beverages
Continent: Europe

Germany
Capital: Berlin
Population: 83 million
Official Language: German
Land Area: 349,223 sq km; 134,835 sq mi
Leading Exports: machinery, vehicles, chemicals, metals and manufactured goods, foodstuffs, textiles
Continent: Europe

Greece
Capital: Athens
Population: 10.6 million
Official Language: Greek
Land Area: 130,800 sq km; 50,502 sq mi
Leading Exports: food and beverages, manufactured goods, petroleum products, chemicals, textiles
Continent: Europe

Holy See (Vatican City)
Capital: Vatican City
Population: 900
Official Languages: Latin and Italian
Land Area: 0.44 sq km; 0.17 sq mi
Leading Exports: no information available
Continent: Europe

Hungary

Capital: Budapest
Population: 10.1 million
Official Language: Hungarian
Land Area: 92,340 sq km; 35,652 sq mi
Leading Exports: machinery and equipment, other manufactured goods, food products, raw materials, fuels and electricity
Continent: Europe

Iceland

Capital: Reykjavík
Population: 279,384
Official Language: Icelandic
Land Area: 100,250 sq km; 38,707 sq mi
Leading Exports: fish and fish products, animal products, aluminum, diatomite, ferrosilicon
Location: Atlantic Ocean

Ireland

Capital: Dublin
Population: 3.9 million
Official Languages: Irish Gaelic and English
Land Area: 68,890 sq km; 26,598 sq mi
Leading Exports: machinery and equipment, computers, chemicals, pharmaceuticals, live animals, animal products
Continent: Europe

Italy

Capital: Rome
Population: 57.7 million
Official Language: Italian
Land Area: 294,020 sq km; 113,521 sq mi
Leading Exports: fruits, vegetables, grapes, potatoes, sugar beets, soybeans, grain, olives, beef, diary products, fish
Continent: Europe

Latvia

Capital: Riga
Population: 2.4 million
Official Language: Latvian
Land Area: 63,589 sq km; 24,552 sq mi
Leading Exports: wood and wood products, machinery and equipment, metals, textiles, foodstuffs
Continent: Europe

Liechtenstein

Capital: Vaduz
Population: 32,842
Official Language: German
Land Area: 160 sq km; 62 sq mi
Leading Exports: small specialty machinery, dental products, stamps, hardware, pottery
Continent: Europe

Lithuania

Capital: Vilnius
Population: 3.6 million
Official Language: Lithuanian
Land Area: 65,200 sq km; 25,174 sq mi
Leading Exports: mineral products, textiles and clothing, machinery and equipment, chemicals, wood and wood products, foodstuffs
Continent: Europe

Luxembourg

Capital: Luxembourg
Population: 448,569
Official Languages: Luxembourgish, French, and German
Land Area: 2,586 sq km; 998 sq mi
Leading Exports: machinery and equipment, steel products, chemicals, rubber products, glass
Continent: Europe

Macedonia, The Former Yugoslav Republic of

Capital: Skopje
Population: 2.1 million
Official Languages: Macedonian and Albanian
Land Area: 24,856 sq km; 9,597 sq mi
Leading Exports: food, beverages, tobacco, miscellaneous manufactured goods, iron and steel
Continent: Europe

Malta

Capital: Valletta
Population: 397,499
Official Languages: Maltese and English
Land Area: 316 sq km; 122 sq mi
Leading Exports: machinery and transport equipment, manufactured goods
Location: Mediterranean Sea

Moldova

Capital: Chişinău
Population: 4.4 million
Official Language: Moldovan
Land Area: 33,371 sq km; 12,885 sq mi
Leading Exports: foodstuffs, textiles and footwear, machinery
Continent: Europe

Monaco

Capital: Monaco
Population: 31,987
Official Language: French
Land Area: 1.95 sq km; 0.75 sq mi
Leading Exports: no information available
Continent: Europe

Netherlands

Capital: Amsterdam and The Hague
Population: 16.1 million
Official Language: Dutch
Land Area: 33,883 sq km; 13,082 sq mi
Leading Exports: machinery and equipment, chemicals, fuels, foodstuffs
Continent: Europe

Norway

Capital: Oslo
Population: 4.5 million
Official Language: Norwegian
Land Area: 307,860 sq km; 118,865 sq mi
Leading Exports: petroleum and petroleum products, machinery and equipment, metals, chemicals, ships, fish
Continent: Europe

Poland

Capital: Warsaw
Population: 38.6 million
Official Language: Polish
Land Area: 304,465 sq km; 117,554 sq mi
Leading Exports: machinery and transport equipment, intermediate manufactured goods, miscellaneous manufactured goods, food and live animals
Continent: Europe

Portugal

Capital: Lisbon
Population: 10.1 million
Official Language: Portuguese
Land Area: 91,951 sq km; 35,502 sq mi
Leading Exports: clothing and footwear, machinery, chemicals, cork and paper products, hides
Continent: Europe

Romania

Capital: Bucharest
Population: 22.3 million
Official Language: Romanian
Land Area: 230,340 sq km; 88,934 sq mi
Leading Exports: textiles and footwear, metals and metal products, machinery and equipment, minerals and fuels
Continent: Europe

Russia

Capital: Moscow
Population: 145 million
Official Language: Russian
Land Area: 16,995,800 sq km; 6,592,100 sq mi
Leading Exports: petroleum and petroleum products, natural gas, wood and wood products, metals, chemicals, and a wide variety of civilian and military manufactured goods
Continents: Europe and Asia

San Marino

Capital: San Marino
Population: 27,730
Official Language: Italian
Land Area: 61 sq km; 24 sq mi
Leading Exports: building stone, lime, wood, chestnuts, wheat, wine, baked goods, hides, ceramics
Continent: Europe

Serbia and Montenegro

Capital: Belgrade
Population: 10.7 million
Official Language: Serbo-Croat
Land Area: 102,136 sq km; 39,435 sq mi
Leading Exports: manufactured goods, food and live animals, raw materials
Continent: Europe

Slovakia

Capital: Bratislava
Population: 5.4 million
Official Language: Slovak
Land Area: 48,800 sq km; 18,842 sq mi
Leading Exports: machinery and transport equipment, intermediate manufactured goods, miscellaneous manufactured goods, chemicals
Continent: Europe

Slovenia

Capital: Ljubljana
Population: 1.9 million
Official Language: Slovene
Land Area: 20,151 sq km; 7,780 sq mi
Leading Exports: manufactured goods, machinery and transport equipment, chemicals, food
Continent: Europe

Spain

Capital: Madrid
Population: 40.1 million
Official Languages: Spanish, Galician, Basque, and Catalan
Land Area: 499,542 sq km; 192,873 sq mi
Leading Exports: machinery, motor vehicles, foodstuffs, other consumer goods
Continent: Europe

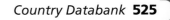

Europe and Russia (continued)

Sweden
Capital: Stockholm
Population: 8.9 million
Official Language: Swedish
Land Area: 410,934 sq km; 158,662 sq mi
Leading Exports: machinery, motor vehicles, paper products, pulp and wood, iron and steel products, chemicals
Continent: Europe

Switzerland
Capital: Bern
Population: 7.3 million
Official Languages: German, French, and Italian
Land Area: 39,770 sq km; 15,355 sq mi
Leading Exports: machinery, chemicals, metals, watches, agricultural products
Continent: Europe

Ukraine
Capital: Kiev
Population: 48.4 million
Official Language: Ukrainian
Land Area: 603,700 sq km; 233,090 sq mi
Leading Exports: ferrous and nonferrous metals, fuel and petroleum products, machinery and transport equipment, food products
Continent: Europe

United Kingdom
Capital: London
Population: 59.8 million
Official Languages: English and Welsh
Land Area: 241,590 sq km; 93,278 sq mi
Leading Exports: manufactured goods, fuels, chemicals, food, beverages, tobacco
Continent: Europe

Latin America

Antigua and Barbuda
Capital: Saint John's
Population: 67,448
Official Language: English
Land Area: 442 sq km; 171 sq mi
Leading Exports: petroleum products, manufactured goods, machinery and transport equipment, food and live animals
Location: Caribbean Sea

Argentina
Capital: Buenos Aires
Population: 37.8 million
Official Language: Spanish
Land Area: 2,736,690 sq km; 1,056,636 sq mi
Leading Exports: edible oils, fuels and energy, cereals, feed, motor vehicles
Continent: South America

Bahamas
Capital: Nassau
Population: 300,529
Official Language: English
Land Area: 10,070 sq km; 3,888 sq mi
Leading Exports: fish and crawfish, rum, salt, chemicals, fruit and vegetables
Location: Caribbean Sea

Barbados
Capital: Bridgetown
Population: 276,607
Official Language: English
Land Area: 431 sq km; 166 sq mi
Leading Exports: sugar and molasses, rum, other foods and beverages, chemicals, electrical components, clothing
Location: Caribbean Sea

Belize
Capital: Belmopan
Population: 262,999
Official Language: English
Land Area: 22,806 sq km; 8,805 sq mi
Leading Exports: sugar, bananas, citrus, clothing, fish products, molasses, wood
Continent: North America

Bolivia
Capital: La Paz and Sucre
Population: 8.5 million
Official Language: Spanish, Quechua, and Aymara
Land Area: 1,084,390 sq km; 418,683 sq mi
Leading Exports: soybeans, natural gas, zinc, gold, wood
Continent: South America

Brazil
Capital: Brasília
Population: 176 million
Official Language: Portuguese
Land Area: 8,456,510 sq km; 3,265,059 sq mi
Leading Exports: manufactured goods, iron ore, soybeans, footwear, coffee, autos
Continent: South America

Chile
Capital: Santiago
Population: 15.5 million
Official Language: Spanish
Land Area: 748,800 sq km; 289,112 sq mi
Leading Exports: copper, fish, fruits, paper and pulp, chemicals
Continent: South America

Colombia
Capital: Bogotá
Population: 41 million
Official Language: Spanish
Land Area: 1,038,700 sq km; 401,042 sq mi
Leading Exports: petroleum, coffee, coal, apparel, bananas, cut flowers
Continent: South America

Costa Rica
Capital: San José
Population: 3.8 million
Official Language: Spanish
Land Area: 51,660 sq km; 19,560 sq mi
Leading Exports: coffee, bananas, sugar, pineapples, textiles, electronic components, medical equipment
Continent: North America

Cuba
Capital: Havana
Population: 11.2 million
Official Language: Spanish
Land Area: 110,860 sq km; 42,803 sq mi
Leading Exports: sugar, nickel, tobacco, fish, medical products, citrus, coffee
Location: Caribbean Sea

Dominica
Capital: Roseau
Population: 73,000
Official Language: English
Land Area: 754 sq km; 291 sq mi
Leading Exports: bananas, soap, bay oil, vegetables, grapefruit, oranges
Location: Caribbean Sea

Dominican Republic
Capital: Santo Domingo
Population: 8.7 million
Official Language: Spanish
Land Area: 48,380 sq km; 18,679 sq mi
Leading Exports: ferronickel, sugar, gold, silver, coffee, cocoa, tobacco, meats, consumer goods
Location: Caribbean Sea

Ecuador
Capital: Quito
Population: 13.5 million
Official Language: Spanish
Land Area: 276,840 sq km; 106,888 sq mi
Leading Exports: petroleum, bananas, shrimp, coffee, cocoa, cut flowers, fish
Continent: South America

El Salvador
Capital: San Salvador
Population: 6.4 million
Official Language: Spanish
Land Area: 20,720 sq km; 8,000 sq mi
Leading Exports: offshore assembly exports, coffee, sugar, shrimp, textiles, chemicals, electricity
Continent: North America

Grenada
Capital: Saint George's
Population: 89,211
Official Language: English
Land Area: 344 sq km; 133 sq mi
Leading Exports: bananas, cocoa, nutmeg, fruit and vegetables, clothing, mace
Location: Caribbean Sea

Guatemala
Capital: Guatemala City
Population: 13.3 million
Official Language: Spanish
Land Area: 108,430 sq km; 41,865 sq mi
Leading Exports: coffee, sugar, bananas, fruits and vegetables, cardamom, meat, apparel, petroleum, electricity
Continent: North America

Guyana
Capital: Georgetown
Population: 698,209
Official Language: English
Land Area: 196,850 sq km; 76,004 sq mi
Leading Exports: sugar, gold, bauxite/alumina, rice, shrimp, molasses, rum, timber
Continent: South America

Haiti
Capital: Port-au-Prince
Population: 7.1 million
Official Language: French and French Creole
Land Area: 27,560 sq km; 10,641 sq mi
Leading Exports: manufactured goods, coffee, oils, cocoa
Location: Caribbean Sea

Honduras
Capital: Tegucigalpa
Population: 6.6 million
Official Language: Spanish
Land Area: 111,890 sq km; 43,201 sq mi
Leading Exports: coffee, bananas, shrimp, lobster, meat, zinc, lumber
Continent: North America

Jamaica

Capital: Kingston
Population: 2.7 million
Official Language: English
Land Area: 10,831 sq km; 4,182 sq mi
Leading Exports: alumina, bauxite, sugar, bananas, rum
Location: Caribbean Sea

Mexico

Capital: Mexico City
Population: 103.4 million
Official Language: Spanish
Land Area: 1,923,040 sq km; 742,486 sq mi
Leading Exports: manufactured goods, oil and oil products, silver, fruits, vegetables, coffee, cotton
Continent: North America

Nicaragua

Capital: Managua
Population: 5 million
Official Language: Spanish
Land Area: 120,254 sq km; 46,430 sq mi
Leading Exports: coffee, shrimp and lobster, cotton, tobacco, beef, sugar, bananas, gold
Continent: North America

Panama

Capital: Panama City
Population: 2.9 million
Official Language: Spanish
Land Area: 75,990 sq km; 29,340 sq mi
Leading Exports: bananas, shrimp, sugar, coffee, clothing
Continent: North America

Paraguay

Capital: Asunción
Population: 5.9 million
Official Language: Spanish
Land Area: 397,300 sq km; 153,398 sq mi
Leading Exports: electricity, soybeans, feed, cotton, meat, edible oils
Continent: South America

Peru

Capital: Lima
Population: 28 million
Official Languages: Spanish and Quechua
Land Area: 1,280,000 sq km; 494,208 sq mi
Leading Exports: fish and fish products, gold, copper, zinc, crude petroleum and byproducts, lead, coffee, sugar, cotton
Continent: South America

Saint Kitts and Nevis

Capital: Basseterre
Population: 38,736
Official Language: English
Land Area: 261 sq km; 101 sq mi
Leading Exports: machinery, food, electronics, beverages, tobacco
Location: Caribbean Sea

Saint Lucia

Capital: Castries
Population: 160,145
Official Language: English
Land Area: 606 sq km; 234 sq mi
Leading Exports: bananas, clothing, cocoa, vegetables, fruits, coconut oil
Location: Caribbean Sea

Saint Vincent and the Grenadines

Capital: Kingstown
Population: 116,394
Official Language: English
Land Area: 389 sq km; 150 sq mi
Leading Exports: bananas, eddoes and dasheen, arrowroot starch, tennis racquets
Location: Caribbean Sea

Suriname

Capital: Paramaribo
Population: 436,494
Official Language: Dutch
Land Area: 161,470 sq km; 62,344 sq mi
Leading Exports: alumina, crude oil, lumber, shrimp and fish, rice, bananas
Continent: South America

Trinidad and Tobago

Capital: Port-of-Spain
Population: 1.2 million
Official Language: English
Land Area: 5,128 sq km; 1,980 sq mi
Leading Exports: petroleum and petroleum products, chemicals, steel products, fertilizer, sugar, cocoa, coffee, citrus, flowers
Location: Caribbean Sea

Uruguay

Capital: Montevideo
Population: 3.4 million
Official Language: Spanish
Land Area: 173,620 sq km; 67,100 sq mi
Leading Exports: meat, rice, leather products, wool, vehicles, dairy products
Continent: South America

Venezuela

Capital: Caracas
Population: 24.3 million
Official Language: Spanish
Land Area: 882,050 sq km; 340,560 sq mi
Leading Exports: petroleum, bauxite and aluminum, steel, chemicals, agricultural products, basic manufactured goods
Continent: South America

United States and Canada

Canada

Capital: Ottawa
Population: 31.9 million
Official Languages: English and French
Land Area: 9,220,970 sq km; 3,560,217 sq mi
Leading Exports: motor vehicles and parts, industrial machinery, aircraft, telecommunications equipment, chemicals, plastics, fertilizers, wood pulp, timber, crude petroleum, natural gas, electricity, aluminum
Continent: North America

United States

Capital: Washington, D.C.
Population: 281.4 million
Official Language: English
Land Area: 9,158,960 sq km; 3,536,274 sq mi
Leading Exports: capital goods, automobiles, industrial supplies and raw materials, consumer goods, agricultural products
Continent: North America

SOURCE: CIA World Factbook Online, 2002

Glossary of Geographic Terms

basin
an area that is lower than surrounding land areas; some basins are filled with water

bay
a body of water that is partly surrounded by land and that is connected to a larger body of water

butte
a small, high, flat-topped landform with cliff-like sides

▲ **butte**

canyon
a deep, narrow valley with steep sides; often with a stream flowing through it

cataract
a large waterfall or steep rapids

◀ **cataract**

delta
a plain at the mouth of a river, often triangular in shape, formed where sediment is deposited by flowing water

flood plain
a broad plain on either side of a river, formed where sediment settles during floods

glacier
a huge, slow-moving mass of snow and ice

hill
an area that rises above surrounding land and has a rounded top; lower and usually less steep than a mountain

island
an area of land completely surrounded by water

isthmus
a narrow strip of land that connects two larger areas of land

mesa
a high, flat-topped landform with cliff-like sides; larger than a butte

mountain
a landform that rises steeply at least 2,000 feet (610 meters) above surrounding land; usually wide at the bottom and rising to a narrow peak or ridge

▶ **glacier**

◄ delta

mountain pass
a gap between mountains

peninsula
an area of land almost completely surrounded by water but connected to the mainland

plain
a large area of flat or gently rolling land

plateau
a large, flat area that rises above the surrounding land; at least one side has a steep slope

river mouth
the point where a river enters a lake or sea

strait
a narrow stretch of water that connects two larger bodies of water

tributary
a river or stream that flows into a larger river

valley
a low stretch of land between mountains or hills; land that is drained by a river

volcano
an opening in Earth's surface through which molten rock, ashes, and gases escape from the interior

volcano ▶

Glossary of Geographic Terms **529**

Gazetteer

A

Acropolis (37°58' N, 23°43' E) a hill in Athens, Greece, on which many temples and archaeological sites are located, p. 186

Aegean Sea (39° N, 25° E) the sea that separates Greece and Turkey and contains many small islands, p. 170

Africa (10° N, 22° E) the world's second-largest continent, surrounded by the Mediterranean Sea, the Atlantic Ocean, and the Red Sea, p. 7

Aksum (14°8' N, 38°43' E) an ancient town in northern Ethiopia; a powerful kingdom and trade center about A.D. 200–600, p. 327

Alexandria (31°12' N, 29° 54' E) an ancient Hellenistic city in Egypt, p. 221

Andes Mountains (20° S, 67° W) a mountain system extending along the western coast of South America, p. 14

Anyang (36°6' N, 114°21' E) capital of the Shang dynasty in ancient China, p. 22

Arabian Peninsula (25° N, 45° E) a peninsula Southwest Asia on which the present-day nations of Saudi Arabia, Yemen, Oman, the United Arab Emirates, Qatar, Bahrain, and Kuwait are located, p. 100

Arctic Circle a line of latitude around Earth near the North Pole, p. 14

Argentina (34° S, 64° W) a country in South America, p. 336

Asia (50° N, 100° E) the world's largest continent, surrounded by the Arctic Ocean, the Pacific Ocean, the Indian Ocean, and Europe, p. 7

Asia Minor (39° N, 32° E) a peninsula in western Asia between the Black Sea and the Mediterranean Sea; within the site of present-day eastern Turkey, p. 40

Assyria (36° N, 43° E) a historical kingdom in northern Mesopotamia around present-day Iraq and Turkey, p. 38

Athens (37°58' N, 23°43' E) a city-state in ancient Greece; the capital city of present-day Greece, p. 175

Atlantic Ocean (5° S, 25° W) the second-largest of the world's oceans; extends from western Europe and Africa to eastern North and South America, p. 49

B

Babylonia (32° N, 44° E) an ancient region around southeastern Mesopotamia and between the Tigris and Euphrates Rivers; present-day Iraq, p. 35

Baghdad (33°30' N, 44°30' E) capital city of present-day Iraq; capital of the Muslim empire during Islam's golden age, p. 302

Bangladesh (24° N, 90° E) a coastal country in South Asia, officially the People's Republic of Bangladesh, p. 383

Bay of Bengal (15° N, 90° E) a part of the Indian Ocean between eastern India and Southeast Asia, p. 107

Belgium (51° N, 4° E) a country in western Europe, p. 437

Benin (6°19' N, 5°41' E) a kingdom in the West African rain forest; major cultural and trading center; may have borrowed traditions from Ile-Ife; located in present-day Nigeria, p. 322

Bethlehem (31°43' N, 35°12' E) the Judaean town where Jesus was said to have been born, p. 260

Bolivia (17° S, 65° W) a country in South America, p. 336

Bosporus (41°6' N, 29°4' E) a narrow strait that separates Europe and Asia and connects the Black Sea with the Sea of Marmara, p. 286

Brazil (10° S, 55° W) the largest country in South America, p. 467

Byzantium (41°1' N, 28°58' E) a city in the Roman Empire; the site of present-day Istanbul, Turkey, p. 275

C

Cahokia (38°34' N, 90°11' W) a village in what is now the state of Illinois; formerly a large, prehistoric city known for its Native American mounds, p. 355

Cairo (30°3' N, 31°15' E) the capital and largest city in Egypt, located on the Nile River, p. 75

Calicut (11°15' N, 75°46' E) city in India that was once a European trading center, p. 457

Canaan (32° N, 35° E) a region occupied by the ancient Israelites, later known as Palestine, located between the Syrian Desert and the Mediterranean Sea; on a site including present-day Israel and part of Jordan, p. 52

Cape of Good Hope (34°24' S, 18°30' E) the southern-most tip of Africa; named in 1488 by Bartholomeu Dias, a Portuguese sailor, p. 457

Caribbean Islands (xx° N, xx° W) islands that lie off the southwest coast of North America, p. 480

Carthage (36°52' N, 10°20' E) an ancient city on the northern coast of Africa that controlled much of the North African coast and other Mediterranean territories; now a suburb of the city of Tunis, p. 233

Ceuta (35°53' N, 5°19' W) a city in North Africa that is controlled by the Spanish, p. 456

Chang River the longest river in China and Asia and the third-longest river in the world (also called the Yzngzi River), p. 137

Chang'an (34°15' N, 108°52' E) a city in northern China; in ancient times the eastern end of the Silk Road; also called Xi'an, p. 365

Chile (30° S, 71° W) a country on the west coast of South America, p. 336

China (35° N, 105° E) a country occupying most of the mainland of East Asia, p. 22

Colosseum (41°54' N, 12°29' E) a large arena built in Rome around A.D. 70; site of contests and combats between people and animals, p. 244

Constantinople (41°1' N, 28°58' E) formerly the ancient city of Byzantium, renamed in A.D. 330 after the Roman emperor, Constantine, who made it the new capital of the Eastern Roman, or Byzantine, Empire; now Istanbul, Turkey, p. 275

Crete (35°15' N, 25° E) an island of Greece, southeast of the mainland, home to the ancient Minoan civilization, p. 170

Cuzco (13°31' S, 71°59' W) a city in Peru; the capital city of the ancient Incan empire, p. 338

D

Damascus (33°30' N, 36°18' E) the capital of and largest city in Syria, p. 262

Delhi (28°40' N, 77°13' E) the third-largest city in India, popularly known as Old Delhi, p. 382

Delphi (38°30' N, 22°29' E) an ancient town in central Greece, site of the oracle of Apollo, p. 183

Denmark (56° N, 10° E) a country in northern Europe; considered part of Scandinavia, p. 396

Djenné (13°54' N, 4°33' W) a city in Mali, Africa; was an important center of Muslim learning in the Kingdom of Mali in the 1300s, p. 320

E

East Africa an eastern region of the continent of Africa that is made up of the countries of Burundi, Kenya, Rwanda, Tanzania, Uganda, and Somalia, p. 12

Ecuador (2° S, 78° W) a country in northwest South America, p. 336

Egypt (27° N, 30° E) a country in North Africa, p. 9

England (53° N, 2° W) an island country in western Europe, p. 412

Ethiopia (9° N, 39° E) a country in East Africa, officially the People's Republic of Ethiopia, p. 69

Euphrates River a river that flows south from Turkey through Syria and Iraq, p. 22

Europe (50° N, 28° E) the world's second-smallest continent; a peninsula of the Eurasian landmass bounded by the Arctic Ocean, the Atlantic Ocean, the Mediterranean Sea, and Asia, p. 6

F

Fertile Crescent a region in Southwest Asia; site of the world's first civilizations, p. 32

Florence (43°46' N, 11°15' E) a city in the Tuscany region of central Italy, p. 433

France (46° N, 2° E) a country in western Europe, p. 233

G

Ganges River a river in northern India and Bangladesh that flows from the Himalayas to the Bay of Bengal, p. 108

Gaul (46° N, 2° E) a region inhabited by the ancient Gauls, including present-day France and parts of Belgium, Germany, and Italy, p. 233

Germany (51° N, 10° E) a country in central Europe, p. 416

Ghana (8° N, 1° W) a country in West Africa; officially known as the Republic of Ghana, p. 319

Giza (30°1' N, 31°13' E) an ancient city of Upper Egypt; site of the Sphinx and the Great Pyramid, p. 84

The Pyramids at Giza

Gobi Desert (43° N, 105° E) a desert in Mongolia and northern China, p. 364

Grand Canal the 1,085-mile (1,747 km) channel connecting the Huang and Yangzi rivers in China; the longest artificially made waterway in the world, p. 366

Great Plains (42° N, 100° W) a mostly flat and grassy region in western North America; home to the Plains Indians, p. 357

Great Wall of China (41° N, 117° E) a wall that extends about 1,400 miles across northern China; built in the third century B.C., p. 150

Great Zimbabwe (20°17' S, 30° 57' E) a former kingdom in the highlands of Southern Africa, located between the Zambezi and Limpopo rivers; founded in A.D. 1100 by the Shona people, p. 329

Greece (39° N, 22° E) a country in southeastern Europe; site of a great ancient civilization, p. 127

Greenland (70° N, 40° W) a large, self-governing island in the northern Atlantic Ocean; part of Denmark, p. 397

Gulf of Mexico (25° N, 90° W) an arm of the Atlantic Ocean in southeastern North America, bordering on eastern Mexico, the southeastern United States, and Cuba, p. 347

H

Harappa (30°38' N, 72°52' E) an ancient city of the Indus civilization; a village in present-day Pakistan, p. 108

Himalayas (the) (28° N, 84° E) a mountain system in south central Asia that extends along the border between India and Tibet and through Pakistan, Nepal, and Bhutan, p. 106

Hindu Kush (36° N, 72° E) a mountain range in central Asia, p. 107

Holy Land (32° N, 35° E) a small region at the eastern edge of the Mediterranean Sea, also known as Palestine, which includes parts of

modern Israel and Jordan; considered holy by Jews, Christians, and Muslims, p. 409

Huang River the second-longest river in China, beginning in Tibet and emptying into the Yellow Sea, p. 22

I

Iberian Peninsula (40° N, 5° W) the peninsula in Europe on which Spain and Portugal are located, p. 455

Ile-Ife (7°30' N, 4°30' E) the capital of a kingdom in the West African rain forest; major cultural and trading center; modern town of Ife is located on top of old city, p. 322

Incan Empire an empire ruled by the Incas that stretched along the Andes Mountains through present-day Ecuador, Peru, Bolivia, Chile, and Argentina; lasted from around the 1300s to the 1500s, p. 336

India (20° N, 77° E) a large country occupying most of the Indian subcontinent in South Asia, p. 17

Indian Ocean (10° S, 70° E) the world's third-largest ocean, lying between Africa, Asia, and Australia, p. 107

Indus River a river that rises in Tibet, crosses the Himalaya Mountains, and flows through India and Pakistan into the Arabian Sea; its valley was the home of India's earliest communities, p. 22

Iraq (33° N, 44° E) a country in Southwest Asia, p. 15

Isthmus of Panama (9° N, 80° W) a strip of land that connects the continents of North America and South America, p. 460

Israel (32° N, 35° E) an ancient kingdom of the Hebrews; a present-day country in Southwest Asia, p. 53

Italy (43° N, 13° E) a boot-shaped country in southern Europe, including the islands of Sicily and Sardinia, p. 229

J

Japan (36° N, 138° E) an island country in the Pacific Ocean off the east coast of Asia, p. 123

Jerusalem (31°46' N, 35°14' E) the capital city of modern Israel; a holy city for Jews, Christians, and Muslims, p. 53

Judah the name of the southern half of the Kingdom of the Israelites (the northern half retaining the name Israel), with Jerusalem as its capital; later called Judaea, p. 453

Judaea (31°35' N, 35° E) a Roman province centered on the ancient region of Judah, Roman Judaea including present-day Israel, Gaza, and the West Bank, p. 260

K

Kemet the term used by ancient Egyptians to describe their land, meaning "the black land," a reference to the dark soil left by the Nile River, p. 71

Kerma (19°38' N, 30°25' E) an ancient Nubian city; a market town in present-day Sudan, p. 97

Kilwa (9°18' S, 28°25' E) a medieval Islamic city-state on an island near present-day Tanzania, p. 326

Knossos (35°20' N, 25°10' E) an ancient city on the island of Crete, occupied by the Minoans, a Bronze-Age civilization, p. 170

Koreas the nations of the Democratic People's Republic of Korea (North Korea) (40° N, 127° E) and the Republic of Korea (South Korea) (37° N, 128° E), which occupy the Korean peninsula in East Asia, p. 123

Kyoto (35°5' N, 135°45' E) a city in west central Japan; was Japan's capital until the late 1800s, p. 376

L

Lake Nasser (22°40' N, 32° E) a lake located in southeast Egypt and northern Sudan, formed by the construction of the Aswan Dam on the Nile River, p. 72

Lake Texcoco (19°30' N, 99° W) a lake, now drained, in central Mexico, where Mexico City now stands; formerly the site of the ancient Aztec capital of Tenochtitlán, p. 344

Lower Egypt (31° N, 31° E) an area in ancient and present-day Egypt, in the northern Nile River region, p. 70

Lower Nubia an ancient region in northern Africa extending from the Nile Valley in Egypt to present-day Sudan; specifically, between the first and second Nile cataracts, p. 69

M

Macedonia (41° N, 23° E) an ancient kingdom on the Balkan Peninsula in southeastern Europe, the site of the present-day nation of Macedonia, northern Greece, and southwest Bulgaria, p. 79

Machu Picchu (13°7' S, 72°34' W) an ancient city in the Andes Mountains built during the Incan Empire; located near the present-day city of Cuzco in Peru, p. 336

Mali (17° N, 4° W) a country in West Africa, officially the Republic of Mali; powerful West African trading kingdom from about 1240 to 1500, p. 318

Marathon (38°10' N, 23°58' E) a village in ancient Greece, northeast of Athens, where the ancient Greeks defeated the Persians in 490 B.C., p. 210

Maurya Empire the Indian empire founded by Chandragupta; empire that began with his kingdom in northeastern India and spread to most of northern and central India, p. 126

Mecca (21°27' N, 39°49' E) a city in western Saudi Arabia; birthplace of the prophet Muhammad; the holiest Muslim city, p. 294

Medina (41°8' N, 81°52' W) a city in western Saudi Arabia; one of the two holiest cities of Islam (the other being Mecca), p. 295

Mediterranean Sea (35° N, 20° E) the large sea that separates Europe and Africa, p. 32

Memphis (29°51' N, 31°15' E) an ancient city in Lower Egypt; capital of many ancient Egyptian dynasties, p. 75

Meroë (16°56' N, 33°43' E) a city in ancient Nubia in present-day Sudan, p. 97

Mesopotamia (34° N, 44° E) an ancient region between the Tigris and Euphrates Rivers in Southwest Asia, p. 31

Mexico (23° N, 102° W) a country in North America, p. 344

Mohenjo-Daro (27°18' N, 68°15' E) an ancient city on the banks of the Indus River in southern Pakistan, p. 108

Moluccas (2° S, 128° E) islands currently part of Indonesia; once known as the Spice Islands, were prized by Europeans for spices such as cloves and nutmeg, p. 466

Mount Olympus (40°5' N, 22°21' E) Greece's highest mountain, site where ancient Greeks believed their gods dwelled, p. 182

Mycenae (37°44' N, 22°45' E) an ancient city on the mainland of Greece, home to one of Greece's earliest civilizations, p. 171

N

Nagasaki (32°48' N, 129°55' E) a city on the island of Kyushu, Japan, p. 474

Napata one of the three most powerful Nubian kingdoms, located between the third and fourth cataracts of the Nile River in Upper Nubia, p. 97

Netherlands (52° N, 6° E) a country in northwestern Europe; also known as Holland, p. 437

New Babylonian Empire a revival of the old Babylonian empire stretching from the Persian Gulf to the Mediterranean Sea, p. 42

Nile River (30°10' N, 31°6' E) the longest river in the world, flowing through northeastern Africa into the Mediterranean Sea, p. 9

North China Plain a large plain in East Asia, built up by soil deposits of the Huang River, p. 137

Norway (62° N, 10° E) country in northwestern Europe, occupying the western part of the Scandinavian peninsula, p. 396

Nubia (21° N, 33° E) a desert region and ancient kingdom in the Nile River Valley, on the site of present-day southern Egypt and northern Sudan, p. 69

O

Orléans (47°55' N, 1°54' E) a city in north-central France; a battle site during the Hundred Years' War where the French under the leadership of Joan of Arc defeated the English, p. 419

P

Pacific Ocean (10° S, 150° W) the largest of the world's oceans; extends from the western Americas to eastern Asia and Australia, p. 347

Pakistan (30° N, 70° E) a country in South Asia between India and Afghanistan; officially, the Islamic Republic of Pakistan, p. 22

Paris (48°52' N, 2° 20' E) the capital of France, p. 407

Parthenon (37°58' N, 23°43' E) the chief temple of the Greek goddess Athena, on the hill of the Acropolis in Athens, Greece, p. 181

Peloponnesus (37°30' N, 22° E) a large peninsula in southern Greece, p. 212

Persia (32° N, 53° E) a vast ancient empire in Southwest Asia; the historical name for the region in and around present-day Iran, p. 157

Persian Gulf (27° N, 51° E) an arm of the Arabian Sea, located between the Arabian Peninsula and southwest Iran, p. 32

Peru (10° S, 76° W) a country in northwestern South America, p. 14

Phoenicia (34° N, 36° E) an ancient region in present-day Lebanon, p. 49

Portugal (40° N, 8° W) a country in western Europe; occupies the Iberian Peninsula with Spain, p. 329

The Parthenon in Athens, Greece

R

Red Sea (20° N, 38° E) a narrow sea located between northeast Africa and the Arabian Peninsula; it is connected to the Mediterranean Sea in the north and the Arabian Sea in the south, p. 71

Rome (41°54' N, 12°29' E) the capital city of Italy; the capital of the ancient Roman Empire, p. 100

Runnymede (51°26' N, 0°34' W) a meadow along the Thames River in England, p. 418

Russia (40° N, 84° W) a country in northern Eurasia, p. 284

S

Sahara (26° N, 13° E) the largest tropical desert in the world, covering almost all of North Africa, p. 71

Silk Road an ancient trade route between China and Europe, p. 156

Sinai Peninsula (29°30' N, 34° E) a peninsula on the northern end of the Red Sea that links southwest Asia with northeast Africa, p. 52

Songhai (16°N, 0°) an ancient empire and trading state in West Africa that reached its peak in the 1400s, p. 321

South Africa (30° S, 26° E) the southernmost country in Africa, officially known as the Republic of South Africa, p. 310

Spain (40° N, 4° W) a country in western Europe; with Portugal, occupies the Iberian Peninsula, p. 233

Sparta (37°5' N, 22°27' E) an ancient city-state in Greece, p. 180

Sumer (31° N, 46° E) the site of the earliest-known civilization, located in Mesopotamia, in present-day southern Iraq; later became Babylonia, p. 30

Sweden (62° N, 15° E) a country in northern Europe, occupying the eastern half of the Scandinavian Peninsula, p. 396

Syria (35° N, 38° E) a country in Southwest Asia, p. 15

T

Taj Mahal (27°10' N, 78°3' E) a spectacular tomb near Agra, India, built by the Mughal emperor Shah Jahan in memory of his wife, Mumtaz Mahal, p. 386

Tanzania (6° S, 35° E) a coastal country in south-eastern Africa, p. 12

Tenochtitlán (19°29' N, 99°9' W) the capital city of the Aztec empire, located on islands in Lake Texcoco, now the site of Mexico City, p. 344

Thames River a river in southern England that flows to the North Sea, p. 418

Tiber River a major river in Italy that rises in the mountains of central Italy and empties into the Tyrrhenian Sea; flows through Rome, p. 228

Tibet (32° N, 88° E) a historical region in central Asia north of the Himalayas; currently under Chinese control, p. 123

Tigris River a river in Iraq and Turkey, p. 22

Tombouctou (16°46' N, 3°1' W) a city in Mali near the Niger River; in the past an important center of Islamic education and a trans-Saharan caravan stop (also spelled Timbuktu), p. 321

Troy (39°57' N, 26°15' E) an ancient city in north-western Anatolia, the Asian part of Turkey; the site of the mythical Trojan War, p. 171

Turkey (39° N, 35° E) a country located in South-west Asia, p. 40

Tyre (33°16' N, 35°11' E) a rich trade port and the major city of Phoenicia, located on the eastern

Mediterranean Sea in present-day southern Lebanon, p. 48

U

Upper Egypt (26° N, 32° E) an area in ancient and present-day Egypt in the Nile Valley, south of the river's delta and the 30th northern parallel, p. 70

Upper Nubia an ancient region in northeastern Africa that extended from the Nile Valley in Egypt to present-day Sudan; specifically, between the second and sixth cataracts, p. 69

Ur (30°57' N, 46°9' E) a city in ancient Sumer in southern Mesopotamia, located in present-day southeast Iraq, p. 22

V

Venice (45°27' N, 12°21' E) a city and major seaport in northern Italy known for its canals, p. 288

Vietnam (16° N, 108° E) a country located in Southeast Asia, p. 123

W

West Africa the countries in the western region of Africa, p. 310

Wittenberg (51°52' N, 12°39' E) the city in Germany where Martin Luther posted his 95 Theses, p. 442

Z

Zimbabwe (20° S, 30° E) a country in Southern Africa, p. 330

Biographical Dictionary

A

Abraham (AY bruh ham) the first leader of the Israelites, who, according to the Torah, led his family to Canaan, where he became the founder of a new nation, p. 51

Akbar (AK bahr) (1542–1605) the greatest of the Mughal emperors and reformers of India, p. 384

Akhenaton (ah keh NAH tun) (died c. 1354 B.C.) a king of ancient Egypt (c. 1372–1354 B.C.) who introduced monotheism; a ruler who lost much of Egypt's territory, p. 82

Alexander the Great (al ig ZAN dur thuh grayt) the king of Macedonia from 356 to 323 B.C.; conquerer of Persia and Egypt and invader of India, p. 79

Alexander the Great

Archimedes (ahr kuh MEE deez) (born 290 B.C.) a Greek inventor and mathematician; calculated the surface area and volume of a sphere, p. 222

Aristarchus (AIR uh STAHR kus) (lived c. 310–230 B.C.) a Greek astronomer who was the first to hold the theory that Earth moves around the sun, p. 222

Aristotle (AIR uh STAHT ul) (384–322 B.C.) a Greek philosopher who was a student of Plato and became a famous teacher; wrote about and taught logic, politics, science, and poetry; author of works that became the basis for medieval church scholarship, p. 216

Asoka (uh SOH kuh) (died c. 238 B.C.) Chandragupta's grandson and last major emperor of India's Maurya empire; credited with having built the greatest empire in India's history; helped spread Buddhism, p. 128

Augustus (aw GUS tus) (63 B.C.–A.D. 14) the first Roman emperor; ruled after Julius Caesar's death in 44 B.C. until his own death; named Octavian, he was awarded the title of Augustus in 27 B.C., p. 235

B

Babur (BAH bur) (1483–1530) a descendant of Genghis Khan and Timur; founder of the Mughal dynasty and emperor from 1526 to 1530, p. 384

Balboa, Vasco Núñez de (VAHS koh NOO nyeth theh bal BOH uh) (1475–1519) a Spanish explorer who discovered the Isthmus of Panama; also led an expedition that reached the Pacific Ocean, p. 460

C

Cabral, Pedro Alvarez (PAY droh AL vuh rez kuh BRAHL) (c. 1467–1520) Portuguese explorer; claimed Brazil for Portugal; later sailed to India, p. 467

Caligula (kuh LIG yuh luh) (A.D. 12–41) a Roman emperor (A.D. 37–41) believed to be insane for much of his rule; responsible for many disturbances during his reign, p. 242

Calvin, John (jahn KAL vin) (1509–1564) the founder of the Calvinist church; preached idea of predestination, p. 447

Champollion, Jean François (zhahn frahn SWAH shahm poh LY OHN) (A.D. 1790–1832) a French scholar; first to decode Egyptian hieroglyphics, p. 92

Chandragupta (chun druh GOOP tuh) (died 297 B.C.) founded India's Maurya empire in 321 B.C.; unified most of India under one ruler, p. 126

Charlemagne (SHAHR luh mayn) (742–814) king of the Franks who conquered much of Western Europe; patron of literature and learning, p. 396

Cicero (SIS uh roh) (106–43 B.C.) the greatest and best-known Roman orator and the author of many famous speeches; also famous as a philosopher and politician, p. 246

Columbus, Christopher (KRIS tuh fur kuh LUM bus) (1451–1506) an Italian navigator who discovered the Americas while looking for a sea route from Europe to Asia, p. 458

Commodus (KAHM uh dus) (A.D. 161–192) a Roman emperor who succeeded his father, Marcus Aurelius; a poor ruler who was assassinated and whose reign marked the beginning of the decline of the Roman Empire, p. 242

Confucius (kun FYOO shus) (551–479 B.C.) a Chinese philosopher and teacher; originator of Confucianism; greatly influenced Chinese life, p. 141

Constantine (KAHN stun teen) (c. A.D. 278–337) the emperor of Rome from A.D. 312 to 337; encouraged the spread of Christianity, p. 270

Cortés, Hernán (hur NAHN kohr TEZ) (1485–1547) a Spanish explorer who reached Mexico in 1519, conquered the Aztecs, and won Mexico for Spain, p. 482

Cyrus the Great (SY rus thuh grayt) (c. 590–529 B.C.) the founder of the Persian Empire in the mid-500s B.C., p. 42

D

da Gama, Vasco (VAHS koh duh GAM uh) (c. 1469–1524) a Portuguese navigator who was the first European to sail to India; his voyage opened the way for the expansion of the Portuguese empire, p. 457

da Vinci, Leonardo (lee uh NAHR doh duh VIN chee) (1452–1519) an Italian artist, scientist, inventor; many of his works, including the Mona Lisa, were not finished, p. 430

David (DAY vid) (died c. 972 B.C.) the king of the Israelites from about 1012 to 972 B.C.; unified the Jews into a settled nation and established a capital at the city of Jerusalem, p. 53

Deborah (DEB uh ruh) (c. 1100s B.C.) a judge and prophet of the Old Testament; started a war against the Canaanites, p. 58

Democritus (dih MAHK ruh tus) (c. 460–c. 370 B.C.) a Greek philosopher who proposed that the universe is made up of atoms, p. 184

Demosthenes (dih MAHS thuh neez) (384–322 B.C.) a Greek orator who issued powerful speeches against King Philip of Macedonia; the speeches became known as *Philipics,* p. 217

Diocletian (dy uh KLEE shuhn) (A.D. 245–316) the emperor of Rome from A.D. 284 to 305; reorganized the Roman government, p. 265

Dias, Bartolomeu (bahr too loo MEE oo DEE us) (c. 1450–1500) a Portuguese explorer, first to sail around southern tip of Africa, p. 457

Donatello (doh nuh TEL oh) (c. 1386–1466) a Renaissance sculptor, p. 433

Durer, Albrecht (AHL brekt DYOOR ur) (1471–1528) German painter; master of woodcuts and engravings; Italian style reflected in his work, p. 437

E

Erasmus, Desiderius (des uh DIHR ee us ih RAZ mus) (1466–1536) a Roman Catholic priest; leading figure of Christian Humanism; mocked certain Church practices, p. 435

Eratosthenes (ehr uh TAHS thuh neez) (c. 275–c. 195 B.C.) a Greek scholar who headed the library at Alexandria; a noted astronomer who wrote about many subjects, p. 222

Etruscans (ih TRUS kunz) an ancient people show lived in Etruria in Italy from at least 650 B.C. to about 500 B.C.; lived before the Romans and influenced their culture, p. 230

Euclid (YOO klid) (c. 300 B.C.) a Greco-Roman mathematician; known for the *Elements,* a book on geometry, p. 222

G

Gautama, Siddhartha (sih DAHR tuh GOW tuh muh) (born after 500 B.C. and died before 350 B.C.) the founder of Buddhism; a prince who left his family and gave up his wealth to try to find the cause of human suffering; also known as the Buddha, p. 119

Gregory VII (GREG uh ree thuh SEV unth) (c. A.D. 1020–1085) a pope who reigned from A.D. 1073 to 1085; considered one of the great papal reformers of the Middle Ages, p. 416

Gutenberg, Johannes (yoh HAHN us GOOT un burg) (died 1468) a German printer who invented movable type, p. 434

H

Hadrian (HAY dree un) (76–138) emperor of Rome from 117 to 138; one of Rome's greatest emperors; worked to unify the empire, p. 242

Hammurabi (hah muh RAH bee) (died 1750 B.C.) the king of Babylon from about 1792 to 1750 B.C.; creator of the Babylonian empire; established one of the oldest codes of law, p. 40

Harun ar-Rashid (hah ROON ar rah SHEED) (A.D. 766–806) the fifth caliph of the Abbassid dynasty; ruled Baghdad at the height of its empire, p. 303

Hatshepsut (haht SHEP soot) (died c. 1458 B.C.) the stepmother of Thutmose III; ruled Egypt as regent and then as pharaoh; achieved economic success, especially in trade, p. 74

Henry (HEN ree) (1394–1460) a prince of Portugal; advanced Portuguese navigation and trade, p. 456

Henry IV (HEN ree thuh fawrth) (1050–1106) a king of Germany and the Holy Roman Empire; argued with Pope Gregory VII and was banned from the Church, p. 416

Henry VIII (HEN ree thuh ayth) (1491–1547) the king of England from 1509 to 1547; had six wives; separated the English Church from Catholicism to begin the English Reformation, p. 446

Herodotus (huh RAHD uh tus) (c. 484–420 B.C.) a Greek author who traveled throughout the known world; wrote about the wars between Greece and Persia in the *History,* the first major historical work of ancient times, p. 68

Homer (HOH mur) (c. 800 B.C.) a Greek poet; credited with composing the epics the *Iliad* and the *Odyssey,* p. 171

I

Iceman (EYES man) one of the best-preserved bodies from prehistory that has ever been found; discovered in the Ötztal Alps on the border between Austria and Italy in 1991; believed to be from Europe's Copper Age (4000-2200 B.C.); also called Ötzi, p. 6

Ieyasu, Tokugawa (toh koo GAH wah, ee yay AH soo) (1543–1616) the founder of the last shogunate in Japan; closed his country off from the rest of the world, p. 378

J

Jahan, Shah (shah juh HAHN) (1592–1666) a Mughal emperor of India and builder of the Taj Mahal, p. 386

Jesus (JEE zus) (c. 6-4 B.C.–c. A.D. 30) the founder of Christianity; believed by Christians to be the Messiah; executed by the Roman government; believed to have appeared to his followers after his death and to have risen bodily to heaven, p. 259

Joan of Arc (john uv ahrk) (c. 1412–1431) a peasant girl who led the French army to victory over the English in the Hundred Years' War, p. 419

John I (jahn thuh furst) (1167–1216) the king of England who was forced to sign the Magna Carta in 1215 under threat of civil war, p. 418

Julius Caesar (JOOL yus SEE zur) (c. 100–44 B.C.) a Roman political and military leader; became dictator for life and was assassinated by Roman senators in the same year; greatly improved the Roman government, p. 234

Justinian (juh STIN ee un) (A.D. 483–565) a Byzantine emperor, responsible for codifying Roman law; his code influenced all later laws, p. 246

K

Kublai Khan (KOO bly kahn) (A.D. 1215–1294) a Mongol emperor of China, p. 37

L

Laozi (LOW dzih) (c. 500s B.C.) a Chinese philosopher and the founder of Taoism, p. 147

Licinius (ly SIN ee us) (died A.D. 325) took control of the eastern part of the Roman Empire in 313; co-emperor with Constantine; continued to allow religious persecution in the east; was defeated in 324 by Constantine, p. 274

Julius Caesar

Liu Bang (LYOH bahng) (256–195 B.C.) the founder of the Han dynasty of China in 202 B.C.; born a peasant; stabilized the government and promoted education, p. 152

Loyola, Ignatius (ig NAY shus loy OH luh) (c. 1491–1556) founded the Society of Jesus; Jesuits worked to educate people and spread Catholicism, p. 448

Luther, Martin (MAHRT un LOO thur) (1483–1546) a German teacher who founded the Protestant Reformation of the 1500s in revolt against the Roman Catholic Church, p. 440

M

Magellan, Ferdinand (FUR duh nand muh JEL un) (c. 1480–1521) a Portuguese explorer whose crew was the first to sail around the world, p. 461

Maimonides (my MAHN uh deez) (1134–1204) a Spanish-born medieval Jewish philosopher and teacher, p. 304

Mansa Musa (MAHN sah moo SAH) (died c. 1332) a Muslim emperor of Mali known for his pilgrimage to Mecca in 1324; encouraged the arts and learning, p. 318

Marcus Aurelius (MAHR kus aw REE lee uhs) (A.D. 121–180) a Roman emperor; generally tolerant and promoter of humanitarian causes, p. 242

Martial (MAHR shul) (c. A.D. 40–104) a Roman poet; wrote poems about the early Roman Empire, p. 252

Menes (MEE neez) (c. 2900s B.C.) the legendary founder of the first Egyptian dynasty; according to tradition, unified Upper and Lower Egypt around 3100 B.C. or earlier and founded the capital of Memphis; possibly King Narmer of the carving known as the Narmer Palette, p. 75

Michelangelo (my kul AN jul loh) (1475–1564) an Italian Renaissance artist; famous for painting the ceiling of the Sistine Chapel, p. 433

Minoans (mih NOH unz) a Bronze Age civilization on the island of Crete; created a large trade net-

Ferdinand Magellan

work; developed a vibrant culture that declined in the mid-1400s B.C., p. 170

More, Sir Thomas (sur TAHM us mawr) (1477–1535) an English writer, author of *Utopia,* a novel that pointed out problems in society, p. 435

Moses (MOH zuz) (c. 1200s B.C.) the Israelite leader who, according to the Torah, led the Israelites from Egypt to Canaan; said to have received the Ten Commandments from God, p. 52

Muhammad (muh HAM ud) (c. A.D. 570–632) the prophet of Islam who proclaimed the message of God; considered by Muslims to be the last of the prophets, p. 292

Mycenaeans (my suh NEE unz) a civilization located on mainland Greece; came into power after the Minoan culture declined; at height of power controlled the Aegean Sea and parts of the Mediterranean; spoke an early form of modern Greek, p. 170

N

Narmer (NAHR mur) the Egyptian king honored in the carving known as the Narmer palette, celebrating the unification of Upper and Lower Egypt; possibly King Menes of Egyptian legend, p. 75

Nebuchadnezzar II (nehb uh kuhd NEHZ uhr thuh SEK und) (c. 630–561 B.C.) the king of the New Babylonian empire from about 605 to 561 B.C., p. 42

Nero (NEE roh) (c. A.D. 37–68) the Roman emperor from A.D. 54 to 68; known for his cruel treatment of the Christians, p. 242

O

Octavian (ahk TAY vee un) (63 B.C.–A.D. 14) Rome's first emperor; strong leader whose rule led to peace and wealth; also known as Augustus, p. 235

Omar Kyayyam (OH mayr ky AHM) (1048–1131) Persian poet, mathematician, and astronomer, p. 300

P

Paul (PAWL) (died c. A.D. 64) a disciple of Jesus; spent his later life spreading Jesus' teachings; helped turn Christianity into an organized religion, p. 262

Peter the Hermit (PEET ur thuh HUR mit) (c. 1050–1115) a French religious leader who led one of the bands of the First Crusade, p. 412

Petrarch, Francesco (frahn CHES koh PEA trahrk) (1304–1374) an Italian poet; first great humanist; loved the works of Cicero and other Latin writers; studied the ancient Romans, p. 432

Pericles (PEHR uh kleez) (c. 495–429 B.C.) an Athenian leader; played a major role in the development of democracy and the Athenian empire, p. 180

Philip (FIL ip) (382–336 B.C.) a king of Macedonia; seized power in 359 B.C.; conquered the Greek city-states; father of Alexander the Great, p. 216

Pizarro, Francisco (frahn SEES koh pea SAHR oh) (c. 1475–1541) Spanish explorer who conquered the Incan empire and claimed Peru for Spain, p. 341

Plato (PLAYT oh) (c. 427-347 B.C.) a Greek philosopher and student of Socrates; founded the Academy of Athens and wrote *The Republic,* p. 185

Polo, Marco (MAHR koh POH loh) (1254–1324) employed by Kublai Khan for 17 years; wrote about his travels after returning to Europe; sparked increased trade between Europe and China, p. 371

Ptolemy V (TAHL uh mee thuh fifth) (died 180 B.C.) the king of ancient Egypt from 205 to 180 B.C., married to Cleopatra; his ascension to the throne is recorded on the Rosetta Stone, p. 92

R

Rabelais, François (frahn SWAH rab uh LAY) (c. 1483–1553) a French Renaissance writer; author of *Gargantua and Pantagruel,* a tale that attacks critics of humanist learning, p. 436

Romulus Augustulus (RAHM yuh lus oh GUS chuh lus) (died c. A.D. 476) the last Roman emperor; ruled from A.D. 475 to 476, p. 276

S

Saladin (SAL uh din) (c. 1137–1193) a Muslim leader who became sultan of Egypt and ultimately defeated the Crusades; was also a man of learning and a patron of the arts, p. 412

Sargon II (SAHR gahn thuh SEK und) (died 705 B.C.) Assyrian king (722–705 B.C.); conquered Babylonia; founded the last great Assyrian dynasty, p. 38

Saul (sawl) (c. 1000s B.C.) the first king of the Israelites, p. 53

Seneca (SEN ih kuh) (c. 4 B.C.–A.D. 65) a writer, philosopher, and statesman of ancient Rome, p. 255

Shakespeare, William (WIL yum SHAYK spihr) (1564–1616) wrote at least 37 verse plays based on plots borrowed from ancient works; interested in the human character, p. 436

Shi Huangdi (shur hwahng DEE) (*c.* 259–210 B.C.) the founder of the Qin dynasty and China's first emperor; ruled from about 221 to 210 B.C., p. 149

Sima Qian (sih MAH chen) (*c.* 135–87 B.C.) a Chinese scholar, astronomer, and historian; wrote the most important history of ancient China, *Historical Records,* p. 159

Socrates (SAHK ruh teez) (*c.* 470–399 B.C.) an Athenian philosopher of the late 400s B.C.; taught by using a method of questioning; helped form many values of Western culture; put to death for challenging Athenian values, p. 184

Solomon (SAHL uh mun) (died *c.* 932 B.C.) the king of the Israelites from about 972 to 932 B.C., after his father King David; built cities, temples and established foreign trade and alliances, p. 53

Solon (SOH lun) (*c.* 630–560 B.C.) an Athenian statesman; made Athens more democratic, p. 175

Sundiata (sun JAH taah) (died 1255) West African king; founded the Kingdom of Mali, p. 320

T

Taharka (tuh HAHR kuh) a prince of Nubia; became king of Nubia and Egypt in 690 B.C., p. 96

Tang Taizong (tahng ty ZAWNG) (A.D. 600–649) second emperor of the Tang dynasty, p. 366

Thales (THAY leez) (*c.* 636–546 B.C.) Greek philosopher; the first recorded Western philosopher; looked for ways to explain the physical world other than with mythological explanations, p. 184

Thutmose III (thoot MOH suh thuh thurd) (died 1426 B.C.) the stepson of Hatshepsut; considered the greatest pharaoh of Egypt's New Kingdom; expanded the empire to include Syria and Nubia; reigned from about 1479 to 1425 B.C., p. 78

Death of Socrates

Timur (tee MOOR) (1336–1405) a Turkish conqueror active in India, Russia, and the Mediterranean, known for his brutality, p. 382

Tutankhamen (toot ahng KAH mun) a king of ancient Egypt from about 1333 to 1323 B.C.; well-known because the excavation of his tomb in 1922 provided new knowledge about Egyptian art and history, p. 77

U

Urban II (UR bun thuh SEK und) (c. A.D. 1035–1099) a pope who developed reforms begun by Pope Gregory VII, began the Crusades, and built political power for the papacy, p. 409

V

Vandals (VAN dulz) a Germanic tribe that captured Rome in A.D. 455, p. 276

van Eyck, Jan (yahn van yk) (c. 1390–1441) a Flemish Renaissance painter; master of realistic portraits, p. 437

Virgil (VUR jul) (70–19 B.C.) a Roman poet and the author of the *Aeneid,* an epic that glorifies Roman ideals in the age of Augustus, p. 240

Visigoths (VIZ ee gahths) a germanic tribe that captured and looted Rome in A.D. 410, p. 276

W

Wudi (woo dee) (c. 156–86 b.c.) the Chinese emperor from 140 to 86 b.c.; expanded the Chinese empire under the Han dynasty; made Confucianism the state religion, p. 152

Y

Yoritomo, Minamoto (mee nah moh toh yoh ree TOH moh) (1147–1199) the founder of the shogunate, a Japanese feudal system that lasted for 700 years, p. 378

Z

Zwingli, Ulrich (ool rik zwing lee) (1484–1531) a religious reformer who believed that the Bible alone contained all religious truth, p. 447

Glossary

A

absolute power (AB suh loot POW ur) *n.* complete control over someone or something, p. 75

acropolis (uh KRAH puh lis) *n.* the fortified, or strengthened, hill of an ancient Greek city; the acropolis of Athens when spelled with a capital *A*, p. 172

afterlife (AF tur lyf) *n.* a life after death, p. 80

agora (AG uh ruh) *n.* a public market and meeting place in an ancient Greek city; the agora of Athens when spelled with a capital *A*, p. 199

ahimsa (uh HIM sah) *n.* the Hindu idea of nonviolence, p. 117

Akbar (AK bahr) *n.* (A.D. 1542–1605) the greatest Mughal leader of India, p. 384

Aksum (AHK soom) *n.* an important East African center of trade, p. 327

Alexander the Great (al ig ZAN dur thuh grayt) *n.* (356–323 B.C.) the king of Macedonia from 336 to 323 B.C.; conqueror of Persia and Egypt and invader of India, p. 79

ally (AL eye) *n.* a country or group that is united with another for a common purpose, p. 491

alphabet (AL fuh bet) *n.* a set of symbols that represent the sounds of a language, p. 50

Anasazi (ah nuh SAH zee) *n.* one of the ancient Native American peoples of the Southwest, p. 355

Andes (AN dees) *n.* a mountain chain in western South America, p. 14

apprentice (uh PREN tis) *n.* an unpaid person training in a craft or trade, p. 407

aqueduct (AK wuh dukt) *n.* a structure that carries water over long distances, p. 244

arch (ahrch) *n.* a curved structure used as a support over an open space, as in a doorway, p. 244

archaeologist (ahr kee AWL uh jist) *n.* a scientist who examines objects such as bones and tools to learn about past peoples and cultures, p. 7

archipelago (ahr kuh PEL uh goh) *n.* a group or chain of many islands, p. 375

aristocrat (uh RIS tuh krat) *n.* a member of a rich and powerful family, p. 174

artisan (AHR tuh zun) *n.* a skilled worker who practices a trade, such as jewelry making, ceramics, or sculpture; in Aztec society, artisans were the third most important class, under the royal or religious leaders and warriors, p. 21

assassinate (uh SAS uh nayt) *v.* to commit murder for political reasons, p. 218

astronomer (uh STRAHN uh mur) *n.* a scientist who studies the stars and other objects in the sky, p. 92

Athens (ATH unz) *n.* a city-state in ancient Greece; the capital of modern-day Greece, p. 198

avatar (AV uh tahr) *n.* a representation of a Hindu god or goddess in human or animal form, p. 115

Aztecs (AZ teks) *n.* a people who lived in the Valley of Mexico, p. 344

B

Babylon (BAB uh lun) *n.* the capital of Babylonia; a city of great wealth and luxury, p. 39

Bantu (BAN too) *n.* a large group of central and southern Africans who speak related languages, p. 310

barbarian (bahr BEHR ee un) *n.* a wild and uncivilized person, p. 216

battering ram (BAT ur ing ram) *n.* a powerful weapon having a wooden beam mounted on wheels; used to knock down walls or buildings, p. 41

bazaar (buh ZAHR) *n.* a market selling different kinds of goods, p. 40

Benin (beh NEEN) *n.* a kingdom in the West African rain forest, p. 322

blockade (blah KAYD) *n.* an action taken to isolate an enemy and cut off its supplies, p. 213

brahman (BRAH mun) *n.* a single spiritual power that Hindus believe lives in everything, p. 115

C

caliph (KAY lif) *n.* a Muslim ruler, p. 302

caravan (KA ruh van) *n.* a group of traders traveling together, p. 40

caste (kast) *n.* a social class of people, p. 111

caste system (kast SIS tum) *n.* a Hindu social class system that controlled every aspect of daily life, p. 111

cataract (KAT uh rakt) *n.* a large waterfall or steep rapids, p. 69

census (SEN sus) *n.* an official count of people living in a place, p. 253

chivalry (SHIV ul ree) *n.* the code of honorable conduct for knights, p. 408

circumnavigation (sir kum nav ih GAY shun) *n.* going completely around the Earth, especially by water, p. 461

circus (SUR kus) *n.* an arena in ancient Rome; also the show held there, p. 255

citadel (SIT uh del) *n.* a fortress in a city, p. 108

city-state (SIH tee stayt) *n.* a city that has its own independent government and often controls much of the surrounding land; Aksum was one of East Africa's ancient city-states, p. 33

civil service (SIV ul SUR vis) *n.* the group of people whose job it is to carry out the work of the government, p. 148

civil war (SIV ul wawr) *n.* a war between different regions of one country, p. 483

civilization (sih vuh luh ZAY shun) *n.* a society with cities, a central government run by official leaders, and workers who specialize in certain jobs, leading to social classes; characterized by writing, art, and architecture, p. 23

clan (klan) *n.* a group of families that trace their roots to the same ancestor, p. 314

clergy (KLUR jee) *n.* persons with authority to perform religious services, p. 403

The Colosseum

code (kohd) *n.* an organized list of laws or rules, p. 44

colony (KAHL uh nee) *n.* a territory ruled over by a distant state, p. 470

Colosseum (kahl uh SEE um) *n.* a large arena built in Rome around A.D. 70; site of contests and combats between people and animals, p. 244

Confucius (kun FYOO shus) *n.* (551–479 B.C.) a Chinese philosopher and teacher whose beliefs greatly influenced Chinese life; originator of Confucianism, p. 141

conquistador (kahn KEES tuh dawr) *n.* a Spanish conqueror of the Americas in the sixteenth century, p. 341

Constantine (KAHN stun teen) *n.* (c. A.D. 278–337) the emperor of Rome from A.D. 312 to 337; encouraged the spread of Christianity, p. 270

Constantinople (kahn stan tun NOH pul) *n.* the capital of the eastern Roman Empire and later of the Byzantine Empire, p. 275

consul (KAHN sul) *n.* one of two officials who led the ancient Roman Republic, p. 232

convert (kun VURT) *v.* to change one's beliefs; in particular, to change from one religion to another, p. 128

covenant (KUV uh nunt) *n.* a promise made by God; a binding agreement, p. 57

Crusades (kroo SAYDZ) *n.* a series of military expeditions launched by Christian Europeans to win the Holy Land back from Muslim control, p. 410

cuneiform (kyoo NEE uh fawrm) *n.* a form of writing that uses groups of wedges and lines; used to write several languages of the Fertile Crescent, p. 46

currency (KUR un see) *n.* the kind of money used by a group or a nation, p. 151

Cuzco (KOOZ koh) *n.* the capital city of the Incan Empire, located in present-day Peru, p. 338

D

delta (DEL tuh) *n.* a triangular plain at the mouth of a river, formed when sediment is deposited by flowing water, p. 70

democracy (dih MAHK ruh see) *n.* a form of government in which citizens govern themselves, p. 175

dharma (DAHR muh) *n.* the religious and moral duties of Hindus, p. 117

diaspora (dy AS pur uh) *n.* the scattering of people who have a common background or beliefs, p. 60

dictator (DIK tay tur) *n.* a ruler who has total control of the government, p. 232

dike (dyk) *n.* a protective wall that controls or holds back water, p. 138

disciple (dih SY pul) *n.* a follower of a person or belief, p. 260

domesticate (duh MES tih kayt) *v.* to adapt wild plants for human use; to tame wild animals and breed them for human use, p. 16

dynasty (DY nus tee) *n.* a series of rulers from the same family, p. 75

E

emigrate (em ih grayt) *v.* to leave one country or region to settle in another, p. 489

empire (EM pyr) *n.* many territories and people controlled by one government, p. 39

encomenderos (en koh men DAY rohz) *n.* Spanish colonists who were granted encomiendas, p. 487

encomienda (en koh mee EN dah) *n.* the right granted by the king to certain Spanish colonists to force the Native Americans to work for them, p. 487

enslaved (en SLAYVD) *v.* made into a slave and treated as property, p. 497

epic (EP ik) *n.* a long poem that tells a story, p. 171

epistle (ee PIS ul) *n.* a letter; in the Christian Bible, any of the letters written by disciples to Christian groups, p. 262

excommunication (eks kuh myoo nih KAY shun) *n.* expelling someone from the Church, p. 403

exile (EK syl) *v.* to force someone to live in another place or country, p. 53

extended family (ek STEN did FAM uh lee) *n.* closely related people of several generations, p. 140

F

famine (FAM in) *n.* a time when there is so little food that many people starve, p. 52

fertile (FUR tul) *adj.* rich in the substances plants need in order to grow well; describes soil and land, p. 16

Fertile Crescent (FUR tul KRES unt) *n.* a region in Southwest Asia; site of the world's first civilizations, p. 32

feudalism (FYOOD ul iz um) *n.* in Europe, a system in which land was owned by kings or lords but held by vassals in return for their loyalty; in Japan, a system in which poor people are legally bound to work for wealthy landowners, p. 377

G

geography (jee AHG ruh fee) *n.* the study of Earth's surface and the processes that shape it, p. 9

Ghana (GAH nah) *n.* the first West African kingdom based on the gold and salt trades, p. 319

Giza (GEE zuh) *n.* an ancient Egyptian city; site of the Great Pyramid, p. 84

gladiator (GLAD ee ayt ur) *n.* in ancient Rome, a person who fought to the death in an arena for the entertainment of the public; usually a slave, p. 255

Great Plains (grayt playnz) *n.* a mostly flat and grassy region of western North America, p. 357

Great Zimbabwe (grayt zim BAHB way) *n.* a powerful East African kingdom, p. 329

guild (gild) *n.* a medieval organization of crafts workers or tradespeople, p. 407

H

Hammurabi (hah muh RAH bee) *n.* (died 1750 B.C.) the king of Babylon from about 1792 to 1750 B.C.; creator of the Babylonian Empire; established one of the oldest codes of law, p. 40

Hellenistic (hel uh NIS tik) *adj.* a term that describes Greek history or culture after the death of Alexander the Great, including the three main kingdoms formed by the breakup of Alexander's empire, p. 220

helot (HEL ut) *n.* a member of a certain class of servants in ancient Sparta, p. 207

hieroglyphs (HY ur oh glifs) *n.* a kind of picture writing in which some pictures stand for ideas or things and others stand for sounds; the written signs and symbols used by the Egyptians, the Mayan people, and other groups, p. 91

history (HIS tuh ree) *n.* the written and other recorded events of people, p. 7

Holy Land (HOH lee land) *n.* Jerusalem and parts of the surrounding area where Jesus lived and taught, p. 409

humanism (HYOO muh niz um) *n.* an interest in the classics, p. 432

Hundred Years' War (HUN drud yeerz wawr) *n.* a series of conflicts between England and France, 1337–1453, p. 419

I

Ile-Ife (EE lay EE fay) *n.* the capital of a kingdom of the West African rain forest, p. 322

immortal (ih MAWR tul) *n.* someone or something that lives forever, p. 182

import (im PAWRT) *v.* to bring in goods from a foreign country, p. 497

Incas (ING kuhz) *n.* the people of a powerful South American empire during the 1400s and 1500s, p. 336

indulgence (in DUL juns) *n.* an official pardon given by the pope in return for money in the Middle Ages; people could pay the Catholic Church to be forgiven for their sins, a practice opposed by Martin Luther, p. 440

inflation (in FLAY shun) *n.* an economic situation in which there is more money with less value, p. 273

irrigation (ih ruh GAY shun) *n.* a method of supplying land with water through a network of canals, p. 20

isthmus (IS mis) *n.* a narrow strip of land connecting two larger areas of land, p. 460

J

Jerusalem (juh ROOZ uh lum) *n.* a city in the Holy Land, regarded as sacred by Christians, Muslims, and Jews, p. 53

Jesus (JEE zus) *n.* (c. 6 B.C.–A.D. 30) the founder of Christianity; believed by Christians to be the Messiah; crucified by the Roman government, p. 259

Justinian (jus TIN ee un) *n.* (A.D. 483–565) one of the greatest Byzantine emperors, p. 246

Justinian's Code (jus TIN ee unz kohd) *n.* an organized collection and explanation of Roman laws for use in the Byzantine Empire, p. 287

K

Kilwa (KEEL wah) *n.* one of the many trading cities on the East African coast, p. 326

kiva (KEE vah) *n.* a round room used by the Pueblo people for religious ceremonies, p. 356

knight (nyt) *n.* a man who received honor and land in exchange for serving a lord as a soldier, p. 394

Kublai Khan (KOO bly kahn) *n.* (A.D. 1215–1294) a Mongol emperor of China, p. 370

Kyoto (kee OH toh) *n.* the capital city of medieval Japan, p. 376

L

Liu Bang (LYOH bahng) *n.* (256–195 B.C.) the founder of the Han dynasty of China in 202 B.C.; born a peasant; stabilized the government and promoted education, p. 152

loess (LOH es) *n.* a yellow-brown soil, p. 138

Lower Nubia (LOH ur NOO bee uh) *n.* an ancient region in northern Africa extending from the Nile Valley in Egypt to present-day Sudan; specifically, between the first and second Nile cataracts, p. 97

M

Magna Carta (MAG nuh KAHR tuh) *n.* the "Great Charter," in which the king's power over his nobles was limited, agreed to by King John of England in 1215, p. 418

maize (mayz) *n.* corn, p. 345

Mali (MAH lee) *n.* a rich kingdom of the West African savanna, p. 318

manor (MAN ur) *n.* a large estate, often including farms and a village, ruled by a lord, p. 397

Mansa Musa (MAN sah MOO sah) *n.* (died *c.* A.D. 1332) a king of Mali, p. 318

martyr (MAHR tur) *n.* a person who dies for a cause in which he or she believes, p. 265

Maurya Empire (MOWR yuh EM pyr) *n.* the Indian empire founded by Chandragupta, beginning with his kingdom in northeastern India and spreading to most of northern and central India, p. 126

Mayas (MAH yuhz) *n.* a people who established a great civilization in Middle America, p. 345

Mecca (MEK uh) *n.* an Arabian trading center and Muhammad's birthplace, p. 294

medieval (mee dee EE vul) *adj.* referring to the Middle Ages, p. 395

meditate (MED uh tayt) *v.* to focus the mind inward in order to find spiritual awareness or relaxation, p. 120

mercenary (MUR suh neh ree) *n.* a soldier who serves for pay in a foreign army, p. 272

merit system (MEHR it SIS tum) *n.* a system of hiring people on the basis of their abilities, p. 367

messiah (muh SY uh) *n.* a savior in Judaism and Christianity, p. 260

Middle Ages (MID ul AY juz) *n.* the years between ancient and modern times, p. 395

migrate (MY grayt) *v.* to move from one place to settle in another area, p. 110

migration (my GRAY shun) *n.* the movement from one country or region to settle in another, p. 310

missionary (MISH un ehr ee) *n.* a person who spreads his or her religious beliefs to others, p. 121

Model Parliament (MAHD ul PAR luh munt) *n.* a council of lords, clergy, and common people that advised the English king on government matters, p. 418

monopoly (muh NAHP uh lee) *n.* the exclusive control of goods or services in a market, p. 469

monotheism (MAHN oh thee iz um) *n.* the belief in one god, p. 51

monsoon (mahn SOON) *n.* a strong, seasonal wind that blows across East Asia, p. 107

Moses (MOH zuz) *n.* (*c.* 1200s B.C.) Israelite leader whom the Torah credits with leading the Israelites from Egypt to Canaan; said to have received the Ten Commandments from God, p. 52

mosque (mahsk) *n.* a Muslim house of worship, p. 295

Mound Builders (mownd BIL durz) *n.* Native American groups who built earthen mounds, p. 352

movable type (MOO vuh bul typ) *n.* individual letters and marks that can be arranged and rearranged quickly, p. 434

Mughal Empire (MOO gul EM pyr) *n.* a period of Muslim rule of India from the 1500s to the 1700s, p. 384

Muhammad (muh HAM ud) *n.* (c. A.D. 570–632) the prophet and founder of Islam, p. 292

mummy (MUM ee) *n.* a dead body preserved in lifelike condition, p. 82

Muslim (MUZ lum) *n.* a follower of Islam, p. 294

myth (mith) *n.* a traditional story; in some cultures, a legend that explains people's beliefs, p. 34

N

nation (NAY shun) *n.* a community of people that shares territory and a government, p. 417

nirvana (nur VAH nuh) *n.* the lasting peace that Buddhists seek by giving up selfish desires, p. 121

nomad (NOH mad) *n.* a person with no permanent home who moves from place to place in search of food, water, or pasture, p. 14

Nubia (NOO bee uh) *n.* a desert region and ancient kingdom in the Nile River Valley, on the site of present-day southern Egypt and northern Sudan, p. 69

O

oasis (oh AY sis) *n.* an area of vegetation within a desert, fed by springs and underground water, p. 293

Omar Khayyam (OH mahr ky AHM) *n.* (A.D. 1048–1131) a Muslim poet, mathematician, and astronomer, p. 300

oracle (AWR uh kul) *n.* in ancient Greece, a sacred site where a god or goddess was consulted; any priest or priestess who spoke for the gods, p. 183

oral history (AWR ul HIS tuh ree) *n.* accounts of the past that people pass down by word of mouth, p. 314

oral traditions (AWR ul truh DISH unz) *n.* stories passed down through generations by word of mouth, p. 8

ore (awr) *n.* a mineral or a combination of minerals mined for the production of metals, p. 97

P

papyrus (puh PY rus) *n.* an early form of paper made from a reedlike plant found in the marshy areas of the Nile delta, p. 91

patrician (puh TRISH un) *n.* a member of a wealthy, upper-class family in the Roman Republic, p. 231

Peloponnesian War (pel uh puh NEE shun wawr) *n.* (431–404 B.C.) a war fought for 27 years between Athens and Sparta in ancient Greece; alliances formed on both sides meant that almost every Greek city-state was involved in the war, p. 212

persecution (pur sih KYOO shun) *n.* causing injury or distress to others because of their religion, race, or political beliefs, p. 474

pharaoh (FAIR oh) *n.* a king of ancient Egypt, p. 74

philosopher (fih LAHS uh fur) *n.* someone who uses reason to understand the world; in Greece, the earliest philosophers used reason to explain natural events, p. 184

philosophy (fih LAHS uh fee) *n.* a system of beliefs and values, p. 146

pilgrim (PIL grum) *n.* a person who journeys to a sacred place, p. 410

plague (playg) *n.* a widespread disease, p. 213

plantation (plan TAY shun) *n.* a large estate or farm, p. 487

plebeian (plih BEE un) *n.* an ordinary citizen in the ancient Roman Republic, p. 231

polytheism (PAHL ih thee iz um) *n.* the belief in many gods, p. 34

prehistory (pree HIS tuh ree) *n.* before history; the events in the period of time before writing was invented, p. 7

prophet (PRAHF it) *n.* a religious teacher who is regarded as speaking for God or a god, p. 59

Protestants (PRAHT us tunts) *n.* Christians who are not members of the Catholic or Orthodox churches; in this text, the people who shared the religious views of Martin Luther and others who protested against the Roman Catholic Church, p. 447

province (PRAH vins) *n.* a unit of an empire; in the Roman Empire, each one having a governor supported by an army, p. 241

pueblo (PWEB loh) *n.* a Native American stone or adobe dwelling, part of a cluster of dwellings built close together, p. 356

pyramid (PIH ruh mid) *n.* a huge building with four sloping triangle-shaped sides; built as a royal tomb in Egypt, p. 84

Q

quipu (KEE poo) *n.* a group of knotted strings used by the Mayas to record information, p. 339

Quran (koo RAHN) *n.* the holy book of Islam, p. 296

R

Reformation (ref ur MAY shun) *n.* the term used to describe Luther's break with the Church and the movement it inspired, p. 443

regent (REE junt) *n.* someone who rules for a child until the child is old enough to rule, p. 78

reincarnation (ree in kahr NAY shun) *n.* the rebirth of the soul in the body of another living being, p. 117

Renaissance (REN uh sahns) *n.* a widespread change in culture that took place in Europe beginning in the 1300s, p. 430

republic (rih PUB lik) *n.* a type of government in which citizens who have the right to vote select their leaders, p. 231

S

samurai (SAM uh ry) *n.* the warriors in Japan who swore to serve their leaders and obeyed a strict code of rules without question, p. 377

salvation (sal VAY shum) *n.* to go to heaven, in religious terms, p. 442

Sahara (suh HAR uh) *n.* a huge desert stretching across most of North Africa, p. 71

savanna (suh VAN uh) *n.* an area of grassland with scattered trees and bushes, p. 311

schism (SIZ um) *n.* a split, particularly in a church or religion, p. 288

scribe (skryb) *n.* in ancient civilizations, a specially trained person who knew how to read, write and keep records, p. 30

serf (surf) *n.* a farm worker considered part of the manor on which he or she worked, p. 399

Shi Huangdi (shur hwahng DEE) *n.* (c. 259–210 B.C.) the founder of the Qin dynasty and China's first emperor, ruled from about 221 to 210 B.C., p. 149

shogun (SHOH gun) *n.* the supreme military commander of Japan, p. 378

siege (seej) *n.* the surrounding and blockading of a town by an army intent on capturing it, p. 482

silk (silk) *n.* a valuable cloth originally made only in China from threads spun by caterpillars called silkworms, p. 158

Silk Road (silk rohd) *n.* a chain of trade routes stretching from China to the Mediterranean Sea, p. 156

silt (silt) *n.* a fine soil found on river bottoms, p. 70

Sima Qian (sih MAH chen) *n.* (c. 145–85 B.C.) a Chinese scholar, astronomer, and historian; wrote the most important history of ancient China, *Historical Records*, p. 159

slash-and-burn agriculture (slash-and-burn AG rih kul chur) *n.* a farming technique in which trees are cut down and burned to clear and fertilize the land, p. 345

slavery (SLAY vur ee) *n.* the condition of being owned by and forced to work for someone else, p. 202

social class (SOH shul klas) *n.* a group, or class, that is made up of people with similar backgrounds, income, and ways of living, p. 24

Song (sawng) *n.* a dynasty that ruled China after the Tang, p. 367

Songhai (SAWNG hy) *n.* a powerful kingdom of the West African savanna, p. 321

Sparta (SPAHR tuh) *n.* a city-state in the southern part of ancient Greece, p. 206

Stone Age (stohn ayj) *n.* a period of time during which people made lasting tools and weapons mainly from stone; the earliest-known period of human culture, p. 13

subcontinent (SUB kahn tih nunt) *n.* a large landmass that juts out from a continent; India is considered a subcontinent, p. 107

Sufis (SOO feez) *n.* a Muslim group that believed they could draw closer to God through prayer, fasting, and a simple life, p. 304

sultan (SUL tun) *n.* a Muslim ruler, p. 382

surplus (SUR plus) *n.* more of a thing or product than is needed, p. 21

Swahili (swah HEE lee) *n.* a Bantu language with Arabic words, spoken along the East African coast, p. 329

T

Taj Mahal (tahzh muh HAHL) *n.* a tomb built by Shah Jahan of India for his wife, p. 386

Tang (tahng) *n.* a dynasty that ruled China for almost 300 years, p. 365

Tenochtitlán (teh nawch tee TLAHN) *n.* the capital city of the Aztecs, p. 344

terraces (TEHR us iz) *n.* steplike ledges cut into mountains to make land suitable for farming, p. 340

tolerance (TAHL ur uns) *n.* the acceptance of differences; Muslims were tolerant of Jews and Christians who accepted Muslim rule during the golden age (about A.D. 800 to 1100), p. 129

tragedy (TRAJ uh dee) *n.* a type of serious drama that ends in disaster for the main character, p. 187

tribute (TRIB yoot) *n.* a regular payment made to a powerful state or nation by a weaker one, p. 181

troubadour (TROO buh dawr) *n.* a traveling poet and musician of the Middle Ages, p. 408

tyrant (TY runt) *n.* a ruler in ancient Greece who took power by force, with the support of the middle and working classes, p. 174

U

Upper Nubia (UP ur NOO bee uh) *n.* an ancient region in northeastern Africa that extended from the Nile Valley in Egypt to present-day Sudan; specifically, between the second and sixth cataracts, p. 97

V

vendor (VEN dur) *n.* a seller of goods, p. 199

veto (VEE toh) *n.* the rejection of any planned action or rule by a person in power; the Latin word for "forbid," p. 232

viceroy (VYS roy) *n.* a governor of a country or colony who rules as the representative of a king or queen, p. 486

villa (VIL uh) *n.* a country estate usually owned by a wealthy family; an important source of food and wealth for ancient Rome, p. 254

W

warlord (WAWR lawrd) *n.* a local leader of an armed group, p. 153

Wudi (woo dee) *n.* (c. 156–86 B.C.) the Chinese emperor from 140 to 86 B.C.; expanded the Chinese empire under the Han dynasty; made Confucianism the state religion, p. 152

Z

Ziggurat (ZIG oo rat) *n.* in ancient Sumeria, the site of the temple to the main god or goddess of a city, p. 34

A ziggurat

Index

The *m, g, q,* or *p* following the number refers to maps (*m*), charts, tables or graphs (*g),* quotes (*q),* or pictures (*p*).

188, 190, 197, 202, 203, 222, 224, 227, 235, 246, 262, 265, 276, 283*m*, 289, 297, 301, 315, 341, 347, 349, 370, 399, 401, 405, 408, 410, 422, 429, 448, 476, 482, 485, 493, 500

define, 62, 188, 306, 358, 386, 388, 399, 408, 422, 487, 498

describe, 19, 24, 26, 42, 47, 85, 93, 102, 118, 130, 132, 148, 151, 153, 162, 167, 190, 203, 213, 222, 224, 246, 258, 276, 306, 311 , 313, 332, 349, 360, 379, 381, 401, 422

evaluate information, 127, 213, 222, 224, 258, 388, 476

explain, 9, 26, 35, 53, 60, 62, 85, 100, 102, 111, 118, 123, 130, 132, 148, 162, 188, 190, 213, 224, 235, 237, 246, 248, 265, 278, 289, 330, 332, 341, 349, 386, 388, 399, 408, 422, 431, 433, 437, 443, 448, 455, 470, 474, 476, 483, 487, 491, 500

explore details, 188

explore main ideas, 35, 132, 246

find main ideas, 413

generalize, 9, 21, 26, 45, 47, 57, 62, 79, 92, 102, 110, 123, 162, 175, 190, 248, 304, 332, 348, 360, 398, 407, 437, 447

identify, 5, 9, 15, 17, 21, 22, 26, 29, 31, 39, 42, 45, 47, 49, 50, 53, 60, 62, 76, 77, 79, 85, 87*p*, 91, 102, 107, 111, 113, 122, 123, 128, 132, 135, 152, 153, 162, 175, 183, 190, 197, 212, 219, 227, 231, 283*m*, 295, 301, 304, 315, 321, 330, 332, 335, 341, 354*m*, 358, 360, 366, 371, 379, 386, 388, 393, 395*m*, 406, 411, 420, 422, 443, 459, 461, 474, 476, 479 , 483, 491, 498, 500

identify causes and/or effects, 9, 24, 26, 50, 53, 62, 73, 98, 102, 111, 123, 130, 132, 141, 155, 162, 190, 222, 248, 289, 297, 306, 323, 358, 360, 379, 386, 388, 399, 408, 413, 420, 422, 433, 450, 498

identify frame of reference, 288, 371, 413, 450

identify main ideas, 53, 62, 100, 118, 235, 258, 272, 276, 278, 433, 470

identify point of view, 491, 500

identify sequence, 224

infer, 5, 9, 17, 19, 23, 24, 26, 32, 35, 47, 51, 59, 60, 69, 76, 77, 82, 87*p*, 89, 115, 123, 132, 141, 145, 150, 152, 158, 160, 162, 175, 188, 190, 203, 212, 213, 218, 219, 222, 231, 237, 248, 258, 264, 265, 278, 285, 287, 302, 306, 311 , 329, 332, 338 , 341, 345 , 349, 354*m*, 358, 360, 363 , 366, 376, 383 , 385*m*, 399, 403, 406, 408, 413, 417, 443, 450, 459, 461, 470, 474, 483, 487, 491, 498

link past and present, 79, 93, 100, 224, 468

list, 73, 93, 102, 148, 160, 190, 235, 246, 278, 323, 332, 408, 437, 447, 448, 450, 491

locate, 289, 304, 332, 375 , 385*m*

name, 24, 62, 162, 246, 258, 399, 420, 436

note, 297

predict, 15, 41, 73, 75, 130, 148, 160, 175, 186, 190, 200, 213, 224, 258, 278, 293, 304, 335, 386, 395*m*, 413, 431

recall, 9, 17, 24, 26, 35, 42, 47, 53, 60, 62, 73, 79, 85, 93, 100, 102, 111, 130, 132, 141, 148, 153, 160, 162, 175, 190, 203, 213, 222, 224, 235, 248, 258, 265, 276, 278, 289, 297, 304, 306, 315, 323, 330, 332, 341, 349, 360, 371, 379, 399, 408, 420, 422, 433, 443, 450, 458, 461, 470, 474, 476, 483, 487, 500

sequence, 26, 53, 85, 190, 358, 413, 476

summarize, 111, 132, 153, 213, 271, 278, 315, 332, 371, 388, 433, 437, 448, 461, 476, 483

synthesize information, 17, 116, 213, 289, 297, 304, 306, 315, 330, 341, 349, 360, 371, 379, 386, 413*p*, 418, 422, 437, 443, 450, 461, 483, 487

transfer information, 129, 148

Croatia, 524

Crusaders
attack on Constantinople, 289

Crusades, 409–413, 410*p*, 411*m*, 412*p*, 417, 421, 455

Cuba, 526

cultural geography, 71—72

cultures
of Africa, 315, 316, 322, 329
of Americas, 359
of ancient China, 139–141, 151
of ancient Egypt, 88–93, 89*p*, 101
of ancient Greece, 170–172, 170*p*, 176–178, 176*p*, 180–187, 181*p*, 220–221, 223
of ancient India, 108–111
of Aztecs, 347–349
of Bantu, 315,
of Byzantine Empire, 287
of China, 365
development of nations and, 417
earliest of humans, 13
in Europe during Middle Ages, 408
guiding question, 1
of Japan, 376
of Mayans, 345–347
of Mound Builders, 353–355
of Nubia, 96–100
project, 502
of Southwest and Great Plains in North America, 355–356
of Sumerians, 33

cuneiform, 46, 46*p*

currency
of ancient China, 151
of Constantinople, 286*p*
of European countries, 466*p*
locations for exchange of, 294
of Phoenicians, 49*p*
use of in Europe, 413

Cuzco, 338

Cyprus, 522

Cyrus the Great, 42, 210

Czech Republic, 524

Q

Qatar, 523

Qianlong (emperor of China), 471

Qin dynasty, 150–151, 152*m*, 161

Quebec, 489

quipus, 339, 339*p*

Quran, 296–297, 297*p*, 305

R

Rabelais, François, 436, 449

radiocarbon dating, 13

Raphael, 432*p*

reading. *See* Target Reading Skills

reading skills
analyze author's purpose, RW
distinguish between facts and
opinion, RW
evaluate credibility, RW1
identify evidence, RW1

reading tables, 124–125, 132

recognizing author's bias, 464–465, 476

Red Sea, 71

Reformation, 440–443, 446–448, 447*m*, 449

regent, 78

reincarnation, 117, 121

religion
of ancient Egypt, 70, 76, 80–85
of ancient Greece, 168, 168*p*, 173, 173*p*, 182–183, 182*p*, 189
of Aryan culture, 111
of Aztecs, 348, 348*p*
of Babylonia, 44*p*
Buddhism, 119–123, 122*m*, 123*p*, 128–130, 129*p*, 130*p*, 131, 133
Christianity, 259–265, 402–405, 440–443, 446–448
Confucianism, 144–148, 146*p*, 161

decline of Byzantine Empire and, 288
founding/origins of, 125*g*
Hinduism, 114–118, 116*p*, 118*p*, 122, 130, 131, 383–384
of Incas, 338–339
of India, 383–384, 385–386
Judaism, 51, 56–60
legalism, 151
of Mayans, 346
of Nubia, 99
of Pueblo peoples, 357
of Romans, 243
Taoism, 147
of Sumerians, 34–35, 34*p*, 63
in world in, 1500, 447*m*

Remus, 228

Renaissance, 429*m*, 431*m*
art and literature of, 430, 430*p*, 432–433, 432*p*
in Italy, 430–433, 449, 450*m*
in northern Europe, 434–437
printing during, 438–439, 438*p*, 439*p*
spread of, 434–437, 449

republic, 231–235

Republic, The (Plato), 185

researching modern societies, 502

revolution, M2, M2*p*

Richard I, king of England, 412, 414, 414*p*, 415*p*

river mouth, 529

roads, 40, 157, 244, 339, 364–365

Robinson Maps, M7, M7*p*

rock paintings, 8*p*

Roman Catholic Church. *See* Catholic Church

Roman Empire, 227*m*, 251*m*
architecture and technology of, 244–245
Christianity and, 259–265, 274–275, 285
daily life in, 252–258, 277

decline and fall of, 270–273, 272*m*, 276, 277, 286, 395–396
emperors of, 240–243, 285
Greek influence in, 243
invasions of, 395, 395*m*
law of, 246
religion of, 243
scattering of Jews by, 59–60, 60*p*
soldiers of, 266–267, 266*p*, 267
See also Italy

Romania, 525

Roman Republic, 231*m*
art of, 231*p*
decline of, 234–235
geography and settlement of, 228–230
government of, 231–233, 236–237, 236*p*, 237*p*
influence of Greece, 247
See also Italy

Rome, 228*p*, 238*p*, 248*m*
area controlled by, 285
burning of, 264, 264*p*
daily life in, 252–258, 252*q*, 253*q*
fall of, 286
myth of founding of, 228
physical geography of, 229

Romulus, 228

Romulus Augustulus, 276

rope bridges, 340, 340*p*

Rosetta Stone, 92*p*

rotation, M2, M2*p*

royal seals, 141*p*

Rudra, 114, 116

Rumi, 304, 304*q*

Runnymede, England, 418, 418*p*

Russia, 284, 417, 512*m*, 525

Rwanda, 521

S

Sahara Desert, 71, 71*p*, 311

Saint Kitts and Nevis, 527

Acknowledgments

Cover Design
Pronk&Associates

Staff Credits
The people who made up **Prentice Hall History of Our World** team— representing design services, editorial, editorial services, educational technology, marketing, market research, photo research and art development, production services, project office, publishing processes, and rights & permissions—are listed below. Bold type denotes core team members.

Penny Baker, **Joyce Barisano,** Peter Brooks, Kerry Lyn Buckley, John Carle, Marianne Frasco, Kerri Hoar, Jen Paley, Deborah Levheim, Raymond Parenteau, **Kirsten Richert, Nancy Rogier,** Robin Samper, Mildred Schulte, Sarah Yezzi

Additional Credits
William Bingham, Jason Cuoco, Ella Hanna, Jeffrey LaFountain, William McAllister, John McClure, Michael McLaughlin, Lesley Pierson, Enrique Sevilla, Michele Stevens, Debra Taffet, The Mazer Corporation, Jeff Zoda

The DK Designs team who contributed to **Prentice Hall History of Our World** were as follows: Damien Demaj, Nigel Duffield, Leyla Ostovar, David Roberts, Pamela Shiels, Rob Stokes, Gail Townsley, Iorwerth Watkins

Maps
Maps and globes were created by **DK Cartography.** The team consisted of: Tony Chambers, Damien Demaj, Julia Lunn, Ed Merritt, David Roberts, Ann Stephenson, Gail Townsley, Iorwerth Watkins

Illustrations
Kenneth Batelman: 78, 285; KJA-artists.com: 18, 18–19, 36, 36–37, 86, 86–87, 112, 112–113, 154, 154–155, 155, 176, 176–177, 186, 186–187, 204, 204–205, 222, 266, 266–267, 298, 298–299, 324, 324–325, 351, 351–352, 380, 380–381, 400, 400–401, 401, 462, 462–463, 492, 492–493; Jill Ort: 232, 271, 279, 291, 292, 300, 364, 374, 382; Jen Paley: 06, 11, 12, 20, 21, 22, 30, 38, 43, 45, 47, 48, 50, 56, 68, 74, 76, 80, 88, 91, 96, 106, 114, 119, 120, 125, 126, 136, 144, 149, 151, 156, 159, 163, 168, 172, 180, 183, 191, 198, 206, 210, 216, 225, 228, 239, 240, 252, 259, 269, 270, 291, 295, 310, 318, 321, 326, 336, 342, 344, 352, 361, 369, 372, 373, 394, 402, 409, 416, 423; Lisa Smith-Ruvalcaba: 146

Photos
Cover Photos
Ron Watts/Corbis; Roger Wood/Corbis

Title Page
Roger Wood/Corbis; Roger Wood/Corbis

Table of Contents
iv–v, Vanni Archive/Corbis; **v t,** George Holton/Photo Researchers, Inc.; **vi,** Woodfin Camp & Associates; **vii,** Réunion des Musées Nationaux/Art Resource, NY; **x,** University of Witwatersrand, Johannesburg, South Africa/Bridgeman Art Library; **viii–ix,** Ric Ergenbright/Corbis

Learning With Technology
xiii tr, bc, Discovery School Channel

Reading and Writing Handbook
Michael Newman/PhotoEdit; **RW1,** Walter Hodges/Getty Images, Inc.; **RW2,** Digital Vision/Getty Images, Inc.; **RW3,** Will Hart/PhotoEdit; **RW5,** Jose Luis Pelaez, Inc./Corbis

MapMaster
James Hall/Dorling Kindersley; **M1,** Mertin Harvey/Gallo Images/Corbis; **M2–3 m,** NASA; **M2–3,** (globes) Planetary Visions; **M5 br,** Barnabas Kindersley/Dorling Kindersley; **M6 tr,** Mike Dunning/Dorling Kindersley; **M10 b,** Bernard and Catherine Desjeux/Corbis; **M11,** Hutchison Library; **M12 b,** Pa Photos; **M13 r,** Panos Pictures; **M14 t,** MSCF/NASA; **M14 l,** Macduff Everton/Corbis; **M15 b,** Ariadne Van Zandbergen/Lonely Planet Images; **M16 l,** Bill Stormont/Corbis; **M16 b,** Pablo Corral/Corbis; **M17 t,** Les Stone/Sygma/Corbis; **M17 b,** W. Perry Conway/Corbis

Guiding Questions
1tl, Bettmann/Corbis; **1br,** Richard Haynes

Unit 1
2–3, American Museum of Natural History

Chapter One
4–5, Philip & Karen Smith/Getty Images, Inc.; **6,** Sygma/Corbis; **7 c,** National Geographic Image Collection; **7 cr,** South Tyrol Archaeology Museum; **7 bl,** South Tyrol Archaeology Museum; **8 tl,** George Holton/Photo Researchers, Inc.; **8 b,** M.&E. Bernheim/Woodfin Camp & Associates; **9,** James Strachan/Getty Images, Inc.; **10 t,** Wolfgang Kaehler/Corbis; **10 b,** The British Museum, London, UK/Dorling Kindersley; **11 cl,** The Granger Collection, New York; **11 br,** Richard T. Nowitz/Corbis; **11 cl,** The Granger Collection, New York; **12,** John Reader/Science Photo Library/Photo Researchers, Inc.; **13 cr,** The Museum of London/Dorling Kindersley; **13 b,** Peter Johnson/Corbis; **14 cl,** Discovery Channel School; **14 b,** Lauren Goodsmith/The Image Works; **16 t,** Peter Adams/Index Stock Imagery, Inc.; **16 cl,** ©Robert S. Peabody Museum of Archaeology, Phillips Academy, Andover, Massachusetts All Rights Reserved/Robert S. Peabody Museum of Archaeology; **17,** J. C. Stevenson/Animals Animals/Earth Scenes; **18 bc,** Lauros/Giraudon/Bridgeman Art Library; **18 br,** Lynton Gardiner/American Museum of Natural History/Dorling Kindersley; **18–19,** The Granger Collection, New York; **19 br,** Ashmolean Museum, Oxford, UK/Bridgeman Art Library; **19 tc,** Peter H. Buckley/Pearson Education/PH College; **19 tr,** D. Finnin/C. Chesek/American Museum of Natural History/Dorling Kindersley; **20,** James R. Holland/Stock Boston/PictureQuest; **21,** Pictures of Record, Inc.; **22,** SuperStock, Inc.; **23 cr,** University Museum of Archaeology and Anthropology, Cambridge/Dorling Kindersley; **23 bc,** University Museum of Archaeology and Anthropology, Cambridge/Dorling Kindersley; **24,** Erich Lessing/Art Resource, NY; **25 tr,** SuperStock, Inc.; **25 bc,** J. C. Stevenson/Animals Animals/Earth Scenes

Chapter Two
28–29, Ed Kashi Photography/Independent Photography Network; **30,** The British Museum, London, UK/Dorling Kindersley; **31,** Nik Wheeler/Corbis; **32–33,** The British Museum, London, UK/Bridgeman Art Library; **33 tr,** Discovery Channel School; **34 tl,** Victor J. Boswell/Oriental Institute Museum/University of Chicago; **34 b,** Hirmer Fotoarchiv; **35,** Bridgeman Art Library; **37 tl,** The Art Archive/Egyptian Museum Turin/Dagli Orti; **37 cr,** Erich Lessing/Art Resource, NY; **37 br,** Ashmolean Museum, Oxford, UK/Bridgeman Art Library; **38,** Musee du Louvre, Paris/SuperStock, Inc.; **39,** Erich Lessing/Art Resource, NY; **40–41,** The British Museum, London, UK; **42,** Bridgeman Art Library; **43,** Musée du Louvre, Art Resource, NY; **44,** Scala/Art Resource, NY; **46 t** The Granger Collection, New York; **48 cl,** Courtesy of P'til Tekhelet,The Association for the Promotion and Distribution of Tekhelet Jerusalem, Israel; **48 bc,** Courtesy of P'til Tekhelet, The Association for the Promotion and Distribution of Tekhelet Jerusalem, Israel; **48 br,** Dr. Davis S. Reese; **46 b,** Steve Gorton/Dorling Kindersley; **49,** Chris Howson/Dorling Kindersley; **50,** Michael Holford Photographs; **52,** Hideo Hagal/HAGA/The Image Works; **53,** Hulton/Getty Images, Inc.; **54 tr,** Eyewire Collection/Getty Images, Inc.; **54 cl,** Bob Daemmrich/The Image Works; **55,** Giraudon/Art Resource, NY; **56,** PhotoEdit; **57 t,** The Granger Collection, New York; **57 c,** The British Museum, London, UK/Dorling Kindersley; **58,** www.asap.co.il; **60,** Erich Lessing/Art Resource, NY; **61 t,** The British Museum, London UK/Dorling Kindersley; **61 cr,** Scala/Art Resource, NY

Unit 2
64–65, Bettmann/Corbis

Chapter Three
66–67, Erich Lessing/Art Resource, NY; **68,** Werner Forman/Art Resource, NY; **69 t,** Bettmann/Corbis; **69 cr,** Discovery Channel School; **70–71,** Wolfgang Kaehler Photography; **71 cr,** John Elk III/Lonely Planet Images; **72,** Richard Nowitz Photography; **73,** Museum of Fine Arts, Boston: Harvard University— Museum of Fine Arts Expedition 21.318; **74,** Araldo de Luca/Corbis; **75,** The Art Archive/Egyptian Museum, Cairo/Dagli Orti; **77,** The Art Archive/Egyptian Museum, Cairo/Dagli Orti; **78,** Miles Ertman/Masterfile Corporation; **79,** Erich Lessing/Art Resource, NY; **80,** Erich Lessing/Art Resource, NY; **81 bc,** The British Museum, London, UK/Dorling Kindersley; **81 bl,** Réunion des Musées Nationaux/Art Resource, NY; **81 br,** Scala/Art Resource, NY; **82 cl,** Manchester Museum/Dorling Kindersley; **82 cr,** Sandro Vannini/Corbis; **83 tl,** L. Mayer/Mary Evans Picture Library; **83 tr,** Dorling Kindersley; **83 b,** Dorling

Kindersley; **84,** Paul Solomon/Woodfin Camp & Associates; **85,** Erich Lessing/Art Resource, NY; **86,** Kenneth Garrett/National Geographic Image Collection; **87,** Peter Hayman/The British Museum, London, UK/Dorling Kindersley; **88,** National Geographic Image Collection; **89,** Erich Lessing/Art Resource, NY; **90 cl,** Gianni Dagli Orti/Corbis; **90 br,** Robert Frerck/Odyssey Productions, Inc.; **91,** Scala/Art Resource, NY; **92 tl,** The British Museum, London, UK/Bridgeman Art Library; **92 c,** Lauros/Giraudon/ Bridgeman Art Library; **92 cl,** The Granger Collection, New York; **93,** The Art Archive/Musée du Louvre, Paris/Dagli Orti; **94 b,** Topham/The Image Works; **94 t,** Scala/Art Resource, NY; **96,** The Granger Collection, New York; **97,** Archivo Iconografico, S. A./Corbis; **98,** Museum of Fine Arts, Boston: Harvard University– Museum of Fine Arts Expedition 13.4081 and 13.40469; **99 cr,** Topham/The Image Works; **99 br,** Tim Kendall; **100,** from K. Lepsius, Denkmaeler aus Aegypten and Aethiopien . . . (Berlin: Nicolaische Bunchhandlung, 1842–45), Abt. 5, pl. 56.; **101 t,** Werner Forman/Art Resource, NY; **101 cr,** The Granger Collection, New York

Chapter Four
104–105, Dinodia; **106–107,** Zane Williams/Panoramic Images; **108 cl,** Bridgeman Art Library; **108 b,** Jehangir Gazdar/Woodfin Camp & Associates; **109 b,** Jehangir Gazdar/Woodfin Camp & Associates; **109 tr** Charles & Josette Lenars/Corbis; **110,** Chris Lisle/Corbis; **111,** Victoria & Albert Museum, London/Art Resource, NY; **113,** Harappan National Museum of Karachi, Karachi, Pakistan/Bridgeman Art Library; **114,** Corbis Digital Stock; **115,** Jacob Halaska/Index Stock Imagery, Inc.; **116,** Woodfin Camp & Associates; **117,** The British Museum, London, UK/Bridgeman Art Library; **118,** Eve Arnold/Magnum Photos; **119,** Lee Boltin/Boltin Picture Library; **120–121,** John W. Banagan/Getty Images, Inc.; **122,** Ashmolean Museum/Dorling Kindersley; **123,** Hugh Sitton/Getty Images, Inc.; **124,** AP/Wide World Photos/Aijaz Rahi; **125,** Russ Lappa; **126,** Flammarion/Musée Guimet, Paris, France/Bridgeman Art Library; **127,** Burstein Collection/Corbis; **129 tr,** Discovery Channel School; **129 b,** Chris Lisle/Corbis; **130,** Bushnell/Soifer Stone/Getty Images; **131 t,** Jehangir Gazdar/Woodfin Camp & Associates; **131 cl,** The British Museum, London, UK/Bridgeman Art Library; **131 cr,** Burstein Collection/Corbis

Chapter Five
134–135, David Allan Brandt/Getty Images, Inc.; **136,** Wolfgang Kaehler Photography; **137 tr,** The Granger Collection, New York; **137 b,** AP/Wide World Photos/Greg Baker; **138 tr,** Chris Stowers/Panos Pictures; **138 b,** Gina Corrigan/Robert Harding World Imagery; **139,** H. Rogers/Trip Photographic; **140 tl,** The Granger Collection, New York; **140 br,** The Great Bronze Age of China/Metropolitan Museum; **141,** Réunion des Musées Nationaux/Art Resource, NY; **143 tr,** Michael Newman/PhotoEdit; **143 b,** Julia Waterlow; Eye Ubiquitous/Corbis; **144,** Victoria Vebell Bruck; **145,** The Granger Collection, New York; **146 tl,** The Granger Collection, New York; **146 tc,** Reed Kaestner/Corbis; **146 tr,** Carlos Spaventa/Getty Images, Inc.; **146 cr,** The Art Archive/The British Museum London, UK; **146 bl,** Bettmann/Corbis; **147 tl,** Bonnie Kamin/PhotoEdit; **147 br,** Archives Charmet/Bridgeman Art Library; **148,** Bridgeman Art Library; **149,** Keren Su/China Span; **150 tl,** Alvis Upitis/SuperStock, Inc.; **150 bl,** Discovery Channel School; **151 tr,** Giraudon/Art Resource, NY; **151 bc,** Réunion des Musées Nationaux/Art Resource, NY; **152,** The British Museum, London, UK/Bridgeman Art Library; **153,** Giraudon/Bridgeman Art Library; **155,** The Art Archive/Musée Cernuschi Paris/Dagli Orti; **156,** Keren Su/China Span; **157,** Réunion des Musées/Art Resource, NY; **158 cr,** Cary Wolinsky/Aurora & Quanta Productions, Inc.; **158 tl,** The Granger Collection, New York; **159 tr,** The British Museum/ Dorling Kindersley; **159 cr,** Alan Hills and Geoff Brightling/Dorling Kindersley; **159 br,** Geoff Brightling/Dorling Kindersley; **160,** The Metropolitan Museum of Art, Purchase, The Dillon Fund, 1977. (1977–78) Photograph by Malcom Varon. Photograph ©1990 The Metropolitan Museum of Art; **161 tr,** China Span; **161 cl,** The Granger Collection, New York

Unit 3
164–165, Zephyr Picture/Index Stock Imagery

Chapter Six
166–167, Picture Finders, Ltd./Leo De Wys Stock Photo Agency/eStock Photography; **167,** James Hall/Dorling Kindersley; **168,** Erich Lessing/Art Resource, NY; **169,** Colin Paterson/SuperStock, Inc.; **170 b,** Gianni Dagli Orti/Corbis; **170 t,** Gianni Dagli Orti/Corbis; **171 t,** Discovery Channel School; **171 b,** Ulf Sjostedt/Getty Images, Inc.; **172,** The British Museum London, UK/Dorling Kindersley; **173 tr,** Archivo Inconografico, S.A./Corbis; **173 c,** Richard Bonson/Dorling Kindersley; **174,** Réunion des Musées Nationaux/Art Resource,

NY; **175 t, b,** The Art Archive/Agora Museum Athens/Dagli Orti; **177 tr,** Donald Cooper/Photostage, Ltd.; **177 b,** Scala/Art Resource, NY; **178 tl,** The Art Archive/The British Museum London, UK/Eileen Tweedy; **178 bl,** David Young-Wolff/PhotoEdit; **179,** Bettmann/Corbis; **180,** The Granger Collection, New York; **181 tr,** The British Museum, London, UK /Dorling Kindersley; **181 b,** The Art Archive/Archaeological Museum Spina Ferrara/Dagli Orti; **182,** David Lees/Corbis; **183 tl,** Steve Vidler/SuperStock, Inc.; **183 tr,** Bridgeman Art Library; **184–185,** Alinari/Art Resource, NY; **186–187,** Vanni Archive/Corbis; **187 tc,** The Art Archive/Dagli Orti; **187 tr,** The Art Archive/Archaeological Museum Piraeus/Dagli Orti; **188 tl,** Hulton Archive/Getty Images; **188 c,** Gianni Dagli Orti/Corbis; **189 tr,** Gianni Dagli Orti/Corbis; **189 cl,** David Lees/Corbis

Literature
192, Alinari/Regione Umbria/Art Resource, NY; **193,** Ivor Kerslake/The British Museum, London, UK/Dorling Kindersley **194,** Erich Lessing/Art Resource, NY; **195 tl,** Joe Malone Agency/Jon Arnold Images/Alamy Images; **195 cr,** Gustavo Tomsich/Corbis

Chapter Seven
196–197, Bernard Van Berg/Image Bank/Getty Images, Inc; **198,** Scala/Art Resource, NY; **199 t,** Richard T. Norwitz/Corbis; **199 b,** The Art Archive / Musée du Louvre Paris/Dagli Orti; **200 tl,** Liz McAulay/British Museum; **200–201,** Erich Lessing/Art Resource, NY; **201 tr,** Réunion des Musées Nationaux/Art Resource, NY; **202,** The British Museum, London, UK/Dorling Kindersley; **203,** The Art Archive/Agora Museum Athens/Dagli Orti; **205,** Erich Lessing/Art Resource, NY; **206,** Gian Berto Vanni/Art Resource, NY; **207,** The Art Archive/Dagli Orti; **208 t,** Karl Shone/The British Museum; **208–209,** Jose Miralles/S.I. International; **211,** Erich Lessing/Art Resource. NY; **212c,** The British Museum, London, UK/Dorling Kindersley; **212 b,** Discovery Channel School **213,** Erich Lessing/Art Resource, NY; **214 tr,** Liz McAulay/British Museum/Dorling Kindersley; **214 bl,** Wolfgang Kaehler/Corbis; **216,** Gianni Dagli Orti/Corbis; **217 cr,** Réunion des Musées Nationaux/Art Resource, NY; **217 b,** Bettmann/Corbis; **218 cl,** The Granger Collection, New York; **218 b,** David Lees/Corbis; **220 c,** Bettmann/Corbis; **220 tr,** Alistair Duncan/Dorling Kindersley Media Library; **221,** Art Resource, NY; **222,** Pearson Learning Group; **223,** Erich Lessing/Art Resource, NY; **224 c,** Jose Miralles/S.I. International; **224 b,** The Granger Collection, New York

Chapter Eight
226–227; David McLain/Aurora Photos; **228,** Enzo & Paolo Ragazzini/Corbis; **229,** Tim Thompson/Corbis; **230,** The Granger Collection, New York; **231,** Scala/Art Resource, NY; **233,** The Metropolitan Museum of Art, Rogers Fund, 1965 (65.183.2) Photograph ©1984 The Metropolitan Museum of Art; **234,** Bettmann/Corbis; **235,** Raymond V. Schoder/Pearson Education U.S. ELT/Scott Foresman; **236 t,** The Art Archive/Jan Vinchon Numismatist Paris/Dagli Orti; **236–237,** Scala/Art Resource, NY; **237 t,** Araldo de Luca/Corbis; **237 b,** Tom Carter/PhotoEdit; **238,** Michael S. Yamshita/Corbis; **239 br,** Christi Graham and Nick Nichols/British Museum/Dorling Kindersley Media Library; **240,** Richard T. Nowitz/Corbis; **241 cr,** Stock Montage; **241 b,** The British Museum, London, UK/Dorling Kindersley; **242,** Nimatallah/Art Resource, NY; **243 cr,** Alinari/Art Resource, NY; **243 bc,** Vanni Archive/Corbis; **244 bl,** Discovery Channel School; **244 cl,** Dallas and John Heaton/Corbis; **245 t,** Max Alexander/Dorling Kindersley; **245 b,** Dorling Kindersley; **247 tr,** The Granger Collection, New York; **247 cr,** Richard T. Nowitz/Corbis

Chapter Nine
250–251, Richard Glover/Corbis; **252,** The Metropolitan Museum of Art; **253,** Christy Graham and Nick Nichols/The British Museum/Dorling Kindersley; **254 tl,** The British Museum, London, UK/Dorling Kindersley; **254 b,** Pearson; **255,** Réunion des Musées Nationaux/Art Resource, NY; **256,** Erich Lessing/Art Resource, NY; **257 bl, br,** Dorling Kindersley; **258 t,** The British Museum, London, UK/Dorling Kindersley; **258 bc,** Discovery School Channel; **259,** Erich Lessing/Art Resource, NY; **260 tl,** Scala/Art Resource, NY; **260–261,** Scala/Art Resource, NY; **262,** Arte & Immagini srl/Corbis; **263,** Scala/Art Resource, NY; **264,** Hubert Robert (1733–1808). The Burning of Rome. 0.76 x 0.93 m. Oil on canvas. Musee des Beaux-Arts Andre Malraux, Le Havre, France. Giraudon/Art Resource, NY; **265,** The Art Archive/Palazzo Barberini Rome/Dagli Orti; **266 cl,** Erich Lessing/Art Resource, NY; **266 b,** Erich Lessing/Art Resource, NY; **267 bl,** The Art Archive/Museo Civico Riva del Garda/Dagli Orti; **268,** Spencer Grant/PhotoEdit; **269 t,** The Art Archive/Dagli Orti; **269 b,** Panorama Images/The Image Works; **270,** Robert Frerck/Odyssey Productions, Inc.; **271 cl,** The Granger Collection, New York; **271 tr,** The British Museum, London,

UK/Dorling Kindersley; **271 cr,** Bridgeman Art Library; **272,** Reunion des Musees Nationaux/Art Resource, NY; **273,** Archivo Iconografico, S.A./Corbis; **274,** Vanni Archive/Corbis; **275,** Richard T. Nowitz/Corbis; **276,** The Granger Collection, New York; **277c,** Scala/Art Resource, NY; **277 t,** Réunion des Musées Nationaux/Art Resource, NY; **277 b,** Richard T. Nowitz/Corbis

Unit 4
280–281, Ric Ergenbright/Corbis

Chapter Ten
282–283, Robert Frerck/Woodfin Camp & Associates; **284,** The Granger Collection, New York; **285 tr,** Topham/The Image Works; **285 b,** Historical Picture Archive/Corbis; **286 tl,** Discovery Channel School; **286 tr,** Chas Howson/The British Museum, London, UK/Dorling Kindersley; **286 bl,** The Granger Collection, New York; **287,** Robert Frerck/Getty Images, Inc; **288,** Paul H. Kuiper/Corbis; **289,** Photos12.com-ARJ; **290 tr,** Corbis; **290 bl,** Jeff Greenberg/The Image Works; **292,** The British Library, London, UK; **293,** Christine Osborne/Agency Worldwide Picture Library/Alamy Images; **294,** Explorer, Paris/SuperStock, Inc.; **295,** Paul Chesley/Stone/Getty Images, Inc.; **296 t,** Latif Reuters New Media Inc./Corbis; **296 cl,** The British Library, London, UK/The Art Archive; **297,** The Granger Collection, New York; **298,** Alan Hills/Dorling Kindersley; **299,** Dorling Kindersley; **300,** Scala/Art Resource, NY; **301,** Archivo Iconografico, S.A./Corbis; **302,** Lauros/Giraudon/Bridgeman Art Library; **303 t,** The Granger Collection, New York; **303 c,** The Granger Collection, New York; **303 b,** Giraudon/Art Resource, NY; **304,** Stuart Cohen/The Image Works; **305 tl,** The Granger Collection, New York; **305 cr,** Lauros/Giraudon/Bridgeman Art Library

Chapter Eleven
308–309, M. & E. Bernheim/Woodfin Camp & Associates; **310,** Tim Rock/Lonely Planet Images; **311,** Chris Anderson/Aurora Photos; **312–313,** SuperStock, Inc.; **314,** Walter Bibikow/Jon Arnold Images/Alamy Images; **315 tc,** Geoff Dann/Dorling Kindersley; **315 tr,** Geoff Dann/Dorling Kindersley; **316,** Werner Forman/Art Resource, NY; **317,** Getty Images, Inc.; **318,** The Granger Collection, New York; **319 cr,** Nik Wheeler/Corbis **319 b,** Ariadne Van Zandbergen/Lonely Planet Images; **320,** David Jones/Alamy Images; **321 t,** Werner Forman/Art Resource, NY; **321 b,** Werner Forman Archive/Art Resource, NY; **322,** Lars Howlett/Aurora Photos; **323,** Christie's Images/Corbis; **325 b,** The Art Archive/Musée des Arts Africains et Océaniens/Dagli Orti; **326,** Marc & Evelyne Bernheim/Woodfin Camp & Associates; **327 t,** David Else/Lonely Planet Images; **327 cr,** D. Harcourt-Webster/Robert Harding; **328 t,** Dave Bartruff/Corbis; **328 cl,** Ariadne Van Zandbergen/Lonely Planet Images; **329 tr,** Discovery Channel School; **329 b,** Mitch Reardon/Lonely Planet Images; **330,** I. Vanderharst/Robert Harding World Imagery; **331,** Christie's Images/Corbis

Chapter Twelve
334–335, SuperStock, Inc.; **336,** Philippe Colombi/Photodisc Green/Getty Images, Inc.; **337;** The British Museum, London, UK/Dorling Kindersley; **338,** Anthony Pidgeon/Lonely Planet Images; **339 t,** Charles & Josette Lenars/Corbis; **339 cr,** The Granger Collection, New York; **340,** Woodfin Camp & Associates; **341,** The British Museum, London, UK/Dorling Kindersley; **343 tl,** The Art Archive/Archaeological Museum Lima/Dagli Orti; **343 br,** The Art Archive/Archaeological Museum Lima/Dagli Orti; **344,** Bodleian Library; **345 t,** Angel Terry/Alamy Images; **345 b,** Robert Fried Photography **346,** Private Collection/Bridgeman Art Library; **347 tr,** Discovery Channel School; **347 b,** Robert Frerck/Getty Images Inc.; **348 t,** Michel Zab/Dorling Kindersley; **348 cl,** Michel Zab/Dorling Kindersley; **349,** Michel Zab/Dorling Kindersley; **351 t,** Werner Forman/Art Resource, NY; **352,** Werner Forman/Art Resource, NY; **353,** Tony Linck/SuperStock, Inc.; **354 cl,** Werner Forman Archive/Art Resource, NY; **354 br,** Richard A. Cooke/Corbis; **355,** Dewitt Jones/Corbis; **356 cl,** David Muench/Corbis; **356–357,** George H. H. Huey Photography, Inc.; **358,** Peter Gridley/Getty Images, Inc.; **359 tr,** Michel Zab/Dorling Kindersley; **359 bl,** David Muench/Corbis

Chapter Thirteen
362–363, B. Davis/Woodfin Camp & Associates; **364–365,** The British Museum, London, UK/Topham-HIP/The Image Works; **365 tr,** Werner Forman/Art Resource, NY; **366,** The Granger Collection, New York; **367,** Honolulu Academy of Arts; **368 cr,** Alan Hills and Geoff Brightling/The British Museum, London, UK/Dorling Kindersley; **368 bl,** The Granger Collection, New York; **369 tl,** The Art Archive; **369 cr,** Lawrence Pardes/Dorling Kindersley/The British Library, London, UK; **369 tr,** ChinaStock; **370,** Werner Forman/Art Resource, NY; **371 tl,** Bettmann/Corbis; **371 cr,** Discovery Channel School; **372–373,** Anthony Bannister; Gallo Images/Corbis; **373 tr,** Burstein Collection/Corbis; **374,** Fitzwilliam Museum, University of Cambridge, UK/Bridgeman Art Library; **375,** Adina Tovy Amsel/Lonely Planet Images; **376,** Akira Nakata/HAGA/The Image Works; **377 cr,** Lee Boltin/Boltin Picture Library; **377 b,** Pearson Education U.S. ELT/Scott Foresman; **378,** The Art Archive; **379,** Fujifotos/The Image Works; **380 b,** Leeds Museums and Art Galleries (City Museum) UK/Bridgeman Art Library; **380 cl,** Victoria & Albert Museum, London, UK/Art Resource, NY; **382,** The Granger Collection, New York; **383,** John Kelly/Getty Images, Inc.; **384,** The Granger Collection, New York; **385,** Gwalior Fort, Madhya Pradesh, India/Bridgeman Art Library; **386,** David Sutherland/Getty Images Inc.; **387 t,** Bettman/Corbis; **387 br,** Fujifotos/The Image Works

Unit 5
390–391, Joel W. Rogers/Corbis

Chapter Fourteen
392–393; Steve Vidler/eStock Photography; **394,** Giraudon/Art Resource, NY; **395,** The Art Archive/Bargello Museum Florence/Dagli Orti; **396;** Gianni Dagli Orti/Corbis; **397 t,** Robin Smith/PhotoLibrary.com; **397 b,** Gianni Dagli Orti/Corbis; **398 t,** The Granger Collection, New York; **398 cl,** New York Public; **398 bl,** Discovery Channel School; Library/Art Resource, NY; **399,** Scala/Art Resource, NY; **401,** The Granger Collection, New York; **402,** Adam Woolfitt/Corbis; **403,** The Granger Collection, New York; **405 t,** The Art Archive/Bibliothèque Municipale Laon/Dagli Orti; **405 b,** The Art Archive/Bodleian Library Oxford/The Bodleian Library; **406,** The British Museum, London, UK/Topham-HIP/The Image Works; **407 tr,** AKG London Ltd **407 bl,** The Art Archive/Museo Civico Bologna/Dagli Orti; **408,** Gianni Dagli Orti/Corbis; **409;** Archivo Iconografico, S.A./Corbis; **410 t,** North Wind Picture Archives; **410 b,** The Granger Collection, New York; **412,** Archivo Iconografico, S.A./Corbis; **413,** Bettmann/Corbis; **414,** Library of Congress; **415 t,** The Granger Collection, New York; **415 bc,** Snark/Art Resource, NY **416,** Scala/Art Resource, NY; **417,** Derek Croucher/Corbis; **418,** ARPL/Topham/The Image Works; **419,** Morton Beebe/Corbis; **420,** Sunday Mirror/Topham/The Image Works; **421,** The Art Archive/Bargello Museum Florence/Dagli Orti

Literature 424, The Art Archive/British Library/British Library; **425;** Reprinted with permission of Atheneum Books for Young Readers, an imprint of Simon & Schuster Children's Publishing Division from *The Boy's King Arthur* by Sidney Lanier, illustrated by N.C. Wyeth. Copyright 1917 Charles Schribner's Sons; copyright renewed 1954 N.C. Wyeth.; **426,** Reprinted with permission of Atheneum Books for Young Readers, an imprint of Simon & Schuster Children's Publishing Division from *The Boy's King Arthur* by Sidney Lanier, illustrated by N.C. Wyeth. Copyright 1917 Charles Schribner's Sons; copyright renewed 1954 N.C. Wyeth.; **427,** Copyright, Pittsburgh Post-Gazette, V.W.H. Campbell Jr., 2002, all rights reserved. Reprinted with permission.

Chapter Fifteen
428–429, Lee Frost/Robert Harding World Imagery; **430,** Leonardo da Vinci "Mona Lisa" ©Musee du Louve/Reunion des Musees National/Art Resource; **431,** The British Museum/Dorling Kindersley Media Library; **432 t,** School of Athens, from the Stanza della Segnatura, 1510–11 (fresco), Raphael (Raffaello Sanzio of Urbino) (1483–1520) Vatican Museums and Galleries, Vatican City, Italy, Giraudon/Bridgeman Art Library; **432 b,** Discovery Channel School; **433,** Christie's Images/Corbis; **434,** Inc, Martin Paul Ltd./Index Stock Imagery; **435,** Erich Lessing/Art Resource, NY; **436 bl,** Bettmann/Corbis; **436 br,** Robbie Jack/Corbis; **437,** The Portrait of Giovanni Arnolfini and his Wife Giovanna Cenami (The Arnolfini Marriage) 1434 (oil on panel), Eyck, Jan van (c.1390–1441) National Gallery, London, UK; **438 tl,** *Dress & Decorations of the Middle Ages* - Henry Shaw, 1858 Volume 2, page 46/Mary Evans Picture Library; **438 bc,** Ellen Howdon/Dorling Kindersley; **438–439,** Bettmann/Corbis; **440,** Bettmann/Corbis; **441,** Dorling Kindersley; **442 cl, b,** Bettmann/Corbis; **443,** The Delivery of the Augsburg Confession, 25th June 1530, 1617 (oil on panel) German School (17th Century) Georgenkirche, Eisenach, Germany/Bridgeman Art

Library; **444,** Charles Gupton/Corbis; **445 t,** The Granger Collection; **445 b,** James L. Amos/Corbis; **446,** Hans the Younger Holbein (1497/8–1543), Dutch, "Portrait of Henry VIII", 16th Century/Bridgeman Art Library; **447,** Hulton Archive/Getty Images; **448,** Archivo Iconografico, S.A./Corbis; **449 tl,** The Bridgeman Art Library International Ltd.; **449 tr,** Bettmann/Corbis; **449 bl,** Robbie Jack/Corbis; **449 br,** Hulton Archive/Getty Images

Chapter Sixteen
452–453, Robert Everts/Getty Images Inc./Stone/Allstock; **454 t,** Royal Geographic Society/Dorling Kindersley Media Library; **454 b,** Science Museum/Dorling Kindersley Media Library; **455 cr,** Michelle Garrett/Corbis; **455 b,** Thomas Wyck (1616–77), Merchants from Holland and the Middle East trading in a Mediterrainean port, oil on canvas, 53.6 x 80.7cm. Philiphs, The International Fina Art Auctioneers/ The Bridgeman Art Library; **456,** Granger Collection, New York; **457 tr,** The Granger Collection, New York; **457 bl,** Corbis; **457 br,** University of Witwatersrand, Johannesburg, South Africa/Bridgeman Art Library; **459 t,** Bettmann/Corbis; **459 c,** Peter Dennis/Dorling Kindersley; **459 b,** Corbis; **461,** The Art Archive/Marine Museum Lisbon/Dagli Orti/The Picture Desk; **462,** David Lees/Corbis; **463,** David Lees/Corbis; **464,** Private Collection/Bridgeman Art Library; **465 t,** Colin Prior/Stone Allstock/Getty Images, Inc.; **465 b,** Victoria & Albert Museum, London, UK/Bridgeman Art Library; **466 c,** Archivo Iconografico, S.A./Corbis; **466 b,** Archivo Iconografico, S.A./Corbis; **467,** Hulton Archive/Getty Images; **468–469,** The Art Archive/Museo de la Torre del Oro Seville/Dagli Orti/The Picture Desk; **470,** Hulton Archive/Getty Images; **471,** Judith Miller & Dorling Kindersley LUBBS915O386; **472 cl,** Judith Miller & Dorling Kindersley LUBBS915O497; **472 bc,** Alan Hills/British Museum/Dorling Kindersley **472–473,** Historical Picture Archive/Corbis; **473 cr,** Judith Miller & Dorling Kindersley O048SL924; **473 b,** Discovery Channel School **474,** The Stapleton Collection/Topkapi Palace Museum, Istanbul, Turkey/Bridgeman Art Library; **475 t,** Science Museum/Dorling Kindersley Media Library; **475 c,** Hulton Archive/Getty Images; **475 b,** Judith Miller & Dorling Kindersley LUBBS915O386

Chapter Seventeen
478–479, Randy Faris/Corbis; **480,** Steve Dunwell Photography/Getty Images, Inc.; **481 t,** Duran, Diego (16th century), Codex Duran:Pedro de Alverado (c.1485–1541). Companion-at-Arms of Hernando Cortes (1485–1547) besieged by Aztec warriors (vellum)/Bridgeman Art Library; **481 cr,** Bettmann/Corbis; **482,** Charles & Josette Lenars/Bettmann/Corbis; **483,** The British Museum/Dorling Kindersley Media Library; **484,** The Granger Collection; **486,** Snark/Art Resource, NY; **487,** Alan Pappe/Photodisc/Getty Images, Inc; **488,** Courtesy of the Pilgrim Society, Plymouth, Massachusetts; **489,** Percy Morgan/Courtesy of the Pilgram Society, Plymouth, Massachusetts; **490,** Bettmann/Corbis, **492,** Courtesy of Pilgrim Hall Museum, Plymouth, MA.; **493,** Courtesy of Pilgrim Hall Museum, Plymouth, MA.; **494,** Smithsonian American Art Museum, Washington, DC/Art Resource, NY; **495 bc, b,** Archivo Iconografico, S.A./Corbis; **495 t,** Werner Forman/Art Resource; **496,** Tom Schierlitz/Stone-Allstock/Getty Images, Inc.; **497 b,** The Granger Collection; **497 t,** Discovery Channel School; **498,** Wolfgang Kaehler/Corbis; **499 tl,** Duran, Diego (16th century), Codex Duran:Pedro de Alverado (c.1485–1541). Companion-at-Arms of Hernando Cortes (1485–1547) besieged by Aztec warriors (vellum)/Bridgeman Art Library; **499 tr,** Courtesy of the Pilgrim Society, Plymouth, Massachusetts; **499 bl,** Alan Pappe/Getty Images, Inc; **499 br,** The Granger Collection

Projects
502 t, Richard Haynes; **502 b,** Richard Bickel/Corbis

Reference
503, Liu Liqun/Corbis

Glossary of Geographic Terms
528 t, A & L Sinibaldi/Getty Images, Inc.; **528 b,** John Beatty/Getty Images, Inc.; **528–529 b,** Spencer Swanger/Tom Stack & Associates; **529 t,** Hans Strand/Getty Images, Inc; **529 cr,** Paul Chesley/Getty Images, Inc.

Glossary
281, Dallas and John Heaton/Corbis; **282,** Erich Lessing/Art Resource, NY; **285,** Bridgeman Art Library; **287,** Hirmer Fotoarchive

Gazetteer
532, Bettmann/Corbis, **536,** Zephyr Picture/Index Stock Imagery

Biographical Dictionary
538, David Lees/Corbis; **540,** Bettmann/Corbis; **542,** The Art Archive/Marine Museum Lisbon/Dagli Orti/The Picture Desk; **544,** Alinari/Art Resource, NY

Text

Chapter Two
47, Excerpt from *A History of the Ancient World, Fourth Edition,* by Chester G. Starr. Copyright © 1991 by Oxford University Press. Published by Oxford University Press. **51,** Excerpt from *Everyday Life in Babylonia and Assyria,* by H.W.F. Saggs. Copyright © 1965 by H.W.F. Saggs. **53,** Excerpt from The Avalon Project: The Code of Hammurabi, translated by L.W. King, (http://www.yale.edu/lawweb/avalon/medieval/hamcode.htm). **56,** Excerpt from *The Torah: A Modern Commentary.* Copyright © 1981 by The Union of American Hebrew Congregations. Reprinted by permission of The Union of American Hebrew Congregations.

Chapter Four
112, Excerpt from the Rig-Veda, 1.154, verses 1–3 adapted from *Hinduism* by V.P. (Hermant) Kanitkar, Stanley Thornes (Publishers) Ltd, 1989.

Chapter Six
180, Excerpt from *The Peloponnesian War,* by Thucydides. Copyright © 1951 by Random House, Inc.

Chapter Eight
240, Excerpt from the *Aeneid,* by Virgil (http://www.pbs.org/empires/romans/voices/index.html).

Chapter Ten
300, from *The Concise History of Islam and the Origin of Its Empires,* by Gregory C. Kozlowski. Copyright © 1991 by The Copley Publishing Group. Reprinted with permission from the Copley Publishing Group. **304,** from *Love's Fire; Re-Creations of Rumi* by Andrew Harvey. Copyright © 1988 by Andrew Harvey, published by Mother Meera Publications.

Chapter Thirteen
369, from *China's Examination Hell,* by Ichisada Miyazaki. Copyright © 1981 by Yale University Press. Reprinted by permission of Weatherhill Inc.

Chapter Fourteen
424–427, Reprinted with the permission of Atheneum Books for Young Readers, an imprint of Simon & Schuster Children's Publishing Division, from *Of Swords and Sorcerers: The Adventures of King Arthur and His Knights* by Margaret Hodges and Margery Evernden. Text copyright © 1993 by Margaret Hodges and Margery Evernden.

Country Databank
520–527, CIA World Factbook Online, 2002 Edition.

Note: Every effort has been made to locate the copyright owner of material used in this textbook. Omissions brought to our attention will be corrected in subsequent editions.